Morna Stewart

Glencoe
and the End of the
Highland War

It is singular how obscure ... this decade of Scots history remains, 1690–1700: a deuce of a want of light and grouping to it!

Robert Louis Stevenson.

This is the frame and constitution of our land. They that are great will cari all with them, not what's right, but what they will.

Alexander Brodie of Brodie.

Glencoe
and the End of the
Highland War

PAUL HOPKINS

Research Fellow of Peterhouse,
Cambridge

REVISED REPRINT

JOHN DONALD PUBLISHERS LTD
EDINBURGH

In memory of my father

ISBN 0 85976 490 7 (Paperback Edition)

Printed in Great Britain by Bell & Bain Ltd., Glasgow.

Contents

List of Maps

Preface to the Paperback Edition

This reprint enables me to mention very briefly important changes in the sources, and a few of my worst factual mistakes or omissions, discovered since the original publication. Over-compression and other faults of style, alas, and faults of interpretation must remain. I will, however, advise general readers that there is a good underlying story, though one with a large cast of main characters, clogged by the need to set events in a wide context and correct a thousand previous errors: they should skip ruthlessly, particularly in Chapter 11 between the two main climaxes.

In my most important source, the Breadalbane Papers (SRO GD 112), the sections I most used were GD 112/39 and /40, Correspondence, and /43, State Papers including more correspondence. Since 1986, Dr B.L.H. Horn has produced an excellent complete catalogue of GD 112, entirely rearranging and renumbering these sections in the process. A new GD 112/39 has been created, consisting of all the letters in the old /39 and /40, and the letters (but not orders) from /43 — the most important being Viscount Dundee's letter of 20 July 1689 — rearranged in chronological order. The former reference numbers in the old /39 and /40 are included. The new GD 112/40 is the small section of royal letters, formerly /42; the present /42 consists of miscellanea. The one doubtful policy decision was to break up and disperse between sections the original bundles of letters and documents (in 112/43) assembled for different purposes by Breadalbane's agents while defending him against the 1695 treason charge. The one significant document I used noticeably misplaced is Breadalbane's original plan for a highland regiment, undated but certainly of 1685, catalogued among items of 1715.[1]

This cataloguing of GD 112 has revealed much relevant material for a fuller picture, often left in unexpected bundles by the original estate managers. There is more evidence of the First Earl's ruthlessness in family affairs. He was willing largely to disinherit both his sons by his first wife to strengthen his hold on Caithness by marrying its widowed Countess, reversing this only in 1686 after wedding his second son to an heiress. Thereafter, with her marriage contract 'lost', the Countess struggled to secure her and her son's provision.[2] Predictably, many scattered items modify the picture of the complex relations between the Campbell of Glenorchy family and the Macdonalds of Glencoe. One striking example, with hindsight, is a 1657 bond signed by the future Breadalbane's father and Alasdair MacIain, the chief killed in the Massacre, and other Glencoe Macdonalds, recalling the families' friendship 'past the memorie of men', ignoring, most recently, a bloody 1646 conflict (p. 52). Its main feature is each side's promise to warn the other of any harm they heard of being planned against them, and to give assistance.[3] There were other forms of Campbell-Macdonald co-operation: one 1666 complaint listing Glencoe cattle-raiders included the son of one of Black Sir Duncan of Glenorchy's many bastards.[4] Predictably, none of the many sections contains a trace of the vital correspondence on Breadalbane's 1691 negotiations and the Massacre which vanished between 1857 and 1872.

The Scottish Catholic Archive's Blairs Letters have also been renumbered.

Other major private archives, as they become available, will modify the book in many details. Yet despite their size, the traces left by intrigues and secret activities may be fragmentary. In the Argyll family papers, for instance, only a later copy gives the instructions to and details of the negotiations of Archibald Campbell of Inverawe (MacConnochie), the 10th Earl's agent, in October and November 1691, the crucial period before the deadline (pp. 312–13), with Sir John Maclean and Lochiel (who hid his dealings more successfully, but alienated Argyll by excessive demands). A reported conversation includes the suggestion that Tarbat might be involved in rival negotiations to Breadalbane's, but leaves it unclear whether this was merely the latter's suspicions or reality.[5]

Detached items may often be crucial. A letter from the father of the Jacobite. Mackintosh of Borlum, traditionally overlooked because it is in the British rather than the National Library, gives a detailed account of events surrounding the last private clan battle, at Mulroy in 1688 between Mackintosh and Keppoch (pp. 107–8). It helps explain the Council's violent response by listing the formidable coalition which supported Keppoch in the field, allegedly more than double his 200 clansmen, and over half from other traditionally lawless clans: 200 Camerons and 80 Macmartins, 80 Glengarry and 60 Glencoe Macdonalds, 60 Ardgour Macleans, 30 Macgregors, 60 followers of Forbes of Skellater, even 20 Campbells under Keppoch's brother-in-law.[6]

I made only limited use of official records not directly connected with the events; a systematic survey would tie up many loose ends. For instance, Colonel Sir John Hill, former governor of Fort William, died at Clockmilne (a little suburb northeast of Holyrood) in April 1701. £413 9s 3d sterling owed him by the government was still unpaid in 1717; but he had managed to marry one of his three daughters to a captain in his regiment.[7] Irish official correspondence and Belfast town records, with Hill's own letters and Williamite and Jacobite pamphlets, give details of his Irish career between his two periods commanding a garrison at Inverlochy; but his early life still remains to be traced in English records.

The worst omissions in works like this are often points so basic that the author takes knowledge of them for granted. One is that King William's order to the Privy Council indemnifying all chiefs and other rebels who took the oath of allegiance by 31 December 1691 (p. 232) specified that this must be before the Council themselves or the sheriffs or sheriffs depute of their respective shires. The proclamation reproduced this; it was not stated but assumed that this should be at the head burgh of each shire. This was the crucial provision which made MacIain of Glencoe late in his last-minute hurry to submit.

Probably my worst mistake about the Macdonalds of Glencoe was the assumption (pp. 341n48, 359–60) that William's triumph again made the Argyll family their direct superiors. This sprang from the clause in William's 1691 financial concessions on the pacification, granting £150 to buy the superiority of Glencoe (it is not said from whom (*pace* p. 277), so that MacIain might hold his lands of the Crown, which would annex them to the (then non-existent) jurisdiction of Inverlochy.[8] Several Argyllshire chiefs received charters after the 9th Earl's forfaulture, invalidated by his son's restoration. Glencoe, in contrast, had been sold by the 9th Earl, though to another Campbell. The future Breadalbane, who had also hoped to buy it, accepted that the Appin Stewarts might legitimately regain an interest there. By a contract of 10 April 1672 with their chief, he had agreed, if Argyll sold him Glencoe, to resell it to him for 22,000 merks. Glenorchy's courts were to have jurisdiction there; Appin should attend him in war with 20 men and give him first refusal if he sold.[9] Argyll probably preferred to sell it to Glendaruel (p. 44) mainly because he would receive payment, unlikely in any transaction with Glenorchy. The final purchaser after the forfaulture, John Stewart fiar of Ardsheal, Tutor of Appin, received sasine of the twenty merkland of Glencoe on 2 April 1687. Sasine of his grant of Larich to Stewart of Ballachulish was registered; similar feuings-out to Macdonalds were not (p. 86).[10] The Tutor was fined for the Glencoe men's plundering after the 1685 rebellion, and one inducement with which the 10th Earl of Argyll persuaded him to submit in 1690 was assistance in obtaining recompense from them (p. 248). The 1691 proposal, which separated the feudal superiority from the land, may perhaps have applied to Argyll's ultimate authority as Appin's and Ardsheal's superior; otherwise, it is unclear whether it was intended to protect or undermine the Tutor, and it remains mysterious.

However, the correction further clarifies Breadalbane's attitude to the Glencoe Macdonalds as the Massacre approached. In his grand scheme for a 4,500-strong highland militia, the main goal of his actions throughout, which he finally unveiled about February 1692 (p. 330), the Laird of Appin was set down for 50 men, the Tutor for 30 more. Had both contingents been Appin men, it would have been a ridiculously high quota from so small a clan; and there was no historical or practical pretext (as with the Macleans) for the division. Ardsheal's men, then, would be drawn from the non-Stewart possession he held as landlord, Glencoe: this avoided naming the Macdonalds, whose reputation would have provoked protests. Breadalbane, therefore, was working to smuggle the Glencoe Macdonalds into the great militia with which he planned to dominate the Highlands — if only to avoid leaving them free to rob during crises — while Dalrymple and Livingston were organising their destruction.[11]

After the Massacre, one early step in the recovery of Glencoe was a grant from the Tutor to the new chief Iain MacIain under a charter of 17 February 1693 of the two merkland of Polveig, the two merkland of Carnoch, and Glen

Lecknamoy (where the chief's summer home was). Ranald Macdonald of Inverrigan, the settlement which had probably lost most men in the Massacre, granted sasine for him. Registration of this may have reassured the Macdonalds, inevitably suspicious, that the Tutor could not now legally evict their chief, even under government pressure, nor any enemy destroy, evidence of his rights (as may have happened during the Massacre). Other Macdonalds granted feus still preserved the deeds less formally — and less safely.[12]

The Tutor had acted throughout on his chief's behalf, and, in a series of sasines in July 1701, Glencoe was transferred to Robert Stewart of Appin.[13] His ability to count the Macdonalds among his followers made the disproportionate pension he received in Lord Treasurer Oxford's 1711–14 highland scheme, a variant on Breadalbane's, less ridiculous (p. 496). For the scheme, Iain MacIain in 1711 bought weapons to re-arm his clan, brought back from Darien, ironically by Captain Thomas Drummond's brother; for it was claimed that their previous ones had been found and carried off during the Massacre.[14] Forfaulted after the '15, Appin protested at Argyll's granting feus to Glencoe men, though it was done mainly to forestall any irrevocable grant of his estate to an outsider.[15] In 1745, the then Argyll and Breadalbane, staunch Hanoverians, restored Robert's son Dougal to his estate, including Glencoe. This doubtless made it easier, when another Ardsheal led the Appin regiment that autumn to join the Jacobites, to persuade the then MacIain of Glencoe (Appin's brother-in-law) to be its lieutenant-colonel.[16]

My most serious omission, as to both the story and analysis, arose from failing, after a surfeit of the weaker side of John Prebble's *Glencoe*,[17] to read his next, better work, *The Darien Disaster*. He had shown, contrary to my assumption (p. 437) that there was a significant highland involvement in the Scottish East India Company's two catastrophic expeditions to colonise 'Caledonia' on the Isthmus of Darien, in 1698–9 and 1699–1700; most relevantly, that the officers formerly of Argyll's regiment in the first fleet included Glenlyon's brutal second-in-command at Glencoe, Captain Thomas Drummond, who was transformed in Scottish eyes from villain to hero, and later, falsely, to martyr, by his involvement with three successive dark spots in Scottish history. There are other thematic connections. William's reaction against the act establishing the Company had destroyed the last real hope of constitutional reform (p. 422); his hostile acts against the colony, again under pressure from increasingly uncontrollable English parliaments, earned him widespread Scottish hatred and discredited his ministries. As over Glencoe, Scottish denunciations have usually overlooked the international situation. William was attempting, by the secret Partition Treaties dividing the Spanish Empire, to save Europe (Scotland included) from another war, and dared not risk offending the Spaniards further by apparent selfish aggression. Yet enough remains to justify Scottish hostility towards him, and towards the English, when his colonial governors strove to enforce prohibitions against trade with the settlers. Disease, logistical problems, immense communications difficulties,

Spain's vital strategic need to control the Isthmus, and the Company's almost supernatural ability to pick the wrong men for the highest posts (duly stressed by Prebble) would ultimately have doomed the colony; but the English imperial boycott made a fearful difference to the death-toll, still being largely enforced as, twice, leaky ships filled with sick and starving colonists abandoned Darien seeking to return home. As before Glencoe, the King's orders had failed to provide for changed circumstances.

Comparatively few highlanders contributed to the £400,000 subscriptions — made in early 1696, when the Company was still considering many promising alternative means of improving the economy — apart from the Campbells, several branches of whom subscribed. Glenorchy, temporarily his family's head, promised £2,000, £500 more than Argyll, though he actually paid little beyond the first one-quarter instalment, £593 6s 8d in all.[18] Tarbat, who subscribed £1,000, vainly warned the directors in 1697 against committing all their funds to a full-scale colony.[19] Tullibardine's £500 was originally to enable him, like other ministers, to meddle on William's behalf; but, after his dismissal, he realigned himself with his Hamilton in-laws, major oontributors and firm supporters; and his ever-luckless brother Mungo died on service in Darien.[20] Several officers of Hill's, the one regiment regularly paid, subscribed over £1,500, perhaps at the instigation of a former comrade, Major James Cunningham of Eickett (one of Hill's confidants before Glencoe), a Councillor in the first expedition — and the first to desert.[21] Many of the disbanded and unpaid officers and soldiers who formed most of the first expedition, disguised as 'overseers' and 'planters', were highlanders, including several officers of Argyll's/Lorne's former regiment. A minister on the second complained that nearly a third of its members were 'wild higlanders that cannot speak nor understand Scotch'.[22]

Robert and Thomas Drummond, younger sons of a Perthshire family which had sunk from being medieval Stewards of Strathearn to landlessness, had their own way to make. Robert took to the sea. For eight years, he was a master in American waters, Boston his main base, probably as an interloper defying the English Navigation Acts. Thomas may have assisted him. He first appears, however, in August 1688 as gunner to Robert, who was master and part-owner of a Glasgow merchantman with 16 guns — needed against North African pirates — sailing from Amsterdam to Marseilles and chartered to bring back wine. The English Navy, facing William's invasion, seized her at Dover for a fireship, and, after the Revolution, bought her for one.[23] Prudently, both brothers left the Scottish merchant marine, devastated during the war, for William's expanded army. Thomas Drummond was a lieutenant in Argyll's from at least November 1689, a captain from January 1691, of the crack grenadier company. Robert by 1697 was a lieutenant in Lord Jedburgh's dragoons.[24]

Thomas Drummond's main enemy, James Byres, claimed that when he first approached the Company, they refused to employ him because of Glencoe. If so, the influence of Robert, whose American experience gained him promotion to command the great ship *Caledonia* on the first expediton, overcame this. However, in the constant feuding, in which both brothers joined vigorously, the reproach was revived: one opponent called them and 'the present Gang' a 'Glencoe Council', and years later, Robert was mistakenly nicknamed 'Glencoe Drummond'.[25]

At Darien, in early 1699, Thomas drove the sick, half-starved colonials ruthlessly to build Fort St Andrew, vital for the settlement's survival — and its one solid relic. Unlike his brother, he strongly opposed the first expedition's decision to abandon Caledonia, but, once it was taken, saved the cannon from the fort. Most of the survivors reached New York; Robert Drummond, though cruel to them, by his seamanship brought the battered *Caledonia* to Scotland. Thomas, determined to return from New York to Darien to assist any Scottish reinforcements to re-establish the colony, illegally obtained a sloop with provisions. An admirer declared that:

> besides his capacity in giving good advice, his singular application to business, his indefatigableness in action and exercise, together with his universall mechanicall genius, with his particular skill in fortification, gunnery, and navigation, have carved him out purposely for this undertaking.[26]

He was waiting with provisions when the second expedition arrived on 30 November 1699; but for this encouragement, they would probably have fled, and Byres, their usurping leader, never forgave him. Knowing that the Spaniards were certain to attack, Drummond proposed pre-emptive strikes, in alliance with the local Indian tribes. He was among the strongest supporters of friendship with them — 'this I have seen, that he hath a greater strok with the Indians than all that are here' wrote one observer— and denounced Byres for 'vilipending' them as monkeys.[27] When Byres claimed that the colony could not support its numbers, he offered to take 150 volunteers and live with the Indians. Byres had him imprisoned for an imaginary plot. Captain Alexander Campbell of Fonab, his old comrade of Lorne's, arriving to command the Company's armed forces on 11 February 1700, released him, and he took a leading part in planning the expedition in which Fonab, with Indian help, defeated the advancing Spaniards. Drummond left to defend himself against Byres in Scotland, but, when the enemy besieged the colony, he ran their blockade with two Company supply ships from Jamaica on 1 April, to find that the colonists had just agreed to surrender. He vainly urged them to fight on, since the Spaniards also were short of provisions, and denounced the latter for seizing the colony's closest Indian ally. After the evacuation, he cruised to windward to warn any later provision ships.[28] He returned to Scotland a hero; in the 1700–1 parliament, Tullibardine, who had led the Glencoe inquiry, named him with Fonab (p. 469) in a resolve as having served the nation well.[29]

In March 1701, Captains Robert Drummond and Stewart proposed an inexpensive scheme to the financially crippled company for a profitable trade in the Indian Ocean. Refitting the two supply ships Thomas had taken to Caledonia, they would exchange European goods with the mainly English Pirates who swarmed off Madagascar for stolen East Indian produce, and also ship black slaves from Madagascar to nearby European-owned plantation islands. Such voyages had been crucial in New York's recent prosperity. They also hoped to found a trading post on the African mainland. With Thomas Drummond supercargo, they sailed in May 1701.[30] Pirates at St Mary's Island off Madagascar supplied them with slaves for the plantations on Réunion. There, in June 1702, Robert Drummond unwisely proposed to a shipwrecked pirate, Bowen, a joint attack on an English East Indiaman, giving him ideas. He then sailed to Maratanga (modern Matatene) on Madagascar, where Thomas Drummond died. Bowen, pursuing, carried off both ships and their crews, leaving the captains stranded.[31]

What with distance and pirates, the Scots remained unaware of this. Exasperated by fresh English provocation, they trumped up a charge that an English East Indiaman, the *Worcester*, whose cargo the Company wished to plunder, had pirated the ships and beheaded the Drummonds, and hanged three of its officers, despite last-minute evidence from seamen who had escaped from Bowen.[32] A 1729 book by Robert Drury, a cabin-boy enslaved for thirteen years on Madagascar, published Robert Drummond's real fate; but the modern literary mania for claiming that all interesting travel books or autobiographies by obscure figures are fictions by Daniel Defoe created doubts until one author found confirmation in the Cape Town Dutch archives. Captured by an inland chief, Drummond led the shipwrecked crew of another English East Indiaman in a daring escape attempt. He and Stewart slipped away rather than trust their pursuers' promises of safe-conduct; those who did were massacred. But Drummond could not escape from Madagascar. Embarking on a pirate ship, as Stewart did, would make him legally a pirate. Other ships called haphazardly, and most charged high prices for passage. If he got word home, the Company probably preferred a dead hero to a live encumbrance. He sank into a beachcomber, and was killed by a black Jamaican.[33]

A modern argument claims that attitudes towards Celtic peoples within the British Isles shaped colonialist treatment of other races in the Empire and American West. This wide-ranging story is a reminder that it can be applied too simplistically, especially in the early stages. Thomas Drummond slaughtered highland fellow-Scots. He allied himself closely with the Darien Indians, the wisest step in an infant colony. He treated some black Africans as commodities. Had the mainland trading post been established, he would have wooed others to buy Scottish cloth. Circumstances rather than fixed attitudes determined his actions; the parallel with Drake and Hawkins is close. The road from Glencoe to Wounded Knee or Amritsar is not straight and clear. Racial barriers are often more obvious, historians would admit, in preventing any idea of sympathy between fellow-sufferers. Drury used his painfully-acquired knowledge of Madagascar, his one asset, in the slave trade to the far crueller plantations.[34]

The old view of the Massacre rested on mythical absolute polarisations, not only Campbells *v.* Macdonalds but Campbells *v.* Jacobites. This revisionist work's fitting conclusion is therefore the '15, in which Clan Campbell was split in two; and my qualifications (pp. 421, 498) on Breadalbane's involvement should mostly be removed. His death in May 1717, like Campbell of Calder's, saved his family from serious trouble. Admittedly, he had occasionally changed sides in Anne's reign, and, like everybody, had submitted in 1714. He had formally transferred his estates to Glenorchy, who remained blamelessly in Caithness throughout; but, as so often, family political 'balancing' reflected personal hostility. Blanket destruction of correspondence merely leaves conspicuous Breadalbane's October 1715 orders raising two battalions, one commanded by Barcaldine's son, and urging them forwards on the western campaign. Setbacks and disappointments as to numbers sprang largely from last-minute defections by the then Campbells of Lochnell and Auchinbreck, and counter-measures by Glenorchy's supporters. Duncan Menzies again acted for Breadalbane in the main camp.[35] Doubt of his initial commitment derives from the vivid description in the Master of Sinclair's cynical *Memoirs* of his visit to the Jacobite camp at Perth while the rising floundered, ironically advising them, since they would not fight, to print propaganda, and with 'a way of laughing inwardlie which was verie perceptible.' Yet the laughter was probably largely directed at himself: to have stayed on the fence despite Dundee, and then, at eighty, to come off it for Mar, merited ridicule.[36]

NOTES

All references to the Breadalbane Papers use the new numbering. Abbreviations will be found later in the book. Sources used only here are not in the bibliography.

1. SRO GD 112/43/25/3, Proposed regiment and auxiliaries, [1685].
2. *Ib.*, /3/74/7, /3/75/1, 3, 5–6, /3/76/9–10, 12, /3/78/3–4, /3/84/7, /3/88/2.
3. *Ib.*, /43/10/11, Bond, 21 Jan. 1657.
4. *Ib.*, /2/141/36, Supplication by James Menzies of Shian, [1666].
5. Inveraray Castle, Argyll Papers, bundle 50, Argyll to cousin, 25 Nov. 1691; *ib.*, bundle 473 no. 220, Copies of Instructions, etc., in Argyll's 1691 transaction with Maclean, [copy after 1701]. (I owe these references to Major Nicolas Maclean Bristol.)
6. BL Add. 39,200 fols. 2–3, 4–8, W. Mackintosh of Borlum to Duke of Gordon, 17 Aug. 1688 + 19thc. copy.
7. SRO CC 8/8/86 fols. 322v–323, Testament dative, 20 June 1717.
8. *CSPD 1690–1*, 492, Financial concessions, 17/27 Aug. 1691.
9. SRO GD 112/43/12/3, Articles of agreement, Glenorchy the younger and D. Stewart of Appin, 10 Apr. 1672.

10. SRO RS 10/2 fols. 184–5.

11. Dalrymple, *Memoirs*, ii, 220, Breadalbane, 'Proposals concerning the Highlanders', [Jan.–Feb. 1692].

12. Macdonald, *Clan Donald*, iii, 217–18; SRO RS 10/2 fols. 382–3.

13. *Ib.*, RS 3/79 fols. 296–303.

14. PRO SP 55/1, 28–31, A. Macdonald of Bracklett's petition, and proceedings, Dec. 1713.

15. SRO GD 112/39/279/27, P. Campbell of Barcaldine to A. Campbell of Monzie, 25 Dec. 1720.

16. A. Stewart, 'The Last Chief: Dougal Stewart of Appin (died 1764)', *SHR*, [xxvi, (1977), 205&n. 13, 20&&n. 33.

17. For instance: even if the idea that the meaning of the name 'Glencoe' refers to 'weeping' is wrong, it is misleading to sneer at his — our — fellow non-Gaelic speaker Macaulay as having invented it from sentimentality. A priest who was there with Montrose in 1645, well before the Massacre, was told that it meant 'moist, as with tears or rain.' Prebble, *Glencoe*, 22; Forbes Leith *Scottish Catholics*, i; 317. No review pointed out my ignorance of *The Darien Disaster*.

18. Prebble, *The Darien Disaster*, (London, 1968), 57, 59; NLS MS Adv. 83.1.6 p. 27; *The Darien Papers...1695–1700*, ed. J. Hill Burton, (Bannatyne Club, 1849), 391–2, 395–6, 401–2, 405.

19. *Ib.*, 375, 378; NLS MS Adv. 83.7.4 fol. 58, Tarbat to Drumelziar, 3 Dec. 1697.

20. Prebble, *Darien Disaster*, 93, 163, 290, 310–11.

21. *Ib.*, 59, 102, 150, 156; *Darien Papers*, 375, 385, 396, 416; NLS MS Adv. 83.1.6 pp. 3, 14, 24, 26–7; SRO GD 406/bundle 633, Hill's deposition, 2 July 1695. However, Cpt. James Montgomerie, Councillor on the first expedition, was not one of Hill's officers but a wartime deserter to the Jacobites in Flanders. Major John Lindsay, Councillor on the second, was not the Lt Lindsay who had taken part in the Massacre. Dalton, *English Army Lists*, iii, 44–5; Prebble, *Darien Disaster*, 110, 229n.

22. *Ib.*, 91–2, 99–101, 250.

23. William Drummond Viscount Strathallan, *The Genealogy of the Most Noble and Ancient House of Drummond*, (Glasgow, 1883), 39–50; *CTB*, ix, 100, 137; *Darien Shipping Papers, 1696–1707*, ed. G. P. Insh, (SHS, 1924), 117; NLS MS Adv. 83.7.5 fol. 50, R. Drummond to Company, 29 Dec. 1699; *ib.*, MS Adv. 83.7.3, nos. 1–4.

24. *APS*, xi, App., 61.

25. James Byres, *A Letter to a Friend at Edinburgh from Roterdam*, (1701), 151; Sir R. C. Temple, *New Light on the Mysterious Tragedy of the 'Worcester' 1704–1705*, (London, 1930), 319; SRO RH 4/135/1 (Journals of Company's Court of Directors, microfilm)/1, pp. 395, 495; *ib.*, GD 45/1/159, W. Murdoch to J. Anderson, 19 Oct. 1699 (apparently the origin of Prebble's 'the Glencoe Gang', *Darien Disaster*, 103, 125 etc.)

26. *Darien Papers*, 156–7, S. Veitch to W. Veitch, 20 Sept. 1699; lb., 144–5, 152–6, 158–9, 181, 189, 192–5, 197–200; Prebble, *Darien Disaster*, 102–3, 110–11, 124–7, 131, 142, 150, 152, 156, 170, 184–92, 195, 198–202, 206, 208, 210–15.

27. *Ib.*, 237–8; *Darien Papers*, 220, 233, 250.

28. *Ib.*, 200–1, 203–6, 210–13, 218–28, 232–40, 250–1, 258–9, 302, 311, 313, 317–18, 322, 332, 353–4; Prebble, *Darien Disaster*, 238–46, 251, 264–5, 298–9, 301, 304–5, 327.

29. *Ib.*, 310.

30. SRO RH 4/135/1/3, 1, 4 Mar., 18 Apr. 1701; *Darien Shipping Papers*, xxi; H.C.V. Leibbrandt, *Precis of the Archives of the Cape of Good Hope: Letters Despatched 1696–1708*, (Cape Town, 1896), 186–7; University of London Library, MS 63 no. 12, [anon], 'Proposals to the Honourable Companie of Scotland...for Establishing a trade to Madagascar', [*c.* 1700].

31. Temple, 134–7, 267, 271–3; A.W. Secord, *Robert Drury's Journal*, (Urbane, Ill., 1961), 28–9.

32. Prebble, *Darien Disaster*, 1–9, 312–14.

33. For Defoe, see p.224n49. Secord, 28–37, 43–4, 58–9.

34. *Ib.*, 39–41; B. Lenman, *The Jacobite Clans of the Great Glens*, (London, 1984), 195–6, 199–200, 205; J. Hunter, *Glencoe and the Indians*, (Edinburgh, 1996), 52–3, 67, 73, 109–10, 123–6. This uses, *ib.*, 60–1, the old rather than the true immediate context of the Massacre to bolster its argument.

35. SRO GD 112/39/272/25–6; *ib.*, 112/43/25/1–2, 8–9; *HMCR Stuart*, iv, 17; *lb.*, 46–9, 51, John Cameron of Lochiel's paper, 24 June 1716.

36. Master of Sinclair, *Memoirs*, 185–7, 260.

Introduction: Sources and Acknowledgements

The Massacre of Glencoe has been much written about and little studied; and the state of the sources is both a cause and consequence of this.

The primary source for our knowledge has always been the Report prepared by the Scottish government in 1695 and unofficially published in 1703. Manuscript copies circulated of the two relevant orders signed by King William, the letters of Secretary Sir John Dalrymple, Master of Stair, and varying numbers of other letters produced before the 1695 Commission. However, the sworn depositions and other items it studied — including some which might otherwise survive among the Privy Council records — remained with Alexander Munro of Bearcrofts, Clerk to the Commission, whose uprooted descendants would scarcely keep irrelevant archives.[1] Besides giving fresh information, this material might indicate the Report's real bias. It has always been assumed that its main political purpose (besides whitewashing William himself) was to discredit Dalrymple, and that evidence implicating the other main suspect, the Campbell Earl of Breadalbane, was merely incidental — and therefore the more damaging. In fact, it was the damning information about Dalrymple which was, in one sense, incidental. The Report was shaped to attack Breadalbane, and its framers communicated the suspicions they failed to prove to historians, who needed an Iago with private motives to remove the blame still further from William.[2] A counter-tradition of Jacobite propaganda portrayed the Massacre as typical of William, and, later, of the whole post-Revolution government in Scotland. Its first reports ensured that the Massacre would not go unnoticed outside the Highlands; but, after these, it provided no fresh information. With one exception: Prince Charles Edward during his occupation of Edinburgh published in the *Caledonian Mercury* not only existing Jacobite pamphlets but the 1695 parliamentary Address and minutes.[3]

The most comprehensive known copy of the orders and letters, possibly belonging to the Stair family, was acquired by an early nineteenth-century antiquarian, who made transcripts of other relevant items, chiefly from the Register House. In 1845, after his death, the Maitland Club printed his collection, with additions. The volume, including the 1695 Report, has been the central source for later writers; a dangerous one, telling a coherent story, leaving the illusion that no more major items remained to find, and overlooking some already printed which hinted at the less coherent truth.[4]

The other main source for the Massacre, as for many highland events, has been Gaelic oral tradition, which at its best can preserve not only the memory of major events but details unexpectedly confirmed by later research. This has almost always portrayed the Massacre as the result of Campbell clan hatred for the Macdonalds. Yet even the oldest tradition on the causes of an unforeseen treachery

1

must be deduction rather than certainty. If the true cause was outside the knowledge of the stunned survivors, trying to understand why they had been singled out, they might, and their successors certainly would, shape events within their knowledge into a misleadingly logical pattern leading up to the horror.

Another nearby miscarriage of justice provides a clear example of this reshaping of the past. The judicial murder of James Stewart, 'James of the Glens', tried as accessory to the assassination of Campbell of Glenure before the Duke of Argyll and a Campbell jury, has obscured the fact that, until government orders forced Glenure to start evicting the tenants on the forfeited estates, he and James were friends. The prosecution's papers show far more plausible suspects 'remembering' by degrees in prison threats James had allegedly made long before against Glenure. Yet these threats have passed into tradition and literature as exemplifying their relations.[5] Hindsight affected the Glencoe traditions even of the events of the Massacre, with stories of soldiers warning their hosts long before, historically, they themselves knew of the plan. And, in telling and re-telling, other original memories received the satisfactory rounding-out of folklore. The relations of a clansman MacIain, the chief, had once killed happened to enlist in the company which was to commit the Massacre; the soldier who spared the baby had to cut off its finger, making possible a later recognition scene.

Even on subjects less controversial than Glencoe, the same problem in using tradition as a historical source exists, the gradual change in memories. 'Tradition has no power of preserving History entire', wrote one of the most constant and scrupulous highland collectors.[6] When an event's historical significance was obvious, constant re-telling may produce many, sometimes contradictory, variants. When its wider meaning could not be known locally, the vivid detail may be all the historical fact that survives: Mull tradition, which remembered that a marauding English frigate shipwrecked in 1690 drifted to her doom stern-first (a fact archaeology has confirmed), claims that she was sent from Spain to avenge the destruction of the Tobermory Galleon and was sunk by witches.[7] Another element in this oral culture, the Gaelic poetry written by contemporaries, is historical evidence as good as most documents; but the traditions attached to poems, explaining and commenting on the events they treat, often contradict plain statements in the poems themselves.[8]

The distinction just made between written sources and tradition is, of course, a partly artificial one. The earliest and most valuable 'traditions' about the Massacre were taken down three years later to form the basis of the Report. The culture of highland gentry was, in a greater or lesser degree, written and Scottish as well as oral and Gaelic. Their views of Glencoe (and, through them, those of many ordinary highlanders) would be influenced by the Jacobite propagandists, who made it one of their staple topics, and by information from the Report and interested lowlanders. One of the most fruitful forms of historical research in the Highlands, the combining of written evidence and oral tradition, was already flourishing in the 1730s, when John Drummond of Balhaldie wrote the life of his grandfather Sir Ewen Cameron of Lochiel, employing the family papers, clan traditions and poetry, some central government records — and a Latin epic on

Dundee's 1689 campaign, an example of another culture highlander and lowlander might share.

Yet Jacobitism and family piety gravely distorted Balhaldie's work. He turned Lochiel, who during much of his long career preserved his and his clan's prosperity by profitable balancing between the Stuarts and their enemies and between the Campbells and the Macdonald–Maclean coalition opposing them, into a constant loyalist and a straightforward, reliable supporter of his neighbours. The text sometimes revealed the strain.[9] This also, unfortunately, became a tradition. Much writing on the highland past has been in the form of clan histories. These usually ignored the wider context of general changes in the Highlands, and partly as a result, many until comparatively recently were uncritical defences, minimising or simply ignoring unflattering evidence about the more dubious episodes, and relying excessively on the clan's own favourable traditions.

Small-scale studies outside the clan strait-jacket were often more valuable. In 1886, a Glenlyon man combined the glen's Gaelic traditions and some surviving papers of Robert Campbell of Glenlyon, the officer commanding at the Massacre, to throw lurid light on his and Breadalbane's financial relations, and to find reasons for the Massacre in recent local grudges over Jacobite raids, rather than general Campbell–Macdonald hatreds — in his words 'Some Historical Reasons why Campbell of Glenlyon and the Earl of Breadalbane hated the Macdonalds of Glencoe'. His book has provided the framework for every study since.[10] Unfortunately, another collection of Glenlyon's papers shows that the local traditions about his ruin and those responsible, though perhaps contemporary, were mistaken guesswork; and that in formally listing his Jacobite oppressors in 1690, he was capable of forgetting the Glencoe men.[11] The moral, that a study of fragmentary evidence may produce misleading results, is a platitude in historical study; but it is particularly important in dealing with highland history in the late seventeenth century, a period of extreme ruthlessness and cunning intrigue masked by vigorous protestations of honesty and legal forms. Individual sources may provide unique glimpses of plots and counter-plots unrecorded elsewhere.

As Breadalbane's part in the affair is the most mysterious, one obvious place to seek a partial solution is his papers. Their existence and possible significance has been known since the later eighteenth-century historian Sir John Dalrymple published his *Memoirs of Great Britain*, printing vitally important documents from state and private archives. The Breadalbane items consisted largely of a selection from Secretary Dalrymple's letters to Breadalbane in late 1691, ending with several expressing such intense hostility towards the highlanders that it seemed natural to assume that Breadalbane's missing replies must have been equally violent to have provoked them.[12] Later historians' treatment of the collection has been strange. The then Marquess of Breadalbane offered to let Macaulay use it for the passage in his *History* on Glencoe. Macaulay replied warning him that he had already formed his hostile view of the Earl, and, although he accepted the invitation, failed in the event to consult the documents. He gained permission for John Hill Burton to print two more of Dalrymple's letters in his *History of*

Scotland, but, as Hill Burton admitted, the relevant passages in his text were finished before he saw them.[13] Macaulay's account elaborated the standard Williamite interpretation in which the wicked Breadalbane from private vindictiveness secretly plied Dalrymple with accusations and misrepresentations against the Macdonalds until he was roused to a furious determination to punish them, unsuspected by William or other Scots.[14] The collection was made available to the reviewer of Macaulay for the *Edinburgh Review*, who printed another selection of documents from late 1691 which made this view untenable — or would have done, if they had not been overlooked ever since.[15]

It was the last chance to consult the complete political correspondence, for, at some time before the Historical Manuscripts Commission studied the collection in 1872, a large proportion — how large is uncertain, for lack of a catalogue — was quietly creamed off and sold; and although items exist in Scottish public collections, the whereabouts of the rest, including nearly all previously printed letters, is unknown.[16] The bulk of the collection is in the Scottish Record Office, including Breadalbane's confidential letters to his Edinburgh writer. These were first used in 1938 by a local historian to question the accepted story.[17] His lead has occasionally been followed; but, in comparison to the collection's estate records, the correspondence has been neglected.

Elsewhere, also, there is evident this dead response to possible leads to new information, such as that in the 1887 Historical Manuscripts Commission report on the Duke of Hamilton's manuscripts: 'a few papers relating ... to the Glencoe massacre' — one of them the missing 1693 report.[18] The strong emotions which Glencoe still arouses apparently find other expressions. With a few honourable exceptions, writers on it have been amateurs in the sense of not using academic historians' methods, but not in the sense of feeling a burning personal determination to do the subject full justice. This has passed unnoticed largely because popular Scottish history has always rested more on a mingling of several exceptionally strong (though sometimes contradictory) popular traditions — (diluted) highland, Covenanting, border, pre-Enlightenment Edinburgh — than on documentation. One consequence of the nineteenth-century opening of archives was the ferocious battles over fundamental differences of interpretation — 'Bloody Claver'se' or 'Bonnie Dundee', for instance — between historians upholding popular traditions and opponents relying on newly unearthed documents, whose authority they often upheld with unhistorical literal-mindedness. The arguments over Glencoe often had their unconscious ironies: when Macaulay depicted the glen as a grim 'valley of the shadow of death', made for tragedy — the (unconscious) corollary being that it was his hero William's bad luck that he was the man chosen to provide one — his chief opponent emphasised its prosperity and fertility by describing the loud bleating of the sheep.[19] Yet both sides went to the *Highland Papers* for their basic facts, and the startling new material the disputes had uncovered went unnoticed. Even in recent years, academic historians have very seldom challenged the popular writers' accounts of the Massacre or its background.[20] This is partly because William's reign has been, until recently, a generally neglected and puzzling area; partly because academics have become, to a dangerous extent, 'too proud to fight'; but mainly because the subject is so bound up with Jacobitism.

There are major difficulties in studying the first period of Jacobitism, from 1688 until the death of James II and VII in exile in 1701. The main archive for the period until 1713, deposited in the Scots College at Paris, was almost totally destroyed in the French Revolution.[21] Except perhaps for one incident, the 'Montgomerie Plot', no independent Scottish printed collections match those for Anne's reign, the 'Scots Plot' papers, Hooke's *Negotiations*, Lockhart's *Memoirs*. Yet the well-documented official biography of James, and a Scottish Undersecretary's papers, the most important of which were printed by James 'Ossian' Macpherson, provide a focus round which large amounts of scattered material in Britain and France could be assembled to construct a fairly coherent picture.[22]

However, English historians determined to defend the credit of politicians and other prominent persons involved in negotiations with the Jacobites have long denied the validity of the material, claiming that it is either forged — as is all the evidence government spies produced against them — or the groundless imaginings of optimistic Jacobites; or that the prominent figures were merely 'reinsuring' themselves by insincere advances in case of a restoration; for, after all, the Jacobite movement, except when foolish Scottish highlanders momentarily gave it life, was of no real political significance. Modified for some periods, this is still very much the orthodoxy for the 1690s. Examples certainly exist of false accusations and of insincere advances; they do not prove that all accusations were false or that other men's advances — or even the same men's, in radically different circumstances — were insincere; yet this is the convenient assumption made. Even if the early Jacobite movement was, ultimately, insignificant at a national level, it might be of vital importance for understanding a famous individual, a parliamentary session or a campaign. When, in these special cases also, the possibility is not even noticed and no knowledge is shown of the evidence, it becomes clear that the dismissive general judgements are not based on rational assessment, constantly checked against fresh findings, but on dogmatic, complacent ignorance. The normal research method to test unusual statements, checking other relevant source collections for any confirmation, is laid aside. These historians restrict themselves to Macpherson and the *Life of James* to make total dismissal of their (inevitably incomplete) evidence easier. To the new material which nevertheless occasionally appears, they apply the Maclean tactics of 1689–90 against pursuing cavalry — knock the facts individually on the head as they straggle up, rather than waiting for them to assemble in order before testing their strength.

In consequence, there has been almost no study of the Jacobite movement of the 1690s, and of its British and European context. This immediately devalues the Highland War of 1689–91, since it was largely that context which gave it meaning. The English, French and Irish Jacobite sources have remained largely uncharted; and it has inevitably been a hit-or-miss business whether Scottish writers on the war and the Massacre can discover the relevant material. It is tempting to assume that the only outside events of importance were those already known, and that everything can be explained in purely Scottish terms. As the evidence on the lowland Jacobite movement is buried in English sources, its intrigues, which several times crucially influenced highland events, must largely be omitted.

Even if such limitations are allowed for, no balanced study has been made of the war. The reasons are artistic rather than historical. Rather than mounting to some tragic Culloden for a climax, it petered out, so that the catastrophe of Glencoe scarcely seems connected with it; and the most important figure, Dundee, was killed almost at the start. His biographies have trotted round the Highlands at his horse's heels, without explaining his more general strategy or hopes; and, after Killiecrankie, other accounts take a flying leap for the Massacre of Glencoe, with contemptuous glances downwards at the defeats at Dunkeld and Cromdale.

The explanation usually given for this gap is that the war was unimportant, since the Jacobite defeat was inevitable. This may well be true, but it should not remove the need for an account: defeat reveals truths about causes and their supporters which prosperity hides; and an investigation would at least throw new light on the preliminaries of Glencoe. Yet, even if the final outcome was certain, some historians show a desperate eagerness to declare the Jacobite cause stone-dead: from the start, after Killiecrankie, after Dunkeld and (with more justification) after Cromdale. This may be partly an understandable reaction against the might-have-beens of sentimental Jacobitism, and they make the same labour-saving assumption about other rebellions of the period, such as Argyll's; but they emphasise the hopelessness of the Jacobite cause with alarming vehemence, and with some distortion of facts. Some imply that the supporters, ultimately inadequate to reconquer a kingdom, who joined Dundee were the only ones who ever could have joined him — as if, in one extreme case, an angel with a flaming sword would have checked Clan Chisholm's march to join him if the collapse of his north-eastern campaign had not — without adding the necessary qualification that areas which had refused him recruits furnished them to his successors. They always accept a dismissive remark about Jacobite activity at face value, even when the circumstances of the utterer — for example, an outmanoeuvred general denying that his successful opponent's plans were at all dangerous — make it suspect. They not only emphasise the Jacobites' defeats, but argue, implausibly, that they had no logical reason for turning up at the battlefields. When the motives of one side are presented as continuously irrational, it indicates that no attempt has been made to understand them.

These historians' arguments may be discounted for two reasons. The first is that they have not grasped the basic shape of the war. Certainly, as they mention, Dundee's incompetent successors dealt the Jacobite cause devastating blows. But this was not a case, as in the months before Culloden, of the existing regime reviving in power as a rebellion declined. Instead, the Jacobite rebellion and the new, unpopular, impoverished Williamite regime declined in strength together, and it remained an open question until fairly late which of the two would collapse first. Many who would not join the Jacobite cause from support for James did so, after its worst defeats, from hostility to the 'presbyterian' government. The second is that too little basic research has been done until now on the war to give generalisations about it much value. The Highland Army's main archives, for instance, captured at Cromdale, are in the Scottish Record Office, containing much evidence on the'chiefs' actions and attitudes after Killiecrankie: they have not been examined. One consequence of this lack of research is that, in a shooting war lasting for under two years and confined almost entirely to the highland areas of six or seven shires, historians have succeeded in totally or almost totally overlooking four campaigns. When the basic account of events contains such gaps, it is unlikely that the more difficult task of placing the Highland War and the Massacre of Glencoe in their real Scottish and European contexts has been carried out. The uncovering of new material is unlikely to change the consensus, for it is the emotional conviction, that the Jacobites *could* never have succeeded, which forms its real basis.

Study of Glencoe and its background must, then, be freed from three unconscious assumptions, two amateur, one academic; they may appear absurd when set out, but the warning is necessary, since the dangerous familiarity of the incident directs thought into well-worn channels. The first is that there was a Massacre of Glencoe scheduled months in advance for 13 February 1692, and that persons whose actions helped bring it about, even indirectly, must have performed them with that intention. The second is that documents which are in print and famous are *automatically* of superior authority to those of the same class still in manuscript or printed in obscure places; thus the deductions drawn from Dalrymple's notorious letters to Breadalbane of how Breadalbane must have replied need not be modified by the recent discovery of the actual replies. The third is largely founded on the academic bias in favour of dullness: that because Dundee was a handsome man on a fine horse, he was obviously 'romantic' and impractical, and that therefore cunning politicians such as Breadalbane could never seriously consider joining him, even as one possibility among several; that his skilful exploitation of shoestring resources and sublimation of his own interests in tireless exertion for a cause could not even temporarily cast doubt on the final triumph of the various egomaniacs, bigots and embezzlers who ruled the roost at Edinburgh.

This introduction has unfortunately had to concentrate on shortcomings; and my own are also relevant. Dealing with a matter of emotional interest to Scots, I am not a Scot; I have very little personal familiarity with the Highlands; most serious of all, I know no Gaelic. The highlanders expressed their feelings on events primarily in their poetry, but I can study only those poems and extracts which others have translated. For this reason, there will doubtless be some inconsistency in my use of the conventions used for transliteration of Gaelic names into English, and my choice between these transliterated Christian names and their English equivalents: the murdered chief of Glencoe's son and heir, for instance, is for the sake of easier recognition always called Iain MacIain, even though he inscribed J.M. for John Macdonald on his new house.

My first thanks must be to the Masters and Fellows of Peterhouse for electing me to a Stone Research Fellowship, which made possible the writing of this book;

and to my late father, for financial and moral support during my first researches, when it seemed that enough unknown material might exist on Glencoe for a short article. I owe particular thanks to the staff of the Scottish National Register of Archives for the considerable time and trouble they have taken to help me; to the staffs of the Scottish Record Office, the National Library of Scotland, and other libraries and archives where I have worked; and to Trinity College Library, Cambridge, for allowing the long loan of books which I needed to consult constantly. For pointing out out-of-the-way sources to me, I thank Dr. Evelyn Cruickshanks, Dr. Jeremy Black, Ian Fisher, Mrs Zélide Cowan and (*fiat justitia*) Professor Edward Gregg. I am obliged to Dr. John Maclean for permission to use his translations of Gaelic poems, from his Ph.D. thesis 'The Sources, particularly the Celtic sources, for the history of the Highlands in the seventeenth century'; and, for permission to use, cite and quote from the manuscripts, to the Duke of Atholl, the Dukes of Buccleuch and Argyll, the Marquess of Bute, the Earl of Moray, the Earl of Cawdor and the Trustees of the Portland Estate and Nottingham University Department of Manuscripts; and to Major-General Sir Humphry Tollemache (although, from lack of time, I have seen only the extracts in the typescript catalogue of his collection). One major collection, that of the Duke of Argyll, is at present unavailable to researchers.

I have made particular use of three previous books in writing this one. The first is David Stevenson's *Alasdair MacColla and the Highland Problem in the Seventeenth Century*. The second is P. W. J. Riley's *King William and the Scottish Politicians*, from which I have borrowed the terms 'presbyterian' and 'episcopalian' as applied to members of the political factions using religion for their rallying-cry. The third, John Prebble's *Glencoe: the story of the Massacre*, is the best and most influential of the popular histories, and therefore, ironically, the one whose statements I most often have to contradict; but Prebble first raised several very important questions, even though I often have to disagree with his answers.

Finally, I thank my typist, Mrs. Audrey Brooks, for successfully producing the typescript of this book, despite the Balzacian extent of my rewriting.

NOTES

1. Scottish Record Office (SRO) GD 406 (Duke of Hamilton) bundle 633, 'Memorial of the proceedings in parliament in relation to the affair of Glencoe ... 1695'; A. Mackenzie, *History of the Munros of Fowlis* (Inverness, 1898), 310–35.

2. G. Burnet, *History of his own time*, ed. M. J. Routh, 6 vols. (Oxford, 1833), iv, 157–61.

3. *Recueil des Nouvelles Ordinaires et Extraordinaires (Gazette de France)*, 12 Apr. 1692(NS), 175–6, Edinburgh report, 23 Mar. (NS); C. Leslie, *Gallienus Redivivus* ('Edinburgh', 1695); *Caledonian Mercury*, Nos. 3899–3910.

4. For some reason, they omitted the last of Dalrymple's letters to Hill. *Papers Illustrative of the Political Condition of the Highlands of Scotland (Highland Papers)*, ed. J. Gordon (Maitland Club, 1845), iii–v, 52; Glasgow University Library (UL), MS Gen. 1274, W. Macgregor Stirling transcripts; *ib.*, MS Gen. 1577, Contemporary copies of letters.

5. Lt-Gen. Sir W. MacArthur, 'The Appin Murder', *The Stewarts*, ix (1952), 88–90f, 93, 96, 102–5; *The Dewar Manuscripts, Vol. I*, trans. H. Maclean, ed. Rev. J. Mackechnie (Glasgow, 1964), 205, 208–9.

6. J. F. Campbell of Islay. *Ib.*, 25–6.

7. See Chapter 7, pp. 248–9, 260n121.

8. For example, Iain Lom's fiery poem of joy at the avenging in 1665 of the Keppoch murder makes it clear that he was still in exile after being driven from Keppoch for his calls for justice; but detailed traditions portray him as taking a leading part in the actual fight — a logical storyteller's development. *Orain Iain Luim, Songs of John Macdonald, bard of Keppoch*, ed. A. M. Mackenzie (Edinburgh, 1964), 128–31, 'An Ciaran Mabach'; Rev. A. & Rev. A. Macdonald, *The Clan Donald*, 3 vols. (Inverness 1896––1904), ii, 637, iii, 573.

9. His account of Lochiel's part in Argyll's feud with the Macleans, for instance, could not survive even a bare statement of its dates. J. Drummond of Balhaldie, *Memoirs of Sir Ewen Cameron of Locheill, (Memoirs of Locheill)*, ed. J. MacKnight (Maitland Club, 1842), 165–6, 200–4, 308.

10. D. Campbell, *The Lairds of Glenlyon. Historical Sketches relating to the district of Appin, Glenlyon and Breadalbane* (Perth, 1886), 31–65; G. Gilfillan, etc., *The Massacre of Glencoe* (Stirling, 1912), 50.

11. SRO GD 170/133/117, Glenlyon's petition to Parliament, 1690.

12. Sir J. Dalrymple, *Memoirs of Great Britain and Ireland*, 3 vols. (London, 1771–88), ii, 'Appendix to Part II', 210–21.

13. *The Letters of T. B. Macaulay*, ed. T. Pinney, v (Cambridge, 1981), 313–14, Macaulay to J. Hill Burton, 26 Feb. 1853; J. Hill Burton, *A History of Scotland . . . 1689–1748*, 2 vols. (London, 1853), i, 525–8.

14. T. B. Macaulay, *A History of England from the Accession of James II*, ed. Sir C. Firth, 6 vols. (London, 1913–15), v, 2143–66; Sir G. O. Trevelyan, *The Life and Letters of Lord Macaulay* (London, 1908), 503–4.

15. [Sir James Moncreiff], Review, '*A History of England . . . by . . . Macaulay, Vols. III and IV'*, *Edinburgh Review*, ([Moncreiff], 'Macaulay's *History*', *ER*), cv (Jan.-Apr. 1857), 172–8.

16. Collections containing items include SRO GD 50 (John Macgregor Collection), National Library of Scotland (NLS) MS 3134. *Historical Manuscripts Commission Reports (HMCR) 4th Report*, 513; SRO GD 112 (Breadalbane Collection) /43/1/1/49, list of papers on the Massacre and Breadalbane's trial, 1872.

17. W. A. Gillies, *In Famed Breadalbane* (Perth, 1938), 166–71.

18. *HMCR. Hamilton*, 194.

19. Macaulay, *History*, v, 2146–7; Trevelyan, *Macaulay*, 497; J. Paget, *The New Examen* ([London], 1934), 42–3.

20. One odd exception has been the dispute between Ferguson and Prebble over the religion of the Glencoe Macdonalds. W. Ferguson, 'Religion and the Massacre of Glencoe', *Scottish Historical Review (SHR)*, xlvi (1967), 82–7; J. Prebble, 'Religion and the Massacre of Glencoe', *ib.*, 185–8; W. Ferguson, 'Religion and the Massacre of Glencoe', *ib.*, xlvii (1968), 203–9. Prebble, the amateur, seems here to be right.

21. Some tiny fragments are in the Edinburgh Scottish Catholic Archives (SCA) Blairs Letters.

22. *Life of James II*, ed. J. S. Clarke, 2 vols. (London, 1816); J. Macpherson, *Original Papers containing the secret history of Great Britain*, 2 vols. (London, 1775).

1

The Highlanders and the Nation (1590–1660)

At Charles II's restoration in 1660, the bulk of the nobility and greater gentry of Scotland, the nation's traditional rulers, faced financial ruin. Even in the pre-war period, their indebtedness had been increasing. Then came nearly two decades of warfare, in which they equipped and maintained armies, directly or through loans and taxes, and often had their estates ravaged: the Bishops' Wars, the armies in Ulster and England, Montrose's campaigns, the Engagement, the resistance to Cromwell, Glencairn's Rising — several of them civil wars in which Scottish resources were wasted on both sides. The Cromwellian regime deliberately set out to break their power. The rigorous laws of debt allowed 'apprisings', compulsory 'wadsets' (mortgages) of estates, which made the raising of redemption money very difficult, and it was the new judges' enforcement of these which drove many nobles in despair to join Glencairn. The rising forced General Monck to modify the policy and allow them some share in government. Yet in 1658 Robert Baillie lamented:

> Our Noble families are almost gone; Lennox hes little in Scotland unsold; Hamilton's estate ... is sold; Argyle can pay little annuel rent for seven or eight hundred thousand merkes, and he is no more drowned in debt than publict hatred, almost of all, both Scottish and English; the Gordons are gone; the Douglasses little better ... many of our chief families states are crashing; nor is there any appearance of any human relief ... [1]

Even after Charles's return restored their status, the problem remained. In the impoverished and humiliated nation to which they referred almost automatically as 'poor Scotland' and 'our poor country', with its comparatively backward agriculture, undeveloped economy and restricted overseas trade, few could reduce their debts to a safe level and secure their family positions by normal exploitation of their estates. One noble realistically prayed to be preserved from ill-gotten gain, 'for if my hands once get it, my heart will never part with it'. Most of them heaped up further debts by large-scale rebuilding and purchase of luxuries, often imported at great expense from England: this was partly a conscious policy of re-establishing their status before the public through conspicuous consumption, but it further undermined their financial foundations.[2]

Immediately on regaining authority, this ruling class moved to crush anyone who might ever again threaten it. The presbyterian church, blamed as the root of all disorder, was replaced by episcopacy; and, when the bishops imagined that this gave them independent spiritual authority, an Act of Supremacy whipped them into place. The lesser gentry might again seek power, through Parliament: the government-controlled guiding committee, the Articles, was given almost total power over it. The royal burghs might show independence: dictatorial, corrupt

Provosts were imposed on them. Besides fear, the ruling class felt anxiety to restrict access to three potential sources of fortune. The first was the profits of high office, which no other form of income could match. The second was repayment of wartime expenditure; as Charles had, at one time or another, recognised almost every regime as legitimate, this would be done by favour, not logic. The third, fines and forfeitures, must provide the bulk of the rewards for eager nobles, 'mostly younger, bred in want, when their fathers were pinched by their creditors, ... having no hope but in the king's favour'. In Scotland, with its tiny revenue, they could not, like their English counterparts, hope for rewards from other sources (except, briefly, for commissions in a large permanent army to be employed in holding down the Presbyterians). They knew that they must ruin and destroy others, or be destroyed by their own debts, and the knowledge drove them constantly to instigate more prosecutions, for real and technical treasons, for 'reset of' (conversation with) traitors, for nonconformity — from which to obtain fines or forfeitures, sometimes promised to them in advance. Successful prosecutions for treason caused the most widespread suffering (and provided the richest pickings); landholding in Scotland was feudal, and when the feudal superior was 'forfaulted' (forfeited), his vassals lost all their rights in the land they held of him, and could, theoretically, be evicted — a royal prerogative even the lawyers admitted was unjust. A similar ruthlessness was shown in normal factional politics and private dealings: 'this kingdome is as a troubled sea, and the small fish are devored of the great', wrote one lawyer.[3] The normal safeguard for 'small fish' in politics was to link themselves to the faction of one of the great noble families of the kingdom, such as Hamilton or Huntly. However, these houses had had the heaviest fall during the Interregnum; and the long years needed to repair the damage, and the political skill of Charles's chief minister, Lauderdale, stunted the growth of these political 'interests', and delayed their complete dominance until after his fall.

One of the great uncertainties in 1660 was the nature of future relations between this regime and the apparently alien society in the Highlands, where perhaps nearly a third of the Scottish population lived. Highland and lowland society had diverged sharply in the Middle Ages, and the rift was at its widest in the reign of James VI. Highlanders were conspicuously different in everything, from their dress, which lowlanders considered indecent, to their religion, which they concluded contained neither true faith nor its fruits in a Christian life (as measured by the Kirk), but widespread surviving catholic and even pagan customs and superstitions. One of the two most important differences was in social structure. Highlanders lived in clans identified to outsiders by the family names (in their various versions) of the chiefs who headed them, and followed them, apparently without scruple, in private warfare and plunder, often against other clans. Most lowlanders believed that this state of war and rapine was the norm for them, that they reckoned their daughters' dowries in cattle to be stolen, and that their bards' poetry was chiefly a celebration of past, and incitement to future, slaughter. The poetry was, of course, in Gaelic; and, now that Gaelic had died out in the Lowlands, the difference in language was the most serious. It encouraged lowlanders and highlanders to believe in another difference, which had less real basis, that of race. Lowlanders referred to Gaelic (and, by implication, to its speakers) as 'Irish'; the fact that its culture was oral, not written, merely confirmed its barbarousness. Many highlanders saw the lowlanders as alien invaders who had robbed them of the fertile plain country — a convenient belief, which justified perpetual cattle-raiding and robbery. On a higher level, linguistic and cultural isolation encouraged the highland elite, although they preserved a concept of Scotland as one nation, to give their deeper emotional loyalty to Scottish Gaeldom, whose political and cultural centre until 1493 was the court of the Macdonald Lords of the Isles, and sometimes to the greater Gaelic community including Ireland.

The practices which lowlanders found alien were not, of course, equally strong throughout the Highlands. Generally, the eastern clans were, by Edinburgh standards, the most civilised and peaceful. Admittedly some on the 'highland line' like the Macgregors and Farquharsons were notorious for ferocity, but their immediate lowland neighbours could match them. The further west, the greater the differences: the sight of a Lochaber clan in full battle array was as nightmarish a shock in 1688 to a Gaelic-speaking highlander from near Inverness as to a lowlander.[4] Such clans' readiness for warfare and raiding arose partly from their social circumstances. They were predominantly a pastoral people, with their main wealth in cattle and other animals, necessarily living at a level of great poverty and simplicity. In war, they could retreat to the mountains with their cattle — often not much worse than what happened normally each summer, when a high proportion of most communities moved to 'shielings' — settlements near the upper cattle pastures — and they could replace what was destroyed more easily than a richer arable-farming society, another grievance for the lowlanders, whose retaliation for highland raids could never inflict comparable material damage. Yet this comparative poverty explained many features of highland society outsiders merely condemned as 'barbarous', such as the state of religion: many areas simply could not afford the cost of any established church. Other such features, arising from the need of protection in an insecure society, had existed until recently in the Lowlands, still lingering on the Borders. Indeed, the change had often been in appearance rather than essence; but those involved would naturally be the last to see this. The Hamiltons massed on the benches of Parliament, normally voting as the Duke, the head of their 'name', required, rather than as they perceived the national interest, felt no affinity between the barbarous Macdonalds, following their chiefs without scruple in private wars and defiance of the government, and themselves — or even their great-grandfathers, who had done exactly the same in the days of feuds.

During the seventeenth century, as the Irish Gaels were finally subdued and memory of the Lords of the Isles faded, the chiefs and major clan gentry were becoming more closely involved with Scottish elite society, both in culture — adopting lowland manners, language and dress — and in political activity. In the Civil Wars, many clans previously known for fighting only among themselves appeared in arms for Charles I and his son, gaining spectacular victories under Montrose. This was a natural reason for the restored regime to sympathise with them and offer them a closer alliance. Yet the highlanders' savage appearance and occasional acts of extreme violence on their lowland campaigns sometimes alienated even their official allies, and some clans plainly fought primarily for Gaelic or catholic ends rather than the Crown; this made it easier, if desired, to undervalue their services. Just possibly, the predatory ruling class might go further and, extending James VI's policies, seek to confiscate highland estates for development or extort fines from chiefs as well as Presbyterians. There was a partial parallel: in its illogical Act of Settlement, the restored regime in Ireland largely confirmed the Cromwellian confiscation for rebellion of the estates of most Catholic landowners (Gaelic and English), even though many had been royalists. Opportunities certainly existed: some chiefs led a Jekyll-and-Hyde life, with their status as law-abiding gentlemen at the mercy of their clansmen's conduct or other men's independent decision to enforce the laws of debt or property. They might suddenly be obliged to abscond, to become (technically) outlaws, even to appear in arms defying formal government authority to protect their clans' very existence; and then, normally, came a compromise, and they resumed intercourse with their peers — until the next time.

The traditional explanation of these anomalies is that they arose from clashes between a 'clan system' and an irreconcilable (and irrational) 'feudal system' imposed upon it; this concept historians are increasingly questioning.[5] One of them, David Stevenson, gives a (simplified) summary of the other, traditional view of a clan: 'a body of people related by blood, descended from a common ancestor, inhabiting a clan territory, ruled by a chief who is head of the kin, . . . and all having the same surname' — although some of the sub-divisions or 'septs' might take different ones. The chief's rule was 'patriarchal', that of a father over his family; although his clansmen owed absolute obedience to his orders, he was expected to take the advice of the leading clan gentry, the *daoine uaisle*, who had perhaps elected him from among rival candidates and might depose him for conspicuous misgovernment. Social divisions within the clan, although sharp, were surmounted by institutions such as fostering, which could create ties as strong as blood. In contrast, feudalism, originally the grant of land in return for military service (although it soon began the metamorphosis into the concept of individual property and inheritance) began with the King's arbitrary division of the nation among his tenants-in-chief, creating illogical boundaries: a chief might come to owe service to several different lords, some of them his or each other's enemies. If an enemy came to own a clan's traditional lands, he had a legal right — though not always the power — to evict them. A chief lost the power of criminal justice over his clan necessary for maintaining order if he were a vassal or if a heritable right of justiciary over an area had been granted to a family, perhaps his hereditary enemies. Within the clan, also, feudal principles of ownership and succession did harm. The grants of land, made to the chief as an individual, strengthened succession by primogeniture, even of the incapable, and weakened the informal mechanism of a chief's accountability for his use of the land.

Modern historians do not deny these hardships; but they argue that, whatever the theoretical differences, in practice clanship and feudalism usually worked in concert; for both, rather than imposed 'systems', were attempts to organise the existing reality of power and the need for protection. The most important revision is to the traditional picture of a clan. Even when the chief was of genuine Celtic or Norse origin, the bulk of those living under him bore no relation to him; that they did was a useful myth to create unity, since blood-relationship was one of the most reliable bonds in times of disorder. For that reason, a chief would by degrees replace the petty chieftains in any area he controlled with members of his family; and, every few generations, his successor would remove them in their turn to make way for his own close relatives. Finally, some of these *daoine uaisle* secured a more permanent claim to such lands; by the late seventeenth century, most of them held by written tacks (leases) and were known as tacksmen. Meanwhile, they and other descendants of the chiefs multiplied and intermarried with older families: the clans were more truly related by blood in the eighteenth century, on the eve of their abolition, than in the mythical past. Feudal barons used similar grants to their kin to strengthen themselves; and most East Highland chiefs were the descendants of such barons, who increasingly stressed the power they derived from kin rather than that from royal grants, and partly adopted their followers' culture. The idea of relationship was seemingly less important at the ordinary clansmen's level: lists from the seventeenth century, when surnames were becoming fixed, show comparatively little preference among them for the chief's name. Septs with their own names were, as often as not, the older ruling families of an area, forced into submission by more powerful chiefs, much as feudal magnates in remote areas forced independent royal vassals to accept them as superiors. The greater protection afforded by written rights in the East Highlands may explain why two groups of ruling families which were late in gaining power there, the Gordons and the Murrays, never quite gelled into clans.

If feudal barons found the kinship bonds of the clan an attractive device, chiefs were willing to strengthen their positions by accepting royal grants, and issuing feudal charters themselves. The Lords of the Isles, whose court was the centre of Gaelic culture, and whose rule was seen as a golden age by comparison with the anarchy which followed, relied largely on feudal methods. No source for strengthening power or security was to be despised. Chiefs emphasised the real or mythical family connections between themselves and lowland houses to gain their support at Court. They secured the support of highland equals and inferiors by bonds of friendship and manrent, which they continued to use (even for securing unwavering support when plotting murders) long after they were obsolete in the Lowlands. They gave refuge to fugitives and men from broken clans, and absorbed them into their own. The government, for its part, could seldom afford to despise power, and adapted itself to some of the chiefs' and clans' needs and desires in dealing with them. It usually did not, for instance, try to enforce strict rules of succession when this was unacceptable; the passing over of the 'rightful' branch among the Glengarry Macdonalds was accepted without comment as late as 1680.

The Camerons and Clan Chattan serve as examples of this revised view. The Camerons have traditionally been seen as a 'natural' clan whose troubles all arose from alien landlords and superiors. Yet a high proportion bore sept names, and a hostile historian can, exaggeratedly, depict the clan as little more than these older septs, kept in subjection by the unscrupulous Cameron of Lochiel family's cunning and force. This submerged hostile tradition within the clan emphasises some truths: every chief's relation with his clan gentry was more or less political, partly a struggle for supremacy which sometimes led to violence, partly mediation between the various branches or septs. Relations with the clan's second most important family, the Macmartins of Letterfinlay, were usually difficult. Ewen of Lochiel was fostered with them to create a closer bond, but unsuccessfully. After the Restoration, the Macmartins were apparently closer to the Macdonalds than to the Camerons, even giving Lord Macdonell a bond of manrent in 1663. Yet, largely perhaps because they might at any time have to defend clan territory against a legal owner, the Camerons remained fairly united.[6] In contrast, the Clan Chattan confederation in the North-East, of which Lachlan, chief of the Mackintoshes, was Captain, had declined by the 1660s from the apparent unity of a 1609 bond to near-disintegration. Every time he called for their armed support for his claims in Lochaber, including his rights over Cameron lands, the tacksmen and lesser chiefs responded with demands for massive concessions before they would stir, increasing them still further, without regard for Clan Chattan's prestige, once the expeditions had actually started. Most such demands were private, for lands or money; but Cluny, chief of the Macphersons, also wanted an acknowledgement that his clan was independent of Mackintosh, intending ultimately to claim the headship of Clan Chattan himself. The two clans once nearly fought a battle. Yet these demands received encouragement from the Gordons, Mackintosh's feudal superiors and enemies. And Cluny in his turn was imposing unprecedented control and unity on the various Macpherson families, and some of them intrigued against him, appealing to Mackintosh and the Council.[7] If, ideally, 'artificial' authorities could have been abolished to free the 'natural' clan system from distortion, it is not clear at what level in the existing clans abolition would have ceased. It would have varied considerably according to the qualities of individual chiefs. Both Ewen Cameron and Lachlan Mackintosh were to succeed in imposing far greater unity on the Camerons and Mackintoshes, not least because both continued to rule all through the Restoration period and William II's reign. Success against internal and external enemies still depended on this, far more than in lowland families: the Macleans were ruined during two long minorities.

The revisionist view, by concentration on the mechanism of control, may be pushed too far. Clan spirit and the tradition of obedience to the chief, although not so universal as the sentimentalists claimed, did exist, and were generally of value for the clan's survival and prospering as a society in a ruthless world. Some 'Camerons' might chafe under Lochiel's rule; but many inhabitants of Ardnamurchan and Morvern, which had been under his control for only short periods, persistently considered themselves his clansmen. A chief's duty to protect 'his' clan extended to those elsewhere in the Highlands supposedly descended from it: the classic example occurred in 1662 when some Macleans in Strathglass, Chisholm tenants for centuries, were threatened with judicial murder for witchcraft, and appealed to Sir Alan Maclean for help. Yet a 'clan myth' of common origin was not necessary to create clan loyalty: the most spectacular late seventeenth-century example was provided by the Frasers, whose chiefs not only admitted but emphasised their French origins and arrival as conquerors. Highlanders might ignore clan surnames in daily life, but still treasure them in the appropriate context; it would not otherwise have been necessary to prohibit the name Macgregor.[8]

Ownership of land, with power over its distribution among tacksmen, was the chief's most important means of maintaining his authority. Grants were by feudal tenure to chiefs as individuals. Councils of clan gentry were sometimes asked to approve expensive undertakings, and they occasionally intervened unasked, as the Macdonalds of Sleat did in 1678 over the financially ruinous quarrels between Sir James and his son; but only too often chiefs ruined themselves unchecked, while tacksmen and tenants lamented and paid their rents. Almost the only situation which would rouse an entire clan was when the marriage of a chief's daughter and heiress to an outsider threatened a transfer of the chiefship, or the lands which supported it, out of the clan. Whatever the disadvantages, the power given by this monopoly helped to keep the clan united: exceptionally, four or five Maclean families besides the chief were independent landowners, and they often failed to act in concert until late in the clan's decline.[9] Even a chief such as Lochiel or Keppoch, whose clan occupied land owned by others, was determined that the tacksmen's grants must come from him; if they gained titles as good as, perhaps better than, his, they might throw off his authority. When, in 1614, Huntly granted independent titles to the Camerons in his part of Lochaber (who allegedly at once began to plot), Lochiel retaliated by slaughtering them; clans under alien superiors often suffered the worst damage, not directly but from the reactions into which the chiefs were forced. Keppoch merely destroyed a similar grant to Macdonald of Inverlair, the one major clansman living on Huntly's land; but it was to be the Inverlair family who murdered the young chief of Keppoch in 1663.[10]

The rest of the Keppoch Macdonalds lived on land for which the Laird of Mackintosh had charters. The only status they could claim was that of 'kindly tenants', with a moral claim to remain on the land from their long previous occupation; but their persistent failure to pay rent ensured that Mackintosh would disregard it. Their real title, of which they were proud, was that attempting to expel them would be too dangerous:

> There is one in Glen Roy, whose only right to his land is a few people who will rise at his whistle.[11]

Mackintosh also owned Glenloy and Locharkaig, occupied by the Camerons, and had equally little reason to show forbearance to them.

Such disputes between the legal owners and real occupants, the main cause of highland disorders by the seventeenth century, arose from several different causes. The one traditionally blamed, the granting away of lands whose owners lacked written rights, or had technically forfeited them, by a distant monarch acting from ignorance or malice — after James VI's 1597 act for producing land titles, for instance — has been exaggerated. Another method, brought to a fine art by the Earls of Argyll, was to exploit the laws of debt. Yet the aggression did not always come from those with the charters. Some quarrels in Lochaber apparently arose because Mackintosh's feudal hold had weakened; the Lochiel family seized the chance to establish their *de facto* independence, but could not obtain a rationalising legal title. Ewen of Lochiel still followed the same policy, on a small scale, after 1660. Exploiting the presence of Camerons among the outsiders who 'came to Rannoch [a wild area] not for building of kirks', he began to grant leases and even wadsets on the lands — a fact the legal owner, Robertson of Struan, discovered only by accident.[12]

After landownership, the best weapon for imposing authority on a clan or highland property was a heritable power of criminal jurisdiction, 'cum fossa et furca, *lie* pit and gallows'. Although most barons possessed the right, lowlanders by the Restoration period almost automatically sent capital cases before the Sheriff. In the Highlands, in contrast, the power was constantly of value against recalcitrant clansmen, either to execute them outright, as (traditionally) Lady Seaforth did the Brahan Seer, or, as in Simon Lord Lovat's sophisticated system, to make them accept transportation overseas rather than face condemnation on rigged charges. There was little outside check, and some chiefs, such as Lachlan Mackintosh, were notoriously harsh. Yet public courts could equally be abused: the Chisholms, having failed to destroy the Strathglass Macleans as witches, prosecuted their sons as thieves.[13] It was not altogether a misfortune that every highland baron was, to a large extent, his own Braxfield, and every highland landlord his own Patrick Sellar; in both capacities, the knowledge that he might soon need his tenantry's armed support restrained him from abusing his powers too far. It is no coincidence that the worst traditional stories of tyranny in private courts concern bailies and other subordinate officials, often men who had bought their places. One of these, Gordon of Brackley, who used a warrant against salmon-fishers for extortion, was the victim of a famous Restoration murder, killed by John Farquharson of Inverey in a skirmish in 1666. Huntly and the Gordons crushed several attempts to have Inverey pardoned. Yet, although he lived so close to the Lowlands that the murder was celebrated in a ballad rather than a Gaelic poem, he remained outlawed but untroubled in 1689.[14] It was a slight example of the lack of control which the government had long been trying to solve — with indifferent success.

James IV's forfeiture of the rebellious Lords of the Isles in 1493, by destroying the one institution capable of controlling the West Highlands, brought about the most violent and unstable hundred and fifty years in recorded highland history. An increasing proportion of the trouble arose from the abuse of delegated and feudal power by the families on which the Crown relied as royal Lieutenants to keep order from the late fifteenth century: the Earls of Argyll, chiefs of the Campbells, in the South-West Highlands, the Earls of Huntly, heads of the Gordons, in the North-East. With almost no local check on them, they rapidly increased their estates and influence, sometimes forcing royal vassals to accept them as intermediate lords, and by the mid-sixteenth century posed a threat to the Crown. However, the Huntlys remained Catholics or crypto-Catholics. Although James VI favoured them, and secretly used them to curb Argyll, they seldom received major new official powers. The protestant Earls of Moray became their hereditary rivals (and Argyll's allies) in the North-East. The only expansionist branch of the Gordon family in the late seventeenth century was a protestant one which had inherited the earldom of Sutherland. Yet Huntly's estates, superiorities and jurisdictions, stretching from Strathbogie to Loch Linnhe, provided many opportunities for internal exploitation.[15]

The Campbells' expansion, in contrast, was spectacular; and it was achieved largely at the expense of Clan Donald. The forfeiture had left at least eight significant branches, Sleat, Clanranald, Keppoch, Glengarry, the MacIains of Ardnamurchan, and the MacIains of Glencoe (Clan Donald North), and the Clan Iain Mor of Kintyre and Islay and the Macdonnells of Antrim (Clan Donald South). The great feud between the Macdonalds and the Campbells, symbolically the heads and the betrayers of Gaeldom, did not break out before the late sixteenth century, though poetry on both sides foreshadowed it. Destructive internal struggles made Clan Donald South vulnerable; the Campbells in contrast prospered largely because they carefully maintained clan unity. The one great exception, the assassination in 1592 of the seventh Earl's Tutor, the first step in a plot by several leading Campbells to murder the Earl, caused misfortunes, including a serious defeat at the hands of Huntly (one of the plotters) and a generation of mistrust between chief and clan, which served as a warning to their successors. Having narrowly escaped bloody disintegration themselves, they were used by James VI to punish other clans for excessive violence. They were constantly accused of encouraging rebellions by other clans and then receiving royal commissions to suppress them and rewards for doing so, often truly; but unsuccessful rebels automatically used the accusation to excuse their own conduct, such as the Clan Iain Mor's persistent failure to settle their internal feuds as the Campbells had theirs. Argyll frequently acted unscrupulously, but on James's, more than his own, initiative.[16]

James's highland policy had two contradictory strands. His laws created a basic framework, on which future governments were to build, for ruling and keeping order in the Highlands, relying largely on the clans as existing institutions: they established (however crudely) land titles, and obliged landlords and chiefs to give yearly bonds making themselves responsible for their tenants' and clansmen's conduct and robberies. Yet James had a violent hatred of the uncivilised highlanders, particularly the 'barbarous cannibals' of the Isles, which several times from 1597 onwards broke out blindly in plans for wholesale extermination. The Statutes of Iona of 1609, notorious as an attack on such features of Gaelic society as chiefs' large households and bards, and an attempt to impose lowland values instead, were a compromise imposed on James by the persistence of his Council, whose underlying aim, to tame even the inhabitants of the Isles into obedient subjects, was liberal compared to his.[17] Though not by the Statutes' cruder methods, more civilised behaviour had spread by the Restoration period, on both sides. The Council no longer broke its safe-conducts to chiefs, as James's had habitually done; and the clans no longer — except in one notorious instance — allowed internal wars and murders over succession disputes, a change which, by removing the main excuse for intervention, made highland society better able to resist direct lowland pressure. In one vital respect, however, its stability was fatally undermined. The costs of yearly appearances before the Council in Edinburgh, crown dues, fines, forfeited bonds, legal proceedings and the new luxuries they encountered for the first time, plunged many chiefs deep into debt, nearly every debtor in his own right dragging a kite-tail of cautioners after him.

James's ruthlessness sprang partly from hope that the lowland Scots would use their colonising energies (later diverted to Ulster) to settle the Highlands profitably. The suicidal civil wars of the Macleods of Lewis made him grant the island to the 'Fife Adventurers'; and he made more grandiose plans for settlement of other islands, 'not by agreement with the countrey people, bot by extirpation of them'. The chief of the Mackenzies (a clan matching the Campbells in ruthless expansion), who had secretly encouraged the revolts in Lewis against the Adventurers, was granted the island and conquered it. He and his descendants, as Earls of Seaforth, became the government's chief agents in the North Highlands.[18]

At least one previous monarch, James V, had ordered the extermination of an entire clan, the Clan Chattan; but he did not persist in it. James VI's orders in 1603 that the Macgregors, whose misdeeds, murder of their enemies and fighting clan battles, had occurred conspicuously near the Lowlands, should be destroyed as a clan and forbidden to use the surname, were carried out, with extreme and widespread brutality. The survivors of the broken and landless clan, permanently forbidden in 1633 to use their name, were forced even more than before to live by cattle-raiding: in the late seventeenth century, a disproportionate number of identified robbers were called Macgregor. Argyll, their chief persecutor, had earlier secretly protected and encouraged them (his descendants were to do so again). James feared Argyll's growing power, as his intrigues with Huntly indicate, and the bribe with which he won him over showed how far his hostility towards the Macgregors overwhelmed his political prudence — a grant of Kintyre and Jura, confiscated from the Clan Iain Mor. When factions within this clan disputing the ownership of its last major possession, Islay, exposed the weakness of the Council's preferred agents in a series of revolts in 1614, James, despite their protests, commissioned Argyll to crush the Macdonalds and granted Islay to his follower Campbell of Calder. His policy of colonisation always underestimated opposition and overestimated profits. High feu duties (feudal rents paid to the Crown), and the unexpected costs of holding Kintyre, Islay and Lewis against later attempts to recover them, helped drive the Argyll, Calder and Seaforth families deep into debt, a cause of future instability.[19]

Charles I confirmed the Argyll family's dominance in the West Highlands by agreeing that the future Marquess, on surrendering the heritable office of Justice-General of Scotland, should retain full justiciary power over Argyllshire and the Isles, a control over criminal cases more complete than their feudal power. In practice, they avoided disputing Seaforth's influence in Lewis and, increasingly, in Skye. Yet their superiorities extended to the Outer Hebrides and Kintail. They had dispossessed a Macdonald sept of Ardnamurchan and Sunart. In Lochaber, Clan Cameron formed their north-eastern bastion. The Camerons' support for Montrose at Inverlochy, when the Marquess's highland power had become stifling, and their later Jacobite traditions have obscured the fact that they were basically a pro-Campbell clan surrounded by anti-Campbell ones. Old Alan of Lochiel collaborated in transferring Cameron territory to Argyllshire, and the Marquess reared Alan's half-Campbell grandson, the great Ewen. Cameron relations with the Macdonalds and Macleans were often strained and suspicious, even after 1688. The revival of catholicism was a further irritant, for the Camerons, exceptionally in the general highland religious vagueness, were consciously protestant.[20]

When the Marquess of Argyll, provoked by Charles's intrigues against him, joined the Covenanting Revolution, the Campbells' immense highland power and reputation of near-invincibility made him its most important leader. He used his clan unscupulously to crush highland opponents and rivals, but not in the Lowlands. The clans were brought directly into national politics — provoking a lasting polarisation in lowland views of them — by the royalists Montrose and Alasdair MacColla, the latter a catholic Macdonald with roots in both the Hebrides and Ulster. The Marquess of Antrim, who claimed to be chief of Clan Donald South, organised Alasdair's expedition, three experienced Irish regiments. Montrose's royal commission provided legitimacy and gained support for them outside the West Highlands. They achieved success in battle through the use of a new tactic invented or adapted by Alasdair, the 'highland charge'; it was this which enabled the clans to influence British, and even European, politics. The clans which made up the highland force marched and fought together under their own chiefs or, at least, some of the clan gentry; they would otherwise refuse to serve. Choosing, where possible, to attack from a height to which they could easily retreat if repulsed, they would advance rapidly with loaded guns, ignoring the enemy's fire. Pouring in one volley at close range and flinging down their firearms, they charged at top speed, armed mainly with broadswords and round targes, sometimes with Lochaber axes and similar weapons, uttering wild shouts to spread panic, and bursting upon the enemy with great impetus before they had time to inflict serious casualties with their fire. Few lowland armies could stand against such a shock.[21] Within a year Montrose and Alasdair won half-a-dozen victories, usually against heavy odds, which revived Charles's cause and gained Montrose, Alasdair's Irish and the clans widespread fame and credit as royalist heroes. Yet the atrocities they committed in the Lowlands, particularly the sack of Aberdeen, confirmed hostile Scotsmen's worst opinion of these barbarians — and of Montrose and the royal cause for employing them. Such critics, automatically accepting a double standard, paid little attention to atrocities in the Highlands.

Montrose's and Alasdair's crushing victory over the Campbells at Inverlochy was their most important, shattering the illusion of Argyll's invulnerability in his own country and greatly reducing his influence in national politics. Yet, when Alasdair ravaged Argyllshire before the battle, and returned some months later (as

Montrose unwisely advanced to Philiphaugh) for nearly two years' campaigning, his primary aim was not to assist Charles I's cause but to re-establish the Clan Iain Mor. To achieve this, Campbell power must be broken for ever, and at times the Macdonalds attempted to kill all male Campbells of military age, whether or not they resisted the ravaging. One of the severest blows to the Campbell empire was that the small Argyllshire and Perthshire clans who had seemingly accepted conquest and absorption, the Kintyre Macdonalds, the Lamonts, Macdougalls, Macgregors and MacNabs, one by one erupted without warning, once there seemed real hope of regaining freedom. Like Alasdair, they were royalists largely because Argyll was not: motives similar to theirs made the subject inhabitants of Lewis support the English garrison in the 1650s against the royalist Mackenzies.[22]

Even with Montrose's commission and prestige, the royalists had succeeded in raising significant forces only in the West Highlands (with Macleod of Dunvegan neutral and Macdonald of Sleat very lukewarm), Atholl and Badenoch, with intermittent support from the Gordons. Once Charles's surrender to the Scots had forced the eastern clans and Montrose to submit, it became comparatively easy for a covenanting army returning from England finally to drive Alasdair from Kintyre to Ireland. On their side also, it was a war of extermination. Montrose's Irish had been slaughtered after surrender at Philiphaugh, and the Campbells now made sure that the small clans could never threaten them again: the Lamonts were massacred at Dunoon, the Macdougalls and Kintyre Macdonalds at Dunaverty, and they never recovered in number. Argyll refused to destroy the Macleans as well, but extorted from imprisoned royalist chiefs grants of land and acknowledgements of imaginary debts.[23] Elsewhere in the Highlands, also, his opponents' failures increased his power. Partly from personal distrust and jealousy, Huntly and Seaforth had not given Montrose effective support — Seaforth had fought against him at Auldearn — but after Philiphaugh they started belated royalist risings, permamently discrediting themselves with the Covenanters. Huntly was finally executed in 1649 and the regime bestowed his estates on Argyll as his principal creditor, seemingly extinguishing the house of Gordon. To secure his title, Argyll continued to buy up Huntly's debts. His enemy Montrose was executed, and Charles II came to Scotland only on the Presbyterians' terms.

Cromwell, however (fresh from crushing the Irish Gaels), completed Alasdair's work: by invading Scotland and defeating the 'godly' on whom Argyll relied for support, he finally destroyed him as a first-rank political figure. When the crisis of 1651 finally forced the Presbyterians to let former royalists fight for the nation, those highland clans who joined Charles's army formed, he said, 'the flower of his forces'. Already, thanks to Montrose's campaigns, they were often seen as the true loyalists, in contrast to the Campbells. Yet, even when they justified this, the unique status given them by the victories they had won using the highland charge was ebbing away. In July 1651, the Macleans under their young chief Sir Hector were almost exterminated, fighting heroically to prevent the Cromwellians from crossing the Forth at Inverkeithing. The Macleods of Skye were destroyed after a similar desperate struggle at Worcester in September. But both were defensive battles; and both were defeats. For two years, 1653–5, the Highlands supported Glencairn's and Middleton's rising against Cromwell. Yet, from the start, it was half-paralysed by quarrels; the chiefs seemed incapable of co-operation. Their successes were gained in raiding, ambushes and small-scale skirmishes (the most spectacular of which, Lochiel's victory over a far larger party from the Inverlochy garrison at Achdalieu, began with a tiny highland charge).[24] Even when the royalists had several thousand men in arms, they avoided pitched battles, and those they were forced to fight were disastrous defeats. A fort to tame Lochaber was successfully established at Inverlochy, and Generals Monck and Morgan penetrated to the depths of the Highlands in the spectacular marches which crushed the rising.

As the highlanders' lustre faded, the English regime redirected attention to their more familiar role, as a people to be kept in order and prevented from stealing, by showing for the first time that this could be done without bloodshed, treachery and abuse of power. Lieutenant-Colonel Hill, the last pre-Restoration Governor of Inverlochy, gained a reputation for trustworthiness still influential thirty years after. Later nostalgia for the period's peace and order overlooked the regime's advantages and exaggerated its beneficence. The system of garrisons, Inverlochy, Inverness and smaller ones, was supported by crushing taxation. The military rulers could ignore many existing rights. The enormous jurisdiction of Inverlochy, which made possible the effective prosecution of thieves, was erected by simple *fiat* from the remote areas of three shires; later a new shire, Lochaber, was created. Litigants prosecuting highlanders in the civil or criminal courts were ordered not to proceed if the judgement was likely to cause disorder. The government followed a policy of discriminating between, and within, clans. Lochiel was the most obviously favoured. His clan was still allowed to carry arms when others were forbidden, so that many outsiders acknowledged him as chief to gain his licence. The shire taxation was altered to benefit him. Monck halted prosecutions against him for past thefts. He prevented Mackintosh from evicting him from Glenloy and Locharkaig, instead applying pressure to make him grant a lease, but he let Lochiel take over Glengarry's lands. It was worth going to great lengths to keep such concessions; and Balhaldie admits that Lochiel used ruthless methods to force his clan to give up the plundering habits made worse by war. Argyll also was allowed some power over enemies, having the Macleans' estates adjudged to him in 1659.[25]

Charles II at the Restoration conspicuously failed to redress or reverse this discrimination. He left the Macleans, helpless under Sir Hector's child brother Sir Alan, to be ruined, though the one major clansman who had followed Argyll was heavily fined. He did nothing for the Macleods, who never again fought for the Stuarts, partly, it seems, from resentment for this ingratitude. Sir James Lamont, whose clan had been massacred, competed with the Duke of Hamilton for a Campbell forfeiture: Hamilton obtained it. Angus Macdonald of Glengarry, the most indefatigable of loyalists, had fought at Inverlochy, returned with Charles II from the Continent, held out longest in Glencairn's rising, conspired afterwards and was forfeited and imprisoned. He received a peerage, Lord Macdonell and

Aros, and a pension; but he claimed that Charles had made, and failed to honour, a promise to create him Earl of Ross, which might have revived dangerous memories of the Lords of the Isles.[26]

Some failures to reward past sufferings arose from bad luck and highlanders' lack of the long purse necessary for successful Court solicitations. When Sir Norman Macleod of Bernera, the clan's commander at Worcester, sought reward at Whitehall in 1663, Neil Macleod, last of the Macleods of Assynt, was on trial before Parliament for betraying Montrose. Charles promised Sir Norman (Neil's next heir) his forfaulture if he was convicted, and, if not, recompense from the fines. Sir Robert Moray, Charles's friend, recommended Sir Norman and Macleod of Raasay most strongly to Lauderdale for favour. Neil, however, was acquitted through bribery, and the long delays over the fines forced Sir Norman to return home with only his knighthood. Charles forgot; Moray died. Meanwhile, Seaforth bought up Neil Macleod's debts, obtained decreets, drove him treasonably to garrison his house, and had him robbed and illegally imprisoned. At nearly every step, the old charge of betraying Montrose was used to deny him justice; and the Mackenzies obtained Assynt.[27]

Such disasters and disappointments for clans which committed themselves either way encouraged the well-known Scottish family tradition of having members on both sides in civil wars. It will be argued later that this is too often made a catch-all explanation for every division. Yet it undoubtedly existed, and was particularly necessary in the Highlands, where the stronger feudal bonds might often drag vassals into doomed causes. In Argyll's 1685 rebellion, many Campbell families had their first sons with him and their second with the government forces. Lochiel, the mainstay (under Dundee) of highland Jacobitism in 1689, had his second son in William's army.[28] Alternatively, obligations might be ignored: the Farquharsons still boasted in 1730 of the trickery they had used to dodge their Erskine superiors' orders to join the army marching to Worcester, while retaining their loyalist reputations. Such tales formed part of a cynical highland tradition which, although leaving few traces compared to the heroic tradition it counterbalanced, was often more influential. Chiefs frequently boasted, openly and rather naively, of their successful tricks, 'repeat[ing] their scurvy, ungenerous, dishonourable maxims by way of vindication and showing their parts and dexterity'. The unbalanced fury which this increasingly aroused outside the circle of highland mutual admiration, as the developing 'polite' veneer on lowland society separated the two cultures, was partly hypocritical: the reporter indignant at the Farquharsons was Erskine of Grange, who had his wife kidnapped illegally and imprisoned in the Western Isles until her death. Yet the anger existed; and it helped bring about the Massacre of Glencoe. In 1691, boasting by highlanders (perhaps including the Earl of Breadalbane and Glengarry, both notorious for it) about their shallow trickery over the proposed pacification enraged lowland politicians, while complacently blinding their own eyes to the deeper traps the lowlanders were laying for them.[29]

However, the Civil Wars had made possible more sympathetic attitudes towards the clans. Montrose and his followers were now seen as heroes; and in

1651 highlanders and lowlanders had fought together for Scotland (and, after Worcester, had been enslaved indiscriminately). During Glencairn's rising, lowlanders would give the English garrisons supposedly protecting them against highland raids no information. Most young Restoration politicians began their careers then, campaigning in all parts of the Highlands, an episode they later emphasised to prove their royalism. Some developed greater sympathy for highland society and culture. The bias in existing laws, and the problems of highland disorder, might edge the government back towards the crude older views, but clan services to the Stuart cause, recognised in Glengarry's peerage and the reinstatement of the name Macgregor, barred the way. On the highland side, poets had referred to the King only as a distant figure; now they linked his service with their heroes' greatest deeds, cursed his enemies, and mentioned lowland, even English, politics. Iain Lom Macdonald, whose poem on the battle of Inverlochy overlooked Montrose, was eventually to consider a recent small fire in Whitehall relevant material for a political poem.[30]

The new category of 'loyal clans' was conveniently arbitrary: spectacular single services outweighed generally dubious records. Lochiel had fought vigorously in Glencairn's rising; but in 1651 he had invaded Glengarry's lands rather than join the royal army, and he had been a major collaborator. Yet, once he had evaded the initial reaction, his exploits gained greater credit for the Camerons than the Mackintoshes, who had supported Charles more consistently but less conspicuously, could obtain. Pinned down by an English officer at Achdalieu, he had torn out his throat with his teeth. It saved him then, and helped win him favour now; a touch of barbarism could be an asset.[31]

Once again, the Scottish colonising impulse — whose strength can be gauged by the co-operation in it of Episcopalians, Presbyterians and Quakers, even during the worst persecutions — was diverted from the Highlands, this time to the new North American colonies; and a better source for systematic fines and forfeitures was found in the Presbyterians, most of whom were concentrated in the Western lowlands. They were comparatively few in highland shires, but the Earl of Moray, for instance, when he felt the need of a fine, would automatically investigate the ex-Covenanter Brodie of Brodie's finances, while conniving at frequent Fraser clan riots against the crypto-presbyterian Forbes of Culloden. Religious differences exacerbated existing feuds: their nonconformity further handicapped the Lords Forbes in their centuries-old struggle with the house of Huntly. This persecution, by isolating the north-eastern sufferers in a resentful, self-aware minority, would have unforeseen results in 1689.[32] The ruling nobles' hostility to the Presbyterians was, of course, far more than a pretext for extracting fines. They desperately feared a return of the Covenanters to challenge the whole newly re-established society. Although it was largely as a result of their persecution that this fear was justified, and that the Cameronians, the followers of the extremist Presbyterian preacher Richard Cameron, declared war against the state in the 1680s, the danger did always exist in some strands of presbyterian thought. Once the regime, despite its wiser ministers' efforts, became committed to almost continuous confrontation with the Presbyterians, alarming consequences could be foreseen; and already by 1666 some religious exiles were plotting with the Dutch army in wartime. In comparison with this danger, the disorders in the Highlands were of little importance, since, once the political links with Gaelic Ireland were broken, the chiefs' ultimate loyalty was certain. The regime treated the highlanders mildly not only because the field army, kept small by the limited revenue, was occupied in holding down the West and unavailable for any systematic operation elsewhere, but because they were anxious for rough and not too scrupulous armed supporters. This grew, it is not certain how soon, into the wish to use them in force to subdue and terrorise the West. For the first time, 'the clans' were, in lowland eyes, committed to supporting one faction in the State; there would be a new danger to them if that faction's opponents ever gained power.

The Presbyterians considered this threat of invasion by the Highlanders still more horrific and unpardonable because so many of them were followers of the Popish Antichrist. Highland Catholics, although a small minority, were proportionately far stronger than lowland ones (one priest estimated 12,000 out of a total of 14,000 in Scotland) and better able to survive and proselytise despite penal laws. In the West Highlands, Franciscan missionaries had revived a disintegrating catholicism early in the century, giving an extra crusading zeal to many of Montrose's men; but the Covenanting and Cromwellian victories brought it to a low ebb. Gaelic-speaking priests after 1660 were few, usually Irishmen who retired after a few years, exhausted by the constant hardships. In many areas, all religion had only a superficial hold: the mission to the Isles, where Clanranald's and MacNeil of Barra's people had, officially, been reclaimed, reported that the people generally were neither protestant nor catholic, although more inclined to catholicism. The Macdonalds were the one 'old' catholic clan, but the Sleat branch was becoming predominantly protestant. Religion had given the clan continental links — MacIain of Glencoe was educated at Paris, the murdered Keppoch brothers partly at Rome — but the Glengarry and Keppoch heirs in the 1670s received Scottish protestant educations and succeeded as Protestants.[33] Catholicism's traditional stronghold was the Huntly family's north-eastern estates round Strathbogie. The young Marquess rode out the government's attempt to convert him and destroy catholicism from above. Individual proselytising had some spectacular successes: one priest converted most of the Chisholms of Strathglass, and another, without support from any major Farquharsons, much of Braemar. They gave lowlanders inconveniently plain evidence of the highland 'growth of Popery'.[34]

The highland chiefs were becoming more deeply involved in the nation's economic life. The cattle trade was already important in the South Highlands before the Civil War, and Lochiel and others in the North were involved. Now, with the growth of lowland, and perhaps English, markets, it became almost universal. Major market-towns arose just inside the Lowlands for the massive cattle-sales. The profits from the trade were vital for the highland economy: part was used to buy lowland grain and meal in exchange, since arable farming in the Highlands could not produce enough to feed the inhabitants; part enabled tenants to pay their landlords' money-rents. Normally, landlords, tacksmen and tenants contracted with professional highland drovers to buy the cattle at fixed prices, or themselves bore the risk. Yet already in the 1660s lowland partnerships were buying cattle in advance on credit from remote chiefs.[35] It might be hoped that the trade would quietly erode the traditional culture of violence and robbery. A generation earlier, the first Macdonald to take up droving in Skye had been universally despised, although he was the clan's greatest warrior; a generation later, the chief's brother was in charge of the great droves which swam, tied nose to tail, to the mainland. The droves, on which so many chiefs' prosperity for the year so largely depended, took place in the early autumn, the traditional main season for cattle-raiding, and were vulnerable targets, suffering not merely in remote areas like Lochaber but in Menteith, close to the markets. Chiefs might, therefore, increasingly find it in their interest to cease any protection of local robbers and support some impartial justiciary which could secure peace and order throughout the Highlands.[36]

Some chiefs also began to exploit their possession of one resource which had almost vanished elsewhere in Scotland, forests. Even the English navy might be a customer. They established sawmills, and overcame the main obstacle which paralysed industry and trade in goods within the Highlands, the lack of roads, by floating the timber down the lochs and rivers. It has been shown that the 'Gentle Lochiel' of the '45 managed his estate and timber as a skilled businessman. His grandfather Ewen was far less sophisticated in exploiting his forests, but he was even more enterprising. In 1678, he commissioned a blast-furnace near his home at Achnacarry (the first to be initiated by a purely highland landlord). By 1688, it was producing and selling first-class iron; but it was probably destroyed in the 1690 campaign.[37]

In purely social terms, the chiefs might probably have been assimilated into the Scottish elite now with less damage to Gaelic culture than was possible earlier, or later when the assimilation actually occurred. The highland magnates, whether of Celtic origin or not, were still careful not to become too distant from the roots of their power. Although the first language of nearly all was Scots (one exception, apparently, being the third Earl of Seaforth, who was also said to have the second sight), and they referred to Gaelic as 'Irish', they took care to have their sons taught it as a vital part of their education, particularly necessary to establish the close relations with their clansmen or vassals that would ensure their loyalty in wars and crises. The undogmatic Restoration spirit of free inquiry which influenced part of the Scottish elite encouraged them to examine aspects of Gaelic culture without automatic hostility or condescension — for instance, the second sight, which would earlier have been denounced as diabolism, and would later be dismissed as superstition.[38]

Yet, despite their new sources of income, the main effect on most chiefs of closer relations with lowland society was to increase their debts. The Council could not have governed the Highlands without the power to issue a protection from arrest to almost every inhabitant they summoned, but these summonses themselves encouraged chiefs to make prolonged stays in Edinburgh, despite the further strain on their purses. Some visited Court, or Europe; some, including even Macdonell, established second homes in the Lowlands. Lowland or English luxury goods and clothes, more elegant and seductive than ever, were still further beyond their means than the lowland nobility's, as the bards lamented. A wise chief like Iain Breac Macleod could successfully mix the two worlds. He visited Edinburgh, and used lowland clothes and luxuries, but he made Dunvegan Castle a centre of traditional hospitality and Gaelic poetry and music, and still succeeded by careful management in paying off most of the family debts. Yet such a balance was precarious: in a few years of lowland extravagance, his son doubled the remaining debt.[39]

At the height of Iain Breac's prosperity, his estates legally belonged under an apprising to other men. This was merely a technical security for creditors, who, in an age without alternative safe investments, were content to receive their annualrent (interest). A Highland landowner's debts, therefore, might be less disastrous than the sum-total suggested; comparatively few major estates changed hands; but there was still danger. A large overlooked debt which had rapidly accumulated interest could shake even the Atholl estate. Moreover, some prominent highlanders had abandoned the old tradition, of leading private armed raids against their enemies, only for a more roundabout means of harassment, in which Argyll was the past master, buying up their debts and prosecuting on them. In extreme cases, they might obtain apprisings and organise armed invasions, as in former days, but with legal backing. To prevent such commissions from being hurried through secretly, to manage the frequent lawsuits with which every Scottish estate was afflicted and the additional ones caused by clansmen's and tenants' robberies, and generally to look after their interests, all chiefs and many lesser highland gentry hired an Edinburgh writer (law agent), often a highlander himself. The 'pension' paid him and the high cost of proceedings were a further burden, and the more distant highlanders, whose letters might be seriously delayed or even intercepted, were at a dangerous disadvantage in lawsuits. In contrast, an aggressive chieftain and landlord like Campbell of Glenorchy would be fighting simultaneously two dozen or more actions, several of which would ruin him if he lost, over estates, teinds, robberies, jointures, wadsets — and, particularly, delaying actions against creditors.[40]

Most highland estates were totally incapable of bearing this social and legal expenditure. To raise large sums locally, the landlords could grant out land in feu-farm, perpetual fixed-rent tenure. Expansionists like Argyll and Glenorchy often did so to finance massive further land purchases, but it required delicate balancing: too much feuing would destroy their hold over their original estates. Farming returns were low, and still paid largely in kind. Clan obligations, to both tacksmen and ordinary tenants, and the need to keep men on the land as a fighting force, restricted commercial possibilities. Despite this protection, the average clansman's life was desperately hard, in strong contrast with his chief's comparative luxury. Many observers, including, surprisingly, James VI and Sir John Dalrymple, saw them with a double vision, both as wild barbarians blindly following their chiefs, and, pityingly, as downtrodden slaves scratching a living under adverse conditions. Every year was a struggle to accumulate a surplus against starvation, ending with a hungry period early in the year; a slight additional misfortune might mean catastrophe. With a few exceptions, such as hunters' flintlock muskets, they lacked the tools and goods of their lowland counterparts: when, rather than tip-and-run cattle raids, the western clans were able to plunder the South-West or the richer areas of Kintyre at leisure, they carried off tools, household goods and clothes, ironwork of all sorts and fishing nets. Chiefs or landlords could not, in reason, demand much more from them. Most highland debts acquired in the seventeenth century remained a burden as apparently inescapable as a hereditary curse, with interest swelling them, until the families were ruined or resorted to the Clearances. In the 1730s, when the Highlands seemed peaceful, the Duke of Argyll resorted to a similar 'advanced' policy, evicting tacksmen and demanding rack-rents: one factor which forced a reversal was the need to raise the clan in arms for the '45. Late seventeenth-century disorders may have been an indirect security for the ordinary highlander's position.[41]

Taxation caused further impoverishment and disruption. The annual revenue of £40,000 a year voted to Charles in 1661, although widely considered too burdensome, was increased by later parliaments and conventions. Even so, the government was engaged until 1688 in a constant struggle to make ends meet. Gradual expansion of foreign trade, unnoticed except when war checked it, eased the burden; but only the hardships were immediately visible. The highlanders also suffered from 'revenue' measures passed mainly to benefit Lauderdale's cronies: a salt monopoly temporarily forced them to use sea water, which caused widespread illness and death.[42] The land tax, the 'cess', exacerbated the hostility of the lowland parts of shires and towns like Inverness, which were regularly forced to make up the deficiencies of highland areas. The powerful could have it imposed unequally to afflict their enemies, as Argyll did against the Macleans. The worst burden, however, was quartering. From 1666, parties of troops were sent to extract arrears (including some from before the Civil Wars) by living at free quarter in deficient areas until the full sum was paid, a convenient means of providing free subsistence for much of the army. Charles referred to this far-reaching legal power to justify the Highland Host. The soldiers who 'prey'd so uncontrollably upon the remoter parts of the kingdom which were far distant from the seat of justice, that in effect these shires payed still a double share', and who sometimes even committed murder unpunished, were often the only representatives of authority to penetrate remote areas.[43] In 1669, Lochiel, the Camerons and Keppoch rose and forced back the meddlesome Sheriff-depute of Inverness, who had obtained a commission to collect arrears and was supported by soldiers. The government reacted with self-conscious mildness, accepting Lochiel's excuse that he had convened his clan only to catch a murderer; but troops were quartered to obtain more immediate arrears.[44]

Tax collection had been more efficient, as well as more just, when there were Cromwellian garrisons in the Highlands. So had the prevention or punishment of cattle-raiding, although the Restoration regime suffered unfairly from nostalgia for the late Interregnum as a time when stray cows could wander safely into Lochaber: Monck, with all his advantages, had increasingly had to resort to professional watches and other traditional measures.[45] But disorder revived rapidly after 1660, when the shire and jurisdiction of Lochaber were abolished, its territory reverted to being the most inaccessible tracts of three shires, and the English soldiers demolished and departed from Inverlochy, Inverness and the other forts. Some ministers would have been glad to keep these, but the highlanders were now rejoicing at their escape from the 'closed pens' in which the laws against travelling without passes and bearing arms had imprisoned them, and it would have been politically impossible to maintain such symbols of English slavery among them while those elsewhere were demolished.[46] Besides, no detachment could have been spared from the Scots army.

So the unpoliced glens again became places to which a highlander's troublesome creditor or a lowlander's unwanted wife could safely be kidnapped.[47] Cattle-raiding soon became almost universal, but the pattern differed from the pre-war one. The huge, vulnerable droves provided a new target, and also gave 'caterans' (highland robbers) a chance to penetrate the Lowlands disguised as drovers (forcing the Council in 1671 to order genuine drovers to carry passes). Most raiding now was the work of 'broken men', members of clans destroyed by their neighbours' expansion earlier in the century or by war, or individuals socially or psychologically uprooted by decades of violence (including surplus males, detained at home by the Civil Wars, who would otherwise have joined foreign armies) or by quarrels within clans. Apparently, many outcasts who might earlier have been absorbed into other clans were not, because land was not available or chiefs dared not bind themselves for their conduct. The most famous of those who deliberately chose the cateran's way of life, later in the century, Domhnall Donn Macdonald of Bohuntin, cattle-raider and poet, had quarrelled with his chief Keppoch and other clansmen. Some lesser men remained independent like him; others lived under the protection of chiefs who would no longer undertake conspicuous full-scale clan raids in the old style, but who might still want to profit from raiding or harass their enemies.[48]

Although the caterans, of whom Donald Macdonald the 'Halket Stirk' (Spotted Bullock) was the most conspicuous in 1660 (he was also to be the most persistent and longest-lived),[49] were the most obvious cattle-thieves, there were three clans, Sir John Campbell of Glenorchy wrote in 1660, who, besides sheltering caterans, had long been notorious for their own raiding, the Camerons and the Macdonalds of Keppoch and Glencoe. In 1660, none of the three had secure tenure of their lands, and none of their chiefs possessed justiciary powers. Those of Lochaber were in the hands of Lochiel's and Keppoch's enemy Mackintosh, but an impartial court would have been almost equally unacceptable: Lochiel opposed the establishment of one as long as he could, though he might hang thieves ruthlessly to gain credit when there was a garrison at Inverlochy. All three chiefs faced internal troubles in their clans, and the young chief of Keppoch's fate was an (unneeded) warning not to attempt to curb their clansmen's traditions of cattle-raiding. A parody 'thieves' grace', perhaps of this period, thanks Lochiel and his tacksmen for giving them free passage and hiding places.[50] Despite the justification feuds gave for inter-clan raids, robbing the Lowlands was evidently seen as a morally less dubious activity: in a famous letter of 1645, Alan Cameron of Lochiel apologised to the Laird of Grant for a robbery on his land by a party en route for 'Morrayland quhair all men taks thair prey'.[51]

It was not merely the Lochaber chiefs who provided protection. The allegiance of the Macgregors, a landless, broken clan (although they still acknowledged a chief), was competed for by Argyll, Glenorchy,[52] Atholl, Montrose and Perth. Patrick Roy Macgregor, the most savage cateran of the 1660s, who imposed a reign of terror in the North-East, and was finally captured after a fight while extorting black-mail (protection money) from the town of Keith, was protected by the unscrupulous Earl of Aboyne, Tutor of Gordon (that is, guardian of his young grand-nephew the Marquess of Huntly, head of the Gordon family). Patrick Roy kidnapped and hanged some gentlemen not merely, it was believed, for having borne witness against him, but for being Aboyne's local opponents.[53] Lowlanders would hire groups of highlanders to take the lead in riots. One common type occurred when a landowner died and his widow continued to occupy the family house and lands, creating the danger that she might remarry and unjustly divert them from the rightful heir. He (usually her stepson) and his party would ritually seize the house, with a great show of violence — hence the highlanders — but almost none in reality.[54]

Yet the old highland tradition of real violence and admiration for violence lurked close below the surface. Modern research has apparently discredited the black legend about the early seventeenth-century Raid of Kilchrist, that on it the Macdonalds burned a church full of Mackenzie worshippers; but it was the Macdonalds themselves, not the supposed victims' clan, who perpetuated and celebrated the story in poetry and pibroch.[55] The violence broke surface in its ugliest form in the Keppoch Murders of 1663, which seemed to confirm the lowlanders' harshest opinions: it could not be foreseen that this would be atypical of Restoration highland society. When the young chief returned from abroad with his brother, their uncle and Tutor could not endure surrendering control of the clan. His sons drew up a band to murder them with the Macdonalds of Inverlair whom Keppoch, like his predecessors, was harrying to curb their independence. The two brothers were murdered in their home, riddled with stab wounds. The poet Iain Lom, who furiously denounced the murderers, was driven into exile. Almost no other clansmen showed concern, since Keppoch had tried to suppress their traditional habits of cattle-raiding — a lesson other chiefs, and lowlanders, would not forget. Despite Iain Lom's passionate appeals, Macdonell, the self-proclaimed head of Clan Donald and wadsetter (mortgagee) of Keppoch, took no action. Only after two years did Sir James Macdonald, who had brought up the youths, accept a commission of fire and sword and send a party under his brother, who avenged the murders on the Inverlair family. Yet the wicked uncle remained undisturbed as chief, and his son Archibald, who had signed the band, succeeded him peacefully — although their new Keppoch House was well provided with bolt-holes. The avengers waved the murderers' severed heads before Macdonell's face, as a reproach for his indifference, a reproach with which lowland observers agreed.[56] 'Black Donald' of Clanranald (chief 1670-85) shot clansmen casually.

Most highland estates outside Lochaber, and lowland estates or communities close to the highlands, had long organised watches, in which tenants, under carefully selected captains, served according to rosters. They were often paid for their trouble, and it was common to hire professionals, often Macgregors with experience on both sides of the law. Not surprisingly, the income paid them was often, in effect, illegal black-mail. Attempts to recover stolen cattle naturally strayed into a grey area of semi-legality: 'tascal money', paid to obtain secret information of them, naturally shaded into 'theft-bote', the compounding (again illegal) with the actual thief (particularly when the watch captain was in league with him) for which informers sometimes prosecuted. It may be argued that, in declaring these activities illegal, the Edinburgh lawyers were attacking a rival tradition for regulating disputes which they did not understand, as, to some extent, was the case even when they suppressed the lowland blood-feud. Most compensation for raids was obtained by informal agreement, with recourse to the courts only a threat to obtain settlement; between clans, assessors were often appointed according to former agreements.[57] However, many sufferers probably used this method less from any liking for it than from the pitfalls of the alternative. At a time when Sir James Lamont could extort money from Argyllshire people by threatening to summon them all the way to Edinburgh merely as witnesses, no ordinary tenant could have afforded to prosecute before the Session or Justice-Court, with their drawn-out proceedings: his only chance of recovering anything was to assign his claim to his landlord. The more remote the raiders — and many of those attacking the South Highlands came from beyond Loch Ness — the less the chance of any real compensation. Charges might be met with skilled counter-charges; although, as chance remarks show, 'highland witnesses' were generally suspected to swear whatever their chiefs wanted, only convicted criminals could be excepted against. Arrested thieves often escaped from the inadequate local tolbooths, and they, or the relatives of the comparatively few who were hanged, might take revenge on the prosecutors — a danger particularly clear in the 1660s.[58] Even the Laird of Grant, who, on the ruling Committee of Estates' orders, in late 1660 captured the 'Halket Stirk', feared massive retaliation from his Macdonald kinsmen in Glengarry and Glencoe, and wanted him released on security.[59] Victims therefore compounded with the thieves or their chiefs, but their resentment grew. 'It is a burthen even to receav a favour from such men,' wrote the Laird of Brodie, a man by no means blind to highlanders' merits, when negotiating with Keppoch.[60]

The central government was naturally concerned with the problem of robbery: the 1660 Committee of Estates, the 1661 Parliament and the new Privy Council carried out investigations and appointed special watches.[61] The only new legislation was a general 1662 act binding the inhabitants of parishes where robberies occurred and those through which the thieves retreated to pursue them, on pain of making good the loss, and otherwise making liable the inhabitants of the parish where the booty was divided. Normally, the government relied on James

VI's laws, which made landlords and chiefs give security, with lowland cautioners, for the peaceful behaviour of their vassals and tenants, renewed yearly, and the vassals in turn give bonds to them. This enabled victims of robbery to sue the landlords, and them to recover the value from the actual criminals. Broken and masterless men were theoretically left without rights, equated with thieves and left to commissions of fire and sword. Some such injustices were inevitable given the clumsiness of the system, and fitting landless Clan Gregor into it was a perennial problem. Yet, despite its faults, it did provide some check on thieving, and the government, like Monck, automatically used it. In the short term, it strengthened and gave added legitimacy to the clans involved: the counter-securities which chiefs who had bound themselves for their clansmen's peaceable behaviour were entitled to take from them increased their authority over them.[62] Macdonell and Sir James Macdonald therefore were sometimes rivals in giving security for other branches of Clan Donald. This could cause trouble: Donald the fiar (heir) of Sleat, who imprudently gave security to obtain the 'Halket Stirk's' release in 1660, was abruptly ordered in 1671 to produce him or forfeit £12,000.[63] Ultimately the system, by obliging the chiefs of the most disorderly clans to pay massive compensation, would plunge them still deeper in debt, increasing instability. More immediately, although landlords were occasionally excepted from giving security for areas they did not control, it was a further motive for Mackintosh to take extreme measures in Keppoch, or Argyll in Glencoe.

The Council in the early 1660s issued several commissions of fire and sword to capture particular robbers, or try those already captured, but there was no group or individual with special overall concern for preventing highland robberies, although the similar but lesser problems of the Borders were referred from 1662 to a Commission. The first committees appointed to consider highland matters were composed entirely of lowlanders — probably not from a sinister motive, as was the case when the Scottish clergy were excluded from the discussions on restoring episcopacy, but from a justified fear that the highland magnates, though they had the knowledge to advise on policy, would twist and misrepresent facts unscrupulously for their selfish interests.[64] Yet inevitably, as a result, the committees were no innovators and acted only with immense delays, while the raids, particularly on Moray, grew severe. In December 1664, the Council decided to establish garrisons in Braemar, Ruthven and Inverlochy. Ruthven at least was temporarily occupied, but the rest came to nothing, and in mid-1665 a private watch had to be established to protect the North-East.[65]

In the twenty-five years until the Revolution the government was at intervals again to be attracted to various Grand Designs for securing order in the Highlands whose main feature was the re-establishment at Inverlochy of a garrison (in the mediaeval castle) and a justiciary commission. The plans were prepared frequently — yearly, in troubled times; occasionally, orders were given for forces to march; but they were never carried out. Instead, the government, like the Cromwellians before them, resorted to traditional measures, for which there was strong local pressure, the summoning of chiefs to give bonds for good behaviour, to be renewed annually.[66] Ineffectual before, this proved ineffectual again. To punish serious disobedience or real crime, the Council had to rely mainly on clumsy 'commissions of fire and sword' granted to groups of local nobles and gentry. Like much 'barbarism' on the highland side, these commissions were more alarming in appearance than practice. The Council indemnified the recipients fully in advance for killing men or burning houses, while normally (except when issuing commissions against known criminals) not expecting them or wishing them to do either, and relying on their showing discretion even in dealing with their personal enemies — a dangerous legal fiction. If no suitable persons were ready to accept a commission, the government might be unable to punish even flagrant crimes, as the Keppoch Murders showed.

Commissions of fire and sword were most dangerous when granted by right as part of the legal process. This in effect left it to the discretion of private subjects like Mackintosh whether or not there should be civil war in the Highlands. They could further involve the government by demanding support from soldiers; Mackintosh in 1663 called for a garrison at Inverlochy.[67] Unlike Monck, the government could not halt lawsuits by military *fiat* in the interest of keeping the peace; but, even when no private interest like Argyll's was involved, it might evade granting or sabotage a commission, like Mackintosh's against Keppoch, for several years. This built up hostility, particularly when the regime was using highlanders to terrorise opponents. To critics, and some conscience-ridden supporters, this was an injustice no different in kind from corrupt favouritism for others of Lauderdale's cronies. To them, basing their assumptions on lowland property laws, and lowland power over tenants, it was Mackintosh who was 'the poor oppressed gentleman', Keppoch 'his oppressor'; that the latter's Macdonalds had lived on the land for centuries merely made the oppression worse. One later Chancellor was to write:

> It is strange to me, that a subject can be suffered to possess another man's inheritance, whether he will or not, by plain violence: and ... if such a possessor's offer, to pay what he is able for bygones, and to find caution for the future rent, is thought reasonable to oblige the proprietor to let his lands to him, whether he wishes or not ... [68]

In contrast, Rothes, the Restoration Lord Commissioner (royal representative in Parliament) and Lord Chancellor, a political fixer of genius, was usually anxious to arrange such compromises. As Stevenson emphasises, in confrontations between clans now, the aggressor would normally have legal decreets and official sanction to justify him.[69] Yet confrontations did not provoke fights to a finish; government pressure, and an increasing reluctance among clans, even the Campbells, to fight for their chief's property rights limited bloodshed, and inconclusive campaigns were followed by winter discussions at Edinburgh to reach a compromise. Despite the constant strain Argyll's self-righteous determination placed on the Council's attempts to prevent the letter of the law from leading to bloodshed, these failed disastrously only twice, in 1680 and 1688. Lawyers, in contrast, emphasised the letter; and it was to be the first lawyer since the Restoration to become Secretary, Sir John Dalrymple, who by enforcing it caused a worse disaster.

NOTES

I owe several significant points in this chapter to Dr. A. I. Macinnes, 'Repression and Conciliation: the highland dimension', a paper read at a historical conference on Restoration Scotland at Glasgow University in September 1982 since published, *SHR*, LXV, (1986), 167-95.

1. F. D. Dow, *Cromwellian Scotland* (Edinburgh, 1979), 56-7, 112-13, 163; *The Letters and Journals of Robert Baillie*, ed. D. Laing, 3 vols. (Bannatyne Club, 1841-2), iii, 387; A. Cunningham, *The Loyal Clans* (Cambridge, 1932), 21.

2. R. K. Marshall, *The Days of Duchess Anne* (London, 1973), 86-7, 150-9.

3. J. Kirkton, *Secret and True History of the Church of Scotland*, ed. C. K. Sharpe (Edinburgh, 1817), 69, 79-80; Sir J. Lauder of Fountainhall, *The Decisions of the Lords of Council and Session*, 2 vols. (Edinburgh, 1759), i, 182-3; *HMCR Laing*, i, 376, W. Douglas to Lauderdale, 6 Aug. 1669.

4. *Justiciary Records 1661-78*, ed. W. G. Scott-Moncrieff, 2 vols. (Scottish History Society (SHS), 1905), ii, 153; E. Burt, *Letters from a Gentleman in the North of Scotland*, ed. R. Jamieson, 2 vols. (London, 1818), ii, 3; Donald McBane, *The Expert Sword Man's Companion* ... (Glasgow, 1728), 76-7; Rev. J. MacInnes, 'Clan Unity and Individual Freedom', *Transactions of the Gaelic Society of Inverness (TGSI)*, xlvii (1971-2), 343-56.

5. D. Stevenson, *Alasdair MacColla and the Highland Problem in the Seventeenth Century* (Edinburgh, 1980), 8-20.

6. S. MacMillan, *Bygone Lochaber* (Glasgow, 1971), 110-12, 121, 163-4; *Register of the Privy Council of Scotland*, 3rd series (*RPCS*), i, 196; *The Scots Peerage*, ed. Sir J. Balfour Paul, 9 vols. (Edinburgh, 1905-14), v, 564; Sir W. Fraser, *The Chiefs of Grant*, 3 vols. (Edinburgh, 1883), ii, 89, Macdonell to Tutor of Grant, 29 June 1667; *Memoirs of Locheill*, 67-8, 153.

7. W. Macfarlane, *Genealogical Collections*, ed. J. T. Clark, 2 vols. (SHS, 1900), i, 337-8, 343-6, 387-94; Sir Aeneas Macpherson, *The Loyall Dissuasive and other papers concerning the affairs of Clan Chattan*, ed. Rev. A. D. Murdoch (SHS, 1902), xxxviii-xlii, 56-9, 61-2, 63-8, 78-9 & n.

8. *Memoirs of the Life of Simon Lord Lovat, written by himself in the French Language* (London, 1797), 315-19; Rev. J. Fraser, *Chronicles of the Frasers: the Wardlaw Manuscript*, ed. W. Mackay (*Wardlaw MS*; SHS, 1905), 31-2, 54-6; R. W. Munro, 'The Clan System; fact or fiction?', Inverness Field Club, *The Middle Ages in the Highlands* (Inverness, 1981), 122-3; MacInnes, 'Clan Unity', *TGSI*, xlvii, 352-4.

9. *Ib.*, 363; Sir W. Fraser, *The Earls of Cromartie; their kindred, country and correspondence*, 2 vols. (Edinburgh, 1879), i, 27-9, Macdonalds to Tarbat, 2 Feb. 1678; F. J. Shaw, *The Northern and Western Islands of Scotland* (Edinburgh, 1980), 16-21, 31-2; Munro, 'Clan System', *Middle Ages*, 122.

10. *Memoirs of Locheill*, 56-7; A. Campbell, 'The Keppoch Murders', *TGSI*, xxxix-xl (1942-50), 168-9; NLS MS 1305 fol. 56, Keppoch to J. Mackenzie of Delvine (hereafter 'Delvine'), 23 Aug. 1698.

11. J. A. Maclean, The Sources, particularly the Celtic Sources, for the History of the Highlands in the Seventeenth Century, (Aberdeen Ph.D., 1939), 234, Iain Lom's son, 'Latha Raon-Ruairidh'; Cunningham, *Loyal Clans*, 39.

12. *Bygone Lochaber*, 22-3, 47-9; B. Lenman, *The Jacobite Risings in Britain, 1689-1746* (London, 1980), 247; *RPCS*, ii, 219-20; *ib.*, iii, 370-1, 470.

13. *Ib.*, i, 545-6; Burt, *Letters*, i, 50-1; C. Fraser-Macintosh, *Antiquarian Notes* (1st

series) (Inverness, 1865), 71; T. Kirk, etc., *Tours in Scotland 1677 & 1681*, ed. P. Hume Brown (Edinburgh, 1891), 23–4.

14. *RPCS*, ii, 199; *ib.*, v, 188–9; *HMCR 6th Report*, 534, Memorandum, 24 Jan. 1677; Macfarlane, *Gen. Colls.*, i, 377–80; British Library (BL) Additional MS (Add.) 23,125 fol. 94, Huntly to Lauderdale, 26 Sept. 1666.

15. E. R. Cregeen, 'The Changing Role of the House of Argyll in the Scottish Highlands', *Scotland in the Age of Improvement*, ed. N. T. Phillipson & R. Mitchison (Edinburgh, 1970), 1–4; *The Black Book of Taymouth*, ed. C. Innes (Bannatyne Club, 1855), xxxiin; Sir W. Fraser, *The Sutherland Book*, 3 vols. (Edinburgh, 1892), i, 308–9.

16. E. J. Cowan, 'Clanship, kinship and the Campbell acquisition of Islay', *SHR*, lvii (1979), 133–4, 136, 144–7; J. MacInnes, 'Gaelic Poetry and Historical Tradition', *Middle Ages*, 148–9; Stevenson, *Alasdair MacColla*, 23–7.

17. *Ib.*, 28–30, 48; M. Lee, *Government by Pen* (Urbana, 1980), 77–9.

18. I. F. Grant, *The Macleods; the history of a clan, 1200*-1956 (London, 1959), 192–6, 201–8.

19. Cowan, 'Clanship', *SHR*, lviii, 150–1, 153–5; Stevenson, *Alasdair MacColla*, 35–48; Shaw, *Northern & Western Islands*, 32; *The Book of the Thanes of Cawdor*, ed. C. Innes (Spalding Club, 1859), xxvi–xxviii.

20. Cunningham, *Loyal Clans*, 22; MacMillan, *Bygone Lochaber*, 117–18; *The Highlands of Scotland in 1750*, ed. A. Lang (London, 1898), 89; W. Cameron, 'Clan Cameron and their chiefs: Presbyterians and Jacobites', *TGSI*, xlvii, 404–5.

21. D. Stevenson, 'The Highland Charge', *History Today*, xxxii, Aug. 1982; Correspondence, *ib.*, Nov. 1982; *HMCR 6th Report*, 681, Order, 16 June 1685; Stevenson, *Alasdair MacColla*, 82–4.

22. *Ib.*, 147–8, 149, 214, 218–19; *The Spottiswoode Miscellany*, ed. J. Maidment, 2 vols. (Edinburgh, 1844), ii, 196.

23. H. McKechnie, *The Lamont Clan 1235*-1935 (Edinburgh, 1938), 202–6, 228; Stevenson, *Alasdair MacColla*, 226–7, 236–7, 240.

24. *Wardlaw MS*, 379, 406–7; C. H. Firth (ed.), *Scotland and the Protectorate* (SHS, 1899), xxxix–xliii; *Memoirs of Locheill*, 117.

25. *Ib.*, 107, 148–55, 159–62, 194; Dow, *Cromwellian Scotland*, 137–8, 140, 144–6, 155, 181–2, 225; MacMillan, *Bygone Lochaber*, 119–20; Stevenson, *Alasdair MacColla*, 274–7.

26. *Ib.*, 258, 277–8; *Acts of the Parliament of Scotland*, ed. T. Thomson, etc., 12 vols. (*APS*; Edinburgh, 1814–75), vii, 429; *Highlands in 1750*, 46–7; Grant, *The Macleods*, 307; McKechnie, *Lamont Clan*, 217; *Scots Peerage*, v, 562–4; Firth, *Scotland & the Protectorate*, 29, 31; BL Add. 23,130 fol. 7, Macdonell's petition, 1663.

27. *Ib.*, Add. 23,129 fol. 45, [Sir R. Moray] to [Lauderdale], 19 June 1663; *ib.*, fol. 46, [same] to [same], 20 June 1663; Sir G. Mackenzie, *Memoirs of the Affairs of Scotland*, ed. T. Thomson (Edinburgh, 1821), 132; Grant, *The Macleods*, 307; C. Fraser-Macintosh, 'Neil Macleod, last of the Macleods of Assynt', *TGSI*, xxiv (1899–1901), 370–81.

28. Fountainhall, *Historical Notices of Scotish Affairs*, ed. D. Laing, 2 vols. (Bannatyne Club, 1848), ii, 692; Nottingham University Library (NUL), Manuscripts of the Duke of Portland (Portland MSS), PwA 675, Hill to Portland, 30 Apr. 1696.

29. *Records of Invercauld*, ed. Rev. J. G. Michie (New Spalding Club, 1901), 324–5, Grange to Erskine of Pittorchy, 22 Mar. 1730/1; NLS MS 2955 fol. 18, Airlie to Lauderdale, 30 May 1666.

30. *Spottiswoode Miscellany*, ii, 144, 164; *Orain Iain Luim*, 204–7, 'Oran air Righ Uilleam agus Banrigh Mairi'; MacInnes, 'Gaelic Poetry', *Middle Ages*, 147, 152–3.

31. *Memoirs of Locheill*, 119, 166–7; Macfarlane, *Gen. Colls.*, i, 306, 314, 322;

Macpherson, *Loyall Dissuasive*, 57-8; Stevenson, *Alasdair MacColla*, 272, 277; *Memoirs of Locheill*, 119, 166-7.

32. Major-Gen. H. Mackay, *Memoirs of the War carried on in Scotland and Ireland, 1689-1691*, ed. J. M. Hog etc. (Bannatyne Club, 1833), 242-3, Mackay to Melville, 20 July 1689; A. & H. Tayler, *The House of Forbes* (3rd Spalding Club, 1937), 208, 218-9; *The Diary of Alexander Brodie of Brodie*, ed. D. Laing (Spalding Club, 1863), 357, 390, 394; *Wardlaw MS*, 511-13.

33. D. Maclean, *The Counter-Reformation in Scotland, 1560-1930* (London, 1931), 146; *RPCS*, ii, 323; J. Prebble, *Glencoe, the story of the Massacre* (London, 1966), 36; Campbell, 'The Keppoch Murders', *TGSI*, xxxix-xl, 167; M. Martin, *A Description of the Western Islands of Scotland*, ed. D. J. Macleod (Stirling, 1934), 150-1, 160; Rev. C. Giblin, 'The 'Acta' of Propaganda Archives and the Scottish Mission, 1623-1670', *Innes Review* (*IR*), v (1954), 60-1, 63-4, 66-9, 72. For doubts on one alleged scandal, the hanging by the tyrannical Donald Macdonald of Clanranald of a priest caught in adultery with his wife, Mons. D. MacRoberts, 'The Death of Father Francis White', *ib.*, xvii (1966), 186-8.

34. A. C. MacWilliam, 'The Jesuit Mission in Upper Deeside, 1671-1737', *ib.*, xxiii (1972), 22-6; MacWilliam, 'A Highland Mission: Strathglass, 1671-1777', *ib.*, xxiv (1973), 76-83.

35. I. Whyte, *Agriculture and Society in Seventeenth-Century Scotland* (Edinburgh, 1979), 190-1, 228-9, 234-7, 240-2; Shaw, *Northern & Western Islands*, 114-16, 155-9; *APS*, viii, App. 21-2; Fountainhall, *Journals*, ed. D. Crawford (SHS, 1900), 184; Sir J. Nisbet of Dirleton, *Some Doubts and Questions in the Law* (Dirleton, *Doubts*; Edinburgh, 1698), (2nd pagination), 5; Sir J. Dalrymple of Stair, *The Decisions of the Lords of Council and Session*, 2 vols. (Edinburgh, 1683-7), i, 329; *Memoirs of Locheill*, 133.

36. *The Justiciary Records of Argyll and the Isles, 1664-1705*, ed. J. Cameron (*Argyll Just. Recs.*, Edinburgh, 1949), 157-61, 166-7; Macdonald, *Clan Donald*, iii, 500-3; J. Dunlop, 'A Chief and his Lawyer', *TGSI*, xlv (1967-8), 277-8; SRO GD 201/1/139, Highland Justiciary decreet, 19 June 1683.

37. *Ib.*, GD 170/629/8, Breadalbane to Barcaldine, 16 Mar. 1688; GD 1/658, 48, 53-4, 69; Sir W. Fraser, *The Melvilles Earls of Melville and the Leslies Earls of Leven*, 3 vols. (*Melvilles & Leslies*; Edinburgh, 1890), ii, 124, Cannon, 'Iron Mills', 23 December 1689; Lenman, *Jacobite Risings*, 247; J. M. Lindsey, 'The iron industry in the Highlands: charcoal blast furnaces', *SHR*, lvi (1977), 54-5; *Wardlaw MS*, 485.

38. *Black Book*, xviii-xx; J. Duke of Atholl, *Chronicles of the Atholl and Tullibardine Families*, 5 vols. (Edinburgh, 1908), i, 477; C. Fraser-Macintosh, *Letters of Two Centuries* (Inverness, 1890), 102, Seaforth to Inches, 14 Nov. 1678; S. Pepys, *Private Correspondence . . . 1679-1703*, ed. J. R. Tanner, 2 vols. (London, 1926), i, 219-23, 370.

39. *Wardlaw MS*, 456-7; *The Blind Harper*, ed. W. Matheson (Edinburgh, 1970), 58-73, 131-5, 'Oran do Mhac Leoid Dhun Bheagain'; Grant, *Macleods*, 345-8, 358-63, 365-77.

40. *Papers from the collection of Sir William Fraser*, ed. J. R. N. Macphail (*Fraser Papers*; SHS, 1924), 259-60, Band of pension, 23 Aug. 1681; *The Book of Dunvegan*, ed. Canon R. C. Macleod, etc., 2 vols. (3rd Spalding Club, 1938-9), i, 17-18; Stevenson, *Alasdair MacColla*, 280-1; Dunlop, 'A Chief and his Lawyer', *TGSI*, xlv, 258, 262-3; Blair Castle, Manuscripts of the Duke of Atholl (Atholl MSS), Box 44/VI/159, Murray to Middleton [1690].

41. *RPCS*, ii, 469-70; Martin, *Western Islands*, 104, 349-50, 353; Shaw, *Northern & Western Islands*, 32, 43-6; Grant, *Macleods*, 209; E. L. Cregeen, 'The Tacksmen and their Successors. A Study of Tenurial Reorganisation in Mull, Morvern and Tiree in the Early 18th Century', *Scottish Studies* (*SS*), xxiii (1969), 93-144.

42. M. Flinn (ed.), *Scottish Population History* (Cambridge, 1977), 156; Mackenzie, *Memoirs*, 241-3.

43. *Ib.*, 29-32; *RPCS*, ii, 207; *The Lauderdale Papers*, ed. O. Airy, 3 vols. (*Laud. Papers*; Camden Soc., 1884-5), ii, 100-1, Arran to Lauderdale, 28 Mar. 1678; BL Add. 23,124 fol. 53v, Bellenden to same, 10 Feb. 1666; Burt, *Letters*, ii, 54; Grant, *Macleods*, 315-16; *Memoirs of Locheill*, 204-5.

44. *Ib.*, 204; *RPCS*, ii, 586-8, 607; *ib.*, iii, 6, 8-9, 10-11, 31, 66-7, 640-1; 'Letters from John, Second Earl of Lauderdale, to John, Second Earl of Tweeddale, and others', ed. H. M. Paton, *Miscellany of the Scottish History Society*, vi (*Misc. SHS*, vi; 1939), 195, Lauderdale to Tweeddale, 23 Jan. 1669; NLS MS 7003 fol. 118, Moray to same, 14 Jan. 1669; *ib.*, fol. 134, same to same, Mar. 1669.

45. Firth, *Scotland & the Protectorate*, xxvi-xxviii; Dow, *Cromwellian Scotland*, 143-4, 188; *The Mackintosh Muniments, 1442-1830*, ed. H. Paton, (Edinburgh, 1903), 111, Scroll petition.

46. *RPCS*, i, 62; *Orain Iain Luim*, 76-7, 'Crunadh an dara Righ Tearlach'; Stevenson, *Alasdair MacColla*, 183.

47. W. Mackay, *Urquhart and Glenmoriston* (Inverness, 1914), 181-5; SCA, J. Thompson, 'History of the Roman Catholic Mission', 2 vols., i, fol. 149.

48. Stevenson, *Alasdair MacColla*, 281-3; S. Mac Gill-Eain, 'Domhnall Donn of Bohuntin', *TGSI*, xlii (1953-9), 91-3, 99-103; *RPCS*, iv, 361-2.

49. The 'Halket Stirk', Donald Macdonald *alias* Gavine Cuin, was already the outstanding cateran by 1660, and not only he but his sons were active in the 1670s. The 'Haked Steir' alias *Angus* Macdonald to whom a 1700 document refers was presumably one of them; but references in the 1690s may well still be to the father, for in 1697 Hill is still talking of the 'haucked stirks son', whom he had arrested but who, in the family tradition, broke prison. *Ib.*, iii, 388, 580; *Chiefs of Grant*, i, lxxxix; *Historical Papers Relating to the Jacobite Period, 1699-1750*, ed. Col. J. Allardyce, 2 vols. (New Spalding Club, 1895), i, 21, Bond, 26 Apr. 1700; Blair, Atholl MSS, Box 29 I (9) 282, Hill to Tullibardine, 14 Aug. 1697; SRO GD 112/39/940, Sir J. Campbell to Glencairn, 12 Sept. 1660.

50. *Ib*; MacMillan, *Bygone Lochaber*, 36.

51. *Chiefs of Grant*, ii, 76, Lochiel to Grant, 18 Oct. 1645.

52. Which may explain his failure to mention the Macgregors among the predatory clans. Macinnes, 'Repression and Conciliation', *SHR*, LXV, 174-5.

53. *Wardlaw MS*, 486-9; *Just. Recs.*, i, 133, 198-200, 260; *RPCS*, i, 598; *ib.*, ii, 265-6, 278-80, 410, 448, 489.

54. E.g., *ib.*, 242-3.

55. One caveat: nearly all the most discredited and obviously implausible similar myths of the later seventeenth century in this book have, by belated discovery of evidence, been proved true. S. Johnson, *A Journey to the Western Islands of Scotland*, etc., ed. R. W. Chapman (Oxford, 1979), 44 (giving wrong victims); K. Macdonald, 'A Modern Raid in Glengarry'. *TGSI*, xv, (1888-9), 11-24.

56. *RPCS*, i, 150-1, 220; *ib.*, ii, 62-3; *Orain Iain Luim*, 88-91, 'Murt na Ceapaich'; *ib.*, 112-13, 'Cumha ... '; *ib.*, 268-74; *Wardlaw MS*, 461-3; *Highlands in 1750*, 101; Campbell, 'Keppoch Murders', *TGSI*, xxxix-xl, 167-75; SRO GD 112/39/960, Sir J. Campbell to Glencairn, 12 Sept. 1660.

57. Burt, *Letters*, ii, 123-5, 130-1, 142; *Argyll Just. Recs.*, 82-3; Whyte, *Agriculture & Society*, 15-16; *Annals of Banff*, ed. W. Cramond, 2 vols. (New Spalding Club, 1891-3), i, 120; J. Wormald, *Court, Kirk and Community: Scotland 1470-1625* (London, 1981), 36-7; Atholl, *Chronicles*, i, 158, Struan to Nairn, 28 Aug. 1667.

58. *Ib.*, 341–2, Ardvorlich to Murray, 18 Jan. 1694; *RPCS*, iii, 312–13; *Just Recs.*, i, 108, ii, 124–5; *Argyll Just. Recs.*, 188; *Inventory of Lamont Papers (1231*–1897), ed. Sir N. Lamont (Edinburgh, 1914), 242; *Urquhart & Glenmoriston*, 177–9; BL Add. 23,130 fol. 78, [Tweeddale] to Lauderdale, 15 Oct. 1668; *ib.*, Add. 23,135 fol. 120, [Kincardine] to same, 21 Dec. 1671.

59. *Chiefs of Grant*, ii, 19–20, 20–1, Committee to Grant, 29 Aug., 9 Oct. 1660; *ib.*, i, 281–2, Grant's instructions, 1660.

60. Brodie, *Diary*, 362.

61. *APS*, vii, 281, 286; *Chiefs of Grant*, ii, 21–2, Commission, 13 Oct. 1660; SRO GD 112/39/960, Sir J. Campbell to Glencairn, 12 Sept. 1660; *RPCS* i, xxx.

62. *Ib.*, iii, 52–7, 553; *APS*, vii, 382–3; Burt, *Letters*, ii, 11–12.

63. *RPCS*, iii, 360, 385, 388, 599; *ib.*, iv, 177–8.

64. In 1665, for instance, Argyll, commenting on an intercepted letter to Lord Macdonell, suggested, from malice or ignorance, that Ranald Macdonald of Scotus, a respectable member of the Glengarry clan, was one of the Keppoch murderers, and that Macdonell was trying to obtain a remission for him. Macinnes's paper, to which I owe the point about the first committees, argues that the motive was sinister. *Ib*; J. Buckroyd, *Church and State in Scotland, 1660*–1681 (Edinburgh, 1982), 25; BL Add. 23,122 fol. 251, [Argyll] to Lauderdale, 26 Jan. 1665; Macinnes, 'Repression and Conciliation', *SHR*, LXV, 175–7; *RPCS*, i, 11, 634.

65. *Ib.*, 511–15, 638; *ib.*, ii, 68; *Wardlaw MS*, 457; C. Fraser-Macintosh, 'The Mackintoshes of Kellachie', *TGSI*, xix, (1893–4), 104–5.

66. *Lairds of Grant*, i, 281, Grant's instructions, 1660; Dow, *Cromwellian Scotland*, 106.

67. *HMCR Laing*, i, 338–9, Mackintosh to Lauderdale, 22 Oct. 1663.

68. *A Selection from the Papers of the Earls of Marchmont*, ed. G. H. Rose, 3 vols. (*Marchmont Papers*; London, 1831), iii, 118, Polwarth to Tullibardine, 28 Nov. 1696; *ib.*, 123, same to Ogilvie, 14 Jan. 1697.

69. Stevenson, *Alasdair MacColla*, 280–1.

2

Restoration without Settlement: the Campbells and their Enemies (1660–1680)

The appointment of royal lieutenants with power and experience in the Highlands might seem a solution to many problems there exacerbated by the government's lack of understanding. Yet it was the Earl of Argyll, whose position, the work of Secretary Lauderdale, made him virtually equivalent to one, who caused the worst highland disorders of the Restoration period.

The essence of Lauderdale's policies was ambiguity. It was never clear whether his major successes, even the removal of the English garrisons, were intended primarily to benefit Scotland or himself. His bullying, extremist rhetoric often masked comparatively moderate measures. While compelled to enforce an episcopalian church policy, which he secretly disliked, with increasing severity, he worked for a compromise with moderate Presbyterians. Although a monarchist, even a supporter of absolutism, he was on bad terms with the extremist 'Cavaliers' (as they called themselves), the ex-royalist out-and-out supporters of Crown and Episcopacy. Their leaders, the Earl of Middleton (who had actually left the Covenanting side later than he) and Sir George Mackenzie of Tarbat, attempted to drive him from power by the Billeting Act, which declared permanently incapable of holding office a dozen ex-Covenanters, chosen by a secret parliamentary ballot which naturally named him at the head. But they had deceived Charles about its terms, and Lauderdale, counter-attacking, instead drove them out of politics, Middleton permanently and Tarbat for fifteen years. He prevented their hungry noble followers from sucking the country dry through fines and a massive standing army. His best subordinates, such as the Earl of Tweeddale, had, like himself, been Covenanters; loyalists considered that his policy was 'to destroy Middleton and poor suffering Cavaliers'.[1] In most respects, historians consider, his policies were beneficial compared to his opponents'. However, the Cavalier leaders he overthrew were the chief advocates of the 'loyal clans', and, in his support for the Earl of Argyll, he showed total indifference for justice or peace in the Highlands.

The traditional view of highland troubles, that the house of Argyll was indispensable for 'bearing down the insolencies of the remote, rebellious, lawless men', could not save the Marquess from execution for treason in 1661 for his leadership of the Covenanters and collaboration with Cromwell. The 'Cavaliers', most of whom blamed their sufferings on him, founded a new cliche, that the family was incorrigibly disloyal and presbyterian and therefore took wicked pleasure in oppressing the loyal clans in their power. The Marquess's son shattered this convenient generalisation: as Lord Lorne, he served in Glencairn's rising, defying his father, and continued to intrigue with Charles after submitting. Yet, although cynics were presumably wrong to think this a family balancing act, his adherence on the whole weakened the loyalist cause: besides his quarrels with other leaders, it robbed them of a simple anti-Campbell rallying cry. He was also (probably more decisively) Lauderdale's relation by marriage, and Lauderdale saved him when the Middletonians, exploiting an imprudent private letter, condemned him in 1662 for an imaginary treason. Lauderdale could not, however, prevent one decision catastrophic for Lorne, who, despite his royalism, always remained as convinced as his father of their right to the Huntly estates. Now Charles restored the estates to the new Marquess of Huntly, a child, without charging them with the real sums Lorne's father had laid out. Even if he could regain all his other lands and powers, Lorne was ruined.[2]

Restoration seemed hopeless in Middleton's ministry, although nothing else was impossible in public and private affairs. The 'Cavaliers' who avoided annexing the Argyll forfaulture to the Crown planned to divide it (including the Huntly lands) among themselves.[3] The one preferred creditor, the second Marquess of Montrose, was granted Cowal outright in 1661 as recompense for his father's losses. Argyll soon reached an informal agreement with him to buy it back once the debt was satisfied, and terms were decided in 1667; but he remained uneasy at any local power, even a watch, being granted to Montrose, as a dangerous precedent. 'Loyal' Argyllshire clans, demanding restoration of lands and fictitious debts the Marquess had extorted from them during the wars, inserted many earlier, legitimate, transactions. A royal warrant was even drafted at one point granting Islay to Glengarry — which would have reversed the verdict not only of the Civil Wars but of the 1614–15 struggle.[4]

Lauderdale steered Argyll's interest through all these dangers. While he attended the 1663 Parliament, Sir Robert Moray in London prevented Charles from cancelling the Captain of Clanranald's massive debt and vassalage to the Argyll family, and was ready to do the same against Maclean. Lauderdale might argue in justification that their debts were needed to satisfy the Marquess's creditors. That October, Charles restored Argyll (under restrictions for payment of family debts) to his earldom, estates and heritable jurisdictions, including that of Justice-General of Argyllshire and the Isles (covered by a deliberately vague general clause) without properly considering the implications.[5] Lauderdale went further, employing Argyll as the government's chief representative in the South Highlands, and Argyll's brother-in-law Moray in the North-East and North, rather than Seaforth — for Tarbat's Billeting Act had intensified an old Maitland–Mackenzie feud. When the Pentland Rising of the south-western Presbyterians temporarily discredited the bishops and remaining 'Cavaliers', whose harsh policies had driven them to desperation, Lauderdale, Tweeddale and Argyll formed a ruling triumvirate.[6]

Even so, Argyll was insecure. The 'Cavaliers'' hostile view was a near-orthodoxy in London and Edinburgh — 'his father's name stinks there as well as here' — however faithfully he supported the regime. He was indifferent over church government, but was persistently suspected of crypto-presbyterianism and was denied a chance of proving his loyalty against the Pentland Rising.[7] His conduct over the family debts confirmed the 'Cavaliers'' hostility and raised fresh enemies. Even in an age of defaulting nobles, he was notorious for his unscrupulousness towards creditors (including charitable institutions). In the 1672 Parliament, he prevented an act to make apprisings in the Highlands easier. The Court of Session, particularly after Lauderdale's nominee Sir James Dalrymple of Stair became President, showed strong bias in favour of him and others of the ruling faction. Such bias was normal, and Stair was probably the best candidate available; but this was an aspect of Lauderdale's regime which both 'Cavaliers' and Whigs were to find almost impossible to forgive.[8]

By giving Argyll authority in the Highlands, Lauderdale destroyed all hope of stability there; for, struggling to escape destruction himself, he was driven to abuse his powers to ruin others. The settlement of his estates gave forewarning. Charles's grant guaranteed to him unburdened lands producing £15,000 Scots, perhaps a third of the Argyll estates' value; and the third of the total family debt of a million merks for which he was personally bound was secured on other lands producing £12,900. An official committee which managed his affairs might sell off the rest (reserving the superiorities) to satisfy the creditors. In selecting the scattered lands to make up the £27,900, Argyll carefully included nearly all the frontier lands of the Campbell empire, and bridgeheads in other clans' territory, in Mull, Ardgour, the Outer Hebrides and Ardnamurchan, while leaving Jura liable to be sold.[9] He would evidently in practice continue the family tradition of expansion; the alternative, to renounce its legacy of hatred and consolidate only the older family lands, was probably financially impossible. Some of his opponents might, from fellow-feeling, have partly excused the aggression to which debts drove him, had he walked more warily. Instead, although a more sympathetic figure than his father, he was self-righteous, felt entitled to his utmost legal rights, and treated his friends' warnings as disloyalty. He failed to understand how much hostility the spectacle aroused of a traitor's son evading his gigantic debts while exploiting the machinery of state and law to entangle and destroy less well-placed debtors. He shamelessly used his father's forfaulture to invalidate his acquittances, and prosecuted his vassals for non-performance of feudal duties in periods when the regime the Marquess supported had abolished them. Exploiting technicalities to destroy their security of tenure, he argued that 'Since His Majesty had fully and absolutely entrusted them to him, they ought to have rested upon His Kindness and Generosity, and not have made all this Clamour'.[10] The strong hostility to him appeared in the 1669 Parliament, when Charles's past grants were ratified only by Lauderdale's violent intervention as Commissioner. Tweeddale 'thought that Lauderdale wasted too much of his favour with the King in maintaining Argyll against so much opposition', urged him to drop him, and attempted to have the Earl deprived of his justiciary power in Argyll and the Isles; but this contributed to his own fall from favour.[11]

Argyll's main preoccupations in the 1660s were to settle Argyllshire and check thieving. In Kintyre, he greatly raised his lowland tenants' rents; elsewhere he demanded feudal dues. He evicted one important tenant, MacCoul of Lorn, from the island of Kerrera, driving him to turn robber. There was already much cattle-theft, which reached alarming levels in 1664. Argyll complained that his motives in trying to suppress it were given sinister innuendoes, and that the Middletonians and Macdonell were trying to create chaos, using the small Argyllshire clans and the Macleans.[12] Most of the small clans, however, had been shattered by the massacres of 1646–7, remaining inactive even in 1689. The one chief who openly opposed Argyll, Colonel Alexander Macnachtan, came from a clan which, although financially ruined, had not joined Alasdair and been crushed. Those who accepted absorption into Argyll's regime received the benefits, such as a justice-court fairly successful in checking robbers; opponents might have reason to fear not merely prosecution for feudal dues, like Macnachtan, but those justiciary powers. When a popular Campbell was killed in an Inveraray tavern scuffle, it was seriously feared that Argyll might immediately execute the actual killer's master, the rich Colonel Menzies of Culdares, Perthshire.[13] Local opponents could hardly succeed against Argyll unless Macdonell succeeded in his persistent attempts to regain Islay, perhaps by purchase from the bankrupt Calder. The possibility made Argyll, who was even less capable of paying the purchase price, demand first refusal. He meanwhile worked to obtain the superiority of Macdonell's lands and bought up his debts as means of harassment. Macdonell's rise drove Argyll and Seaforth to settle a traditional hostility, since both had far stronger hereditary feuds against the Macdonalds of Glengarry. Macdonell complained in 1666 that they were buying up superiorities over his lands in concert.[14]

In North Lorn there remained two unbroken clans who were Argyll's vassals but had opposed him strongly in the Civil War — the Stewarts of Appin and the Macdonalds of Glencoe. The latter, whose chief's family was also known as MacIain, were the smallest independent sept of Clan Donald. They occupied the south shore of Loch Leven, Glencoe itself, running south-east from the loch to Rannoch Moor, and Dalness, in a valley to the south-west. By the late seventeenth century, there were perhaps 200 families, and they could normally send about 100 men to war. They had almost incessantly been vassals of other clans, first the Stewarts, then the Glenorchy or the Argyll Campbells. By the 1650s, the Marquess of Argyll was their direct superior and landlord, using rents from Glencoe for interest and security in transactions elsewhere. His son in the 1660s granted a tack of it to the Campbells of Glenorchy, emphasising the preservation of deer and woods, and young Glenorchy was to claim in 1695 that 'in Glenco, the inhabitants ... hav[e] for the most part their dependence upon himself'; but Argyll was prepared to yield it to the creditors.[15] (See Preface p. vii)

However, in the Civil Wars the Glencoe Macdonalds had persistently followed Montrose, Alasdair and their successors in warfare against the Campbells. When Argyll denied in 1666 that any full-time thieves lived on his estates, his exception probably referred to them: 'some [on the fringes] who were greatest enemies to me in my trouble and if I should deall harshly vith them it would be said to be upon that account ... they would be receate by my nighbours and would steall from me'. In the 1660s, robberies caused the main strain on relations. Glenorchy the elder in 1660 considered the broken men of Clan Iain one of the three main groups of highland thieves.[16] In 1666, some Macdonalds involved in the Keppoch

Murders who had fled south led a band 80–100 strong in a major raid in Aberdeenshire. Most were Huntly's tenants, but six were from Glencoe, and part of the spoil was divided there. The Council therefore adjudged Argyll as landlord liable, despite his protests that he could not control what happened there, to pay full damages, and Glenorchy, as tacksman, similarly liable — the first application of that law in forty years.[17] In other raids the Glencoe men took the lead, exploiting the thieves' roads on Rannoch Moor and their 'wyld rockish countrey' which included a hidden corrie suitable for stolen cattle. Their raiding provoked a curious shift in South Highlands tradition which blamed them for a notorious Macgregor murder of 1589. When Alasdair MacIain, twelfth chief of Glencoe, escaped in 1674 from imprisonment on Argyll's warrant in Inveraray Tolbooth, the Council gave warning that he and his chief tacksman, Macdonald of Achtriachtan, had committed several murders and depredations, and that the country would probably now suffer.[18]

MacIain's arrest may have been on a charge which made him notorious even outside the Highlands, the murder, in person or at his orders, of two of his own clansmen. One version, that this was for giving information about a robbery, was preserved in the Dalrymple family, and Sir John referred in 1692 to 'the murderer McIain' while planning the destruction of Glencoe.[19] Yet, even on the most hostile interpretation, MacIain became notorious partly because he headed a small vassal clan, unable either to use heritable jurisdiction to dispose of clansmen who challenged his authority under a pretence of justice or arrange an apparently unrelated killing, as a more important chief could: he had to commit the slaughter openly. One cause of the notoriety, Argyll's attempt to prosecute him for it, was (like Mackintosh's 1671 indictment of alleged accomplices in the Keppoch Murder) largely an attempt to gain a legal hold over him, probably to counterbalance his strong ties to Lord Macdonell (who appointed him an executor) and to Sir James Macdonald. If the Glencoe men had been his supporters, Argyll might have proceeded more discreetly, as he did over some murders among the Camerons in 1667.[20]

Many Lowlanders, who knew less of the Macdonalds than of any other major clan south of Loch Ness, gained the impression (shared by some later writers) that the Clan Iain were merely a glorified robber band, and Glencoe their stronghold, where lowland and Campbell law never penetrated. In reality, Argyll visited Glencoe on business, and MacIain in 1673 safely attended the Inveraray justice-eyre even after his part in substituting an impostor for one defendant was known.[21] Although more liable than other chiefs to be fined for his clan's robberies, he held a respected place in highland society. The Macdonalds and their allies respected him as a wise counsellor, a brave warrior and a cultured chief. His family had friendships with East Highlands families, Grants and Farquharsons, and hereditary friendships with some Campbell neighbours, such as Inverawe. A Macdonald of Achnacone in Glencoe obtained (presumably through Atholl's influence) a wadset over part of Campbell of Glenlyon's estate, which, ironically, he still held three years after the Massacre.[22] Such links did not prevent conflict, or even atrocities, between clans, but came into their own as an alternative tradition in peaceful periods. Maybe Iain Lom's tireless and pitiless hatred of the Campbells actually reflected a more realistic understanding of the long-term dangers of their expansion; but even in his own Keppoch clan there were poets who told him to stop his obsessive harping on the slaughter of the wry-mouths (particularly inappropriate since Keppoch's hereditary bodyguards came from a group of Campbell families long settled in Brae-Lochaber).[23] One potential source of local hostility to the Glencoe men was strangely overlooked: they were Catholics. However, the glen, like most of the west Highlands, could not support a priest, which made its religious affiliations less conspicuous.[24]

Argyll tried to pass on the problem of the cattle-raiding in 1673 by selling Glencoe to Campbell of Glendaruel, who in turn began to transfer it to Sir James Campbell of Lawers. However, when Argyll's seizure of Mull provoked MacIain, as the Macleans' ally, into making major raids on Argyllshire, Argyll furiously attempted to buy it back 'and to wast it once [i.e. by eviction] and reinhabite it with friendly honest men by this I lose from the time comeing 4000^{lb} [purchase price] and 100^{lb} of few duty and it might one day yeeld my sone 1000^{lb} or 1200^{lb} by yeare'. Fortunately for the Macdonalds, Lawers' bargaining for terms dragged on until Argyll's fall. Historians depicting the Macdonalds primarily as thieves have argued that Glencoe was too barren to support them otherwise; their opponents, that, as it was fertile enough for crops and legitimate cattle-raising to support the inhabitants, accusations against them are exaggerated. Argyll's figures suggest a third alternative; that the Macdonalds, in their concentration on cattle-robbing, were not fully employing the glen's resources — not a case of insecurity of tenure driving a clan to raiding (as has been argued in the cases of the Camerons and Keppoch Macdonalds), but of raiding jeopardising its tenure. Fairly certainly, Argyll's plan made no impression on his son Lorne, who was then languidly disclaiming interest even in the proceedings against the Macleans, on which the family fortunes depended.[25] (See Preface, p. ix)

Argyll, while still settling Argyllshire, embarked on policies which dipped the Highlands into civil war. The Macleans, once the Campbell's expansionist rivals, had been in decline since 1600, although they still held Mull, Ardgour and Morvern on the mainland, and lands in southern islands including Jura. Although the chiefs were in grave financial difficulties by 1637, the foundation of Argyll's claim was his father's purchase of the arrears of taxes which Sir Lachlan (who followed Montrose) owed the Covenanting regime. The Marquess imprisoned him until he acknowledged a grossly inflated debt, all payments on which were ignored. His son Sir Hector concluded an even worse agreement to protect Mull from Campbell attack when the Macleans joined the royal army in 1651 — which should, after Inverkeithing, have obliged Charles to protect the clan. Instead, Argyll's grant included the debt, now estimated at £121,000 Scots, mostly interest. Sir Alan's rental was under £1,000 sterling, and he had other creditors.[26]

Argyll declared his intention of transferring Maclean's and Clanranald's debts to his father's creditors and leaving them to reach a settlement. Certainly, the Tutors, and later Sir Alan himself, deserved some blame for missing the opportunity: 'he is a long eared beast comonly called ane ass' complained Argyll after one negotiation. Yet it was with the creditors that the decision rested, and, apparently, they who finally refused, lacking Argyll's power to enforce claims in the Highlands.[27] While Argyll declared, perhaps sincerely, his willingness to compromise, he was tightening the screws on the Macleans and increasing their debts. He had himself infeft in (formally granted) the estates, bestowed Maclean outposts like the Garvellach Islands on his followers, virtually for conquest, and led provocative expeditions to dive on the Tobermory Galleon for treasure.[28] Having the power to apportion the shire cess, he imposed unfair amounts on Mull, and quartered troops there to impoverish the Macleans still further. This drove Sir Alan, who had originally co-operated, to desperation, and in 1667 he fled to London to seek redress from Charles. The government's attempts to arrest him in the Lowlands failed, but Lauderdale blocked access.[29] On his return, he continued negotiations with Argyll and the creditors, attracting the contempt of bolder dissidents. Yet he was trying to create a united front among the Macleans for the day when Argyll would enforce his claims by invasion — a difficult task, since some clan gentry, landowners in their own right, had a tradition of independence and considered his orders oppressive, while others were Argyll's feudal vassals and hesitated to oppose him. To ensure their support, Sir Alan relied partly on holding their bonds for debts, some even purchased from Campbells; but Argyll could match this financial pressure with decreets against them obtained in his regality courts and demands for feudal fines and wardship — often from the heirs of men killed at Inverkeithing.[30]

The Macleans' most important highland supporter was Lord Macdonell, whose assistance to them, like his attempts to purchase Islay, was partly a means of staking a claim to be chief of all Clan Donald. Many Macdonalds considered their lack of one dominant chief a stigma; but most branches and the government recognised the Sleat family as at least titular heads. The Glengarry branch had originally been a minor sept of Clan Ranald, and they were still at best the third largest. Yet Macdonell's royalist record and consequent credit made him a serious rival to Sir James, who had collaborated with the English. His peerage was a unique advantage, now clan links with the Antrim family were fading; as Earl of Ross he would have been irresistible. He exploited his limited resources to increase his credit among Macdonalds, persistently obtaining wadsets of Keppoch from Mackintosh, hoping finally to gain possession. He rebuilt his castle at Invergarry, destroyed by Monck; this was, indirectly, to preserve his clan in 1692.[31] He also tried to extend his power outside the Highlands, over Inverness, near which he usually now lived, an unwelcome neighbour. When a 1665 market riot turned into an unprovoked attack on the Macdonalds, in which several were killed, he raised his clan and threatened to destroy the town unless the magistrates surrendered the culprits and signed a very one-sided bond of alliance with him. The Council, who finally settled matters, in their distrust of burgh independence presumably overlooked Macdonell's raising of his clan. But such violence now needed a veil of legality to succeed permanently: Macdonell's persistent weakness was his inability to find one.[32]

His ambition was not the sole reason for the failure to form a united Macdonald front against the Campbell advance; Clanranald was hopelessly in debt to Argyll and his vassal for some estates, and he was also one of Sir James Macdonald's creditors, partly by inheritance, partly by purchase.[33] Yet it did cause a serious breach, driving Sir James to obtain an acknowledgement of his chiefship from Clanranald, MacIain and the Kintyre Macdonalds (while Macdonell, appropriately, signed a bond of mutual recognition with Cluny). The Sleat family had long been allies of the Mackenzies — Tarbat, Sir James's nephew by marriage, was a constant supporter — and in 1676 Sir James applied through Seaforth for an earldom. To scotch this, Macdonell employed a hereditary ally, who, from an even stronger hereditary enmity towards Argyll, became the Macleans' most important lowland sympathiser: the Earl of Atholl.[34]

Atholl was reconstructing his family interest after the damage of the Civil Wars, handicapped by massive debts and the fact that the Murrays were not a clan: his power over his followers, mainly Stewarts and Robertsons, was basically feudal. In the absence of automatic clan loyalty, it was particularly unfortunate that he lacked any gift of personal leadership. Even in the most sympathetic period of his career, when he led dashing youthful attacks to recapture his castles from the English during Glencairn's rising, he was unable to raise a significant following.[35] He could rely instead on his position as the chief natural supporter in the Highlands of monarchy and episcopalianism (strengthened by his marriage to the martyr Earl of Derby's daughter) to ensure support in Atholl, a reliance which backfired disastrously in 1689. His chief officials, Patrick Steuart of Ballechin the bailie and his brother Alexander the chamberlain, served him from this mixture of family loyalty (their elder brother had been killed saving his life) and Stuart loyalism. Parties of Atholl highlanders under Ballechin were considered the most effective deterrent against conventicles in Perthshire.[36]

Parties under him also carried on semi-legal harassment against neighbours whom Atholl wanted to force to become his vassals, like Robertson of Struan, chief of the Robertsons, or to sell him their estates, like Campbell of Glenlyon. Argyll's followers slanderously accused Atholl of trying to use judicial murder also. His power over his actual vassals, strengthened by a grant of the fines imposed on local former rebels, enabled him, 'then in his pomp', to extort large sums from them and buy land and superiorities from them at his own rates. His enemy Simon Fraser Lord Lovat probably exaggerated when he claimed that the Stewarts and Robertsons hated the Murrays and were always secretly ready to mutiny; but Atholl's need for money and blustering in enforcing his feudal powers did cause alienation.[37] To win followers outside his immediate neighbourhood, in contrast, he followed a policy of sympathising and help. He tried to help Inverey obtain a pardon for Brackley's murder. When Huntly in the early 1680s was maltreating the Macphersons, he offered to sell cheaply to Cluny estates in Atholl where he could settle as his vassal, transferring the clan's allegiance even though most of them would remain on Huntly's lands. His most important protégés in the Highlands were the Macdonalds (who, according to tradition, were related to the Murrays), in particular Macdonell.[38] A similar ancient link united the house of

Argyll and the Frasers, and the apex of Atholl's influence in the North Highlands came only after Argyll's fall, when in 1685 the young Lord Lovat married his daughter Amelia. By the contract, the peerage and estates were to pass to any child of the marriage, male or female. As the Lovats were a notoriously short-lived race, a long minority under Atholl domination was probable. This alienated the Tarbat family, which through a similar minority had controlled the Lovat interest until the marriage. Seventy years earlier, the then Lord Lovat had refused James VI's offer of the earldom of Atholl because it was burdened with vast debts and an insubordinate people; after this ironic reversal, the Frasers had good reason to fear that Atholl, notoriously driven by his inherited debt to 'unwarrantable shifts of rigor and oppression', would make permanent his family's grip on the Lovat estates as a financial milch-cow.[39]

Argyll's most important acquisition of the 1660s, which Atholl and Macdonell failed to prevent, also showed how an adroit chief could exploit national politics and highland divisions. Lochiel's position in 1661 seemed desperate, with his patron Argyll executed, a pre-war judgement in force for his eviction from Mackintosh's lands of Glenloy and Locharkaig, and Macdonell emphasising his record of collaboration. He adroitly joined Middleton's faction, even signing their petition against restoring Lorne, and they supported him, ignoring Macdonell (with whom they had quarrelled) and overruling Parliament's decision in Mackintosh's favour. They twice introduced him at Court, and Charles urged the Council to arrange a compromise. When Lauderdale triumphed in 1663, Mackintosh received a commission of fire and sword: it seemed that Lochiel had made a fatal false step. By 1664, however, he had made his peace with Argyll. Supporters of Lauderdale who had previously assisted Mackintosh, such as Moray, now secretly turned against him, while Middletonians changed sides too late to help, and other potential supporters were too frightened of Cameron raids. When Mackintosh nevertheless assembled a force in 1664, Lochiel promised to settle peacefully, and, at a meeting of both sides in arms across the River Ness, agreed to buy the lands — only to break the agreement, probably at Argyll's instigation, when Mackintosh's force had dispersed.[40]

That winter Lord Commissioner Rothes tried to bring them to compromise at Edinburgh. Mackintosh refused, considering the offer contemptible, and Rothes could not (as he clearly wished) compel him; but the pressure, and some indirect official sabotage of his preparations, continued through 1665. The decisive factor, however, was that Clan Chattan was reduced to impotence by internal divisions (fanned by Lochiel), while Clan Cameron (despite the Macmartins' recent relations with Macdonell, who supported Mackintosh) was not. From late 1664, Cluny was refusing to accompany Mackintosh against Lochiel unless he would acknowledge the Macphersons' independence. Others of his followers, including several Mackintoshes, also refused unless he would make them major grants or wadsets of land — to be taken from other clansmen. Only Mackintosh's youthful fury against Lochiel made him persist. Once the expedition was on the march, he was more at his followers' mercy, and had to make some unreasonable grants, including a virtual admission of Macpherson independence; despite this, when, in

September 1665, they faced across the River Arkaig a smaller force of Camerons (assisted by Glencoe men and Macgregors), they refused to fight if any settlement, even an unfavourable one, was possible. This enabled young Campbell of Glenorchy, who arrived with 200 men, to bring about one for the sale of Glenloy and Locharkaig to Lochiel, for under three-quarters of what Mackintosh had been offered a month earlier, by declaring that he would impartially take sides against whichever of the chiefs (both his relations) proved recalcitrant.[41]

In reality, since the purchase price was far beyond Lochiel's means, the buyer, who had been negotiating terms with him for months, would be Glenorchy's principal, Argyll. Knowledge of this had presumably increased Mackintosh's hostility to previous offers, since Argyll was hopelessly in debt and had the repurchase of Cowal as a more urgent priority. He paid Mackintosh the first instalment, but later defaulted, for which his sureties (including Glenorchy) suffered — another example, to the public, of his amorality.[42] Although the only alternative offer, Atholl's (his refusal of which made Atholl his lifelong enemy) was far worse, Lochiel accepted Argyll's terms reluctantly, less for the actual conditions on which he held Glenloy and Locharkaig, light feu-duties and feudal service, than for other demands. For some years, he had held Ardnamurchan and Sunart, on a wadset the Marquess had granted his Tutor. Now he had to surrender them, although the inhabitants continued to count themselves Camerons, and Argyll granted them to the Campbells of Lochnell. Lochiel possessed the feudal superiority over Macdonell's lands in Knoidart, and had given him a bond to sell it back to him. Now Argyll insisted on buying it, cheaply, to exploit them against him. Indeed, Macdonell, who had opposed the settlement, but had been distracted by his feud with Inverness, was perhaps the chief sufferer; for with Argyll's first instalment Mackintosh redeemed his wadset over Keppoch.[43]

The struggle between Argyll and his opponents now shifted to controlling the measures taken against highland robbers. Argyll might have been of great service in framing these — 'if it were seriously gone about, few need be hanged, though some must', he wrote — but he was excluded out of fear that he would introduce distortions to further his own interests, and even suspicion that he himself was instigating raids. 'The braes of the Highlands are fallen very broken,' he complained in 1666, 'the cry will be at Glenurchy, and so at me: but it concerns no subject more to have them peaceable.'[44]

By September that year, the Council was considering three alternative methods of quelling the robbers. One was to raise regular armed companies; but it was suspected that they might become a permanent charge even after the crisis subsided. Another was to give control to a single magnate, who could use his private resources; but he might exploit it in his own interest. A third was to employ a lesser person, backed by the royal authority. He must, emphasised Argyll (who favoured this plan), have local knowledge, enabling him to discover without using severity (as strangers must) 'who of one, two or three races of people tooke [cattle] and wher they are receate and by what ways they drove them'. That autumn, it was almost agreed to appoint Colin Campbell of Ardkinglas, but instead policing was left to the troops sent to quarter for arrears.[45]

In August 1667, however, the Council after much debate granted Atholl a general commission for a year and a half (a shorter period than that proposed for the lesser man) covering all counties from Inverness-shire round to Dunbarton-shire. Seaforth received a similar one for the North. Argyll refused one, and would not sign Atholl's, which granted him £200 a year to raise a standing watch to guard particular passes and patrol the braes. Agents were appointed at Ballachastell in Strathspey (Grant's home), Ruthven, Braemar, Blair and Glengey near Stirling, and Huntly promised his support. If informed within thirty-six hours of the theft of cattle or goods, Atholl's watch must regain them or repay the value, theoretically from the forfeited possessions of convicted thieves. Those they captured might be tried before the Justice-Court or local jurisdictions.[46]

Outwardly, the commission seemed successful. In February 1668, the Council reported the country free from depredations. Their only reforms were to appoint a commission to sit with heritable judges in their jurisdictions in trying thieves — although cases with landed men as defendants must be referred to the Council. Atholl, being Justice-General, could reduce friction between the commission and the Justiciary Court.[47] The increase in his normal highland influence might recompense him for his expenditure, but he was suspected of developing it by dubious means. Lauderdale was warned in 1669: 'last yeare the theefes were only quiet because they were imployed to keep the rest from stealing & for that hade great liberties allowd them, & besides many thefts were not complained of because they uold not offend the person uho was ansuerable for them, being too great for such an imployment'. Argyll hinted that, if dismissed, Atholl might even encourage the thieves.[48]   The Council shared this distrust. Although Atholl was repaid expenses when his commission expired, it was not, as he had hoped, renewed. Instead, the committee proposed a new, stricter bond for landlords and chiefs, including obligations not to give or take black-mail and to recover or compensate for goods their tenants had taken. Most objected; Argyll was nearly imprisoned for refusing, and Lochiel was unable to find lowland cautioners. All delayed giving the bonds because there were reports that highland thieves employed by magnates, perhaps including Atholl, were preparing massive raids.[49] Partly to mollify him, he was made commander of the Troop of Guards. Tweeddale, having turned against Argyll, groomed him as an alternative, and the two highland magnates became rivals for government favour throughout the 1670s.[50]

In Atholl's place, the Council decided,

> there shall be a privat gentleman found who shall be bound to refound the theft or produce the theef, who shall be bound lykewise to produce deade or alive all the theefes of the Highlands acording to a list ... And who shall serve thus for one yeare without any condition but what the councell shall please after the proof of his service.[51]

They were careful not to replace Atholl's direct with Argyll's indirect dominance in their nominee, Sir James Campbell of Lawers on Loch Tay. His father had been killed fighting against Montrose at Auldearn, and the financial involvement with the Covenanting cause which left Sir James hopelessly in debt, finally ruining the family, had forced him to comply with the English invaders: he first showed his widespread highland influence by organising a plot to kidnap Middleton. Paradoxically, this helped to obtain the commission, since 'he hath no dependence but upon the King's favour and the Councells countenancing him, for all the great men of the Highlands hate him, especialy his cheef'; Argyll tried to sabotage the grant.[52] In September, Lawers was ordered to collect bonds from heads of highland families and track down some named thieves, mostly Macgregors. In November, he received a commission for a year, similar to Atholl's but including Argyllshire. He would receive £100 and £300 expenses, and protection from his debts may have compensated him for any additional costs. The subordinate agents and their stations were changed.[53] His swift success in capturing some notorious Cameron thieves drove Argyll to similar efforts. Naturally, in making captures and recovering goods he used agents and methods of dubious legality, although he gave bond not to employ common thieves. The Justiciary Court hanged one intermediary he employed to recover stolen goods, suspected of organising the robberies himself but convicted merely of compounding with thieves and receiving a commission on goods recovered.[54]

Lawers's success by mid-1670 encouraged the Council to order Moray, as Sheriff of Inverness-shire, to hold a court at Inverlochy. Mackintosh, as Steward of Lochaber, had prior rights, but had exercised them only once, after a 1667 Brae–Lochaber cattle raid. Cluny and several Mackintosh vassals had attempted fresh extortion, and Huntly had even persuaded the Camerons to assemble to frighten him. Mackintosh had held the courts, but would not expose himself to Clan Chattan blackmail again.[55] Moray may have intended to forestall trouble between the Camerons and Macdonalds, probably a result of Lochiel's transfer to Argyll of the rights over Knoidart. If so, he failed disastrously. At the meeting, Lochiel, fearing the establishment of permanent courts and a permanent garrison, indirectly stirred up his Camerons to a violent riot against the Macdonalds, in which two men died, and courteously escorted Moray (or his depute) out of Lochaber.[56]

In early 1671, Lawers, who had captured eight notorious thieves, had his conduct approved and his commission renewed, as it was in 1672 and 1673. The Council ordered that all drovers coming from the Highlands should have passes proving their respectability. When, in early 1671, they decided to revive the Justiciary Circuit Courts, and Argyll offered to allow one conditionally at Inveraray and to persuade other holders of shire regalities, it seemed that the possibility of trying cattle-thieves speedily and cheaply would be a further deterrent. Instead, the circuits were postponed from year to year, and sat only in Anne's reign.[57]

Tweeddale's suggestion that Lawers should receive a company in the army for quieting the Highlands came to nothing, and the Council had no means to prevent the further clashes that summer between the Camerons and Macdonalds. They attempted to make Lochiel and Macdonell bind themselves for their clans, but

Macdonell, surprisingly, denied being chief of the Macdonalds. Meanwhile, a party of troops was ordered to Inverlochy, to protect the courts to be held there, but greater priority was given to their other tasks, ejecting from Menzies's Rannoch lands the defiant occupants (who included some Keppoch Macdonalds and the Laird of Macgregor) and quartering for arrears, and they apparently never arrived.[58] In the autumn, Cameron raids caused further fighting, and the Clan Ranald became involved. By December, the Council feared that the struggle would spread and jeopardise the peace of the Highlands. Despite long hearings, they were unable to settle the dispute, but, by imprisoning the chiefs until they found lowland caution, they seem to have prevented further open fighting. Instead, Macdonell revived his complaints over Lochiel's Interregnum conduct in the 1672 Parliament.[59]

In 1674, Lawers was superseded in the commission by the Laird of Grant's uncle, Major George Grant, Deputy-Governor of Dumbarton Castle, who held it for three years. This mysterious change defied the criteria established in choosing Lawers, for Grant was apparently the candidate of the Huntly interest under Aboyne. Several of the agents at his seven local stations were more distinguished than Lawers', including Ballechin's brother at Blair, Farquharson of Invercauld (and the outlaw Inverey) at Braemar and his own brothers at Ballachastell and Ruthven. In September, an imposing court composed of Sheriffs and their deputes was established to try the thieves he caught — forty in the first year. Yet Grant's public and private record of dishonesty made him otherwise a bad choice, and he exploited the commission to make illegal seizures.[60] His main fault, however, seems to have been simple failure to protect the North-East adequately. In November 1675, Moray landowners felt obliged to make a private contract, on the official model, for a watch, and, perhaps in response, the Sheriff-depute of Inverness-shire was added in the 1676 reshuffle of Grant's local agents. Throughout Grant's tenure, outside causes made his task hopeless. Snowstorms in early 1674 caused disastrous loss of life among cattle, and, after the one catastrophic harvest of the Restoration period, there was famine in some areas and widespread shortages throughout 1675. The exchange of cattle for grain on which the highland economy depended must have been almost totally disrupted. And, as the Highlands began to recover from this, they were more persistently disturbed by Argyll's advance, which provoked a minor civil war.[61]

Argyll's chief adviser was John Campbell of Glenorchy, of the main cadet branch of the family, which had expanded from the head of Loch Awe north-eastwards into Perthshire. The most successful and aggressive chieftain, Sir Duncan, 'Black Duncan with the cowl' in James VI's reign, was notorious even in that age for his unscrupulousness, particularly his part in the campaign to exterminate the Macgregors; and his evil reputation coloured perceptions of his great-grandson's activities.[62] The existing accumulation of debt upon the estate grew rapidly under his second son Sir Robert, who had a large family. The marriages of Sir Robert's daughters made his eldest grandson John, born about 1635, first cousin to the Campbells of Glenlyon, Ardkinglas and Inverawe, and to

Lochiel (born in the old family castle of Kilchurn), with whom he always maintained close relations.[63]

During the Civil War, the family naturally adhered to Argyll. In December 1644, Montrose marched the length of their estates to invade Argyllshire, totally devastating them, although their half-dozen castles held out. Sir Robert estimated his losses at 1,200,000 merks, and by 1649 his estates were in his creditors' hands. Their shape, a long, thin arc 'but 9 miles from lochaber in some places & no parte of it is a nyts march' away, made them terribly vulnerable to raids. Young John recalled 'having [in the 1640s] seen my Uncle and near relatives and hundreds of our men killed and all our Estate brent and Harried'. The worst raid was in 1646, when an interrupted wedding-party, launching a rash pursuit of Keppoch and Glencoe raiders, was defeated with the loss of eighteen Campbell gentry. The young chief of Keppoch was also killed. Yet the later Glenorchy tradition was of comparatively friendly relations with Keppoch; their chief Macdonald enemies were apparently the Scotus family of Glengarry.[64]

Glencairn's rising caused further devastation. The family, now managed by Sir Robert's son Sir John, again sided with Argyll — and the English invaders. Monck helped them crush the MacNabs and destroy their clan castle. Exceptionally, when most young nobles and gentry prominent after 1660 were with Glencairn, young John of Glenorchy began his career as 'a highland star to Monck', guiding him on his marches and cunningly influencing the Campbell gentry not to rise at Lorne's summons. Going to London to petition Cromwell for reward, he succeeded in marrying an heiress.[65] In 1660, he received control of the estates, but immediately provoked a decade-long quarrel with his father (who survived until 1686) by trying to cheat him and his own numerous siblings out of their burdensome rights. Sir John also distrusted his gambler's policy of buying land and accumulating fresh debts (and dangerous lawsuits) rather than reducing the existing ones. His complaining letters showed an ambivalence which many others were to share: extreme respect for his son's intellect and abilities; extreme distrust of his honesty.[66]

Young Glenorchy did not suffer in 1660 for his past record, not least because he gained Glencairn's own favour.[67] His abilities were soon noticed, particularly in the advice and help in negotiations he gave Argyll in settling Argyllshire, with the agreement between Lochiel and Mackintosh as his greatest success. Argyll was often told that his cousin was 'the best feather of [his] wing'.[68] Despite his youth, Glenorchy sat in Parliament for Argyllshire from 1662.[69] The Council soon listened to his advice and appointed him to special commissions to try thieves. Yet at least one was withdrawn on suspicion that he would abuse it. In his public career in the Highlands, Glenorchy almost always preferred to work by conciliatory negotiation. He may have been far more ruthless on his estates, pursuing, for instance, a vigorous hereditary quarrel with Lawers, with whom he co-operated on general questions of settling the Highlands. Suspicions of his conduct at a local level would explain MacIain of Glencoè's apprehension of his vengeance after a quarrel over some cattle-thieves in 1691.[70]

Glenorchy was determined to continue the expansionist tradition which had placed the family home at Balloch, at the north-eastern extremity of the estates, and disinherited his eldest son, whose simple-mindedness made him unsuitable for maintaining a dynasty. However, expansion from Balloch was blocked by Atholl's and Menzies of Weem's estates.[71] In Argyllshire, where the family possessed a third of Lorn, only limited gains at the expense of declining Campbell families were possible.[72] Glenorchy's models must be the Campbells of Calder (Cawdor) with their scattered estates, Cawdor in Nairnshire gained by marriage to an heiress, Islay by conquest; and accident turned his attention to the shire of Caithness.

Caithness was held mainly by gentry of one name, the Sinclairs, but was socially and economically a lowland shire beyond the Highlands, an extremely fertile arable country, 'the girnells of the north', with a flourishing export trade. Its people wore lowland clothes, only half spoke Gaelic, and many had a contempt, which was to prove disastrous, for highlanders.[73] The head of the Sinclairs, George, sixth Earl of Caithness, who succeeded as a child in 1643, had his immense family debts greatly increased by loans to Middleton, English ravaging of the shire and his traditional aristocratic lifestyle. His marriage to the Marquess of Argyll's daughter was an obvious disadvantage after the Restoration, when he even at first failed to become Sheriff of Caithness. An appeal to Lauderdale with mention of their relationship, a promise of support and a douceur, helped to recover the post, but not the lost ground.[74] The most quarrelsome of the quarrelsome race of Sinclair, William Sinclair of Dunbeath, who had persecuted the Earl since the early 1650s, had meanwhile obtained a deputation, and held courts to harass him and his servants. Council pressure made Dunbeath pretend to reach an agreement with him, but in 1663 he prevented him even from sitting as a J.P.[75]

The Council could do little to prevent this or worse illegalities. Distance alone would have made the people of the North — 'we yt lives at ye back of gods elbow', as Seaforth said — hard to control, and disorders rooted in the past probably made the area the most unstable in the Highlands throughout the 1660s. Fear and suspicion had always been the staples of family politics there. An experienced adviser in the 1620s warned his chief to maintain spies in rival chiefs' houses, and to assume that his hereditary enemies, however friendly their behaviour, were always working to destroy him. This attitude persisted: 'they are so doubtfull amongst themselves that they are always preparing for the worse, especially in prouiding armes', reported a Macdonald in 1665, when the Mackenzies were convinced that Macdonell was about to launch an attack on them.[76] The fresh feuds created by the Civil War and the Covenanting Sutherland family's expansionist policy were continued in raids and counter-raids. The bitterest, between Strathnaver and Caithness, were provoked by the chance killing of a Mackay chieftain in Caithness in 1649. The Council's intervention might do more harm than good: a commission of fire and sword it granted was used to justify fresh raids. It could only assist the private pacifications between chiefs which by degrees from 1661 limited the disorder.[77]

By the late 1660s, however, Caithness, financially crippled and credulous, had drifted under Dunbeath's influence — a dangerous one, since he was the chief organiser of raiding, and was privately backed by Seaforth, the hereditary enemy of the Caithnesses. Caithness was childless, and secretly settled the earldom's estates on Dunbeath, to be surrendered by September 1668.[78] He himself joined in the raids, partly to enforce an obsolete hereditary jurisdiction over Sutherland. In early 1668, the Council urged a peaceful settlement, but Caithness and Dunbeath immediately led 1,200 men across northern Sutherland, plundering and kidnapping gentlemen, one of whom, William Mackay of Scourie, died of ill-treatment. Caithness then directly defied the central government: when some troops quartering for arrears (characteristically, its only direct representatives locally) committed irregularities and were seized by the Thurso townsfolk, he declared that he would try them and threatened the Council messenger sent to forbid this with hanging.[79]

Finally appearing at Edinburgh, Caithness was very briefly imprisoned in the Castle, and attempts began to settle matters between him and Strathnaver. Lauderdale obtained a remission, 'necessary for so near a friend', but he and Tweeddale wanted it kept as a 'pokquet pistole' for emergencies, fearing an outcry if Caithness used it to stop the accumulating Justiciary prosecutions. He reached an agreement in December with the Sutherland family to forgive previous raids.[80] Dunbeath had conveniently separated his case from Caithness's, and enabled the Council to ignore his claims on the estate, by fleeing Edinburgh in August and fighting against a party pursuing him, killing William Mackay's brother Hector (which unexpectedly diverted the Scourie succession to their brother Hugh, a professional soldier then in Crete, later Dundee's adversary). In December a commission of fire and sword (originally balanced by one against the Strathnaver raiders) was issued against him and his chief accomplice, and committed to Caithness, Strathnaver, other northern gentry, Argyll and Glenorchy, but was delayed for fear of provoking fresh instability in the North.[81]

Dunbeath, though outlawed, continued to act as Sheriff-depute and defy Caithness. Finally, on 29 July 1669, Glenorchy, probably chosen chiefly as Argyll's representative, was commissioned to bring him to justice, raising armed men and planting garrisons. He marched with 300 men, including a party of regulars. A supporter warned him that many thieves intended to follow him north, where their robberies would be blamed on him. He garrisoned Dunbeath House, but Dunbeath himself roved the country in safety, always one day ahead of him, abetted by the Sinclair gentry — 'I never see men more waded to a person then they ar all to Dunbeath,' he wrote. He therefore imprisoned for three months a dozen gentry who refused a bond that they and their tenants would not shelter him. Others, cited before the vindictive Caithness, temporarily fled from the shire, and Dunbeath, with his support removed by these drastic measures, retired into Ross. He was soon unsuccessfully offering Caithness £6,000 not to oppose a remission. Glenorchy returned south. Although the Council ignored Sinclair complaints against him, he had made himself very unpopular in Caithness.[82]

The Earl, with his finances 'putt in great confusione' by Dunbeath's activities and quartering for arrears which seemed likely to become permanent, was no

sooner freed from one Sinclair than he became the dupe of another, Sir Robert
Sinclair of Longformacus, of a lowland branch, a very prominent and
unscrupulous advocate.[83] In 1668, with great professions of family loyalty, he
offered his assistance with the creditors, and, by buying up the debts at great
discounts, by 1670 he had Caithness financially at his mercy. He himself claimed
to be a poor innocent whom the Caithnesses fraudulently lured into pledging his
credit; but already in 1669, before his largest purchase, he was proposing that
Caithness should grant him the estates and live on a small annuity. In 1670,
Lauderdale made an award reducing Sir Robert's claims, and making him allow
Caithness three years to pay them.[84] Almost immediately, Sir Robert broke the
agreement to buy up no more debts, and tried to obtain an Exchequer grant of the
estate. Glenorchy and the Countess believed that Tarbat and other hostile
Mackenzies were financing him.[85]

Glenorchy had meanwhile also been buying up Caithness's debts, for himself
and, apparently, Argyll.[86] In 1672, Sir Robert again nearly forced Caithness to
sign away his estates. Instead, in October, he granted them to Glenorchy, his
wife's cousin, whose claims and advances to him (which Glenorchy himself had to
borrow) soon, with interest, reached £3,800 sterling. He was to receive them after
Caithness's death, meanwhile managing them to pay off creditors and allowing
him an annuity. He himself claimed to 'pitie and compassionat ... ane ancient
familie ... opprest & all uith ye Colour of Law'. Although he desired the peerage,
there was a redemption clause, with which he and Caithness hoped alternatively to
obtain better terms for themselves from Sir Robert.

They had miscalculated. He reacted to this 'setlment on strangers' by openly
declaring that he would ruin Caithness — a promise a first-rank lawyer could keep.
He started or encouraged several dozen lawsuits to exhaust the money Caithness
had raised to pay him, and used his agents to disrupt the estate until the tenants
refused to pay their rents.[87] One result was to drive the Caithnesses, not only
financially but emotionally, into closer dependence on Glenorchy. He too faced
ruin. Even with land sales, the estates could not pay the annuities and creditors'
interest. The Sinclairs declined to relieve their chief, never having forgiven his
treatment of Dunbeath.[88]

Glenorchy turned for help to Lauderdale's second wife, whom he had married
in 1672. The Duchess had great influence over her husband, and used it
unscrupulously and harmfully. Although the increasingly clear failure of his
policy of Indulgence towards Presbyterians was the main cause of his alienation
from his abler and more honest supporters, her extreme ambition and greed
played a part, and her quest for husbands for her daughters strongly influenced his
choice of new favourites. She was apparently responsible for his disastrous use as
his deputy in Scotland of his dishonest brother Halton (whom she herself
despised), a sign of the regime's increasing corruption, and she accepted large
bribes to exploit her influence.[89] Glenorchy's first request, however, was fairly
legitimate. He was willing to leave Sir Robert the title and estates if he could
honourably escape from the affair with repayment of his outlays. Rather than
furnish an excuse for the ruining of the Caithnesses, he declared, he would

reluctantly cancel half his claim. If, however, she would persuade Sir Robert to grant Caithness the same terms he himself had, and pay his claim, he 'humbly offer[ed] on thousand pounds ... touards my sweet Lady Catherns portion', meanwhile promising £500 for a necklace to her. He strongly hinted, though not as a formal condition, that the Duchess should obtain a peerage for him as compensation for the lost earldom. The proposal came to nothing, and his own agreement with Caithness remained valid, but he remained one of the Duchess's protégés.[90]

Argyll, however, whose own remarriage had provoked a quarrel with Lauderdale, had no such security. He would gladly have been reconciled; but his rival Atholl gained the Duchess's favour, possibly even before her marriage, and prevented it. Appointed Privy Seal in 1672 as a reward for his parliamentary support for new taxes, and unlikely ever to rise higher by his own abilities, Atholl therefore concentrated on ingratiating himself with her. Rothes wrote that he 'has nothing else to stand by but her favour', which gained him a marquisate. In 1673–4, he and Argyll vied in displaying their loyalist zeal, and both received preferment to the Treasury and Session. Yet Argyll found the Duchess unfriendly; and she might, under Atholl's influence, succeed in turning Lauderdale against him.[91]

Argyll urgently needed firm Court support, for in 1674 his affairs with the Macleans reached a crisis. His final legal steps to dispossess them were proceeding rapidly that spring when Sir Alan died young, leaving a four-year-old son, Sir John. Maclean of Lochbuie and Maclean of Torloisk immediately became Tutors, but Sir Alan's death inevitably disrupted his measures for resistance, giving Argyll his opportunity. He bought ammunition and provisions and summoned the Argyllshire gentry to meet him at Inveraray. A regular company he had quartered in Mull for the excessive public dues attended the messengers who in August unsuccessfully summoned Maclean of Brolas to surrender Duart and then crossed to join Argyll at Dunstaffnage.[92] He had assembled a formidable invasion force including Glenorchy, Calder, Lochnell, Stewart of Appin — and Lochiel, despite the dangerous illness from which he suffered that year.[93] Even the Macdonalds took part, Clanranald as a vassal, and Sir James as a visitor. On the other side, Torloisk and most of the leading Macleans remained neutral.[94]

In early September, Argyll received a commission of fire and sword, but also the Council's offer of indemnity. Brolas's one hope was that Argyll might tie himself down on landing in besieging Duart, and he drove off the cattle to the hills. Instead, the invaders landed on 16 September in three parties, ruthlessly houghing (hamstringing) cattle in Iona. Glenorchy and Lochnell, both sympathetic to the Macleans, intervened to negotiate a pacification on 18 September. The rebels were to submit, surrender Duart and acknowledge Argyll's legal rights. In return, he would pardon them their rebellion and payments of rent to Sir Alan, treat them well as tenants and grant Brolas a wadset over his own lands. The infant Sir John was nowhere mentioned.[95] Duart was handed over; the Macleans hoped to recapture it soon, but during all the later rebellions it was to remain a Campbell garrison.[96] Peace seemed likely if Argyll treated the Macleans

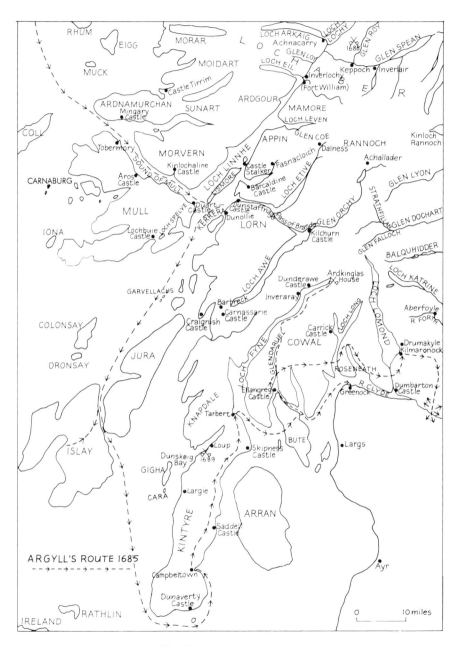

RHUM
EIGG
MORAR
MUCK
MOIDART
Castle Tirrim
ARDNAMURCHAN
SUNART
Mingary
Castle
COLL
Tobermory
MORVERN
Kinlochaline
Castle
Aros
Castle
CARNABURG
MULL
IONA
Lochbuie
Castle
GARVELLACHS
COLONSAY
ORONSAY
JURA
ISLAY
GIGHA
CARA
IRELAND
RATHLIN

L
O
C
H
LOCH ARKAIG
Achnacarry
1688
GLEN LOY
GLEN ROY
GLEN SPEAN
LOCH EIL
Keppoch
Inverlair
Inverlochy
(Fort William)
E
R
ARDGOUR
MAMORE
LOCH LEVEN
APPIN
GLEN COE
RANNOCH
Dalness
Kinloch
Rannoch
Castle
Stalker
Fasnacloich
Achallader
Barcaldine
Castle
GLEN LYON
Duart
Castle
Dunstaffnage
Castle
Pass of Brander
GLEN ORCHY
STRATHFILLAN
GLEN DOCHART
Dunollie
LORN
Kilchurn
Castle
GLEN FALLOCH
BALQUHIDDER
LOCH AWE
Dunderawe
Castle
Ardkinglas
House
LOCH KATRINE
Barbreck
Inveraray
Aberfoyle
R FORTH
Carnassarie
Castle
Craignish
Castle
Carrick
Castle
COWAL
LOCH LONG
LOCH LOMOND
Drumakyle
Kilmaronock
ROSENEATH
Dumbarton
Castle
Ellangreg
Castle
Greenock
R CLYDE
KNAPDALE
Tarbert
BUTE
Largs
Loup
Skipness
Castle
Dunskeig
Bay
1689
Largie
KINTYRE
ARRAN
Saddell
Castle
Ayr
Campbeltown
Dunaverty
Castle

SOUND OF MULL
LOCH LINNHE
LISMORE
LOCH SPELVE
KERRERA
LOCH ETIVE
LOCH FYNE
GLENDARUEL

ARGYLL'S ROUTE 1685

0   10 miles

The South-West Highlands

well, and Lochiel, whose wife was Sir Alan's sister, went despite his sickness to Inveraray (accompanied by suspicious clansmen who feared that Argyll might have his throat cut) to receive his assurances.[97]

Negotiations between Argyll and some leading Macleans that winter, however, aroused their suspicion. In April 1675, he decided to return to Mull, having obtained fresh letters of ejection against Torloisk and several hundred lesser tenants, presumably as a means of applying pressure. Glenorchy warned him that he must first calm the Macleans' groundless suspicions; otherwise, his journey would only spread alarm more widely. Argyll replied furiously 'he should goe if it wer in a farie [ferry] boat'.[98] His journey provoked Brolas and other Maclean gentry to swear a league, garrison the impregnable island-fortress of Carnaburg, off the west coast of Mull, occupy Tiree and drive away Argyll's Maclean bailie as a collaborator. Of other leading Macleans, Coll, Torloisk, and Lochbuie remained neutral, but their sons and the mainland chieftains Ardgour and Kinlochaline were with Brolas. During Argyll's brief stay, large armed parties stood on guard, and Brolas went to consult Lord Macdonell. The Macleans boasted of their determination, if necessary, to devastate Morvern and withdraw its cattle into Mull. Argyll returned, fatuously pleased at having 'discovered' the rebellion.[99]

Glenorchy's advice to show moderation merely alienated Argyll from him — 'I am so great a complyer with the McLeans that I am a suspected person' — and his persistence widened the breach, since Argyll considered all such advice merely a sign of indifference to his interests.[100] Yet, although the objections reflected Glenorchy's reluctance to assist Argyll, they were sound. The most obvious was the cost. Once the Macleans were united and found allies, Argyll had to mount regular campaigns against them, supporting permanent garrisons, large forces in the summer, and even a flotilla of armed ships. The yearly expense was £5–600, 'no small mater to a Scots estate', forcing him to borrow and wadset other estates.[101] Since the Macleans offered rewards for supporters, he must make counter-offers. In return for Clanranald's support or neutrality, he eventually promised not to demand payment of his debt. MacCoul of Lorn supported Brolas in 1674, and to win him over Argyll had to grant him a good estate. Lochiel in May 1675 informed Argyll that the Macleans had approached him and were tempting his second son to take a tack of Morvern and Ardgour, and in June Argyll granted a contract rewarding him for attendance with fifty men. His own creditors had less chance than ever of repayment.[102]

The effect on Argyll's reputation was still more disastrous, although his self-righteous conviction that he was upholding the principles of legality and property blinded him to this. As the troubles with the western Presbyterians moved towards a crisis, he, a supposed pillar of the government, employed his power exclusively in a highland war and frequently demanded regular forces to assist him.[103] His actions on returning from Mull exemplified the obvious injustice of his methods. Using his justiciary power, he summoned the Macleans to answer for their rising at Inveraray, before his depute deep in his country. When, not surprisingly, they failed to appear, he had them declared outlaws. He greatly damaged his credit at Court by so frequently demanding commissions bearing 'that dreadfull name of fire and sword'. Caterans took advantage of the disruption his activities caused, and landowners blamed him for the raids. Atholl's influence might even shake Lauderdale's support.[104]

The 1675 campaign showed that subduing Mull would be far more difficult than Argyll anticipated. In July he received his commission of fire and sword. The Campbells including Glenorchy, Appin, Lochiel, Clanranald and the Macleods were expected to support him, and regular troops were sent to assist, although he was again urged to offer an indemnity. In September, Argyll assembled 1,500 men at Dunstaffnage and began to ship them to Duart. Clanranald had joined him, but Lochiel unexpectedly wrote that the Camerons refused to serve him on the terms he had granted. He soon afterwards raised them to join Lord Macdonell, who was gathering a force to 'mediate'. In mid-September they crossed together from Morvern with 1,100 men and joined the Macleans, outnumbering Argyll. He sent a flotilla to land elsewhere as in 1674, but was driven back by a tremendous storm, allegedly raised by a witch — not the last time the Macleans would receive such help against invaders. Argyll admitted defeat and withdrew to the mainland, but had to station 900 men to protect Argyllshire and its islands from raids.[105]

The Macleans had granted to Lochiel, as to other supporters, a pension, 1,420 merks, to attend yearly with his clan to assist them. They evaded the laws on conspiracy by officially describing the pensions as 'interest' on imaginary debts. Argyll, who nicknamed Lochiel 'the Bishop of Munster' after a notorious contemporary prince-condottiere, clearly believed that he had changed sides merely for the bribe. He may also, as Balhaldie suggests, always have intended to give Argyll merely nominal support, and, since their contract contained a promise of arbitration, he or his clan may genuinely have objected to the outlawing of the Macleans. One other main inducement to the Camerons was the opportunity for plunder. Raids were made that winter on Ardnamurchan, Lorn, Lismore and other islands, and, when Lochiel was satiated, he staged a false night-alarm to disperse the force.[106]

During 1676 and 1677, affairs in Mull remained stalemated. Macdonald yearly assembled and led there a force of Macdonalds and Camerons large enough to forestall Argyll. He could not unite Clan Donald in his 'confederacy' against the Campbells: Clanranald and Sleat remained neutral or hostile, and he was followed only by the men of Glengarry, Keppoch (whose new chief Archibald evidently succeeded by this in reconciling those within his clan who remembered his share in the Keppoch Murders) and Glencoe.[107] The force caused severe shortages of provisions in Mull, and the Camerons' plundering provoked a quarrel between Lochiel and the Macleans in 1676. They blockaded Duart, but Glenorchy warned that, unless they attacked it, it would be politically disastrous to retaliate. Through his command of the sea, Argyll could keep Duart supplied and send treasure-hunting expeditions to Tobermory. In 1677, Macdonell planned to buy an armed frigate to challenge him. There were occasional clashes and casualties; but both sides claimed to be law-abiding.[108]

On the mainland, however, raiding by the Macleans' allies and caterans was out of control. Some, like the Cameron raids on Campbell estates in Lorn late in 1676, were directly connected with the dispute, but most merely arose from the encouragement it gave to armed disorder, coming soon after the disasters of 1674–5. In early 1676, Lochaber men were already raiding Badenoch, Strathspey and Glen Urquhart. By July, some of Clan Ranald were in upland Moray seeking their share of the plunder, but Cluny disbanded the Badenoch watch although the most dangerous season lay ahead.[109] Early that autumn, parties of Camerons and Macdonalds (including the 'Halket Stirk'), advanced into Perthshire, raised some of the MacNabs, and launched raids as far afield as Fife. Some MacGibbons kidnapped Lawers and made him give bond to pay a ransom. The disorder was so serious that Glenorchy, always hostile to garrisons, made Finlarig Castle available for an army detachment sent in September to guard the braes. A watch was organised; but Lawers caught his kidnappers for execution only by tricking them with a forged remission.[110] In June 1677, the Sheriff of Inverness reported that he was to meet MacIain and Keppoch about their followers, 'who are now turned avowedly louse wtout any regaird to King or Lawe'; Keppoch's had already committed a slaughter in Glen Urquhart. Arms were being distributed in Stirlingshire and Moray to meet raids.[111]

In January 1677, Lawers, instead of Major Grant, again received the commission to prevent highland thieving, but in September this was changed to a joint one with Lord Macdonell. A garrison was to occupy Inverlochy the instant it was repaired, and a justiciary court, Argyll, Moray, Glenorchy/Caithness and Aboyne (for the Huntly interest) was to judge captured thieves there. The garrison was intended to give Argyll a major advantage against the Macleans, and the strange appointment of Macdonell may have been intended to redress the balance, and re-establish authority in areas where Lawers would be resisted. He took the task seriously, and began to obtain fresh bonds from the Macdonalds.[112] His efforts were jeopardised by a proposal to give Mackintosh a commission of fire and sword against the Keppoch Macdonalds. Mackintosh had planned since 1672 to 'improve' his estates, evidently by evicting them, but the Council then had refused the commission. The grant now, ostensibly a punishment for their raiding, was presumably intended to prevent one ally of the Macleans from helping them further. But it, and the whole garrison project, were frustrated by the crisis in the South-West.[113]

Balhaldie misleadingly criticises Brolas for increasing Maclean's debts with pensions to allies.[114] In fact, only such a military (and financial) setback for Argyll could rally his enemies to support the Macleans and obtain any justice. In late 1675, Seaforth was sent to persuade the Macleans to behave peaceably, and in 1676 he, Atholl and Macleod supported Macdonell when the dispute came before the Council, who well into 1677 avoided any decision. Argyll retaliated by starting a lawsuit to evict Macdonell from that portion of his estate over which he had obtained the superiority from Lochiel.[115] Yet his own position was by no means secure. Atholl, who had agreed by 1676 to marry his heir Lord Murray to the Duchess of Lauderdale's second daughter, was using her influence to attack his rivals for power, even Lauderdale's brother Halton. He was the Macleans' chief supporter on the Council committees, and Argyll dared not even conciliate him by settling their direct family differences, since such 'weakness' would give the Macleans fresh heart.[116]

Negotiations between Argyll and the Duchess in early 1677 to marry Lorne to her elder daughter averted the danger that she would try to ruin him. Yet Atholl, despite promises to her, still headed all opposition to him, and persuaded James Duke of York to go to law with him, unsuccessfully, over the ownership of the Tobermory Galleon. The two men's factions on the Council were almost equally balanced, and they nearly fought a duel.[117] On the committee appointed to settle the dispute with the Macleans, however, there was only Atholl to counterbalance Lauderdale, Halton and Stair. They therefore decided that the entire debt Argyll claimed was valid; and their suggestion that the King should forgive the Macleans £3,000 arrears of feu-duties and teinds would more immediately have favoured him, since he had given bond for them on his infeftment. Argyll, who had been brought to negotiate at all only by Glenorchy's persuasions, offered to grant £200 sterling a year from the estate to Sir John, his mother and Brolas. The Macleans refused the offer.[118] Argyll's success was confirmed when Atholl broke off the proposed marriage, and the Duchess had him deprived of the Guards.[119]

Glenorchy's affairs, in contrast, had at first gone smoothly. Caithness died in March 1676. As the next heir, his cousin George Sinclair of Keiss, was a minor under the Earl's care, his family lands were being administered with the Caithness estates. Glenorchy quietly embezzled them, leaving him penniless, but from the start he had Sinclair support. In September 1676, he was in Edinburgh, where Glenorchy had just been appointed to the Council, hoping to exploit Glenorchy's failure to ask Charles's permission for the conveyance.[120] To obtain this and a proclamation forbidding George Sinclair to assume the title, Glenorchy again turned to the Duchess of Lauderdale. According to later articles against her, she demanded £2,000 sterling — a plausible figure in the light of his 1673 offer. Half, hastily borrowed from a money-lending Tayside laird, was paid when the title was granted, and he was unsuccessfully trying to raise the rest from 1678 onwards. This immense additional strain on his finances left him very close to ruin throughout his career, and may largely explain why he gave various Campbell relatives who were ruined, Glenlyon and Barbreck, much legal but little financial aid. In return, Charles was persuaded in February 1677 to grant a proclamation which forbade George Sinclair to use the title, without hearing his claims, and in June to make Glenorchy Earl of Caithness.[121]

Caithness immediately began working to conciliate the Sinclairs and the rest of his new people, labouring in the Session to thwart prosecutions against them for the raids of the 1660s and sending them assurances that he and his would assume the name of Sinclair. A meeting of Sinclairs replied thanking him, but postponing an answer to his specific requests until absentees were present. Dunbeath carried his letter, for Caithness noticeably relied chiefly on the very faction which he had attacked in 1669. Calder, ominously, recommended a potential Sheriff-depute as a loyal supporter of Campbell interests, right or wrong. The sales of land, the 'Caithness bargains', continued, though without recompensing his outlays and bribes.[122] In April 1678, he married the widowed Countess of Caithness. This arose naturally from his role as her protector against Sir Robert, but the peerage and marriage naturally alienated Argyll further from his upstart cousin. In September 1677 George Sinclair began his counter-attack, landing in Caithness and occupying his family lands.[123] (See Preface, p. vii)

Caithness could not retaliate immediately, for he was involved in the incident which proved decisive, for the Restoration period, in crystallising the hostile lowland view of the clans: the Highland Host. The immediate provocation was the refusal of the western gentry to accept a bond making them liable for their tenants' — religious — misdeeds; highland landlords had never had any other choice over tenants' possible thieving. It is still uncertain whether Lauderdale and his ministers genuinely believed the West so close to presbyterian rebellion that a large force must be stationed there, almost entirely at free quarter. The massive precautions taken to have the Irish army ready to send help might suggest so. However, the latest study of Lauderdale's policies sees it as part of his carrot-and-stick policy towards Presbyterians, a particularly violent and clumsy application of stick, as an attempt to ruin their secular allies — and as a miscalculation, since the protests afterwards at London forced even Charles, despite his fear of rebellion, to accept some Opposition charges.[124]

The employment of the highlanders, whose culture, language and habits made them in lowland eyes 'a barbarous savage people, accustomed to rapine and spoil', was obviously intended to terrorise the South-West, and make the occupation harsher. It was feared in late 1677 that the clans summoned would be those with the Mac- prefix (including 'McForbesses'), the most Gaelic and therefore the least civilised.[125] In fact, the 5,000 highlanders (out of a total force of 8,000, including regular troops and horse and foot militia) who rendezvoused at Stirling on 24 January 1678, were drawn almost entirely from the south and east, the followers of Atholl, Caithness, Moray (from his Menteith properties only), Perth and Mar. Huntly, who was originally ordered to prepare his tenants to join, was eventually told to stay and, with his vassal Grant, Macdonell and Lawers, to protect the country from robbers. Evidently, employing a Catholic's followers to coerce disobedient Protestants was considered too open to criticism.[126] The most openly outlandish members of the Host, as it settled on free quarter first round Glasgow and then in Ayrshire, were the Macdonalds of Glencoe, who marched with a heather-bush, the Clan Donald emblem, on a pole as an ensign. Caithness's is the only contingent in which they can have come, and the inducement was evidently not any real obligation of vassalage (for which he showed little regard when gathering followers) but his willingness to employ men who might otherwise raid his estates in his absence, and the prospect for them of legitimate plunder. They may sometimes have acted under the command of Caithness's impecunious cousin Campbell of Glenlyon.[127]

The occupying forces were meant to punish the defiant and spare the obedient, but their lack of military discipline and ignorance or half-knowledge of Scots made the highlanders an inappropriate instrument for distinguishing the 'Fig' (as they called the Whigs) from others. They plundered indiscriminately, and there was little hope of redress from the Western Committee controlling the operation, which was composed largely of their commanders. Not all the contingents behaved alike. Caithness's was apparently one of the worst, while Atholl's and Moray's were, initially at least, restrained. The militia also plundered, and two of its commanders, Airlie and Strathmore, who could hardly plead in excuse the highlanders' bad example, were said to have profited most. The West was a fairly backward area of the Lowlands, but it was estimated that Ayrshire alone suffered £200,000 Scots damages.[128] It was noticeable that the highlanders did not attempt to drive off cattle and sheep in any significant numbers, and were accused of slaughtering them wastefully: horses, for baggage-carrying, were the only animals widely confiscated. Instead, they seized everyday items in short supply in the Highlands: shoes, so persistently that the Committee was obliged to have some made for them, iron and ironwork, even the coulters from ploughs in the fields, household goods — and, of course, money. They exacted luxurious and wasteful quarters, and charged for many more men than existed.[129] Although worse misdeeds were generally far less serious and widespread than had been feared, some were committed: the extortion of ransoms by threats to kill people or burn towns, some burning of houses and cornstacks, wounding or maiming of persons who resisted plundering, several sexual assaults, apparently even one or two murders not officially recorded — the only one which was was of one of Caithness's highlanders, killed by a mob in Stirlingshire when returning homewards.[130]

The greater part of the Host remained in the West for under a month, and then returned, leaving only 500 of the highlanders (who themselves apparently stayed only briefly). One reason was that robbery by Caithness's and Mar's followers disrupted the markets round Ayr, creating a shortage of provisions for the forces and the Committee. No active resistance had been discovered, and a novel legal means of proceeding against those who refused the bond was under way.[131] Having seriously disrupted the West's ploughing season, the highlanders were anxious to return for their own. So, for various reasons, were their leaders. Caithness, for instance, despite his precaution of taking the Glencoe men with him, suffered a raid on his property in Strathfillan. More alarmingly, George Sinclair was consolidating his position. Caithness courteously left the decision on withdrawing his final contingent to the Duchess as his chief creditor.[132] Atholl and Perth, having been the foremost in offering their contingents for the Host, now claimed to have been misled, and joined the opposition to Lauderdale. One enemy accused them of starting to allow conventicles in the Perthshire Highlands.[133]

During 1678, Argyll tried to blockade the Macleans who defied him and fired on his flotilla at Tobermory.[134] In Edinburgh, his enemy Tarbat returned to favour as Archbishop Sharp's protégé; yet Lorne's marriage to the Duchess's elder daughter (and that of Moray's son to the younger) decisively strengthened his position. The alliance naturally generated its own difficulties and quarrels, but it ensured the Lauderdales' support for his family's vital interests.[135]

The first-fruit came in September, when Charles ordered a total change in the organisation opposing highland raids. Argyll and Caithness were to raise two independent highland foot companies, commanded by Colonel Menzies and

Lawers. An alternative commission, for Caithness himself, was signed but ultimately left in Argyll's hands, causing further predictable friction. Officially, these and a Guards company were supposed finally to establish the Inverlochy garrison and justiciary commission, which now consisted of Argyll, Moray, Caithness, Mackintosh and the military commanders, leaving neither Macdonell nor Huntly any influence. Enforcement of Argyll's and Mackintosh's claims was among their first business. Two-thirds of the 150 landlords, chiefs and heads of families now ordered to give yearly bonds, including Keppoch, MacIain, Appin and Cluny, were to do so at the garrison, a step intended to paralyse Argyll's opponents. The Council took the proposed garrison seriously, granting Menzies 9,000 merks to establish it, and ordering Grant to send men to assist. Argyll, however, intended to use the companies entirely against the Macleans, and Lawers feared that guarding the braes was 'despysed and neglected'. The Council renewed Argyll's commission of fire and sword, despite some opposition and a further unsuccessful offer of indemnity.[136]

Meanwhile, the confederacy was disrupted. Even in 1676, Lochiel's ties with the Macleans had been loosened by his wife's death and disputes between them and the Camerons. In Edinburgh that winter, after (according to Balhaldie) almost shooting Argyll on impulse for his misdeeds, he tried to negotiate a settlement.[137] Argyll's confidence that he would leave the confederacy for the next campaign was mistaken, but Macdonell, remembering the old feud, was turning the Macleans against him. After summer-long negotiations employing Caithness, Argyll in October 1678 bribed Lochiel into making a final change of sides by cancelling a 40,000 merk debt. 'Ewen has lost his God, but the Earl his money,' declared the Macleans.[138]

A month later, Caithness, Lochiel and Colonel Menzies were tossing aboard Argyll's frigate in Loch Linnhe near Inverlochy. Seven to eight hundred Macleans were in Mamore, and the Glengarry and Keppoch Macdonalds under Macdonell suddenly advanced to Loch Leven, close to a confrontation with Argyll in Appin, and sent parties into Lismore. They were revenging themselves on Lochiel's territory for his treachery, though still using legal pretexts. Argyll had written to Mackintosh to march with his men to Inverlochy. Yet the danger of full-scale highland war was less than appeared. The Council had made Argyll promise not to use his commission of fire and sword. He failed to obtain one for Mackintosh against Keppoch, and without it not enough of Mackintosh's men would join him. Caithness had hoped that Lochiel's change would help to bring Lord Macdonell and through him the Macleans to a settlement, and began negotiations with Macdonell in late November. Argyll watched these with extreme suspicion, and sent a party to Mull to collect the year's rent.[139] Soon afterwards, when Caithness had returned to Argyll's camp, the Macdonalds and Macleans planned a night attack on it, since a successful surprise was, militarily speaking, their only chance of success. Caithness claimed that they nearly caught Argyll's force sleeping, but that his orders saved it while Argyll and Campbell of Auchinbreck were quarrelling over command. He then persuaded Macdonell to agree to a cessation of arms with Argyll at the start of December and return home.

Soon afterwards, he quarrelled with Argyll and left him, infuriated at an attempt to reduce his company, but left a hundred men to accompany Argyll to Mull.[140]

Landing there with perhaps 1,500 men in mid-December, Argyll met no active resistance. He agreed to pardon the tenants on mild terms, but not the tacksmen, and seized Lochbuie and his castle. His brother Lord Neil invaded the mainland, where Lochiel joined him with 400 men, and Maclean of Ardgour retreated into Kinlochaline Castle in Morvern.[141] Brolas from the impregnable island fortress of Carnaburg, and the Macdonalds, Camerons, Stewarts and MacCouls from the mainland, launched constant cattle-raids on Mull by boat. The Glencoe Macdonalds were still doing so in April.[142] Throughout the expedition, Argyll invariably gave Caithness's men the hardest tasks and refused them their pay and clothing, driving them to mutiny and plunder. Relations between the two Earls reached their lowest point.[143]

The 'Popish Plot' in England further benefited Argyll. No attempt was made to manufacture a Scottish equivalent for political advantage, although some agents used against the Presbyterians would have been willing tools. Congratulating Charles on his escape, the Council emphasised that no Scots were involved, probably in the hope that this would partly wipe out the shame of the surrender of his father to the Roundheads in 1647. However, a proclamation for the disarming of Papists was naturally issued. Macdonell, still working to raise a Macdonald force, defied the Council's orders to attend with his usual violent spirit and put himself in the wrong. In April 1679, Argyll obtained a special commission to disarm him, Keppoch, and the defiant Maclean leaders, whom he had also managed to represent (falsely) as Papists, or at least rebels.[144]

Argyll, in his over-confidence, never considered that this might drive the confederacy to desperate action, which he was unprepared to meet. Campbell of Inverawe, more far-sighted, hastily renewed his bond of friendship with MacIain. Argyll lacked meal even for the force he had already raised, and the regular detachment with him mutinied over its starvation diet. Caithness, at Finlarig, would not raise his tenants or reassemble his ill-treated independent company. He was not merely nursing grievances, for Lawers warned him, 'In all appeirance the E. A[rgyll] will not cease till the Highlands be in a combustione'.[145]

Argyll knew by mid-May that the Maclean leaders had again reoccupied Mull, but trusted his frigate to stop them crossing to the mainland. When they nevertheless joined Macdonell in Lochaber, he called on the Council to send an army to Inverlochy. The idea was absurd — it was just after Archbishop Sharp's murder — and Rothes relished refusing: 'if he has brewn well, let him drink the better'. Yet Argyll dismissed Macdonell's followers as 'broken men', and advanced to Kilchurn on 24 May.[146] Macdonell had actually gathered a force, including the men of Glencoe and Rannoch, better organised and perhaps larger than Argyll's; Caithness claimed that they were 2,000 strong. Argyll's anti-catholic allegations were partly justified, for two priests served as captains, evidently considering it a crusade. Early on 24 May, the leaders were still at Keppoch, where MacIain divided his Maclean pension to bind another Macdonald family to the cause. They then advanced south, swarmed across Loch

Leven in captured boats, and by early next morning were in the braes of Glencoe, a few miles from the unprepared Argyll. Suddenly, it seemed possible that the Campbells were facing destruction.[147]

Argyll was at first blindly determined to fight, relying on local reinforcements, and remained at Kilchurn until 30 May. The Macdonells and Macleans, though sending out raiding parties through Lorn, refrained from attacking him, the first indication that they might not push matters to extremes. On the 30th, Argyll retired to Inveraray and hastily gathered reinforcements.[148] Macdonell's force advanced to the slopes of Beinn Bhuidhe near the head of Loch Fyne, but, to Iain Lom's regret, did not advance to do battle, although parties raided Glen Shira and Glen Aray. Some raiders penetrated far south, and local guards were hastily raised.[149] Others occupied Caithness's Glenorchy and Strathfillan lands, blocking reinforcement from the east. Caithness ignored Argyll's emphatic orders to join him with all his followers. Besides fearing for these estates, he knew that Argyll would then certainly fight, and his ill-prepared force would probably be defeated, ruinously for Clan Campbell. Even an (inevitably bloody) victory would arouse widespread hostility (and start a feud between the houses of Glenorchy and Glengarry). If bloodshed could be averted, the setback might prove a blessing, forcing Argyll to listen to his moderate supporters and accept a compromise with the Macleans.[150]   On 26 May, Caithness had written to Macdonell offering to act as intermediary. He encouraged Argyll's brother and chief supporters to put pressure on him, and on 1 June the infuriated Earl reluctantly allowed him to negotiate with Macdonell.[151] The latter's willingness to listen after the 1678 cessation had proved so fruitless suggests that he never intended to go to the lengths of an old-fashioned clan battle against an enemy holding the government's commission, which ultimately might only damage the Macleans' cause. Caithness's most effective argument was an appeal to his long record of loyalty. The Covenanters had risen, and temporarily held even Glasgow. If he continued his campaign now, it would further weaken the government during the worst crisis since 1660, giving grounds for Argyll's claim that he was a rebel, and even for accusations that he was in league with the Whigs. There was some truth in the first point: although the Sheriff-depute of Inverness-shire, who had just raised 1,200 men to help Argyll, dismissed them to join the host against the rebels, they, with all Moray and Strathspey, were paralysed by the rumours Whig sympathisers spread that Macdonell was about to invade the country. Convinced by Caithness, Macdonell and the Macleans wrote to the Council that they had convened only in self-defence, and offered to join the royal army if Argyll would remain inactive, 'which he hath ever done when his majesty had any thing to do'. Some of the Council wished to accept the offer, but, at the height of the Popish Plot, they dared not. Instead, in early June Macdonell's force began to retire from Argyllshire.[152]

Caithness was hopelessly over-optimistic about Argyll's professed willingness to take his friends' advice. He counted as 'friends' only his unquestioning supporters during the crisis, which he blamed entirely on Caithness's own failure to join him. On receiving arms and ammunition from Edinburgh (just before the rebels cut communications), he disregarded the negotiations 'betwixt the two highland Princes EC and L McD', and, once Macdonell had left the shire, set out in vindictive pursuit, totally ignoring the crisis in the West.[153] Caithness was prevented from intervening by the Council's repeated orders to march against the rebels. His 600 men reached Stirling the day the Duke of Monmouth won the battle of Bothwell Bridge. There were some eastern highlanders at the battle, and others cut off a party of Fife rebels, but their part in the campaign was small.[154]

The Macleans had returned to Mull, and the Macdonalds alone could not resist effectively when Argyll entered Lochaber and advanced to Keppoch, where the flooded Spean checked him. He had written to Mackintosh on 30 May, suggesting that he invade Keppoch while the warriors were absent, but Moray and Huntly sabotaged this out of hostility to Mackintosh. Argyll's parties seeking for the enemy's cattle ranged as far as lowland Moray and Knoidart. He sent his vanguard up the Great Glen, hoping finally to smash the opposing alliance, but the Council's order to march against the western rebels, although he disregarded it, made him recall them when they were approaching Loch Ness. Without an enemy's country to live off, his forces suffered badly from hunger and soon dispersed. Leaving one party with Lochiel, Argyll sailed to Mull with another.[155] Lochiel's continuing raids on Macdonald lands stung Macdonell and Keppoch into planning counter-attacks, probably making him more sympathetic than usual to the idea of an Inverlochy garrison, for which he made preparations. However, the soldiers and Argyllshire men gave forewarning of its probable disadvantages, seizing from the Camerons the cattle they had just stolen from Morar.[156]

Most of the Macleans put up no resistance to Argyll; he was confident that, if they did, he could call on Clanranald and Sir Donald Macdonald for help. Maclean of Ardgour held out in Kinlochaline until late July, but it surrendered before Lord Macdonell with 600 men arrived to relieve it. The Macleans held out only in Carnaburg, which Argyll unsuccessfully besieged with his flotilla. He prudently pardoned the lesser Maclean tenants, but he divided Mull up between Campbell tacksmen, and granted Morvern, whose inhabitants were mainly Camerons, to Cameron of Glendessary. Outwardly, the government supported him, approving his conduct as prudent and moderate (which Charles blindly endorsed). Yet he had ignored a national crisis for one his own selfish interests had created, and this was remembered.[157]

Although Argyll had invaded Keppoch, he had done nothing to advance his nominal ally Mackintosh's interests. Mackintosh, convinced he would never receive a commission of fire and sword, decided to compromise with Keppoch. He wanted a large armed force to assist negotiations, but his tacksmen's extortion in 1665 and 1667, Cluny's refusal, and recent bloodshed which made taking the Farquharsons too explosive a risk, thwarted him. He led only a small following to Keppoch in August, and an easy settlement was quickly reached. He increased the rent, and agreed to pay the public taxes from it, if the Macdonalds reimbursed previous arrears. He at first sincerely tried to make the settlement succeed.[158]

Any hope this gave of peace in the Highlands was drowned in the rising flood of cattle-raiding. In September, the Council felt obliged to scatter 400 troops in small parties round from Dunbartonshire to Sutherland, guarding passes and braes.

Argyll and Lawers, who was trying to protect Argyllshire with the independent companies, still held the fading hope of garrisoning Inverlochy, but feared that their men would soon desert for lack of pay. The Glencoe Macdonalds, who received Argyll's protection and offered to disclaim any rebellious intentions, raided deeply that winter into Argyllshire and Dunbartonshire.[159]

Although Lauderdale remained Secretary despite the Bothwell Bridge rising, there was a major political change, the arrival in December 1679 of Charles's brother, James Duke of York, retreating from the 'Popish Plot'. In Scotland, his rights would remain before the English public, his activity as Charles's representative could dispel hysterical alarms about him, and (he privately thought), if Exclusion succeeded, he could make the country his base for a civil war. He had always taken an interest in Scottish affairs, supposedly with a secret antipathy to Lauderdale, and he acted on the warning not to let gratitude for recent help commit him to his faction. James continued Monmouth's policy of indulgence and moderation and brought Lauderdale's opponents back on to the Council, winning support on nearly all sides.[160] He naturally made Huntly, as the head of the Scottish Catholics, a favourite, and one of his main secret motives in forming policy during the next few years was to benefit him, but he dared not openly advance him. This was unfortunate, for Huntly, though high-handed in his private affairs, was a political moderate, and was alarmed as James began to show a desire for harsher, more divisive policies: his moderation had been largely a means of stealing Monmouth's thunder. After his first return to England in early 1680, a new severe policy towards the Presbyterians was initiated. James's regime was still to be, in some sense, a reforming one, but on a far more partisan basis than had at first been hoped. Most of the reconciled peers, having opposed Lauderdale as much for his neglect of 'loyalists' as for his harsher policies, easily made the change.[161]

Often, indeed, it was their advice which altered James's policies, after an original willingness to accept Lauderdale's ambiguous legacy. Argyll was among those who at first objected to his sitting in Council without taking the oath, and made difficulties over the select militia proposals. Yet James wrote: 'I find him a man of very good parts, and both willing and able to serve his Ma[jesty]'. Argyll could appeal to his strong fear of social disorder by emphasising that the Campbells had kept the Highlands peaceful for the Crown, 'therefore all the broken men and their patrons, were enemies to him'. He flattered his vanity by proposing that he should call most leading highlanders involved in disputes before him and the Council to explain and, if possible, settle their conflicting claims through his impartial wisdom.[162]

Caithness, unlike Argyll, failed to attend James's arrival — an imprudent step, since James's own position made him feel strongly for George Sinclair.[163] It made matters worse that he was absent preparing an invasion of the shire. After legal proceedings that summer failed, he sent Campbell of Kinloch with a small party (who plundered unscrupulously in Sutherland) to garrison Castle Sinclair and await his coming. George Sinclair starved them out in a fortnight and took full possession of the earldom, collecting the rents and exporting the victual. In

November, Caithness obtained the Council's commission and began raising 1,200 highlanders to march north. A protest over this from Sutherland may have brought the affair to James's attention. Both Caithness, ordered to suspend executing his commission, and George Sinclair were among those summoned on 29 December before the Council. Argyll told Caithness that this could do no harm, and another Councillor remarked: 'it will be happy for yow if yow can setle befor Caithnes turne Mull'. His official position was strengthened when George Sinclair failed to appear. Instead, occupying Thurso and conscripting the inhabitants to work for him, he demolished or slighted three of the Earl's houses or castles.[164]

One of James's main priorities in this brief first stay was to 'preserue that antient and Loyal Clan of the Maclanes', not least because Argyll's total triumph would make him 'greater than it were fit for a Subject to be'. He at first proposed that Charles should pay off Argyll's claims. Argyll necessarily consented, but cash was unavailable, and he refused the offer of forfeited estates. Instead, he revived the proposal to grant Sir John Maclean an estate in Tiree worth £200 a year.[165] Soon after James's departure, the Macleans damaged their position by invading Tiree from Carnaburg — so conveniently for Argyll that the Council obviously suspected provocation; while their patron Macdonell showed his violent, 'barbaric' temper in a quarrel over his pension.[166]

The Macleans' action was ill-timed, since the two independent Campbell companies faced disbandment. James, anxious to prevent highland robbery and disorder 'vithout vhich ... the King is not entirely King of the whole kingdome', found them useless, with 'scarce a man in constant pay' except when they were employed for Argyll's and Caithness's private ends. Complaints were exposing the terror tactics they used, including the murder of untried prisoners 'to prevent rescue'.[167] His alternative proposal, chiefly intended to gain power and prestige for Huntly, was to divide the Highlands, for policing purposes, among four magnates, Argyll, Atholl, Huntly and Seaforth. When given good warning, they were to regain stolen cattle or other livestock within forty days or make recompense. They and their deputes would have full power to hold courts, though landed men's sentences remained with the Council. Argyll's district stretched from Stirlingshire and Breadalbane to Kintail; Atholl's was the rest of Perthshire and Angus; Huntly's, from the Mearns round to Loch Ness, Badenoch, and Lochaber; Seaforth's, Inverness-shire north of Loch Ness, the North, Skye and Lewis.[168]

There were rational objections to these 'foure high & mighty Thief catchers', as Lauderdale sarcastically called them. Fountainhall foresaw that 'these great men will not be very accessible' to victims. Argyll saw the plan as harming his interests. The Earl of Mar protested that it would leave 'my interest in the Highlands ... intirely broken, and my men a prey to nighbours, that uould be glad to see it', Huntly and Atholl. The one successful objection, however, was that too much power was given to a Papist, and half Huntly's division was transferred to Moray. Their commissions, with £200 a year salary each, were to last for a year from 1 May 1680, but that passed without its coming into effect, although Tarbat and Atholl struggled for it.[169] As they warned Lauderdale, raiding was increasing. By October, Montrose alone was forced to raise a hundred men to protect

Stirlingshire, and professional organisers of watches were demanding exorbitant terms. The main obstacle was that Argyll and Caithness were still employing the highland companies, whose pay was needed for the salaries, on their private affairs. On 3 July, Lauderdale obtained Charles's order to postpone the disbandment and the establishment of the districts, which finally lapsed. James would not look very kindly on those who had thwarted his plans for Huntly.[170]

In April, Argyll sent Colonel Menzies to Tiree with 200 of the highland companies to relieve the garrison. However, his expedition to Mull that summer, leaving Lawers to guard the braes, was almost entirely treasure-hunting at Tobermory.[171] Meanwhile, a compromise solution was reached. Charles agreed to purchase lands worth £300 a year to add to Argyll's promised £200 a year. The estate was to be in Tiree, and Argyll began to set artificially high rents there in order to minimise the grant's real value. In 1681, the Treasury warned Charles of this trap, and he ordered the extra £300 to come from Argyll's feu duties.[172]

The Macleans' chief protector, Lord Macdonell, died in December 1680. He was childless, and his peerage lapsed. His arrangements for the Glengarry succession showed that, despite the settlement, he still expected a perilous and insecure future for the Highlands. The clan's need for a chief whose military ability and political cunning matched his own was urgent enough to justify the risk of starting a feud. Totally bypassing the legitimate heirs, the Achtera family, he chose Ranald Macdonald of Scotus, not for himself but because his son Alasdair had these qualities; and, although Ranald survived through the 1690s, Alasdair from the start ruled the clan.[173] Atholl, as patron of the clan, played a major part in the choice and in persuading the Achtera family to acquiesce: in the crisis of 1697-8 he was openly to lament having done so. The tie was further strengthened when Glengarry married Lovat's sister. While making himself popular with the ordinary clansmen, Glengarry ruled almost entirely without consulting the chieftains and gentry, but he made an exception of one of the Achtera family.[174]

The most conspicuous highland disruption in 1680 was brought about by the Earl of Caithness. In June, Charles wrote ordering the Council to send him with his highland company to restore order in the shire. Yet his position was increasingly precarious. The dispute was now attracting almost as much attention at Court as Argyll's with the Macleans, and Charles was aware that his grant had been unjust. Tarbat protested in Council against giving a virtual commission of fire and sword against men who had not been declared rebels. Therefore, the select force of Campbells, Macgregors and Macintyres which Caithness mustered in late June under several Campbell captains, Kinloch, Glenlyon, Inneryeldie and Barcaldine his son, and Toshach of Monivaird, consisted of only 500 men in all; and they avoided plundering in Sutherland.[175]

Although most Sinclair gentry probably favoured George Sinclair, only a few openly supported him. In early July, he marched to Thurso with about 300 Caithness and Strathnaver men and pressed a reluctant contingent of 100 townsmen. His party had also two cannon, and its leader, Major William Sinclair, clearly relied on the traditional fear barbarous highlanders were supposed to feel for 'Muskie's mother'. As Caithness approached, they marched to the shire borders to meet him, but he doubled south and marched towards Wick. On 9 July at Spital, Sinclair's force opened a heavy cannon and musket fire from a hill beside the road on the Campbells as they passed, and they begged Caithness to let them attack. 'You men are ill natured,' he replied, 'they are all my owne tennents and vassals.' He was confident that, if he could avoid fighting the Sinclairs for two or three days, they would disperse. Besides landlord's interest and any humane motives, he knew that a serious fight would further provoke Court disapproval. His men angrily marched off, to the enemy's cheers. That weekend, he sent messengers to order the enemy to disperse and to encourage his supporters, including Dunbeath.[176]

Caithness could not find provisions for his force at Wick, and on 13 July had to march again. Still wanting to avoid the Sinclair forces, posted on the high road, he inquired for, and took, another route. His Fabian strategy very nearly succeeded: that morning, the Thurso contingent tried to desert Sinclair, and was stopped only by cannonfire. Unfortunately, it had only confirmed the rest of the enemy in their contempt for highlanders and over-confidence, despite their inferior numbers. Coming up with the rear of Caithness's force at Allt nam Mearlach near Wick, they loaded their cannon. The invaders later claimed they were forced to fight or run; and Caithness could not have kept his clan's respect after any further retreat now. Both sides drew up, and the Sinclairs fired a cannon and musket volley, killing one man and wounding others. The Campbells returned the fire and charged; and the Sinclairs almost immediately broke and fled. Caithness began to call to his men to give quarter, but for some minutes could not restrain them. They killed at least 107 people, including a fifth of the luckless Thurso contingent and a child, and captured 100, losing two dead. By an extreme irony, it was not the obstinately aggressive Argyll but the incessantly conciliatory Caithness whose actions had caused major bloodshed in the Highlands. The Sinclairs later explained their failure with a convenient tradition that Caithness had cunningly allowed them to capture a waggonload (or shipload) of whisky the previous night, and that they had not recovered.[177]

Caithness reoccupied Thurso, planted garrisons and began to organise the collection of rents. At first, the government appeared to accept his actions. He and Menzies were ordered to quarter their companies for arrears in Badenoch, Lochaber and the Isles.[178] By September, however, the Council were writing in dismay to Caithness that his action under their commission 'was very far from their intention and thoughts' when they granted it, relying on his 'prudence and all possible moderation, whereunto your owne interest seemed to oblidge yow'; they would have to hold an inquiry.[179] Never before had he so needed Lauderdale's support. But in October Lauderdale, worn out and discredited, resigned as Secretary; and his successor Moray, although his loyal follower, was politically a mere shadow.

NOTES

1. Macpherson, *Original Papers*, i, 367, Dundee to Melfort, 28 June 1689.

2. Fraser-Macintosh, *Letters*, 74, Lorne's petition; Stevenson, *Alasdair MacColla*, 278–9; *APS*, vii, 374, 411–12; Mackenzie, *Memoirs*, 71–2; *Spottiswoode Miscellany*, ii, 156–7; *Wardlaw MS*, 439.

3. *HMCR Laing*, i, 374–5, W. Douglas to Lauderdale, 6 Aug. 1669; *A Complete Collection of State Trials*, ed. T. B. Howell, 23 vols. (*State Trials*; London, 1809–26), viii, 860.

4. *APS*, vii, 337–41, 383, 419, 499; *Register of the Great Seal of Scotland, 1660-1668*, (*RGSS*), 57,553; BL Add. 23,124 fol. 58, [Argyll] to Lauderdale, 14 Feb. 1666; *ib.*, Add. 23,125 fol. 132, [same] to same, [c. Nov. 1666]; *ib.*, Add. 23,126 fol. 126, Montrose to same, 12 Mar. 1667; Buckminster (Grantham), Tollemache MSS, Lauderdale Papers, 4294, Draft warrant granting Islay to Glengarry, n.d. [?1660].

5. *RGSS*, 271–3; BL Add. 23,120 fol. 34, [Sir R. Moray] to Lauderdale, 28 Sept. 1663; *ib.*, Add. 23, 119 fol. 46, [same] to [same], 20 June 1663; *ib.*, fol. 51v, [Lauderdale] to [Sir R. Moray], 23 June 1663; Blair, Atholl MSS, Box 29 I (3) 77, Clanranald to Atholl, 20 Jan. 1682.

6. Mackenzie, *Memoirs*, 179; *Wardlaw MS*, 451–2.

7. Yet it was his enemy Macdonell whose correspondence the government intercepted. M. Napier, *Memorials and Letters . . . of John Graham of Claverhouse, Viscount Dundee*, 3 vols. (Edinburgh, 1858–62), i, 363, Rothes to Queensberry, 25 Mar. 1678; *Letters from Archibald Earl of Argyll to John Duke of Lauderdale*, ed. C. K. Sharpe & Sir G. Sinclair (Bannatyne Club, 1829), 14 (14 Feb. 1665), 62–4 (1 Feb. [1667]); BL Add. 23,125 fol. 196, Argyll to Dalyell, 24 Nov. 1666.

8. Mackenzie, *Memoirs*, 221–2; Brodie, *Diary*, 369; Fountainhall, *Hist. Notices*, i, 13, 342; *Journals*, 213–14.

9. *RGSS*, 464–7; Argyll, *Letters*, 5 (25 June 1664), 25 (22 Sept. 1665); BL Add. 35,125 fol. 126, Argyll to Lauderdale, 18 Nov. 1665.

10. Fountainhall, *Hist. Notices*, i, 11–13, 15–16; Dirleton, *Doubts*, 203–4; Stair, *Decisions*, i, 627–8; *HMCR Laing*, i, 373–4, Tweeddale to Lauderdale, 22 July 1669.

11. BL Add. 23,132 fol. 62, [same] to same, 10 Aug. 1669; *Misc SHS*, vi, 188, Lauderdale to Advocate, 7 Jan. 1668/9; *APS*, vii, 581–3; Mackenzie, *Memoirs*, 177–80.

12. Rev. R. Law, *Memorialls*, ed. C. K. Sharpe (Edinburgh, 1818), 83; Cregeen, 'Tacksmen', *SS*, xiii, 104; Argyll, *Letters*, 14 (14 Feb. 1665), 29 (12 Oct. 1665); *Laud. Papers*, i, 201, Argyll to Lauderdale, 30 Sept. 1664.

13. The alarm was partly justified; Argyll hastily sent for his chief adviser, Campbell of Glenorchy the younger, to support him against the dead man's friends. *RPCS*, iii, 326–7; *HMCR 6th Report*, 699–700, Macnachtan to [?Weem], 1 Apr. 1671 (2); Dirleton, *Doubts*, 203–4, 213; D. McNaughton, *The Clan McNaughton* (Edinburgh, 1977), 25–7; SRO GD 112/40/4/2/18, [Argyll] to Glenorchy, 5 Apr. 1671; *ib.*, 39/1029, same to same, 23 June 1670.

14. *Ib.*, 1037, same to same, n.d; NLS MS 7003 fol. 94v, [same] to Tweeddale, [?May 1668]; *ib.*, MS 7037 fol. 108, 'Memorandum concerning the Highlands'; Argyll, *Letters*, 14–15 (14 Feb. 1665), 31 (18 Nov. 1665); BL Add. 23,122 fol. 260, A. Macdonald to Macdonell, 19 Jan. 1665; *ib.*, Add. 23,124 fol. 107, Macdonell to Lauderdale, 26 Mar. 1666.

15. Macdonald, *Clan Donald*, ii, 189-201; Prebble, *Glencoe*, 24-33, 37; D. J. Macdonald, *Slaughter under Trust* (London, 1965), 13-23, 148; *The Argyll Sasines*, ed. H. Campbell, 2 vols. (Edinburgh, 1933-4), ii, 324-6; *RGSS*, 467 (misprinted Glenroan); *The Rawdon Papers*, ed. Rev. E. Berwick (London, 1819), 430, Case of the Earl of Breadalbane, 1695; NLS MS 7003 fol. 94, [Argyll] to Tweeddale, [May 1673]; SRO GD 112/39/1012, [same] to Sir J. Campbell, 19 Apr. 1667; *ib.*, 957, MacIain to same, 18 Dec. 1662.

16. *Ib.*, 940, Sir J. Campbell to Glencairn, 12 Sept. 1660; BL Add. 23,125 fols. 102–3, [Argyll] to Lauderdale, [?1666].

17. *Ib.*, Add. 23,137 fol. 156 [Sir R. Moray] to same, 26 July 1667; Edinburgh UL (EUL) MS Laing III, 354 fol. 145, Sir P. Wedderburn to same, 27 July [1667]; *RPCS*, ii, 329–32, 564.

18. The new version of the 1589 story was apparently being told by 1700. *Ib.*, 331; *ib.*, iv, 177–8; A. G. Murray Macgregor, *History of the Clan Gregor*, 2 vols. (Edinburgh, 1898–1901), i, 213–18.

19. Prebble (*Glencoe*, 61) gives the only known document on this (a similar list in Breadalbane's papers (SRO GD 112/43/1/1/16) accuses MacIain and his followers of murdering two other men). A version of the tradition collected at Fort William in 1762, with the predictable storyteller's twist of the murdered men's heirs enlisting and participating in the Massacre, shows that the Dalrymple version was not a mere family invention. *Calendar of State Papers Domestic (CSPD) 1690–*1, 497, Remission for MacIain, 20/30 Aug. 1691; Dalrymple, *Memoirs*, i, 190; NLS MS 7014 fol. 8, Dalrymple to Tweeddale, 16 Jan. 1692; *Selections from the Letters and Correspondence of Sir James Bland Burges, Bart.*, ed. J. Hutton (London, 1885), 357 (I owe this reference to the kindness of Dr. Jeremy Black).

20. *Just. Recs.*, ii, 59; Argyll, *Letters*, 83 (10 June 1667); *RPCS*, iv, 177–8; *ib.*, vii, 694.

21. *Ib.*, vi, 43 (lowland ignorance); BL Add. 23,125 fol. 275v, [Argyll] to Lauderdale [c.1666]; *Argyll Just. Recs.*, 26, 32–3.

22. *Ib.*, 33; Maclean, 'Celtic Sources', 355–6, 359–60, 'Muck Bard' (for whom see Prebble, *Glencoe*, 222n), 'Murt Ghlinne-Comhann' (translated by Maclean); *Records of Invercauld*, 252, Bond, 13 Apr. 1680; J. Aubrey, *Three Prose Works*, ed. J. Buchanan-Brown (Fontwell, 1972), 121; NLS MS 1672 fol. 40, Bond of friendship with Inverawe, 20 July 1669; Blair, Atholl MSS, Box 62/II/149, Wadset, 3, 7 June 1678; *ib.*, 309, Disposition, 14 May 1695.

23. Mac Gill-Eain 'Domhnall Donn', *TGSI*, xlii, 94; MacMillan, *Bygone Lochaber*, 157–8.

24. The conclusive evidence of this is SCA, Blairs Letters, Box B¹, 108, A. Mongan to [W. Leslie], 13 Dec. 1694, a letter from one of the Irish priests in the Highlands in 1692 which counts the victims of the Massacre as catholic martyrs. It was incorporated in a later account of the Scottish Mission (W. Forbes Leith, *Memoirs of Scottish Catholics during the XVIIth and XVIIIth Centuries*, 2 vols. (London, 1909), ii, 171. Their religious allegiance had evidently become clearer since 1645, when the priest accompanying Montrose's army reported them as 'not averse' to Catholic customs. In 1711, a government spy's report on the clans (which he had visited) describes Iain MacIain, son of the murdered chief, as 'a papist, a good-natured, honest, sort of a man'. *Ib.*, i, 317; *HMC Portland*, x, 370–1, Cpt. Ogilvie's report on the Clans, 26 May 1711. Supplementary evidence appears in Prebble, 'Religion and the Massacre of Glencoe', *SHR*, xlvi, 185–8.

25. SRO GD 112/39/1038–9, [Argyll] to Glenorchy, [?c.1674–7]; *ib.*, 40/4/2/30, Glendaruel to same, '10 Apr. 1673' [?1703]; Paget, *New Examen*, 41–3; Macinnes, 'Repression and Conciliation' *SHR*, LXV, 175-6.

26. *Highland Papers*, i, ed. J. R. N. Macphail (SHS, 1914), 245–8, 320; *Eachann Bacach and other Maclean Poets*, ed. Colm O Baioill (Edinburgh, 1979), xxxviii–xlii; *RPCS*, vi, 319; *Memoirs of Locheill*, 193–5.

27. *Ib.*, 195–6; SRO GD 112/39/1037, Argyll to Glenorchy, [c.1665]; BL Add. 23,135 fol. 11v, same to Lauderdale, 7 Mar. 1671; Argyll, *Letters*, 4–5 (25 June 1664), 25–6 (21 Sept. 1665).

28. _Ib._, 99 (6 May 1669); _Highland Papers_, i, 248; _Argyll Sasines_, ii, 432; Cregeen, 'Changing Role', _Scotland in the Age of Improvement_, 8.

29. _RPCS_, iv, 208, 246; _ib._, viii, 393–4; _ib._, xiii, 191–2; BL Add. 23,125 fol. 105, [Argyll] to Lauderdaule, [c.1666]; _ib._, Add. 23,126 fol. 101, Rothes to same, 2 Mar. [1667]; Macfarlane, _Gen. Colls._, i, 138 (misdated); Argyll, _Letters_, 73–4 (2 Mar. 1667).

30. _Ib._, 90 (11 Nov. 1667), 94 (Dec. 1668); _Highland Papers_, i, 335–7; Fountainhall, _Hist. Notices_, i, 108; SRO GD 112/39/1029, Argyll to Glenorchy, 23 June 1670; _ib._, 1065, same to same, 22 May 1675.

31. Burt, _Letters_, ii, 117–18; Argyll, _Letters_, 31 (18 Nov. 1665); Macdonald, _Clan Donald_, ii, 372–3, iii, 67; Dow, _Cromwellian Scotland_, 89, 127; _Mackintosh Muniments_, 105, 107, 117; D. Macgibbon & T. Ross, _The Castellated and Domestic Architecture of Scotland_, 5 vols. (Edinburgh, 1887–92), iii, 620–1.

32. _RPCS_, ii, 150–2; _Wardlaw MS_, 457, 479–80; _Records of Inverness_, ii, ed. W. Mackay & G. Smith Laing (New Spalding Club, 1914), 223–6, 228–9; BL Add. 23,124 fol. 57, [Argyll] to Lauderdale, 14 Feb. 1666.

33. Shaw, _Northern & Western Islands_, 43–4; NLS MS 7037 fol. 108, Memorandum on the Highlands.

34. Macdonald, _Clan Donald_, iii, 654–5, Declaration of chiefship; _Collectanea de Rebus Albanicis_ (Iona Club, 1839), 207–8, Bond of friendship, 20 Oct. 1673; Buckminster, Lauderdale Papers, 2651, [Atholl] to [Duchess of Lauderdale] (hereafter 'Duchess'), 25 Aug. [1676].

35. _Spottiswoode Miscellany_, ii, 150; SRO GD 26/ix/274, Hill, 'Ane acompt how the highlanders were brought to . . . Civilitie' [6 Oct. 1690]; Dow, _Cromwellian Scotland_, 88–9.

36. Napier, _Dundee_, ii, 183, Lady Braco to Braco, 4 Nov. 1678; Lenman, _Jacobite Risings_, 140; R. M. Steuart, 'The Steuarts of Ballechin, Perthshire'; _The Stewarts_, xii, (1966), 193.

37. _RPCS_, iv, 570–6; _ib._, vii, 46–8, 73–4, 85–7; Atholl, _Chronicles_, i, 179–80; _Just. Recs._, ii, 128–32, 137–8; Lovat, _Memoirs_, 8; Rev. J. Robertson, _The Barons Reid-Robertson of Straloch_ (Blairgowrie, 1887), 25–6.

38. Macpherson, _Loyall Dissuasive_, 133–7; Blair, Atholl MSS, Box 42 (1) 29, Memorandum for Inverey, 1679; _Orain Iain Luim_, 154–5, 'Blar Tom a 'Phubaill'.

39. _Scots Peerage_, v, 534–7; _Wardlaw MS_, 134, 243–4, 253, 467, 482, 513–15.

40. _Ib._, 453–4; _APS_. vii, 295–9; _ib._, viii, 21; _RPCS_, i, 256, 398, 410–15; _Memoirs of Locheill_, 174–84; _Mackintosh Muniments_, 114, Agreement, 15 June 1664; Macfarlane, _Gen. Colls._, i, 328–37.

41. _Ib._, 337–76; Macpherson, _Loyall Dissuasive_, 79 & n; Argyll, _Letters_, 10 (31 Jan. 1665), 22–4 (21 Sept. 1665); _Mackintosh Muniments_, 114–15; _Memoirs of Locheill_, 184–92; A. M. Mackintosh, _The Mackintoshes and the Clan Chattan_ (Edinburgh, 1903), 257–9; BL Add. 23,122 fol. 306, [Rothes] to Lauderdale, 9 Mar. 1665.

42. Fraser-Macintosh, _Letters_, 85–6, Argyll to Mackintosh, 17 Apr. 1666; SRO GD 112/39/974, Argyll to Glenorchy, 13 Jan. [1665]; _ib._, 1079, same to same, 26 Dec. 1676.

43. _Ib._, 978, same to same, 21 Oct. 1665; BL Add. 23,137 fol. 77v, [same] to Lauderdale, [1675]; _Memoirs of Locheill_, 167–8, 192–3; Dirleton, _Doubts_, 197–8; Macfarlane, _Gen. Colls._, i, 376–7; NLS MS 7037 fol. 108, Memorandum concerning the Highlands.

44. Argyll, _Letters_, 34 (30 Jan. 1666), 38 (23 Aug. 1666).

45. Doune, Moray MSS, Box 6, 886, Douglas of Spynie to Moray, 3 Nov. 1666; Argyll _Letters_, 62, Argyll to Lauderdale, 1 Feb. [1667]; BL Add. 23,125 fols. 101–3, same to same, [1666]; _Laud. Papers_, i, 243, Bellenden to same, 9 Oct. 1666; EUL, MS Laing III, 354, fol. 143, Sir P. Wedderburn to same, 24 Sept. 1666.

46. Buckminster, Lauderdale Papers, 1820, same to same, 1 Aug. 1667; BL Add. 23,127 fol. 178, [Sir R. Moray] to same, 3 Aug. 1667; _ib._, Add. 23,129 fols. 25v–26, [Argyll] to

same, [Mar. 1668]; Atholl, *Chronicles*, i, 161, Huntly to Atholl, 27 Oct. 1667; Marchioness of Tullibardine, *A Military History of Perthshire 1660*-1902 (Perth, 1908), 28-30; *RPCS*, ii, 324-8.

47. *Ib.*, 414, 421-4; *Just. Recs.*, i, 264, 290-7.

48. Blair, Atholl MSS, Box 74/II/83, Instruments, 26 May 1680; BL Add. 23,129 fol. 86, [Argyll] to Lauderdale, [Mar. 1668]; *Laud. Papers*, ii, 137, Kincardine to same, 24 June 1669.

49. *Ib.*, 136; *ib.*, 131-2, same to same, 11 June 1669; *Misc. SHS*, vi, 214, Lauderdale to Tweeddale, 20 July 1669; *RPCS*, ii, 594-5, 599-602; *ib.*, iii, 32, 34, 52-9, 105.

50. Mackenzie, *Memoirs*, 179, 187; *HMCR Laing*, i, 373, Tweeddale to [Lauderdale], 22 July 1669.

51. *Laud. Papers*, ii, 136, Kincardine to same, 24 June 1669.

52. *Ib.*, 136; *HMCR Laing*, i, 380-1, same to same, 12 Jan. 1671; BL Add. 23,132 fol. 62, [Tweeddale] to same, 10 Aug. 1669; *A Collection of the State Papers of John Thurloe, Esq.*, ed. T. Birch, 7 vols. (London, 1742), vi, 80, Monck to Thurloe, 26 Feb. 1656/7; Dow, *Cromwellian Scotland*, 139; Gillies, *Breadalbane*, 242-3.

53. *RPCS*, iii, 73-6, 85-6, 115; *Laud. Papers*, ii, 199, Tweeddale to Lauderdale, 2 Sept. 1669; BL Add. 23,132, fol. 62, [same] to same, 10 Aug. 1669.

54. Buckminster, Lauderdale Papers, 2154, [Argyll] to same, 1 Apr. 1670; NLS MS 7004 fol. 16, Lawers to Tweeddale, 18 Apr. 1670; *Just. Recs.*, i, 315-19; *RPCS*, iii, 644-5.

55. *Ib.*, 222-3; Macfarlane, *Gen. Colls.*, i, 380-7; Fraser-Macintosh, *Letters*, 86-7, Mar to Mackintosh, 26 Nov. 1667.

56. *Just. Recs*, ii, 67; *Memoirs of Locheill*, 208-9 (misdated); *RPCS*, iii, 222, 236.

57. *Ib.*, 270-1, 301-3, 471; *ib.*, iv, 14-15; NLS MS 7005 fol. 38, [Sir R. Moray] to Tweeddale, 24 June 1671; BL Add. 23,135 fols. 3-4, 13, Argyll to Lauderdale, 4 Mar. 1671.

58. *Ib.*, fol. 76, T. Hayes to same, 1 Aug. 1671; *ib.*, fol. 30, Highland committee's report, 9 Mar. 1671; *RPCS*, iii, 341, 351, 356, 367, 370-5, 403; Brodie, *Diary*, 317; Buckminster, Lauderdale Papers, 2234, [Tweeddale] to Lauderdale, 31 Jan. 1671.

59. *Laud. Papers*, ii, 220, Kincardine to same, 14 Dec. 1671; *ib.*, 221, same to same, 21 Dec. 1671; *APS*, viii, App., 21; *RPCS*, iii, 399, 419, 430, 471-2, 478, 490-2, 540.

60. *Ib.*, iv, 135-6, 276-7, 378, 551-2, 646-7, 670; *ib.*, v, 168, 187-8; *Chiefs of Grant*, i, 238, 283-4; I. M. M. MacPhail, *Dumbarton Castle* (Edinburgh, 1979), 119-21; Law, *Memorialls*, 161-2.

61. *Ib.*, 74; *RPCS*, iii, 552; *A Genealogical Deduction of the Family of . . . Kilravock*, ed. C. Innes (Spalding Club, 1848), 362-3, Contract, 1 Nov. 1675; *ib.*, 371, Calder to Kilravock, 19 July 1674; Flinn, *Scottish Population History*, 114, 159-60.

62. Gillies, *Breadalbane*, 125-42; J. Macdiarmid, 'Folklore of Breadalbane', *TGSI*, xxvi, 148-50; *Coll. de Rebus Albanicis*, 135-6; *Black Book*, 49-54, 69, 71.

63. *Ib.*, 80, 96; *Memoirs of Locheill*, 67, 154-5; *Scots Peerage*, ii, 200.

64. *Ib.*, 189; Gillies, *Breadalbane*, 145-8; *Dewar MSS*, 242-3, 361-2; Stevenson, *Alasdair MacColla*, 148-9, 215; SRO GD 112/40/4/2/26, [Breadalbane] to [Carwhin], 7 [Dec. 1689]; *ib.*, 43/1/1/8, Breadalbane, Information for Loudoun, [1705-7].

65. *Ib.*, 39/1019, Sir J. Campbell to [Sir R. Moray], Dec. 1667; *Thurloe State Papers*, vi, 352, Monck to Thurloe, 16 June 1657; *Earls of Cromartie*, i, 46, Breadalbane to Queensberry, 20 May [1685]; *A Book of Scotish Pasquils, 1568-1715*, ed. J. Maidment (Edinburgh, 1868), 277, Verses on Hamilton and Breadalbane, [1693]; Gillies, *Breadalbane*, 99-103, 158-9.

66. *RPCS*, ii, 597; *Argyll Sasines*, ii, 328; *The Red Book of Menteith*, ed. Sir W. Fraser, 2 vols. (Edinburgh, 1880), ii, 161, Sir J. Campbell to Earl of Airth, 13 Sept. 1660; *ib.*, 162-4,

same to same, 1 Jan. 1661; SRO GD 112/40/3/1/38, Glencairn to Sir J. Campbell, 20 July 1662.

67. Sir Robert's survival until 1657 may have averted formal responsibility from his son and grandson. Although they were not fined, their Perthshire chamberlain was. *APS*, vii, 426.

68. SRO GD 112/39/976, Argyll to Sir J. Campbell, 17 Oct. 1665; NLS MS 7003 fol. 94, [same] to Tweeddale, [?May 1668].

69. It has always been assumed that this was his father, and that he did not sit until 1669, but the inconsistent parliamentary references to the new member (elected 1661, but not attending the first session) and a clearer one in a petition to the Council show that it was he. *APS*, vii, 372, 390, 438–9; *RPCS*, i, 506.

70. *Ib.*, 394, 397; *ib.*, iii, 315–16; Stair, *Decisions*, i, 558–9; *Highland Papers*, 101, Report, 20 June 1695; Gillies, *Breadalbane*, 240–3, 247, 251; BL Add. 19,254 fol. 119, Perth to Blair Drummond, 21 Oct. 1687; *ib.*, Add. 23,112 fol. 310, Argyll to Lauderdale, 11 Mar. 1665; SRO GD 112/40/3/1/110, Tweeddale to Glenorchy, 18 Apr. 1669.

71. Local tradition claimed that his first son really forfeited favour by a marriage into the Lawers family; if so, a precocious one, for he was only eighteen when his father was first allowed to exclude him. *Scots Peerage*, ii, 205–6; Gillies, *Bradalbane*, 121–3, 176.

72. *Argyll Sasines*, i, 162–3, ii, 433–4, 492–3; Shaw, *Northern & Western Islands*, 20.

73. *RPCS*, xv, 260; Gillies, *Breadalbane*, 162; J. E. Donaldson, *Caithness in the Eighteenth Century* (Edinburgh, 1938), 14–16, 26, 54–5; J. Brand, *A Brief Description of Orkney, Zetland, Pightland-Firth and Caithness* (Edinburgh, 1701), 149–50.

74. Kirkton, *Secret History*, 156, 157–8nn; *Wardlaw MS*, 439, 450, 482; BL Add. 23,115 fol. 75, Caithness to Lauderdale, 15 Feb. 1661; *ib.*, Add. 23,116 fol. 112, same to same, 25 Aug. [1661]; *ib.*, fol. 63, Middleton to same, 20 May 1661; *ib.*, Add. 23,124 fol. 124, Countess of Caithness (hereafter 'Countess') to same, 21 Apr. 1666.

75. *Ib.*, Add. 23,120 fol. 153, Caithness's information, [1663]; *RPCS*, i, 187–8, 225–6, 403, 435–7, 452–3; J. Henderson, *Caithness Family History* (Edinburgh, 1884), 85–6.

76. BL Add. 23,122 fol. 260, A. Macdonald to Macdonell, 19 Jan. 1665; NLS MS 7003 fol. 115, Seaforth to Tweeddale, 22 Dec. 1668; *Sutherland Book*, ii, 348–9, 351, 367, Sir R. Gordon's letter.

77. *Ib.*, 186–9; W. Macgill (ed.), *Old Ross-shire and Scotland*, 2 vols. (Inverness, 1909–11), ii, 16, Caithness to Balnagown, 4 Nov. 1664; Mackenzie, *Munros of Fowlis*, 90–1; A. Mackay, *The Book of Mackay* (Edinburgh, 1906), 146, 149, 153–4; *RPCS*, ii, 242–7, 299–300, 316–18, 357–8, 405–6, 433–4.

78. Henderson, *Caithness Family History*, 85, 87; Aubrey, *Three Prose Works*, 95–6; BL Add. 23, 129 fol. 268v, [Tweeddale] to Lauderdale, 8 Aug. 1668; *ib.*, fol. 98, Countess to same, 24 June [1668].

79. Mackay, *Book of Mackay*, 289–90; NLS MS 7003 fol. 80, Caithness to Tweeddale, Apr. 1668; *ib.*, fol. 98, Countess to same, 24 June [1668]; *RPCS*, i, 149–50; *ib.*, ii, 396, 404–6, 433–4, 437–8, 461, 463–5, 496–9, 566–7.

80. *Ib.*, 510–11, 512, 518, 552–3, 560–1, 571–2, 574; *Just. Recs.*, i, 264, 289, 291, 295; *Sutherland Book*, iii, 201–3, Articles of agreement, 9 Dec. 1668; *Misc. SHS*, vi, 170, Lauderdale to Tweeddale, 17 Nov. 1668; BL Add. 23,130 fol. 112, [Tweeddale] to Lauderdale, 14 Nov. 1668; *ib.*, fol. 78, [same] to same, 28 Oct. 1668.

81. *Ib;* *ib.*, Add. 23,129 fol. 268v, [same] to same, 8 Aug. 1668; *ib.*, fol. 296, T. Hay to same, 18 Aug. 1668; *ib.*, Add. 23,131 fol. 3, [Tweeddale] to same, 3 Dec. 1668; *ib.*, fol. 170, Cpt. H. Mackay's petition; EUL, MS Laing III 354 fol. 52, T. Hay to Lauderdale, 17 Nov. 1668; *RPCS* ii, 517–18, 566–7, 584.

82. *Ib.*, iii, 11, 13–14, 93–5, 123–4, 134–8, 144–5, 157, 174; NLS MS 7003 fol. 162, Glenorchy to Tweeddale, 20 Sept. 1669; *ib.*, fol. 164, same to same, 25 Sept. 1669; *ib.*, MS 7004 fol. 78, Caithness to same, 7 June [1670]; SRO GD 112/40/3/1/109, R. Campbell to Glenorchy, 19 Aug. 1669.

83. *Ib.*, 40/3/2/17, Sir R. Sinclair to same, 9 Feb. 1671; *RPCS*, iii, 137; *The Complete Baronetage*, ed. G. E. C[ockayne], 6 vols. (Exeter, 1900–9), iii, 351; Fountainhall, *Journals*, 213–14, 219: *Misc. SHS*, vi, 151, Lauderdale to Tweeddale etc., 28 Jan. 1668.

84. SRO GD 112/40/3/1/114, Sir R. Sinclair to Countess, 15 Sept. 1668; EUL, MS Laing III 354 fol. 115, same to Lauderdale, 9 Mar. 1671; *ib.*, fol. 21, Stair to Duchess, 4 June 1673; Buckminster, Lauderdale Papers, 5165, Agreement on arbitration, 5 Sept. 1670; BL Add. 23,133 fol. 38, Countess to Lauderdale, 5 Mar. 1670; *ib.*, Add. 23,135 fol. 238, Caithness's petition.

85. *Ib; ib.*, fols. 32v–33, Kincardine to Lauderdale, 9 Mar. 1671; *ib.*, fol. 257, Glenorchy to Duchess, 8 Mar. 1673; *ib.*, fol. 259, Countess to same, 11 Mar. 1673.

86. SRO GD 112/40/3/2/2, R. Andrews to Glenorchy, 22 Mar. 1670; *ib.*, 5, [Argyll] to same, 16 Dec. 1670.

87. By June 1673, at least, Sir Robert was being offered the succession if he would give Caithness the same terms as Glenorchy. *Ib.*, 39/1053, Glenorchy to Duchess, 2 Aug. 1673; BL Add. 23,135 fol. 220, same to same, 12 Dec. 1672; *ib.*, Add. 35,125 fol. 357, same to same n.d; Edinburgh EUL, MS Laing III 354 fol. 117, Sir R. Sinclair to same, 11 Apr. 1673; *ib.*, fol. 21, Stair to same, 4 June 1673; *APS*, viii, 368; *Scots Peerage*, ii, 203; *CSPD 1672–3*, 158, Protection to Caithness, 12 Nov. 1672.

88. SRO GD 112/40/3/2/35, [Caithness] to Lord Duffus, 19 Feb. 1674; *ib.*, 36, Calder to Glenorchy, 24 Dec. 1674; *ib.*, 41, R. Murray to same, 27 July 1674; *ib.*, 42, Duffus to Caithness, 9 Apr. 1674.

89. Mackenzie, *Memoirs*, 217, 239; Burnet, *History*, i, 546–7; D. Cripps, *Elizabeth of the Sealed Knot* (Kineton, 1975), 91–5, 98–9, 127–31.

90. The suggestion (J. M. Graham, *Annals and Correspondence of the Viscount and the . . . Earls of Stair*, 2 vols. (Edinburgh, 1875), i, 62n) that Lauderdale previously had claims on the Caithness estate is wrong. BL Add. 23,135 fol. 236, Glenorchy to Duchess, n.d; *ib.*, Add. 35,125 fol. 357, same to same; SRO GD 112/39/1053, same to same, 2 Aug. 1673; *CSPD 1673–5*, 254, Warrant, 19 May 1674.

91. Fountainhall, *Journals*, 223, 232; Mackenzie, *Memoirs*, 180–1, 227–8, 314, 320–1; Burnet, *History*, i, 547, 618, 622; Napier, *Dundee*, i, 362, Rothes to Queensberry, 4 Oct. 1677; SRO GD 112/39/1038, [Argyll] to [Glenorchy, ?1674–7].

92. *Ib.*, 1058, same to same, 22 July 1674; *RPCS*, iv, 208, 245–6; *ib.*, viii, 393; Macfarlane, *Gene. Colls.*, i, 138; *Highland Papers*, i, 249, 260–71.

93. Balhaldie's account, probably deliberately, misdates Lord Macdonell's expeditions to defend Mull as being in 1669–74, muddles the order of Lochiel's actions in the 1670s and suppresses facts he knew to obscure the context and motives of Lochiel's changes of side in 1675 and 1678. *Ib.*, 273–277; *Memoirs of Locheill*, 196–200; *RPCS*, iv, 272–4.

94. Clanranald may have taken part reluctantly, for he soon afterwards contracted with one of his tacksmen to perform the bulk of his vassal duty to Argyll. Macdonald, *Clan Donald*, iii, 655–8, Contract, 6 Nov. 1674; *HMCR 6th Report*, 629, Cases of Ardgour & Torloisk; Doune, Moray MSS, Box 7, 685, [Argyll] to [Moray], 19 Sept. 1674.

95. *Ib; RPCS*, iv, 272–4; *Highland Papers*, i, 275–7, Articles of agreement, 18 Sept. 1674; *ib.*, 277–95, Rental; Law, *Memorialls*, 81; Rev. A. Maclean Sinclair, *The Clan Gillean* (Charlottetown, 1899), 202–3.

96. *Royal Commission on Ancient and Historical Monuments of Scotland (RCAHMS)*

Argyll, 4 + vols., (HMSO, 1971-), iii, 192, 197-8; SRO GD 112/39/1061, Argyll to Glenorchy, 30 Apr. 1675.

97. *Memoirs of Locheill*, 201-3 (apparently misdated; for date, *HMCR 6th Report*, 620, Lochiel to Argyll, 2 Sept. 1675).

98. *Highland Papers*, i, 296-303; *Thanes of Cawdor*, 332, Glenorchy to Calder, 7 May 1675; SRO GD 112/39/1065, Argyll to Glenorchy, 22 May 1675.

99. *Ib.*, 1061, same to same, 30 Apr. 1675; *Highland Papers*, i, 305-8; *HMCR 6th Report*, 622, 632, L. Maclean to Argyll, 1675, 1676; *Thanes of Cawdor*, 332, Glenorchy to Calder, 7 May 1675.

100. *Ib*; NLS MS 975 fol. 25, [same] to Argyll, 14 Feb. 1675.

101. *Ib.*, fol. 18, Bond, 5 Aug. 1675; SRO GD 112/39/1082, [Argyll] to Lauderdale, 9 Jan. 1677.

102. As Lochiel's second son was at most ten years old, this was a broad hint. Balhaldie attributes the agreement to pressure from Camerons secretly corresponding with Argyll. *Memoirs of Locheill*, 200, 202; *Law, Memorialls*, 83; Shaw, *Northern and Western Islands*, 44; NLS MS 975 fol. 16, [Lochiel] to Argyll, 17 May 1675.

103. *Ib.*, fol. 25, [Glenorchy] to same, 14 Feb. 1677.

104. *Highland Papers*, i, 303-8; Napier, *Dundee*, ii, 183, Lady Braco to Braco, 4 Nov. 1678; SRO GD 112/39/1144, R. Maitland to 'Caithness', [?1679].

105. *RPCS*, iv, 432-5, 439; *Law, Memorialls*, 82-3; BL Add. 23,137 fols. 77-8, [Argyll] to Lauderdale, [Sept. 1675]; *HMCR 6th Report*, 617, same to Linlithgow, 14 Sept. 1675, same to Macdonell, 10 Sept. 1675; *ib.*, 620, Lochiel to Argyll, 2 Sept. 1675.

106. Balhaldie impudently claims that Lochiel's opposition to the raids on Argyllshire (misdated to 1674) led to his 1675 contract with Argyll. Balhaldie's Inventory mentions his 1675 contract with the Macleans, but the month (which would help establish his motives) seems illegible. *Ib.*, 627-8, Papers on raids; *RPCS*, v, 361-4; *Memoirs of Locheill*, 198-9, 202-4; SRO GD 1/658, 31-2; GD 112/39/1083, Argyll to Glenorchy, 22 Jan. 1677 (identifying the nickname).

107. *Ib; ib*, 1067, same to same, 31 Oct. 1676; *Memoirs of Locheill*, 196, 198-9; Mac Gill-Eain, 'Domhnall Donn', *TGSI*, xlii, 94-5; Fort William, West Highland Museum, Manuscripts, A21, MacIain's bond, 24 May 1679.

108. *HMCR 6th Report*, 618-19, Inverawe to Argyll, 27 Feb., 23 May 1677; NLS MS 975 fol. 23v, [Glenorchy] to same, 16 Jan. 1677; SRO GD 112/39/1083, Argyll to Glenorchy, 22 Jan. 1677; Brodie, *Diary*, 395.

109. *Ib.*, 352, 362; E. Dunbar Dunbar, *Social Life in Former Days* (Edinburgh, 1865), 292-3, Cluny to Sir R. Gordon, 6 July 1676; *RPCS*, v, 87-9.

110. *Ib.*, 36-8, 43-5, 84; BL Add. 23,138 fol. 21, Glenorchy to Duchess, 7 Sept. 1676; Fountainhall, *Hist. Notices*, i, 125, 136-7.

111. *Ib.*, 178; *Thanes of Cawdor*, 335-6, Calder to W. Duff, 19 July 1677; Doune, Moray MSS, Box 6, 528, A. Chisholm to Moray, 9 May 1677; *ib.*, 539, same to same, 21 June 1677.

112. SRO GD 112/40/3/2/58, Macdonell to 'Caithness', 24 Nov. 1677; *ib.*, REF 310.044 (GD 44; MS of projected HMC report), 51, T. Gordon to Huntly, 24 Sept. 1677; *RPCS*, v, 92-5, 243-51.

113. *Ib.*, 239, 251-2; *ib.*, iii, 553-564; Macfarlane, *Gen. Colls.*, i, 395-6.

114. *Memoirs of Locheill*, 196.

115. *RPCS*, iv, 483-4, 491, 527; *ib.*, v, 3-5, 11, 17, 49, 57-62, 73, 182-3; Fountainhall, *Hist. Notices*, i, 108-9; Dirleton, *Doubts*, 197-8; Stair, *Decisions*, ii, 478-9; *Law, Memorialls*, 83, 88, 94.

116. Mackenzie, *Memoirs*, 314, 320-1; Brodie, *Diary*, 384.

117. *Ib.*, 388, 391; Fountainhall, *Hist. Notices*, i, 169–72; Cripps, *Elizabeth*, 215, Atholl to Duchess, 8 Sept., 22 Dec. [1676]; Napier, *Dundee*, i, 359, Rothes to Queensberry, 16 Aug. 1677.

118. That winter, Argyll obtained a remission of the arrears of feu-duties. *RPCS*, v, 228; *ib.*, vi, 318–19; *CSPD 1677–8*, 505–6; BL Add. 23,241 fol. 29, Glenorchy to Duchess, 20 Feb. 1677; Napier, *Dundee*, i, 359, Rothes to Queensberry, 20 July 1677.

119. *Ib.*, 362, same to same, 4 Oct. 1677; Atholl, *Chronicles*, i, 174, Hickes to ?, 23 Oct. 1677; Fountainhall, *Historical Observes of Memorable Occurents in Church and State*, ed. A. Urquhart & D. Laing (Bannatyne Club, 1840), 122.

120. *APS*, viii, 368; *RPCS*, v, 32; *ib.*. vi, 275; *Scots Peerage*, ii, 345; SRO REF 310.044 (GD 44), 115, Gordon's memoirs, 2; BL Add. 23,138 fol. 21v, Glenorchy to Duchess, 7 Sept. 1676.

121. *Ib.*, fols. 21v–22; *RPCS*, v, 115–16, 120, 237–9; *Scots Peerage*, ii, 203; Fountainhall, *Hist. Notices*, i, 148–9; *Red Book of Grandtully*, ii, 233, Glenorchy to J. Steuart, 14 June 1677; *ib.*, 237, same to same, 21 May 1678; *ib.*, 240, same to same, 29 June 1678; Drumlanrig, Queensberry Papers, vol. 128, 19, Articles against Duchess, [?1681].

122. *RPCS*, iii, 93; *Earls of Cromartie*, i, 24–5, [Glenorchy] to Laird of Cromartie, 18 May 1677; Henderson, *Caithness Family History*, 221–2; SRO GD 112/39/1085, Calder to Glenorchy, 2 June 1677; *ib.*, 1086, Sinclairs to 'Caithness', 28 Aug. 1677.

123. *APS*, viii, 368; *RPCS*, v, 378, 440–1, 446, 500; *ib.*, vi, 14–15; Fountainhall, *Decisions*, i, 407, 465–6, 470; *Scots Peerage*, ii, 206.

124. J. R. Elder, *The Highland Host of 1678* (Glasgow, 1914), 8–12, 19–30; Buckroyd, *Church and State*, 124–7, 128–9.

125. *HMCR Buccleuch (Drumlanrig)*, i, 230, L.G. to Hamilton, [Oct. 1677]; R. Wodrow, *The History of the Sufferings of the Church of Scotland*, 4 vols. (Wodrow, *Church History*; Glasgow, 1829), ii, 375.

126. Part of the 1,000-strong Angus foot militia would also have been composed of highlanders. Elder, *Highland Host*, 45–7; W. Mackay, 'The Highland Host (1678)', *TGSI*, xxxii (1924–5), 72; *Chiefs of Grant*, ii, 23, Huntly to Grant, 22 Dec. 1677; *RPCS*, v, 272–3, 291, 297, 300–4.

127. *Ib.*, 335; Wodrow, *Church History*, ii, 427; 'A Copie of a Letter from the Host about Glasgow', 1 Feb. 1678, *Blackwood's Magazine*, i (1817), 68.

128. *Ib.*, 69; Kirkton, *Secret History*, 390–1; Elder, *Highland Host*, 129–30.

129. This was apparently not merely for travel in or from the Lowlands; Caithness's party with Argyll in Mull in January 1679, veterans of the Host, did the same. *Memoirs of Mr William Veitch and George Brysson*, ed. T. M'Crie (Veitch, *Memoirs*; Edinburgh, 1825), 518–19; Wodrow, *Church History*, ii, 412–13, 425–8; *RPCS*, v, 336–7, 547–8; 'Letter from the Host', *Blackwood's*, i, 68; SRO GD 112/39/1100, Barcaldine to 'Caithness', 11 Jan. 1679; Lt.-Col. W. Cleland, *A Collection of Several Poems and Verses* ([Glasgow], 1697), 38, 'A Mock Poem Upon the Expedition of the Highland-host'.

130. One killing is mentioned in Cleland's poem, the last part of which seems to be a (bad) versification of a genuine protest presented by the Ayrshire gentry to the Committee. It is not particularly surprising that it was not recorded; the cossacks-and-peasants relations prevailing between the regular forces and presbyterian country-folk a few years later, of which we occasionally get glimpses (e.g. Veitch, *Memoirs*, 520–2) did not find their way into official reports. Cleland, *Poems*, 35, 37–9, 42; Wodrow, *Church History*, ii, 388, 422, 429–31; Elder, *Highland Host*, 134; 'Letter from the Host', *Blackwood's*, i, 69; *RPCS*, v, 578–9.

131. *Ib.*, 365–6, 547; Atholl, *Chronicles*, i, 176–7, Murray to Marchioness of Atholl

(hereafter 'Marchioness'), 20 Feb. 1678; Napier, *Dundee*, ii, 169–70, Perth to Queensberry, 20 Feb. 1678.

132. SRO GD 112/39/1087, same to 'Caithness', 14 Mar. 1678; *RPCS*, v, 378, 440–1, 446, 518.

133. *Laud. Papers*, iii, 93, Perth to Lauderdale, 9 Dec. 1677; Napier, *Dundee*, ii, 172–3, Rothes to Queensberry, 16 Apr. 1678; *ib.*, 174–6, Bishop Paterson to Primrose, 24 Sept. 1678; Wodrow, *Church History*, ii, 423.

134. *HMCR 6th Report*, 627, Notorial instruments, 7 Sept. 1678; SRO GD 202/18, 87–8, Argyll's warrant, 17 June 1678.

135. Cripps, *Elizabeth*, 152–3, 170–1, 225; Brodie, *Diary*, 400, 402.

136. *Ib.*, 405; *RPCS*, vi, 1–2, 10, 18, 34–51, 58–9, 74–5, 468; C. Dalton, *The Scots Army 1661-1688* (London, 1909), 108; Fountainhall, *Hist. Notices*, i, 204–5, 409; *Highland Papers*, i, 309–11; Buckminster, Lauderdale Papers, 2779, [Argyll] to [Moray], 19 Oct. 1678; SRO GD 112/39/1094, [same] to 'Caithness', 29 Oct. 1678; *ib.*, 40/3/2/77, Lawers to same, 18 Jan. 1679.

137. *Ib.*, 39/1067, Argyll to same, 31 Oct. 1676; *ib.*, 1083, same to same, 22 Jan. 1677; *Memoirs of Locheill*, 198 (misdated).

138. *Ib.*, 198, 204; SRO GD 1/658, 24; Macfarlane, *Gen. Colls.*, i, 138; NLS MS 975 fol. 27, Lochiel to A. Campbell, 25 July 1678; Doune, Moray MSS, Box 6, 265, 'Caithness' to Moray, 12 Nov. 1678.

139. *Ib; ib.*, 51, [Argyll] to same, 27 Nov. 1678; Rev. A. E. Anderson, 'Notes from the Presbytery Records of Lorne', *TGSI*, xxxvi, 121–2; NLS MS 975 fol. 30, 'Caithness' etc. to Argyll, 23 Nov. 1678; *ib.*, fol. 43, Mackintosh to same, 11 Feb. 1679; *ib.*, fols. 33, 35, Lochiel to same, 30 Nov. 1678 (2).

140. *Ib.*, fol. 37, same to same, 4 Dec. 1678; Brodie, *Diary*, 407; SRO GD 112/40/3/2/95, Macdonaid to 'Caithness', 7 June 1679; *ib.*, 39/1104, 'Caithness' to ?, 15 Feb. 1679; *ib.*, 1095, Barcaldine to 'Caithness', n.d; *ib.*, 1097, Macdonell to same, 2 Jan. 1679.

141. *Ib.*, 1098, [Argyll] to same, 10 Jan. 1679; *ib.*, 1103, same to same, 19 Jan. 1679; *ib.*, 40/3/2/68, [same] to same, 24 Dec. 1679; *ib.*, 62, J. Campbell to same, 20 Dec. 1679; *ib.*, 71, ? to same, 22 Dec. 1679; *RCAHMS Argyll*, iii, 226; *HMCR 6th Report*, 629, Argyll's condescendence, 7–8 Aug. 1679; *Thanes of Cawdor*, 339–40, D. Campbell to Calder, 2 Jan. 1679; *Highland Papers*, i, 317.

142. SRO GD 112/39/1103, [Argyll] to 'Caithness', 19 Jan. 1679; *ib.*, 1109, ? to same, 22 Apr. 1679.

143. *Ib.*, 1100, Barcaldine to same, 11 Jan. 1679; *ib.*, 1101, same to same, 19 Jan. 1679; *ib.*, 1104, 'Caithness' to ?, 15 Feb. 1679; *Thanes of Cawdor*, 344, Calder to Countess, Apr. 1679.

144. *RPCS*, vi, 58, 70–1, 75–6, 101–4, 165–6, 169–73; Burnet, *History*, ii, 162–5; Doune, Moray MSS, Box 6, 541, A Chisholm to Moray, 12 Feb. 1679.

145. SRO GD 112/39/1116, [Argyll] to 'Caithness', 6 May 1679; *ib.*, 1117, Lawers to same, 7 May 1679; *ib.*, 40/3/2/76, 'Caithness' to Argyll, 13 May 1679; Buckminster, Lauderdale Papers, 2853, [Argyll] to Moray, 29 May 1679; NLS MS 1672 fol. 41, Bond of friendship, 2 May 1679; Napier, *Dundee*, i, 316, Rothes to Queensberry, 28 May 1679.

146. *Ib; RPCS*, vi, 203–5; SRO GD 112/39/1118, Argyll to 'Caithness', 12 May 1679; *ib.*, 1143, [same] to same, 'Sunday' [25 May 1679].

147. *Ib; ib.*, 1120, ['Caithness'] to [Moray], 26 May 1679; *Orain Iain Luim*, 154–5, 'Blar Tom a 'Phubaill'; MacWilliam, 'A Highland Mission', *IR*, xxiv, 84; Fort William, West Highland Museum, MSS, A21, MacIain's bond, 24 May 1679; Buckminster, Lauderdale Papers, 2853, [Argyll] to Moray, 29 May 1679.

148. Only Brodie's diary, written in Moray, mentions bloodshed, on both sides. *Ib;* *Mackintosh Muniments*, 131, same to Mackintosh, 30 May 1679; SRO GD 112/39/1126, [same] to 'Caithness', 30 May 1679; Brodie, *Diary*, 412–13; *HMCR 6th Report*, 629, Reports of depredations, 1679.

149. *Ib.*, 628–9; *Orain Iain Luim*, 152–7, 'Blar Tom a 'Phubaill' (date corrected); Sir W. Fraser, *The Chiefs of Colquhoun and their country*, 2 vols. (Edinburgh, 1869), i, 291.

150. SRO GD 112/40/3/2/85, 'Caithness' to brother, 8 June 1679; *ib.*, 102, same to Rothes, June 1679.

151. *Ib.*, 39/1122, same to Macdonell, 26 May 1679; *ib.*, 1130, same to same, 2 June 1679; *ib.*, 1123, same to Macdonald of Fersit, 26 May 1679; *ib.*, 1125, same to Ld. N. Campbell, 29 May 1679; *ib.*, 1132, [Argyll] to 'Caithness', 1 June 1679.

152. If Caithness's negotiation alone were responsible for Macdonell's withdrawal, and its unfortunate results, Iain Lom would presumably have denounced him vigorously in his poem on the expedition. *Ib.*, 40/3/2/95, Macdonell to same, 7 June 1679; *ib.*, 98, R. Macdonald to same, 7 June 1679; *ib.*, 85, 'Caithness' to brother, 8 June 1679; Wodrow, *Church History*, iii, 88–9; *RPCS*, x, 409, 477–8, 501–4; Brodie, *Diary*, 413.

153. SRO GD 112/40/3/2/97, [Argyll] to Countess, 1 June 1679; Doune, Moray MSS, Box 6, 48, [Argyll] to Moray, 5 June 1679; *ib.*, 49, [same] to same, 28 June 1679.

154. Tullibardine, *Military History*, 116–17; NLS MS 3186 fols. 18v–19, Balhaldie's petition; *RPCS*, vi, 205, 223–4, 238, 253.

155. *Ib.*, 222; Brodie, *Diary*, 415; *Mackintosh Muniments*, 131, Argyll to Mackintosh, 30 May 1679; Doune, Moray MSS, Box 6, 49, [Argyll] to Moray, 28 June 1679.

156. NLS MS 975 fol. 47, Lochiel to Argyll, 27 June 1679.

157. *HMCR 6th Report*, 629; Cregeen, 'Tacksmen', *SS*, xiii, 97–8; *RCAHMS Argyll*, iii, 189, 208; Doune, Moray MSS, Box 6, 47, [Argyll] to Moray, 21 Aug. 1679; *ib.*, 49, [same] to same, 28 June 1679; *ib.*, 53, [same] to same, 5 Aug. 1679; *RPCS*, vi, 304, 312, 318–19, 333–4.

158. *Ib.*, 421–2; *Mackintosh Muniments*, 131, Tack of Keppoch, Aug. 1679; Macfarlane, *Gen. Colls.*, i, 397–404; NLS MS 975 fol. 49, Mackintosh to Argyll, 22 Oct. 1679.

159. *Ib*; *RPCS*, vi, 324; *HMCR 6th Report*, 619, Lawers to Argyll, 22 Oct. 1679, 10 Dec. 1679; *Chiefs of Colquhoun*, ii, 214–15; Doune, Moray MSS, Box 6, 50, [Argyll] to Moray, 27 Sept. 1679.

160. Fountainhall, *Hist. Observes*, 74–5; *Life of James*, i, 569, 580; Napier, *Dundee*, ii, 173, Rothes to Queensberry, 16 Apr. 1678; Buckroyd, *Church & State*, 131–3.

161. *Ib.*, 133–5; SRO GD REF 310.044 (GD 44) 115, Gordon's memoirs, 1, 12.

162. *RPCS*, vi, 344, 371–2; *Life of James*, i, 575–8; *Laud. Papers*, iii, 181–2, Argyll etc. to Lauderdale, 6 Nov. 1679; BL Add. 23,245 fol. 35, James to same, 20 Dec. [1679]; SRO GD 112/39/1142, [Argyll] to 'Caithness', 29 Dec. 1679.

163. SRO REF 310.044 (GD 44), 115, Gordon's memoirs, 2.

164. *RPCS*, vi, 337, 348–9, 372, 373–4, 411, 598–9; SRO GD 112/43/1/6/44, Articles & answers, 10 Aug. 1683; *ib.*, 51, G. Sinclair to inhabitants of Thurso, 16 Jan. 1680; *ib.*, 39/1145, R. Maitland to 'Caithness', 30 Dec. 1679; *ib.*, 1142, [Argyll] to same, 29 Dec. 1679.

165. *Ib.*, 1156, same to same, 24 May 1680; BL Add. 23,246 fol. 49, same to Lauderdale, 15 June 1680; *Life of James*, i, 707, James's report (misplaced: Stevenson, *Alasdair MacColla*, 288).

166. *RPCS*, vi, 432, 437, 438–9, 450–1, 495–6; *Laud. Papers*, iii, 197, Halton to Lauderdale, 13 Mar. 1680; Fountainhall, *Hist. Notices*, i, 263; *Miscellany of the Spalding Club (Spalding Club Misc.)*, ed. J. Stuart, iii (1846), 220, James to Huntly, 13 Mar. [1680].

167. *RPCS*, vi, 393; SRO GD 112/43/1/1/24, Queries; *Life of James*, i, 705.

168. *Ib.*, 706–7; *RPCS*, vi, 382, 392–8; SRO REF 310.044 (GD 44), 115, Gordon's memoirs, 1–2.

169. *Ib; RPCS*, vi, 394, 428–9; Fountainhall, *Hist. Notices*, i, 261; *Spalding Club Misc.*, iii, 220, James to Huntly, 13 Mar. [1680]; *Laud. Papers*, iii, 195, Sir G. Mackenzie to Lauderdale, 17 Feb. 1680; BL Add. 23,246 fols. 9–10, Mar to same, 20 Mar. 1680; Doune, Moray MSS, Box 7, 461, [Lauderdale] to Moray, 4 Mar. 1680.

170. *RPCS*, vi, 428–30, 446, 457, 466, 470, 474–5, 490–1, 493, 562; *Laud. Papers*, iii, 200–1, Bishop Paterson to Lauderdale, 17 June 1680; *HMCR 6th Report*, 619, Lawers to Argyll, 3 May 1680, Sir J. Colquhoun to same, 2 Oct. 1680; SRO REF 310.044 (GD 44), 56, [Tarbat] to Huntly, 26 June 1680; *ib.*, GD 112/40/3/3/8, Sir A. Forrester to 'Caithness', 3 July 1680.

171. *Ib.*, 39/1153, [Argyll] to same, 26 Apr. 1680; *ib.*, 1155, same to same, 19 May 1680; *ib.*, 1158, same to same, 27 May 1680.

172. *CSPD 1679–80*, 487, Lauderdale to Argyll, 20 May 1680; *ib.*, 544, Charles to Scottish Treasury, 10 July 1680; *RPCS*, vi, 490, 537; Fountainhall, *Hist. Notices*, ii, 533; *Hist. Observes*, 13; *HMCR 6th Report*, 633, 'Council' [Treasury] to Moray, 1 Oct. 1681, Charles to [Treasury], 19 Oct. 1681.

173. As Alasdair remembered that his father was, theoretically, chief only when chiefs had to take the allegiance and assurance to William in 1693, he will be referred to as 'Glengarry'. Tradition claims that Alasdair was the second son, and that the peaceable elder quietly accepted the decision, a further indication that the urgency of the need was obvious. Macdonald, *Clan Donald*, ii, 449, 454, iii, 321; NLS MS 7015 fol. 106, Glengarry to Hill, 11 Sept. 1693.

174. *Scots Peerage*, v, 534; *Memoirs of Locheill*, 260–1; Lovat, *Memoirs*, 10–11; *Leven and Melville Papers: Letters and State Papers chiefly addressed to George Earl of Melville*, ed. W. L. Melville (*Leven & Melville*: Bannatyne Club, 1843), 632, Tarbat to Melville, 25 July 1691; SRO GD 170/629/75, Breadalbane to Barcaldine, 14? [1698]; Blair, Atholl MSS, Box 29 I (3) 96, J. McDonell of Achtera to Atholl, 15 Sept. 1682.

175. *CSPD July–Sept. 1683*, 276, Pardon to Breadalbane, 10 Aug. 1683; *RPCS*, vi, 467–9, 490; *Laud. Papers*, iii, 201, Paterson to Lauderdale, 17 June 1680; *Red Book of Menteith*, ii, 185–6, Claverhouse to Menteith, 3 July [1680]; Murray Macgregor, *Clan Gregor*, ii, 227; Campbell, *Lairds of Glenlyon*, 334; Gillies, *Breadalbane*, 161; SRO GD 112/39/1161, [Argyll] to 'Caithness', 15 June 1680; *ib.*, 43/1/6/44, Articles & answers, 7 Aug. 1683; GD 170/629/2, Breadalbane to Barcaldine, 2 Apr. 1683.

176. *Scotish Pasquils*, 104 (belief about cannon); Henderson, *Caithness Family History*, 26; SRO GD 112/43/1/6/46, J. Oswald's declaration, 14 Nov. 1680; *ib.*, 65, Depositions, 23 Nov. 1680.

177. Another tradition, that he planted an ambush beforehand, is wrong in some details and seems improbable. *Ib; ib.*, 53; *ib.*, 56, Wick magistrates' declaration, 4 Oct. 1680; GD 170/629/2, Breadalbane to Barcaldine, 2 Apr. 1683; Gillies, *Breadalbane*, 161–2; Campbell, *Lairds of Glenlyon*, 333–5.

178. SRO GD 112/43/1/3/2, Sir W. Sharp to 'Caithness' & Menzies, 19 Aug. 1680; *ib.*, 3, 'Caithness' to Barcaldine, 18 Oct. 1680; *ib.*, 4, Menzies to 'Caithness', 18 Nov. 1680.

179. *RPCS*, vi, 544–5.

3

The Loyalist Revenge (1680–December 1688)

James Duke of York was now unquestionably the focus of all Scottish political life. By the time he returned permanently to England, his vigorous administration and firm support (despite personal catholicism) for the established church had won him widespread loyalty among the governing classes — and driven the presbyterian extremists further towards civil war. He was popular partly because he was, in one sense, a reformer, sweeping away what 'Cavaliers' saw as Lauderdale's heritage, shady favouritism and compromise towards Presbyterians and ex-rebels, and the corruption and abuse of power maintaining this — by, for instance, breaking (though for other reasons) Stair's Court of Session. He was later to warn his son, 'Trust none in the [Scottish] Government but those of the Antient loyal familys that haue had no taint of the Presb: or accustom'd to Rebell'.[1] The chief ministers he chose, Gordon of Haddo, created Earl of Aberdeen, Queensberry, Perth and his brother Melfort, were from such families, and were vigorous in sniffing out hereditary disloyalty — a charge to which both major branches of the Campbells were vulnerable.

The 1681 Parliament seemed a reforming one, as grievances against Lauderdale's regime were aired. In reality, of course, there had been no such complete break in principles, and James, distrusting criticism from below as harmful to authority even when he agreed with it, prevented their proceeding further. It was the contrary trend which prevailed in the Parliament, the increase of government and royal power by acts rushed through the subservient Articles, particularly the Test Act with its self-contradictory non-resistance oath.[2] The new regime was, especially after James's departure, as corrupt and oppressive in everyday matters as its predecessor, although the choice of oppressors and victims had somewhat altered. One new disadvantage for highland nobles, whom Lauderdale had not personally troubled, was heavy pressure from Aberdeen and Perth, with their own highland interests, to yield them vital feudal superiorities.[3]

The Parliament showed how much James's advisers of the moment dominated him, and some observers concluded that 'he had neither great conduct nor a deep reach in affairs, but was a silly man'.[4] Events largely confirmed this. Through Charles's control, even Lauderdale's regime had retained a balance of sorts, with past and potential enemies like Rothes still in apparently high office. James let his favourites monopolise him, but this seldom lasted; and the prospect of gaining such power encouraged instability in Scottish politics. His self-proclaimed strongest virtue was his loyalty to servants. Yet, over five years, he allowed the other ministers to destroy Lauderdale's brother, Aberdeen's colleagues to overthrow him by bribing Charles's mistress, and Perth and Melfort to undermine Queensberry with obvious misrepresentations. His ministers, therefore, desperate to win or retain his favour, dared not give him disinterested advice.[5] His most notorious characteristic was firmness — or obstinacy — and he violently resented and overrode direct opposition to his policies. Yet, except over a few basic matters, adroit advisers could manoeuvre him into accepting series of *faits accomplis* which left him pursuing the opposite policy but eerily unaware that he had changed.

The truth seems to be that James, while possessing very strong principles and prejudices, lacked the capacity to make a logical system of them, although most of them, being authoritarian, had a family resemblance which concealed the fact. As he could not even perceive their frequent contradictions, there was no check on his acting upon whichever individual prejudice was being played on. As a result, though usually sincere, he frequently broke his word or overlooked obvious obligations without any idea that he was doing so. Scotland, where he believed the monarch absolute, was spared further complications — and hopes — from his occasional English expressions of belief in the King-in-Parliament. Yet it was largely this inner incoherence which made him overlook his deep distrust of Scottish Presbyterians and Whigs when he imposed a toleration in 1687 and in a 1690 plot offered control of the government to Whig Jacobites.[6] To an exceptional degree, court intrigue replaced real policies. James's abrupt changes of direction appear clearly in his treatment of the Earl of Argyll in 1681.

The new regime encouraged the hostility against both major Campbell families to explode. Caithness, naturally, was the first attacked. In September, the Council granted an investigation at George Sinclair's petition, on James's return a committee was appointed, and in December the charges and counter-charges were heard. Caithness thought that it 'uas designed to hav reached my lyf and fortoune'. In January, at the Council's command, a prosecution for treason was started against him, but, thanks to Lord Advocate Mackenzie, who where possible still served the Lauderdale interest, it did not go far.[7] As Parliament approached, Sinclair petitioned to sit as Earl of Caithness, and the Council persuaded Charles to remove the 1677 ban. He took his place without opposition, and Glenorchy was consoled with a new earldom, Breadalbane, enabling him also to attend. However, when the new Earl of Caithness petitioned Parliament to restore his family lands so that he could finance his lawsuits against Breadalbane for the Caithness estates, which might have encouraged the anti-Campbell forces to go further, Mackenzie managed to have it referred back to the Council, which merely ordered the land restored.[8] Articles which were prepared against the Duchess of Lauderdale for her many extortions, but never presented to Parliament, included Glenorchy's bribe. She had frequently declared in 1680 that she would not accept his £1,000 until the earldom was securely his. Yet she passed the bond to her son-in-law Lorne, who possessed it as a weapon against Breadalbane throughout the 1690s.[9] Breadalbane's loss of favour aroused his creditors, and he had to retire from the Council for over a year, losing other posts. His local activities in the early 1680s have invited sinister interpretations on the assumption that Argyll's fall, by making him the leading Campbell, increased his power and influence. It was actually a disaster to him as to other Campbells, leaving him exposed to financial ruin or worse.[10]

Argyll, in contrast, remained in apparent favour that winter. Lorne became a Privy Councillor. The Council forced the Macleans to surrender their last stronghold, Carnaburg, despite their plea that it was a private residence. Yet the main danger to him, from the Argyll family's loyalist creditors anxious to reverse the settlement of 1663, was so threatening that the Duchess of Lauderdale wished he would sell his estates.[11] Their ostentatious loyalty appealed to James, but he had apparently attempted clumsily to persuade Argyll to turn Catholic as a personal favour which could also make him 'the greatest man in Scotland'.[12] His refusal and anti-papist activity early in Parliament tilted the balance of James's mixed feelings about him towards hostility, and he orchestrated the creditors' attacks.[13] Yet, when they produced their acts, one for a committee with full powers to overturn the grant of Argyll's estate, and another to deprive him of his heritable jurisdictions, James, openly regretting his previous support, prevented it, 'upon the first principle that hee wold neither suffer the Kings servants nor his ... patents to be calld in question befor the parlt.' His tenderness towards Argyll as a royal servant has caused surprise, but the speed with which the English Parliament had progressed from Charles's imprudent encouragement to impeach Clarendon to its recent violent attacks on any of Charles's ministers who would not support Exclusion deeply influenced his attitude. Argyll obtained confirmation of the barony of Duart, apparently ending Maclean hopes.[14]

Yet, after vetoing in Parliament the idea of a commission on Argyll's affairs, James's mind was directed back to it that autumn. Argyll, having, as he thought, obtained his consent, took the Test with a qualification hinting that it was inconsistent. He may possibly have hoped to rally and head a 'protestant' opposition (although his own account suggests that, with Lauderdale's old faction increasingly under pressure, he was on the defensive throughout). In that case, it was remarked, James would have been wise to accept his oath, discrediting him for ever with the Presbyterians. Instead, having first seemed pleased, then angrily satisfied that Argyll had 'cheated himself' into taking it, he was afterwards persuaded (apparently by Tarbat and Haddo) to have him arrested and tried for treason. He and Charles intended Argyll's predictable condemnation as a very crude instrument for depriving him legally of his heritable jurisdictions, 'too much for any one Subject', after which he could be restored. Argyll, however, not daring to trust to Charles's clemency, or at least James's use of it when influenced by court intrigues, escaped in December. He went south partly to appeal to Charles, but was already en route conciliating the extreme Presbyterians. Charles unexpectedly had to forfault Argyll entirely. James characteristically wrote, once the prosecution was in progress, as if impartial law, not politics, would decide it, and could not see why he was blamed in England for instigating it.[15]

'Lord Lorne' (who also lost his title) and the Lauderdales tried to obtain another almost full restoration, claiming that the superiorities were merely small financial rights, but Charles determined to annex them and the heritable offices to the Crown (finally done in 1685). 'Lorne' was granted £15,000 Scots a year from the estates, and Argyll's younger children were provided for, but they did not regain Inveraray or any solid territorial base. Loyal clans ruined or being ruined by the family received partial or full compensation, and the remaining estates — not much after this, it was anticipated — would be employed paying off the creditors in an order determined by the Lords of Session.[16] In 1683, discovery of Argyll's part in Whig plots and pressure from Scottish politicians made Charles alter these terms for the worse. He was legally unable to make the children's tenure more precarious, as he originally intended, but decided that the rest of the estate, never to be restored, should be wadsetted to the creditors. Atholl, Perth and other politicians bought up vast Argyll debts and had themselves ranked ahead of genuine creditors. Argyll's vassals had, theoretically, been forfaulted with him. When the government denied that the 1682 grants exposed their estates to the creditors' claims, it was suspected that they were being reserved for the politicians; and in mid-1684 Charles ordered an estimate of which were traditionally loyal, which disloyal.[17]

The creditors' demands meant that in 1682 Sir John Maclean could be awarded only the £500 a year sterling previously agreed on, and that Mull was still burdened with unjust demands Argyll had transmitted to others and with much of his children's provision. The judges, Breadalbane claimed, evaded this by decreeing that Mull, Morvern and both ends of Coll together did not produce the full £500, while they laid the children's claim on Tiree, using the impossibly high rental Argyll had concocted to evade meeting Sir John's own claims.[18] Macnachtan regained his Argyllshire lands and local power, enabling his son Iain to marry Breadalbane's sister in 1683, the year he succeeded. Iain was to be a major link between his brother-in-law and the Jacobites. Macdougall of Dunollie's grant caused complaints among the creditors, and was not passed until 1688.[19] Charles's original proposal to cancel Clanranald's debt to Argyll had to be abandoned, but the lands of Glengarry and Knoidart comprised from Lord Macdonell were restored to Glengarry. Atholl had probably sponsored both proposals.[20] Other debts, including Lochiel's, were at the creditors' disposal. He received no favour, being considered more Argyll's ally than a loyalist. The Campbell tacksmen in Mull who in early 1682 were evading government orders to surrender Duart and other strongholds, an ironical parallel to the Macleans a year earlier, included Cameron of Glendessary.[21]

The Appin Stewarts benefited less directly from Argyll's fall. Lawers was now able to sell his rights over Glencoe to the Earl of Perth, who re-sold them to John Stewart of Ardsheal, Tutor of Appin. He began feuing out the land to the Glencoe gentry to recover the purchase-price, but 6,000 merks were still owing in 1690. In other ways, also, it proved a dear bargain. The political climate allowed the Stewarts to exploit less legal advantages. In the 1630s, they had lost their fortress, Castle Stalker, for debt to the Campbell family of Airds. Now they claimed it back as having been seized by the Marquess in the Civil Wars; and, sometimes playing on Airds's insecurity as a vassal of Argyll, sometimes actually besieging the castle, they had it back by 1686.[22] (See Preface, p. ix)

These grants, liable to be reversed if forces hostile to James triumphed and restored Argyll, provided a basis of self-interest for the western clans' support for James after 1688. It has been traditionally claimed that this alliance was far deeper, and that there was a natural bond of sympathy between the personal rule of Stuart monarchs and the 'patriarchal' chiefs of the 'loyal clans' which had supported the

Crown in the 1640s and 1650s. The major feudal superiorities of one clan over another were dangerous to both, enabling Argyll and others to call out reluctant vassals against the Crown, and oppress them perpetually if they refused; and James, particularly aware of this, was anxious, as he often told Lochiel, that chiefs like him should hold directly of the Crown. The traditional, mystical monarchy of Scotland and the clan system with its Gaelic culture naturally stood and fell together.[23]

More recent historians, in contrast, emphasise how strange a figurehead James was for the West Highland clans. He turned to them, after the Crown's neglect in the years of comparative security since 1660, when he might need their armed help in gaining and holding the throne. He showed hostility towards Gaelic culture in Ireland (where, admittedly, it was directly subversive, as it was not in Scotland), and there was no simple connection between it and Jacobitism: Iain Breac Macleod, a chief particularly famous for maintaining traditional hospitality and support for the arts, remained conspicuously neutral in 1689.[24] As James's suggestion over the Highland Justiciary showed, he was a strong believer in social hierarchy, with little understanding of what oppressions it made possible. He had no objection to a loyal magnate exploiting his feudal powers to raise men. Despite a suggestion in the 1685 Act of Annexation, he pursued no coherent policy of making 'loyal' clans hold directly of the Crown. Such a policy, though clearer after the Revolution, was betrayed once in 1690, and is still qualified in his 1692 'Advice to his Son': 'be Kind to the Highlanders, especially to those Clans who have allways stuck to the Crowne, lett their Cheef dependance be on the Crown, without doing wrong to such of the Nobility as have interest in those parts'.[25] He made a special case of Lochiel, who had convinced him of his loyal conduct in the 1650s, and frequently declared it a pity that he should not have command of his own clan, but his actions showed the prevalence of court intrigue over policy mentioned earlier. Gordon was granted the lands of Lochiel by charter in January 1685, and James, succeeding soon after and being petitioned by Lochiel, considered annulling this, granting Gordon compensation; instead, in January 1686, he confirmed Gordon's signature without any necessary safeguards, a step it took great trouble to undo.[26]

James was also a bureaucratic centraliser, with little sympathy for the liberties and irregularities of peripheral areas. Probably only the increasing violence in the West, which tied down the army there, prevented the government, which planned an Inverlochy garrison in the early 1680s, from trying to control the Highlands by military rule, for which James had a general predilection. This, by enforcing government claims and legal rights like Mackintosh's in the regime's increasingly high-handed style, would progressively have set it at odds with the Lochaber clans.[27] James's most ostentatiously 'loyalist' and most influential chief ministers, Perth and Melfort, had, despite their own highland links, 'small faith in tartan trews'. Perth took the lead in the Secret Committee's hysterically savage orders for punishment of Argyllshire rebels and their families, which they would not have applied to lowlanders, and in 1688 he ordered fire and sword against his fellow-Catholics, the Keppoch Macdonalds.[28]

Yet revisionism is pushed too far. Whatever James's centralising tendencies, his entourage was largely drawn from the peripheries — borderers, for instance, providing most of his Household circle — and even the Celtic peripheries: his liking for Irish Catholics caused trouble throughout Charles's reign, and, symbolically, the three sea-captains who followed him into exile were a Cornishman, a Welshman and an Antrim Macdonnell.[29] James's centralising plans and reliance on social hierarchy contained contradictions which even he might be unable to ignore, since Charles's 'highland policy', largely a lazy willingness to use the imperfect tools to hand —magnates like Argyll — was so obviously inefficient. Adroit lesser chiefs, although out of sympathy with the ultimate centralising aims, might exploit the clash. Even James's extraordinary mental processes had advantages, leaving him, for instance, after his unsuccessful Dissenting alliance, with a new and lasting belief in religious toleration. However accidental Argyll's forfeiture, it encouraged James to establish as the vital criterion for treatment of the clans their 'loyalty' in the Civil Wars — in the highly simplified versions they themselves presented, luckily for such as Lochiel. This attitude, unlike Charles's memory of sacrifices, might, as Lochiel predicted in 1690, survive after a restoration. Disloyalty was treated almost as something tangible, a hereditary disease likely to afflict the most outwardly healthy descendant, and the discrimination practised on this basis made it a self-fulfilling prophecy. James even planned in the 1685 Parliament to proscribe the name of Campbell, like that of Macgregor in 1633, although he changed his mind when Breadalbane and other Campbells were campaigning against Argyll for him.[30] Even if the government often did not see its employment of the western clans, 'the Mackes', against Whig rebels as a natural alliance, its opponents did, even supposing that it had connived at normal cattle-raiding to fit the clans for the task of imposing popery and slavery; and their hatred contributed to bind both sides together.[31]

Clans might not support an absolutist monarch from the supposed resemblance of his powers to a patriarchal chief's. They might, however, support him, even if he sometimes carried out punitive acts like the ravaging of Keppoch, for the same reason the catholic minority supported even a protestant Stuart who had bursts of priest-hanging: his powers were needed to protect them against a largely hostile society and legal system, which, if left unchecked, was far more certain to destroy them. One streak in James's character, inconsistent with the rest but fostered by his catholicism, made him at times particularly effective in this role as common father, at once head of the state and protector of those at odds with it. This partly explains his patronage of Lochiel.[32] The Revolution, besides restoring Argyll, threatened to increase the hostile elements in lowland society and strip the monarch of these necessary powers. Yet, particularly for upper-class highlanders, that society was only partly alien, and they shared the feelings — and disagreements — of other Scots. The bards justifying Jacobitism spoke not in terms of the highlanders' special needs but of James's divine right and the wrongs done him, sometimes with biblical precedents.[33]

The glamour of the Stuart cause, which so maddens modern nationalists, was already important. It influenced Lochiel, who 'had Montrose alwaise in his mouth' (where a purely highland tradition would have placed Alasdair) — never so constantly as his biographer claimed, but significantly.[34] The poets, and the chiefs themselves, increasingly accepted the simplified tradition of their past loyalty (though without forgetting the cynical underground tradition). In 1689, they expressed this vigorously in declarations and bonds not to submit without general agreement; and, to some extent, their rhetoric trapped them. Lochiel had one son serving under William, and from late 1690 he was anxious to submit 'if he Could Come of with honor & some advantage'; but, after his undaunted speech to a council of war that spring, the honourable pretext proved more difficult to find than the government bribe, keeping him in arms for over a year. Even if such concern for reputation was hypocritical, it contrasted sharply with Lochiel's own fairly shameless changes of side for money in the Argyll–Maclean struggle.[35] The strength of the tradition appears, surprisingly, in the conduct of the most unscrupulous chief of the next generation, Simon Fraser Lord Lovat, in 1715. He had abused the Jacobite Court's trust to carry out his private revenge, it had ruthlessly imprisoned him for a decade and he had spied on it; his one rational chance of pardon and power was to bring the Frasers over to the Hanoverian side; yet his reluctance to take arms against the Stuarts was visible to his companions.[36]

This tradition was not foreshadowed in James's and the Council's attitude to the highlanders in 1681. Although the two Campbell independent companies were replaced by regular ones attached to Mar's regiment, the March proclamation renewing landlords' obligations to give bond reflected hostility to the 1679 Macdonald rising in its emphasis on suppressing insurrection and its threats of forfeiture against those who resisted government forces. It also declared that a garrison would occupy Inverlochy, and in September their orders were issued.[37] However, the only troops to enter Lochaber were a party quartering for deficiency of cess. In February 1682, several hundred Camerons under Lochiel's cousins themselves garrisoned Inverlochy against them and disarmed and stripped them, after (according to Balhaldie) they killed a woman who opposed their taking her cows. The sequel showed the development of the tradition, and the instability of court favour as its basis. When Lochiel came to Edinburgh, James was fascinated (though perhaps, as Stevenson suggests, with an undercurrent of distrust) with his 'loyalist' past and adventures, and knighted him. After James's departure, however, he and the rioters were heavily fined in January 1683, and some were unsuccessfully indicted for treason. This was intended to put pressure on him to submit in Lochaber to James's other favourite, Huntly.[38]

Argyll's fall had naturally transformed the balance of power in the Highlands and the influence this had on the distribution of office. The young Marquess of Montrose ruled Argyllshire as Lieutenant. Atholl, with his lifelong rival removed, expected to be made Chancellor, to which his parliamentary service gave him some right. He sulked deeply when James unexpectedly appointed the new President of the Session, Gordon of Haddo, both as a loyalist 'new man' likely to do his bidding, and as the representative in office of his catholic chief Huntly.[39] Not immediately realising this link, Sir George Mackenzie suggested that Haddo should ally with the young Earl of Seaforth and support himself with his highland interest. Instead, the Chancellor, made Earl of Aberdeen in December 1682, made Seaforth compound for his superiorities with Huntly. He later threatened to deprive the Earl of Mar of his hereditary governorship of Stirling to make him surrender his Braemar superiorities, so that Huntly should be supreme in the North.[40]

To extend his power in Lochaber, Huntly in 1683 negotiated to buy the hereditary Stewartry from Mackintosh and erect it into a regality, though the bargain apparently fell through. He put pressure on Lochiel, already his vassal for Mamore, to acknowledge his superiority also for the lands he had held from Argyll, but Lochiel, although making smaller concessions, refused.[41] Argyll's forfaulture involved Lochiel in other difficulties. By voluntarily declaring his own debts to him he at first obtained preferential treatment, but Argyll's creditors began to prosecute him. One of them in January 1685 informed the courts that Lochiel was planning to settle his estates on his son John and emigrate to New Jersey. Although a startling claim, this would explain his incongruous third marriage, that month, to the daughter of a Quaker family. Her brother, Robert Barclay, through his favour with James and leading ministers, had organised the establishment of a largely Scottish colony, and some Campbells, including Argyll's brother Lord Neil, emigrated there at least temporarily in the mid-1680s. The first attempt to obtain a charter to John, in 1684, apparently failed through a covert attempt to include some of Gordon's lands.[42]

The advance of the Gordon interest, which so gravely inconvenienced Lochiel, threatened Breadalbane with total ruin. In early 1683, Aberdeen revived the Justiciary Court process for treason against him and six of his subordinates for their actions in Caithness. He could not be prosecuted for his clearest misdeeds, in which Charles and his government were involved. So the actual slaughter at Allt nam Mearlach was bolstered with charges based on misrepresentation, illegally garrisoning houses and levying private taxes, and others utterly fantastic, ravaging Sutherland (by pulling down derelict huts for camp-fires) and even employing a necromancer.[43] The prosecution, however, was entirely in earnest, and the intention was to forfault Breadalbane permanently, at least in his Caithness lands. Although denying knowledge, James would not intervene and let Aberdeen exploit his name. A trial might be averted by conceding some lands to those behind the prosecution, and the Countess started negotiations with Huntly. Aberdeen, however, by now had ambitions to build up his own estates and interest, and intervened on his own behalf, demanding, Breadalbane later claimed, that he sell him the Caithness lands at a mere two and a half years' purchase, in return for favourable representation at Court.[44] Perth expressed great sympathy with Breadalbane, but secretly bought up his debts to obtain a claim if the estate were forfeited — by a trial at which he would preside as Justice-General.[45]

Breadalbane's most powerful ally was Atholl, whose lasting grudge against Aberdeen made him give vigorous help all spring; Breadalbane acknowledged that it was he who saved him. He, therefore, presumably cleared the way for him to go to Court in June and submit to James. In July, an order came down to stop the prosecution. On 7 August, Breadalbane produced his proofs and affidavits on the invasion of Caithness before Charles and James, and he and his subordinates received a full remission.[46] His submission came in the nick of time. In June, the Rye House Plot was exposed, including Argyll's plans for a rising. The fresh discredit to the name of Campbell might have proved fatal in a trial. Instead, Charles in December appointed him to the Highland Justiciary, and he became its moving spirit when Perth was promoted Chancellor.[47] For it was not Breadalbane who fell but Aberdeen himself. The nobles' hostility to him as an upstart and autocratic lawyer had provoked him to a hurried and ruthless attempt to establish an independent interest, causing widespread resentment. Huntly's alienation from him over his independent extortion from Breadalbane and his attempt to regain some popular credit by opposing further straining of the law were the final straw, and he was dismissed in June 1684.[48]

Breadalbane had vainly requested a pension in London, for his financial difficulties were enormous, driving him in Caithness to use legal tricks to defraud even his own supporters. When he was favoured with a protection against his creditors in late 1684, James was startled at the outcry it caused.[49] This, and his dependence on Atholl's support, may partly explain why Breadalbane did so little to save a kinsman and neighbour from the latter's aggression.

The Campbells of Glenlyon, north of Loch Tay, a cadet branch of the Glenorchy family, provided a protective outpost for them, as they themselves did for Argyll.[50] Breadalbane's slightly older cousin Robert Campbell, succeeding as a child, was in serious financial difficulties before 1660. He served on the Caithness raid, but otherwise wasted what remained of his estate in drink, gambling and building, and attempted to restore his finances by marketing his woods.[51] Glenlyon tradition, which deeply distrusted Breadalbane and admired Colonel Menzies of Culdares as a soldier of fortune who had risen from nothing, suspected Breadalbane's responsibility for all that followed; but it was Menzies whom Glenlyon and his son blamed for their ruin. Menzies lent money, his original capital probably the £1,000 he received for capturing the Marquess of Huntly (afterwards executed) in 1647. Glenlyon was soon deep in debt to him, the Provost-dictator of Perth, and many others, including Atholl. In 1674, it was agreed that Atholl should buy up other creditors' apprisings, granting a backbond that this should merely be to secure his own debts and ease Glenlyon. It was 'a most exuberant trust' for someone who so often mislaid vital documents to grant.[52] The web wound tighter as a partnership, including Atholl's baillie Ballechin, contracted to establish a sawmill in the glen. Its extreme destructiveness drove Glenlyon in 1677 to riot against it, which eventually cost him damages.[53]

In 1681, Glenlyon signed a bond declaring himself easily deceived, and promising to do nothing without Argyll's and 'Caithness's' advice. Soon neither was in a position to assist him, and, as Atholl continued to take out apprisings, he made fresh agreements with him. He had other troubles. The Highland Justiciary frequently ordered him to present the many Glenlyon men, including his own brother, who were accused of cattle-raiding, and in 1684 he and Menzies were seized, and interrogated in Edinburgh on suspicion of communicating with

Argyll.[54] The legend claims that, in disgust at Breadalbane's neglect, Glenlyon chose to sell his estate to Atholl. According to Glenlyon himself, visiting Dunkeld in August 1684, he was arrested for debt — for theft, claimed Ballechin — and, fearing a long imprisonment, he agreed to the sale. If he could pay £39,000 in two instalments, at Whitsun 1687 and 1690, he could redeem it. If not, Atholl would pay him £26,000 for absolute possession.[55] To Breadalbane, Atholl explained that he was merely securing his debt. He showed his real aim secretly that autumn when Cluny was considering moving to become his vassal, offering him the baronies of Glenlyon and Comrie to settle in.[56] Atholl, allowed part of the glen to pay off the debt, occupied more; and, when a lease of Glenlyon's woods elsewhere expired, his men remained in possession. Somehow, Glenlyon raised half the money in 1687, and offered it on condition that half the estate should be returned to enable him to raise the rest. This was refused, and he paid nothing.[57]

In 1688, a committee of Campbells was established to manage Glenlyon's affairs, but it was Breadalbane, not one of them, who increasingly intervened. His motives are uncertain. His enemies suspected that he himself intended to cheat Glenlyon out of the estate, and this may at times have been true: in 1692, his son Glenorchy wrote of buying it from Murray. Yet, as Breadalbane wrote privately that year: 'its my interest to continow ... a laird of Glenlyon' — not least as a buffer against Atholl.[58] He perhaps failed to act earlier partly because, as a cautioner for some of Glenlyon's debts, he feared that proceedings would be started, finally wrecking his finances, if he made trouble. This was probably the grievance which made him in 1685 support Queensberry against Atholl.[59]

Paradoxically, the government which, at a higher level, was carrying out such an unscrupulous scramble for highland estates, produced probably the Restoration regime's most effective and honest attempt to check highland robberies. In 1681 and early 1682, constant raiding, impairing the people's ability to pay taxes, was reported along the southern edge of the Highlands and in the North, where Seaforth complained: 'to resist a uhol country of robers [Lochaber] is not in my power vithout the King's authority'. Glenorchy tried to protect his estates in January 1681 by a bond of manrent (witnesses to which included Glenlyon and MacIain of Glencoe) from Keppoch.[60] Finally, in August 1682, a Commission of Highland Justiciary was issued on new lines. It at first contained no magnates and peers (except the Officers of State), only about seventy-five gentry and chiefs, including Lochiel and Glengarry. There were four Commissions, for: the North; Ross, Inverness-shire and Moray; the North-East; and from Perthshire to Argyllshire. They could hold courts largely where they thought fit, being encouraged, though not explicitly authorised, to extend their jurisdiction over suspects living in the less efficient regalities. They could try murderers, thieves or resetters and declare accused persons who failed to appear fugitives. Rules were made that no highlander might sell cattle at market without certificates or travel over seven miles from home carrying firearms without a pass. A company of soldiers was to garrison Inverlochy and other posts, but, as usual, this failed to happen.[61] The southern Commission, the most vigorous, began its circuits that autumn, usually presided over by Lieutenant-General Drummond, collecting accusations, holding a few trials and making landlords give bonds. However, the Inverness-shire one, the most essential for the scheme's success, failed to meet, supposedly for lack of a clerk.[62]   Older, cruder, means were simultaneously being used. Mackintosh's relations with the Keppoch Macdonalds broke down by early 1681, and that September he obtained a commission of fire and sword. Only in July 1682, however, did he convene 1,100 men and march to Keppoch. The inhabitants all remained in hiding, and he built a little fort on the site of the murdered chief's house and left a garrison there. He succeeded so easily largely because Archibald of Keppoch was dying. On his death, his son Coll, then a student at St Andrews, returned home, passing through Inverness in January 1683. Mackintosh persuaded the magistrates to imprison him, and they did so eagerly, hoping to extract the enormous deficiencies of cess from his lands which they had had to make up. When the Council, thanks to Huntly's influence, ordered that he be bailed, they reluctantly obeyed. Coll very quickly captured the fort, and, when Mackintosh collected a force and began to march, he demolished it and retired. Mackintosh decided to wait and see what the Justiciary would do.[63]

In 1682, the southern Commission had remained fairly close to the Lowlands. However, they planned their June 1683 meeting to be at Loch Rannoch, and asked their Inverness-shire colleagues to sit simultaneously at Inverlochy for greater effectiveness against thieves. The Council strengthened their hands by empowering them to try men living outside their jurisdiction for crimes committed there; and that year's unsuccessful plan for an Inverlochy garrison, a major one of 4–500 men, for which Lawers and Colonel Menzies were to prepare the fort,[64] emphasised the help it could give the Commission. Justice-General Perth attended the courts at Loch Rannoch and Achallader, from which he went on progress to Glencoe, which the Commission had previously noted as the home of many thieves.[65] Although the north-eastern Commission had met at Braemar, the Inverness-shire one had failed to assemble at Inverlochy (or at all). Perth, escorted by troops under Lieutenant-General Drummond, therefore held court there for four days in August, and symbolically hanged a Cameron for theft. Having organised the Inverness-shire Commissioners there, he returned through Appin and Lorn.[66]

Executions, although the 'newly errected gibbets' were striking 'as monuments of justice but verie extraordinarie in those countreys', were not typical of the southern Commission's methods: its records indicate that in three years it hanged only sixteen men for theft (besides one shot resisting arrest). Its significance was in providing accessible and inexpensive means of prosecuting thieves or their landlords for compensation. Many men, who became fugitives when summoned, later became willing to surrender and make restitution. The Commissioners were willing to receive them, and to let landless thieves surrender for banishment rather than trouble the country.[67] They took several hundred bonds for securing the peace and lists of men living on the givers' property, not merely from chiefs and major landlords but from lesser men, though they were reluctant to weaken the old-style clan bonds once these were given.[68]

In 1684, the southern Commission reported that 'the task to banish away theeffing and robeing is not soe dificult as wes supposed', and that they had restricted it, even in Lochaber, to 'some few fugitives and intercomuned persones'. Two harvests, the worst periods for robbery, had passed peacefully, and they awaited the third confidently. Doubtless, this contained much exaggeration and self-deception, for the legacy of the mutual raiding and oppression in the Campbell–Maclean dispute was not so easily forgotten. They themselves admitted that their colleagues were less satisfactory, the Aberdeenshire ones lukewarm and irregular, the northern ones never meeting. The Inverness-shire Commission depended on a tiny quorum, but acted vigorously, strengthening the hand of other jurisdictions. In 1684, the Sheriff-depute was planning to hold a court in Skye, where there had been none for fifteen years.[69]

There were good reasons why the Commissioners obtained more success than previous measures. They were almost all lesser men, without the magnates' obvious intent of extending their power. They could hold courts throughout the Highlands, including Argyll's former regality. Their decreets were inexpensive and swift (although the Council and Session soon started to impose delays), and were an effective weapon to frighten highlanders into conformity, 'this restitutione being ane greater awe band then hanging'. They had, or could easily obtain, local knowledge, and, even when their policy was basically the same as the Council's, could act far more flexibly. By offering the clans a criminal indemnity for past thefts (once civil compensation was paid) they hoped to make them hand over a few of the 'broken men' who committed most actual robberies, breaking the tacit alliance between them and the chiefs.[70] Of course, Commissioners with private interests might exploit the courts. The Council took seriously Macmartin of Letterfinlay's charge that his enemy Mackintosh was doing so, and took excessive precautions to secure a fair trial. In fact, Macmartin adroitly exploited their concern, to escape from imprisonment for debt and join Keppoch in fresh disturbances against Mackintosh.[71]

In 1684, Mackintosh petitioned the Council for military aid against Keppoch, but 'It was thought not safe at this tyme to send away any of the standing forces so far of, or to irritate the Macdonalds to break the Hylands', so they were merely charged under pain of treason.[72] The Highland Commissioners had no suggestions for resolving the dispute, which emphasised a major difficulty in their attempt to bring law to the Highlands. The more successful it was, the more isolated Keppoch's position would be, driving him to desperation. They reported in 1684 that it was vital to establish a garrison at Inverlochy; but Mackintosh would certainly call on this to enforce his legal rights. More generally, their initial success might encourage litigants to revive vast claims for past losses which would confront the Lochaber clans with ruin, as happened during the 1690s. However, their failure came about the opposite way. Not only could no garrison be spared for Inverlochy; by June 1684, Charles wanted a force raised from the North and Highlands to suppress commotions, to be maintained by the West — a permanent Highland Host. Their actual employment, against the Campbells, was even more certain to destroy the newly-established discipline.[73]

The unease Charles's government had frequently shown about the loyalty of

Argyllshire reached a head in early 1684 when Montrose died and investigations began to show widespread Scottish participation in the Whig plots. Charles appointed new Lieutenants throughout Argyllshire, and in May a proclamation was issued ordering various nobles and chiefs to have 4,100 highlanders ready to march to specified areas and give any assistance necessary.[74] No invasion or rising took place, but the Secret Committee of the Council, the small cabinet which ruled in Edinburgh, chose Atholl as the appropriate new Lord Lieutenant to ensure that the shire was thoroughly subdued. Despite again failing to become Chancellor, he was gratifyingly loyal: although he had recently married his heir Lord Murray to Duke Hamilton's daughter, some supposedly 'disloyal' disobedience now made him try, until 1688, to disinherit him as far as possible. He was a hereditary enemy of Argyll, and could raise a massive private force of highlanders to overawe the shire. He had just been allotted a massive 'locality' on the estates for his claims as a creditor, and received a tack of Inveraray for lieutenancy expenses.[75]

Atholl's instructions were to arrest several leading Campbells, including Ardkinglas, Ellangreg, Inverawe, Barbreck and Dunstaffnage — and Cameron of Glendessary. He was to disarm the disaffected, demolish the castles and examine the indulged presbyterian ministers, to find pretexts for withdrawing their licences. In August, he marched with 1,000 highlanders, and entered Argyllshire without opposition. Ardkinglas was arrested for supplying Argyll with money, and the ministers were silenced, but Atholl acted with moderation. Rather than try other suspects and make them desperate with sentences he had no authority to commute, he made them give bond to appear before the Council. He collected weapons from the militia and the disaffected, but unsuccessfully suggested to the Committee that the country people should be allowed to keep their arms. He obtained the heritors' promise to support the Inveraray garrison (but in the event, had to pay for it himself) and demolished no castles as yet. Then he returned, leaving Steuart of Ballechin as his deputy with a small force.[76]

Argyll's invasion did not come until May 1685, after James's succession. It was far too soon, allowing no time for James's folly to start alienating his supporters, but Argyll and the Scots forced Monmouth and the English exiles to agree. The story of Argyll's expedition has often been told from the viewpoint of those involved: the sailing of three small ships from Amsterdam on 2 May; the imprudent landing at Orkney which alerted the government; Argyll's insistence, despite his lowland colleagues' protests, on landing not in the West, as they wished, but in Argyllshire, relying on promises of support he communicated to nobody else; the failure to raise a large force in Kintyre and the constant deadlock disputes between Argyll and his Whig colleagues; the trapping of the flotilla behind Bute by English warships; the futile march towards Glasgow, the final dispersal beside the Clyde on 18 June, and Argyll's capture. Seen like this, it was not only impossible that Argyll's rising could ultimately succeed, but inevitable, once diverted to the Highlands, that it should collapse as ignominiously as it did. Study of the government side of the hill, however, indicates that Argyll might at least have won sufficient early successes and have held out long enough to encourage Monmouth's rebellion strongly — even, perhaps, have given the

English Whigs heart to launch the secondary Cheshire rising that was intended to prevent concentration against Monmouth.

By chance, the most important of Argyll's earlier secret contacts is known. The Irish army marched to Ulster to suppress any rising among the Scots–Irish, who were in contact with the rebels, and, if necessary, to cross and help Atholl.[77] Their commander Lord Granard, a comrade of Argyll's under Glencairn, had agreed with him in 1682 on a joint rising. It is uncertain whether Argyll knew that Granard had been implicated by the Rye House Plot investigation, and blackmailed by the pro-catholic party into supporting them — so absolutely that he became the last Irish protestant peer to abandon James.[78] Otherwise, outside Argyll's imagination, there was never any hope of matching the enemy in numbers, even, after the first surprise, locally. The government expected to muster 60,000 men, standing forces, militia and heritors. Even potential sympathisers would not dare to remain neutral. Grant, for instance, having just been heavily fined, was warned that he must now show special loyalty, and hastened to raise his clan.[79] Yet even the enemy's numbers might bring unexpected benefits.

Argyll's decision to land in Argyllshire, doubtless made for the wrong reasons, was probably correct if followed up vigorously. Certainly, there were more men ready to rebel in the West, and Government control was imperfect: small armed bands roamed the interior for months. But a landing, which involved unloading Argyll's large cargoes of arms, was a different matter, for the bulk of the regular army was stationed on the coast. Even after Argyll's landing, James would not allow it to move.[80] He was confident that any rising could be extinguished by 'puringe in the Hyelanders upon them'; but he and the Council assumed that the rising would be only in the West. In April, the Council ordered 1,100 highlanders, 300 of them Breadalbane's and the rest from the areas best suited to oppose an Argyllshire landing, to be sent to Mauchline in Ayrshire to track down Whigs. As invasion approached, other experienced Perthshire highlanders were called up for the militia regiments, which were concentrated at Stirling. Breadalbane was extremely uneasy, with justice, over the quality of the men left, after this double creaming off, for the first stages of any Argyllshire campaign.[81] The attempt in late May and June to remedy this by 'puringe in' as many highlanders as possible carried its own dangers. Early rumours, exploited by Atholl's enemies, that Argyll had captured Inveraray and a large magazine of provisions, stood on its head the real problem: there was no adequate magazine to support an army even for a few weeks. Tarbat, who tried to ship meal to Atholl, warned him early 'necessity of dissipating for want of bread is what I feare most ... Beleive it, if yow call more men as yow can provyd, yow break'.[82] Yet neither Atholl nor, as hysteria gripped them, the Secret Committee, did enough to avoid this. If Argyll could score early successes in the weeks before English warships (unready when he sailed) arrived, and then maintain a force in being until Atholl's swollen host dissolved from hunger, he might establish himself.[83]

In March, Atholl was ordered to take 500 Perthshire men to demolish the castles and secure the shire, but this was apparently cancelled. As Breadalbane privately told him, Argyllshire was shamefully ill-prepared to resist a direct attack.[84] Breadalbane himself, although apparently worried about this, was in London, organising a coup which might ultimately solve his financial problems, the marriage of his son Glenorchy to one of the daughters and co-heiresses of the magnate Duke of Newcastle. He returned only in mid-April for the Parliament.[85] Lochiel also was in London. Huntly, created Duke of Gordon the previous winter, applied for a grant of Argyll's old superiority over Glenloy and Locharkaig. Lochiel came up to get it transferred instead to him (or his son) according to James's vague promises, and to regain Sunart and Ardnamurchan from Campbell of Lochnell. There was little hope of this, since they were one of the 'localities' granted to Atholl to satisfy his claims and Lochnell paid him rent until 1688. A grant of Lochiel's estate and superiorities to Gordon passed in January, but Lochiel by May had persuaded James to reconsider. However, before it could be carried out he was summoned back, leaving London only after Argyll's landing in Lorn.[86]

The first effect of Argyll's protestant rebellion was to enable James to appoint Catholics to high office with little objection: the Earl of Dumbarton to command the regular army, the Duke of Gordon Lord Lieutenant of the North to command the highlanders there.[87] The Council ordered the 'northern' clans to rendezvous under him 4,200 strong at the head of Loch Ness on 9 June. If the delay was necessary, in such a crisis, to accommodate Caithness and Strathnaver contingents, they should not have included the Macdonalds of Sleat and Macleods. Atholl protested, and got the Macleans, Camerons and Macdonalds of Glengarry, Clanranald and Keppoch, less than a thousand, ordered to join him — at Inverlochy! The disproportion made him suspicious, and Tarbat soon had to caution him against flying into unnecessary rages.[88] Atholl himself left Edinburgh only on 18 May, and began collecting his vassals. To replace the commanders serving in the militia, he received some professional officers of Mar's regiment, including Captain Mackenzie of Suddie of its highland company. Breadalbane parted from Atholl and reached Balloch only on 20 May. He planned to gather his men at Kilchurn, his castle at the head of Loch Awe, an excellent strategic rallying point.[89]

When, therefore, Argyll's ships arrived off Dunstaffnage Castle on 13 May and landed his son Charles to call out the clan, there was no leader to organise local opposition. The obvious candidate, Macdougall of Dunollie, had just died, almost a hint from Providence to exploit the opportunity. Instead, representatives were elected for a council.[90] Certainly, the news Charles Campbell brought was disappointing. A dozen potential supporters, such as Campbell of Dunstaffnage and Campbell (MacConnochie) of Inverawe, had been detained at Edinburgh. Others even refused to see Argyll. One source alleges that Campbell of Lochnell promised to join, then sent Argyll's letters to the Council; certainly, by 26 May he was in Ardnamurchan raising men for Atholl and complaining that Lochiel was claiming them as his followers. Argyll's lowland colleagues were contemptuous of the result, and Argyll was dismayed.[91] Yet the haphazard government detentions often weakened their own side. Most of Inverawe's men joined his cousin Breadalbane. Campbell of Calder was refused permission to send his son to organise Islay against Argyll, but the inhabitants' later attitude indicates that he might have succeeded. Instead, Ballechin with 450 men, almost the whole government force in the shire, was occupied in disarming them, and risked capture when Argyll sailed there on 14 May, leaving Charles Campbell to raise Lorn and Mid-Argyll.[92] In Holland, Argyll had apparently understood that the campaign must begin with 'making the best of a few men in partyes', but a main reason for his collapse was his attempt to raise a large force and fight a conventional campaign. One of Atholl's officers remarked on his total failure to exploit the highland landscape for delaying actions or ambushes.[93] Pressure to prepare for a southern rendezvous prevented Charles Campbell from pressing his advantages in Lorn before Breadalbane could arrive, even from garrisoning Dunstaffnage, to which Breadalbane sent a party.[94] Yet otherwise he acted skilfully on the principles of such irregular warfare, working not merely to raise men himself but to deprive the enemy of them and of initiative. Sir Duncan Campbell of Auchinbreck, and Campbell of Barbreck (Breadalbane's brother-in-law), Kilberry the younger, Ellangreg and others joined him. His parties ranged into Knapdale and Cowal, and he may in all have raised 1,200 men.[95] Most of these, of course, were forced out under threat of losing their cows and were unarmed, but their numbers still kept the loyalists on the defensive. Campbell of Craignish, who tried to join Breadalbane, was besieged in his castle, and other loyalists took to theirs. Breadalbane, who temporarily believed that 'ther [were] hardly four of the name of Campbell but have joyned them', collected only 300 men, not summoning more from fear of exhausting provisions, since Atholl had set an alarmingly late date for the general rendezvous and the 'Maks and Clans' had failed to appear. He even half-believed Charles Campbell's propaganda claims that MacIain, other Macdonalds, or, most persistently, the Camerons under Glendessary had joined the rebels.[96]

In contrast to his son's, Argyll's recruiting campaign was a disaster. Ballechin retreated from Islay in time, Calder's bailie tried to arm the people against him, and he gained (besides pressed men) only eighty volunteers, most of whom soon deserted.[97] In Kintyre, they did well among the lowland colonists, but highland recruitment remained disappointing (although they gained a surprising number in Gigha). Argyll's financial conduct before his forfeiture had partly alienated his vassals, as he realised, inserting in his personal declaration a promise to pay his and his father's debts. Besides this resentment, and fear, a third motive restraining many may have been that the Campbells had created a self-justifying clan image of themselves as the chief highland support of Crown, government and law which was hard to break.[98] Argyll and his lowland colleagues were at loggerheads. They caballed against him, and spread exaggerated reports of the supporters ready in the West; he took precautions against their sailing off, and sometimes suggested dividing the force, only to change his mind. Either an immediate advance on Inveraray, or an immediate decision that some or all should invade the West, might have a chance; but always, rather than directly confront his opponents, Argyll used delay to thwart them when his one chance lay in rapid action.[99]One man who might save the rebellion was Ballechin. His best-trained men had stayed with the McAlisters and other small clans, who garrisoned castles in Kintyre (provoking widespread rumours that they had joined Argyll). During his absence in Islay, young Campbell of Kilberry, still pretending to be loyal, had nearly captured Inveraray Castle by bluff. Ballechin had only about 500 men, mostly raw Argyllshire recruits, but was anxious to attack and 'chease them to the sea'.[100] By letters from Kilchurn, Breadalbane tried to teach him his strategic alphabet. It was Argyll's interest to 'ventur all on the first brush having no way to be recruited ... but in a desperat game' in which any success would have an immense effect, and theirs to temporise until Atholl arrived. He should either leave a strong garrison to hold Inveraray and fall back, carrying all available provisions, to join him or Atholl, or destroy Inveraray and the other castles and retire with his entire force; in either case, without last-minute hurry. He himself increasingly favoured total evacuation, which the Secret Committee had advised, and which Atholl finally ordered.[101] Ballechin stood his ground, considering Breadalbane hopelessly timid. Yet he himself admitted that a night alarm caused a major panic, and that he dared not openly leave his men to consult Atholl for fear most should run away. His decision succeeded only because it was not until 28 May that Argyll joined Charles Campbell and most of his forces at Tarbert, 1,800 men together, and openly declared his intention of attacking Inveraray by land and sea. His lowland colleagues objected, and persuaded the Campbell gentry to agree to cross to the Lowlands. Meanwhile, Atholl, setting out with 2,000 highlanders before his proclaimed rendezvous, and collecting Breadalbane, reached Inveraray on 30 May, 3,000 strong in all.[102]

Argyll, whose forces were already hungry, shipped them to Bute, largely hostile Stewart-owned territory where he could plunder as well as recruit. On 1 June, Charles Campbell landed in Cowal, but was surprised and driven back to his boats by Suddie Mackenzie, and a belated reconnaissance in force across the Clyde was also repulsed.[103] Atholl within a week received massive reinforcements, 400 Braemar men, 300 under Lochiel, who sent back others foreseeing a shortage of provisions, the Tutor of Appin with 100 Stewarts and MacIains, Glengarry and Keppoch with 300, 400 Macleans and some loyal Campbells, and knew that Argyll's force was far smaller. Yet he made no move except to send Ballechin and 500 men to protect Tarbert against reinforcements allegedly coming from Islay under Campbell of Airds. He feared that, if he committed himself by marching into Cowal, Argyll, still having command of the sea, would cross Loch Fyne and take Inveraray or escape into the North Highlands.[104] A repulse would still have a dangerous effect in the country, where the militia was already breaking out in mutinies and mass desertions. All his correspondents, including the Secret Committee, urged Atholl to show caution, 'for much of all the three Kingdoms' affairs depends on that Important first Rencounter', and the Committee showed their panic in their hysterically savage orders: 'All men who joyned, and are not come off ... are to be killed, or disabled ever from fighting again; and burn all houses except honest men's, and destroy Inverarra ... Let the Women and Children be Transported to remote Isles'.[105]

Once the approaching warships secured the West, Dumbarton would send forces from Glasgow, and Gordon sensibly started on 8 June with 1,100 men, leaving Lord Strathnaver to bring the clans mustered at Loch Ness southwards later.[106] Yet, even a few days' delay threatened Atholl's force with hunger, and an enemy later claimed that he was simply incompetent:

> If ever there was a cause under heaven . . . , in which he wold have stretched himself and bended all his power and strength, was when . . . Argyle landed. He was then imployed he and his wer entertained at the publick Cost he had Locheill and the most eminent of the [1689] Rebells to assist him, and yet he never made any tollerabl appearance, nor did any man stay with him, but went and came as they pleased, and if it had not bene for some litle pettie folk regnis about My L: Argyle who had a mind to keep there heads whole, he had eate up M: Atholl.[107]

Atholl had another justification: he could not be certain of the loyalty of all his forces, as young Kilberry's attempt on Inveraray showed. The many Campbell second sons with him while their elder brothers accompanied Argyll might merely be following the normal prudent policy, like 'Lorne', who offered to James in London to serve against his father (only to be detained in the Tower):[108] but their purpose might be more sinister. Several had briefly appeared for Argyll before changing sides, and on 30 May the Secret Committee sent the report of an alleged meeting of Cowal Campbells. Those who joined Atholl promised to betray him at a crisis, and had hopes of the non-Campbell Argyllshire clans, Colonel Menzies and Breadalbane's followers, though Breadalbane himself might be loyal.[109] The chief suspect, however, was Lochiel, even though Atholl had not yet heard from prisoners the reports a 'spy' spread in Argyll's camp, that Lochiel and Glendessary had arranged through him that the Camerons and Macleans (!) should join the rebels. Others later repeated this, including Charles Campbell *after* he was out of danger of a summary hanging. Lochiel's real conduct in the 1650s and since made it reasonable at least for the hostile Atholl to believe this: if Argyll's fall had ultimately driven Lochiel to plan emigrating, he may now have considered joining him, or at least temporising. Atholl suppressed the charges in his report, but then began to collect accusations from persons in his power in anger at Lochiel's later criticisms of his generalship.[110] Yet the details of the depositions suggest that Argyll, following up his son's propaganda, deliberately spread the 'secret' to encourage his followers and, through Atholl's spies in his camp, disrupt the enemy — his one flash of ability in the whole affair.[111]

His strategy showed less and less. Despite the lowlanders' protests, and with the highlanders deserting, he shifted his base to Ellangreg Castle, in Loch Riddon north of Bute, where, within a few days, the English warships easily blockaded his flotilla.[112] Meanwhile, Lochiel's offer to advance and attack Argyll with only the Camerons and Macleans had, by its implications, violently offended Atholl. On the night of 9 June, at the news that Argyll was planning an attack, Lochiel was sent out with 200 Camerons to scout. There were already three outposts placed, but none knew of the others — some indication of the confusion in the camp. After two narrow escapes, Lochiel by mistake attacked some Perthshire gentry and killed half a dozen before the truth was realised. According to Balhaldie, the Camerons and Macleans (a few of whom were implicated in the skirmish) remained in arms outside the camp all next day, and Atholl's council of war considered attacking them to seize Lochiel before deciding to treat it as an accident.[113] If fighting did break out, Breadalbane might take Lochiel's side, and he claimed later that Glengarry, his hereditary enemy, therefore offered to have him assassinated.[114]

If Argyll had attacked that day, the consequence might have been catastrophic, and one account claimed that he received the news by 8 a.m.[115] Yet it was only the next day that he sent an advance guard to Ardkinglas House, near Loch Fyne-head. On the 12th, Atholl, imagining that they had retreated, sent Mackenzie of Suddie with 300 men to reconnoitre. Running into Argyll's vanguard, soon reinforced by the Earl himself, they were driven back in a skirmish. As Atholl, although he sent Suddie reinforcements, remained paralysed at Inveraray, from fear of Argyll's crossing Loch Fyne or of treachery (which made him prevent Lochiel from joining Suddie), Argyll might have won a minor victory but for Suddie's skill in withdrawing his dangerously over-optimistic followers and the lowlanders' refusal to support an Inveraray campaign. Argyll's fear that they would leave in his absence damped his enterprise.[116]

On 13 June, Atholl, having at last heard that Argyll's flotilla was blockaded, marched round Loch Fyne. Yet his over-cautious advance and trust in Lamont reports that Argyll was entrenching in Glendaruel enabled the enemy to slip away on the 14th, and, when its garrison abandoned Ellangreg as English warships approached, he wasted two days in occupying it. This was probably one of Lochiel's later criticisms against him.[117] His supporters made counter-accusations: Atholl sent Lochiel late on 15 June with 600 Camerons, Macleans and others to pursue Argyll, and his failure to catch him proved his incompetence or treachery. In fact, the task was impossible, for Argyll crossed Loch Long that very evening. The next day, Lochiel captured the Campbells of Ellangreg and other stragglers from the garrison; but, almost immediately afterwards, his party, apart from 40–50 men, disintegrated and began to plunder.[118]

They were not unique. In early June, Atholl had hoped to prevent robbers from operating as 'soldiers', but by mid-June, when all attempts to send adequate meal had failed, the army marched with 'Lowing of herds of cows, and bleeting of sheep, and shriking of women following them in to oure camp'. Necessary seizures easily passed into open pillaging. The problem grew worse as Gordon's and Strathnaver's forces poured into Argyllshire, although Gordon soon continued towards Stirling.[119] Even Argyll's lowland gadfly Hume now suggested that the imminent dispersal of Atholl's army from hunger gave him an opportunity to return to Argyllshire and fight a guerilla war; but Argyll now insisted on pressing on towards the Lowlands, to his own force's collapse and his capture and beheading.[120]

Atholl could not control followers 'nether under pay nor discipline', and the highlanders — 'such a paick as I would not have thoght hade been on arth' declared one Perthshire officer — dispersing through Cowal, Roseneath east of

Loch Long and other parts, supposedly to round up rebels, plundered cattle, horses, other animals, corn, household goods and fishing boats and nets. Strathnaver's northerners did the same. They met little opposition, since most of the Campbell gentry were absent, with Argyll, detained in Edinburgh, or even with Atholl, which was no protection. On 23 June, the Council ordered them to return home, but they continued to plunder as they drifted back.[121] The Appin and Glencoe men were among those who robbed indiscriminately in Cowal, Roseneath and on the west coast on their way home, at least once in collaboration with Campbell of Lochnell's party. They could not have foreseen that the raid which was to bring the most serious trouble on them was on the estate of an undoubted rebel, Barbreck.[122] Breadalbane and his tenants, whose lands lay on Gordon's and Strathnaver's paths into the shire and the Lochaber clans' way home, were especially heavy sufferers.[123] Of course, it was not merely outsiders who plundered. The gentry of the small local clans, who had retreated into garrisons as Argyll passed, showed great rapacity, particularly the McAlisters and MacNeils.[124] Nor was it merely highlanders: Perthshire gentry and Atholl's lieutenants benefited, and Atholl himself carried off some of Argyll's trees from the Inveraray plantations.[125]

Despite the end of real danger, the news that many rebels were returning to Argyllshire made Perth on 23 June send Atholl even more violent orders: he was to execute all the heritors he caught and a hundred ringleaders from among the common people. Almost any policy Atholl followed would in comparison be merciful. The dispersal of his hungry forces had left him only the Clanranald men, delayed in joining him by the death and burial of the Captain, and the Macleans, sustained by hope of revenge and plunder.[126] The one remaining centre of resistance was Auchinbreck's home Carnassarie, where about eighty men were holding out and even raiding. Atholl sent Suddie Mackenzie with a party of Macleans and loyal Argyllshire men to besiege it. Their method was simple: a Lamont officer whose father the Campbells had executed in 1646 rounded up several Campbell gentlemen as hostages. After at least one, and perhaps more, had been hanged, the garrison surrendered on terms. However, a fanatic tried to blow up the house and the victors together. The explosion merely burned the house, but the furious Macleans lynched Auchinbreck's loyalist uncle before they could be stopped. They afterwards plundered the estate ruthlessly, but the terms were kept with the garrison.[127]

Atholl and his deputes conformed to Perth's orders by executing at Inveraray seventeen of the 120 heritors they had captured. One of them, a Major Campbell, particularly active in the rising, was sentenced (after Atholl's departure) to have his arms cut off before death. Charles Campbell, who had slipped back to Argyllshire, was captured while sick, and it was reported that Atholl had wanted to hang him at the gates of Inveraray; but Atholl was then in Edinburgh, and replied to the charge that only his protest prevented the Secret Committee from ordering the execution. Charles and another of Argyll's sons, John, were banished instead.[128] Auchinbreck and about thirty-five other heritors were forfaulted. About 150 rebel commoners, highlanders and Kintyremen, were transported that summer to the plantations, chiefly Jamaica, along with the survivors of the notorious 'Whigs' vault' at Dunnottar and other Presbyterians (although, unlike many of these, they did not lose an ear for refusing to own James's authority). Many of those transported were among the 215 commoners whose livestock Atholl declared forfeited at a court that October. Nevertheless, the rising was suppressed with less savagery than Monmouth's, though the Secret Committee deserved no credit.[129]

When Atholl returned from Argyllshire in early July, he left 500 freshly arrived Perthshire men under Ballechin to secure the country, demolish castles and, by degrees, shepherd the roving bands of highlanders homewards. They were often too weak to oppose them directly, and several times recovered cattle were simply seized again. The Macleans and Keppoch Macdonalds, in particular, remained plundering for most of July.[130] The shire courts resumed, and began to pass verdicts against the robbers. Ironically, Breadalbane, who violently demanded that order should be restored, was one of the first sufferers. His, Lochnell's and Inverawe's men were found guilty of carrying off a fellow-Campbell's cows. They protested that the real raiders, Macdonalds, returning through their lands, had also plundered them, and that their tenants had recovered a mixture of their own and other people's cattle, while half the rest was carried to Glencoe, half to Brae-Lochaber.[131] Lochnell and Inverawe must anyway have had uneasy relations with other Campbells after their men joined the forces which ravaged the shire, even though his loyalty gave Breadalbane power to influence the government in favour of the gentry detained in Edinburgh.[132] The division now may partly explain why Lochnell and Inverawe followed Breadalbane into Jacobite plotting in 1689.

Passing an indemnity for seizures made from military necessity caused problems. Atholl presented a general proposal against which Breadalbane protested as too wide — 'it may be supposed that our K: uould not bestow my goods upon Lochziall or Glencoa Theeves' — and as ammunition for Queensberry's enemies if he let it pass. In practice, the courts took the dispersal of Argyll's army as the date after which seizures were illegal, but the indemnity James finally sent down in February 1686 extended this to 1 August, probably for Gordon's benefit.[133]

As Breadalbane remained in London that summer as Queensberry's agent against Melfort's misrepresentations, he was obsessed with the idea — since Atholl was plainly incapable of dominating the Highlands — of doing so himself. His instrument would be a fusilier regiment of ten plaided companies, drawn from various clans as far north as the Frasers, each commanded by a chief or his representative. He naturally would be Colonel, Atholl would be placated by making his son Lord William Murray, who had served against Argyll, Lieutenant-Colonel, and Lochiel was proposed as Major, but demoted on the accusations against him. Keppoch was the only Macdonald captain. Each chief would engage a force of several hundred auxiliaries (in which, ironically, MacIain of Glencoe, under Keppoch, and Campbell of Glenlyon would have served together) to support the regulars, making a total force of well over 4,000 men, 'for a materiall and effectuall [re]enforcing of the King's Armie', and to restore order in the Highlands 'without 6 pence of Expense'. He proposed this to Queensberry, naturally denying any self-interest in it, 'being sensible of the trouble and Expence of it if don right ... for I uill be so vaine as to assert that I know best the affair of any of our Language'. James at first appeared interested; but, with Queensberry's fall, the idea vanished. It was the first of many similar schemes from Breadalbane and others; the next was decisively to influence the earl's conduct in 1691–2.[134]

Lochiel in Edinburgh imprudently criticised the generalship of Atholl, to whom troublemakers exaggerated what he had said. Atholl retaliated by collecting accusations that Lochiel had corresponded with Argyll and that he had deliberately let him escape. The rest of the Secret Committee were apparently embarrassed by the affair. Breadalbane wrote to Lochiel that he was still in favour. To Queensberry, he claimed to have warned Lochiel that he himself would become his enemy if he came to London, since further accusations would merely bring about a messy *post mortem*.[135] Atholl, however, planned to prosecute Lochiel for the deaths of the Perthshire gentlemen, and gave Suddie Mackenzie, marching his company through Lochaber to Inverness early that autumn, a warrant to arrest him. Lochiel evaded him and rode to Court, but, from fear or (probably in Breadalbane's case) disapproval, found nobody to introduce him. Lieutenant General Drummond, evidently influenced by his co-operation with the Highland Justiciary in 1683, finally did so. James assured him that he understood the accident, and made Lochiel a grotesque favourite, with clumsy jokes about the 'King of Thieves', until his departure home. Then, with his own almost clockwork illogicality, James renewed the grant of his estate and superiority to Gordon.[136]

In early 1686, Perth and Melfort, having conveniently become Catholics, got Queensberry dismissed after a particularly unscrupulous campaign. Gordon initially benefited, obtaining the governorship of Edinburgh Castle. Atholl's and Perth's clashing highland interests made them also natural enemies, and Atholl lost his Lord Lieutenancy of Argyll.[137] Breadalbane avoided disfavour on Queensberry's fall, perhaps by supporting James's unsuccessful attempt to introduce toleration for Catholics in the 1686 Parliament. He afterwards became more prominent in the Council. The long setback to his career since 1680 would have one advantage: unlike his northern counterpart (and enemy) Tarbat, who had taken the lead in proposing the severities of the 'Killing Time', he 'never dipped in [presbyterian] blood', and this was remembered in the 1690s.[138]

The government had tried to maintain the Highland Justiciary despite the rebellion, leaving part of Mar's regiment to quarter in the Highlands and appointing substitutes for Commissioners on active service. In July 1685, the Commission was renewed, specifically including abuses committed by the Highland auxiliaries, and it met from September. However, decreets which it issued against the Macleans and others for plundering after the campaign was officially over were ignored or suspended by the Council.[139] The liberty allowed then, the Commissioners admitted in early 1686, had largely undone their past work. A bad year evidently assisted. Glencoe and Lochaber raiders were exploiting a shortage of fodder which forced their neighbours to keep cattle on the mountains, and parties of a dozen came down to Fife 'thigging' in arms and stealing. Suspects, particularly in Lochaber, defied summonses and officers. Commissioners were reluctant to sit at their own expense, but Breadalbane's proposed bill in the 1686 Parliament for a rate on neighbouring counties for their expenses and a salary for the watches was defeated.[140] The less vigorous Inverness-shire Commission's efforts were enormously strengthened by the orders given Suddie's company at Inverness to pursue robbers and enforce the laws, but, although the Council agreed to the southern Commission's request for the regiment's other highland company, it never came.[141]

One major problem was that some rebels were still lurking in arms in Argyllshire, often joined by mere robbers. In September 1686, Drummond was sent with an armed force to settle the shire, provoking a protest from Atholl against a possible retrospective attack. Drummond's instructions mainly concerned financial consequences of the rebellion, but he carried an indemnity for the common people (excluding robbery since the rising) and a commission of justiciary. In November, he claimed that his activities 'had now reduced the Highlands to full quiet and peace' — a gross exaggeration.[142] The Highland Justiciary achieved some improvement by 1688, but the failure to repress highland robberies was still made one of the Grievances in the Convention.[143] A very deliberate attempt was made to turn Argyllshire into a bastion of the regime, both military and financial, by granting forfeited estates to reliable supporters, such as Ballechin, with fairly high feu duties. However, the new owners often found difficulty in taking possession. The Sheriff of Bute, granted Campbell of Barbreck's estate, had to apply to its former plunderer the Tutor of Appin to collect the rents — in seized cattle. In 1687, the Tutor bought it, and he and Macdonald of Achnacone planted it with Appin and Glencoe men.[144]

Meanwhile, despite failure in Parliament, James's catholicising policies were pressed ahead, and, while gaining comparatively few new converts, they made his religion far more conspicuous, in Highlands as well as Lowlands. The Popish Plot, and the reluctance of Irish priests to endure the hardships for more than five years, at one time had reduced the mission in the Central and West Highlands and Isles to two priests.[145] By 1688, the Highland Mission, with a £200 pension from James, had a dozen working, sick, or arriving, and it could afford to station one in Sir Donald Macdonald's outwardly protestant country of Sleat.[146] Some episcopalian clergy apparently accepted the priests' activity in traditionally catholic areas.[147] Another mission, by Father Cornelius Con to Lewis, had great temporary success. However, in the most notorious of highland catholic scandals Con seduced the daughter of Seaforth's uncle Mackenzie of Kildun (officially the only Lewis Catholic), apostatised, and married her. The Catholics thereupon imprisoned him at Seaforth's castle of Eilean Donan, later claiming as a legal justification that a previous affair with her aunt made this incest.[148]

It was only in this revival that the heads of two traditionally catholic clans conformed. Alasdair of Glengarry was apparently a Protestant until after 1685. His change may have been inevitable sooner or later to satisfy his clan, but it greatly shocked his patrons the Atholl family. An (otherwise unreliable) 1690 rumour had him denying his catholicism.[149] Coll of Keppoch, after schooling with the Atholl children, was at St Andrews — and therefore at least a nominal Protestant — when his father died, and, like Glengarry but unlike the Tutor of Clanranald, did not appear in the November 1685 list of Catholics excused the Test. He wore his new catholicism fairly lightly, claiming, when it was convenient in 1692, to be a Protestant.[150]

Other conversions had no such clan rationale. There were very few catholic Mackenzies, but by 1685 Seaforth had converted under the influence of his father-in-law, the Marquess of Powys, and had influenced his younger brothers John of Assynt and Alexander to do likewise. This gained him some rewards and helped check the erosion of his 'interest', by Tarbat and others, but it had few immediate Scottish implications, since his family debts compelled him to live in England. However, it probably made the Mackenzies more reluctant to rise with him when he returned in 1690.[151] Among the Macleans, 'the deaths of the three Lachlans', Brolas, Torloisk and Coll (at least one a strong Protestant) in 1686–7 left Sir John largely in royal hands. He was won over at the Scots College, Paris, in 1688, while engaged in 'further education' in France — doubtless James's main reason for sending him. A very self-conscious catholicism was to be one element of his strong Jacobitism.[152] That degree of enthusiastic commitment was most obvious in 1689 in Catholics who were largely isolated in protestant society — Grant of Ballindalloch, Macdonald of Largie, Chisholm of Knockfin.[153] The traditionally catholic clans probably took their religion more calmly. Yet it, and the presbyterian threat to it, obviously played a major part in making them rise for James, and an even greater one in preventing their submission. The Irish priests provided encouragement to fight on — by spreading lies, claimed the Williamites — and in 1691 prohibited any submission which involved taking the oath of allegiance to William.[154]

Most conversions in James's reign, however, were from fashion or self-interest. The most blatant was that of 'Lord Lorne', in the vain hope of regaining the Argyll title and estates. When this failed, he crossed to join William of Orange in late 1688.[155] The most futile was Moray's, a bid to stop Melfort from monopolising favour. The worst timed was in November 1688 by an enemy of Seaforth's, the Master of Tarbat, who hoped to gain Lewis. The cynical assumptions these revealed were too often justified: that James would reverse his most important policies to please a convert, or sacrifice the previous convert to the more recent.[156]

Or sacrifice the genuine Old Catholic to the convert. For, although James had for so long quietly favoured Gordon, whose supporters in late 1685 expected great power for him, it was only in November 1686, eight months after he received the Castle, that he gained places in the Council and Treasury (which he hesitated to accept), and he rose no further. Perth and Melfort, hating a genuine catholic noble above all other rivals, slandered him as a half-wit.[157] As they encouraged James in his most extreme policies with the claim that he was absolute monarch in Scotland, and yet suppressed their lifelong hatred of Presbyterians to collaborate in his policy of toleration, his moderate supporters, prompted by Gordon's loyal but ill-rewarded vassal, the lawyer Sir Aeneas Macpherson (another convert), hoped to establish Gordon as acknowledged head of the catholic interest in Scotland, cutting the ground from under the brothers' feet.[158]

Gordon, however, lacked essential qualities for this. As his supporter William Penn said, he 'has sense, and some very good links in him, but 'tis impossible to make a chain of ym'.[159] His worst failing was to cling obstinately to his full legal rights over estates James had granted him, showing himself harsh and unscrupulous, rather than relying on royal favour to recompense him for concessions. Lochiel's case was only the most notorious.[160] Breaking assurances to James, Gordon sued to evict Lochiel from both the lands he formally held of Argyll, since he was technically forfaulted as a vassal, and those held of Gordon himself, since he had not gained the Marquess of Argyll's confirmation during his Interregnum possession — now declared illegal — of the Huntly estates! Through Barclay, Lochiel appealed to James for protection. In mid-1688, James finally declared that he should only pay Gordon feu-duty for the lands, and the Duke's obstinacy provoked him into erecting an independent jurisdiction, 'for he would have Locheill master of his own Clan, and onely accountable to him or his Councill for them'. Evidently, this was to be a special case rather than a general policy.[161] Gordon's obstinacy had laid him open to general attacks. Melfort eroded his powers in Edinburgh Castle, driving him by September to offer to resign.[162]

Lochiel received still further favours. James wrote stopping a creditor of Argyll's from prosecuting him, an infringement on property rights. And Lochiel had no scruples about exploiting the same feudal laws which had placed him in Gordon's grasp when they instead benefited him. In 1687–8, Atholl's final claims on the Argyll estates were extinguished by Treasury payments, and his 'localities' were redistributed, apparently on permanent terms. The Earl of Balcarres received Sunart and Ardnamurchan, displacing Campbell of Lochnell despite his services in 1685. James decided to buy them for Lochiel, and Balcarres wrote to Sir John Drummond of Machany, Sheriff of Argyllshire, to give support in case Lochiel had any difficulty in occupying Mingary Castle.[163] Yet it was symbolic of the ambiguous position of a clan chief that, at this height of prosperity, Lochiel had suddenly to hide in the Tolbooth to escape arrest by the Council for his clansmen's activities.[164]

In February, the Council renewed Mackintosh's 1681 commission of fire and sword, and ordered Mackenzie of Suddie with the Inverness independent company to arrest and imprison Keppoch until he gave bond to answer the law. According to Keppoch, Mackintosh obtained the renewal now because arbitrators were about to suggest a compromise, a two-fifths rent increase, which would not satisfy him but would justify government refusal to assist him.[165] If he thought that the rest of Clan Chattan would be more enthusiastic than on previous occasions, he was mistaken. He could raise only 4–500 men, but was so confident that he took his wife and daughter with him. In July, Suddie's company joined him at Keppoch, and they began, as before, to build a fort. Realising their small numbers, the Macdonalds camped across the flooded Spean and sent for their supporters. They themselves, Suddie estimated, could muster only 200, so the remainder of their final force, equal to or larger than their opponents, came from neighbouring clans, particularly the Macmartins of Letterfinlay and the Camerons of Glen Nevis. Lochiel left for Edinburgh just before the battle, giving the Council cause to suspect that he had planned it.[166] (See Preface, p. viii)

On 7 August 1688, when the Spean fell, the Mackintoshes and Suddie crossed and advanced up Glen Roy to punish the insolent rebels. At Mulroy, as they climbed the hill, Keppoch (who claimed they fired first) launched a classic highland charge, one volley and an attack with swords and Lochaber axes. Suddie was mortally wounded, half-a-dozen Clan Chattan gentry and many others were killed, and a large number were carried wounded to Inverness. By threatening their prisoners, the Macdonalds captured Mackintosh, his family and a large booty in his fort, and forced him to make a written agreement, 'Then detaining him Captive till he was rescued by his friends and ther followers' — according to one tradition, the Macphersons, to another the Grants — at whose approach they released him.[167]   'The unhappie accident I had wt Mckintoshe at Millroy', as Keppoch later called it,[168] is remembered as the last private clan battle. The significance at the time, however, was that royal troops had been attacked and some, including a well-connected captain (for whose protection Keppoch, later sources claim, had given orders) had been killed.[169] The Council decided (again) to establish a garrison in Lochaber. Meanwhile, 150 foot and 60 dragoons under Captain Straiton were ordered to ravage Keppoch — and, fairly certainly in the light of Perth's hysterical brutality in 1685, to kill Macdonalds mercilessly, though perhaps not, as was much later claimed, to spare neither man, woman nor child. Breadalbane was ordered to gather men at Achallader to accompany Straiton. He set a date, but protested that Keppoch's men would flee south into Rannoch, make the way north too dangerous, and attack his estates, and that Mackintosh and his vassals were the proper instruments. He warned Straiton to beware of night attacks, and advised Lochiel to help the expedition. It is uncertain whether he managed to avoid sending his men. Although Keppoch and most of his people had withdrawn into the mountains, the troops killed some who remained, besides burning houses and corn, until the reports of invasion recalled them.[170]

From September, William of Orange's threatened invasion made it vital for Scotland's stability that the major political interests should be united behind James. Instead, his obsession had brought about an exceptionally unrepresentative government, 'a strange mixture of rogues and converts to Roman Catholicism', as Lenman says, the former including Tarbat, Breadalbane and Stair's son Sir John Dalrymple. This naturally tempted Atholl, the only one of magnate status, to make trouble and withdraw hoping that events would help him to supplant them.[171] Yet Perth and Melfort continued to harass a major natural supporter of James: Gordon. He returned in near-disgrace to command Edinburgh Castle, but the main Scottish arms magazine was transferred to Stirling, ostensibly for its strategic position between northern and southern Scotland, actually to humiliate him. An expensive pleasure; for the Earl of Mar, Governor of Stirling, who had suffered for opposing James's catholicising policy, could, unlike Gordon, consider serving William. Without the transfer, the army which opposed Dundee could not have been armed.[172]

The invasion threat did not moderate government attitudes to Keppoch and his followers, who were excluded from James's indemnity. Perth wrote to Breadalbane linking them and the invasion as threats obliging the Commissioners of Justiciary to inflict double the normal punishments.[173] When the regular army had marched to England to help repel the invasion — a step Balcarres blamed on Melfort[174] — the Council called out the select militia and on 31 October, after some hesitation, 1,000 highlanders to remain on government pay at Stirling, provided chiefly by Atholl and his neighbours, Breadalbane and Mar. Gordon's, the main northern contingent, did not arrive in time.[175] Lochiel and his Camerons were sent instead to Argyllshire, where Sir John Drummond was garrisoning Inveraray. With local supporters, he could muster 1,200 men in all to prevent any rising on behalf of 'Lord Lorne'. Presumably this led the Council to allow several of Keppoch's major accomplices, chiefly Camerons, to give formal securities to appear, but in mid-November Perth emphasised to Breadalbane that the Commission must not relax in its activities.[176]

Breadalbane was then organising the highlanders at Stirling. Since these and the militia were already proving a strain on the revenue, half of them were sent home in late November. In Argyllshire, only the Camerons and some Appin Stewarts remained.[177] This was not because the crisis seemed less acute. William landed in the West of England on 5 November. The interception of messages to London and treachery of messengers forced one of the most loyal ministers, Balcarres, to journey up to reassure James, when his presence was badly needed at Edinburgh. Tarbat and Dalrymple (not, at first, Breadalbane, who had gone home) used Atholl as a figurehead while working to undermine Perth, whom they persuaded that the expense and the need to conciliate William on his rapid triumph in England made it necessary to disband nearly all the forces. Perth was hoodwinked; the highlanders started home on 3 December, and the disbandment of the militia was ordered on the 7th. Atholl and his party immediately warned Perth that as a Catholic he must no longer sit in Council.[178]

Growing anti-catholicism further alarmed Perth, and, although Gordon offered him refuge in the Castle, on 10 December he fled to Drummond Castle. He wrote to Lochiel at Inveraray to march his Camerons there and escort him to Lochaber, from which he would embark for Ireland with Lochiel's eldest son John. This indicates that Perth hoped to obtain help from Tyrconnell to send back. Just possibly, if Perth had gone to the Highlands and taken a resolute lead, Sir John Drummond and the local loyalists might have kept control over disarmed Argyllshire until this arrived, greatly increasing the chances of a successful counter-revolution. However, Perth, as he admitted, was gripped by blind panic as his tenants turned against him, and he desperately adopted another plan, to escape from Fife by sea. Lochiel, advancing through the snow, heard the news at Comrie, and immediately returned home.[179] Drummond, presumably already ordered to disband his garrison, must almost immediately have abandoned Inveraray, allowing the Campbells to seize the administrative machinery. Yet it was not until February that the Tutor of Appin, having refused to surrender Castle Stalker, was driven from the estates of Barbreck, losing cows and a crop.[180] Perth's choice of flight by sea, which ended in capture and imprisonment, symbolised the distrust and neglect which was one of the alternative attitudes of James's regime towards the highlanders.

NOTES

1. *Life of James*, i, 580, 707; *ib.*, ii, 634–5; *State Trials*, vii, 863.

2. *Ib.* , 1261–70; *APS*, viii, 368–9; Fountainhall, *Hist. Notices*, i, 310, 313–4, 320, 323.

3. Aberdeen's demands were made on behalf of his chief Huntly. *Ib.*, 440–1; Napier, *Dundee*, ii, 323–4; BL Add. 19,254 fol. 114, Breadalbane to Perth, 21 Oct. 1687; *ib.*, fol. 119, R. Drummond to Blair Drummond, 21 Oct. 1687.

4. Huntly was later told that excluding him from office was the primary aim of James's extremist advisers in the Test. SRO REF 310.044 (GD 44), 115, Gordon's memoirs, 12–16; Fountainhall, *Hist. Notices*, i, 327.

5. *Ib.*, ii, 745; *Hist. Observes*, 78–9, 131.

6. Such concessions might, admittedly, be necessary in 1690; but James seems to have overlooked rather than rejected the arguments against. *Leven & Melville*, 506–10, Annandale's confession, 14 Aug. 1690; P. A. Hopkins, Aspects of Jacobite Conspiracy in England in the reign of William III, (Cambridge Ph.D., 1981), 41–5.

7. *RPCS*, vi, 547, 572–3, 597–600, 618; *ib.*, vii, 6–7, 10–13; Fountainhall, *Hist. Notices*, i, 276, 279–80; BL Add. 23,247 fol. 65, 'Caithness' to Duchess, 28 Dec. 1680; *Laud. Papers*, iii, 218, Sir G. Mackenzie to same, [1680].

8. *Ib.*, 225, same to same, [17 Sept. 1681]; *APS*, viii, 231, 243, 368–9; *RPCS*, vii, 160, 184–5, 200–2; Fountainhall, *Hist. Notices*, i, 302, 328; *Scots Peerage*, ii, 203.

9. Cripps, *Elizabeth*, 235, Duchess to Moray, 2 Mar. 1679/80; *Life of James*, i, 684–5; BL Add. 23,248 fol. 13, 'Caithness' to Duchess, 2 May 1681; SRO GD 170/133/142, D. Campbell to Breadalbane, 23 Apr. 1698; Drumlanrig, Queensberry Papers, Vol. 128, 19, Articles against the Duchess of Lauderdale, [c. 1681].

10. *HMCR Buccleuch (Drumlanrig)*, ii, 14, Moray to Queensberry, 6 July 1682; Campbell, *Lairds of Glenlyon*, 41–2; *RPCS*, vii, 387.

11. *Ib.*, vi, 551, 615–6, 618; *ib.*, vii, 35; A. Lang, *Sir George Mackenzie* (London, 1909), 217.

12. This implies that James would largely have abandoned Huntly's interests. J. Willcock, *A Scots Earl in Covenanting Times* (Edinburgh, 1907), 249.

13. Fountainhall, *Hist. Notices*, i, 312–13; *State Trials*, viii, 846–59.

14. *Ib.*, 859–61; *APS*, viii, 257–9, 446; J. M. Miller, *James II: a Study in Kingship* (Hove, 1978), 53; Stevenson, *Alasdair MacColla*, 289; *Laud. Papers*, iii, 225, Mackenzie to Duchess, [17 Sept. 1681].

15. *State Trials*, viii, 861–8, 985, 987–8; *Life of James*, i, 709–10; Fountainhall, *Hist. Observes*, 54–5; *Hist. Notices*, i, 335–6, 342; Burnet, *History*, ii, 318–19, 320–1; Lang, *Mackenzie*, 321–7; Willcock, *Scots Earl*, 288–9; Stevenson, *Alasdair MacColla*, 289–90.

16. *APS*, viii, 493; *CSPD 1682*, 130–1, Warrant, 17 Mar. 1682; *Life of James*, i, 711, 712–13; *Letters . . . to George Earl of Aberdeen*, ed. J. Dunn (Spalding Club, 1851), 6–7, Perth to Haddo, 14 Mar. 1682; Fountainhall, *Hist. Notices*, i, 350.

17. *Ib.*, 455–6; *ib.*, ii, 478, 507, 524, 533; *Decisions*, i, 265, 273, 279; *HMCR Buccleuch (Drumlanrig)*, ii, 139–40, Paper on the Annexation of the Argyll estate, Sept. 1683; *CSPD 1684–5*, 57, Instructions to Treasurer, 14 June 1684.

18. *Ib.*, 59, Grant to Maclean, 14 June 1684; *ib. 1682*, 130, Warrant, 17 Mar. 1682; *RPCS*, viii, 393–4; *ib.*, xi, 393–4; *ib.*, xii, 546–7; Fountainhall, *Hist. Notices*, ii, 533; Macfarlane, *Gen. Colls.*, i, 138; Cumnock, Dumfries House, Manuscripts of the Marquess of Bute, bundle A517/13, [Breadalbane] to [Dalrymple], 19 Nov. 1691 (for identification of addressee, see Chapter 8,n. 52).

19. *Letters to Aberdeen*, 13, Tarbat to Haddo, 25 Apr. 1682; *ib.*, 84, same to same, 4 Oct. 1682; *Earls of Cromartie*, i, 57–8, Macdougalls to Tarbat, Apr. 1688; *Scots Peerage*, ii, 202; McNaughton, *The Clan McNaughton*, 27; *CSPD 1684–5*, 60, Charter to Macnachtan, 14 June 1684; *ib. 1682*, 130, Warrant, 17 Mar. 1682.

20. *Ib.*, 130–1; *ib. July*–Sept. 1683, 184, Signature for Clanranald, 21 July 1683; *HMCR Buccleuch (Drumlanrig)*, i, 186, James to Queensberry, 27 Mar. 1683; Blair, Atholl MSS, Box 29 I (3) 77, Clanranald to Atholl, 20 Jan. 1682; *ib.*, 86, Glengarry to same, 13 June 1682.

21. *Letters to Aberdeen*, 25, Tarbat to Haddo, 29 Apr. 1682; *RPCS*, vii, 381–2, 395, 400.

22. *Ib.*, xv, 486, Articles for surrender of Castle Stalker; Macdonald, *Clan Donald*, iii, 222; J. G. Dunbar, 'A Siege of Castle Stalker', *The Stewarts*, xiii (1968), 29–32; SRO GD 112/40/3/2/30, James Campbell of Glendaruel to Breadalbane, '10 Apr. 1673' [?1703].

23. *Memoirs of Locheill*, 210; Cunningham, *The Loyal Clans*, 196, 306, 353–4, 496; Lenman, *Jacobite Risings*, 127–9, 133; Stevenson, *Alasdair MacColla*, 12–13.

24. *Ib.*, 287, 297–8; Lenman, *Jacobite Risings*, 49; *The Blind Harper*, xlv–liii.

25. For the 1690 betrayal, see Chapter 6, p. 219. Lochiel's claim, in the 1691 negotiations with Breadalbane, that James had made a general promise (*Memoirs of Locheill*, 301) was an exaggerated bargaining point; see Chapter 8, p. 278. *APS*, viii, 493; *Life of James*, ii, 635.

26. See pp. 104, 107.

27. For James's liking for military rule, J. Childs, *The Army, James II and the Glorious Revolution* (Manchester, 1980). Lenman, *Jacobite Risings*, 51–2; Fountainhall, *Hist. Notices*, ii, 553–4.

28. Melfort, at least, later gained a more favourable opinion of the highlanders. *HMCR Buccleuch (Drumlanrig)*, ii, 67, Moray to Queensberry, 14 May 1685; *ib.*, 148, Lundin to same, 12 Oct. 1683; Atholl, *Chronicles*, i, 244, Perth to Atholl, 23 June 1685; Stevenson, *Alasdair MacColla*, 292.

29. *CSPD 1686–7*, 53, Grant to Cpt. R. Macdonell, 10 May, 1687; Colin, Earl of Balcarres, *Memoirs touching the Revolution in Scotland*, ed. Lord Lindsay (Bannatyne Club, 1841), xx; Hopkins, Aspects of Jacobite Conspiracy, 71–3, 407; *Life of James*, ii, 273–6.

30. *Ib.*, 634–5; *Memoirs of Locheill*, 292–3; *RPCS*, xi, 399–400; *HMCR Buccleuch (Drumlanrig)*, i, 91, Instructions to Queensberry, 25 Mar. 1685; *ib.*, 104, James to same, 1 June 1685.

31. *Culloden Papers . . . from the year 1625 to 1748*, ed. H. R. Duff (London, 1815), 14, [D. Forbes], 'Memoir . . . for preserving the Peace of the Highlands' [1690]; Stevenson, *Alasdair MacColla*, 292–3.

32. This characteristic is far clearer in James's special relationship with the Quakers.

33. *Ib.*, 296, 298; *Orain Iain Luim*, 202–7, 'Oran Air Righ Uilleam agus Banrigh Mairi'; Maclean, 'Celtic Sources', 255–8.

34. Lenman, *Jacobite Risings*, 20–2; *Memoirs of Locheill*, 86, 114.

35. *Ib.*, 292–4; *APS*, ix, App. 60, The Chiefs to Mackay, 17 Aug. 1689; SRO GD 26/ix/274, Hill to Melville, 2 Nov. 1690; Cumnock, Dumfries House, Bute MSS, bundle A517/12, [Breadalbane] to [Dalrymple] 16 Nov. 1691.

36. *Major Fraser's Manuscript*, ed. A. Fergusson, 2 vols. (Edinburgh, 1889), i, 179–80; ii, 12, 83.

37. *RPCS*, vii, 74–84, 204–5.

38. *Ib.*, 354, 361–3, 590; *ib.*, viii, 7–8, 42; *Letters to Aberdeen*, 15, Tarbat to Haddo, 29 Apr. 1682; *Memoirs of Locheill*, 204–6; Stevenson, *Alasdair MacColla*, 294; Fountainhall, *Hist. Notices*, i, 378, 384.

39. According to Huntly himself, often an ungrateful one. *Hist. Observes*, 68–9; SRO REF 310.044 (GD 44), 115, Gordon's memoirs, 2, 12, 15–16.

40. *Letters to Aberdeen*, 54, Sir G. Mackenzie to Haddo, [May–June 1682]; Fountainhall, *Hist. Notices*, i, 440–1.

41. *Mackintosh Muniments*, 136, Articles of agreement, 23 Feb. 1683; SRO GD 44/25/1683, Lochiel's renunciation of salmon-fishing, 5 June 1683; *Memoirs of Locheill*, 209–10.

42. Lochiel might have married partly for the sake of Barclay's more general favour at Court, but in 1684–5 the general persecution against Dissenters made that very unsure. *Ib.*, 210; *CSPD 1684–5*, 59, Charter to J. Cameron, 14 June 1684; Fountainhall, *Hist. Notices*, ii, 550, 599–600; *HMCR Buccleuch (Drumlanrig)*, i, 215, James to Queensberry, 16 July 1685; MacMillan, *Bygone Lochaber*, 121; BL Add. 19,254 fol. 116, D. Toshach to Perth, 17 Mar. 1685.

43. SRO GD 170/629/2, Breadalbane to Barcaldine, 2 Apr. 1683; GD 112/43/1/6/44, Articles of treason, 1683.

44. A reference by Fountainhall suggests that Breadalbane may have granted him some lands, but evidently not enough. *Ib.*, 39/1169, [Carwhin] to Breadalbane, 16 Mar. 1683; *ib.*, 1170, Grahame to same, 23 Mar. 1683; *ib.*, 1173, A. Dunbar to Countess, 3 Apr. 1683; *HMCR Buccleuch (Drumlanrig)*, ii, 131, Lundin to Queensberry, 5 Sept. 1683; Fountainhall, *Hist. Observes*, 129.

45. SRO GD 112/40/3/3/30, [Countess] to Breadalbane, 16 June 1683; GD 170/629/13, Breadalbane to Barcaldine, 29 Mar. 1683; Blair, Atholl MSS, Box 29 I (3a) 8, same to Atholl, n.d.

46. *Ib.*, (5) 131, same to Murray, 29 June 1688; *CSPD July–Sept. 1683*, 108, Charles to Justiciary, 12 July 1683; *ib.*, 275–6, Remission, 10 Aug. 1683; Fountainhall, *Hist. Notices*, i, 447; SRO GD 112/43/1/6/44, Articles of treason, 1683.

47. *RPCS*, ix, 187–8.

48. Burnet, *History*, ii, 425–7; Fountainhall, *Hist. Notices*, ii, 469–70; *Hist. Observes*, 127–31.

49. *Decisions*, i, 465–6, 469–70, 494; *HMCR Buccleuch (Drumlanrig)*, i, 213, James to Queensberry, 22 Dec. 1684; *ib.*, ii, 155, Lundin to same, 18 Oct. 1683.

50. SRO GD 112/43/1/1/8, Breadalbane, Memorial to Loudoun, [1705–7].

51. *Ib.*, GD 170/133/124, Inventory of Glenlyon papers, 1691; *RPCS*, iii, 448; Blair, Atholl MSS, Box 29 I (5) 160, Glenlyon to Murray, 29 July 1689; *ib.*, Box 45 (1) 232, J. Flemyng to same, 14 Aug. 1701; *Lairds of Glenlyon*, 29–32.

52. *Ib.*, 41–2, 85–91; SRO GD 170/133/3, J. Corse to Glenlyon, 7 Aug. 1691; *ib.*, 12, The grounds of Atholl's apprisings; *ib.*, 104, Information for Glenlyon, 15 Apr. 1690; *ib.*, 138, J. Campbell's petition.

53. *RPCS*, v, 264; *ib.*, vii, 46–8; *Lairds of Glenlyon*, 33–5.

54. *Ib.*, 39–41, Agreement, 5 Aug. 1683; *RPCS*, vii, 635–6, 638, 640; *ib.*, viii, 532, 544; Fountainhall, *Hist. Notices*, ii, 544–5; SRO GD 170/133/138, J. Campbell's petition.

55. *Ib; ib.*, 104, Information for Glenlyon, 15 Apr. 1690; *Lairds of Glenlyon*, 45, 71; Blair, Atholl MSS, Box 29 I (5) 59, Ballechin to J. Flemyng, 6 May 1688.

56. Macpherson, *Loyall Dissuasive*, 133; SRO GD 170/133/31, Interrogatories, 1698.

57. *Ib.*, 104, Information for Glenlyon, 15 Apr. 1690; *ib.*, 109, same, 3 Feb. 1697.

58. *Ib.*, 159, Glenlyon's declaration, 10 May 1688; GD 112/40/4/1/14, Glenorchy to

Breadalbane, 2 Jan. 1691/2; *ib.*, 40/4/3/6, Breadalbane to Carwhin, 6 Feb. 1692; Atholl, *Chronicles*, i, 333, Murray's diary.

59. The £5,000 bond he is recorded as owing Glenlyon may be a backbond in one of these transactions. *Lairds of Glenlyon*, 42–3; *HMCR Buccleuch (Drumlanrig)*, ii, 50, Moray to Queensberry, 13 Apr. 1685; SRO GD 112/40/3/4/34, Atholl to Breadalbane, 3 May 1688; Blair, Atholl MSS, Box 29 I (5) 57, Glenlyon to Threipland, 25 Apr. 1688.

60. *More Culloden Papers, i, 1626–1704*, ed. D. Warrand (Inverness, 1923), 173–4, Inverness-shire petition for watch, 1681; Fraser-Macintosh, *Letters*, 106, A. Chisholm to Provost of Inverness, 25 Nov. 1681; *Black Book of Taymouth*, 261–2, Bond of Manrent, 26 Jan. 1681; *Letters to Aberdeen*, 36, Perth to Haddo, 17 July 1682; *ib.*, 71, Seaforth to same, 25 Sept, 1682.

61. *Ib.*, 20, Moray to same, 24 June 1682; *ib.*, 30–1, same to same, 6 July 1682; *RPCS*, vii, 419, 507–15.

62. *Ib.*, 632–48; *ib.*, viii, 534.

63. *Ib.*, 23–4, 36–7, 106; *ib.*, vii, 191–2; *Records of Inverness*, ii, 313; Mackintosh, *Mackintoshes*, 277–8; *Mackintosh Muniments*, 136, Articles of Agreement between Huntly and Mackintosh, 22 Feb. 1683; Doune, Moray MSS, Box 6, 463, Mackintosh to Moray, 31 Mar. 1681; *ib.*, 465, same to same, 25 April 1684.

64. SRO GD 112/43/1/3/12, Contract for Inverlochy garrison, 2 Feb. 1683.

65. *RPCS*, vii, 613–14, 647–8; *ib.*, viii, 531–4, 536–8; *ib.*, ix, 189.

66. Balhaldie, who places here the (1670) riot which drove away the 'Sheriff of Invernesshire', was plainly wrong: the Highland Justiciary's records show several days' successful activity. *Ib.*, 189–90; *ib.*, viii, 534–5, 538–9; *Memoirs of Locheill*, 208–9.

67. *RPCS*, viii, 572, 587–8; *ib.*, ix, 132, 190, 194, 195–6.

68. *Ib.*, viii, 535, 539; *ib.*, x, 211–14.

69. *Ib.*, viii, 93; *ib.*, ix, 190–1, 197–8; Doune, Moray MSS, Box 6, 537, A. Chisholm to Moray, 10 June 1684.

70. *RPCS*, ix, 191, 199–200.

71. *Ib.*, 132; *ib.*, viii, 104–5, 419; *ib.*, x, 182; *ib.*, xi, 134; *Records of Inverness*, ii, 321–5; MacMillan, *Bygone Lochaber*, 17; *Mackintosh Muniments*, 138, Petitions, 1685.

72. Fountainhall, *Hist. Notices*, ii, 554.

73. *RPCS*, ix, 198; *CSPD 1684–5*, 55, Add. Instructions to Secret Committee, 14 June 1684.

74. *Letters to Aberdeen*, 84, Tarbat to Haddo, 4 Oct. 1682; *HMCR 5th Report*, 617, Aberdeen to Sheriff of Bute, 31 July 1683; *RPCS*, viii, 508–10; *ib.*, x, 372–4.

75. *Ib.*. 81–3, 96; Atholl, *Chronicles*, i, 185–6, Atholl to James, Werden, 29 July 1684; *ib.*, 188–90, 265; *ib.*, 268, Graeme to Murray, 29 Sept. 1686; Blair, Atholl MSS, bundle 1622, Murray's diary, 31 July 1688; Fountainhall, *Hist. Notices*, ii, 547.

76. *Ib.*, 545, 553, 556; *CSPD 1684–5*, 104–5, Instructions to Argyll, 26 July 1684; *RPCS*, ix, 318–20, 323–32; Atholl, *Chronicles*, i, 190, Secret Committee to Atholl, 28 Aug. 1684; *ib.*, 191–2, same to same, 6 Sept. 1684; *ib.*, 195–6, Sir G. Mackenzie to same, 17 Sept. 1684; *ib.*, 192–3; *ib.*, 196–8, Atholl's report.

77. Atholl later tried to claim some credit for keeping the dreaded 'Irish' troops out of Scotland; but these were, of course, protestant Anglo-Irish. *Ib.*, 228–9, Secret Committee to Atholl, 5 June 1685; *ib.*, v, App., clxxi, Vindication of the Marquess of Atholl, 1699; *Marchmont Papers*, iii, 50, Sir P. Hume's narrative, 1685.

78. *HMCR 2nd Report*, 213–14, Lord Mountjoy's Memoirs; Willcock, *Scots Earl*, 302–4.

79. Fountainhall, *Hist. Observes*, 165–6; *Chiefs of Grant*, i, 306, Sir G. Mackenzie to Grant, [May 1685]; *ib.*, 25, Grant to PCS, 5 June 1685; *Marchmont Papers*, iii, 22–3, Hume.

80. *RPCS*, xi, 25–7; Wodrow, *Church History*, iv, 291–2; Veitch, *Memoirs*, 337–41; *HMCR Buccleuch (Drumlanrig)*, i, 110, James to Queensberry, 31 May 1685.

81. *Ib.*, ii, 60, Moray to same, 30 Apr. 1685; *RPCS*, xi, 40–2, 281, 284–5; Fountainhall, *Hist. Notices*, ii, 636; *Hist. Observes*, 165–6; P. Walker, *Six Saints of the Covenant*, ed. D. Hay Fleming, 2 vols. (London, 1901), i, 296–7; SRO GD 112/40/3/3/47, General Douglas to Breadalbane, 16 May 1685; Blair, Atholl MSS, Box 29 I (4) 54, Breadalbane to Atholl, 'Sunday' [24 May 1685] (The dates given in Atholl, *Chronicles*, are mistaken; the corrected ones were provided by the cataloguer of the Atholl MSS).

82. *Ib.*, 38, Kintore to same, 22 May 1685; *Earls of Cromartie*, i, 41, Tarbat to same, [May 1685].

83. *HMCR Buccleuch (Drumlanrig)*, i, 109, James to Queensberry, 25 May 1685; *ib.*, 135, Secret Committee's Instructions, [1685].

84. He specifically mentions this in a later letter to Queensberry which might be hindsight, but his remark to Atholl that he will lose 'no tyme yt ye can recover' suggests that he had made the reproach. *Ib*; Drumlanrig, Queensberry MSS, Vol. 122, 39, Breadalbane to same, 28 July 1685; Atholl, *Chronicles*, i, 208, same to Atholl, 23 May 1685.

85. *Ib.*, 211, same to same, 'Sunday' [24 May 1685]; *Scots Peerage*, ii, 207; SRO GD 112/40/3/3/38, Sunderland to Newcastle, 11 Apr. 1685; *HMCR Buccleuch (Drumlanrig)*, i, 106, James to Queensberry, 11 Apr. 1685.

86. *Ib.*, ii, 36, Moray to same, 18 Nov. 1684; *ib.*, 65–6, same to same, 12 May 1685; *CSPD 1684–5*, 288–9, Charter to Gordon, 15 Jan. 1685; *Memoirs of Locheill*, 209–10, 218; Atholl, *Chronicles*, i, 203–4, Secret Committee to Atholl, 21 May 168[5]; *ib.*, 265, Argyll's claims, 1699; J. Cameron, 'The Camerons in the Rising of 1715', ed. W. Mackay ('The Camerons in the '15'), *TGSI*, xxvi (1904–7), 65–6; SRO GD 1/658, 34.

87. Fountainhall, *Hist. Notices*, ii, 640; *The Siege of the Castle of Edinburgh, 1689*, ed. R. Bell (*Siege*; Bannatyne Club, 1828), 2–3.

88. The Council Register would suggest that they forgot to write to Keppoch; but he came anyway. They set no date. *RPCS*, xi, 31–2, 38–42, 43–5; *Earls of Cromartie*, i, 41, Tarbat to Atholl, [May 1685].

89. *Ib.*, 44–7, Breadalbane to Queensberry, 20 May 1685; Atholl, *Chronicles*, i, 203, Secret Committee to Atholl, 21 May 1685; *ib.*, 204–5, J. Flemyng to Marchioness, 22 May 1685; *ib.*, 250, Atholl's report, 9 July 1685.

90. J. Erskine of Carnock, *Journal 1683–7*, ed. Rev. W. Macleod (SHS, 1893), 116–7.

91. One of Iain Lom's poems may be hinting at this accusation. *RPCS*, xi, 40, 112; *Marchmont Papers*, iii, 41, Hume; Wodrow, *Church History*, iv, 287–90; *Orain Iain Luim*, 180–1, 'Tuirneal a' Chnatain'; Blair, Atholl MSS, Box 29 I (4) 51, Lochnell to Atholl, 26 May 1685.

92. *Thanes of Cawdor*, 382, Calder's petition to PCS; Erskine, *Journal*, 117; SRO GD 112/39/1194, Secret Committee to Breadalbane, 14 June 1685.

93. *Marchmont Papers*, iii, 13, Hume; Atholl, *Chronicles*, i, 240, [Dollery] to 'cousin', 16 June 1685.

94. Surprisingly, they also retired when the Captain's wife said she intended to deliver it to Maclean of Brolas. *Ib.*, 202, Breadalbane to Atholl, 'Sunday' [24 May 1685]; *ib.*, 208, same to same, 23 May 1685.

95. The hostile Hume indicates that Argyll's estimate was accurate. Ballechin, who claimed Mid-Argyll furnished only 400, always underestimated the enemy. Breadalbane thought Argyll at his height had 2,000. Proceedings afterwards discovered 1,100 rebels, but, as informers' lists showed, many would escape unnoticed. *Ib*; *ib.*, 199, Kilberry to Lamont, 20 May 1685; *ib.*, 209, Ballechin to Atholl, 'Thursday' [28 May 1685]; *Marchmont*

Papers, iii, 44–5, Hume; *Scots Peerage*, ii, 201; D. C. Mactavish, *The Commons of Argyll: Name Lists of 1685 and 1692* (Lochgilphead, 1935), 1–16; *Rawdon Papers*, 279, Breadalbane to Albemarle, 4 June 1685; *RPCS*, xi, 305–7.

96. Glendessary, who had helped cheat the Argyll children out of their rights in Tiree, would have made an odd fellow-rebel. *Ib.*, 142–3, 593–4; Atholl, *Chronicles*, i, 201, Breadalbane to Ballechin, '9 at night'; *ib.*, 208, same to Atholl, 23 May 1685; *ib.*, 211, same to same, 'Sunday' [24 May 1685]; *ib.*, 214, same to same, 'Tuesday' [26 May 1685]; *ib.*, 205–6, Ballechin to same, 22 May 1685.

97. *Ib.*, 205; *Thanes of Cawdor*, 373–4, Court, 1 Sept. 1685; Erskine, *Journal*, 117–18, 120.

98. *Ib.*, 118–20; H. C. Foxcroft (ed.)., *A Supplement to Bishop Burnet's History of his own time* (Oxford, 1902), 158; Mactavish, *Commons*, 17; Maclean, 'Celtic Sources', 220–1, Ballad to the Earl of Argyll (*Leabhar na Féinne*); *ib.*, 222, 225, An t-Aos-dàna Mac Shithich, 'Cumha do Iarlu Earra-Ghàidheal' (translated by Maclean); Wodrow, *Church History*, iv, 291n.

99. *Ib.*, 298; *Marchmont Papers*, iii, 42–4, Hume; Erskine, *Journal*, 119–21.

100. Blair, Atholl MSS, Box 29 I (4) 47, Secret Committee to Atholl, 25 May 1685; Atholl, *Chronicles*, i, 205–6, Ballechin to same, 22 May 1685; *ib.*, 220*–221, McAlisters to same, 2 June 1685; *ib.*, 201, Breadalbane to Ballechin, '9 at night'.

101. *Ib.*, 200–2; *ib.*, 202–3, same to Atholl, 'Sunday' [24 May 1685]; *ib.*, 200, Secret Committee to Atholl, 20 May 1685; SRO GD 112/39/1185, Atholl to Breadalbane, 26 May 1685; Blair, Atholl MSS, Box 29 I (4) 53, Breadalbane to Ballechin, 'Sunday' [24 May 1685].

102. *Ib.*, 55, Ballechin to Atholl, 'Thursday' [28 May 1685]; *ib.*, 56, same to same, 27 [May 1685]; Atholl, *Chronicles*, i, 209, same to same, 'Thursday' [28 May 1685]; *ib.*, 217–18, J. Flemyng to Marchioness, 30 May 1685; *ib.*, 250, Atholl's report, 9 July 1685; Erskine, *Journal*, 120–1; *Marchmont Papers*, iii, 45–6, Hume.

103. Atholl's report misdates the skirmish. *Ib.*, 46–8; Erskine, *Journal*, 121–4; Atholl; *Chronicles*, i, 223, J. Flemyng to Marchioness, 3 June 1685; *ib.*, 250–1, Atholl's report, 9 July 1685.

104. *Ib.*, 250, 252; *Memoirs of Locheill*, 211–12.

105. Fountainhall, *Hist. Observes*, 168; Erskine, *Journal*, 127; *Earls of Cromartie*, i, 38–9, Tarbat to Atholl, 27 May 1685; Atholl, *Chronicles*, i, 219*–220, Secret Committee to Atholl, 31 May 1685.

106. *Ib.*, 230, Gordon to same, 8 June 1685; *ib.*, 237–8, same to same, 14 June 1685; *Sutherland Book*, ii, 311–12, same to Strathnaver, 8 June 1685.

107. NLS MS 7012 fols. 204v–205, [Sir A. Bruce (Bruce)] to Tweeddale, 8 Nov. 1690; Fountainhall, *Hist. Observes*, 187.

108. *Hist. Notices*, ii, 692; Willcock, *Scots Earl*, 356; SRO GD 112/40/3/3/50, 'Lorne' to Breadalbane, 31 June 1685.

109. Atholl, *Chronicles*, i, 215–17, Secret Committee to Atholl, 30 May 1685; *ib.*, 224, A. Clark's deposition, '3 June' 1685 (date, from internal evidence, wrong).

110. Breadalbane, writing in August, seemed to look on it as an affair of escalating counter-charges. Atholl, believing the charges true, was far less unscrupulous than Perth, who isolated prisoners to get them to accuse Queensberry and Tarbat; but if, as he claimed, he had saved Charles Campbell's life, the obligations might make him confirm the charge. Atholl left the earlier evidence with Tarbat: it may still exist. *Ib.*, 224–5; *ib.*, 261–2, C. Campbell to Atholl, n.d; *ib.*, 262–4, Depositions, 1 Oct. 1685; SRO GD 112/40/4/7/58, [Atholl] to Breadalbane, 4 Aug. [1685]; Fountainhall, *Hist. Notices*, ii, 661; Drumlanrig, Queensberry Papers, Vol. 122, 42, Breadalbane to Queensberry, 4 Aug. 1685.

111. Another possibility is that the danger of being attacked by Atholl after the affair of 9 June forced Lochiel to open communications with Argyll, which would explain the involvement of the Macleans. However, one story, of Argyll ostentatiously reading a *legibly* signed letter from Lochiel, proves (unless it is the witness's embroidery) that Argyll was playing a trick. For Atholl's spies and Argyll's knowledge of them, MacTavish, *Commons*, 11; Wodrow, *Church History*, iv, 298. Atholl, *Chronicles*, i, 262–4, Depositions, 1 Oct. 1685.

112. Or Eilean Gheirrig; but it is best known in the corrupted form applied to its owner. *Ib.*, 251, Atholl's report, 9 July 1685; *Marchmont Papers*, iii, 49–51, Hume; Erskine, *Journal*, 125.

113. The contemporary documents contain no trace of this, but it has left traces in the (otherwise absurd) local folklore on the rising. *Ib.*, 128; Atholl, *Chronicles*, i, 233, J. Flemyng to Marchioness, 10 June 1685; *Memoirs of Locheill*, 212–15; Marquess of Lorne, *Adventures in Legend* (Westminster, 1898), 251–5; Maclean, 'Celtic Sources', 218, Domhall Ban Bard, 'Oran do Shir Eoghann Camshron' (translated by Maclean).

114. The one fleeting reference to this plot does not give the precise context, but this seems the only plausible occasion. SRO GD 112/40/4/8/21, [Tarbat], Notes on procedure for objecting to [Breadalbane's] trial, [1695].

115. Atholl, *Chronicles*, i, 262–3, Depositions, 1 Oct. 1685.

116. *Ib.*, 250–2, Atholl's report, 9 July 1685; Wodrow, *Church History*, iv, 293–4; *Marchmont Papers*, iii, 51–2, Hume; A. Brown, *Memorials of Argyleshire* (Greenock, 1889), 399–402; Maclean, 'Celtic Sources', 213–16, A. Robertson, 'Latha Cheann Loch-Fine' (translated by Maclean); *Memoirs of Locheill*, 215.

117. *Ib*; Atholl, *Chronicles*, i, 239–40, [Murray of Dollery] to 'Cousin', 16 June 1685; *ib.*, 241–2, J. Haldane to Lanrick, 16 June 1685; *ib.*, 252–3, Atholl's report, 9 July 1685.

118. *Ib.*, 253; *ib.*, 260, Tarbat to Atholl, 6 Aug. 1685; *ib.*, 260–1, Officers' declaration, 17 Aug. 1685; *Marchmont Papers*, iii, 54, 57, Hume; *Memoirs of Locheill*, 215–16; 'The Camerons in the '15'. *TGSI*, xxvi, 66; *An Account of the Depredations committed upon the Clan Campbell and their followers during the years 1685 and 1686*, ed. [A. Kincaid], (Edinburgh, 1816), 12, 14, 30, 43, 65, 79–80, 87.

119. *Ib.*, 1–6, 23, 30, 51–2; *RPCS*, ix, 348–9; Atholl, *Chronicles*, i, 221–2, Atholl to Macnachtan, 2 June 1685; *ib.*, 240–1, [Dollery] to 'cousin', 16 June 1685; *ib.*, 247, Tarbat to Atholl, 24 June 1685; Erskine, *Journal*, 131–1.

120. *Marchmont Papers*, iii, 55–6, Hume.

121. Atholl, *Chronicles*, i, 241, [Dollery] to 'cousin', 16 June [1685]; *ib.*, v, App., clxiv, Memoir for the Marquess of Atholl, 1699; *RPCS*, xi, 83.

122. *Ib.*, xii, 167; Prebble, *Glencoe*, 69–71; MacTavish, *Commons*, 61; *Account of the Depredations*, 3–4, 8, 13–14, 51–2, 64, 69, 85.

123. Although some of them of course took part in the plundering elsewhere. *Ib.*, 57; *Sutherland Book*, i, 314, Breadalbane to Strathnaver, 20 June 1685; Drumlanrig, Queensberry Papers, Vol. 122, 40, same to Queensberry, 30 July 1685; Atholl, *Chronicles*, i, 256, same to Atholl, [July 1685].

124. *Ib.*, 258–9, D. MacNeil & J. McAlister to same, 15 July 1685; *Account of the Depredations*, 45, 69, 84, 90, 95, 97–9, 105.

125. *Ib.*, 18–19, 75, 118; *RPCS*, xi, 425; Atholl, *Chronicles*, i, 265–6, Argyll's claims, 1699; *ib.*, v, App., clxiv–clxv, Memoir for the Marquess of Atholl, 1699.

126. The year usually given for Clanranald's death, 1686, is mistaken. *Ib.*, clxviii, Vindication of the Marquess of Atholl; *ib.*, i, 235, A. Maclear [sic] to Atholl, [c. June 1685]; *ib.*, 246–7, Perth to same, 23 June 1685; *ib.*, 253, Atholl's report, 9 July 1685.

127. Some of Argyll's followers had similarly tried to blow up Ellangreg and some

hostages with it. By 1699, Atholl was claiming that he was there and the intended victim. *Ib.*, 253–4; *ib.*, v, App., clxix–clxx, Vindication; *APS*, ix, App., 44–5; *RPCS*, xi, 142–3, 156, 272; *ib.*, xii, 291–2.

128. *Ib.*, xi, 122, 592; Atholl, *Chronicles*, i, 247n; *ib.*, 261–2, C. Campbell to Atholl, n.d; *ib.*, v, App., clxx–clxxi, Vindication; Fountainhall, *Hist. Notices*, ii, 655, 661.

129. *Ib.*, 692, 694; *Hist. Observes*, 220; MacTavish, *Commons*, 18–22; *RPCS*, xi, 114–15, 119, 123–4, 126–7, 129–30, 136–8, 187, 444.

130. *Ib.*, 101; *Account of the Depredations*, 40, 41, 48–50, 61–2, 63, 65, 117; *RCAHMS Argyll*, i, 159, 161; *ib.*, ii, 210; Atholl, *Chronicles*, i, 254, Atholl's report, 9 July 1685; *ib.*, 257–8, Ballechin to Atholl, 11 July 1685; *ib.*, 258, Lochnell to Ballechin, 14 July 1685.

131. *Ib.*, 257, 258; *ib.*, 256, Breadalbane to Atholl, [July 1685]; *Account of the Depredations*, 92–3; *RPCS*, xi, 129, 225–6, 390–1.

132. SRO GD 112/39/1195, Secret Committee to Breadalbane, 16 June 1685.

133. *RPCS*, xii, 29; Fountainhall, *Hist. Notices*, ii, 656, 695–6, 710; *HMCR Buccleuch (Drumlanrig)*, i, 133–4, Secret Committee's instructions; Drumlanrig, Queensberry Papers, Vol. 122, 40, Breadalbane to Queensberry, 30 July 1685.

134. SRO GD 112/43/1/1/23, Proposed strength of regiment and auxiliaries, [1685 — date established by the mention of Lord William Murray (at sea until 1685, Lord Nairne from 1690), and of Maclean of Torloisk (died 1687), and by the sudden demotion of Lochiel]; Drumlanrig, Queensberry Papers, Vol. 122, 35, Breadalbane to Queensberry, 11 July 1685; *ib.*, 38, same to same, 25 July 1685; *ib.*, 43, same to same, 11 Aug. 1685.

135. *Ib.*, 42, same to same, 4 Aug. 1685; *ib.*, 44, same to same, 18 Aug. 1685; Atholl, *Chronicles*, i, 260, Tarbat to Atholl, 6 Aug. 1685; *ib.*, 260–1, Officers' declaration, 17 Aug. 1685; *ib.*, 262–4, Depositions, 1 Oct. 1685; *Memoirs of Locheill*, 216–17; Fountainhall, *Hist. Notices*, ii, 661.

136. *Hist. Observes*, 217; *APS*, viii, 613; *Memoirs of Locheill*, 217–22; 'The Camerons in the '15', *TGSI*, xxvi, 65; Stevenson, *Alasdair MacColla*, 295; *Records of Inverness*, ii, 334.

137. Fountainhall, *Hist. Notices*, ii, 713, 716; SRO REF 310.044 (GD 44), 115, Gordon's memoirs, 18–19.

138. *HMCR Buccleuch (Montagu)*, ii, 194, Johnston to Shrewsbury, 21 June 1695; *Culloden Papers*, 333–4, 'Memorandum anent the Viscount of Tarbat', 1701.

139. *RPCS*, xi, 16, 57, 61, 103–4, 170–1, 275, 395, 400; *ib.*, xii, 467; *ib.*, xiii, 9–10; *Account of the Depredations*, 53–4.

140. R. Steele (ed.), *Tudor and Stuart Proclamations, 1485*–1714, 2 vols. (Oxford, 1910), ii, S2667; Fountainhall, *Hist. Notices*, ii, 732; *RPCS*, xii, 1–3, 136, 467–8.

141. *Ib.*, 3, 337; *ib.*, xi, 201, 251.

142. *Ib.*, xii, 314, 401, 461–5, 525; Atholl, *Chronicles*, i, 267–8, Melfort to Atholl, 29 Sept. 1686; Mactavish, *Commons*, 62.

143. *APS*, ix, 45; *RPCS*, xiii, 291–2.

144. J. H. J. & Lt-Col. D. Stewart, *The Stewarts of Appin* (Edinburgh, 1880), 132–3, Memorandum; SRO SP 4/11, 227, 4/12, 290–2, Grant & Charter to Ballechin.

145. MacWilliam, 'A Highland Mission', *IR*, xxiv, 83; SCA, Thompson, 'History', i, fols. 165, 171, 177.

146. *Ib.*, fols. 243–6, 259; *CSPD 1689–90*, 383, List of pensions; Forbes Leith, *Scottish Catholics*, ii, 148–9.

147. This seems indicated by Dean Fraser of the Isles' matter-of-fact references to a priest on Eigg. [Rev. D. Macleod], 'Theophilus Insulanus', *A Treatise on the Second Sight* (Edinburgh, 1763), 74–5.

148. *HMCR Athole*, 55, Steuart to Tullibardine, 21 Oct. 1697; *The Blind Harper*, 219–21;

Martin, *Western Islands*, 27; M. Dilworth, 'The Scottish Mission in 1688-9', *IR*, xx (1969), 71; Dilworth, 'The Blind Harper and Catholicism', *ib.*, xxii (1971), 113-14; Blair, Atholl MSS, Box 29 I (9) 315, Seaforth to Tullibardine, 22 Sept. 1697.

149. The evidence of Glengarry's omission from the November 1685 list of exemptions from taking the Test is confirmed by Atholl's later claim that he had not corresponded with Glengarry, directly or indirectly, since his apostasy, since he was with him in Argyllshire in 1685. MacIain of Glencoe is also not named; but his clan's exploits that year made him seem more than usually a robber chief rather than a potential candidate for public office; and Chisholm of Knockfin, whose catholicism was inconspicuous, was also omitted. *RPCS*, xi, 213; *Est. Procs.*, ii, 163; Blair, Atholl MSS, Box 44/VI/173, [Atholl] to Lady Murray, [1693].

150. *Ib*; NLS MS 7014 fol. 6, Hill to Tweeddale, 14 Jan. 1692; *RPCS*, viii, 36, *ib.*, xi, 213.

151. *Ib; ib.*, xii, xxiii; *HMCR Buccleuch (Drumlanrig)*, i, 130, Tarbat's memorial, 1685; D. Warrand, *Some Mackenzie Pedigrees* (Inverness, 1965), 21-3, 28, 31; BL Add. 28,239 fol. 120, Countess of Seaforth to 'Gentlemen' [18th century]; Fountainhall, *Hist. Notices*, ii, 759.

152. *Ib.*, 735; *Eachann Bacach*, 66-70, Maighstir Seathan, 'Ge grianach an latha'; SCA, Blairs Letters, Box T, 57, Seaforth to L. Innes, 23 Aug. 1688; SRO GD 26/viii/39, Sir J. Maclean to Melfort, 12 Sept. 1689; *RPCS*, xiii, xlvii.

153. *Ib.*, xi, 213; MacWilliam, 'A Highland Mission', *IR*, xxiv, 77.

154. The priest David Burnet carried James's to Buchan in late 1690. Mackay, *Memoirs*, 289, Mackay to Melville, 15 Oct. 1689; SCA, Blairs Letters Box U, 1690, 2, Burnet to Innes, 27 May 1690; *ib.*, 18, same to same, 1/10 Oct. 1690; Cumnock, Dumfries House, Bute MSS, bundle A517/12, [Breadalbane] to [Dalrymple], 16 Nov. 1691.

155. *The Lockhart Papers*, ed. A. Aufrere, 2 vols. (London, 1817), i, 63; Childs, *The Army, James II & the Glorious Revolution*, 161.

156. Grant, *Macleods*, 204; *HMCR 11th Report* App. 7, 24, ? to [Seaforth], 22 Nov. 1688. Of course, some conversions, which brought worldly loss, were presumably sincere. *Seafield Correspondence from 1685 to 1708*, ed. J. Grant (SHS, 1912), 42-3, Earl of Findlater to James Ogilvie, 18 June 1688.

157. *RPCS*, xiii, xxvii, xxxvi; *Siege*, 5; NLS MS 1384 fol. 20, Ae. Macpherson to Delvine, 19 Dec. 1685; Fountainhall, *Hist. Notices*, ii, 713, 759, 762.

158. *Ib.*, 767; *HMCR Laing*, i, 443, Perth to James, 29 Dec. 1685; NUL, Portland MSS, PwA 2161, James Johnston to ?, 23 May 1688; Macpherson, *Loyall Dissuasive*, 151-7 (chronology muddled).

159. *Ib.*, 165.

160. For another, *RPCS*, xii, xxvi; NUL, Portland MSS, PwA 2120, spy's letter, 21 Dec, 1687; *ib.*, 2149, same, Mar. 1688.

161. *RPCS*, xiii, xxxix; *Memoirs of Locheill*, 220-8; Fountainhall, *Hist. Notices*, ii, 787, 840; Stevenson, *Alasdair MacColla*, 295; SRO GD 1/658, 35, 180-1.

162. *Siege*, 8-11.

163. *RPCS*, xiii, xxvii, xxxv, xliv, xlviii; Fountainhall, *Hist. Notices*, ii, 852, 869; SRO GD 1/658, 34; *Memoirs of Locheill*, 229, 231.

164. *Ib.*, 230-1.

165. *Mackintosh Muniments*, 140, Commission of Fire & Sword, 23 Feb. 1688; NLS MS 295 fol. lv, 'Information of the grounds of the differences betwixt ... MacIntosh and Keppoch', [1695].

166. Both sides overestimated enemy numbers. *Ib.*, fol. 2; *RPCS*, xiii, ix; *ib.*, 299-300, Suddie Mackenzie to Sir W. Paterson, to General Douglas, 3 Aug. 1688; *ib.*, Mackintosh to

Perth, 3 Aug. 1688; *ib.*, 352, 354; SRO GD 112/40/3/4/56, Carwhin to Breadalbane, 18 Aug. 1688.

167. McBane, *The Expert Sword Man's Companion*, 76–7; *Memoirs of Locheill*, 229–30; Maclean, 'Celtic Sources', 237–41, Iain Lom's son, 'Latha Raon-Ruairidh'; Macdonald, *Clan Donald*, ii, 644–5; Mackintosh, *Mackintoshes*, 281–2; SRO PC 1/51, 380; NLS MS 295 fol. 2, 'Information'.

168. Blair, Atholl MSS, Box 29 I (9) 281, Keppoch to Tullibardine, 12 Aug. 1697.

169. *Memoirs of Locheill*, 230; Cpt. J. Creichton & Jonathan Swift, *Memoirs of Captain John Creichton*, Swift, *Miscellaneous and Autobiographic Pieces*, ed. H. Davis (Oxford, 1962), 160–1.

170. *Ib.*, 161; *RPCS*, xvi, 90; Maclean, 'Celtic Sources', 242–3, Aonghus Mac Alasdair Ruaidh, 'Deoch-Slainte Colla na Ceapaich'; SRO GD 112/40/3/56–7, Carwhin to Breadalbane, 18 Aug. 1688; GD 170/629/10, Breadalbane to Barcaldine, 24 Aug. 1688; *ib.*, 12, same to Straiton, 24 Aug. 1688.

171. Lenman, *Jacobite Risings*, 28–9; Balcarres, *Memoirs*, 6–8; Fountainhall, *Hist. Notices*, ii, 877; *RPCS*, xiii, xxvi.

172. *Ib.*, xxv–xxvi, 1; *Melvilles & Leslies*, iii, 192, Notes of events in 1688; *Siege*, 11–13.

173. *RPCS*, xiii, x; SRO GD 112/40/3/4/58, Perth to Breadalbane, 22 Sept. 1688.

174. Balcarres, *Memoirs*, 11–12; C. S. Terry, *John Graham of Claverhouse, Viscount Dundee* (London, 1905), 233–5.

175. *RPCS*, xiii, lii, 355–6; *Chiefs of Grant*, ii, 27, Gordon to Grant, 2 Nov. 1688; Tullibardine, *Military History*, 29; SRO GD 112/40/3/4/59, 61, 62, Perth to Breadalbane, 1, 19, 31 Oct. 1688.

176. *Ib.*, 64, same to same, 14 Nov. 1688; *Memoirs of Locheill*, 231; *RPCS*, xiii, xxiii, xxvi, li, 352, 354; 'The Camerons in the '15', *TGSI*, xxvi, 66.

177. *Ib; RPCS*, xiii, 349–50, 355–6, 360.

178. *Ib.*, xii, 364–5; Balcarres, *Memoirs*, 13–15; *Melvilles & Leslies*, iii, 192, Notes of events in 1688; SRO GD 112/40/3/4/66, Breadalbane to D. Campbell, 1 Dec. 1688; *Letters from James, Earl of Perth*, ed. W. Jerdan (Camden Society, 1845), 7–8, Perth to Melfort, 31 Dec. 1688.

179. *Ib.*, 8–9; *Siege*, 16–17; 'The Camerons in the '15', *TGSI*, xxvi, 66; *Memoirs of Locheill*, 231–2.

180. Stewart, *The Stewarts of Appin*, 133, memorandum; SRO GD 26/viii/102, Tutor of Appin to Macnachtan for James & Melfort, [Sept. 1689].

4

'The Last and Best of Scots'
(December 1688–July 1689)

On 10 December, after Perth's flight, the Council added several members, including Breadalbane, to their Secret Committee, who at once disinterestedly voted themselves £400 sterling each. That evening, the guards at Holyrood Abbey fired against some rioting youths, killing a few — including, ironically, young Maclean of Coll, who would otherwise have fought for James six months later. Four Privy Councillors, Atholl, Breadalbane, Tarbat and Dalrymple, signed an order for the city forces to disarm them, and, after some fighting, the mob sacked the Abbey. The Council, meeting under Atholl's presidency on the 12th, commissioned Breadalbane to go and explain the 'most unaccountable' riot to James.[1]

Although this proved the decisive step in the Revolution in Scotland, the Council intended it as a demonstration to James that he must abandon his catholic ministers and policies and return to employing 'natural' Scottish political leaders. They expected a compromise, with James retaining the throne but William having a major say in British affairs. All factions therefore courted Sir John Dalrymple, who, with Tarbat, carried up a letter urging James to call a free parliament, because his father Stair was with the Prince. Yet, even by the time Breadalbane left on 17 December, the situation was changing dramatically.[2] James's first flight, return and final escape gave the Council's continuous activity a different meaning. Most of them accepted a prospective change of kings with apparent indifference. They sent William an address on 24 December urging him to call a free parliament.[3] The Earl of Mar was committed involuntarily by imprisoning the captured Perth at Stirling Castle, on the Council's order. Going south in January, he left a recently intruded loyalist deputy in charge, and had declared neither way, but he must anticipate James's anger for imprisoning his chief Scottish minister.[4]

The nobles progressively disregarded past constitutional 'principles' as the intense rivalry between them made each hope to exploit the political vacuum to establish a monopoly of power. The main struggle, between Atholl, temporarily in control of the government, and Queensberry, still without even a Council seat, began as soon as Perth fled.[5] Its most drastic effect was on control of the Castle. The Duke of Gordon was poorly supplied with ammunition and provisions. His 120-strong garrison was always close to mutiny, and his attempt to supplement them with some of his own highlanders caused such alarm in Edinburgh that he had to abandon it. From mid-December, the Council was demanding that he surrender the Castle. With James's cause apparently collapsing for good, Gordon considered restoring the Castle to the Governor deprived in 1686, Queensberry. A majority of the Council would have endorsed it, but Atholl, as he himself wrote, wrecked the plan rather than see his rival benefit. From factiousness he named a rival candidate, and Gordon wrote to James and then William for orders. It was Atholl's fault that, when he and the rest abandoned Edinburgh, the Castle was still in catholic hands.[6]

It was obvious from the start that power and office would be obtained only in London, and most Councillors left immediately, despite the increasing chaos in Scotland. Atholl temporarily delayed, hoping to enhance his reputation with William as the noble patriot sacrificing personal interest to protect the nation. However, his friends warned him that only his presence in London would benefit him. Breadalbane, the most pressing, wrote frankly; 'I am convinced . . . it uer proper for ye good of the Cuntree yor Lop uer ther, but yr relations desyring it as yor oun particular advantage . . . , I uish yor lop uas her'. Atholl immediately altered his policy. When the Edinburgh authorities warned him and other Privy Councillors on 31 December and 1 January that a multitude of the Cameronians who were then ejecting episcopalian ministers in the West were planning to march on Edinburgh, they replied that, not being a quorum, they could not give orders or advice. On 8 January Atholl went, leaving a successor whose commands nobody obeyed.[7] The country was almost totally without government. The College of Justice, the conservative body of lawyers, maintained order in Edinburgh, but William's Declaration for a Convention, read on 13 February, ordered their disbandment.[8]

Meanwhile, in England James's rule had collapsed with unbelievable suddenness. Having advanced in mid-November to Salisbury to join his army, he was panic-stricken by the rapid desertion of officers, and retreated, abandoned by others including Queensberry's son Lord Drumlanrig, the 'proto-rebel' among the Scots. Leaving his army stationed west of London, James opened negotiations with William, while many of his favourites fled to France, Melfort first. Driven by exaggerated fears of murder or execution, James himself disastrously attempted to flee on 11 December, leaving the army and administration without a head, and was ignominiously captured. Returning to Whitehall, he was forced by William to retire to Rochester, and on the 22nd escaped to France. In January, Seaforth jumped bail (given by William's general, Mackay) in London when ordered to join him.[9]

The most significant Scottish loyalist remaining in England was Colonel John Graham of Claverhouse, recently created a major-general and Viscount Dundee, a distant relation of the great Montrose. He had first served under the Prince of Orange, whose ingratitude to him probably strengthened his later Jacobitism with personal feeling — the case with several of William's notable opponents.[10] He received a Scottish commission in 1678, and wrote that few men had 'toyld so much for honor as I have don, thogh it has been my misfortun to atteen but a small shear'. Yet his service until 1688 against the south-western Presbyterians consisted chiefly of inglorious and often dirty duties. Like his Cavalier generation, he believed in the policy of repression, and unhesitatingly enforced it, becoming a black legend among the Covenanters. But, unlike most 'Cavaliers', he showed, here and in his political career (which was built, like those of greater men, on plundering the fallen Maitlands), the virtues of his principles: some concern for acting within the law, willingness to forego financial benefits to make royal policy a success, and the courage which led him to challenge Queensberry at the height of his power. James, whose patronage had enabled Claverhouse to form a regiment of horse, automatically supported the magnate against a subordinate. Claverhouse was rehabilitated only when Perth and Melfort turned against Queensberry, and, since his ambitions gave them no cause for jealousy, his alliance with them still existed at the Revolution.

Dundee took part in the futile Salisbury campaign, and may have advised James vainly to fight, see William personally or retire to Scotland. However, around Reading on 9–10 December the Scots Army failed to reverse the tide, and Dundee himself, perhaps hesitant from fear of treachery, acted feebly.[11] On 11 December, as the scattered army, deserted by James, necessarily applied to William, Dundee, with Lord Livingstone, commander of the troop of Guards, and Atholl's most fervently loyalist son Lord Dunmore, Colonel of the dragoons, wrote from Watford vainly asking his leave to march the Scottish force home.[12]

The events from mid-December until the start of Dundee's rising are usually treated as if his final course was long predictable and planned. In fact, his intentions remained fluid for some time. Not only his alleged conference with James at Rochester but the story that James gave him and Balcarres charge over Scottish affairs about 17 December are false. Balcarres' own memoirs indicate that James's first instructions to them came at the start of February.[13] Balcarres himself was not the paragon he later implied; he frequently attended on William, and on 31 January applied indirectly for an English peerage.[14]

Therefore, when a meeting of Scots notables in early January formally asked William to assume the administration and summon a convention, Dundee avoided attending and opposing, not merely from prudence, lest William detain him in England, but from uncertainty. In case James's cause was permanently ruined, he checked that he would be unmolested if he lived quietly in Scotland without swearing allegiance. William emphasised that his policy was to drive nobody to desperation by refusing the exiles' first demand that five men — Queensberry, Tarbat, Lord Advocate Mackenzie, Dundee and Balcarres — should be permanently incapacitated from office.[15]

The news that James allowed them to attend a convention and was himself crossing to Ireland gave Dundee and Balcarres their cue. Their first duty was unpleasant. Both were Melfort's allies; but the hostile reception his signature drew upon James's letters to the English convinced them that the King must leave him in France. They sent this advice to James and Melfort himself, with a conciliatory letter promising reforms for James to send to the Convention. Then, evading pressure to promise William support, both returned to Scotland. Part of Dundee's troop defiantly escorted him. William intended the regiment, with the Guards and Dunmore's dragoons, for a force to secure Ireland, but it disintegrated.[16]

Unlike Dundee, most Scots (and English) politicians about London then acted from self-interest, shifting allegiance shamelessly in blundering pursuit of their ambitions. The Earl of Annandale, who changed sides five times in five months, was exceptional; but the Scots Commander-in-Chief, Lieutenant-General Douglas, Queensberry's brother, nearly matched him in inconsequential treason. The rotten English officer corps corrupted him in November, and he suggested to Dundee that they should change sides. Yet his Scots Guards' desertion to William humiliatingly defied the pattern, set by English regiments, of losing nearly all their officers and almost no men. Douglas's officers remained loyal while his men, embittered by his maltreatment, revolted despite him. He took service under William; but, coming to Edinburgh early in 1689, he conspicuously drank James's health, promised Dundee to make atonement, and was briefly imprisoned by the Convention. Returning to London, he again became a Williamite, notorious for plundering in Ireland. Yet his reasons were not entirely cynical, including admiration for William as a soldier and, surprisingly, a desire to atone for his activities against the Covenanters, which made him champion the Scots–Irish presbyterian forces.[17]

William himself greatly increased the confusion by two major, often overmastering, characteristics. He shared his uncles' monarchical prejudices and fear of revolutionaries, and felt, as Charles's legitimate heir, entitled to his entire prerogative, though conscientiously obliged to use it better. Therefore, despite his propaganda against 'evil counsellors', he was anxious wherever possible to retain the pre-Revolution ministers in office, even (had they accepted him) the Scottish bishops. This obsession affected his Scottish policy for several years. Partly in consequence, he showed violent, often wildly imprudent, resentment against those supporters who demanded office and rewards as their right for services in the Revolution. Whigs and Presbyterians naturally suffered most; but the first Scottish victim was Atholl. He had seemed ready to accept the change of kings; but when, arriving in London, he mistakenly sought William's favour by exploiting his actions on the Privy Council and his wife's Nassau descent, he was rebuffed so violently that he began to commit himself to the Jacobites.[18]

His role was assumed by his lowland counterpart, the Duke of Hamilton, another magnate who, largely from political incompetence and a hectoring personality, had failed throughout the changes of Charles's and James's reigns to gain real political power. After conspicuously changing sides three times in London during the invasion, he chaired the meeting of Scottish notables which asked William to call a convention. His episcopalian and his Duchess's presbyterian connections made him in some respects an appropriate chief agent. His demands for favours, like Atholl's, alienated William; but the King did not openly show this until the autumn, by which time Hamilton had committed himself still further by his services. The delay was probably crucial: despite frequent (and often justified) fury at William's treatment of him, he seems never to have intrigued with the Jacobites.[19]

Cynics might argue that he had no need. His eldest son, the courtier Earl of Arran, made an unsupported plea for James's restoration at the meeting of notables, was arrested in February, and remained in the Tower until November.[20] He was to be a Jacobite leader in both kingdoms. This seemed to exemplify the Scottish aristocratic tradition of balancing during civil wars. 'As for my Lord

Arron', snarled Melfort, 'if ye K. rely on ye old trick of father knave & son honest God have mercy.'[21] Yet the cynics' idea of fairly overt Master of Ballantrae pacts overlooks immense differences between cases. In one sense, William himself was protecting Stuart family rights from the republicanism James's folly had aroused, but they hardly acted in collusion. In lesser families also, choice of sides might reflect personal hostility between magnates and their heirs. Arran's revolt was against Hamilton's laborious way of life, rebuilding the family fortunes. His Jacobitism, like his previous Court place, was partly an excuse for not settling down responsibly. It was unconsciously collusive on Arran's side, in that he could afford his Jacobite zeal, which left St Germain in 1702 with the ruinous illusion that he was the movement's Bayard, because 'his' estates were safe from confiscation in his parents' possession, and because Hamilton, who several times prevented his arrest at crises, and his father-in-law Sunderland could obtain his personal pardon.[22] He became generally more cautious after succeeding as Duke; yet his unpredictable contortions in Anne's reign to avoid jeopardising real or illusory Hamilton interests in four countries show that conscious attempts at balancing could ultimately be self-defeating.

This applied also when the division was between family members. Magnates like Hamilton were intriguers, but usually also undisciplined, violent-tempered and blindly reacting into opposition, politically short-sighted, and ambitious for power and profit for themselves, not their posterity, changing sides in 1688–9 as shamelessly as those without sons to exploit. Whatever the theoretical future safety of a divided family (and it had not ultimately saved either of the Argylls), it was usually a grave present liability. Accusations of 'ye old trick' were among the most effective weapons enemies could use to deny its members political advancement. This was clear to Hamilton, whose family connections of all religious and political shades made him particularly vulnerable.[23] This Namierite malignity was ignored at lower levels, where Colonel John Buchan served against his Jacobite brother Major-General Thomas throughout 1690 without arousing alarm.

Different degrees of unconscious or conscious collusion doubtless existed, and family members would exploit divisions they did not create. Queensberry, forestalled by Atholl in Scotland and Hamilton in London, openly leaned towards the Jacobites, but privately, through Drumlanrig at Court, he assured William that he would (indirectly) work for him by supporting Union. Yet differing attitudes were to cause a genuine breach in the family's solidarity at the crisis of the Montgomerie Plot.[24]

Breadalbane followed an opposite course to Queensberry. He obtained an audience with William; he signed the notables' address; and he later claimed that Stair recommended him as the fittest man to be Chancellor. This alienated Hamilton, who had earmarked that office (among others) for himself. His hostility probably helped alienate Breadalbane from the nobles' proceedings. He returned to Scotland, and advised the bishops not to attend the Convention.[25] Tarbat, as one of the five men proposed for incapacitating, naturally kept his Jacobite links, writing to James in France even before Dundee, and later to Ireland — both times advising him to dismiss Melfort. However, when he found that William trusted his presbyterian cousin Lord Melville, whose life he had saved in 1683, he applied himself to win the King's favour and strengthen his regime. William naturally admired so shrewd and cultivated an upholder of episcopacy and aristocracy, and, after Hamilton imprudently frightened him from Edinburgh in June, constantly took his advice and seriously considered him for Secretary.[26]   It was certainly unfortunate that William should choose a confidant who, that spring, in guilty terror, 'stood up in Parliamt confessing ... that he had been ane ill man; crying out was there no mercy for a penitent siner?' However, he was the only adviser who fully realised the threat the highlanders, particularly the western clans alienated by the prospect of Argyll's restoration, might pose to the new regime, and the possibility of keeping them peaceful by a distribution of money.[27] It was becoming clear, despite Hamilton's and Stair's mistaken opposition, that troops must be sent to Scotland, since the time when Gordon 'was willing to surrender' the Castle 'to anybody' had been let slip. William ordered down by land Dunmore's former dragoons, now under the Dutch-born Scot Sir Thomas Livingston. Many officers and men, including their Lieutenant-Colonel, William Livingstone, were determined not to serve against James.[28] Major-General Hugh Mackay was ordered to ship the three Scottish regiments of the Anglo-Dutch Brigade, his own, Balfour's and Ramsay's (still paid from England) to Leith. They had a very high reputation; but William's transfers of seasoned soldiers to fill up his Dutch regiments left them only at one third strength, 1100 in all. Presumably at Tarbat's prompting, Mackay approached Gordon's former agent Sir Aeneas Macpherson, whom the Revolution had plunged into poverty, allegedly offering him a colonel's commission if he would persuade Cluny to join the Grants in supporting William. He refused.[29]

In fact, the first steps in planning a highland rising were already being taken, encouraged by events in Ireland. The catholic Lord Deputy, Tyrconnell, had, while temporising with William, raised an enormous catholic army and consolidated his hold on the country. However, since late 1688 the Ulster Protestants, most of whom had strong Scottish links, had been preparing for self-defence against supposed papist aggression. In December, the gates of Londonderry had been shut against the Earl of Antrim — the head of the Irish Macdonells, brother and successor of the Marquess who had organised Alasdair's expedition to Scotland in 1644. There was no immediate retaliation, and by late February, when the Protestants' over-confident volunteers controlled most of Ulster, it seemed they might be too strong to attack. Yet some Scottish Macdonalds sent to Antrim, who had partly maintained the old links, offering, if Irish troops were shipped to their aid, to raise 25,000 men to join them. Their exaggeration backfired: Tyrconnell 'desird and prest my lord of Antrim to make use of his interest in the highlands of Scotland, to prevaill with them to send over hither 1500 men to assist the popish pairty to reduce the north of Ireland'.[30]

Meanwhile, in February and March, Lochiel was organising a rising. Private interest as well as principles prompted him. Argyll's restoration would not ruin him, as it would the Macleans, but he would lose his independent regality and ownership of Sunart and Ardnamurchan. However, that alone would scarcely have made him take the risk of plotting when he had no idea even where James was. He consulted first with Glengarry, then with the Tutor of Clanranald in Moidart, finally with the leading Maclean gentry in Mull, since young Sir John was abroad. Argyll's activities in Argyllshire, raising men to 'protect' the forthcoming Convention, emphasised the danger. Nothing could be done while the country was buried under snow; so they appointed a rendezvous for 18 May, on Lochiel's lands in Lochaber.[31] However, the appalling weather did not prevent the men of Glencoe, reinforced from Lochaber to a strength of 2–300, from setting out in February to plunder their co-religionist Perth's unprotected estates.[32]

Other Macdonalds behaved similarly, with more excuse. Keppoch, when Dundee met him on 1 May outside Inverness, had not, as Balhaldie supposed, been sent there deliberately by other chiefs. He and his followers may have lived by raiding all winter: the loss of their corn and cattle left them little choice. They were certainly in arms by mid-March. Gordon proposed including them in an indemnity, and Inverness sent representatives to ask the Convention for means to defend the town against them. And, though James's government had devastated Keppoch's lands, this realignment meant that he would, at least nominally, support James. In late March, Perth's chamberlain, wiser than his master, urged him to raid Strathearn Williamites to persuade wavering gentry that a Jacobite rebellion was possible.[33]

A far more important ally, Gordon, altogether failed to act. He might possibly have surrendered the Castle in February but for Dundee and Balcarres. Early in March, a messenger from France called Brady brought him verbal instructions to leave the garrison under his deputy and retire to the North to await orders to raise his men. However, he had nothing written; Melfort had, perhaps deliberately, mislaid the instructions, and Gordon would not obey without them. He could argue truthfully that only his personal authority prevented a surrender. This unimaginative dutifulness was convenient for his own safety from both sides.[34]

The ungoverned nation had remained fairly orderly because both sides were concentrating on elections for the Convention. James's supporters, relying chiefly on pressure from above, were disappointed almost everywhere, outside the North. Even Dundee burgh elected a strong Presbyterian, to the fury of its Viscount-Provost. The bulk of the nobility, which outnumbered either barons or burghs, were conservative and might have redressed this result. However, Dundee and Balcarres could not inform enough of them of James's authorisation to attend, and others still dared not come even to serve James — constant straining of the letter of the law in prosecutions under Charles and James now brought its just punishment. Yet Dundee, James's most vigorous manager, won back others by promises that James would grant reforms and dismiss Melfort from office.[35]

When the Convention met on 14 March, the revolutionaries had brought into Edinburgh well over a thousand armed 'Cameronians' from Glasgow and the West and Argyll's highlanders, nominally under the command of Melville's son the Earl of Leven. Obviously, at crucial moments they would overawe the Convention: equally obviously, but for their presence Dundee's troopers and the many officers and soldiers who had straggled back from England to Edinburgh would have done so.[36] Some forfeited Williamites, Argyll in particular, took their seats. Nearly all the peers who were to be prominent in Jacobite activity attended; but Breadalbane, although he came to Edinburgh, pretended to be ill to avoid sitting.[37] Hamilton was the Williamite candidate for President. As Queensberry had not yet returned, and failed to get the Convention delayed for his convenience, James's supporters had to nominate Atholl. Atholl himself, though already reacting into Jacobitism, would not become the official leader of opposition to William, and his personal following's vote helped secure Hamilton's victory.[38]

The Convention immediately summoned Gordon to surrender. He had just purged his mutinous garrison, had received no orders from James, and even some Jacobites were advising him to capitulate. That night he gave his brother-in-law the Earl of Dunfermline, who was leaving the Convention, an authorisation to raise the Gordon vassals in the North for the king and to use his money and horses. Yet the next day he offered reasonable terms for surrender. Dundee and Balcarres hastily sent him, as he had demanded, a signed declaration that his holding out was vital for James's service, and he wrecked the negotiation by demanding that the indemnity he had requested be extended to all the highland clans, particularly Keppoch.[39]

On 16 March came the decisive moment. A messenger, Crane, appeared with a letter from James — though without an advance copy for the loyalists. Gambling everything on the presumption that he would satisfy grievances, they let Hamilton read a smooth letter from William, and signed an agreement not to dissolve the Convention. Gordon, doubtless by arrangement, threatened, atypically, to bombard the city — a hint of mailed fist to supplement the expected velvet promises. Then the letter was read, and shattered James's party. The warnings to James against carrying him to Ireland had led Melfort to suppress all Dundee's and Balcarres' letters — including their draft to be sent to the Convention. He himself scribbled the replacement aboard ship at Brest, at top speed without time for thought or revision. The letter was largely patriotic blarney, offered no concessions but a parliament to fulfil James's existing 'promises' and pardon to all returning to duty by 31 March, and modulated into unmistakably Melfordian threats of 'infamy and disgrace . . . in this world and the Condemnation due to the Rebellious in the nixt'. The Convention was lost.[40]

The sole consolation was that the letter and Crane confirmed that James was bound for Ireland. Empowered by a more rational letter which he sent ahead, the remaining loyalists decided to withdraw and establish a rival convention at Stirling to act as a rallying-point until he could arrive. The Earl of Mar was willing to protect them, from Stirling Castle. Atholl, growing more vigorous in the Jacobite cause now that he would not have to lead, offered to raise his highlanders to guard them, and Dundee believed, from what Lord Murray had said at London, that he would second his father. He himself had a special reason for going — evidence of a Cameronian plot to murder him and Lord Advocate Mackenzie, which the Convention had pointedly disregarded. A rendezvous was set for Monday 18 March. Tarbat, by his own account, set himself to destroy the conspiracy, and won back several of those involved. Atholl at the last moment demanded another day's delay. The others agreed, and prepared to attend the Convention to be less conspicuous. However, Dundee, not having been informed, appeared in the Canongate with fifty horsemen and, having arranged to meet others outside Edinburgh, would not change his plans — probably wisely. Checking that the Convention was determined not to answer James's letter, he marched down Leith Wynd. That evening, Lord Livingstone and others followed him.[41]

Dundee climbed the rock at the west side of the Castle and spoke with Gordon outside the postern. He reported the disastrous reception of James's letter, but what followed is uncertain. Gordon, much later, claimed that Dundee said 'he designed to go to the King in Ireland', and that he himself then suggested a convention at Stirling, to be guarded by 'Capuch with his Highlanders who was yn in Arms for the K:'. Gordon was certainly partly mistaken. Yet Dundee may have considered, if the loyalists failed to follow him to Stirling, retiring to Ireland — one report mentions his asking the Convention for a pass — and Gordon's mention of Keppoch may have been the first time that he heard the Lochaber clans seriously suggested as potential supporters. It is not clear whether Gordon made any specific promises to hold out until, or Dundee to relieve him before, a definite date. Dundee rode off towards Queensferry.[42]

When the news reached the Convention, Hamilton immediately had the doors locked, and the Cameronians mustered. Leven within two hours raised a first-class regiment of 800 men to blockade the Castle, filled chiefly with western Whigs.[43] Hamilton produced a letter from the Ulster leaders, the first mention of possible danger from the Highlands. An irregular committee of members with highland interests was appointed to make a report. Breadalbane was included, evidently in the hope that this would draw him into attending and supporting the Convention. The next day, the militia and fencible men were ordered to make ready.[44]

Dundee spent the night at Linlithgow, evidently awaiting other loyalists — a fatal delay. Mar left Edinburgh, possibly with the Convention's warrant, but God knows with what intentions. A Cameronian guard under William Cleland arrested him. While he was detained 'sick' at Edinburgh, Tarbat arranged for his Whig relative Erskine of Alva to go that night in his place. Therefore, although Stirling town was believed hostile to the Revolution, when Dundee arrived on the 19th, Alva kept both it and the Castle firm against him. He had no immediate alternative policy. Livingstone, although he now retired to Glamis, wrote submissively to the Convention and failed to join Dundee when he rose. Dundee himself, accompanied by his troopers, rode home. At Dunblane, Drummond of Balhaldie met him with a report of his own father-in-law Lochiel's consultations among the clans. From then, at least, Dundee's main course was clear. However, the prolonged winter made it necessary to postpone action until as close as possible to the clans' rendezvous. This would give James time to send him formal powers from Ireland. He returned to his home near Dundee, where his wife was about to give birth, hoping to temporise with the Convention's summons.[45]

In the Convention, loyalist opposition had largely collapsed. Outside, plotting momentarily revived when Queensberry reached Edinburgh on 20 March, to find

Hamilton in full control. Dunmore, who accompanied him, roused his and Atholl's Jacobite side. Atholl took the lead in a wild project to make Gordon bombard Edinburgh until the Convention was forced to move elsewhere, causing chaos. Not surprisingly, Gordon refused without specific orders from James. At this, most of the true loyalists left Edinburgh. Queensberry and Atholl began to attend the Convention occasionally, avoiding controversial debates including James's forfaulture, but voting for making William King.[46] Gordon, meanwhile, continued negotiations for surrender really intended to emphasise that James was in Ireland. His ceremonial feu-de-joie for this on 22 March developed into the first major exchanges of fire with Leven's men. While sparing the city, he frequently fired on the suburbs, though hesitating to slaughter the Cameronians in their amateurish siege works.[47]

On the 25th, Mackay finally began to land his regiments at Leith and to relieve the western men, who were publicly thanked and marched home. The Estates commissioned him their general. Knowing of Mar's involvement with Dundee, he sent a detachment to Stirling, reinforcing it with Livingston's dragoons when they arrived. With more tact than he usually displayed, he persuaded Mar to accept a reliable garrison without showing him that he was distrusted. This finally won him over, and it was no risk when the Convention confirmed him in his post in April.[48] Other garrisons were investigated. The Bass was still loyal to James. The harsh reply to its original offer to submit needlessly prolonged its resistance until August. The Lieutenant-Governor of Dumbarton survived a security investigation, but a prisoner taken that summer warned that he was secretly purging the garrison of non-Jacobites, and in December he was dismissed.[49]

The certainty that James had landed in Ireland on 12 March produced a burst of energy. Muskets, pikes and ammunition were transferred from the magazine at Stirling to Glasgow and distributed in the south-western counties. Two Glasgow frigates, the *Pelican* and *Janet*, were armed to cruise on the coast. The militia was reorganised. Yet the possible danger from the Highlands was overlooked. The militia further north than Argyll and Perthshire was ignored. Leven's regiment, once relieved by Mackay, was sent into Fife, its task supposedly done. Most surprising of all, the representatives from Inverness were content to receive the money for arms to repel Keppoch indirectly in tax concessions, not immediately in cash. Clearly the Convention, when it declared Dundee a rebel on 30 March, had little idea what danger it was provoking.[50]

Dundee was not seriously troubled for nearly four weeks after his return home, and had time to consider his plans for starting and maintaining a war for James in Scotland. Although he could not yet know every relevant fact, the main points were mostly clear.

From Lochiel's message, he knew that he could primarily rely on the clans of Lochaber and the Isles, although a few individual chiefs might default (as, in the event, Macleod did). These were all medium-sized to small clans, and several which might be expected to join them from other parts, like the Macgregors, were marginal. The largest could not raise a thousand men. Tarbat emphasised in early

June that no magnates were actively involved, 'and some of these alone are of more interest then all who are engadged'. The latter, he estimated, could raise at the most 3–4,000 men, but would probably bring to the fields 2,500. This was an underestimate — Dundee at that moment had that number, though neither the Macleans nor the Macdonalds of Sleat had joined him — but certainly he had smaller total forces at his disposal than the commanders in the other major highland risings — Montrose's, Glencairn's, the '15 or the '45.[51] One common factor linking clans who rose was hostility to Argyll's restoration, which would harm them in various degrees — totally ruining the Macleans, depriving Lochiel of his new independence and large estates, once again exposing Clanranald and Glengarry to the combination of debt, superiorities and jurisdiction through which the familiar web might be woven about them. Another common factor was the surprising number of Jacobite chiefs under age — Clanranald, Sir John Maclean, Stewart of Appin, Robertson of Struan, Macdonald of Largie — which gave more experienced ones, especially Lochiel, great influence.[52] Some writers, therefore, rapidly conclude that Dundee's rising was doomed from the start, a mixture of bankrupts and schoolboys without the weight to change the obvious course of Scottish history; and dismiss it with graceful rhetoric on the fortunate leader whom a bullet at Killiecrankie killed before disillusionment could.

They are far too rapid. They quote Tarbat's conclusions, but overlook that his list of magnates 'in no wayes joined in it' includes Seaforth and Gordon, and Atholl whose people joined Dundee spectacularly two months later. 'Neutrality' was not unchangeable: both sides wrote reproachfully to Cluny, but the Macphersons wavered close to joining the Jacobites, twice at least sending them substantial contingents. A highland rising needed time to develop impetus. Dundee's successfully survived in June and early July the doldrums which might have destroyed it; and the victory at Killiecrankie brought a predictable rush of support, which Dundee's incompetent successors wasted.

Lochaber was a good cradle for a rising, but it was always obvious that it must expand or perish — probably from actual starvation. Although the harvest of 1688 had been fairly good, an extremely severe and long winter — there were heavy snowfalls even in late May — doomed the 1689 crop and disrupted the exchange of cattle for grain, on which the Highlands relied. Political instability naturally made this worse, and there was almost no bread left in Lochaber that autumn.[53] Ammunition also would be a problem: Dundee had only 50 lb of powder, and was making unsuccessful covert attempts to buy more from the seaports. He lacked money, and the sums later remitted from France did not reach him. All these problems would be reduced if the Jacobites could seize the lowland towns and take over the machinery of shire government, collecting revenue and levying men.[54]

There were three areas in northern Scotland where Dundee might obtain the additional strength necessary to sustain the rising. The most promising was the North-East, where he first concentrated his efforts — partly from necessity, since conditions in Lochaber, which endangered his precious handful of cavalry even in mid-May, delayed operations there.[55] If Gordon's vassals rose, Dundee would have an army. Half Montrose's battles had been fought in the North-East, partly

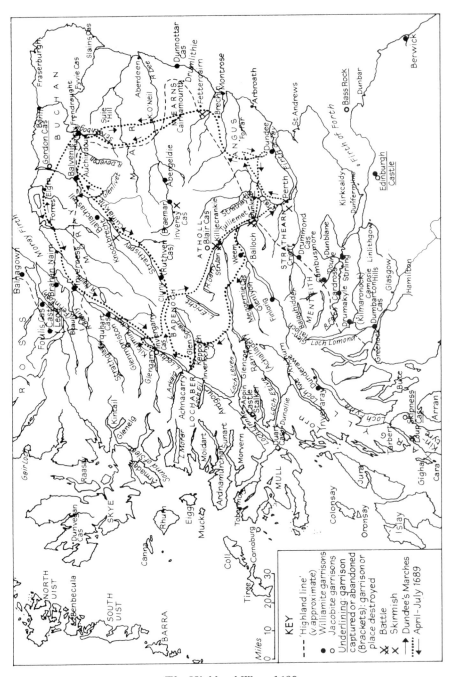

The Highland War, 1689

to secure the Gordon family's support. The lowland lairds there could furnish the vital mounted men his army would otherwise lack. A generation later, they provided the '15 with its military and financial base while the Lochaber clans were still hesitating. Religion was one main motive for this, since the area was strongly episcopalian, and remained so: the north-easterner Forbes of Culloden frankly defended presbyterianism as the religion of a revolutionary minority.[56] This motive at first worked against Dundee. Many Episcopalians remained neutral until it became clear that neither Parliament nor William would prevent the imposition of a bigoted presbyterian church. Mackay commented on the change between the North-East's passivity in 1689 and its Jacobite vigour in 1690.[57]

The North was the least promising. Seaforth was with James, which roused the anti-Mackenzie clans, the Rosses and Munros, under their presbyterian heads. The Mackenzies, in contrast, 'were not a stirring people at any time', as one prominent member, Sir Alexander Mackenzie of Coul, assured Mackay. There was a sharp difference between most of the Mackenzie gentry, who lived in the Lowlands, and Seaforth's highlanders in Wester Ross, particularly the wild Macraes of Kintail, and many gentry feared that a rebellion would encourage the common people to shake off all authority.[58] The only would-be Jacobite leader, the Master of Tarbat, an unstable convert, lacked any influence. The Dowager Countess's brother Tarbat worked from Edinburgh to quiet them, and told Mackay that, even if Seaforth returned, he could easily overturn his projects.[59] Further north, the ex-Covenanting Sutherland interest was organised for William by Lord Strathnaver, but the loyalist families which had then fought against it were no longer a counterbalance. Lord Reay was a minor under Williamite guardianship, and all Mackays supported the Major-General. The Earl of Caithness was insignificant. Only the constant troublemaker Sinclair of Dunbeath promised Dundee in June to raise 200 horse and 800 foot.[60]

The third area was Perthshire and Argyllshire. Atholl's intentions were now uncertain, but Dundee presumably received messages from some of his vassals. Breadalbane sent his promises of support by Carleton, a messenger he was dispatching to James with proposals including the restoration of Argyll. Dundee disapproved of most of them. Secretly, Breadalbane and Balcarres had instructed Carleton to press for Melfort's dismissal, and on reaching Dublin he falsely claimed Dundee's endorsement.[61] In mid-April, Breadalbane slipped away from Edinburgh to his estates without warning the Convention. Argyll and others wrote that his enemies would exploit this. Breadalbane probably did intend to join Dundee — if he could start a promising rising. If, however, like the late Argyll's, it merely provided another pretext for the Lochaber clans to plunder Argyllshire, he would oppose it. Argyll's departure for London as one of the delegation to offer the Crown to William forced the Argyllshire gentry to consult frequently about defence, and he took a vigorous part. Meanwhile, through his two most trusted subordinates, his chief chamberlain in Argyll, Campbell of Barcaldine, and his Edinburgh writer, Campbell of Carwhin, he maintained contact with local Jacobite clans and with lowland plotters.[62]

Dundee presumably grasped that Breadalbane's promises were conditional, but the possibility of his organising an alliance between loyal Campbells and other clans necessarily formed a major part of Jacobite strategy. If he failed, it was only a matter of time before Argyll united Argyllshire, cowing opponents, and raised a major Williamite force. The Lochaber clans would then face simultaneous advances by this and a regular army from different sides, and would not be strong enough to fight both — the actual situation which developed in July. To have some hope of success, Dundee needed accurate knowledge of government decisions; and Williamites complained that he and his successors received this constantly from Privy Councillors. William's first Council, appointed in May, contained few obvious sympathisers. Sir Hugh Campbell of Calder, who had married his son to Cluny Macpherson's daughter in March, was the chief suspect, although he had a strong and very recent grievance against James.[63]

Many lowland Jacobites sent Dundee promises, then or later, but almost none of them would dare to rise unless either his or James's army was present to protect them. The one possible exception was the Borders, where the debt-ridden Earl of Home and Sir Patrick Maxwell of Springkell vigorously plotted with lairds and moss-troopers. On the English side, many of James's inner court circle of Household officials and soldiers had strong family links in Northumberland and Cumberland, and came north in early 1689 to organise in preparation for his landing.[64] However, Montrose's example would warn Dundee against committing himself too far to Border allies. The English ones shot their bolt in March, and soon surrendered or drifted away for good. Home was arrested in June. The borderers were useful as a distraction to William's government, since their activities, mustering, riding armed, and cutting communications with England, revived at every crisis.[65] They could do no more in 1689, since from March onwards William quartered English and Dutch regiments along the English side, 8–9,000 men by late April.[66] These served as a pool of reinforcements for Scotland: Dundee's every success was penalised by the summoning of two or three experienced English regiments. Fortunately for his hopes, Scotland could not support a large English force. Scotland lacked hay, and English cavalry therefore could not operate until spring grass had grown without high losses of horses, while their infantry could not endure the Scottish standard of living, and retaliated by plundering.[67]

Even if Dundee could not reconquer Scotland by military means, by holding out and adding to the Scottish people's new burdens he helped create a disaffection which might cause the overthrow of William's government. It had been widely felt that Charles's and James's royal revenue was a crushing burden. The common people in many areas in 1688–9 assumed that taxes would now be abolished; and Tweeddale hoped that William would disband the standing army.[68] By degrees it became clear that the new regime demanded a far higher rate of permanent taxation — including one innovation of 1690, the Hearth Tax, just abolished as oppressive in England — from a nation impoverished by a harmful war with France. An enormous and destructive new standing army was raised, and yearly drafts of pressed men were shipped to Flanders for campaigns which, occasionally, the English claimed that the Scots were fighting only as auxiliaries.[69]

During Glencairn's rising, the '15 and the '45, both the executive government and legislature were in London — too distant to be overthrown save by miracles or English help. During Montrose's wars, the executive was totally controlled by the Estates. In 1689, however, one of the strongest Jacobite advantages was a breach between Parliament, no longer fettered by the Articles, and William's government. The prevailing party in the Convention, over-trustful of him, left a dangerous number of necessary reforms to his goodwill. Like the peers before them, the parliamentarians were disillusioned, by William's actions upon accepting the crown and by his appointments — Melville as sole Secretary, Sir John Dalrymple as Lord Advocate, his father Stair as President of the Session. In William's first Parliament that summer, held under Hamilton as inadequately instructed Commissioner, a mixture of frustrated radical principles and envy caused the majority of members, led by Sir James Montgomerie, baron for Ayrshire and the chief political influence on Argyll, to form the 'Club', a Scottish equivalent of the English 'Country Party'.[70] The latter was a loose parliamentary alliance supposedly defending traditional liberties against the encroachments of a corrupt Court, usually by negative means such as the refusal of supply.

A 'Country Party' was at its worst when facing the pressing emergencies of war, which the 'Court' automatically exploited to deny reforms and demand massive taxation. The 'Country' Opposition normally reacted by denying the existence of danger. In England, with the Channel and the Navy between them and the French, this might be plausible, but the 'Country' position drove the Club to discount the danger when there was civil war in Scotland. Club leaders holding commissions, including the experienced soldier Lord Ross, refused to leave Parliament to serve with their units. Even Killiecrankie was seen almost as a government trick to distract attention.[71] This, in turn, fed one of William's worst characteristics, his willingness to let Scottish affairs slide. He was by nature reluctant to make decisions and a bad administrator. His impatience burst out in the unforgivable remark that autumn to Hamilton: 'I believe you have a mind to be King of Scotland; I would you were'.[72] This division might at least prevent the grant of supplies for the army; if it developed it might even furnish the constitutional machinery for restoring James, a disaffected parliament.

Dundee also calculated on help from Ireland. In March, the 'Break of Dromore' shattered the Ulster Protestants' forces. As his armies advanced on Londonderry, James had apparently regained the initiative, and his first priority was to succour Scotland. In the event, the forces he succeeded in shipping over were trivial beside the Marquess of Antrim's semi-private expedition of 1644. But nobody, least of all James, could have believed that in March. His train included Seaforth; two young highlanders recruited in France, Sir John Maclean, and Donald Macdonald of Sleat bound for the wars in Hungary; some minor catholic nobles; and, unfortunately, Melfort.[73] His presence confirmed hostile Scots' conviction that James was incorrigible and alienated waverers like Atholl. He quarrelled bitterly even with fellow-Jacobites in Ireland, Seaforth and Gordon's in-laws.[74] From the start, James and he were determined to cross almost immediately to Scotland — or even England — with an army. Modern historians agree with the neglected Irish, in whom this inspired contempt for James and burning hatred for Melfort. Yet, wrong in most lesser matters, they were probably right in this. Although their incompetence increased the chaos, the basic problem in Ireland was structural, and insoluble: the vital technical skills needed to make the kingdom defensible had been monopolised by Protestants, who had now fled. William in England faced administrative confusion and a major reaction against him, neither likely to last, but temporarily as grave as James's problems: possibly, whichever king pushed first might overthrow the other.

Unfortunately, the first definite Scottish news which James received in March was sent at that misleading moment when Atholl was a violent Jacobite and Mar seemed about to declare for him.[75] Therefore, the mass of letters and orders which Brady carried back rested on optimistic illusions. The loyalists were to rise and form regiments under Lieutenant-General Dundee, to protect a loyal Convention meeting at Stirling. Once Ireland was in order, he would send 5,000 men. Balcarres was to raise two regiments in Fife. Gordon was given the choice of staying in the Castle or going to raise his vassals as Lord Lieutenant of the North. Atholl and other magnates (many of them Williamites) were ordered to raise their followers, chiefs their clans. James's English borderer courtiers were to co-operate. A general proclamation offered to pardon all except those who voted against James in the Convention, came over with William, or remained obdurate now. To Dundee and Balcarres, however, he promised to 'let the ancient Cavalier party know that they are the only true basis the monarchy can rest upon in Scotland; and wee have found such effects of our mercy in times past, as will make us now raise our friends, upon the ruine of our ennemys'.[76]

None of these letters reached their destinations, and James's cause never fully recovered.[77] Brady, who was directed to go to Dundee and Balcarres, was captured with his papers at Greenock early in April. Mackay had already sent Sir Thomas Livingston to seize Dundee, but Balcarres and some Fife neighbours with whom he was plotting were arrested and brought to Edinburgh. When the Convention considered the evidence on 18 April, they were roused to hysteria by a passage from Melfort's letter to him: 'Experience has Convinced Our Master that some folks Must be Made Gibeonitts And that ther are Great men Most be made Examples of Which you and I hav thought Long to Deserv it'. Gibeonites were hereditary 'hewers of wood and drawers of water', and the Convention under Hamilton hysterically assumed that Melfort and Balcarres had planned their destruction. Queensberry saved him by arguing that Melfort perhaps intended the letter to be captured and ruin Balcarres. Balcarres, expecting retaliation for his attempts to remove Melfort, himself believed this.[78]

Although Melfort did sometimes self-deceivingly harm the Jacobite cause to damage his rivals, the charge was groundless. He might well expect Balcarres, with other Cavaliers, to want a clean sweep, unlike 1661, of all who, Dundee later wrote anxiously, 'long at the King's restoration to have a Lauderdale to destroy Middleton and poor suffering cavaliers'.[79] Melfort, besides, was obsessed with punishment for traitors and rewards for loyalists, subjects on which his letters dwelt whoever the recipient. His incredible self-deception, envy and malice were expressed in a vivid and effective style — he was a master of the unforgettable and unforgivable phrase. His only Scottish rival in this combination of savage thought and brilliant style was Sir John Dalrymple, and it is no coincidence that they have the worst reputations among even late seventeenth century Scottish politicians. Their clarity condemns them. The lesson of this incident, that bloodthirsty expressions in letters do not necessarily reflect the recipient's sentiments, throws light on what Dalrymple wrote to Breadalbane in late 1691.

Brady's capture hastened preparations for defence. On 18 April, a levy was ordered from the shire militia of 500 horsemen to form ten troops. Volunteers raised two more, and Lord Cardross a six-troop dragoon regiment. Offers were accepted from five west-country peers and Argyll, Mar, Grant and Strathnaver to raise infantry regiments — all 600 strong except the young Earl of Angus's at 1200.[80] More immediately, however, there was a lack of available troops, and a refugee Irish company was ordered on 24 April 'to marche and clear the braes of Stirling shyre of lowse and ill affected men, . . . And therafter . . . to serve as a garisone in Drumond casle'. The establishment of a garrison actually attracted raiders — an effect which soon became familiar. Yet the Convention did not think it necessary to conciliate highlanders who might be wavering (unlike William, who was willing to distribute £5–6,000 among them), and the Committee which governed from 30 April planned merely to summon the chiefs to give the usual bond.[81]

Already, in mid-April, Dundee, accompanied by 50–60 horsemen, had raised James's standard outside the town of Dundee and ridden off for the North-East. Sir Thomas Livingston's dragoons arrived a day too late to arrest him. Lady Dundee, in entertaining the officers, discovered that Lieutenant-Colonel Livingstone and several others hoped to carry the regiment over to her husband, to whom she sent immediate word. He received it about 25 April at Forres, to which he had ridden through the North-East writing to potential supporters to join him, and instantly started back, sending the news to James. At the Cairnamounth Pass south of Dee, however, he intercepted letters showing that Mackay himself had joined the dragoons with several hundred men and was advancing. Although hopelessly outnumbered, Dundee waited until the last possible moment before returning north, and then feinted up the Dee as if he planned to dodge south past Mackay — intending, by delaying him, to give the north-eastern Jacobites additional time to raise their men.[82]

Mackay had grasped that the danger of invasion from Ireland was not immediate, and that Dundee might raise a formidable force from the Duke of Gordon's lands unless he was crushed — which, Mackay thought, would take a fortnight. Unaware of the dragoons' conspiracies, he left Lieutenant-Colonel Livingstone with two troops in Dundee to overawe the disaffected shire, and advanced with 450 men — 200 fusiliers from the Brigade, the rest of Livingston's dragoons and Colchester's newly-arrived English cavalry regiment, which was soon largely immobilised by bleak Scottish conditions. Atholl and Mar promised to prevent hostile movement on his highland flank. He hoped that Grant would hold the line of the Spey, trapping Dundee in the North-East, but Grant would not tear himself away in time from the Convention.[83]

Mackay was an able and experienced general. The contemporary opinion that he was a model subordinate but a hesitant independent commander, the apparent contrast between Dundee's rapid movements and Mackay's slower ones, and Killiecrankie have gained him a reputation as a plodder. In fact, in May and June he, on the whole, outgeneralled Dundee, thwarting his main aim of gaining control over the North-East, and sometimes making bold defensive stands with smaller forces. As William and the Council, fearing invasion, became increasingly doubtful about his protracted northern campaign, he confidently defended it.[84] This self-confidence shaded into extreme vanity. Even in his pious *Memoirs*, he emphasises the obvious intervention of Providence to bring about the two victories where he did not command, Dunkeld and Cromdale: his own successful skirmish at Perth alone was won by purely human means. Twice, before Killiecrankie and Dunkeld, this fault made him over-confident.[85] Writers emphasise the contrast between Dundee's considerable scruples over ravaging lands — rewarded by the concoction of atrocity stories — and the highlander Mackay's professional lack of hesitation in carrying out threats — for instance, 'burn[ing] 12 miles of a very fertile Highland countrey at least 12 or 1400 houses'. He shared the Edinburgh government's view of the highlanders as 'barbarians'. Tarbat protested at the double standard in their orders to him to destroy not only those in rebellion but any who would not join him against them — a policy they would never have pursued against lowlanders.[86] Indeed, almost the only sign of Mackay's highland origin was his clan hatred of the Mackenzies. Though he considered the highlanders the finest untrained soldiers in Scotland, he did not understand their manner of fighting, and had an incredibly crude and mechanical picture of a chief's powers, writing and acting as if they were literally absolute and no clansman or vassal dared act independently in important matters. If, therefore, any of them joined Dundee, it was because they had been ordered to; and if most of their fellows acted differently, it was merely a trick to hide the fact. He applied this equally to a real chief and to a magnate with purely feudal powers, like Atholl; and assumed that their control was as absolute when exercised from Edinburgh, or England, as when their followers were under their eye. This ridiculous principle repeatedly made him alienate potential supporters.[87]

It helps explain his frequent claim that the whole North-East and North was hostile, apart from a few Whig presbyterian families. He himself was a Presbyterian, and the claim was also partly an expression of crusading zeal against popery, partly an unscrupulous device to establish his co-religionists in power since, as he privately admitted, he could easily have organised a majority even of Williamite Episcopalians in the nation.[88] The truth was that, for various reasons, the north-eastern clans were largely neutral. Mar, by now Mackay's dependable ally, unexpectedly died in May, and was succeeded by a minor. The chief of the Farquharsons, Invercauld, was also a minor. Cluny, who had just married his only child to Campbell of Calder's son, was at odds with the Macphersons, who suspected that he intended to entail the chiefship on him and on 14 March had signed a bond to protect the next Macpherson heir's interests against him. Mackintosh, still licking his wounds after Mulroy, was unlikely to appear in arms for anybody; but in April he ignored Dundee's promises that if he rose for James he would be 'established in all your ancient rights'; and he later gave Gordon's vassals false orders from the Duke to submit to the government.[89] As Mackay later more honestly admitted, the North-East in 1689 lacked Jacobite enthusiasm. The Williamites, the Master of Forbes in Aberdeenshire and Sir George Gordon of Edinglassie, Sheriff of Banffshire, in contrast showed energy.[90]

Dunfermline had employed the Duke of Gordon's authority to make his officials muster his tenants, and Dundee hoped to raise 1,300 of them; but late in April cracks began to show. The 300 best men selected at Huntly refused to leave the area. The men of Strathavon, Glenlivet and other highland areas, organised to rise at twenty-four hours' notice, had few arms, 'grudge[d] exceedingly to be takin out in beare seed tyme', and were made mutinous by a paper. Only John Grant of Ballindalloch, a defiant cadet of the Whig family, accompanied Dunfermline, who joined Dundee with 40–50 gentlemen at Castle Gordon on 1 May. However, hope of a real accession of strength hurried him that night to Inverness.[91]

The threat from Keppoch, which Inverness had neglected, suddenly materialised. With 8–900 men, mostly Cameron, Stewart and Macgregor 'volunteers' anxious for booty, he advanced ravaging Mackintosh lands in Stratherrick and Strathnairn, and encamped outside the open town, threatening to burn it for imprisoning him in 1683 unless it paid a 4,000 mark ransom. The raid alienated the crypto-Jacobite Rose of Kilravock, who raised 300 men to defend Nairnshire. The magistrates appealed to Dundee, who denied responsibility for Keppoch's action and gave a bond that the ransom would be repaid on James's return. Privately, he stingingly rebuked Keppoch.[92] Nevertheless, he was confident that the Macdonalds would follow him, and wrote to Elgin to prepare quarters for them. The magistrates of Elgin, who had loyally drunk with Dundee on 1 May, abruptly altered their attitude on finding that he intended to quarter a highland clan on them and sent to Mackay for help. He hurried his force to Elgin and, although finding himself outnumbered and the North-East neutral, held his ground, trusting that forces from the North under Ross of Balnagown, to whom he had written from Edinburgh, would advance on Inverness.[93]

Meanwhile, Keppoch and his men, anxious to carry home their booty, refused to obey Dundee's orders to advance, the Camerons making the excuse that they must ask Lochiel's permission, and retired, soon followed by Keppoch. Without him Dundee could do nothing, and he left Inverness on 8 May.[94] Mackay advanced from Elgin and occupied it without trouble. Strathnaver went north to raise his regiment, Balnagown brought 500 Rosses, and Mackay got him made Sheriff. He was a cavalier's caricature of a Presbyterian, impotent, wife-dominated, cowardly, expressing his extreme malice in unscrupulous slander. He swore to torment the Mackenzies, and Mackay obstinately listened to his allegations that they were disaffected (although they made no trouble when he arrested the Master of Tarbat), because they would not join him. Mackay also suspected the Frasers, although Lovat's absence in Edinburgh explained their inactivity and his chief agent Fraser of Kinnaries' retirement to Inverness for safety showed that they would not join Dundee as a clan. Despite these paranoid fears, Mackay was confident that he could secure the north with 600 more of the Dutch Brigade, whom he ordered Colonel Ramsay to bring to him via Atholl and Badenoch.[95]

Meanwhile, Dundee's force rode up Loch Ness and, after paying Glengarry a flying visit, across Badenoch into Atholl. En route, he confirmed the rendezvous of the clans on 18 May, for which Lochiel was numbering and preparing his clan. On Dundee's orders he visited others, such as the Stewarts of Appin.[96] Dundee may have been in contact with Atholl's baillie Steuart of Ballechin, but they did not appear openly in collusion. On 10 May, Dundee entered Dunkeld and seized some revenues being collected. In the small hours of the 11th, he surprised the city of Perth, captured the Laird of Blair, who was raising a troop of horse, and several other Williamite officers, seized the cess and excise and left in the morning. After symbolically collecting a Jacobite cess, on 13 May he came before Dundee, hoping that Lieutenant-Colonel Livingstone would bring over the two troops of dragoons there. A Williamite officer, however, stopped Livingstone from sallying out as a pretext, and Dundee withdrew to the Highlands, temporarily scattering part of Mar's regiment. His brief raid had put heart into the Lowlands Jacobites, but he had gained only the adherence of an insignificant peer, Lord Dunkeld, the giant Halyburton of Pitcur and several other minor local lairds with a few followers each, £300 in Williamite taxes and a few useful prisoners, whom he carried with him for a month for lack of a secure base.[97]

All the coastal towns were thrown into panic, and the Committee was rattled enough to issue some extraordinary orders. However, it recovered and summoned into Scotland, to his horror, Sir John Lanier, the commander at Berwick, with his cavalry regiment, Berkeley's dragoons and Hastings' and Leslie's regiments of foot, the last three of which were quartered in Perthshire and Angus to prevent another raid. Atholl was told to investigate Dundee's passage through his country but Ballechin easily deceived him.[98] Meanwhile, the new regiments were taking shape. The largest, Angus's, was to be raised from the Cameronians on his father the Marquess of Douglas's estates, under the real command of Lieutenant-Colonel William Cleland, the son of Douglas's gamekeeper. As a teenager, Cleland had written a contemptuous satire on the Highland Host, and had helped win the Covenanting victory at Drumclog. In 1685, he had lurked ready to raise men if Argyll had reached the West. The Cameronian General Council at Douglas on 13–14 May raised so many difficulties that the project would have collapsed if Cleland and the preacher Shields had not swayed the mustered companies by their appeals, temporarily silencing objections. Only half the companies were true Cameronians, the rest being recruited more normally; but there were strong Cameronian elements in two other regiments, Leven's, and Cardross's dragoons. Of the other south-western regiments, two almost entirely consisted of Irish Protestants.[99] The four 'highland' regiments suffered either from lack of arms — like Strathnaver's and Grant's, which was still without proper muskets after Killiecrankie — or of men — Mar's death blighted his regiment. Argyll had guaranteed only that he could raise 300 men, and his regiment did not have all its companies for well over a year. Most regular forces were still so unready that the

Committee gladly accepted highland offers to guard against raids by voluntary groups — including the Macfarlanes west of Loch Lomond, once such thieves themselves that the moon was known as 'Macfarlane's Lantern'.[100]

Meanwhile, on 6 April Alexander Maclean, Sir John's cousin, had reached Dublin, sent by the clans, who did not know of James's arrival, to ask Tyrconnell for help. He told James that if 2,000 regular troops and supplies of arms were landed, 5–6,000 highlanders would join them, and overestimated in detail the numbers the western clans could raise at 4,400, including 500 Macleods and a giant regiment, 900 strong, under himself. As Commissary of Argyll, son of the late bishop, and owner of a forfeited Campbell estate, he had widespread links in Argyllshire; and the regiment was to include the Stewarts of Appin and all the small clans of mid-Argyll and Kintyre, a regiment 'strong, effectual & of good continuance'. He raised two Irish companies as a nucleus.[101] James and his cabinet decided to send three good regiments immediately — sending more, when there was such a shortage of arms, would jeopardise Ireland's safety — to maintain resistance until James himself landed. He knighted Alexander Maclean and Donald Macdonald and dispatched them and Sir John Maclean, carrying letters and commissions — in which Melfort undermined Gordon's and Seaforth's authority by appealing directly to their vassals.[102]

The three regiments were Antrim's, Cormac O'Neill's — both raised in Ulster, an exploitation of old links — and the Scot Brigadier-General Ramsay's. Their commander was to be Major-General Thomas Buchan, an Aberdeenshire Catholic convert who had served in France, Holland and Scotland.[103] However, Londonderry must submit before they could leave; and on 18 April, while its citizens still hesitantly considered Richard Hamilton's generous terms, James's blundering approach with his army aroused their fears of papist treachery, tipping the balance towards resistance.[104] Over the next three months the Scots watched the siege with agonised concern. Not only were most people inside Londonderry of Scottish descent, but its outcome would determine whether James could invade Scotland. Buchan and the three regiments were fully occupied; and Ramsay and his officers were slaughtered resisting the great sortie of 6 May.[105] When James had returned to Dublin, and the French had snubbed his plea to help him land 10,000 men at Troon, he altered his plan. He would ship over 1,200 men, all that could now be spared, in small boats in two stages.[106]

For boats plying a shuttle service and in danger from warships, the obvious landing-place was Kintyre. Despite the massacres of 1647 and the subsequent plantation, several non-Campbell clans survived in the north of the peninsula, unable to resist alone for long — since most local castles had been destroyed in 1647 or 1685 — but anxious to rise. Dundee knew Kintyre's strategic importance. In June, hoping that he had tricked the government troops into marching out, he wanted the second wave of reinforcements landed there, and was willing to fight his way down through Argyllshire to meet them.[107] In May, however, he could not influence the struggle. Only small numbers took part, and it has passed unnoticed,[108] but it was strategically vital.

The Kintyre lairds in power in 1688 had not been deposed like those on the mainland. When supply for the new forces was voted on 27 April, McAlister of Loup and Macdonald of Largie, representatives of its former Macdonald rulers, were almost the only non-Campbell commissioners for Argyllshire. When, in late April, a French merchantman commandeered by Irish refugees arrived, Loup joined Angus Campbell of Kilberry in seizing and guarding her.[109] The Convention planned to send part of Angus's new Cameronian regiment to garrison Kintyre, and authorised Campbell of Calder to raise 600 men for local defence in Islay and Jura. Yet it was more immediately concerned with the danger to the South-West.[110]

On 2 May, young Sir Donald Macdonald landed in Cara, and that night the beacons blazed along the coast. The Macleans arrived a few days later. Sir Alexander made MacNeil of Gallachallie, in Gigha, his lieutenant-colonel, and, leaving him and Sir Donald to organise the Kintyre clans, sailed with his Irishmen and Sir John to Mull. Mobilising all Gigha, Gallachallie was joined by McAlister of Loup, his cousin McAlister of Tarbert, young Macdonald of Largie and his Tutor, and the few remaining Islay and Jura Macdonalds, in seizing Skipness Castle (which the McAlisters had held in 1685). The Tutor secretly obtained for Largie a colonel's commission over his tiny sept.[111] Sir Alexander and Sir Donald had established contact with Sir James Stewart, the Sheriff of Bute, who was in Edinburgh, hoping that he would return and raise his island. However, Cleland intercepted the boat carrying his replies at Greenock, and the Committee imprisoned him.[112]

The Committee, hearing on 7 May of the landing, ordered eight of the companies nearest completion from three regiments being raised in the West to march or cross by sea to Kintyre. They were 500 strong, but raw men still lacking some equipment, particularly bayonets. Their commander was Captain William Young, an excellent choice.[113] Argyll's lieutenant-colonel Auchinbreck was at Inveraray raising companies for his regiment, but only one — ironically of Macaulays, not Campbells — was ready. Auchinbreck, sick and alarmed at the rising, tried to avoid provocations that might make neighbouring clans, Macnachtans or Macdougalls, join it. He was ordered to march as many as possible of his men south into Kintyre.[114]   Despite Dundee's raid on Perth, the campaign went forward. Twelve large boats were hired at Largs. Although the Scots Navy was out of touch destroying birlinns on the Irish coast, Captain Rooke's arrival with English frigates in Greenock indicated that the sea was clear.[115] On 15 May, Young disembarked his men at Tarbert, and next day began to march them towards Kilchalmanel, a clachan in Dunskeig Bay on the west coast. In 1647, David Leslie had outwitted Alasdair by invading Kintyre by land when he was expected by sea, and Young may have obtained a similar surprise in reverse: as he marched, nine barks full of armed men, who had presumably been waiting to surprise him in Knapdale, crossed Loch Tarbert to the south shore. Just beyond Loup, three hundred men under Gallachallie, young Sir Donald, Largie and McAlister of Loup opened a heavy fire from a precipitous hill overlooking the road. Young immediately put his men into battle order and led them up the 'precipices'. They fought well, and, without suffering loss, killed two men and captured others. The Jacobites were pursued and dispersed, some to the mountains and some back to their boats. This almost bloodless skirmish ended resistance in the peninsula, and Macdonald of Largie, who had been holding Skipness, soon abandoned it.[116]

Most of the defeated force reached Gigha. McAlister of Loup instantly began negotiations for surrender, and on 21 May the Convention authorised Young to promise protection to all rebelling heritors and tenants. However, both McAlister lairds, Loup and Tarbert, had already fled to Ireland without telling their comrades. Young, reinforced by local men and a detachment of Argyll's regiment, gathered 1200 men on the coast opposite Gigha. Campbell of Calder expected the attack to succeed, but still feared for the safety of his tenants' cattle in Islay.[117]

In mid-May, some Macleans in birlinns dashingly carried off the French merchantman to Mull and armed her with cannon. It was the start of a distinguished clan flotilla, although this ship, sent to Ireland with messages for James, was immediately burned by Rooke.[118] The raiders probably reported the Kintyre Jacobites' plight to Sir Alexander Maclean. Sir John lent him a hundred Macleans to supplement his Irishmen, and, in their concentration on the rescue, they ignored the general rendezvous set for 18 May.[119]

Sir Alexander sailed on 21 May. The *Janet*, which he unsuccessfully tried to capture by boarding, pursued him, and Rooke's squadron, summoned by Young, was approaching from the south, but he arrived safely. Secretly contacting Largie and his followers, who had been in Arran, he successfully shipped them over on the 26th, bringing his strength to 400. A few hours later, Rooke approached Gigha and opened a cannonade, but vigorous small-arms fire prevented his boats from cutting out anything but one small bark. At 8 p.m., after twelve hours' fighting, Rooke retired to transport Young's invasion force. Sir Alexander, having confused the smaller English ships with boat manoeuvres, quickly embarked his forces at the north end of Gigha, after an evening chase up its coast. Rooke had to rely on long-range gunfire, and, although he sank or captured seven of the twenty boats, wounded only one man. The rest landed safely in mainland Argyll, dispersed some fencible men, re-embarked, and reached Mull on 31 May — an exploit which, as Glencairn's regiment arrived to join Argyll's, could not be repeated. Fifty Macdonalds and McAlisters who took ship for Ireland were less lucky: the Scots frigates captured them.[120]

Sir Alexander Maclean had brought off the Kintyre clans when they seemed encircled and doomed. His hope of forming a 'strong, effectuall' regiment from them was destroyed when the two McAlisters in Ireland got colonels' commissions for themselves and, for consistency's sake, for Macnachtan, Macdougall and Appin — all, except the last, 'ridiculous collonells and worse regiments'. However, he could furnish Dundee with a force of 200 highlanders always available for duty, since they could not, like others, disperse to their homes, and were certain to fight desperately to regain them.[121]

The disadvantage from his expedition was only temporary: preparation for it, followed by Sir John's sickness, prevented the Macleans from attending most of Dundee's Strathspey campaign. However, Young's crushing of the premature

Kintyre rising was a victory more permanent than anything Dundee had yet achieved. Argyll could now advance on Mull and Lochaber with less need for cautious glances over his shoulder. More significantly, it was too dangerous to send Irish reinforcements to the nearest friendly territory — Mull — in small boats in the face of Williamite frigates. The lack of larger ships, and Melfort's incompetence, made it uncertain when a reinforcement could be sent.

On 18 May, the rendezvous of the clans was held. Dundee's poetical standard-bearer was to celebrate the chiefs and their followings in an appropriately Homeric catalogue, including many who were still absent. For all their picturesque appearance, the chiefs were glad to receive the commissions brought from Ireland, which gave them official status and some guarantee that their expenses at least would be repaid. Commissions also served other ends. Although the Macdonalds of Sleat were absent, they carefully obtained Keppoch's written consent to be Sir Donald's Lieutenant-Colonel — an implicit acknowledgement of his headship.[122] After vainly waiting for the Macleans until 25 May, Dundee set out for Badenoch on hearing from Ballechin that Ramsay was marching up through Atholl to rendezvous with Mackay at Ruthven Castle, where Mackay had placed a company of Grant's new regiment. Ramsay, however, was a brave soldier but a timid commander and did not know the country. Seeing Ballechin in arms with the Atholl men, and finding that he was intercepting his correspondence and in contact with Dundee, he spent the night hesitating and on 25 May retreated to Perth. Lanier immediately sent some English regiments north through the Lowlands, and, once Lord Murray had reported Atholl quiet, Ramsay started again with 900 men.[123]

Dundee's forces, already hungry, plundered in Badenoch, and some men joined him as an alternative to fleeing to the hills. Others, however, refrained only from fear that they might be raided in their absence by Atholl men or the Ruthven garrison, which Dundee set Keppoch to besiege. Cluny, though not daring to declare openly, 'stented' his lands to raise 200 Macphersons who joined Dundee without advertising their presence — for which Cluny later irrelevantly pleaded his ill-health to Mackay.[124] Dundee had besides, according to a spy (whose estimates exceed Dundee's own made at his rendezvous), Lochiel with 600 Camerons, the Tutor of Clanranald and Glengarry with 400 Macdonalds each (200 and 300), Keppoch with 300 (200), an incredible 500 Appin and Glencoe men (200), 120 Frasers under Fraser of Foyers (including the Frasers of Beaufort), and 60 Grants from Glenmoriston north of Loch Ness. Lord Murray prevented support from Atholl, but from Braemar John Farquharson of Inverey, undaunted after twenty-three years as an outlaw, joined him with 50 men about 3 June. The total was reported as 2,600 men, the largest army Dundee commanded; and even by his report (which ignores late arrivals) it would be over 1,900.[125]

Mackay, leaving Balnagown in charge of Inverness with 400 of the northern clans — soon increased by reinforcements to over a thousand — to guard against the imagined danger from the Mackenzies and Frasers, had set out to meet Ramsay with his 450 regulars and 200 Mackays and Rosses. Although, on hearing of Ballechin's conduct, he expected all Atholl's and his son-in-law Lovat's followers to join Dundee, he boldly marched across to Strathspey to block Dundee's advance into the North-East. He hoped that Ramsay had merely made a detour to the east, and was confident that his mounted troops could defeat any number of highlanders. The armies came in sight on 28 May. Dundee, on reconnoitring and discovering that Mackay had not brought the northern clans, wished to launch an attack, which, if the dragoons had deserted, might have destroyed Mackay's force; but a misunderstanding with Lochiel, who withdrew the clans several miles on Dundee's first, cautious orders, and, perhaps, a false rumour of enemies to the south, delayed it, and Mackay came to his senses and withdrew to Culnakyle, to cover the Grant country.[126]

Probably doubtful after this of his forces' ability to face cavalry despite their numerical superiority, Dundee halted awaiting Sir Donald and Maclean until Ruthven, which had no store of provisions, surrendered. Keppoch burned not only the castle but Mackintosh's nearby mansion of Dunachton, provoking another furious rebuke from Dundee. However, his cateran's ability to discover cattle hidden in the hills when the army needed food soon reconciled Dundee to 'Coll of the Cows'.[127] The delay, although it enabled the Grants to join Mackay, was also necessary to establish contact with Lieutenant-Colonel Livingstone, whose two troops had rejoined their regiment, and arrange how the dragoons were to desert. Livingstone was less enthusiastic than some of his subordinates, and Dundee did not entirely trust him.[128]

Deserters warned Mackay that his dragoon officers were plotting with Dundee. He dared not then arrest them, but trusted by constant supervision to give them no opportunity and remained in his camp. However, he realised that when Dundee advanced he must retreat, abandoning Grant's country and letting his people, apart from a garrison in Ballachastell, disperse to save their goods. On 2 June, accordingly, hearing of Dundee's approach, he began a rapid night march with a hungry army — characteristic of the tactics which made him so unpopular with his troops — turning aside to halt only at Balvenie. Gordon of Edinglassie and the Master of Forbes met him with some hastily-raised men. Mackay had not dared retreat by Glenlivet and Glen Rinnes, Huntly's country, and feared that Dundee would cut him off that way from the English reinforcements. He got his hungry army marching again that evening eastwards. Dundee's army just failed to intercept them. The highlanders flung off their plaids for battle, but Mackay managed to delay them with a disorganised (and partly disloyal) cavalry screen until darkness fell, giving him some protection. The Frasers harassed his rear, but at Edinglassie near the Deveron Dundee checked the pursuit. The highlanders' fear of cavalry attack in Strathbogie, which influenced him, must have been strong. Mackay's army staggered south-east and collapsed across the upper Bogie at Suie Hill, where Leslie's foot and Berkeley's dragoons joined him on 4 June.[129]

The North-East momentarily seemed open to Dundee, and he apparently intended to hold it, placing a garrison in Gordon Castle (which fled when summoned soon after). However, he was falling sick with dysentery, and could not prevent the highlanders from plundering not only Sheriff Gordon's Edinglassie — legitimate prey — but many of the Duke's and his vassals' lands in Strathbogie, from which Dundee hoped to be joined by recruits. Most of his three troops of horse, being near their homes, dispersed.[130] The dragoon officers sent warning late on the 4th that Mackay had been reinforced and was advancing, and that they themselves would have to fight. Dundee decided to retreat into Badenoch, and on 5 June marched back all the way to Cromdale (where, ironically, there was a false night alarm). The haste and his illness relaxed discipline. The highlanders plundered vigorously, and many straggled. Mackay followed cautiously, pausing at Edinglassie to arrest the treacherous dragoon officers (who were imprisoned for a time, but not further punished). Sir George Gordon and Grant exploited their powers of jurisdiction to hang stragglers whom they caught, particularly Camerons, as if they were common robbers.[131]

As Dundee retreated slowly up the Spey near Boat of Garten about 7 June, the first 2–300 Macleans arrived under Sir John's Lieutenant-Colonel, young Maclean of Lochbuie, to join him, but began to make up for lost time by plundering the country indiscriminately. MacIain of Glencoe, whom Dundee had sent to guide them to camp, had himself obtained a buff coat as spoil at Edinglassie, but objected to their harming friends, and he was trying to prevent this in the evening when a second-sighted man warned him that danger was at hand. He retired, and soon afterwards Sir Thomas Livingston appeared with over 200 dragoons. They chased the Macleans, cutting down stragglers and capturing their baggage. Yet the Macleans, with their conquer-or-die tradition, showed, as at Cromdale, that they could keep their heads under attack by cavalry. About 100 rallied on a steep hill, Knockbrecht. The dragoons over-confidently began a night attack, and Lochbuie launched a miniature highland charge, killing a captain and a dozen men. The infuriated dragoons slaughtered forty Maclean prisoners, but spared Lochbuie's brother. The Macleans collected their stragglers and rejoined Dundee without further trouble.[132]

Mackay hoped that Ramsay, at his second attempt, would enter Badenoch above Dundee, forcing him, at best, to disperse across the hills; but Ramsay, moving slowly, merely joined Mackay. Dundee, retreating through Badenoch, resolved, despite his illness, to continue to Rannoch, from which he could threaten the Lowlands. But as the clans melted away in large groups with their cattle and booty, he thought it best to take them into Lochaber and dismiss them formally. The Chisholms, sent out by their chief under John Chisholm of Knockfin to join him, straggled disconsolately home.[133]

Mackay, having advanced to Ruthven and confirmed the dispersal by scouts, returned with his exhausted army to Inverness. Despite agitated orders from William and the Council to march south for fear of invasion, he stayed to settle the North. He placed Sir Thomas Livingston at Inverness, with his dragoons, Leslie's regiment and detachments, 1,000 soldiers in all, backed by Strathnaver's and Grant's raw regiments. He disbanded the northern clansmen, apart from 200 Rosses and Mackays to garrison the Mackenzie houses, Brahan and Castle Leod. In the crisis, he had had Tarbat and Lovat arrested on suspicion, and, not surprisingly, the Mackenzies and Frasers remained unwilling to serve him. Under his suspicious eye, the cattle-watch the Mackenzies were organising collapsed.

The only resistance came from a poltergeist at Brahan; but Mackay and Balnagown could scarcely have made greater efforts to turn lukewarm supporters into enemies.[134] Mackay, meanwhile, considered the lessons of the campaign. He saw the need for greater strategic co-ordination, criticising the forces in Argyllshire for not attacking Lochaber in the clans' absence; but he developed a dangerous contempt for the highlanders, and an exaggerated trust in his own and his experienced troops' ability to defeat them whatever the odds. He overlooked that after his and his officers' vigorous recruiting to restore his mainstay, the Dutch Brigade, to full strength, two-thirds of the men would be raw — apart from a few men, in a draft from Grant's regiment, who had fled at Mulroy.[135]

Dundee's lack of success so far was emphasised by the surrender of Edinburgh Castle on 13 June, after three months' siege. Gordon, with a small and still partly disaffected garrison, had not dared to make sorties or impose siege rationing. Although he was short of ammunition and most equipment, the besiegers lacked heavy cannon, and their batteries were frequently silenced. The mortars sent by sea from London shifted the balance in May; but, though their bombs damaged the buildings (and the nation's records) and drove the garrison into the unhealthy vaults, they inflicted no casualties. While Gordon avoided firing on the city, but threatened to do so whenever barricades were raised there, the besiegers did not bombard the Castle from that side, the only one where a normal storming was possible. Mackay instead had the Nor' Loch drained, to affect the Castle's wells and (theoretically) make its north side more vulnerable. The besiegers felt some pleasure, as Scots, that their Castle was impregnable.[136]

Gordon's Edinburgh agent sent messengers to Ireland to warn that the Castle must surrender after 1 June. One of them, William Mackintosh of Borlum the younger (the general of the '15), falsely claimed to bear warnings from James's chief supporters against Melfort. Melfort accused him of spying for William and imprisoned him — causing widespread alarm in the Highlands.[137] He also used his influence to prevent James from replying; but on 17 May the king finally sent a brief approbation of Gordon's conduct. Other letters followed; but even if Melfort relented, his Edinburgh correspondent, a lady, did not, and never delivered them. Gordon and his allies saw the silence as proof of Melfort's vindictiveness.[138] One despairing report from Ireland, and a message from Dunfermline after the Perth raid reached him, but none of Dundee's promises of relief. The French tried harder than James to establish contact with him. In April, they sent a spy to settle in Edinburgh, communicating with France through the privateer who carried him; but the privateer fled from Leith in needless panic. Mary of Modena's letter of 24 May, assuring Gordon of her and Louis' favour, came too late.[139]   A mass desertion on 31 May informed the besiegers of the Castle's shortages and Gordon's network of supporters in Edinburgh, who were arrested. To ensure his garrison's safety while he still had supplies to bargain with, he opened negotiations on 12 June. When they were broken off, Sir John Lanier forced Hamilton to authorise him to mount batteries in the city. Gordon inflicted heavy casualties on the troops building them, but at a rate that would exhaust his ammunition in a week. Unknown to him, the government's expenditure of ammunition made

William write on 13 June forbidding further firing until Mackay returned. That day Gordon surrendered, obtaining indemnity for the garrison and its correspondents. Showing the 'good links but not a chain' characteristics which ruined his career, he asked no guarantees for himself from respect for the half-Stuart William, an unwise gesture when William, to conciliate his turbulent Parliament, a month later was ready to repeal all forfeitures since 1660 — which would restore the Marquisate of Argyll and its rights to the entire Gordon estates. Meanwhile, other Jacobites shunned him, and Melfort thoroughly prejudiced James against him.[140]

Ramsay's retreat had naturally made the Council demand an investigation of what was happening in Atholl. This had no connection with the Marquess's earlier Edinburgh intrigues: he might join other major politicians in a combination elsewhere which might swiftly restore a grateful James, but would not enter a hazardous rising which might cause the devastation of his estates. When in late May illness (and prudence) made him go to Bath, infefting his son, Lord Murray, with his authority and leaving orders for the Atholl men to resist Dundee, he did not expect excessive zeal: when Hamilton earlier urged him to raise them, he declared that they would refuse to rise unless the government paid their charges. Yet he did assume they would obey; he would hardly otherwise have made himself an involuntary hostage. His family was divided, with his sons Dunmore, William (later Lord Nairne) and Mungo (a captain in Dumbarton's regiment when it revolted in March) the obvious Jacobites, but there is no sign of conscious collusion.[141] Murray, who increasingly received control of the family estates, would have been unsuitable as a party to it. A strong, moralistic, somewhat priggish religious belief partly checked his inherited magnate pride and violent temper. He long remained undecided about the Revolution, writing in a frank private prayer in 1692, when he feared that an invasion might force him to choose irrevocably, that 'the want of clearnes what was my duty has been the reason of my backwardnes in acting ether in one side or the other'. He consciously attempted to decide exclusively on religious grounds (ignoring, for instance, that James had encouraged Atholl to disinherit him in favour of Dunmore), balancing loyalist episcopalianism against fear of the persecuting catholicism he had witnessed in France. He was influenced through his marriage, constantly by his presbyterian wife and Williamite father-in-law Hamilton, occasionally by the Jacobite Arran. Only in 1694, when Johnston had brought him into William's service, could Lady Murray definitely thank God for preventing 'his joyning wt thy Enemys' the Jacobites.[142] Yet Murray's 1692 prayer implies that he did not see unenterprising obedience to Edinburgh's orders for local defence as making a decisive choice; and throughout 1689 he did his utmost to keep the Atholl men loyal to William.

The summer of 1689 was the first of two occasions in William's reign when the near-regal power of the Atholl family collapsed at a touch. The reasons probably included some secret resentment of Robertsons and Stewarts at their feudal overlord, and the country people's desire for plunder. Yet Dundee's warning to Murray that he could no more make the Atholl men fight against James than Hamilton could make his Cameronian tenants fight for him, contained truth as well as rhetoric. Just as local Whigs whose fathers' houses Montrose had burned steeled themselves to endure Dundee's burning theirs, so equally strong traditions from Montrose's and Glencairn's campaigns swayed loyalists.[143] The most fanatical family was the one to which Atholl had given most power, largely for their loyalty — Patrick Steuart of Ballechin, his bailie, Ballechin's brother Alexander, his chamberlain, and their sons. Their Jacobitism persisted: Ballechin's son was in the '15, his grandson in the '45. Although there were Jacobite members of the Atholl family in both risings, the Ballechins could expect only maltreatment from its vindictive pro-government heads — imprisonment in the 1690s, blackmail in 1716 — and kept office largely because Atholl was in debt to them.[144]

Murray, coming to investigate, reached Dunkeld on 28 May. Both sides of his character — aristocratic disbelief that Ballechin could disobey orders, secret guilt over a youthful affair with his daughter — blinded him. He accepted, and made the Council accept, his plausible story that the musterings which had so frightened Ramsay were merely provoked by his soldiers' plundering.[145] Murray had some reason for complacency: he quieted the overt Jacobites, such as the teenage Robertson of Struan who, after making spectacular preparations to march with 300 men on 31 May and join Dundee, instead came in and submitted. Local lairds, including Menzies of Weem and Glenlyon, engaged to bring in their followers, some of whom had nearly accompanied Struan. Murray put a small garrison into Blair, organised watches, in which Ballechin and his brother naturally held important places, and returned satisfied to the Lowlands. Dundee wrote to him in vain.[146] Even his discovery, on holding a court in Balquhidder in late June, that the minister, Robert Steuart, Alexander's son, had sent round the fiery cross did not alert him. Nor did a suspicious visit his own brother William made to Ballechin just afterwards.[147]

Dundee, meanwhile, recovered his health at Lochiel's house. He sent his prisoners to Mull under Maclean's charge. On 22 June, his position was strengthened when a much-delayed messenger brought his commission as Lieutenant-General, authority to assemble a committee of Privy Councillors with the Council's full powers and to summon a convention, and a proclamation for levying war against the Williamite one.[148] He wished to give the Highlanders conventional military training, and his lowland officers and some young chiefs, following fashion in war as in peace, agreed. However, when Lochiel explained in detail why the clans should be allowed to fight in the traditional highland fashion, Dundee accepted his advice, and instantly saw how highland tactics — one volley and then a charge with broadswords and targes — could counterbalance his worst shortage, lack of powder, now only 20 lb.[149] This willingness to adapt to highland needs was a main cause of Dundee's success in maintaining a rising without money or provisions to back it. The name of Graham, and his relationship to the great Montrose, were another. Yet Dundee, a career official rather than an aristocrat, reared in the simplicities of a polarised creed, was a less complex figure than Montrose — and, probably, a more effective leader for a rising in its present doldrums: the fiasco in Strathspey, for instance, might have provoked Montrose to dangerous recriminations.[150]

That fiasco, however, was now working to his advantage in the Lowlands, confirming the traditional impression of the highlanders as contemptible figures interested primarily in plunder. Although their mountainous haunts made it difficult finally to crush them now, they were unlikely, now they had satiated themselves and dispersed, ever to assemble under Dundee again. In early July, the English asked for their regiments back.[151] This attitude was important because one important factor in the 'highland charge's' success in Scottish battles for over a century was the gap of a generation between the wars in which it was used, giving time to forget its lessons. In the Restoration period, the Highland Host had been particularly effective in making the highlanders appear mainly as thieves and barbarians, even giving a false impression of their weapons. In 1668, the Perthshire highlanders generally possessed flintlocks (ahead of the army), and by 1689 the Lochaber clans also did so, though the Kintail men still relied largely on matchlocks. Highland broadswords were far superior to regulation army swords. Yet for the Host, perhaps because it was seen largely as making a show, they had decked themselves out with obsolete weapons and armour. Some carried both targes and giant two-handed swords, and one observer was grotesquely torn between Whig indignation and antiquarian enthusiasm at their armour.[152] In some respects, regular troops had become less equipped to meet a highland charge. The proportion of pikemen in regiments had been reduced to a third, no longer wearing the half-armour and helmets that would have protected them from many dreadful broadsword strokes. Musketeers had plug bayonets which took time to ram into musket-barrels, and which, once in, might be chopped off through the plug like Donald McBane's at Mulroy. The desperate search for available muskets and drafts between regiments were starting to create a situation where there was no uniformity of calibre, even within companies.[153]

Dundee's strategy was to alarm the government and Mackay into transferring the army entirely to the West for fear of an invasion from Ireland, while James's actual force should land at Inverlochy to join him. In his letters and conversation, even with friends to whom he revealed who secretly intended to join him, he repeated that James would invade the West, and he coolly brought about the Dowager Countess of Erroll's arrest to get such letters discovered. Before 1688, the disaffected western shires had been allowed no foot militia, and Dundee probably overlooked the effect now of the widespread distribution of arms among the Presbyterians there. Mackay, however, was the main obstacle to his attempts to panic the government, and he himself unintentionally strengthened Mackay's hand. When Clanranald and MacNeil of Barra landed from the Outer Hebrides, he may have called a rendezvous for 26 June, possibly already planning to enter Kintyre to meet a second force from Ireland. If so, he cancelled it because Sir Donald Macdonald was still absent. A rumour that he intended to march north from it to raise the Mackenzies and Frasers reached Inverness, and subordinates' pleas gave Mackay justification, when he finally marched south, for leaving Livingston's whole garrison at Inverness and most of Berkeley's dragoons guarding the North-East.[154] On his march, he detached on 2 July a small party of foot and horse under the Master of Forbes up the Dee to garrison Braemar Castle and seize Farquharson of Inverey, who had been raiding the country since his return from Strathspey. Forbes, though guided by Inverey's hereditary enemy Gordon of Brackley, bungled his orders, and Inverey, 'the Black Colonel', though forced to flee from home in his shirt, instantly gathered a force, frightened him from Braemar by a surprise attack and burned it. Mackay returned in force and established a garrison at Abergeldie, lower down the Dee, but this delayed his return to Edinburgh until 12 July.[155]

Clanranald and MacNeil put additional pressure on the resources of Lochaber. For lack of meal, which Dundee attempted to obtain by threats from areas as far apart as Stratherrick and Weem, they fed on the local cattle, still very thin. Lochiel's promise that Dundee's followers should not want while there was a cow in Lochaber was approaching literal fulfilment. Raiding made up some losses; but this created a great danger for a rising that was failing to expand, surrounding it with an increasingly wide band of potential supporters alienated by their losses. The situation was worst in Ross, where the Mackenzies were caught between a regime which still believed them on the point of revolt and Jacobite raiders who stole hundreds of cows every week. These included Lochiel's and Glengarry's men, Glenmoriston Grants, Chisholms and Frasers. The Kintail men, who suffered raids and casualties in late June, were by late July themselves sallying out in parties of 60, with pipe and colours, to raid Balnagown's, 'the enemy's country'.[156]

The most notorious raid took place on 28 June. A party of 40 Camerons, unauthorised according to tradition, with Dundee's order claimed Lochiel when prosecuted in 1695, raided the Laird of Grant's lands in Glen Urquhart, both to avenge the hangings in Strathspey and to obtain cattle. As they retreated with a hundred cows, a local party under the Grants of Shewglie, brothers believed to sympathise with the Jacobite cause, came up with them. The Camerons tried to avoid fighting, but, when the pursuers would not leave them, they killed or mortally wounded a dozen of them, including the Shewglie brothers, and then drove off the cows. The crime shocked all Ross. It disrupted Dundee's camp as well, for they had also killed a Macdonald fighting with the Grants. Glengarry, to satisfy his clan's expectations, made a violent fuss demanding satisfaction on the Camerons. Dundee responded with rational arguments which could officially satisfy him.[157]

With supplies dwindling and no help from Ireland, Dundee's leadership had its dubious side. Mackay commented that autumn that the catholic priests had assumed his task of spreading lies among the clans. Time and again, he wrote letters declaring on his honour that Londonderry had fallen and that help had sailed from Ireland, and he confessed late in June that he was no longer believed. Moreover, he had to keep secret his most promising plans and hopes, since security was so poor. The delay gave time for omens to demoralise some clans. Keppoch admitted to a spy the day before the Killiecrankie campaign began:

> that hitherto he had little [reward from following Dundee], that he was a brocken man and wanted a master, but if Argyll wull take him by the hand, and preserve his

estate, he would willingly serue him, butt was affraid, though the offer wer made . . . [Argyll] wodd not accept of it.[158]

Most Williamites hoped that the highlanders could be brought to submit peacefully, and agreed that it was worth some expenditure. Argyll told William in May that he could buy all the clans with £4,000, and in July tried to sound Lochiel's attitude, though convinced that he would not listen without 'the readie pennie'. Tarbat had the most sophisticated scheme — to buy out for £5,000 Argyll's pretensions over all clans but the Macleans, for whom the 1680 agreement might be revived. He worked loyally for William, plying Lochiel with offers of money, a commission, the governorship of Inverlochy; and he had the subtlety necessary in such a negotiation. Yet Mackay, because he did not make the Mackenzies rise for William (which he had never claimed he could), accused him of treachery; and Hamilton, his old enemy, arrested him, Lovat and (with more reason) Dunmore. Tarbat was soon released, but for fear of Hamilton fled to England, just as William sent a commission for him to negotiate. Hamilton unsuccessfully suggested Campbell of Calder instead.[159] Various Williamites made cruder approaches: Mackay wrote to Glengarry, who sarcastically recommended to him to emulate Monck; Livingston had Strathnaver warn Dundee himself to surrender; and when the Council on 18 July issued a proclamation putting a price on Dundee's head, Dalrymple expected the clans to betray him for it.[160]

Dundee on his side worked to rally more supporters, by fair means or foul. The most conspicuous neutral clan were the Macleods (apart from Macleod of Raasay and his devoted followers). Possibly Iain Breac's positive political opinions, as well as continuing resentment over Stuart ingratitude to the clan after Worcester and doubts about Dundee's chances of success, contributed to this, for Tarbat was confident very early that he would not join, and he exiled his protégé the Blind Harper from Dunvegan for his Jacobitism. In 1690 (when an Irish invasion seemed possible) he at least seemed less determined, and the Jacobites remained on friendly terms with him afterwards. This was not the case in 1689. Sir Donald Macdonald, having raised his men, spent much of July in Skye trying to force the Macleods, and still more the Mackinnons who had no Dunvegan to retire to, to join Dundee. Meanwhile, Dundee and Glengarry wrote to Mackenzie of Coul, who had declined to rise, that, if he did not, his property would be ravaged worse than Edinglassie's.[161]

Dundee sent to Edinburgh for professional soldiers, causing several panics over 'plots' in July.[162] He summoned the non-Campbell clans of Argyll, writing to Macnachtan on 28 June: 'it will be hard for you to rease your regiments houever doe your best . . . and march them this way. Concert with Makdougall that you may come together and then apen [Appin] may come with you'. His hopes were disappointed. Macnachtan and his uncle John joined him, but most of his tenants refused to follow him — despite which, Argyll ravaged his lands. Macdougall of Dunollie excused himself as surrounded by his enemies. Small parties of septs from Cowal and a Lamont cadet joined him; but Lamont himself, though declining a company in Argyll's regiment, served in a local one in 1690; and his brother accepted a commission in Glencairn's for fear of Argyll, though he sent Dundee information. The Laird of Macfarlane, offered a colonel's commission, was already committed to William.[163]

Dundee's most important correspondent in Argyllshire, however, was Breadalbane — a fact which transforms our understanding of the Killiecrankie campaign. They had, says Carwhin's biography, 'kept Constant Correspondence', in which Breadalbane had been useful 'pa[rticular]ly in mainageing the highlanders ... so Cautiously ... that the Govern could not get the least pretence of destroying his Country'. This is obviously ambiguous; and Breadalbane retired to Kilchurn Castle and declared that he was suffering from gout and would meddle on neither side. Dundee would not have concentrated his campaigning in the North-East if he had solid hopes of so important a recruit. By late June, however, Breadalbane could see that Dundee's rising would not collapse. Meanwhile, his agent in Dublin, Carleton, reported that James was willing to accept some of his proposals, even to restore Argyll on terms; and was privately campaigning for Melfort's dismissal. On 23 June, Dundee supposed that Breadalbane 'now will come to the feelds', though he naturally wrote little of Carleton's employer to Melfort. The basis of his confidence was presumably the authority he had just received from James, enabling him 'to act uith ye pouer of our uhole councell', and thus to make authorised agreements.[164] Their correspondence became frequent and conspicuous. Their intermediaries included Macnachtan, and Major Duncan Menzies of Forneth (near Dunkeld), Colonel Menzies's son-in-law. Duncan Menzies had by 1688 been a professional soldier for a decade, serving in Thomas Buchan's regiment and, in 1685, under Atholl, in whose household he had relatives. He was recognised as Breadalbane's man, but was an active Jacobite, fighting at Killiecrankie and openly questioning Breadalbane's word when highland interests demanded it.[165]

By late July, Dundee relied on 'a deliberate and well founded desyne ... of the E. of B. his joyning him with 1600 of his men. To which also he had prepared Argyleshire and a Good part of Perthshire who were all ready to ryse with him'. On the 20th, Dundee wrote:

> My Lord what was said ... of the king's opinion of you I dout no ways of and I hop every day will confirm him mor for if things succeed your lordship has in hand you will be the great ingyn of his business here. I am very glaid to hear that the gentry of argyl shyr are lyk to be wyse and take right measures for their own good. I ... shall play to your hand tho I dare tell it here to nobody no not that I have a good opinion of you as I really have, for fear what you are about bee seen throw.

The chief agents whom Breadalbane, 'sitting with soar foot at the fyr seyd' used in his preparations were two of his chamberlains, Campbell of Barcaldine, in Argyll and Lismore, and Toshach of Monivaird in Perthshire; Campbell of Lochnell, the most zealous Jacobite, and Campbell (MacConnochie) of Inverawe. Lochnell's and Lochiel's rival claims to Sunart and Ardnamurchan caused difficulties. When Lochiel arranged for a Jacobite garrison supporting him to be placed at Mingary Castle, Breadalbane explained matters to Dundee, who wrote assuring Lochnell that he would not let the decision be prejudged.[166]

Breadalbane might soon be put to the test. On 27 June, Mackay from Elgin advised the Council to establish a force of 2,000 men in Argyllshire, to overawe the Breadalbane and Atholl areas and attack the rebels' homes if they marched north. On 3 July the Council gave orders for the force, Argyll's, Glencairn's and Angus's regiments, Young's detachment from Kintyre, and four troops of horse. Argyll, having attempted, as a leader of the Club, to discredit Sir John Dalrymple, set out on 12 July. In his discussions at Edinburgh, he had planned to advance immediately into enemy territory and live off the country, without fear of 'anie rable Dundee can Have of Highlanders', although he soon knew that they were anxious to fight him. The Council, however, alarmed by the reinforcements from Ireland for Dundee, ordered him not to advance or risk fighting, and were emphatically confirmed by Mackay, who 'esteem[ed] the Highlanders as good as their troupes, their number greater, and better officer'd'. Argyll protested that his force would rapidly exhaust the country round Inveraray and starve.[167]

Dundee agreed that Breadalbane should try to persuade Argyll to change sides and disarm his lowland regiments; it was the last chance he would have. If he did, 'your Lordship Dunfermling and I make a comitty of Councell with pouer of full counsell, soe will grant him all the councel used to doe in lyk caices'. James would doubtless restore him, though perhaps without his superiorities, and with compensation elsewhere for his claims against the Macleans. Yet, secretly hostile, Dundee cautiously tempted Breadalbane: 'there are few considerable cadets so just to their chief if Argyl wer out of the way Bredalben would be all in these contreys and have the wholl name to follow him'. This emphasises one unexpected trait in Breadalbane also visible in 1691. Despite his personal unscrupulousness, he did not exploit public negotiations to ruin enemies or rivals. The Campbells' traditional self-restraint, reinforced by clan experience in the early 1680s after the late Argyll's forfeiture, probably influenced him. Yet Argyll showed him no such consideration in 1691. Knowing that even Lauderdale had strained his influence supporting an Argyll who had done the King some service, Breadalbane must have realised that he would exhaust whatever favour his own Jacobite activities accumulated supporting his cousin, who had done none, in the 'white terror' likely to follow James's restoration. Argyll was not then prepared even to temporise with the Jacobites, writing, 'I have no Back door God knows but I see most people have it', and passing to Hamilton evidence of Breadalbane's correspondence. On 25 July, the Council modified its restrictions, allowing Argyll to advance and quarter round Kilchurn, and Hamilton, uncovering Carleton's mission from Breadalbane, secretly ordered Argyll to arrest him. Unless the threat of military locusts spurred him to declare for Dundee, it seemed Breadalbane would soon be a prisoner — in either case, an overt Jacobite. Then came Killiecrankie.[168]

On Mackay's return, he had found the newly-raised troops 'guarding' and plundering the Perthshire and Stirlingshire lowlands far too numerous to maintain for long. The one reliable highland outpost was Weem, which Robert Menzies the younger held with a company of clansmen — though Blair was also assumed to be safe. Mackay determined to transform the war by marching through Atholl straight to Inverlochy to plant a Cromwellian-style garrison as the one means of subduing the rebellious Lochaber clans. He suggested it to Melville in mid-June, but to the Council only when diverted to Abergeldie on 4 July. The government, preoccupied with an uncontrollable Parliament, merely appointed a committee. After his return, therefore, there were frantic discussions in Council and then Parliament on baggage horses, provisions, 2,000 pioneers — whom Mackay supposed Edinglassie could provide from the North. He was dangerously naive about the possibility of planting a garrison exclusively by land: Monck had done so by sea. Yet preparations were pushed ahead after it was known that Dundee had been reinforced from Ireland.[169]

Writing to Melfort in late June, Dundee, while denouncing Carleton, had regretfully advised him that the hostility to him in Scotland, however unjust, probably made his resignation necessary. Later Jacobites claimed that this made Melfort starve Dundee's rising of support. In reality, Melfort's strongest self-delusion, which cracked only when an irrevocable step like leaving him in France was raised, was that he was unselfishly ready to sacrifice himself the moment his presence harmed James. He repeatedly promised this in letters to Dundee, and circulated rather than suppressing Dundee's replies.[170] Military reality, not intrigue, explains the failure to send adequate help. The army round Londonderry was so weakened and demoralised that its generals decided in July to make no further attacks and merely starve the city out. An English army arrived off Londonderry in mid-June, landed in a nearby island in early July, and, but for over-caution, could have relieved the city. When, therefore, James finally sent to Carrickfergus in early July three large frigates loaned by the French, the only regiment he dared spare was Purcell's, 400 raw men. An older, conventionally-trained regiment would have complemented the qualities the clans possessed; Alasdair's regiments had fought in the highland fashion with the skill of professional soldiers; but Purcell's seemed to the more sophisticated clans rather barbaric: a Maclean bard who fought next to them at Killiecrankie praised their bravery but compared their charge to a stampede of cattle. Brigadier-General Cannon shipped the nucleus of a dragoon regiment to be completed in Scotland, the catholic Scots Lords Buchan and Frendraught, Sir William Wallace (Melfort's brother-in-law) and Sir George Barclay carried commissions for future regiments, and about seventy-five junior officers went to serve with them or the clans.[171]

On 10 July, the three large frigates sailed from Carrickfergus. Off Kintyre, they sighted the Scots Navy, and after a bloody, one-sided fight captured both ships. Most of the ever-luckless Cannon's embryo regiment was captured by Auchinbreck. The French landed the remaining forces in Mull and sailed for southern Ireland, sending the Scots Navy to Dublin. On the 17th, Rooke's squadron appeared off Mull. Cannon ferried Purcell's regiment and most of the supplies, including thirty-five barrels of powder, into Morvern, but Rooke captured much equipment and provisions in two small prizes, from which the Scottish officers fled inland. He bombarded Duart for several hours, but merely 'dung doun som skleats', strengthening the Macleans' confidence, before retiring for good from Scottish waters, which allowed Purcell to cross Loch Linnhe.[172]

The smallness of the succour caused widespread dismay. To compensate, Dundee spread fresh reports of the fall of Londonderry and a French invasion fleet, which he probably believed himself this time. They created a great effect in Atholl, but less elsewhere: in Dundee's correspondence from Cluny he fell within eight days from demanding 400 men to calling for provisions (for which he gave a bond) to prevent disorders as he passed.[173] Waiting for reinforcements had apparently placed him in a desperate position. If he did not muster the clans and take the offensive against Mackay, they might become demoralised, and Mackay and Argyll could organise simultaneous advances. If he did, Argyll was dangerously close, had spies in his camp and could make preparations, while the clans' full strength assembled, to invade Lochaber as soon as they marched. If he attacked Argyll, Mackay might enter Lochaber and garrison Inverochy unopposed. The only solution was to muster, march and strike before Argyll could realise that he was gone. This meant that not all the clans would join him, and these would not be at full strength — far from the 4,000 he boasted of. There was much debate in the camp where the next campaign should be, Lochiel wishing to return to Strathspey to avenge his hanged clansmen, all the rest to invade Argyllshire, and Dundee gave out that this was what he intended. Mackay, however, assumed that he meant to return to Strathspey.[174] His real aim was to raise Atholl and Braemar for James before Mackay could overawe them — an audacious gamble, for he set it in motion on 9 July, before he knew of the succour from Ireland.

Halyburton of Pitcur went with orders to Ballechin to take possession of Blair Castle, which he did by sending in 'reinforcements'. Dundee wrote on the 10th to the gentry of Atholl ordering them to rise in James's name, promising them the support of his whole army and threatening to treat as traitors those who refused. He sent Sir Alexander Maclean's regiment, which had been his guard for the past month, to throw in a small additional garrison and march to Braemar to assist Farquharson of Inverey. Gallachallie's first attempt, with sixty men, was beaten off by the local gentry, who had hurriedly assembled to blockade Blair, but on 13 July Sir Alexander arrived with his whole 300 men, and they retired. He then marched for Braemar, and on 19 July he and Inverey attacked down the Dee and burned Gordon of Brackley's lands, skilfully outmanoeuvring the Master of Forbes.[175] Murray heard of the seizure on 14 July. After warning Mackay, he hurried to Atholl. Ballechin, though he apparently told hesitant vassals that James would make him Marquess of Atholl, still wrote to Murray (who had declared both Steuart brothers dismissed) as a dutiful bailie, trusting that he would now declare for James. Dundee, who was really uncertain whether Murray's threats against Ballechin were 'mowes or earnest', wrote similarly. Murray raised 1,000 Atholl men and blockaded Blair. Lacking even a petard to blow open the gate, he could do no more.[176] Both he and Ballechin, however, were very reluctant to bring war upon the countryside. Ballechin wrote asking Dundee if it was vital to hold the Castle, and received a firm reply on 25 July. Murray's messenger asked Mackay if he could not avoid Atholl in marching to Inverlochy. Mackay replied that he could not leave Blair in unfriendly hands, would hang Ballechin unless he surrendered, and, if Murray did not continue the siege, would ravage the country.[177]

Dundee had set a general rendezvous for 28 or 29 July, genuine or to mislead spies. The sudden raising of a force beforehand was made easier when the Macdonalds of Sleat at last landed, although illness almost immediately made old Sir Donald retire, leaving command to his son. They were at the head of Loch Eil on 16 July, reaching the camp at the weekend. The army marched on 23 July, so suddenly that a spy who was in the camp that morning did not know of it.[178] Even Lochiel, whose well-organised clan had formed such a proportion of the army in Strathspey, could collect only 240, from Lochaber, and had to leave his son and Lieutenant-Colonel to gather the rest. The only other major mainland chief present, Glengarry, raised 5–600 men, probably including the Grants of Glenmoriston. Keppoch apparently failed to join, though the army marched through his lands of Glen Roy; but some of his men were in Sir Donald's battalion. The clans of the Isles, Maclean and Clanranald, were prominent in the army partly because they could not go home so easily.[179] Dundee's total numbers at Killiecrankie were probably slightly under 2,000, besides about forty horse. The provisions he ordered from Cluny were for 1,500 men, though he declared that others were already provided for, and Sir Alexander Maclean's regiment only rejoined him later. However, the army's morale was high, and maintained by Dundee's brief but emphatic words of encouragement.[180]

From Glen Roy the army marched to the Spey, into Badenoch. Murray reported this, but Hamilton assumed that Dundee was again going north. Cluny's provisions were ready, but the Camerons did some plundering. The Macphersons remained inactive. Alexander Steuart met the clans and guided them into Atholl on 26 July. They found only the women at home, the men fled to the hills. Murray's men began to melt away, chiefly to drive their cattle to safety, and with the remaining 3–400 he retreated through the Pass of Killiecrankie, leaving a guard at the top. He was realising that he could not rely on any of them to fight against Dundee, not only because their property was at his mercy, but from genuine support for him. A source of this was Ballechin's son Charles, whom Murray had made one of his commanders, incorrigibly believing his protestations. Dundee's army camped above Blair, and Dundee slept there.[181]

Mackay, not believing that Dundee could intervene in Atholl, left it to Murray to settle that country, while he prepared for the Inverlochy expedition and inspected the troops which were to guard Stirling in his absence. He arrived at Perth on 25 July. His force was to consist of one battalion from each of the three regiments of the Brigade, 1800 strong, Hastings' English foot, Leven's and Kenmure's, nearly 4,000 in all. Colchester's regiment needed time to recover; he was given eight troops of Scottish horse and dragoons, but marched when only two, Annandale's and Belhaven's, had arrived, leaving the others to guard the Lowlands against raids. He received three little leather cannon, suitable for mountain campaigning — from the Army of the Covenant's artillery train. Twelve hundred baggage horses had been gathered with the utmost difficulty, but only a fortnight's provisions.[182]

As Mackay began his march on the 26th, Robert Menzies sent warning that Dundee was approaching Atholl, but Mackay disbelieved it, and was, besides, too over-confident to wait for the other six troops. That night he reached Dunkeld, and, warned by Murray, sent 200 musketeers under Lieutenant-Colonel Lauder to guard the head of the Pass of Killiecrankie, from which the Atholl guard had vanished, and wrote to Perth for the six troops. Marching up the next morning, he was joined by Robert Menzies and his highland company. Murray, however, who was with his remaining followers at Moulin below the pass, warned him that they would not join him, although he believed that, by himself remaining at their head, he could stop them from joining Dundee, who was at Blair with 2,000 men. Mackay placed Hastings' regiment and Annandale's troop behind the baggage to stop the Atholl men from plundering it, but disregarded Murray's main warning and marched on through the pass, untroubled except (according to tradition) by a single sniper.[183]

Dundee had just dispatched a party to attack Lauder's detachment when he heard, in the early afternoon, that Mackay's main army was emerging from the pass. A hasty council of war was held. The regular officers argued that the highlanders were very inferior in numbers (for Ballechin, made colonel of the Atholl men, had no time to gather them[184]), hungry and exhausted, and should have their confidence built up by skirmishes before risking a battle, but Dundee trusted Glengarry's and Lochiel's judgement that they should fight immediately. He refused, however, their request that he should not risk his own life, replying that the highlanders would not respect him unless he fought in person in at least one battle. He had evidently considered the matter, preparing a Gaelic phrase to back his arguments; and the contrary example of Cannon at Dunkeld indicates that he was right. Sir William Wallace provided a jarring note by unexpectedly producing an order from his brother-in-law Melfort that he, rather than the trusted Dunfermline, should command the cavalry.[185] While skirmishing parties on the direct road to the pass delayed and distracted Mackay, the whole army marched, almost running in the heat, north round the Hill of Lude and back over the pass east of it, and deployed eastwards on the slopes below Creag Eallaich, a steep hill to which they could retreat safely if repulsed.[186]

Mackay, while ammunition was distributed to his infantry, who had marched with dangerously little, reconnoitred to find a site for a battle near the river Garry, and unexpectedly saw Dundee emerge. He hastily made his men turn simultaneously to the right in their marching order and advance up through thickets past the house of Raon Ruairidh to a plateau, where he drew them up. He had prevented Dundee from surprising him on the march, but now had close behind his line a steep slope to the river plain. Dundee remained still, perhaps to tempt Mackay into attacking, and to give his troops time to recover from their march and postpone an attack until the sun was no longer in their eyes. Mackay's extreme left, Lauder's 200 musketeers, was on a wooded hill, but he feared that he would be outflanked to his right, cutting him off from the pass. To lengthen his line he reduced his regiments (except the most inexperienced, Kenmure's[187]) to three ranks' depth — the worst formation for receiving a highland charge — and

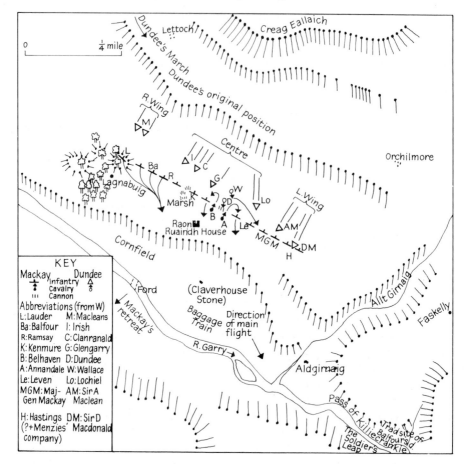

Killiecrankie, 27 July 1689

when the delay allowed Hastings' regiment to arrive, rather than keeping it in reserve, he sent it to the far right. Next to it was Mackay's, then Leven's. Behind the large gap before the next, Kenmure's, he stationed his two troops of horse, not daring to expose them directly to Dundee's cavalry, but hoping, when the clans advanced, to attack those on either side in the flank. He realised his greatest mistake: with eight mediocre troops rather than two, he might have daunted the clans. A bog interrupting communications beyond Kenmure's forced him to leave the left wing to his second-in-command, Brigadier Balfour. His speech to his troops was scarcely inspiring, emphasising chiefly that if they ran away they would be slaughtered by the clans or Atholl men.[188]

Dundee could not spare any troops for a reserve, and also feared being outflanked if he attacked only Mackay's centre. He therefore left gaps between his left wing, the Macdonalds of Sleat, under young Sir Donald and Sir George Barclay (one of the few professional officers the clans admired), and to their right Sir Alexander Maclean's regiment; the centre, Lochiel, Glengarry, Clanranald and Purcell's Irish; and the right wing, Sir John Maclean's, divided in two. Each regiment marked a Williamite one opposite. All were 'deep in file' to ensure that their charge would break through the points it struck in Mackay's line. For two hours from 5 p.m., the armies faced each other. Mackay opened fire with his three cannon, in the centre, but did little harm: one ball allegedly struck a Glenmoriston man full on the targe, but merely knocked him over unharmed. Skirmishers on both sides advanced and fired on the enemy lines, the highlanders inflicting greater casualties. Dundee rode along his lines, encouraging the men.[189]

At seven, he gave the order to attack.[190] The highlanders advanced, the left half of their army faster than the right. Sir Alexander Maclean and Lochiel converged on Mackay's regiment, accidentally, because the Camerons at first outran Lochiel, or because it had such a reputation. His brother, the Lieutenant-Colonel, had trained it well in musketry, and it managed to fire at least two devastating volleys before the highlanders returned fire and closed; while Leven's, left unopposed, fired at close range into the Camerons' flank.[191] Sir William Wallace pointlessly wheeled to the left and joined the highlanders attacking Mackay's, while Dundee with a handful of horsemen charged and silenced the cannon.[192] As Glengarry advanced on Kenmure's, which had fired vigorously, Mackay led out Belhaven's troop to charge him in the flank, but nearly all except Belhaven suddenly fled through Kenmure's regiment. This, according to one account, broke when the charging highlanders shouted, and they poured into the gap. Annandale's leaderless troop, which was intended to attack Lochiel, and part of Leven's regiment also fled. Mackay's left, as the Jacobite right came down on it, suddenly broke and ran, much of it without firing, with the clans quickly in the fugitives' midst cutting them down. Lauder was one of those who escaped down the pass. As the clans struck Mackay's regiment, which had no time to fix bayonets, it fled before them, leaving the Lieutenant-Colonel, the officers and a few pikemen to be killed or wounded. 'In the twinkling of an eye', both generals were left almost alone in the same area. Half Leven's regiment remained unbroken; but Dundee's only force remaining in the field was the Macdonalds of Sleat on the far left who, with Sir Donald fighting at their head, were forcing what was left of Hastings' regiment backwards downhill. As he rode over to take command, he was shot and fell mortally wounded. Colonel Hastings wheeled his regiment back so that the Macdonalds would continue past him downhill, and they, with many leaders wounded or killed and seeing the pursuit below, took the bait, leaving him to climb back to the battlefield.[193]

The pursuit of the fugitives continued, amid screams and cries for quarter, through the baggage-train and down the Garry. Fleeing for the pass and not knowing the country, many were trapped and slaughtered just above it where the river, running between precipitous rocky banks, was hardest to cross. Brigadier Balfour was one of them, killed (according to tradition) by Ballechin's nephew

Rev. Robert Steuart after insultingly refusing his offer of quarter. One fleeing soldier saved himself by leaping from a high rock clean across the river at its narrowest. Night ended the clans' pursuit, but not their plundering. As the first fugitives came down the pass, Murray marched his rapidly-disintegrating force across the hills to Tulliemet, taking it away from the temptations on the line of flight — all he could do. Charles Steuart was among the first to slip away with his men to attack the fleeing soldiers, but even Murray's most loyal subordinates could not prevent theirs from plundering them, and many of the country people murdered as well as robbing. The Williamites claimed that numerically they did more harm than the clans. At Tulliemet, Murray disbanded those who remained and left for Edinburgh to make his explanations.[194]

On the battlefield, a Jacobite party returning under Dunfermline discovered Dundee on the point of death, and were carrying him away when Leven's advanced and fired, mortally wounding Pitcur and driving them off. Dundee died, and his body was stripped and robbed in the night by some Camerons.[195] Mackay brought together the remains of Leven's and Hastings', 400 in all, and, when it was clear that none of the fugitives would return, prepared to march off after sunset. Dunfermline, even with the Gaelic-speaking Balhaldie's help, could not gather enough men to attack them. Mackay marched to the river above the battle area, crossed and was joined by Ramsay with 200 unarmed fugitives he had rallied. Fearing that, though the highlanders were plundering, Dundee and his cavalry might pursue him, he marched over the hills with Robert Menzies to his house at Weem, losing many stragglers to be killed or captured, and from there, by late on 28 July, to Drummond Castle.[196]

Dunfermline claimed that Mackay had left 1,200 casualties on the field, besides perhaps as many more in the flight. The Atholl men brought in 4–500 prisoners, who, apart from the officers, were released — apparently without having to swear not to bear arms against James again.[197] The horrific wounds of the dead and living — smashed skulls, chopped-off arms, bodies split from shoulder to entrails — showed that the broadsword was the clans' most effective weapon. The regulars' was the musket, whose effects, despite victory, gave clear notice that the days of the 'highland charge' were numbered: many of the Gaelic poems on Killiecrankie lamented rather than rejoiced. The most horrific casualty rate was that of the Camerons, half of the 240 present. The Macdonalds of Glengarry and Sleat also suffered heavily, the right scarcely at all. Balhaldie estimated total Jacobite losses at a third of the entire force, about 700 (and the spurious Dundee 'last letter' even higher, at 900). Almost 200 badly wounded men were carried to Blair.[198] Because the gentry of a clan charged at its head, the loss was particularly heavy among them. Mackay's officer casualties, with a general, two lieutenant-colonels and several captains and subalterns killed — his own regiment suffered particularly — or captured, were still light in comparison. The Macdonalds were worst hit. Glengarry lost one brother and another was wounded. In Sir Alexander Maclean's regiment, Macdonald of Largie was killed and his Tutor mortally wounded. Several of Sir Donald's close relatives were killed, or wounded like his second-in-command Barclay.[199]

Everyone, however, from William and Hamilton to the Gaelic poets, admitted that the one decisive death was Dundee's, and that the victory was not worth his loss to the Jacobite cause. Personal achievements and relations were far more important among the highlanders than on the Williamite side. Dundee's had been decisive in creating and sustaining the Highland Army (as it now called itself); and no remaining Scottish Jacobite could match his combination of qualities — soldier, politician, gentleman of honour (vital for a negotiator giving guarantees about James's future conduct) — or his ability to adapt, with Lochiel's help, to an unfamiliar Gaelic society. Some speculation on what would have happened had he survived is justified, for his death leading his troops was not Providence's punishment for romanticism but an occupational hazard of the type of war he had to fight, just as Mackay's in 1692, obeying a superior's command which he knew to be disastrous, was of his. Everything between the Tay and Inverness (which, with the Williamite northern clans, would have been totally isolated for lack of sea communication) would have gone over to Dundee. The rising arranged with Breadalbane would have prevented Argyllshire from being a government bastion, as in the '45. Others who had made vaguer promises would have declared themselves after such successes; in the period of uncertainty before Dundee's death was known many Williamites at Edinburgh prepared, through application to prisoners there, to turn their coats again. Had Dundee and the Highland Army forced the line of Forth, defended by Lanier whose heart was not in Scottish service, Hamilton would have abandoned Edinburgh.[200] However, whether or not he captured Edinburgh, William's next step would abruptly have checked his impetus — sending to Scotland Schomberg's army, assembled for the reconquest of Ireland. The western Presbyterians would have rallied to it in vast numbers — 14,000 were to rise on a lesser emergency in 1690. Dundee's hopes of further success would have depended on matters too uncertain for speculation: how far Schomberg, who disliked irregular warfare, and an army unprepared for privations could have redressed the balance, and how the Lowlands would have reacted to them; whether the Jacobite rally in Ireland that winter could have established itself permanently if Ulster had not already been lost to Schomberg; and whether the English would have continued to support, at unprecedented expense, a usurper who had practically lost half the Three Kingdoms. For Scotland's fate ultimately depended on that English decision.

All this was now might-have-been; but the elegiac note was overdone. Many opponents who now declared Dundee the soul of the rising had a few weeks earlier dismissed him as an almost comic figure deserted by his barbarians. Now, when they declared the danger over, their relapse into faction, corruption and incompetence might help to falsify their prophecy.

NOTES

1. Balcarres, *Memoirs*, 15–17; *Siege*, 17–19, 97–8; *Extracts from the Records of the Burgh of Edinburgh 1681–1689 (Edinburgh Records 1681–9)*, ed. M. Wood & H. Armet (Edinburgh,

1954), 252–4; Sinclair, *Clan Gillean*, 376; NLS MS 7026 fols. 81–3 [Tweeddale] to [Yester], 11 Dec. 1688; SRO GD 112/40/3/4/67, Council to James, 12 Dec. 1688.

2. *Ib.*, 86, PCS minute, 14 Dec. 1688; *ib.*, 88, Dalrymple to Breadalbane, 14 Dec. 1688; *ib.*, 43/1/2/99, 'History of part of the late Earl of Breadalbane's Life' (Breadalbane's Life), 1; *HMCR 11th Report App. 7*, 23,? to Dundee, Nov. 1688; *RPCS*, xiii, liv; Balcarres, *Memoirs*, 17; P. W. J. Riley, *King William and the Scottish Politicians* (Edinburgh, 1979), 11; NLS MS 7026 fol. 85v, [Tweeddale] to [Yester], 16 Dec. 1688.

3. *Melvilles & Leslies*, iii, 193, Notes of events in 1688.

4. *HMCR Buccleuch (Montagu)*, ii, 40, Melfort to Perth, 29 Mar. 1689; Balcarres, *Memoirs*, 18; Dalton, *Scots Army*, 163; BL Add. 19,254 fol. 122, ? to Laird of Banff, 10 Jan. 1689.

5. *HMCR 11th Report App. 7*, 23, ? to Dundee, Nov. 1688; NLS MS 7026 fol. 93v, [Tweeddale] to [Yester], 28 Dec. 1688; Blair, Atholl MSS, Box 29 I (5) 82, Atholl to Murray, 22 Dec, 1688.

6. *Ib.*, 73, same to same, 29 'Nov.' [Dec. 1688]; *Siege*, 15–16, 19–25; NLS MS 7026 fol. 85v, [Tweeddale] to [Yester], 16 Dec. 1688; *ib.*, fol. 87v, same to same, 18 Dec. 1688; *ib.*, fol. 100, same to same, 3 Jan. 1689.

7. *Ib.*, fol. 75, same to same, 4 Jan. 1688[/9]; *ib.*, fol. 84, same to same, 16 Dec. 1688; *ib.*, fol. 119, same to same, 31 Jan. 1689; Riley, *King William*, 12; Atholl, *Chronicles*, i, 271–2, Marchioness to Murray, 3 Jan. 1689; Blair, Atholl MSS, Box 29 I (5) 85, Breadalbane to Atholl, 29 Dec. 1688; *Edinburgh Records 1681–9*, 256–8.

8. *Ib.*, 263–4; *RPCS*, xiii, lv; Balcarres, *Memoirs*, 23; NLS MS 7026 fol. 105, [Tweeddale] to [Yester], 31 Jan. 1689; *ib.*, fol. 143, same to same, 22 Feb. 1689.

9. *State Trials*, xiii, 1447.

10. This tradition, denounced and often 'disproved' by Dundee's biographers, is basically confirmed by a comment of Tweeddale's in February, *before* Dundee's campaign had given it suspicious 'poetic' point: 'in short [Dundee] resents soe much the displeasur he had in holland from the prince of orange as he wold willingly mak a uar upon the king of england'. NLS MS 7026 fol. 143, [Tweeddale] to [Yester], 22 Feb. 1689; Terry, *Claverhouse*, 24–7, 30–3.

11. T. Morer, *A Short Account of Scotland* (London, 1702), 96; *The English Currant*, No. 1, 12 Dec. 1688; C. Huygens, *Journaal*, 2 vols. (Utrecht, 1876), i, 41–2, 43–4; *Correspondentie van Willem III en van Hans Willem Bentinck*, ed. N. Japikse, 5 vols. (The Hague, 1927–37), ii, 631, Verhuel van Onse Marche; *ib.*, 2nd Part, iii, 80–1, Bentinck to Herbert, 10/20 Dec. 1688.

12. *Ib.*, 83, Livingstone, Dundee & Dunmore to William, 11 Dec. 1688; Terry, *Claverhouse*, 243; NLS MS 7026 fol. 88, [Tweeddale] to [Yester], 20 Dec. 1688.

13. James's own list of those who visited him at Rochester disproves the first story, and the silence of Balcarres' own memoirs contradicts the otherwise possible story in his son's. *Life of James*, ii, 268; Macpherson, *Original Papers*, i, 299; Balcarres, *Memoirs*, xvii–xviii, 20, 22; *Correspondence of Henry Hyde, Earl of Clarendon*, ed. S. W. Singer (*Clarendon Corr.*), 2 vols. (London, 1828), ii, 258–9; Terry, *Claverhouse*, 12, 242–4; NLS MS 7026 fol. 85, [Tweeddale] to [Yester], 16 Dec. 1688.

14. Huygens, *Journaal*, i, 78–9 (all dates New Style); Blair, Atholl MSS, Box 29 I (5) 91, Lady Murray to Murray, 5 Jan. 1689.

15. *An Account of the Proceedings of the Estates in Scotland, 1689*–1690, ed. E. W. M. Balfour-Maitland (*Est. Procs.*), 2 vols. (SHS, 1954), ii, 293–6; Burnet, *History*, iv, 39; Balcarres, *Memoirs*, 19, 21; SCA, Blairs Letters, Box T, 1689, 103, C. Whyteford to W. Leslie, 31 Jan. 1689 (NS).

16. For stories of both Dundee and Balcarres parting on hostile terms from William, Morer, *Short Account*, 97; Balcarres, *Memoirs*, xviii–xix (his son's memoirs). *Ib.*, 22–3, 28; *APS*, ix, App., 37; *CSPD 1689–90*, 28, list, 18 Mar. 1689; *Correspondentie*, i, 62, Lijst van de Regimenten . . . , c. 4 Jan. 1689; *Clarendon Corr.*, ii, 251, 259; Creichton, *Memoirs*, 166.

17. *Ib.*, 161–3, 169; *Correspondentie*, ii, 627, 631–2; Marchesa Campana de Cavelli, *Les Derniers Stuarts à St Germain en Laye*, 2 vols. (Paris, 1871), ii, 375; Balcarres, *Memoirs*, 10–11, 23, 31–2; Mackay, *Memoirs*, 132; Creichton, *Memoirs*, 169; Macpherson, *Original Papers*, i, 363, Dundee to Melfort, 27 June 1689; Drumlanrig, Queensberry Papers, Vol. 121, 41, Douglas to Queensberry, 24 Apr. 1690; *ib.*, 45, same to same, 4 July 1691; NLS MS 7026 fol. 143, [Tweeddale] to [Yester], 22 Feb. 1689.

18. William would recall the Atholl-Nassau link as a reason for favour when not pressed to do so, as when he was appointing Lord Murray Secretary in 1696. *Ib.*, fol. 79, same to same, 8 Jan. 1688[/9]; Balcarres, *Memoirs*, 23; Riley, *King William*, 12; Blair, Atholl MSS, Box 44/II/22, 'Memorial des Emplois' [post 1714]. Lenman's summary of the attitudes of Atholl and his family during 1689 (*Jacobite Risings*, 37–8) relies on too narrow a range of sources.

19. Balcarres, *Memoirs*, 19–20; *Clarendon Corr.*, ii, 206; H. C. Foxcroft, *Life and Letters of Sir George Savile, first Marquis of Halifax*, 2 vols. (London, 1898), ii, 205; Riley, *King William*, 14.

20. Creichton's story that the arrest was made on Hamilton's own advice is groundless. *CSPD 1689–90*, 11, warrant, 28 Feb. 1689; *Life of James*, ii, 268; Balcarres, *Memoirs*, 21–2; *Clarendon Corr.*, ii, 265–6; Creichton, *Memoirs*, 165; House of Lords Record Office (HLRO), Willcocks MSS, Section VI, 26, Yester to Tweeddale, 28 Feb. 1689; *ib.*, 27, same to same, 2 Mar. 1689.

21. Riley, *King William*, 14–15; BL MS Lansdowne 1163C, 214, Melfort to Innes, 11 Nov. 1690(NS).

22. There is, noticeably, evidence that Sunderland used Arran to apply to James, none that Hamilton did. *Journals of the House of Lords*, (*LJ*) (London, n.d.), xvi, 599, Melfort to Perth, 17 Feb. 1700/1; Marshall, *Days of Duchess Anne*, 169–70, 186; Blair, Atholl MSS, Box 29 I (7) 68, Arran to Murray, 17 Apr. 1694.

23. *Leven & Melville*, 213, Lockhart to Melville, 30 July 1689; SRO SP 3/1 fol. 85v, Johnston to Ormiston, 27 Dec. 1692.

24. *CSPD 1691–2*, 201, Melville to William, 26 Mar. '1692' [1690]; Balcarres, *Memoirs*, 22–3; Riley, *King William*, 13–14; Drumlanrig, Queensberry Papers, Bundle 1185, 4, 'Memoriall for My sone'; NLS MS 7026 fol. 108, [Tweeddale] to [Yester], 22 Jan. 1689.

25. *Ib.*, fol. 138, same to same, 16 Feb. 1689; Foxcroft, *Halifax*, ii, 203; SRO GD 112/43/1/2/98, Carwhin's draft biography of Breadalbane (the fair copy 'Breadalbane's Life', *ib.*, 99, misreads 'Chancellor' as 'Counsellor').

26. *Leven & Melville*, xiiin; *ib.*, 14–15, exoneration for Tarbat, 25 Apr. 1689; *ib.*, 23–4, J. Steuart's opinion, 24 May 1689; *ib.*, 96, Sir P. Hume to Melville, 27 June 1689; Foxcroft, *Halifax*, ii, 220, 233; BL MS Lansdowne 1163A, 162, Melfort to Innes, 23 Apr. 1690(NS); NLS MS 7026 fol. 98, [Tweeddale] to [Yester], 1 Jan. 1689; *HMCR Buccleuch (Montagu)*, ii, 45–6, Melville to [William], 16 Apr. 1689.

27. *Ib.*, 41–2, [Tarbat] to Melville, 13 Apr. 1689; *Culloden Papers*, 334, Memorandum anent the Viscount Tarbat, [1701]; *Leven & Melville*, 16, Portland to [Melville], 25 Apr. 1689.

28. Creichton claimed that the regiment never took the new oaths, but he had reason to lie. *Ib.*, 4–5, Stair to same, 27 Mar. 1689; Foxcroft, *Halifax*, ii, 212; *Est. Procs.*, i, 199–200; NLS MS 3740 fol. 80, Mackay to Blathwayt, 2 Feb. 1688[/9]; Sir J. Reresby, *Memoirs*, ed.

A. Browning (Glasgow, 1936), 558; Balcarres, *Memoirs*, 23; Creichton, *Memoirs*, 166–8; Mackay, *Memoirs*, 3.

29. *Ib.*, 4–6, 59, 119; *ib.*, 221–2, Instructions to Mackay, [7 Mar. 1689]; *Leven & Melville*, 6, Portland to Melville, 1 Apr. 1689; *ib.*, 13, Stair to same, 21 Apr. 1689; Macpherson, *Loyall Dissuasive*, 9–10, 164.

30. *APS*, ix, 12, Lord Mountalexander etc to Hamilton, 22 Feb. 1689; Campana de Cavelli, ii, 539, Memoire de M. de Pointis, Feb. 1689; NLS MS 7026 fol. 163, Convention minutes, 18 Mar. 1689.

31. Both Balhaldie and John Cameron of Lochiel accidentally undervalue Sir Ewen's action by assuming that he knew of James's arrival in Ireland; in fact the clans still did not know that he was coming when they sent a messenger at the end of March. The letter from James which Balhaldie cites would have arrived much later even had it not been intercepted. *Memoirs of Locheill*, 233–4; 'The Camerons in the '15', *TGSI*, xxvi, 66–7; Mackay, *Memoirs*, 4; *Négociations de M. le Comte d'Avaux en Irelande*, ed. P. Hogan, (D'Avaux, *Négociations*; Irish Manuscripts Commission (IMC), 1934), 76, d'Avaux to Louvois, 16 Apr. 1689(NS); Macpherson, *Original Papers*, i, 354, 'News from Scotland with Mr Hay', recd 7 July 1689; NLS MS 7026 fol. 143v, [Tweeddale] to [Yester], 22 Feb. 1689; *ib.*, MS 1672 fol. 42, Argyll to Lochnell, 9 Mar. 1689.

32. SRO REF 310.044 (GD 44), 97, Perth to Gordon, 9 Feb. 1689; *Spalding Club Misc.*, v, 195, Countess of Errol to Dr Fraser, 22 Feb. 1689.

33. *HMCR Hope-Johnstone*, 188, 'Information against Mr Thomas Crighton'; *APS*, ix, 31; *Memoirs of Locheill*, 236–7; J. Dowden (ed.) 'The Siege of Edinburgh Castle, 1689', *Northern Notes & Queries (NNQ)*, i (1886), 4.

34. *Ib.*, 5; Balcarres, *Memoirs*, 23–4; *Siege*, 26–8; HLRO, Willcocks MSS, Section VI, 26, Yester to Tweeddale, 28 Feb. 1689; NLS MS 7026 fol. 147v, [Tweeddale] to [Yester], 28 Feb. 1689.

35. *Ib.*, fol. 145, same to same, 26 Feb. 1689; *ib.*, fol. 149, same to same, 2 Mar. 1689; Balcarres, *Memoirs*, 22–4; Macpherson, *Original Papers*, i, 367, Dundee to Melfort, 28 June 1689; Lenman, *Jacobite Risings*, 39–41; Drumlanrig, Queensberry Papers, bundle 1185, 6, Memorandum about the ensuing Convention, 1689.

36. The loyalists in the first days of the Convention tried to obtain a proclamation banishing all strangers from Edinburgh, but discussion was always put off. *APS*, ix, 23; *Est. Procs.*, i, 21; *ib.* 33–4, Dundee to Hamilton, 29 Mar. 1689; Mackay, *Memoirs*, 4; Balcarres, *Memoirs*, 24, 31; *Siege*, 29, 37; NLS MS Adv. 33.7.8 (Minutes of the Convention), 4, 7, 11; *ib.*, MS 7026 fol. 158, [Tweeddale] to [Yester], 14 Mar. 1689.

37. *APS*, ix, 4–5; SRO GD 112/43/1/2/99, Breadalbane's Life, 1; *ib.*, 43/1/4/8, A. Campbell to Breadalbane, 23 Apr. 1689.

38. *APS*, ix, 6; Balcarres, *Memoirs*, 24–5; Riley, *King William*, 12; NLS MS 7026 fol. 156v, [Tweeddale] to [Yester], 12 Mar. 1689; *ib.*, fol. 158, same to same, 14 Mar. 1689.

39. Balcarres' claim that Dundee himself visited the Castle to encourage Gordon must be wrong. *APS*, ix, 6–8; Balcarres, *Memoirs*, 26; *Siege*, 28–34, 39; 'Siege of Edinburgh Castle', *NNQ*, i, 4; SRO REF 310.044 (GD 44), 96, William to Gordon, 6 Feb. 1688/9; NLS MS Adv. 33.7.8, 7.

40. *APS*, ix, 9–10n; *LJ*, xvii, 404, Sir J. Maclean's discovery, [1703]; Balcarres, *Memoirs*, 26–8; D'Avaux, *Négociations, Supplement*, ed. J. Hogan (IMC, 1958), 4–5, d'Avaux to Louvois, 11 Mar. 1689(NS); NLS MS Adv. 33.7.8, 12; SCA, Blairs Letters, Box T, 1689, 54, W. Innes to [L. Innes], 26 Apr. 1689.

41. *APS*, ix, 5; *Est. Procs.*, i, 11, 14; *ib.*, 33–4, Dundee to Hamilton, 27 Mar. 1689; *Siege*, 33, 35; Balcarres, *Memoirs*, 26–8; *Leven & Melville*, 54, Lord [Murray] to Melville, 11 June

1689; *Memoirs of the Lord Viscount Dundee* (London, 1714), 22; Terry, *Claverhouse*, 253–5; SRO GD 26/xiii/78 fol. 59, Tarbat's memorial [1689]; NLS MS 7026 fol. 175, minutes, 28 Mar. 1689; *Thanes of Cawdor*, 381–2, ? to Lady H. Campbell, [Mar. 1689].

42. It seems certain that Dundee did climb the rock (after originally calling up), since not even the garrison overheard his secret agreement with Gordon. *Ib; Siege*, 38, 69–70; Balcarres, *Memoirs*, 30; *Memoirs of Dundee*, 22; 'Siege of Edinburgh Castle', *NNQ*, 4; *Est. Procs.*, i, 7, 11; Terry, *Claverhouse*, 257–8; NLS MS Adv. 33.7.8., 18.

43. *Ib.*, 15–17; Balcarres, *Memoirs*, 30–1; *Est. Procs.*, i, 8; *Calendar of Treasury Books (CTB)*, ix, 897–8; SCA, Blairs Letters, Box Y, unsigned, Diary of the Convention; *APS*, ix, 11, 18.

44. *Ib.*, 12–13; *Est. Procs.*, i, 7.

45. *Ib.*, 7, 9, 34; *APS*, ix, 14, 16, 32–3; *Leven & Melville*, 113, Tarbat to Melville, n.d; *Memoirs of Locheill*, 235; NLS MS 7026 fol. 175, Minutes, 28 Mar. 1689; SCA, Blairs Letters, Box Y, unsigned, Diary of the Convention; Balcarres, *Memoirs*, 34–5.

46. *Ib.*, 34–6; *Leven & Melville*, 11–13, Queensberry, Atholl to William, 13 Apr. 1689; *Est. Procs.*, i, 9–10, 14–15, 16–17, 29, 33, 36; Riley, *King William*, 12–13; NLS MS 7026 fol. 167, [Tweeddale] to [Yester], 23 Mar. 1689; *ib.*, fol. 170, same to same, 26 Mar. 1689; *in.*, fol. 184, same to same, 4 Apr. 1689.

47. *Ib.*, fol. 167, same to same, 23 Mar. 1689; *ib.*, fol. 170, same to same, 26 Mar. 1689; *Siege*, 38–45; *Memoirs of Dundee*, 39; *Est. Procs.*, i, 12, 15, 22.

48. *Ib.*, 18, 21; *RPCS*, xiii, 334; Mackay, *Memoirs*, 4–7; *Siege*, 45; *APS*, ix, 23, 67–8; NLS MS 7026 fol. 176, [Tweeddale] to [Yester], 30 Mar. 1689.

49. However, the prisoner who accused him was being examined by Argyll, and it was Argyll's uncle who succeeded him. *APS*, ix, 78–9; *ib.*, App. 6, 26, 31; *RPCS*, xiii, 457; *ib.*, xiv, 28, 591; *Leven & Melville*, 192–3, Dalrymple to Melville, 24 July 1689; *Est, Procs.*, i, 90, 93, 107; SRO GD 406/M9/194, H. Farquhar's confession, ? 24 July 1689.

50. *APS*, ix, 17–18, 20–1, 25–6, 31–3; *HMCR Buccleuch (Montagu)*, ii, 36, Tyrconnell to Hamilton, 15 Mar. 1689.

51. The Macdonalds, of course are not counted as one clan in these estimates. The *Grameid*, the epic of the rising, claims that both Camerons and Macleans mustered a thousand men, but more prosaic documents show that this was an exaggeration. J. Philip, *The Grameid*, ed. A. D. Murdoch (SHS, 1888), 130, 140; Lenman, *Jacobite Risings*, 44–7; SRO GD 26/viii/71, Number of highland men with Dundee, [June 1689]; *Leven & Melville*, 38, Tarbat to Melville, ? 1 June 1689.

52. *Ib.*, 38–9; Mackay, *Memoirs*, 18–19; *CSPD 1690–1*, 491–2, Concessions to highlanders, 17/27 Aug. 1691; Lenman, *Jacobite Risings*, 46–7; Macdonald, *Clan Donald*, ii, 340, iii, 384; Macfarlane, *Gen. Colls.*, i, 138; BL MS Lansdowne 1163C, 238, Melfort to Mary of Modena, 25 Nov. 1690 (NS).

53. *Siege*, 54–5; *Est. Procs.*, ii, 38, 47, 63; *Grameid*, 91–2; Perth, *Letters*, 1, Perth to Countess of Erroll, 29 Dec, 1688; R. Mitchison, 'The Movements of Scottish Corn Prices in the Seventeenth and Eighteenth Centuries', *Economic History Review (Ec.HR)*, 2nd Series, xviii, 280–1; Blair, Atholl MSS, Box 29 I (5) 96, Lady Murray to Murray, 14 Jan. 1689.

54. Burnet was mistaken in supposing that an agent had carried £5–6,000 to Scotland that spring (*History*, iv, 31–2). Macpherson, *Original Papers*, i, 362, Dundee to Melfort, 27 June 1689.

55. *Grameid*, 75–8.

56. *HMCR Roxburghe*, 118, Forbes to Sir P. Hume, 22 Aug. 1689; Lenman, *Jacobite Risings*, 55–7, 61, 127–38; A. & H. Tayler, *Jacobites of Aberdeenshire and Banffshire in the Rising of 1715* (Edinburgh, 1934), vii.

57. Mackay, *Memoirs*, 111.

58. NLS MS 1329 fol. 76, Sir A. Mackenzie of Coul to Delvine, 10 Aug. 1689; *ib.*, fol. 82, same to same, 1 June 1689; *ib.*, fol. 102, same to same, 26 Dec. 1689.

59. *HMCR Buccleuch (Montagu)*, ii, 42, Tarbat to Melville, 13 Apr. 1689; *Leven & Melville*, 38, same to same, ? 1 June 1689; *Earls of Cromartie*, i, clviii–clxxi, same to [Master of Tarbat], n.d.; *ib.*, cxcvi–vii, Mackay to Major Mackay, 11 May 1689; Mackay, *Memoirs*, 25.

60. *Ib.*, 232, Mackay to Hamilton, [May] 1689; Dundee, *Letters*, ed. G. Smythe, (Bannatyne Club, 1826), 42, Dundee to Macleod, 23 June 1689; Stevenson, *Alasdair MacColla*, 269; Mackay, *Book of Mackay*, 160.

61. Macpherson, *Original Papers*, i, 360–1, Dundee to Melfort, 27 June 1689; Balcarres, *Memoirs*, 38; *Melvilles & Leslies*, ii, 108, Carleton to Breadalbane, 18 June 1689; SRO GD 112/43/4/6, [Dundee] to same, 20 July 1689.

62. *Ib.*, G.D 170/711, Sir J. Maclean to same, 20 May 1689; GD 112/40/3/3/81, Argyll to same, [? 1689]; *ib.*, 39/1206, same to same, 28 Apr. 1689; *ib.*, 40/3/4/72, Breadalbane to Barcaldine, 30 Apr. 1689; *ib.*, 43/1/2/99, Breadalbane's Life, 2.

63. In November 1688, James had abruptly and unilaterally revoked the grant by Charles I to his family of the feu duties of Islay, on technical grounds, despite past ratifications. The justification for this action, likely to ruin the Calder family, was the pressing need for money in the emergency; yet a few days later the duties for 1688 were granted to Melfort. In May 1689, Calder was expressing the hope that all who opposed the protestant religion would be destroyed. Mackay, *Memoirs*, 19, 45–6; *HMCR Hope-Johnstone*, 161, Hill to Crawford, 16 Nov. 1690; *ib.*, 173, Lt-Col Hamilton to same, 10 Sept. 1691; *Thanes of Cawdor*, 379, Calder to bailie of Islay, 29 May 1689; SRO SP 4/13, 327–30, 348–9, 359–60, papers on the resumption.

64. Balcarres, *Memoirs*, 25; *HMCR Buccleuch (Montagu)*, ii, 163, S. Weeld's answers, 8 Dec. 1694; Hopkins, 'Aspects of Jacobite Conspiracy', 71–3.

65. *Ib.*, 407; *Est. Procs.*, i, 132, 138, 161; *HMCR Le Fleming*, 286, newsletter, 21 Aug. 1690; Oxford, Bodleian Library (Bodl.), MS Carte 228 fols. 188–9, Col. Langston to T. Wharton, 1 Aug. 1689.

66. SRO REF 310.044 (GD 44), 99, Mackay to Gordon, 23 Apr. 1689; NLS MS 7026 fol. 211, [Tweeddale] to [Yester], 16 Apr. 1689.

67. *APS*, ix, App., 13, 21; Mackay, *Memoirs*, 8, 12; *ib.*, 239, Mackay to Hamilton, 27 June 1689; Whyte, *Agriculture & Society*, 82; SRO GD 112/40/4/2/2, Breadalbane to Carwhin, 19 Feb. 1690; NLS MS 3740 fol. 88, Lanier to Blathwayt, 29 May 1689.

68. *Ib.*, MS 7026 fol. 106v, [Tweeddale] to [Yester], 19 Jan. 1689; *ib.*, fol. 143, same to same, 22 Feb. 1689; *Spalding Club Misc.*, v, 198, Countess of Erroll to Dr Fraser, 22 Mar. 1689.

69. MacIain in 1692 offered to send to Flanders any of his clansmen who would not submit to the government. *Highland Papers*, 106–7, Report, 20 June 1695; R. Wodrow, *Analecta*, 4 vols. (Maitland Club, 1842), i, 205; A. Fletcher, *Selected Political Writings and Speeches*, ed. D. Daiches (Edinburgh, 1979), 34, 37.

70. Balcarres, *Memoirs*, 8; *Culloden Papers*, 31920, 'State of Things in 1696'; J. Halliday, 'The Club and the Revolution in Scotland', *SHR*, xlv (1966), 143–59. I hope shortly to produce a biography of Montgomerie.

71. *Leven & Melville*, 176, Crawford to Melville, 18 July 1689; *ib.*, 195–6, Dalrymple to same, 25 July 1689; *ib.*, 215, same to same, 30 July 1689. All, of course, biased.

72. Foxcroft, *Supplement to Burnet*, 192–3; BL Add. 51,511 (Lord Halifax's notebook), fols. 24v, 43v, 47.

73. *CSPD 1687-9*, 185, Pass for N. Macleod & D. Macdonald, 12 Apr. 1688; *RPCS*, xiii, xlvii; Macpherson, *Original Papers*, i, 180, 'Journal of what passed in Ireland', 12 Mar.–18 July 1689; Macfarlane, *Gen. Colls.*, i, 139; Dunlop, 'A Chief and his Lawyer', *TGSI*, xlv, 259; E. B. Powley, *The Naval Side of King William's War*, (London, 1972) 242; HLRO, Willcocks MSS, Section VI, 25, Yester to Tweeddale, 26 Feb. 1689.

74. *Leven & Melville*, 223n, Dundee to Murray, 19 July 1689; BL MS Lansdowne 1163B, 26, Melfort to Innes, 6 June 1690 (NS); D'Avaux, *Négociations*, 180, d'Avaux to Louis, 27 May 1689(NS).

75. *Ib.*, 48–9, same to same, 4 Apr. 1689(NS); *ib.*, 244, Louis to d'Avaux, 2 June 1689(NS); Balcarres, *Memoirs*, 29, 38; *HMCR Hamilton Supplement*, 113, Sir A. Kennedy to Balcarres, 29 Mar. 1689; *HMCR Buccleuch (Montagu)*, ii, 40, Melfort to Perth, 29 Mar. 1689; *ib.*, 43, Melville to [William], 16 Apr. 1689.

76. *Ib.*, 38–9, James to Balcarres, 29 Mar. 1689; Dundee, *Letters*, 35–7, same to Dundee, 29 Mar. 1689; *HMCR Hamilton*, 178–9, same to Atholl; NLS MS 3194 fol. 120, same to Lochiel; *ib.*, MS 1031 fol. 28, Hamilton to Selkirk, 18 Apr. 1689; *HMCR Lords 1689-90*, 152–5, James's proclamation, 1 Apr. 1689; Macpherson, *Original Papers*, i, 179–80, 'Journal'; *Siege*, 115–6, James to Gordon, 29 Mar. 1689.

77. *Ib.*, 116, same to same, 17 May 1689.

78. Both Balcarres and the *Proceedings*, quoting from memory, made the offending passage more sinister. *RPCS* xv, 148; *Est. Procs.*, i, 33, 38, 42, 43–4, 46–7, 56, 61; *HMCR Buccleuch (Montagu)*, ii, 43–4, Melville to [William], 16 Apr. 1689; Mackay, *Memoirs*, 7; Balcarres, *Memoirs*, 36–9; Joshua c.9 vv.21–7; SRO GD 26/xiii/78 fol. 178v, Melville's note; GD 406/1/3509, Instructions to Brady; *ib.*, 9138, Melfort to Balcarres, 30 Mar. 1689.

79. Macpherson, *Original Papers*, i, 367, Dundee to Melfort, 28 June 1689.

80. *APS*, ix, 47–8, 50, 52, 54–6, 58–9.

81. *Ib.*, 31, 44, 61–2, 77; *RPCS*, xiii, 385–6; *Est. Procs.*, i, 64; *HMCR Buccleuch (Montagu)*, ii, 47–8, William to Hamilton, [Apr. 1689].

82. Terry, *Claverhouse*, 265–72; *Grameid*, 45–50; Macpherson, *Original Papers*, i, 352–3, 'News from Scotland with Mr Hay', recd 7 July 1689; *Seafield Corr.*, 49, F. Ogilvie to Findlater, 2 May 1689; *Analecta Hibernica*, xxi, ed. L. Tate (IMC, 1959), 104, Melfort to Louvois, 29 May 1689; *Est. Procs.*, i, 199; Creichton, *Memoirs*, 170; W. D. Simpson, 'The Early Castles of Mar', *Proceedings of the Society of Antiquaries of Scotland (PSAS)*, lxiii (1928–9), 121–2; NLS MS 1329 fol. 79, Sir A. Mackenzie to Delvine, 30 Apr. 1689; Mackay, *Memoirs*, 7–8.

83. *Ib.*, 8–13; *ib.*, 235, Mackay to Hamilton, 27 June 1689.

84. Burnet, *History*, iv, 48, 176; *The Scots Brigade in the Dutch Service*, ed. J. Ferguson, i (SHS, 1899), 471–2; *RPCS*, xiii, 420; *Melvilles & Leslies*, ii, 127–8, Melville to Hamilton, 4 June 1689; SRO GD 406/1/3607, Mackay to same, 4 July 1689.

85. NLS MS 7012 fol. 205v, Sir A. Bruce to Tweeddale, 8 Nov. 1690; Mackay, *Memoirs*, 63–4, 69–70, 94–5.

86. *Ib.*, 255, Mackay to Hamilton, 29 July 1689; *ib.*, 346, same to Melville, 29 Aug. 1690; *Leven & Melville*, 37–8, Tarbat to same, ? 1 June 1689; *Est. Procs.*, i, 116, 138–9, 155–6.

87. NLS MS 7012 fols. 205v–206, Sir A. Bruce to Tweeddale, 8 Nov. 1690; Atholl, *Chronicles*, i, 310, Mackay to Murray, 4 Aug. 1689; Mackay, *Memoirs*, 230, same to Melville, 14 June 1689; *ib.*, 232, same to Hamilton, [June] 1689; *ib.*, 236, same to same, 27 June 1689.

88. *Ib.*, 228, same to Melville, 13 June 1689; *ib.*, 232, same to Hamilton, [June] 1689; *RPCS*, xv, 671–2, same to Grant, 4 Dec. 1690.

89. *Thanes of Cawdor*, 377, Macpherson bond, 14 Mar. 1689; Fraser-Macintosh, *Letters*, 119–20, Dundee to Mackintosh, 24 Apr. 1689; A. Macpherson (ed.), 'Gleanings from the

Charter Chest at Cluny Castle', *TGSI*, xx, 225, same to Cluny, 20 July 1689; Mackay, *Memoirs*, 9–10.

90. *Ib.*, 8, 13; *APS*, ix, App., 2; SRO GD 406/1/3569, Mr of Forbes to Hamilton, 18 June 1689.

91. *APS*, ix, App., 57, J. Osburne's deposition, 14 May 1690; *HMCR 1st Report*, 115; *Seafield Corr.*, 49, F. Ogilvie to Findlater, 2 May 1689; *Grameid*, 53–4; Fraser, *Chiefs of Grant*, i, 520–1; SRO GD 26/viii/12, ? to ?, 2 May 1689; *ib.*, 72, ? to Dunfermline, 27 [Apr.] 1689; NLS MS 1329 fol. 80, Sir A. Mackenzie to Delvine 7 May 1689.

92. *Ib*; Terry, *Claverhouse*, 273–4; *RPCS*, xiv, 272–3; *Grameid*, 54–5; *Memoirs of Locheill*, 237; Macpherson, *Original Papers*, i, 353, 'News from Scotland'; *Family of Kilravock*, 379.

93. Mackay, *Memoirs*, 13–16; *APS*, ix, 86; *The Records of Elgin*, ed. W. Cramond, 2 vols. (New Spalding Club, 1903–8), i, 346–8, 352; Macgill, *Old Ross-shire*, ii, 22–3, Mackay to Balnagown, 12 Apr. 1689.

94. The Camerons' excuse confirms that Keppoch had *not* been sent by the Clans. Macpherson, *Original Papers*, i, 353, 'News from Scotland'; *APS*, ix, 207 (? misdated claim); *Grameid*, 55–6; *Memoirs of Dundee*, 23; Terry, *Claverhouse*, 277.

95. *APS*, ix, App., 33; Mackay, *Memoirs*, 16–17, 121; *ib.*, 229–30, Mackay to Melville, 14 June 1689; *RPCS*, xiii, 407; *ib.*, xiv, 593–4; *ib.*, xv, 178–9; *Earls of Cromartie*, i, cxcvi–vii, Mackay to Major Mackay, 11 May 1689; *ib.*, 62, same to Tarbat, 8 May 1689; *ib.*, 62–3, same to same, 20 May 1689; *Leven & Melville*, 38, Tarbat to Melville, ? 1 June 1689; Fraser-Macintosh, *Antiquarian Notes* (1st ser.), 59–61; NLS MS 1329 fol. 81, Sir A. Mackenzie to Delvine, 21 May 1689; *ib.*, fol. 82, same to same, 1 June 1689; *ib.*, MS 1332 fol. 40, A. Mackenzie to same, 21 May 1689.

96. Stewart, *The Stewarts of Appin*, 206, A. Stewart of Ballachulish to Stewart of Invernahyle, [1690]; *Grameid*, 56–8; SRO GD 406/M9/194, H. Farquhar's confession, 24 July 1689; Macpherson, *Original Papers*, i, 353–4, 'News from Scotland'.

97. *Ib.*, 354; Terry, *Claverhouse*, 277–82; *APS*, ix, App., 19, 22, 24, 37; *ib.*, 54–6, Lt. J. Colt's deposition, 12 May 1690; *ib.*, 57, J. Osburnes deposition, 14 May 1690; *ib.*, 58–9, C. Steuart's deposition, 14 May 1690; *Est. Procs.*, i, 67; *Grameid*, 58–75; *HMCR Roxburghe*, 117, Rollo to Sir P. Hume, 14 May 1689, n.d; *Scots Peerage*, iii, 380–1; Lenman, *Jacobite Risings*, 47; Atholl, *Chronicles*, i, 277, ? to Murray, 11 May 1689.

98. *Ib.*, 283, Atholl to same, 23 June [1689]; NLS MS 3740 fol. 86, Lanier to Blathwayt, 25 May 1689; *APS*, ix, 86; *ib.*, App., 19–20, 23, 27, 33.

99. *RPCS*, xv, 107–8, 148–9; Wodrow, *Analecta*, i, 189–90; [M. Shields], *Faithful Contendings Displayed* (Glasgow, 1780), 390–405; Erskine, *Journal*, 140, 144; SRO GD 26/ix/225, T. Turnbull to [Cardross], 27 July 1689; *ib.*, 334, [W. Lawrie to Melville, 12 Aug. 1689]; Mackay, *Memoirs*, 298, Mackay to Melville, 9 Nov. 1689.

100. *Ib.*, 286, same to same, 12 Oct. 1689; *APS*, ix, 92; *ib.*, App., 11, 20, 22, 25–6; *RPCS*, xiv, 5–6; *Est. Procs.*, i, 41; SRO GD 26/ix/291, muster rolls Argyll's reg., Jan. 1690.

101. D'Avaux confusingly refers to the messenger as 'Le Chevalier Macklean', which should logically mean Sir John. *Grameid*, 138n; Macfarlane, *Gen. Colls.*, i, 149; Sinclair, *Clan Gillean*, 303; SRO GD 26/viii/20, Sir A. Maclean to Macnachtan, 27 June 1689; D'Avaux, *Négociations*, 79–80, Maclean's memoire, 16 Apr. 1689 (NS); *ib.*, 60, d'Avaux to Louis, 16 Apr. 1689 (NS); *ib.*, 76, same to Louvois, 16 Apr. 1689 (NS); Drumlanrig, Queensberry Papers, Vol. 122, 46, Breadalbane to Queensberry. 12 Jan. 1686; *Eachann Bacach*, 234–8.

102. *LJ*, xvii, 495, Campbell [of Glendaruel]'s interrogation, [1704]; D'Avaux, *Négociations*, 60, d'Avaux to Louis, 16 Apr. 1689 (NS); *ib.*, 77, same to Louvois, 16 Apr.

1689 (NS); *ib.*, 180, same to Louis, 27 May 1689 (NS); Macpherson, *Original Papers*, i, 180, 'Journal of what passed in Ireland', 12 Mar.–18 July 1689.

103. *Ib.*, 189; J. D'Alton, *Illustrations . . . of King James's Irish Army List*, 2 vols. (Dublin, 1860), ii, 2, 160–2, 352–4; Dalton, *Scots Army*, 115, 155, 165; The Buchans of Auchmacoy (typescript, SRO NRA(S)), 20, 22, 85–6.

104. Hamilton's alleged final offer of surrender on 18 April (reprinted C. D. Milligan, *History of the Siege of Londonderry, 1689* (Londonderry, 1951), 128–9) specifically mentions that Gordon is holding the Castle and 'Dundee is in Armes'; but the peculiar tone of this and the garrison's alleged reply indicates that both are later forgeries invented when the city vainly appealed to the ungrateful English parliament to repay its immense losses.

105. *Ib.*, 187–9; Macpherson, *Original Papers*, i, 192–3, 'Journal . . . ', 12 Mar.–18 July 1689; *Analecta Hibernica* xxi, 99–100, Rosen to [Louvois], 20 May 1689 (NS); Buchans of Auchmacoy, 87, Melfort to Buchan, 10 June 1689.

106. D'Avaux, *Négociations*, 150–1, James's memorial, 16 May 1689 (NS); *ib.*, 189, d'Avaux to Louis, 5 June 1689 (NS).

107. Macpherson, *Original Papers*, i, 364–5, Dundee to Melfort, 27 June 1689.

108. It is overlooked in A. McKerral, *Kintyre in the Seventeenth Century* (Edinburgh, 1948).

109. *APS*, ix, 73, 77–8; *Est. Procs.* i, 57–8, 60, 99; *Memoirs of Locheill*, 363, J. Campbell to A. Campbell of Kilberry, 1 May 1689; *HMCR Finch*, ii, 212, Rooke to Nottingham, 1 June 1689; *DNB*, sub, 'King, Robert, second Baron Kingston'.

110. *APS*, ix, 17, 22, 64, 79; *ib.*, App., 3, 6, 8, 13, 23–4; *Est. Procs.*, i, 60, 66, 92–3.

111. *Ib.*, 71, 77; *APS*, ix, App., 11, 19; *Grameid*, 119; Macpherson, *Original Papers*, i, 358, 'Relation of what passed in Scotland', 2–23 June 1689; Maclean, 'Celtic Sources', 296, Aonghus Mac Alasdair Ruaidh, 'Latha Raon Ruairidh' (translated by Maclean); SRO GD 26/viii/20, Sir A. Maclean to Macnachtan, 27 June 1689; *ib.*, ix/241, Cpt. Young to Col. Balfour, [16 May] 1689; GD 406/M9/194, H. Farquhar's confession, 24 July 1689.

112. *RPCS*, xiv, 414–15; *Est. Procs.*, i, 77–8; *APS*, ix, App., 16.

113. *Ib.*, 9, 10, 11, 14, 33; *APS*, ix, 83; *London Gazette*, No. 2456, 23–27 May 1689.

114. *Est. Procs.*, i, 78; SRO GD 112/39/1207, Auchinbreck to Breadalbane, 23 May 1689; *APS*, ix, App., 9, 10, 11, 17, 26.

115. *Ib.*, 11, 13, 34; *RPCS*, xiii, lvii; Powley, *Naval Side*, 141, 220–1.

116. J. Blaeu, *Atlas Major*, xii (Scotland), (Amsterdam, 1662), map of Kintyre; SRO GD 26/ix/241, Cpt. Young to Col. Balfour, [16 May] 1689; Stevenson, *Alasdair MacColla*, 232–5; *APS*, ix, 83; *Est. Procs.*, i, 100; Macpherson, *Original Papers*, i, 358, 'Relation of what past in Scotland', 2–23 June 1689.

117. *Ib.* (Loup as 'Lurip'); *APS*, ix, 82–3; *Thanes of Cawdor*, 378–9, Sir H. Campbell to bailie of Islay, 29 May 1689; *Est. Procs.*, i, 95–6.

118. *Ib.*, 96; *APS*, ix, App., 34; *HMCR Finch*, ii, 212, Rooke to Nottingham, 1 June 1689.

119. Macfarlane, *Gen. Colls.*, i, 139; Macpherson, *Original Papers*, i, 354, 'News from Scotland'.

120. *Ib.*, 358–9, 'Relation of what past in Scotland', 2–23 June 1689 (dates wrong); *ib.*, 368, 'An account of the engagements . . . ', 15 Dec. 1689; *HMCR Finch*, ii, 212–13, Rooke to Nottingham, 1 June 1689; *London Gazette*, No. 2461, 10–13 June 1689; *RPCS*, xiii, 382, 402; *Thanes of Cawdor*, 378, Sir H. Campbell to bailie of Islay, 29 May 1689; SRO GD 112/39/1207, Auchinbreck to Breadalbane, 23 May 1689; NLS MS 1031 fol. 41v, Hamilton to Selkirk, 28 May 1689.

121. Of the 400 men Sir Alexander had in Gigha, 100 were Macleans now restored to Sir John. He himself estimated that he had three Kintyre companies under Gallachallie, and

two Irish ones. Macpherson, *Original Papers*, i, 368, 'Account of the engagements', 15 Dec. 1689; *ib.*, 357, 'News from Scotland'; SRO GD 26/viii/20, Sir A. Maclean to Macnachtan, 27 June 1689.

122. It was, of course, young Sir Donald who had obtained these commissions. *Grameid*, 118–64; Macdonald, *Clan Donald*, ii, 787–8, Keppoch's obligation, 18 May 1689; Macpherson, *Original Papers*, i, 354, 'News from Scotland'.

123. *Ib.*, 354–5; Mackay, *Memoirs*, 17–18, 20–2, 122–4; *ib.*, 231–2, Mackay to Hamilton [May] 1689; *Est. Procs.*, i, 114–15; *RPCS*, xiii, 381, 384, 387; NLS MS 7011 fol. 188, Sir P. Moray to Tweeddale, 30 May 1689; Blair, Atholl MSS, Box 29 I (5) 113, Hamilton to Murray, 27 May 1689.

124. The Macphersons' caution has also deceived historians. In Lord Murray's copy of the list of Dundee's numbers, they are added to the Camerons' strength. *Ib.*, 157, List of highlanders; SRO GD/26/viii/71, same [June 1689 — date from mention of Inverey]; Macpherson, *Loyall Dissuasive*, 212; *Grameid*, 168–9, 172–3; Macpherson, 'Gleanings', *TGSI*, xx, 221–2, Dundee to Cluny, 19 May 1689; *ib.*, 229–30, Mackay to same, 21 May 1689; *Melvilles & Leslies*, ii, 114, Cluny to Mackay, 25 June 1689; Mackay, *Memoirs*, 237, 241, Mackay to Hamilton, 27 June 1689; *ib.*, 224–5, Murray to same, 4 June 1689.

125. *Ib; APS*, ix, App., 55–6, Lt J. Colt's deposition, 12 May 1690; *ib.*, 57, J. Osburne's deposition, 14 May 1690; Lovat, *Memoirs*, 221; W. C. Mackenzie, *Simon Fraser, Lord Lovat* (London, 1908), 4–5; Terry, *Claverhouse*, 292; SRO GD 26/viii/71, Number of highland men with Dundee [June 1689]; Macpherson, *Original Papers*, i, 354, 'News from Scotland'.

126. The date is calculated from Mackay's indications. Dundee's biographers have followed the *Grameid*'s presumably poetic rearrangement by which action begins only after the Restoration celebrations; but Dundee's own account puts it before the formal siege of Ruthven, which began that day. Yet Terry is probably right in connecting it with the *Grameid*'s description of a false alarm. *Ib.*, 355; Terry, *Claverhouse*, 293–4; M. Barrington, *Grahame of Claverhouse* (London, 1911), 397–8; Balcarres, *Memoirs*, 40; *Grameid*, 170–2, 176–7; Fraser-Macintosh, *Antiquarian Notes* (1st series), 65–6; Mackay, *Memoirs*, 21–4; *ib.*, 231–4, Mackay to Hamilton, [May] 1689; *ib.*, 238, same to same, 27 June 1689.

127. *Ib.*, 30; *APS*, ix, 190–1; *ib.*, App., 56, Lt J. Colt's deposition, 12 May 1690; *RPCS*, xv, 674–82; *Grameid*, 172–6; *Memoirs of Locheill*, 242–3, 244.

128. *Est. Procs.*, i, 196–7, 200; Balcarres, *Memoirs*, 41; Mackay *Memoirs*, 26–7; *ib.*, 244, Mackay to Melville, 20 July 1689.

129. *Ib.*, 27–36; *Est. Procs.*, i, 130–1, letter 9 June 1689; *ib.*, 197; *Grameid*, 182–6, 197–8; *Memoirs of Locheill*, 244; SRO GD 406/1/3606, Mackay to Hamilton, 19 June 1689; Macpherson, *Original Papers*, i, 355, 'News from Scotland'.

130. Not only the Jacobite clans plundered friends in this campaign; the Grants ravaged Gordon of Gordonstoun's lands. *Ib.*, 356–7; *Est. Procs.*, i, 131–2, letter 9 June 1689; *ib.*, 197; *RPCS*, xvi, 376–7; SRO GD 406/1/3605, Mackay to Hamilton, 13 June 1689.

131. Mackay, *Memoirs*, 37–8; *Grameid*, 199–209; *Est. Procs.*, i, 198; Balcarres, *Memoirs*, 41; *Memoirs of Locheill*, 244; Macpherson, *Original Papers*, i, 356, 'News from Scotland'.

132. *Ib.*, 356–7; *ib.*, 360, 'Relation', 2–23 June 1689; *ib.*, 368, 'An Account of the engagements', 15 Dec. 1689; *APS*, ix, App., 55, Lt J. Colt's deposition, 12 May 1690; *RPCS* xiii, 509; Aubrey, *Three Prose Works*, 121–2, ? to J. Garden, 1694; *ib.*, 398–9; Macfarlane, *Gen. Colls.*, i, 139; *Memoirs of Locheill*, 244–5; *Highlands in 1750*, 75; NLS MS 1332 fol. 44, A. Mackenzie to Delvine, 12 June [1689]; Mackay, *Memoirs*, 38–9.

133. *Ib.*, 39–40; Macpherson, *Original Papers*, i, 357, 'News from Scotland'; *ib.*, 359–60, 'Relation', 2–23 June 1689; *Est. Procs.*, i, 143–4; NLS MS 1329 fol. 83, Sir A. Mackenzie to

Delvine, [June 1689]; *ib.*, MS 1332 fol. 49, A. Mackenzie to same, 2 July 1689; SRO GD 406/1/3606, Mackay to Hamilton, 19 June 1689.

134. *Ib; CSPD 1689*-90, 133, Melville to Mackay, 4 June 1689; NLS MS 1332 fol. 46, A. Mackenzie to Delvine, 18 June 1689; *ib.*, fol. 48, same to same, 9 July 1689; Mackay, *Memoirs*, 40; *ib.*, 237-8, Mackay to Hamilton, 27 June 1689.

135. *Ib.*, 46, 59; Atholl, *Chronicles*, i, 309, Mackay to Murray, 4 Aug. 1689; SRO GD 406/1/3605, same to Hamilton, 13 June 1689; McBane, *Expert Sword Man's Companion*, 78.

136. C. S. Terry, 'The Siege of Edinburgh Castle, March–June 1689', *SHR*, ii, 163-72, overlooks the Bannatyne Club account by one of the garrison, and fails to understand Gordon's difficulties. *Siege*, 29-30, 36-7, 46-7, 51-4, 56-8, 60, 66-7, 82-3; *Memoirs of Dundee*, 40; *Est. Procs.*, i, 22, 27, 46, 57, 84, 115; *HMCR Leyborne-Popham*, 268-9, Dr G. Clarke's autobiography.

137. *HMCR Lords 1689*-90, 148, 'C. Powell' [W. Bromfeild] to 'J. Lane' [W. Penn], 10 June 1689; *Melvilles & Leslies*, ii, 237, Lady Dunfermline to Dunfermline, 3 Oct. [1689]; *Siege*, 36.

138. The lady is unknown — not the Countess-Dowager of Erroll, through whom the Jacobites had communicated with the Castle in March. *Siege*, 114; *ib.*, 116-17, James to Gordon, 17 May 1689; D'Avaux, *Négociations*, 180, d'Avaux to Louis, 27 May 1689 (NS); Balcarres, *Memoirs*, 35; *Est. Procs.*, i, 136, 138; BL MS Lansdowne 1163B, 157, Melfort to Innes, 18 July 1690 (NS); SCA, Blairs Letters, Box Y, 'E.G.' to 'Mr Lewis' [Innes], 1 June 1689.

139. *APS*, ix, App., 9, 30; *Siege*, 38, 53, 57; *Spalding Club Misc.*, iii, 226-7, Mary of Modena to Gordon, 24 May [1689, ? NS]; Campana de Cavelli, ii, 586-7, 'Memoire ... au sieur qui doit passer a Edimbourg', 18 Apr. 1689 (NS); J. Doublet, *Journal*, ed. C. Breard (Paris, 1883), 153-60, 163 (misdated by over two years and the spy bowdlerised into an 'engineer' for the Castle); Macpherson, *Original Papers*, i, 358, 'News from Scotland'.

140. *Ib.*, 211, 'Journal ... ', 12 Mar.-18 July 1689; *CSPD 1689*-90, 189, Additional instructions to Hamilton, 17 July 1689; *Est. Procs.*, i, 111-14, 125-6; *Edinburgh Records 1689-1701*, ed. H. Armet (Edinburgh, 1962), 9; *HMCR Leyborne-Popham*, 268-9; SRO GD 26/vii/48, A. Strachan's examination, 18 Feb. 1690; *Leven & Melville*, 57, Melville to Col Balfour, 13 July 1689; *ib.*, 191-2, Dalrymple to Melville, 24 July 1689.

141. *Ib.*, 21-2, Atholl to Melville, 21 May 1689; NLS MS 7012 fol. 205, Bruce to Tweeddale, 8 Nov. 1690; Atholl, *Chronicles*, i, 275-7; *ib.*, 283, Atholl to Murray, 23 June [1689].

142. Murray's later ecclesiastical position, stressed by Lenman, developed through pressure from his beloved, bigoted wife and the political presbyterianism in which Johnston involved him. The evidence on Murray's views discredits the picture of self-interest overcoming Jacobitism which his enemy Simon Lord Lovat painted. However, it does not necessarily apply after his resignation in 1698; and emphatically not after Lovat's attempt to have him condemned for treason on false evidence, apparently supported by the government, in 1703 — an injustice often held to cancel the bond of allegiance. *Ib.*, 185, same to James, 29 July 1684; *Lockhart Papers*, i, 72-3; Lovat, *Memoirs*, 9, 13-16; Blair, Atholl MSS, bundle 1621, prayer, 8 May 1692; *ib.*, bundle 1622, prayers, 14 Oct. 1688, 11 Mar. 1692; *ib.*, bundle 1631, Lady Murray's diary, 13; Lenman, *Jacobite Risings*, 62-5.

143. Lenman's argument that the Atholl men had no fixed views (*ib.*, 38) is based on a misreading (see Chapter 5 n.8) *Leven & Melville*, 222n, Dundee to Murray, 19 July 1689; Atholl, *Chronicles*, i, 302, Ld James Murray to same, 28 July 1689; Mackay, *Memoirs*,

223–4, Murray to Hamilton, 4 June 1689; Robertson, *Barons Reid-Robertson*, 45–6; Stevenson, *Alasdair MacColla*, 121, 126; Lovat, *Memoirs*, 7.

144. *Ib.*, 7–8; Steuart, 'The Steuarts of Ballechin, Perthshire', *The Stewarts*, xii, 192–7; Blair, Atholl MSS, Box '71' II C 14, C. Steuart's receipt, 6 May 1696; *ib.*, bundle 56, *Catalogue of . . . The Valuable Collection of MSS from Castle Menzies* (Edinburgh, 1914), 72, No. 1316.

145. *Ib.*, bundle 1624, Murray's diary; *ib.*, bundle 1627, meditation, 28 Dec. 1707; *ib.*, Box 29 I (5) 116, Hamilton to Murray, 30 May 1689; *ib.*, 122, Atholl to same, 7 June [1689].

146. Mackay, *Memoirs*, 223–5, Murray to Hamilton, 4 June 1689; *Leven & Melville*, 54, [Murray] to Melville, 11 June 1689; Atholl, *Chronicles*, i, 278, Lady Struan to Robertsons, 25 May 1689; *ib.*, 279, same to Murray, 29 May 1689; *ib.*, D. Robertson to Struan, 26 May 1689; *ib.*, 280–2, Murray's notes; NLS MS Adv. MS 13.1.8 fol. 79, Memorial.

147. *Melvilles & Leslies*, ii, 116, Cleland to Melville, 25 July 1689; Blair, Atholl MSS, 125, Minutes of Balquhidder court, 22 June 1689; *ib.*, 129, Ballechin to Murray, 27 June 1689.

148. *HMCR Lords 1689–90*, 155–6, James's proclamation, 4 May 1689; SRO GD 26/viii/115, James to [Dundee], 17 May 1689; *APS*, ix, App., 57, Lt J. Colt's deposition, 12 May 1690; Dundee, *Letters*, 40, Dundee to Macleod, 23 June 1689.

149. *Ib.*, 47, 64–5, same to Melfort, 27, 28 June 1689; *Memoirs of Locheill*, 250–2.

150. Stevenson, *Alasdair MacColla*, 171–2, 204–5; *Est. Procs.*, ii, 67–8.

151. *Ib.*, i, 138, 147, 169; *Melvilles & Leslies*, ii, 133, Melville to Hamilton, 2 July 1689; Blair, Atholl MSS, Box 29 I (5) 118, Hamilton to Murray, 3 June 1689.

152. *RPCS*, ii, 458; Mackay, *Memoirs*, 51–2; Morer, *Short Account*, 10; Cleland, *Poems*, 13; Letter from the Host, 1 Feb. 1678, *Blackwood's Magazine*, i, 66; C. Blair, 'The Word Claymore', *Scottish Weapons and Fortifications*, ed. D. Caldwell (Edinburgh, 1981), 386; SRO GD 26/viii/68, Glengarry to Cannon, Dec. 1689.

153. Col. C. Walton, *History of the British Standing Army, 1660*–1800 (London, 1894), 344–5, 354–5. 427–30; McBane, *Expert Sword Man's Companion*, 77; Drumlanrig, Queensberry Papers, bundle 1185, 1, 'Remarks upon the State of the Army in Scotland', 16 Oct. 1691; Mackay, *Memoirs*, 52.

154. *Ib.*, 10–11, 41; *ib.*, 237–8, Mackay to Hamilton, 27 June 1689; Dundee, *Letters*, 40–1, Dundee to Macleod, 23 June 1689; *ib.*, 51–3, same to Melfort, 27 June 1689; *Est. Procs.*, i, 136, 138, 165; *RPCS*, xiii, 440–1; SRO GD 26/ix/255/1, Livingston to Mackay, [26 June 1689]; *Melvilles & Leslies*, ii, 113–14, Balnagown to same, 25 June 1689.

155. *Ib.*, 168, Mar's representation; Mackay, *Memoirs*, 41–3; *RPCS*, xv, 71–3; SRO GD 406/1/3607, Mackay to Hamilton, 4 July 1689; *ib.*, 3659, Mr of Forbes to same; J. Grant, *Legends of the Braes o' Mar* (Aberdeen, n.d), 99, 110–12, 115–16.

156. *RPCS*, xiii, 456; *Melvilles & Leslies*, iii, 208, Cannon's Instructions to Achtera & Widdrington, [Dec. 1689]; *More Culloden Papers*, 206, Dundee to Fraser of Culduthel, 11 June 1689; *Memoirs of Locheill*, 247–8; *Orain Iain Luim*, 184–5, 'Oran air feachd Righ Seumas'; SRO GD 406/M9/198, 'Information from the breas', [July 1689]; NLS MS 1329 fol. 86, Sir A. Mackenzie to Delvine, 18 July 1689; *ib.*, fol. 97, same to same [July 1689]; *ib.*, MS 1332 fol. 51, A. Mackenzie to same, 30 July 1689; *ib.*, fol. 49, same to same, 2 July 1689.

157. Local tradition cloaked the incident by claiming that Shewglie fought at Killiecrankie and that the raid took place after the war. *Ib;* *ib.*, MS 1329 fol. 85, Sir A. Mackenzie to same, 3 July 1689; *ib.*, MS 7019 fol. 125, Lochiel to Tweeddale, 11 Nov. 1695; *Memoirs of Locheill*, 252–5; Mackay, *Urquhart & Glenmoriston*, 199–202, 221–4; SRO GD 112/43/1/4/3, 'A true Information of the death of Grant of Shewglie', [1695].

158. Dundee, *Letters*, 39–40, Dundee to Macleod, 23 June 1689; *ib.*, 64, same to Melfort,

28 June 1689; Stewart, *The Stewarts of Appin*, 207, Ballachulish to Invernahyle, [1690]; SRO GD 406/M9/198, 'Information from the breas', [July 1689]; Mackay, *Memoirs*, 289, Mackay to Melville, 15 Oct. 1689.

159. *Ib.*, 18–19, 21; *CSPD 1689–90*, 131, Commission, 1 June 1689; Dundee, *Letters*, 49, Dundee to Melfort, 27 June 1689; 'The Camerons in the '15', *TGSI*, xxvi, 67; *HMCR Hamilton*, 183, Argyll to Hamilton, 20 July 1689; *ib.*, 193–4, Tarbat to same, 3 June 1689; *HMCR Buccleuch (Montagu)*, ii, 42, same to Melville, 13 Apr. 1689; *Leven & Melville*, 39–40, same to same, ? 1 June 1689; *ib.*, 33, Hamilton to same, 1 June 1689; *ib.*, 103, Dalrymple to same, 28 June 1689.

160. *Ib.*, 193, same to same, 24 July 1689; *Est. Procs.*, i, 173; Dundee, *Letters*, 68–9, Strathnaver to Dundee, 3 July 1689; *More Culloden Papers*, 206–7, Glengarry to Mackay, 12 June 1689.

161. *Leven & Melville*, 38, Tarbat to Melville, ? 1 June 1689; *Book of Dunvegan*, i, 142–3, James to Macleod, 29 May 1690; *ib.*, 145, 3rd Viscount Dundee to same, 28 Apr. 1691; *The Blind Harper*, lvi–lviii; *Grameid*, 146–8; Martin, *Western Islands*, 215 (Raasay); Grant, *The Macleods*, 324–7, 338–9; NLS MS 1332 fol. 47, A. Mackenzie to Delvine, 9 July 1689; *ib.*, MS 1329 fol. 97, Sir A. Mackenzie to same, [July 1689]; *ib.*, fol. 87v, same to same, 23 July 1689.

162. *Est. Procs.*, i, 155, 157–62, 166–7, 178–9.

163. BL Add. 12,068 fol. 137, Dundee to Macnachtan, 28 June 1689; *RPCS*, xiii, 554–5; 'Journal of a Soldier in the Earl of Eglinton's Troop of Horse', ed. G. Neil, *Transactions of the Glasgow Archaeological Society*, (*TGAS*), i (1868), 43; *Grameid*, 153–6; *HMCR Hope-Johnstone*, 194–5, Information, 23 March 1691; *Inventory of Lamont Papers*, 278 (misdated — correct date from NLS MS 3138 fol. 36); McKechnie, *The Lamont Clan*, 252–3; SRO GD 26/viii/39, Sir J. Maclean to Melfort, 12 Sept. 1689; *ib.*, 60, Macdougall to Cannon, 3 Dec. 1689; *ib.*, 104, I. Macnachtan to Macnachtan, 17 July 1689; GD 406/1/3562, ? to [Argyll], 18 July 1689; *ib.*, 3566, Argyll to Hamilton, 20 July 1689.

164. Carleton was afterwards lost crossing to France in a ship with other enemies of Melfort, who commented: 'It is a good thing to depend upon God, who is a friend at a distance and can execute his will at all ye Corners of the earth'. *Melvilles & Leslies*, ii, 108, Carleton to Breadalbane, 18 June 1689; Dundee, *Letters*, 42, Dundee to Macleod, 23 June 1689; *ib.*, 44, 48, same to Melfort, 27 June 1689; SRO GD 26/viii/15, James to [Dundee], 17 May 1689; BL MS Lansdowne 1163A, 136, Melfort to Innes, 18 Apr. 1690 (NS); SRO GD 112/40/3/4/74, Breadalbane to D. Campbell, 4 July 1689; *ib.*, 43/1/2/99, Breadalbane's Life, 1–2.

165. *APS*, ix, App., 57, J. Osburn's deposition, 14 May 1690; Atholl, *Chronicles*, i, 204, J. Flemyng to Marchioness, 22 May 1685; *ib.*, 260–1, Officers' testimony, 17 Aug. 1685; *Red Book of Grandtully*, ii, 186, Sir T. Steuart to J. Steuart, 10 Feb. 1669; Dalton, *Scots Army*, 113–16, 155–6; SRO GD 112/43/1/1/50, J. Macnachtan to Breadalbane, 2 Aug. 1689; GD 170/629/17, Breadalbane to Barcaldine, 18 Nov. 1689.

166. Dundee's letter or 'Breadalbane's Life', standing alone, might imply merely self-delusion or a wish to delude others. Together, they confirm each other, and are further confirmed by the tone of Breadalbane's more secret letters to Barcaldine. *Ib.*, 159, same to same, [c. Dec. 1689]; GD 112/43/1/1/50, J. Macnachtan to Breadalbane, 2 Aug. 1689; *ib.*, 43/1/4/6, [Dundee] to [same], 20 July 1689; *ib.*, 43/1/2/99, Breadalbane's Life, 2; GD 26/viii/64, Appin to Cannon, 21 Dec. 1689; Shaw, *Northern & Western Islands*, 20; *RPCS*, xiv, 236–7.

167. *Ib.*, xiii, 482, 489–91, 497–8, 512–13; Mackay, *Memoirs*, 239, Mackay to Hamilton, 27 June 1689; SRO GD 406/1/3609, same to same, 26 July 1689; *ib.*, 3568, 3566, 3564,

3565, Argyll to same, 14, 20, 22, 25 July 1689; *ib.*, 3561, Council of War, 22 July 1689; *Est. Procs.*, i, 162–6; *Leven & Melville*, 158, Sir W. Lockhart to Melville, 11 July 1689.

168. *Ib.*, 189, Crawford to same, 23 July 1689; *ib.*, 194, Hamilton to same, 25 July 1689; *RPCS*, xiii, 552–4; SRO GD 112/43/1/4/6, [Dundee] to [Breadalbane], 20 July 1689; GD 406/1/3564, Argyll to Hamilton, 22 July 1689; *ib.*, 3562, ? to [Argyll], 18 July 1689; *ib.*, M9/198, Information from the breas, [July 1689].

169. Mackay claimed that he gave the Council his plans, and that he returned to Edinburgh, earlier than he actually did, to throw the blame on them for all that went wrong. *APS*, ix, 104; *RPCS*, xiii, 479, 491–2, 499, 510–11, 519–20, 530, 535; Mackay, *Memoirs*, 41, 43–6; *ib.*, 230, Mackay to Melville, 14 June 1689; SRO GD 406/1/3607, same to Hamilton, 4 July 1689; *HMCR Athole*, 38, Gleneagles to Murray, 21 June 1689; 'Journal of a Soldier', *TGAS*, i, 42; *Memoirs of Locheill*, 110; Blair, Atholl MSS, Box 29 I (5) 134, R. Menzies to Murray, 3 July 1689.

170. D'Avaux, *Négociations*, 218, d'Avaux to Louis, 26 June 1689 (NS); *ib.*, 248, same to same, 10 July 1689 (NS); *Leven & Melville*, 223–4nn, Dundee to Murray, 19 July 1689; Macpherson, *Original Papers*, i, 361–2, 366–7, same to Melfort, 27, 28 June 1689; *ib.*, 217–18nn, Council of War before Derry, 20 July 1689; A. & H. Tayler, *John Graham of Claverhouse* (London, 1939), 261 (quoting a highlander writing c. 1720); SCA, Box T, 1689, 86, Nairne to [Innes], 10 July 1689; *Analecta Hibernica*, iv, Letter-Book of Tyrconnell, ed. L. Tate (IMC, 1932), 136–7, Glengarry to Tyrconnell, [July 1689]; Powley, *Naval Side*, 224–9, 233–7.

171. *Ib.*, 148, 150, 241–2, 272; *Melvilles & Leslies*, ii, 33–4, James to Cannon, 1 July 1689; Macpherson, 'Gleanings', *TGSI*, xx, 223, Dundee to Cluny, 18 July 1689; D'Alton, *King James's Irish Army List*, ii, 766; Maclean, 'Celtic Sources', 301–2, Iain Mac Ailean, 'Coille Chnadaigh' (translated by Maclean); SRO GD 26/ix/170, Commissions for Cannon's regiment, 17 May 1689; GD 406/1/3535, Rooke to Hamilton, 20 July 1689.

172. *Ib; APS*, ix, App., 55–6, Lt J. Colt's deposition, 12 May 1690; *ib.*, 60, The Chiefs to Mackay, 17 Aug. 1689; *RPCS*, xvi, 309–10; *Memoirs of Locheill*, 257; *Est. Procs.*, i, 166, 168, 175; Macpherson, *Original Papers*, i, 214–15, 'Journal . . . ', 12 Mar.–18 July 1689; Powley, *Naval Side*, 240–4; Macpherson, 'Gleanings', *TGSI*, xx, 222–3, Dundee to Cluny, 14 July 1689; *ib.*, 223, same to same, 18 July 1689; SRO GD 112/43/1/4/6, [same] to [Breadalbane], 20 July 1689.

173. He still demanded that Cluny join him, but gave him the bond after he failed to do so. *Ib*; Macpherson, 'Gleanings', *TGSI*, xx, 222–3, same to Cluny, 14 July 1689; *Ib.*, 225, same to same, 22 July 1689; Fraser-Macintosh, *Letters*, 107n; Atholl, *Chronicles*, i, 322, Murray to Ld James Murray, '24' [4] Aug. 1689.

174. SRO GD 406/1/3562, ? to [Argyll], 18 July 1689; GD 112/43/1/4/6. [Dundee] to [Breadalbane], 20 July 1689; *ib.*, RH 15/1/16/12. Mackay to Edinglassie, 14 [July] 1689.

175. *RPCS*, xv, 71–3; *Rawdon Papers*, 308–9, H. Smith to Sir A. Rawdon, 7 Aug. 1689; Atholl, *Chronicles*, i, 284–5, Dundee to L. & J. Robertson, 10 July 1689; *ib.*, 284, L. Robertson to Murray, 14 July 1689; *ib.*, 287, Ballechin to same, 17 July 1689; *ib.*, 293–4, same to same, 25 July 1689; *ib.*, 293, Hamilton to same, 24 July 1689; *London Gazette*, No 2475, 29 July–1 Aug. 1689; *Est. Procs.*, i, 180, 182; Robertson, *Barons Reid-Robertson*, 34–6, 44–6; Macpherson, *Original Papers*, i, 357, 'News from Scotland'; *ib.*, 369, 'Account of the engagements', 15 Dec. 1689; Blair, Atholl MSS, Box 29 I (5) 195, Murray's Representation to the Council, 1689.

176. Murray's diary shows that the claim in his Representation that he went twice to Atholl, once with a handful of men, once with 1,000, is false. *Ib*; *ib.*, bundle 1624, Murray's diary; Mackay, *Memoirs*, 47; *Leven & Melville*, 222–4nn, Dundee to Murray, 19 July 1689;

SRO GD 112/43/1/4/6, [same] to Breadalbane, 20 July 1689; Atholl, *Chronicles*, i, 289, Lady Murray to Murray, 22 July 1689; *ib.*, 286–7, Ballechin to same, 17 July 1689.

177. *Ib.*, 287; *ib.*, 293–4, same to same, 25 July 1689 (2 letters); *ib.*, 295–6, ? to same, 25 July 1689; *ib.*, 296, Mackay to same, 25 July 1689.

178. Mackenzie of Coul thought Sir Donald had 300 men, his son thought 700. *Ib.*, 292, Hamilton to same, 24 July 1689; *Orain Iain Luim*, 184–7, 'Oran air feachd Righ Seumas'; *Memoirs of Dundee*, 24–5; SRO GD 406/M9/198, 'Information from the breas', [July 1689]; NLS MS 1329 fol. 97, Sir A. Mackenzie to Delvine, [July 1689]; *ib.*, MS 1332 fol. 47, A. Mackenzie to same, 9 July 1689.

179. *Proelium Gillicrankianum*, a Latin rhyming poem on the battle (*HMCR Laing*, 462–5) has caused great confusion by naming as present several clans which were not. However, some, such as Macleod of Raasay and MacNeil of Barra, which are not mentioned in other sources, fairly certainly were there, commanded by more important chiefs as their colonels only; for several of the formations at Killiecrankie were a cross between a clan and a regiment. This probably helps explain the contrast between the numbers of the Camerons, a genuine clan regiment, and Glengarry who could expect additional men from several other clans. The Glencoe bard implies that he had a right to expect such support from the Glencoe and Keppoch Macdonalds, but one Keppoch Macdonald known to have fought, Iain Lom, was in Sir Donald's battalion, *APS*, ix, App., 57, J. Osburne's deposition, 14 May 1690; *Memoirs of Locheill*, 256; *Grameid*, 144–8; Maclean, 'Celtic Sources', 290–1, Aonghus Mac Alasdair Ruaidh, 'Lath Raon-Ruairidh'; *ib.*, 193, Mac do Iain Lom, 'Latha Raon-Ruairidh' (translated by Maclean); *Orain Iain Luim*, 186–7.

180. *Ib.*, Terry, *Claverhouse*, 331; Macpherson, *Original Papers*, i, 369, 'Account of the engagements', 15 Dec. 1689; Blair, Atholl MSS, Box 29 I (5) 157, List of Highlanders, June [1689]; *ib.*, 195, Representation, 1689; Macpherson, 'Gleanings', *TGSI*, xx, 225, Dundee to Cluny, 22 July 1689.

181. *Ib*, 232, Cannon to same, '20' [? 29] July 1689; *APS*, ix, App., 58, J. Malcome's deposition, 14 May 1690; *Orain Iain Luim*, 186–7; *Leven & Melville*, 225–6, Murray to Melville, 1 Aug. 1689; Blair, Atholl MSS, Box 29 I (5), 195, Representation, 1689; *ib.*, 152, Hamilton to Murray, 27 July 1689.

182. *Ib*; *RPCS*, xiii, 516, 530; Atholl, *Chronicles*, i, 295, ? to Murray, 25 July 1689; Mackay, *Memoirs*, 46–9, 50, 55; Tullibardine, *Military History*, 258n; SRO GD 406/1/3608, Mackay to Hamilton, [24 July 1689]; *ib.*, 3609, same to same, 26 July 1689.

183. *HMCR 6th Report*, 700, same to R. Menzies, 26 July 1689; Atholl, *Chronicles*, i, 309–10, same to Murray, 4 Aug. 1689; *ib.*, 278n, 299–300; Mackay, *Memoirs*, 49–50, 61; *ib.*, 263–4, Mackay, 'Short Relation', 17 Aug. 1689; EUL, MS Laing II fol. 338v, 'A true account'; *Orain Iain Luim*, 192–5, 'Cath Raon-Ruairaidh'.

184. There is no evidence supporting the tradition that Robertson of Struan and his clan were at Killiecrankie, and the poets' complaints indicate that no major Atholl group were — except perhaps the (Fergusson and Rattray) Strathardle men. Dundee, *Letters*, 78–9nn, Commission to Ballechin, 21 July 1689; Fergusson, 'Early History of Strathardle', *TGSI*, xxiii, 157; Maclean, 'Celtic Sources', 305–8, Aonghus Mac Alasdair Ruaidh, 'Lath Raon-Ruairidh' (translated by Maclean).

185. *Memoirs of Locheill*, 258–65, 268; Balcarres, *Memoirs*, 46; Macpherson, *Original Papers*, i, 369, 'Account of the engagements', 15 Dec. 1689.

186. For this, the traditional site, Tullibardine, *Military History*, 268–70, confuting Terry, *Claverhouse*, 336–8. While the field of the clans' final defeat, Culloden, is being carefully restored as far as possible, a dual carriageway is being driven through the site of

their most spectacular triumph, Killiecrankie. *Orain Iain Luim*, 185–7, 'Oran air feachd Righ Seumas'; Mackay, *Memoirs*, 50.

187. An inference from a poem's mention of Glengarry, stationed opposite it. *Ib.*, 59; Maclean, 'Celtic Sources', 290–1, Aonghus, 'Latha-Raon Ruairidh' (translated by Maclean).

188. Lochiel's second son was apparently serving in Mackay's regiment (though his first recorded commission was in 1692), and, according to tradition, Mackay sneered at his father's 'wild savages' to him; if so, he changed his tune on seeing them deploy (see Chapter 1, p. 23). Mackay, *Memoirs*, 50–1, 52–4; *ib.*, 264, Mackay, 'Short Relation', 17 Aug. 1689; Morer, *Short Account*, 102; Foxcroft, *Supplement to Burnet*, 325; Terry, *Claverhouse*, 339n; NUL, Portland MSS, PwA 675, Hill to Portland, 30 Apr. 1696; *Memoirs of Locheill*, 267.

189. *Ib.*, 265–7; Macpherson, *Original Papers*, i, 369, 'Account of the engagements', 15 Dec. 1689; *Ib.*, 378, Buchan to James, 14 Feb. 1690; Macfarlane, *Gen. Colls.*, i, 139; Balcarres, *Memoirs*, 46; *APS*, ix, App., 59, Lt J. Hay's deposition, 14 July 1690; Mackay, *Urquhart & Glenmoriston*, 201–2 (which names the man hit by the ball as Grant of Shewglie, killed a month earlier by the Camerons).

190. SRO GD 26/39/1208, Dunfermline to Breadalbane, 29 July 1689.

191. Macpherson, *Original Papers*, i, 370, 'Account of the engagements', 15 Dec. 1689; *Memoirs of Locheill*, 269, 271; McBane, *Expert Sword Man's Companion*, 78–9; Mackay, *Memoirs*, 55, 59.

192. The wheel to the left for which the Jacobites blamed Wallace is obviously the same recorded by Mackay, who uses it to claim Dundee and the other mounted Jacobite casualties for his regiment's fire. Since Dundee's handful did not apparently encounter either of Mackay's troops, the cannon (which, however comic at a distance, might be harmful at short range) may have been to the left of Kenmure's. *Ib.*, 265, Mackay, 'Short Relation', 17 Aug. 1689; Balcarres, *Memoirs*, 46; *Memoirs of Locheill*, 268.

193. Balhaldie's detail on Dundee's fall and the Macdonalds of Sleat seems largely designed to answer charges interpolated into the 1714 printed version of Balcarres: there is no mention by eye-witnesses of their delaying their charge. Although Balcarres and the author of the 'Account of the engagements' agree that Dundee was riding to the left wing, a local laird wrote that he was 'shot dead one the head of his horse'. This may be an assumption, like Balhaldie's, from the last time they saw him in action; but it does admittedly tally rather better with his dying question how the day went. *Ib.*, 272–3; *APS*, ix, App., 56, Lt J. Nisbet's deposition, 14 May 1690; Balcarres, *Memoirs*, 46–7; Macpherson, *Original Papers*, i, 370, 'Account of the engagements', 15 Dec. 1689; Mackay, *Memoirs*, 56–9; Atholl, *Chronicles*, i, 304, T. Stewart to Murray, 29 July 1689; EUL, MS Laing II fol. 338v, 'A true account'; *Orain Iain Luim*, 192–5, 'Cath Raon-Ruairaidh'.

194. *Ib.*, 190–3; *ib.*, 188–9, 'Oran air fechd Righ Seumas'; Mackay, *Memoirs*, 58–60; *ib.*, 266, Mackay, 'Short Relation'; Atholl, *Chronicles*, i, 310, Mackay to Murray, 4 Aug. 1689; *ib.*, 313, A. Stewart to A. Douglas, 9 Aug. 1689; McBane, *Expert Sword Man's Companion*, 79; Fergusson, 'Early History of Strathardle', *TGSI*, xxiii, 162–5; Maclean, 'Celtic Sources', 277–81, 'Soraidh do na Ghaidheal a bha ann am Blar Raon-Ruairidh'; Blair, Atholl MSS, Box 29 I (5) 195, Representation, 1689.

195. Dunfermline wrote: 'my lord Dundie was killed in the filde'. This decides the question against the authenticity of his 'last letter'. The dispute over whether or not his death was instantaneous has usually turned on whether (as rival reports claimed) his wound was in the body or the face near the eye. Interestingly, an officer writing from Perth less than a fortnight after the battle reported that he had two, having been 'shot under his armour into the belly, and betwixt the eye brows': the first may have been the mortal

wound, the second the *coup de grace*. The identity of the plunderers appears from a letter from Dundee's brother asking Cannon to reinforce Lochiel's authority to regain what was taken. *Orain Iain Luim*, 192-3; Dundee, *Letters*, 83n; *Rawdon Papers*, 310, H. Smith to Rawdon, 7 Aug. 1689; *SHR*, v, 503-5, vi, 63-70, controversy; Maclean, 'Celtic Sources', 314; SRO GD 26/viii/41, D. Graham to Cannon, 19 Sept. 1689; *Memoirs of Locheill*, 269.

196. *Ib.*, 270; Mackay, *Memoirs*, 57-61; *ib.*, 265-6, Mackay, 'Short Relation', 17 Aug. 1689; Atholl, *Chronicles*, i, 303, Ld James Murray to Murray, 28 July 1689.

197. Cannon wrote: 'wee haue freelie set at liberty all the common souldiers', contrasting this with the hanging of the highlanders in Strathspey. The messenger who carried the first news to James in Ireland claimed that there were 800 prisoners. *Ib.*, 304, T. Stewart to Murray, 29 July 1689; *Melvilles & Leslies*, ii, 118, Cannon to Mackay, 5 Aug. 1689; Macpherson, *Original Papers*, i, 370, 'Account of the engagements', 15 Dec. 1689; SRO GD 112/39/1208, Dunfermline to Breadalbane, 27 July 1689; *Rawdon Papers*, 309-11, Smith to Rawdon, 7 Aug. 1689; *Franco-Irish Correspondence, December 1688–February 1692*, ed. S. Mulloy, 3 vols. (IMC, 1984), iii, 85, Fumeron to Louvois, 15 Oct. 1689 (NS).

198. *Memoirs of Locheill*, 270-1; Dundee, *Letters*, 84; SRO GD 26/viii/24, A. Steuart to Cannon, 31 July 1689; *Orain Iain Luim*, 218-19, 'Cumha do Shir Domhnall Shleite'; Maclean, 'Celtic Sources', 290-1, 297-8, 'Latha Raon-Ruairidh' (translated by Maclean).

199. *Ib.*, 284-5, 289-91, 294-5; Macpherson, *Original Papers*, i, 370, 'Account of the engagements', 15 Dec. 1689; Atholl, *Chronicles*, i, 304, T. Stewart to Murray, 29 July 1689; *Orain Iain Luim*, 194-5, 'Cath Raon Ruairidh'; *ib.*, 218-19, 'Cumha do Shir Domhnall Schleite'; *Memoirs of Dundee*, 27-8; Mackay, *Memoirs*, 59.

200. *Ib.*, 248, Mackay to Melville, 24 July 1689; *ib.*, 252, Hamilton to same, 29 July 1689; Balcarres, *Memoirs*, 48; SRO GD 26/ix/229, Cardross to [Melville], Aug. 1689 (for the phrase 'the Highland Army').

5

Dunkeld (July–September 1689)

As evidence that Dundee was dead, some of Mackay's men claimed to have seen Brigadier-General Cannon, late in the battle, taking command and drawing back some forces; and the messenger who carried the news to Ireland gave him excessive credit for the victory.[1] His orders, like Dunfermline's, can have had little effect, for he knew no Gaelic. Cannon, a Galloway man, had spent his career in the Anglo-Dutch Brigade. By early 1685, he, like Dundee before him, was seriously at odds with William, and James employed him on permanent loan in England for most of his reign. In 1687, he became Colonel of the Queen's Regiment of Dragoons when the Duke of Somerset was dismissed for opposing James's catholicising practices, but in late November 1688 almost all his officers went over to William.[2] He had some conventional military skill; but he was sent from Ireland not only because he was a Protestant but because the abler Scottish generals, Buchan and Wauchope, were with the army before Londonderry. He was Dundee's successor by formal military seniority, not by any commission to command the Highland Army, 'an old unactive Man', who, Mackay thought, commanded only 'provisionally'. The logical commander, since a chief would have been unacceptable, would have been Dunfermline, Dundee's confidant, Gordon's representative, and a Privy Councillor. The two therefore collaborated. They presumably realised that cabals applying to them separately might breed serious quarrels, for one prisoner remarked: 'wherever he saw the one of these two he saw the other'.[3]

Another alternative did exist. Carwhin's biography claimed that Dunfermline and most of the chiefs sent Breadalbane a signed commission inviting him to be general, 'But he uisely uaived it In regard it did not proceed imediately from K. Ja. himself'. However, surviving letters from Dunfermline and others merely urge him to join them immediately — a demand he ignored. The French agent Hooke (then in the Tower) claimed years later that, but for Melfort, he would have been appointed and would have raised 4,000 men. In fact, Dundee had probably told Melfort nothing of his dealings with Breadalbane, for fear of his hostility; and the crisis of the campaign was over before James could have made any appointment. Breadalbane might have made a good leader — had he been younger in 1715, many would have chosen him rather than Mar — but the story merely shows what he would have liked to happen.[4]

Practically, Cannon was in a favourable position. One major problem, the shortage of provisions, should easily have been solved: the regiment guarding Perth had fled, leaving Mackay's stores exposed. Cannon was even spared one pitfall which frustrated much finer commanders of highland armies: having obtained, as Dunfermline wrote, 'such a plunder that I never thought a Scots army would have had the like', the highlanders did not, for the most part, disperse but packed it on hundreds of captured baggage-horses and remained.[5] Indeed, the army was soon joined by clans and parties whom Dundee's rapid advance had left behind. According to Balhaldie, on the 30th there arrived 500 Camerons under Lochiel's son John, 250 Macphersons (still, presumably, incognito),[6] about 150 Keppoch Macdonalds, some Macgregors, and about 300 Appin Stewarts and Glencoe men — a few Stewarts were even in time for Killiecrankie. The last two clans' arrival was a tribute to their loyalty and to Dundee's influence over them, since they had left their lands lying open to Argyll's force at Inveraray. They were allowed to return home immediately, but the danger was already over. The Council, in its first belief that Mackay was dead, had summoned the force back, and its march from Inveraray through difficult country to Glasgow in atrocious weather, coming after the irregular pay and provisions of the expedition, temporarily ruined the three regiments.[7]

Atholl produced the most new recruits and a figurehead to lead them. Hurrying to the Lowlands to justify himself, Lord Murray left his brother James at Tulliemet to restrain the vassals from joining the rebels.On the 28th, Lord James was warning them that Dundee's death doomed the rising; early on the 29th he admitted that all the Atholl men were nevertheless joining; and, going that day to Dunkeld (occupied the previous evening), he did so himself. Expressions in his and Lord Murray's letters indicate that he acted not only, as everybody claimed afterwards, to preserve Dunkeld House from destruction, but, since Atholl's vassals were rising anyway, to ensure that if this came to anything there would be somebody present to reap benefit for him from it.[8] Lord Murray's furious letters are a useful reminder that such apparent family balancing acts were often neither concerted nor approved by other members; and he was right to be furious. Far from securing the family's future on both sides, Lord James's action, while not particularly helpful to the Jacobites, wrecked its credit for good among most Wiliamites. Murray's failure to join Mackay before Killiecrankie and his men's inhumanity towards the fugitives afterwards — almost the main impression left by the battle — had created a suspicion that he, on Atholl's instructions, had been carrying out a plan to lure Mackay to destruction (which Mackay himself endorsed as an excuse); and this confirmed it. The most obvious consequence was Atholl's arrest at Bath and his imprisonment in London for several months, from which he was released only on heavy bail. In the longer run, the Atholl family could 'never purge the Gilliecrankie blood, taken in either sense'. The events of three months blighted their chances of political success for a generation.[9]

Lord James Murray's arrival gave the semblance of family authority for the imposition of a formal levy in Atholl, and he called out his brother's tenants in Balquhidder; but he was not trusted with real command over those who joined. Despite threats, few gentlemen did so, and they were fortified by Murray's reproachful appeal to vassals, authorised by the Council.[10] Robert Campbell of Glenlyon, who had refused to join Murray before Killiecrankie because Colonel Menzies had misrepresented him and because he did not consider himself a vassal, was not troubled, and Cannon gave his wife a protection for the estate.[11]

The first news, that Mackay and his army were cut off, made the Edinburgh government fear that all Scotland beyond Tay. and probably Fife also, was lost; and, although they sent Lanier to gather all available forces at Stirling, they were uncertain if demoralised troops could hold even the line of Forth. William, hearing this first news, ordered to Scotland forces from the Border and even those at Chester intended for Ireland.[12] Then, early on 29 July, Mackay arrived at Stirling with the few hundred men of his army who still kept together. His actions over the next fortnight show him at his best as a general. Even before he knew of Dundee's death, he determined to preserve Scotland benorth Tay, and brushed off the challenge which Lanier, emboldened by the defeat, hoped to offer, representing not only jealousy of his chance seniority but the defeatist policy of making Leslie's and Berkeley's regiments retreat from the North.[13] Mackay had the self-confidence to order from England, of the forces available, only Heyford's dragoons and two infantry regiments (one only momentarily); and to refuse help from the western Presbyterians, who had assembled in arms at the news, since acceptance would give additional weight to their bigoted demands. News on the 30th that Dundee was dead, confirmed by the lack of enterprise the Jacobites had shown since, determined him to reoccupy Perth immediately with his cavalry. He set off next day with Colchester's regiment and eight Scottish troops, 400 in all, to be followed by two infantry regiments. Cannon, lying at Dunkeld, failed to foresee this. Instead of advancing on Perth in strength, he sent a party of 300 Atholl men, largely Robertsons under Struan, with a few horse, to carry off the meal stored there. Early on 1 August, Mackay surprised them as they tried to escape from Perth or lay drunk there, killing or capturing over a hundred of the party.[14]

This trivial skirmish revived confidence on the Williamite side. On Mackay's suggestion, the Council thought it worthwhile to make a special offer of pardon to the Atholl men. However, a major setback occurred next day in Edinburgh. The news that Londonderry had just been relieved and that Dundee was dead enabled the Country opposition in Parliament again to concentrate exclusively on their unsatisfied grievances. When Hamilton on 2 August asked for a supply, they decided, after meaningless calculations, that enough remained for several months, refused, and were immediately adjourned until October. Even as a means of putting pressure on William, it was ineffective. As a soldier, he would scarcely favour politicians who showed so little concern for the defence of their country. Within three months, all forces on Scots pay would start to disintegrate for lack of money.[15]

Yet for the moment they were formidable. Lochiel and the other chiefs, who had forgotten their caution before cavalry in Strathspey after the Scots horse fled at Killiecrankie, were willing to fight in the plain. Breadalbane allegedly sent Cannon advice to remain in the hills until his army was stronger — to William's later amusement. Cannon was probably right then not to give way to the clans. Mackay's English regiments, although rapidly losing their horses, were experienced professional soldiers. A battle in the Lowlands, where the clans could not break off immediately on a setback, might end disastrously.[16]

There were far stronger reasons for the clans' other wish, to turn south along the edge of the Highlands. Recruits were eagerly awaiting them: young Lord Strathallan, for instance, was raising Strathearn and Balquhidder. Confident parties were raiding the Lowlands as far south as Campsie. Most important, although Carwhin's biography says that Dundee's death 'brocke' Breadalbane's plan to rise, his selfish prudence did not immediately overcome his hopes for such a 'deliberate and well-founded desyne': on 2 August, his chamberlain Toshach of Monivaird brought Cannon and Dunfermline his appeal 'to assist [him] from Argyll his oppression'. They seemed favourable, and it was once actually planned to march into Balquhidder. Yet, about 4 August, the Highland Army instead began to move north-east along the edge of the hills, accompanied by a small Atholl force under Lord James Murray and Ballechin. Cannon was determined to relieve Farquharson and other Braemar Jacobites from the Abergeldie garrison. He had already decided on 31 July, when he ordered Alexander Steuart to provide him with four cannon from Blair for a siege. He may have hoped en route to seize Dundee, but Berkeley's regiment, warned by the magistrates, came to the rescue, and he retired to the hills on hearing of Mackay's advance.[17]

The news of Killiecrankie created consternation in the North. Apart from some robbing, the Ross highlanders were quiet but expecting an opportunity to rise, and Seaforth's brother was among them. However, Sir Thomas Livingston, having concentrated his forces, was confident that he could defend Inverness. To raise Williamite spirits, he sent Strathnaver with 500 foot and some dragoons to ravage Glenmoriston. They broke into and burned John Grant's house, Invermoriston, and drove off all the clan's cattle, nearly ravaging Strathglass also. Further south, the Master of Forbes sensibly took supplies to Abergeldie, then fell back and raised forces in the Lowlands.[18] Mackay, marching north-east from Perth in the plain parallel to Cannon, heard on the 8th at Forfar that he had crossed into Braemar. He boldly decided to advance with the mounted troops he had with him into Aberdeenshire and defend the North-East with them and a backing of local forces. A foot regiment and Berkeley's dragoons were at Dundee, and Lanier was to bring his regiment and Heyford's dragoons to defend Angus. Argyll was to command a massive garrison of several infantry regiments at Perth; an even larger one, including the wreckage of the Killiecrankie army, was to hold the Stirling area.[19] This was the chief weakness of Mackay's plan. He had reacted from over-confidence in the Dutch Brigade into mistrust of all his infantry, and intended to leave them on the defensive for the remainder of the campaigning season, even though the Highland Army was elsewhere. Argyll's detachment seemed to justify his doubts. Mutinies and mass desertions tore apart Glencairn's, and Angus's, the remains of which were sent to Doune; while Argyll, quarrelling with his lieutenant-colonel, Auchinbreck, remained at Glasgow. Ramsay therefore commanded at Perth.[20]

Mackay arrived at Aberdeen on 10 August, to find that Cannon was quartering on Forbes's lands and ravaging other Whigs' estates. Aberdeenshire and Banffshire supporters could easily join him. Glengarry was blockading Abergeldie, and the garrison of Balvenie fled when a Jacobite party approached, abandoning a magazine of provisions.[21] Mackay summoned Livingston's dragoons from Inverness and Heyford's from Angus, thinking that then, with 1200 mounted men, he would be able to drive back Cannon's forces, estimated at 4,000 foot and 150 horse. His strategy was unpopular in the army — 'a *Cavalcade*, or *Progress*, more than War' — but had so far prevented any leading figures from joining Cannon. Jacobite sympathisers like the Earls of Strathmore and Aberdeen dutifully came to Edinburgh. Lord Livingstone, with Lords Callendar and Duffus and several armed troopers, after consulting Breadalbane, rode to Blair — only to drift away indecisively into Moray. Colin Mackenzie, Seaforth's uncle, joined Cannon; but, expecting Seaforth himself to land and raise the Mackenzies any day, he came alone. Many Aberdeenshire highlanders had joined 'the first to overpour them' under Inverey; and enough Jacobite gentry had come in to increase the previously insignificant horse to about 300; but results had not justified Cannon.[22]

When, after he marched north to Strathbogie, Mackay advanced to within five miles, safely joined Livingston and encamped, with Gordon of Edinglassie's daredevil daily scouting to protect him from attack, the highlanders' discontent erupted. On the pretext of outdated orders from James to Dundee to attack Argyllshire and Kintyre, they obtained a council of war, held in Auchindoun Castle. Lochiel and the chiefs first argued that the professional officers should not vote, since they had brought no actual followers to the army. Defeated in this, they demanded to attack Mackay, since only a success would bring the North-East to join them. They had more reason than in Perthshire. Gordon's local tenants would bring them information, and the marshy and woody countryside would protect their retreat if they were repulsed. Colchester's regiment was losing its horses, and most of Mackay's other troops were new, but he would certainly soon receive reinforcements. Lochiel even offered to fight with only the Camerons and the horse; but Cannon, Dunfermline and the professional officers carried it against him. Tired and disgusted, he retired to Lochaber, but left his clan with the army, under his son John and Glendessary. Sir Donald did likewise. Keppoch, however, left with his followers, and within a fortnight he was offering, through Campbell of Calder, to submit to the government. It seemed likely that more would follow him.[23]

Meanwhile, on 12 August, the Council ordered Angus's regiment to march from Doune to Dunkeld, a dangerous plan which has also usually been called pointless, giving the paranoid Cameronian claim that it was a deliberate attempt to betray them to destruction some plausibility. Hamilton, who headed the Council that day (eight days before leaving for London with Murray), had long declared that the regiment, which was notorious for silencing episcopalian ministers, should be disbanded, and allegedly wanted to forbid it to communicate with Perth or Dundee if attacked. However, the Council (one of whom had a son in the regiment), who ordered Cleland to report to Lanier at Forfar and Ramsay at Perth, had good reasons for ordering the march. Mackay's later denial that there was 'the least prospect of advancement to the service by their being posted there' was untrue.[24]

A force at Dunkeld could check raids from Atholl on the Perthshire lowlands (which Mackay's disposition of forces left exposed) and preserve the town, as the base for an advance against Blair. The Council had suggested to Mackay on the 9th that the forces left in Perthshire and Angus under Lanier should attack Blair before the rains started and made it a safe base for raiders all winter. Anticipating a favourable reply, they ordered the two regiments under Argyll from Glasgow to Stirling, and, three days later, the march of Angus's regiment. Leven protested in Council that this was too dangerous unless horsemen accompanied them. However, Mackay had taken nearly all the horse and dragoons to join his or Ramsay's forces, outside the Council's direct authority, and the only two remaining troops were guarding the line of Forth against raids. The risk existed only until Mackay allowed Lanier to proceed; but his pursuit of Cannon northwards delayed his reply. The Council could give Lanier orders only on the 19th.[25]

As Mackay complained, the Cameronians were the worst possible regiment to send to an episcopalian highland area, but they were the Council's only force within striking distance. Dunkeld might become a death-trap if attacked in strength, but there seemed little chance of that. From Murray, Hamilton had a truer idea than Mackay of conditions in Atholl. Murray's appeal to the vassals had had considerable success, and they were irritated by the plundering of the Irish garrison left in Blair under Alexander Steuart. On 14th August the government issued an offer of full indemnity to all those who laid down arms within eight days of its proclamation locally and took an oath of allegiance by 10 September. It would restrain most Atholl men, even if the Cameronians committed some outrages.[26] The rest could not by themselves endanger the regiment. Cannon's force was far away and, it was confidently reported, a drifting rabble that would obey neither him nor Dunfermline. Mackay, ordered to keep within a day's march of them, reported that they would soon disperse. His later denunciations concealed the fact that danger arose only because Cannon, encumbered with an enormous baggage train, successfully slipped away from him despite his immense superiority in cavalry.[27]

Dunkeld, on the north bank of the Tay, is overlooked by a ring of high hills and some lower ones closer at hand, one of these latter beside the river to the east. From its foot, the main street ran west to the Cross (where a side-street, Scots Raw, branched north-west) and onwards, finally passing the south wall of the half-ruined cathedral. Only the chancel and solitary north-west tower of this were in use, but the walls of the unroofed nave were intact. Around the cathedral were the houses of the chapter, the largest of the townsbuildings. Some faced it across the main street, with their gardens sloping to the Tay. The rest formed an irregular semi-circle to the north round its graveyard. On the site of one of them, a short way north-east of the cathedral, stood the splendid mansion Sir William Bruce had designed for the Marquess of Atholl a dozen years earlier, forming a square round a courtyard. Its north-east face was on Scots Raw, and, although it already had 'yards', it was hemmed in by the buildings over which it towered. Atholl planned by degrees to absorb the other canons' properties, and had just bought from townsmen for demolition the north-east side of Scots Raw and part of a similar street which formed the north-west boundary of the town: he was to be saved the trouble. East of the House, Shiochies Hill, a narrow, abrupt mount divided by dykes, ran north from behind the buildings at the Cross. From opposite the west end of the cathedral, the empty hill where the bishop's palace had stood ran down to the Tay, where the foundation-piles of the wrecked mediaeval bridge still formed a ford across the river.[28]

The two battalions of Angus's regiment, still without uniforms, were reduced by desertion to 7-800 men, a high proportion of them Cameronian 'madd men not to be Governed even by mastr Shiels ther orachle'. Besides general hardships, they were discontented with Cleland and his major — not only for imposing experienced but profane officers, and turning out fanatics, but for embezzling pay and provisions and clothing money. Both men were killed before they could answer; but Cleland complained that the Marquess of Douglas's factor, Lawrie of Blackwood, was trying to ruin him so he could plunder the regiment as its agent at pleasure. As Blackwood wrecked Douglas's marriage to keep his grip on the estates; as he plainly saw the regiment as of his own raising; and as he helped draft the officers' articles of complaint, on which he then made his 'impartial' report,

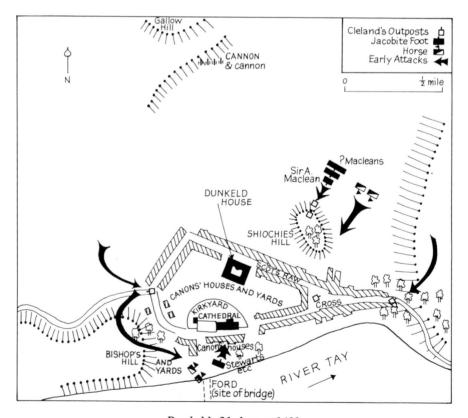

Dunkeld, 21 August 1689

Cleland was probably justified.[29] Nevertheless, the discontent was strong, and, on reaching Dunkeld on 17 August, many men argued that they were betrayed and demanded to retreat. Their officers and the many west-country gentry volunteers who accompanied them quieted them.[30]

Although the Cameronians, convinced that they were among enemies, began to fortify the yard-dykes behind Dunkeld House, the first force to appear, on the 18th, was a local defensive watch headed by gentry, which took no part in the later fighting. The leaders tried to frighten the Cameronians out of their supposed intention of burning Dunkeld and committing massacres, which had made most of the inhabitants flee. Cleland proclaimed the indemnity, but his soldiers' plundering destroyed its effect.[31] He reported to Ramsay that he could hold Dunkeld if he had ammunition and provisions, and Ramsay sent a little, which caused further paranoid fears. Ramsay also ordered Lord Cardross with five troops of horse and dragoons to Dunkeld, where he arrived early on Monday 19th, drove off some small parties from nearby hills, and took prisoners.[32]

The Jacobite response was weakened because the problem was seen as local. The Stewarts of Appin, returning 120 strong now Argyll's offensive had collapsed, had reached Blair on their march. They insisted on continuing to join Cannon, although they agreed to ravage Strathardle en route for its failure to supply the garrison. The people of Strathardle rose and faced them during the afternoon and night of the 19th. The Stewarts then departed with a gratuity, and unexpectedly met Cannon a few hours later.[33] Meanwhile, Alexander Steuart collected 600–1000 Atholl and Strathtay men overnight by the fiery cross. On the 20th, Cardross received Ramsay's alarmed order to return at once but defied it when Steuart's men, horse and foot appeared on the hills.[34]

After reconnoitring, Cardross, as senior officer, led the forces in a sally upstream, leaving 150 men in Dunkeld House. At their head were small groups of fusiliers, horsemen and halberdiers, like old-fashioned 'forlorn hopes', to break the first impetus of a highland charge (and compensate for a dangerous lack of bayonets). Cleland presumably helped plan these tactics, which he adapted next day for defence. Mackay condescendingly called him 'a sensible, resolute man, though not much of a souldier', but, though he had called highland warriors 'monkeys' in a 1678 poem, he had studied the lessons of Mackay's own defeat. However, the highlanders confined themselves to laying abortive ambushes, and the troops spent the day in successful skirmishing, and killed a dozen men — breaking off sharply that evening as Cannon's vanguard appeared.[35]

Cannon's march to Dunkeld is his one action as Commander-in-Chief that justifies his previous reputation. His campaign had been a disaster; and, unless he achieved something decisive before the remaining clans dispersed for the harvest, they would be hard to reassemble. His only advantage was the over-confidence which Mackay, after his past fortnight's achievements, was again feeling. Somehow, Cannon reasserted control. On 17 August, as Mackay was reinforced and confidently expected the news of Londonderry's relief to make the clans disperse before his eyes, they slipped away from Strathbogie on the first of their 'extraordinary long marches'. By night, they had crossed the Dee. Mackay tried to trick them into delay by summoning them formally to battle, and pursued them to Kincardine O'Neil; but, not daring to follow them into the mountains, he had to go round via Aberdeen, and by the 22nd had only reached Drumlithie.[36]

Cannon, of course, knew nothing yet of Angus's regiment and hoped to break into the Mearns. Lanier, who had already destroyed one ferocious Jacobite raiding party on the 15th near Brechin, was on the alert, and repulsed his reconnaissance at Fettercairn.[37] However, the news from Dunkeld gave Cannon a golden opportunity. He turned south-west, and Lanier, marching parallel in the plain, informed Ramsay at Perth. Ramsay's timidity as commander made him commit a terrible mistake. Having always feared that the Jacobites would cut Cardross off from him, he peremptorily ordered him to retire from Dunkeld; yet, because Lanier 'knows of Angus regiment being there', he ignored that it also was under his own command and sent it no order. He did (according to Mackay) send to Lanier for instructions, which Lanier, not knowing the country, delayed to give until he could consult him.[38] As the cavalry retired, the Cameronians mutinied and declared that they would go with them rather than be butchered in 'an open, useless place'. Cleland, privately sharing their fears of treachery, 'charged those retiring dragoons with the loss and blood of that regiment'. Yet he and the other officers, by dramatically offering to shoot their horses to prove their own determination, finally persuaded them to stay. Cannon's instinct in returning to an area where overlapping commands caused confusion was fully justified. Had his tactics matched his strategy, or had he faced a normal regiment and commander, he would have won an annihilating victory, reviving Jacobite hopes and frightening the newly-raised forces off highland service for good.[39]

Besides the Atholl men, the first major contingent of Macgregors under Glengyle (Rob Roy's father) joined Cannon, and Robertson of Struan, the Appin and Glencoe men rejoined him. The clans which had fought at Killiecrankie were still present in strength, even those from the Outer Hebrides which would have farthest to travel before harvest, Macdonald of Sleat's men from North Uist, Clanranald's men under the Tutor (Benbecula) and MacNeil of Barra. The North-East had strengthened the cavalry to four fine troops.[40] Estimates of Cannon's force varied between 2,500 (from episcopalians belittling the Cameronians' achievements). Balhaldie's 3,000 (the only figure from the Jacobite side), 4,000 (official) and 5,000 (including 1,000 Atholl men), given by prisoners and involuntarily confirmed by Mackay.[41]

At dawn on 21 August, this army appeared on the hills round Dunkeld, while a vast baggage-train carried its plunder towards Blair. Balhaldie's argument that Cannon should instead have lured out the Cameronians on another sortie and have overwhelmed them seems groundless. Unlike many of his men, Cleland knew, from the boasts of prisoners and Ramsay's orders, that this was the Highland Army, and would not have risked a sortie without cavalry cover. If any opportunity was missed, it was on Tuesday, before the vanguard could be identified; but the highlanders then were exhausted by long marches and hunger.[42] However, Cannon would now have to commit the clans to street fighting, for which they were unsuited. He and his officers made the decision without proper consultation, and Sir John Maclean protested at it.[43] Yet Cleland still had some reason to fear a highland charge. Although the dykes in much of his main perimeter round the mansion and cathedral were high, they contained breaches, and included 'low gardens, not above four feet high'. The highlanders' initial impetus might enable them to break through here. Cleland's solution was again to check this through small skirmishing parties. These would certainly be forced back, and he explained in detail how they should retreat, to prevent panic. The regiment was short of powder and very short of bullets, so squads were set to work stripping the lead off Dunkeld House roof and melting it into slugs.[44]

At 7 a.m. the battle began. The four Jacobite cannon — leather ones, according to one source — were placed on the Gallowhill, just north of the town and House. Cannon's initial plan of attack was at least original. From east of the Gallowhill, a hundred of Sir Alexander Maclean's regiment, the usual shock troops, carrying swords, and protected by helmets, half armour and targes, ran forward towards Shiochies Hill. The rest of the regiment followed with firelocks, giving covering fire, and behind them came a larger force, perhaps Sir John Maclean's. To their left advanced two troops of horse.[45] On Shiochies Hill Cleland had stationed Captain Hay and a party, who defended it dyke by dyke. The east end of the town was indefensible, with the hill overhanging it and a wood on the slopes mingling with the first houses; so the outpost there, when attacked, merely made a token resistance, burned the houses and retreated to a barricade at the Cross. Besides assisting the attacks there and on Shiochies Hill, the two troops of horse were plainly stationed to prevent escape eastwards; and two more, fired on by a detachment at the west end of town, crossed Bishop's Hill and guarded the ford. Plainly, Cannon started the battle confident that he could annihilate the trapped regiment. Everywhere, the highlanders followed their usual practice of firing one volley and then attacking with sword and target. The barricade at the Cross was rushed and the commander killed as he tried to withdraw his men. Hay's force was driven back by degrees to the House, and both he and Sir Alexander Maclean suffered broken legs. The detachment to the west, attacked by overwhelming numbers, retreated to the cathedral, where there were a hundred soldiers and those inhabitants who had not fled before. In these retreats, some soldiers were trapped in houses and killed.[46]

The highlanders now attacked vigorously in four places at once. On the riverbank, they deployed under point-blank fire, stormed from the rear the houses south of the cathedral, and, headed by the Appin Stewarts, attacked the cathedral itself so vigorously that help had to be brought it. Very soon, the soldiers were driven back until they held only Dunkeld House, the cathedral and a few canons' houses — only three by the end of the battle. Most of the highlanders advanced to the dykes and fought with sword and target against the pikemen and halberdiers — for the Cameronian musketeers had neither swords nor bayonets. Some, however, entered the captured houses and opened fire from them. About 8 a.m., Cleland was shot dead near the House and the Major was mortally wounded. Command passed to the senior captain present, Munro, the appointment of Cleland's most strongly opposed by the Cameronian General Meeting.[47]

Yet the Jacobite attack was losing its impetus, as each fresh group fired its one volley and joined the crowds pressing round the walls, jostled by the corpses of those the last volley had killed. The Glencoe poet lamented:

> They were not accustomed to stand against a wall for protection, as was done at Dunkeld. The stalwart young men fell ... felled by bullets fired by cowherds.[48]

Cannon was commanding from the rear. This inevitably roused the clans' fury at 'a devil of a commander who was out of sight of his enemies'; and it should in compensation have enabled him to make and carry out fresh plans after the attack had started, a possibility seldom open to commanders who charged with their men.[49] He was particularly criticised for not exploiting his artillery. Even if (and it is not certain) they were only leather guns, they could have been effective in close-range bombardment of the House and, particularly, of the gaps in the dykes, filled with loose stones, through which the highlanders several times nearly forced their way unaided. Instead, those firing them, after having a month to train, 'wer so il guners that they did no execution'. Cannon could certainly have obtained from Blair or the spoil at Killiecrankie cannonballs of the right calibre. Instead, he was almost without them, and, unlike the Cameronians melting Dunkeld House roof for slugs, the only bullets they had after 9 a.m., he was unable to improvise. Aonghus Mac Alasdair Ruaidh may have been wrong in arguing that Dundee would never have made the clans attack a town; but certainly Dundee would have made every possible preparation beforehand, and when the first attack faltered, would have changed his tactics. The poet's conclusion was justified:

The day of the fight at Dunkeld showed that Claverhouse was dead.[50]

However, the snipers in the captured houses were harassing the defenders and, Balhaldie claimed, were gaining the upper hand and preventing the Cameronian musketeers from taking proper aim.[51] At about 9.30, Munro, seeing the danger, organised sorties by small parties carrying blazing faggots on their pikes, who set fire to the houses, killed some highlanders, and locked others in to burn to death — sixteen in one house, they claimed. The highlanders retaliated by setting other houses alight to drive out the defenders. Yet the attacks continued amidst the smoke, flames and screaming.[52] By 11 a.m., the regiment's powder was running out. Its most desperate leaders were planning a suicidal last stand in the House, when the highlanders suddenly drew off. Later Cannon was blamed for this, as for everything; but Lt. Blackader, writing the same day, reported a prisoner's admission that the officers had tried to make the clans return to the attack, but they had refused to fight any more against 'mad and desperate Men' (others called them 'devils', and the name stuck). Mackay commented that the troops the highlanders had routed at Killiecrankie would have continued the attack. Cannon claimed that the highlanders themselves were out of ammunition. Episcopalians everywhere preferred to believe that they had groundlessly feared the arrival of Lanier's cavalry.[53]

The highlanders at first remained on the hills north-west of the town. The Cameronians prepared for their return by building up breaches in the yard-dykes with stones and the church seats, and by cutting down trees, under cover of which snipers had galled them. Then they sang psalms and waited. In the afternoon, Cardross returned, finally allowed by Ramsay to bring his dragoons to the rescue. At his approach, the highlanders retreated up the Tay, abandoning their dead and plundering. At midnight, Ramsay himself suddenly set off for Dunkeld, just before Lanier reached Perth.[54]

Both sides, incongruously, made the same claims about casualties: about twenty of their own men killed. and about three hundred of the enemy. The Cameronians' claims were nearer to the truth, though they probably omitted some soldiers who had been trapped in houses and killed by the first highland rush, and their bodies burned: after the recent mutinies and desertions, they cannot have known exactly who was with the regiment. The prolonged sniping had caused heavy officer casualties: besides Cleland and his major, a captain and a lieutenant were killed and at least three captains wounded.[55] Having restored Scottish presbyterianism's tarnished reputation in Britain, the regiment became temporarily unfit for service, torn by internal reproaches, feelings of betrayal and mass desertions, and Mackay hastily withdrew them from active service.[56]

On the Jacobite side also, there were heavy casualties among leading men. Sir Alexander Maclean nearly died and had to leave permanently for Ireland for treatment. His captain-lieutenant was killed, as were two of Sir John Maclean's captains, and Maclean of Ardgour's mainland detachment suffered particularly heavily. The Tutor of Appin lost two brothers there, with many other Stewarts. John Cameron, who had fought at the head of his clan, reported that the Camerons suffered considerable loss — though nothing like the slaughter of Killiecrankie. There were also killed 'some other officers of note'.[57]

Cannon had one quality of the successful general, the ability to conceal failures from his superiors. His report suggested that the clans had stormed a walled town, killing the regiment's officers and 200 men, and that the rest escaped only by fleeing into 'the castle and the great church'; despite which, the clans unreasonably took a 'distaste ... at Cannon's conduct'. James was deceived, and sent Cannon his warm thanks. However, he could not deceive the clans, who were now also demoralised by the certainty, which they had previously refused to believe, that Londonderry had been relieved — and, just afterwards, that Marshal Schomberg with a large English army had landed in Ulster.[58]

Obviously, Cannon must let his disheartened forces disperse for harvest, but after such a sequence of disasters it was doubtful whether they would reassemble under a commander who had so totally lost their respect — something admitted even by those who argued that he did not deserve this. Therefore, on 24 August a bond was drawn up at Blair and signed by most of the chiefs present, agreeing to muster in September with an agreed minimum force. The numbers set down amounted in all to 1,810, but the first detachment mentioned, the Atholl men to be commanded by Lord James Murray and Ballechin, had none filled in, neither man signed the bond, and the place of rendezvous (Lochaber) and exact date were left blank.[59] With the Highland Army on the point of dispersal and an overwhelming force gathering at Perth, it was obvious that the Atholl rebels must either submit, face destruction, or abandon their homes — a course only the obdurate Ballechin, his brother and their families would follow. Yet Ballechin's son Charles went to Perth on 25 August to inquire on what terms Atholl could submit, took the oaths, and even testified in the forfeiture proceedings — probably a family compromise. The Highland Army would naturally have destroyed Blair on leaving it, if Mackay had not threatened to burn every house and cornfield above Dunkeld if they did. Lord James Murray persuaded the highlanders to spare the castle — his last action before going to submit. As on other occasions, the Jacobites' scrupulousness, in contrast to Mackay, brought them serious disadvantage — the planting of a garrison that could keep Atholl, 'a large Third parte of the rebells strength', subdued.[60]

The army retreated along Loch Rannoch, and dispersed about 29 August. Not only Williamites but also Lord James Murray believed that it would never reassemble. They had some reason, for it was torn by intrigues. Sir William Wallace was caballing against Dunfermline, because, ludicrously, he wished to supplant him as commander of Dundee's non-existent regiment. Glengarry temporarily led the opposition to Cannon. He therefore was probably the chief of the 'persons of note' who, even more grotesquely, warned the catholic professional officers that Cannon intended to massacre them for their religion. They naturally disbelieved this, but he persuaded Cannon, who proceeded to Inverlochy, that the chief catholic officers were working to undermine him. Cannon and Dunfermline avoided quarrelling, but drowned their sorrows together in aquavitae. The proposed date of rendezvous in September passed without result, and a bond that was drawn up for the chiefs on 3 October remained without signatures.[61]

Discredited though Cannon was, one series of orders he gave was promptly obeyed. Very early in September, Macgregor of Glengyle, his youngest son Rob Roy, and a party of 140 Macgregors raided Stirlingshire and lifted 162 cows. Everything possible was done to give it official status. They plundered only the tenants of the Williamite colonel Lord Cardross; they declared to their pursuers that they had Cannon's commission and that the cows were not for themselves but for their 'masters'; and two lowland Jacobite gentlemen accompanied them. Frequent raids of this sort would be necessary for the clans to survive the winter. The disruption of normal trade in victuals all that year, the large amounts consumed at Dundee's gatherings and the continuous rains now starting, which must have ruined an already bad harvest, left the Highlands on the verge of starvation. Cannon wrote urgently begging Lord Melfort to send supplies, 'for other ways I kno not what sal becom of all of us hear'.[62]

Mackay, who had arrived at Perth on 25 August, took no chances this time. He assembled an enormous army (which plundered unmercifully), took with him seven infantry battalions, two regiments of horse, two of dragoons and three independent troops, and left a large garrison. Setting out through the rains on 26 August, he reached Blair two days later without incident and established a garrison 500 strong. He allowed the Atholl men to take the indemnity, but only on surrendering their arms, and ignored all claims from those who had opposed the Jacobites and were now exposed to their raids. Assuming that all Atholl was disloyal, he wrote to Hamilton that only the latter's relation to Murray had made him act so mildly. The inhabitants, however, were 'amazed yt they find soe litle shelter under ye indemnity, yt . . . they are ruined intirely'. But Mackay, though he thought the Atholl men deserved badly, was horrified by the worst devastations, which Argyll's regiment carried out in revenge for the treatment of their shire in 1685. They burned houses and lands, cut down most of the trees round Blair and Dunkeld, and plotted to blow up Dunkeld House. Argyll encouraged them, even making his horse dung on the dining-table there to fulfil a prophecy, and told the outraged Mackay that he could not prevent his men from devastating Atholl. Mackay retorted that he was abusing the King's service for private revenge. The hope shared by Lord Murray and Ballechin that July that the war could be made to bypass Atholl had been cruelly disappointed.[63]

The rain became torrential. Robertson of Struan apparently relied on this to prevent Mackay from advancing from Blair the few miles to his house, and was even confident enough to keep some Killiecrankie prisoners there. However, Mackay sent out a detachment with Glenlyon, who had accepted a commission in Argyll's regiment before Killiecrankie, acting as guide. After some firing, Robertson, Dundee's brother and Sir George Barclay were captured in the house. All were exchanged that winter.[64]

South of Blair, Mackay reinforced Menzies's garrison at Weem, near the foot of Loch Tay. He had hoped to plant another in Breadalbane's castle of Finlarig at its head, but the rains forced him back to the Lowlands. There, he had to organise the departure of nearly all the English forces which had given him his crucial superiority in mounted men over the past months — three regiments under the overjoyed Lanier to embark from the west for Ireland, two to England for recruitment. Leslie's, still at Inverness stayed only because 'it is hard to get a Scotch lord march with his Reg^{mt} soe farr North'. In other ways, also, the balance was swinging against him. The Treasury was almost empty. After October, those forces not paid from England would not even receive subsistence, and would deteriorate rapidly. The Club leaders, with whom Mackay sympathised, were going to London to confront William, but there was no real prospect of an agreement and a parliament willing to vote supplies. William favoured the obvious solution, disbanding a large part of the army. Yet Mackay, forced on to the defensive for the winter, had to maintain much larger forces than the highlanders would be using — garrisons all along a 250 mile semi-circle round the area in rebellion, sustained by several armies to meet large-scale attacks.[65]

However, this could not efface the impression his success had created. Jacobites flocked to Edinburgh to take the indemnity before it expired on 10 September. They included several lowland gentry from Angus and Aberdeen; peers from the same area such as Strathmore, who had sympathised with Dundee but had not risen; Lord Livingstone, who nearly had; some McAlisters from Kintyre, a sign that Sir Alexander Maclean's regiment was disintegrating; and Breadalbane's chief Campbell subordinates in plotting his rising. Some highland lairds appeared in Edinburgh to submit. None of the major chiefs were among them, despite constant rumours, but Mackay hoped to detach Sir John Maclean, breaking the confederacy, if he were empowered to offer him terms that would save him from ruin. By employing mild pressure rather than severity against Jacobites whose treason had not received formal notice, the Council later made several more submit, including even Lochiel's son-in-law Drummond of Balhaldie.[66]

Breadalbane had genuine need of an indemnity: one of Carleton's letters proving his intrigues with James was in Hamilton's hands. He exploited this to excuse himself to the Jacobites. However, it covered a more general doubt whether their success was possible, on which he had been acting since Dundee's death (and, perhaps, his own failure to become general). In mid-August, well before Dunkeld, he applied to Sir John Dalrymple to obtain Melville's protection for him. Dalrymple sent a reply that his best means of gaining favour would be to break the combination of the clans. After Dalrymple left for London, Breadalbane corresponded with him via Carwhin, protesting his blamelessness and promising to work for peace. Possibly Dalrymple was already calculating that, if a political struggle came between him and Melville, he would need an agent for highland negotiations to match Melville's Tarbat.[67] In early September, Breadalbane hastened from Kilchurn to Edinburgh, and after the zealous Annandale — a Jacobite six months earlier and six months later — had raised difficulties, was carried in a chair to the Council bar and took the oath. Waverers in the highland camp, including Macdonald of Achnacone in Glencoe (Achtriachtan's brother) applied to him for help in submitting. His urgent dissuasion may have prevented Macnachtan from setting out for Ireland with important dispatches for James.[68]

Yet news circulating at Edinburgh within a few days probably gave him second thoughts. Melfort had left his position as James's Secretary and had retired to France (where his Jacobite opponents, adroitly playing on Louis XIV's admiration for his qualities, got him sent on a mission even further off, to Rome). His departure began a strong Jacobite rally in Ireland after the disasters of the summer. And, although it would not benefit the clans directly, it removed one of the genuine obstacles which had prevented magnates and politicians from working, even indirectly, for James's restoration. Even on the presbyterian Club it had its effect. In reality, Melfort had fled for fear of assassination by the Irish, and had deliberately not resigned as Secretary. Ignorant of this, Club leaders, obsessed with their struggle against William, who seemed incorrigible in choosing bad advisers and infringing the nation's rights, secretly wondered whether James's dismissal of his evil genius might not indicate that adversity had brought him wisdom — a dangerous thought as they journeyed south to negotiate with his rival.[69]

NOTES

1. *London Gazette* No. 2476, 1-5 Aug. 1689; *Franco-Irish Corr.*, iii, 85, Fumeron to Louvois, 15 Oct. 1689 (NS).

2. C. Dalton, *English Army Lists*, 6 vols. (London, 1892-1904), i, 216, ii, 54, 107, 230; Ferguson, *Scots Brigade*, i, 481-4; *Correspondentie*, ii, 627, Verhuel van Onse Marche; SRO GD 26/xiii/14, Middleton to Skelton, 20 Mar. 1684/5.

3. *APS*, ix, App., 56, Lt. J. Nisbet's deposition; Atholl, *Chronicles*, i, 303, Ld James Murray to Murray, 29 July 1689; Mackay, *Memoirs*, 259, Mackay to Hamilton, 2 Aug. 1689; Dundee, *Letters*, 67, James to Dundee, 7 July 1689; Macfarlane, *Gen. Colls.*, i, 139.

4. *Correspondence of Colonel N. Hooke*, ed. W. D. Macray, 2 vols., (Roxburghe Club, 1870–1), i. 49–50, 'Memoire Sommaire sur les Affaires d'Ecosse', 2 Feb. 1704; SRO GD 112/39/1208, Dunfermline to Breadalbane, 29 July 1689; *ib.* 40/3/4/76, J. Macnachtan to same, 2 Aug. 1689; *ib.*, 43/1/1/50, Macnachtan to same, 2 Aug. 1689; *ib.*, 43/1/2/99, Breadalbane's Life; GD 406/M9/194, H. Farquhar's confession, 24 July 1689 + list of nobles said in Ireland to be for King James.

5. Mackay, *Memoirs*, 238, Mackay to Hamilton, 29 July 1689; *ib.*, 259, same to same, 2 Aug. 1689; Atholl, *Chronicles*, i, 317, *The Exact Narrative of the Conflict at Dunkeld*; SRO GD 26/viii/24, A. Steuart to Cannon, 31 July 1689; GD 112/39/1208, Dunfermline to Breadalbane, 29 July 1689.

6. However, Balhaldie may be wrong: in a (misdated) letter from Blair, Cannon ordered Cluny, who was hanging back on a complaint of some injury done by the Camerons, to join him with all his men. Macpherson, 'Gleanings', *TGSI*, xx, 232, Cannon to Cluny, '20' [?29] July 1689.

7. *Memoirs of Locheill*, 283; *APS*, ix, App., 60, Lt J. Hay's deposition, 14 May 1690; *RPCS*,xiii,565–6; 'Journal of a Soldier', *TGAS*, i, 43; Stewart, *The Stewarts of Appin*, 208, Ballachulish to Invernahyle [1690]; SRO GD 406/1/3558, Argyll to Hamilton, 2 Aug. 1689.

8. Lenman misreads a passage in Lord James's letter of 11 August, 'all the Atholl men wold joyne whou ever' to mean that they 'had no particular prejudices, either way, in the conflict'; it is actually his spelling of 'however', and means that they would have joined the Jacobites whatever he himself did. Lenman, *Jacobite Risings*, 38; Atholl, *Chronicles*, i, 302–3, Ld James Murray to Murray, 28 July 1689; *ib.*, 303, same to same, 29 July 1689; *ib.*, 304, T. Stewart to same, 29 July 1689; *ib.*, 326, Sir P. Moray to same, 3 Sept. 1689; *ib.*, 321–2, Murray to Ld James Murray, '24'[4] Aug. 1689; Blair, Atholl MSS, Box 29 I(5) 173, Ld James Murray to Lady Murray, 11 Aug. 1689; *ib.*, 184, same to Murray, 5 Sept. 1689; *ib.*, 195, Representation, 1689.

9. *APS*, ix, 109; *Leven & Melville*, 204, 205, Lockhart, Dalrymple, to Melville, 28 July 1689; *Est. Procs.*, i, 186–7; *State Papers and Letters addressed to William Carstares*, ed. J. M'Cormick(*Carstares S.P.*; Edinburgh, 1774), 275, Argyll to Carstares, 21 Mar. 1696; Foxcroft, *Halifax*, ii, 230; Atholl, *Chronicles*, i, 310, Mackay to Murray, 4 Aug. 1689; *ib.*, 312, Marchioness to same, 8 Aug. [1689]; *ib.*, 313–14, same to same, 13 Aug. [1689]; *ib.*, 321–3, Murray to Ld James Murray, to Atholl vassals, '24'[4] Aug. 1689.

10. An additional reason for believing that Murray's objections were sincere was that the attempt to transfer his inheritance to Dunmore had left him acutely sensitive about any of his brothers giving orders to his vassals. *Ib.*;*ib.*, 308, Col. Menzies to Murray, 2 Aug. 1689; *ib.*, 311, various Robertsons to same, 8 Aug. 1689; *RPCS*, xiv,7–8

11. Atholl, *Chronicles*, i, 305–6, Glenlyon to Murray, 29 July 1689; Campbell, *Lairds of Glenlyon*, 48, Cannon's protection, 2 Aug. 1689.

12. Even when William countermanded some of these orders, he left more troops available than Mackay required. *RPCS*, xiii, 565–9, 573; *ib.*, 14–15; *Leven & Melville*, 203–4, Hamilton to Melville, 28 July 1689; *ib.*, 205–7, same to same, 29 July 1689; *ib.*, 207, Lockhart to same, 29 July 1689; Mackay, *Memoirs*, 61–2.

13. *Ib.*, 62; *ib.*, 255–6, Mackay to Hamilton, 29 July 1689; *Leven & Melville*, 239, Dalrymple to Melville, 7 Aug. 1689; Morer, *Short Account*, 101; NLS MS 3740 fol. 96, Lanier to Blathwayt, 3 Aug. 1689.

14. *Ib.*, fol. 98, Mackay to same, 11 Aug. 1689; Mackay, *Memoirs*, 62–4; *ib.*, 259–60, Mackay to Hamilton, 2 Aug. 1689; *ib.*, 266, Short Relation, 17 Aug. 1689; *RPCS*, xiv, 38; *CTB*, ix, 1144; *Est. Procs.*, i, 190–1; *Memoirs of Lochiell*, 283; Macpherson, *Original Papers*, i, 370–1, Account of the engagements, 15 Dec. 1689; SRO GD 406/1/3610, Mackay to Hamilton, [30 July 1689].

15. *APS*, ix, 138; *Est, Procs.*, i, 191; *Leven & Melville*, 160–1, Sir W. Lockhart to Melville, 11 July 1689; *ib.*, 228, Sir J. Dalrymple to same, 2 Aug. 1689.

16. *Melvilles & Leslies*, ii, 118–19, Cannon to Mackay, 5 Aug. 1689; *Memoirs of Lochiell*, 285 (Council of war misdated); Dalrymple, *Memoirs*, i, 189n.

17. 'Journal of a Soldier', *TGAS*, i, 43; SRO GD 26/viii/24, A. Steuart to Cannon, 31 July 1689; *ib.*, 27, examination of C. Campbell, 6 Aug. 1689; *ib.*, 102, Tutor of Appin's Information, [Sept. 1689]; *ib.*, ix/105, J. Mackdougall to Mackay, 12 Aug. 1689; GD 112/43/1/1/50. J. Macnachtan to Breadalbane, 2 Aug. 1689; *ib.*, 43/1/2/99, Breadalbane's Life, 2; Blair, Atholl MSS, Box 29 I (5) 173, Ld James Murray to Lady Murray, 11 Aug. 1689; *Rawdon Papers*, 310, Smith to Rawdon, 7 Aug. 1689.

18. *RPCS*, xiv, 5–6, 27; *Sutherland Book*, i, 318, Memoir of Earl of Sutherland, 1715; Mackay, *Urquhart and Glenmoriston*, 204–6; NLS MS 1329 fol. 76, Sir A. Mackenzie to Delvine, 10 Aug. 1689; *ib.*, MS 1332 fol. 53, A. Mackenzie to same, 13 Aug. 1689; SRO GD 406/1/3570, Mr of Forbes to Hamilton, 5 Aug. 1689.

19. *Ib.*, 3611, Mackay to same, 4 Aug. 1689; *ib.*, 3612, same to same, 8 Aug. 1689; *ib.*, 3617, 'Reasons for the measures which Major–General Mackay resolves to take', 8 Aug. 1689; Mackay, *Memoirs*, 65–6; Simpson, 'Early Castles of Mar', *PSAS*, lxiii, 116–17.

20. *RPCS*, xiv, 3, 16–17; *Leven & Melville*, 252, Dalrymple to Melville, 13 Aug. 1689; SRO GD 406/1/3559, 3560, Argyll to Hamilton, 5 Aug. 1689.

21. *APS*, ix, 182, 447; *RPCS*, xv, 152; Mackay, *Memoirs*, 66; SRO GD 26/ix/105, J. Mackdougall to Mackay, 12 Aug. 1689.

22. *APS*, ix, App., 59, Lt. J. Hay's deposition, 14 May 1690; *RPCS*, xiv, 14, 24–5, 219–20; *Est. Procs.*, i, 201, 205, 208, 210, 215; *Leven & Melville*, 282–3, Livingstone to Melville, 12 Sept. 1689; *ib.*, 291n, same, Callendar & Duffus to Hamilton, 5 Aug. 1689; Morer, *Short Account*, 102; SRO GD 26/viii/38, C. Mackenzie to Seaforth, 29 Aug. 1689; GD 406/1/3570, Mr of Forbes to Hamilton, 5 Aug. 1689; Mackay, *Memoirs*, 66, 68; *Memoirs of Lochiell*, 285.

23. The printed Clans' Letter to Mackay and Bond of 24 August would seem to contradict Balhaldie, since they include Lochiel's signature; but the original of the latter shows that this is actually 'J. Cameron off Lochyeall'. Similarly, the signature printed as 'D. Mackdonald', supposedly Sir Donald the younger, appears to be 'R.', possibly Macdonald of Achtera. For the possibility that the misreadings were deliberate, see note 59. Keppoch signed neither the letter to Mackay nor the Blair bond, though he was named in the latter, like other absentees. *Ib.*, 284–6; *APS*, ix, App, 60, Chiefs' letter to Mackay, 17 Aug. 1689; *ib.*, Bond, 24 Aug. 1689; SRO GD 26/viii/30, same; *RPCS*, xiv, 667–9; *Memoirs of Dundee*, 29–30; *Seafield Corr.*, 52, A. Ogilvie to Findlater, 15 Aug. 1689; *ib.*, 53–4, same to same 17 Aug. 1689; Mackay, *Memoirs*, 66–7; *ib.*, 266–7, Mackay, 'Short Relation', 17 Aug. 1689; *ib.*, 273–4, same to Melville, 30 Aug. 1689.

24. Sir Patrick Hume, whose son was at Dunkeld and who had no love for Hamilton, reported the battle to him without any suggestion of reproach — indeed, fairly casually. *RPCS*, xiv, 34; Wodrow, *Analecta*, i, 192; Atholl, *Chronicles*, i, 316, *Exact Narrative*; SRO GD 26/ix/334, [W. Lawrie to Melville, 12 Aug. 1689]; GD 406/1/3573, Sir P. Hume to Hamilton, 27 Aug. 1689; Mackay, *Memoirs*, 68–9.

25. *Ib.*; *Melvilles & Leslies*, ii, 121, Sir W. Lockhart to Melville, 23 Aug. 1689; 'Journal of a

Soldier', *TGAS*, i, 43–4; *RPCS*, xiv, 27–9, 34, 62–3, 766–7.

26. *Ib.*, 3, 43–4; Atholl, *Chronicles*, i, 310–11, Atholl gentry to Murray, 6–8 July 1689; *ib.*, 325, Sir P. Moray to Atholl, 3 Sept. 1689; Mackay, *Memoirs*, 69.

27. *Ib.*, 267, 'A Short Relation', 17 Aug. 1689; *RPCS*, xiv, 27, 63; *Est. Procs.*, i, 215.

28. Slezer's views of Dunkeld and the cathedral are the most valuable contempory evidence. No maps of its real shape (as distinct from a proposed Georgian 'New Town') seem to exist from before the early nineteenth century, when Telford's bridge altered its axis. However, the most valuable of these maps, SRO RHP 10560, 'Sites of the old and new mansions at Dunkeld' [1834], gives the former owners and the date of purchase of each piece of ground by the Atholl family, showing, for instance, that Bruce's Dunkeld House was on a recently purchased site, not, as is usually supposed, that of the old Atholl tower-house. The decrepit tower to the left of Slezer's view (at a spot other 19th century maps call Castle Close) was not, therefore, a fragment of the bishop's palace, but the first Atholl house. Slezer's view was taken about 1680; by 1689, the tower-house had presumably been demolished, since it is not mentioned in accounts of the battle — 'the Cassell' being used of Dunkeld House. Shiochies Hill was later landscaped into Mount Stanley, but it is mentioned in pre-1688 deeds and its identity shown by the 1834 map. The trooper of Eglinton's and the *Exact Narrative* mention the ford, and the latter indicates its position. J. Slezer, *Theatrum Scotiae* (London, 1693), plates 24, 25; *Statistical Account*, xii, 317, 323n, 344, 346; H. Fenwick, *Architect Royal* (Kineton, 1970), 20–1; 'Journal of a Soldier', *TGAS*, i, 44–5; J. Hunter, *The Diocese and Presbytery of Dunkeld, 1660–1689*, 2 vols. (London, n.d.), i, 262–3; Atholl, *Chronicles*, i, 317, *Exact Narrative*; *ib.*, 324, Cpt. C. Graham to Lady Murray, 27 Aug. 1689; Blair, Atholl MSS, Box 28 I (3a) 11, Lord Murray to Marchioness of Atholl, [?1676]; SRO, RHP 10560, Sites of the old and new mansions at Dunkeld, [1834]; *ib.*, RHP 10561/1, plan of the Duke of Atholl's lands about Dunkeld, [c. 1809]; *ib.*, RHP 11623, plan of the lines of intended roads from the new bridge at Dunkeld [1802].

29. *RPCS*. xiv, 28; *Melvilles & Leslies*, ii, 115–16, Cleland to Melville, 25 July 1689; Dalton, *English Army Lists*, iii, 406, 'The Complaints of some officers . . . in my Lord Angus regiment . . . ', Aug. 1689; NLS MS 542 fol. 8, draft of same; *ib.*, fol. 12, Lawrie's report, 6 Aug. 1689; *DNB*, sub 'Lawrie, William'; SRO GD 26/ix/227, Lawrie to Melville, 20 Aug. 1689; *ib.*, 334, [same to same, 12 Aug. 1689].

30. Shields, who helped prevent them, was at a conference in Edinburgh by 19 August with the Cameronian senior captain, Ker of Kersland — which shows that the officers did not expect immediate danger. *Ib.*, 229, Cardross to same, 25 Aug. 1689; Wodrow, *Analecta*, i, 192; Shields, *Faithful Contendings*, 411–112; Atholl, *Chronicles*, i, 314, 320, *Exact Narrative*.

31. *Ib.*, 315; *ib.*, 325, Sir P. Moray to Atholl, 3 Sept. 1689.

32. *Melvilles & Leslies*, ii, 119, Ramsey to Cardross, 19 Aug. 1689; *TGAS*, i, 'Journal of a Soldier', 44; Wodrow, *Analecta*, i, 192; SRO GD 26/ix/229, Cardross to Melville, 25 Aug. 1689

33. *APS*, ix, App., 56, J. Nisbet's deposition, 14 May 1690; Robertson, *The Barons Reid-Robertson*, 37–8; Stewart, *The Stewarts of Appin*, 208, Ballachullish to Invernahyle, [1690].

34. *RPCS*, xiv, 82; *Melvilles & Leslies*, ii, 119, Ramsey to Cardross, 19 Aug. 1689; SRO GD 26/ix/229, 251, Cardross to Melville, 25 Aug. 1689; Atholl, *Chronicles*, i, 325, Sir P. Morsay to Atholl, 3 Sept. 1689; *ib.*, 315, *Exact Narrative*.

35. *Ib.*, 315–17; *RPCS*, xiii, 487; Mackay, *Memoirs*, 71; *TGAS*, i, 'Journal of a Soldier', 44–5; SRO GD 26/ix/251, [Cardross] to [Melville, 25 Aug. 1689]; Cleland, *Poems*, 31, 35.

36. *APS*, ix, App. 60, the Chiefs to Mackay, Birse, 17 Aug. 1689; *RPCS*, xiv, 82, 708–9; *ib.*, xv, 632; *Seafield Corr.*, 53, A. Ogilvie to Findlater, 17 Aug. 1689; Mackay, *Memoirs*, 67–8; *ib.*, 226–7, 'Short Relation'.

37. *Est. Procs.*, i, 215, 220; Morer, *Short Account* 7, 104–5; Mackay, *Memoirs*, 69.

38. *Ib.*, 69–71; *Melvilles & Leslies*, ii, 120, Ramsey to Cardross, 20 Aug. 1689.

39. Atholl, *Chronicles*, i, 316–17, *Exact Narrative; Est. Procs.*, i, 223, Blackader's letter; 'Journal of a Soldier', *TGAS*, i, 45; Mackay, *Memoirs*, 70–1; SRO GD 26/ix/251, [Cardross] to [Melville, 25 Aug. 1689] *ib.*, 256, Cleland to Cpt. Erskine, [20 Aug. 1689]; *RPCS*, xiv, 126.

40. Of course, these Hebridean forces were also the ones least able to slip away casually for a time. *Ib.*, 82; *APS*, ix, App. 59, Lt. J. Hay's deposition, 30 May 1690; *ib.*, 60, the Chiefs to Mackay, 17 Aug. 1689; *ib.*, Bond of Association, 24 Aug.1689; Atholl, *Chronicles*, i, 317, *Exact Narrative; From the Farthest Hebrides*, ed. D.A. Fergusson (Toronto, 1978), 35, 'Iain Mac Thormaid 'ic Iain'.

41. Mackay, *Memoirs*, 68; *RPCS*, xiv, 82; *Melvilles & Leslies*, ii, 121, Sir W. Lockhart to Melville, 23 Aug. 1689; *Est Procs.*, i, 221; *ib.*, 224, Blackader's letter; *Memoirs of Lochiell*, 286; Atholl, *Chronicles*, i, 317, *Exact Narrative*.

42. *Ib; Memoirs of Locheill*, 286; *Est. Procs.*, i, 224, Blackader's letter; *Melvilles & Leslies*, ii, 120, Ramsey to Cardross, 20 Aug. 1689; SRO GD 26/ix/229, Cardross to Melville, 25 Aug. 1689; Stewart, *The Stewarts of Appin*, 208, Ballachulish to Ivernahyle, [1690].

43. Maclean, 'Celtic Sources', 319, Aonghus Mac Alasdair Ruaidh, 'Latha Raon-Ruairdh' (translated Maclean). Maclean interprets this as taking place after the battle, and the Macdonalds (on whom Maclean's action apparently 'cast a gloom'), as wishing to continue the campaign; but Aonghus's poem itself shows their strong contempt for Cannon, and Glengarry became temporarily his violent enemy. James Winchester's advice to Dunfermline just before the next major meeting on strategy (SRO GD 26/viii/53, 31 Oct. 1689), that Cannon and he should give their opinions but hear those of the chiefs and accept a majority decision, shows only too well what happened before Dunkeld.

44. Slezer, *Theatrum Scotiae*, plate 25; Mackay, *Memoirs*, 69; *RPCS*, xiv, 126; Atholl, *Chronicles*, i, 317, 319, *Exact Narrative*.

45. The accounts name neither of the hills. However, Blackader mentions that Captain Hay's party fought with some horse, as well as the armoured men described by the *Exact Narrative*. These are certainly not the two troops which blocked the ford at the west end, for the *Exact Narrative* says that they 'marched about the town' to reach it, being fired on by another named outpost, while the men in armour 'marched straight to enter the town'. Therefore the cavalry Hay fought were the two troops the *Exact Narrative* describes as operating near the Cross. Shiochies Hill is the only 'little hill' to suit these conditions, and could, besides, not have been ignored by the defenders, even if smaller than today. Therefore, the hill north of the House (called Gallowhill in the 1834 map) was not the one occupied by the Cameronians. The *Exact Narrative* implied that the force marching straight to attack Shiochies Hill came from the same place from which their cannon 'advanced down to the face of a little hill'. It was not the hill to the east, the attack from which was described separately (and obviously the wrong place to station cannon for the main battle). If it had been the hills to the north-west of the town, the contrast between the cavalry sent to the ford marching 'about the town' and the shock troops marching 'straight to enter' it by Shiochies Hill would not exist. *Ib.*, 317; *Est Procs.*, i, 224, Blackader's letter; *Blackwood's Magazine*, i (1817), 609, 'Some Account of Colonel William Cleland' (quoting an unknown eye-witness account); Macpherson, *Original Papers*, i, 371, 'An Account of the engagements', 15 Dec 1689.

46. *Ib*; *Memoirs of Locheill*, 286; *Est. Procs.*, i, 224; Atholl, *Chronicles*, i, 317–19, *Exact Narrative*.

47. *Ib.*, 318; *Ib.*, 325–6, Sir P. Moray to Atholl, 3 Sept. 1689; *Est. Procs.*, i, 224, Blackader's letter; [Shields], *Faithful Contendings*, 404; Stewart, *The Stewarts of Appin*, 208, Ballachulish to Invernahyle, [1690].

48. Atholl, *Chronicles*, i, 321; Maclean, 'Celtic Sources', 316, Aonghus Mac Alastair Ruaidh, 'Latha Raon-Ruairidh' (translated by Maclean).

49. *Ib*; Stevenson, *Alasdair MacColla*, 261–3.

50. The part the cannon *should* have played was oddly reflected in the first, inaccurate reports of the battle at Edinburgh. *RPCS*, xiv, 126; Atholl, *Chronicles*, i, 319, *Exact Narrative*; *Est. Procs.*, i, 222; *Melvilles & Leslies*, ii, 121, Sir W. Lockhart to Melville, 23 Aug. 1689; Maclean, 'Celtic Sources', 310, *op. cit*; SRO GD 26/viii/24, A. Steuart to Cannon, 31 July 1689; Balcarres, *Memoirs*, 49; *Memoirs of Locheill*, 286

51. However, he mentions this to explain a 'fact' which was not true, the smallness of the Highlanders' casualties. *Ib*.

52. *RPCS*, xiv, 126; Atholl, *Chronicles*, i, 318–19, *Exact Narrative*; *ib.*, 326, Sir P. Moray to Atholl, 3 Sept. 1689; *Est. Procs.*, i, 225, Blackader's letter.

53. *Ib.*, 224–5; Mackay, *Memoirs*, 70; Macpherson, *Original Papers*, i, 371, 'An account of the engagements', 15 Dec. 1689; *Memoirs of Locheill*, 287; *Scotish Pasquils*, 247, 'You're welcome, Whigs'; Rev. R. Kirk 'London in 1689–90', ed. Maclean & Brett Jones, *Transactions of the London and Middlesex Archaeological Society (TLMAS)*, NS vii (1933–7), 305; Atholl, *Chronicles*, i, 319, *Exact Narrative*.

54. *Ib*; *ib.*, 326, Sir P. Moray to Atholl, 3 Sept. 1689; *Melvilles & Leslies*, ii, 120, Sir W. Lockhart to Melville, 23 Aug. 1689; *Est. Procs.*, i, 226; SRO GD 26/ix/251, [Cardross to Melville, 25 Aug. 1689].

55. Only Mackay, typically, accepted the highlanders' low estimates of their own casualties. *RPCS*, xiv, 82, 126; Mackay, *Memoirs*, 70; Macpherson, *Original Papers*, i, 371, 'An Account of the engagements', 15 Dec. 1689; *Memoirs of Locheill*, 286–7; Atholl, *Chronicles*, i, 317–20, *Exact Narrative*.

56. *Ib.*, 320; *ib.*, 324, Cpt. C. Graham to Lady Murray, 27 Aug. 1689; *Melvilles & Leslies*, ii, 121, Sir W. Lockhart to Melville, 23 Aug. 1689; Mackay, *Memoirs*, 290, Mackay to same, 22 Oct. 1689; [Shields], *Faithful Contendings*, 436; *HMCR Roxburghe*, 119, A. Munro to Sir P. Hume, 24 Sept. 1689; Kirk, 'London in 1689–90' *TLMAS*, NS vii, 305; SRO GD 26/ix/232, Cardross to [Melville] 31 Aug. 1689.

57. Macfarlane, *Gen. Colls.*, i, 139–40; Stewart, *Stewarts of Appin*, 130, 132; 'The Camerons in the '15', *TGSI*, xxvi, 68; Maclean, 'Celtic Sources', 316–19, *op. cit.*; SRO GD 26/viii/39, Sir J. Maclean to Melfort, 12 Sept. 1689; *ib.*, 81, Sir A. Maclean to Cannon, 28 Jan. 1690; *ib.*, 102, Tutor of Appin to James & Melfort [Sept. 1689]; Macpherson, *Original Papers*, i. 371, 'An account of the engagements', 15 Dec. 1689.

58. *Ib*; *Leven & Melville*, 333, James to Cannon, 30 Nov. 1689; *Est. Procs.* i, 210; *APS*, ix, App., 60, Chiefs to Mackay, 17 Aug. 1689.

59. The original bond shows that the printed version, besides errors of transcription, includes one name, 'Tho Farqrson', not in the original. Unless there was another copy, it seems that Dalrymple or somebody else was determined to get Inverey convicted — but mistook the name (also printed as 'Tho' from the letter to Mackay). *Ib.*, Bond of Association, 24 Aug. 1689; SRO GD 26/viii/30, same; *ib.*, 42, Macnachtan to Cornet Crawford, Sept. 1689; *ib.*, 53, J. Winchester to Dunfermline, 30 Oct. 1689.

60. *APS*, ix, App., 57–8; Atholl, *Chronicles*, i, 326, Sir P. Moray to Atholl, 3 Sept. 1689; *Est. Procs.*, ii, 1–2; Mackay, *Memoirs*, 71–2; *ib.*, 271, Mackay to Melville, 30 Aug. 1689; *ib.*,

276, same to same, 10 Sept. 1689.

61. *Ib.*, 271, 277–8; *APS*, ix, App., 56, Lt J. Nisbet's deposition, 14 May 1690; *Melvilles & Leslies*, ii, 237, Dunfermline to Melfort, 29 Aug. 1689; *ib.*, 237–8, Lady Dunfermline to Dunfermline, 3 Oct. 1689; Blair, Atholl MSS, Box 29 I (5) 184, Ld James Murray to Murray, 5 Sept. 1689; SRO GD 26/viii/35, Lord Drummond to [Melfort], 29 Aug. 1689; *ib.*, 46, Draft bond, 3 Oct. 1689; *ib.*, 48, J. Fountaine & W. Douglas to Cannon, 12 Oct. 1689; *ib.*, 53, J. Winchester to Dunfermline, 31 Oct. 1689 (for Glengarry's 'Caball' as Cannon's chief opponents).

62. None of the documents addressed to Melfort in August or September ever reached him, since the messenger, the Laird of Macnachtan, failed to go, and they were captured with his baggage at Cromdale. *Ib.*, 38, Declaration of Lord Cardross's tenants, 6 Sept. 1689; *ib.*, 117, Cannon to Melfort, [?29 Aug. 1689]; *Melvilles & Leslies*, iii, 208, Cannon's instructions to Achtera & Widdrington [c. Dec. 1689]; Mackay, *Memoirs*, 72.

63. *Est. Procs.*, ii, 3–5; Atholl, *Chronicles*, i, 326–7, Sir P. Moray to Murray, 3 Sept. 1689; *ib.*, v, App., clxv, Memoir for the Marquis of Atholl, 1699; *ib.*, clxxi–ii, Vindication of the Marquis of Atholl; Mackay, *Memoirs*, 72; *ib.*, 271–3, Mackay to Melville, 30 Aug. 1689; *ib.*, 276, same to same, 10 Sept. 1689; *ib.*, 280, same to same, 16 Sept. 1689; SRO GD 406/1/3616, same to Hamilton, 24 Sept. 1689; GD 26/ix/232. Cardross to [?Melville], 31 Aug. 1689.

64. *APS*, ix, App., 56, J. Nisbet's deposition, 14 May 1690; *RPCS*, xiv, 523, 551; *Est. Procs.*, ii, 4, 66, 77; SRO GD 170/133/117, Glenlyon's petition to Parliament, 1690; Blair, Atholl MSS, Box 29 I (5) 160, Glenlyon to Murray, 29 July 1689.

65. Mackay, *Memoirs*, 72–4, 114; *ib.*, 284–7, Mackay to Melville, 12 Oct. 1689; *ib.*, 306, same to same, 12 Dec. 1689; *HMCR 6th Report*, 701, same to Menzies, 2 Sept. 1689; NLS MS 3470 fol. 106, Lanier to Blathwayt, 12 Sept. 1689; *ib.*, fol. 110, same to same, 15 Sept. 1689.

66. *RPCS*, xiv, 219–20, 225, 230–1, 235–7, 238–9,247, 598; *ib.*, xv, 24; *Est. Procs.*, ii, 10–13; Macpherson, *Original Papers*, i, 363–4, Dundee to Melfort, 27 June 1689; *Memoirs of Locheill*, 287–8; Mackay, *Memoirs*, 279–80, Mackay to Melville, 16 Sept. 1689; *Leven & Melville*, 276, Cardross to same, 9 Sept. 1689; *ib.*, 283–4, Livingstone to same, 12 Sept. 1689.

67. *Ib.*, 194, Hamilton to same, 25 July 1689; *ib.*, 256, Dalrymple to same, 16 Aug. 1689; SRO GD 50/10/1/14, [same] to Carwhin, 8 Sept. 1689; *Melvilles & Leslies*, ii, 108, T. Carleton to Breadalbane, 18 June 1689; Paris, Bibliothèque Nationale (BN), MS Nouvelles acquisitions françaises (Naf) 7492 fol. 281v, [Sir R. Clarke] to [L. Innes], 10/20 Oct. 1689.

68. However, the increasing danger of interception may also have influenced Macnachtan. *RPCS*, xiv, 239; SRO GD 26/viii/104, [I. Macnachtan] to Macnachtan, 11 Sept. 1689; GD 112/39/1209, Macdonald of Achnacone to Breadalbane, 8 Sept. 1689; *ib.*, 43/1/2/99, Breadalbane's Life, 2; *Est. Procs.*, ii, 20.

69. *Ib.*, 16–17; D'Avaux, *Négociations*, 466, d'Avaux to Croissy, 20 Sept. 1689(NS); Burnet, *History*, iv, 63; BL MS Lansdowne 1163C, 109, Melfort to Mary of Modena, 30 Sept. 1690(NS).

6

The Haughs of Cromdale (September 1689–June 1690)

Breadalbane, although taking no risks, still served the Jacobite cause. On receiving a commission to do so, he approached Argyll, offering to reconcile him to James. As the Club were increasingly infuriated against William, Argyll might have been more receptive than before. However, Breadalbane, who had quarrelled more often with his nephew by marriage than most men, was a bad choice: neither trusted the other, and their meeting had no result.[1]

This naturally remained a secret. Breadalbane's submission therefore began to seem sinister when Cardross, exploiting a late September pause in the rains, planted a garrison at Finlarig to bridle the Macgregors. It formed part of a chain intended to protect the Perthshire and Stirlingshire lowlands: Blair, Weem, Drummond Castle, Cambusmore on the Teith (the property of the presbyterian Lord of Session Campbell of Aberuchill), Cardross on the upper Forth and Drumakyle by Loch Lomond. Breadalbane treated this as evidence of government mistrust.[2] Cannon, however, suspected that he had authorised it. If he allowed another garrison in Achallader, his tower-house at the south end of Rannoch Moor, it would make most raiding to the south-west difficult. On 4 October, Cannon ordered a detachment of Lochiel's, Glengarry's, Keppoch's, Glencoe's and Appin's men to burn it. They did so with help from some Glenorchy men, This gained Breadalbane no Williamite sympathy. Mackay wrote that it 'may be burnt by consent, otherwyse he will resent . . . it, which tyme will let vs see. Ther is no great mater for vs, because wee had no desseyn upon it'. Fortunately for Breadalbane's sanity, he did not see that comment.[3]

Writers have assumed that this raid aroused Breadalbane's vindictiveness against MacIain. He urged Barcaldine to discover who gave the order and who took part, but his open anger was directed against his own collaborating tenants, and by December he held Lochiel responsible for the actual burning. Once he knew it was Cannon's order, the question how he could be so misunderstood preoccupied him. He also realistically saw little distinction between raiders and the Finlarig garrison, on whose ravaging of the country his anger became concentrated.[4] His growing obsession with garrisons as the root of all evil soon received fresh justification.

The attack on Cardross began a series of raids to relieve the desperate food shortage in the Jacobite Highlands. The professional officers were worst off: some died of privations, and others bought bread with their uniform buttons (of little value when the highlanders were using gold watch-cases for snuff-boxes). Food was shortest in Mull, where the Macleans had to feed not only the prisoners but the whole Irish regiment, who were quartered on the island. The meagre diet, barley-bread, a little meat and water, hastened the death of the most important captive, the Laird of Blair. An unreliable returning prisoner claimed that by November constant raiding had improved the situation in Lochaber, where they had 'plenty of French Wines, and good store of Beef, but great scarcity of Bread'.[5] Cannon's aim, which had some degree of success, was to avoid indiscriminate raiding, which would alienate potential friends, and attack only properties with Williamite owners or useful to the army.[6]

On 7th October, Mackay ordered Robert Menzies at Weem to establish a subsidiary garrison at Meggernie Castle in Glenlyon. Robert Campbell protested that the house was unsuitable, but in vain. His real grievance was that he himself was not in command, and in late October he protested to Mackay in Edinburgh that the Menzies family favoured Atholl's interest there against him. Mackay replied that he was concerned with William's service, not family disputes. Meanwhile, catastrophe struck.[7]

Writers have portrayed the great October raid on Glenlyon as a private exploit by the freebooting Macdonalds of Keppoch and Glencoe drifting home after Dunkeld, in defiance of Cannon's protection to Lady Glenlyon.[8] In fact, Glenlyon's action at Struan and the new garrison made the glen a legitimate Jacobite target. The raiders presumably had a written order, and Cannon's only later complaint was that MacIain had plundered some Macnachtan lands in the glen. Of course, formal correctness did not exclude practical calculation: a large booty would help to keep Keppoch satisfied and loyal. As the raiders approached, Colonel Menzies sent to him emphasising that his patron Atholl practically owned the glen; but he ignored this. The glen was plundered very thoroughly — according to tradition, even a baby was stripped of its blankets. Glenlyon lost at least £7,500 Scots in cattle and goods.[9] The Meggernie garrison did nothing, and presumably soon withdrew for lack of provisions.

It is uncertain whether Glenlyon could have raised the money to redeem his estates, though Atholl thought it possible.[10] Now he was totally ruined. The family and their tenants nearly starved that winter. Desperation made him increasingly erratic. In February, he attempted to seize the Glenlyon sawmills, and then extorted 'watch money' in Lorn. In August, although a captain of Argyll's, he was to raid Atholl with his soldiers.[11] Naturally, at Whitsun 1690 he could not redeem the estates. He prepared a petition for Parliament. Breadalbane, through Carwhin, increasingly tried to manage his affairs and establish a trust for his son.[12] No doubt Glenlyon felt bitterness over the Glencoe men's part in the raid, but it was scarcely obsessive. His petition omits them in listing the raiders, concentrating, besides Keppoch, on his neighbours, Robertsons, Macgregors, Atholl and Weem tenants — culminating in paranoid claims that Colonel Menzies had organised the attack to secure Glenlyon for Atholl. This was nonsense: Atholl was furious with his old protege Keppoch.[13]

The raid justified Breadalbane's worst prejudices against garrisons. Writers have assumed that it gave him a violent hatred for the Glencoe men. This is disproved by the tone of his comments on another raid, in November. MacIain led, with Cannon's warrant, two officers accompanied him, and the party of 500 was drawn from several clans, to distribute the benefits equally. Their victim was a

Williamite officer, Cochrane of Kilmaronock (Dundee's brother-in-law!) south-east of Loch Lomond. They passed through Strathfillan and Glenfalloch, destroying both but sparing Breadalbane's tenants, frightened indoors the garrison of Drumakyle, very deliberately wasted Kilmaronock, and compelled a local Campbell laird to 'compon ane assythment for on of ye Glencoan men uas hangd in ye peacable time of ye Justice Courts aledging yt he uas active to promote his death'. They then retired, leaving the Council haphazardly to switch garrisons between local houses.[14] Breadalbane showed anger — against not MacIain but the officious Sheriff-depute Campbell of Ardkinglas, who officially informed the government, 'to bring on ye State of Garisons':

> McEan sent ane Expres to Ardkinglas as he past by to assure him yt nayth he nor any in yt Armie designed hurt to Campbels if they uould let them alone and he uas as good as his uord & yet yt creatur most be lying and sending false Alarums to E A[rgyll] to occasion trouble & expence to all of us.[15]

His attitude, recognisable today, that anything the clans did was a response to government provocation in establishing garrisons, made him blame Ardkinglas as attacks on Argyllshire increased: 'it uill be great goodness in them if he is not punished seeing he insolently gave the provocation'. In contrast, he paid a Glencoe woman compensation for cows his tenants had stolen. Naturally he used every sophistry and scrap of influence to prevent his one real stronghold, Kilchurn, from being made a garrison in November.[16]

His diatribes against garrisons were justified. They were too small to oppose major raids, too static to intercept those avoiding normal routes. Local Williamites were kidnapped for ransom under their noses. The Council vainly tried to organise warning beacons to summon fencible men to support them.[17] The garrison near Loch Lomond, which the Macgregors were trying to lure into ambushes, instead captured Macgregor of Glengyle in an imprudent second raid on Kilmaronock in January, but such successes were rare.[18] Raids penetrated as far as Kintyre. In December, the Glaswegians hysterically arrested 'incendiaries' supposedly planning to destroy the city in concert with highlanders hidden nearby.[19]

At the news of MacIain's raid, Mackay and the Council decided to send Argyll with his regiment and half another to protect Argyllshire and 'make a Diversion'. He was to raise auxiliaries (and thus 'render ... Braid Albin ... insignificant'), cut the rebels' communications with Ireland, threaten Mull — and even invade it if a chance arose — and, above all, prevent the Jacobites clans from marching to attack the Lowlands by showing himself ready to invade their lands if they did; the forces at Inverness would do the same if they turned against Argyllshire. Argyll, however, who was maintaining his regiment at his own expense, violently opposed a winter campaign which would wreck it. Hurrying from Glasgow, he forced the Council on 16 December to cancel the order, and needlessly insulted Hamilton and Mackay.[20]

In December, the Council summoned, to give advice on raids, landowners bordering on the disaffected areas, including Breadalbane, Lords Lovat and

Murray, Cluny and the Macphersons, to make them commit themselves. Breadalbane, like the rest, ignored the summons. Earlier, he had refused to unite with the Atholl men in a major watch, which both sides would suspect. He repeatedly ordered Barcaldine not to let tenants join either side, since the harm this did him would outweigh any credit it brought. In practice, he had become neutral, hoping to preserve his estates from both rebel raids and government garrisons.[21]

Of course, he himself did not fully realise this. In his own eyes, he was a loyal Jacobite, forced to play a complex lone hand by circumstances Cannon and Lochiel simply could not appreciate. He used Macnachtan to explain himself to them, and circulated the Council's summons as a forerunner of favours he had nobly refused. Hearing that a letter from James to him was at Edinburgh, he exploited the fact —then disregarded its summons to rise immediately. When the quarrel between Lochiel and Lochnell over Mingary flared up again, he worked to prevent Cannon from installing a Jacobite garrison favourable to Lochiel and, emphatically, Lochnell from calling for a Williamite one. When the Macleans and MacNeil of Gallachallie occupied the Campbell island of Lismore and raided the mainland, he tried to reduce resentment in Argyllshire.[22] He was not altogether convincing. Major-General Buchan reported, on arriving in February, that he had sent him great promises: 'yet, for what I can learn underhand, he is not to be trusted'.[23] Moreover, the Argyllshire rising he still claimed to be preparing was becoming less important in Jacobite strategy.

James's fortunes had revived astonishingly in Ireland. Schomberg, advancing to Dundalk, dared not attack his large force, and encamped. That autumn, the raw, ill-officered English army collapsed horrifically through neglect and disease, until the survivors crept north to winter quarters. To James and the Jacobites, this was God's judgement, more impressive than any merely human victory (though Sarsfield's recapture of Sligo provided one). Furthermore, James's possible return need not raise anxious doubts among supporters, as during Melfort's dominance, since young Seaforth, nobody's enemy, was acting Scottish Secretary.[24]

James's letters of 30 November to his actual and potential supporters were therefore confident. He would almost immediately send Seaforth to raise his vassals in the North, and, as soon as advancing spring allowed the shipping of horse, his young natural son the Duke of Berwick, already an able soldier, with a large Irish force. He advised Cannon meanwhile merely to keep the clans together and on the defensive, recommended to all to avoid faction (easier now Melfort's relations had returned to Ireland), and urged them (and neutrals like Breadalbane) to raise large forces, for which they would be recompensed out of forfeitures.[25] One letter sharply diverged from these generalised promises. James had evidently been warned that Keppoch was wavering, and, without naming names, he apologised to him for Mulroy and promised to establish him at the expense of the 'Rebellious race' of Mackintosh.[26]

The abortive September rendezvous Cannon had planned was for a campaign in the North, ultimately to capture Inverness. Colin Mackenzie, Seaforth's uncle, probably the most dauntless northern Jacobite, returned in mid-September from

Mull to Kintail and tried to raise the inhabitants. They refused, particularly as no Highland Army assembled.[27] The northernmost overt Jacobite outpost remained Glenmoriston, where John Grant the younger had, after Invermoriston was destroyed, built an improvised fort.[28]

However, here also Cannon was still able from October to organise major raids. For instance, while MacIain was operating in Perthshire and Argyllshire, his sons and Stewart of Appin were raiding Dulshangie in the Laird of Grant's Glen Urquhart.[29] The largest raid, in mid-October, was carried out by 500 men (including the Glenmoriston men and the Chisholms of Knockfin) in military organisation with Cannon's warrant to waste Forbes of Culloden's estate of Ferintosh in the Black Isle. They naturally also robbed nearby Mackenzie estates. There was no organised watch in Ross to give proper warning. Strathnaver's regiment was quartered on the country, but an alarm spread of an attack on Easter Ross — allegedly invented to frighten away a burdensome company — and on 13 October Balnagown in alarm summoned the companies to his house, keeping four there and having three break into and garrison Tarbat House. Culloden's brother, a captain in Grant's, preserved some of his Ferintosh property, but the local garrisons refused him help to pursue. Glenmoriston and Braelochaber men soon launched other raids.[30] East of Loch Ness, Moray was also suffering.[31]

Something more became possible for the highlanders when a conference took place early in November. Cannon and Dunfermline took the warning not simply to give the chiefs orders, as at previous ones, but to present their own opinions, ask for others, and accept the majority decision.[32] As a result, Glengarry began to give Cannon vigorous support and advice on the northern campaign. His intelligence system in and around Inverness was of particular value — it was probably he who was to have Livingston's valet steal vital letters from his pocket. He corresponded with his brother-in-law Lovat there, hoping to win him over.[33] Glengarry's activity contrasted with the apparent apathy of Lochiel, who claimed next year 'that hee had noe Great heart to the business ever since Killycranky'.[34] A grand advance on Inverness down both sides of Loch Ness may have been planned: Cannon on the south leading the Camerons, Macdonalds of Keppoch and Glencoe, Macleans and Macphersons, and raising the Stratherrick men as he went, Glengarry on the north with his, Clanranald's and Sir Donald's Macdonalds — (a satisfaction to his claims to primacy) and the Grants of Glenmoriston, Macleod's coerced Glenelg tenants, the Kintail Mackenzies and the Chisholms, a force they optimistically assumed might amount to 4,000 men.[35]

Leslie at Inverness, in Moray and Ross, had at least seven troops of horse and dragoons, his English infantry regiment, and Grant's and Strathnaver's, still badly armed and paid and very troublesome to the inhabitants. He believed that most of the townsfolk were loyal, although some were caught sending brandy and salt to the highlanders.[36] Throughout November, Leslie feared a full-scale highland attack and raised several false alarms. He put an outpost at Urquhart Castle on Loch Ness. In November, he was ordered to protect the country from raiders by placing garrisons at three Moray houses, at Lord Lovat's home Castle Dounie west of Inverness and at the Chisholm's, Erchless in Strathglass; but he dared not garrison Erchless, instead concentrating his forces, including half the garrisons of Castle Leod and Brahan, at Inverness to meet the expected attack.[37]

In late November, Leslie sent a raiding party to Strathglass, and another from Urquhart Castle to Glenmoriston to seize John Grant. Not finding him, they fired on and wounded his wife and daughter.[38] This probably hastened the Jacobite attack. Glengarry and Lord Frendraught advanced to Glen Urquhart, arriving on 3 December, with a force given out as 600 men. In fact, though they kept the Castle blockaded, there were only 120. They would have to retreat, Glengarry warned, unless Cannon speedily raised the main force and followed them. About 400 Glenmoriston men and Chisholms, who marched despite the Chisholm's protests under his uncle Colin of Knockfin, joined Glengarry, and some Glen Urquhart men, including Grant of Corriemony, defied the Laird of Grant to show support. The rest of the barony was so devastated that Grant could draw no rents for several years.[39] However, Lochiel's men, rather than follow Glengarry or Cannon, seized the chance for indiscriminate plunder. Since early November hundreds had poured into the Aird, supposedly to deny provisions to Inverness, robbing Mackenzie and Fraser gentry and plundering Lovat's estates when Glengarry was anxious to conciliate him. Very few had joined the war.[40] They now attacked the lands left vacant by the loyal Glengarry, Glenmoriston, Strathglass and Glen Urquhart men, sometimes pretending to have Cannon's commission. This forced Glengarry to retreat from before Urquhart Castle in mid-December, before the time of rendezvous he had agreed on with Colin Mackenzie.[41]

His retreat was particularly unfortunate, since Colin had assembled 400 men, soon increased to 600, in Kintail. More were certain to join him when Cannon entered Ross, '& noe doubt', Glengarry wrotè, 'it uer uell uorth your pains to gett ... [them] dipped deep'. Colin wrote for ammunition and match, but warned that he had only with difficulty assembled the men after raising and dismissing them once already. If he had to disband them again, they might not assemble the third time. An unsuccessful skirmish may have hastened their dispersal.[42]

Cannon's attempts to call the clans together — 'let the numbers be neuer so feu I will march' —failed: they would not obey him.[43] Momentarily, there seemed a chance when Lochiel appointed a fresh rendezvous for 1 January at Mucomir.[44] Yet this too apparently failed, though probably not entirely from lack of enthusiasm. Cannon reported to James that winter that Dundee's gathering of the clans had cost so much in money and provisions that it could not be repeated without his help, and Lochiel, who would again have been the host, may now have realised this.[45] Bad weather probably cut off island chiefs, particularly Sir John Maclean, who had expressed continuing loyalty even before Cannon's change of policy. Yet Sir Donald, returning from North Uist only in mid-December, inquired like a spectator what the clans were doing:

> The season is soe bad sure it must be more then ane ordinary project ... but if the designe caryes noe more than to pilladge and plunder some of your nighbours it [will] not advance our great Mrs interist ... If ... to incomod Inverness I confess (if practicable) it is more honourable for ... many ... would joyne us soe that yoak were not on their necks.[46]

An apparently welcome contrast to the Lochaber clans' refusal was Cluny's spontaneous declaration in December of his readiness to join Cannon. After failing to do so in November, he perhaps acted on advice to show zeal before Berwick's approaching landing. He failed to attend Cannon's next rendezvous, 8 February, and in March persistently evaded raising his men, using the excuse he made now, that he had no independent colonel's commission. Yet the warrant he desired to command local Mackintoshes and others of Gordon's tenants would, by strengthening his claim to be head of Clan Chattan, encourage him to more active Jacobitism, now James had turned against Mackintosh. As Glengarry advised, granting the warrant would ensure that Cluny would raise 200 men for him, and, when the news leaked, would finally force him to rise for James with all his men.[47]

Inverness was by now even more strongly defended. Sir Thomas Livingston with his regiment and some troops of horse arrived to take command in late December, although he reduced Leslie's excessive concentration to give Ross and Moray some protection.[48] Raids continued, and the troops were 'perpetually harass'd upon Parties, and ... hunting of the Highlanders';[49] but they scored some success. A large party occupied Erchless in February, recapturing corn and cattle from the Jacobites, and raiders who attacked them a month later were crushed by Livingston.[50] The garrisons of course plundered the surrounding country. Leslie had imposed massive requisition for the Inverness magazine, including impossible amounts of corn and straw from Wester Ross, and the people had to buy these elsewhere or face ruin by quartering. All severities were excused with the claim that the Mackenzies and Frasers had been planning to rise. Local Whigs made false lists of Colin Mackenzie's followers, and when the Council on 3 January issued a list of highland and lowland rebels whose rents were declared sequestrated, they included the Chisholm as well as his uncle.[51] Throughout February, it was rumoured that government forces were about to attack the local highlanders who had taken part in raids, ravage their lands and spare neither man, woman nor child — which, observers thought, though formally justified, would expose the government to charges of cruelty.[52]

Many local episcopalian clergy encouraged rebellion, riding about and urging the people to remain faithful to James.[53] Even after Colin Mackenzie's disappointment, Seaforth's own arrival with money and arms might rally a significant force. Very early in January, he sailed from Galway with some officers, but his ship was driven back by contrary winds and her mast broken, and he returned to Dublin. During the next few months, his strong enthusiasm ebbed.[54] In mid-February, Livingston was instructed to treat with Grant of Glenmoriston and Chisholm, obviously in response to their approaches to him.[55] Had Seaforth raised a force, it could not directly have endangered Inverness; but it would have prevented Livingston from concentrating his army against any Jacobite advance into the North-East.

Cannon's latest message to James warned that the professional officers were utterly impoverished and that the chiefs could not afford another long rendezvous, and asked for a commission of justiciary to suppress unauthorised depredations (such as had just wrecked Glengarry's campaign) and an order to make lukewarm supporters declare or be treated as enemies. Yet he also asked for the appointment of Privy Councillors and blank commissions for new supporters to raise regiments, and he urged the sending of Berwick with 6,000 men by claiming that 'as the nobility and gentry stand now presently affected', it could not only win Scotland but provide a diversion to England. In February, he wrote to Tyrconnell that their affairs were going as well as could be imagined.[56] Besides automatic over-optimism, the explanation was the change in the North-East.

As Mackay admitted, that area, having been lukewarm towards Dundee in 1689, was now 'determinately bent' towards the Jacobites.[57] The underlying causes included the misdeeds of the minority regimes he himself, making very different allegations, had established there in 1689 and of the Williamite army; the activity of the episcopalian clergy, facing deprivation and ruin, in the area where their influence, particularly among nobles and lairds, had always been strongest; the similar long royalist tradition; and the highlanders' success in keeping James's cause alive for a year. The immediate agents included the Dowager Countess of Erroll; Lord Frendraught, a catholic Melfordian whose direct contacts with St. Germain gave him special authority among the highlanders, flitting freely through highland and lowland Aberdeenshire and Banffshire;[58] Dunfermline freely returning to his home, Fyvie; and Farquharson of Inverey in Braemar. The troops showed little enterprise. Grant of Ballindalloch safely occupied his home on the lower Spey and some professional officers simply remained about Fraser-burgh. These Jacobites could proselytise important local figures personally.[59]

In Braemar, Abergeldie partly checked highland raids, and new garrisons were established, Aboyne lower down the Dee and Kildrummy on the upper Don.[60] Undaunted by the Lochaber clans' failure to rise, Inverey and Frendraught persuaded a score of crypto-Jacobite gentry, Grants, Gordons, Farquharsons, even Forbeses, to join in a bond drawn up at Tomintoul in Strathavon on 15 January. Inverey hoped to gain more in the three north-eastern counties, and thought that if only 1,000 Jacobites came to the area, they could raise a host.[61] Livingston claimed in January that Lovat had been with Frendraught and Ballindalloch in Buchan, plotting to raise Gordon's tenants.[62] There were setbacks. In mid-February, a captured messenger caused the arrest of the Dowager Countess, evidently James's most trusted lowland loyalist agent. Soon after, cavalry from Inverness captured several careless plotters at Lord Oliphant's Nairnshire home — an accident which should have taught a general lesson.[63]

Gordon was still a prisoner and unable to help the north-eastern plotters directly. In January, he was allowed to London on his parole to do nothing hostile before seeing William. Apparently rebuffed by him, he crossed to France carrying reports on Scotland. William thought that he had broken his word, and long refused to forgive him. He hoped to join James in Ireland, and rumours that he was returning in arms soon began. In fact, James still distrusted him, and had forbidden his agents in Scotland to see him. He was kept in France, and Melfort from Rome urged harsher treatment.[64] Meanwhile, in late 1689, the Club had confronted William over the constitutional reforms it claimed he was bound to grant, and their episcopalian opponents, backed by English Tories, exploited his

The Highland War, 1690–1692

anger and the unsettled state of Scotland to reopen the question which church should be established. Even after presbyterianism triumphed in 1690, church matters provided the main ostensible party division for half William's reign. Yet this cloaked so many struggles between rival political 'interests', previous feuds and constitutional and social issues that P.W.J. Riley's usage of calling the factions 'presbyterian' and 'episcopalian' is the best — not least because their members' private beliefs often bore no relation to their politics. 'Episcopalians' included the godly Presbyterian Stair, the Earl of Lothian when Commissioner to the General Assembly, and, by 1695, Melville, who originally organised the presbyterian settlement; and politics drove the Episcopalians Hamilton and Lord Murray among the 'presbyterians', with odd results.[65] However, the original pejorative use of 'episcopalian', implying tyranny and crypto-Jacobitism, genuinely applied, that autumn and for at least two years, to the group headed by Queensberry and Atholl. They had a strong prejudice in favour of the old order, a Stuart on the throne, an episcopalian church, and themselves and their dependents filling most offices of state. It was scarcely a principle, since hope of office usually made them ignore it, but when disappointed they almost automatically relapsed into Jacobitism. Lacking fear of reprisals from what appeared a weak government,[66] they often dabbled in futile and easily discovered intrigues, knowledge of which overrode even William's bias in favour of pre-Revolution ministers. 'What, do you think I will pull them out of a plot, to put them into the Government?' he replied when Tarbat recommended Queensberry, Atholl and Breadalbane to him. The exclamation shattered the 'episcopalian' political alternative Tarbat had been building; and in 1690 he left William's side for Scotland without struggling, once again Melville's supporter.[67]

Through his chosen intermediaries in all Scottish affairs, his Dutch favourite the Earl of Portland and his presbyterian chaplain William Carstares, William offered the Club concessions and future power if they would accept his past actions; but Montgomerie hurried them into an open breach. He was unknowingly in the net of an experienced Jacobite intriguer, Henry Neville Payne, and a double agent he employed, Simpson alias Jones. To Portland, Simpson reported that Montgomerie was plotting with the Jacobites; to Montgomerie, that the Court was manufacturing evidence for a treason charge against him; and, by playing them off against each other, he soon roused Montgomerie to frenzy. Dragging Annandale and Ross, and more hesitant English Whigs, he formed a real Jacobite plot, drawing up proposals and demands for Simpson to carry via France to James. His plan was to press the Club's demands even more unrestrainedly in the next session, until William dissolved Parliament and called another. Most Club members would by then be so furious and disillusioned with William that when Annandale produced James's patent as Commissioner and instructions to pass the reforms William had refused, they would return to their allegiance. To defend Parliament against the Williamites, he asked the French for arms. This extraordinary scheme depended dangerously on adversity having made James willing to grant concessions. As Melfort emphasised, if he encouraged their activities without committing himself until they finally broke with William, they would then have to accept his terms.[68] Montgomerie also demanded major rewards for the plotters, such as the secretaryship for himself. His ally Argyll was to have not only his father's but his grandfather's forfaulture rescinded, and perhaps also a patent for a dukedom. Argyll (by then back in Scotland) may have known no more of this than of Breadalbane's 1689 dealings for him.[69]

The only loyalist Jacobite Montgomerie had so far consulted was Arran, who left the Tower in November.[70] To succeed in wrecking the next session, he would need support from the 'episcopalians', many of whom had stayed away in 1689. He now approached Queensberry and Atholl, making them think that the plot was for a full-scale rising rather than a parliamentary transformation, and they joined, Atholl enthusiastically carrying money for it to Scotland.[71] The outward explanation was that this was a 'Country' alliance: in return for the 'episcopalians'' support in passing constitutional reforms, Montgomerie would prevent the imposition of presbyterianism. Not surprisingly, this alarmed the 'moderate' leaders Hume of Polwarth and Forbes of Culloden, to whom religion was the vital issue. Their realignment on William's side resulted not merely from his bribery but from genuine alarm at Montgomerie's present associates and arguments.[72]

Clearly, no Parliament willing to vote money for the army was likely for some time; and political rather then military considerations dominated discussions of what to do. Tarbat, determined to obtain a dissolution, argued nonsensically that, besides five regiments paid from England, a mere 1,200 foot and four troops of horse could defeat the highlanders.[73] William had no such illusion of easy victory, secretly refusing to allow the exchange of an important soldier with highland experience.[74] Yet he spoke seriously of disbanding the army if Parliament refused to support it, however disastrous the consequences; and, when in December he established a commission to remodel the army, he at first ordered that the eighteen new troops of horse and dragoons, the type of soldier the highlanders most feared, should be reduced to six. On protest, he limited major changes to the merging of three regiments into one, Cunningham's, and the reduction of Angus's to one battalion.[75] These, Argyll's and Strathnaver's regiments were earmarked for the Irish campaign despite Mackay's need for them, and paid (theoretically) on the Irish establishment, for a year. In practice, like most troops, they were living by free quarter and plundering, which made both soldiers and civilians increasingly hostile to the regime.[76]

William must cross to reconquer Ireland that summer; and Mackay, struggling against the lack of money, wanted to establish a garrison at Inverlochy and pacify the Highlands before he left. He had been promised three English warships to serve off the West of Scotland, and suggested that winter that in late March he should embark with 3–4,000 men at Dunstaffnage and plant a garrison at Inverlochy by sea, as Monck had done. This would avoid the delay until spring furnished forage for a land march to Inverlochy, and also the mountain passes, of which he had grown wary since Killiecrankie. Dalrymple argued in support that the (supposedly) fully clothed troops could endure the cold better than the half-naked highlanders — an odd idea on which he relied in 1691. As William never replied and the Scottish Treasury was empty, Mackay modified his plan. He would ship 600 soldiers to cruise for three months off the Isles as a diversion, preventing the inhabitants, by raids or the mere threat, from joining the Highland Army. The Treasury scraped together the money for this, but a committee of the Council wrote to William on 1 March urging him, successfully, to send £4,000 from England for the Inverlochy expedition immediately. Otherwise, the highlanders, striking from their central position anywhere in the Lowlands, would gain the initiative; the forces would be tied down ineffectually reacting to their raids; and 'the whole northern shires, out of disloyalty or necessity, may be obliged to join your enemies, and furnish them with horses'.[77]

This fear made Mackay particularly suspicious that Tarbat, who proposed delays and negotiations to pacify the clans, did so largely to gain credit with James for preventing the campaign. This merged with his belief that Tarbat and Melville were plotting to replace him as Commander-in-Chief by Leven. Others less paranoid also believed this, but it may merely have reflected his jealousy of Leven's reputation after Killiecrankie.[78] Tarbat could argue that Mackay's purely military plans were over-optimistic. Even if men and money could be scraped together to fortify Inverlochy, it would not in itself end the war, and the nation could no longer afford the cost — £150,000 for 1689, he estimated. A far smaller expenditure might end not only the war but the clan discontents that had made it possible. His activities were scarcely Jacobite 'reinsurance': James, if restored now, would hardly forgive the letters he was writing, 'like a banquire at London', to tempt the clans to submit, offering Lochiel £1,000 and the payment of his debts.[79]

Tarbat's choice of agent indicates some degree of sincerity. Lieutenant-Colonel John Hill had commanded the Cromwellian forts at Ruthven and Inverlochy, maintaining friendly relations with local chiefs like the young Lochiel. After the Restoration, Hill like other Nonconformist ex-officers, made a career in Ireland, but maintained contacts even with Tarbat, whom he asked for Scottish employment in 1688.[80] He was then living in Belfast, and 1689 gave him good practice for complex negotiations, as he worked to avert its plundering or destruction by the Irish army, dealing with the favourable James and Melfort in Dublin (via Pottinger, the usurping Jacobite 'Sovereign' (Mayor)); with a Scottish catholic general anxious not to destroy Belfast even when militarily necessary; and with Irish soldiers who had to be bought off.[81] Even though he would be largely a dependent of Tarbat's, Hill's normal strong conscience and hostility to 'episcopalians' made him unsuitable for his more dubious activities.[82] Tarbat presumably therefore summoned him to Scotland because he genuinely believed that he could help to conclude a real pacification. The year's campaign would end successfully only through a combination of Mackay's and Tarbat's plans, a fort at Inverlochy with Hill, rather than some officer determined to crush the highlanders by force, in command.

On 25 March, Tarbat in London received his warrant to negotiate. He was allowed to offer up to £2,000, and even a peerage, to any one major chief, but he and Hill estimated that the total cost should not be over £10,000.[83] He did not intend a purely pacific policy, approving of the expedition to the Isles, for which the English warships arrived on 26 March. To provide a base for it, the Council ordered that Dunstaffnage Castle should be garrisoned, and Tarbat considered that Hill, rather than some Campbell vulnerable, through his estate, to Jacobite blackmail, should be commander.[84] In Argyllshire itself he secretly employed Auchinbreck to negotiate with Jacobite clans, and by May hoped to bring in the Laird of Luss.[85] His care in choosing Hill makes it uncertain how far he encouraged the employment of Breadalbane in negotiations. Dalrymple and others had kept the latter's name before William, obtaining permission for him to come up (which Carwhin claimed he never received). However, by February Dalrymple was losing faith in him and employing the imprisoned Macgregor of Glengyle, who claimed that Glengarry and Keppoch were ready to submit on terms. Breadalbane's return to Edinburgh, which made William in March order Melville to win him over as an agent, was part of a Jacobite plot.[86]

The Club plotters had returned to Scotland in December. Nearly all the Club were kept in ignorance of their real intentions but were so plied with propaganda and slander against William that Melville, coming down as Commissioner in March, found them violently disaffected. Argyll's position is uncertain. Montgomerie had great influence over him, and English Jacobites believed him involved, but his letters suggest that he repulsed an advance in February.[87] For their military backing, they relied partly on the extreme Cameronians; partly, claimed one informer, on four Scottish regiments, including Grant's.[88] Mackay had appointed to command the detachment for the Isles Major Ferguson of Lauder's regiment, who had been captured at Killiecrankie and exchanged. In April, Jacobites including his brother, the notorious Robert Ferguson 'the Plotter', tempted him, but he repelled them.[89] Melville, nervous at the dangers, required Mackay to concentrate the army round Edinburgh rather than attempt a highland campaign, causing further hostility between them.[90]

There was a major campaign to make nonjuring 'episcopalians' attend Parliament and ally with Montgomerie. The outward pretence used on both sides was that, finding that William could not protect them from the Club, they must earn their forgiveness by joining them to promote 'Country' measures. Some refused to collaborate; but perhaps twenty-five crypto-Jacobites, mostly peers, did so, including Queensberry, Atholl, Breadalbane, Balcarres, Strathmore, Livingstone (now Earl of Linlithgow), Atholl's son Lord Nairne and son-in-law Lovat. Tarbat encouraged them secretly, not for Jacobite ends, but apparently to force William to dissolve this 'presbyterian' Parliament — one dubious reason for his anxiety to settle the Highlands without the army.[91] The Club plotters had the advantage of still being on the Council: they had Balcarres kept in prison until they were sure he would join them, and Breadalbane summoned to Edinburgh immediately under threat of denunciation.[92] Once there, he was initiated into the Plot, and, Montgomerie saw, despite his lack of political weight besides Queensberry and Atholl, 'he was most to be noticed of any and gave the rest ther measures; Arr[an] was ruled by him'. Insofar, that is, as Arran, who was capable of leaving a conspirators' meeting and trying through Mackay to obtain a Williamite pension, could be ruled by anybody.[93]

Meanwhile, Major-General Thomas Buchan had sailed from Dublin on 24 January in the *Janet* to Mull. He was of an Aberdeenshire family — particularly appropriate when the campaign would be decided by a struggle for the North-East — a catholic professional soldier who had served with credit in France, Holland, Scotland and now Ireland. He brought with him several professional officers, a cargo of ammunition and £900, £300 for Cannon (now made Major-General), £100 for Purcell (who, instead, returned to Ireland) and £500 for the Irish regiment (finally distributed among the officers).[94] However, he was not the Duke of Berwick; and, although he repeated James's assurances that Berwick and a large force, perhaps 8,000 men, would soon arrive, the disappointment chilled even those like Glengarry who had been ready to attend Cannon's February rendezvous.[95]

In mid-February, the clans and officers held a council of war at Inverlochy, and some chiefs suggested that James's failure justified their seeking terms. Lochiel turned the tide with an eloquent speech, reminding them that the clans in the 1650s, in far worse conditions, had surrendered only with Charles's permission, and that submitting while James headed an army in Ireland and had many English supporters would discredit them. He also assured them that James intended to keep the clan regiments in pay as standing forces after a restoration — a plan he was certainly considering. Lochiel, Sir Donald, Glengarry, Keppoch, Macnachtan and, apparently, MacIain, signed a letter to James asking for Berwick's arrival but promising to fight on, which Sir George Barclay, whom they all trusted, carried to him. On Sir John Maclean's fanatical determination Buchan could already count.[96] Yet Lochiel's eloquence had its price. Showing Buchan his offers from Tarbat, he submitted a request to James for a grant of Sunart and Ardnamurchan. Buchan, having seen evidence that 'he rules the Highlanders more than any Scotchman does', successfully advised James to grant it. One Jacobite claimed Lochiel dared not negotiate with the government only because the other chiefs kept a suspicious eye on him. Buchan knew that several of them had done so, and feared that all would unless help speedily arrived. In March, he sent old Sir Donald Macdonald as his 'ambassador extraordinary' to ask James for it.[97] James, given confidence by a French army's arrival in Ireland, had responded to Barclay's mission with a letter to the chiefs containing a startling threat: 'ashure your selves uee shall make verey little difference betueen those uee reduce by force and such as are lookers on at this tyme, ffor uee vallow not ther good uishes for us uho uill not hazard any thing uith us'. Yet subsequently he again failed to send the promised help.[98]

If Buchan could start a fire in the Highlands, much of the Lowlands would be tinder. Almost immediately, the Earls of Erroll, Strathmore and Panmure and other noblemen sent to him asking for commissions, although he believed they would never actually rise until Berwick landed. In the North-East, he also established a correspondence with the Earl of Aberdeen. A deputation of episcopalian clergy, uncertain what James's attitude to them really was, is a reminder how much of this Jacobitism was primarily a reaction against the new regime.[99] South of Forth, Buchan was soon corresponding with Arran, who remitted large sums of money to him, Home, who could co-ordinate a rising on the Borders with him, and Breadalbane, who informed him of the Montgomerie Plot and the disruption it must cause.[100]

Yet Buchan would find it difficult to raise an effective highland force. Some gentry who had returned home promising to appear again at the order might not do so.[101] Others were too preoccupied with raiding. Southwards, Argyll's organisation of Campbell watches and the lowland garrisons still left the country sadly vulnerable, and Stewart of Appin was probably not the only Jacobite who would rather continue 'oppress[ing] poor widows' than join the army.[102] The main reason, however, was the extreme shortage of provisions. There was almost no bread, and, although they ploughed their fields as usual when the season came, the highlanders had little seed-corn to plant. They could not make usquebaugh or buy brandy, and lived on fish, flesh and water.[103] No large army could assemble for some time, but the council of war at Inverlochy agreed that each clan should raise a hundred men to provide a force with which Buchan could raid, and perhaps recruit in, the Lowlands before the government cavalry had forage for a campaign. The rendezvous was set for 15 March. However, the weather was so bitter that Sir John Maclean, Sir Donald and others reported that their tenants had been unable to plough their fields, and it was postponed until 1 April.[104] Meanwhile, Buchan travelled to Skye and made advances to Macleod. He promised to rise when James or Berwick landed — temporising, but perhaps a slight softening of his attitude in 1689.[105] Buchan also organised an infantry regiment of his own. It consisted largely of lowland officers and over 120 Irish soldiers, but MacIain's second son Alasdair became a captain.[106]

Even if shortage of provisions finally thwarted the rendezvous, Buchan might still buy time by negotiation. Although Melville's advisers considered that Breadalbane 'walks in the clouds, and is but trimming', he felt obliged by William's orders to employ him. Breadalbane demanded high terms, including £5,000 to distribute — part of which, it seemed clear, he intended to pocket, for he was openly acting from self-interest. His negotiation also had the crypto-Jacobite motives Mackay had suspected in Tarbat. He left Edinburgh in late March for the Highlands, only to return abruptly in mid-April magnifying the power of the clans.[107] The real reason was that Atholl, jealous of anyone else settling the Highlands, had spread suspicions of his sincerity among the other 'episcopalian' Jacobites. Summoned back, he defended himself before them as gaining a cessation until James could send help from Ireland. They were satisfied, and urged him to proceed. But for the delay, he later claimed, he could have prevented Cromdale.[108] Melville, anxious to keep the army in the Lowlands, gave him a warrant to treat with the clans until 20 May. Considering that the main army would probably not be ready until then, he ordered a cessation of arms. Ferguson's force should cruise off the Isles but make no attacks until further orders. It was these orders, given although he openly admitted his distrust of Breadalbane, which, he thought, most turned Mackay against him.[109] Tarbat, unable to go north himself, sent Hill to Inverness to negotiate.[110]

In mid-April Parliament met, beginning serious business on the 22nd. The 'episcopalian' Jacobites were a strange spectacle, supporting Montgomerie, who from the first was demanding the most extreme, 1649, model of presbyterian church government.[111] Hamilton, indignant at being the scapegoat for the unsuccessful 1689 session, mounted an independent opposition, supporting Club measures but criticising any concessions for harming the prerogative. The atmosphere was hysterical, and real grievances, rumours and sudden revolutionary proposals provided material which a master parliamentary tactician like Montgomerie could exploit destructively.[112] It is unlikely that he could have carried out his full plan — he had not even yet received James's reply — but he certainly had good prospects of wrecking the session; and adjournment would certainly plunge the country into chaos, giving Buchan a golden opportunity.

Even before Melville's order, Ferguson was delayed awaiting provisions. Mackay spread the rumour that his force was far larger, and believed that it was the threat this presented which deterred the clans in the coasts and Isles from joining Buchan in full force. As their original plan was made in February, his general claim is wrong; but it may have had some influence on the Isles, even Skye.[113] Sir John Maclean, however, who was ready to destroy Duart rather than let any invader of Mull use it as a base, sent two Maclean companies under his cousin and Sir Alexander's brother.[114] The total force Buchan gathered is, as usual, disputed. Mackay and Buchan himself, both very partial, roughly agree on a low number, 8–900 including Buchan's regiment, and a low estimate of quality, disgraceful in Buchan's case: 'the very worst men amongst the Clanns, the Chiefes never venturing ther best but where they goe themselves'.[115] This was certainly untrue of the Macleans. Some sources (not first-hand) suggest that one chief, Keppoch, came himself — his special gifts were needed[116] — and Buchan's own account shows that the number is absurd for his force at Cromdale itself.[117] One contingent he probably omitted was that imposed on Cluny. It had been raised to 200, and, having tried to evade it into early April, he submitted, under threat of having Badenoch plundered or even burned, and sent them. In Edinburgh, he was reported to be in full rebellion, and the Council commissioned Calder to win him back.[118] Once on the march, the army 'increased as a snow ball daily', and officers captured at Cromdale declared that they were by then 1,400–1,500 men, a number confirmed by later sources — Macleans, Macdonalds, Camerons, Macphersons, Macnachtans, Grants of Glenmoriston and Irish, all foot.[119] On 4 April, Sir Thomas Livingston reported that a large number was in arms, and that their goal was reported to be Moray.[120]

Mackay, after constant arguments with Melville, had assembled at Perth the nucleus of his proposed Inverlochy expedition, horse and foot, to protect the country against a descent on that side, although he could scarcely keep them together for lack of money. It was no check on Buchan's movements, since he knew that Mackay could not advance into the Highlands with horse until the grass grew; but it probably helped restrain Angus, the most Jacobite lowland shire.[121] In the second week of April, the north-eastern Highlands began to threaten Aberdeenshire, just when most mounted forces had been sent off to protect Banff. 'All Braemarr, Strathdon, Strathdee, Strathdown, Glenlivet, most of Strathspey

& Badenoch are joined,' reported Lieutenant-Colonel Buchan at Aberdeen. They intended to raise or burn Strathbogie, and would gain many supporters in lowland Aberdeenshire if they appeared there in strength. Ominously, they were gathering large numbers of horses from sympathisers. Raids began, and some major parties were seen near Aberdeen. The government troops were generally preparing to advance up-country, but such sightings made coast towns like Montrose nervously demand and receive garrisons — a dangerous trend.[122]

General Buchan's most pressing problem was probably still subsistence. A daring attempt by a small party to seize a meal ship for him in Caithness had narrowly failed.[123] He therefore, accompanied by Dunfermline and Cannon, led his force in mid-April to the head of Loch Ness, and the Keppoch Macdonalds (under Keppoch himself, the victims claimed) launched a savage raid up Stratherrick and down Strathnairn close to Inverness, apparently gaining enough meal to solve the army's immediate problems. Livingston marched out in the hope of intercepting him, but failed and returned with his troops in starving condition. Buchan took his army to upper Strathspey, where they remained for ten days.[124]

Marching down the east bank, they held a council of war at Culnakyle on 29 April, to determine the next day's march. They were in Grant's country, and, although he was absent attending Parliament, a company of his regiment under Captain Grant of Easter Elchies garrisoned his home, Ballachastell, near the west side of Spey, and would be in contact with Livingston. They resolved to march to Glenlochy, separated from the plain of Spey by the Hills of Cromdale and containing woods that would secure them against cavalry attacks. Buchan overruled them and, despite their protests, ordered them to march down and encamp at Cromdale, opposite and slightly below Ballachastell, on the river-plain and low foothills, the 'Haughs of Cromdale' (a term strictly applicable only to the alluvial flats). It was contrary to all highland principles to camp in a place so vulnerable to cavalry. If any misfortune happened, Buchan would not be forgiven.[125]

He had secret reasons for his decision. Many of Grant's people had sent him a message that they were anxious to join him, but, with their vindictive chief a strong Williamite, dared not unless he appeared to be forcing them out with threats.[126] Openly encamping opposite the enemy stronghold was probably intended as one means of increasing the confidence of these would-be supporters. He possibly also intended to gather there other supporters from the North-East, most of whom Livingston thought ready to join him. Dunfermline left the camp on a mission on 30 April.[127]

Downstream, Buchan was largely protected from surprise by Ballindalloch, which had beaten off an incompetent Williamite attack early in April.[128] He was aware that the enemy were marching from Inverness towards him, and knew that they might be coming through the hills to Ballachastell. He and some officers therefore sounded the Spey, and found it fordable in only three places. The most important, by Cromdale Church, was at the head of so deep a bend to the north-west (the original 'crom[crooked] dale') that the others, a quarter-mile off on either side, were probably closer to the camp. At each ford he placed a guard forty-five strong under a lieutenant, probably local men as the names of two, Grant and Brodie, indicate. Halfway between them and the main encampment, he stationed 240 men under a lieutenant-colonel. The rest of the army camped in villages or round fires, on the river plain just above Dalchapple (east of Cromdale), round Lethendry Hill with its little ruined castle to the south-east, or elsewhere on the low hills. Keppoch, however, refused to join them, and camped his men half a mile north-east of Dalchapple, where Tom an Uird, a steep hill near the river, gave a closer refuge. Buchan had not seen the weakness of his plan. If enemy horse broke through at a ford and galloped directly for the camp, his own outposts, lacking mounted men, would be unable to give adequate warning.[129] It has been

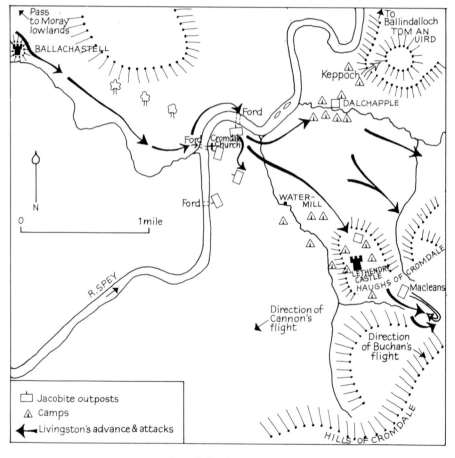

Cromdale, 1 May 1690

assumed that Buchan was totally surprised. The fact that he had some foreknowledge of danger, but, rather than move his camp, took precautions which proved disastrously inadequate, makes the case against him worse.

With the exposure of Glengarry's spy as a good omen, Livingston left Inverness on 27 April.[130] For two days, he had to remain at Brodie, awaiting his baggage-horses and four troops of horse and dragoons from Elgin, but he would not wait for the two regiments Mackay had ordered from Aberdeen to his help. He had 400 of Leslie's regiment, six companies of Grant's, the Mackay highland company, his regiment of dragoons and two cavalry troops — 800 foot and 400 horse. At noon on 30 April, he received Captain Grant's information of the highlanders' camping-place and numbers. He set out southwards over the hills through rough country, and at 2 a.m. on 1 May reached Ballachastell.[131] Captain Grant, since sending the news, had refused to allow out any of the people who had taken refuge there, some of whom would have warned Buchan. While his exhausted men and horses briefly rested, Livingston established the highlanders' position from their campfires, obtained guides and, although warned that the ground was rather boggy, decided to attack if his soldiers had the strength. They eagerly agreed, and marched at 2.30.[132]

Having marched unseen down a hollow to the river, Livingston sent 200 men to create a diversion by attacking the ford at Cromdale Church, and led the rest of his army to the lower ford. The guards there were either negligent or had gone to help beat off the attack at the church, and the Mackay highlanders and two troops of dragoons were across before they were observed. As men ran back to warn the camp, Livingston galloped forward with four troops of horse and dragoons (the rest formed his rearguard), leaving behind all the foot save some Grants who mounted behind dragoons.[133]

As they approached the camp, some parties of highlanders were running up and down in confusion, while others were still asleep. Buchan ordered his nephew and some lowland officers and soldiers to defend Lethendry Castle. He claimed that only the Macleans gathered into a body, although he admitted elsewhere that some of the Badenoch men fought well. Cannon and many highlanders fled in their shirts, others naked. Most of those not immediately killed ran back towards the Hills of Cromdale for refuge. The Macleans, however, kept their heads, and at the hill-foot turned suddenly on their pursuers, hoping to inflict a repulse that would turn the tide. They killed or wounded several dragoon horses with their broadswords, but they were not seconded. When more pursuers came up and were about to surround them, the men threw down their swords and scattered, but the officers, two captains, a lieutenant and an ensign, stood and were taken.[134] The horsemen pursued the highlanders even up the hillside and would probably have killed many more but for a sudden mist which settled on the upper slopes, making the fugitives seem 'rather to be People receiv'd up into Clouds, than flying from an Enemy'. Livingston retired to the plain, drew up his men and began to collect prisoners.[135] Livingston's charge, sweeping bloodily over the camp above Dalchapple, left untouched the Keppoch Macdonalds to the north-east, and Keppoch hastily retreated with them up Tom an Uird. There he, 'who was ever keen for plunder, but never once fought for his King', remained without being attacked or making any attempt to take part in the battle, until Livingston's return to camp enabled him to retire.[136]

Captain Buchan and about sixty men had barricaded themselves in Lethendry and seemed defiant. Livingston surrounded the castle, and began to undermine it and bombard it with grenades, and they surrendered. Captain George Carleton, who carried the messages, claimed that Livingston first loudly declared so that all around could hear that, having shot men after they were offered quarter, they should have none, but then privately told him that, since many were both men's old Dutch Brigade comrades, they should. A trivial incident; but Livingston's implied assumption that ruthlessness was the one effective way of impressing highlanders was to be important when he was Commander-in-Chief at the time of Glencoe.[137] The one reason for doubting it is that Carleton claims that the party had killed two grenadiers, while Livingston's and all other contemporary reports claim that he had no man killed and only three or four wounded, although many horses were dead or disabled. He estimated that they had killed 3–400 of the enemy, and captured (including those in Lethendry and another party in a mill) about a hundred, at least a score of them officers. Buchan brazenly claimed that, besides a dozen officers taken, only thirty men (six of them highlanders) were killed; but the Macphersons alone lost thirty-six men killed, besides at least thirteen prisoners. The Camerons again suffered heavily. Yet besides the Macleans, only one highland officer seems to have been captured, Ensign Macnachtan. Buchan's regiment must have been practically destroyed.[138] The victors found an unexpectedly large booty in the camp, including the Jacobite royal standard, Cannon's, Dunfermline's and Macnachtan's correspondence, which helped to convict the chiefs in the proceedings for treason that summer, 400 bolls of meal and much claret. The victors drank this and returned with their prisoners to camp through the rain, with green branches in their hats to celebrate May Day.[139]

The Jacobites had fled in two directions, like their chiefs, Cannon up the Spey, where Cluny gave him refuge, Buchan eastwards into Glenlivet — it was at Auchindoun, well to the north-east, that the man in the famous song met the fugitive. At first, the main pursuit in the foul weather was up the Spey. A party of Macleans and Camerons who had crossed the river was next day attacked at Granish, and the survivors fled to the mountains. Keppoch, returning up the east bank, made an ineffectual attack on Grant of Rothiemurchus' house. Inhabitants of the southern highlands feared that, now so much of the Williamite army had gone north, parties from Buchan's army would retaliate by raiding them; but most were apparently too demoralised even for that, and drifted home.[140] Livingston advanced, destroying a party of highland reinforcements. On 6 May, he ordered Cluny instantly to send 120 men to join him, and on his refusal briefly arrested him. Short of provisions, he then marched down Spey on 8 May to occupy Ballindalloch, and returned to Inverness.[141] Lieutenant-Colonel Buchan advanced up-country and tried unsuccessfully to intercept his brother and other Jacobites, while troops in Angus seized in Glen Clova some Jacobite plotters who had been awaiting Buchan's success. When, at the start of June, highland raiders attacked the Mearns, the local fencibles assembled under local Whig gentry and drove them back —a strong contrast to their conduct in August.[142]

Many prisoners were kept at Inverness, but the officers and some others were brought to Edinburgh and crowded into the prisons. Keppoch's brother instantly burned the escorting officer's lands, but that was little consolation.[143] Pressure was put on the common soldiers, largely Irish, to enlist for the Continent, and they had to rely on sympathisers' charity. They were at least more fortunate than the Jacobite common prisoners (highland or lowland is not clear) at Aberdeen that autumn, many of whom died of starvation in gaol.[144] The officers remained, also supported by charity, as prisoners of war. The clans were particularly concerned to exchange the Maclean captains, but were unsuccessful. They were delivered to Argyll to be used in pacifying Mull, and finally assisted his January 1692 negotiations with Sir John in rivalry with Breadalbane. Once the Highland Army dissolved, no exchanges could be arranged, and some officers remained prisoners until 1693.[145]

Cromdale was the decisive stage in that dissolution. Making his way back after the disaster, Buchan received recent letters from the chiefs assuring him that they would immediately take the field, and others from lowland nobles calling for highland military backing to allow them to rebel. The chiefs, however, were already very uneasy at the non-arrival of any aid from Ireland, and the news of Cromdale shattered their plans for a general rendezvous. Buchan's insulting comments on the men he had led to disaster probably became known. Although remaining their general, he became, Sir John Maclean recalled later, 'the most ungrateful [unpopular] Man living to the Highlanders'.[146]

A slightly earlier event would, had they known of it, have afflicted the clans more than Cromdale. Simpson's mission succeeded in France, where Louis XIV prepared two shiploads of arms to send Montgomerie.[147] When he reached Ireland, it was already clear that the Jacobite counter-offensive was over. At first, James's ministers merely considered sending Dumbarton rather than Berwick with the Scottish invasion force.[148] By April, however, Tyrconnell, now James's chief adviser, saw little hope of saving Ireland unless a Scottish rising diverted William's invasion. He therefore swiftly persuaded James to accept most of Montgomerie's demands, including the restoration of Argyll. Most of Melfort's belated advice from Rome was sinister, even diabolical; but he emphasised that restoring Argyll would ruin the loyal clans fighting for James, whose interests must come first: ' the fatted Calf may be for ye prodigal, but ye inheritance ought to remain to the elder brother'.[149] James, despite his prejudice, was sometimes surprisingly easy to persuade into endorsing 'Whig' policies. He apparently accepted largely without sharing the fears which made Tyrconnell advise him or considering the consequences, and held himself absolved from the conditions —when Montgomerie failed. Yet he took minute interest in the religious demands affecting his conscience. Should the affair become known, warned Melfort, the clans would desert James. They would have been justified.[150]

Meanwhile, the Club Plot was collapsing in Parliament. Despite frequent attempts to terrorise him, Melville for once showed some courage and flexibility,

winning decisive votes by judicious concessions. Even the Cameronians saw
something odd in the 'episcopalians' supporting high presbytery. Club members,
increasingly trusting Melville rather than Montgomerie, began to change sides,
and the normal time-servers followed.[151] As this was beginning, Simpson reached
Edinburgh with James's replies. First Montgomerie alone, and then he,
Annandale, Ross and Arran removed items the 'episcopalians' would find
offensive, particularly a commission to the four of them and, perhaps, Argyll to
govern the country. On 3 May, a meeting was held, attended by the three Club
leaders, Atholl, Breadalbane, Linlithgow and Balcarres. Queensberry sent his
excuses, and Arran (possibly offended at not being appointed general) was with his
sick wife.[152] The 'episcopalians' were disgusted that James had refused some
demands, that the Club plotters had monopolised the promises of office, and that
they had relied entirely on parliamentary means to restore James, rather than
obtaining arms and reinforcements. Not yet aware of the French promise of arms,
Montgomerie could not moderate this criticism. The meeting broke up, only to
hear the news of Cromdale. Carwhin kept the papers, but Breadalbane,
Montgomerie and Annandale soon burned most of them for security.[153]

The Club plotters and the 'episcopalians', headed by Queensberry, met briefly
again to discuss sending a reply. Montgomerie's suggestion of a blank paper
bearing their signatures on which Simpson, once safe in France, should copy out
their opinions from memory, was badly received. Queensberry suggested that the
Club should make the reply, they that it was the 'episcopalians'' turn, and they
parted without agreement. Montgomerie showed violent determination to reply.
He, Arran and Ross finally sent a demand for an invasion, and Arran surprisingly
persuaded Murray, after a year of thankless and misunderstood attempts to keep
the Atholl men loyal to William's government, to join in endorsing it — his one
positive Jacobite action of this period. Simpson left with Argyll's erratic brother
John.[154]

Despite their disillusionment, the 'episcopalians' continued to vote with
Montgomerie. On 8 May, however, Melville made a decisive concession, the
abolition of the Articles. Committees were elected, including one for the supply.
The 'episcopalians' warned the Club that they dared not oppose William over this,
and by mid-May they were making approaches to Melville. Montgomerie
continued in increasingly desperate opposition. His main tactic was to appeal to
the Presbyterians' extremism and fears, and Melville had to respond with
concessions to them. In consequence, most of the constitutional reforms the Club
had demanded never took place, while the prebyterian church was established
without the safeguards William had wanted. The lopsided settlement, giving
the Scots more scope for expressing their grievances but little more power to affect
William's decisions and choice of ministers, was to cause continued struggles and
instability throughout his reign. On 7 June, the first Supply Act, for 28 months'
cess, was passed, and should have solved the army's problems.[155]

Both Breadalbane and Tarbat were anxious to minimise the significance of
Cromdale. Although they still gave plausible reasons for negotiating, some
justified by events that summer, private interest in controlling so much influence

and money and even more dubious motives might be suspected when they co-operated to delay or even prevent the campaign. Breadalbane suggested arranging a cessation of arms with the clans until 30 November, and Tarbat even recommended it to William, as preventing danger while he was in Ireland, and giving an opportunity to negotiate with individual chiefs and break the confederacy.[156] Melville signed another warrant for Breadalbane. He appointed Barcaldine his agent, and Duncan Menzies was one of the chief Jacobite negotiators. These claimed, untruly, that neither Lochiel, Keppoch nor Glengarry was likely to negotiate with Hill, and that the clans were now gathered and ready to attack the Lowlands, although Buchan indicated to Cluny that they badly needed the cessation. The negotiators suggested as terms for a general submission an indemnity, pensions for all the chiefs and capital sums for purchase of superiorities and to fulfil the 1680 agreement with Sir John Maclean. What proved the critical point in 1691 appeared: 'they will be seeking passes to send men to Ireland to aquainte KJ what they are dooing.' Far from making it easier to deal with individual chiefs, it roused their expectations so greatly that Lochiel and Glengarry broke off negotiations they had started with Hill.[157]

Not surprisingly, in early June Mackay and other officers finally refused to let such negotiations delay the campaign. Breadalbane nevertheless managed to persuade Melville to let him ride to meet William at Chester and obtain a further extension.[158] The Montgomerie Plot was breaking; Neville Payne had been captured in the Borders, and Ross betrayed it to Melville and was sent to Chester. It was therefore believed that Breadalbane, Balcarres and Argyll, who also rode there, intended to confess and gain pardon.[159] Not only Breadalbane but Argyll had a more obvious reason, Argyll's being to object to the clans' demands as infringing his rights. According to Breadalbane, Ardkinglas and Aberuchill, 'his great enemies in all his transactions', persuaded Melville to endorse these objections. Breadalbane reached Chester too late to see William, who would anyway have refused his request, but claimed to have reached an understanding with Argyll. When he returned to Edinburgh, he found the plot exposed and Dalrymple gave warning that a warrant was out for him. Narrowly escaping arrest, he fled to Kilchurn.[160] The justifiable suspicions of crypto-Jacobitism and financial corruption produced by this negotiation were to haunt him in 1691.

Behind him, the conspiracy continued to collapse. Ross, Annandale and Montgomerie in turn approached Melville, and were sent south to confess to Mary. All emphasised the 'episcopalians'' part in the plot. Annandale made a full confession and was pardoned, and Ross was only briefly imprisoned. Montgomerie had originally hoped to make the government promise silence about him in return for his confession, enabling him even to retain his party's confidence. Yet he delayed seeing Mary and finally prevaricated, particularly denying, from pride and fear of their retaliation, all knowledge of his English Whig supporters. He vanished in London, unpardoned, with only the Jacobite cause open to him. He was to be as disruptive there as he had been among the 'presbyterians'.[161]

Melville and Tarbat, still hoping for a peaceful settlement, now sent an

Edinburgh episcopalian minister of a Skye family, Macqueen, previously best known for wearing clothes made from the stolen petticoat of the girl he vainly loved, to persuade Sir Donald Macdonald to submit. This failed entirely. Macqueen instead journeyed to Ireland and France on Melville's money to seek James's help for the clans.[162]

NOTES

1. *Lockhart Papers*, ii, 14; BN Naf 7492 fol. 281v, [Sir R, Clarke] to [L. Innes], 10/20 Oct. 1689; SRO GD 112/43/1/10, [Breadalbane] to [Carwhin]. 2 Dec. 1689.

2. *Ib.*, 43/1/2/99, Breadalbane's Life, 2; *ib.*, 39/1210, Mackay to Breadalbane, 7 Oct. 1689; *APS*, ix, 465; *RPCS*, xiv, 299–300; Mackay, *Memoirs*, 73; *ib.*, 283–4, Mackay to Hamilton, 11 Oct. 1689; *ib.*, 290–1, same to Melville, 22 Oct. 1689; Drumlanrig, Queensberry Papers, bundle 1185, 18, Memorial on reducing the army, 1691.

3. *HMCR 6th Report*, 701, Mackay to R. Menzies, 12 Oct. 1689; *RCAHMS Argyll*, ii, 171–4; Prebble, *Glencoe*, 80–1; NLS MS 3134, 12, Cannon to ?, 4 Oct. 1689.

4. SRO GD 170/629/14, [Breadalbane] to Barcaldine, 10 Oct. 1689; *ib.*, 15, same to same, 16 Oct. 1689; *ib.*, 159, same to same [c. Dec. 1689]; NLS MS 2955 fol. 83, same to Campbell of Duneaves, 11 Oct. 1689.

5. *Est. Procs.*, ii, 38–9, 42–3, 47, 58–9, 61–2, 63; *The Dunlop Papers: Letters and Journals 1663–1889*, ed. J. G. Dunlop (Frome, 1953), 52–3, Dundonald to W. Dunlop, 18 Nov. [1689]; SRO GD 26/viii/51, Sir. J. Maclean to Cannon, 29 Oct. 1689.

6. One reason why the chiefs might obey the despised Cannon in this matter (if the policy was his) was that raiders captured obeying such military orders might have a better chance of surviving as prisoners of war.

7. *HMCR 6th Report*, 701, Mackay to R. Menzies, 7 Oct. 1689, 12 Oct. 1689, 1 Nov. 1689.

8. To make this and the attack on Achallader part of the same drift home, Prebble has to ignore the dates given in his sources. Prebble, *Glencoe*, 80–1; *Lairds of Glenlyon*, 49–51.

9. Glenlyon at one point claimed to have lost £3,000 sterling. *Ib.*, 49–50, 53–7; *Melville & Leslies*, ii, 124, Cannon to MacIain, 23 Dec. 1689; SRO GD 170/629/159, [Breadalbane] to [Barcaldine, c. Dec. 1689]; *ib.*, 133/117, Glenlyon's petition to Parliament, 1690.

10. Blair, Atholl MSS, Box '71' II A 38, memorandum, 10 Oct. 1689.

11. *Ib.*, Box 29 I (6) 18, Atholl to Murray, 24 Aug. [1690]; *Ib.*, Bundle 1624, diary entry, 18 Feb. 1690; *Lairds of Glenlyon*, 47, 57; SRO GD 26/viii/86, A. Macdougall to Macnachtan, 2 Mar. 1690.

12. *Ib.*, GD 112/40/4/2/22, Carwhin to Breadalbane, 6 Jan. 1691; GD 170/133/104, Information for Glenlyon, 1690; *ib.*, 117, Glenlyon's petition to Parliament, 1690.

13. *Ib.*; *ib.*, 118, Reasons and answers for Glenlyon, 1690; *ib.*, 40, Glenlyon to Carwhin, 26 July 1691; Blair, Atholl MSS, Box 44/VI/173, [Atholl] to Lady Murray, [1693]

14. *APS*, ix, 471; *RPCS*, xiv, 530–1, 542–2; *HMCR 8th Report*, 310, Requests for Hamilton of Barns, 1689; *Dunlop Letters & Journals*, 54, Dundonald to W. Dunlop, 30 Nov. [1689]; SRO GD 170/629/18, Breadalbane to Barcaldine, 21 Nov. 1689; GD 112/43/1/1/10, [same] to Carwhin, 2 Dec. 1689.

15. *Ib.*

16. *Ib.*; Prebble, *Glencoe*, 144; SRO GD 170/629/14, [Breadalbane] to Barcaldine, 10 Oct. 1689; *ib.*, 21, same to same, 6 Dec. 1689; *ib.*, 23, same to same, 'Monday night'.

17. *Ib.*, 25, same to same, 'Monday morning'; *APS*, ix, 208; *RPCS*, xiv, 485–6; *HMCR 8th Report*, 301, Requests for Hamilton of Barns, 1689.

18. *Leven & Melville*, 369, Crawford to Melville, 11 Jan. 1690; SRO GD 26/viii/62, ? Macgregor to Dunfermline & Cannon, 16 Dec. 1689; *RPCS*, xv, 138.

19. *Ib.*, 127–9, 149; *Est. Procs.*, ii, 61–2, 69, 72–3, 74.

20. *RPCS*, xiv, 524, 535–6, 563; Mackay, *Memoirs*, 306, Mackay to Melville, 12 Dec. 1689: NLS MS 1031 fol. 73, Hamilton to Selkirk, 22 Jan. 1690; *ib.*, MS 17,498 fols. 65–6, Mackay, Instructions for Argyll, 13 Dec. 1689; SRO GD 170/629/24, Breadalbane to Barcaldine, 'Sunday night'; *ib.*, 159, same to same, [c. Dec. 1689].

21. *Ib.*, 17, same to same, 18 Nov. 1689; *ib.*, 18, same to same, 21 Nov. 1689; *ib.*, 23, same to same, 'Monday night'; GD 112/40/3/4/91, Carwhin to Breadalbane, 27 Dec. 1689; *RPCS*, xiv, 561–2, 591–2; *ib.*, xv, 101.

22. The context sometimes identifies persons given code-names or letters in Breadalbane's correspondence with Barcaldine. G = Lochiel (Mingary dispute, 629/159). F = Macnachtan (with rebels, acting as Breadalbane's intermediary, wife on his property, 15). P = James (his service, 18, 159). X = (presumably) Cannon (in charge, Breadalbane last saw him in England, 159). *Leven & Melville*, 354, Lord N. Campbell to Melville, 24 Dec. 1689; SRO GD 26/viii/103, I. [Macnachtan] to [Macnachtan], 4 Dec. [1689]; *ib.*, 64, Appin to Dunfermline, 21 Dec. 1689; GD 112/42/1, James to Breadalbane, 30 Nov. 1689; GD 170/629/24, Breadalbane to Barcaldine, 'Sunday night'; *ib.*, 25, same to same 'Monday morning'; *ib.*, 159, same to same, [c. Dec. 1689]; *ib.*, 16a, list of code symbols.

23. Macpherson, *Original Papers*, i, 377–8, Buchan to James, 14 Feb. 1690.

24. *Est. Procs.*, ii, 118; *Leven & Melville*, 332, James to Macnachtan, 30 Nov. 1689.

25. *Ib.*, 331–2; *ib.*, 333–4, same to Cannon, 30 Nov. 1689; *CSPD 1689–90*, 338, same to Sir D. Macdonald; SRO GD 112/42/1, same to Breadalbane; NLS MS 3194 fols. 121–2, same to Lochiel. For the Melfordians' whereabouts, Macpherson, *Original Papers*, i, 375, ? to Mary of Modena, 14 Mar. 1689/90; BL Add. 33,924 fol. 74, J. Trench's report.

26. J.A. Smith, 'Notes on original letters of King James II ... ', *PSAS*, vii, Part I (1866–7), 249–50, James to Keppoch, 30 Nov. 1689.

27. As he later claimed to have raised and disbanded his men once already, this hostile report may underestimate his success. *Est. Procs.*, ii, 33, 38; *The Blind Harper*, 28–9, 114, 'Oran Mu Oifigich Araid'; NLS MS 1329 fol. 95, Sir A. Mackenzie to Delvine, 24 Sept. 1689; *ib.*, fol. 96, same to same, 3 Oct. 1689.

28. Mackay, *Urquhart & Glenmoriston*, 206.

29. Cpt. P. Wimberley, 'Selections from the Family Papers of the Mackays of Bighouse (Bighouse Papers)', *TGSI*, xxi, 134–6, Justiciary decreet, 20 Dec. 1695.

30. *CSPD 1689–90*, 324, William to Sir J. Leslie, 19 Nov. 1689; *Melvilles & Leslies*, iii, 197–8, Information on garrisoning of Tarbat Castle, 1689; Macgill, *Old Rosshire*, i, 89, Justiciary case, 1694; *ib.*, 233–4, Sir J. Leslie to Balnagown, 11 Nov. 1690; *ib.*, 384, W. Ross to [same? 1689]; NLS MS 1329 fol. 107, Sir A. Mackenzie to Delvine, 28 Jan. 1690; SRO GD 26/xiii/31, Delvine to [Tarbat], 14 Nov. 1689.

31. HLRO, Willcocks MS, Section VI, 46, A. Hay to Tweeddale, 21 Oct. 1689.

32. SRO GD 26/viii/53, J. Winchester to Dunfermline, 31 Oct. 1689.

33. *Ib.*, 54, Glengarry to Cannon, 15 Nov. 1689; *ib.*, 59, same to same, 3 Dec. 1689; Mackay, *Memoirs*, 303, Leslie to Mackay, 9 Dec. 1689; SRO SP 3/1 fol. 112, Johnston to Tweeddale, 18 Feb. 1693.

34. This was said to Williamites; and the lack of letters from him in the Highland Army's archives may merely mean that he was in company with Cannon, or that he preferred oral messages. *Ib.*, GD 26/ix/274, Hill to Melville, 6 Nov. 1690.

35. These are the forces Sir James Leslie feared *were* attacking him in December, but by then the plan was different. This may have been a trick to distract him from the real attack, or a leak of genuine information from the highland camp; he was certainly apprehensive throughout November. Mackay, *Memoirs*, 301–2, Leslie to Melville, 6 Dec. 1689.

36. *Ib.*, 299–301; *ib.*, 302–3, same to Mackay, 9 Dec. 1689; *ib.*, 305, Mackay to Melville, 12 Dec. 1689; *CSPD 1689*–90, 304, newsletter, 26 Oct. 1689; SRO GD 26/viii/54, Glengarry to Cannon, 15 Nov. 1689.

37. *Est. Procs.*, ii, 53; Mackay, *Memoirs*, 299–300, Leslie to Melville, 6 Dec. 1689; *Seafield Corr.* 56–7, W. Hope to Findlater, 20 Nov. 1689; NLS MS 1353 fol. 58, K. Mackenzie of Redcastle to Delvine, 11 Nov. 1689.

38. NLS MS 1329 fol. 101, Sir A. Mackenzie to same, 10 Dec. 1689.

39. *Ib.*, fol. 101, same to same, 10 Dec. 1689; *ib.*, fol. 102, same to same 16 Dec. 1689; *ib.*, fol. 108, same to same, 5 Feb. 1690; Mackay, *Memoirs*, 299–300, Leslie to Melville, 6 Dec. 1689; *ib.*, 303–4, same to Mackay, 9 Dec. 1689; *Lairds of Grant*, i, 515; Mackay, *Urquhart & Glenmoriston*, 213; SRO GD 26/viii/61, Glengarry to Cannon, 6 Dec. 1689.

40. *Ib.*, 59, same to same, 2 Dec. 1689; *ib.*, xiii/31, Delvine to [Tarbat], 14 Nov. 1689; NLS MS 1329 fol. 77, Sir A, Mackenzie to Delvine, 'Martinmas Day' [11 Nov.] 1689.

41. *Ib.*, fol. 102, same to same, 16 Dec. 1689; SRO GD 26/viii/63, Glengarry to [Dunfermline], 18 Dec. 1689; *ib.*, 112, same to [Cannon, Dec. 1689].

42. *Ib.*, 61, same to same, 6 Dec. 1689; *ib.*, 68, same to same, Dec. 1689; *ib.*, 63, same to [Dunfermline], 18 Dec. 1689; Mackay, *Memoirs*, 304, Leslie to Mackay, 9 Dec. 1689; *Est. Procs.*, ii, 95–6; NLS MS 1329 fol. 102, Sir A Mackenzie to Delvine, 26 Dec. 1689; *ib.*, fol. 110v, same to same, 20 Feb. 1690.

43. SRO GD 26/viii/68, Glengarry to Cannon, Dec. 1689; *ib.*, 108, Cannon to Macnachtan, n.d.

44. *Ib.*, 111, [same] to ?, 25 'Nov.' [Dec. 1689] (month established by mention of Cluny's letter, sent on by Glengarry, *ib.*, 68 and answered by Cannon on 23rd Dec. (*TGSI*, xx, 232)).

45. *Melvilles & Leslies*, iii, 208, Cannon's instructions to Achtera and Widdrington, [c. Dec. 1689].

46. SRO GD 26/viii/51, Sir J. Maclean to Cannon, 29 Oct. 1689; *ib.*, 69, Sir D. Macdonald to [?same], ?18 Dec. 1689.

47. *Ib.*, 68, Glengarry to same, Dec. 1689; *ib.*, 111, [Cannon] to ?, [Dec. 1689]; GD 80/827, same to Cluny, 10 Nov. [1689]; Macpherson, 'Gleanings', *TGSI*, xx, 232, same to same, 23 Dec. 1689; *ib.*, Commission to same, 27 Dec. 1689; *ib.*, *TGSI*, xxi, 392, Frendraught to same, 22 Dec. [1689].

48. Mackay, *Memoirs*, 305, Mackay to Melville, 12 Dec. 1689; *Est. Procs.*, ii, 80; NLS MS 1329 fol. 101, Sir A. Mackenzie to Delvine, 10 Dec. 1689.

49. Cpt. G. Carleton, *The Memoirs of an English Officer* (London, 1728), 40. Carleton's *Memoirs* have usually been considered a fiction of Defoe's, on the grounds that they sound too authentic actually to be so; but Stieg Hargevik, *The Disputed Assignment of Memoirs of an English Officer to Daniel Defoe, Stockholm Studies in English*, xxx–xxxi (Stockholm, 1974), has shown that they were at least based on Carleton's memoirs and partly his actual writing, and that there is no evidence Defoe was involved. Most of the book was written to the orders of the Earl of Peterborough, to justify his conduct in Spain; but Carleton's Scottish reminiscences are unaffected by this.

50. *Est. Procs.*, ii, 87–8, 112, 130; NLS MS 1329 fol. 109, Sir A. Mackenzie to Delvine, 15 Feb. 1690; Mackay, *Memoirs*, 314–15, Mackay to Melville, 31 Dec. 1689.

51. *Ib.*, 316; *ib.*, 303–4, Leslie to Mackay, 9 Dec. 1689; *RPCS* xv, 2–3, 57–8, 643–4; NLS MS 1329 fol. 104, Sir A. Mackenzie to Delvine, 20 Jan. 1690; *ib.*, fol. 108, same to same, 5 Feb. 1690; *ib.*, fol. 110v, same to same, 20 Feb. 1690.

52. *Ib.*, fol. 112, same to same, 17 Feb. 1690; *ib.*, fol. 113, same to same, 29 Feb. 1690.

53. *HMCR Hope-Johnstone*, 155, Livingston to Mackay, [Jan. 1690]; *RPCS*, xv, 66.

54. *Ib.*, 105, James's instructions to Strachan, 25 Jan. 1689/90; *CSPD 1689–90*, Seaforth to Sir D. Macdonald, [17] Jan. 1690; SRO GD 26/vii/48, A. Strachan's examination, 18 Feb. 1690; J. Bernadi, *A Short History of the Life of Major John Bernardi*, (London, 1729), 64–6.

55. *RPCS*, xv, 92.

56. *Melvilles & Leslies*, iii, 207–8, Cannon's instructions to Achtera and Widdrington, [c. Dec. 1689]; T. Thorpe, *Supplement to . . . Catalogue of Manuscripts for 1836* (London, 1836), 147, Cannon to Tyrconnell, 22 Feb. 1689[/90].

57. Mackay, *Memoirs*, 111.

58. *Melvilles & Leslies*, ii, 151, Frendraught to Cannon, 1 Mar. 1690; SRO GD 26/viii/122/2, Mackay to Melville, 29 Mar. 1691; BL MS Lansdowne 1163B, 10, Melfort to Nihill, 6 June 1690(NS); *HMCR Hope-Johnstone*, 201, J. Forbes to ?, 9 Jan. 169[0].

59. *Ib*; *Est. Procs.*, ii, 124, 126; SRO GD 26/viii/55, Grant of Ballindalloch to ?, 16 Nov. 1689; HLRO, Willcocks MSS, Section VI, 63, Yester to Tweeddale, 22 Mar. 1690.

60. The Jacobites preventively burned Corgarff, higher on the Don, now or in April. *RPCS*, xv, 20–1; *Est. Procs.*, ii, 81; *Leven & Melville*, 451–2, Mr of Forbes to Melville, 27 June 1690; SRO GD 26/ix/263, Lt-Col Buchan to Hamilton of Binnie, 21 Jan. 1690.

61. *Ib.*, viii/66, Inverey to Cannon, 29 Dec. 1689; *ib.*, 79, same to same, 26 Jan. 1690; *APS*, ix, App., 60, Tomintoul bond, 15 Jan. 1690; Tayler, *Jacobites of Aberdeenshire*, for some families involved.

62. *HMCR Hope-Johnstone*, 153, [Livingston] to Crawford, 30 Jan. 1690.

63. *RPCS*, xv, 98, 104–5, 113–14; *Melvilles & Leslies*, ii, 150–1, Frendraught to Cannon, 1 Mar. 1690; *Est. Procs.*, ii, 114–18.

64. *Ib.*, 83, 93–4; *RPCS* xv, 22–4; *HMCR Hope-Johnstone*, 178, Grants to Crawford, 23 Feb. 1694; *Siege*, 84–7; SRO GD 26/viii/132, Abstracts of letters found on Gordon, & his report, 1690; NLS MS 7012 fol. 51, Lady Roxburghe to Tweeddale, 17 Apr. 1690; *ib.*, MS 14,408 fol. 286, Johnston to same, 29 Mar. 1694; BL MS Lansdowne 1163A, 244, Melfort to Innes, 16 May 1690(NS); *ib.*, B, 186, same to Mary of Modena, 22 July 1690(NS).

65. Riley, *King William*, 3–7 (though he disagrees about some of the examples).

66. *HMCR 7th Report*, 199, [Blancard] to Dykveldt, 19 June 1691.

67. Halifax, recording this exclamation, gives only initials and no date, and it might seem more appropriate after the Montgomerie Plot. Yet Tarbat did not come to London that winter, and Tweeddale, the only major pro-'episcopalian' 'T' then giving him advice, would not have advised such an extreme measure. Halifax gained his knowledge of Scottish politics because as William's most trusted English minister, he reluctantly investigated disputes; and this ended with his resignation in January 1690. *Leven & Melville*, 110, Tarbat to Melville, [late 1689]; BL Add. 51,511 fol. 24v; Drumlanrig, Queensberry Papers, bundle 1185, 14, 'Papers . . . got from . . . Tarbat at London', 1689.

68. I hope to give a fuller account of this plot in a biography of Montgomerie. *Culloden Papers*, 325–7, 'State of things in 1696'; Burnet, *History*, iv, 61–3; Balcarres, *Memoirs*, 51–2; Macpherson, *Original Papers*, i, 384, Melfort's memorial, 18 Apr. 1690(NS); *Leven &*

Melville, 506–8, Annandale's confession, 14 Aug. 1690.

69. *Ib.*, 509, 512; SRO GD 26/viii/93a/5, Instructions to Annandale, no. 9.

70. *CPSD 1689*–90, 318–19, newsletter, 12 Nov. 1689; Balcarres, *Memoirs*, 51.

71. Riley suggests that Queensberry was too important to let himself be involved; but his 1691 remission and 1693 pardon leave no doubt. *Ib.*, 54–6; Riley, *King William*, 35, 40; Drumlanrig, Queensberry Papers (old catalogue), 956, warrant for remission, 15/25 June 1691 + pardon, 30 Dec. 1693; *Leven & Melville*, 499, Lockhart to Melville, 24 Aug. 1690; *ib.*, 512, Annandale's confession, 14 Aug. 1690.

72. *Ib.*, 365, Sir P. Hume, memorandum, 7 Jan. 1690; *Culloden Papers*, 328–9, 'State of things in 1696'.

73. Drumlanrig, Queensberry papers, bundle 1185, 15, 'Papers . . . got from . . . Tarbat at London', 1689.

74. *HMCR Hope-Johnstone*, 143, Melville to Crawford, 7 Nov. 1689; *Est. Procs.*, ii, 83–4.

75. SRO GD 406/1/6588, [Hamilton] to [Duchess], 21 Nov. 1689; Mackay, *Memoirs*, 82–4; *ib.*, 308–10, Instructions, 18 Dec. 1689; *ib.*, 319–20, Revised Instructions, 4 Jan. 1689/90.

76. *Ib.*, 82–3; *RPCS*, xv, 10; *CTB*, ix, 510, 692; *ib.*, x, 77; *Leven & Melville*, 427, Ranelagh to Melville, 19 Apr. 1690; NLS MS 3740 fol. 143v, Mackay to Blathwayt, 4 'Feb.' [Mar.] 1690.

77. *CSPD 1690*–1, 286–7, Committee of Council to William, 1 Mar. '1691' [1690]; *CTB*, ix, 377; *Leven & Melville*, 367–8, Dalrymple to Melville, 10 Jan. 1690; Mackay, *Memoirs*, 79–81, 84–6, 103–4; *ib.*, 171–2, Mackay to William, 14 Jan. 1690.

78. *Ib.*, 83, 88–90, 106–7; SRO GD 26/xiii/98, [Melville], ' A true account of these things'; NLS MS 7012 fol. 147, Bruce to Tweeddale, 7 Aug. 1690.

79. Macpherson, *Original Papers*, i, 378, Buchan to James, 14 Feb. 1690; *CSPD 1690*–1, 209, Tarbat to William, [May 1690].

80. Firth, *Scotland & the Protectorate*, xl–xliii, 321; Prebble, *Glencoe*, 85–9; *Earls of Cromartie*, i, 58–9, Hill to Tarbat, 19 Aug. 1688.

81. *Leven & Melville*, 415–16, Belfast certificate, 28 Feb. 1689/90; [C. Leslie], *An Answer to a Book, Intituled, The State of the Protestants in Ireland under the Late King James's Government*, [Leslie], *Answer to King*; London, 1692), 148–151; *ib.*, App. 73–6, Letters of James, Melfort and Hill; R. M. Young, *The Town Book of the Corporation of Belfast*, (Belfast, 1892), 242; *An Abstract of Three Letters from Belfast* (London, 1690).

82. Yet he could conquer his principles when it was hopeless to do otherwise, changing in 1659–60 from eager republicanism to being at least nominally 'active and instrumentall in his Matie's happy Restauration'. *HMCR Hope-Johnstone*, 166, Hill to Crawford, 16 Jan. 1691; *Spottiswoode Miscellany*, ii, 160, Hill to Glencairn, 30 Dec. 1653; Worcester College, Oxford, Clarke MSS, cclxvii, same to W. Clarke, 20 June, 15 Dec. 1660; *ib.*, xxxi, fol. 148, certificate, Oct. 1661.

83. *CSPD 1691*–2., 62, Tarbat to William, [July — Aug. 1690]; *Leven & Melville*, 422–3, Warrant to Tarbat, 25 Mar. 1690; Mackay, *Memoirs*, 202, Mackay to Portland, 8 June 1690.

84. *RPCS*, xv, 177–8; *Est. Procs.*, ii, 128–9, 131, 133; PRO ADM 51/345/1 (Log of HMS *Fanfan*), 19, 26 Mar. 1690; *CSPD 1689–90*, 546, Tarbat to William, 9 Apr. 1690; *ib.*, 550, same to same, 13 Apr. 1690.

85. If Tarbat refers to Colquhoun of Luss, this seems the only evidence that he had joined the Jacobites. *Ib*; *ib. 1690*–1, 209, same to same, [May 1690].

86. *Leven & Melville*, 363, Dalrymple to Melville, 4 Jan. 1690; *ib.*, 389, same to same, 31 Jan. 1690; *ib.*, 394–5, same to same, 7 Feb. 1690; *ib.*, 421, William to same, 20/30 Mar. 1690;

SRO GD 112/40/4/2/54, ? to Breadalbane, 21 [Dec. 1689].

87. *Leven & Melville*, 374, Argyll to William, 20 Jan. 1690; *ib.*, 401, same to Melville, 11 Feb. 1690; *HMCR Finch*, ii, 392, J. Grahme's statements, July 1690; *Melvilles & Leslies*, ii, 155, anon. [? Earl of Monmouth] to Melville, 30 May 1690.

88. Presumably a gross exaggeration. *Ib.*, 154; *HMCR Finch*, iii, 318–19, Preston's confession, 13 June 1691; Wodrow, *Analecta*, i, 196.

89. Simon Lord Lovat claimed, surprisingly, that Ferguson was a strong Jacobite by 1703. *Est. Procs.*, ii, 66; Lovat, *Memoirs*, 230–2; Mackay, *Memoirs*, 87, 92; *ib.*, 178–9, Mackay to William, 16 Apr. 1690.

90. *Ib.*, 175, same to same, 9 Apr. 1690.

91. Balcarres, *Memoirs*, 54–8; Riley, *King William*, 38, 39–40; *Leven & Melville*, 508, Annandale's confession, 14 Aug. 1690.

92. *Ib.*, 372–3, Dalrymple to Melville, 16 Jan. 1690; *RPCS.*, xv, 28, 101, 130.

93. Mackay, *Memoirs*, 179–80, Mackay to William, 16 Apr. 1690; SRO GD 26/xiii/78 fol. 178, Melville's notes.

94. Dalton, *Scots Army*, 115, 117–18; Macpherson, *Original Papers*, i, 374–5, ? to Mary of Modena, 14 Mar. 1689/90; *HMCR 4th Report*, 529, James's instructions to Buchan, 18 Jan. 1689[/90]; *RPCS*, xv, 105, same to Strachan, 25 Jan. 1689/90; SRO GD 26/viii/83, Buchan to Cannon, 3 Feb. [1690].

95. *Ib.*, 82, MacIain to Glengarry, 1 Feb. 1690; *RPCS*, xv, 104; Macpherson, *Original Papers*, i, 375, ? to Mary of Modena, 14 Mar. 1689/90.

96. Balhaldie, who misplaces this meeting after Seaforth's arrival, was mistaken in thinking that Clanranald attended; he probably did not yet know of Buchan's arrival. *Ib.*, 377, Sir J. Maclean to James, 1 Feb. 1690; *ib.*, 377–8, Buchan to same, 14 Feb. 1690; *ib.*, 379 Chiefs & Officers to same, [14 Feb. 1690]; Balcarres, *Memoirs*, 53; SRO GD 26/viii/89, A. Macdonald [?Clanranald] to Cannon, 8 Mar. 1690; SCA, Blairs Letters, Box U, 1690, 2, D. Burnet to Innes, 27 May 1690; *Memoirs of Locheill*, 290–4.

97. *Ib.*, 231; *ib.*, 290, James to Lochiel, 31 Mar. 1690; Macpherson, *Original Papers*, i, 378, Buchan to James, 14 Feb. 1690; *Leven & Melville*, 394–5, Dalrymple to Melville, 7 Feb. 1690; NLS MS 1329 fol. 114, Sir A. Mackenzie to Delvine, 17 Mar. 1690; *Est. Procs.*, ii, 124, 126, 130, 146.

98. NLS MS Wodrow Fol. XXXIV fol.62, James to [Chiefs], 31 Mar. 1690.

99. Macpherson, *Original Papers*, i, 378, Buchan to James, 14 Feb. 1690; Mackay, *Memoirs*, 118; *LJ*, xvii, 494, Sir J. Maclean's examination, 11 Mar. [1704].

100. *Ib.*, 493; *Leven & Melville*, 512, Annandale's confession, 14 Aug. 1690; *State Trials*, xii, 1346, B. Blair's confession, 12 Mar. 1695/6; SRO GD 26/viii/129, Copy of cipher captured at Cromdale.

101. Possibly the case with MacNeil of Gallachallie. *Est. Procs.*, ii, 87; SRO GD 26/viii/80, Sir A Maclean to Cannon, 26 Jan. 1690.

102. *Ib.*, 88, J. Macnachtan to same, 8 Mar. 1690; *CSPD 1689–90*, 496, newsletter, 6 Mar. 1690; *ib.*, 568, same, 27 Apr. 1690; *Memoirs of Lochiell*, 388, Argyll to Campbell of Kilberry, etc., Feb. 1690; *Est. Procs.*, ii, 121.

103. *Ib.*, 121, 146.

104. Macpherson, 'Gleanings', *TGSI*, xx, 236, Buchan to Cluny, n.d.; *Memoirs of Dundee*, 31; SRO GD 26/viii/120, Buchan to Cannon, 28 [Feb. 1690].

105. *Ib.*, Macleod, *Book of Dunvegan*, i, 131–2, Buchan to Macleod, 31 Jan. 1690; *ib.*, 132, same to same, 22 Mar. 1690; *ib.*, 142–3, James to Macleod, 29 May 1690.

106. *RPCS*, xv, 266 (Irishmen); SCA, Blairs Letters, Box Y, unsigned, 63, 'An acct of the

affaires of Scotland from ye 1st of May to ye 27th of May 1690', 10 June 1690; *Leven &*
Melville, 632, Tarbat to Melville, 25 July 1691.

107. *Ib.*, 433-4, William to same, 2 May 1690; *CSPD 1691-2*, 202, Melville to William, 26
Mar. '1692' [1690]; *ib.*, 540, extracts from Melville's letters, Apr. [1690]; Mackay, *Memoirs*,
90; *ib.*, 176, Mackay to William, 9 Apr. 1690.

108. SRO GD 112/43/1/2/98, Carwhin's draft biography (the fair copy, 'Breadalbane's
Life', misinterprets 'Marq. A.' as Annandale); GD 26/xiii/78 fol. 17, [Melville], 'View of
Affairs'.

109. *Ib.*, GD 170/3424, Melville to Pottinger, 25 Apr. 1690; *CSPD 1689-90*, 258,
Melville to William, 27 Apr. '1692' [1690]; *Leven & Melville*, 429, same to Breadalbane, 24
Apr. 1690; *ib.*, 433, William to Melville, 2 May 1690; Mackay, *Memoirs*, 105-6; *ib.*, 177,
Mackay to William, 23 Apr. 1690.

110. *Ib.*, 105; *CSPD 1689-90*, 550, Tarbat to William, 13 Apr. 1690; *Est. Procs.*, ii, 152.

111. NLS MS 1332 fol. 59, A. Mackenzie to Delvine, 23 Apr. 1690.

112. For instance the vindictive idea of an 'Act Rescissory', repealing the similar one of
1661 — and thus restoring all the legislation of the 1640s at a stroke, certain to cause chaos.
Est. Procs., ii, 142; *CSPD 1689-90*, 496, Hume & Forbes to William, 6 March 1690.

113. *Ib.*, 560, newsletter, 19 Apr. 1690; Mackay, *Memoirs*, 92-3.

114. Macfarlane, *Gen. Colls.*, i, 140; SRO GD 26/viii/110, Sir J. Maclean to James
Maclean, 14 Apr. [1690]; SCA, Blairs Letters, Box Y, unsigned, 63, 'An acct of the affaires
of Scotland', 10 June 1690 (this is largely a transcript of Buchan's official report).

115. *Ib*; Mackay, *Memoirs*, 93, 104.

116. *APS*, ix, 207; L. Shaw, *History of the Province of Moray* (Edinburgh, 1775), 226.

117. The outposts he records having posted at Cromdale would have been almost as
numerous as the 'main body'.

118. *CSPD 1689-90*, 550-1, Tarbat to William, 13 Apr. 1690; Macpherson, *Loyall*
Dissuasive, 212; Macpherson, 'Gleanings', *TGSI*, xx, 233-4, Dunfermline to Cluny, 5 Apr.
1690; *ib.*, 236-7, Buchan to same, 'Sunday'; *ib.*, 238, same to same, 18 Mar. 1690, 31 Mar.
1690.

119. *Melvilles & Leslies*, ii, 151, Livingston to Mackay, [May 1690]; *A True and real*
Account of the Defeat of General Buchan (London, 1690), [same — postscript omitted
elsewhere]; *Memoirs of Dundee*, 31; Shaw, *Moray*, 225. The priest David Burnet, who left
Buchan on 28 March, reported optimistically that the total he assembled after his departue
was 1,600-2,000. SCA, Blairs Letters, Box U, 1690, 2, D. Burnet to Innes, 27 May 1690.

120. SRO GD 26/ix/255/3, Livingston to Mackay, 4 Apr. 1690.

121. Mackay, *Memoirs*, 94, 97; *ib.*, 180-1, Mackay to Portland, 9 Apr. 1690; *Est. Procs.*, ii,
101-2, 134; SCA, Box Y, unsigned, 63, 'An acct of the affaires of Scotland', 10 June 1690;
SRO GD 26/viii/129, Copy of a cipher captured at Cromdale.

122. *Ib.*, viii/93, Lt-Col Buchan to [Mackay], 7 Apr. 1690; *ib.*, ix/270, same to Melville,
10 Apr. 1690; *Est. Procs.*, ii, 133, 138-9, 142, 146.

123. SRO GD 26/viii/92, Cpt. W. Mackay to Livingston, 4, 7 Apr. 1690.

124. *APS*, ix, 207; *Est. Procs.*, ii, 142; Mackay, *Memoirs*, 93; NLS MS 7012 fol. 51, Lady
Roxburghe to Tweeddale, 17 Apr. 1690; *Memoirs of Dundee*, 31.

125. *Ib*; *Lairds of Grant* i, 318; J.A. Rennie, *In the Steps of the Clansmen*, (London, 1951),
107 (quoting an 18th c. MS account, on which Lachlan Shaw's was based); Mackay,
Memoirs, 96.

126. *Ib.*, 95; *ib.*, 209, Mackay to Portland, [1690]; SCA, Blairs Letters, Box Y, unsigned,
63, 'An acct of the affaires of Scotland', 10 June 1690; *Melvilles & Leslies*, ii, 151, Livingston
to Mackay, [May 1690].

127. *Ib.*, 152; *London Gazette*, No 2556, 8–12 May 1690; Mackay, *Memoirs*, 93.

128. NLS MS 7012 fol. 45v, Lady Roxburghe to Tweeddale, 8 Apr. 1690.

129. *Memoirs of Dundee*, 30–2; Rennie; *Clansmen*, 107; Shaw, *Moray*, 226; SCA, Blairs Letters, Box Y, unsigned, 63, 'an acct of the affaires of Scotland', 10 June 1690.

130. *HMCR Le Fleming*, 270, newsletter, 10 May 1690; *Melvilles & Leslies*, ii, 151, Livingston to Mackay, [May 1690].

131. Mackay's claim, that he intended to camp late at night in the hills, but was persuaded by an officer to continue to Ballachastell, may be true, but as, by emphasising Providence's part in the victory, it reduces Livingston's, it may be an expression of his jealousy, He several times indicates that Livingston had less information than he actually did, *Ib; True and Real Account*; Mackay, *Memoirs*, 93–5, 96.

132. *Ib.*, 95; *Est. Procs.*, ii, 153–4; Shaw, *Moray*, 226; *Melvilles & Leslies*, ii, 151–2, Livingston to Mackay, [May 1690].

133. Livingston and Mackay mention the distance of the second ford. Lachlan Shaw claimed that the ford was below Dalchapple, but this is over a mile below the church. The MS account on which his version is largely based makes it clear that the hidden glen down which Livingston marched brought him out opposite Cromdale Church, but seems to imply that he crossed there. One early report claimed that the ford was upstream from the church. *Ib.*, 152; Mackay, *Memoirs*, 95; *Est. Procs.*, ii, 154; *Memoirs of Dundee*, 32; *HMCR Le Fleming*, 270, newsletter, 10 May 1690; Rennie, *Clansmen*, 107; Shaw, *Moray*, 226; SCA Blairs Letters, Box Y, unsigned, 63, 'An acct of the affaires of Scotland'. 10 June 1690.

134. Later Jacobite and highland writers tried to turn defeat into partial victory by claiming that this stand was general, and that they drove off the dragoons with great slaughter. It was the same impulse which made some Jacobite tack on to the Williamite song 'The Haughs of Cromdale' a happy ending making Montrose's earlier victory at Auldearn an avenging sequel. It was more appropriate than he knew, since, as Stevenson has shown, Montrose came close to being surprised as disastrously as Buchan. *Ib; Macfarlane, Gen. Colls.*, i, 140; Macpherson, 'Gleanings', *TGSI*, xx, 238, Buchan to Cluny, 22 May 1690; Mackay, *Memoirs*, 96; *Memoirs of Dundee*, 32; *Memoirs of Locheill*, 294–6; J. Hogg, *The Jacobite Relics of Scotland* (Edinburgh, 1819), 3–5; Stevenson, *Alasdair MacColla*, 179–80; *Melvilles & Leslies*, ii, 152–3, Livingston to Mackay, [May 1690].

135. *Ib.*, 154; *Est. Procs.* , ii, 154; Carleton, *Memoirs*, 42–3.

136. Rennie, *Clansmen*, 107; Shaw, *Moray*, 226.

137. Carleton, *Memoirs*, 43–4; *Melvilles & Leslies*, ii, 152, Livingston to Mackay, [May 1690].

138. *Ib.*, 152–3; *RPCS*, xv, 304–5; Mackay, *Memoirs*, 96; *Est. Procs.*, ii, 154, 157; Macpherson, *Loyall Dissuasive*, 197; Macpherson, 'Gleanings' *TGSI*, xx, 240, Hill to Cluny, 17 June 1690; 'The Camerons in the '15', *ib.*, xxvi, 68; Shaw, *Moray*, 226; SCA, Blairs Letters, Box Y, unsigned 63, 'An acct of the affaires of Scotland', 10 June 1690; *True and Real Account*.

139. *Ib.*; *APS*, ix, App. 60; *London Gazette*, No. 2556, 8–12 May 1690; Carleton, *Memoirs*, 45; SRO GD 26/viii, passim.

140. *True and Real Account*; *The Scotch and Irish Post* (London, 1690); *Chiefs of Colquhoun*, ii, 218–19, J. Macfarlane to J. Colquhoun, 6 May 1690; Rennie, *Clansmen*, 107; Shaw, *Moray*, 226; Macpherson, *Loyall Dissuasive*, 213.

141. *Ib.*, 197; *Seafield Corr.*, 59, G. Grant to Findlater, 9 May 1690; Macpherson, 'Gleanings', *TGSI*, xx, 236–7, Livingston to Cluny, 6 May 1690; *ib.*, 237–8, Buchan to same, 22 May 1690; *Est. Procs.*, ii, 166–7, 171.

142. *Ib.*, 166–7, 171, 174; *HMCR Le Fleming*, 272, newsletter, 27 May 1690; *RPCS*, xv, 253; Sir W. Fraser, *History of the Carnegies, Earls of Southesk*, 2 vols. (Edinburgh, 1867), i 196, Sir D. Carnegie's memorial.

143. *APS*, ix, 182; *Est. Procs.*, ii, 174, 181; *RPCS*, xv, 304.

144. *Ib.*, 266, 304, 376; SRO GD 26/viii/99, Lt-Col Buchan to Hamilton, 18 Oct. 1690; NLS MS 975 fol. 63, Prisoners' petition to Argyll, [1690].

145. *RPCS*, xv, 264, 514–15; SRO PC 1/49, 188, 192; GD 112/40/4/6/31, P. Birnie to Breadalbane, 13 Jan. 1692; GD 170/3034, A. & J. Maclean to ?, 9 June 1691.

146. *LJ*, xvii, 493, Sir J. Maclean's examination, 11 Mar. [1704]; *Est. Procs.*, ii, 163, 166; SCA, Blairs Letters, Box Y, unsigned, 'An acct of the affaires of Scotland'. 10 June 1690.

147. BL MS Lansdowne 1163B, 27, Melfort to Innes, 6 June 1690 (NS); *ib.*, 34, same to Mary of Modena, 6 June 1690 (NS).

148. *Ib.*, 2, same to Father Maxwell, 6 June 1690(NS).

149. *Ib.*, A, 239–40, same to James, 16 May 1690(NS); *ib.*, 263, same to James, 1 June 1690(NS); *Analecta Hibernica*, iv, 116–17, Tyrconnell to Mary of Modena, 2 Apr. 1690(NS); *ib.*, 132, same to same, 24 June/4 July 1690; SRO GD 26/viii/93a/5, Instructions to Annandale, No. 9.

150. *Ib.*, 93a/1, James to Annandale, 13 Apr. 1690; Macleod, *Book of Dunvegan*, i, 142–3, same to Macleod, 29 May 1690 (for his fatuous optimism); Hopkins, 'Aspects of Jacobite Conspiracy', 45, 341–2, 348–9; BL MS Lansdowne 1163C, 238–9, Melfort to Mary of Modena, 25 Nov. 1690(NS).

151. *Melvilles & Leslies*, iii, 229–30, Montgomerie to James, [1693]; Wodrow, *Analecta*, i, 197; *Leven & Melville*, 508, Annandale's confession, 14 Aug. 1690.

152. Annandale claims that Arran attended, but Breadalbane's letter implies not. *Ib.*, 508–10; SRO GD 406/1/3371, Breadalbane to Arran, 8 May [1690]; Balcarres, *Memoirs*, 61.

153. *Ib.*, 61–2; *Est. Procs.*, ii, 153; *Leven & Melville*, 454, Ross's answers, June 1690; *ib.*, 484n, Mary of Modena to [Club leaders], 1 May 1690(NS); *ib.*, 510–11, Annandale's confession, 14 Aug. 1690.

154. *Ib.*, 511; Balcarres, *Memoirs*, 63; *Melvilles & Leslies*, iii, 230, Montgomerie to James [1693]; Dalrymple, *Memoirs*, ii, 'Appendix to Part II' (all references are to this, the third pagination in the volume), 161, Mary to William, 16/26 Aug. 1690.

155. *Ib.*, 202–3, Tarbat to William, 15 May 1690; *APS*, ix, 134; *Leven & Melville*, 508, Annandale's confession, 14 Aug. 1690.

156. NLS MS 7012 fol. 65v, Lady Roxburghe to Tweeddale, 6 May 1690; *CSPD 1690–1*, 209–10, Tarbat to William, [May 1690]; *ib. 1691–2*, 60–1, same to same, [July–August 1690].

157. *Ib.*, 61–2; Macpherson, 'Gleanings', *TGSI*, xx, 238, Buchan to Cluny, 8 June 1690; *Melvilles & Leslies*, ii, 155, Hill to Melville, 2 June 1690; SRO GD 26/ix/274, same to same, 19 June 1690; GD 112/43/1/1/6, Warrants to Breadalbane and Barcaldine, 23 May 1690; GD 170/629/26, Barcaldine to Breadalbane, 1 June 1690.

158. *Ib.*, GD 50/10/1/19, Breadalbane to Buchan, 7 June 1690; Mackay, *Memoirs*, 196, Mackay to William, 8 June 1690.

159. *Est. Procs.*, ii, 178, 185–6, 198; Burnet. *History*, iv, 111–12.

160. He claimed later, implausibly, that the Presbyterians tried to murder him as he returned. Mackay, *Memoirs*, 108; *ib.*, 199, Mackay to William, 8 June 1690; SRO GD 112/43/1/99, 'Breadalbane's Life', 3; GD 26/xiii/78 fol. 158, Melville's notes; Drumlanrig, Queensberry Papers, bundle 1347, Breadalbane to [Melville], 28 June 1690.

161. Burnet, *History*, iv, 112–13; *Melvilles & Leslies*, ii, 226, Montgomerie to James, [1693]; *Leven & Melville*, 523–5, Narrative on Montgomerie, 6/16 Sept. 1690.

162. *Ib.*, 552–3, Tarbat to Melville, 21 Oct. 1690; Fountainhall, *Historical Observes*, 115–16; *Fasti Ecclesiae Scoticanae*, ed. H. Scott, 8 vols. (Edinburgh, 1915–50), i, 132; SRO GD 26/xiii/78 fol. 178v, Melville's notes.

7

The Williamite Offensive (June–December 1690)

On 30 June, the Anglo-Dutch Fleet was defeated off Beachy Head, providing an excellent opportunity for a French army to invade or for the Jacobites to rise against the few troops left in England. The result suggested that the rebel highlanders were providing a massive diversion from a non-existent main event: the French had no invading force ready, and the English Jacobites no organisation or solid plans for rising. On 1 July, William decisively defeated James at the Boyne. The Irish army rallied in the west, repulsed William at Limerick, and succeeded in prolonging the war for another year. James, however, after ungenerously denouncing them for cowardice, had taken panic flight to France.

On arriving, James established a court at St. Germain. The few men of real political stature among his followers were not appointed to the weak Cabinet of five or six courtiers who decided policy. Father Lewis Innes, the Principal of the Scots College at Paris, had managed Jacobite correspondence in his absence, and James appointed him Secretary for Scotland, despite objections that 'he had very little insight into businesse' and that 'his being a Priest would render him odious ... to the Scotch nation'. He served reluctantly and worked for Melfort's return.[1] Gordon, still harassed from afar by Melfort's ceaseless malice, had only a Bedchamber place, but highlanders might gain informal access to James via him or an Irish Macdonnell colleague.[2]

James and his ministers were anxious to send the highlanders relief, caring little in comparison for the more important war in Ireland. St. Germain, of course, was almost entirely dependent on Louis XIV. They repeatedly urged him to land troops in Scotland, since the English might welcome an invasion from there, but not directly from France or Ireland — or, at least, to keep the clans supplied as a diversion. It nearly always seemed possible that just a little more solicitation, another memorial, might persuade him, totally transforming the situation. One Jacobite minister later described then as 'still lying at the pool to watch when the angel moves the waters' — the imagery of paralytics;[3] and this encouraged a dangerous procrastination in Jacobite policy. However, James could have few such hopes in late 1690. After his flight, the French clearly believed nothing he said. In October, he proposed an invasion by 5,000 troops, but was told that Louis dared not risk his warships so far away as Scotland.[4]

Macqueen's arrival in August with letters from Buchan and the clans, reporting their wretched condition and warning James that they must submit unless sent relief, did persuade Louis to equip two small frigates at Dunkirk to carry messengers with money and letters to Scotland. They sailed in late September, but the captains disobeyed strict orders not to attack merchant shipping, and both ships had to return badly mauled.[5] Even on this level the French were unenthusiastic. The Minister of War demanded back the arms supplied for shipment to Montgomerie, for which the clans still hoped.[6] A later private proposal by Sir Alexander Maclean to establish a base for St. Malo privateers in the Western Isles was unsuccessful.[7] 'The King ... is at this tyme indeuoring to send what help he can to the Hylands, since he cannot ... send what he would,' wrote Mary of Modena to Buchan in August, and he consoled them with military promotions: Sir George Barclay, for instance, was made Brigadier.[8]

Two months before the Boyne, James had eventually organised an expedition which should have relieved the pressure on the Lochaber clans. The captured *Janet* left Dublin carrying Seaforth, now promoted to Marquess and Major-General, some officers, a company of Irish grenadiers as a bodyguard and a cargo of corn and ammunition.[9] After long delays from contrary winds, he landed on 20 May at his castle of Eilean Donan opposite the east end of Skye. Vassals, even from distant isles, and 'Great Numbers of common People came in also well armed, and rejoiced exceedingly at the sight of their Lord'. He sent the Macrae minister of Kintail as his representative to inform the lowland clan gentry of his arrival (upon which a catholic priest allegedly seized the manse). The Fraser country was simultaneously opened to him when its garrison accidentally burned Erchless. He sent Cluny a colonel's commisssion — with threats, Cluny claimed to Livingston, but actually with assurances carried by young Mackintosh of Borlum, Gordon's agent, now rehabilitated. He twice sent his senior professional officer, Major Bernardi, to consult with Buchan, and the Jacobite leaders felt fresh confidence.[10]

Yet meanwhile Seaforth did nothing. He spoke of visiting his estates in Lewis (to which he sent the wretched lapsed priest Con). He summoned several Mackenzies to visit him — but for private, not Jacobite reasons. He claimed to be delaying only until Berwick landed with a large Irish army in Galloway.[11] In fact, according to Hill, after their abortive winter activities, even the western Mackenzies were mostly unwilling to rise except on compulsion, having just refused a demand from Colin. Seaforth himself was in constant contact with a strong Williamite. In February 1689, some Munster Protestants had revolted under Sir Thomas Southwell's command, had surrendered on condition their lives should be spared, but had nevertheless been tried and condemned for treason. Irish pressure prevented James from pardoning them outright and 'there hardly passed a Council day but there was a motion for their execution'. Seaforth, Southwell's friend, could only ensure his safety by carrying him along with him; but it meant that he had him always at his elbow, preaching surrender.[12]

This provided a splendid opportunity for Hill, whom Seaforth trusted as his father's friend. Southwell travelled to Inverness bearing his demands: that he should not have the oaths put to him, and should be allowed to reside at Brahan with the (valueless) garrison removed, and that a Protestant Mackenzie should replace Balnagown as Sheriff. The news that Buchan was negotiating with Breadalbane, and Lochiel and Glengarry with Hill himself, probably satisfied his conscience over this. Hill expected that the demands over Brahan and Balnagown would both be granted. Melville sent a pass permitting him to submit formally, although dubious about allowing him Brahan. By late June, Hill and the Dowager Countess seemed about to secure his submission: he was weary of 'wyld places' and awaited only the removal of the garrison.[13]

Seaforth's arrival had given the Jacobites their last chance to extend and strengthen their rising. They had failed, and, their limited period of grace over, faced attack by large forces from two directions. Forced to disperse to defend their homes, they could resist neither. On 14 May, Major Ferguson's expedition sailed from Greenock, ordered to ravage the rebel islands, destroy all boats and cut communications. He might accept the inhabitants' submission if they disarmed and took the oaths. He should obtain Macleod's support and, if possible, occupy Mull with Campbell help. The ships also carried the materials for the fort at Inverlochy. Their flagship, the 32-gun frigate *Dartmouth*, noted for her manoeuvrability, had engaged the forts to cover the relief of Derry. Her captain, Commodore Edward Pottinger (brother of Belfast's 'Sovereign'), knew highland waters well. So did his Scottish second-in-command, the survivor of the two merchant captains who carried the provisions to Derry. The squadron contained three English warships, the Scots armed ship *Lamb*, hired by the Council, and four merchantmen. Ferguson's 6–800 troops were drawn from Mackay's three 'Dutch' regiments and Argyll's.[14]

Despite Young's victory a year earlier, Kintyre and its islands were still not properly subdued: Argyll arrested men in Jura even in August.[15] Therefore, the islands were raided and houses, corn and cattle destroyed: Gigha (17 May), Cara (18 May), Colonsay and part of Jura (19 May). Some Kintyre gentry who had served with Sir Alexander Maclean, McAlisters of Loup and Kinloch and Macdonald of Largie, had returned defiantly to their homes, but now hurried to Edinburgh to take the oaths with Argyll as cautioner.[16] The squadron then sailed to Mull, and burned areas round Lochbuie and Aros. However, the Macleans had gathered 5–600 men near Duart, and Ferguson, obeying Mackay's strict orders to take no risks, had the Council order Argyll to raise 600 Argyllshire men to join them. These would be ready only in late June, and meanwhile, leaving patrols to cut Maclean's communications, the ships dispersed to raid smaller isles, Coll (probably where Pottinger took prisoner the episcopalian Dean Fraser of the Isles), Rhum, Eigg, where they found only one old man (2 June), and after vainly awaiting the inhabitants' submission, Canna (6 June). 'Upon some Islands,' wrote Pottinger, 'The Souldiers have [left] scarce a beast, nor a Hutt to shelter in.'[17]

The squadron sailed for Skye. Ferguson landed with all his men at Isle Ornsay harbour, while Pottinger scattered 700 Macdonalds with cannon-fire. Old Sir Donald had gone to Ireland to request help, and, even though 200 reinforcements were preparing to cross from the mainland, young Sir Donald, who had always been less enthusiastic, was reluctant to risk further devastation. On 8 June, he came aboard the *Dartmouth* off Armadale and gave his word of honour not to take arms against William's government, nor to assist those who did. Pottinger also began a friendly correspondence with Seaforth and encouraged the Macleods in their loyalty.[18]

Unfortunately, not only had three men from the *Dartmouth* been killed straggling from the boats during the landing; despite young Sir Donald's submission, 'this disorderly Clann', catching a fourth who had hidden a few days later, hanged him; and a boat's crew from Eigg who happened to be in Skye were involved. To avoid driving young Sir Donald back to resistance, Pottinger and Ferguson determined to take revenge only on Eigg, and they returned to the island about 12 June. Although the fighting men were still absent, the other inhabitants, apart from a few who had fled on a second-sighted man's deathbed warning, were there, unsuspecting. The troops and sailors burst upon them and committed murders and rapes, unchecked and even condoned by the commanders. The inhabitants were Catholics, and one of the massacres a catholic priest described may have happened here: discovering their religion from their rosaries, the soldiers bound people to stakes and slaughtered them.[19] The atrocities resembled those Ferguson's grandson was to carry out on his notorious 1746 cruise in the Isles; and, as they are known only by chance from writers on the second sight, it is possible they were repeated elsewhere. Surviving logs omit the massacre, and Pottinger's guilty conscience made him write an extraordinarily hypocritical letter, claiming to have killed only eight highlanders in the whole campaign so far. 'Those under protection (I presume) shelters the women & Children to whom the Souldiers were strictly charged not to molest, either in person or apparell.' Yet Mackay had strictly forbidden any harming of women and children, even when rigorously laying waste the most defiant rebels' islands, and Pottinger clearly feared exposure. An isolated major atrocity might not be noticed, but a series would have been, and, after such a letter, would have blighted Pottinger's career, even outside Scotland.[20]

The ships briefly raided the lochs opposite Skye and, ineffectually, Carnaburg.[21] Provision ships for the Lochaber garrison were arriving, and the Campbells had assembled at Dunstaffnage. Following Mackay's orders, Ferguson took them aboard and, on 26 June, sailed with the *Dartmouth* up Loch Linnhe. According to Balhaldie's original account, Lochiel saw them coming and gathered 200 Camerons. He sent to Keppoch and Glengarry to honour previous promises of help, but they failed to come — not surprisingly, since they awaited Mackay's advance. Lochiel and Buchan helplessly watched the ships land their men at Corpach. Leaving the merchantmen in Loch Eil, Ferguson occupied and entrenched Achnacarry to await Mackay.[22]

Startling news had called Pottinger away. Old Sir Donald Macdonald had returned from Ireland in a French frigate with letters, commissions, '£1,000' to distribute among the clans (and, perhaps, an earl's title for himself), the last communication from James before the Boyne.[23] The frigate put in at Eilean Donan in late June. Sir Donald offered a prize ship filled with meal to Seaforth, but he refused and ordered his men not to touch it on pain of death. Sir Donald carried it to eastern Skye for unloading. Pottinger advised his old acquaintance to follow his son's example; but he was exalted with Jacobite enthusiasm, and young Sir Donald avoided his curse only by persuading him that he had merely made the concession he himself would accept, 'to live quietly till such tyme only, as I see a more fair opportunity to Serue my great Master, then as yet I doe'.[24]

The collapse of Breadalbane's negotiations should have left Mackay ready to march and plant garrisons, including Inverlochy, while the dry season lasted. Ferguson's departure had increased his impatience, and on 17 May he had given the Council a memorial frankly denouncing their irresolution and calling for the borrowing of £5,000 sterling to furnish the army with a month's pay — after which it would march even without proper provisions.[25] There was no real hope that the money would be found: Melville was expending £4,000 William had sent from England for the Fort William expedition on current military expenses. Some regiments were near disintegration, and Argyll's mutinied and had to be quieted by private borrowings. Even though Mackay's 'Dutch' regiments were less in arrears, their higher expectations made them equally liable to mutiny.[26] Heeding, to Mackay's fury, protests from the overburdened shires, the Council ordered for him only 600 baggage horses and 500 pioneers. Here also further delay would only make matters worse, since Melville had appointed an incompetent favourite as commissary. Yet he hindered Mackay's departure with constant obstructions until Mackay wrote directly to William at Chester and obtained his order.[27]

Mackay disregarded Melville's talk of plots and ascribed his attempts to delay his march to (at best) excessive timidity or envy.[28] Yet Melville had rational causes for alarm which he could not reveal to Mackay, too often the Club's dupe. He now knew much, but far from everything, about the Montgomerie Plot and its startling ramifications. Participants now retiring after its parliamentary defeat to the Highlands or the Borders (where disaffected gentry were already absconding to the Cheviots to 'hunt') might be following a careful second-string plan for a revolt. Others were in hiding, as were enough of Dundee's followers for a dangerous little rising. Yet the necessary steps to seize them might drive the 'presbyterians', still fearing the government tyranny the Club had warned them of, into rebellion.[29] William, in a gamble like Mackay's, had stripped England of troops for Ireland, including, despite Mackay's own requests, the regiments (except Berkeley's dragoons) which had formed a reserve on the Borders in 1689.[30] Besides highland garrisons and mounted men (including Drumlanrig's Horse Guards), Mackay left Melville three battalions near Edinburgh, Glencairn's regiment at Perth (under orders to retreat if seriously attacked) and the wreck of Kenmure's at Stirling; but Melville had secretly been warned that three of these regiments supported the Plot.[31] The Master of Forbes, with four troops of horse and dragoons, local militia, and imperfect support in Aberdeenshire must defend the North-East while the infantry regiments joined Livingston.[32]

In one sense, Mackay, who left Perth with seven infantry battalions, the 'Dutch Brigade' and Argyll's regiment, Menzies's highland company, which left a gap at Weem the Jacobites exploited, and four or more troops of horse, at least 4,000 in all (though he, typically, claimed only 3,000), acted very cautiously. Rather than advance directly on Lochaber (his plan in early June), through passes where the highlanders might ambush him — or simply check him until hunger forced his retreat — he sent a false vanguard towards Blair, and then marched on 21 June via Strathardle, Braemar, Strathdon and Strathavon, areas where the highlanders, though rebellious, were dangerous only to small parties, to the Spey. On 27 June, at Culnakyle — as far from Inverlochy as Dunkeld, complained one observer — he held rendezvous with Livingston, who brought his dragoons, Grant's, Angus's and Leslie's foot, two highland companies and 300 Mackays for foraging, in all 2–3,000 men.[33] United, they outnumbered several times any force the Lochaber clans could now raise. Yet Mackay's caution masked a gigantic gamble: that no sudden outside danger would threaten the denuded Lowlands, that the rebellious episcopalian North-East would remain passive under the thinnest military control and that the rebels would act only on the defensive. To be certain of completing its mission quickly, the expedition must be numerically overwhelming; but Melville's later reproach, that Mackay was risking the loss of Scotland to gain Inverlochy, was not entirely hysterical. A somewhat smaller force would still have been overwhelming; but, showing a caution over his own role inappropriate for such a gamble, he reduced the Lowlands forces below the danger-point, though aware that even a slight setback there might provoke a dangerous Jacobite outbreak.[34] When bad news poured in from England soon after he marched, and Cannon and Buchan momentarily showed a flash of Dundee's spirit, he had to fall back on his basic, secret assumption: that once Inverlochy was built and holding down Lochaber, he could on his return retrieve any temporary disaster.

The risks seemed greatest in the North. Although he had always denounced the negotiations of Tarbat (whom he accused of Jacobitism) and Hill with the clans, Mackay nevertheless gambled on their main claim, that Seaforth would not act. If he did, he could raise well over 1,000 Mackenzies (though presumably not the 3,000 Mackenzie of Coul claimed for him), and Mackay had originally planned to have a second army, 1,500 soldiers and clansmen, operating north of Loch Ness to keep him in check.[35] Now although Seaforth was still 'hovering', he left only Strathnaver's regiment to garrison Inverness, Urquhart and Erchless, supplemented by 600 Rosses and Sutherland men, and backed by two cavalry troops at Elgin. Furthermore, the Ross-shire and Inverness-shire governing elites were violently divided. Balnagown was almost universally hated; and all the other local leaders on whom Mackay relied, Strathnaver, Grant, Culloden, even Munro of Foulis, were in Edinburgh for Parliament or other business.[36]

The united force was badly short of provisions. The commissaries had furnished only meal — living off victual rents, they thought it answered everything, said Hill — there were too few baggage horses to carry enough, and it proved rotten. The army was exceptionally dependent on foraging, and to save rations Mackay dismissed the few pioneers, relying on his soldiers to build the fort. Baggage-horses were constantly stolen. Mackay was forced to start up the Spey towards Inverlochy without any certainty that Ferguson and the provision ships had arrived, 'which is som what contrarie to the maxime of war'. Although Strathspey inevitably suffered from the army, he offered to pay even the ambiguous Cluny for cattle and sheep, but threatened to devastate Badenoch unless they appeared.[37]

Mackay also used the demands to deceive the enemy about his intended route. The best and obvious one was to the head of the Spey and down the Roy through Glen Roy. However, the clans must make a stand shortly, and, as Mackay correctly suspected, 800 men awaited him in Glen Roy, hoping for a second Mulroy. On 1

July, while a mounted 'vanguard' made a feint advance up the Spey, Mackay marched south- west from Cluny over the hills towards Glen Spean, difficult country where the army often had to proceed in single file. Some enemy highlanders soon discovered them and opened a heavy sniping fire from the mountain sides, but a party which tried to raid the baggage was repulsed. The army stood to arms under occasional fire all night. Next day, as they came down Glen Spean, 200 highlanders attacked the vanguard but were beaten back, and the clans then scattered to protect their own families, cattle and goods — an easier task since the people were then at the shielings. On 3 July, Mackay reached Inverlochy.[38] When it became clear that he could not be resisted, Buchan rode east with seventy horsemen hoping to raise the Aberdeenshire Lowlands, Cannon south-east with thirty to Perthshire. They took no infantry. Some remnants of the Irish regiment were with Glengarry, since Mackay might be planning to besiege Invergarry, and the bulk with Sir John Maclean in Mull.[39]

Starting on 5 July, Mackay built the new Fort William in eleven days. Lack of time forced him to use the old Cromwellian foundations on Loch Linnhe-side by the River Nevis, although they were insufficiently firm and the site was dominated by nearby hills and without water supply. Although shaped according to the best military rules, it was merely an earthwork with a palisade on top: one of the soldiers building it called it a 'trinch'.[40] Mackay borrowed twelve cannon from Pottinger's squadron, the heavier ones to point towards the sea, for fear of a French attack.[41] To Mackay's anger, the chiefs, buoyed up by reports that Arran and Breadalbane were rising and by Sir Donald's distribution of the money, made no advances to him. As the army badly lacked provisions for its own use and the fort, he sent out parties to make massive seizures of cattle, which penetrated as far as Appin.[42] Although Mackay disbelieved in his policy of negotiating, there was never any doubt that Hill, who knew the area and some of the chiefs and gentry (including his secret paid agents in Cromwell's time),[43] but who would be impartial between them, should be Governor. Contrary to the normal maxims, Mackay appointed the highlander Robert Menzies his deputy. Hill was promised a new regiment, and, until this could be formed, was left for a garrison nine companies of Grant's, four of Angus's, mutinous until promised early recall, four of Argyll's, and Menzies's and Balnagown's highland companies, 1,200 in all, with many close friends or relations among the Jacobites.[44]

But for the Council's repeated orders to return on the disastrous news from England, Mackay would have shipped a large detachment under Ferguson to conquer the Isles, or at least Argyll's regiment to invade Mull. Instead, only a deatchment under Auchinbreck embarked for a brief cruise. Mingary Castle, left unguarded even after James's award to Lochiel, was seized and garrisoned. It was probably also now that Maclean of Coll submitted to the government.[45] Pottinger sailed to Skye and boldly navigated two narrow races to seize Sir Donald's prize. On his approach, Sir Donald burned it, and Pottinger in revenge destroyed Armadale, 'the prettyest house in the Highlands', by bombardment and a landing party covered by his guns, which also carefully burned the home of Sir Donald's mistress. On 21 July, lack of provisions forced Pottinger to sail for Greenock, having, by constant movement and unpredictable raids, prevented the Isles from helping to oppose Mackay.[46]

The Council's orders, shortage of provisions and baggage-horses, and an outbreak of dysentery that soon produced five shiploads of sick men, prevented Mackay from returning via Inverness, besieging Invergarry en route.[47] He began his return march on 18 July. He was still anxious to avoid Glen Roy, and led his army up Glen Gloy to the upper Roy and from there into Badenoch. On the 21st, he took the horse and dragoons to Ruthven Castle, and left the independent company of Mackays there to repair and garrison it. This time, the Jacobites made no attempt to recapture it, and, although some Badenoch men robbed and stripped stragglers, Mackay was not opposed in his return.[48] Meeting Atholl en route, he suddenly became convinced of his sincerity and potential value to William's cause. He reached Perth on 26 July. Dysentery was spreading, but the campaign had gained for Mackay one great advantage, which he had previously lacked — the love and trust of the army.[49]

Although the *Lamb* was hired to carry supplies to Fort William, the Council failed to use the dry weather to send there adequate stocks of provisions and building materials. The soldiers were unruly, and within a few days desertion reduced them to 900.[50] Hill nevertheless opened negotiations with the clans, although their parliamentary forfaulture that month created a further obstacle. Mackay and other officers violently opposed his policy, wanting the rebels' lands wasted until they were terrorised into submitting unconditionally; but Hill knew that doing this in summer would merely drive the clans to the hills, desperate and ready to join Buchan to recoup their losses from the Lowlands.[51] On 21 July, Lochiel sent asking him not to attack them until they had held a meeting to consider whether they could come in on terms. On 31 July, Glengarry, Clanranald, Keppoch, young Sir Donald and MacNeil deputed him to gain more time until they could consult the remaining chiefs. They meanwhile allowed their tenants and clan gentry to submit independently, and most inhabitants of Appin and Glencoe had done so, although not MacIain or Robert Stewart. The Tutor of Appin independently offered to surrender Castle Stalker if he could be recompensed the money he had spent in garrisoning it.[52] Meetings continued throughout August, and Hill suggested that the grant of £5–6,000 to buy the superiorities from Argyll and Gordon and an agreement that Keppoch should be secure and pay rent to Mackintosh would pacify them. The garrison traded with local people, Lochaber was quiet, and, although Sir John Maclean launched attacks on Campbell-held islands, satisfaction was promised.[53]

Deliberating and allowing the common people to submit might, of course, merely be a trick such as Lochiel had played on the first Inverlochy garrison to gain protection from attack until a more favourable opportunity for rising occurred. Although Glengarry was involved in the talks, Hill found him 'too much begotted' towards the Jacobites by the influence of Sir George Barclay, who had stayed with him.[54] Yet, when inflated accounts of Buchan's genuine successes came, he joined Lochiel in assuring Hill they would not rise to support him. Lochiel went further, reminding the young men, who were encouraged by reports that James had landed in England, how often similar claims had proved untrue, and discounting Buchan since, 'tho' all Scotland were in armes for King James, if England were not for him, or nott divided amongst themselves, 'twould all signifie nothinge'.[55] Buchan was furious with him, and swore that Hill's persuasion (which contrasted favourably with his own increasing use of threats), had damaged the Jacobite cause more than any troops.[56] Hill's own negotiations showed him how far Breadalbane's, under the cover of a pacification, had been intended to keep the clans in arms, and inspired a deep dislike and distrust of him.[57]

When Buchan and Cannon launched their raids towards the Lowlands, the French were off England, the English government's order to stop mail at the Borders had left Melville apprehensive in the dark, and the Jacobites were reporting not only Beachy Head but a successful Irish invasion of England under James. The news which should have counterbalanced all this, the Boyne, was neutralised by bold claims that William had been killed there, which were widely believed in the North-East (though not Lochaber).[58] The Borders were in ferment as Home and Maxwell of Springkell organised for a rising. Throughout July and August, groups of horsemen mustered, rode about and occasionally even skirmished with soldiers.[59]

Melville could not know of a blow which destroyed the plot's coherence. Arran, who had campaigned in France, had had a regiment under James, and had vainly trusted Montgomerie to obtain him a lieutenant-general's commission, seemed the obvious choice for leader. Yet from his hiding-place, he several times ordered his supporters to gather for a rising, only to stay away, and when Home sent to him to co-operate, he 'would not give way to it, pretending he had no orders from the King, and so the business was crusht'.[60] He had earlier used that argument when some highlanders begged him to come to the hills as their general, and they appealed to James before the Boyne. From France, he sent a lieutenant-general's commission, and Arran, cornered, refused to accept it until an invading force landed, when he would rise with all his friends. He instead fled briefly to London and begot a bastard on the Duchess of Cleveland's daughter. Several highland chiefs never forgave his desertion.[61]

Arran's defection was a severe blow to Cannon. Another came when he wrote on 4 July from Loch Rannoch-head to Cluny to raise his clan and join him in Balquhidder: Cluny did not stir.[62] He had been acting ambiguously since May, specially applying to James via Sir Donald, but sending his letters from Seaforth to Livingston. He had to temporise, Buchan admitted in May, to preserve his country, and needed also to get the Macpherson prisoners from Cromdale released. Indeed, if retaining Williamite favour was his main aim, he mismanaged it, failing to visit either Livingston or Mackay, which brought his father-in-law Campbell of Calder also under suspicion, and, Hill informed him, was the main reason for planting the Ruthven garrison.[63] Glengarry believed that Cluny's failure now was not on his own initiative but the advice of Sir Aeneas Macpherson, Gordon's former agent.[64] His accusation (confirmed by events in 1691) was plausible, for Macpherson, who had come to Scotland and had been captured and imprisoned with Neville Payne, was secretly, for all his later denials, spying on him for Melville. Macpherson, however, was never a reliable traitor. When the Council decided to torture Payne, he sent them a threatening anonymous letter which made them postpone it for four months.[65]

In early July, Cannon was near the foot of Loch Tay, raiding the Perthshire Lowlands. This helped to create a climate of suspicion, in which highland watches were disarmed or even imprisoned; but it raised no recruits in Atholl.[66] His force, all mounted, included Dundee's brother (now the Viscount), Macnachtan, Robertson of Struan, Ballechin, his brother and their sons, MacCoul of Kindrogan in Strathardle, and Duncan Menzies, about 60 in all. However, having marched south of Loch Tay to Balquhidder, they remained undisturbed there for a week, coercing inhabitants into joining them and gathering Macgregors to obtain 300 foot.[67] They could normally have done nothing; but Melville held the forces paralysed, not daring to commit them even on the Highland Line for fear of a rebellion elsewhere.[68] Cannon, therefore, was able to raid almost unhindered, deliberately concentrating on the lands of known Williamites north and south of Forth, from Campbell of Aberuchill to fairly humble soldiers. Once his force routed some government dragoons and chased them to the Park of Stirling.[69]

Cannon could gain no significant reinforcement from the neighbouring Lowlands. In late June, as the crisis developed, the government had called out the fencible men of the South-West. At least 14,000 immediately assembled, and flocked to Glasgow to oppose the raids in such numbers that the Council on 24 July had to dismiss all but 4,500, whom they stationed at Glasgow, Stirling and Falkirk until Mackay's forces had returned and revictualled. As many were fanatics, the government's relations with them were somewhat uneasy. The party sent to Stirling tried to rabble ministers there.[70] Such incidents added to episcopalian discontent; but Buchan's first foray into Aberdeenshire with seventy horse gave no sign this might matter. Descending to the plain, he was routed, losing the Earl of Buchan and other officers prisoners, by the Master of Forbes, who went on to scatter local rebel parties. In late July, Buchan, with three skeleton troops under himself, Dunfermline and Frendraught, rejoined Cannon, whose Macgregors had dispersed with their spoil. Montgomerie claimed later that vigorous action by Buchan would have brought supporters flocking (as it did just afterwards in Aberdeenshire). Instead, he claimed to have express orders not to fight, and, even before the pursuers set out from Stirling, his party retired north-east. Mackay's Perth forces failed to intercept them at Weem, and he went to Edinburgh, confident all danger was over.[71]

However, Farquharson of Inverey was still in arms in Braemar, and there and in Cromar raised 800 men on Buchan's and Cannon's arrival. Leaving 160 to blockade Abergeldie, they marched across to the garrison of Kildrummy on the upper Don. Mackay had already reinforced the Master of Forbes's four troops of horse and dragoons with four more, and with these he advanced to meet them. Buchan skilfully spread out his foot and mixed baggage beasts with his horse to give the illusion of numbers. Forbes, thunderstruck, held a council of war which agreed to retire to Aberdeen until infantry regiments should arrive. The retreat rapidly became a wild panic flight, from which Forbes's reputation never recovered. Mackay in such circumstances had counter-bluffed and held his position — crucial, the contrast would show, for preventing the spread of rebellion.[72]

Kildrummy was captured and burned.[73] Buchan pursued down through the Garioch, halting close to Aberdeen, which Forbes tried to make defensible with barricades and cannon. His position was more insecure since the magistrates' and inhabitants' strong episcopalian feelings, heightened by the recent stay of Angus's Cameronians, made them susceptible to rebels who declared themselves for James and episcopacy. An almost entirely local army would not arouse memories of Montrose's 1644 sack of Aberdeen. The government's position soon received another blow. The Council had already sent Cunningham with three and a half infantry regiments and a few horse to secure Aberdeen. He, on first hearing of the retreat, declared 'he would not put off his clothes till he got there'; then halted at Montrose for Livingston's dragoons, which encouraged the Jacobites to march south. Livingston himself fell dangerously ill with dysentery, throwing the whole burden on Mackay.[74]

The recruits Buchan gained now were mounted. Hamilton wrote: 'by this number of horse they have got yow may judge of the disaffection of the Countrey, ... where the King had one Enemy here a year & a half ago he has ten now'.[75] Some, like Sir Peter Fraser of Dores, would probably have joined anyway. Most, however, including the most prominent recruit, the Earl of Kintore's son Lord Inverurie, would not, if Buchan had not been able to advance unopposed to Aberdeen. Although the mixture of encouragements and threats which seduced them differed from case to case, the danger to their houses and lands was obviously among the strongest motives. Inverurie, for instance, claimed that he had no Jacobite contacts. Buchan's rapid advance just prevented him from reaching and garrisoning the family home. Receiving Buchan's letter threatening to ravage Kintore's lands, he went to his camp purely to negotiate, but was kept there by threat and persuasions for some weeks. Others forced to join had actually followed Forbes until his flight.[76] Yet more positive motives also influenced the recruits (down to a group of Aberdeen schoolboys): the leaders' constant claims that help was coming from the clans and Ireland, family connections (clearest in Urquhart of Meldrum, Perth's stepson and Buchan's nephew by marriage), Dunfermline's local influence, friends' encouragement, genuine Jacobite or episcopalian beliefs.[77] If the rising could be maintained long enough to commit the new recruits, original force or fraud (both of which helped give the '15 its first footing in the North-East) would not matter.

The enthusiasm and impetus were clearest as Buchan advanced south into the Mearns, with a force rumoured to be 1,800 strong. Sheriff-depute Keith joined him. The Whig gentry entrusted with the fencible men could raise none, and their estates were ravaged. 'Many of our shyre ... have joigned them alreadie, and the rest are upon a whistle', warned one of them. 'I am told ther are severall gentlemen joynd with them which I never imagind. It seems an absolut frenesie has possest them' lamented Kintore. One party summoned Marischal to surrender Dunnottar, and others approached Montrose.[78] If Buchan could have continued his successes, his recruits could have raised infantry, and the important north-eastern peers he had corresponded with might even have declared themselves. However, Mackay with Livingston's dragoons and 1,400 of the Dutch brigade reached Brechin on 17 August. He thought the danger strong enough to warrant calling out the fencibles of the South-West, and, as the government's victualling arrangements increasingly collapsed, his force was close to paralysis. But Buchan dared not oppose him directly, and from Fettercairn he retreated over the Cairnamounth and continued north, shedding recruits with every mile. Mackay marched to Aberdeen to find provisions.[79]

Buchan had temporarily achieved the most constant aim of Jacobite policy since April 1689, the arousing of major lowland support in the North East — two months too late to be decisive. If he could have done so before mid-June, Mackay could never have stripped the Lowlands to form the army that built Fort William; every port-town would have demanded a regiment in garrison. As it was, Hill's garrison did its work. It was the lack of a stronger highland nucleus which prevented Buchan from consolidating his extraordinary advantages. Had he brought 800 men from Lochaber, Hill wrote, he could have raised 10–12,000 more.[80] Yet Mackay's excessive gamble over the expedition gave Buchan a major opportunity. If the rallying of the south-western Presbyterians against Cannon's raids showed on what reserves of strength the regime could rely, Buchan's success showed how fragile its control was in some major shires. The logical conclusion, argued Presbyterians like Forbes of Culloden, was that no Episcopalians should be trusted or employed; but that would mean committing still more power to broken reeds like the Master of Forbes. In late November, a bench of 'presbyterian' JPs was imposed on Perthshire, headed by Argyll — an ironical reversal of 1685.[81] The more they were proscribed, the more likely north-eastern Episcopalian peers and gentry would be to join the Jacobites.

Farquharson of Inverey had retreated to Braemar to blockade Abergeldie. When Mackay turned to relieve it, Inverey, thinking that the ground would protect him, advanced with 200 men to the Pass of Ballater, where Mackay's nephew with sixty dragoons defeated them on 21 August. The 'Black Colonel's' son was captured, but he himself, after lying apparently dead for hours, escaped, leaving his famous blunderbuss. However, his power was broken. While relieving Abergeldie, Mackay burned twelve miles of Strathdee, 12–1400 homes, sparing Braemar only for lack of time. The orders he left, that only those who surrendered their arms and swore allegiance should be allowed to rebuild, had considerable success.[82] Meanwhile the Macgregors, 130 strong, harassed the Cardross garrison, ambushing and destroying a party on 22 August; but a detachment from Angus's at Dunblane overtook and defeated them next day.[83]

The campaign now echoed that of early 1689. Buchan, like Dundee before him, rode rapidly for Inverness with a force reduced to 500, hoping to find highlanders — in this case Seaforth's Mackenzies — who would enable him to continue the campaign. Mackay pursued with his horse and dragoons, leaving the infantry to follow later. The Jacobites passed from Strathdon through the hills and crossed the Spey near Gordon Castle. Lord Doune, Moray's son, and young Mackintosh of Borlum joined them, briefly accompanied by Lord Duffus and Rose of Kilravock. They had plundered Williamites' property along the way, and halted short of Inverness in an unsuccessful attempt to occupy Culloden House. Doune, Kilravock and earlier visitors could all have raised infantry for them if they could have provided a solid nucleus, and Mackay 'found all the north in a design to joyn them'.[84] They might still retrieve a campaign in which victory suddenly seemed still possible — if Seaforth would co-operate wholeheartedly.

This placed Seaforth under great pressure. Hill's sudden transfer to Fort William had disrupted but not ended the negotiations, and the 'Marquess', as his clan called him, still seemed about to submit. In late July, he was visiting Mackenzies in Wester Ross.[85] By late August, however, all the other Jacobites were blaming their setbacks on his failure to rise with them; and he decided (he later claimed), to show James that the utmost he could do would be useless. It was the first of several crises at which he did just enough to alienate the Williamites without really benefiting the Jacobite cause — a characteristic which led to his spending most of his remaining life in prison. Mackay, who had shown such hostility to the Mackenzies in 1689, and remembered his jumping bail in London, was totally unsympathetic to his dilemma, and, perhaps rightly, thought him so easily influenced that his demonstration might become reality.[86]

Apparently just before Buchan's arrival, Seaforth raised the fencible men of Kintail, Lochcarron and Lochalsh. His main supporters were his uncle Colin, his brother Alexander (also a Catholic), and the younger Mackenzies of Gairloch and Hilton (Strathbran). According to Mackenzie of Coul, only one lowland gentleman joined him in arms. The Chisholm, who had submitted in June, secretly entered his camp.[87] Supporters alleged that for this 'sham' Seaforth deliberately limited his numbers, 'fitter for a convoy ... than ane army'.[88] Yet certainly many of his supporters expected to fight. The departure of the garrison companies for Fort William had left lowland Ross-shire vulnerable, and he advanced 8–900 strong to Achilty near Contin.[89] Mackay, arriving unexpectedly, almost surprised Buchan and Cannon near Inverness. They fled into the Aird and attempted to raise the Frasers, unsuccessfully (though young Simon of Beaufort earned a brief imprisonment). The horsemen retreated down the north side of Loch Ness to Glenmoriston.[90]

It was reported in Buchan's camp that Seaforth had written promising to join; but his councils were divided.[91] According to Coul, those for peace included (surprisingly) Colin Mackenzie, the Chisholm and the hesitating Seaforth himself, while the rest were for war. A Mackenzie poet, however, claimed that three bad advisers he would not mention (probably including Coul, certainly not Colin Mackenzie), while declaring that they would follow and fight for Seaforth whatever the consequences, advised him:

> Return yet to your country along with Buchan's cavalry, and disband but some of your clan, so that a way may be opened for you to make your peace with honour, since your can see no better way.

According to Bernardi, Colin Mackenzie was so opposed to surrender that he nearly stabbed Southwell for proposing it; but the belated truth about the Boyne paralysed Seaforth.[92] He sent Coul to Mackay, explaining that he was 'obliged in honour to make some appearance for King James', but had no intention of joining Buchan, and offered the clan gentry as sureties for his future peaceable behaviour. On 28 August, his mother asked leave for him to live at Chanonry. Mackay absolutely refused, giving Seaforth the choice between immediate surrender or the devastation of his country.[93] Certainly, Mackay had to end the persistant vague threat from Seaforth, and feared that he might now withdraw to remote fastnesses. But, determined in no circumstances to make terms with even half-hearted rebels, he acted on the crude assumption that Coul's activity, a natural attempt to save his lands and his chief, was proof that all the lowland Mackenzies also were Jacobites (which was nonsense) and that their lands also could justifiably be ravaged.[94]

Under this threat of devastation, Coul and the Countess negotiated an agreement with Mackay, that Seaforth should save his honour by coming to Chanonry and being 'captured' by troops, and should then be under house arrest at Inverness. Fearing for his health in any imprisonment, Seaforth foolishly broke the agreement. Mackay furiously ordered the raising of 900 Mackays, Rosses and Sutherland men who, with 200 of Strathnaver's regiment, were to destroy the Mackenzie highlands, while he himself with mounted forces devastated the Lowlands. Yet he sent warning of his intention. Buchan had now entered Lochaber, and so could not help.[95] Under pressure from many of his men, Seaforth disbanded them on 2 September, with others of them weeping. Yet Mackay refused to recall his orders unless Seaforth surrendered. Seaforth momentarily considered accompanying Colin Mackenzie, who guided the professional officers into Lochaber to join Buchan, but Sir Thomas Southwell and others persuaded him to submit, and on 3 September at Strathpeffer he did so, to save the Mackenzies from ruin. Coul, however, blamed his mother's concern for her private interest for making him come in without adequate terms.[96]

Mackay remained at Inverness only long enough to settle a garrison, and then returned through the North-East, quartering troops at intervals to prevent any repetition of Buchan's exploits.[97] Orders were given in mid-October to transport Seaforth prisoner to Edinburgh, whence he was not to return until five years later, a fugitive. Buchan and Cannon allegedly dropped hints to make his captors harsher towards him, in retaliation for his desertion. The Mackenzies, however, felt deep shame that his clan had failed him and, in effect, handed him over to the enemy. Coul was generally blamed, and in late September there were false rumours that some of the Lochaber raiders (who were to kill women on a cattle-raid a month later) planned to murder him. The threats continued, and in early 1691 he sent to Buchan and Glengarry to deny the charge.[98]

In Lochaber, Glengarry, Lochiel and Keppoch briefly visited Buchan, but refused outright to join him. He marched 300 strong to Glen Dochert, met the Campbell laird (Breadalbane's first cousin) and Stewart of Appin and gathered 200 foot in Balquhidder.[99] However, the Council had regained confidence since July. On 5 September, when he approached Dunblane, they immediately sent

Drumlanrig with a massive cavalry and infantry force to Stirling to attack him. If the crisis passed, Argyll with his regiment (from Perth) and half Glencairn's should proceed to reduce the Isles.[100] On 8 September, Drumlanrig advanced hoping to surprise Buchan in Menteith, but sympathisers gave warning and he retreated through Balquhidder.[101] Order there seemed restored by November, but Macgregors and other Jacobites remained active, burning Aberuchill's house of Cambusmore as soon as a reorganisation transferred the garrison.[102]

After rumours that he intended for Argyllshire, Buchan was sighted late on 11 September passing Crieff, with 400 horse and 100 foot, 'a very unusual proportion . . . in an Highland-Army'. They might intend surprising Perth, and Drumlanrig rapidly marched from Stirling, hoping to duplicate Mackay's victory a year earlier. However, the Jacobites no longer had the necessary vigour. They were suffering severely from lack of food and forage. Buchan and Cannon were strongly criticised, and there were frequent desertions. On 12 September, they dismissed their foot and turned north-westwards at Methven. Drumlanrig followed them past Weem until provisions gave out.[103] Although they had split into several parties, Buchan and Cannon still hoped to raise Braemar and Badenoch. However, on 15 September Mackay, returning south, ordered Cunningham to march from Aberden with 800 men to disarm or destroy upper Braemar just after harvest. The Farquharsons dared not stir.[104] Buchan and Cannon still collected 200 foot, for they had hopes from Badenoch, but their appeals to the Macphersons and some Mackintoshes failed entirely. When Cunningham entered Badenoch on one side (ravaging it when the Macpherson gentry scrupled to take the oaths) and a large force from Inverness advanced up the Spey, they disbanded their remaining followers in late September.[105] They evidently accepted that the Robertsons at least were too firmly subdued to rise next spring, for they gave young Struan letters of recommendation to James. He slipped away to St. Germain.[106]

Yet the Jacobites refused to abandon even the Lowlands entirely. Already Major Duncan Menzies, with Lord Dunkeld, several Angus gentry and sixty men had descended and seized a small island castle in Loch Clunie near Dunkeld. Menzies mounted small cannon on the castle, 'intend[ing] . . . to hold it out ys winter', gambling on the weather breaking as in 1689 and making government counter-attacks impossible. He knew the area intimately, and in one raid captured a party from the Blair garrison. However, Atholl, who had recently returned to the area, wrote warning Mackay. Lauder's regiment surrounded the lake before sufficient provisions were gathered, and the castle had to surrender about 9 October. The Jacobites were sent prisoners to Dundee, from which Lord Dunkeld and others (presumably including Menzies) escaped.[107]

On 28 September, Lord Frendraught, with about forty gentlemen, officers and servants, rode deep into Buchan and occupied Fedderate Castle, 'the strongest House in all the County, having very thick Walls, and double Vaulted', surrounded by a morass. They evidently hoped to keep alive resistance in the North-East, and must also have been anxious to avoid a highland winter of hunger and privations harsher than the last. They built up a major magazine by raiding, but, on 1 October, Lieutenant-Colonel Buchan arrived, drove back the raiders and blockaded the castle. No more was possible without large cannon and mortars, and the Jacobites' calculations were almost proved right by a violent storm on 9 October.[108] However, a siege train made its slow way from Edinburgh, and, seeing Buchan preparing an assault, the Jacobites surrendered on terms on 18 October, on Buchan's promise to seek permission for them to leave Scotland or live peacefully on giving security. The bigot Earl of Crawford, then heading the Council, revoked these terms, and the Jacobites long remained prisoners of war like those taken at Cromdale. Frendraught, the last (and the most trusted by the highlanders), did not gain bail until June 1694.[109]

As they surrendered, another party was reported to have seized the castle in the Lake of Menteith; but they probably withdrew on hearing of the surrenders.[110] The failure further encouraged the north-eastern peers and gentlemen who had joined Buchan that summer to submit. Lord Inverurie was the first, and was specially recommended to William's mercy. Most of the gentry involved came in voluntarily to Lieutenant-Colonel Buchan, some as to a relation (a motive which had made them rise with his brother), although a few had to be seized. Next spring, he was allowed to bail most of them. A trickle of further submissions continued through the winter.[111]

Security in the Highlands was dwindling, as Hill extended his influence, Argyll turned towards Mull and the *Dartmouth* began another cruise on 27 August. The constant wear on his cables from rough weather alarmed Pottinger, and he refused Hill's order to sail north about and collect the only available £1,000 which the government had allotted Fort William — from Orkney revenues. He took aboard some soldiers, and may even have raided Uist, but a small surprise landing at Armadale was a failure: young Sir Donald hastily gathered twenty-four men, and drove the invaders back to their boats.[112] The *Dartmouth*, with the *Lark*, sailed for a third time for Eigg, arriving on 9 September, and landing forty soldiers. This time, the fighting men were at home, outnumbering them, and had obtained some cattle to replace those destroyed in June. Pragmatically overlooking the past atrocity, they gave warning that any further destruction would make them fight ruthlessly, but that, if granted protection, they woud surrender their arms. Pottinger promised it, and they took the oath of allegiance.[113] Then, in mid-September, back to Skye, cutting off young Sir Donald on the mainland.[114] Large gatherings of Macdonalds often prevented landings, but rumours spread that Pottinger's force was enormous. Old Sir Donald in alarm asked for a twenty-day cessation of arms. Pottinger made him give his word of honour to apply to the government to submit, and, releasing his captured brother as a gesture, gallantly retired on 21 September (really for lack of provisions).[115]

Sir Donald accordingly wrote to Mackay at Edinburgh, offering to surrender in return for an indemnity, a pension to enable him to live with his debts, and a peerage. Even this last was probably not a deliberate wrecking demand: his Jacobite title provided a bargaining point, and he exploited his linked claim to primacy over the Macdonalds, having his agent claim that he could bring in Keppoch and Clanranald with him. Mackay, once again over-confident, replied that Sir Donald must submit unconditionally, although he offered a safe-conduct for discussions and informally promised him William's favour. Captain Hugh Macdonald of Mackay's warned him that his agent had leaked his mission, so that both sides would denounce him if he fought on, while Mackay, Argyll and his wife's cousin Morton were ready to introduce him at Court, where he could finally outdistance Glengarry. Tarbat, although sending similar warnings, secretly suggested to Melville that the concessions would be a small price to prevent another campaign. His warning was ignored, and he complained in November that Seaforth's imprisonment in Edinburgh Castle after voluntarily submitting was discouraging others.[116]

If Skye was temporarily neutralised, Mull was not. In late September Sir John Maclean was planning to attack the Laird of Coll for his earlier submission.[117] On 11 September, Argyll had again set out with the Council's orders to collect a force in Argyllshire and reduce Appin, Glencoe, Morvern, Ardnamurchan and Mull. Argyll sensibly shipped the six companies of Glencairn's granted him from Dunstaffnage to Fort William, having received thence in exchange the four companies of his regiment.[118] Gathering the Argyllshire gentry, he gained their agreement to levy a force, which he was to pay. At the rendezvous at Dunollie, his regular regiment was supplemented by two local ones, Ardkinglas's of 850 men and Auchinbreck's of 550, 100 gentlemen volunteers and 100 followers, and 200 men to row 40 birlinns pressed from all along the coast. Bad weather delayed them, but the *Dartmouth* was in the Sound of Mull cutting communications. A Maclean messenger unexpectedly arrived claiming that Sir John, and still more some gentry such as the Tutor of Torloisk, were willing to submit. Argyll sent gentlemen to negotiate, and, he claimed, Sir John offered to grant all his private demands, even to blow up Duart, if in return he would avoid disarming them. Obviously, he wished to rise for James again when circumstances improved, and Argyll refused.[119]

The Tutor of Appin holding Castle Stalker was willing to submit, as his earlier messages to Hill indicated, and on 9 October he came to Dunollie and signed terms. He was to surrender the castle, complete with cannon and birlinns, next day, and was to join Argyll in reducing the inhabitants of Glencoe to submit to the government. In return, Argyll promised to obtain an indemnity for him, and to assist him to avoid paying Perth the remainder of the purchase price for Glencoe and to obtain recompense from the Glencoe men for damages adjudged against him for their 1685 raids. Argyll wrote to Mackay for instructions on dealing with chiefs anxious to submit. Glencoe may have been his next objective. If so, as most of the inhabitants had already submitted and his employment of Stewart indicated friendly intentions, it was, ultimately, their misfortune that the storm of 9 October changed his plans.[120]

Ordered to co-operate with Argyll, the *Dartmouth* was cruising in the Sound of Mull. Pottinger was hoping to leave 'this melancholy station' for good in a month. According to legend, he had threatened meanwhile to sweep Mull with a besom, but failed to add 'with God's help'. This gave the Mull witches their opportunity. When the *Dartmouth* anchored in Scallastle Bay on 9 October, they cast a spell to wreck her, and to match Pottinger's counter-spells (unusual in an Ulsterman) they summoned other witches in crow and cat form, from Glencoe, from Moy in Lochaber, even from Kintyre and Cowal. A 'hurricane' (as Hill at Fort William called it) struck the *Dartmouth* from the south-west, the worn cable parted, and she drove stern-first across the Sound, struck an islet off the Morvern shore and sank with Pottinger and nearly all hands.[121] The witches' united effort, of which the Jacobite chiefs were by then incapable, scored the last highland success of the campaign, and had longer-term results. If the frigates ordered to cruise off Mull in 1691 had shown Pottinger's diligence, they could, in collaboration with Williamites ashore, have brought the highlanders to submit early that summer. Instead, their one haphazard week's excursion to Mull was the first blow against Breadalbane's pacification.[122]

The storm emphasised the urgent need to occupy Mull before the weather broke; and there was no sufficient force to meet Argyll. Lochiel and Glengarry had previously promised assistance when it was needed. In early October, Sir John crossed the sound and came guarded within two miles of Fort William to speak to Lochiel about it, but he refused, having already promised Hill not to join him. Sir John, 'heady and zealous for his M[aste]r' James and facing private ruin, spoke of going abroad.[123] Argyll landed on 16 October in Loch Spelve on Mull with 1,900 foot and 60 dragoons. The Macleans retired to the mountains with their cattle. On 21 October, Argyll advanced on Duart, burning the country as he went, while another part of his forces encamped at Aros Bay. On 22 October, he sent the Tutor of Torloisk to Lochbuie, Ardgour and other Maclean cadets who were discussing submitting, telling them to surrender their forts and arms and take the oath of allegiance to gain his protection, and giving them twenty-four hours to consider. The wasting gave fresh alarm to the mainland chiefs, although the most to which Buchan could bring Lochiel, Glengarry and Clanranald was an agreement to combine against Argyll when he landed in Ardnamurchan, while the Macleans harried his rear. They sent Lady Lochiel to inform Hill, who dissuaded Lochiel and Glengarry and warned Argyll of the need for moderation.[124]

He took the warning, and showed a mildness in pressing his own interests that won Hill's praise. By early November, most Macleans had (with Sir John's permission) submitted, taken the oaths and surrendered arms, though Hill grumbled that they had merely 'deliver[ed] some old rusty trash' while hiding their real weapons, and might rebel again. Argyll in fairly rapid stages released the prisoners he had taken. Duart held out, and Sir John remained in the mountains with 170 Irish and some clansmen, waiting to descend and reconquer the island when Argyll advanced.[125] The mainland chiefs were determined to fight to the last should he land there, and, although 'the people generally were willing to sitt downe quiet ... they persuad ym that my Lord argyle comes to Insleve them'. Argyll had already decided to besiege Duart instead, and Hill promised to send him two siege guns, grenades and petards. However, bad weather encouraged sickness as his forces lay for ten days in the fields before Duart, and he had no boats fit to carry cannon. On 8 November, therefore, he embarked with the bulk of his force, particularly his regiment. He left (and paid for) garrisons at Lochbuie, and at Mingary on the mainland to the north (besides Castle Stalker), and a reserve of 250 at Aros to operate against Sir John Maclean. Sir John, unable to make head against such odds, retreated with his followers into the near-impregnable island of Carnaburg.[126]

Hill's position at Fort William remained precarious. The garrison lived on meal, water and salt herrings, liable to starve in case of a French blockade or prolonged contrary winds.[127] The men's pay was too low for so desolate and costly a country, and almost no money arrived.[128] Deals were shipped to him, but no nails or timber. Maclean of Ardgour was willing to sell him timber, but he lacked boats to transport it. The soldiers were still under canvas in October and remained without proper quarters.[129] Winter rains made large sections of the earth ramparts collapse. This recurred every winter, a special misfortune in 1691 when an impressive appearance was particuarly needed.[130]

Harsh conditions and poor food caused much sickness and death. Robert Menzies, who was developing into a valuable second-in-command, undertook a journey on garrison business while sick, and died in early October.[131] Almost all the two highland companies afterwards deserted.[132] The detachment of Angus's, Hill's most reliable force, declared it would not remain after October.[133] His worst troubles were with Grant's, which was constantly close to mutiny — not entirely owing to its sufferings, since it had frequently caused trouble at Inverness. Fortunately, he had its major, Hugh Mackay, to assist him in watching day and night to crush the first outbreak. Mutineers nailed up the touchholes of the cannon pointing inland, intending to seize and plunder the officers and march off in a body during solemnities for William's birthday on 5 November. They approached Angus's companies to join them, but principles overcame grievances in most Cameronians. Hill was warned, and thwarted the plot, which, he wrote coolly, they would probably try again in three weeks. It was claimed that desertion and death had reduced the garrison by over half, to 600, most of them sick.[134] However, the danger shocked the Council into providing £1,000, a month's pay for the garrison. The immediate crisis passed, and after some disciplining, including a hanging or two, even the Grants became loyal. The Council thereafter at least made greater efforts for the garrison than for the rest of the army, and Hill became a favourite of Crawford at the Treasury, not least for his distrust of Episcopalians' loyalty.[135] Yet the Council's attempt to secure the garrison an income, by authorising Hill on 25 November to collect the rents of forfeited Camerons, Macdonalds, MacIains, Stewarts and Macleans, had to be disregarded, since it would obviously ruin all negotations for submission.[136]

William had originally intended to break only Kenmure's and Glencairn's regiments to form Hill's, but their wastage was such that in November he unexpectedly added, besides Menzies's company, Grant's. Lack of money soon made him deprive the dismissed officers even of half pay, and Grant, left little hope of recovering his immense regimental expenses, temporarily became violently hostile to William.[137] Although so many of his 1,100 men were highlanders, Hill in nominating their officers followed his and most advisers' normal rule of avoiding highland gentry likely to work for private or clan interests

— like Mackintosh, who showed his first active interest in the war by asking to be given an independent company stationed at Keppoch.[138] However, Hill made a surprising exception, asking for Campbell of Ardkinglas as his Deputy-Governor and Lieutenant-Colonel. William refused, leaving the post vacant, and, in his reluctance to appoint men with local connections, for some time resisted making Culloden's brother John Forbes the regiment's major. Hill, who had emphasised the Lochaber clans' hostility to Argyll, probably intended to conciliate him by a nomination he intended to fail.[139] Yet it was just possibly connected with Hill's main ambition, which he was to press throughout his governship: to revive the Cromwellian shire and jurisdiction of Inverlochy, stretching from Glengarry and Arisaig to Rannoch and Appin, overriding all heritable jurisdictions, the one means of controlling 'the Greate theife holes of ye highlands'. As a less punitive means of spreading civilisation, he obtained for the settlement founded by the Cromwellian garrison, now called Gordonsburgh, a royal charter as 'Maryburgh' (his suggestion). Many local highlanders hoped a school for their children would be founded.[140]

Although Hill, when requested, explained to Mackay that only a winter campaign, when their corn and cattle were in, could force the highlanders to submit,[141] he was confident that negotiations and some distribution of money would pacify them, even though Buchan and Cannon had returned. Both briefly remained with Glengarry, but in late October Cannon, Dunfermline and sixty protestant officers crossed to Sir Donald in Skye, while Buchan and the Catholics remained at Invergarry. Later events showed that not only religious convenience and the need to avoid 'eating up poor Glengarry' with too large a company but increasing hostility between the two generals was behind this.[142]

One officer, Major Bernardi, feeling that Seaforth's surrender had ended his mission, asked Buchan for help to retire to Edinburgh. Buchan summoned MacIain of Glencoe, who came to Invergarry with forty men to serve as Bernardi's escort. The Fort William garrison delayed their journey south, since 'it was impossible to pass them', even across the lower slopes of Ben Nevis, 'but when asleep, and their gate lock'd'. After spending a week in late October in Glencoe, whose total population he estimated at almost 1,000, he was escorted by forty Macdonalds, travelling at night to escape attack from the Williamite garrisons, to the Braes of Menteith, where there were Jacobite contacts to help him on his way.[143]

Although Glengarry in October agreed, like Lochiel, to allow free passage for Hill's men from Inverness,[144] and allowed his people to trade with the garrison, he showed the strongest determination to hold out. Hill regretted it, considering him generous, a man of his word, and, with Lochiel, able to control the other chiefs.[145] Sir Donald's friends again tried to bring him in with warnings that Glengarry relied on supplanting him if another revolution should restore James.[146] Secret encouragement from Privy Councillors and constant expectations of help from France also encouraged some chiefs, though the latter had failed so often that even Buchan 'begins to swear there's nothing but lies on all hands'.[147]

Lochiel, by his subtlety and advice, was the most influential of the chiefs, and,

Hill considered, the most promising, since 'nothing but interest can lead him he is covetous and the hopes of promised advantages ma[de] him stick so Close to K. Ja.', and he was anxious to break off if it could be done with honour and some advantage. To Hill's representatives he claimed that gratitude had made him support James, but that he was now convinced that his ultimate aim had been to bring in popery, and was anxious to lie quiet.[148] He had taken the lead in frustrating the plans to unite against Argyll, increasing Buchan's fury against him.[149] Keppoch was more forward than Lochiel, coming to the garrison himself and offering to submit, even to serve William, if he could be given some means of supporting himself.[150] Further straws in the wind were the applications of priests wishing to go abroad and professional soldiers wishing to submit to or even enlist under William. Hill expected that in any settlement the clans would insist on Cannon and Buchan receiving free passage to join James.[151] Such a settlement seemed close in December. Lochaber was peaceful, an oath was taken among the people not to steal, and Lochiel, establishing his respectability, hanged a man for theft. He and Keppoch summoned a meeting of the chiefs to vote whether or not to submit, and told Hill they were confident of gaining a majority. Hill and Tarbat urged that granting some reward to Lochiel, Keppoch and Sir Donald would make them submit, also bringing in Clanranald and leaving the rest insignificant.[152] Yet cynics might point out that, for all the months of negotiations since July, despite the many small concessions and the increasingly peaceful atmosphere, the chiefs had taken no irrevocable step, and could, if they had good hopes of success, make the many ordinary clansmen who had sworn the oaths break them. Time and again, Hill had reported that Lochiel and others were on the brink of total submission. Yet the clinching surrender never came. Sir Thomas Livingston, the new Commander-in-Chief, expressed this view: 'flater them as much as you wil, the least prospect or incouragement the[y] schal get from the contrair party, but the[y] wil laf at you and cut your throat with your one knyf'.[153]

Negotiations were abruptly checked when Hill fell dangerously ill in early 1691, not fully recovering until April. There were rumours of his death, and pretenders applied for the post. Dalrymple lamented that he knew no man capable of filling it. Unfortunately, Hill was unaware of this opinion a year later.[154] None of the 'presbyterians' then controlling the Edinburgh government was likely to take up Hill's policy of granting money to 'barbarous' tribes which were costing the Lowlands so much by their raiding. Petitions to Parliament about depredations had finally produced in September only an act making the inhabitants of parishes adjoining raided areas liable for the value of stolen cattle, an unreasonable law when the raiders were full war parties. That winter, several exposed areas asked for the burdensome troops 'protecting' them to be removed — laying themselves open to further raids. Although machinery for estimating losses was established, the only person to gain any effective compensation from the government was Forbes of Culloden, who, by gaining a fixed-rate farm of the excise on his devastated estate of Ferintosh, was able to set up the famous distilleries.[155] Any policy of pacifying the clans with money must originate elsewhere.

Meanwhile, the Jacobites at St Germain had remained unable to obtain effective French support. Their own over-optimistic claims backfired, representing Cannon and Buchan that autumn as strong enough to fight Mackay and scoring major victories in the North-East — able, therefore, to survive alone.[156] In November, a French frigate finally carried James's letters to Buchan to Scotland.[157] Macqueen's urgent protests and James's solicitations made Louis promise two provision ships. A vessel that ran into Larne and surrendered in December may have been the first.[158] The other, a French privateer carrying Macqueen and Lieutenant-Colonel William Charteris with a cargo of flour, salt, brandy, lead, flints and medicines, was intended to leave Nantes in November. Yet it sailed only in March, in company with another supply ship bound for Ireland. James made humiliatingly clear his preference for the highlanders over the Irish. Tyrconnell, trying to maintain an army almost entirely without money and supplies, was ordered to give Charteris, who sailed via Galway, twenty barrels of gunpowder and £1,000 sterling — £200 of this for ejected episcopalian clergy! A council of war, with Cannon, Buchan and Dunfermline or two of them a quorum, was to distribute the rest among the clans and officers. James promised help once Louis had gained the mastery of the seas that summer; but, 'too tender of their lives to expose them . . . by pretending to doe more than he was really able', he consented

> that if they cannot any longer . . . stand out but are forced by the pursute . . . of the rebells to some kind of Outward submission or Complyance, we shall not think the worse of ym for keeping quiet, but shall compassionate & not condemne yr suffering condition, being perfectly assured of their hearts at all tymes, and of their hands too, whenever the Condition of Our affairs shall require ym to appear for us. And as to those of our officers who cannot bend . . . to any kind of complyance & perhaps would not be receaved . . . tho they should, we desire all such to make use of . . . the ship . . . to retire to . . . Ireland.[159]

NOTES

1. J. Macky, *Memoirs of the Secret Service of John Macky* (London, 1733), xxvii-xxviii; BL MS Lansdowne 1163C, 240, Melfort to Innes, 23 Nov. 1690(NS); Westminster Cathedral, Westminster Diocesan Archives (WDA), MSS of Secretary of State Henry Browne (Browne MSS), 239, 240, unsigned letters, [1690]; *Carstares S.P.*, 152, List of King James's Household, [1690].

2. *Ib*; Macpherson, *Loyall Dissuasive*, 193; BL MS Lansdowne 1163B, 186, Melfort to Innes, 22 July 1690(NS); *ib.*, C, 172, same to same, 28 Oct. 1690(NS).

3. Bodl. MS Carte 256 fol. 68v, Middleton to Bishop Turner, 15 Nov. 1694(NS).

4. *Life of James*, ii, 431-2; Paris, Archives des Affaires Etrangères (AAE), Correspondance Politique (Corr. Pol.) Angleterre, 172, fols. 54-5, Memorial, 13 Oct. 1690(NS); *Carstares S.P.*, 149, 151-2, [Macky], Information for Lord Sydney, [c. Jan. 1691].

5. *Ib.*, 148-9; Doublet, *Journal*, 161-6 (misdated); SCA, Blairs Letters, Box U, 1690, 13, Burnet to W. Leslie, 2 Sept. 1690(NS); *ib.*, 17, same to Innes, 22 Sept. 1690(NS); *ib.*, 18, same to same, '1/10' Oct. 1690.

6, *Leven & Melville*, 540, Crawford to Melville, 9 Oct. 1690; Paris, Archives Nationales, Marine B₃, 62, fol. 29, Louvois to [Pontchartrain], 6 Nov. 1690(NS).

7. WDA, Browne MSS, 253, Memorial, n.d; J.S. Bromley, 'The Jacobite Privateers in the Nine Years War', *Statesmen, Scholars and Merchants*, ed. A. Whiteman, Bromley & P.G.M. Dickson (Oxford, 1973), 19.

8. *HMCR 4th Report*, 529, Mary of Modena to Buchan, 23 Aug. [1690 NS]; NLS MS 14,266 fol. 103, (31 Jan. 1696).

9. *RPCS*, xvi, 598; *HMCR Le Fleming*, 273, newsletter, 7 June 1690; BL MS Lansdowne 1163B, 26, Melfort to Innes, 6 June 1690(NS); SCA, Blairs Letters, Box Y, unsigned, 63, 'An acct of the affaires of Scotland', 10 June 1690; *State Trials*, xiii, 1448.

10. *Ib.*, 1447; *Melvilles & Leslies*, ii, 156, Hill to Melville, 2 June 1690; *Est. Procs.*, ii, 193; Macpherson, 'Gleanings', *TGSI*, xx, 238, Buchan to Cluny, 22 May 1690; Bernardi, *Life*, 68, 72; NLS MS 1329 fol. 117, Sir A. Mackenzie to Delvine, 26 May 1690; *ib.*, MS 1353 fol. 6v, Mackenzie of Redcastle to same, 28 May 1690.

11. *Ib.*; *ib.*, MS 1329 fol. 117, Sir A. Mackenzie to Delvine, 26 May 1690 *ib.*, fol. 119, same to same, 28 May 1690; Blair, Atholl MSS, Box 29 I (9) 315, Seaforth to Tullibardine, 22 Sept. 1697.

12. *CSPD 1691-2*, 91, Southwell's petition; Bernardi, *Life*, 66-7; *HMCR Finch*, ii, 466-7, Tarbat to Nottingham, 1 Oct. 1690; W.H. Whelpy, 'The Galway Prisoners and 'Doctor' William Bromfield', *Notes & Queries*, clviii (1930), 3-5, 39-40, 42; *Melvilles & Leslies*, ii, 156, Hill to Melville, 2 June 1690.

13. *Ib.*, 155-6; *Earls of Cromartie*, i, 64, Seaforth to Hill, 30 May 1690; *ib.*, 64-6, Hill to Seaforth, 19 June 1690 (2); *ib.*, 66-7, Countess Dowager to Tarbat, 28 June 1690; Macgill, *Old Ross-shire*, i, 238, Leven to ?, 12 Sept. n.y; *Est. Procs.*, ii, 215-16; NLS MS 1329 fol. 127, Sir A. Mackenzie to Delvine, 18 July 1690; SRO GD 26/ix/274, Hill to Melville, 19 June 1690.

14. *Ib.*, same to same, 8 Oct. 1690; Mackay, *Memoirs*, 108; *ib.*, 322-4, Mackay's Instructions to Ferguson & Pottinger, [Apr. 1690]; *RPCS*, xv, 179-80, 358; *ib.*, xvi, 4; Powley, *Naval Side*, 247-8, 250, 254-5, 273-4; C. J. M. Martin, 'The Dartmouth, a British frigate wrecked off Mull: the ship', *International Journal of Nautical Archaeology (IJNA)*, vii (1978), 29-31, 54; NLS MS 3138 fol. 35, Argyll's report to PCS, 25 Nov. 1690; PRO ADM 51/345/1, 14 May 1690.

15. *Ib.*, 51/3890/4 (Log of HMS *Lark*), 27 Aug. 1690.

16. Fortunately for his tenants, Sir James Stewart of Bute had shown no signs of such wavering for a year. *Ib.*, 16, 19 May; *ib.*, 51/345/1, 16, 17, 18, 19 May; *HMCR 5th Report*, 617, Raith to Stewart, July 1690; *RPCS*, xv, 267, 727; *Est. Procs.*, ii, 178-9.

17. *Ib.*, 193, 249; *Memoirs of Locheill*, 389, Argyll to Campbell of Kilberry, 4 June 1690; [Macleod], *Second Sight*, 75; PRO ADM 106/399 fol. 355, Pottinger to Navy Board, 19 June 1690; *ib.*, ADM 51/3890/4, 20, 21, 25, 28 May; *ib.*, 51/345/1, 29 May, 1, 2, 4, 6 June.

18. *Ib.*, 7, 8, 9, 10, 11 June; *Leven & Melville*, 471, Ferguson to Melville, 19 July 1690; *Est. Procs.*, ii, 219.

19. The other atrocity the priest mentioned was Glencoe. [Macleod], *Second Sight*, 74-5; Martin, *Western Islands*, 345-6; SCA, Blairs Letters, Box B¹, 108, A. Mongan to [W. Leslie], 13 Dec. 1694 (quoted in Forbes Leith, *Scottish Catholics*, ii, 170-1); PRO ADM 51/345/1, 13, 14, 17 June; *ib.*, ADM 106/399 fol. 355, Pottinger to Navy Board, 19 June 1690.

20. *Ib*; Mackay, *Memoirs*, 324, Instructions to Ferguson & Pottinger.

21. *Ib.*, PRO ADM 51/345/1, 19, 20, 21 June; *ib.*, ADM 51/3890/4, 17, 19, 20, 21 June.

22. Balhaldie may have omitted this passage because it was a mistake, confused with an

unsuccessful agreement with an earlier Glengarry and Keppoch, in 1654; or because it was inconveniently true. *Ib.*, 24, 26 June; *ib.*, ADM 51/345/1, 10 July; *Leven & Melville*, 463, Melville to William, 6 July 1690; 'Journal of a Soldier', *TGAS*, i. 48; *Memoirs of Locheill*, 103–4; NLS MS 3194 fol. 16.

23. There is no formal trace of the alleged earldom, but Jacobite peerage records for this period are very defective. *Ib.*, fol. 114v, James to Cluny, 29 May 1690; SRO GD 26/xiii/52, [R. Menzies] to Melville, 10 July 1690; NLS MS 7012 fol. 114v, Sir A. Bruce to Tweeddale, 10 July 1690; *ib.*, MS 1329 fol. 122, Sir A. Mackenzie to Delvine, 2 July 1690.

24. *Ib.*; *ib.*, fol. 127, same to same, 18 July 1690; PRO ADM 106/399 fol. 357, Pottinger to Navy Board, 10 July 1690; *ib.*, fol. 138 [same] to [Sir D. Macdonald], 28 June 1690, Sir D. Macdonald to [Pottinger], 2 July 1690; *ib.*, ADM 51/345/1, 27, 30 June.

25. *RPCS*, xv, 238–40; Mackay, *Memoirs*, 185–6, Mackay to Portland, 29 May 1690.

26. *Ib.*, 182–3, same to William, 14 May 1690; *ib.*, 208, same to Portland n.d.; *CTB*, ix, 377, 692; SRO PC 1/48, 159–60; GD 26/ix/299, Accounts of the £4,000, May 1690; NUL, Portland MSS, PwA 2347, Melville to [d'Allonne, 21 June 1690].

27. *RPCS*, xv, 249–50, 271–2, 305–6; *Leven & Melville*, 441–2, William to Melville, 9 June 1690; Mackay, *Memoirs*, 91–2; *ib.*, 189–90, Mackay to William, 5 June 1690.

28. *Ib.*, 197–8, same to same, 8 June 1690; *ib.*, 108–9.

29. *RPCS*, xv, 274–5; *Leven & Melville*, 445, Atholl to Mackay, 19 June 1690; *ib.*, 463, Melville to William, 6 July 1690; SRO GD 26/ix/305, depositions, [1690]; NLS MS 7012 fols. 92–3, Bruce to Tweeddale, 26 June 1690; NUL Portland MSS, PwA 2347, Melville to [d'Allonne, 21 June 1690].

30. *Ib.*, PwA 2359, Mackay to Mary, 7 June 1690; Mackay, *Memoirs*, 184, same to William, 14 May 1690.

31. Probably untruly. *Ib.*, 109; *ib.*, 200–1, Instructions for [Scipio] Hill, [5] June 1690; *Melvilles & Leslies*, ii, 157, anon. [?Earl of Monmouth] to Melville, 30 May 1690; NLS MS 7012 fols. 137v–8, Bruce to Tweeddale, 31 July 1690.

32. *Leven & Melville*, 451–2, Mr of Forbes to Melville, 27 June 1690; Mackay, *Memoirs*, 100, 109; *ib.*, 200, Instructions for [S.] Hill, [5] June 1690; *ib.*, 330, Mackay to PCS, 28 June 1690.

33. Sir Alexander Bruce was mistaken in claiming that Mackay had actually reached the Spey at Ruthven and then retreated down it. *Ib.*, 98; *ib.*, 201–2, Instructions for [S.] Hill, [5] June 1690; *ib.*, 204, Mackay to Portland, 26 July 1690; *ib.*, 326–7, same to 'Hamilton' [Melville], 18 June 1690; *ib.*, 327–8, same to 'same', 23 June 1690; *ib.*, 329, same to PCS, 28 June 1690; *HMCR 6th Report*, 701, same to R. Menzies, 20 June 1690; 'Journal of a Soldier', *TGAS*, i, 47; NLS MS 7012 fol. 114, Bruce to Tweeddale, 10 July 1690.

34. *Ib.*, fol. 93, same to same, 26 June 1690; NUL, Portland MSS, PwA 2359, Mackay to Mary, 7 June 1690; Mackay, *Memoirs*, 337, same to 'Hamilton' [Melville], 24 July 1690.

35. *Ib.*, 200, Instructions to [S.] Hill, [5] June 1690; *ib.*, 202, Mackay to Portland, 8 June 1690; *ib.*, 329–30, same to PCS, 28 June 1690; MacGill, *Old Ross-shire*, i, 238, Sir A. Mackenzie to Tarbat, n.d.

36. NLS MS 1329 fol. 124, same to Delvine, 8 July 1690; *ib.*, MS 7012 fol. 133v, Bruce to Tweeddale, 31 July 1690; *RPCS*, xv, 305–6, 319–20, 388–9; Mackay, *Memoirs*, 339, Mackay to 'Hamilton' [Melville], 26 July 1690; *ib.*, 340–1, same to PCS, 28 July 1690.

37. *Ib.*, 329–31, same to same, 28 June 1690; *ib.*, 343, same to 'Hamilton' [Melville], 30 July 1690; Macpherson, 'Gleanings', *TGSI*, xx, 230, Mackay to Cluny, 27 June 1690; *ib.*, 241, Hill to same, 29 June 1690; *Est. Procs.*, ii, 224; *Seafield Corr.*, 65, Grant to Lord Boyne, 22 Sept. 1690; NLS MS 7012 fol. 141, Bruce to Tweeddale, 31 July 1690; *ib.*, fol. 146v, same to same, 7 Aug. 1690.

38. *Ib.*, MS 1329 fol. 124, Sir A. Mackenzie to Delvine, 8 July 1690; Carleton, *Memoirs*, 40–1; 'Journal of a Soldier', *TGAS*, i, 47–8; Mackay, *Memoirs*, 98; *ib.*, 204, Mackay to Portland, 26 July 1690.

39. *Ib.*, 332, same to PCS, 7 July 1690; *ib.*, 109; *Leven & Melville*, 496, Hill to Leven, 21 Aug. 1690; SRO GD 26/ix/274, same to [Mackay], 2 Nov. 1690.

40. The fort was on Gordon's land, but nobody bothered about that. Mackay, *Memoirs*, 98–9; *ib.*, 332–4, Mackay to 'Hamilton' [Melville], 10 July 1690; 'Journal of a Soldier', *TGAS*, i, 48; BL, Map Room (MS) K. L.37.1a, J. Elphinstone, Fort William and environs, 1748; W.T. Kilgour, *Lochaber in War and Peace* (Paisley, 1908), 336, 'Information of the Abuses committed by the Governors of Fort William'.

41. *More Culloden Papers*, 213–14, Hill to Melville, 2 Nov. 1690; Drumlanrig, Queensberry Papers, bundle 500, 'Ane accompt off ye Artillery ... of ffort Wm', 7 Dec. 1691; Mackay, *Memoirs*, 337, Mackay to 'Hamilton' [Melville], 24 July 169[0]; *ib.*, 335, same to same, 10 July 1690.

42. *Ib.*, 334–5; *ib.*, 331, same to PCS, 7 July 1690; *CSPD 1690-1*, 48, Hill to ?, 4 'July' [Aug.] 1690; *Est. Procs.*, ii, 237; SRO GD 26/xiii/52, [R. Menzies] to Melville, 10 July 1690.

43. *Ib.*, ix/274, Hill 'Ane accompt how the highlanders were brought to ... Civilitie', [Oct. 1690], Hill to [Mackay], 2 Nov. 1690.

44. *Ib.*, same to Tarbat, 21 July 1690; Mackay, *Memoirs*, 99; *ib.*, 205, Mackay to Portland, 26 July 1690; *ib.*, 334–6, same to 'Hamilton' [Melville], 10 July 1690.

45. *Ib.*, 335; *ib.*, 331, same to PCS, 7 July 1690; *ib.*, 99; PRO ADM 51/345/1, 10, 15, 16 July ('Argyll's castle' must, from the location, be Mingary); *ib.*, 51/3890/4, 21 July, 8, 22 Sept.; *ib.*, ADM 106/399 fol. 357, Pottinger to Navy Board, 10 July 1690.

46. *Ib.*, fol. 361, same to Sir R. Beach 31 July 1690; *Leven & Melville*, 470–1, same to Melville, 19 July 1690; *ib.*, 473, same to Mackay, 21 July 1690; NLS MS 1329 fol. 127, Sir A, Mackenzie to Delvine, 18 July 1690.

47. PRO ADM 51/345/1, 19 July; Mackay, *Memoirs*, 332, Mackay to PCS, 7 July 1690.

48. *Ib.*, 205, same to Portland, 26 July 1690; *ib.*, 338, same to 'Hamilton' [Melville], 24 July 169[0]; *ib.*, 99; Macpherson, 'Gleanings', *TGSI*, xx, 241, Hill to Cluny, 5 Aug. 1690; 'Journal of a Soldier', *TGAS*, i, 48.

49. Mackay, *Memoirs*, 214–15, Mackay to William, [c. Aug. 1690]; *ib.*, 340, same to PCS, 28 July 1690; NLS MS 7012 fol. 147, Bruce to Tweeddale, 7 Aug. 1690.

50. *RPCS*, xv, 358; Mackay, *Memoirs*, 339, Mackay to 'Hamilton' [Melville], 26 July 1690; *Leven & Melville*, 477, Hill to same, 26 Aug. 1690; *ib.*, 496–7, same to same, 21 Aug. 1690; SRO GD 26/ix/274, same to [Tarbat], 21 July 1690.

51. *Ib*; *APS*, ix, App., 61–3; Mackay, *Memoirs*, 331, Mackay to PCS, 7 July 1690; *CSPD 1691-2*, 61–2, Tarbat to William, [July-Aug. 1690].

52. The 'MacNeil' involved in the conferences may be Barra or Gallachallie. *Ib. 1690-1*, 48, Hill to ?, 4 'July' [Aug.] 1690; SRO GD 26/ix/274, same to [Tarbat], 21 July 1690; *ib.*, viii/102, Tutor of Appin to Macnachtan [for James & Melfort, Sept. 1689]; *HMCR 6th Report*, 702, Hill to Sir A. Menzies, n.d.

53. *Ib.*, 701, same to same, 11 Aug. 1690; *ib.*, 702, same to same, 28 Aug. 1690; *CSPD 1690-1*, 48, same to ?, 4 'July' [Aug.] 1690; *Leven & Melville*, 496–7, same to Leven, 21 Aug. 1690.

54. *Ib*; *Memoirs of Locheill*, 126.

55. *HMCR 6th Report*, 701, Hill to Sir A. Menzies, 11 Aug. 1690; *ib.*, 702, same to same, 28 Aug. 1690; *Leven & Melville*, 496, same to Leven, 21 Aug. 1690.

56. SRO GD 26/ix/274, same to Melville, 8 Oct. 1690, same to [Tarbat], '13' [11] Oct. 1690, same to same, 23 Oct. 1690.

57. Prebble, *Glencoe*, 106.

58. *Est. Procs.*, ii, 227, 275–6; *Culloden Papers*, 15, 'Memoir ... for preserving the Peace of the Highlands', [1690]; *Leven & Melville*, 465–6, Carstares to [d'Allonne], 9 July 1690; *ib.*, 475, Melville to Mary, 24 July 1690.

59. *Ib.*, 472, Billingsley to Melville, 19 July 1690; *ib.*, 468, Nottingham to same, 13 July 1690; *CSPD 1690–1*, 50, same to Governor of Carlisle, 5 July 1690; *Est. Procs.*, ii, 251–2; 'Journal of a Soldier', *TGAS*, i, 48–9; *HMCR Le Fleming*, 286, newsletter, 26 Aug. 1690; Northants RO, Buccleuch (Shrewsbury) MSS Vol. 63, 2, (*HMCR Buccleuch (Montagu)*, ii, 163), S. Weeld's Answers, 8 Dec. 1694.

60. *Ib.*; Balcarres, *Memoirs*, 61; NLS MS 7012 fol. 133, Bruce to Tweeddale, 31 July 1690.

61. *Carstares S.P.*, 149, [Macky], Information for Sydney, [c. Jan. 1691]; *ib.*, 647–8, Argyll to Carstares, 15 Sept. 1700; Marshall, *Days of Duchess Anne*, 188; SRO GD 26/ix/305, Depositions, [c. June 1690].

62. *Leven & Melville*, 469, Carstares to [d'Allonne], 13 July 1690; Blaeu, *Atlas Major*, xii, map of Breadalbane etc. (Dunan = Downen); Macpherson, 'Gleanings', *TGSI*, xx, 231, Cannon to Cluny, 4 July '[1689]' [1690].

63. *Ib.*, 238, Buchan to same, 22 May 1690; *ib.*, 240, Hill to same, 17 June 1690; *ib.*, 241, same to same, 5 Aug. 1690; NLS MS 3194 fol. 114v, James to same, 29 May 1690; *Est. Procs.*, ii, 193.

64. SRO GD 26/viii/96, Glengarry to Sir Ae. Macpherson, 18 July 1690.

65. *Est. Procs.*, ii, 178, 185–6, 252–3; Macpherson, *Loyall Dissuasive*, 183–90, 204–5; NUL, Portland MSS, PwA 2347, Melville to [d'Allonne, 21 June 1690].

66. NLS MS 7012 fol. 114v, Bruce to Tweeddale, 10 July 1690; Blair, Atholl MSS, Box 29 I (6) 18, Atholl to Murray, 24 Aug. [1690]; *RPCS*, xv, 463, 546–8.

67. *Ib.*, 332; *HMCR Hope-Johnstone*, 93–4, W. Reoch's narrative, 25 Oct. 1690; *Leven & Melville*, 173, Murray to Sir W. Anstruther, 17 July [1690]; *ib.*, 469, Carstares to [?d'Allonne], 13 July 1690; NLS MS 7012 fol. 114v, Bruce to Tweeddale, 10 July 1690; Mackay, *Memoirs*, 342, Mackay to 'Hamilton' [Melville], 30 July 1690.

68. *Ib.*, 109; NLS MS 7012 fol. 139, Bruce to Tweeddale, 31 July 1690.

69. *HMCR Hope-Johnstone*, 94, W. Reoch's narrative, 25 Oct. 1690; *APS*, ix, 208; Veitch, *Memoirs*, 449; *Memoirs of Dundee*, 33; *RPCS*, xv, 332.

70. *Ib.*, 279–80, 330–1, 332, 349–50; NLS MS 7012 fols. 113v–114, Bruce to Tweeddale, 10 July 1690; *ib.*, fols. 137–8, same to same, 31 July 1690; *Est. Procs.*, ii, 208, 246, 249–50.

71. *Ib.*, 232, 241–2, 247–9; *CSPD 1690–1*, 83, newsletter, 31 July 1690; *RPCS*, xv, 346; Mackay, *Memoirs*, 99–100; *ib.*, 342–3, Mackay to 'Hamilton' [Melville], 30 July 1690; *Scots Peerage*, ii, 274; SRO GD 26/i/4/166/2 p.8, Montgomerie's memorial, [? 1693]; *HMCR Hope-Johnstone*, 94, W. Reoch's narrative, 25 Oct. 1690.

72. *Ib*; Mackay, *Memoirs*, 42, 100; *ib.*, 340, Mackay to PCS, 28 July 1690; Macpherson, *Original Papers*, ii, 118, 'An Account of the Highland Clans', 1709; *Est. Procs.*, ii, 224, 253, 257; *Memoirs of Dundee*, 32–3.

73. *Melvilles & Leslies*, ii, 168, Representation of Mar's losses.

74. *RPCS*, xv, 363–4; *ib.*, xvi, 197; *CSPD 1690–1*, 100–1, newsletter, 21 Aug. 1690; *Leven & Melville*, 494, D. Carnegie to Mackay, 16 Aug. 1690; Mackay, *Memoirs*, 100; *Est. Procs.*, ii, 257–8, 260–1; NLS MS 1031 fol. 103, Hamilton to Selkirk, 13 'Aug.' [Sept.] 1690.

75. *Ib.*, fol. 102v.

76. *RPCS*, xv, 623–5; NLS MS 7036 fol. 7, Lord Inverurie's declaration, 1690; *HMCR Hope-Johnstone*, 94, W. Reoch's narrative, 25 Oct. 1690.

77. *Ib*; H. Tayler, *The Family of Urquhart* (Aberdeen, 1946), 152; NLS MS 7036 fol. 7, Inverurie's declaration, 1690; *RPCS*, xvi, 81–2, 204, 229–30.

78. *Ib*., xv, 253, 339–40, 454; *HMCR Le Fleming*, 286–7, newsletters, 26, 28 Aug. 1690; *Fraser Papers*, 53; *Leven & Melville*, 493–4, D. Carnegie to Melville, 16 Aug. 1690; *ib*., 494–5, Kintore to same, 17 Aug. 1690; Mackay, *Memoirs*, 343–4, Mackay to PCS, 17 Aug. 1690.

79. *Ib*., 343–5; *ib*., 101; *RPCS*, xv, 345; *Est. Procs.*, ii, 260–1.

80. SRO GD 26/ix/274, Hill to Melville, 8 Oct. 1690.

81. *Culloden Papers*, 15–16, 'Memoir … for preserving the Peace of the Highlands', [1690]; *RPCS*, xv, 539–40.

82. The most famous legend about Farquharson, his riding his horse up the side of the Pass to escape, may be based on this defeat. Mackay, *Memoirs*, 101; *ib*., 346, Mackay to Melville, 29 Aug. 1690; *ib*., 349–50, same to PCS, 1 Sept. 1690; Macphèrson, *Original Papers*, ii, 118, 'An Account of the Highland Clans', 1709; *Seafield Corr.*, 64, Sir J. Abercromby to Findlater, 22 Aug. 1690; Grant, *Legends of the Braes o' Mar*, 106–7; *Est. Procs.*, ii, 263–4.

83. *Ib*., 262–3; *RPCS*, xv, 405, 448.

84. *HMCR Hope-Johnstone*, 94–5, W. Reoch's narrative, 25 Oct. 1690; Mackay, *Memoirs*, 101; *Est. Procs.*, ii, 266.

85. *ib*., 223, 248; NLS MS 1353 fol. 11, Mackenzie of Redcastle to Delvine, 26 July 1690; *ib*., fol. 14, same to same, 30 July 1690; *Leven & Melville*, 497, Hill to Melville, 21 Aug. 1690.

86. SRO GD 26/ix/274, same to [Tarbat], 13 Oct. 1690; *ib*., 279, Mackay to [Leven], 2 Sept. 1690; *State Trials*, xiii, 1447.

87. *Ib*., 1448; Maclean, 'Celtic Sources', 323–5, anon. 'Oran' [1690] (Fernaig MS; translated by Maclean); Warrand, *Some Mackenzie Pedigrees*, 31, 118, 127–8; *Est. Procs.*, ii, 216; NLS MS 1329 fol. 134, Sir A. Mackenzie to Delvine, 10 Sept. 1690; Macgill, *Old Ross-shire*, i, 238, same to Tarbat, n.d.

88. *Ib*; *Leven & Melville*, 502, Countess Dowager of Seaforth to Melville, 28 Aug. 1690.

89. Only Bernardi supports the estimate in the later indictment of Seaforth of 1,500. Mackenzie of Coul publicly claimed that there were only 700, but privately estimated 8–900. *State Trials*, xiii, 1448; Macgill, *Old Ross-shire*, i, 234, Sir A. Mackenzie to Tarbat, n.d; NLS MS 1329 fol. 133, same to Delvine, 9 Sept. 1690; Bernardi, *Life*, 72–3; Mackay, *Memoirs*, 351, Mackay to PCS, 1 Sept. 1690.

90. There is an unfortunate lack of precise dates in the sources. *Ib*., 346, same to 'Melville' [Leven], 29 Aug. 1690; *ib*., 101–2; *Est. Procs.*, ii, 266–7; Lovat, *Memoirs*, 11–12; *HMCR Hope-Johnstone*, 95, W. Reoch's narrative, 25 Oct. 1690.

91. It was later claimed that fear that the Munros would attack his country if he advanced further was one major factor. *Ib*., SRO GD 220/5/630/6/15, Sir R. Munro to Cpt. Munro, [1716].

92. Bernardi, *Life*, 73–4; Maclean, 'Celtic Sources', 323–4, 326, anon. 'Oran' [1690] (translated by Maclean); NLS MS 1329 fol. 134, Sir A. Mackenzie to Delvine, 10 Sept. 1690.

93. *Ib*., fol. 133, same to same, 9 Sept. 1690; *Leven & Melville*, 501–2, Countess Dowager to Melville, 28 Aug. 1690; Mackay, *Memoirs*, 102; *ib*., 346–7, Mackay to 'Melville' [Leven], 29 Aug. 1690.

94. *Ib*., 347; *State Trials*, xiii, 1448.

95. Mackay, *Memoirs*, 102; *ib*., 349–51, Mackay to PCS, 1 Sept. 1690; *ib*., 353–4, same to same, 2 Sept. 1690.

96. *Est. Procs.* ii, 270; Bernardi, *Life*, 74; *HMCR Finch*, ii, 466–7, Tarbat to Nottingham, 1 Oct. 1690; *State Trials*, xiii, 1448; Maclean, 'Celtic Sources', 324–5, anon. 'Oran' (translated by Maclean); NLS MS 1330 fol. 1, Sir A. Mackenzie to Delvine, 15 Jan. 1691; SRO GD 26/ix/279, Mackay to Melville, 2 Sept. 1690.

97. *Ib.*, same to [Leven], 11 Sept. 1690.

98. *Est. Procs.*, ii, 273–4; Maclean, 'Celtic Sources', 321–2, D. Macrae, 'Gre Orain'; *ib.*, 323–6, anon 'Oran' (translated by Maclean); NLS MS 1329 fol. 135, Sir A. Mackenzie to Delvine, 30 Sept. 1690; *ib.*, fol. 137, same to same, 20 Oct. 1690; *ib.*, MS 1330 fol. 26, same to same, 6 May 1691; *ib.*, MS 1353 fol. 17, Mackenzie of Redcastle to same, 15 Oct. 1690.

99. *HMCR Hope-Johnstone*, 95, W. Reoch's narrative, 25 Oct. 1690; *Scots Peerage*, ii, 199–200; *Est. Procs.*, ii, 280.

100. *Ib.*, 267–8; *RPCS*, xv, 423–4, 427.

101. *Ib.*, 428; *Est. Procs.*, ii, 270, 273, 277; *Leven & Melville*, 528–9, Drumlanrig to Melville, 10 Sept. 1690.

102. *APS*, ix, 464–5; *RPCS*, xv, 377–8, 518, Blair, Atholl MSS, Box 29 I (6) 31, Orders to Balquhidder watch, 10 Nov. 1690.

103. *HMCR Hope-Johnstone*, 95, W. Reoch's narrative, 25 Oct. 1690; *Est. Procs.*, ii, 274–5, 277–8; NLS MS 7012 fol. 177, Sir A. Bruce to Tweeddale, 1 Oct. 1690; Drumlanrig, Queensberry Papers, Vol. 115, 6, E. Bryce to Drumlanrig, 11 Sept. [1690]; *ib.*, Vol. 126, 10, same to same, 12 Sept. [1690]; *ib.*, 11, Mackay to same, 15 Sept. 1690; Mackay, *Memoirs*, 355–6, same to 'Hamilton' [Melville], 15 Sept. 1690.

104. *Ib.*, 356; *Melvilles & Leslies*, ii, 158, Cunningham to [same], 15 Sept. 1690; *Est. Procs.*, ii, 280, 285.

105. *Ib.*, 288–9; *HMCR Le Fleming*, 294, newsletter, 30 Sept. 1690; Macpherson, 'Gleanings', *TGSI*, xx, 230, Mackay to Cluny, 20 Oct. 1690; SRO GD 26/xiii/56, G. Gordon to D. Scrimseor, 1 Oct. 1690.

106. NLS Adv. MS 13.1.18 fol. 3, Struan to his mother, [late 1690]; *ib.*, fol. 81, 'The Behaviour of Alexander Robertson of Struan'; WDA, Browne MSS, 49, Cannon, Dunfermline & Dundee to [James], 27 Sept. 1690; *ib.*, 207, Buchan to same, 25 Sept. [1690].

107. One report claimed that Robertson of Struan was among those captured, but this must be a mistake. *RPCS*, xv, 471, 487–8; *ib.*, xvi, 150; *Est. Procs.*, ii, 288, 290; Atholl, *Chronicles*, i, 331, Marchioness to Murray, 29 Sept. [1690]; *HMCR Le Fleming*, 297–8, newsletters, 14, 18 Oct. 1690; Macgibbon & Ross, iii, 589–90.

108. *Ib.*; i, 357–8; *Est. Procs.*, ii, 285–6, 287, 290–1; *The Statistical Account of Scotland, 1791–1797*, ed. Sir J. Sinclair, (D. J. Withrington & I.R. Grant), 20 vols., (Wakefield, 1975–83), xv, 116.

109. *RPCS*, xv, 559; *ib.*, xvi, 27–8; *Leven & Melville*, 557, Crawford to Melville, 28 Oct. 1690; *HMCR Le Fleming*, 298–9, newsletter, 18 Oct. 1690; *Scots Peerage*, iv, 132; SRO GD 26/viii/99, Lt-Col Buchan to Hamilton, 18 Oct. 1690 + terms + list of prisoners; *London Gazette*, Nos. 2605, 27–30 Oct; 2606, 30 Oct.–3 Nov; 2607, 3–6 Nov. 1690.

110. *Ib.*, No. 2606.

111. *RPCS*, xv, 476, 484–5, 618, 620–1; *ib.*, xvi, 81–2, 148–9, 204; *Leven & Melville*, 523, Kintore to Melville, 2 Sept. 1690; *ib.*, 549–50, same to William, 18 Oct. 1690; *ib.*, 550, Crawford to Melville, 18 Oct. 1690; SRO GD 26/viii/99, Lt-Col Buchan to Hamilton, 18 Oct. 1690.

112. *RPCS*, xv, 406; *More Culloden Papers*, 215–16, Hill to Culloden, 8 December 1690; *Statistical Account*, xx, 210; NLS MS 1329 fol. 134, Sir A. Mackenzie to Delvine, 10 Sept. 1690; PRO ADM 106/399 fol. 363, Pottinger to Navy Board, 2 Sept. 1690.

113. *Ib.*, fol. 364, same to same, 4 Oct. 1690; *ib.*, ADM 51/345/1, 27 Aug; *ib.*, 51/3890/4, 9, 11 Sept.

114. Going, one (dubious) report claimed, to join Cannon. *Gazette de France*, 28 Oct. 1690(NS), 571, London report, 17 Oct. (NS).

115. PRO ADM 51/3890/4, 16, 17, 20, 21 Sept; *ib.*, ADM 106/399 fol. 364, Pottinger to Navy Board, 4 Oct. 1690.

116. *Leven & Melville*, 553–5, Tarbat to Melville, 21 Oct. 1690; *ib.*, 566–7, same to same, 6 Nov. 1690; *ib.*, 567, same to same, 8 Nov. 1690; *RPCS*, xv, 517; Rev. A. Macdonald, 'Gleanings from the Charter Chests of the Isles; Sleat', *TGSI*, xxxviii, 367–9, Cpt. H. Macdonald to Sir D. Macdonald, 23 Oct. 1690.

117. PRO ADM 51/3890/4, 22 Sept.

118. *RPCS*, xv, 430–2, 487; SRO GD 26/ix/274, Hill to Melville, 8 Oct. 1690, same to [Tarbat], '13' [11] Oct. 1690, 23 Oct. 1690; NLS MS 3138 fol. 35v, Argyll's report, 25 Nov. 1690.

119. *Ib.*, fols. 35, 36; *Inventory of Lamont Papers*, 278, Ardkinglas's regiment (misdated); *Leven & Melville*, 537, Hill to Melville, 2 Oct. 1690; *More Culloden Papers*, 215, same to Culloden, 8 Dec. 1690; PRO ADM 51/3890/4, 3, 4, 9 Oct.; *RPCS*, xv, 562.

120. *Ib.*, 485; *ib.*, 486–7, Articles for the surrender, 9 Oct. 1690; *HMCR 6th Report*, 702, Hill to R. Menzies, [1690].

121. As the legend represents Pottinger as sent by the King of Spain to avenge the destruction of the Tobermory Galleon, other points in it may be inaccurate. *London Gazette*, No. 2605, 27–30 Oct. 1690; Lorne, *Adventures in Legend*, 188–9; N. Macleod, *Reminiscences of a Highland Parish* (London, 1911), 179, 186–9; Martin, 'The Dartmouth, ... the ship', *IJNA*, vii, 30–1, 33, 39–40; SRO GD 26/ix/274, Hill to [Tarbat], '13' [11] Oct. 1690, same to Melville, '6' [16] Oct. 1690; PRO ADM 106/399 fol. 361, Pottinger to Sir R. Beach, 31 July 1690; *ib.*, fol. 364, same to Navy Board, 4 Oct. 1690.

122. See Chapter 8, pp. 273, 275–6, Chapter 9, p. 286.

123. Macfarlane, *Gen. Colls.*, i, 140; SRO GD 26/ix/274, Hill to [Tarbat], '13' [11] Oct. 1690.

124. *Ib.*, same to same, 23 Oct. 1690, same to Melville, '6' Oct. 1690; *Culloden Papers*, 13, same to Culloden, 24 Nov. 1690; PRO ADM 51/3890/4, 16, 18, 19, 21 Oct; *HMCR 6th Report*, 629, Argyll to Maclean cadets, 22 Oct. 1690.

125. *Ib.*, 634, Instructions to J. Campbell of Jura, C. Campbell of Bragleine, [Oct.–Nov. 1690]; PRO ADM 51/3890/4, 30 Oct., 2, 7, Nov.; NLS MS 3138 fol. 35v, Argyll's report, 25 Nov. 1690; *ib.*, MS 975 fol. 55, Hill to Argyll, 26 Nov. 1690; *Leven & Melville*, 617, same to Melville, 3 June 1691; SRO GD 26/ix/274, same to [Mackay], 2 Nov. 1690.

126. *Ib*; *ib.*, same to Melville, 2 Nov. 1690; *Culloden Papers*, 13, same to Culloden, 24 Nov. 1690; Macfarlane, *Gen. Colls.*, i, 140; *RCAHMS Argyll*, iii, 177, 208, 217, 226; NLS MS 3138 fol. 35v, Argyll's report, 25 Nov. 1690; PRO ADM 51/3890/4, 8 Nov; *RPCS*, xv, 561–2.

127. SRO GD 26/ix/114, Estimates of freights of ships; NLS MS 7012 fol. 222, Bruce to Tweeddale, 29 Nov. 1690; *HMCR Hope-Johnstone*, 197, Hill to Crawford, 15 Dec. 1690; *Culloden Papers*, 13, Hill to Culloden, 24 Nov. 1690.

128. *Ib.*, 12.

129. *More Culloden Papers*, 217, same to same, 8 Dec. 1690; SRO GD 26/ix/274, same to [Tarbat], '13' [11] Oct. 1690; NLS MS 7012 fol. 222, Bruce to Tweeddale, 29 Nov. 1690.

130. Drumlanrig, Queensberry Papers, bundle 500, 'An account of ye Artillery ... of ffort Wm', 7 Dec. 1691.

131. Prebble, *Glencoe*, 109–10; SRO GD 26/ix/274, Hill to Melville, 8 Oct. 1690.

132. *More Culloden Papers*, 214, same to [same], 2 Nov. 1690; *HMCR Hope-Johnstone*, 187, same to Crawford, 15 Dec. 1690.

133. NLS MS 7012 fol. 215, Bruce to Tweeddale, 15 Nov. 1690; SRO GD 26/ix/274, Hill to [Tarbat], 23 Oct. 1690.

134. *Ib.*, same to Melville, 8 Oct. 1690, same to [Mackay], 6 Nov. 1690; *RPCS*, xv, 516; NLS MS 7012 fol. 222, Bruce to Tweeddale, 29 Nov. 1690; *More Culloden Papers*, 208, Livingston to Culloden, 19 Nov. [1690].

135. *Ib.*, 215, Hill to same, 8 Dec. 1690; *Earls of Cromartie*, i, 72–3, same to '[Queensberry]', [Melville], 25 Dec. 1690; *RPCS*, xv, 523, 545.

136. *Ib.*, 548–9; *HMCR Hope-Johnstone*, 161, Hill to Crawford, 16 Nov. 1690; *ib.*, 166, same to same, 16 Jan. 1691.

137. *Ib.*, 194, Information, 23 Mar. 1691; *RPCS*, xv, 575–6; *ib.*, xvi, 9; *Leven & Melville*, 522–3, William's order, 2 Sept. 1690.

138. *Ib.*, 565, Tarbat to Melville, 1 Nov. 1690; *Culloden Papers*, 17, 'Memoir . . . for preserving the Peace of the Highlands', [1690]; SRO GD 26/xiii/59, Mackintosh to Countess of Melville, 24 Nov. 1690.

139. Tarbat suggested as much. *Ib.*, 58, Docquet of letters arrived, 19 Nov. 1690; *Leven & Melville*, 567, Tarbat to Melville, 8 Nov. 1690; *Culloden Papers*, vii; *More Culloden Papers*, 217–18, Hill to Culloden, 8 Dec. 1690.

140. *Earls of Cromartie*, i, 73, same to '[Queensberry]' [Melville], 25 Dec. 1690; *APS*, viii, 504; Kilgour, *Lochaber in War & Peace*, 330–1, charter of Maryburgh, 13 Nov. 1690; SRO GD 26/ix/274, Hill, 'Ane accompt how the highlanders were brought to . . . Civilitie', [Oct. 1690].

141. *Ib.*, Hill to [Mackay], 2 Nov. 1690.

142. *Ib.*, same to Melville, 8 Oct. 1690; *Culloden Papers*, 13, same to Culloden, 24 Nov. 1690; NLS MS 1329 fol. 139v, Sir A. Mackenzie to Delvine, 28 Oct. 1690.

143. Bernardi, *Life*, 75–83 (misdated; correct year from *Carstares S.P.*., 150–1).

144. SRO GD 26/ix/274, Glengarry to Hill, 25 Oct. 1690; *Culloden Papers*, 13, Hill to Culloden, 24 Nov. 1690.

145. *Leven & Melville*, 585, Tarbat to Melville, 18 Dec. 1690; SRO GD 26/ix/274, Hill to [Mackay], 2 Nov. 1690, same to Melville, 6 Nov. 1690.

146. Macdonald, 'Gleanings', *TGSI*, xxxviii, 370, Cpt. H. Macdonald to Sir D. Macdonald, 2 Jan. 1691.

147. *HMCR Hope-Johnstone*, 161, Hill to Crawford, 16 Nov. 1690; *Culloden Papers*, 13, same to Culloden, 24 Nov. 1690; SRO GD 26/ix/274, same to Melville, 2 Nov. 1690.

148. *Ib.*; *ib.*, same to same, 6 Nov. 1690, same to [Mackay], 2 Nov. 1690.

149. *Ib.*, same to [Tarbat], 13 Oct. 1690, same to Melville, 8 Oct. 1690.

150. *More Culloden Papers*, 217, same to Culloden, 8 Dec. 1690.

151. *Ib.*, 214–15, same to [Melville], 2 Nov. 1690; *Leven & Melville*, 538, same to same, 2 Oct. 1690; SRO GD 26/ix/274, same to [Mackay], 6 Nov. 1690.

152. *HMCR Hope-Johnstone*, 187, same to Crawford, 15 Dec. 1690; *Earls of Cromartie*, i, 73, same to '[Queensberry]' [Melville], 25 Dec. 1690; *Leven & Melville*, 565, Tarbat to same, 1 Nov. 1690; *ib.*, 584, same to same, 18 Dec. 1690.

153. *More Culloden Papers*, 209, Livingston to Culloden, 19 Nov. [1690].

154. *CSPD 1690-1*, 298–9, newsletter, 7 Mar. 1691; *Leven & Melville*, 601, Livingston to Melville, 2 Apr. 1691; SRO GD 26/ix/316, Dalrymple to same, 24 Feb. 1691.

155. *APS*, ix, 220–1, 233–4; *ib.*, App. 68; *RPCS*, xv, 503, 517–18, 527, 537.

156. Hooke, *Negotiations*, i, 498–512, Earl of Lauderdale, 'L'Etat de l'Ecosse', 1690; *Gazette de France*, 26 Aug. 1690(NS), 436, London report, 15 Aug. (NS); *ib.*, 2 Sept. 1690,

450, same, 22 Aug. (NS); *ib.*, 23 Sept. 1690, 498, same, 8 Sept. (NS); *ib.*, 14 Oct. 1690 (NS), 533, same, 26 Sept. (NS).

157. SCA, Blairs Letters, Box U, 1690, 21, Burnet to Nicholson, 29 Nov. 1690; *Carstares S.P.*, 148, [Macky], Information for Sydney, [c. Jan. 1691].

158. *Earls of Cromartie*, i, 73, Hill to '[Queensberry]' [Melville], 25 Dec. 1690.

159. *Life of James*, ii, 433–4, 451–2, 468–9; *Carstares S.P.*, 149–50, [Macky], Information for Sydney, [c. Jan. 1691]; NLS MS 3194 fols. 114v–115, James's Instructions [to Charteris, Nov. 1690]; *Franco-Irish Corr.*, ii, 288, Fumeron to Louvois, 23 May 1691(NS).

8

The Road to Achallader (November 1690–June 1691)

On 2 August, Sir William Hamilton wrote from Edinburgh:

> The breach betuixt the tuo Dalrimples and M[elville] is greater than ever. Young D. they say hes joyned with D. Q[ueensberry] and M. A[tholl] for beating doune of M[elville] and presbytrie together; and yesterday eight dayes they sent away ... to the King ... The morrow after W. Carstairs was sent by M. to counter them.[1]

It marked the emergence of a new political alignment which was predictable, but which the Montgomerie Plot had delayed. The Officers of State had been obliged to stand together publicly against an Opposition in which 'episcopalian' plotters insincerely supported Montgomerie's (equally insincere) demands for the extreme presbyterian settlement of 1649. When the plot collapsed, Melville claimed, Dalrymple strengthened his ties with the 'episcopalians' by warning Arran and Breadalbane of warrants against them, and he continued to see Arran when he was in hiding.[2]

The coalition Dalrymple could assemble to attack Melville's ruling faction was broad. Queensberry and Drumlanrig had been on opposite sides during the plot, but they were now co-operating, and Melville was wildly denouncing them.[3] Stair was a Presbyterian in religion, but supported his son's 'episcopalian' policies from necessity as well as family ambition: the 'presbyterian' members had led the attack on him for his judicial record, and for now making William appoint, unconstitutionally, a weak Session to ensure his own dominance as President. Having to manage a parliament infuriated by this grievance had made Melville, like Hamilton the year before, very hostile to Stair. Tweeddale, who had settled in London in 1689, was Dalrymple's chief intermediary at Whitehall. He was not really committed to bringing in the 'episcopalians', suggesting in late 1690 that the ambassador to Brandenburg, James Johnston —no less a Whig 'presbyterian' than Melville, but intelligent and financially scrupulous — should become joint Secretary. However, his reputation as an honest politician — by Scottish standards —made him a valuable ally.[4] Mackay, who went to London in November, by now hated Melville blindly, seeing every delay or obstruction during 1690 as deliberately intended to discredit him. Belatedly realising that he had needlessly increased his difficulties in 1689 by suspicions of Atholl, he began to recommend him enthusiastically, though unable to guarantee his loyalty to William.[5]

Dalrymple's policy of bringing 'episcopalian' nobles into office was, from one viewpoint, a predictable development: from another, it was lunacy. Attempting it had wrecked Tarbat's independent career; and since then the 'episcopalian' peers had plunged into the Montgomerie Plot, and Annandale had revealed their involvement. Dalrymple's persistence under these circumstances reveals a vital truth about his character.

Dalrymple was certainly an unscrupulous politician. In Charles's reign, he helped organise a false accusation of treason. In a classic example of a Scottish family's balancing, he became Advocate under James, saving the estate which Stair's involvement wtih Argyll in exile had forfeited; Stair made him retain office when he wanted to resign. Yet, despite his former protection of local Presbyterians, he now strained the law to convict Covenanters. His extreme ambition made him uphold the absolutist basis of James's policy of toleration — he afterwards rationalised this, to the horror of good Jacobites, as intended to ruin him.[6] After the Revolution, he denied that the Claim of Right was binding on William, and took credit for blindly defending his prerogative. Yet in the 1689 session he tried to curry favour with his Club opponents, and Melville believed, from a document captured at Cromdale, that he and Stair had tried to 'reinsure' themselves with the Jacobites.[7] Most writers have therefore portrayed him as a cool-headed Machiavellian, moved by rational self-interest and therefore supporting a union with more 'civilised' England — at whatever cost.[8]

Though this contains some truth, Dalrymple, like his notorious 'Machiavellian' contemporary Sunderland, was not a far-sighted, calm intriguer. The superstitious belief in a diabolical taint running through the family symbolises his other side. He was 'stiff, peremptory and very proud, and would hear no reasoning when he took up a pique and was disobliged'. His policy often merely rationalised these feelings, and sometimes erupted into unthinking, ruinous violence. The second most notorious example was at Anne's cabinet meeting on the 'Scots Plot' in 1704, when he burst out that Scotland was already virtually in rebellion, and that she must send an army, paid from England, to hold it down.[9] He was naturally a gambler, as even his youthful secret marriage to an heiress shows. Not only had her reputation suffered from a rape; her stepfather, the powerful Lord Register, who had intended his son to marry the estate, became a mortal enemy to Dalrymple and Stair.[10] Both these traits encouraged and shaped his commitment to 'episcopalian' policy from 1689; his old tutor Veitch, who saw him that April still quivering with shock after presbyterian second thoughts had nearly deprived him of the chance to offer the crown to William, thought that that incident gave him an ineradicable grudge.[11]

There were always, of course, good pragmatic reasons for any politician to peddle the 'episcopalian' line to William. By late 1690, the appeal of the 'natural rulers' was somewhat tarnished. However, Melville's alternative regime, a small, unrepresentative clique, was discredited. He and his followers, insecure in their offices, exploited them unscrupulously to make speedy fortunes, further increasing William's displeasure and their own insecurity. This seriously reduced the revenue available for the war. One instance was Leven's regiment, of high quality when first raised, but by 1691 reduced by his embezzlements to mutiny, 'ye worst in ye Armie'.[12] Relying for support on presbyterian extremists, Melville could not prevent them from enforcing the religious settlement harshly in the (dubiously legal) General Assembly, its committees, and the Council, where Crawford could still conjure up bigoted quorums. Warnings from moderates at Court were disregarded. The religious issue had the advantage of bringing into play English bishops and politicians, needed to counterbalance Portland and Carstares, who, impressed by Melville's supposed influence among Presbyterians, supported him long after he became insignificant. William had never forgiven Melville his religious concessions in parliament; but his own natural reluctance to make decisions regarding a country that scarcely affected him directly was increasing. Religion, on which appeals from Englishmen would supplement Dalrymple's, was the lever most likely to move him.[13]

English politics justified William in at least balancing the 'presbyterians' with some 'episcopalians' in government. Even after his original 'trimming' gave way to a mainly Tory ministry, he carefully kept several important posts for Whigs. A party totally excluded from favour could sabotage war supplies in parliament; its members' resentment at exclusion from office, or fear of being judicially murdered through false witnesses (which a skilful Jacobite had aroused in Montgomerie in 1689) might even make them appeal to James.[14] Mixed ministries, though unstable, worked fairly well between reshuffles. William's hopes of similar results in Scotland were to fail because the two sides were so intent on fighting each other that they had little energy for anything else. In late 1690, however, Dalrymple's scheme seemed plausible.

The first step, however, was decidedly a gamble: to bring touchy nobles involved in a major conspiracy to Court, prove their penitence and obtain their remissions. William had silently decided to ignore nearly all plotting before the Boyne, but his rebuke to Tarbat must always have been in Dalrymple's mind. He must now choose between the two incompatible magnates who had supported him, and decided against Atholl. Atholl lacked a surviving network of supporters like Queensberry's, but the negative reasons were still stronger. As one Queensberry man said, 'The nation is too little to satisfy that family': Atholl and Dunmore alone would expect positions bringing £5–6000 a year, and the other sons would also demand office.[15] The general belief that Atholl and his family had acted treacherously in the Highlands throughout 1689 and were responsible for Killiecrankie was an extra burden of prejudice which might wreck Dalrymple's plan. Mackay, besides, wanted Atholl to pacify the Highlands, the role for which Dalrymple had long groomed Breadalbane.[16]

Breadalbane had planned to be one of the 'episcopalian' representatives to William, and sent his wife ahead to London, but his friends persuaded him not to come. Linlithgow and Balcarres set out for London, to 'sound the ford'.[17] Queensberry, who was expected to lead them, also remained in Scotland. The scheme relied on his magnate interest, the others reported their progress to him throughout 1691, and his supporters made extravagant claims of office for him; but, whether from increasing illness, lingering fears of James's restoration or other reasons, he himself took comparatively little part. The warrant for his remission for treason, necessary if he were to re-enter politics, was obtained in June 1691, but he never had it passed, and took out a formal pardon for the same crimes only in late 1693.[18] This gave an unexpected importance to Dalrymple, the active faction leader, and to his particular protégé Linlithgow, who strengthened his position by giving the Presbyterians an impression of conversion. It was hoped to turn Leven out of the Castle in his favour; and Dalrymple may already secretly have had the further ambition he admitted in May — to have him made Chancellor.[19]

However, Jacobite connections threatened everything. Hamilton complained that Dalrymple persuaded William that Arran, if he surrendered, should be bailed only if he took the oath of allegiance, at the request of Queensberry, Linlithgow and the rest, 'that he might be as deep in as they for they go mad to think he should be in other circumstances then theirs' — only meaningful if they expected a restoration.[20] Balcarres was the most extreme. As he went south, his long 'Memoirs touching the Revolution in Scotland' were sent across to St. Germain. He considered fleeing there himself, and Melfort from Rome launched panic-stricken denunciations to discredit him. He finally went to London only because 'since wee are brought in a foolish afair [the Montgomerie Plot] noe body can blaim us to extricat our selfs as weal as wee can'.[21] Indeed, he supported Dalrymple's plans only on his assurance that he himself was putting the 'episcopalians' into office merely to bring about James's restoration. Balcarres solemnly sent James the news. Of course, Dalrymple was insincere: he would use similar claims when he needed the support of Whig Jacobite leaders later. Yet there was great danger that the story would fall into the hands of an enemy who would take it literally — as actually happened. Dalrymple may have been no more sincere in his support for episcopalianism than for James; but, even if the motive that drove him was purely negative, hatred for the Whigs and Presbyterians, it made him take enormous risks to put the 'episcopalians' into office — a far cry from the colourlessly ambitious figure presented by Riley, with 'little in mind but using other peoples' backs to reach higher and higher ledges'.[22]

Linlithgow and Balcarres found the English Tory ministry ready to help them for religious reasons. Its head, Lord President Carmarthen, was an ambiguous figure, but Secretary Nottingham was more blindly sincere in his commitment to whatever political groups claimed to represent episcopalian interests — 'party sense in person', one hostile observer called him. However, Melville blocked access to the king, on the grounds that Linlithgow and Balcarres were implicated in Montgomerie's plot. Portland told them that William could not in honour see them until they took out remissions for it, though they need not confess anything. Linlithgow complained to Queensberry that if he had been there the demand would not have been made. After further obstruction by Melville, Linlithgow and Balcarres saw William and reported on the condition of Scotland. Linlithgow correctly predicted to Queensberry that William would appoint Dalrymple as joint Secretary and declare his willingness to employ both 'episcopalians' and 'presbyterians', but would make no more changes until his return from the great Allied conference at the Hague, for which he was to leave in January. 'This is mutch more then could have bein expected . . . , nor indeed can on ansuer for any thing untill they sie it in blake and whitt'. That instability of Court decisions made

Dalrymple's appointment in December a necessary preliminary to any further 'episcopalian' advance.[23]

Balcarres' blunders were the main threat. To justify himself, he described Dalrymple's promise to serve James to leading Jacobite agents, and also to Argyll (his mother's stepson) hoping to win him over. Argyll's brother James had forcibly married an English child-heiress, and his adviser Sir John Johnston was betrayed, tried, and hanged on 23 December. He denied that they had used force, and was seen as a victim of English prejudice: 'The Scotch Nation take it so much to themselves, yt it has had a more generall effect than a privat case can be thought to have'. Argyll vainly solicited William and Parliament to pardon Johnston. The general Scottish sympathy for the abductors would reappear in a more notorious case.[24] Balcarres' approach was therefore not total lunacy, but it still failed. Argyll reported it fully to Melville, and soon confirmed that Balcarres had also told the Jacobite agents — so it was not a trick to convert him. Argyll at first refused to let William know that the information came from him, evidently fearing the king would assume he had done something to justify the confidence. Here was a rift which a more skilful Jacobite might exploit. However at present, though William presumably disbelieved the charges, 'episcopalian' activities suffered discredit, especially as Balcarres was supposed to be close to Dalrymple.[25]

Mackay had left Scotland for ever, although he served in 1691 in Ireland. On his recommendation, Sir Thomas Livingston rather than the more senior Ramsay was made Commander-in-Chief. He received rank as brigadier-general and a seat on the Privy Council only in March, and until then had to preside, with a junior colonel's commission, over a major reorganisation of the army.[26] Ramsay sailed with four regiments, including Angus's, to Flanders. Besides the three regiments amalgamated into Hill's, Strathnaver's foot and Cardross's dragoons were broken — the latter probably for its Cameronian connections. The Scottish establishment now contained two regiments of dragoons, formed from the independent troops of horse, three foot regiments, Argyll's, Buchan's and Hill's (the largest), and independent companies at Finlarig, Blair, Abergeldie, Ruthven and Ballindalloch. Paid from England, but at the inadequate Scottish rate, were Livingston's dragoons and Leven's and Lauder's foot. There was also the English regiment of Sir James Leslie, who succeeded Livingston as Governor of Inverness (besides another, Beveridge's, in Edinburgh since 1689).[27]

The immediate result was a rash of mutinies, particularly among troops facing disbandment or reduced status, whose arms and accoutrements were their only lever for obtaining their arrears. Despite Parliament's grants, the troops in November were six months further in arrears than in March 1690, and were ruining the country with free quarter, the garrisons being the worst. The officers, almost never paid, often lived by cheating their men. Even without the government's corruption and incompetence, the revenue, though William reserved it almost entirely for the army's subsistence, was hopelessly insufficient. Powder and arms were almost exhausted; Livingston made grandiose plans for fortifying Inverness or preparing campaign magazines in the garrisons, but could scarcely keep Fort William supplied. When invasion seemed possible in April, he warned: 'we schal not be in a condition to drau together; for no provisions, ... scars of amonition, no bagage horsis; ... so that we schal be a great deal wors provyded as thoas that coms to invade us'.[28]

Fortunately, the enemy remained quiet. James's letters to Buchan apologised for not sending supplies in 1690 and promised some for the spring — and perhaps also the landing of forces. Yet Buchan remained at Invergarry and Cannon in Skye. They believed that they still had many supporters in the Lowlands — Duncan Menzies that autumn was to list some, including almost 'the whole shires of Angus and Mearns' — but, unlike the previous year, no attempt was made to rouse them.[29] The only real military activity came from the Macleans. In January, their Carnaburg flotilla captured a provision ship bound for William's Irish army, their Duart flotilla one bound for Fort William. In February, they re-entered Mull and fought a desperate skirmish against the Aros garrison. However, by April Sir John was negotiating with Hill to surrender Duart.[30]

In Dunbartonshire, Stirlingshire and Perthshire, parties chiefly of Macgregors continued raids indistinguishable (apart from a special animus against Williamites) from normal thieving: when winter prevented them from lifting cattle, they stole household goods. In late January, the Council re-established a garrison at Cardross Castle, but all garrisons were too small even to protect local sympathisers. Parties of up to forty raiders openly quartered round Doune. In February, the Stirlingshire and Dunbartonshire gentry organised a watch under other Macgregors, including Glengyle's son John, evidently as part of a bargain to free his father. Several suspect Stirlingshire lairds were put under bond to prevent their collaborating. Yet in mid-April there were further major Macgregor raids near Stirling, possibly with Glengyle's other son, Rob Roy, taking part.[31] In May captains of watches in Menteith and Atholl were found to be in contact with rebels. There were raids all round the borders of the disaffected areas, the largest in Moray in late March. Occasionally, raiders were killed, and frequent special commissions were issued for trying robbers — some of whom doubtless considered themselves legitimate solders.[32].

The new impulse came from the Lowlands. William intended to let the bygones of the Montgomerie Plot be bygones — except for the unfortunate Neville Payne, whom he tortured and then imprisoned, illegally, for over ten years. In January, he let Seaforth be freed, and Arran and Home emerge from hiding, on bail.[33] Arran instantly resumed intriguing. It was more dangerous because the government, exceptionally, had two good spies. Melville, a credulous foreigner, was normally the dupe of the feeblest of the London plot-forgers, modelling themselves on Titus Oates, who pestered ministers. Now there appeared two agents, John Macky and Alexander Higgens, who had been at St. Germain and had the full confidence of British Jacobites. Working independently, they sometimes crossed purposes; but they provided much accurate information, all indicating that the 'episcopalian' nobles were untrustworthy. The plotting revolved round Arran and the worldly Archbishop Paterson of Glasgow. In late March, a clear message arrived from St Germain that the French could spare no forces until the autumn; but Paterson's circle, who were hopelessly optimistic, became convinced, with 'no other grounds than what their own fancies dictated to them', that an invasion from Dunkirk under the Dukes of Berwick and Gordon was imminent, at first with only a token force, which was soon embroidered into several thousand men. The rumour spread through the Lowlands and, via the clans' most trusted correspondent Lord Frendraught, to the Highlands, where it was eagerly swallowed.[34]

The highlanders had also more solid reasons for encouragement. On 29 March, after a three-week siege, Louis XIV captured the great city of Mons, while William's army was still unready. This demonstration of French power rang through Europe, as Louis intended. It made plausible the hopes of French assistance, even the story about Berwick and Gordon. Glengarry began to fortify Invergarry with earthworks and palisades. Lochiel and the other chiefs treating with Hill broke off, making him suggest angrily that, if they rose, the south-western Presbyterians and the Williamite clans should be loosed on them 'till they be utterly rooted out'. Iain Lom's triumphant and savage 'Oran an Righ Uilleam agus Banrigh Mairi' shows the new confidence the news aroused. Dunfermline, whom the clans sent in early May to seek help from James, carried an oddly divided message: complaints of the crypto-Jacobite nobles' inactivity and a warning that unless the southern Scots joined them, or he sent help, they must submit; a claim that they were still firm Jacobites and could assemble 10,000 strong if they were only given arms and victuals.[35]

Meanwhile, the spies' reports reflected devastatingly on Dalrymple's schemes. Both episcopalian archbishops had been ready to sign an invitation to James, though Darymple persuaded William that St Andrews was not worth arresting. Queensberry was deeply involved with Paterson, Tarbat more ambiguously so; and Balcarres and Linlithgow, Macky reported, were privy to all business concerted for James. Queensberry, Linlithgow and Breadalbane delayed their April journey to London to await the fate of Mons, and Breadalbane tried to see Arran secretly, employed a Jacobite agent whom Arran had, typically, abandoned and meddled in Paterson's affair. Had Melville been able to let the intrigue unfold further, the 'episcopalian' leaders might have committed themselves irrevocably; and Dalrymple was probably relieved in mid-April to countersign William's order for the arrest of Paterson, which broke it off sharply.[36]

Breadalbane had previously remained on his estates since Montgomerie's plot collapsed. On 9 September, the Council had ordered him and the Earl of Menteith to Edinburgh to receive orders for preventing highland raids. He had excused himself as fearing arrest for debt; but he actually feared that it was a pretext to seize him and try him for treason. He was naturally concerned to prevent highland raids into Argyllshire; but he would have been reluctant to promise, as did Menteith, to co-operate with troops sent to the area: he would do nothing to encourage soldiers.[37] He was still scribbling angry protests about the Finlarig garrison's plundering. In March 1690, the commander had protested that a siege of three or four days would starve it out, but the Council did nothing. After stealing meal and burning Breadalbane's plantations until November, almost all the garrison mutinied, bound their officers, and marched off, declaring that they were starving but had oppressed the country round them for too long already. The Council merely sent them to Fort William, but an independent company soon filled the gap.[38]

Glenlyon, now a serving captain in Argyll's regiment, was a particular menace. He collected rents in Atholl's part of Glenlyon, alienating Lord Murray. In December, he mustered 240 Argyllshire men for a raid on a supposed Jacobite's lands, and they made their way plundering through Glenorchy and Strathfillan before discovering that he had no warrant. He then proposed ravaging Glenlyon itself, but his followers came to their senses on the march and dispersed. 'Glenlyon ought nou to be sent to Bedlam, as Sr Duncan used his great Grandfh' wrote Breadalbane furiously.[39]

The ravaging by both sides naturally turned Breadalbane's attention to the means of pacification. 'I have seen many proposals made', he wrote, 'for setling the highlands by lowland politicians on Topick wherof was that no highlanders should hav a vote in it, but all proved yet ineffectual except, On' — his own between Lochiel and Mackintosh.[40] Considering the possibilities of a settlement, he developed a design for achieving primacy in the Highlands: that a semi-permanent highland militia, 4000 strong, should be maintained, under a 'principal person' drawing general's pay —himself. It arose from the scheme for a highland regiment which he had proposed in 1685. Perhaps Lochiel's claim in early 1690 that James had promised that after a restoration he would keep the highlanders in military pay (which must have been a bargaining point in Breadalbane's 1690 negotiations) had revived it.[41] It made Breadalbane a more reliable collaborator in Dalrymple's plans than Dalrymple himself realised; for, beside the hope of attaining such a position, questions of allegiance seemed trivial. The depth and persistence of Breadalbane's commitment to this dream are shown in the obstinacy with which he proposed it at the start of 1692, when the highlanders' conduct had made it impossible;[42] and, even more, in stone and mortar.

From late 1690, despite his enormous debts, he was rebuilding Kilchurn Castle on a massive scale — 'one of the last major essays in private fortification in Britain'. It is not surprising that the renewed fighting and insecurity should have made him repair his one real stronghold as a refuge for himself, his tenants and their goods. Yet this need makes inexplicable the form the rebuilding took: 'a large block of barracks, suitable for the accommodation of a private army ... of more than two hundred men' — the likeliest means, in this or any future crisis, to bring upon Kilchurn the fate Breadalbane most dreaded, a government garrison. Already in November 1689 one had been planned, and Breadalbane had used all his influence and sophistry to prevent its being installed. Yet he was willing to take this risk to have a barrack ready for his share of the projected force.[43] Obviously, such a scheme had no place for Fort William. This was the one real difference between Breadalbane's plan of pacification and Tarbat's, which gave the governor there a similar position of supervisor over the western clans largely because he had no highland links and might therefore be impartial. This in itself would probably be juster and more satisfactory to the clans; but it was based on the admission that they were the government's enemies, Breadalbane's scheme on the assumption that they could become its supporters. Once his intentions became known, Hill, financially dependent on his pay and already Melville's partisan, would become a dangerous enemy.[44]

Breadalbane continued to rebuild Kilchurn despite a major family disaster. Lord and Lady Glenorchy, marooned for years in Caithness caring for Breadalbane's interests, mutinied and set out for England, giving as justification her need for English medical care in her pregnancy. In Aberdeenshire she fell ill and died on 4 February. Her inheritance as co-heiress of her father Newcastle (who died that autumn) was lost. Breadalbane now needed the profits of office still more urgently. The danger of ruin also made him promote even more vehemently the 'Caithness bargains', a scheme for selling lands there that wronged his wife's jointure rights. These rights, interpreted unfavourably, could easily ruin him; and, when the Countess was in Edinburgh in January 1690, he had ordered Carwhin to shut off secretly all access to her except by his friends. Now he entered into bargains which, if they went wrong, might leave her penniless.[45] He showed similar ruthlessness in trying to introduce new methods of administering his estates, nearly driving Barcaldine to resign. Yet Breadalbane never feared that his grievance might make him betray the Earl's Jacobite double dealings: 'I can trust my lyf & fortoun to his honesty', he wrote.[46] (See Preface, p. vii)

Normal estate business that December included the seizure of three of Campbell of Ardchattan's followers who had stole a tenant's cows. Breadalbane imprisoned the thieves at Balloch until full compensation was paid — unless Ardchattan's violent protests should force him to hang them. They were apparently originally from Glencoe, for on 29 December Breadalbane wrote about the case to Barcaldine: 'If you find any of the Clan ean medle in this affair of resenting my apprehending of theives who stealls my gear, send for Ion roy in Achinryrie Imediatly to come up to yow & send him with the Incloased to mc ean'. This was probably the start of Breadalbane's dispute with MacIain, which erupted in a violent quarrel at the Achallader meeting in June.[47] However, Breadalbane had other connections with the Glencoe men that spring. The minister of Glenorchy was an Episcopalian. Already in 1690 the pre-1662 presbyterian minister, though settled elsewhere, had unsuccessfully tried to re-establish himself. Now largely through the officiousness of Sheriff-depute Campbell of Ardkinglas, the synod deprived the Episcopalian by a trick and appointed another Presbyterian in March 1691. Breadalbane, as one of a faction emphasising its own lawfulness and its opponents' 'rabblings', could not keep him out by force. However, while the Glenorchy people merely refused to hear the minister, a party of Lochaber and Glencoe men appeared and abducted him, 'telling him he behoved to see Buchan & Cannon in the Ile of Skye or he returned'. They were pursued and, after theatrical exchanges of threats, released him on his promise never to return. Breadalbane made Carwhin spread the news that none of his own men had joined in the kidnapping, but he must at least have connived at it.[48]

After some delays, Queensberry, well furnished by his faction with reports on Scotland's grievances, set out in early April with Linlithgow. Breadalbane still cautiously avoided Edinburgh, and met them on the road. They formed just one of several groups representing all Scotish factions who assembled in London to meet

William on his return.[49] Dalrymple might reasonably have expected a change of ministry. Instead, William departed for Holland again on 1 May without making alterations. The Melville clique, surviving through his indifference to Scottish affairs, not his favour, was forced by insecurity to rely still more on presbyterian bigots. Dalrymple's proposals had already failed by 28 April, and Breadalbane (whose pardon for the Montgomerie Plot William signed at Harwich) decided to spend the summer in London.[50]

The hitch arose largely because William, remembering past 'episcopalian' plots, was determined to observe their conduct over the summer before entrusting them with office. Time was on Dalrymple's side, provided that his protégés behaved well. However, on past form, if the invasion scare was justified, or if Louis sent aid to Scotland after the Flanders campaign, some 'episcopalians' would misbehave, wrecking his bid for power as they had Tarbat's. Massive desertions to the enemy by Scottish officers in Flanders were an evil portent. Success in pacifying the Highlands, however, would remove France's incentive to invade and would be a catalyst to bring the 'episcopalians' safely into office before they could be further tempted.[51]

Dalrymple therefore resumed soliciting after William's departure. Mary, a strong Anglican advised by Carmarthen and Nottingham, already favoured him. He used the invasion scare, believed in England longer than in Scotland itself, to persuade her to authorise Breadalbane in negotiating with the clans. His own attitude to the rumour was to be important. Until March he openly disbelieved it, since the French had failed to exploit their existing foothold in Ireland. However, the constant corroborations converted him to belief in the danger. Breadalbane later appealed to his clemency by emphasising its reality — a futile step unless he thought Dalrymple sincere. When, after crossing to Flanders, Dalrymple found that the Duke of Berwick was in the French camp, his attitude was that the story, though itself false, had expressed a general truth. The French would send military aid to the clans when they had the chance; and therefore the war must be ended, by pacification or, if that failed, by force.[52]

He could argue that the army was unfit for a highland campaign. He obtained cannon and ammunition for it, but on 28 April — at a time when his hopes of employing Breadalbane had collapsed — he ordered Livingston not to provoke the clans into activity, since there was no money for a field army.[53] The increasing consensus among Mary's advisers on attempting a peaceful settlement was reflected by Breadalbane's rival. Samuel Souton belonged to a syndicate that had dived on the Tobermory Galleon in James's reign, wanted to have their grant confirmed despite Argyll's restoration, and hoped to strengthen their case with proposals on ending the war, rapidly altered to suit Court attitudes: on 27 April, a seaborne invasion of the Isles (run largely on credit); on 1 May, a landing in Lochaber, but only after money had been offered to pacify the chiefs; on 8 May, negotiations with warships in the background. One suggestion, 'that men may be raysed in the Highlands for the King and Queene's service',may indicate that similar ideas to Breadalbane's already vaguely existed.[54]

It was decided that Breadalbane should negotiate with the chiefs for their submission to William, who would in return buy out the troublesome superiorities with money from the English Treasury, enabling them to hold directly of the Crown. His instructions left the sum blank, but a limit of £12,000 was verbally agreed at his suggestion. He borrowed £2000 of it and set off. Earlier in May, the Admiralty had ordered three warships to the west coast of Scotland. Dalrymple had then thought that they might attack and subdue the Isles, so long as this did not rouse the mainland clans to united action, but had admitted that Hill thought it would. Now they coud be used to blockade the coast — a reminder of the force backing Breadalbane's negotiation. Dalrymple, serving as Scottish Secretary in Flanders, persuaded William to confirm everything.[55]

This success finally alienated the Duke of Hamilton, who had arrived too late to meet William. Although in his own way a supporter of 'episcopalian' policies, he resented Dalrymple's high-handedness and his own exclusion from decisions, and opposed the preferment of former conspirators to high office, particularly — since he had earmarked the post of Chancellor for himself since 1689 — Dalrymple's suggestion for it of Linlithgow. All this drove him to reconciliation and co-operation with Melville, despite his religious policy. As Secretary and President of the Council, they could easily sabotage or misrepresent the negotiations. Dalrymple therefore established an informal chain of communication with Breadalbane, Solicitor Lockhart in Edinburgh and Nottingham in London. If the 'presbyterian' ministers had any scruples about opposing his scheme, this removed them.[56]

The gathering of Scottish politicians in London jostling for William's favour had enabled Sir James Montgomerie, undaunted as Milton's Satan, to start recruiting for a fresh Jacobite 'Club' among the losers. It included malcontent English Whigs, 'some men', wrote Carmarthen, 'not to be made honest by obligations', to whom Montgomerie abused William without revealing his support for James. He may possibly have approached Breadalbane unsuccessfully; but his main Scottish recruits were the two men most hostile to a pacification achieved by anyone but themselves, Argyll and Atholl.[57] Argyll had betrayed Balcarres' Jacobite approaches to Melville in January, but now Montgomerie, his old mentor and Club comrade, had better success, although Argyll remained cautious. Dalrymple wrote soon afterwards that opposition by him to the highland pacification would 'make clear to the world his engagements elsewhere'. In May, he left for Argyllshire, where the many upheavals since 1681 had left his estates in urgent need of reorganisation.[58] Montgomerie could use Arran (once the latter's troubles were over) to foster his Jacobitism. Argyll and his regiment might be used to support a lowland rising among the extreme Presbyterians, some of whom were stirring.[59]

It is unlikely that Atholl and Argyll met as fellow-conspirators —fortunately, in view of the events of 1685, though Argyll could always sacrifice clan resentment to current self-interest. Probably aware that he had been excluded from Dalrymple's scheme, Atholl reached London only after William's departure. His sole benefit from the scheme was a formal pardon for treason. He claimed to be the natural leader of the 'episcopalian' interest, but a government favouring it which did not include him would soon destroy that asset. Unlike the other Scottish politicians, therefore, he seldom waited on the Queen, though remaining in London until July. He committed himself to Dunmore, the strongest Jacobite among his sons, who constantly took him among Tory and Whig plotters. An agent of the Dutch warned Dunmore (whom he mistook for Murray) that conspiracy was dangerous, but he merely laughed, saying 'que s'il faisoit quelque chose il ne seroit pas plus malheureux que les autres et que le gouvernement ne punit personne'. That the Jacobites, while declaiming against William's regime as tyrannical, should privately have come to rely automatically on its mercy — or weakness, as they called it — was more dangerous than they realised. This atititude, adopted by the Court of St. Germain, was to be one main cause of the Massacre of Glencoe.[60]

Atholl enthusiastically plunged into Montgomerie's plot, and began proselytising for his 'Club', while Montgomerie, in a last desperate effort to regain the Williamite side where he naturally belonged, was betraying its doings to Mary. Not surprisingly, Atholl was offered no part in Breadalbane's mission, to which he reacted with blind fury. He had never forgiven Keppoch, his former protégé, for the raid on Glenlyon, and now 'offered . . . yt if ye Governmt would give him noe remission I would bring him in yt he might be hangd for his murder & theft'. Before this, he had been on fairly good terms with Breadalbane, and the Marchioness, suspecting no change, was to report to him on the Achallader negotiations without any hostility; but Atholl now wanted to ruin Breadalbane.[61]

To restrain the Scottish Jacobites from discrediting Breadalbane's mission, Mary and Dalrymple made Sir Thomas Livingston demand of Arran, Seaforth and Home their word of honour not to rebel or conspire before 1 October. Seaforth agreed, Home refused and was imprisoned, Arran absconded but then gave Livingston his promise. Hamilton, whom the order further irritated against Dalrymple, declared it illegal. It was certainly eccentric and, like a search of Edinburgh in May which netted the ostentatious plotter Sir Peter Fraser of Dores (and, unnoticed, Sir Aeneas Macpherson), encouraged the Jacobites to hope.[62]

The Council could argue by early June that they had — inadvertently — made Breadalbane's negotiation superfluous. Before going south, Hamilton had had a Secret Committee of 'presbyterians', including Crawford, Melville's sons, Stair, the judge Campbell of Aberuchill and Livingston, chosen to manage affairs. Livingston, unlike Mackay, vigorously embraced the 'presbyterians' and was soon on bad terms with Dalrymple. It was to stop their grandiose plans for a joint attack by Livingston and Hill on the clans, for which there were no funds, that Dalrymple wrote on 28 April.[63] The Committee, perhaps in retaliation, ordered Hill to attack and destroy all highlanders near him who did not take the oath of allegiance and surrender their arms — which would expose them to destruction from their neighbours. On hearing of the order, William had it revoked, though the clans did not know this. Hill, given room to manoeuvre, adroitly exploited the alarm it had caused to persuade the highlanders to take the allegiance, or at least an oath not to take up arms. Nearly all the Camerons insisted on submitting, and Lochiel allowed them. He declared that he himself waited till other chiefs should join him, 'that they should not accuse him as the first to break the ice', but he peacefully built a sawmill close to the garrison. The Catholics usually refused to take the oath of allegiance, and Glengarry continued to fortify Invergarry; but Hill thought that he would soon have to fight alone. Many Keppoch Macdonalds and some Macleans came in. At the start of June, he agreed that Stewart of Appin and MacIain of Glencoe should take the oaths before Argyll, but many of their followers submitted to him. Hill made large purchases of timber from the Tutor of Appin, and continued to do so all summer. In persuading the highlanders, he had declared 'what he was like to bear from the Government for his lenity towards them, which reproach he behoved to repair upon their ruines if they submitted not'. He meant it literally; but, unfortunately, the clans had forgotten the threat by the winter.[64]

Breadalbane reached Edinburgh at the start of June, to find his mission already known and some in the government raising objections to treating with, rather than crushing, the highlanders. He asked Tarbat to go north and use his influence there. Tarbat, doubtless aggrieved that Breadalbane had supplanted him, could justify staying in Edinburgh: his son was being tried for murder. Yet he wrote to Melville that he was soliciting for Breadalbane's success. They both feared that the highlanders' irrational hopes based on the French succour to Ireland might wreck the negotiations.[65]

By 5 June, Breadalbane was in the Highlands, and summoned Buchan and the chiefs to talks. He ignored as insignificant the eastern Jacobites, Farquharson of Inverey and the lesser Badenoch gentry, although his settlement was to allot £150 for satisfying the feud between Inverey and Gordon of Brackley. Very surprisingly, he also omitted Sir Donald Macdonald — which might legitimately have alienated Tarbat. One possible reason was that in the Isles, apart from Mull, the problem was not superiorities (though Clanranald was Argyll's vassal in some lands) but simple debts, which were not yet causing public disorder. Restoring Sir Donald to any financial stability would have consumed most of the £12,000. The only concession to claims from the Isles (besides the Macleans) in the final agreement was £600 to pay a debt from Clanranald to Argyll — a further injustice to Sir Donald, who was now Clanranald's chief creditor. This naturally created a party against Breadalbane. However, they might be too scattered for effective action, and many Sleat Macdonalds were determined to submit and to make Sir Donald, the chief malcontent, refrain from rising. The malcontents' claim that 'of all the Clans in the Highlands he [Breadalbane] had but three deserve the name of a family' was absurd. His appeal was to the clans of Lochaber and northern Argyll. He was also anxious to win over Ballechin and Colin Mackenzie, whose personal followings had dispersed, but who influenced the Lochaber clans, and on their refusal to attend continued to write to them.[66]

Hill complained that, when Breadalbane's mission became known, it gave fresh confidence to the clans, which had been — yet again — on the point of final submission. This time, the claim contained more truth, for the Secret Committee's order had frightened the chiefs. Yet Breadalbane's promises had been intended to contrast with a threat from the English frigates ordered to blockade the coast. They did not appear, making his offer seem a result of

William's weakness, not his clemency: their captains preferred piracy against Scottish shipping.[67]

As a result, early in June the French ship carrying Charteris, which had not arrived at Galway until mid-May (when Dunfermline was passing through Ireland towards France), finally succeeded in reaching Skye. Buchan had it taken to Eilean Donan Castle, which both sides had forgotten since Seaforth left it. It was surrendered after a few token shots. The provisions were stored there, and Seaforth appointed as governors Ballechin and Colin Mackenzie.[68] Even without Breadalbane's negotiation, the ship's arrival would have wrecked Hill's hopes. Highland rumour instantly converted it into a squadron of four French warships carrying Dunfermline, officers, arms and money, and revived the expectation of Gordon's and Berwick's invasion force. This influenced the clans more than a genuine little Jacobite success. On 15 June, the prisoners on the Bass Rock seized control. Reinforced and provisioned from privateers, they were to hold out until April 1694, a standing reminder — since a small naval force could have starved them out — of the low priority Scottish affairs had for William. However, the Bass was entirely independent of the Highland Army, and the affair merely made Dalrymple order — belatedly — that Eilean Donan be garrisoned.[69]

Ironically, Charteris's arrival should have assisted Breadalbane. He had only two barrels of gunpowder from Ireland to show for months of delay, and he carried instructions which conditionally authorised submission. However, these were eight months old, and the fall of Mons might have made them obsolete. Buchan was an easily influenced man. His letter of 10 June to James from Eilean Donan dwelt exclusively on implausible hopes for fighting on:

> my Lord Sieforth does all he can for your màjestis servis under hand and hes given ane order to Mr Collen his unkelle and to Liutt Coll: broun to haue all his frinds and follours redie when ever annie partie apirs for your majestie and is to mak his esskept to hied them himsellff ... the duke off bervick is ... dessyred by all to coemand ...

No mention of Breadalbane's first approach; yet within a few days his best subordinate, Sir George Barclay, who believed that the clans could no longer hold out unaided, had persuaded him to take part in the negotiation. He could not use the instructions Charteris had brought, however, to sway his Council of War, because they declared that its quorum must include Dunfermline (now well on his way to France) or Cannon. Cannon, who was in Skye with Sir Donald, plainly disliked his fellow-commander. He 'was at this tyme sicke neither did he then countenance Bredalbin and Buchan transaktion', although he may have written to Breadalbane. Even if the other professional officers had made a united decision to submit, the clans might have disregarded it; but in fact several refused all dealings with Breadalbane. If Buchan in these circumstances used James's instructions as excuse for a final submission, he would be accused of disloyalty at St Germain and probably ruined.[70]

At 'his hous at Glenurchy', Kilchurn, Breadalbane met individual chiefs and officers, particularly Lochiel, Maclean, Glengarry, Buchan and Barclay. Then, later in June, all the chiefs gathered at his destroyed castle at Achallader, where five hundred highlanders camped at his expense.[71] He 'managed his business', Duncan Menzies reported, 'so as, which ever of the two governments stood, he would be great'. He told the chiefs that he was still a Jacobite, entering the government only to undermine it like a sapper. As for the negotiation,

> what induced him to it, was the affection he bore to ... the captains of the Highland clans; that they were to be immediately attacked by Sir Thomas Livingston with fire and sword; and there being no other appearance of relief, he thought they could not do better than sue for a cessatione, which would be a breathing to them, and give them time to represent their circumstances to King James; which, if he could not relieve he could not blame them to submit.

His claim that the settlement would include the destruction of Fort William was widely repeated by Menzies, and reached Hill.[72]

Not surprisingly, such claims made the chiefs, particularly his cousin Lochiel, distrust him. He told them that the money he promised them was locked in a chest at London, but they suspected, reasonably, that unless he paid them then and there, he would embezzle some, and the final agreement did not totally reassure them. In reality, playing for higher stakes, he omitted even to cover his expenses. He had a violent quarrel with MacIain of Glencoe over the theft of cows by the latter's men, and threatened to do him a mischief; and MacIain withdrew, telling his sons and followers that he feared a mischief from nobody so much as him. Yet in the agreement Breadalbane duly obtained for him £150 to purchase the superiority of Glencoe, and pardon for a murder.[73] (See Preface, p. ix)

Lochiel put the highlanders' counter-proposals. They demanded that William should pay them £20,000 to refund their war expenses, since the clansmen were so impoverished that they must otherwise live by raiding, and should also buy out the superiorities at the public expense. They should have a full indemnity, take only the oath of allegiance, and be allowed to wear their arms. A messenger must be sent to ask James's permission to submit, and the officers must have the right to stay in Scotland or go to France.[74] Breadalbane's chief success in arguing with the clans was to beat the sum down to his authorised limit of £12,000, nearly all of it to be spent on purchasing the superiorities. Both sides apparently overlooked the need to cancel the arrears of taxes since 1689 theoretically owed by Jacobite clans. Lochiel's terms were not accepted by all the chiefs: the catholic ones declared that they would not take the oath of allegiance. Breadalbane declared that they must, but failed to press the point.[75]

His most important discussions were with Buchan, whose self-justifying summaries of the points agreed formed the basis of the five 'private articles' circulated two months later by Breadalbane's enemies. These written 'articles' were a forgery — by whom, the next chapter will show. Menzies declared: 'They had nothing under Bredalbin's hand but a double of the cessation'. Yet Breadalbane's most trusted defenders when he was accused in 1695 admitted that 'it was in the treatie but not in the Conclusions'.[76] Buchan would have been failing in his duty if he had not insisted on the first four conditions: that the cessation should be null if there were an invasion or Lowlands rising, if James objected to it (which made necessary the dispatch of messengers to seek his permission), or if William shipped abroad the troops the highlanders were holding down. The Marchioness of Atholl's report, the first and fairest, shows that, by the last condition, the cessation was also to be null if any of James's followers left Scotland — theoretically a balanced agreement, although there was no real danger that the handful of Jacobite officers or clans would intervene in the Irish war.[77] The fifth 'article' was that, if William rejected the agreement, Breadalbane should join the rebels with a thousand men — an absurd limitation for a man staking his neck, as he later remarked. In the defence he prepared in 1695, after conventional denials, he justified it as a penalty clause, like the giving of hostages, to obtain a cessation which, he argued, ensured the end of the highland rising.[78] The clans could no longer live by raiding — it was agreed, the Marchioness reported, that any depredations they committed during the cessation must be repaid threefold. They therefore had to disperse, encouraged by protections allowing them to return home unmolested: they were to accept William's indemnity and give security before the cessation expired. Buchan was to be allowed an escort of forty horse to accompany him during the cessation. Afterwards, he and his officers, and those in prison, should be allowed to live unmolested or be given passes to France.[79]

The individual negotiations with the chiefs ran alongside these general ones, and Breadalbane achieved a major breakthrough on 24 June, persuading Keppoch, always the most openly selfish chief, to sign a separate cessation. Sir John Maclean also naturally supported an agreement which would save some of his estates. Buchan, who depended on the Catholic chiefs, was put in a weak bargaining position, since, on the other hand, Glengarry violently opposed the negotiation. Apparently the humiliation to Sir Donald did not outweigh his own hereditary enmity towards Breadalbane (and Lochiel). About 20 June, he launched a major raiding party, 500 strong, against Ross of Balnagown's lands to disrupt negotiations. Leslie and the Inverness garrison repulsed them, but large parties of Lochaber men caught Nairnshire and Moray off guard in the next week. These raids, reported to the Council, must have increased its members' cynicism about a cessation.[80]

Breadalbane's division of the £12,000 inevitably caused great discontent. £3,000 was to be used, in accordance with the 1680 agreement, to buy back from Argyll for Sir John Maclean estates worth £300 a year, to which Argyll was to add others worth £200 a year. The most controversial grant was £2800 to enable Lochiel to buy Sunart and Ardnamurchan of Argyll, to be held of the Crown. Dalrymple, while defending this, privately admitted that Lochiel had no real right to the lands: it was partly an act of normal family favouritism in Breadalbane, like the £300 to pay off Argyll's pretensions on his brother-in-law Macnachtan's estate. Yet he could argue that Lochiel's influence over other chiefs justified special treatment; and, similarly, that the £3000 which he promised to buy out Mackintosh's superiority over Keppoch was some reward for his 'breaking the ice'. He had also a more formal justification. Lochiel had initially demanded that William should buy out all grievous superiorities 'as King James was to have done, for which they produced his Letters'. In fact, only Lochiel and Keppoch had such letters, and clearly used them as bargaining levers: Breadalbane seems to have taken Keppoch's as documentary justification.[81]

Glengarry, though aggrieved, accepted £1500, to buy Knoidart of Argyll for him and settle a debt the Earl had bought affecting his estate. £600 was to pay off a debt of Clanranald's to Argyll; £150 for clearing the latter's pretensions on Stewart of Appin's estate; £150 for MacIain; £150 to Gordon of Brackley as assythment for the murder of his father by Inverey, who was to receive a pardon. Ballechin, despite his refusal to attend, would receive £150. In all, Breadalbane promised £11,800.[82] On 28 June, he wrote to Nottingham of his confidence that he was on the brink of settlement, despite 'great pains and art used to obstruct this work, and by some who would not be thought to have such ill principles'. A last-minute dispute arose. Dalrymple had originally set Lammas — 1 August — as the deadline for final submission. When Breadalbane agreed on 24 June on an independent cessation with Keppoch, he had to extend this to 1 September. Now Buchan insisted on having still longer, to enable James to send aid. After a deadlock, Breadalbane on 30 June agreed to extend the deadline again, to 1 October, giving three months in which to achieve a final settlement.[83] Two messengers were to be sent to James, Lieutenant-Colonel Charteris and Duncan Menzies, whose close relations with Breadalbane Buchan had not grasped. Breadalbane considered a proposal that Buchan himself and Barclay should go instead. The chief's bonds not to break the cessation were hastily drawn up and signed. Breadalbane wrote to Hill informing him of the cessation. Then he mounted and departed, reaching Achmore, near Finlarig, that night; while the chiefs rode off in the other direction, towards Glencoe.[84]

NOTES

1. *Seafield Corr.*, 62, Sir W. Hamilton to Sir J. Oglivie, 2 Aug. 1690.

2. SRO GD 26/xiii/78 fol. 173v, Melville's notes; NLS MS 7012 fols. 132v–133, Bruce to Tweeddale, 31 July 1690.

3. *Ib.*, fol. 136; Drumlanrig, Queensberry Papers, Vol. 128, 51 [Drumlanrig to Prince George, 1690].

4. Riley, *King William*, 16–17, 19, 22–3, 48–50, 59–60.

5. Mackay, *Memoirs*, 9, 88–9, 105; *ib.*, 214–15, Mackay to William, [1690]; SRO GD 26/xiii/68/1, same to Sir T. Livingston, 1 Jan. 1691; NLS MS 7012 fol. 204v, Bruce to Tweeddale, 8 Nov. 1690.

6. Fountainhall, *Hist. Notices*, i, 310; *ib.*, ii, 772, 794–5; *Lockhart Papers*, i, 88; *Scotish Pasquils*, 185, Pasquil on the Stair Family; *HMCR Hamilton Supplement*, 102–3, Mountgrenan's declaration 13 Aug. 1681; SRO GD 26/xiii/78 fol. 173v, Melville's notes.

7. *Ib*; *Culloden Papers*, 313, 'State of things in 1696'.

8. E.g. Prebble, *Glencoe*, 121–7; *Lockhart Papers*, i, 88–9.

9. Atholl, *Chronicles*, ii, 20, Tullibardine to Duchess of Atholl, 20 Jan. 1704; Wodrow, *Analecta*, i, 335; *Scotish Pasquils*, 183–4, 187–9, op cit. For Sunderland, J.P. Kenyon, *Robert Spencer, Earl of Sunderland* (London, 1958), 329–32.

10. *Laud. Papers*, ii, 116–17, Tweeddale to Lauderdale, 30 July 1668; Mackenzie,

Memoirs,241; *pace* Prebble, *Glencoe*, 123.

11. Wodrow, *Analecta*, i, 335; *Culloden Papers*, 320-1, 'State of things in 1696'.

12. NLS MS 7013 fol. 33, Bruce to Tweeddale, 2 Apr. 1691; Drumlanrig, Queensberry Papers, Bundle 1185, 1, 'Remarks upon the State of ye Armie in Scotland', 16 Oct. 1691; Riley, *King William*, 57-8.

13. *Ib.* 55-6, 57-8, 62-5; *RPCS*, xv, 671-2; Sir W. Fraser, *Memoirs of the Maxwells of Pollok*, 2 vols. (Edinburgh, 1863), ii, 91, Crawford to Pollok, 8 Oct. 1690.

14. Burnet, *History*, iv, 61-2.

15. NLS MS 7012 fol. 205, Bruce to Tweeddale, 8 Nov.1690.

16. *Leven & Melville*, 558, Tarbat to Melville, 19 Dec. 1690.

17. SRO GD 112/40/4/2/27, [Countess] to Breadalbane, 16 Oct. 1690; *ib.*, 43/1/2/99, Breadalbane's Life, 4; *ib.*, GD/26/xiii/78 fol. 158, Melville's notes.

18. Riley, *King William*, 59-60; Drumlanrig, Queensberry Papers (old catalogue), 956, warrant for remission, 15/25 June 1691 & pardon, 30 Dec. 1693.

19. The garbled story recalled, at third hand, in Wodrow, *Analecta*, ii, 171-2, must refer to this visit, and seems to have some basis of fact, since it refers to the idea of making him Chancellor; but the main claim that illness and seriousness had made him a 'presbyterian' is nonsense. NLS MS 7012 fol. 226, C. Hay to Yester, 2 Dec. 1690; *ib.*, MS 1031 fol. 125, Hamilton to Selkirk, 31 May 1691.

20. *Ib.*, fols. 113v-114, same to same, 16 Dec. 1690.

21. BL MS Lansdowne 1163C, 237-8, Melfort to Mary of Modena, 11 Nov. 1690(NS); SRO GD 112/40/4/2/11, Balcarres to Breadalbane, 4 Dec. 1690.

22. *Ib.*, GD 26/xiii/78 fol. 178, copy of [Argyll's] information (Argyll identified from *ib.*, 65, Argyll to Melville, n.d.); Riley, *King William*, 60.

23. SRO SP 4/15, 106-8, Linlithgow's and Balcarres' remissions, 22 Dec. 1690; GD 26/xiii/78 fol. 158, Melville's notes; GD 112/40/4/2/10, Linlithgow to Breadalbane, 4 Dec. 1690; Drumlanrig, Queensberry Papers, Vol. 122, 50, same to Queensberry, 25 Dec. 1690; Riley, *King William*, 59-61.

24. Huygens, *Journaal*, i, 382-3; WDA, 60a [W. Penn] to [?James], 29 Dec. 1690; *The Argyll Papers*, ed. J. Maidment (Edinburgh, 1834), 52-5; *Leven & Melville*, 577, Argyll to Melville, 25 Nov. 1690.

25. SRO GD 26/xiii/65, same to same, n.d; *ib.*, 78 fol. 178, copy of [Argyll's] information; NLS MS 7013 fol. 8v, Lady Roxburghe to Tweeddale, 24 Jan. 1691.

26.Mackay, *Memoirs*, 127-9; *More Culloden Papers*, 207-8, Livingston to Culloden, 19 Nov. [1690]; NLS MS 7012 fol. 198, Bruce to Tweeddale, 4 Nov. 1690; *RPCS*, xvi, 181, 196.

27. *Ib.*, 8-13, 15-16, 18; *CSPD 1690-1*, 227, William to Scottish Treasury, 16 Jan. 1691; *ib.*, 235, Blathwayt to Nottingham, 27 Jan. 1691; *ib. 1691-2*, 33-4; *CTB*, ix, 970; SRO GD 26/ix/315, Livingston to Melville, 13 Jan. 1691; Drumlanrig, Queensberry Papers, Bundle 1185, 1, 'Remarks upon ye State of ye Armie', 16 Oct. 1691.

28. *Ib.; ib.*, 18, Memorial on reducing the army, [1691]; *ib.*, 19, Sir A. Bruce's memorial [Apr.] 1691; *RPCS*, xvi, 36, 59-60, 78-9, 100, 147, 162-3, 202, 213, 264; Mackay, *Memoirs*, 216-17, Mackay to Portland, 4 Nov. 1690; *Leven & Melville*, 586-7, Tarbat to Melville, 18 Dec. 1690; *ib.*, 601, Livingston to same, 2 Apr. 1691; *The Blind Harper*, 22-5, 'Oran mu Oifigich Araid', 105-6; NLS MS 7013 fol. 14, Bruce to Tweeddale, 26 Feb. 1691.

29. *Ib.*; Luttrell, ii, 169; *Carstares S.P.*, 133, Macky to Melville, '11' Apr. 1691; *ib.*, 139, [same] to [same], 21 Sept. 1691; SRO GD 26/viii/124, J. Edmonstone to 'John', 17 Jan. 1691.

30. *RPCS*, xvi, 115; *Leven & Melville*, 611, Hill to Melville, 12 May 1691; Macfarlane,

Gen. Colls., i, 140; *Gazette de France*, 10 Mar. 1691 (NS), 127, Edinburgh report, 12 Feb. 1691 (NS); SRO GD 202/18, 91-2, Ardkinglas to Tutor of Dunstaffnage, 28 Feb. 1691; SCA, Blairs Letters, Box Y, unsigned, 67, 12 Feb. 1691.

31. *CSPD 1690-1*, 347, newsletter, 25 Apr. 1691; SRO GD 26/viii/128, 'Informatione anent the Robberies', 1691; *RPCS*, xvi, 70, 99-100, 124, 148, 247-8, 255.

32. The reports that Cannon commanded some of these parties were mistaken. *Ib.*, 86-7, 196, 238, 278-9, 282, 286, 338-9; Atholl, *Chronicles*, i, 332; *HMCR Le Fleming*, 320, newsletter, 14 Mar. 1691; *ib.*, 323, same, 31 Mar. 1691; *ib.*, 324, same, 4 Apr. 1691.

33. *RPCS*, xv, 596-7, 616-17; *ib.*, xvi, 4, 7-8, 13, 54-5.

34. Hopkins, 'Aspects of Jacobite Conspiracy', 185-93, 196-7, 203-5; *HMCR Finch*, iii, 20, Nottingham to Sydney, 20 Feb. 1690/1; *ib.*, 58, same to same, 12 May 1691; *ib.*, iv, 4, Higgens's memorial; *Carstares S.P.*, 134, Macky to Melville, '11' Apr. 1691; *ib.*, 148, [Macky], 'Information for my Lord Sidney'; *ib.*, 129, 131, 132, 133-4, Macky to Melville, 6, 13, 19 Mar., '11' Apr. 1691; SRO GD 26/viii/122/2, same to same, 29 Mar. 1691.

35. Internal evidence shows that Iain Lom's poem was written in April before the news of the fall of Mons was confirmed. *Life of James*, ii, 468; *Franco-Irish Corr.*, ii 288, Fumeron to Louvois, 23 May 1691 (NS); *Leven & Melville*, 610, Hill to Melville, 1 May 1691; *HMCR Hope-Johnstone*, 167, J. Ferguson to Livingston, [1691]; *Orain Iain Luim*, 202-13; NLS, Adv. MS 13.1.8 fol. 2, Struan to his mother 21 Apr. [1691] (NS).

36. *HMCR Finch*, iii, 36-7, Sydney to Nottingham, 3 Apr. 1691; *ib.*, 167, 'Scotish Affairs', 20 July 1691; *ib.*, 174, Dalrymple to Breadalbane, 23 July 1691; *ib.*, 234, anon. letter, 25 Aug. 1691; *Carstares S.P.*, 129, 130, 132, Macky to Melville, 6, 10, 19 Mar. 1691; SRO GD 26/viii/122/10, same to same, n.d; Blair, Atholl MSS, Box 44/VI/169, Arran to Murray, 6 Apr. [1691]; *HMCR Hamilton Supplement*, 116, Dalrymple to Hamilton, 20 Apr. 1691 (NS); *RPCS*, xvi, 261.

37. *Ib.*, xv, 428, 453-6, 462-3; *Leven & Melville*, 530, Breadalbane to Melville, 17 Sept. 1690; SRO GD 112/43/1/2/99, Breadalbane's Life, 3-4.

38. *Ib.*, 40/4/2/13, Breadalbane to Carwhin, [late 1690]; *ib.*, 56, same to same, 12 Dec. 1690; *RPCS*, xv, 156-7, 563, 577; *HMCR Hope-Johnstone*, 167, J. Ferguson to Livingston, [1691]; NLS MS 7012 fols. 228-9, Bruce to Tweeddale, 8 Dec. 1690.

39. *Lairds of Glenlyon*, 58, ? Campbell to Glenlyon, 28 Sept. 1690; Blair, Atholl MSS, Box '71' II D 8, Lady Glenlyon to Murray, 27 Mar. 1691 + reply; SRO GD 112/40/4/2/4, Breadalbane to Carwhin, [Dec. 1690].

40. *Ib.*, 1, same to same [Dec. 1690].

41. *Memoirs of Locheill*, 292.

42. Breadalbane's 'Proposals concerning the Highlands' (Dalrymple, *Memoirs*, ii, 217-20) can be firmly dated to January-February 1692 by the first sentence and by the mention (219) of Lochiel as being in London. *Highland Papers*, 53-6, 'Proposalls offered by the Earle of Broadalban' [c. Feb. 1692].

43. *RCAHMS Argyll*, ii, 28, 236-9; SRO GD 112/40/4/2/26, [Breadalbane] to [Carwhin], 7 [Dec. 1689]; *ib.*, 43/1/1/10, same to same, 10 Dec. 1689. I owe the original mention of this point to Mr. Ian Fisher.

44. *CSPD 1691-2*, 61-2, Tarbat to William [1690]; *Leven & Melville*, 565, same to Melville, 1 Nov. 1690; Riley, *King William*, 67.

45. *The Scots Peerage*, like all reference works, gives Lady Glenorchy as dying on 4 February 1690, the Countess on 4 February 1691. In fact, this is the same date — that of Lady Glenorchy's death — in the Scottish and English systems of dating. The Countess of Caithness survived until about December 1699. The Breadalbane papers include a letter she wrote that summer and Tarbat's letter of condolence to the Earl. *Scots Peerage*, ii,

206-7; SRO GD 112/39/1214, Lady Newcastle to Glenorchy, 25 Feb. 1690 [/1]; *ib.*, 1215, P. Urquhart to Breadalbane, 4 Feb. 1691; *ib.*, 1216, Glenorchy to same, 7 Feb. 1691; *ib.*, 40/4/7/44, Tarbat to Breadalbane, 30 Dec. 1699; *ib.*, 61, Countess to Carwhin, 3 July 1699; *ib.*, 40/4/2/3, Breadalbane to same, 27 Jan. 1690; *ib.*, 15, Glenorchy to same, 2 Dec. 1690; *ib.*, 19, Breadalbane to same, 13 Dec. 1690; *ib.*, 51, same to same, 15 Jan. 1691.

46. *Ib; ib.*, 1, same to same, [Dec. 1690]; *ib.*, 22, Carwhin to Breadalbane, 6 Jan. 1691.

47. *Highland Papers*, 101, Report, 20 June 1695; SRO GD 112/40/4/2/1, [Breadalbane] to [Carwhin, Dec. 1690]; *ib.*, 6, same to Barcaldine, 29 Dec. 1690.

48. *Ib.* 29, same to Carwhin, 9 Mar. 1691; Story, *Carstares*, 217, Carstares to Dunlop, 17 Aug. 1691; *Fasti Ecclesiae Scoticanae*, ed. H. Scott, 8 vols. (Edinburgh, 1915–50), iv, 86.

49. *HMCR 7th Report*, 197, [Blancard] to Dykveldt, 19 May 1691; NLS MS 7013 fol. 24, Bruce to Tweeddale, 17 Mar. 1691; *Ib.*, fol. 39v, Sir P. Murray to same, 4 Apr. 1691; Blair, Atholl MSS, Box 44/VI/169, Arran to Murray, 6 Apr. [1691]; Drumlanrig, Queensberry Papers, Vol. 122, 51, Linlithgow to Queensberry, 20 Feb. 1691.

50. SRO GD 112/40/5/11, Breadalbane to Mrs Campbell of Carwhin, 28 Apr. [1691]; *ib.*, SP 4/15, 208–10, Remission of Treason for Breadalbane, [2 May] 1691.

51. CSPD 1690-1, 350, newsletter, 28 Apr. 1691; A. Browning, *Thomas Osborne, Earl of Danby*, 3 vols., (Glasgow, 1944–51), ii, 200–1, Carmarthen to William, 22 May 1691; Hill Burton, *History*, i, 526, Dalrymple to Breadalbane, 27 Oct. 1691; *HMCR Finch*, iv, 2, same to Nottingham, 8/18 June 1691.

52. *Ib; HMCR Hamilton, Supplement*, 116, same to Hamilton, 17 Mar. 1691; *ib.*, 117, same to same, [July 1691]; *ib.*, 120, same to same, 27 Aug. 1691 (NS); SRO GD 26/ix/316, same to same, 17 Feb. 1690/1, 16 Mar. 1691; *RPCS*, xvi, 357; HLRO, Willcocks MSS, Section VI, 97, Yester to Tweeddale, 27 June 1691; Cumnock, Dumfries House, Bute MSS, bundle A517/14, Breadalbane to [Dalrymple], 25 Nov. 1691. The three letters of Breadalbane's in this bundle, Nos. 12–14, are unaddressed, but Dalrymple in his letter of 2 December (Dalrymple, *Memoirs*, ii, 214) acknowledges the receipt of Breadalbane's of 16 and 19 November, and Breadalbane's of 25 November answers a remark about Glengarry in Dalrymple's of the 3rd (Hill Burton, *History*, i, 527). The recipient has not been identified because Breadalbane began the letters 'My Lord'; but the Officers of State were *ex officio* peers, and Breadalbane was by then anxious to conciliate Dalrymple even with that scrap of flattery. For the usage, NLS MS 1031 fol. 162, Hamilton to Selkirk, 8 Nov. 1692.

53. Luttrell, ii, 233, 235; *Annandale Book*, ii, 46, Dalrymple to Livingston, 28 Apr. 1691; *ib.* 47, same to same, 4 May 1691.

54. *CSPD 1695*, 170–1, 'Propositions to the final reduction of such highlanders', 27 Apr. 1691; SRO GD 112/vii/280, 'Concerning the Spanish wreck ship at Mull'; *HMCR Finch*, iii, xlviin, Souton's proposal; *ib.*, 42, 'The Affaire of Scotland'; *ib.*, 390, 392; information, Mrs. Z. Cowan.

55. *Ib.*, 174, Dalrymple to Breadalbane, 23 July 1691; *ib.*, iv, 2, same to Nottingham, 8/18 June 1691; *Annandale Book*, ii, 48, same to Livingston, 6 May 1691; SRO GD 112/40/4/1/1, Lord Glenorchy to Mrs. Campbell, 29 Sept. [1691]; PRO ADM 8/2 (disposition lists), 1 May, 1 June, 1 July, 1 Aug. 1691.

56. *HMCR 7th Report*, 197, [Blancard] to Dykveldt, 19 May 1691; Riley, *King William*, 68, 70–1; NLS MS 1031 fols. 110–11, Hamilton to Selkirk, 4 Dec. 1691; *ib.*, fol. 122, same to same, 15 May 1691; *ib.*, fols. 125–6, same to same, 31 May 1691; *ib.*, fol. 130, same to same, 29 Aug. 1691.

57. The suggestion about Breadalbane is based only on his appearance in Montgomerie's list of Jacobite code-names. Browning, *Danby*, ii, 207, Carmarthen to William, 11 Sept.

1691; WDA, Browne MSS, 101, Ord's report, 20 May 1691; *ib*., 257f, Montgomerie's code-names [July 1691]; NUL Portland MSS, PwA 2698b, 3, Langton to [James], 18 Aug. 1691.

58. *HMCR 4th Report*, 472, Argyll to agents, 24 Aug. 1691; Dalrymple, *Memoirs*, ii, 211, Dalrymple to Breadalbane, 24 Aug. 1691; *The Clan Campbell*, ed. Rev. H. Paton, 8 vols. (Edinburgh, 1913–22), i, 5–6.

59. Macpherson, *Original Papers*, i, 390, Major Holmes's Paper, Oct. 1691; Luttrell, ii, 228; *State Trials*, xii, 1346, B. Blair's confession, 12 Mar. 1695/6; *Gazette de France*, 21 Apr. 1691 (NS), 203, Scottish report, 6 Apr. 1691 (NS); SRO GD 112/40/4/5/29, Countess to Carwhin, [12 Nov. 1691].

60. The younger son's title of Earl evidently caused the agent's mistake. Colonel Hill was also mistaken in reporting that Atholl had returned to the Highlands by late June. *CSPD 1690–1*, 415, Atholl's pardon, 15/25 June 1691; *HMCR 7th Report*, 197, [Blancard] to Dykveldt, 19 May 1691; *ib*., same to same, 19 June 1691; *Leven & Melville*, 625, Hill to Melville, 26 June 1691; SRO GD 26/viii/122/8, Macky to same, n.d.; *ib*., GD 170/612/3, Carwhin to Barcaldine, 22 May 1691; NLS MS 7013 fol. 53, Lady Roxburghe to Tweeddale, 21 Apr. 1691; Blair, Atholl MSS, Box 29 I (6) 14, Marchioness to Atholl, 8 July [1691].

61. *Ib*.; *ib*., Box 44/VI/173, [Atholl] to Lady Murray [?1693]; Macpherson, *Original Papers*, i, 390, Major Holmes's Paper, Oct. 1691; Thomas, Earl of Ailesbury, *Memoirs*, ed. W.E. Buckley, 2 vols., (Roxburghe Club, 1890), i, 302–3 (misdated and muddled).

62. Sir Peter Fraser's plot, to start a rising in the North-East with a manifesto for the restoration of episcopacy, though doubtless largely fantasy, emphasises the Jacobite concern with the area throughout the war. *RPCS*, xvi, 281, 283–5, 287, 357, 549; *HMCR Finch*, iii, 116–17, Nottingham to Dalrymple, 16 June 1691; *ib*., 118–19, Dalrymple to Nottingham, June 1691; *ib*., 134, same to same, 30 June 1691; *ib*., 210–11, [Payne] to 'Aunt', 15 Aug. 1691 (James Hamilton = Arran); *Leven & Melville*, 614–16, Arran to Raith, 25 May 1691; NLS MS 7013 fol. 67, Bruce to Tweeddale, 26 May 1691; SRO PC 1/48, 619–20.

63. The choice of Stair, and the unprotesting part he took in the Committee's proceedings, suggests that he may not always have been in close concert with his son's plans. HLRO, Willcocks MSS, Sect. VI, 87, Yester to same, 21 Apr. 1691; *RPCS*, xvi, 255–6; *Annandale Book*, ii, 46, Dalrymple to Livingston, 28 Apr. 1691; *ib*., 47, same to same, 4 May 1691.

64. *HMCR Finch*, iii, 100, Breadalbane to Nottingham, 5 June 1691; SRO GD 112/40/4/5/47, same to Carwhin, 5 May 1691; Fort William, West Highland Museum, MS B1, Hill, 'An Accompt off Moneyes Laid out', 23 Jan. 1692; *HMCR Hope-Johnstone*, 168–9, J. Stewart to Crawford, 3 June 1691; *Leven & Melville*, 611–12, Hill to Melville, 12 May 1691; *ib*., 613, same to Melville, 15 May 1691; *ib*., 617–18, same to same, 3 June 1691.

65. *Ib*., 619, Tarbat to Melville, 4 June 1691; *HMCR Finch*, iii, 100, Breadalbane to Nottingham, 5 June 1691.

66. Barcaldine, writing in September, lumps Sir Donald, Ballechin and Mackenzie together as excluded from the negotiations, but Buchan's letter of 16 July shows the difference. *Ib*.; *CSPD 1691–2*, 492, concessions to the highlanders, 17/27 Aug. 1691; Shaw, *Northern and Western Islands*, 44; SRO GD 26/xiii/78 fol. 179v, Sir D. Macdonald etc. to Sir Ae. Macpherson, 28 Aug. 1691; GD 112/40/4/8/31, [Barcaldine] to [Carwhin], 13 Sept. 1691; GD 170/3046, Buchan to D. Menzies, 16 July [1691]; *Leven & Melville*, 627, Hill to Melville, 26 June 1691.

67. *Ib*., 623, same to same, 18 June 1691; *ib*., 624–5, PCS to same, 23 June 1691; *HMCR Finch*, iii, 101, Breadalbane to Nottingham 5 June 1691; *ib*., 123, Nottingham to Sydney, 23

June 1691; *HMCR Hope-Johnstone*, 169, J. Stewart to Crawford, 3 June 1691.

68. *Ib.*, 170–1, Hill to same, 18 June 1691 (2 letters); Macpherson, *Loyall Dissuasive*, 194; SRO GD 26/viii/122/5, Macky to Melville, n.d. (facts wrong); *Franco-Irish Corr.*, ii, 288, Fumeron to Louvois, 23 May 1691 (NS); *ib.*, 310–11, Bouridal to same, 21 July 1691 (NS); WDA, Browne MSS, 206, Buchan to James, 10 June [1691].

69. *RPCS*, xvi, 338, 340; *HMCR Hamilton Supplement*, 117, Dalrymple to Hamilton, [July 1691]; *ib.*, 117–18, Hamilton to Dalrymple, 1 Aug. 1691; *Leven & Melville*, 620, Hill to Leven, 9 June 1691; NLS MS 7014 fol. 17, same to Tweeddale, 27 Feb. 1692; SRO GD 26/ix/323, A Fletcher to Melville, 16 June 1691.

70. *HMCR Hope-Johnstone*, 170, same to Crawford, 18 June 1691; SRO GD 26/xiii/78 fol. 179v, Sir D. Macdonald etc. to Macpherson, 28 Aug. 1691 + Melville's note; GD 112/40/4/8/31, [Barcaldine] to [Carwhin], 13 Sept. [1691]; NLS MS 3194 fol. 115, James's instructions to [Charteris, Nov. 1690]; Blair, Atholl MSS, Box 29 I (6) 14, Marchioness to Atholl, 8 July [1691]; WDA, Browne MSS, 206, Buchan to James, 10 June [1691].

71. *HMCR Finch*, iii, 131, Breadalbane to Nottingham, 28 June 1691; *ib.*, iv, 239, same to same, 16 June 1692; *Leven & Melville*, 626, Hill to Melville, 26 June 1691.

72. *Ib.*, 648, same to Breadalbane, 17 Oct. 1691; *Carstares S.P.*, 136, [Macky] to J. Melvill, 11 Sept, 1691; *ib.*, 138, same to [Melville], 21 Sept. 1691; SRO GD 26/xiii/78 fol. 179, Glengarry to Raith, 12 Sept. 1691.

73. *CSPD 1691–2*, 492, Concessions, 17/27 Aug. 1691; *ib.*, 497, remission for MacIain, 20/30 Aug. 1691; *Highland Papers*, 100–1, Report, 20 June 1695; *Leven & Melville*, 625–6, Hill to Melville, 26 June 1691; MacGill, *Old Ross-shire*, i, 237, same to [? Balnagown, ? July 1691].

74. These terms appear as a near-transcript of a formal document in *Memoirs of Locheill*, 301, but have a different shape in Balhaldie's first draft (NLS MS 3194 fol. 102), and may therefore only be his faulty reconstruction of the final settlement. However, the major differences between it and the final terms suggest that he had a real document and did not know its significance; and the fifth article is clearly a reaction to the Secret Committee's order of May to Hill, of which Balhaldie could not know because it is not among the Council records.

75. Hill Burton, *History*, i, 526, Dalrymple to Breadalbane, 27 Oct. 1691; NLS MS 7013 fol. 108v, Bruce to Tweeddale, 23 Oct. 1691.

76. *Carstares S.P.*, 136, [Macky] to J. Melvill, 11 Sept. 1691; SRO GD 112/43/1/2/28, Tarbat's objections to Glengarry [1695]; *ib.*, 68, [Carwhin] note 'ant the process of treason' [1695].

77. Blair, Atholl MSS, Box 29 I (6) 14, Marchioness to Atholl, 8 July [1691]; *HMCR Finch*, iii, 242, 'Private articles'.

78. *Ib; HMCR Hamilton Supplement*, 121, Melville to Hamilton, 22 Sept. 1691; SRO GD 112/40/4/8/28, Breadalbane's draft speech [c. 30 June 1695]; *ib.*, 43/1/5/1, *Answers for the Earl of Breadalbane*, [1695], 4–5.

79. *Ib.*, 3; *Carstares S.P.*, 138 [Macky] to [Melville], 21 Sept. 1691; Blair, Atholl MSS, Box 29 I (6) 14, Marchioness to Atholl, 8 July [1691].

80. *Leven & Melville*, 626 Hill to Melville, 26 June 1691; *Thanes of Cawdor*, 387, Sir H. Campbell to Hay of Park, 29 June 1691; Dalrymple, *Memoirs*, ii, 220–1, Keppoch's cessation, 24 June 1691.

81. It came to the Society of Antiquaries of Scotland from a collection part of which clearly came from the Breadalbane Papers. *Ib.*, 215, Dalrymple to Breadalbane, 2 Dec. 1691; *Memoirs of Locheill*, 231, 290, 301; *PSAS*, vii, 249–50, James to Keppoch, 30 Nov.

1689; *ib.*, 248–9; *CSPD 1691–2*, 491–2, Concessions, 17/27 Aug. 1691.

82. *Ib*; SRO GD 112/43/1/5/32, Barcaldine to Breadalbane, 12 July [1695].

83. *Ib; HMCR Hamilton Supplement*, 117, Dalrymple to Hamilton, [July 1691]; Dalrymple, *Memoirs*, ii, 220–1, Keppoch's cessation, 24 June 1691; *Highland Papers*, 21–2, Cessation, 30 June 1691.

84. There is a dilemma here. Breadalbane's defence against the treason charge in 1695 depended largely on an alibi, that he was not at Achallader after 30 June, and Barcaldine's private letters to him then indicate that this was the truth. Yet the copy of his letter to Hill which the latter included in letters within a month or two is dated Achallader, 3 July 1691. It seems most probable that this date or place-name was falsified. *Ib.*, 22, 'Private articles'; *HMCR Finch*, iii, 174, Dalrymple to Breadalbane, 23 July 1691; SRO GD 112/43/1/5/32, Barcaldine to same, 12 July [1695]; GD 170/3046, Buchan to D. Menzies, 16 July [1691]; Macgill, *Old Ross-shire*, i, 237, Breadalbane to Hill, '3 July 1691'.

9

Ratification and Sabotage (July–October 1691)

When Sir John Maclean returned to Mull, he may have witnessed the first breach of the cessation. Some English warships and merchantmen, with Argyll aboard, arrived and made a night attack on the two prizes, a Dutch ship and a Leith bark, which were the chief strength of the Macleans' flotilla, 'under yr castle walls' at Duart. The Macleans had to burn one and scuttle the other next morning rather than allow their recapture. The English sailed onwards and on 2 July anchored in Tobermory Bay. They prepared to dive for the supposed treasures of the Armada wreck, which the Macleans considered rightly theirs. A week later, another of the flotilla was captured.[1]

Ever since the Argyll family was first granted the 'Tobermory Galleon' in 1641, they had been financing expeditions, hoping for a discovery that would help pay their debts. In 1677 and 1678, the Macleans, increasingly convinced of the wreck's value, dug trenches round the bay and fired on the salvage ships. This and divers' exaggerations in turn strengthened the myth that the wreck contained 'thirty millions of Cash'.[2] The tenth earl, his chaotic affairs made worse by the debts incurred in his Mull campaign, desperately needed such a windfall. In London during March 1691 he secured support from City financiers, granted shares of the findings to followers like Campbell of Calder and awarded the contract for the expedition to Goodwin Wharton. Wharton, secretly a hopeless madman who had constant dealings with the fairies, was outwardly a respected Whig MP and an expert in marine treasure-hunting. He was also the cousin of the heiress for whose abduction Captain Johnston had suffered. During the expedition, several Campbell gentlemen in Mull tried to provoke him to a duel over this.[3] Yet Argyll, who received many offers, chose him as most likely to recover the treasure, without regard for clan sentiment.

The expedition's arrival just as the cessation began was apparently an accident. Argyll, informing Breadalbane of his contract, had expected to start in mid-June, but Wharton was delayed awaiting a (fairy) diver. Carwhin, although he suspected Argyll's motives in launching the expedition, reported that it was the English (including the two frigates, encountered by accident) who first attacked at Duart, obliging him to give support. Yet Argyll showed his hostility to the cessation when Livingston informed him of it, 'desyring the Councells distinct ansuer how he is to carry therin, since he knowes not but some may pretend to possess pairt of his estate under pretence of cessatione'.[4] Sir John Maclean promised Breadalbane not to retaliate, and only (allegedly) sent a request by the messengers to James for a Dunkirk privateer to be dispatched against Wharton's ships.[5]

Argyll was not yet openly attacking the cessation; but his jealousy of Breadalbane's prospects and willingness to oblige his new ally Atholl made him sacrifice Glenlyon, a Campbell and a captain in his own regiment. He offered to persuade him, rather than press the lawsuits he was starting to annul the sale of his estate, to submit his claims to Arran and Argyll himself, agreeing to accept their decision. Murray felt conscientious scruples about accepting such arbitrators, one his brother-in-law and both (he may have guessed) his father's fellow-conspirators. Argyll swept these aside, writing on 23 July: 'I am proud of our Garrauntie the E. of Arran. I am sure everiething must be honorable he has a finger in'.[6] The proposal had a strong flavour of Montgomerie's Jacobite conspiracy. Argyll had no previous reason to favour Atholl, and Arran was an odd choice for an arbitration which might one day come before a Williamite Session: within a week of Argyll's letter, he was asking James's permission to flee to France.[7]

On 12 July, Dalrymple wrote warning Tarbat that, unless news of an agreement came within a week, he would have to order the army to march, although he feared for the result. That evening, he received the first news of Breadalbane's success, along with the capture of Athlone in Ireland. 'I think the back both of the campaign and of the war may be broke' he wrote. He expected that Breadalbane would have to cross to Flanders to ensure William's consent. Breadalbane, however, had written on 28 June suggesting that Dalrymple should cross to London with instructions authorising him to make the necessary modifications in the final agreement. Thinking he would, Breadalbane remained in Edinburgh with Linlithgow and Lockhart, boasting openly of his success, until 10 July.[8] Arriving in London a week later, he easily convinced Mary and Nottingham about the agreement. Nottingham had no second thoughts even when, in early August, he intercepted a major Jacobite's letter stating, in transparent 'allegorical' language, that the 'episcopalians' intended to enter William's service only to work and spy for James, and that there were rumours (probably spread by Breadalbane himself) that he had James's authorisation for the cessation.[9]

Buchan had changed his mind about using Menzies as one of his messengers on discovering how closely he was involved with Breadalbane, and Sir George Barclay was chosen instead. On 18 July, Breadalbane obtained passes from the Highlands to London for Barclay, Charteris and Menzies (whom he intended to employ himself, if the need arose), and sent them off. The highlanders, however, decided to replace Barclay with Lieutenant-Colonel William Rattray, a Catholic banished by the Council in 1689 on pain of death. It was on James's orders that he returned next year from Ireland with Seaforth, but he might still legitimately be hanged after any general capitulation. For greater safety, he sailed in the French privateer as it returned to Ireland and France. Strangely, the Third Viscount Dundee (Dundee's brother), who accompanied him, still carried Buchan's uncancelled letter of 10 June, with its optimism about further resistance. Charteris, who intended to travel via Holland, suffered a paralytic attack at Edinburgh.[10]

From mid-July, the 'presbyterian' majority on the Council was doing its utmost to destroy the cessation. The party had some justification for hostility. They believed that Dalrymple's scheme would restore to power all the 'episcopalian' persecutors, even Atholl. Presbyterian preachers justly complained of blind favour shown to treacherous nobles. Reports of Breadalbane's Jacobite remarks at Achallader circulated, and Hill wrote to William accusing him.[11] He had let slip something of his plans for a highland military force, which made him a real danger to the nation. If, as they believed, nearly all 'episcopalians' were crypto-Jacobites, they would use this force to restore James once William's perverse susceptibility to bad advice had allowed them to take power. Even if Breadalbane were not now a Jacobite, the danger was real. The 'presbyterian' statesmen had seen enough of William's arbitrary side in 1689–90 to fear the prospect of his having a permanent 'Highland Host' at his disposal should he ever wish to crush their liberties. They naturally did not write this down, though a sour joke of Melville's hints at it, but it influenced them.[12]

Yet — and this is the most damning comment on their later activities — the Council at first did nothing against the cessation. Crawford, who often presided, concentrated on punishing episcopalian riots. On 25 June, they received a letter of the 15th(OS) from William, ordering that Livingston should march his forces to the borders of the Highlands, without starting hostilities, as a threat to encourage the clans to submit. Dalrymple and Breadalbane probably sent private advice that the negotiations might make the march unnecessary, for the Council gave no orders. Crawford wrote on 11 July: 'our Highlanders . . . are in a good way to make submission, their leaders and chiftains having lately engadged for their quiet and good behaviour for thrie moneths to come, which . . . may be introductive of a good setlement in these parts'. Livingston was allowed to inform Argyll of the cessation, and on 14 July the earl's protesting reply was 'layd asyde without ansuering'.[13] Two days later, the Duke of Hamilton presided, and the Council's highland policy was transformed.

Hamilton had intended to remain in London until William's return, but in late June Mary imprudently persuaded him to return to Scotland. He was inflamed by disapproval of Dalrymple's policies and resentment over his own exclusion from them and the treatment of Arran; and he had formed a far closer alliance with Melville than had existed when they were William's chief ministers in 1689.[14] On his return, he received a conciliatory letter from Dalrymple, explaining that the army would attack the clans if Breadalbane failed, but that 'the first steps against them may be easy and plain but the sequell may be doubtfull . . . if they lay by we can not root them out and to provock them and leav them in despair will make them call for thes assistances from France'.[15] Unfortunately, it mentioned the order for Livingston, which Hamilton decided to enforce. Lockhart privately protested: 'the Highlanders, who are a jalous pople, will beleive . . . that Breadalban's wholl bussiness was a sham', but Hamilton replied 'that the Counsell was not concerned what was the bussines of privatt men, and that nather King nor Queen had said anay thing of that to him,.[16] The Council's previous acts made nonsense of this argument, but Hamilton established his personal dominance there, and probably soon convinced the 'presbyterians' that Breadalbane's success would produce a fatal change of ministry. At the 16 July meeting, he had the Council order Livingston to march — at which Stair left in protest — and made other preparations for open warfare.[17]

His third move that day proved the most decisive. Sir Aeneas Macpherson, seized in the search in May, petitioned offering to go into exile. Hamilton must have heard from Melville of his previous spying, for the Council freed him and recommended him to the Treasury for a 'a competent soume to releive his present straits'. A bargain was soon struck. In return for £100 and a promise of future reward from Melville, he was to go to the Highlands and obtain signed evidence of the nature of Breadalbane's dealings.[18] His broader mission is uncertain. Both before and after, hostile Privy Councillors were accused of hiring agents to encourage Jacobite resistance — which, in the event, Macpherson did. However, in August Hill reported that he was trying to pacify the clans, but was hindered by their oath to do nothing without each others' consent. The 'presbyterians' recommended him openly to William that autumn, a dangerous course if he might be exposed as their *agent provocateur*. Macpherson, when captive in 1695, claimed (when hinting the opposite would have been more effective) to have used his interest to pacify the clans. If the 'presbyterians' could break Breadalbane's cessation and themselves bring about a submission, they might regain William's favour. They claimed that Hill had nearly succeeded, and Macpherson was an obvious instrument to complete his work.[19]

The order to Livingston began an ingenious campaign, maintained all summer, to undermine the cessation. It bore the marks of Hamilton's mind, attention to protocol and pedestrian cunning. The Council, defying the spirit of royal orders, never disobeyed their letter, but, as they blocked one line of attack, instantly switched to another. Warned by Lockhart, Mary, despite Melville's opposition, got the Duke of Leinster, who had been left as Commander-in-Chief in England, to order Livingston on 22 July not to march. She herself wrote to Hamilton confirming this — fortunately, for the Council denied that Leinster's authority extended to Scotland, but passed on her order.[20]

The Council already had a new means of provocation. Stewart of Appin had detained a soldier from a provision boat going to Fort William who struck down an Appin man during a drinking session. Before the cessation, Hill would have been conciliatory to the young chief. Now, desperate to ruin Breadalbane and keep his employment, he was prepared to destroy the peace he had worked to create. After an exchange of angry letters, he sent 400 men, who met no resistance, to seize Stewart and his guests. The conveniently mixed bag included MacIain's son Alasdair and Macdonald of Achtera, Glengarry's trusted kinsman. On 29 July, the Council decided to transfer the prisoners to Glasgow, although Stair and other judges protested that the highlanders would assume it was intended to try them as rebels. The Council again refused to recognise the cessation, despite the queen's letter to Hamilton.[21] On 4 August, she wrote giving official notice of it, ordering the release of Stewart and the other prisoners, and enclosing a backdated commission extending Leinster's powers to Scotland, hastily obtained from William — a step certain to alienate Livingston further.[22] The Council already had their next move ready.

By then, Breadalbane had made his greatest mistake: he had set out for Flanders to gain William's agreement. His allies agreed with Dalrymple that the latter must remain at William's side, lest Portland, Carstares and other hostile advisers on Scotland should persuade him to repudiate not only Breadalbane's mission but the whole 'episcopalian' scheme. Nottingham agreed, and suggested that Mary be authorised to settle everything. Dalrymple, on receiving Breadalbane's first brief announcement, wrote to Nottingham: 'I hav not yett the particulars, and I doubt the King will go on blindly to giv full pouers to conclud till he knowes the tearms and in my opinion it might do weill that Breadalbin cam over hither weill instructed and recommended from thence'.[23]

This advice probably determined Breadalbane to cross to Flanders. It appealed to his love of making dramatic, rushed journeys to settle business, like his ride to Chester in 1690, and to his main intellectual interest, geography: he hoped to combine his mission with a tour in Holland even in August, despite 'our affaris requyring heast'.[24] By 21 July he had decided to go, and reports of the Council's order to Livingston only delayed him briefly to advise on counter-measures.[25] Meanwhile, Dalrymple had exerted his full powers of persuasion, arguing that any delay might encourage the clans to listen to Jacobite proposals, and, contrary to his own expectations, persuaded William (who disliked dealing with even the most vital domestic business on campaign) to send an authorisation for concluding the settlement to London.[26]

Just afterwards, Dalrymple received his first long letter from Breadalbane since the cessation, and was horrified. He had never been blindly committed to the negotiation. Alongside the fear of French assistance for the clans, already mentioned, his correspondence had shown, since Berwick's invasion proved a false alarm, a growing regret over the very favourable terms offered to them. Charteris' arrival, showing that the French did value highland resistance, temporarily checked this.[27] Breadalbane's letter gave no details of his negotiation, not even making it clear that the agreement over the money was concluded, but demanded a larger sum than £12,000 for distribution and permission for not only Barclay but Buchan to cross to France to get James's permission for the professional officers to leave Scotland. In a revulsion of doubt, Dalrymple wondered whether Breadalbane was not still an active Jacobite, spinning out negotiations until the campaigning season was over. He had William write to Livingston that he trusted the troops were now encamped close to the Highlands awaiting orders. Yet he obtained the warrant for Mary to ratify Breadalbane's articles, signed and sent off on 23 July.[28] The next day Breadalbane, who had no reason to expect this, sailed from Greenwich with General Douglas, having borrowed another £200 of the £12,000 for the journey. The warrant arrived on the 28th, useless.[29] The delays on the journey in awaiting warships or land convoys, necessary for protection against French raiders,[30] prevented Breadalbane's return for nearly two months — months during which his settlement began to collapse. If he had been windbound until the warrant arrived, there would have been no Massacre of Glencoe.

Almost immediately, the government unknowingly missed another opportunity. A messenger from the Highlands, Captain Thomas Dunbar, had arrived at St. Germain on 15 May(NS) to ask for food and money. As usual, the Jacobite ministers put off having to make an unfavourable reply, sending him back only in late July. James's letters carried by him were intercepted in London, and showed 'how little they may expect from France and how easy therefore it will be to appease all disorders in Scotland if by the ill practises of some in authority there they be not driven to despair'.[31] Sent to Flanders by Nottingham, the letters probably smoothed Breadalbane's explanations. They were not sent to Scotland or mentioned there, since James's influence over the highlanders could not be officially recognised. Yet, arriving then, they would have seemed almost a reply to Rattray's mission. Had Breadalbane been in London, he would have found some excuse for it. As Dunbar remained in London collecting money for the clans, they knew nothing of James's admission of helplessness.[32] William's letter to Livingston now gave the Council an advantage in the duel with Mary. Though not daring to enforce it, they wrote on 3 August urgently demanding instructions. Mary, herself now uncertain of William's intentions, awaited the outcome of Breadalbane's mission before replying, and so could not intervene to prevent less overt harassment of the highlanders.[33]

Breadalbane reached William's camp, far south-east of Brussels, on 10 August(OS). General Douglas (until his sudden death) and Drumlanrig, both unquestionably Williamite 'episcopalians', gave him useful support. Over the next week, as William feverishly manoeuvred to bring the French to battle before lack of forage ended the campaign, Breadalbane made his explanations at snatched intervals, 'by degrees knowing that Kings lov not to be surfeted or chokt, but gently Entertaind'.[34] Events elsewhere favoured him. The spy Higgens, escaping from France, brought (erroneous) news that Louis was ready to send 10,000 more troops to Ireland; but the decisive Williamite victory there at Aughrim in July made it likely that, if France intended to maintain a bridgehead in Britain, she must turn to the Highlands.[35] Breadalbane found William receptive, won over Portland and persuaded Carstares at least to be neutral. They discussed other Scottish matters with him, including, as he vainly assured Argyll that November, a very friendly conference on his affairs.[36] In the evenings, Breadalbane dined at William's table, largely to emphasise to the foreign envoys in the camp (and, through the gazetteers, to the Dutch public) that the pacification would allow the king to use the Scottish army next year in Flanders. On 16 August, to Breadalbane's delight, William spoke to him chiefly about Kilchurn Castle — though the intention expressed in the financial concessions to annex Glencoe to the jurisdiction of Inverlochy shows that Breadalbane kept hidden his private plans for Kilchurn and Fort William. The king also made 'his company at table merry with his asking at my Lord Breadalban, if there were any wolves in the Highlands, and upon his answering in the negative, with telling him that they had enough of two-footed wolves to need any four-footed ones'. It was only a joke, then.[37]

The next day, the main business was concluded. The letter Dalrymple prepared for William to send the Council probably reflected Breadalbane's emphasis in describing the highlanders' 'willingness to render themselves in subjectione to our authority and laues, humbly asking our pardone for what is past' — a language very unlike that actually used at Achallader. Despite his joke, William fairly certainly felt the romantic attraction of having the clans as his direct feudal subordinates.[38] He approved the £11,800 financial concessions. Breadalbane, unless he obtained another grant, would have to repay the £2,000 of the promised money he had borrowed in May. He had apparently given the financial settlement insufficient thought, for he forgot to ask William to forgive the rebels their vast arrears of cess since 1688, which hostile officials could exploit to ruin highlanders who submitted, remembering it only while returning to London. Although William could not openly have proclaimed this, he might have made a private promise.[39]

The Council were ordered to issue a proclamation indemnifying and restoring all rebels who took the oath of allegiance to William. The deadline for this was extended, since Breadalbane's journey had caused such delay, to the end of the year, a major concession which he obtained by personally engaging for the clans that they would not break the cessation. This was a far cry from Dalrymple's original expectation that everything would be settled by Lammas. Clearly, Breadalbane secretly intended to give James ample time to reply to the messengers. As the Council would plainly use every roundabout means to wreck the agreement, William ordered the army to winter quarters, and his letter to the Council contained some explicit warnings, including the astonishing one to garrison commanders 'that they shew noe more zeall against the highlanders after their submissione then they have ever done formerly when these were in open rebellione'.[40] (See Preface, p. viii)

The letter then changed tone sharply. Thefts were blamed largely on the Macgregors, 'who have little proppertie of inheritance to be a pledge for them', and the Council were to issue a proclamation 'certifying our good subjects of the dainger they incurr by intertaining that clan' and requiring all landlords to give special sureties for depredations committed by those living on their lands. Naturally, within a few months some landlords, rather than risk fines, were anxious to evict all Macgregors on their property, even the chief.[41] The order was the first example of full-fledged Court hostility to any particular highland clan, the first step on the road to Glencoe (and to the renewed proscription of the name Macgregor after 1693); but the reason for it can only be conjectured.

This reason was certainly not any traditional hatred in Breadalbane for the clan the Campbells had done most to destroy a century earlier; that was not only past but dead history.[42] The bulk of the landless clan now looked to Argyll and Breadalbane for protection, particularly since a recent quarrel with Atholl, and Argyll saw the proclamation as an indirect attack on him.[43] Breadalbane would not have harmed the Glenlyon Macgregors, useful potential allies for Robert Campbell against Atholl. The young Rob Roy, whom he was to protect for some years against Lord Murray, had just (according to tradition) rescued some of his cows as his first notable deed.[44]

William's joke about 'two-legged wolves' helps to explain the proclamation. Nothing would cast more doubt on the highlanders' sincerity than continued raids on the Lowlands during the cessation, and a major one was reported in July. Buchan and the chiefs saw the danger, and in mid-August, at the report of robberies in the north, they held a meeting and passed severe resolutions against all who committed them.[45] Possibly, the decisive event was Rob Roy's first major exploit, the 'herriship of Kippen'. Its exact date in 1691 is uncertain. The (contradictory) modern accounts suggest after harvest, but, if it was one of the known raids — the one by the Macgregors near Stirling reported in April, or, worse still, the one in July — the spectacular burning of villages south of Forth may have aroused William's and Dalrymple's hostility to the clan.[46] The Macgregors had, anyway, made themselves conspicuous by their raiding all winter and spring. They had not been at Achallader, and Breadalbane could not answer for them. The purchase of superiorities, by giving chiefs jurisdiction over their clans, would justify demanding stricter securities of them for their clansmen's behaviour, and such a tightening of obligations would drive a landless clan still further outside the law. Whatever his feelings, Breadalbane did not think the order enough of a defeat to stop him from describing his negotiations as completely successful.

He momentarily planned to carry the letter to the Council himself to forestall their sabotage. However, his business was not finished. Only after three more days of army manoeuvring could he obtain William's signature to remissions for MacIain, Achtriachtan and Farquharson and an approbation for himself. From Dalrymple, he got passes to France for Buchan and his officers, among which he silently included ones for Barclay, Charteris and Menzies.[47] He then set off with a convoy to Holland. Dalrymple wrote to Queensberry explaining that William, concentrating on the war and averse to thinking on Scottish business, would not follow up the success by immediately appointing an 'episcopalian' ministry. Four days later, he wrote to Breadalbane himself to hurry back to Scotland. Assuming that he could easily persuade the clans, he advised him to secure Argyll's consent, the one remaining problem, by blackmailing reminders that William knew of his Jacobite connections. However, a confusion over shipping detained Breadalbane at Rotterdam. He was there on 26 August when the Council received William's orders. Dalrymple's conciliatory covering letter to Hamilton emphasised that the concessions, paid for by England, would end the danger of French assistance and make heavy taxation less necessary.[48]

The Council's counter-stroke was ready. Sir Aeneas Macpherson had written to highlanders opposed to the cessation, and on 24 August Sir Donald Macdonald, Major A. Gordon and other disaffected officers replied denying the importance of Breadalbane's negotiations and attributing Jacobite weakness to Melville and Hill — a letter they probably intended him to forward to Melville. Gordon was probably the 'Lieutenant-Colonel Gordon', Buchan's nephew, to whom he sent a list of the terms he had verbally agreed with Breadalbane, to vindicate himself — a weapon Gordon could use against the cessation. He gave it to Macpherson, who used it as a basis to forge formal 'private articles' between Breadalbane and Buchan, a copy of which he gave to Hill at Fort William.[49] Hill eagerly sent them to Livingston — later arguing, implausibly, that Macpherson might have been an *agent provocateur* ready to denounce him if he did not — and Livingston gave them to Hamilton. Another version from Gordon reached a councillor, Lord Kintore, an 'episcopalian' involved in Dalrymple's scheme who nevertheless, through some misapprehension, also laid them before the Council. Glengarry has usually been blamed for the forgery, but he did not turn against Breadalbane until a fortnight later. Some copies included the date (probably from Buchan's letter to Gordon) 2 July 1691, for which Breadalbane had alibis. Glengarry would not have made this mistake, although he was repeatedly to perjure himself to support it.[50] The 'articles' omitted everything which might suggest that Breadalbane intended a genuine settlement, and there were differences between copies, often intended to implicate him further. Early in September, somebody studying the fifth article realised that (as he himself soon pointed out) if he sincerely intended to join the Jacobites, he would hardly limit himself to raising a thousand men. The copy Glengarry sent in on 12 September changed this to 'all his men'.[51]

On 29 August, the Council sent William Hill's copy of the 'private articles' without comment. Their reply argued that the highlanders might use the indemnity merely to seduce fresh recruits; but they were privately confident enough of 'things being in such peace and quiet everie wher in the kingdome' to adjourn on 31 August for a month, during which Hamilton, left in control, retired to the country.[52] The proclamation, issued on 27 August, carefully reproduced from William's letter the humiliating mention of the highlanders' 'subjectione' and 'humbly asking our pardone'. They warned that William's order to garrisons not to show more hostile zeal after the clans' surrender than before, 'being somewhat unclear may perhapps be otherwayes understood by these officers then your Majestie intends it' — and then had Livingston transmit it verbatim.[53] On 29 August, they made him summon the Bass garrison to surrender immediately or lose all benefit of the indemnity. That might be excused, since it was independent of the highlanders; but on 31 August Argyll was ordered to summon Duart and Carnaburg on these terms, a direct defiance of William's deadline. The Council had also named Invergarry and Eilean Donan as places which must be garrisoned to secure the western Highlands, but Glengarry and Colin Mackenzie received no summons. Argyll, who had just left Mull, returned and summoned Carnaburg. A refusal must have been expected, since so impregnable a fort could not justifiably be surrendered without orders. The aim was plainly to make the Macleans despair of safety from the cessation, whose opponents would soon show that they believed Sir John's choice would decide its success or failure.[54]

The troubles in Mull had died down during the summer. Failure of equipment and his workmen's hostility constantly frustrated Goodwin Wharton's diving at the Tobermory Galleon. Bad weather in mid-August drove him to the easier wreck of the *Dartmouth*. He believed that the Macleans had intended to raise the fourteen guns he retrieved and mount them at Duart (as they may already have done with two), commanding the entrance to Loch Linnhe and cutting off Fort William. Yet, although the wreck was opposite Duart, there were no further clashes. The expedition returned to Liverpool in September out of pocket, and Wharton presented the guns to Mary.[55] His activities and Argyll's summons had not disheartened Sir John Maclean. On 8 September he replied to a letter of

Breadalbane's from Flanders, promising not to resent such attacks and to encourage the clans to keep the prolonged cessation.[56]

On the mainland, however, patience had dwindled. Stewart of Appin and the other prisoners were not released for some weeks, for Hill shipped them off for Glasgow the day before the order arrived. The troops harassed highlanders who had peacefully returned to their homes on the cessation, and Hamilton made prisoner several who had Dalrymple's passes, 'alledging, that the passes must be forged, for they could never be granted to such villains'. By early September, raids were starting again, and Williamite defenders of the cessation had to argue that only clans which had refused it were involved.[57] Some highlanders now doubted whether Breadalbane had genuinely had William's authority to negotiate, and it was decided to send out fresh messengers. In early August, Barclay asked to meet Barcaldine before leaving for England. Yet, although he left the Jacobite army, he apparently did not travel south for over a month. Breadalbane wrote that the clans were persuaded that he was in prison in London when he was still in Argyllshire.[58] In late August, Menzies reached Edinburgh en route for London, 'sent ... by the generals and other gentlemen in the Highlands, to know whether my Lord Bredalbane had a power to treat with them; and, if he had, why the said treaty was not observed by the council of Scotland'. Charteris had recovered, and on 31 August presented his passes to Hamilton for confirmation. Hamilton was secretly not even certain that Breadalbane had not been authorised to let the clans appeal to France, but he mounted searches for Menzies and had Charteris prevented from leaving. Menzies obtained a pass from the Holyrood postmaster and rode south. Hamilton briefly imprisoned his helpers. Menzies reached London safely, and 'entered a complaint ... against the Duke of Hamiltone, as the onlie occasion of the not keeping of the cessatione'.[59]

Barcaldine, though delighted by his audacity, feared that 'there will be great missing now' of him and Barclay in the Jacobite camp, 'G: M: B[uchan] being a very easy man fflexible to men (if not to all mens advyses)'.[60] When Breadalbane finally reached London on 9 September, after five days' voyage, a storm and brushes with French ships, he was dismayed to find that no highlanders had taken the indemnity. A letter from Lochiel justified Barcaldine's foreboding: he warned that the clans were dissatisfied with the oath of allegiance in the Indemnity, and that 'the major generall sayes he can doe nothing till he gets the kings order'.[61]

At first however, Breadalbane's main problems were private: Glenorchy's insistence on immediately setting out on a promised Grand Tour, and a major crisis over the Caithness bargains. The preparations had roused Breadalbane's creditors to expect immediate payment: failure would probably ruin him. He and Carwhin had deliberately kept the Countess in ignorance throughout, hoping that she would sign the papers without question. On 17 September she refused, unless she could have other securities for her jointure, but he demanded unconditional submission.[62] The scheme was certainly dishonest. Her present advisers, the Argyll family, besides wishing to embarrass Breadalbane, wanted to safeguard her as Argyll's aunt, and, above all, their own expectations from her, over which they bullied her as ruthlessly as Breadalbane. He had to leave for Scotland with the business still undone, and during October this, rather than the highland negotiations, was probably his main preoccupation. Throughout that month the Countess scribbled curses on Carwhin, the original proposer, and worked herself into illnesses which nearly killed her. Finally, she submitted with justifiable bitterness.[63] Yet, simultaneously, she was sending balanced and important warnings of political intrigues against Breadalbane, particularly Montgomerie's. Sick and housebound, she got better intelligence from her friends than Melville from all his paid spies except Macky.

Nevertheless, Breadalbane in September could be optimistic. His supporters had already persuaded Mary to disbelieve the 'private articles'. The Earl of Cassilis' attempts to prepare the way for a deputation from the Council to accuse him failed.[64] Dalrymple wrote that, although William had not yet seen the 'articles', he was not so changeable as to believe such nonsense, and Argyll would be prevented from meddling in Mull. There was some difficulty in obtaining the £12,000 from secret service funds. The officials of the empty Treasury made difficulties, and even Dalrymple suggested that William's promise to pay should satisfy the chiefs, calmly assuming that they would share his high opinion of the usurper's trustworthiness. However, Breadalbane was confident of success and reward. He 'treat[ed] Melville familiarly in all companyes', and rumours spread that he would be made Secretary or Chancellor.[65]

Meanwhile, he looked to his interests with James. Rattray had reached St. Germain and reported the negotiation, stressing Breadalbane's Jacobite professions. At first, James's court seemed likely to drift into compliance. Macky on 30 August passed on a report 'that Scotland was looked upon as lost at that Court neither did he hear of anie designes of ever making head there again'. Menzies now planned to start a correspondence with Rattray. Meanwhile, other Jacobites hoped to prevent Breadalbane's enemy Melfort from regaining power at St. Germain. Cockburne of Langton, a prisoner of war about to be exchanged and go to France, had some authority, as Sir George Mackenzie's son-in-law, to speak for the 'episcopalians', and the Tory Jacobite leaders in England intended to send James warning by him that Melfort's return would wreck the movement.[66]

Suddenly, Breadalbane faced ruin. A messenger from St. Germain produced a letter from James to Cannon — Buchan was evidently in disgrace for Achallader — 'to endeavour what in him lay to break this negociation betwixt the Highlanders and Breadalbane, till the latter end of Januarie or beginning of Februarie, against what time they should be certainly supplied'. Langton, about to send this down express, showed it to Menzies, who exploded;

> that all the letters King James could wryte would take no effect with the Highland clans, seeing he sent them very large promises, the year before, of supplies; and, when they came, proved to be but a small ship with a little flower and wine: But, as for what officers were in the Highlands, they being, by the articles ... to get passes to goe abroad, he could pass his word, that my Lord Braedalbane should delay their being transported till after the time appointed by King James for their relief; and, if they pleased, for their further encouragement, they might send them word of King James's promise; but he feared there was hardly subsistence for them this winter in the Highlands.[67]

On 21 September, Menzies offered to carry the letter himself. Langton and his comrades evidently doubted his intentions, for they made him swear to deliver it.[68] Their suspicions were correct. Breadalbane and he had decided to suppress the letter, and Hamilton's disruption of communications enabled them to do so successfully. Yet concealment alone was useless: as Lochiel had reported, Buchan would only submit on a positive order. If the pacification collapsed, Breadalbane risked not only failure to gain office but prosecution for treason by his aroused enemies. Melville, for instance, was so preoccupied in seeking evidence of his Jacobitism in Macky's report that he missed its basic point — that James disapproved of the cessation. Dalrymple's fresh assurances of William's favour, hinted, disquietingly, that it depended on Breadalbane's getting 'evidence you both have dealt sincerely, and are able, in despite of opposition, to conclude the Highland affair'.[69] Even his hopes of long-term safety forced him to take a greater gamble. He sent Menzies, using his legitimate pass, to St. Germain to assure James that the pacification was in his interest and persuade him to assent. Meanwhile, he himself on 25 September received the £12,000, converted it to bills of exchange and three days later posted north.[70] The 'private articles' were meanwhile laid before William, with other evidence of Breadalbane's Jacobite activity since 1689, but he dismissed them, allegedly saying 'Men who manage treaties, must give fair words'.[71]

The immediate reason for James's change from the hopelessness of July was the French decision to send a small fleet to relieve Limerick. The Jacobites had no independent ability to send help: Innes privately admitted that they had failed, despite promises, even to supply the Bass. In reality, their hopes from the French were groundless. Melfort, the one minister who might influence Louis, had been recalled but had not yet left Rome. Louis and his advisers had secretly agreed to send only enough supplies to keep the Irish war alive as a diversion. And, showing the incompetence which both Williamites and Jacobites overlooked when estimating French power, they sent the convoy too late to prevent the surrender of Limerick.[72] Yet some minor setbacks which ended William's land and sea campaigns in September seemed to outsiders to strengthen the possibility that the French might consider an expedition to Scotland on purely strategic grounds.

However, one main reason for St. Germain's sending the highlanders the order to fight on was pressure from Scottish Jacobite groups there and in London and Edinburgh. Lacking responsibility or accurate knowledge, these groups were more optimistic than either the highland chiefs or James's ministers, and served as a distorting medium between them. No government, particularly one in exile, willingly orders its forces in a major theatre of war to surrender while any hopes of supporting them remain. The submission of the Highlands would shake, perhaps even destroy, the already weakened English Jacobite movement. The catholic Cabinet was the more reluctant because its timid members feared accusations of incompetence or treachery. The highlanders' widely-reported refusal to take the indemnity immediately might merely mean that they awaited James's permission, but it could be interpreted otherwise; the catholic Cabinet would hardly dare order the surrender of men willing to fight on.

In October, the Scot Robert Ferguson, an expatriate since 1655, wrote from London calling for an invasion of Scotland with 10,000 men, and promising a rising under Arran, Atholl, Argyll and Home. He considered that the cessation was beneficial, despite Breadalbane's untrustworthiness. He might have been trusted with the truth that such an invasion now seemed impossible, but the vague reply suggested only that it 'depend[ed] upon time and circumstances'. Alexander Robertson of Struan wrote unofficially from St. Germain to Scotland with poetic licence that a large French force under Berwick and Gordon was actually embarking at Dunkirk. James's suppressed letter to Cannon would have done less harm.[73]

Montgomerie's group was particularly hostile to Breadalbane. Though a Jacobite, he was still a 'presbyterian' politician, as reluctant as Melville to see Dalrymple's 'episcopalians' get office. He was a dangerous enemy, for in August James publicly declared that he would hear no accusations against him. On 28 July he wrote asking if Breadalbane had had James's authorisation for his negotiation. This may have influenced the letter to Cannon.[74] As suspicions of his own treachery grew, he accused in early August an 'episcopalian' Jacobite agent freshly come over, Sir William Sharp (the archbishop's son) of being a traitor employed by Nottingham and Breadalbane. This prevented Sharp's mission to Scotland and destroyed his usefulness there. Langton's detective work cleared his name at St. Germain, and Montgomerie retaliated with similar accusations against Langton.[75] Breadalbane was the next target. Montgomerie's circle wrote claiming that Menzies's mission had been ordered by William, and advising James to repulse or imprison him, and they believed that James had agreed. They sent over a messenger to propose transferring the highland negotiation to Arran and Home, who would protract it until help could come. It was not explained how William would be persuaded to accept overt Jacobites as mediators. However, Montgomerie's English followers were already leaving him. Ferguson, who discovered his communications with Mary, warned St. Germain, and James's favour rapidly changed to the conviction that Montgomerie was working for a republic.[76]

Montgomerie's 'Club' had more success in Scotland. William's endorsement of Breadalbane raised Atholl's jealousy to fever-pitch. He rationalised it by blaming him, rather than the Atholl men's treachery, for his own imprisonment in England in 1689.[77] At the start of September, he invited several Jacobite chiefs, including Lochiel, to his house at Tulliemet in the hills between Killiecrankie and Dunkeld. Glengarry, whom Atholl had avoided since his conversion to catholicism, was the only one who came. He held out for a day or two, during which Atholl presumably appealed vainly to past ties and favours. This drove the Marquess to allege falsely that Breadalbane intended to give him only £1,000 out of the £1,500 promised him at Achallader, and Glengarry changed sides on the spot.[78] The lie reforged their political alliance, which Lord Murray would later exploit during his brief ministry. It now made Glengarry write to Melville's son Raith declaring that the 'private articles' were authentic, and, simultaneously, react into violent Jacobitism and do his utmost to make the chiefs break the cessation. He wrote to Keppoch and went to Eilean Donan to see Lochiel.[79] Atholl may possibly have been the 'great and good friend' behind a letter from Dundee's former chaplain to Lochiel, warning him that 'there was never any thing that troubled the King more than the late cessation' and that 'yow can never receive your master's countenance, friendship, or favour, if yow make any capitulation till yow receive his orders'. It concluded with false optimistic news and promises of large rewards.[80]

Atholl was defying William's wishes even more openly than the Council did. He perhaps hoped that the threats he made against anybody who reported his actions, particularly Breadalbane, would keep the truth from the king. Yet the effect of the Tulliemet conference on Glengarry was too obvious to hide, and suggests that Atholl's main hopes were now Jacobite. Dalrymple doubted this: 'If the Marq. of A. knew what a reverend opinion they have of him, either at St. Germain or Versailles, he would stickle non, and really I ... think his lordship does not so much obstruct this settlement in favour of KJ as to have some interest in the doing of it to recommend himself to King William, in which case he's to be excused'. Breadalbane, however, wrote privately: 'The M: is hounded out by such as ar angry at K:W: but not for lov to K:J:' — an accurate assessment of Montgomerie.[81]

Montgomerie's group complained that Argyll was more timorous. However, the preamble to the Concessions, which seemed to attack the principle of feudal superiorities on which his power rested, had revived his suspicions of the settlement. Montgomerie completely dominated his weak brother John Campbell, who at his orders wrote to Argyll alarmist letters which seriously influenced him. Argyll's influence might be decisive against Breadalbane in the West Highlands.[82]

Meanwhile, the Privy Councillors continued to sabotage the indemnity, delaying the release of prisoners like Macgregor of Glengyle who had taken it. Through agents, they assured the chiefs that if they remained in office through its failure, they would favour them, and played on their vanity, emphasising that Breadalbane had attributed humiliating sentiments to them, and that their submission would 'give him the advantage off sayeing, he could guide and lead the Highland Clans as he pleased, being, ... saveing his title, noe better a man then some off themselves' and would enable him 'to raise and aggrandise himselfe by inslaueing them as if he had all their heads under his girdle'.[83] Only one of Breadalbane's rivals acted to help him. Tarbat, though still feeling a natural jealousy, wrote sharply to Glengarry and Sir Donald Macdonald that only Breadalbane's influence had saved them from attack the previous summer, and that the politicians who were persuading them to refuse his terms were, to his certain knowledge, planning their destruction; but Breadalbane, suspecting his motives, seems not to have forwarded the letters.[84]

Fort William remained peaceful: some of those captured in the Appin raid even called there on their return from Glasgow. After Macpherson brought the 'private articles', Hill allowed him free passage between the Fort and the clans. By mid-October, he was offering to carry up a copy authenticated by Cannon to London, where the Council's emissary Lord Cardross was singing his praises.[85] Carwhin had discovered that Melville was paying Macpherson, but his warnings merely served 'to expose yr authors to just contempt and laughter'. Barcaldine hoped that he would influence only the less important Jacobites of Badenoch and the North Highlands, and that those who had signed the cessation would remain firm. On 26 September, Carwhin heard that Buchan as yet paid little attention to him. Breadalbane might still forestall him.[86]

Breadalbane reached Edinburgh on 2 October. He called Queensberry, Linlithgow and Kintore to a conference, and advised them to go to London, do what they could underhand, but not move in business publicly until he came up. On 7 October he reached Balloch, and sent out invitations to meet him there, or a week later at Glenorchy, to the chiefs, including some, such as Sir Donald Macdonald, who had not been at Achallader. He hoped that those who had would meet him, take the oaths in their shires, and return for their money. However, a troublesome widowed niece's private affairs further delayed him, and he was probably unwilling to venture too far off while the Caithness bargains remained unsettled. While he delayed, Macpherson acted.[87]

The deed that most won him the highlanders' trust was particularly two-faced. While encouraging other clans to resist, he obtained for Cluny and the Macphersons full credit for Jacobite loyalty while adroitly ensuring that they did nothing to offend the government. He brought Cluny's promise to appear when summoned with a full regiment of Macphersons instead of the detachments which had fought under lesser men in 1689 and 1690, representing his zeal so convincingly that Buchan himself wrote urging Cluny to risk nothing until James's orders arrived. Cluny remained so quiet that the government in December unhesitatingly summoned him to march against the rebels; and Buchan was brought to endorse even this.[88] Macpherson then travelled between Jacobite houses collecting testimonials and encouraging opposition to the settlement: on 13 October, at Armadale with Cannon and Sir Donald; on the 19th, at Eilean Donan with Ballechin (who had just refused Breadalbane's summons) and Colin Mackenzie (who was implausibly rumoured to have raised 800 Mackenzies furious at the clan's being ignored in Breadalbane's terms); on the 24th, at Invergarry with Glengarry. He reported to Hill; but his proposed journey to London with the 'articles' was merely the cover for one to St. Germain to prove to James his 'great service in coming among his name and friends, in taking away divisions among them, and making 'em unanimous to serve the King ... and encouraging severall others to the same effect who were rather enemies than friends formerly'. He would have been far away when the chiefs he had roused had to face the government's wrath.[89]

Dalrymple cursed 'that Rogue M'Pherson' as the chief agent in creating opposition, but this soon built up its own momentum. Breadalbane found that the chiefs had bound themselves by 'ane unhappie Ingadgment ... (befor my return) that they uould not accept uithout the joynt consent of ye pluralitie at least some of the most considerable'.[90] Buchan had changed sides before a divided meeting about the indemnity held at Invergarry not later than 11 October, where he 'endeavour[ed] all he could to rase mischeif and poyson afress all whome he apprehended had any inclination to it'.[91] Robertson of Struan's letter and a forged 'French King's Manifesto' promising not to sheath the sword until James was restored, written in late 1690 and revived now, were circulated. Breadalbane reported that the catholic priests — all Irishmen, since the starvation diet in the West Highlands since 1689 had kept out the less hardy lowlanders — were 'possessing such of ym as are Papists not to take the oath of Alledgance upon ye account of conscience, And such of them as are protestants ar advysed that it is dishonorable for them, & that if they accept of the kings bounty it is the selling of ther king'.[92] Some highlanders openly told Hill that they had accepted the cessation only to benefit the Jacobite cause, giving him justification for his activities against it. Yet simultaneously several chiefs — even, Sir Alexander Bruce claimed, Lochiel himself — felt that too much of the £12,000 was going to the Macleans, and that their shares were too small. All 'vow they will not take the oaths and doe declare they never gave Bradalbane any the least ground to think they would or to offer in their name'. Finally, another meeting in late October determined, despite Lochiel's and perhaps Keppoch's reluctance, to have no further dealings with Breadalbane. He wrote in despair: 'they ar ruind and abused uith lyes that children of 10 years age could not beleev and they talk as if they uer to giv terms & not to receav them but they uill find yt a great mistak in feue ueeks notuithstanding of all My Endeavours to the Contrarie'.[93]

It is generally assumed that in the autumn of 1691 the highland chiefs were willing to submit and were prevented only by the non-arrival of James's permission. If the events leading to the Massacre are to be judged fairly, it must be made clear that by late October the policy of pacification appeared to be collapsing. The chiefs were, outwardly, far more eager to fight than they had been a year earlier. The cessation had, as had been predicted, merely given them time to recover, and their comments now, which reached Dalrymple, suggested that they had acted insincerely from the start. In fact, their resolution was hollow. The Highlands were too impoverished to support another campaign without outside supplies, and, for all the promises Cluny and others made, the chiefs would probably be unable to raise an effective army. They were listening to the offers of 'presbyterian' politicians, their traditional enemies, to secure safety and rewards for them, and apparently wished to have both the credit for Jacobite loyalty and the financial benefits of submission. This gave some hope that Breadalbane's delayed counter-representations might succeed, if backed by Lochiel and Sir John Maclean who stood to benefit most from the cessation. But, if he failed, a winter campaign would be necessary; and the government and the soldiers, blaming all the extra hardships which this entailed on the treachery of the clans, would be anxious for vengeance.

NOTES

1. SRO GD170/612/4, Carwhin to Barcaldine, 20 July 1691; BL Add. 20,007 (G. Wharton's diary), fol. 80v; PRO ADM 51/4285/1 (Log of HMS *Pembroke*), 30 June–10 July 1691; *ib.*, 51/3796/4 (Log of HMS *Conception*), 30 June–9 July 1691.

2. The implausible Maclean legend that a suicidal Maclean hostage, rather than the secret agent Smollett, blew up the ship was probably an attempt to strengthen their claims to the

treasure. R. P. Hardie, *The Tobermory Argosy* (Edinburgh, 1912), 12–13, 18–20; *HMCR 6th Report*, 619, A. Campbell to Argyll, 23 May 1677; *ib.*, 625–7, papers on the Tobermory Galleon.

3. *Ib.*, 627, retrocession by A. Campbell of Calder to Argyll, 22 Dec. 1694; Cawdor Castle, Lord Cawdor MSS, bundle 584, agreement between Argyll, Sir S. Evance & W. Dockwra, 19 Mar. 1690/1; BL Add. 20,007 fols. 79v–80v.

4. *Ib.*, fols., 80v–81; *RPCS*, xvi, 411; SRO GD 112/40/4/2/33, [Argyll] to Breadalbane, 4 June 1691; GD 170/612/4, Carwhin to same, 20 July 1691.

5. BL Add. 20,007 fol. 80v; SRO GD 170/3032, Sir J. Maclean to [Barcaldine], 29 July 1691.

6. *Ib.*, 629/31, Breadalbane to same, 24 Oct. 1691; Blair, Atholl MSS, Box 44/VI/256, Argyll to Murray, 23 July [1691]; *ib.*, Box '71', D 9, A. Douglas to same, 30 June 1691.

7. Macpherson, *Original Papers*, i, 388, Major Holmes's Paper, Oct. 1691; WDA, Browne MSS, 208, Jacobite cabinet minute, 30 Aug. 1691 (NS).

8. MacGill, *Old Ross-shire*, i, 238, Dalrymple to [Tarbat], 12 July 1691; Drumlanrig, Queensberry Papers, Vol. 126, 6, same to Queensberry, 13/23 July '1690' [1691]; HLRO, Willcocks MSS, Section VI, 93, Yester to Tweeddale, 11 'June' [July] 1691; *HMCR Finch*, iii, 131, Breadalbane to Nottingham, 28 June 1691; *ib.*, 136, Linlithgow to same, 2 July 1691; *ib.*, 159, Lockhart to same, 16 July 1691.

9. *Ib.*, 200–1, 'J. Scott' to 'J. Watson', 10 Aug. 1691; WDA, Browne MSS, 208, Jacobite cabinet minute, 30 Aug. 1691 (NS).

10. *RPCS*, xiv, 247–8, 617; *Carstares S.P.*, 136, [Macky] to J. Melvill, 11 Sept. 1691; MacGill, *Old Ross-shire*, i, 237, Hill to [?Balnagown, ?July 1691]; PRO SP 44/342, 89, passes, 18 July 1691; *Franco-Irish Corr.*, ii, 311, Bouridal to Louvois, 21 July 1691 (NS); Bodl., MS Carte 180 fol. 451, Rattray's memorial; SRO GD 170/3046, Buchan to D. Menzies, 16 July [1691]; GD 406/1/6623 (M1/246), memorandum, 31 Aug. 1691.

11. *Leven & Melville*, 647, Breadalbane to Hill, 10 Oct. 1691; *HMCR Finch*, iii, 211, [Neville Payne] to 'Aunt', 15 Aug. 1691.

12. Its existence is shown by an alternative rumour: that William intended to ship the Scottish army overseas, replacing them with foreign troops. *HMCR Hamilton Supplement*, 121, Melville to Hamilton, 22 Sept. 1691; NLS MS 7013 fol. 80, Bruce to Tweeddale, 13 Aug. 1691.

13. *RPCS*, xvi, 357, 411; Dalrymple, *Memoirs*, ii, 210, Dalrymple to Breadalbane, 15/25 June 1691; *HMCR Hope-Johnstone*, 172, Crawford to Lords Justices of Ireland, 11 July 1691.

14. NLS MS 1031 fol. 130, Hamilton to Selkirk, 29 Aug. 1691; *HMCR Hamilton Supplement*, 116–17, same to William, 20 June 1691.

15. As he used the same argument to the friendly Tarbat, he presumably believed it. *Ib.*, 117, Dalrymple to Hamilton, [July 1691]; MacGill, *Old Ross-shire*, i, 238, same to [Tarbat], 12 July 1691.

16. *HMCR Finch*, iii, 159, Lockhart to Nottingham, 16 July 1691.

17. *Carstares S.P.*, 136, [Macky] to J. Melvill, 11 Sept. 1691; *Leven & Melville*, 628–9, Hamilton to Melville, 21 July 1691; *RPCS*, xvi, 420–1, 423.

18. He looked to Melville as his employer, then and later — the one clear proof that Melville actively sabotaged the cessation as well as passively deploring it. *Ib.*, 251–4, 283–4, 295–6, 360, 421–2; *HMCR Finch*, iii, 270, 'Edgar' to ?, 18 Sept. 1691; SRO GD 26/viii/130, A. Gordon to Sir Ae. Macpherson, 6 Jan. 1692; *ib.*, xiii/415, Sir Ae. Macpherson to [Melville], 6 June 1692.

19. *Ib.*, 78 fol. 179, Sir D. Macdonald etc. to Sir Ae. Macpherson; *Leven & Melville*, 641,

Hill to Raith, 22 Aug. 1691 (Gillis = Macpherson); SRO GD 112/40/4/5/31, Countess to Carwhin, 5 Nov. 1691; Macpherson, *Loyall Dissuasive*, 204; *RPCS*, xvi, 451–2.

20. *Ib.*, 446, 451; *HMCR Hamilton*, 178, Mary to Hamilton, 22 July 1691; *Melvilles & Leslies*, ii, 149, Melville to same, 29 July [1691]; *HMCR Finch*, iii, 171, Nottingham to Lockhart, 22 July 1691; *ib.*, 171–2, Leinster to Livingston, [22 July 1691].

21. *Ib.*, 184–5, Lockhart to Nottingham, 29 July 1691; *Leven & Melville*, 631–2, Tarbat to Melville, 25 July 1691; *HMCR Hope-Johnstone*, 58, Sir W. Hamilton to Annandale, 6 Aug. 1691; SRO GD 170/612/5, Carwhin to Barcaldine, 26 July 1691; *RPCS*, xvi, 447, 451–2.

22. *Ib.*, 488–90.

23. *HMCR Finch.*, iii, 135, Lockhart to Nottingham, 2 July 1691; *ib.*, 155, Dalrymple to same, 13/23 July 1691; *ib.*, 152, Nottingham to Breadalbane, 11 July 1691; *ib.*, 172–3, same to Portland, 25 July 1691; *HMCR Roxburghe*, 122, Carstares to Polwarth, 6 Aug. 1691.

24. SRO GD 50/10/1/24, Breadalbane to Countess, 17 Aug. [1691]; GD 112/40/4/2/2, same to Carwhin, 19 Feb. 1690; *ib.*, 40/4/5/8, same to same, 26 Sept. 1691; *ib.*, 43/1/5/3, same to same, Oct. '1696' [1695].

25. *HMCR Finch*, iii, 169, Nottingham to Lockhart, 21 July 1691; *ib.*, 171, same to same, 22 July 1691.

26. *Ib.*, 166–7, Dalrymple to Nottingham, same to Breadalbane, 20/30 July 1691.

27. *Ib.*, 134, same to Nottingham, 30 June 1691.

28. *Ib.*, 174–5, same to same, same to Breadalbane (2), 23 July 1691; *RPCS*, xvi, 464; *CSPD 1690-1*, 458, William to Mary, 23 July 1691.

29. *Ib.*, pass for Breadalbane, 23 July 1691; *HMCR Finch*, iii, 166, 175; *ib.*, 176, Nottingham to Dalrymple, 24 July 1691; *ib*, 188, same to same, 31 July 1691; Drumlanrig, Queensberry Papers, Vol. 121, 47, General Douglas to Queensberry, 22 July 1691; SRO GD 112/40/4/1/1, [Glenorchy] to Mrs Campbell, 29 Sept. [1691].

30. *Ib.*, 40/4/5/15, Breadalbane to Countess, 25 Aug. [1691]; Story, *Carstares*, 217, Carstares to Dunlop, 3 Aug. 1691.

31. *HMCR Finch*, iii, 188–9, Nottingham to Sydney, same to Dalrymple, 31 July 1691; Marquis de Sourches, *Mémoires*, ed. Comte de Cosnac & E. Pontal, 13 vols. (Paris, 1882–92), iii, 420; BL Add. 37,662 fol. 110, Cpt. Knightley to H. Browne, 2 May 1691 (NS).

32. SCA, Blairs Letters, Box U, 1691, 10, 'J. Murray' [T. Dunbar] to [Innes], 6 Oct. 1691; *ib.*, 11, same to same, 23 Nov. 1691.

33. *RPCS*, xvi, 464, 552; *HMCR Finch*, iii, 194–5, Lockhart to Nottingham, [c. 4 Aug. 1691]; *ib.*, 197, Nottingham to Lockhart, 8 Aug. 1691.

34. SRO GD 50/10/1/22, Breadalbane to Carwhin, 13/23 Aug. 1691; Drumlanrig, Queensberry Papers, Vol. 122, 48, same to Queensberry, 13/23 Aug. 1691.

35. Huygens, *Journaal*, i, 481; *HMCR Hamilton Supplement*, 119–20, Dalrymple to Hamilton, 27 Aug. 1691 (NS).

36. *HMCR Finch*, iii, 213, same to Nottingham, 17/27 Aug. 1691; Cumnock, Dumfries House, Bute MSS, bundle A517/13, Breadalbane to [Dalrymple], 19 Nov. 1691; Story, *Carstares*, 217–8, Carstares to Dunlop, 17 Aug. 1691.

37. *Ib.*, 218; *CSPD 1690-1*, 492, Concessions, 17/27 Aug. 1691; SRO GD 50/10/1/24, Breadalbane to Countess, 17 Aug. [1691]; GD 112/40/4/5/15, same to same, 25 Aug. [1691]; *ib.*, 40/4/8/30, speech, [1695].

38. This can be deduced from a remark he made in 1692 about Argyll's regiment, showing an — equally groundless — confidence in their feudal loyalty to him. *RPCS*, xvi, 536; SRO SP 3/1 fol. 60v, Johnston to Tweeddale, 26 Nov. 1692.

39. *CSPD 1690-1*, 491–2, Concessions, 17/27 Aug. 1691; Dalrymple, *Memoirs*, ii, 212,

Dalrymple to Breadalbane, 18/28 Sept. 1691; NLS MS 7014 fol. 156, Hill to Tweeddale, 24 Aug. 1692.

40. *HMCR Finch*, iii, 211, Portland to Nottingham, 17/27 Aug. 1691; SRO GD 50/10/1/28, [Sir J. Maclean] to Breadalbane, 8 Sept. 1691; *RPCS*, xvi, 526-7.

41. *Ib.*, 537-8, 540-1, 615-16.

42. See Chapter 1, pp. 19, 30, 37n52.

43. SRO GD 112/40/4/8/31, [Barcaldine] to [Carwhin], 13 Sept. [1691].

44. The tradition may be partially confirmed by the mention of a special payment Barcaldine was to make to 'the Macgregors' in May 1691. *Ib.*, 43/1/2/11, list of those taking the Indemnity, [1692]; Atholl, *Chronicles*, i, App., xliii-xliv, Murray to Marchioness, 21 May [1695]; H. Howlett, *Highland Constable* (Edinburgh, 1959), 22-5; SRO GD 170/612/3, Carwhin to Barcaldine, 22 May 1691.

45. *Ib.*, 7, same to same, 8 Aug. 1691; GD 50/10/1/25, [Barcaldine] to Carwhin, 26 Aug. 1691; *Gazette de France*, 11 Aug. 1691 (NS), '515-16', London report, 31 July 1691.

46. Kippen Church was destroyed, but the Minutes of the Presbytery of Dunblane, which might have made a more exact date possible, are lost for this period. Murray Macgregor, *Clan Gregor*, ii, 274-5; Howlett, *Highland Constable*, 26-9; *Statistical Account*, ix, 525. Hership/herriship = devastation, plundering, spoil.

47. In 1695, to confuse the issue at his trial, he was to claim in one defence that Barclay and Menzies also had official passes to return from France. Yet it is clear from Dalrymple's late 1691 letters that he remained opposed to letting the highlanders communicate with James and unaware of Menzies's relations with Breadalbane. *CSPD 1690-1*, 496-7, discharge to Breadalbane, remissions, pass for Buchan, 20/30 Aug. 1691; SRO GD 112/43/1/5/1, *Answers for the Earl of Breadalbane*, 6; *ib.*, 25, Breadalbane to Buchan, 16 Nov. 1691; *ib.*, 27, [Carwhin] to 'Mrs Pringle', 27 Aug. 1691; Dalrymple, *Memoirs*, ii, 215-16, Dalrymple to Breadalbane, 2 Dec. 1691.

48. *Ib.*, 211, same to same, 24 Aug. 1691; *HMCR Hamilton Supplement*, 119-20, same to Hamilton, 27 Aug. 1691 (NS); Drumlanrig, Queensberry Papers, Vol. 126, 7, same to Queensberry, 24 Aug. '1692' [1691]; *RPCS*, xvi, 536-8; SRO GD 112/40/45/15, [Breadalbane] to [Countess], 25 Aug. [1691].

49. Hill declared in 1695 that it was Macpherson who gave him the 'articles'. *Ib.*, 43/1/2/34, Carwhin's notes on the libel of exculpation, [1695]; GD 26/xiii/78 fol. 179v, Sir D. Macdonald etc. to Sir Ae. Macpherson, 24 Aug. 1691; *HMCR Stuart*, i, 73, lists of Scots officers, 1692; *RPCS*, xvi, 550.

50. *Ib; HMCR Finch*, iii, 280, Breadalbane to Nottingham, 3 Oct. 1691; *Leven & Melville*, 648-9, Hill to Breadalbane, 17 Oct. 1691; *HMCR Hope-Johnstone*, 173-4, same to Crawford, 14 Sept. 1691; SRO GD 112/43/1/5/32, Breadalbane to same, 12 July [1695]; GD 26/xiii/78 fol. 179, Glengarry to Raith, 12 Sept. 1691 + 'private articles', 2 July 1691.

51. *Ib; HMCR Finch*, iii, 242-3, Hill's copy 'private articles'; *HMCR Hamilton Supplement*, 121, Melville to Hamilton, 22 Sept. 1691; SRO GD 112/43/1/5/1, *Answers for the Earl of Breadalbane*, 4-5.

52. *RPCS*, xvi, 550, 553-4.

53. The Jacobite biographer Drummond of Balhaldie certainly misunderstood the order, seeing it as William's preliminary plan for the Massacre. *Ib.*, 541, 550; *Memoirs of Locheill*, 305.

54. *RPCS*, xvi, 551-2, 554; SRO GD 50/10/1/25, [Barcaldine] to Carwhin 26 Aug. 1691; GD 112/40/4/2/37, summons to Cairnburgh, 7 Sept. 1691; NLS MS 7014 fol. 79, Hill to Tweeddale, 2 May 1692.

55. *HMCR 7th Report*, 202, [J. Blancard] to Dykveldt, 18/28 Sept. 1691; P. McBride,

'The Dartmouth ... 3. The guns', *IJNA*, v, (1976), 189–95; BL Add. 20,007 fols. 80, 81v.

56. SRO GD 50/10/1/28, [Sir J. Maclean] to Breadalbane, 8 Sept. 1691.

57. *Ib.*, 25, [Barcaldine] to Carwhin, 26 Aug. 1691; *Carstares S.P.*, 135–6, [Macky] to J. Melvill, 11 Sept. 1691; *Leven & Melville*, 645, Livingston to Leven, 11 Sept. 1691; *Gazette de France*, 13 Oct. 1691 (NS), '592–3', London Report, 2 Oct. 1691 (NS).

58. SRO GD 170/591, Barclay to Barcaldine, 5 Aug. 1691; *ib.*, 629/30, Breadalbane to same, 24 Oct. 1691.

59. *Carstares S.P.*, 135–7, [Macky] to J. Melvill, 11 Sept. 1691; *Leven & Melville*, 645, Hamilton to Melville, 11 Sept. 1691; SRO GD 406/1/6623 (M1/246), memorandum, 31 Aug. 1691.

60. SRO GD 112/40/4/8/31, [Barcaldine] to [Carwhin], 13 Sept. [1691].

61. *Ib.*, 40/4/5/41, Countess to Mrs. Campbell, 10 Sept. 1691; GD 170/629/29, Breadalbane to Barcaldine, 15 Sept. 1691; GD 50/10/1/29, [Lochiel] to Breadalbane, 11 Sept. 1691.

62. SRO GD 112/40/4/1/1, [Glenorchy] to Mrs Campbell, 29 Sept. [1691]; *ib.*, 40/4/2/36, same to Breadalbane, 29 Sept. 1691; ib., 40/4/5/18, Countess to Mrs Campbell, 3 Oct. 1691; *ib.*, 32, Breadalbane to Countess, 31 Oct. 1691; *ib.*, 37, same to Carwhin, 5 May 1691; *ib.*, 40/4/2/34, Glenorchy to [Carwhin], 17 Sept. 1691.

63. *Ib.*, 50, [Countess] to Carwhin, 2 Nov. 1691; *ib.*, 64/2/1/3, same to same, 3 Nov. 1691; *ib.*, 40/4/5/31, same to Mrs Campbell, 5 Nov. 1691.

64. *Ib.*, 36, Glenorchy to same, 6 [Sept. 1691]; NLS MS 7013 fol. 82, J. Dickson to Tweeddale, 24 Sept. 1691.

65. *Ib.*, fol. 86v, same to same, 10 Oct. 1691; *CTB*, xvii, 1505–6; Dalrymple, *Memoirs*, ii, 211–12, Dalrymple to Breadalbane, 18/28 Sept. 1691; *ib.*, 212, same to same, 20/30 Sept. 1691; SRO GD 112/40/4/5/9, Breadalbane to Carwhin, 22 Sept. 1691; *HMCR Finch*, iii, 270, 'Edgar' to ?, 18 Sept. 1691; Blair, Atholl MSS, Box 29 I (6) 46, [Dunmore] to Murray, 15 Sept. [1691].

66. *Gazette de France*, 25 Aug. 1691 (NS), '539', London report, 9 Aug. 1691 (NS); Ailesbury, *Memoirs*, i, 274; *Carstares S.P.*, 137, [Macky] to J. Melvill, 11 Sept. 1691; *ib.*, 138, same to [Melville, 21 Sept. 1691]; SRO GD 26/viii/122/12, same to same, n.d; *ib.*, 127, same to same, 30 Aug. 1691.

67. *Carstares S.P.*, 137–8, same to same, [21 Sept. 1691].

68. *Ib.*, 138.

69. *HMCR Hamilton Supplement*, 121, Melville to Hamilton, 22 Sept. 1691; Dalrymple, *Memoirs*, ii, 213, Dalrymple to Breadalbane, 20/30 Sept. 1691.

70. *HMCR Buccleuch (Montagu)*, ii, 202, Johnston to Shrewsbury, 19 July 1695; *HMCR Finch*, iii, 280, Breadalbane to Nottingham, 3 Oct. 1691; SRO GD 112/43/1/2/2, Breadalbane's receipt, 25 Sept. 1691.

71. Dalrymple, *Memoirs*, i, 188–9.

72. *Carstares S.P.*, 137 [Macky] to [Melville, 21 Sept. 1691]; C. Nordmann, 'Louis XIV and the Jacobites', *Louis XIV and Europe*, ed. R. Hatton (London, 1976), 84; NLS MS 14,266 (Sir D. Nairne's Journal) fol. 28 (4 Sept. 1691 (NS)); SCA, Blairs Letters Box U, 1691, 46, Innes to Talon, 4 Sept. 1691 (NS); Macpherson, *Original Papers*, i, 386.

73. *Ib.*, 388–9, Major Holmes's paper, Oct. 1691; *ib.*, 392, Instructions to Ferguson, 1691; *LJ*, xvii, 411, Ferguson's narrative, 27 Dec. 1703; *HMCR Hope-Johnstone*, 176, Hill to ?, 19 Oct. 1691, same to Crawford, 29 Oct. 1691.

74. SRO GD 26/viii/127, Macky to Melville, 30 Aug. 1691; WDA, Browne MSS, 208, Jacobite cabinet minute, 30 Aug. 1691 (NS).

75. Yet some honest Jacobites had mistrusted Sharp earlier. *Ib.*, 5 Aug., 30 Aug., 12 Sept.

1691 (NS); *ib.*, 260, 'W. North' to [J. Caryll, July 1691]; *HMCR Finch*, iii, 275,? to 'Mr Lewis' [Innes], 22 Sept. 1691; NUL, Portland MSS, PwA 2698, Langton to James, 14, 18 Aug. 1691.

76. *Archives de la Bastille*, ix, 372–3, Renaudot to Croissy, [Nov. 1692]; Macpherson, *Original Papers*, i, 390, Major Holmes's paper, Oct. 1691; WDA, Browne MSS, 208, cabinet minute, 12 Sept. 1691 (NS); BN Naf 7847 fol. 163, 'Memorial of several Measures taken by Melfort since he came from Rome', [1692].

77. SRO GD 112/40/4/5/38, Carwhin to Breadalbane, 26 Sept. 1691.

78. *Ib; ib.*, 40/4/8/30, draft speech by Breadalbane, [1695] (cancelled passage); *ib.*, 31, [Barcaldine] to [Carwhin], 13 Sept. [1691]; Dalrymple, *Memoirs*, ii, 216, Dalrymple to Breadalbane, 3 Dec. 1691; *Memoirs of Locheill*, 260–1; NLS MS 7013 fol. 108v, Bruce to Tweeddale, 23 Oct. 1691; Blair, Atholl MSS, Box 44/VI/173, Atholl to Lady Murray, [1693].

79. SRO GD 26/xiii/78 fol. 179, Glengarry to Raith, 12 Sept. 1691; GD 50/10/1/31, M. Campbell to Carwhin, 13 Sept. 1691; GD 112/40/4/8/31, [Barcaldine] to [same], 13 Sept. [1691]; *Memoirs of Locheill*, 307.

80. Dundee's chaplain was Charles Edward, of the Fife clerical and map-making dynasty. *Ib.*, 310–11; Scott, *Fasti*, v, 367–8; Lenman, *Jacobite Risings*, 65–7; SRO PC 1/50, 478.

81. Hill Burton, *History*, i, 527, Dalrymple to Breadalbane, 27 Oct. 1691; Blair, Atholl MSS, Box 29 I (6) 54, Lord James Murray to Murray, 11 Nov. 1691; SRO GD 112/40/4/5/45, Breadalbane to Carwhin, 31 Oct. 1691.

82. *Ib.*, 33, same to same, 16 Oct. 1691; *ib.*, 43/1/5/27, [Carwhin] to 'Mrs Pringle', 27 Aug. 1691; Cumnock, Dumfries House, Bute MSS, bundle A517/13, Breadalbane to [Dalrymple], 19 Nov. 1691; *HMCR Finch*, iii, 275, ? to 'Mr Lewis' [Innes], 22 Sept. 1691 ('Anderson' = Argyll, WDA, Browne MSS, 257f).

83. *Ib.*, 280, Breadalbane to Nottingham, 3 Oct. 1691; *RPCS*, xvi, 572–3; *HMCR Hope-Johnstone*, 176, Hill to ?, 19 Oct. 1691; *Leven & Melville*, 649, same to Raith, 29 Oct. 1691.

84. Linlithgow suggested to Breadalbane that Tarbat was merely seeking to take credit if the negotiation succeeded, but he himself then cared little for its success. Tarbat later had his son the Master appeal to Sir Donald. *Ib.*, 644, Tarbat to Melville, 29 Aug. 1691; [Moncrieff], 'Macaulay's History', *ER*, cv, 172; *ib.*, 173, Linlithgow to Breadalbane, 17 Oct. 1691; NLS MS 1330 fol. 58, Sir A. Mackenzie of Coul to Delvine, 10 Nov. 1691; SRO GD 112/40/4/2/38, Tarbat to Glengarry, 4 Oct. 1691, n.d., same to Sir D. Macdonald, 10 Oct. 1691.

85. *Ib.*, 40/4/5/31, Countess to Mrs Campbell, 5 Nov. 1691; *ib.*, 38, Carwhin to Breadalbane, 26 Sept. 1691; *HMCR Hope-Johnstone*, 173, Hill to Crawford, 14 Sept. 1691; *Leven & Melville*, 649, same to Raith, 29 Oct. 1691.

86. Macpherson, *Loyall Dissuasive*, 192; SRO GD 112/39/1219, Breadalbane to Carwhin, 15 Sept. 1691; *ib.*, 40/4/8/31, [Barcaldine] to [same], 13 Sept. [1691]; *ib.*, 40/4/5/38, Carwhin to Breadalbane, 26 Sept. 1691.

87. *Ib.*, 33, Breadalbane to [Carwhin], 16 Oct. 1691; *ib.*, 43, same to same, [8 Oct. 1691]; GD 26/viii/122/13, Macky to Melville, Nov. [1691]; *HMCR Finch*, iii, 280, Breadalbane to Nottingham, 3 Oct. 1691; Macdonald, *Clan Donald*, iii, 76.

88. Macpherson, *Loyall Dissuasive*, xxi, [Buchan] to [Sir Ae. Macpherson], 6 Jan. [1692]; *ib.*, 192, 196–7, 212–13; Macpherson, 'Gleanings', *TGSI*, xx, 246–7, Dalrymple to Cluny, 13 Dec. 1691.

89. Macpherson, *Loyall Dissuasive*, 192–6; SRO GD 112/40/4/4/6, Ballechin to

Breadalbane, 15 Oct. 1691; NLS MS 7013 fol. 108, Bruce to Tweeddale, 23 Oct. 1691.

90. *Highland Papers*, 48, Dalrymple to Lt-Col Hamilton, 1 Dec. 1691; Cumnock, Dumfries House, Bute MSS, bundle A517/13, Breadalbane to [Dalrymple], 19 Nov. 1691.

91. *HMCR Hope-Johnstone*, 174, Lt-Col Hamilton to Crawford, 16 Oct. 1691.

92. *Ib.*, 176, Hill to same, 29 Oct. 1691; Forbes Leith, *Scottish Catholics*, ii, 148, 151, 169–70; SRO GD 103/2/250, 'The French King's Manifesto in favour of King James'; Cumnock, Dumfries House, Bute MSS, bundle A517/12, Breadalbane to [Dalrymple], 16 Nov. 1691.

93. *Leven & Melville*, 648, Hill to Breadalbane, 17 Oct. 1691; *ib.*, 649–50, same to Raith, 29 Oct. 1691; NLS MS 7013 fol. 108, Bruce to Tweeddale, 23 Oct. 1691; SRO GD 170/629/30, Breadalbane to Barcaldine, 24 Oct. 1691.

10

The Massacre (October 1691–February 1692)

From the Hague, Dalrymple wrote on 2 October to Queensberry that several days earlier he had believed that the highland affair would fail, unjustly branding the 'episcopalians' as insincere; but, now that Breadalbane had 'extricat himself out of the toills', it need not cause Queensberry to come to London:

> I am not for pushing any thing nou till ... Breadalbin may return in triumph for upon that much depends and according as the king takes his resolutions [on the civil government] the orders to the kirk [for the General Assembly] must be peremptor or easy ... I do not Beleiv any body will find it fitt to disturb ther church goverment wtout Bishops bot if they will not depend upon the king they hav nather interest nor security if the king signify the least indifferency to any parl: he can call.

If any 'episcopalians' had expected Dalrymple to push the attack against the Presbyterians further, this was a tacit withdrawal. However, it caused no such disillusionment as realisation of his anti-Jacobitism had done that summer to Balcarres, who abandoned political activity.[1]

On arriving in England, Dalrymple was dismayed that Breadalbane had not yet succeeded, although the negotiation had at least shown to what unpatriotic extremes the 'presbyterians' would go to thwart it. However, a positive success was badly needed, and Dalrymple exposed the financial corruption of Melville's regime, which was about to farm the excise well below value to the Treasury Commissioners' favourites. He ensured that a rival group would bid higher, and sent Tweeddale with special powers to Edinburgh, where he concluded the bargain. This justified some governmental changes, which would convert waverers. Queensberry and Linlithgow arrived in late October to support Dalrymple, and William gave them assurances.[2]

However, they had dangerous opponents. Tarbat came up after loudly declaring that the 'presbyterians'' incorrigibility had driven him into Dalrymple's camp. Yet, while temporising, he on the whole worked for his cousin Melville, and although — perhaps because — he did not try to discredit the highland negotiation, his influence rapidly grew.[3] Dalrymple had muffled Hamilton's hostile complaints all year by deluding his courtier son and representative, Selkirk, but this could not last.[4] Crawford and other hostile Privy Councillors, who were now implausibly promising that the Presbyterians would show exemplary toleration, concentrated on begging William to delay changes until he saw the result of Breadalbane's negotiation. 'It is now the only defence our high-flown boys have against the settling of the Government that the highlands are not, and will not, be got settled,' wrote Linlithgow on 10 November. Their emphasis made the negotiation the Scottish affair that was most discussed in London throughout

November, and Dalrymple was constantly busy defending Breadalbane. Disappointed by Sir Aeneas Macpherson, they exploited Glengarry's detailed accusation of Jacobitism against the Earl. Personal rulers and non-bureaucratic ministers inevitably had short memories for detail, and the 'presbyterians' temporarily convinced Portland that Breadalbane had not received the chiefs' written promises. Even if their mere importunity did not irrationally persuade William that their previous sabotage had been justified, the conflicting allegations might, as they had that spring, make him consider it simply too troublesome to decide on changes. 'If once that miserable resolution of our kingdom be taken to hold all there, then there will be little thanks for a pitiful necessary submission', Dalrymple warned Breadalbane on 10 November.[5]

The Treaty of Limerick on 3 October, which ended the Irish war, marked a decisive stage in hardening attitudes towards the highlanders. It released a major army for the war against France, in which the Allies had stood on the defensive for three years. In 1692, they planned offensives, in Flanders, across the Channel, and in Savoy. If this did not win the war, it would probably be lost, either through the English parliament's refusing vital supplies — the Opposition was almost uncontrollable in the present session — or, if the unprecedented burden on England continued, by financial collapse: no politician then could have foreseen that this would be staved off until 1696–7. And, once the war was lost, Louis could concentrate on restoring a vengeful James. The campaign of 1692, then, would probably be neck or nothing. Yet, on the national level, the treaty marked the end of serious Jacobite military hopes, and showed the futility of French assistance. The chiefs should realise this, Dalrymple considered, rather than prolong a hopeless war whose burden would merely ruin Scotland. The Treaty had also made their defiance more conspicuous. Dalrymple's enemies repeatedly stressed that the war would be over if, rather than dishonourably offering concessions to treacherous enemies, he had allowed in summer the campaign which must now be fought in nightmare winter conditions. Mackay, with Irish successes enhancing his reputation, was the most dangerous critic.[6]

Although William might ignore Scotland's domestic problems, strategic considerations made him take an interest in the highland settlement, dangerously limiting Breadalbane's freedom of negotiation. He must prove that the civil war in Britain was over to bring the Allies heartily into the 1692 campaign. He must be able to take four more regiments for it from Scotland; but how ensure the kingdom's quiet once its defences were cut to the bone?[7] On Breadalbane's arrival in the Highlands, several professional officers approached him asking for passes to France, and he wrote for them. William refused them for any but the leaders, since, as Dalrymple explained, 'it's not fit to let too many go, who will always ... maintain correspondence to ruin the Hylands with vain delusions, which, after this indemnity, would be severely punished ... That part of the treaty with Limerick we do not like, and you will see ways will be taken that few shall get abroad'. He foresaw the immediate disadvantage: 'these who have no way for subsistence left will endeavour to keep up the clans, but this is not in my power to alter'. Had passes been granted, the officers might have won Buchan to

Breadalbane's side at the crisis in November. Instead, Breadalbane had lamely to justify his inability to fulfil the June agreement.[8]

William was increasingly angry that the chiefs delayed their promised submission, making it uncertain by mid-November whether he could withdraw the regiments from Scotland. He would make no further concessions, such as allowing the Catholics not to take the oath. He took credit for not repudiating the concessions now the balance had tilted decisively in his favour, although this would arouse fresh 'presbyterian' protests and suspicion of his supposed Highland-Host tendencies. Dalrymple wrote to Breadalbane:

> there is no Prince alive but ours whose success should not have tempted him to hearken to ... his government there, rather to have made the Hylanders examples of his justice by extirpating them (... as much some men's designe, as it's now practicable, tho' perhaps it was not so likely when you entered in this negotiation) ... he can gratify many by destroying them with as little charge. And certainly, if there do remain any obstinacy, ... by their ruin, he will rid himself of a suspicious crew.[9]

Linlithgow wrote on 31 October: 'push the Clans to do one thing or other, for such as will stand it out must not expect any more offers, ... the last standers out may pay for all, and besides I know the K. does not care that some do it that he may make examples of them'.[10] William considered the matter from the cold viewpoint of a lifelong Continental professional soldier — which had made him consider a French design for drowning his homeland, Holland, legitimate warfare. A clan whose defiance caused a ruthless attack could hardly suffer a worse fate than, every year, Flemish peasants did who merely lived in the path of campaigns.[11]

Yet this was not a 'conspiracy' for a 'general massacre', as writers quoting Dalrymple's — sinister enough — violent expressions assume.[12] A war was still in progress, and the chiefs seemed determined to refuse very favourable peace terms. That they lacked resources to continue fighting, and secretly might not expect to have to make good their boasts merely made matters worse: even regular troops who persisted in hopeless resistance might be refused quarter. The war against the Irish Gaels had been conducted with ruthlessness, and they had submitted; that against the Scottish Gaels with comparative restraint, and, though unable to assemble an army, they stood out. The clemency William had shown to Jacobites in England and Scotland had merely provoked fresh conspiracies which exploited and mocked his 'weakness'. Only some act of ruthless punishment would break the circle, and overt highland Jacobites might suffer partly for the treachery of English or Scottish conspirators, including Breadalbane in 1690 and Atholl now.[13] Yet the highlanders had done likewise. Lochiel, for instance, had been ostentatiously about to surrender ever since Fort William was built, while remaining able to resume the war at any real opportunity. Some highlanders rationalised breaking the Achallader agreement by claiming that it had only been a trick to avoid a summer campaign. If their promises were that meaningless, their voluntary submission might be positively dangerous.[14] They could await in safety the moment to join a French invading force or, once the army was reduced, exploit the widespread lowland disaffection to threaten the regime. If William considered that an example of terror was necessary to produce genuine submission, it was a logic the clans themselves had often acted on, most recently in 1685. The most sinister aspect was that their increasing weakness revived the attitude, intermittent since 1689, that they were merely rebels and robbers. Dalrymple, no longer fearing immediate French aid for them and regretting the favourable terms he had authorised Breadalbane to offer, shamelessly revealed the reasons behind the change in his praise of William.

Breadalbane was nevertheless allowed to use William's desire for examples, along with his other arguments, to persuade all the clans to submit. He could hardly object directly to it. His scheme had caused the government's dilemma. The truth about his Jacobite connections was still secret — Dalrymple thought Menzies a mere slanderer[15] — but, if it were fully revealed, he might be lucky to escape the block. Furthermore, if his negotiation failed, there was no alternative to a winter campaign, which would inevitably be bloody, squalid and merciless. Breadalbane would have to support this with men and preliminary advice, as he had the equally nasty 1685 campaign against his fellow-Campbells. 'Those who have been their friends must act with the greatest vigour against them,' wrote Linlithgow on 31 October. And he, a near-rebel in 1689 and a conspirator in 1690, added on 5 November 'I wish some of the most obstinate of them would stand it out, that they might be made examples of'.[16]

Dalrymple several times hinted that Breadalbane might be ordered to break off, but it was not merely a wish to wind up an unsatisfactory negotiation. He was genuinely determined on a permanent settlement of the Highlands; but from the start, furious against the chiefs whose unreliability was jeopardising his political career and willing to see them punished as rebels, he linked the idea with at least partial extirpation. His reply to Breadalbane's letter of 7 October, *before* the chiefs' boycott became known, modulated into a startling mixture of incitement to clan hatred and bigoted mysticism:

> All the papist chieftains stand forfaulted by act of Parliament, and it ought to be made effectuall. My Lord, you have done very generously, being a Campbell to have procured so much for McDonalds, who are the inveterate enemies of your clan; and both Glengary and Keppoch are papists, and that's the only papist clan in the Hylands. Who knows but by God's providence they are permitted to fall into this delusion, that they only may be extirpate, which will vindicate their Majesties' justice, and reduce the Hylands without further severities to the rest?

Then he resumed talk of the need for Lochiel and Glengarry to submit quickly. Writers have assumed that Breadalbane worked to inflame Dalrymple with special hatred of the Macdonalds; the opposite is the grotesque truth. It was not surprising Breadalbane told Ardkinglas that the Macdonalds would suffer for destroying the pacification, though Ardkinglas later saw the remark as sinister.[17] Dalrymple's letters showed an alarming indifference whether the settlement came by negotiation or extirpation, and he once demanded that the chiefs who did submit should 'concur, as the crowes do, to pull down Glengary's nest this winter'

— an impossible affront to their sense of honour.[18]

However, Breadalbane in early November broke the boycott. The chiefs agreed to meet him on the 10th, and he moved to Kilchurn. The money was ready in an Edinburgh merchant's hand. Although he needed a fortnight to be certain, he was fairly confident of persuading all the chiefs but Glengarry, who, he agreed, was likely to ruin himself.[19] (For next section, see Preface, p. viii)

Meanwhile, the strangest combination against him, Argyll's Jacobite intrigue, was collapsing. Breadalbane feared that John Campbell, primed by Montgomerie, would come north, spurring his brother to worse excesses against him, and ordered Carwhin to intercept him at Edinburgh.[20] All that year Argyll's regiment, usually commanded by Major Robert Duncanson, a lifelong follower of the family, had been quartered at Stirling, with companies manning the Forth and Perthshire lowland garrisons in rotation. Montgomerie hoped to employ it to support a rising by south-western presbyterian extremists. However, Argyll was anxious, since he and his officers had paid the regiment since 1689 largely from their own pockets or borrowings, to place it on the sounder English establishment. In early November, he wrote to William offering it for Flanders, 'at wch report John was lik to fly in the air'. On 15 November, John Campbell left London with Montgomerie's orders 'to stop his brother from Coming hither, and also to devert him from sending his Regiment abroad'. No appeal so damaging to Argyll's self-interest could succeed, and he left for London, anxious to be reconciled to Dalrymple — and supplant Breadalbane.[21] His intended Jacobite commander, Arran, did not venture to London, but nevertheless showed typical unreliability. He had determined to marry an heiress. In November, he was making ardent proposals for one of Newcastle's daughters; in December, with a lunacy even he never surpassed, for Portland's, while asking James's permission for the match.[22]

As Breadalbane hurried to Kilchurn, he lost his trump card. John Maclean, an Edinburgh Writer to the Signet who since 1689 had alternately been imprisoned for his contacts with his clan and employed in arranging exchanges of prisoners,[23] had carried a message to Sir John Maclean. The 'person in great favor with king William or uas to be in great favor & had great friends about K.W.' who sent it is unknown, but was apparently influential on the Council, to which John Maclean vainly looked for favour.[24] He promised that, if Sir John repulsed Breadalbane, he would get enforced the decree of the 1680s, after the late Argyll's forfeiture, which allotted to Sir John Mull, Morvern and Coll, leaving Argyll only Tiree for compensation. 'This uer to exchange E. Ar[gyll] for Mclane' remarked Breadalbane. It was utterly incredible that the 'presbyterians', always enemies to the western clans, would alienate Argyll by keeping such a promise after Sir John's temporary usefulness ended. Admittedly, he did not totally rely on it; but he trusted John Maclean as an adviser and opposed Breadalbane at the meeting despite his promises.[25] Although this was decisive in seducing Sir John, he was simultaneously using the same intermediaries to negotiate with Argyll, who, after all, knew the Macleans' affairs better than anyone else outside the clan, and whose consent would be necessary for any settlement. He responded eagerly, and exploited the negotiation to gain favour at Court. Yet Sir John again overlooked the weakness of his position: once the general pacification failed, the government need not make great concessions to a chief the bulk of whose clan had submitted in 1690.[26] Argyll's known opposition to the settlement weakened its general chances and roused the other superior involved, Mackintosh, to demand a higher price.[27]

For a week from 10 November, Breadalbane met the chiefs. Buchan was absent from sickness, Glengarry from hostility. Breadalbane vainly argued that the protestant chiefs might take the money despite their honour and the catholic chiefs the oath despite their religion. His one active supporter was Lochiel, who 'would fain be at the sillr [silver] but poynt of honr troubles him' over the agreement to submit only on a majority decision, while reluctance to be the first restrained others who wanted the money. They hoped to be able to take it with honour if James's permission (a consideration Breadalbane now first mentioned to Dalrymple, omitting his own complicity) arrived at any time before 1 January, and he vainly warned them that, as they were disrupting the nation's concerns, the money would not be on offer as long as the Indemnity. A solution seemed possible when the catholic chiefs, Maclean, Glengarry and Clanranald, declared that, rather than offend their consciences, they would go abroad and leave their tenants to the mercy of the government, but the meeting ended in failure.[28]

Lochiel sent to Breadalbane urging him to keep the offer of the money open until 1 January, since he had hopes of winning over Maclean, young Sir Donald and Glengarry. However, a final meeting about 23 November, attended only by Lochiel, Keppoch, Maclean and a son of MacIain, also failed, though Breadalbane warned them of William's anger.[29] The saboteurs in Edinburgh were winning over Lochiel, like Maclean, with their extravagant offers. While Glengarry prepared with Buchan at Invergarry for war, he wrote to Tarbat at Court passing on Atholl's story that Breadalbane intended to give him only £1,000 of the promised £1,500.[30] All Breadalbane's negotiations had persuaded only Farquharson of Inverey to submit, and Gordon of Brackley was paid the £150 assythment for his father's murder. Even Breadalbane's brother-in-law Macnachtan was defiant. In desperation, he offered some money to men not originally named, such as MacNeil of Gallachallie. He vainly requested the imprisoned Perth to use his influence with the clans, and wrote to Dalrymple that he wished their political enemies would settle the Highlands, if they could.[31]

Breadalbane has been suspected of instigating the Massacre chiefly because it is assumed (as with Melfort's letters to Balcarres in 1689) that the violence of those Dalrymple wrote to him must have been provoked by a corresponding violence in his. Breadalbane's actual letters of 16, 19 and 25 November, flatteringly addressed to 'My Lord' [Secretary],[32] actually attempted to calm him — indirectly, for neither Breadalbane's insecure position nor the facts allowed of a direct contradiction. He admitted William's right to destroy rebels, but emphasised the fresh glory mercy would bring him, and doubted that they could cause any serious disturbance. His suggestion that the catholic chiefs might go abroad, and had no families, tacitly made extirpating their clans unnecessary. Once already, he had restrained Dalrymple from giving orders for 'another method with Glengarry … ', playing on his reluctance 'to have kept all the forces there, and to have laid the best part of the great scheme to an after day'.[33] Breadalbane omitted to mention the last unsuccessful meeting, and pleaded afterwards that if the chiefs submitted at the last moment 'let ther be no stumbling at ther coming in'. That letter necessarily emphasised military punishment, promising advice on the preliminary steps necessary before attacking Glengarry. He wrote that winter was the season for reducing the clans, which would not form the least impediment to William's shipping regiments for Flanders: this was of course nonsense, for a winter campaign would certainly leave the troops involved temporarily unfit for any other service.[34] The one aspect that aroused his noticeable enthusiasm was the chance to annoy Argyll by getting his cosseted regiment sent to guard the Argyllshire braes and Glenlyon against raids from Lochaber.[35] However, he hinted at a scheme —which he must wait to explain until he saw Dalrymple — which would totally prevent the clans from rebelling in future or making plundering raids, would apply whether they surrendered or were crushed, somehow depended on the 'episcopalians' being in office, and was connected with the pre-Revolution army size of 3,000. His proposals in February 1692 give the vital clue: this was a version of his perennial scheme for a highland militia. It was not surprising that he kept the language so vague, to prevent Dalrymple from furiously rejecting it before he had the chance to employ his powers of persuasion. This, however, led Dalrymple, whose mind was running on blood, to take it for a 'scheme for mauling them.'[36]

Dalrymple, despite his previous violent language, had never expected the negotiation to fail totally, and the news increased his anger. The chiefs' conduct seemed to him more inconsistent than it actually was, since Breadalbane had successfully concealed how vital a part of the Achallader agreement the appeal to James was. This would not have mollified him, since it was unacceptable that the chiefs should remain loyal to James.[37] Contrary to legend, though, the real problem was less flattering. After agreeing to submit on terms, the chiefs had listened to higher offers from rival factions, scarcely a mark of unspotted loyalty; and, while rejoicing in their petty cunning, had failed to see that their 'presbyterian' enemies, with deeper cunning, were making these obviously incredible promises merely to ruin them. 'I perceive half sense will play a double game, but it requires solidity to embrace an opportunity', he wrote.[38] To his personal resentment, a lawyer's attitude to enforcing the letter of the law and willingness to treat the chiefs as rebel savages, he now added the conviction that they were too stupid to understand their own interest — and therefore dangerously unreliable.

Dalrymple found a sounding-board for violent thoughts in Hill's Lieutenant-Colonel, James Hamilton. Hamilton first appears in July 1689, when appointed Major in Bargany's regiment. He was, like most men in it, an Irish protestant refugee, probably with the usual fear of Gaelic Papists, and the double standard by which these 'barbarians" presumed determination to destroy or ruin Protestants by any means justified Protestants in doing likewise to them — first. When Bargany's was absorbed into Richard Cunningham's new infantry regiment in 1690, he became its Lieutenant-Colonel, leaving in June 1691 to become Hill's Lieutenant-Colonel and Deputy-Governor.[39] Hill's illness had shown one was needed, and Major Forbes, 'no Souldier but a talkative idle fellow' who made his men settle all disputes by fighting duels, was incapable of tackling the problems. Hamilton soon built himself a reputation as 'a fyne man, a good Officer & a discreett man', so pleasing the Muster-Master that the latter totally omitted to mention Hill in his report on the regiment.[40]

In seeking a patron, Hamilton, like Hill, naturally first turned to Crawford at the Treasury. When the 'episcopalians'' apparent hostility to the garrison appeared, he sent him at London a rosy picture of its condition and evidence that Breadalbane's negotiations were failing.[41] Then, in November, he decided that Dalrymple would win, and must be deliberately starving Fort William of money and supplies in revenge for Hill's opposition. And Hill was provoking him further, sending to London (with additional requests for the garrison) Forbes, who testified there that Glengarry had told him of Breadalbane's Jacobite contacts. In November, Hamilton wrote to Dalrymple directly and indirectly, providing useful information about Macpherson's intrigues and begging him not to ruin the garrison for Hill's faults. Dalrymple replied denying any vendetta, asking for advice on details for a highland campaign 'to maul them in the cold long nights', and revealing to this stranger his willingness that the catholic Clan Donald should be destroyed as an example. After writing on 1 and 3 December, he apparently dropped direct correspondence. However, Hamilton's skilled sycophancy had convinced him that he was 'a discreet man', and he recommended him immediately to Breadalbane and later to Livingston, rationalising this as necessary because Hill was too old for active service in midwinter. Hamilton had again shown his ability to undermine his superior, which, with Hill's reaction to it, would be crucial in bringing about the Massacre.[42]

However, Dalrymple might still have escaped notoriety, for his fury was concentrated on Glengarry, whose combination of ostentatious Jacobitism and unscrupulous efforts to overturn the pacification for selfish reasons made him a justifiable choice for punishment, and who would need a legitimate siege to overthrow him. That some example must be made was generally accepted. Tarbat, the self-appointed champion of the Macdonalds, merely suggested Keppoch rather than Glengarry; but, Dalrymple wrote, 'he hath not a house so proper for a garison, and he hath not bein so forward to ruin himself and all the rest. Bot I confess boths best to be ruined'.[43]

Breadalbane retired in late November, but only to Achmore, hoping for a last-minute change of heart by the chiefs. He knew that he was jeopardising his chance of office by ignoring the clear deadline, the end of November, which Dalrymple had earlier set for his coming to London, and a later warning to leave the Highlands. His own 'episcopalian' colleagues would show him little sympathy for it; but he stayed.[44] He staked everything on Duncan Menzies's triumphant return, writing on 24 November:

> DM has wreat of ye 4th instant from the far end of his journay desyring Z [Breadalbane] not to stir out of his Countre untill his return which he thought would be as soon as his letter, that he is ... made welcome and hops to mak all right, this ... induces me not to mak great heast out of this place nor to be at Edr.

intill ... the 15 ... consider if it be not fitt Loche[il] knou this wherby they may express ther willingness the sooner that I may hav yt to say that its yr own inclination after consideration ... [45]

In November, Barclay had unexpectedly joined Menzies from London. The Countess reported:

Sir G. barclay went over to france latlie the Contrivance having been made to send him by som who are too great men for me to nam ... al the hiland afair doth now depend on his return and the answer he doth bring no other being to be trusted but he, and this is don to let it be seen that uho is in Scotland that knows beter how to order hiland afairs then E.B.[46]

Unfortunately there is no known proof to show who these 'great men' were: if, as her words imply, 'presbyterians', they had particular need to keep it secret, since they were simultaneously hoping to ruin Breadalbane for Jacobite dealings. Barclay certainly also had excellent protectors around London, as was proved four years later after the Assassination Plot.[47] He was probably carried to France by Jacobite-controlled Kentish smugglers — a route shortly disrupted by an economical Scot who refused to pay them his fare.[48]

Barclay and Menzies co-operated fully, and the Duke of Gordon threw his influence behind them. However, they faced great difficulties. The Jacobite Cabinet was increasingly incapable of taking any decision unacceptable to its English correspondents. Rumours against Innes, probably started by Montgomerie, so destroyed his confidence that he resigned suddenly at the end of November (NS). Earlier that month, Melfort reached St. Germain, but his wife's illness on the road instantly recalled him. Scottish business must have been paralysed for weeks.[49]

Meanwhile, a genuine chance of sending assistance to Scotland suddenly appeared. It became known that the Treaty of Limerick allowed the Irish army to be transported to France, and that (despite the government obstacles Dalrymple had desired) at least ten thousand were coming. The Jacobites realised that their possession of such a force would at last make Louis take them seriously. At the most cynical estimate, he would desire to tie down William's forces in another diversion. In fact, it inspired him that May to launch a full-scale invasion of England. Now, rather than evading James's proposals (as he had done since the Boyne), he asked him if the Irish could be used for a descent on Scotland. Melfort's first duty on becoming Secretary was to prepare a plan. It suggested that Louis should strengthen the Irish forces with their compatriots already in French service, remount their cavalry, and supply transports, an escorting fleet, arms for Scottish supporters and artillery. The expedition should sail from a western port, pass through the Irish Sea, and land at Ayr or Dumbarton. The army should march straight on Edinburgh, assisted by the highlanders and lowland Jacobites.[50]

The plan's faults are obvious. It overlooked the deplorable condition of the Irish troops after a long campaign without money or supplies, although James knew they needed 'quarters of refreshment'. It proposed to send them on a long, stormy winter voyage through dangerous hostile waters.[51] Yet, only three years after

William's winter invasion, the opportunity to embark an Irish army for a landing in Scotland — compensating for chances lost through French caution in 1689–90 — was too promising to miss. Even an army at the end of its tether might succeed if it surprised the enemy and the campaign was short; and the alternative was the surrender of the last part of Britain loyal to James. The fault most obvious now is that the highlanders would be exposed unaided to the government onslaught during the period necessary for preparing the expedition. Yet the memorial's talk of warning them to rise showed that James and Melfort assumed that the army would be occupied guarding the west coast. Even Barclay and Menzies did not yet understand the danger.

James presented the memorial, presumably on 2 December(NS), but was unsuccessful. The reason was probably not the plan's drawbacks, which Louis must have anticipated, but advice from his ministers, who remained sceptical about all James's schemes and claims about supporters. If so, Louis overcame their arguments by January, and began asking James about a descent on England; but his abortive Scottish project had caused a fatal delay in replying to the clans.[52]

Although hopes of French assistance were over, most Jacobites still found the alternative unacceptable. Sir William Sharp had arrived empowered by a London group to support Menzies, but a letter from Montgomerie's faction immediately claimed that Nottingham had sent him. The full burden of the decision rested on Melfort, who had dismissed the catholic Cabinet and monopolised power. If he let the highlanders submit, perhaps starting a chain reaction among Jacobites, it might reawaken his unpopularity at the very start of his ministry. Accusations of mismanagement, even treason, might, if James's existing suspicion of Sharp's loyalty were exploited skilfully, shake his trust, on which Melfort's power depended; and they did, in fact, help alienate the French ministers.[53] However, one of Melfort's few good qualities was his appreciation of the highlanders' services, which had made him warn James in 1690 not to sacrifice them to the Club's demands. Now he persuaded him to release them. A warrant to Buchan to allow the clans to do what was necessary for their safety was signed on 12 December — *that is, 2 December by British reckoning.* Menzies claimed that James said 'He would never order any body to swear; but that He left every one to judge for himself what he could best do ... [Menzies] understood this for a tacit Compliance'; also that he verbally ordered that only Buchan and Cannon, of the professional officers, should return to France.[54] Barclay and Menzies had a month to reach Scotland by sea from Dunkirk and bring in the clans, a dangerously, but not impossibly, short time.

They did not hurry, leaving St. Germain only on 15 December(NS), the day James departed for Brest to review the Irish troops.[55] The reaction to the warrant among the Scots exiles justified the objection that it would ruin Jacobite morale. Menzies informed Breadalbane: 'our cuntrie people in France ... were, at my way coming, willing to give cautione and com home to Leive peacablei ... I am shure that they wold not truble the peace of the kingdoms'. Dunfermline gave him a letter to Breadalbane, begging help in gaining a pardon, and left St. Germain to await the reply.[56] A Dunkirk privateer was to carry the messengers to Scotland. A similar one, sent just before to relieve the Bass, made a successful passage, but the messengers were unlucky. An English warship captured them off Dover on 12 December(OS), and the warrant was discovered. Brought to London, they were released next day after writing to Dalrymple. He apparently attached little importance to their arrival, for William that day had 'adjusted the march of the troops towards a winter hyland campain'.[57]

Only Dalrymple's self-justifying 1695 account gives details of this meeting. William

> did call severall of his Privy Councill, both in England and Scotland, and most of the officers of the Scots forces that were in England for the tyme, to deliberat what should be done, and how the execution might be effectuall of what should be determined. All aggreid that forfeited and obstinat rebells might be cut off by military execution.

Melville, though still nominally Secretary, was excluded. Portland took charge of the military preparations.[58]

The master plan was for a double thrust into Lochaber from Inverness and Fort William. Most of the troops in the North-East, from as far down as Perth, should concentrate at Inverness: Buchan's regiment, seven companies of Leslie's, four of Cunningham's dragoons, and 150 men from the Abergeldie, Ballindalloch and Ruthven garrisons — 1,340 soldiers. Five hundred auxiliary highlanders with a fortnight's provisions were to be furnished by Grant, Tarbat, Lovat, Mackintosh and Cluny, Balnagown and Munro of Foulis, and baggage horses by the country. Siege cannon and ammunition were to be shipped there, for this force, advancing up the Great Glen, was to carry out the main task of the campaign, the siege of Invergarry. Meanwhile, Major Duncanson was to march 400 of Argyll's regiment from Stirling to Dunstaffnage, where Hill would provide boats to carry them to Fort William. Half the Blair and Finlarig garrisons — one hundred men — were to march directly there — ironically, the general peacefulness of the country was assumed if so tiny a force was to arrive safely. These, 600 of Hill's regiment — 1,100 soldiers in all — 300 of Argyll's followers, 100 of Breadalbane's and 100 of Atholl's, would form the second force. The campaign was to be run on a desperate shoestring: Leslie and Hill received only £230 between them to buy meal, aquavitae, tobacco and other necessities, and, although the Treasury was ordered to distribute £2,100 arrears among the regiments, Dalrymple admitted that this was only a pious hope until the Treasury Commission was reformed. The Inverness force would have provisions (including what the highlanders brought themselves) for only four weeks. Its regular troops were dangerously ignorant of the Highlands; after two years at Inverness, some still believed that the Lochaber clans, whom they had seen only at their summer shielings, were nomads. Although the siege of Invergarry would itself be fairly easy, since a hill overlooks the castle within cannon-shot, having to transport the heavy guns beforehand for forty roadless miles through the snow-blocked, storm-ridden Highlands might well turn the campaign into an ignominious disaster.[59]

Definite instructions could not be issued until it was known which chiefs would take the Indemnity; but that evening Dalrymple sent Hill his preliminary orders and the chiefs their summons to produce their contingents by 1 January. The letters were so delayed by bad weather that few of the chiefs could obey them on time. The Council could probably have managed the matter better, but Dalrymple persisted throughout in bypassing them when issuing orders. After their conduct that summer and some members' present dealings, it is not surprising that he did not trust them to show the necessary secrecy and support. Yet, as the Council were in the best position to query unwise orders, this removed a vital check on his proceedings. He destroyed another by ordering Livingston, who was travelling to London, to return to Scotland for the campaign without seeing William. The reason for so treating the commander who must execute the plan was probably muddle rather than malice — summoning him in time to participate would have emphasised Breadalbane's failure. However, Dalrymple's assurances could not convince Livingston that this was not the first step towards his dismissal for having supported the 'presbyterians'. He therefore did not antagonise Dalrymple further by objecting to any order — certainly not to ones against the highlanders, whom he too hated. Had he gone on to London, command would have devolved on Sir James Leslie, who shared neither that fear nor that hostility.[60]

On their release, Barclay and Menzies still did not understand how dangerous the government's new mood made delay, and 'resolve[d] for Scotland some time this week'. Late on Monday 14th, they were rearrested and their papers were confiscated. The government hoped that James's orders would convince William's allies that his regime was now stable, and that he could fully commit his army against France. Dalrymple had written: 'the reputation through the world of their submissiones is of more importance than any thing can be promised from their honesties'.[61] The English Privy Council closely examined Barclay and Menzies to ensure that they were not exceeding their instructions, and the foreign envoys in London were shown their papers. However, although willing to exploit James's authorisation, the government would not recognise it in any way. It merely increased distrust of the highlanders since, as Dalrymple had emphasised, their submitting 'after they get KJ allowance, is worse than their obstinacy; for those who lay down arms at his command, will take them up by his warrant'.[62]

On 15 December, therefore, the marching orders were issued for the troops. Major Forbes was sent away with some small concessions for Hill and his garrison.[63] The messengers were forbidden to carry their news north unless they themselves took the oaths. Barclay refused, and was kept prisoner. Menzies agreed, and was released on 15 December. The news of his mission had already spread consternation among the Jacobites: 'The misfortunes in Ireld were great, but this is worse'. According to Montgomerie's faction, he deliberately increased it, 'declar[ing] it to be his Maties meaning, by that order, that all his subjects should' submit. Nevertheless, after being detained for another council on 17 December, he started his midwinter journey north with a desperate haste which shows he had at last realised how dangerous the government's attitude had become.[64]

Breadalbane had declared that, expecting Menzies's arrival, he would not return to Edinburgh before 15 December, but Glenlyon's affairs forced him. Argyll and Arran had duly decided the dispute over the estate entirely in Atholl's favour. Glenlyon wrote to Breadalbane on 20 November that he must, in his condition, accept the propositions unless Breadalbane could produce a better alternative, but he would sign nothing for eight days. In fact, that same day he agreed with Murray that he and his teenage son should sign a conclusive renunciation in return for a bond of 45,000 marks (less deductions) — a generous bargain, Murray self-righteously recorded; the next day, that he would sell him another estate. One reason for his docility was fear: he had believed during the highland raids in July that Colonel Menzies had hired the 'Halket Stirk' to kidnap him to Lochaber. Breadalbane, returning in early December, persuaded Glenlyon to break the appointment for signing the agreements, and, for greater security, to hand over his son, whom he immediately sent to Kilchurn, in case Glenlyon relapsed. Breadalbane probably never considered that, in persuading Glenlyon to forego a solid financial agreement on the strength of uncertain promises, he was behaving in private affairs like his enemies in the highland business.[65]

Conflicting priorities distracted Breadalbane, A warning from Queensberry made him feverishly hire a coach to hurry to Court. Dalrymple's letters of 2 and 3 December, advising him, after his failure, to stay away until the reshuffle was complete, naturally increased his desire to go. 'I think the Clan Donell must be rooted out, and Lochiel' wrote Dalrymple: the ruthless reference to Breadalbane's cousin shows how his influence was shrinking. Yet it also made him delay, striving to save his scheme and his relatives. On 10 December, hearing that Lochiel's eyes were opened, he put off departing and secretly sent him extracts from Dalrymple's letter indicating that Glengarry was making his own peace. Lochiel appointed to meet Barcaldine; but hostile emissaries brought him three formal articles, which they promised would be made good to him and 'his Nighbor', and he relapsed.[66]

Murray, having returned and interrogated Glenlyon, confronted Breadalbane on 14 December, demanded that he hand over Glenlyon's son, and challenged him to a duel, of the savage type where the seconds also (Murray's was his brother James) fought to the death. Breadalbane, according to Murray, informed the authorities. Next day he left for London. His policy had had one slight success. Farquharson of Inverey took the oaths at Edinburgh, his clansmen at Aberdeen, and the few remaining Perthshire lowland rebels at Perth. Glenlyon rejoined the detachment of Argyll's which marched on December 25, financed by a loan from Stirling, for Argyllshire (where the minister of Glenorchy's prophetic dreams of death and destruction seemed to forebode evil from their arrival). Breadalbane's meddling had destroyed a settlement which would have left him less totally dependent on his captain's pay.[67]

Menzies met Breadalbane on the road, and accompanied him for a mile discussing his mission. He reached Edinburgh on 21 December and his home, Cardney House, on the 22nd, utterly exhausted. From Edinburgh, and Cardney, he sent off letters: to Buchan; to Macnachtan and other Jacobites to meet him on the 26th; to Lochiel that Glengarry, for all his claims, was not well regarded at St. Germain; to others denouncing Sir Aeneas Macpherson as Melville's agent; and to

Atholl denying that he had spoken ill of him, and claiming misleadingly to have travelled from Paris in twelve days. He made copy after copy of the warrant to convince the chiefs.[68]

Menzies's news obviously played some part in making the clans submit, and writers have simply assumed that it was decisive. He, like Carwhin, certainly did not think that what he had done by 1 January would produce much effect and wrote to Livingston asking for permission to visit the chiefs afterwards. The Council rejected the request.[69] Menzies had good reason for pessimism. He had been prevented from bringing James's original order from London, and there was only his word that the copies were genuine. He was widely distrusted as Breadalbane's agent, and this might be seen as another trick. John Maclean WS refused to transmit his letter to Sir John. He lamented to Breadalbane:

> it appers they have Little credit for me notwithstanding of what I have done in that affair, which ... makis me verie circumspect either to meit or corespond with any of them for ... I am heated by all p[ar]tys ... bein Looked on as infected by the pest or some wors deseas ...

A widespread report at Edinburgh that he had joined the rebels and was urging resistance indicates his failure.[70]

Balhaldie claimed that Buchan at Invergarry (supposedly through Glengarry's influence) did not pass on Lochiel's copy of the warrant until thirty hours before the deadline. If so, Balhaldie himself has exposed his hero; for Lochiel submitted to Hill at Fort William on 25 December, and immediately set out for Inveraray to take the oaths — arriving, Balhaldie alleged, only on 31 December. The facts are uncertain, since Balhaldie clearly draws on a direct letter from Menzies to Lochiel, probably of the 22nd; but it seems unlikely that this could have reached him across the snow-bound Highlands within three days. Lochiel's letter to Barcaldine of 25 December merely claims that, having met with some of his neighbours, he had resolved to go on with Breadalbane. The case seems clearer with Keppoch. He had to travel through the snow to Inverness, the length of the Great Glen, to take the oaths; yet by 31 December, the news reached Hill. He must have started before Menzies's news arrived.[71]

The chiefs submitted almost on the deadline mainly — in some cases, only — because, as Hill wrote, 'this winter campaign put the Highlanders under great consternation, and they were much affrighted, and are all very submissive and humble'. They had not really believed in it, relying not only on French assistance but, increasingly, on protection and better offers from their 'friends' at Edinburgh. The failure of these hopes produced a panic.[72] Even if James's orders alone had caused their surrender, it should not have affected the agreement that none should submit unless the majority agreed: a united front now would be the best means of ensuring that all were pardoned. However, the weather would have prevented a general meeting until the Indemnity had expired, and several chiefs dared not risk that. Keppoch, at least, apparently did not inform his allies.[73] At Inveraray, Campbell of Ardkinglas received the submissions of Lochiel,

Macnachtan, Gallachallie and the Stewarts of Appin — though the chief, too ill to come himself, sent a written promise. Ardkinglas wrote to Argyll a report of who had submitted, and returned home.[74]

Glengarry could not shed his obligations so lightly. He had not only been the main instigator of resistance, but had Buchan and his officers at Invergarry (though Cannon was still apparently in Skye). In addition, he still objected to the oaths, unlike Keppoch, who soon cheerfully claimed to be a Protestant. On 30 December, his confidant Macdonald of Achtera brought to Hill his conditional offer of submission. If Buchan, Cannon, and their followers and servants — up to twenty-four — received passes to go overseas, Glengarry and his followers would submit and the Catholics among them would give security for future behaviour. If this was refused, Buchan wrote to Macpherson, 've ville goe to all extremety'. Keppoch and MacIain were to be covered by the submission. Since Glengarry was obviously ignorant of Keppoch's journey and MacIain came in separately, he had no authorisation from them. Their inclusion was partly an indirect means of posing as head of Clan Donald. Yet he also intended to save from the dangerous consequences those whom he had persuaded to hold out — a welcome contrast with the panic rush of other chiefs. Disastrously, however, this condition was stated not in the document which Achtera signed, but in Hill's letter to Melville, which Melville, dismissed before it arrived, did not pass on to Dalrymple with the document.[75]

Soon after Hill wrote on 31 December, MacIain of Glencoe entered Fort William, the hindmost of that first panic rush to surrender. He had played no part in the autumn's intrigues, being too unimportant to be worth deluding: he seems merely to have followed Glengarry's lead.[76] Yet his refusal of Breadalbane's terms, emphasised by his son's presence at the last unsuccessful meeting, must have increased his uneasiness over the quarrel at Achallader. He several times said 'that he fear'd a mischief from no man so much as from the Earl of Braidalbin', or reckoned up blood shed in the two families' past quarrels. The second-sighted man who had saved him from being surprised in June 1689 warned him that he would be murdered by night in his own house, probably increasing his apprehensions.[77] As the deadline approached, he decided to take the oath; and, ignorant that Hill lacked power to administer it, and failing to ask his better-informed Stewart neighbours, he travelled many miles in the wrong direction to the Fort.[78] Hill sent him to Ardkinglas with a letter arguing that 'it was good to bring in a lost sheep at any time'. MacIain would obviously be unwise to rely on Hill's own hope of obtaining a prolongation of the general Indemnity through Tarbat, or the offer from Glengarry, the chief most likely to be denied mercy. MacIain, now desperately alarmed at his danger, began a hurried journey south through a snowstorm, not even turning aside to visit his own house.[79]

The detachment of Argyll's had found no boats at Dunstaffnage, and moved towards Fort William by land. The Captain of Grenadiers, Thomas Drummond — the one competent officer, the Muster Master had claimed, perhaps also the most ruthless — seized MacIain and, despite Hill's letter, detained him in Barcaldine Castle for twenty-four hours. Released then, he reached Inverarary on 3

January; but Ardkinglas had gone home, and the storm prevented his return for three more days.[80]

Despite the letter, Ardkinglas, having heard that the Indemnity would be applied literally, at first refused to give the oath to his recent enemy. MacIain even wept as he pleaded, and, in a last display of autocratic chieftainship, promised that any of his people refusing it would be imprisoned or sent to Flanders as recruits. Ardkinglas administered the oath, made MacIain sign a certificate, and sent this to his sheriff-clerk Colin Campbell, then at Edinburgh, asking him if the Council would accept the oath. He wrote to Hill how he had received 'the great lost sheep Glenco' (a grotesque metaphor), and ordered him to prevent harm to the Glencoe men until William's or the Council's pleasure was known. He himself remained at Inveraray to continue negotiations with a chief who asked more than MacIain, but whose potential usefulness to Argyll's interest at Court made it unthinkable to enquire the Council's pleasure or worry about intercommuning — Sir John Maclean. Ardkinglas's dislike of Breadalbane increased his pleasure. Sir Alexander Maclean's brother brought a message from Sir John, and, after consulting Ardkinglas's 'club', left for Edinburgh to equip John Maclean WS for a mission to Argyll in London. He secretly carried a letter to Breadalbane from Sir John, who plainly hoped to make the two earls bid against each other for his support.[81]

The storm had made the ferry at Ballachulish, across the mouth of Loch Leven, impassable. Therefore, while MacIain was still away, Argyll's regiment marched to Glencoe. The only report merely says that 'they were ceivilie and kyndlie intertain'd'. Their arrival must have caused great alarm, but the peace was apparently kept. As only part of the force could be quartered in the glen, Duncanson could select Argyllshire captains grateful for MacIain's forbearance in the 1689 raids and send Glenlyon elsewhere. This passage presumably made it easier for MacIain, on his return, to persuade his people to live peaceably.[82] They should have been doubly protected, by MacIain's oath and Glengarry's terms (if these were accepted). Achtriachtan and several other clansmen also had protections taken out from Hill, some of them months earlier.[83]

Colin Campbell presented the roll of certificates to the two Clerks of Council, but they refused to receive it because MacIain's certificate was dated after the Indemnity expired. He might now have laid it, with Hill's and Ardkinglas's letters, before the Council. Yet, if they decided unfavourably, that would formally emphasise that Ardkinglas had intercommuned with a rebel — had, at best, exceeded his powers. Both of them were already notorious for this: Breadalbane had complained over taxation: 'that zealous Clerk Colin and Ardkinlas doe make acts of parliamt & Instructiones of yr own'. Colin therefore had Campbell of Aberuchill collect informal opinions from fellow Privy Councillors, particularly Stair, whether he should apply openly. They replied that it could not be received without the King's warrant 'and that it would neither be safe to Ardkinlas, nor profitable to Glenco, to give in the certificate'. Colin Campbell erased MacIain's oath, and in this state the paper was accepted.[84]

The 1695 commissioners claimed that the advisers 'seem to have had a malicious design against Glenco', but showed their partiality by not blaming the Clerks for their original rejection, which alone made consultation necessary.[85] Private resentment may, of course, have influenced the advice. MacIain's second son seems to have led a raid on Aberuchill's estate in late 1690, and he was vindictive.[86] However, the suggestion of a deliberate plot by Campbells and Dalrymples was misleading. Aberuchill was a 'presbyterian', soon to be removed from the Council, and was meddling in the highland negotiations against Breadalbane.[87] So was Ardkinglas, and applying for William's warrant would enable Dalrymple to accuse him of intercommuning. The advisers doubtless cared nothing that their priorities were unjust to MacIain; but they had no reason to suppose him in greater danger than his neighbour Appin. Even Stair presumably did not mention it to Dalrymple when there were ministerial changes and the General Assembly to discuss. As the Council had refused Menzies's request, their decision would probably have been unfavourable; but again they had the luck to avoid formal involvement. Indeed, a favourable decision might not have averted tragedy unless they had publicised it before formally examining the certificates in late February.[88] For Dalrymple never attempted to consult these, and his secret orders bypassed the Council.

On 16 January, the Council received orders to issue a proclamation to forbid all intercommuning 'upon the highest penaltie the law alloues' with 'these obstinate rebells', who were to be 'cutt off'.[89] Yet it was generally believed that late submissions would be accepted, and that there would be no campaign. This, the weather and the late arrival of orders encouraged the chiefs not to provide auxiliaries unless they had special reasons. Atholl, to regain credit with William, wrote to the Council emphasising that his contingent was ready and his neighbours' were not. It was useless: his intrigues with Glengarry had discredited him, and he had so little political value left that even Montgomerie dropped him from his intrigues in favour of an approach to the new power, Queensberry.[90] Cluny, in contrast, avoided jeopardising his credit with either side. On 1 December, he signed a bond of friendship with Glengarry, a sign that he would not act vigorously for the government. Through Sir Aeneas Macpherson, who was lurking at Inverness as a spy, he now got Buchan's permission to obey the order and avoid punishment, and he indirectly applied to his feudal superior, the House of Gordon, for authorisation. Meanwhile, he reported his readiness to Cunningham at Inverness, who thanked him but hoped that he would not be needed.[91] This hope gladdened the army officers, many of whom had protested on receiving their orders that a highland campaign in this weather was impossible, and would totally ruin the forces. 'If his Ma[tie] ... accept[s] the offer, Glengarie has made,' Sir James Leslie wrote on 14 January, 'we are like to have no winter Campaigne, for this Kingdome will be wholly at peace.' But Leslie was not Commander-in-Chief.[92]

Priorities had changed in London. If the Scottish issue of greatest interest there in November was the highland negotiation, from December onwards it was the Assembly and the possibility of reconciling the communions. A conference marked the most open interference of English ministers in Scottish affairs of William's reign — even the Archbishop of Canterbury took part. Portland defended presbyterianism, but was out-argued by Carmarthen.[93] To both William and Dalrymple, the highland campaign, including the order which caused the Massacre, was to be of secondary importance. The shift of emphasis extended to persons. Dalrymple, who had originally proposed Lord Carmichael as Commissioner to the Assembly, now intended him as conjoint Secretary — a Presbyterian for balance but without a masterful personality. He probably took Breadalbane's intended place.[94]

Yet even this revised scheme was endangered throughout December in a fluctuating struggle which privately extinguished Dalrymple's remaining temper and balance, constantly reminding him that it was ultimately the highland chiefs' unreliability that had exposed him to this. In early December, Queensberry nearly returned home discouraged; and in mid-month he was informed that William could not bring him into the government yet, although in compensation he would put Drumlanrig on the Treasury Board. The reasons were not merely Queensberry's past persecution of Presbyterians and recent Jacobitism. Once in power, he would have been an overwhelming patron; and Dalrymple, exploiting his former inertia, suddenly switched to opposing his appointment. Almost at once he regretted this, as their enemies' attacks on the 'episcopalians' increased, and he joined Queensberry's friends in trying via the English Tory ministers to reverse the decision.[95] Exerting all his influence, Dalrymple thought that he had ensured that Linlithgow would be Chancellor. Linlithgow, however, believing that he was not to have it, burst out in a fury, and the offended William excluded him from consideration.[96] In his place, William's advisers, including Archbishop Tillotson, proposed Tweeddale — not Dalrymple's choice, but he must support him for fear of getting Tarbat. When Crawford, so notorious for his bigotry, impressed William by staking his credit that the Assembly would act moderately, Dalrymple momentarily feared that 'the high sort of the Club' would gain power. This was defeated, and on 26 December William ordered him to draw warrants for Melville as Privy Seal, Tweeddale as Chancellor and Carmichael as Secretary, a victory of sorts.[97] Then, unexpectedly, Carmichael refused to be Secretary, since he found the new religious policy too pro-episcopalian. The predictable alternative candidate was James Johnston, supported, again, by Tillotson and other non-Scottish advisers, a strong Whig and a strong character. Vital points had been achieved: Melville had been kicked upstairs, and Tweeddale's appointment would certainly drive Hamilton to self-destructive resignation.[98] Yet the unexpected failures filled Dalrymple with fury which he dared not, with Linlithgow as a warning, expend in lowland affairs.

Throughout the critical period, Dalrymple showed an eerie mixture of vindictiveness and absent-mindedness in dealing with highland measures. He could not prepare formal orders until he knew who had submitted at the last moment, but on 7 January he wrote to Livingston that he wanted Lochaber, Appin and Glencoe destroyed, and expected that the cold would keep the enemy trapped in their settlements. 'I hope the souldiers will not trouble the Government with prisoners,' he wrote, justifying his harshness, then and in his next letter, with the argument that 'those deluded devils' must be crushed before the French assistance on which they obviously depended could arrive.[99] Having interrogated Menzies and kept James's original warrant, he should have known that for some months at least there was no danger; but he had not only refused officially to recognise Menzies's mission, but had failed to incorporate its significance in his mental framework.

Breadalbane grasped the ruthless mood that prevailed on his arrival, and emphasised in his letters to Carwhin that he had no part in the planning. This emphasis has been considered suspicious enough to suggest that he had; but there were good reasons for excluding him.[100] Although he was on good terms with Dalrymple (and even Argyll, whom he belatedly convinced of his honesty towards Glenlyon), he could not expect office, and it might be feared that he would leak some of the plans in retaliation. Melville was also excluded. William had decided to create a balanced ministry, with only one 'episcopalian' to two 'presbyterians'. When Dalrymple on 7 January made his remaining nominations, Drumlanrig and Linlithgow for the Treasury, Breadalbane made plans to settle in London.[101]

Two days later, the first reports of the rush to take the Indemnity reached London. Breadalbane and his supporters spread it without waiting for confirmation, and he wrote, though with no great hopes, urging Lochiel to come up.[102] The first reports mistakenly claimed that MacIain had submitted; disastrously, this concentrated Dalrymple's regrets upon the division among the papist Macdonalds that put Keppoch and MacIain out of reach, and the good reasons that existed for rooting them out.[103] However, they were safe: and the submissions had left divided and isolated the areas that still held out, Glenmoriston, Glengarry and the Macdonald parts of Skye (besides Eilean Donan, Duart and Carnaburg). On 11 January, Dalrymple drew up Livingston's orders to attack the rebel areas 'by fire and sword', burning their houses, destroying their goods and killing all the men. They were to capture and garrison Invergarry. Chieftains, tacksmen and other leading men should be allowed to surrender, but only as prisoners of war, safe from death but not forfeiture; but the ordinary highlanders, if they took the allegiance, surrendered their arms, and agreed to take new tacks of their land from the government, should be untouched. Dalrymple deliberately had William both superscribe and subscribe these Instructions, contrary to custom and law; possibly, to ensure that Livingston, having helped sabotage so many of the government's orders during 1691, would obey; apparently also as the start of a general policy.[104] It was certainly not to throw the 'blame' on William, as Dalrymple's opponents suggested from 1693; the Instructions, more restrained than his letters, were for a war, which, so far as he knew, was still in progress — a point hostile Inquiries later obscured.[105] The one objection among those few in the secret came from Carmarthen, who was having to use all his political skill to dodge attacks from English Opposition factions in Parliament. He feared that they might exploit the words 'fire and sword' (formal usage in Scotland) as the basis for an accusation of excessive harshness — scarcely logical, after they had just tried to make him responsible for excessive kindness to other Jacobite 'barbarians' in the Articles of Limerick, but likely enough in Parliament.[106]

Despite Dalrymple's vindictiveness against the clans, he intermittently sympathised with the plight of ordinary highlanders, who, he knew, had no choice but to follow their chiefs. He evidently hoped that, once these and the tacksmen were forfeited, the common people would not only provide 'a perpetuall subsistence to the garrisones' from their rents but, granted better leases, would become peaceful, prosperous farmers — 'yeomen', he sometimes incongruously called them. This, insofar as it was a coherent plan, was the opposite of the one he had supported all summer, to strengthen the chiefs' authority by rationalising the upper end of the feudal structure. Recurring even in the violent letter of 30 January which ordered the attack on Glencoe, it shows that his hostility towards highland society sprang partly from the hope for economic 'improvement' so common a century later — but, by the chances of politics, with greater concern than those 'improvers' showed for the interests of ordinary highlanders.[107] It was not an entirely absurd idea, for the loss of the war after years of privation created widespread passive discontent. Hill was to report:

> the Midle sort of Gentry & commons (yt have anything) ... all say, they have never got anything but hurt by following the Lairds, for if there be reputation or money got (by their stirring) the Lairds have it, & they are sure to get nothing, but ye Losse off yr life, & the hassard off all they have.[108]

Yet Dalrymple, who felt grim amusement that the chiefs were being forced to do what they might once have got money for, also on 11 January hinted to Tweeddale that 'all ther tennents even of thos who hav taken the oaths ar in mercy bot ... at present ... its not necessary to mention that' — a clear breach of the spirit of the Indemnity.[109]

While Dalrymple was writing on 11 January to Livingston, Argyll reported that the authentic list of those who had submitted at Inveraray did not include MacIain. Dalrymple added to the letter an encouragement 'to be exact in rooting out that damnable sept, the worst in all the Highlands' — but also a warning that those who had taken the oaths must be unharmed, which, unknown to him, might have warranted their preservation. Summoning Breadalbane, he ordered him and Argyll to ensure that the Glencoe men should be debarred a retreat in their lands — a promise Breadalbane fulfilled by writing to Carwhin that night to circulate the Council's general proclamation against reset.[110] Thinking that only Glengarry, Glencoe and Clanranald were standing out, he did not, to judge from the self-glorifying paragraph he prepared for the *Gazette*, expect fighting: as they had declared in November, these Catholics would go into exile with Buchan, leaving their clans to surrender.[111]

Dalrymple's main enemy was still Glengarry, and the main military operation was still to be the siege of Invergarry. Then, about 16 January, he received the proposals Glengarry had given to Hill. And, for the first time, he realised the difficulties of the campaign. His grave underestimation of them had made him exaggerate the highlanders' perversity in resisting. Even on 11 January, he was confident that the campaign would be over in time for the forces to reach Flanders by April.[112] Yet its most vital preliminary, the shipping of the siege train from

London to Inverness, had totally fallen through. He had ordered Livingston to furnish cannon and other necessities from Edinburgh Castle, but the Council authorised the Treasury to hire a ship only on 19 January.[113] He therefore prepared Additional Instructions on 16 January, dealing almost entirely with how far Livingston (through Hill, the obvious negotiator) should relax the terms offered to Glengarry. Buchan, Cannon and twenty 'servants' would be allowed passes abroad. Glengarry and his followers would be assured of their lives, though not their estates, if they surrendered Invergarry. Yet, in deepest secrecy, Hill was reluctantly authorised 'rather than be baffled, and after the hardship the troops must suffer' to grant them better terms, even security for their estates. Dalrymple added a final instruction, 'If M'Kean of Glencoe, and that tribe, can be well separated from the rest, it will be a proper vindication of the publick justice to extirpate that sept of thieves', and laid the document before William, who superscribed and subscribed it.[114]

The claims by William's defenders, Burnet's that he signed the paper without reading it (a defence more alarming than the accusation) and Macaulay's that he did not take 'extirpate' literally, are both nonsense.[115] William did often work off accumulated arrears of Scottish business (usually postponed decisions rather than totally unseen matters) in rushed signing sessions; but he would certainly examine any orders affecting the availability of troops for Flanders. He had signed orders on 11 January to 'cutt off the men' of clans still resisting; having felt a need since the autumn to make an example, he would assume that Dalrymple had selected some appropriate 'two-legged wolves'. Yet hostile writers' reconstruction of a significant confrontation in which king and minister glimpsed each others' souls are equally groundless.[116] Dalrymple drew up the Additional Instructions so carelessly that, as he later admitted, he forgot to include his King Charles's Heads, Eilean Donan and the Bass; and William overlooked the omission.[117] His mind, certainly had little time then for Scottish business. Besides the normal press of affairs, he was close to a total breach with the Earl of Marlborough, who was organising a strike of English army officers against foreign generals, alienating the heir-presumptive Anne from William and intriguing with the Jacobites. Four days later, William was abruptly to disgrace him, risking a possible coup, or at least a refusal to pass supplies by Parliament, in which Marlborough had in October hoped to lead a Jacobite–Whig Opposition.[118] With this preoccupation, he would have given Dalrymple's proposals only superficial attention. Little more seemed needed, for both men were determined not to extend or alter the Indemnity, even when (as by catholic chiefs giving security rather than taking an oath their priests denounced) it might strengthen the settlement, since granting better terms to those who resisted would be a fatal precedent. Both assumed that the war, though increasingly one-sided, was still in progress, and William signed commissions appointing a Scottish Secretary at War and filling the vacancies in the regiments. Their orders assumed that two legally distinct classes of chiefs existed, those who had taken the Indemnity and those who (though perhaps deluded by promises of better terms) had definitely refused it and so were committed to fight on. Neither apparently considered the problem of borderline cases.[119]

Dalrymple, when later accused of exceeding these Instructions in his covering letters, answered sarcastically, 'which letters must do, as sermons exceed texts'.[120] Certainly, the claim in the 1695 report that the Instructions did not encourage Livingston and Hill to discriminate unfavourably between the Glencoe men and other highlanders was whitewash.[121] Yet that clause did remain conditional; and their obvious first priority, to which others might be sacrificed, was to obtain the surrender of Invergarry with the fewest concessions possible. Dalrymple's covering letters 'intreat[ing] that for a just vengeance ... the theeving tribe of Glencoe may be rooted out' and suggesting that Argyll's detachment and a party posted in Castle Stalker should carry out the attack, were significant (in the context of his previous letters to Livingston) in shifting this balance, making him and Hill see that as the touchstone over which opposition might ruin them and co-operation win them favour. Dalrymple should have grasped that the more positive his words made this Instruction seem, the more he weakened their hands for bargaining over Invergarry and realising his general scheme for forfeiting Jacobite chiefs and tacksmen and favouring ordinary clansmen; but his vindictive feelings blinded him. Even before military considerations forced him to spare Glengarry, he had begun to realise how appropriate a target for his random vindictiveness was 'the murderer McIain' and his 'sept of thieves', too incorrigible to transform into yeomanry; and it spilled over, irrelevantly, into his letter to Tweeddale. And the tone of his 'sermons', insisting that no favour must be shown to the obstinate the more vehemently as he allowed individual exceptions, was important in blurring the difference between an enemy people, to be attacked, even when excluded from quarter, within certain limitations, and a band of robbers, individually notorious, against whom any strategem was legitimate.[122]

That evening, Lochiel arrived at Breadalbane's lodging, a living proof of the clans' submission and his influence. Breadalbane presented him to William on the 19th, and had the *Gazette* report it; and his hopes revived of office, and even, if sufficient others followed Lochiel, of part of the £12,000 being distributed.[123] He had to admit, however, that opinion at Court was violently hostile to the highlanders. William and Portland were unimpressed by Sir John Maclean's letter, and a courtier commented that it was not worth £500 a year to keep a chief whose clan had already submitted from going to France. Breadalbane hoped that Argyll would have better success. His isolated solicitations merely lost him favour and attracted contempt that he should still speak for persons who had done him such injury.[124] He worked to get Barclay freed and got him a pass to return to France on 19 February. Keppoch unexpectedly arrived in London on 24 February, and Breadalbane presented him also at Court. His brother was anxious for an army commission, in return for which he would bring many Macdonald recruits, and Breadalbane was successful in obtaining one; but not in gaining Keppoch's promised money, for which Mackintosh vainly waited.[125] Nevertheless, Breadalbane had regained his old swagger. He wrote to Tweeddale declaring that if he had been Chancellor sooner his own task of pacification would have been far easier, and promising advice on controlling the Highlands. Tweeddale, who had opposed the whole negotiation and particularly the offer of money as derogatory to the government, and whose proposed ministry excluded both Breadalbane and Tarbat, was not impressed.[126]

Now, at last, Breadalbane decided to bring forward his proposals for a 4,000 strong highland militia, in a memorial to William:

> The last opinion given ... concerning the settling of the Highlanders, having had good success, by their submitting to your government, ... and taking the oath of allegiance; it remains now to propose ... how to make them ... take up arms for Your Majesty in case of insurrection at home, or invasion from abroad ...

Based on the law about calling out all fencible men, the militia was to be furnished in set proportions by the chiefs, commanded by an unnamed general (obviously himself) with Lochiel (paid the sum promised him) as second-in-command, both working in close concert with an 'episcopalian' government, and with forty captains under them — these being paid only while the militia was active. Supplementing the standing forces, they would suppress any rebellion at home and, perhaps, furnish a highland regiment (armed and disciplined in their own fashion) for service in Flanders. Not surprisingly this met objections: of about 4,500 men allotted from various chiefs and chieftains in proportion, nearly 1,100 had openly fought against William, and 750 more were provided by hostile chiefs. Breadalbane was on the defensive in a memorial on what to do with the £12,000: suggesting either that it should be laid out at interest in Scotland to finance a 3,000 strong highland militia; or part paid to those who had submitted in time — a device to benefit Lochiel, since he deliberately overlooked Keppoch's claims; or at least part used to pay his own expenses at Achallader.[127] This militia scheme on which he so doggedly spent effort and money is, with his private letters, the best proof that Breadalbane was not involved in the Massacre. Although he was to continue hoping and spending money on Kilchurn afterwards, that terrorist 'example' destroyed the sleight-of-hand on which the whole scheme relied, the assumption that simply by submitting the highlanders had become, and would be treated as, William's loyal subjects. In fact, Dalrymple's and Breadalbane's highland 'policies', one determined largely by fury and the other by ambition, were by now diametrically opposed. (See Preface, p. ix)

Hill at Fort William knew that no campaign was needed. Even before the deadline, he had been receiving requests to punish thieves, as if peace was established.[128] On 14 January, he reported to Dalrymple and Tweeddale that Lochaber was as quiet as the streets of London or Edinburgh. Argyll's regiment and the independent companies were quartering peacefully on 'rebel' lands, including Keppoch's. Glenmoriston and Fraser of Foyers had submitted with Keppoch at Inverness. Old Sir Donald Macdonald died on 5 February; but already, having prevented his son from yielding within the time, he had had a deathbed change of heart, and sent him hurrying to Inverness. He took the oaths about 23 January, and waited there while Leslie inquired whether he could accept him. Clanranald's mainland tenants sent offering to submit, and Clanranald himself, now detained by weather in Uist, would do likewise.[129]

Hill therefore took no action on Livingston's letter of 14 January (prompted by

Dalrymple's of 7 January) that he should destroy Glencoe, 'that nest of Theives', and Appin, if they had not submitted; nor on William's orders of 11 January, accompanied by a general order from Livingston of the 17th to march against those who had not taken the Indemnity and to take no prisoners. Ominously, Livingston also wrote to Lieutenant-Colonel Hamilton, who 'must be the principall actor', a step which made Hill feel insecure.[130] On 20 January, Hill wrote to Livingston explaining that MacIain had taken the oath but, as Ardkinglas had now written, the Council had not accepted it, leaving him theoretically outside the Indemnity.[131]

This letter merely weakened Hill's position by rousing Livingston's contempt for his mildness towards highlanders. When he forwarded the fatal second set of Instructions on 23 January, he therefore wrote not to Hill, 'knowing how slow he was in the execution of such things', but to Hamilton:

> I understand that the Laird of Glenco, coming after the prefixed time, was not admited to take the oath, which is very good news here, being that at Court it's wished he had not taken it, ... for the Secretary in three of his last letters hath made mention of him, and it is known at Court he has not taken it. So Sir, here is a fair occasion for you to show that yor garrison serves for some use; ... begin with Glenco, and spair nothing which belongs to him, but do not trouble the Government with prisoners.

These were the formal orders on which the Massacre took place.[132] Livingston was shielded from blame at the 1695 Inquiry with the excuse that he had returned from London too recently to understand the situation, and this has usually been accepted. In fact, his responsibility was great. As Commander-in-Chief, he had some discretionary power to alter or question orders; and he knew, as Dalrymple did not, the truth about MacIain's attempts to submit. Even if he would not risk the Secretary's favour by directly challenging a project on which he had plainly set his heart, he might have represented the facts indirectly at London via Tweeddale or Melville, to whom he wrote that nothing worth telling him had occurred, dismissing the whole highland campaign as 'ane insignificant busines'. He felt only eagerness to recommend himself, for he was as hostile as Dalrymple to the highlanders, and to the Glencoe men as thieves.[133]

Hill, on the spot, knew that the order to destroy the Glencoe men was a wanton atrocity, 'a nasty durty thing'. He was under more obligation to prevent it than is usually realised. He had given protections to Achtriachtan and others, had pursued the negotiation with Glengarry, whose original offer assumed that any agreement would safeguard MacIain, and (the Additional Instructions implied) now had power to administer the oaths. However, Hill feared that any protest after his opposition that summer would make Dalrymple (whom he was trying to propitiate with a scheme for recapturing the Bass) get him dismissed in favour of Hamilton. He was an old man with dependent daughters, had expended his savings in preserving Belfast, and feared destitution. In June, he had warned the clans that, if his forbearance endangered his post, he would secure himself by destroying them; and he had balanced his advice that the government should accept belated offers of submission with protestations that he would do whatever it ordered.[134] Therefore, he replied to Livingston that the attack must be delayed until negotiations were complete for the surrender of Invergarry.[135] He dared not write to Tweeddale, nor, apparently, to Dalrymple about Glencoe; but he seems to have hoped that the delay would enable Dalrymple to gain a true picture of the peaceable state of affairs from his letter of 14 January, the Council's account of MacIain's belated submission and other sources. If no revised orders came, he could resign his commission then.[136]

Meanwhile, he left it to Hamilton and Duncanson (since Dalrymple's letter specified Argyll's regiment) to concert a plan of attack. He told Hamilton of MacIain's submission, and Hamilton, the outsider, who, according to a much later (and unreliable) source, openly sneered in a conference of officers at his commander's scruples, was probably the man who suggested the unforgivable feature of the plan, that troops should be quartered in the glen and then kill their hosts. However, Hill dared not veto it — a decisive capitulation, after which he complained to sympathetic subordinates. Nor did Duncanson, who, as Procurator-Fiscal in Argyll's courts, should have had some legal scruples to temper his military obedience; and he must have selected to command the force Glenlyon, whose relationship by marriage to young Alasdair MacIain would disarm suspicion, and whose resentment over the 1689 raid might overcome his objections at the crisis.[137] Two companies of Argyll's were to quarter in Glencoe, the rest under Duncanson about Ballachulish to the west. When the order was given, they were to enter the glen, while Hamilton with 400 of Hill's marched from Fort William to Kinlochleven, the east end of the sea-loch, to start the killing there.[138] The high rock walls on either side preventing escape made Glencoe itself an excellent scene for slaughter — apart from the passes on the south side, of which Hamilton and Duncanson received details from a Lieutenant Campbell of Argyll's, probably Robert Campbell of Drummond's grenadiers.[139] This, as well as the need of a ruthless and efficient subordinate for Glenlyon, presumably prompted the choice of Drummond's as the second company. He and his officers were probably in the secret: one person who was not, as the final order shows, was Glenlyon.[140]

On 1 February, Argyll's regiment marched to Ballachulish and Glenlyon's detachment continued towards Glencoe — his company, with Lieutenant Millan and Ensign John Campbell, Drummond's, the regimental 'aide-major' (quarter-master) Lieutenant Lindsay, and at least one officer, Ensign Lundie, from another company.[141] As they approached Glencoe, Iain MacIain with about twenty armed men met them and asked their purpose. Lindsay showed Hill's orders for quartering (for which arrears of taxes gave theoretical justification), and Glenlyon and two other officers, presumably those of his company, gave their — sincere — word that they intended no harm. They had, after all, done none in Keppoch. They were welcomed to the glen, and some leading inhabitants who had fled returned.[142] The 120 men were quartered in the settlements up and down the glen, MacIain, his sons, Achtriachtan and other prominent men each having a dozen in

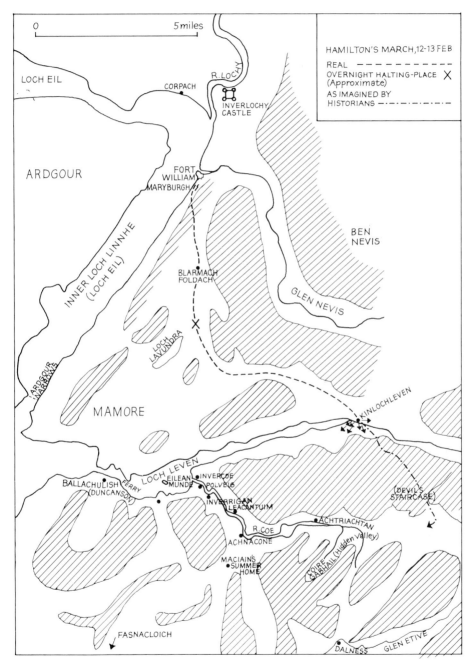

The Massacre of Glencoe, 13 February 1692

their homes, with three or five in some smaller huts.[143] Glenlyon himself quartered at Inverrigan, a short way up the glen from Polveig, MacIain's home. MacIain took only two precautions: to send several young unmarried girls to his summer home to be safe from the soldiers, and, disastrously, to hide most of the clan's weapons at a distance in case Glenlyon had orders to disarm them.[144] The days passed in courteous entertainment, and the close quarters at which they lived made it seem increasingly improbable that the soldiers could have secret plans.

Meanwhile, Hill negotiated with Glengarry for the surrender of Invergarry. Glengarry, his determination stiffened by Buchan's resolution to 'go to all extremity' if refused passes to France, held out obstinately;[145] and Hill, because over half his force was already tied down by the order about Glencoe, had to yield point after point. Buchan received passes for himself, Cannon, twenty officers and their servants to be shipped from Leith, the concession whose refusal had helped wreck Breadalbane's negotiation. In return, he gave orders for Eilean Donan's surrender — he had no control over the Bass. Glengarry no longer stipulated for MacIain's inclusion in the terms: there seemed no need, now that he, like Keppoch, had submitted and seemed to be accepted. Dalrymple's one adamant condition for the Glengarry negotiations was that those who submitted must take the oaths. On 4 February, Glengarry came to the fort, did so — another 'insuperable' obstacle of the past autumn evaporated — and agreed to surrender Invergarry in eight days. He had bargained so firmly that Hill had to give him a written promise to evacuate it — within a month, Glengarry claimed.[146] This was not fulfilled; but it shows how grossly Dalrymple's vindictiveness had undermined his radical plan for destroying Glengarry's power, and the government's whole highland policy.

He wrote again to Livingston and Hill on 30 January, still apparently unaware of MacIain's submission — although his remark to Livingston, 'I am glade that Glenco did not come in within the time prescribed', might suggest otherwise.[147] The Council had sent him no information on the Indemnity. Breadalbane knew something of MacIain's action by 6 February, Argyll presumably earlier.[148] Yet there was no reason why anyone not aware of Dalrymple's special animosity against Glencoe — apparently recorded first on 9 January, and since then only in secret orders and letters, whose recipients left it to others to inform him — should spontaneously have given him special information about a fairly minor sept, which general reports like Hill's letter of 14 January simply overlooked. However, Hill's report that Lochaber was as quiet as the streets of London failed to alter his vindictive resolution, and the truth (except about the quartering) might not have done so. Preoccupied with the Assembly, he wanted highland affairs ended quickly, and yet insisted that William would offer no new terms to the highlanders — though young Clanranald might be received and bred a Protestant. He gave few detailed commands, except about Eilean Donan and Glencoe: 'Pray when any thing concerning Glenco is resolved, let it be secret and suddain, otherwayes the men will shift you, and better not meddle with them than not to do it to purpose'. He repeated that Argyll's regiment, which he supposed still in Keppoch, should be used.[149]

It is doubtful whether, in the bitter storms, Dalrymple's letter reached Hill by 12 February, destroying his last hope of a countermand.[150] The crisis was, anyway, at hand. The previous day, he had sent troops to occupy Invergarry and an independent company with Buchan's orders to surrender Eilean Donan. Argyll's regiment must shortly march to Edinburgh to embark. Some of Hill's officers were openly and mutinously rejoicing that Livingston's orders were being sent to Hamilton rather than their unpopular Colonel. His excuse for delay was gone, and the need to maintain his authority provided one for letting Hamilton proceed. Drugging his conscience with the consideration that this might be Providence's indirect means of punishing the Glencoe men for past bloodshed, he did so, protecting himself by the wording.[151]

Hamilton faced one major difficulty. Even in the harsh weather, the fort was under observation by day, and the alarm would run ahead of any large party which left before the gates were shut for the night. His 400 men could only start afterwards, and therefore might be delayed; but he sent Duncanson orders nevertheless to attack Glencoe at 5 a.m. He spontaneously emphasised that neither 'the old fox, nor none of his cubs' must be allowed to escape, and added that he should take no prisoners, and spare nobody under seventy — setting no lower age limit.[152] Duncanson repeated these ruthless points in his order to Glenlyon, who must start the killing even if Duncanson had not arrived from Ballachulish by 5 — possibly, since he did not face Hamilton's difficulties, wishing to avoid an involvement which might bring feuds upon him.[153]

Glenlyon faced a more hopeless dilemma than Hill. Duncanson's order threatened to treat him as 'not true to King nor Government' and get him cashiered if he refused to act; and, with Hamilton's, showed that King, Commander-in-Chief and Hill were all involved.[154] Atholl had taken out hornings against him, and somewhere in the storm a messenger was bringing him a mocking letter from Murray that he would gladly save the large sums promised by the November agreement.[155] He made his choice, and, until the Massacre began, lulled suspicions with unhesitating hypocrisy. The two officers who had given their word with him decided differently, refused to act and were arrested, afterwards being sent prisoners to Glasgow.[156] This must have made still more difficult the covert issuing of commands in a developing blizzard to troops scattered along the glen. Nothing apparently was done on Duncanson's order to secure the passes. Many soldiers heard the command only minutes before the Massacre began, but others knew earlier. Those quartered on young Iain MacIain slipped away to prepare, while others came and called at his window to warn him; for several common soldiers went beyond the mere refusal of the honest officers.[157] It is striking that the traditions of a community which suffered such a treacherous attack should consist so largely of tales of warnings given beforehand. The fact that many of them, implying greater advance knowledge than the soldiers had, cannot be true, merely emphasises their favourable bias. Yet such warnings could have only limited effect. If there is truth in the story of a soldier obliquely giving one by addressing a stone, and if the stone is the one shown today, it was within a pebble's-throw of MacIain's house; but he suspected nothing.[158]

Once the watchers outside Fort William's gates were off guard, they reopened, and Hamilton and Forbes set off with 400 men. However, they

> were no sooner a myle from the Garison then fell a most hidious Storme of wind and snow in the men's faces such as no man could stand against So that after great toill and Injury to many of the men by the cold wind, snow and often falls they gott, they were fain to house four myles of till to morrow.[159]

Glenlyon mustered his men at Inverrigan some time before 5 a.m., explaining to the curious Iain MacIain that they were to march against some of Glengarry's men. At the hour, he sent parties of twenty back to the other settlements — a cumbersome procedure which must have alerted many Macdonalds — with orders to enter the main houses and open fire on those present. At Polveig, Lindsay, Lundie and their soldiers entered MacIain's house. He greeted them, and, as he rose to dress, they poured a volley point-blank into his back, killing him. They also murdered two of his servants, and left a badly wounded third man — possibly, with the lunatic logic of military obedience, because he was not a Glencoe man but a letter-carrier from Braemar. MacIain's widow was robbed of her rings and stripped naked, as were women elsewhere. Lindsay's party started up the glen to catch MacIain's sons; but they, warned by servants less trustful of the soldiers, fled and met on the hillside. A party under a sergeant marched to Achnacone, where Macdonald of Achnacone, his brother Achtriachtan and seven others were sitting round the fire, and instantly opened fire, killing Achtriachtan and four more; but the other four, though wounded, broke away and escaped. Such volleys alerted nearly everyone else in the settlements, enabling them to flee. Occasionally, the soldiers saved ammunition by braining their victims with their musket-butts, but they showed equal incompetence in this: the eighty-year old Archibald Macdonald in Leacantuim survived such an attack (only to be burned when the houses were set alight). A few men were killed while still asleep.[160]

At Inverrigan, Glenlyon had nine men who had been bound (presumably to prevent their giving warning) brought out and shot one by one; and he personally gave the coup de grâce with a bayonet. Yet, unlike one of his Glenlyon recruits, who worked himself into a frenzy with memories of the 1689 raid, or the soldiers infected by the excitement of killing who smeared corpses with dung, he could not drown his guilt and, afterwards, stood watching in frozen despair. Twice, he tried to spare victims, a youth and a boy, and twice the thug Drummond came up and had them shot — the boy, allegedly, with the brutal joke that a nit, if spared, would grow into a louse. Even at Inverrigan, incompetent organisation allowed several men to escape, and the soldiers instead killed a sixty-year old woman and a child.[161] Elsewhere, also, having failed to kill more than a few able-bodied men, they turned on the very old. There was no lower age limit set, and it is said that at least one soldier was ordered to discover a baby's sex (and lied about the result).[162]

Some traditions allege that fugitives with dirks managed to kill one or two pursuers who followed them too far; but it is more probable that the only weapons were adzes and other household tools used to parry blows as men fled.[163] Many inhabitants, on finding that they were not pursued, remained hidden on the slopes.

Some from Achtriachtan, the highest major settlement in the glen, may have crossed to Dalness in the next glen, the one area overlooked in the plan for massacre, but they probably dared not remain there. Most survivors, however, attempted to escape through passes further west, into Appin. Glenlyon had failed to post guards, but they met the full force of the storm which had stopped Hamilton's force in its tracks. MacIain's widow, although her sons had found and helped her, was one of many women who died of exposure:

> nothing left them, and their houses being burnt, and not one house nearer than six miles; and to get thither they were to pass over mountains, wreaths of snow, in a vehement storm ... poor stript children and women, some with child, and some giving suck, wrestling against a storm in mountains and heaps of snow, and at length overcome, and give over, and fall down and die miserably.[164]

The clan never declared how many women and children died; but the first garbled report of the Massacre to reach the North Highlands claimed that of forty-five killed, all but thirteen were women.[165]

Duncanson's force advanced late into the glen to find almost all the inhabitants escaped. Campbell of Airds's company discovered at Achnacone an overlooked man dying of fever and his five-year old son, and killed both. They later guiltily threw the child's corpse into the river; but it was so mangled that one hand fell off.[166] Finally, at 11 a.m., Hamilton's command reached Kinlochleven after a two hour march; but his encamping and the alarm from the main glen had enabled the inhabitants to escape eastwards, and the parties he sent out killed only one old man. All the houses were thoroughly plundered and then burned with the barns. The force then returned to Fort William, driving the Macdonalds' cattle — 400 cows, besides sheep and goats, according to Hill's report. In 1695, the Macdonalds claimed to have lost 1,500 cows and 500 horses; cows which the soldiers sold cheaply in the nearby countryside may form some part of the discrepancy.[167]

Hamilton left no guards on the glen, and some survivors returned that day to collect their dead. There were about 200 families in Glencoe, who, in normal conditions of warfare — not emergencies — sent out 100 fighting men. Hill reported that MacIain, Achtriachtan and thirty-six other men were killed — presumably excluding the boys of five, but including the old men. The first printed report, in the Paris *Gazette*, claimed that four women also were killed. MacIain's and Achtriachtan's sons and most of the lesser clan gentry (apart from Macdonald of Inverrigan) had survived. The bodies were later carried to Eilean Munde in the loch, to 'sleep in the Isle till the Day of Judgement'.[168]

Livingston was confident that nobody would dare to shelter the survivors; but Dalrymple's insistence on secrecy now began to work in their favour. There had been no formal proceedings against them, although Hill now unsuccessfully asked Dalrymple for a proclamation. It was not clear whether they came within the prohibition against intercommuning, since MacIain had submitted, and the first reports were uncertain whether the Massacre was authorised or an outbreak of Campbell clan hostility.[169] Only direct fear of the troops might prevent assistance being given. The Stewarts of Fasnacloich, who were in the fugitives' path, gave generous help. Despite the part played by Campbell of Airds's company, a strong *Macdonald* tradition asserts that the Airds family at Castle Stalker did likewise. Some Macdonalds displayed clan solidarity: when the news reached the farmer-seamen of the island of Heisgeir off North Uist, the tacksman loaded a birlinn with meal and steered it through the winter seas to feed them.[170]

Some survivors, with their world shattered, may have fled from the area for ever, settling elsewhere or becoming 'broken men'.[171] The remainder gathered again under MacIain's sons. They prepared an armed party of fifty men, and there were false rumours that they had attacked Glenlyon. In fact, they attempted no retaliation, although the Glencoe bard, not surprisingly, included in his elegy a hope for James's restoration to punish the killers.[172] Nor, contrary to Balhaldie's claim, did the other recently-submitted clans show any sign of resistance at the news.[173] Instead, despite the treachery with which MacIain's submission had been rewarded, those who had stood out hastened to take the oaths. Young Stewart of Appin, still sick, was carried by boat to have them administered by Hill (who evidently now felt empowered by the Instructions of 16 January). Clanranald's mainland tenants were taking it four days after the Massacre, and at the end of February Clanranald himself, like Glengarry ignoring his previous catholic protestations, did so. Only the remote MacNeil of Barra remained, and Hill had sent for him. Although most of these had already been preparing to submit in mid-February, the lesson to be drawn from Glencoe seemed clear to many in the government, and the new Secretary Johnston summed it up: 'Thus it is evident severity is the way to deal with them tho the manner here has been odde'.[174]

Hill at first attempted to gain credit for carrying out his orders. The hostile Breadalbane claimed that his first letter to Dalrymple 'valu[ed] himself on it as his deed & regrait[ed] the storm yt hindered all to be cutt of'. However, he felt some guilt, as the dishonesty of his defence to Tweeddale shows; and by 28 February he was writing to Portland to suggest that enough Glencoe men had been killed for an example, and to ask for permission to receive the rest into mercy — a request in which he determinedly persisted for months.[175] He apparently ignored Livingston's orders of 24 February to send out constant parties to harass and kill them, particularly MacIain's sons. Even Hamilton was too mild for Livingston, who criticised him for having, a few days after the Massacre, taken prisoner some Lochaber men rather than shooting them on the spot.[176]

To many of those involved, including, probably, almost all of Hamilton's detachment, the Massacre was not an event of particular importance.[177] One of the few who were really conscience-stricken was Glenlyon. Now the desolate Highlands were peaceful, Argyll's regiment marched from Fort William for Edinburgh in late February. By early March, he was drinking and defending his conduct in the taverns and coffee-houses there, showing Hamilton's and Duncanson's orders (of which the Jacobites took copies), sometimes declaring that he would stab anybody at the king's command without asking the reason, sometimes lamenting that he had had to kill his landlord at Inverrigan with a protection in his pocket.[178] Having broken the basic laws of Christianity and hospitality, he evidently felt that he could defy military instructions, and left his company at free quarter on Murray's tenants in Glenlyon. He was mistaken: Sir James Leslie sent him a rebuke and orders 'to see all your quarters payed & not to stay above tuelve dayes'.[179]

NOTES

1. Balcarres' letter of 20 July to Queensberry, welcoming him to Edinburgh and announcing his own retirement from politics, may date from 1691 or 1692, but the former, from Queensberry's date of arrival, seems more probable. SRO PC1/48, 164; Drumlanrig, Queensberry Papers, Vol. 117, [53], Balcarres to Queensberry, 20 July [? 1691]; *ib.*, Vol. 126, 8, Dalrymple to same, 2/12 Oct. 1691.

2. Hill Burton, *History*, i, 525, same to Breadalbane, 27 Oct. 1691; *ib.*, 528, same to same, 3 Nov. 1691; Riley, *King William*, 71–3.

3. NLS MS 7013 fol. 132v, J. Dickson to Tweeddale, 7 Nov. 1691; [Moncreiff], 'Macaulay's *History*', *ER*, cv, 173, Linlithgow to Breadalbane, 13 Oct. 1691; Dalrymple, *Memoirs*, ii, 216, Dalrymple to same, 3 Dec. 1691; *ib.*, 204, 'Ld. B. Hamilton' [Selkirk] to Hamilton, 12 Dec. 1691 (correct identification by R. K. Marshall).

4. *Ib*; NLS MS 1031 fol. 133, Hamilton to Selkirk, 23 Oct. 1691.

5. [Moncreiff], 'Macaulay's *History*', *ER*, cv, 176, Linlithgow to Breadalbane, 5 Nov. 1691; *ib.*, 177, same to same, 10 Nov. 1691; *ib.*, 175, Dalrymple to same, 31 Oct. 1691; *ib.*, 176, same to same, 10 Nov. 1691; *ib.*, 177, same to same, 22 Nov. 1691; SRO GD 112/40/4/5/40, Countess to Mrs Campbell, 7 Nov. 1691.

6. The memorial in French, PRO SP 8/11/6 (calendared *CSPD 1691–2*, 62–3), is not in Mackay's writing, and bears no attribution; but, from some persistent themes of his in it, such as the lament that neither Presbyterians nor Episcopalians have any disinterested views, it seems to be his. *Ib*; Dalrymple, *Memoirs*, i, 188; Hill Burton, *History*, i, 528, Dalrymple to Breadalbane, 3 Nov. 1691.

7. *Ib.*, 527; *Highland Papers*, 48–9, same to Lt.-Col. Hamilton, 1 Dec. 1691.

8. Hill Burton, *History*, i, 526, same to Breadalbane, 27 Oct. 1691; *ib.*, 527, same to same, 3 Nov. 1691; [Moncreiff], 'Macaulay's *History*', *ER*, cv, 174, Linlithgow to same, 31 Oct. 1691; SRO GD 112/43/1/5/25, Breadalbane to Buchan, 16 Nov. 1691; *ib.*, 40/4/5/33, same to [Carwhin], 16 Oct. 1691.

9. *Ib.*, GD 170/629/31, same to Barcaldine, 24 Nov. 1691; Hill Burton, *History*, i, 525–6, Dalrymple to Breadalbane, 27 Oct. 1691; [Moncreiff], 'Macaulay's *History*', *ER*, cv, 176, same to same, 10 Nov. 1691.

10. *Ib.*, 175, Linlithgow to same, 31 Oct. 1691.

11. For a 1693 example in which Argyll's regiment was involved, Walton, *Standing Army*, 245–6; Prebble, *Glencoe*, 291–2. Burnet, *History*, iv, 566n.

12. Prebble, *Glencoe*, 165–7; Macdonald, *Slaughter Under Trust*, 72, 81–2.

13. See Chapter 8, p. 274. If, therefore, the attempts during 1691 to bring to trial the major figures behind Lord Preston's English plot, including the Queen's uncle, had not collapsed, William might have felt less eagerness to make a highland example, Hopkins, 'Aspects of Jacobite Conspiracy', 183–4.

14. Occasionally, Dalrymple admitted that Breadalbane's having dealt with the clans as equals and having portrayed them to William as suppliants exaggerated the contrast between their conduct then and now; but it was still great. *CSPD 1691–2*, 62–3, [Mackay], Memorial, [1691]; *Highland Papers*, 57–8, Dalrymple to Livingston, 7 Jan. 1692;

[Moncreiff], 'Macaulay's *History*', *ER*, cv, 177, same to Breadalbane, 22 Nov. 1691.

15. Dalrymple, *Memoirs*, ii, 217, same to same, 3 Dec. 1691.

16. [Moncreiff], 'Macaulay's *History*', *ER*, cv, 174, Linlithgow to same, 31 Oct. 1691; *ib.*, 176, same to same, 5 Nov. 1691.

17. SRO SP 3/1 fol. 181, Johnston to Carstares, 1 July 1693; Hill Burton, *History*, i, 526-7, Dalrymple to Breadalbane, 27 Oct. 1691.

18. *Ib.*, 527, same to same, 3 Nov. 1691.

19. [Moncreiff], 'Macaulay's *History*', *ER*, cv, 176, same to same, 10 Nov. 1691; *HMCR Finch*, iii, 297, Breadalbane to Nottingham, 5 Nov. 1691; *ib.*, iv, 495, Breadalbane, 'Representation' [Oct. 1692]; SRO GD 26/xiii/78 fol. 17, Melville's note; GD 112/40/4/5/29, Countess to Carwhin, [12 Nov. 1691].

20. *Ib.*, 22, same to Mrs Campbell, 22 Oct. 1691; *ib.*, 45, Breadalbane to Carwhin, 31 Oct. 1691.

21. *Ib.*, 7, Countess to Mrs Campbell, 24 Nov. 1691; *ib.*, 22, same to same, 'thursday' [12 Nov. 1691]; *ib.*, 40, same to same, 7 Nov. 1691; Dalton, *English Army Lists*, iii, 53-4; Cumnock, Dumfries House, Bute MSS, bundle A 517/13, Breadalbane to [Dalrymple], 19 Nov. 1691; SRO E 100/14/18-55, muster rolls, 1691; *ib.*, PC 1/48, 159-61.

22. *HMCR Finch*, iv, 9-10, [J. Simpson] to 'Mrs Jones', 10 Jan. 1692 (NS); SRO GD 112/40/4/5/17, Countess to Mrs Campbell, 10 Dec. 1691; GD 406/1/7613, Arran to R. Murray, 12 Nov. 1691; *ib.*, 6299, Ld G. Hamilton to Arran, 2 Feb. 1692.

23. *APS*, ix, App., 31, 131; *RPCS*, xiv, 37-8, 42-3, 181, 518, 545.

24. This description appears to rule out Atholl, for instance. By the time John Maclean made his application (which left no trace in the registers) to the Council, their membership had been altered. SRO GD 112/39/1221, Breadalbane to [Carwhin], 14 Nov. 1691; *ib.*, 1253, same to same, 5 Apr. 1692; Cumnock, Dumfries House, Bute MSS, bundle A517/13, same to [Dalrymple], 19 Nov. 1691.

25. *Ib.*

26. SRO GD 112/40/4/3/4, same to Carwhin, 23 Jan. 1692; *ib.*, 40/4/5/28, Countess to Mrs Campbell, 8 'Nov.' [Dec.] 1691; *ib.*, 40/4/6/31, P. Birnie to Barcaldine, 13 Jan. 1692; *ib.*, 33, J. Macnachtan to Breadalbane, 13 Jan. 1692; Dalrymple, *Memoirs*, ii, 215, Dalrymple to same, 2 Dec. 1691.

27. *Ib.*, 216, same to same, 3 Dec. 1691; SRO GD 112/40/4/2/49, Mackintosh to same, 26 Dec. 1691; *ib.*, 39/1221, Breadalbane to Carwhin, 14 Nov. 1691.

28. *Ib*; *ib.*, 43/1/5/25, same to Buchan & Glengarry, 16 Nov. 1691; *HMCR Finch*, iii, 301, same to Nottingham, 16 Nov. 1691; Cumnock, Dumfries House, Bute MSS, bundle A517/12, same to [Dalrymple], 16 Nov. 1691; *ib.*, 13, same to same, 19 Nov. 1691.

29. SRO GD 170/629/31, same to Barcaldine, 24 Nov. 1691; *HMCR Roxburghe*, 123, Hill to Polwarth, 25 Nov. 1691.

30. Dalrymple, *Memoirs*, ii, 216, Dalrymple to Breadalbane, 3 Dec. 1691; Macpherson, *Loyall Dissuasive*, 193.

31. *Highland Papers*, 56, 'Proposals ... for delaying to return the money', [1692]; SRO GD 112/40/4/3/4, Breadalbane to Carwhin, 23 Jan. 1692; *ib.*, 40/4/4/5, Blair Drummond to Breadalbane, 19 Dec. 1691; *ib.*, 40/4/2/48, J. Campbell to same, 29 Dec. 1691; Cumnock, Dumfries House, Bute MSS, bundle A517/14, Breadalbane to [Dalrymple], 25 Nov. 1691.

32. See Chapter 8, n52.

33. [Moncreiff], 'Macaulay's *History*', *ER*, cv, 177, Dalrymple to Breadalbane, 22 Nov. 1691; Cumnock, Dumfries House, Bute MSS, bundle A517/12, Breadalbane to [Dalrymple], 16 Nov. 1691.

34. *Ib; ib.*, 14, same to same, 25 Nov. 1691.

35. *Ib.*, 13, same to same, 19 Nov. 1691.

36. *Ib.*, 12, same to same, 16 Nov. 1691; *ib.*, 14, same to same, 25 Nov. 1691; *HMCR Finch*, iii, 301–2, same to Nottingham, 16 Nov. 1691; Dalrymple, *Memoirs*, ii, 216, Dalrymple to Breadalbane, 3 Dec. 1691.

37. *Ib.*, 215–16, same to same, 2 Dec. 1691.

38. *Ib.*, 215.

39. *RPCS*, xiii, 533; Mackay, *Memoirs*, 290, Mackay to Melville, 22 Oct. 1689. Prebble wrongly suggests that Hamilton served in Cunningham's regiment on the shameful expedition that retired and left Londonderry to its fate in early 1689; that his presence on this clouded his career; and that Dalrymple secured him the post at Fort William largely because he could always bring him to heel by recalling it. The English regiment under Colonel John Cunningham on the Londonderry expedition had no connection with Colonel Richard Cunningham's Scottish one, not founded until December 1689. Hamilton's appointment at Fort William took place in a series of transfers whose original aim was apparently to part the quarrelling Argyll and Auchinbreck. Dalrymple was not concerned — 'I had never the good fortune to be acquainted with you,' he wrote — and the 'lapses of single persons' he mentioned refer, as his next letter makes plain, to Hill's intrigues against Breadalbane's negotiation, nothing to do with Hamilton. *Highland Papers*, 49, Dalrymple to Lt-Col Hamilton, 1 Dec. 1691; *ib.*, 52, same to same, 3 Dec, 1691; Prebble, *Glencoe*, 163; Dalton, *English Army Lists*, iii, 5, 90, 97, 211; Bland Burges, *Selections*, 357, Anecdotes about Glencoe, 1762.

40. *RPCS*, xvi, 532; Prebble, *Glencoe*, 163–4; McBane, *The Expert Sword Man's Companion*, 80; Drumlanrig, Queensberry Papers, bundle 1185, 1, [Sir A. Bruce], 'Remarks upon the State of ye Armie in Scotland', 16 Oct. 1691.

41. *HMCR Hope-Johnstone*, 173, Lt-Col Hamilton to Crawford, 10 Sept. 1691; *ib.*, 174, same to same, 16 Oct. 1691.

42. *Highland Papers*, 48–9, Dalrymple to Lt-Col Hamilton, 1 Dec. 1691; *ib.*, 52–3, same to same, 3 Dec. 1691 (meaning of passages on the Macdonalds corrected from the original, Glasgow UL MS Gen. 1577); *ib.*, 51, same to Breadalbane, 2 Dec. 1691; *ib.*, 57, same to Livingston, 7 Jan. 1692 (substituting 'Hamilton' for the second 'Cunningham', a copyist's mistake); SRO GD 26/ix/119, 'Memoir . . . anent the Garison of Fort William', [Nov. 1691]; GD 170/629/33, Breadalbane to Barcaldine, [Dec. 1691].

43. [Moncreiff], 'Macaulay's *History*', *ER*, cv, 178, Dalrymple to Breadalbane, 3 Dec. 1691 (postscript, omitted elsewhere); Dalrymple, *Memoirs*, ii, 214, same to same, 25 Nov. 1691.

44. *Ib*; Hill Burton, *History*, i, 528, same to same, 3 Nov. 1691; SRO GD 170/629/33, Breadalbane to Barcaldine, [Dec. 1691]; *ib.*, 31, same to same, 24 Nov. 1691.

45. *Ib.*

46. SRO GD 112/40/4/5/20, [Countess] to Mrs Campbell, Nov. 1691 (date mutilated).

47. After the exposure of his 1696 plot to assassinate the king, despite the most rigorous search of which the government was capable (which netted most of his accomplices), he remained untraced for over a year and finally escaped to France, *Memoirs of Locheill*, 312; NLS MS 14,266 fols. 102v (27 Jan. 1696), 116 (18, 19 Aug. 1696), 131, (13, 18 July 1697).

48. SCA Blairs Letters, Box V, 1692, 37, 'H. Burd' [Cpt. Griffith] to Innes, 15 Dec. 1691.

49. *Ib.*, 1691, 3, 'Com. fr. fr.' [C. Lawton] to same, 10 Oct. 1691; *ib.*, 4, same to same, 8 Dec. 1691; *ib.*, 56, Renaudot to same, 28 Nov. 1691 (NS); *ib.*, 65, 'J. Wood' [J. Simpson] to same, 20 Nov. 1691; *ib.*, 38, Melfort to W. Leslie, 19 Nov. 1691 (NS); NLS MS 14,266 fol. 29; SRO REF 310.044 (GD 44) No. 106, Pleas of Gordon's advocates, July 1693.

50. Macpherson, *Original Papers*, i, 394–6, Memorial ('delivered a little time before the arrival of the troops from Ireland', news of which arrived on 8 December: Sources, iii, 480).

51. The mention of the landing at least creating a diversion was merely to allure Louis: Melfort was always over-optimistic. *Ib.*, 395–6; Luttrell, ii, 322, James to the Irish, 27 Nov. 1691 (NS).

52. Marquis de Dangeau, *Journal*, ed. Soulié *et al*, 19 vols. (Paris, 1854–60), iii, 437; Macpherson, *Original Papers*, i, 396, 'A memorial to the King of France', Dec. 1691 or Jan. 1692; AAE Corr. Pol. Angleterre, 172 fol. 144v, questions & answers on French policy, [14 Dec. 1691 (NS)].

53. SCA Blairs Letters, Box V, 1691, 69, J. Thompson to W. Leslie, 3 Dec. 1691 (NS); BN Naf 7487 fol. 163, 'Memorial of Several Measures taken ... by Melfort'; *Archives de la Bastille*, ix, 373, Renaudot to Croissy [Nov. 1692]; SRO REF 310.044 (GD 44) No. 115, Gordon's memoirs, 36–8; *HMCR Stuart*, vi, 63–4, T. Sheridan's narrative.

54. *Ib.*, i, 66, Warrant 12 Dec. 1691 (NS); *LJ*, xvii, 494, Sir J. Maclean's paper, 20 Feb. 1703/4; *Memoirs of Locheill*, 311–12. Balhaldie forgot to allow for the difference between British and Continental dating, and has been followed by later writers. By 12 December (OS), James was no longer at St. Germain.

55. Dangeau, iii, 442; *Carstares S.P.*, 140, [Macky] to Melville, [14 Dec. 1691].

56. *Ib*; SRO GD 112/40/4/6/28, Menzies to Breadalbane, 17 Feb. 1692; *ib.*, 43/1/2/5, Dunfermline to same, 15 [Dec.] 1691.

57. *RPCS*, xvi, 601; SCA, Blairs Letters, Box U, 1691, 15, Sir J. Geraldine to Innes, 9 Dec. 1691 (NS); *ib.*, 16, same to same, 31 Dec. 1691 (NS); *ib.*, Box V, 1692, 37, 'H. Burd' [Griffith] to same, 15 Dec. 1691; Bodl. MS Carte 76 fol. 169, newsletter, 15 Dec. 1691; NLS MS 7013 fol. 154, Dalrymple to Tweeddale, 13 Dec. 1691; SRO GD 170/612/9, Carwhin to Barcaldine, 21 Dec. 1691.

58. *HMCR Hamilton*, 123–4, Melville to Hamilton, 19 Dec. 1691; *Highland Papers*, 155, [Dalrymple], 'Memorial of some affairs of state', [1695]; NUL Portland MSS, PwA 2435, 'Memorie Expeditie in de hoogelanden van Schotlands', Jan. 1691/2.

59. *Ib;* *CSPD 1691–2*, 32–4, Warrants and orders, 15 Dec. 1691; Carleton, *Memoirs*, 40; Macpherson, 'Gleanings', *TGSI*, xx, 246–7, Dalrymple to Cluny, 13 Dec. 1691; NLS MS 7013 fol. 154, same to Tweeddale, 13 Dec. 1691; *Highland Papers*, 57, same to Livingston, 7 Jan. 1692.

60. *Ib.*, 56–7; *CSPD 1694–5*, 509, [Johnston] to [William], 26–8 June 1695; *HMCR Hamilton Supplement*, 124, Melville to Hamilton, 5 Jan. 1692; *Leven & Melville*, 652, Hamilton to Melville, 26 Dec. 1691; NLS MS 1031 fol. 142, same to Selkirk, 24 Dec. 1691.

61. *Carstares S.P.*, 140, [Macky] to Melville, [14 Dec. 1691]; SCA, Blairs Letters, Box V, 1692, 37, 'H. Burd' [Griffith] to Innes, 15 Dec. 1691; *Highland Papers*, 48–9, Dalrymple to Lt-Col Hamilton, 3 Dec. 1691.

62. Dalrymple, *Memoirs*, ii, 215–16, same to Breadalbane, 2 Dec. 1691; L. von Ranke, *History of England*, 6 vols. (Oxford, 1875), vi, 174, F. Bonnet to Court of Brandenburg, 29 Dec. 1691/8 Jan. 1692; BL Add. 17,677LL fols. 322v–323, T. Baden to States General, 15/25 Dec. 1691; *ib.*, fol. 324, J. Hop to same, 15/25 Dec. 1691.

63. *Highland Papers*, 57, Dalrymple to Livingston, 7 Jan. 1692.

64. Ranke, vi, 174, Bonnet to Brandenburg, 29 Dec. 1691/8 Jan. 1692; *Archives de la Bastille*, ix, 373–4, Renaudot to Croissy, [Nov. 1692]; BN Naf 7487 fol. 163, 'Memorial of several measures'; SCA, Blairs Letters, Box V, 1692, 37, 'Burd' [Griffith] to Innes, 15 Dec. 1691; SRO GD 170/612/10, Carwhin to Barcaldine, 22 Dec. 1691.

65. *Ib.*, 11, same to same, 31 Dec. 1691; *ib.*, 629/31, Breadalbane to same, 24 Nov. 1691; *ib.*, 133/17, agreement on Kilmorich, 21 Dec. 1691; *ib.*, 20, Glenlyon to Breadalbane, 20

Nov. 1691; *ib.*, 40, same to Carwhin, 26 July 1691; GD 112/39/1222, Breadalbane to Carwhin, 2 Dec. 1691; Atholl, *Chronicles*, i, 332–3, Murray's diary.

66. Dalrymple, *Memoirs*, ii, 215–17, Dalrymple to Breadalbane, 2, 3 Dec. 1691; SRO GD 170/693/6, ? to Barcaldine, 17 Dec. 1691; *ib.*, 629/32, Breadalbane to same, 10 Dec. 1691; *ib.*, 34, same to same, 5 Jan. 1692; Drumlanrig, Queensberry Papers, Vol. 117, [38], same to Queensberry, 5 Dec. 1691.

67. Atholl, *Chronicles*, i, 333, Murray's diary; Blair, Atholl MSS, bundle 1621, same (erased passage); SRO PC 1/48, 127; *ib.*, GD 170/592, P. Birnie to Barcaldine, 28 Dec. 1691; *ib.*, 629/9, Carwhin to same, 21 Dec. 1691; *ib.*, 11, same to same, 31 Dec. 1691.

68. *Ib.*, 9, same to same, 21 Dec. 1691; *ib.*, 10, same to same, 22 Dec. 1691; *ib.*, 12, same to same, 7 Jan. 1692; *ib.*, 681/1, Menzies to same, 22 Dec. 1691; *ib.*, 681/2, same to?, n.d; Blair, Atholl MSS, Box 29 I (6) 61, same to Atholl, 22 Dec. 1691; Atholl, *Chronicles*, i, 334, *Memoirs of Locheill*, 312, copies of warrant; SRO GD 26/viii/130, A. Gordon to Sir Ae. Macpherson, 6 Jan. 1692. For the letter to Lochiel, see n. 71.

69. *Highland Papers*, 56, PC register, 5 Jan. 1692; SRO GD 170/612/11, Carwhin to Barcaldine, 31 Dec. 1691.

70. *Ib.*, 10, same to same, 22 Dec, 1691; *ib.*, 12, same to same, 7 Jan. 1692; GD 112/40/4/6/28, Menzies to Breadalbane, 17 Feb. 1692 (repeating remarks from an earlier, lost letter); *Gazette de France*, 9 Feb. 1692(NS), 66, Edinburgh report, 18 Jan. 1692(NS); NLS MS 7029 fol. 36v, Tweeddale to William, 11 June 1695.

71. Yet Mackenzie of Coul reported that he submitted only on 1 January. The existence of a letter from Menzies to Lochiel can be deduced from Balhaldie's misleading claim that Menzies had made his way from Paris in eleven days, matching a passage in Menzies's existing letter to Atholl. *Memoirs of Locheill*, 311–12; *Melvilles & Leslies*, ii, 166, Hill to Melville, 28 Dec. 1691; SRO GD 170/595, Lochiel to Barcaldine, 25 Dec. 1691; NLS MS 1330 fol. 70, Sir A. Mackenzie to Delvine, 5 Jan. 1692.

72. The first orders for the campaign, Carwhin reported on 21 December, were 'the street rumour yesterday' in Edinburgh, but Dalrymple's violent letters, passed on by friends like Breadalbane, would already have been affecting them. *CSPD 1691–2*, 154, Hill to Portland, 28 Feb. 1692; SRO GD 170/612/9, Carwhin to Barcaldine, 21 Dec. 1691.

73. This seems clear from Glengarry's inclusion of him in his own terms. *Melvilles & Leslies*, ii, 166, Hill to Melville, 31 Dec. 1691.

74. *Ib; HMCR Finch*, iv, 8, Breadalbane to Nottingham, 12 Jan. 1692; *Highland Papers*, 62, Dalrymple to Livingston, 11 Jan. 1692; *ib.*, 102, Report, 20 June 1695.

75. *Melvilles & Leslies*, ii, 166–7, Hill to Melville, 31 Dec. 1691; *ib.*, iii, 219, Achtera's paper, 30 Dec. 1691; Macpherson, 'Gleanings', *TGSI*, xx, 238, 'J. Forbes' [Buchan] to 'Villiamson' [Sir Ae. Macpherson], 6 Jan. [1692]; NLS MS 7014 fol. 6, Hill to Tweeddale, 14 Jan. 1692.

76. Johnston, making the assumption on first seeing in 1693 Dalrymple's January 1692 letters, his cousin Burnet (elaborating the claim between his 1693 draft and the published *History*) and Macaulay, exaggerating Burnet still further, claimed that MacIain led the resistance to Breadalbane's negotiation. No source that autumn (including Breadalbane's private letters) gives any support for that view: all agree that Glengarry was the main saboteur. Burnet and Macaulay, determined to find Breadalbane guilty of the Massacre, wished to find a motive for him in some proportion to the atrocity. Burnet, *History*, iv, 157–8; Foxcroft, *Supplement to Burnet*, 371–2; Macaulay, *History*, v, 2147–8; SRO SP 3/1 fol. 189v, Johnston to Carstares, 4 Aug. 1693; NLS MS 7014 fol. 52, Hill to Tweeddale, Mar. 1692.

77. Aubrey, *Three Prose Works*, 122, ? to J. Garden, 1694; *Highland Papers*, 101, 103, Report, 20 June 1695.

78. In a letter defending himself against the first protests at the Massacre, Hill claimed that MacIain had come to him and agreed to surrender, but was then dissuaded by Glengarry and merely wrote to Inveraray. Having received Ardkinglas's letter of 9 January, he must have known that this was false — it was Appin who sent the paper. He may have conflated an earlier application with that of 31 December, but in that case, MacIain should have known that Hill could not administer the oath —unless Hill refers to a visit in June, just before Breadalbane's arrival (See Chapter 8, p. 275). *Ib.*, 102–3; NLS MS 7014 fol. 52, Hill to Tweeddale, Mar. 1692.

79. [Leslie], *Answer to King*, App., 58, 'A Letter from a Gentleman in Edinburgh to his Friend in London after the Massacre', [20 Apr. 1692]; *Earls of Cromartie*, i, 83, Hill to Tarbat, 28 Dec. 1691; *Highland Papers*, 101–2, Report, 20 June 1695.

80. *Ib.*, 102; Drumlanrig, Queensberry Papers, bundle 1185, 1, 'Remarks upon the State of the Armie', 16 Oct. 1691.

81. Neither of Breadalbane's agents who reported on this thought to mention MacIain's action. [Leslie], *Answer to King*, App. 58–9, 'Letter'; SRO GD 112/40/4/6/31, P. Birnie to Barcaldine, 13 Jan. 1692; *ib.*, 33, Macnachtan to Breadalbane, 13 Jan. 1692; *Highland Papers*, 102–3, Report, 20 June, 1695.

82. The first (1693) official report on the Massacre claims that MacIain first returned to Fort William; but no other source mentions this, and the report makes several mistakes. *Ib.*, 102; Blair, Atholl MSS, Box 43/VI/15, 'Information of the murder of the Glenco men 1692' ([Murray], 'Information'; for its provenance, see Chapter 10, n. 81); SRO GD 406, bundle 633, [J. Steuart], 'An Impartiall Account of the Slaughter of Glenco and his men upon the 13th of ffebery 1692', 1 ([Steuart], 'Impartiall Account, [1693]; for authorship, SRO SP 3/1 fol. 189v, Johnston to Carstares, 4 Aug. 1693).

83. [Leslie], *Answer to King*, App., 61, 'Letter'; *Highland Papers*, 108, Report, 20 June 1695.

84. *Ib.*, 103–4; SRO GD 112/40/4/2/51, Breadalbane to [Carwhin], 15 Jan. 1691.

85. *Highland Papers*, 114, Report, 20 June 1695.

86. As a captain in Buchan's regiment, Alasdair MacIain the younger was the logical 'Alexander Macdonald' to be leading a small mixed force of highland foot in late 1690. Prebble alleges that Colin Campbell perhaps had a grievance against the Glencoe men for a dozen cows taken in the harrying of Argyll in 1685. In fact, though the pursuers caught up with the raiders in Glencoe, they were all men from the Strontian area of Sunart, dependents of Campbell of Lochnell. *HMCR Hope-Johnstone*, 93–4, W. Reoch's narrative, 25 Oct. 1690; *Account of the Depredations*, 70–1; Prebble, *Glencoe*, 192–3; SRO GD 112/40/4/2/51, Breadalbane to [Carwhin], 15 Jan. 1691.

87. There was, admittedly, some solidarity between Campbells: when Aberuchill was dismissed, for his conduct in the Assembly, Breadalbane vainly interceded for him. *Ib.*, 39/1247, same to same, 12 Mar. 1692; *ib.*, 40/4/1/14, Glenorchy to same, 2 Jan. 1691/2; *HMCR Finch*, iv, 20, 'putt out'.

88. SRO PC 1/47, 579–80; *ib.*, 1/48, 80–1.

89. *Highland Papers*, 63–4, PC register, 16 Jan. 1692.

90. Only Montgomerie's list of code-names survives. This cannot show what success his approaches to Queensberry or others had; but it does show whom he considered important. *Ib.*, 67–8, same, 19 Jan. 1692; BN Naf 7487 fol. 155, list of codenames [1692].

91. Macpherson, 'Gleanings', *TGSI*, xx, 238, 'J. Forbes' [Buchan] to 'Villiamson' [Sir Ae. Macpherson], 6 Jan. [1692]; *ib.*, 247, Cunningham to Cluny, 11 Jan. 1692; *Spalding*

Club Misc., iv, 165, R. Mackay to Duchess of Gordon, 3 Jan. 1691[2]; SRO GD 80/229, bond of friendship, 1 Dec. 1691.

92. SRO GD 112/39/1226, Breadalbane to Carwhin, 5 Jan. 1692; NLS MS 3740 fol. 158, Sir J. Leslie to [Blathwayt], 14 Jan. 1692.

93. Ranke, vi, 174, Bonnet to Brandenburg, 29 Dec. 1691/8 Jan. 1692; NLS MS 7014 fol. 5, Dalrymple to Tweeddale, 11 Jan. 1692; *ib.*, MS 1320 fol. 28, R. Mackenzie to Delvine, 29 Dec. 1691.

94. Only in rumours did definite statements appear of what post was suggested for Breadalbane. It was not Chancellor, which was earmarked for Linlithgow, but it was far higher than the place on the Treasury Commission he finally received. He was the only 'episcopalian' whose stock fell drastically during the period in which Carmichael's rose. SRO GD 112/40/4/1/10, Glenorchy to [Carwhin], 26 Mar./6 Apr. 1692; NLS MS 7013 fol. 86v, J. Dickson to Tweeddale, 10 Oct. 1691; *ib.*, fol. 88, A. Johnston to same, 13 Oct. 1691; *ib.*, fol. 158, Dalrymple to same, 26 Dec. 1691; Drumlanrig, Queensberry Papers, Vol. 126, 8, same to Queensberry, 2/12 Oct. 1691.

95. SRO GD 112/40/4/5/28, Countess to Carwhin, 8 'Nov.' [Dec.] 1691; GD 406/1/11029, 11033, 11035, 11036, [Selkirk] to [Hamilton], 15, 24, 31 Dec. 1691, 2 Jan. 1692.

96. We know of this only because Johnston mentioned it to Annandale three years later, so the exact date is uncertain. Rumours that the choice still lay between Tweeddale and Linlithgow still circulated when Tweeddale had actually been chosen; but Selkirk indicates that by 19 December Tweeddale was the only serious candidate. On 12 December, William said that he was undecided whether or not to have a Chancellor; but this might be after the fiasco. Hamilton in one letter suggested that Linlithgow had been discarded by early November, but Carmichael was later being asked whether he would rather see him or Tweeddale in the post. *Ib.*, 11037, [same] to [same], 5 Jan. 1692; Dalrymple, *Memoirs*, ii, 204–5, [same] to [same], 12, 19 Dec. 1691; *Annandale Book*, ii, 93, Johnston to Annandale, 17 Jan. 1695; NLS MS 1031 fol. 149, Hamilton to Selkirk, 31 Dec. 1691; *ib.*, fols. 139v–140, same to same, 17 Dec. 1691.

97. *Ib; Annandale Book*, ii, 113, Johnston to Annandale, 18 Apr. 1695; SRO SP 3/1 fol. 11v, same to A. Fletcher, 14 Mar. 1691/2; 'Letters to J. Mackenzie of Delvine from Rev. Alexander Munro, 1690–8', ed. W. K. Dickson, *Misc.SHS*, v (1933), 220–1, 23 Dec. 1691; NLS MS 7013 fol. 157, Dalrymple to Tweeddale, 22 Dec. 1691; *ib.*, fol. 158, same to same, 26 Dec. 1691.

98. *Ib.*, MS 7014 fol. 2, same to same, 5 Jan. 1692; SRO GD 406/1/11035, 11037, 11039, [Selkirk] to [Hamilton], 31 Dec. 1691, 5, 9 Jan. 1692; GD 112/39/1228, Breadalbane to Carwhin, 7 Jan. 1692; Riley, *King William*, 102n1.

99. *Highland Papers*, 57–8, Dalrymple to Livingston, 7 Jan. 1692; *ib.*, 59, same to same, 9 Jan. 1692.

100. For the main accusation that Breadalbane instigated the Massacre, Foxcroft, *Supplement to Burnet*, 371–2; Burnet, *History*, iv, 158. Breadalbane's mistaken claims, that Forbes, who left London on 15 December, carried the orders for the Massacre, and that Hill used Argyll's regiment deliberately to start a feud, could both easily be disproved in the Highlands for which they were intended — which indicates that he believed them. Had he been involved in the Massacre, he would not have employed Campbells. D. Wimberley, 'Selections from the Family Papers of the Mackays of Bighouse', *TGSI*, xxi, 133, Breadalbane to Barcaldine, 26 May 1692; SRO GD 112/40/4/3/11, same to Carwhin, 26 Mar. 1692; *ib.*, 39/1226, same to same, 5 Jan. 1692.

101. *Ib.*, 1225, same to same, 2 Jan. 1692; *ib.*, 1228, same to same, 7 Jan. 1692; *ib.*, SP 3/1

fol. 4, Johnston to Tweeddale, 5 Mar. 1692; *HMCR Hamilton Supplement*, 124, Melville to Hamilton, 5 Jan. 1692.

102. SRO GD 112/39/1229, Breadalbane to Lochiel, 9 Jan. 1692; *ib.*, 40/4/3/1, same to Carwhin, 9 Jan. 1692; *ib.*, 2, same to same, 11 Jan. 1692.

103. *Highland Papers*, 58-9, Dalrymple to Livingston, 9 Jan. 1692; *ib.*, 62, same to same, 11 Jan. 1692.

104. He wrote on 20 February to Lothian, the late Commissioner to the General Assembly, 'I send you inclosed the first letter I believe ever King William subscribed to Scotland'. *Ib.*, 60-1, Instructions to Livingston, 11 Jan. 1692; *ib.*, 61, Dalrymple to Livingston, 11 Jan. 1692; Graham, *Stairs*, i, 179, same to Lothian, 20 Feb. 1692; *Annandale Book*, i, cclxxxiii-cclxxxv.

105. Burnet, *History*, iv, 159; SRO GD 406/bundle 633, [Steuart], 'Impartiall Account', [1693], 2-3.

106. C. Leslie, *Gallienus Redivivus*, 6 (stripping the story of the humanitarian aspects Carmarthen later gave it); *Highland Papers*, 109, Report, 20 June 1695.

107. *Ib.*, 61-2, Dalrymple to Livingston, 11 Jan. 1692; *ib.*, 66, same to same, 16 Jan. 1692; *ib.*, 71-2, same to Hill, 30 Jan. 1692.

108. NLS MS 7015 fol. 104, Hill to Tweeddale, 20 Sept. 1693.

109. *Ib.*, MS 7014, fol. 5, Dalrymple to same, 11 Jan. 1692.

110. This at first seems particularly sinister, because it appears in the 16 January letter to Hill, with the clear orders to attack Glencoe; but Dalrymple did not write to Hill on 11 January, and Breadalbane's letter of 11 January to Carwhin is clearly the relevant one; that of 16 January makes no mention of the requirement. *Highland Papers*, 62-3, Dalrymple to Livingston, 11 Jan. 1692; *ib.*, 67, same to Hill, 16 Jan. 1692; SRO GD 112/40/4/3/2, Breadalbane to Carwhin, 11 Jan. 1692.

111. *HMCR Finch*, iv, 8, same to Nottingham, 12 Jan. 1692.

112. NLS MS 7014 fol. 5, Dalrymple to Tweeddale, 11 Jan. 1692; *Highland Papers*, 62, same to Livingston, 11 Jan. 1692.

113. *Ib.*, 57, same to same, 7 Jan. 1692; SRO PC 1/48, 580; GD 80/835, Col. Cunningham to Cluny, 26 Jan. 1692.

114. *Highland Papers*, 65, Additional Instructions, 16 Jan. 1692; *ib.*, 67, Dalrymple to Hill, 16 Jan. 1692.

115. Burnet, *History*, iv, 153-4; Macaulay, *History*, v, 2157-8.

116. Prebble, *Glencoe*, 201-2.

117. *Highland Papers*, 69, Dalrymple to Livingston, 30 Jan. 1692.

118. Hopkins, 'Aspects of Jacobite Conspiracy', 274-5, 277-9.

119. *CSPD 1691-2*, 102, Commissions, 16 Jan. 1692; *Highland Papers*, 66, Dalrymple to Livingston, 16 Jan. 1692; Graham, *Stairs*, i, 168, same to Lothian, 16 Jan. 1692.

120. NLS MS 7027 fol. 39, [Johnston], 'Our Conference', [Dec. 1695].

121. The 1693 report even argued that its conditional clauses meant that it was not an order at all. SRO GD 406/bundle 633, [Steuart], 'Impartiall Account', [1693], 3; *Highland Papers*, 114-15, Report, 20 June 1695.

122. *Ib.*, 68-9, Livingston to Lt-Col Hamilton, 23 Jan. 1692; *ib.*, 66, Dalrymple to Livingston, 16 Jan. 1692; *ib.*, 66-7, same to Hill, 16 Jan. 1692; NLS MS 7014 fol. 8, same to Tweeddale, 16 Jan. 1692.

123. *London Gazette* No. 2733, 18-21 Jan. 1691/2; SRO GD 112/39/1231, Breadalbane to Carwhin, 16 Jan. 1692; *ib.*, 1232, same to same, 21 Jan. 1692.

124. *Ib.*, 1234, same to same, 26 Jan. 1692; *ib.*, 1235, same to same, 28 Jan. 1692; *ib.*, 40/4/3/4, same to same, 23 Jan. 1692.

125. Keppoch's brother, like Lochiel's second son, was formally commissioned only after Steinkirk, in Mackay's regiment. *Ib.*, 39/1238, same to same, 9 Feb. 1692; *ib.*, 1243, same to same, 25 Feb. 1692; *ib.*, 1244, same to same, 28 Feb. 1692; *ib.*, 1251, [Carwhin] to Breadalbane, 22 Mar. 1692; GD 170/612/13, same to Barcaldine, 6 Feb. 1692; *ib.*, 669, A. Macdonald to same, 17 Jan. 1692; *ib.*, 629/34, Breadalbane to same, 5 Jan. 1692; *CSPD 1691–2*, 141, Pass to Barclay, 19 Feb. 1692; Dalton, *English Army Lists*, iii, 281.

126. SRO SP 3/1 fol. lv, Tweeddale to Johnston, 23 Feb. 1691/2; *ib.*, fol. 3, Tweeddale's proposed ministry; Blair, Atholl MSS, Box 29 I (6) 69, P. Murray to Murray, 17 Feb. 1692.

127. The second memorial may possibly date from after 27 February, when the news of the Massacre came; but Keppoch's arrival would seem to make its neglect of his claims in Lochiel's favour too blatant. Dalrymple, *Memoirs*, ii, 217–20, Breadalbane, 'Proposals concerning the Highlanders', [Jan.–Feb.]; *Highland Papers*, 53–6, Breadalbane, 'Proposals offered ... for delaying to returne the money from Scotland', [? Feb. 1692].

128. Blair, Atholl MSS, Box '71' II D 11, Murray to Hill, 10 Dec. 1691.

129. Dunlop, 'A Chief and his Lawyer', *TGSI*, xlv, 260; SRO GD 112/40/4/3/5, Breadalbane to Carwhin, 30 Jan. 1692; NLS MS 7014, fol. 6, Hill to Tweeddale, 14 Jan. 1692; *ib.*, fol. 9, same to same, 23 Jan. 1692; *ib.*, MS 1330 fol. 70, Sir A. Mackenzie of Coul to Delvine, 5 Jan. 1692; *ib.*, fol. 71, same to same, 8 Jan. 1692; *ib.*, fol. 72, same to same, 23 Jan. 1692; *ib.*, fol. 73, same to same, 27 Jan. 1692.

130. *Highland Papers*, 68, Livingston to Lt-Col Hamilton, 18 Jan. 1692; SRO GD 406/bundle 633, [Steuart], 'Impartiall Account' [1693], 2, same to Hill, 14 Jan. 1692; *ib.*, 4, same to same, 17 Jan. 1692.

131. The date of this letter is not certain. The surviving copy of Hill's 1693 declaration gives 20 January. The 1693 report gives 26 January, but there are careless mistakes elsewhere in it; Livingston's order of 23 January indicates that he already knew the facts about MacIain, and a later letter of his claims that Hill's reply to this was an excuse for delay; and some special reason is needed to explain his ignoring the chain of command by sending the orders direct to Hamilton. *Ib.*, 5; *ib.*, copies of letters + Hill's declaration; *Highland Papers*, 91, Livingston to Lt-Col Hamilton, 8 May 1693.

132. Parliament's 1695 address to William claimed that there were later orders to Hamilton; but Hamilton, who handed over every document which could justify him, would certainly have produced these had they existed. The claim in the address was one means of reducing Hill's responsibility. (See Chapter 12, p. 408 for the implicit bargain to protect him in 1695.) *Ib.*, 90 (corrected from the original, Glasgow UL MS Gen. 1577); *ib.*, 68–9, same to same, 23 Jan. 1692; *ib.*, 147, Address by the Parliament, 10 July 1695.

133. He described Glencoe as 'that nest of Theives' in a letter to Hill *before* any of Dalrymple's letters containing similar expressions reached him. *Ib.*, 113, Report, 20 June 1695; SRO GD 26/ix/335, Livingston to Melville, 28 Jan. 1692; SRO GD 406/bundle 633, [Steuart], 'Impartiall Account', [1693], 2.

134. *Ib.*, Hill's deposition, 2 July 1695; *HMCR Hope-Johnstone*, 169, Cpt Stewart to Crawford, 3 June 1691; Prebble, *Glencoe*, 224; *Highland Papers*, 69, Dalrymple to Livingston, 30 Jan. 1692; *ib.*, 88, Hill to Culloden, 9 Oct. 1692.

135. *Ib.*, 91, Livingston to Lt-Col Hamilton, 8 May 1693.

136. For the question whether Hill did write to Dalrymple about MacIain's surrender, see n. 147. SRO GD 406/bundle 633, Hill's deposition, 2 July 1695.

137. *Ib; Argyll Just. Recs.*, 141–5; *Highland Papers*, 106, 111–12, Report, 20 June 1695; *The Delaval Papers*, ed. J. Robinson, (Newcastle [c. 1890]), 108, 'History of Glencowe', 7 Mar. 1716 (NS) (based on Atholl family traditions; I owe this reference to the kindness of Dr E. Cruickshanks).

138. It was at Kinlochleven that Hamilton sent out his parties during the Massacre, not, as is persistently claimed, the head of Glencoe itself. Had they attempted to descend the 'Devil's Staircase' in the storm, the Massacre would have been partly avenged almost before it began. *Ib.*, 108; *ib.*, 73, Hill to Hamilton, 12 Feb. 1692; Prebble, *Glencoe*, 242–3; Macdonald, *Slaughter under Trust*, 105–6.

139. Hamilton's mention of 'the avenues, minded by Lievt. Campbell on the south side' uses 'minded' in the sense of 'remembered'. Parliament in 1695 questioned Hill particularly about who gave the information on the country, evidently hoping to implicate Breadalbane. SRO GD 406/bundle 633, Hill's deposition, 2 July 1695; *Highland Papers*, 74, Lt-Col Hamilton to Duncanson, 12 Feb. 1692; Prebble, *Glencoe*, 314.

140. *Ib.*, 223, 227; *ib.*, plate 7, Duncanson to Glenlyon, 12 Feb. 1692.

141. Most writers assume that Lindsay and Lundie were now Glenlyon's officers. Yet Lindsay is mentioned as carrying the orders for quartering — appropriately for an 'aide-major'; and Glenlyon received a new ensign in March. Two officers gave their word with him on 1 February and refused to break it — not Hamilton's lieutenants, who had not yet arrived; hardly Drummond's subordinates, either strangers or accomplices; so presumably Glenlyon's. The one account to give names, a late, unreliable, one based on Atholl sources names James Menzies (a captain of Hill's) and a 'Captain Archbold.' *Ib.*, 219, 312; *Delaval Papers*, 108–9, 'History of Glencowe' 7 Mar. 1716 (NS); Macdonald, *Slaughter under Trust*, 89, 134; Dalton, *English Army Lists*, iii, 275; [Leslie], *Answer to King*, App., 64, 'Letter'; SRO GD 406/bundle 633, [Steuart], 'Impartial Account', [1693], 1.

142. *Ib; Highland Papers*, 104–5, Report, 20 June 1695; [Leslie], *Answer to King*, App., 59, 'Letter'.

143. *Ib.*, 61; Blair, Atholl MSS, Box 43/VI/15, [Murray], 'Information'.

144. *Highland Papers*, 106, Report, 20 June 1695; [Leslie], *Answer to King*, App., 62, 'Letter'; Macdonald, *Slaughter under Trust*, 93.

145. Breadalbane in a reply to Carwhin's letter.of 23 Jan. is pleased to hear that 'Glen.' has chosen to accept, and trusts that those who are holding out, particularly two of his mother's kin, will not do harm. Though this probably refers to Glengarry, it may possibly be a private business affair. Macpherson, 'Gleanings', *TGSI*, xx, 238, [Buchan] to [Sir Ae. Macpherson], 6 Jan. [1692],; SRO GD 112/40/4/3/5, Breadalbane to Carwhin, 30 Jan. 1692.

146. *Highland Papers*, 77, PC register, 22 Mar. 1692; NLS MS 7014 fol. 9, Hill to Tweeddale, 23 Jan. 1692; *ib.*, fol. 11, same to same, 4 Feb. 1692; *ib.*, fol. 17, same to same, 27 Feb. 1692; Blair, Atholl MSS, Box 45 (4) 129, P. Smith to Atholl, 4 Apr. 1704; *ib.*, 130, Glengarry to same, 4 Apr. 1704.

147. The 1693 report states definitely that Hill did write to inform Dalrymple. However, the declaration by him on which this section is based, though claiming to have written the facts several times, specifically mentions only Livingston. If he did write anything to Dalrymple, it was hopelessly unclear; for the Secretary's letter of 5 March shows that he did not even understand that Hill was not empowered to give the oath. (His shamelessness over the matter ensures that this was not a trick — as it might have been with, say, Breadalbane.) SRO GD 406/bundle 633, [Steuart], 'Impartiall Account', [1693], 5; *ib.*, copies of letters + Hill's declaration; *Highland Papers*, 70, Dalrymple to Livingston, 30 Jan. 1692; *ib.*, 75, same to Hill, 5 Mar. 1692.

148. My original note rested on the mistaken idea that Argyll now again owned the glen (see Preface, p. ix). *Ib*; SRO GD 112/40/4/6/34, Carwhin to Breadalbane, 28 Jan. 1692; *ib.*, 40/4/3/6, Breadalbane to Carwhin, 6 Feb. 1692.

149. Hill's mention in his letter of 14 January that Argyll's regiment was at Keppoch (*ib.*, 5, same to same, 30 Jan. 1692) explains the 'Letrick' or 'Letrickweel' of some versions of Dalrymple's letter to Livingston (Prebble, *Glencoe*, 204n) as misreadings. *Highland Papers*, 69–70, Dalrymple to Livingston, 30 Jan. 1692; *ib.*, 70–2, same to Hill, 30 Jan. 1692; Graham, *Stairs*, i, 171–4, same to Lothian, 30 Jan. 1692.

150. Hill's letter of 14 January took fourteen days to reach London; but snowstorms in early February greatly increased the time taken even between London and Edinburgh. Hill in 1695 declared that he could not remember when the letter came. *Ib.*, 168, same to same, 16 Jan. 1692; *ib.*, 174, same to same, 2 Feb. 1692; SRO GD 406/bundle 633, Hill's deposition, 2 July 1695.

151. *Highland Papers*, 73, Hill to Hamilton, 12 Feb. 1692; *ib.*, 82, PC register, 28 Apr. 1692; NLS MS 7014 fol. 13, Hill to Tweeddale, 14 Feb. 1692; *ib.*, fol. 52, same to same, Mar. 1692; SRO GD 406/bundle 633, Hill's deposition, 2 July 1695; *ib.*, [Steuart], 'Impartiall Account', [1693], 7, Hill to Livingston, 14 Feb. 1692.

152. *Ib; Highland Papers*, 74, Hamilton to Duncanson, 12 Feb. 1692.

153. Prebble, *Glencoe*, 227–8; *ib.*, plate 7, Duncanson to Glenlyon, 12 Feb. 1692.

154. Duncanson evidently enclosed a copy of Hamilton's order, since it was through Glenlyon that both were 'leaked' to the Jacobites.

155. SRO GD 170/133/13, letters of horning, 2 Feb. 1692; *ib.*, 29, Murray to Glenlyon, 11 Feb. 1692.

156. [Leslie], *Answer to King*, App., 64, 'Letter'.

157. Blair, Atholl MSS, Box 43/VI/15, [Murray], 'Information'; *Highland Papers*, 105, 107–8, Report, 20 June 1695.

158. Some versions of the tradition, however, place the stone near Inverrigan. (The suggestion that MacIain's house was not on the site of the present monument seems to arise from the fact that his son Iain rebuilt the house later; but at the time of the Massacre, Iain was living somewhere between Inverrigan and Achnacone, since he heard the firing at both places.) *Ib.*, 106; Prebble, *Glencoe*, 231–2; Macdonald, *Slaughter under Trust*, 94–6, 99–100.

159. SRO GD 406/bundle 633, [Steuart], 'Impartiall Account', [1693], 7, Hill to Livingston, 14 Feb. 1692; *Highland Papers*, 108, Report, 20 June 1695.

160. *Ib.*, 105–6, 107; [Leslie], *Answer to King*, App., 61–2, 'Letter'; Blair, Atholl MSS, Box 43/VI/15, [Murray], 'Information'; Maclean, 'Celtic Sources', 351–2, 'Muck Bard', 'Murt Ghlinne-Comhann' (translated by Maclean).

161. Even the Glencoe bard recorded Glenlyon's watching the killing, rather than vigorously joining in. *Ib.*, 349–50, Aonghus Mac Alasdair Ruaidh, 'Murt Ghlinne-Comhann'; *Highland Papers*, 106–7, Report, 20 June 1695; Blair, Atholl MSS, Box 43/VI/15, [Murray], 'Information'; Prebble, *Glencoe*, 234n; Campbell, *Lairds of Glenlyon*, 50; *Delaval Papers*, 109, ['History of Glencowe']; Bland Burges, *Selections*, 358.

162. Lorne, *Adventures in Legend*, 271; the versions given in Prebble, *Glencoe*, 245, Macdonald, *Slaughter under Trust*, 102–3, seem to be developments of this.

163. The bards mention no killings of soldiers, merely emphasising how differently a fair fight would have gone. *Ib.*, 107; Prebble, *Glencoe*, 242; Lorne, *Adventures in Legend*, 271; Maclean, 'Celtic Sources', 348, 'Muck Bard', 'Murt Ghlinne-Comhann' (translated by Maclean); Stewart, *The Stewarts of Appin*, 155–6. (See Preface, p. x)

164. *Highland Papers*, 105, 107–8, Report, 20 June 1695; [Leslie], *Answer to King*, App., 62–3, 'Letter'.

165. NLS MS 1330 fol. 80, Sir A. Mackenzie of Coul to Delvine, 24 Feb. 1692.

166. The main account of this seems to claim that Airds did the killings himself. Blair,

Atholl MSS, Box 43/VI/15, [Murray], 'Information'; *Highland Papers*, 107, Report, 20 June 1695.

167. The 'Letter' in April claimed 900 cows and 200 horses. *Ib.*, 107–9; *ib.*, 119, Glencoe petition, 26 June 1695; [Leslie], *Answer to King*, App., 62, 'Letter'; SRO GD 112/40/4/3/8, Breadalbane to Carwhin, 5 Mar. 1692; GD 406/bundle 633, [Steuart], 'Impartiall Account', [1693], 7, Hill to Livingston, 14 Feb. 1692.

168. *Ib*; NLS MS 7014 fol. 13, same to Tweeddale, 14 Feb. 1692; *Grameid*, 124; [Leslie], *Answer to King*, App., 61–2, 'Letter'; Maclean, 'Celtic Sources', 355–6, 'Muck Bard', 'Murt Ghlinne-Comhann' (translated by Maclean); Blair, Atholl MSS, Box 43/VI/15, [Murray], 'Information'; *Gazette de France*, 12 Apr. 1692 (NS), 176, Edinburgh report, 23 Mar. (NS).

169. *CSPD 1691–2*, 154, Hill to Portland, 28 Feb. 1692; NLS MS 1330 fol. 80, Sir A. Mackenzie of Coul to Delvine, 24 Feb. 1692; SRO GD 406/bundle 633, copies of letters, Livingston to Hill, 24 Feb. 1692.

170. Stewart, *The Stewarts of Appin*, 155–6; Macdonald, *Clan Donald*, ii, 222; information, A. L. Campbell yr of Airds.

171. Macdonald, *Slaughter under Trust*, 113.

172. Maclean, 'Celtic Sources', 349–51, Aonghus, 'Murt Ghlinne-Comhann'; SRO GD 112/40/4/3/7, Breadalbane to Carwhin, 1 Mar. 1692; Blair, Atholl MSS, Box 29 I (6) 74, Lady Murray to Murray, 2 Apr. 1692.

173. *Memoirs of Locheill*, 322–3.

174. SRO 3/1 fol. 21, Johnston to Portland, 1 Apr. 1692; *ib.*, GD 112/39/1247, [Breadalbane] to Carwhin, 12 Mar. 1692; NLS MS 7014 fol. 15, Hill to Tweeddale, 17 Feb. 1692; *ib.*, fol. 17, same to same, 27 Feb. 1692; *CSPD 1691–2*, 153–4, same to Portland, 28 Feb. 1692.

175. *Ib*; NLS MS 7014 fol. 52, same to Tweeddale, Mar. 1692; SRO GD 112/40/4/3/12, [Breadalbane] to Carwhin, 31 Mar. 1692.

176. *Highland Papers*, 74–5, Livingston to Hamilton, 26 Feb. 169[2]; SRO GD 406/bundle 633, copies of letters, same to Hill, 24 Feb. 1692.

177. Donald McBane was a member of Forbes's company, and therefore presumably accompanied him, under Hamilton's command on the expedition; and he passed his last years at Fort William. Yet his frank autobiography contains no mention of the Massacre.

178. *Highland Papers*, 108, Report, 20 June 1695; [Leslie], *Answer to King*, App., 65, 'Letter'; SRO GD 26/xiii/80, ? to Countess of Melville, 8 Mar. [1692].

179. Blair, Atholl MSS, Box '71' II D 13, Menzies of Comrie to Murray, 17 Mar. 1692; *ib.*, 14, Leslie to Glenlyon, 19 Mar. 1692.

11

The 'Episcopalian' Ministry (February 1692–October 1694)

While Glenlyon's men were still plundering houses and gathering cattle in Glencoe, the General Assembly was dissolved in Edinburgh. It had met on 15 January instructed by William to admit into the church former episcopalian clergy who acknowledged its authority. Agreement, even if insincere, would have obtained a mainly 'presbyterian' civil government and have exposed the Jacobite basis of many episcopalian ministers' defiance.[1] However, the members were assured from London that, if they unanimously refused, William would abandon his demand, and Privy Councillors like Crawford, who had promised William presbyterian tolerance, led the opposition. Finally, early on 13 February, the Commissioner, Lothian, declared it dissolved without naming any date for its successor, and the Moderator, amid tumult, named August 1693.[2] There was widespread presbyterian disaffection, but its only immediate results were a few treasonable speeches, and slight Cameronian outbreaks.[3]

In his fury at the Assembly's bigotry, William discarded his idea of a predominantly 'presbyterian' ministry but, typically, kept his choices (apart from Johnston) secret until he left for Flanders on 4 March.[4] Tweeddale, Queensberry, Linlithgow, Strathmore, Breadalbane and Tarbat were among those inserted on the Privy Council; and seven 'presbyterian' members, including Crawford, Grant and Aberuchill, were struck off for their conduct in the Assembly. Now there was a Chancellor, Hamilton was demoted to be Lord Admiral. Tarbat was restored as Lord Register, and, now Melville was eclipsed, threw in his lot with the 'episcopalians'. The Treasury Commission under Tweeddale balanced the 'presbyterian' survivors Raith and Cassillis with Drumlanrig, Linlithgow and Breadalbane — a predictably inadequate reward, wrote Glenorchy, which would not repay the expenses of living in Edinburgh to perform the duties. Lauder of Fountainhall, an honest 'episcopalian', was made Advocate.[5] Queensberry remained excluded; the greater changes evidently made it more necessary not to push the Presbyterians too far. It was some slight consolation that his English counterpart Rochester, in William's simultaneous swing towards the Tories, was also made a Privy Councillor only, although plainly one of the ministry's leaders — but no real cause for hope, since Rochester's real influence came from his strategic position at the English Court. From the start, Queensberry was alienated from the ministry his 'interest' had helped bring to power.[6] The 'presbyterians' in Scotland feared even more unfavourable changes.[7]

It was while all Scottish attention at London was absorbed in awaiting William's decision that the news of Glencoe arrived. Breadalbane, who first heard it about 27 February from Barcaldine's report to Carwhin, was shocked and hoped that it might be exaggerated. From the start, his dismay arose largely from fear that his estates and those of other Campbells, whether involved or not, would be attacked in retaliation for the use of Argyll's regiment, though Argyll (who had not had the news) fatuously trusted that the government would protect them. Breadalbane protested vigorously at Court at the injustice and imprudence of the Massacre, declaring that he would have warned the victims had he known in time, and that he would make his tenants restore the cows the soldiers had sold them from the plunder.[8] He made very little impression. Nobody would believe that the troops had been quartered on the Macdonalds, and he noted that the Massacre 'makes no noyse here nor was it noticed by ye Court even at the first report'. It is not clear how much William heard in the crowded week before he embarked.[9] Most people in London refused to believe that there had been a massacre. The newsletters reported: 'Wrote from Edinburgh, the earle of Argiles regiment in their march thither from the highlands kill'd about 60 of them who refused to submit to their majesties government'.[10]

Tarbat agreed with Breadalbane that it was 'precipitat & Injust', but made no major protest. The one politician besides Breadalbane to do so was Fountainhall, who refused to become Advocate unless he was authorised to prosecute Glenlyon and the other officers for murder. Dalrymple had no alternative candidate ready, and the post remained unfilled — probably the only consequence of the Massacre he regretted.[11] Writing to Hill on 5 March, he was unaffected by the first, confused, reports that MacIain had belatedly taken the Indemnity, and lamented only 'that any of the septe gote away, . . . there is necessity to prosecute them to the utmost'.[12]

Perhaps the worst political result of the Massacre — and also the one most harmful to Breadalbane — was that it enabled the highlanders to suppose that all government policy since Achallader had not been a 'profound plan' of 'bygons to hav been bygons' but insincere from the start — the most damaging belief imaginable for its future credit. They suspected not only Breadalbane but Lochiel, who had always urged submission, and had then followed Breadalbane to London, doubtless to concert the Massacre.[13] It was predictable that they should believe so, rather than confront the unbearable truth about the opportunity they had thrown away. Their self-justifying suspicions of Breadalbane were strengthened, he was informed (but could not believe), by letters from Atholl and the Countess of Argyll to Glengarry accusing him.[14] Breadalbane repeatedly declared his innocence to all around him, and sent messengers to MacIain's sons offering to obtain a remission for them if they would confirm this. Ironically, the fact that he was the only person anxious to do so merely implanted a conviction of his guilt in a formidable group of both lowlanders and highlanders, which eventually included Melville, Johnston and his cousin Bishop Burnet, Hamilton, Murray, MacIain's sons and Iain Lom.[15]

Breadalbane, of course, had many other preoccupations. He feared retaliation particularly upon two Londoners he had hired to extract turpentine from his Argyllshire firwoods.[16] After his appointment, his lamentations to Carwhin mingled with instructions about Edinburgh lodgings and coach-horses. He continued his efforts to have some of the money paid to the chiefs who had submitted in time. Dalrymple seconded this, from a wish to create jealousies among the chiefs over their different fortunes, rather than from any favour for them. One exception was the Macleans, 'never a robbing, thieving people, nor ever deserved ill at the hands of its countrey', for whom he momentarily hoped to obtain good terms from Argyll. However, William's urgent need of money made him order the return of the £12,000 to London, wrecking these hopes. Dalrymple crossed to Flanders and Lochiel and Keppoch returned home. Breadalbane hoped for a while that the Scottish Treasury could dissuade William from recalling the money.[17] When that failed, he claimed expenses of £2,300, and was treated generously. He was tacitly allowed £2,000, and £500 more was lost by the exchange in returning the rest.[18]

Hill also had many preoccupations besides Glencoe. William had Dalrymple write to Tweeddale to prepare a grant of a jurisdiction for Fort William extending from Glencoe to Keppoch, but the lawyers made difficulties and frustrated it. Hill began a long series of applications to Tweeddale for such a jurisdiction as the one means to prevent highland thieving.[19] When some of the Irish catholic priests, disheartened by the submission of their flocks, applied for passes to go abroad, he seized the opportunity to rid the Highlands of them.[20] Ignoring Dalrymple's orders to 'prosecute' the remaining Glencoe men, he argued that enough had been killed for an example, and presented the pardoning of the rest as a logical part of this settlement, first to Tweeddale and then to Dalrymple. Already in early March Argyll at Court had been offering to obtain remissions for them if they would go abroad. In mid-April, Hill was sent orders to seize on the remaining survivors until they could be transplanted; but he wrote again, pushing Dalrymple to the furthest concession he would for the moment make. Writing to Hill on 30 April, when he knew the full story, he still considered it 'a thing so necessary to rid the Countrey of thieving' that his only qualification was 'that in the execution it was neither so full nor so fair as might have been'. Glengarry, Clanranald and Sir Donald, who had taken the oaths long after MacIain, were to receive remissions, but he gave Hill William's permission to pardon 'these irreclaimable Thieves' only on condition that they went abroad to Ireland (for which the anti-catholic government there would scarcely thank him), to the plantations (a journey for which they had no money),

> or to any place they please If you think fit to take Caution from them to live honestly & peaceably anywhere except Glencoe, But that Quarter is so advantageous to their thieving Trade, that his Maty doth not allow any of them to return to Glenco ... If after all wee come to slack and yeild, the work that's well begun will come to ill effect.[21]

Dalrymple did not believe reports that the French were planning an invasion; he might otherwise have been less unrelenting, and more aware that Sir John Maclean was still holding out in Carnaburg and Duart. Argyll came north in mid-March with an order to attack these castles with 300 of Hill's regiment, if Sir John would not negotiate. He was very willing to do so, applying to Argyll and the

Council for safe-conducts and to Tarbat for advice. He adroitly remained always on the point of surrendering and setting off for Court; but by 2 May nothing had changed, and Argyll was preparing the expedition. Doubt whether Carnaburg could be captured without a warship to bombard it was one reason for the forbearance shown, but most of those involved wished to help Sir John: Hill, for instance, knowing Dalrymple's prejudices, wrote claiming that he had never been a Catholic.[22] Sir John was outwardly delaying the surrender of the castles, his last bargaining points, partly from hope (absurd in the circumstances) that he might be allowed Carnaburg as a home, partly to prevent troops from being sent to quarter in Mull for vast arrears of taxes and destroying his people. Secretly, he may still have expected to retrieve something in London, or even from a French invasion.[23]

On 12 April(NS), the French official *Gazette*, whose editor had close links with the Jacobite court, printed a brief report of the Massacre in a mid-March report from Edinburgh. It was fairly accurate, although over-emphasising Hill's part in ordering it and omitting the most scandalous circumstance of all, Glenlyon's troops being guests in Glencoe.[24] After the initial disregard, 'Major Duncanson's Christian order' was circulated in Edinburgh and London by mid-March, and a month later Dalrymple's Undersecretary was exhibiting his register of out-letters to avert accusations.[25] Dalrymple remained contemptuous, sneering at the coffee-house complaints of 'our humoursome people at home' who showed 'so much regreet for such a sept of theevs', and he wrongly blamed Hill for making his orders public.[26] Late in April, the alarm of invasion distracted the public attention in both kingdoms.

What was known about Glencoe had already attracted the interest of the Secretary left in Britain, James Johnston. He did not exploit it immediately, although he was seeking a weapon against Dalrymple. Johnston had been William's chief resident secret agent in Britain shortly before the revolution. A Club sympathiser, he admired William largely because he expected him, with some reason, to uphold legality and liberty, and even, once bad advisers were prevented from misrepresenting them and playing on his habit of delaying difficult decisions, to support major reforms. Therefore, besides the obligatory whitewashing, he was genuinely puzzled by the contrast between William's normal clemency — excessive, he himself thought — and the savage illegality of Glencoe.[27] Johnston, although Warriston's son, was personally no Presbyterian; he was rather an English Whig of a recognisable type, a Court supporter from his trust in William, but otherwise an extremist, seeing most leading Tories and 'episcopalians' as simply crypto-Jacobites, and willing to use Popish Plot methods to prove this. He believed that, ultimately, English politics were the dog and Scottish politics only the tail; but the 'presbyterians' were his constituency, the nearest thing to Whigs in Scotland, who welcomed him for his father's sake, and he worked vigorously for what he considered their interests.[28] His close links with successive Archbishops of Canterbury, Tillotson and Tenison, who were erastians, willing to support a presbyterian national church in Scotland if it would only receive into it the loyal 'conformist' clergy, gave him considerable room for manoeuvre in obtaining a church settlement acceptable in England: they trusted him even when he truckled to bigots. Believing that 'the Church must go to the civill Government or the civill Government return to it', he found a strong ally in Carstares, alienated by the unforeseen extent of the 'episcopalian' success. They shared a low opinion of Tweeddale and his attempts to balance between the two sides, sniped at by both.[29] Johnston's opposition to the 'episcopalians' did not arise gradually from the natural power struggle between Secretaries: from the start, he was determined to destroy them. To Portland, who was talking of giving up Scottish business in disgust at presbyterian folly, he wrote on 28 April that Linlithgow and Breadalbane were communing with notorious Jacobites, doubtless to win them over — although they were thought to be incorrigible. The innuendo in Breadalbane's case was probably justified. Johnston soon convinced his cousin Bishop Burnet, who had played a part in bringing in the 'episcopalians', that they were openly Jacobite.[30] Yet, in building a coalition against them, he himself intended to appeal to Jacobites, particularly magnates' heirs like Arran.[31]

In March, the Council under Tweeddale had confirmed Hill's grant of passes to Buchan, Cannon and those officers (including Lords Dunkeld and Dundee) who followed them, and had allowed those wishing to remain in Scotland to find security rather than taking the oaths. Buchan and Cannon came to Edinburgh, where Tweeddale gave them a dinner, as a courtesy due to enemy generals — a recognition in odd contrast to the massacre of former followers. They were visited by their Edinburgh supporters, and supposedly tried to proselytise in the army.[32]

In mid-April they landed at Havre, and the sequel justifies William's original reluctance to release them. James and Melfort had at last persuaded Louis, and had assembled Irish and French troops at the Hogue for a full-scale invasion of England. They immediately ordered Buchan (still noticeably in disgrace for his negotiation with Breadalbane) to march his officers to Dunkirk, where most Scots with military experience (except the Duke of Gordon, who remained with James) were assembled, including Dunfermline, Barclay, Sir Alexander Maclean, Robertson of Struan and officers who had deserted William in 1691 — about a hundred in all. When James's main invasion force sailed, they were to embark on two frigates commanded by the famous privateer Jean Bart. They were to land either at Dunnottar Castle in the Mearns or Slains Castle in Aberdeenshire, to whose occupants, Erroll and Lord Keith (Marischal's son) James wrote expressing (apparently unwarranted) confidence that they would hand them over and join Buchan.[33] Melfort prepared a Declaration for Scotland. It denounced the Massacre in its preamble, and the long list of persons excepted from pardon included (besides the Melvilles, Argyll, Annandale, Tweeddale, Tarbat, Stair and those prominent in fighting or financing the Williamite campaigns) Dalrymple, Major Duncanson and Glenlyon — and Duncan Menzies for having encouraged Jacobites to submit.[34] Obviously, the Jacobites hoped to raise the North-East and other lowland areas — James sent three special letters to Queensberry, Arran and Aberdeen — but they must also have relied largely on the clans rejoining Buchan. If Jacobite affairs had gone according to plan in both December and May, then, the chiefs would have kept their solemn allegiance to William for just five months.

Johnston remained in London to reassure the Scottish government that its needs were not forgotten at Court, though he explained that the English, convinced (correctly) that the threat was against them, could not satisfy its demands for arms or troops.[35] He gained considerable credit for the secret information he obtained from spies, including John Macky, who brought early warning of the invasion, and Sir Aeneas Macpherson, who, deciding to await James's return in London, and failing to obtain his promised reward from Melville, wheedled secrets from Jacobite prisoners for money.[36] However, Johnston's secret intelligence was far less extensive and accurate than he claimed in retrospect. He feared a widespread conspiracy, and scarcely mentioned any major Tory without suspicion. In fact, even the most conspicuous Jacobite activity, the raising of regiments around London, in which many Scottish Jacobite officers were involved, was haphazard and disrupted by government arrests. Dunmore was involved, and was seized in hiding with the expatriate Earl of Middleton, a leading Jacobite moderate.[37]

On 19 May, the French, misled by Jacobite spies, attacked the far larger Anglo-Dutch fleet, and over the next few days they were decisively defeated. Although a strong rumour that Louis had swiftly transferred 4,000 men to Dunkirk for an invasion of Scotland needlessly prolonged apprehension there,[38] the disaster destroyed his trust in Jacobite promises. That autumn, lack of money forced James to send off most of the Scottish officers as a company in the French army. They were to fight bravely in Catalonia and Alsace; but James, typically, picked an unjust officer to command them.[39] A campaign had begun, organised by Montgomerie, to bring Middleton over to be James's chief minister. Melfort, discredited and on the defensive, still had enough interest to harass the Duke of Gordon until he retired altogether from France into Germany. He was seized there and handed over to William.[40]

Although James sent a professional soldier to Scotland, as he did to several English counties where regiments were forming, it is not clear whether the Scottish Jacobites had any organisation for a rising. Johnston's claim that Arran had a commission as Lieutenant-General to head one seems only a conjecture: he had recently written offering to remain quiet, he for once remained openly in Edinburgh, and he was on bad terms with Home, the obvious leader of any Border movement — who surrendered himself only after news of the victory.[41] In late April, Johnston sent down warning of a plot to seize the Castle, causing great alarm; but the only solid proof found was of an outside plan for Neville Payne's escape.[42] The prisoners who briefly seized the Canongate Tolbooth claimed afterwards to be protesting against the keeper's corruption; Lord Fraser, the minor peer who proclaimed King James at Fraserburgh, that he had been blind drunk.[43]

Even at their most apprehensive, the Council feared comparatively little from the Highlands, leaving Hill's regiment and local supporters to keep the peace while the remaining forces moved south to form an army. Seaforth, who fled from confinement in Edinburgh on 6 May (and was recaptured ten days later) apparently acted only from vague hopes, and groundless fears of being tortured in the 'boots'.[44] Hill reported that, despite the invasion rumours, he expected the

Highlands to be the last area to stir. The chiefs were divided, and the middle ranks of the clans wished to remain quiet. Lochiel came in to Fort William offering support and declaring a hatred of popery. Clanranald set out to present himself to Mary without awaiting the result of the crisis. The danger that the Glencoe survivors might gather several hundred broken men made the Council on 3 May authorise Hill to promise them temporary protection until William's pleasure was known, and they remained quiet.[45] The one exception was Sir John Maclean. As he continued to find excuses for delaying the surrender of Duart and Carnaburg, it became clear to the disillusioned Hill that he was playing for time in case the invasion succeeded. Only in July, when all hopes (including rumours of a fleet off Skye) were long over, did he surrender his castles, which Hill's regiment occupied, and belatedly set out for William's camp.[46] His conduct shows the problem which had driven William's government into the course which produced the Massacre: had it continued its mild policy of mid-1691, most of the clans would have temporised as Maclean did.

The only active Jacobitism reported in or about the Highlands, however, was a meeting near Dumbarton in mid-May, the participants in which sent their horses there. They allegedly included Glencairn and Cochrane of Kilmaronock, who had fought for William; and, although this was never confirmed, it emphasised the government's problem.[47] In the invasion crisis, its English counterpart could be sure that, although there might be some treachery among politicians and officers, the mass of the people was trustworthy; the Scottish government could not. The Jacobites posed no active independent threat; but the nation was, as Johnston said, 'like a woman who is ill with her husband but scruples to take another man ... tho she will not take she may be easily taken'.[48] The Jacobite highland rising had achieved at least the negative success that the burdens of civil war had alienated the people's hearts from William; the costly and damaging European war increased the grievances; and the change of ministry brought on a crisis. The 'presbyterians' were alienated, convinced that the new ministers planned to betray the country, and often disaffected. The most conspicuous non-Jacobite example was the Duke of Hamilton. Even Fletcher of Saltoun, then, as usual, a violent opponent of official policy, begged him to co-operate with the ministry until the danger was past; but instead, although he came to Edinburgh at the crisis, he ostentatiously refused even to attend Council.[49] Meanwhile, the new ministers were denied the vital time they needed to persuade their fellow-'episcopalians' to take the oaths. Lacking a secure power-base at the crisis, they acted indecisively; and they never fully recovered from this setback.

One disadvantage was that several straggled back from London belatedly — Queensberry first attending Council on 2 May, Breadalbane and Drumlanrig later, Tarbat only on the 16th. Even then, despite the dismissals, the 'presbyterians' could often outvote them, and they still considered themselves very much a minority in the government. Being emphatically instructed not to alienate the 'presbyterians' further, they abandoned other measures which they might have carried, weakening their policies still more.[50] However, although a bi-partisan committee for security was appointed when the first warning of invasion arrived on 26 April, 'episcopalian' policy guided the first major decision — and irretrievable mistake. They called out not the militia, who were in confusion and whose officers were mainly Presbyterians, but the heritors and fencible men. As many of these would be disaffected, the proclamation finally issued ordered those who would not take the allegiance and assurance and serve to surrender their arms and take an Engagement (drawn up by Stair) not to join the invaders. The startling confession of government weakness encouraged very many heritors, including the Midlothian ones, to refuse even this.[51]

Even before this shock, the government's conduct was weak. Johnston declared that there was greater panic in Scotland, which was not in danger, than in England, which was, and that Tweeddale had lost his head. The Council had immense powers but did not effectively press the execution of orders against suspects. On 8 May, they tried to recall the three regiments shipped at Leith under orders for England, but the commanding officer refused to obey. Thus Argyll's regiment landed in London — to find that the xenophobic Treasury Commissioner Sir Edward Seymour had stopped their English pay on the pretence that half of them had deserted.[52]

To supplement the regular forces, the Presbyterians in the western shires and the Lothians offered to raise volunteer unpaid regiments, if they were allowed to choose their own officers, as in previous crises. The 'episcopalian' ministers, who feared a coup, represented this condition as rampant republicanism. However, William, who accepted that the Cameronian regiment obeyed its chaplain rather than its officers and (in 1693) that Argyll's regiment, while fighting bravely for him, drank James's health, was pragmatic in military matters, and took the offer kindly.[53] A counter-offer of six regiments without such a condition made, somewhat later, by 'episcopalian' ministers including Breadalbane (from himself and Argyll) and Linlithgow, was similarly maligned by the 'presbyterians' as made only when all danger was over, a crypto-Jacobite trick.[54]

The 'assurance' was a declaration that William and Mary were 'lawfull undoubted' sovereigns which all those liable to take the allegiance, including parliamentary electors, must sign, which was rushed through a thin Parliament in July 1690, as unacceptable to the High Presbyterians, in declaring uncovenanted monarchs lawful, as to the Jacobites.[55] The 'episcopalian' ministers knew that the bulk of the nation would not take it without long preliminary preparation, but that saying so would arouse accusations that they did not wish people to take the oaths. This was absurd, for they not only desired sufficient electors to qualify themselves to elect an anti-presbyterian parliament, but, having taken the oaths themselves, wanted company. As one bitter Jacobite put it:

> Why should Tories live free from death and damnation,
> More than the first Peers and wise men of the nation?[56]

Now, however, they found themselves obliged to put the allegiance and assurance to heritors, starting with the Midlothian ones, in circumstances which ensured refusal. The 'presbyterians', meanwhile, afraid that their high-fliers would refuse while hostile electors qualified, played an adroit double game, blaming the 'episcopalians' as Jacobites in Britain for imposing it so that vast refusals would expose the government's weakness, in Flanders for opposing it. Meanwhile the 'episcopalians' began putting only the allegiance to those summoned before them, and obtained some success.[57]

Their enemies, however, would not let them slip off the hook, and despite Dalrymple, who lamented being 'a cypher in my post', persuaded William to send on 14 July a harsh letter declaring that gentle methods had failed and must be replaced by severity. They must put the allegiance and assurance to all heritors, and must prosecute for treason Seaforth — who was to pay dearly for that futile escape — Gordon and other Jacobites in France.[58] Many heritors who had accepted the allegiance now refused the assurance, and the prisons were soon full. Had the letter come just after the Hogue, Dalrymple thought, there might have been a chance, but now the Allies' earlier hopes were crumbling. News of William's bungled attempt to surprise the French at Steinkirk on 24 July, which caused Mackay's death and the cutting to pieces of three Scottish regiments, encouraged refusals.[59] Even Johnston protested that there was no hope of success, but, having received orders, the best the Council could do was to proceed very slowly. Their adjournment in mid-August provided a cover for dropping the attempt, although William formally countermanded it only in November.[60] Although 'presbyterian' pressure had made William give the order, the 'episcopalians' suffered for it. The accusations of treason against them received a welcome counter-balance in mid-August, when the lunatic fringe of the Cameronians issued a declaration at Sanquhar declaring William deposed and the Duke of Monmouth's son king. It was so opportune that Dalrymple wondered if Drumlanrig had connived at it. However, rather than make dangerous martyrs, the Council merely imprisoned the fanatics for a few months.[61]

One area where the 'episcopalians' had expected to show William their superiority was the Treasury. Their first major report to him, though emphasising difficulties, was confident — dangerously so — that, if he prevented them from being swamped by arrears, they could raise the revenue and pay the army punctually: 'if We enter upon a clean floor, We will be answerable to keep it so'.[62] The invasion threat had shown how fragile their hopes were: within six months they issued extraordinary precepts for a quarter of the total revenue. Their position became impossible as branch after branch of the revenue bent and broke under the burden of war, trade depression, and finally famine. Some of them, particularly Breadalbane, were accused of corruption, but, even if true, this made little difference.[63] One slight extra difficulty came that December when Dalrymple imposed on the overburdened invalids' fund — soldiers' pay retained to finance their treatment in sickness — a large pension for Lieutenant-Colonel Hamilton.[64]

The Glencoe men had avoided committing thefts, merely travelling in small parties and civilly begging for a little meal to keep them from starving. Hill continued to plead for clemency for them to Portland, Dalrymple, Johnston and Argyll. In August, his persistence was rewarded by authorisation to receive them into mercy and resettle them. Ardkinglas, acting for Argyll (not now their immediate superior), gave security for their good behaviour.[65] They were without cattle or other possessions, and remained very close to starvation. Yet although they continued, like other clans, to produce thieves, most of them remained so orderly under hardship that Stewart of Ballachulish was able to open and operate a commercial slate quarry just along the coast in 1693.[66] (See Preface, p. x)

Many other highland areas were being reduced more peaceably to almost equal poverty. The tax-collectors arrived demanding that the people, impoverished by the war and hard winters, should immediately pay the arrears of cess and other taxes owing since the Revolution or well before — in some cases, since 1640. They ruthlessly quartered troops on defaulters, giving them no time even to sell their goods; but the people, 'the meaner sort being the psons in thes ptes yt bear ye burden', remained submissive. The Macleods, who had merely been cut off from the mainland administration, were treated as rigorously as their Jacobite neighbours. In September, all the landowners in Skye protested to the Council against the subcollectors' ruthlessness. Finally, in December, the Treasury obtained William's permission to forbid quartering for public dues before Candlemas (2 February) 1691; but by then Lochaber, Appin, Ardgour and some of the Isles had paid a staggering twenty-four months' cess, which Hill hoped would be allowed from future taxes.[67] Presbyterian hostility may have increased the determination of lowland collectors. Yet when the Treasury, on Breadalbane's suggestion, withdrew the inland excise of Argyll from the farm and granted the collection to Barcaldine, on the grounds that this would avoid destructive quartering, within five months he was summoning Hill's soldiers to Appin. Breadalbane, who forced him to accept, presumably benefited financially himself.[68]

Crushing taxation, coming after the major economic and social dislocation caused by the war, presumably encouraged widespread and frequent thefts and robberies. Already on 1 March 1692, the Council was asking for troops to control the broken men in the braes of Perthshire.[69] Hill noted a major change in the nature of robberies in Lochaber: '(tho they take up no herships) yet they Comitt Lesser thefts one upon another'. In the southern Highlands, Stewart of Ardvorlich confirmed the observation in 1694: no major raids, but incessant thefts of horses and cattle; poor people unable to afford prosecutions, even when they caught criminals redhanded; and the thieves banding into unofficial watches, to whom tenants paid black-mail of up to 5% of their rents. MacCoul of Kidrogan, the most notorious robber in Atholl during 1691, returned to his Strathardle home and had his cattle-lifting done by Badenoch men, while he himself merely stole sheep, disposed of in an ingenious underground kitchen.[70]

In the North-East, however, there was at least one major raid in mid-1693 by Keppoch Macdonalds and Frasers on Strathspey, with the watch there, headed by local gentry, secretly conniving. Keppoch showed willingness to make some redress, but the Frasers, despite casualties, recaptured their share of the stolen cattle from troops sent to seize it.[71] The Blind Harper, exiled for his indiscreet Jacobitism by Macleod to mainland Glenelg, tried to preserve his cattle by flattering the clans most likely to steal them — Camerons, Macdonalds of

Keppoch and Glengarry, Mackenzies, Macraes, and the broken Macphees and Macmillans beside Loch Arkaig.[72] Domhnall of Bohuntin, a kinsman of Keppoch, was probably now at the height of his career, raiding over a very wide area — probably mostly in the North — without a permanent base.[73] According to tradition, there was boat-borne cattle raiding in the Outer Hebrides in 1694.[74]

As a first step to establishing a court capable of checking robberies, the Council confirmed Hill's acceptance in March 1692 of a deputation from Mackintosh as Steward of Lochaber. Mackintosh's authority, however, covered only a quarter of the country. In August, Hill put forward his detailed plans for reviving the jurisdiction of Inverlochy. He warned emphatically that the Council must fix a limit beyond which retrospective prosecutions were forbidden, and decide how far the Indemnity or Jacobite orders could cover wartime raids; otherwise, the establishment of a court would merely drive the clans to desperation and increase disorder. Meanwhile, he sent notorious thieves whom he had no authority to hang as levies to Flanders.[75]

The Council prepared to revive a Commission of Justiciary on the 1680s model, and on 28 July appointed a committee headed by Breadalbane and Tarbat to prepare one, checking sheriff courts until the Commission's guidelines on the Indemnity were decided. On 11 August the proposals were presented to the Council, suggesting as commissioners Argyll, Breadalbane, Hill and Tarbat (replaced, when he refused, by Mackenzie of Coul). Loosely drawn, they gave so much power to single members — a deliberate plan by Breadalbane to dominate the Commission — that Fountainhall and Stair doubted their legality. Argyll protested at the inclusion of his regality, Argyllshire, though offering to give private commissions to those named. 'I wish you Could adjust that matter by his deputation to hill,' wrote Johnston to Dalrymple. In November, Tweeddale had strong hopes that the Commission would pass, but it was stuck: William was very reluctant to grant one which excluded Argyllshire, but could find no alternative precedent except during the forfeiture.[76]

Breadalbane's hope of dominating the Commission was merely one branch of his scheme for a highland militia 3,000 strong, to be maintained on the savings from disbanding the independent companies. He did not present it to William (who rejected a similar lowland scheme), but, as continued peacefulness in the Highlands obscured the effects of Glencoe, he continued to hope and rebuild Kilchurn. His opponents were aware of his scheme, and suspected it of having Jacobite aims.[77] This encouraged Johnston, who had a lowlander's opinion of highland honesty, to accept the old 'presbyterian' argument that the Achallader agreement had been unnecessary, and that its terms should therefore be restricted — or ignored. Even Farquharson of Inverey and his followers, who had duly fulfilled the requirements of the Indemnity, were harassed until 1693.[78] Breadalbane naturally became its champion in Council, and worked for mildness even towards those who had refused it. In August, for instance, he introduced a petition from his old opponents Ballechin, his brother and Colin Mackenzie, who were still absconding in the Highlands, endorsed their nonsensical claim that remoteness had prevented them from hearing of the Indemnity, and obtained a session to receive their submission. They failed to attend. Colin Mackenzie finally surrendered only in 1694. By May 1693, both Steuart brothers had been committed at separate times, probably through the Atholl family's influence, to the Canongate Tolbooth, where they remained until July 1697. The Reverend Robert Steuart, however, who had submitted in time, re-established himself in Balquhidder parish despite Lord Murray.[79]

Breadalbane's scheme lost credibility in October 1692 when the Captain of Clanranald, despite a favourable reception at Court, crossed to St. Germain. Hill, who had trusted him, wrote demanding that he be made an example, and both Secretaries responded. Johnston obtained a fund of £150 a year for Fort William out of the estate; but, after two years, Sir Donald Macdonald, who had a wadset over Moidart and Arisaig, and other creditors with claims took over nearly all the lands.[80] Dalrymple's scheme was more extravagant. Sir John Maclean had managed to get his delay in surrendering overlooked. As Hill had said, he was 'really the finest Gentleman of his age ... both for person, partes & breeding ... in all the highlands, & I have Confidence when the King sees him, he will be kynd to him, (as most yt know him are)'.[81] William was anxious to preserve his family — claiming to be Charles's legitimate successor, he had assumed the responsibility to recompense them for Inverkeithing — but had no money to pay Argyll. Dalrymple suggested that the Macleans should instead be given the Clanranald estates, which would force them to become loyal Williamites. Sir John tactfully raised only the practical objections: as the Macdonalds thrice outnumbered the Macleans, he could never hold it, and his throat would be cut. Alternatively Argyll might transfer his claims wholesale to the Clanranald estate and conquer it, which would merely continue his existing feud with the Macdonalds over Kintyre; but Argyll refused. In either case, Dalrymple declared, an example must be made, to prevent other chiefs from following the Captain: 'it seems good that sept ... of that dangerous clan of M'Donald, wherof the yeomans ar as weill papists as the heritors and chiftan, ... wer rooted out for the rest of the hylands who ar unruly for the disapointment of the mony aught'. The outrageous proposal, echoing in attitude and even language the orders which had led to the Massacre, shows how deep-rooted was Dalrymple's hostility to the Macdonalds — and how closely connected with their catholicism, for he added his hope that the papists Gordon and Seaforth should be forfaulted for treason. His alternative to Breadalbane's scheme indicated how far apart their attitudes were: the Williamite Mackays and Forbeses should be granted Dunfermline's estate, which would enable them to raise 1,200 reliable men.[82]

Hill was ordered to garrison Clanranald's Castle Tirrim, and did so. When the independent companies were absorbed into forces raised for Ireland, his regiment alone occupied the Highlands, with outposts also at Duart, Carnaburg, Eilean Donan, Invergarry, Inverness, Ruthven and (until 1694) Blair and Finlarig. This was a restricted military presence in comparison with Cromwell's days, when there had been garrisons at Stornoway and Thurso, and it reflected the comparatively limited area of open rebellion. Yet it was the first more than haphazard government control the Central Highlands had known for thirty years.

Although the government still theoretically feared a highland rising, large drafts were taken from Hill's regiment from 1692 onwards, which, with the heavy losses from sickness, left it composed mainly of reluctant recruits.[83] Military occupation probably created less instability than office-holding by pro-Revolution heads of minority clans in neighbouring shires, like Balnagown's tyranny over the Mackenzies in Ross.[84]

Meanwhile, the 'episcopalians' played into their enemies' hands. Groundless rumours had reached William that the £12,000 had never left London and that Breadalbane had embezzled the £500 lost in the exchange. In August, Dalrymple wrote to him that unless he vindicated himself he would have to repay the £2,000 also, and would never be trusted again. He decided to go to London. Tarbat accompanied him, allegedly to disprove accusations of favouring Jacobites, really, it seems, to present an address from the episcopalian clergy. In mid-September, William's normal prohibition to Privy Councillors to leave Scotland (and bother him, understood) arrived, and they hurriedly departed before Tweeddale could officially inform them. Breadalbane, at least, might have pleaded justification, but they foolishly lied to Mary that they had not known of the prohibition. Their enemies exposed the lie, and, although the accusations against Breadalbane were dropped, William saw them only to order them home.[85] Within a few months, the 'episcopalians' had lost much of their original favour, and the initiative had passed to Johnston, who had constantly claimed that only the 'presbyterians' were really loyal to William.

Johnston had organised William's English intelligence network before the Revolution, and his strongest card was his exploitation of secret information. What he obtained was actually rather poor. Macky had blown his cover in giving warning of the invasion, and Johnston employed mainly the same worthless perjurers who had deceived Melville. Johnston was only partly deceived; but he used them. This made him fairly exceptional among William's ministers, who did not knowingly instigate false accusations; but since Titus Oates's time it had been common among some sections of Opposition Whigs, Johnston's English allies. He had been spied on himself for supposed links with Montgomerie, and had no scruples about retaliating in kind.[86] His scapegrace brother Alexander largely managed his intelligence activities for him, and developed a fine skill in entrapping and bullying suspects.[87] Perhaps because Alexander served as a buffer, and because the rogues Johnston used were small-minded, they never by flattering his prejudices tricked him into unconsciously dancing to their tune, as Simon Fraser did the Second Duke of Queensberry in 1703.

To gain a true understanding of Jacobitism, however, Johnston proceeded

> not by downright informations, which a man rarely gets and which come only by knaves, who often impose, but . . . by laying together in ones own mind a multitude of matters of fact . . . which require much thought and observation to reason upon them, but when a man does yt right the conclusion follows naturally and a man is scarcely deceived.[88]

Following these principles led Johnston to construct and believe, like most intelligence agencies, a picture of a tireless, coherent, omnipresent and dangerous enemy movement far more alarming than real Jacobitism.

To make both investigation and exploitation of Jacobitism effective, Johnston needed to have his men in the key posts of Advocate and Justice-Clerk. After Fountainhall's refusal, every lesser 'episcopalian' candidate feared that becoming Advocate would turn all his own abler rivals against him. Johnston's candidate was always James Steuart, 'Jamie Wylie', a former Whig collaborator with James, a rogue despite his high reputation among Presbyterians. Against violent Tory opposition, he got him chosen in November.[89] On 1 December, he persuaded William to appoint as Justice Clerk Cockburn of Ormiston, an extreme bigot, to carry out at the Edinburgh end Johnston's police duties.[90]

Johnston was now preparing his decisive stroke. He made a conciliatory approach to Queensberry — a sign of the gap between the 'episcopalian' ministry and its original magnate supporter. On 2 December, he wrote a crucial letter to Tweeddale, to be carried by Steuart. Breadalbane, Tarbat and Dalrymple, he warned, had attacked him. Bad advisers were betraying him. Despite the 'presbyterians" obvious faults, he must join them to overthrow the crypto-Jacobites, and, if possible, detach Queensberry from his colleagues to counterbalance Duke Hamilton, whom William considered it in his interest to bring back into the government.[91]

Just afterwards, Johnston learned, to his incredulous horror, that a dispute over the Edinburgh city elections, which the 'presbyterians' had shamelessly rigged, had come before the Council, and that Tweeddale and the majority had decided against them and allowed an immediate fresh election. William's letter ordering them to wait arrived soon afterwards.[92] Johnston's plan of overthrowing the 'episcopalians' was temporarily shattered. He considered that Tweeddale, for whom he immediately substituted a bowdlerised version of his former letter, had betrayed him, and did not fully trust him again until 1695.[93] He instantly set himself to force through a reversal of the decision, undermining William's belief in Tweeddale's impartiality. As he once frankly admitted, he cared nothing for the legal rights of the case. He inquired whether the election was any more illegal than usual, but refused to believe evidence that it was. The conciliatory re-election of most of those chosen previously did not mollify him.[94] By exploiting all his influence he managed to get dismissed from their posts and the Council two 'episcopalian' officeholders, one for alleged Jacobite connections — a man excepted from pardon in James's last Declaration.[95]

As so often, the real Jacobites unintentionally came to Johnston's aid, retrospectively justifying a dubious policy. On 24 December, he rejoiced: 'a matter of moment is come into my hands, as it were from heaven'.[96] During December and January, there were constant rumours of a coming invasion from Dunkirk under Jean Bart. In fact, Montgomerie's accusations had so turned the French against Melfort, and James for employing him, that such a mission was unthinkable. Johnston, however, badly misinformed about St. Germain, believed that Louis had supported Melfort, that the danger was real, and, consequently, that there was deep significance in the flurry of conspicuous Jacobite intrigue in

Scotland that winter.[97] Arran and Home staged a reconciliation. Messengers flitted to and fro across the Borders, and Johnston rehabilitated his cousin and chief Annandale by setting him to catch some.[98] Neville Payne wrote asking that an Edinburgh benefactor should be made town clerk there: 'a Line from your Brother [James] doth it'. It was this that Johnston intercepted. He used it as final proof that 'the affair of Edinburgh is a downright plot, and what ever the King doe in it he knows it. The proofs are unanswerable' — a plausible but false logical jump from part to the whole.[99] The supposed plot made him even less sympathetic towards the highlanders, since 'the uniting of the popish highland interest in Scotland with the Lancashire ... popish interest in Engl together is their present project'.[100]

The appointment of Steuart and Ormiston, extending Johnston's intelligence network, alarmed the Jacobites, and, having furnished him much useful information, they subsided even before the invasion alarm died down. Arran even made indirect approaches to Johnston. The Archbishop of Glasgow, lying untried in Edinburgh Castle since 1691, was their other potential leader. William was determined to persist in prosecuting Gordon and other Jacobites, particularly Seaforth and Clanranald; but he naturally wished to avoid trying a leading churchman, and through Tweeddale persuaded Paterson in late January to accept voluntary banishment from Scotland.[101]

Johnston persuaded William not to delay changes. The most important was to bring Hamilton back into the ministry, where, Johnston was confident, despite his episcopalian faith he might be a vital reinforcement for the 'presbyterians'. Yet, although William accepted his return as necessary to counterbalance Queensberry and to strengthen the government, his absence during the crisis had taken much explaining away. Johnston and Portland warned that his delays in returning to Council now while he made further personal demands risked permanently alienating William, 'and the offers of others who offer ther whole families will be accepted he cannot offer but a half of his'.[102] Finally he came on 19 January. He was to be restored to the Treasury as part of the bargain, and Dalrymple hoped that this would cause the dismissal of either Linlithgow or Breadalbane.[103] This was almost the only point in which he failed. 'The prize is wone. The tyde is turned', rejoiced Alexander Johnston on 2 February. William ordered that the second Edinburgh election should be reversed, and that Tweeddale must find a formula to save the Council's face. Annandale was restored to the Council. Hamilton was to preside in Tweeddale's absence and be Commissioner if there was a parliament; Tweeddale complained that William must be frightened of the Duke. The only sign of balance was William's insistence that Sir James Ogilvie should be Solicitor, 'to have his Lawyers presbiterian and Episcopall'.[104]

At the start of March, William was hesitating whether to hold a Parliament, a short session under Hamilton after his own departure. Dalrymple and his English supporters struggled vainly to dissuade him. Breadalbane wrote to Nottingham that there was little real danger of invasion and therefore no need. The changes had left three 'presbyterians' to every 'episcopalian' in the government, and they now had a head, Hamilton, who would be 'the most unacceptable man in the nation' as Commissioner.[105] Nottingham was so concerned over Scottish affairs that he was taken by surprise when William appointed members of the Whig Junto in England. Johnston rejoiced: 'So if English must medle in our affairs ther will be fair play at least'. Carmarthen admitted to Breadalbane, 'his majesty consults the affairs of that nation with none of this', and Johnston's unscrupulous interception of the 'episcopalians'' correspondence soon made them stop writing to the Tory ministers.[106]

There were conflicting opinions as the instructions for the session were hastily prepared, although all agreed that an act was needed to make the Church admit former episcopalian clergy on easier terms. William considered a paper from Hamilton which suggested reversing some important concessions made in 1690, enabling the Officers of State to vote on committees, and replacing the fining and imprisonment of Papists and Nonjurors by merely the payment of double cess.[107] The open or secret instructions drawn up by Johnston with advice from Hamilton in Scotland incorporated the attempts to restore the prerogative, and called for the raising of more standing forces, perhaps compensated by temporarily disbanding the militia. Proposals (presumably Johnston's) in the drafts to compensate instead by appointing a Committee of Public Accounts — like the one which formed the nucleus of the English Country Opposition — and to bring about a union between England and Scotland at least in peace and war (already in practice the case) and trade, were ignored, but anticipate some of his policies in 1695. However, Jacobites and Nonjurors were to be shown no favours, correspondence with France was to be forbidden, and going and staying there made treason.[108]

An act was to clarify to whom the allegiance and assurance should be put, including all clergy who had not yet taken them. Johnston, seeing the danger from immediate confrontation, proposed that the Council should have discretion whether to put them to ministers, but Dalrymple insisted that the Episcopalians would certainly take them if they were also put to the Presbyterians. He was probably gambling that the latter would break out in some spectacular disavowal of William's authority that could be represented as rebellious.[109] To reconcile ordinary Presbyterians to the church acts, William gave instructions for a more genuinely democratic election of parish ministers by the heritors than the notorious 1690 act allowed.[110]

The secret instructions, besides ordering the act to empower William to call and dissolve General Assemblies and permitting reforms in the Session but not a challenge to its composition, directed Hamilton to discover from the leading members whether eight months' cess for life could be obtained for William (an obsession with him, since James had received a life cess in 1685); but, if it was unlikely, he was to hinder anybody from proposing it, 'for above all things you are to mind the point of reputation'. Another emphasised that he must prevent any misunderstanding between King and Parliament; and this sensitivity made Johnston add an instruction which the Jacobites had inspired.[111]

In mid-April 1692 the Edinburgh Jacobites had written a short, fairly accurate account of the Massacre, incorporating Hamilton's and Duncanson's orders. Perhaps lacking a press of their own, they sent it to Charles Leslie, a Scots-Irish Anglican cleric in London, and Johnston reported early in May that it was being prepared for printing.[112] However, the Jacobites thought such propaganda unnecessary when James himself was about to return and avenge Glencoe. Only after recovering from the shock of the Hogue did they return to it. An Irish cleric, King, had produced a grossly dishonest book on the Irish Protestants' sufferings under James, particularly valuable to the regime as indicating that adversity had not reformed him. Leslie inserted the 'Letter from a Gentleman in Scotland' in a massive *Answer* to King, the most important book the Jacobites produced that decade on the factual side of their case. On 30 June, he visited Argyll's regiment at Brentford to confirm the story. However, constant harassment of the presses delayed the printing, and the first major pamphlet to mention the Massacre was Sir James Montgomerie's *Great Britain's Just Complaint*, which created a sensation in September 1692.[113]

Montgomerie, a Jacobite for purely negative reasons, had little real belief in the cause, and the pamphlet's biting, valid criticisms were set in a framework of lies. The brief mention of the Massacre his intrigues had helped bring about contrasted the undue favouring of Irish Papists in the Treaty of Limerick with the murder of supposed Scottish Protestants. The Dean of Durham, the hack who produced the official reply in January, ploddingly denouncing both lies and truths, claimed of William's instructions 'A milder and juster Order was never given', and took the instance as a test of Montgomerie's credibility: William had directed that if examples were made, they should be of men guilty of murder and robbery as well as rebellion, and one such clan which had not submitted was accordingly attacked. The one benefit of the immense delay in publishing Leslie's *Answer*, which finally appeared almost a year after the Massacre, was that the 'Letter' refuted this claim instantly.[114] It was merely one of two dozen miscellaneous Appendices of documents supporting pro-Jacobite points, and it was not properly used in the main text. Anti-Catholicism made Leslie a strange Jacobite controversialist. Privately, he criticised King for wholesale lying when the truth about Jacobite Ireland was damning enough — he himself could have written it. The argument exploiting the Massacre was similarly contorted: just as William was presumably not responsible for the Massacre, although he did not punish the soldiers, so James could not personally be blamed for misconduct by his catholic Irish troops. In death, as in life, the Glencoe men were used as pawns to benefit the supposed broader interests of Jacobitism.[115]

However, the 'Letter' had a devastating effect, and Mary felt keenly the imputation against her husband. She and a committee of bishops, who were preparing a formal answer to Leslie, pressed Johnston for an official inquiry, confident that the truth would prove creditable to William. Although Johnston was told that William was fully informed about it and that he would risk losing favour by mentioning it, the pressure made him suggest cautiously that there should be one. William agreed, and Hamilton's secret instructions included one 'with the concurrence of the Chancellor and our Secretary and Advocate or Solicitor ... , to enquire thoroughly into the business of Glencoe and then to resolve what in prudence is to be done for the vindicating the honour of our Government which is so much aspersed upon that account'.[116]

The 'presbyterians' had already been preparing for another session since late 1692, with Sir William Hamilton of Whitelaw organising the burgh members.[117] The real 'manager' was Johnston, rather than the blundering Duke. The Presbyterians, realising that their intransigence had alienated William, were ready to be more conciliatory; yet one chief tactic of Johnston was to pander to their bigots to an extent, a report claimed, which alarmed even Crawford.[118] His main policy, however, was to exploit Jacobitism. He had increased his knowledge since December from Neville Payne's incautious boasting in prison and more intercepted letters. These may have included one from Buchan at St. Germain to Breadalbane reporting that he and Linlithgow were in great favour there and encouraging them to persevere, for in February Johnston wrote to him strongly hinting that William knew of his misdeeds.[119] Ironically, although the government changes had inspired charges that Johnston, a supporter of the Club in late 1689, was bringing the whole Montgomerie Plot into office, it was Dalrymple who now made advances to his old enemy Montgomerie in the hope of gaining some support from the Whig members he still influenced, outflanking Johnston — as insincere a manoeuvre as his 1691 Jacobite promises to Balcarres.[120] For Dalrymple's failure either to attend Parliament (although he refused the offer, to avoid publicly exposing ministerial differences) or to accompany William to Flanders severely shook his credit. One observer considered that Breadalbane took his place as 'episcopalian' leader in Parliament, the 'Highland Czarr' capable of matching the 'Lowland Czarr' Hamilton.[121] This encouraged Johnston in his policy, to discredit the 'episcopalian' leadership as crypto-Jacobite while building an alliance against them of those excluded from power, including even the episcopalian Atholl family and Queensberry.

As an important Jacobite report intercepted that summer showed, this was ironically almost the opposite of the truth. Despite Dalrymple's flirtation with Montgomerie, the Stairs were 'mortal' anti-Jacobites, and Dalrymple's influence over Breadalbane and Linlithgow was so strong that they could not be trusted; while almost all those with whom Johnston was attempting to ally gave some ground for Jacobite hopes, including Tweeddale — 'only he is worse than Proteus' — and Steuart.[122] The report even claimed to be sure of support from Argyll's interest in Scotland and his regiment in Flanders. Yet, whoever the regiment drank to, once they had made their disorderly way there they fought gallantly for William, helping in July to force the French lines at Dottingnies, where Drummond's grenadiers suffered heavily.[123] Although Dalrymple had some influence over him, Johnston managed to gain his support throughout the session. He wrote that, if Argyll would apply himself, he would signify far more politically; but instead he concentrated upon private money-making schemes. Showing complete lack of concern for Scotland's interests, he commissioned a privateer to prey on the Glasgow trade with France. This, being necessary to both the economy and William's revenue, had been connived at, but, if it became notorious, would have to be stopped. His example inspired the English to make similar raids.[124]

Johnston continued his approaches to Queensberry, suggesting that his semi-retirement arose largely from distrust of the 'episcopalian' politicians he had previously supported.[125] Johnston exaggerated this isolation, and Queensberry voted with the 'episcopalians' in Parliament. The intercepted report indicates that he was the crypto-Jacobite, not they, although some of his activity may merely have been precautionary. The one major Williamite influence on him was Drumlanrig, one of Johnston's strongest opponents at Court that winter. He was nevertheless brought into Parliament as 'Lord Treasurer', presumably in the hope that, being primarily a courtier, he would make part of the family interest obey the 'managers'; but he mutinied.[126]

The Jacobite report also claimed that Atholl and Murray would do their utmost for James, but admitted that they professed otherwise. It became one of Johnston's main policies to bring Murray into the government (which involved ensuring that Atholl was neutral) and even to win Arran to the Williamite side. He acted partly to oblige Hamilton, but knew the risk involved, warning him in December that his wisest course for his and both young men's interests would be to ask William to imprison them until the spring was over.[127] Yet Johnston also had strong motives of his own for persevering, the need to secure the backing of some magnate interest for the 'presbyterians' and — a characteristic again visible in his ignominious 1704 return to politics — a desire that young nobles should develop their talents in serving their country and the Revolution regime rather than wasting them on plotting. Like Andrew Fletcher (who, predictably, hated him), he could sometimes inspire them with his own ideals and energy. If Murray could be persuaded to take the oaths, he could be relied on, for he was known for keeping his word and he would bring enough support for the regime, when combined with Argyll's, to secure it in the Highlands.[128] By pointing out to Atholl that the family's enemies would certainly accuse Murray of complicity in Arran's intrigues, but that he and Lord James Murray were willing to take the oaths, Johnston obtained his permission for them to do so and his own written word of honour not to conspire.[129] Arran wrote to Johnston of his desire to submit. Prudent Williamites and Jacobites both avoided trusting him; but, to conciliate Hamilton and his father-in-law Sunderland (a possible English Secretary), and in case he might be reclaimed, Johnston avoided arresting him for the moment, even though it was largely with evidence of his intrigues that he hoped to mould the session.[130]

Parliament assembled on 18 April. The extent of disaffection was visible in the roll: the heritors of Angus had totally refused to elect shire members, and only threats of punishment later coerced a small quorum into doing so.[131] A Committee for the Security of the Nation, twenty-seven strong, was chosen, composed almost entirely of 'presbyterians'. Johnston claimed that he had wanted to balance them with Queensberry and others, but was warned that it would cause controversy. Hamilton immediately laid before them a memorial emphasising (like his speech) the dangers of invasion and the need for fresh forces and supplies.[132]

Johnston managed the Committee's activities. He informed them that the rumours of invasion were no government trick; the evidence was entirely convincing but largely confidential. A sub-committee of three, including Annandale, examined it and reported their general impression. The Committee was satisfied and made its report, calling for the grant of £105,000 sterling over eighteen months (the time the war was expected to last) in addition to the taxes already being collected — an incredible sum by pre-war standards — to pay for raising six new regiments of foot and dragoons, bringing the standing forces up to 6,000, the number allegedly mentioned for the proposed invading army. Their subsidiary report claimed that they had proof that an invasion had been planned, that rebel forces had been organised for a rising and manifestos concerted, and that Jacobite interests had been behind the Edinburgh election disputes.[133] Even though the main financial recommendations were accepted, this claim provoked major controversy. Stair and other 'episcopalians', secretly assured by Jacobite contacts that the letters were forgeries, demanded their production. On 2 May, Payne's and other letters and the sub-committee's report were read: Johnston spoke for three hours on Jacobite plots, with the rules of debate specially suspended. When he explained that the sub-committee's claim about Edinburgh meant only that James's interests had been carried on in a hidden manner, Parliament accepted the report by three to one.[134]

The letters provided genuine evidence of intrigues; but there was justification also for 'episcopalian' scepticism over 'our grand Plot' ('Noe man did ever see it, /Till Johnston christened it by vote'), and for Dalrymple's warning that inventing sham plots might drive men into real ones.[135] The rumours, boasts and irrational acts typical of many Jacobites were blended with more solid evidence to create a picture of a coherent, alarming conspiracy. The alleged manifesto, discovered among the Nonjuring cleric Robert Calder's papers that March, was one example. He had actually written it for Sir Peter Fraser's fantasy plot in 1691.[136] Claiming that the rebels' aim was merely to defend episcopacy, not to overthrow William, it was useless for a rising which was to start on a French invasion. Yet Johnston, rather than admit this, convinced himself that Calder was not the real author, although remaining determined to convict and even hang him if he would not confess. On William's orders, the prosecution continued even when all others collapsed; but the judges fortunately refused to stretch the law.[137]

Johnston's policy was, his letters show, partly deliberate alarmism to divert Parliament from attacking William's 'episcopalian' ministers, particularly Stair for biased judgements and Dalrymple for 'illegal orders', including Glencoe. Instructions from Flanders further limited the 'managers'' options: 'since nothing is to be done to gratify the parliament, I mean, nothing that they reckon a gratification, there remained no handle by which to work on them, but to begett in them a conviction of the danger they are in', although he knew that the supposed invasion plans had collapsed several months earlier.[138]

However, Johnston was not acting cynically; his capacity for suspecting Jacobitism made that unnecessary. He became genuinely convinced in April that the danger of invasion had revived. Lord Middleton crossed to St. Germain to become chief minister for James, who then issued a liberal Declaration. The French had exerted pressure for both. In fact, no longer intending to give him military support themselves, they wanted him to make compromise terms for a restoration with English politicians; but it seemed far more plausible to both Jacobites and ministers, including Dalrymple, that this heralded an invasion.

Even rumours of one intended in the West which the ministers disbelieved (but must still guard against) increased the tension.[139] An alleged page of Melfort's, captured in April, gave details of supposed recent plotting implicating the 'episcopalians' — and, inconveniently, Annandale and Queensberry. Johnston, although admitting that some of his statements were certainly lies, used others to supplement information on Payne's plot.[140] He may originally have intended to behave as a conventional Court 'manager', imparting Hamilton's instructions to Tweeddale, Queensberry and Stair, but his spymaster's attitude, inflaming his Whig distrust of 'episcopalians', quickly drove him into more ambiguous relations with Parliament. He prevented addresses against ministers, but his own accusations to Carstares, for instance, that Tarbat was trying to sell his place because he knew Middleton's invasion plan, served the same purpose.[141]

The immense supply Johnston frightened Parliament into granting had this ambiguity. Some 'episcopalians' at first organised opposition to taxation and the raising of troops. This insincere 'Country' alliance, their one chance of gaining a majority (and sabotaging the session) Johnston destroyed with his evidence of Jacobitism.[142] The 'episcopalian' leaders then pressed Hamilton to obtain William a cess for life. Important members agreed that after the eighteen months grant this was impossible, justifying him by his instructions in preventing any attempt. When Linlithgow nevertheless made one, Queensberry stayed away, Breadalbane left, Parliament refused even to minute it and Tweeddale, who had been Linlithgow's ally, broke with him as merely trying to discredit the 'presbyterians' with William at the risk of discrediting William. Johnston wrote that they dared not make such a grant with 'episcopalian' traitors in the Treasury.[143] There was probably some truth in the 'episcopalians'' counter-claim that the 'managers' had introduced their grant partly to make impossible serious discussion of one which would make William independent of Parliament, without directly defying him.[144] Johnston emphasised that the money, though not formally appropriated, was assumed to be for new regiments, and wrote at length on the choice of colonels, 'presbyterians' who could defend Scotland against treachery as well as invasion. His suggestions included Murray and the reluctant Grant, since their regiments and followers, with Argyll's, could keep the Highlands secure.[145]

Not all clashes with the 'episcopalians' were deliberate. Hamilton furiously denounced in Parliament Stair's bland lies about his legal malpractices, but the 'managers' prevented the reforms which these made necessary from becoming attacks on him.[146] However, the act for putting the allegiance and assurance to clergy, officeholders and some others (including nobles and their eldest sons, to prevent the traditional balancing act) emphasised the rift, though in an unexpected form. The 'episcopalians', finding that the presbyterian clergy were not likely, as they had supposed, to refuse, which would leave episcopalian clergy and other Nonjurors vulnerable, opposed it, temporarily winning over Hamilton. Yet, failing in this, they tried to have it put to all heritors, hoping that enough would be forced to qualify to provide an electorate which might choose an 'episcopalian' parliament. Hostile heritors were already organising, and Johnston, remembering the 1692 débâcle, instead had the act empower the Council to put the allegiance and assurance to what heritors they chose, fining refusers up to a year's valued rent (which gave great scope for vendettas). The 'episcopalians' assumed that Johnston feared creating an electorate favourable to them; he, that they wanted a public mass refusal to weaken William's regime.[147] Each side really hoped to use the act to discredit the other with William.

The 'episcopalians' had an unexpected tactical ally. Melville, alienated by the Johnston ministry's failure to restore him to some power, unsuccessfully tried to unite the more extreme Presbyterians against the act. Fresh mortifications for his family that autumn drove him on, but his private hostile notes on other politicians still show greater mistrust of the 'episcopalians', as crypto-Jacobites.[148] However, his relations with Tarbat encouraged his drift, and his tactic to gather an 'interest', appealing to the 'presbyterians'' church interests at the expense of the more Whiggish political feelings Johnston exploited, suited one of the 'episcopalians'' strongest concerns, defence of the prerogative. Melville's family followed him in his volte-face without hesitation.

Johnston also made concessions to the bigots. There was no attempt to give William power over General Assemblies, because, he claimed, this would have exposed Dalrymple's responsibility for illegally dissolving the 1692 one. The act reforming the election of parish ministers was drafted but went no further.[149] Johnston might argue that sacrifices were necessary to make possible the act for settling the church, passed on 8 June. He claimed that he relied on 'episcopalian' folly for its success: Linlithgow and Tarbat spoke so violently against it that the Presbyterians assumed it must be good and blindly voted for an erastian act which allowed Parliament ultimate authority over the composition of the ministry. It admitted all who accepted the Confession of Faith and presbyterianism as 'the only government of this church'; and Johnston minimised in his justifications the importance of the one remaining loophole, the power to reject scandalous and disorderly ministers.[150]

Accused of raising 'heats', Johnston claimed that his exposure of plotting had frightened the crypto-Jacobites into obedience within Parliament. He was determined to follow it up and, if possible, execute some recent conspirators, since 'the lenity of the government encourages men to go on from plot to plot, which at last must end in a rebellion'. An act was passed making going to or remaining in France treason. Neville Payne, who knew the secrets of all Jacobite factions, must be convicted, to confess or be made the example. Since the Jacobite codenames in his letters, although transparent, could not be proved in the regular courts, he must be tried in Parliament.[151] So must Gordon and Seaforth, since Gordon's international stature and his arrest within the Empire made publicity obligatory. When Hamilton's reluctance to harm his cousin Gordon made William send orders to try both, not only Hamilton but Tweeddale protested that Gordon's moderation in 1689 would make it unpopular.[152] Meanwhile, the heaviest blow against Scottish Jacobite organisation was dealt, for all Johnston's boasting, accidentally. Arran had promised not to conspire, and Johnston was still trying to win him over. Hamilton, on Steuart's and others' advice, had left him free, but, summoned before the Council to take the allegiance and assurance, he absconded on 22 May, fearing imprisonment and, perhaps, examination for Payne's trial. Again leaving his Jacobite underlings in the lurch, he fled to England and Sunderland's protection, not returning to Scotland until 1699.[153] For all his faults, he was indispensable as Jacobite leader. Jacobites at St. Germain allegedly could only suggest Home, Southesk and Sinclair, as a stopgap.[154] Payne's trial would have concluded the session dramatically, but, the night before, he sent out messages threatening, if condemned, to denounce all 'from the greatest to the Lowest in parlt' who had had Jacobite dealings. Those not afraid for themselves, including Hamilton and Tweeddale, feared for their sons, and, despite Johnston's protests, they drew out proceedings and finally remitted him, Gordon and Seaforth, to the Justice Court.[155] Parliament then drew up a letter to William which, without definite charges, warned him that the session would be fruitless unless he animated his government with a well-disposed spirit, obviously implying dismissal of the 'episcopalians'. It also requested a Scottish title for Portland.[156]

One major act was passed after the letter. William's instructions, inspired by the Council's pleas, left to Parliament settling the bounds of the Highland Justiciary and creating a jurisdiction at Fort William. The 'presbyterian' Committee for Security brought forward an act on that last crowded day. It decreed that Argyll and other holders of regalities should, for two years, grant private commissions to the persons named in the official ones. It extended the landlords' and chiefs' obligation to give bond for preventing depredations to ones for maintaining public peace. And, abruptly, it restored the 1633 act against the Clan Gregor, once again banning the name of Macgregor. No opposition is recorded, although Argyll, the Macgregors' patron, was on the committee. Rather than being provoked by fresh clan activity, this was probably merely the harshest of the conventional measures to which regimes hostile to the highlanders automatically turned. The act was rushed, since William's offer to let Parliament appoint the urgently needed Commissioners of Justiciary was not taken up. The ban did not prevent the Macgregors from electing a new chief a few months later.[157] The instructions also suggested that Parliament should find means of recompensing wartime sufferers, perhaps from the forfeited estates; but it merely gave a list of them to the Council.[158] Sessions concerned with investigation usually neglected legislation.

Meanwhile, a very different inquiry begun at the same time as Johnston's Jacobite scare had been proceeding. Some members anxious to attack Dalrymple had declared that they would investigate Glencoe in Parliament, and Hamilton anticipated this by holding an authorised inquiry. Livingston ordered Hill to send copies of his orders and an account of his proceedings. In early May, it was decided that he should come to Edinburgh to testify, and Livingston wrote to Lieutenant-Colonel Hamilton revealing his contempt for the inquiry — 'It is not that any body thinks that thieving tribe did not deserve to be destroyed' — and for Hill's reluctance to execute the orders in 1692. In Edinburgh, Hill showed the orders and letters sent him — more than he would reveal in 1695 — and Livingston displayed those sent him. The inquiry went no further.[159]

Late in June, a further request from the bishops anxious to answer Leslie made

Johnston and the other officers of state examine the documents — the first time they had seen any orders higher than Lieutenant-Colonel Hamilton's. Johnston was shocked at the tone of Dalrymple's letters but admitted that he could not be linked with the manner of execution. Both he and Hamilton believed that Breadalbane was also responsible, deducing this, despite his 1692 protestations, from the references in Dalrymple's January letters and an interview with Ardkinglas. From this in turn they deduced that MacIain must have been prominent in overthrowing the negotiation.[160] However, although the good 'presbyterian' Livingston's critical order to Lieutenant-Colonel Hamilton and letters to Hill showed clearly enough his attitude, Johnston assured him that winter 'The business of Glenco can never concern you'. In 1695, he would make good this guarantee.[161] William's orders of 16 January took the ministers somewhat aback. Johnston wrote: 'The King can be easily acquited of the affair of Glenco. The Instructions if publisht would do that, but then if others be not persuaded all recurrs'. Hamilton emphasised that Dalrymple had illegally made William both superscribe and subscribe the Additional Instructions. Lord Advocate Steuart, instructed to draw up a report based on the documents (careless, as well as tendentious), exploited this. He argued that William's order about the Macdonalds, being restricted by previous clauses to apply merely if they still held out, was thus so conditional that it was only a statement, not an order. In case this sophistry was unconvincing, he argued that Dalrymple had made William sign the Instructions twice 'on purpose to decline the odium which he foresaw would Inshew upon the badd use that some were to make of these papers', and that he had known that MacIain had taken the oath.[162] Steuart's 'Impartiall Account' was sent to Archbishop Tillotson; but the English bishops presumably shared Johnston's doubts over the Instructions, for no reply to Leslie's *Answer* appeared. On returning to London in August, however, Johnston spoke to Mary about Glencoe, naming some officers who he thought should be cashiered. She replied that they should be hanged.[163]

The real Jacobites rejoiced over the session as having deepened the divisions within Scotland. Some disruptions probably arising from Johnston's emphasis on invasions and plots, such as outbreaks of irrational Jacobite optimism and use of charges of Jacobitism in private vendettas, were accidental;[164] others were not. The Council began to put the allegiance and assurance to those on bail, imprisoning dozens who refused. On 27 May they issued a list of others to be summoned, highland and lowland. The underlying intention to discredit the 'episcopalians' was shown most clearly by the inclusion of Balcarres, whose close contacts with former colleagues, particularly Linlithgow, would implicate them in his refusal. The result was even more satisfactory: Balcarres fled abroad, even though he was obliged to drift about Holland and Denmark for a year, not daring to go to St. Germain until his enemy Melfort was dismissed in mid-1694.[165] The highlanders named were chiefly those in the North on the edge of the inconclusive 1689–90 campaigns or too far off for Hill to summon effectively to Fort William. Sir John Maclean, the only chief from Lochaber they named had, admittedly, been in Edinburgh; but they had a more sinister purpose.[166]

After the ridiculous Clanranald proposals were dropped, William, as usual, postponed a decision. The Maclean historians claim, implausibly, that he offered Sir John a regiment. Finally, the morning that he left for Holland, he informed Johnston that he had decided to fulfil the 1680 agreement, and that meanwhile Sir John should receive £500 a year from his estate. When he arrived in Edinburgh in late April, the order was challenged as inadequate, and Johnston would not enforce it. It was later claimed that he threatened to send him to the Castle. Declaring his intention to appeal to William in Flanders, Sir John hastened his departure on 26 May to avoid having the allegiance and assurance put to him. In London, Mary allegedly told him that she had been sent reports that he had gone to raise a rebellion in the Highlands. He left for Flanders on 10 June.[167] However, Johnston's treatment had driven him to despair that William's intentions would be fulfilled, and he slipped away to St. Germain. Ironically, Sir John's panegyrists have been unjust to him in claiming that this was a snap decision made in the expectation that William's crushing defeat at Landen on 19 July (where Clanranald fought among the French) would lead to a restoration. In fact, on 14 July (NS) Sir Alexander Maclean wrote from the French army that Sir John was already at St. Germain. Alexander Johnston claimed that he had carried messages from other British Jacobites. At St. Germain he applied to Melfort, to the regret of the anti-Melfordian Sir Alexander.[168]

This, of course, ended all William's plans for preserving any Maclean independence. The clan appealed for advice to Hill, and he told them to settle with Ardkinglas, who was acting as Argyll's representative. That summer, Argyll again had Goodwin Wharton diving, unsuccessfully, at Tobermory. In September, Ardkinglas was in Mull, which he reported peaceful. He proposed that the Macleans should compound for the long arrears they theoretically owed Argyll with two years' rent, but accepted their counter-offer of one year's. Only one minor gentleman was defiant.[169] Several Macleans were commissioned in William's army in 1696–7. They had few alternatives, for Argyll's policy was to make his tacksmen refuse to lease land to the clan gentry.[170] In early 1698, Sir John applied in Paris to Portland for permission to return, but was peremptorily refused. An attempt in 1703 caused his capture in England.[171] The Macleans remained in despair, with their chief exiled, their gentry driven out, and their episcopalian ministers silenced.[172] Yet visitors did not see this inner disorientation reflected outwardly. It was in 1698 — not 1688 as always believed — that the romantic William Sacheverell, also treasure-hunting at Tobermory, admired the people, who were apparently still allowed to carry arms, for their 'generous air of freedom, and contempt of these trifles, luxury and ambition, which we so servilely creep after'.[173]

On 27 June, the Council ordered Hill to administer the allegiance and assurance to the chiefs, and to imprison refusers. Most could not swallow the assurance. Dalrymple wrote that all except Lochiel, who hoped for present favours from William, had absconded from alarm at Maclean's usage; the order was folly if there *was* a danger of invasion. Cluny's refusal forfeited the credit from his elaborate double dealing during 1691, for at the next crisis, in 1696, he was treated as an enemy.[174] Sir Donald Macdonald, certain that either prison or having to pay a year's valued rent would ruin him, pretended to be sick in Uist and wrote offering to give bail instead. Hill encouraged the idea, and emphasised that the Highlands were peaceful, entirely occupied in getting together the cess.[175] With a governor less sympathetic to the clans and less trusted by them, the order might have caused needless unrest. By January 1694, most of the chiefs were ready to offer lowland bail. Stewart of Appin, who abused one of Hill's officers, was the only one to suffer long imprisonment, and, transported to Edinburgh, found it wisest to submit in July.[176] The Catholics faced, if anything, a lesser problem, since few expected them to take the assurance. The Glengarry Macdonalds assured Hill of their peaceable intentions, and Glengarry himself offered Atholl and Lovat as his securities. Keppoch did likewise, explaining that he dared not visit the fort. A negotiation with Mackintosh about settling the dispute by his selling Lochaber had recently fallen through, and he feared he would get him imprisoned. However, in October he came in and took both allegiance and assurance.[177] He changed his mind largely because Atholl, who had still not forgiven him and Glengarry for their conduct during the war, violently refused to be their bail. He claimed that it was a plot by Hill to discredit him; let him and Breadalbane look after their 'creatur' Keppoch. Murray, in contrast, was aware of the family's need to rebuild its influence in the Highlands, and on returning next spring, he arranged Glengarry's securities. He applied to Johnston for some favour for him and their brother-in-law Lovat, though without success, and as a good Protestant he provided the unhappy convert with controversial books to win him back.[178] At least by mid-1693, he was also corresponding with MacIain of Glencoe, perhaps merely restoring a pre-Revolution link.[179]

Hill continued working to make Fort William a centre for the West Highlands. He had thieves captured within his limited jurisdiction hanged or sent to Flanders, and, with the help by the local gentry, forced others outside it to restore their spoil.[180] Lochiel and his people were on friendly terms with him. In early 1694 William authorised £30 a year out of the bishops' rents for a school at Fort William for the sons of chiefs and gentry, to instil lowland civilisation and counteract the effects of the catholic schools.[181] It was clear that Breadalbane's highland ambitions no longer threatened the garrison. He began to sell provisions to it from his estates. His defence of the Indemnity, necessary if the Highlands were not to be driven to desperation, increasingly united him and Hill in a quiet rapprochement against lowland 'presbyterians' who expressed constant distrust of the clans. Already in May 1693 Johnston was bracketing 'Inverlochy and Broadalbine' as part of a 'Highland interest ... a bugbear', which Argyll and Murray, united, could make superfluous.[182] Opposition to Murray was a further link. His support for Glengarry's interests brought him into conflict with Hill, and the continuing dispute over Glenlyon made him and Breadalbane increasingly hostile.[183]

Since May, the 'episcopalians' had been undermining Johnston's ecclesiastical policy. Tarbat forged parliamentary minutes and persuaded the northern clergy to stand out — which made them legally liable to deprivation. Dalrymple, though probably wanting the clergy to take the oaths, began a barrage of misrepresentations against the Parliament, over the army, Payne's trial, the chances of a cess for life. In the most notorious instance, he misled Tillotson about the Church Act, and transmitted his first exclamation, that this was an exclusion rather than a comprehension, to influence William.[184] However, William had probably already made his worst Scottish mistake that summer, an order of 8/18 June cancelling almost all the new regiments, which deranged the 'managers" whole patronage network and convinced many 'presbyterians' that the alarm had been merely a trick.[185] Otherwise William (admittedly preoccupied by his defeat at Landen) did nothing to exploit Parliament's actions, and disillusionment spread. Encouraged by Dalrymple, he even ignored the date for which the rebellious 1692 Assembly had appointed its successor. However, leading Presbyterians voluntarily adjourned it to winter — a concession, Johnston wrote, which they would have made for no other monarch.[186] Murray, who had desired a government post rather than a pension, had been promised a Council seat, and had made Lovat take the oaths, but he was now delaying taking them himself, and Johnston feared that he might even finally refuse. The Advocate, always a weathercock, flirted with the Dalrymples. The results of the session were endangered.[187]   Johnston struck back violently, exploiting hints of treason. His agents showed that Dalrymple and his Undersecretary had granted passes overseas to known catholic proselytisers and Jacobite agents.[188] Nottingham was the only English statesman still supporting Dalrymple's allegations. A naval disaster had provoked widespread suspicions that he (almost the only major Tory who apparently *never* made application to James) was a traitor. Johnston had even convinced himself that most Jacobite correspondence with St. German passed through his office.[189] He believed that English changes must precede Scottish ones, and the English Whigs wished to use his methods. Alexander Johnston's false witnesses knew, even unprompted, what was wanted. In October they supplied Wharton, the most unscrupulous of the Junto, with tales of treason for an impeachment. When William returned, Johnston presented to him their charges of stifling plots. William disregarded this, but, to save Nottingham from the impeachment, had to dismiss him.[190]

William heard Hamilton's and Johnston's reports. He 'was inquisitive to know fully that matter of Glenco'. Hamilton informed him, emphasising Dalrymple's failure to countersign the fatal orders. William told Johnston that he could not think about Glencoe without horror; but he took no steps against Dalrymple.[191] Yet Dalrymple's position was weak. Only Breadalbane of his major supporters, by visiting Bath, had escaped the prohibition to leave Scotland. Their tactics included claiming that Murray, then attending in London, was a crypto-Jacobite, an ironic slur since Breadalbane was supposed to be the Scot with most influence at St. Germain.[192] That December, Sir George Barclay secretly approached him. Melfort, under increasing attack from Middleton, wanted to bolster his position with reports from prominent British supporters that the policy he favoured — an immediate French invasion — would succeed. Replying was not necessarily a sign of Jacobite commitment, and Breadalbane, although suggesting that troops might be sent to Scotland (after giving him advance warning) made the soberest reply:

the English Parliament would probably take control of the fleet and improve its effectiveness — a warning Melfort garbled.[193] It brought him no benefit. In 1694, he was dismissed and replaced by Middleton, a lifelong expatriate, who relied on English contacts for a peaceful restoration. Serious Scottish Jacobite activity became even less likely.

The Church Act had angered William against Johnston, and his incredibly foolish self-justification, telling Mary that her husband had either forgotten his own Instructions or changed his mind since, nearly brought about his instant dismissal. Hamilton had hastily to smooth matters for him. Dalrymple's November hopes of a turn towards the 'episcopalians' proved groundless: William admitted that 'the last setlment he had made had not answered his expectation'.[194] However, Johnston's campaign against them collapsed as Hamilton surprisingly turned against him and many fruits of the past session. Johnston's claim that this was merely his familiar ill-temper and personal and family ambition and greed was not the whole truth. He himself proved skilful at obtaining places for supporters, and used Hamilton's temper as a catch-all excuse. Intoxicated by power and guided by Johnston, who, he now realised, had 'tooke more upon him to say things then he had any good warrant for', Hamilton had obtained his majorities from the parliamentary groups he most distrusted, extreme presbyterians and independent barons, and his deep hierarchical prejudices made some reaction certain. Having passed a Church Act likely to destroy the episcopalian clergy, he hoped before the General Assembly to organise moderate Presbyterians to push through a resolution favouring them.[195]

Yet the accusation was largely true, as appeared most clearly in his constant attempts to overthrow Tweeddale and become Chancellor.[196] These drove Tweeddale to attempt an independent alliance with Queensberry, and delayed any expression of his increasing alienation from the 'episcopalians', caused by Dalrymple's rival attempts to make Linlithgow Chancellor.[197] Johnston still wooed Queensberry through appointment to the Session (with Annandale — the first noble intrusion since the Revolution) and to commissions which affected his interests. Coolness towards other 'episcopalians', particularly when they allied with Hamilton, might make him turn to Johnston.[198] However, Hamilton's changes baffled such political calculations. In early December, he let the 'episcopalians' obtain William's promise not to dismiss them and hinted at another session. Their need of one to undo the work of the last — and, therefore, of a Commissioner — was their strong attraction.[199] The appointment to the Session of his relation Sir William Hamilton to counterbalance Stair temporarily carried him back into Johnston's camp, but by February he was again with Dalrymple: he changed sides every month.[200] Meanwhile, in Scotland, Linlithgow managed through Tarbat to make the Melville family support the 'episcopalians'.[201]

Dalrymple remained politically far weaker than this would imply; for, whatever the realignments, Hamilton still worked for Murray's advancement, necessarily in alliance with Johnston.[202] They persuaded William to raise two of the proposed infantry regiments, one under Murray, the other, to Tory dismay, under Crawford's son Lord Lindsay. Murray also received a Council place.[203] He returned to Scotland, where Johnston's patronage of him provoked some protests, and raised his regiment, asking Hill for trained recruits. Lovat was one of his captains, and young Simon Fraser of Beaufort unsuccessfully applied to be another, finally obtaining a commission as lieutenant in 1695. But Murray was still not trusted with the Blair garrison.[204] Raising regiments as a security measure logically suggested other steps, 'disarming all Highlanders, and dismounting all Lowlanders', as Breadalbane complained. Orders for seizing Nonjurors' horses were enforced so unscrupulously that plough-horses were taken. Such actions had been called proofs of tyranny under Charles. Hamilton led the denunciations of the enforcement of acts he himself had just passed as Commissioner.[205]

The decisive struggle came over the General Assembly. William was undecided about holding it, and a debate was held between 'presbyterians', 'episcopalians' and English bishops, with Hamilton excluded — and, at first, Breadalbane, until Bishop Compton demanded him. All 'episcopalian' propaganda for another session, however, broke down on the one point — their clergy would not take the oaths. William at last hurriedly decided to hold it.[206] However, Dalrymple and (from a distance) Tarbat strongly influenced the instructions. The critical point was an order for the ministers to take the allegiance and assurance before the Assembly might sit. It soon became clear that they would not take such an erastian oath; but the order stood, and may have been repeated. For the first time since presbyterianism was established in 1690, there was a real possibility that a fatal breach might develop between Church and King. On both sides were long arrears of mistrust and resentment; even Johnston's Church Act was being portrayed as an 'episcopalian' plot; and, once William's obsession with the prerogative and the Church's with its intrinsic power were aroused, they might easily become trapped in a cycle of rebellion and repression. Carstares or Johnston (probably the former) besieged William in his nightshirt and had the order recalled. The Assembly was a success. The 'episcopalians'' trump card had failed.[207] In April the ambiguous Hamilton died while returning to Scotland (broken-hearted, Johnston claimed, at Dalrymple's lying reports of what William said of him), mourned chiefly by the 'episcopalians'. From then on, Johnston was confident that Dalrymple's dismissal was merely a matter of time.[208]

A Commission of Justiciary for the Highlands was signed by William on 30 December, sent off with many blank names to be filled by the Council, and finally issued on 13 February.[209] It was urgently needed as other legal means proved inadequate. The 'Halket Stirk', for instance, although at last captured in the North-East in 1693, seems to have escaped punishment.[210] Many highland officials probably emulated Breadalbane's chamberlain, who hanged a known murderer without authority rather than risk leaving him to the haphazard central courts.[211]

The Commission, to last for two years, divided the Highlands into northern, middle and southern districts, with Lovat and Grant conveners of the northern, Murray and Breadalbane of the southern. The Commission contained major highland and nearby lowland proprietors, including Argyll and half a dozen leading Argyllshire gentry. The inclusion of magnates and other peers was the

main difference from 1682. However, the only commissioners in Lochaber were
Hill, Hamilton and Cameron of Glendessary, since the government rejected Hill's
nominations, including other Camerons and the Tutor of Appin. The first
meeting, intended for Fort William, lapsed for want of a quorum, and the Council
appointed another for Inverness. Hill's frequently expressed desire 'in the heart of
all the theif holes, to . . . break the neck of robbing and stealing' was again
frustrated.[212] Forbes of Culloden dragged a quorum to Fort William in August,
but by then a greater problem was visible. Innumerable prosecutions against the
highlanders for robberies committed since long before the Indemnity were
revived,

> so that . . . twenty tymes the moveables of all Lochaber will not make vp the
> restitution; and . . . imploy[ing] Colonel Hill's regiment vpon the poynding, wee
> must immediately have a thousand sterveing divills brought to ane absolute necessity
> of stealing to fill ther bellys, and ready to joyn with any change that can better ther
> fortune . . . men must fall into ther old slavery of paying black meall . . . [213]

Glengarry had given his bond answering for his followers with the other chiefs,
but at these lawsuits he began to draw back, urging Lochiel and Keppoch to do
likewise, and in mid-August resumed cattle-raiding. Yet, Forbes argued, the bulk
of highlanders were anxious to live peaceably, and, if this were possible, the chiefs
and gentry would, by their bonds, deliver up the remaining incorrigible thieves.
On the Cromwellian precedent, it would be worth the government's while to buy
out Mackintosh's claims against Keppoch, the main single cause of instability,
even to impose a cess to pay off legitimate recompense for past thefts. In August,
the southern court at Crieff split over the question whether the 1691 Indemnity
'remitts the cryme but not the restitution'. Murray, with the majority, agreed;
Breadalbane opposed. Their personalities and political allegiances matched their
attitudes; but Forbes considered that both also hoped by their interpretations to
increase their highland power, Murray (despite the harm to protégés like
Glengarry) by 'stretching [the jurisdiction] so as multitudes must be made
desperate', Breadalbane 'by enervateing of it so as bad men may dispyse it'. When
both sides applied to William for his definitive interpretation, Forbes warned —
superfluously — against his making a hasty answer. Breadalbane also appealed to
Johnston in London, but he avoided replying. Somehow, the Courts continued to
function.[214]

Despite the government's generally hostile attitude to the highlanders,
permission was given to some of their leaders to return from exile. Since
sequestrated highland estates, 'to which there hath not been tutus accessus', often
produced little profit, there was no significant financial pressure for further
forfaultures. On 19 July, the Advocate was ordered to prosecute Jacobites in
France, including, besides politicians and soldiers, Sir John and Sir Alexander
Maclean, Clanranald and Robertson of Struan.[215] Perth, now banished, was
warned that Lord Drummond would also be indicted. Drummond therefore left
St. Germain for Holland, where he obtained William's pardon and pass in
October. He reached Scotland in February 1695.[216] Although spared the oaths,

he had promised to live quietly; but he became the active head of the Highland Jacobites, remaining so until the '15. In some ways he was unsuitable for the position, as he quickly showed by squandering money and proposing for the most vigorously presbyterian of Hamilton's daughters.[217] In early 1695 Clanranald, having met with 'disappointments' in France, left for Flanders. He could claim that his Jacobite activities while still a minor were the fault of 'evil company'; his Mackenzie bride's sister had married into the Villiers family;[218] and his friends borrowed £40,000 Scots security in England. In 1696 he was allowed back to Scotland, and in 1697 his estates were restored, and he established his elegant (but burdensome) little court in South Uist.[219] Robertson of Struan's mother was permitted to write to him, but, having been forfaulted in 1690, he neglected the opportunity to return.[220]

Two highland magnates greater than Drummond — Gordon and Seaforth — remained in prison after Parliament rose, although their prosecutions were not pursued. William became less implacable towards Gordon on discovering that he had not, as he had supposed, broken his word in 1690. In December 1694, since his health was suffering, he was released into confinement within Edinburgh.[221] Seaforth, although likely if tried to be acquitted, remained a prisoner, perhaps through difficulties over security for £2,000 feu duties he owed for Lewis. In January 1695, when most of the Council favoured his petition for bail, Annandale got it rejected. In August, they wrote to William recommending his release; but, with characteristic bad timing, he chose that month to escape from Edinburgh Castle, not being missed for several days. He fled to his own country; but the lack of hue and cry after him indicates that little danger from simple highland Jacobitism was now felt.[222]

NOTES

1. Story, *Carstares*, 223–5; *HMCR Laing*, i, 472–3, ? to Sir R. Anstruther, 1692; Graham, *Stairs*, i, 171–3, Dalrymple to Lothian, 30 Jan. 1692.

2. *Ib.*, 167–8, same to same, 16 Jan. 1692; *ib.*, 175–6, same to same, 10 Feb. 1692; *Marchmont Papers*, iii, 401, Polwarth to Portland, 26 Jan. 1692; *Ib.*, 403–4, same to same, 13 Feb. 1692; *ib.*, 405–6, same to same, 16 Feb. 1692; Wodrow, *Analecta*, i, 203–4; Riley, *King William*, 74–5.

3. *HMCR Finch*, iv, 283, Information v. Provost of Rutherglen; *Gazette de France*, 22 Mar. 1692 (NS), 138–9, Edinburgh report, 1 Mar. (NS); *ib.*, 29 Mar. 1692 (NS), 152–3, Edinburgh report, 8 Mar. (NS); SRO PC 1/48, 70–1.

4. *London Gazette* No. 2744, 25–29 Feb. 1692; SRO SP 3/1 fol. 4, Johnston to Tweeddale, 5 Mar. 1692; *ib.*, GD 112/40/4/3/8, Breadalbane to Carwhin, 5 Mar. 1692.

5. *Ib.*, 40/4/1/10, Glenorchy to same, 26 Mar. 1692; *ib.*, SP 3/1 fols. 6v–7, Johnston to James Steuart, 10 Mar. 1691/2; *CSPD 1691–2*, 166–7, Commissions, 3 Mar. 1692; *HMCR Finch*, iv, 20, list 'putt out'; Graham, *Stairs*, i, 173, Dalrymple to Lothian, 30 Jan. 1692; Riley, *King William*, 75.

6. Burnet, *History*, iv, 210–11; *Scotish Pasquils*, 314–15, Verses on Breadalbane and Queensberry; SRO SP 3/1 fol. 13, Hallsyde's memorial to William, 16 Mar. 1691/2.

7. *Gazette de France*, 19 Apr. 1692 (NS), 188-9, Edinburgh report, 29 Mar. (NS); Luttrell, ii, 396.

8. SRO GD 112/39/1244, Breadalbane to Carwhin, 27 Feb. 1692; *ib.*, 1246, same to same, 8 Mar. 1692; *ib.*, 40/4/3/7, same to same, 1 Mar. 1692; *ib.*, 8, same to same, 5 Mar. 1692.

9. Dalrymple mentioned Hill's report of the Massacre, and a letter from him asking for pay as Governor which he showed to William, as separate items. *Ib; ib.*, 39/1244, same to same, 27 Feb. 1692; *Highland Papers*, 75, Dalrymple to Hill, 5 Mar. 1692.

10. Luttrell, ii, 384; [Leslie], *Answer to King*, App., 58, 'Letter'.

11. *Ib.*, 65; Fountainhall, *Journals*, xxiii; SRO SP 3/1 fol. 17, Johnston to Portland, 22 Mar. 1692; GD 112/40/4/3/10, Breadalbane to Carwhin, 22 Mar. 1692.

12. *Highland Papers*, 75, Dalrymple to Hill, 5 Mar. 1692.

13. SRO GD 112/40/4/3/8, Breadalbane to Carwhin, 5 Mar. 1692; *ib.*, 9, same to same, 17 Mar. 1692.

14. Wimberley, 'Bighouse Papers', *TGSI*, xxi, 133-4, Breadalbane to Barcaldine, 26 May 1692.

15. *Highland Papers*, 109, Report, 20 June 1695; Atholl, *Chronicles*, i, 335, Murray to [Marchioness], 29 May '1693' [1695]; *Orain Iain Luim*, 198-201, 'Murt Ghlinne Comhann'; Foxcroft, *Supplement to Burnet*, 371-2; SRO SP 3/1 fol. 189v, Johnston to Carstares, 4 Aug. 1693; GD 26/xiii/78 fol. 172, Melville's notes; Blair, Atholl MSS, Box 29 I (7) 141, Ld B. Hamilton to Murray, 31 May 1695.

16. SRO GD 112/40/43/3/11, Breadalbane to Carwhin, 26 Mar. 1692.

17. *Ib.*, 9, same to same, 17 Mar. 1692; *ib.*, 10, same to same, 22 Mar. 1692; *ib.*, 12, same to same, 31 Mar. 1692; *Highland Papers*, 76, Dalrymple to Hill, 5 Mar. 1692.

18. *CTB*, xvii, 653; *HMCR Finch*, iv, 239-40, Breadalbane to Nottingham, 16 June 1692; *ib.*, 495, Breadalbane's representation to William, [Oct. 1692].

19. *Highland Papers*, 75-6, Dalrymple to Hill, 5 Mar. 1692; NLS MS 7014 fol. 42, Hill to Tweeddale, 28 Mar. 1692; *ib.*, fol. 61, H. Dalrymple to same, 5 Apr. 1692.

20. *Ib.*, fol. 17v, Hill to same, 27 Feb. 1692; SRO PC 1/48, 112-13.

21. *Ib.*, SP 3/1 fol. 27, Johnston to Cardross, 15 Apr. 1692; *ib.*, GD 112/39/1246, Breadalbane to Carwhin, 8 Mar. 1692; NLS MS 7014 fol. 42v, Hill to Tweeddale, 28 Mar. 1692; *ib.*, fol. 52, same to same, Mar. 1692; *ib.*, fol. 77v, Dalrymple to same, 30 Apr. 1692; Glasgow UL, MS Gen. 1577, same to Hill, 30 Apr. 1692.

22. *Ib; CSPD 1691-2*, 160-1, William to Hill, 1 Mar. 1692; *Highland Papers*, 81-2, PC warrant, 26 Apr. 1692; SRO GD 112/39/1251, [Carwhin] to Breadalbane, 22 Mar. 1692; NLS MS 7014 fol. 81, Hill to Tweeddale, 2 May 1692; *Earls of Cromartie*, i, 84-5, Sir J. Maclean to Tarbat, 30 Mar. 1692.

23. *Ib;* SRO GD 112/39/1255, Breadalbane to Carwhin, 12 Apr. 1692; NLS MS 7014 fol. 107, Hill to Tweeddale, 16 June 1692; *ib.*, fol. 109, Sir J. Maclean to [Hill], 4 June 1692.

24. *Gazette de France*, 12 Apr. 1692 (NS), 175-6, Edinburgh report, 23 Mar. (NS); Hopkins, 'Aspects of Jacobite Conspiracy', 62-3.

25. SRO SP 3/1 fol. 4v, Johnston to Broomhall, 10 Mar. 1691/2; *ib.*, fol. 20, same to Tweeddale, 26 Mar. 1692; *ib.*, fol. 20v, same to Dalrymple, 1 Apr. 1692; *ib.*, fol. 28, same to same, 22 Apr. 1692.

26. *Ib.*, fol. 24v, same to same, 8 Apr. 1692; *ib.*, fol. 33, same to same, 10 May 1692; *Highland Papers*, 115-16, Report, 20 June 1695; NLS MS 7014 fol. 77v, Dalrymple to Tweeddale, 30 Apr. 1692.

27. SRO SP 3/1 fols. 4v-5, Johnston to Broomhall, 10 Mar. 1691/2; *ib.*, fol. 25v, same to Tweeddale, 9 Apr. 1692.

28. *HMCR Finch*, iv, 283, Sir W. Lockhart to Nottingham, 2 July 1692; Foxcroft, *Supplement to Burnet*, 370; SRO SP 3/1 fol. 62, Johnston to Queensberry, 1 Dec. 1692.

29. Riley, *King William*, 81-3; SRO SP 3/1 fol. 6v, Johnston to Steuart, 10 Mar. 1691/2; *ib.*, fol. 28v, same to Carstares, 22 Apr. 1692.

30. *Ib.*, fol. 28, same to Portland, 22 Apr. 1692; Burnet, *History*, iv, 133-4, 155; Riley, *King William*, 81.

31. SRO SP 3/1 fol. 22, Johnston to Carstares, 5 Apr. 1692.

32. Melville believed that Tweeddale secretly drank Jacobite toasts with Buchan and Cannon. *Ib.*, fol. 21, same to Portland, 1 Apr. 1692; *ib.*, fol. 22, same to Tweeddale, 5 Apr. 1692; *Highland Papers*, 77-8, PC register, 22-3 Mar. 1692; *Gazette de France*, 19 Apr. 1692 (NS), 188, Edinburgh report, 29 Mar. (NS); SRO GD 26/xiii/78 fol. 173, Melville's notes.

33. *HMCR Stuart*, i, 72, James to Buchan, May 1692; *ib.*, same to Erroll & Keith, May 1692; *ib.*, 73, memorandum; *HMCR Buccleuch (Montagu)*, ii, 292-3, Cpt J. Scott's discovery, 18 Jan. 1695/6; Sourches, *Mémoires*, iv, 28; C. de la Roncière, *Histoire de la Marine Française*, vi (Paris, 1932), 136; SCA, Blairs Letters, Box V, 1692, 19, T. Dunbar to Innes, 19 May 1692; SRO SP 3/1 fol. 34v, Johnston to Tweeddale, 10 May 1692.

34. Lieutenant-Colonel Hamilton may have been omitted on the technical point that he was Irish. One odd exception was that of Sir Hugh Campbell of Calder, formerly suspected of passing Council information to the Highland Army. Steele, *Proclamations*, ii, S2933; *HMCR Finch*, iv, 280, 'J. Scot' to 'R. Fitzgerald', 11 July 1692 (disregarding editorial misidentifications).

35. SRO SP 3/1 fol. 28, Johnston to Portland, 22 Apr. 1692; *ib.*, fol. 29, same to Tweeddale, 23 Apr. 1692; *ib.*, fol. 34v, same to same, 12 May 1692.

36. *Ib.*, fol. 39v, same to Carstares, 29 May 1692; *ib.*, GD 26/xiii/415, Sir Ae. Macpherson to [Melville], 6 June 1692; Macpherson, *Loyall Dissuasive*, 195; Macky, *Memoirs*, iii–v; NUL, Portland MSS, PwA 1375, [A. Johnston], Intelligence expenses.

37. *Ib; Carstares S.P.*, 209-10, same to Carstares, 10 Aug. 1694; Macky, *Memoirs*, 205; SRO SP 3/1 fol. 29v, Johnston to Tweeddale, 26 Apr. 1692; *ib.*, fol. 36v, same to same, 17 May 1692; *ib.*, fol. 40v, same to Broomhall, 31 May 1692; *ib.*, fol. 82v, same to Ormiston, 27 Dec. 1692.

38. *Ib.*, fol. 38, same to Tweeddale, 26 May, 1692; *HMCR Finch*, iv, 151, Nottingham to Blathwayt, 13 May 1692.

39. The accounts of the maltreatment of Cannon and Dunfermline for being Protestants given in Macky's *View of the Court of St Germain* are untrue or exaggerated: it is a dishonest work. Macky, *Memoirs*, xxiv–xxvii; *HMCR Stuart*, i, 73, memorandum; *HMCR Buccleuch (Montagu)*, ii, 293-4, Cpt J. Scott's Discovery, 18 Jan. 1695/6; *Memoirs of Dundee*, 92-132.

40. *HMCR Finch*, iv, 474, Blathwayt to Nottingham, 7 Oct. 1692 (NS); *ib.*, 475, same to same, 9 Oct. 1692 (NS); SRO REF 310.044 (GD 44), 115, Gordon's memoirs, 35, 39.

41. *Carstares S.P.*, 219, A. Johnston to Carstares, 4 Sept. 1694; *Melvilles & Leslies*, iii, 225, Warrant, 9 June 1692; Macky, *Memoirs*, 177; *Nevil Payn's Letter* (London, 1693), 14; SRO SP 3/1 fol. 29, Johnston to Tweeddale, 23 Apr. 1692; *ib.*, fol. 30, same to Arran, 30 Apr. 1692; *ib.*, fol. 33, same to Dalrymple, 10 May 1692; fol. 39v, same to Carstares, 29 May 1692; *ib.*, PC 1/48, 166, 311-12; Drumlanrig, Queensberry Papers, Vol. 117, (3), Home to Queensberry, 27 May 1692; *ib.*, (4), same to same, 18 June 1692.

42. Dalrymple, *Memoirs*, ii, 208, A. Fletcher to Hamilton, 29 Apr. 1692; SRO SP 3/1 fol. 29, Johnston to Tweeddale, 23 Apr. 1692; *ib.*, fol. 32, same to Leven, 4 May 1692; *ib.*, PC 1/48, 162, 175-6, 206, 230-1, 240-1.

43. *Ib.*, 182-3, 187, 436-7; *ib.*, 1/49, 32-3.

44. *Ib.*, 1/48, 141, 170-1, 190-3, 196-7, 199-200, 218, 220; *Seafield Corr.*, 80, Tweeddale

to Grant, 27 Apr. 1692; *ib.*, 85, A. Fella to Ogilvie, 9 May 1692; *ib.*, 86–7, same to same, 17 May 1692.

45. *Highland Papers*, 82–3, PC register, 3 May 1692; *HMCR Finch*, iv, 240, Hill to Tweeddale, 29 May 1692; NLS MS 7014 fol. 90, same to same, 16 May 1692; *ib.*, fol. 92, same to same, 21 May 1692.

46. *Ib.*, fol. 107, same to same, 16 June 1692; *ib.*, fol. 118, same to same, 4 July 1692; *ib.*, fol. 121v, same to same, 26 July 1692; *ib.*, fol. 109, Sir J. Maclean to Hill, 4 June 1692; *HMCR Finch*, iv, 213, Hill to Tarbat, 6 June 1692.

47. SRO PC 1/48, 226.

48. *Ib.*, SP 3/1 fol. 31, Johnston to Carmichael, 3 May 1692; fol. 53, same to Sydney, 18 Oct. 1692.

49. Dalrymple, *Memoirs*, ii, 208, [Selkirk] to Hamilton, 19 May 1692; *ib.*, Fletcher to same, 29 Apr. 1692; SRO PC 1/48, 201; NLS MS 1031 fol. 156v, Hamilton to Selkirk, 12 May 1692; *HMCR Finch*, iv, 344, Dalrymple to Nottingham, 27 July 1692.

50. *Ib.*, 352, Breadalbane to same, 29 July 1692; *ib.*, 364, Lockhart to same, 3 Aug. 1692; Drumlanrig, Queensberry Papers, Vol. 115, 14, Dalrymple to Drumlanrig, 7/17 July 1692; SRO PC 1/48, 164, 170, 186, 196.

51. *Ib.*, 156, 164, 177–82, 306–8, 383; *Highland Papers*, 83, PC register, 5 May 1692; SRO SP 3/1 fol. 36v, Johnston to Tweeddale, 17 May 1692; *ib.*, fol. 42, same to Dalrymple, 10 June 1692.

52. Argyll himself, however, received some compounded arrears from the last time it had been on English pay, 1690. *Ib.*, fol. 33, same to same, 10 May 1692; *ib.*, fol. 35, same to Tweeddale, 12 May 1692; *ib.*, fol. 35v, same to Dalrymple, 13 May 1692; *ib.*, fol. 37, same to Tweeddale, 17 May 1692; *ib.*, fol. 39v, same to Carstares, 29 May 1692; *ib.*, PC 1/48, 174–5; *CTB*, ix, 1524, 1535.

53. *HMCR Finch*, iv, 263, Tarbat's information, June 1692; *ib.*, 282, Lockhart to Nottingham, 2 July 1692; *ib.*, 332, Nottingham to Dalrymple, 22 July 1692; Wodrow, *Analecta*, i, 203; Dalton, *English Army Lists*, iii, 416; SRO PC 1/48, 334.

54. *Ib.*, 274, 384, 393–5; *HMCR Finch*, iv, 263, Tarbat's information, June 1692; *ib.*, 240, Breadalbane to Nottingham, 26 June 1692; *ib.*, 365, Lockhart to same, 3 Aug. 1692; *ib.*, 498, Tarbat to same, 5 Nov. 1692.

55. *APS*, ix, 223.

56. *Scotish Pasquils*, 315, Verses on Breadalbane & Queensberry; *HMCR Finch*, iv, 364, Lockhart to Nottingham, 3 Aug. 1692; *ib.*, 351, Breadalbane to same, 29 July 1692.

57. *Ib.*, 352; *ib.*, 332–3, Nottingham to Dalrymple, 27 July 1692; SRO SP 3/1 fol. 38v, Johnston to Tweeddale, 26 May 1692; *ib.*, fol. 41v, same to same, 7 June 1692; *ib.*, PC 1/48, 291, 306–9.

58. *Ib.*, 333–6; *HMCR Finch*, iv, 343–4, Dalrymple to Nottingham, 27 July 1692.

59. *Ib.*, 313, same to same, 14/24 July 1692; SRO PC 1/48, 337, 340; *ib.*, SP 3/1 fol. 49, Johnston to Dalrymple, 6 Aug. 1692; *ib.*, fol. 60v, same to Tweeddale, 26 Nov. 1692.

60. *Ib.*, fol. 48, same to 'My Lord', 2 Aug. 1692; *HMCR Finch*, iv, 351–2, Breadalbane to Nottingham, 29 July 1692; *ib.*, 404–5, Lockhart to same, 18 Aug. 1692; SRO PC 1/48, 392–3, 473.

61. *HMCR Finch*, iv, 393, Breadalbane to Nottingham, 14 Aug. 1692; Luttrell, ii, 545; Sir W. Fraser, *The Scotts of Buccleuch*, 2 vols. (Edinburgh, 1878) i, 483; SRO PC 1/48, 395, 405, 411–12; *ib.*, 1/49, 21; Drumlanrig, Queensberry Papers, Vol. 115, 13, Dalrymple to Drumlanrig, 25 Aug. 1692.

62. *Ib.*, Vol. 111, 7, Treasury to Secretaries + William's answers, 14 July 1692; *HMCR Finch*, iv, 296, Breadalbane to Nottingham, 5 July 1692.

63. A. L. Murray, 'The Scottish Treasury, 1667–1708', *SHR*, xlv, 101, 104; SRO PC 1/48, 383; *ib.*, SP 3/1 fol. 166, Johnston to Portland, 10 June 1693; Drumlanrig, Queensberry Papers, bundle 559, note of payments, 30 Mar.–16 Sept. 1692.

64. *Ib.*, 'An accompt of ... those belonging to the invalids', 1693; *ib.*, 'The present state of the Invalids', 1694.

65. *Highland Papers*, 85–6, protection to A. Macdonald, 3 Oct. 1692; *ib.*, 87, Hill to Culloden, 9 Oct. 1692; NLS MS 7014 fol. 121v, Hill to Tweeddale, 26 July 1692; *ib.*, fol. 151, same to same, 8 Aug. 1692; *ib.*, fol. 160, same to same, 10 Sept. 1692; *ib.*, fol. 155, J. Macdonald to Hill, 13 Aug. 1692; SRO SP 3/1 fol. 41, Johnston to Dalrymple, 7 June 1692; *ib.*, fol. 49, same to same, 6 Aug. 1692.

66. Lenman, *Jacobite Risings*, 54; *RCAHMS Argyll*, ii, 277; *HMCR Roxburghe*, 124, Hill to Polwarth, 14 July 1694; NLS MS 7014 fol. 163, same to Tweeddale, 17 Sept. 1692.

67. *Ib.*, fol. 156, same to same, 24 Aug. 1692; *ib.*, fol. 180, same to same, 17 Dec. 1692; *ib.*, MS 14,407, fol. 186, same to same, 24 July 1692; *ib.*, fol. 188, warrant; Macleod, *Book of Dunvegan*, i, 134–6, letters & papers on taxes, Aug.–Oct. 1692; SRO PC 1/48, 401–3, 474.

68. *Ib.*, GD 112/39/1259, [Carwhin] to Breadalbane, 30 Sept. 1692; NLS MS 7015 fol. 19, Hill to Tweeddale, 31 Jan. 1692/3; NLS MS 7030 fol. 16, Tweeddale to Johnston, 11 Jan. 1696; Drumlanrig, Queensberry Papers Vol. 129, 32, commission to Barcaldine, 13 Aug. 1692.

69. PRO PC 1/48, 88.

70. *HMCR Hope-Johnstone*, 166–7, J. Ferguson to Livingston, [Apr. 1691]; Atholl, *Chronicles*, i, 341–2, Ardvorlich to Murray, 18 Jan. 1694; Fergusson, 'Early History of Strathardle', *TGSI*, xxiv, 197–200; NLS MS 7014 fol. 180, Hill to Tweeddale, 17 Dec. 1692.

71. *More Culloden Papers*, 234, Cuthbert of Castlehill to Culloden, 25 Apr. 1693; *ib.*, 235–6, J. Forbes to Culloden, 5 July 1693; Fraser-Macintosh, *Letters*, 124–5, J. Gordon to Sir R. Gordon, [1693]; Dunbar Dunbar, *Social Life*, 1st series, 295–6, Keppoch to L. Gordon, 8 Aug. 1693.

72. *Blind Harper*, 36–45, 115, 119–24, 'A' Cheud Di-luain de'n Raithe'.

73. Sorley Maclean has shown how little solid information on Domhnall's cattle-raiding career can be extracted from the poems attributed to him; but the dating of his execution to the late 1690s (see Chapter 13 n.37) indicates that many of his exploits must have occurred now. Mac Gill-Eain, 'Domhnall Donn of Bohuntin', *TGSI*, xlii, 99–102.

74. Fergusson, *From the Farthest Hebrides*, 34, 37.

75. *Seafield Corr.*, 136, J. Anderson to Sir J. Ogilvie, 6 Apr. 1694; NLS MS 7014 fol. 42, Hill to Tweeddale, 28 Mar. 1692; *ib.*, fol. 156, same to same, 24 Aug. 1692; *ib.*, fol. 180v, same to same, 17 Dec. 1692; *ib.*, fol. 158, paper on settlement of the jurisdiction, Aug. 1692; SRO PC 1/48, 342–3.

76. Among several special commissions issued for trials in these years (for lack of circuit courts), only one, in October 1692, was for a highland robber. *Ib.*, 340–1, 385, 395, 426–8, 473, 477; *Highland Papers*, 84–5, PC register, 9, 11 Aug. 1692; SRO SP 3/1 fol. 50v, Johnston to Dalrymple, 13 Aug. 1692; *ib.*, fol. 60v, same to Tweeddale, 26 Nov. 1692; *ib.*, fol. 72v, same to Breadalbane, 8 Dec. 1692; NLS MS 7015 fol. 7v, Dalrymple to Tweeddale, 14 Jan. 1693; *HMCR Finch*, iv, 392, Breadalbane to Nottingham, 14 Aug. 1692.

77. *Ib.*, 392–3; *Highland Papers*, 86–7, Hill to Culloden, 9 Oct. 1692; SRO PC 1/48, 384, 473.

78. *Ib.*, SP 3/1 fol. 72v, Johnston to Breadalbane, 8 Dec. 1692; GD 112/39/1265, Dalrymple to same, 21 Mar. 1693; *ib.*, 1267, Inverey to R. Fulles, 11 May 1693; *ib.*, 1268, same to Breadalbane, 11 May 1693.

79. _Ib._, PC 1/48, 356; _ib._, 1/49, 95, 173–4, 342, 357; _ib._, 1/50, 129; _ib._, 1/51, 231–2; Fountainhall, _Decisions_, i, 539; Lovat, _Memoirs_, 8; Blair, Atholl MSS, Box 29 I (9) 378, Ormiston to Tullibardine, 27 Oct. 1697.

80. SRO SP 3/1 fol. 44v, Johnston to Broomhall, 13 Oct. 1692; _ib._, fol. 69v, same to Hill, 7 Dec. 1692; _ib._, PC 1/48, 474; Fort William, West Highland Museum, MS B3, Hill to Treasury, 29 Feb. 1695/6; NLS MS 7014 fol. 180, same to Tweeddale, 17 Dec. 1692.

81. _Ib._, fol. 81, same to same, 2 May 1692.

82. Balhaldie's account of Argyll's intended generosity to Sir John is therefore, not surprisingly, greatly exaggerated. _Ib._, MS 7015 fol. 7v, Dalrymple to same, 14 Jan. 1693; _Highland Papers_, 78–81, [Dalrymple], 'Memoriall to the King', [Jan. 1693 — misdated in book]; _Memoirs of Locheill_, 326–7; SRO SP 3/1 fol. 93, Johnston to Tweeddale, 17 Jan. 1693.

83. _CSPD 1691–2_, 539, warrant to Hill, 31 Dec. 1692; _More Culloden Papers_, 221–2, J. Forbes to Culloden, 22 Jan. 1693; Atholl, _Chronicles_, i, 350, Major Hay to Murray, 11 Aug. 1694; _ib._, 354; Tullibardine, _Military History_, 43.

84. PRO PC 1/48, 299.

85. _HMCR Finch_, iv, 495, Breadalbane, 'Representation', [Oct. 1692]; _Selections from the Family Papers preserved at Caldwell_, ed. W. Mure (_Caldwell Papers_, Maitland Club, 1854), 186, W. Stewart to W. Hamilton, 3 Jan. 1692/3; SRO PC 1/48, 416–17; _ib._, SP 3/1 fol. 52, Johnston to Tweeddale, 13 Oct. 1692; _ib._, vo, same to C[arstares], 14 Oct. 1692; NUL, Portland MSS, PwA 2437, 'Case of the Addressing Clergy'; _Annandale Book_, ii, 55, A. Johnston to Annandale, 25 Oct. 1692.

86. _Ib._, 94, Johnston to same, 19 Jan. 1695; P. A. Hopkins, 'Sham Plots and Real Plots in the 1690s', _Ideology and Conspiracy: Aspects of Jacobitism, 1689–1759_, ed. E. Cruickshanks (Edinburgh, 1982), 94–5.

87. _Carstares S.P._, 199, A. Johnston to Carstares, 29 June 1694; _Annandale Book_, ii, 94–5, Johnston to Annandale, 19 Jan. 1695.

88. SRO SP 3/1 fol. 82, same to [Ormiston], 27 Dec. 1692.

89. _Ib._, fol. 17v, same to Portland, 22 Mar. 1692; _ib._, fol. 56, same to Tweeddale, 19 Nov. 1692; _ib._, 58, same to Broomhall, 24 Nov. 1692; _ib._, fol. 62, same to Queensberry, 1 Dec. 1692.

90. _Ib; ib._, fol. 74, same to Ormiston, 17 Dec. 1692; _ib._, fol. 82, same to [same], 27 Dec. 1692; _Carstares S.P._, 227–9, warrants to Ormiston, 17 Dec. 1694, 12 Mar. 1695/6; Macky, _Memoirs_, 224–5.

91. _Annandale Book_, ii, 56, J. Fairholme to Annandale, 1 Dec. 1692; SRO SP 3/1 fol. 61, Johnston to Hamilton, 1 Dec. 1692; _ib._, fol. 61v, same to Queensberry, 1 Dec. 1692; _ib._, fols. 64v–65, same to Tweeddale, 2 Dec. 1692; _ib._, fol. 69v, same to Broomhall, 6 Dec. 1692.

92. _Edinburgh Records 1689–1701_, 107–10; _ib._, 299, Johnston to Tweeddale, 6 Dec. 1692; _ib._, 301, same to same, 17 Dec. 1692; _ib._, 303, same to same, 1 Feb. 1693; _Caldwell Papers_, 185–6, W. Stewart to W. Hamilton, 3 Jan. 1692/3; SRO PC 1/48, 503–5.

93. SRO SP 3/1 fol. 69, Johnston to Steuart, 6 Dec. 1692; _ib._, fol. 71, same to same, 8 Dec. 1692; _ib._, fol. 73, same to Tweeddale, 2 Dec. 1692 (revised version).

94. _Edinburgh Records 1689–1701_, 300, same to Broomhall, 6 Dec. 1692; _ib._, 300–1, same to McLurg, 8 Dec. 1692; _ib._, 302, same to Sir P. Murray, 27 Dec. 1692; _ib._, 304, same to Hamilton, 2 Feb. 1693; SRO PC 1/48, 503–5.

95. Graham, _Stairs_, i, 378–9, Dalrymple to Lothian, 22 Dec. 1692; Riley, _King William_, 83; NLS MS 7015 fol. 21v, Dalrymple to Tweeddale, 11 Feb. 1693; Blair, Atholl MSS, Box 29 I (7) 43, Sir P. Murray to Murray, 16 Dec. 1693; SRO PC 1/48, 575; _ib._, SP 3/1 fol. 79, Johnston to Annandale, 20 Dec. 1692; _ib._, fol. 84, same to Sir P. Murray, 27 Dec. 1692;

ib., fol. 100, same to Broomhall, 2 Feb. 1693; *ib.*, fol. 112, same to Tweeddale, 18 Feb. 1693.

96. *Ib.*, fol. 81v, same to Steuart, 24 Dec. 1692.

97. Johnston may have been misled by the false claims Melfort himself spread in Jacobite circles. *Caldwell Papers*, 185, W. Stewart to W. Hamilton, 3 Jan. 1692/3; Hopkins, 'Aspects of Jacobite Conspiracy', 325–6, 330–5; NLS MS 7015 fol. 7, Dalrymple to Tweeddale, 14 Jan. 1693; SRO SP 3/1 fol. 83v, Johnston to [Ormiston], 27 Dec. 1692; *ib.*, fol. 93v, same to same, 17 Jan. 1692.

98. *Ib.*, fol. 79, same to Annandale, 20 Dec. 1693; *ib.*, fol. 95v, same to Steuart, 19 Jan. 1693; *ib.*, fol. 152v, *Carstares S.P.*, 171 (explanations of Payne's code-names — a mistake in the latter, since Home = Littlejohn); *Nevil Payn's Letter*, 10–11, Dr Gray to M. Brown, 4 Dec. [1692]; *ib.*, 21, same to 'Mrs Little', 25 Dec. 1692; *ib.*, 14, Payne to 'Aunt', 3 Dec. 1692.

99. *Ib.*, 17–18; SRO SP 3/1 fol. 95, same to Broomhall, 17 Jan. 1693; *ib.*, fol. 83, Johnston to [Ormiston], 27 Dec. 1692.

100. *Ib.*, fol. 82v.

101. *Ib.*, fol. 93v, same to same, 17 Jan. 1693; *ib.*, fol. 48, same to Portland, 26 July 1692; *ib.*, fol. 104, same to Arran, 9 Feb. 1693; *ib.*, fol. 107, same to Countess of Seaforth, 14 Feb. 1692; *ib.*, fol. 115v, same to Ogilvie, 21 Feb. 1693; *ib.*, PC 1/48, 473–4, 569–70; *Nevil Payn's Letter*, 15, Payne to 'Aunt', 3 Dec. 1692.

102. *HMCR Hamilton Supplement*, 125, Ormiston to Hamilton, 3 Jan. 1693; SRO SP 3/1 fol. 61, Johnston to same, 1 Dec. 1692; *ib.*, fol. 65, same to Tweeddale, 2 Dec. 1692; *ib.*, fol. 80v, same to Ormiston, 20 Dec. 1692; *ib.*, fol. 85v, same to same, 27 Dec. 1692; *ib.*, fol. 88, same to Broomhall, 31 Dec. 1692.

103. *Ib.*, fol. 90v, same to same, 12 Jan. 1693; *ib.*, PC 1/48, 558.

104. *Ib.*, 575; *ib.*, 1/49, 17; *ib.*, SP 3/1 fol. 98v, Johnston to Ormiston, 2 Feb. 1693; *ib.*, fol. 110v, same to Tweeddale, 18 Feb. 1693; *Edinburgh Records 1689*–1701, 303–4, same to same 1 Feb. 1693; *ib.*, 304–5, same to same, 2 Feb. 1693; *ib.*, 115; *Annandale Book*, ii, 57, A. Johnston to Annandale, 2 Feb. 1693.

105. Graham, *Stairs*, i, 186, Dalrymple to Lothian, 1 Apr. 1693; SRO SP 3/1 fol. 122v, Johnston to Melville, 2 Mar. 1693; *ib.*, fol. 125, same to Tweeddale, 21 Mar. 1693; *HMCR Finch*, v (transcripts for projected volume at Historical Manuscripts Commission, Quality House, Chancery Lane, London) No. 105, Breadalbane to Nottingham, 11 Mar. 1693.

106. *HMCR Finch*, iv, 536, same to same [1693]; [Moncreiff], 'Macaulay's *History*', *ER*, cv, 169n; SRO SP 3/1 fol. 125v, Johnston to Tweeddale, 28 Mar. 1693; *ib.*, fol. 126, same to Hamilton, 28 Mar. 1693.

107. *Marchmont Papers*, iii, 409–11, Polwarth, Project, Jan. 1693; *HMCR Hamilton Supplement*, 125, Hamilton to Portland, 18 Feb. 1693; *CSPD 1693*, 450–1 (SRO GD 406/bundle 634/9), Mem: of business to be done the next session.

108. *Ib.*, 35, Instructions, Nos. 2, 4, 5, 13, 21 Mar. 1693; *ib.*, 36, 37, drafts of Instructions; *ib.*, 38, Secret Instructions, No. 3, 23 Mar. 1693.

109. SRO SP 3/1 fol. 165, Johnston to Portland, 10 June 1693; *ib.*, GD 406/bundle 634/35, Instructions, No. 5, 21 Mar. 1693.

110. *Ib.*, No. 7.

111. *Ib.*, 38, Secret Instructions, Nos. 1, 3–5, 8, 23 Mar. 1693.

112. SRO SP 3/1 fol. 33, Johnston to Dalrymple, 10 May 1692; [Leslie], *Answer to King*, App., 58–65, 'Letter' [20 Apr. 1692].

113. *Ib.*, 'To the Reader', 1; *ib.*, App., 65; Hopkins, Aspects of Jacobite Conspiracy, 308–9.

114. The 'Letter' could easily have been published separately earlier; but there is no trace of this. *Great Britain's Just Complaint*, *Somers Tracts*, ed. Sir W. Scott, 13 vols. (London,

1809-15), x, 451-2; [T. Comber], *The Protestant Mask Taken off from the Jesuited Englishman* (London, 1692/3), 36-7; [Leslie], *Answer to King*, To the Reader, 1-2.

115. *Ib.*, 151-2; Northamptonshire RO, Buccleuch (Shrewsbury) MSS, Vol. 63, 7, J. Cooper's memorandum on meetings with Leslie, 6-10 June 1696, 2.

116. Johnston, writing to Tweeddale, names the person who warned him only (ironically) as 'your friend'. SRO SP 3/1 fol. 184, Johnston to Stevenson, 11 July 1693; NLS MS 7027 fol. 40, [Johnston], Our Conference, [Dec. 1695]; SRO GD 406/bundle 634/38, Secret Instructions No. 6, 23 Mar. 1693.

117. *Marchmont Papers*, iii, 400, [Polwarth], Memorial [late 1692].

118. Foxcroft, *Supplement to Burnet*, 391; NUL, Portland MSS, PwA 2445, ? to 'Mr Crow' [Lauderdale], 11 July 1693.

119. *Nevil Payn's Letter*, 5-7, 19-20, 31-2; *HMCR Buccleuch (Montagu)*, ii, 195, Johnston to Shrewsbury, 21 June 1695; SRO SP 3/1 fol. 80, same to Lt-Gov. Erskine, 20 Dec. 1692; *ib.*, fol. 95v, same to Steuart, 19 Jan. 1693; *ib.*, fol. 116, same to Breadalbane, 21 Feb. 1693.

120. *Ib.*, fol. 118v, same to Steuart, 23 Feb. 1693; *Archives de la Bastille*, ix, 447, Renaudot to Croissy, 10 Feb. 1694 (NS); *HMCR Finch*, v, No. 200, Kingston to Nottingham, c. 2 May 1693.

121. *Carstares S.P.*, 154, Johnston to Carstares, 18 Apr. 1693; *Scotish Pasquils*, 276-7, Satire upon Hamilton & Breadalbane, [1693]; SRO GD 112/39/1266, [Dalrymple] to Breadalbane, 1 Apr. 1693.

122. NUL, Portland MSS, PwA 2445, ? to 'Mr Crow' [Lauderdale], 11 July 1693.

123. *Ib; CTB*, ix, 1810; Dalton, *English Army Lists*, iii, 416; Walton, *Standing Army*, 241-6.

124. NLS MS 7015 fol. 17, Dalrymple to Tweeddale, 26 Jan. 1693; *ib.*, fol. 94, same to same, 19 'Apr.' 1693; SRO SP 3/1 fol. 60v, Johnston to same, 26 Nov. 1692; *ib.*, fol. 108v, same to same, 14 Feb. 1693; *Carstares S.P.*, 183, same to Carstares, 'May' [24 June] 1693.

125. SRO SP 3/1 fol. 113v, same to Broomhall, 19 Feb. 1693.

126. *Ib; APS*, ix, 249; *Carstares S.P.*, 194, A. Johnston to Carstares, 19 Sept. 1693; *Earls of Cromartie*, i, 91, Queensberry to Tarbat, 23 Feb. 1693; Drumlanrig, Queensberry Papers, Vol. 115, 18, Dalrymple to Drumlanrig, 3 Aug. 169[3]; NUL, Portland MSS, PwA 2445, ? to 'Mr Crow' [Lauderdale], 11 July 1693.

127. *Ib*; SRO SP 3/1 fol. 85v, Johnston to Ormiston, 27 Dec. 1692; *ib.*, fol. 97v, same to Hamilton, 2 Feb. 1693.

128. *Ib.*, fol. 98, same to Murray, 2 Feb. 1693; *ib.*, fols. 175v-176, same to Portland, 24 June 1693; *Carstares S.P.*, 172, same to Carstares, 16 May 169[3].

129. *Ib.*, 172; SRO SP 3/1 fol. 133, same to Atholl, 26 Apr. 1693.

130. *Ib.*, fol. 93v, same to Ormiston, 17 Jan. 1693; *ib.*, fol. 104v, same to same, 9 Feb. 1693; *ib.*, GD 406/1/7721, Arran to Johnston, 21 Feb. [1692/3]; NUL, Portland MSS, PwA 2445, ? to 'Mr Crow' [Lauderdale], 11 July 1693.

131. *Ib.*, PwA 329, [Dalrymple] to William, 11 July 1693; *APS*, ix, 250, 282; *ib.*, App., 73, 79.

132. *Ib.*, 70, 72; *Carstares S.P.*, 172, Johnston to Carstares, 16 May 169[3].

133. *Ib.*, 154, same to same, 25 Apr. 1693; *ib.*, 157, same to same, 27 Apr. 1693; *ib.*, 175, same to same, 16 May 169[3]; SRO SP 3/1 fol. 130v, same to William, 22 Apr. 1693; *APS*. ix, App., 74; SRO GD 112/43/1/2/25, Report of the Subcommittee for Security, 2 May 1693.

134. *Ib; APS*, ix, 253; *ib.*, App., 75; *Carstares S.P.*, 157, Johnston to Carstares, 27 Apr. 1693; *ib.*, 158, same to same, 29 Apr. 1693; *ib.*, 160, same to same, 4 May 1693; *ib.*, 163, same to same, 6 May 1693; SRO SP 3/1 fols. 134v-135, same to Locke, 2 May 1693.

135. *Scotish Pasquils*, 411; NUL, Portland MSS, PwA 327, Dalrymple to William, 30 May 1693.

136. See Chapter 8, p. 283 n62.

137. *APS*, ix, 250; *HMCR Laing*, i, 476–9, Fountainhall to Dalrymple, 8 Sept. 1693; NLS MS 1946 (Justiciary records), 592–6; SRO PC 1/48, 619–20; *ib.*, 1/50, 116–18; *ib.*, SP 3/1 fols. 198v–199, Johnston to Rankeillor, 20 Sept. 1693; *Carstares S.P.*, 167, same to Portland, 11 May 1693.

138. *Ib.*, 153–4, same to Carstares, 18 Apr. 1693; *ib.*, 159, same to same, 4 May 1693; Riley, *King William*, 86; SRO SP 3/1 fol. 124, same to Tweeddale, 14 Mar. 1693.

139. *Ib.*, fol. 139v, same to Portland, 4 May 1693; *ib.*, fol. 151, same to Stevenson, 23 May 1693; *ib.*, fols. 151v–153, same to Mary, 24 May 1693; *CSPD 1693*, 143, Tweeddale to William, 30 May 1693; Hopkins, 'Aspects of Jacobite Conspiracy', 342–3, 350; NUL, Portland MSS, PwA 327, Dalrymple to William, 30 May 1693; *Carstares S.P.*, 161, Johnston to Carstares, 4 May 1693.

140. The page's allegations so concentrate on lists of letters and minor agents, lacking the big scenes which usually expose false witnesses, that it is hard to tell whether they have any basis of truth; but they have a very dubious air. *Ib; ib.*, 157, same to same, 27 Apr. 1693; *ib.*, 173, same to same, 16 May 169[3]; SRO SP 3/1 fol. 202v, same to Steuart, 24 Oct. 1693; GD 112/43/1/1/45, 'The Declaration of James McGill, pretended page to my Ld Melfoord'; *Nevil Payn's Letter*, 22.

141. *Carstares S.P.*, 154, Johnston to Carstares, 18 Apr. 1693; *ib.*, 159, same to same, 4 May 1693; *ib.*, 173, same to same, 16 May 169[3].

142. *Ib.*, 154, same to same, 18 Apr. 1693; *ib.*, 158, same to same, 27 Apr. 1693; SRO SP 3/1 fol. 130v, same to William, 22 Apr. 1693.

143. *Ib.*, fols. 154–5, same to Portland, 27 May 1693; *ib.*, fol. 158v, same to Stevenson, 1 June 1693; *Carstares S.P.*, 158, same to Carstares, 29 Apr. 1693; *ib.*, 165–6, same to same, 6 May 1693; Riley, *King William*, 87.

144. They claimed that a speech by Polwarth gave the game away. NUL, Portland MSS, PwA 217, Memorial, [1693 — misdated in catalogue].

145. *Carstares S.P.*, 171–2, 176, Johnston to Carstares, 16 May 169[3]; *ib.*, 178, same to same, 19 May 1693.

146. *Ib.*, 167, same to Portland, 11 May 1693; SRO SP 3/1 fol. 160, same to Stevenson, 3 June 1693; *ib.*, fol. 167, same to same, 13 June 1693.

147. *Carstares S.P.*, 177, same to Carstares, 16 May 169[3]; *ib.*, 178–80, same to same, 19 May 1693; *APS*, ix, 262–4; NLS MS 7016 fol. 121, Dalrymple to Tweeddale, 26 Apr. 1694.

148. Riley, *King William*, 87; *Melvilles & Leslies*, iii, 229, Sir J. Montgomerie's report, [1693]; SRO GD 26/xiii/78 fols. 172–3, Melville's notes, [1693–4]; *Carstares S.P.*, 177–8, Johnston to Carstares, 16 May 169[3].

149. SRO SP 3/1 fol. 192, same to same, 11 Aug. 1693; *ib.*, GD 406/bundle 634/30, draft act on election of ministers.

150. *APS*, ix, 303; Riley, *King William*, 87; SRO SP 3/1 fols. 163v–165, Johnston to Portland, 10 June 1693; *ib.*, fols. 181v–182, same to Burnet, 1 July 1693.

151. *Carstares S.P.*, 165, same to Carstares, 6 May 1693; *ib.*, 166–7, same to same, 11 May 1693; SRO SP 3/1 fol. 159, same to Stevenson, 1 June 1693; *APS*, ix, 266.

152. NUL, Portland MSS, PwA 375, Hamilton to Portland, 27 May 1693; *ib.*, 547, Tweeddale to same, 30 May 1693; SRO GD 406/bundle 634/39, Additional Instruction, 18/28 May 1693; *Carstares S.P.*, 164, Johnston to Carstares, 6 May 1693; *ib.*, 184, same to same, 27 May 1693.

153. *Ib.*, 164, same to same, 6 May 1693; *ib.*, 170, same to same, 16 May 169[3]; *ib.*, 183, same to same, 24 May 1693; SRO SP 3/1 fol. 150v, same to Stevenson, 23 May 1693; *ib.*, fol. 221v, same to Tweeddale, 2 Jan. 1693/4; Ailesbury, *Memoirs*, ii, 481–2; NUL, Portland MSS, PwA 327, Dalrymple to William, 30 May 1693; Blair, Atholl MSS, Box 29 I (7) 17, Lady Murray to Murray, 7 Aug. [1693].

154. Macky, *Memoirs*, xxxix.

155. Foxcroft, *Supplement to Burnet*, 392–3; SRO SP 3/1 fols. 167v–168, Johnston to Stevenson, 15 June 1693; *ib.*, fols. 172v–173, same to Locke, 20 June 1693; *APS*, ix, 308, 323.

156. *Ib.*, 323–4.

157. *Ib.*, 324; *ib.*, App., 83, 93; *Highland Papers*, 89–90, PCS to Johnston, 15 Mar. 1693; SRO PC 1/49, 2; *ib.*, GD 112/39/1281, [Carwhin] to Breadalbane, 6 Jan. 1694; GD 406/bundle 634/35, Instructions to Hamilton, No. 15, 23 Mar. 1693.

158. *Ib.*, No. 17; *APS*, ix, App., 92.

159. *Highland Papers*, 90, Livingston to Lt-Col Hamilton, 21 Apr. 1693; *ib.*, 90–1, same to same, 8 May 1693.

160. Foxcroft, *Supplement to Burnet*, 371–3; Blair, Atholl MSS, Box 29 I (7) 141, Ld B. Hamilton to Murray, 31 May 1695; SRO SP 3/1 fols. 180v–181, Johnston to Carstares, 1 July 1693; *ib.*, fol. 183, same to same, 11 July 1693; *ib.*, fol. 189v, same to same, 4 Aug. 1693; *ib.*, fol. 184, same to Stevenson, 11 July 1693.

161. *Ib.*, fol. 207, same to Livingston, 9 Nov. 1693.

162. *Ib.*, fol. 183, same to Carstares, 11 July 1693; *ib.*, fol. 184v, same to Stevenson, 11 July 1693; *ib.*, GD 406/1/7331, [Hamilton] to [Duchess], 28 Nov. 1693; *ib.*, bundle 633, [Steuart], 'Impartiall Account', [1693], 3, 5, 8.

163. SRO SP 3/1 fol. 189v, Johnston to Carstares, 4 Aug. 1693; *ib.*, fol. 192, same to same, 11 Aug. 1693.

164. *Seafield Corr.*, 105, Findlater to Ogilvie, 20 June 1693; SRO GD 112/39/1283, [?Linlithgow] to Breadalbane, 13 Jan. 1693; NUL, Portland MSS, PwA 2445, ? to 'Mr Crow', 11 July 1693.

165. *HMCR Buccleuch (Montagu)*, ii, 295, Cpt. Scott's Discovery, 18 Jan. 1695/6; T. Thorpe, *Catalogue of the Southwell Manuscripts* (London, 1834), 51, J. Butts to Blathwayt, 15 July, 1693; *ib.*, 469, Sir P. Rycaut to same, 4 Aug. 1693; SRO GD 26/xiii/78 fols. 172–3, Melville's notes; *ib.*, PC 1/49, 51.

166. Stewart of Appin also slipped away from Edinburgh; but, if his name was on the list, it was taken off. *Ib.*, 50–1, 119; *Seafield Corr.*, 111–12, J. Anderson to Ogilvie, 2 Aug. 1693; SRO SP 3/1 fols. 157v–158, Johnston to Stevenson, 30 May 1693.

167. *Ib.*, fol. 157v; NLS MS 1320 fol. 60, R. Mackenzie to Delvine, 18 Apr. 1693; *ib.*, fol. 66, same to same, 13 June 1693; SRO GD 406/1/8317, Sir J. Maclean to Hamilton, 27 May 1693; Macfarlane, *Gen. Colls.*, i, 140–1.

168. *Ib.*, 141; *Memoirs of Locheill*, 327; *Carstares S.P.*, 186, A. Johnston to Carstares, 7 July 1693; *ib.*, 375, A. Stevenson to same, 6 June 1698; *HMCR Finch*, iv, 430, ? to [Portland, Aug. 1692]; WDA, Browne MSS, 215, [Sir A. Maclean] to [H. Browne], 14 July [1693, NS]; NLS MS 7015 fol. 94, Dalrymple to Tweeddale, 19 Aug. 1693.

169. *Ib.*, fol. 104, Hill to Tweeddale, 20 Sept. 1693; *ib.*, fol. 107, Ardkinglas to Hill, 7 Sept. 1693; BL Add. 20,007 fol. 86v.

170. *CSPD 1697*, 114, 134; Dalton, *English Army Lists*, iii, 323; *ib.*, iv, 105, 136, 154, 189; W. Sachaverell, *An Account of the Isle of Man . . . With a Voyage to I-Columb-kill* (London, 1702), 144; Cregeen, 'Tacksmen', *SS*, xiii, 97.

171. *Carstares S.P.*, 374–5, A. Stevenson to Carstares, 6 June 1698; Macfarlane, *Gen. Colls.*, i, 141.

172. *Eachann Bacach*, 90–9, Maighstir Seathan, 'Ge grianach an latha'; *ib.*, 311–12, J. Beaton, 'Upon the Revolution, and silencing the Episcopal ministers in Mull'; J. L. Campbell (ed.) *A Collection of Highland Rites and Customes* (Cambridge, 1975), 102–3.

173. Sacheverell, *Account*, 128–9. For the date, Hopkins, 'The Date of William Sacheverell's Voyage to Iona', *Notes & Queries of the Society of West Highland and Island Historical Research*, xxv (Dec. 1984), 17–21.

174. *Highland Papers*, 91–2, PC Register, 27 June 1693; Macpherson, 'Gleanings', *TGSI*, xx, 242, Hill to Cluny, 22 July 1693.

175. Dunlop, 'A Chief and his Lawyer', *ib.*, xlv, 261, 263–4; NLS MS 7015 fol. 104, Hill to Tweeddale, 20 Sept. 1693; *ib.*, MS 7016 fol. 3, same to same, 3 Jan. 1693/4; *ib.*, fol. 4, Sir D. Macdonald to Hill, 16 Oct. 1693; Cumnock, Dumfries House, Bute MSS, bundle A 517/17, [Dalrymple] to [William, July 1693].

176. NLS MS 7016, fol. 34, Hill to Tweeddale, 30 Jan. 1693/4; SRO PC 1/49, 342–33; *Highland Papers*, 92–4, PC Register, 7 June–3 July 1694.

177. *Mackintosh Muniments*, 143; NLS MS 7015 fol. 104, Hill to Tweeddale, 20 Sept. 1693; *ib.*, fol. 124, same to same, 11 Oct. 1693; *ib.*, fol. 106, Glengarry to Hill, 11 Sept. 1693.

178. Blair, Atholl MSS, Box 29 I (7) 63, same to Murray, 12 Mar. 1694; *ib.*, 57, Marchioness to same, 17 Feb. [1694]; *ib.*, 81, Murray to Glengarry, 15 July 1694; *ib.*, Box 44/VI/173, [Atholl] to Lady Murray, [1693]; *ib.*, 192, Johnston to same, [1694].

179. *Ib.*, 182, Ld James Murray to Murray, 29 July [1693].

180. NLS MS 7015 fols. 104v–105, Hill to Tweeddale, 20 Sept. 1693; *ib.*, MS 7016 fol. 3, same to same, 3 Jan. 1693/4.

181. Kilgour, *Lochaber in War and Peace*, 77; *HMCR Roxburghe*, 128–9, Hill to Polwarth, 22 Mar. 1696; *Memoirs of Locheill*, 332–6; SRO GD 1/658, 53.

182. *Carstares S.P.*, Johnston to Carstares, 16 May 1693; Shaw, *Northern & Western Islands*, 159; SRO GD 112/40/4/7/106, Breadalbane to Barcaldine, 15 Apr. 1695.

183. *Ib.*, 39/1287, [Carwhin] to Breadalbane, 22 Jan. 1694; Atholl, *Chronicles*, i, 345n; Blair, Atholl MSS, Box 29 I (7) 39, Sir P. Moray to Murray, 9 Nov. 1693; *ib.*, 76, Breadalbane to same, 5 June 1694.

184. *Annandale Book*, ii, 59–60, Note of quarrel; Riley, *King William*, 85–6, 88; NUL, Portland MSS, PwA 217, Memorial, [1693]; *Ib.*, PwA 328, Dalrymple to William, 20 June 1693; *Carstares S.P.*, 172, Johnston to Carstares, 16 May 169[3]; *ib.*, 182–3, same to same, 'May' [24 June] 1693; *ib.*, 185, A. Johnston to same, 7 July 1693.

185. Besides retaining one dragoon regiment, he transferred to the Scottish establishment two infantry regiments just raised for service in Ireland; but this did not conciliate officers whose commissions were cancelled. *Ib.*, 168, Johnston to same, 11 May 1693; SRO SP 3/1 fol. 171, same to Stevenson, 20 June 1693; *ib.*, fol. 184v, same to A. Johnston, 11 July 1693; *ib.*, PC 1/49, 83; Foxcroft, *Supplement to Burnet*, 393.

186. *Ib*; NUL, Portland MSS, PwA 331, Dalrymple to William, 8 Aug. 1693; SRO SP 3/1 fol. 191v, Johnston to Carstares, 11 Aug. 1693; *ib.*, fol. 193, same to Steuart, 12 Aug. 1693; *ib.*, fol. 194, same to Stevenson, 25 Aug. 1693.

187. *Ib.*, fol. 176, same to Portland, 24 June 1693; *ib.*, fol. 186, same to Stevenson, 4 Aug. 1693; *ib.*, GD 406/1/3774, Carstares to Hamilton, 22 May 1693; Blair, Atholl MSS, Box 29 I (7) 11, Lovat to Murray, 17 June 1693; *ib.*, 18, Murray to Lady Murray, 11 Aug. 1693; *ib.*, 27, Lady Murray to Murray, 2 Sept. [1693].

188. *Carstares S.P.*, 189–91, A. Johnston to Carstares, 4 Aug. 1693; *ib.*, 191–2, Macky to Melville, 24 Aug. 1693; *HMCR Finch*, v, No. 200, Kingston to Nottingham, c. 2 May 1693.

189. The 'park-keeper' Johnston took to mean Nottingham was actually an obscure Captain Williamson — a sign of how far his judgement was affected. *Seafield Corr.*, 115, Steuart to Ogilvie, 11 Aug. 1693; Ailesbury, *Memoirs*, i, 347; SRO SP 3/1 fol. 151, Johnston to Stevenson, 23 May 1693.

190. *Annandale Book*, ii, 61–2, same to Annandale, 19 Oct. 1693; *HMCR Downshire*, i, 530, Kingston to Trumbull, 10 Aug. 1695; *HMCR Finch*, v, Nos. 411, 419, R. Holland's informations, 8–22 Oct. 1693.

191. SRO GD 406/1/7331, [Hamilton] to [Duchess], 28 Nov. 1693; *ib.*, SP 3/1 fol. 219, Johnston to Ormiston, 19 Dec. 1693 (codenames identifiable from context on fol. 217v).

192. *Ib.*, fol. 189v, same to Carstares, 4 Aug. 1693; GD 26/xiii/78 fol. 172, Melville's notes; Blair, Atholl MSS, Box 29 I (7) 36, Lady Murray to Murray, 11 Oct. [1693]; *ib.*, bundle 1619, Murray's prayers at London 1693–4, 'when falsely arenged, & malicious enemies raised up against me'.

193. Macpherson, *Original Papers*, i, 464 (Bodl. MS Carte 181 fol. 530), Sir G. Barclay's memorial, 28 Dec. 1693 (NS); Hopkins, 'Aspects of Jacobite Conspiracy', 375–6.

194. *Earls of Cromartie*, i, 101, Dalrymple to Tarbat, 24 Nov. 1693; SRO SP 3/1 fol. 209v, Johnston to Steuart, 14 Nov. 1693; *ib.*, GD 406/1/7325, [Hamilton] to [Duchess], 14 Nov. 1693; *ib.*, 7326, [same] to [same], 16 Nov. 1693; *ib.*, 7328, [same] to [same], 21 Nov. 1693.

195. *Ib; ib.*, 7835, [same] to [same], 2 Jan. 1693/4; *ib.*, SP 3/1 fol. 211, Johnston to Polwarth, 25 Nov. 1693; *Earls of Cromartie*, i, 103, Breadalbane to Tarbat, 7 Dec. 1693; *HMCR Hamilton Supplement*, 127–30, Papers on General Assembly, Dec. 1693; *ib.*, 132, Hamilton's memorandum, 25 Mar. 1694.

196. *Ib.*, 132–3; *Annandale Book*, ii, 63, Annandale to Johnston, 31 Oct. 1693; SRO GD 406/1/7303, [Hamilton] to [Duchess], 21 Oct. 1693; *ib.*, 7454, same to same, 22 Feb. 1694; Riley, *King William*, 89.

197. *Ib.*, 91; NLS MS 7028 fol. 23, Tweeddale to Sir A. Murray of Blackbarony, 10 Feb. 1694: *ib.*, MS 7016 fol. 5v, Queensberry to Tweeddale, 4 Jan. 1694.

198. *Ib.*, fol. 5; *ib.*, fol. 83, same to same, 12 Mar. 1694; SRO SP 3/1 fol. 221, Johnston to same, 2 Jan. 1693/4; Fountainhall, *Decisions*, i, 571; *Annandale Book*, ii, 78, Annandale to Johnston, 13 May 1694; *Earls of Cromartie*, i, 106, Queensberry to Tarbat, 19 Mar. 1694.

199. *Ib.*, 101, Dalrymple to same, 24 Nov. 1693; *ib.*, 102–3, Breadalbane to same, 7 Dec. 1693; SRO GD 112/39/1278, [Tarbat] to Breadalbane, 26 Dec. 1693.

200. Riley, *King William*, 86; *HMCR Hope-Johnstone*, 96, Johnston to Annandale, 22 Mar. 1694; NLS MS 7016 fol. 5, Queensberry to Tweeddale, 4 Jan. 1694; *ib.*, MS 7028 fol. 36, Tweeddale to Blackbarony, 23 Feb. 1694; *ib.*, fols. 55v–56, same to same, 17 Mar. 1694.

201. *Ib.*, fol. 45, same to Johnston, 10 Mar. 1694; *Annandale Book*, ii, 70, Annandale to same, 15 Mar. 1694.

202. Murray was even hinted at for Secretary in Dalrymple's place. NLS MS 7016 fol. 23v, Blackbarony to Tweeddale, 18 Jan. 1694.

203. *HMCR Hope-Johnstone*, 177, Johnston to Crawford, 6 Dec. 1693; *Annandale Book*, ii, 69, same to Annandale, 1 Mar. 1694; SRO SP 3/1 fol. 221, same to Tweeddale, 2 Jan. 1693/4; *ib.*, PC 1/49, 358; *ib.*, GD 406/1/7457, [Hamilton] to [Duchess], 1 Mar. 1693/4.

204. The letters show that Simon Lord Lovat's later story that first Lovat and then he were tricked into joining the regiment by Murray and Glengarry with the claim that it was being raised to benefit James must be a lie. Atholl, *Chronicles*, i, 347, P. Murray of Dollery to Murray, 12 Mar. [1694]; *ib.*, 350, Major Hay to same, 11 Aug. 1694; *ib.*, 354–5; Blair, Atholl MSS, Box 29 I (7) 80, Hill to same, 14 July 1694; Lovat, *Memoirs*, 8–15; *Annandale Book*, ii, 77, Annandale to Johnston, 13 May 1694.

205. *Ib.*, 74, same to same, 17 Apr. 1694; *HMCR Hope-Johnstone*, 96, Johnston to

Annandale, 29 Mar. [1694]; Steele, *Proclamations*, ii, S3003, S3008; *Maxwells of Pollok*, ii, 93–4, Steuart to Pollok, 10 Apr. 1694; *Earls of Cromartie*, i, 105, Breadalbane to Tarbat, 8 Mar. 1694.

206. *Ib*; NLS MS 7016 fol. 44, Blackbarony to Tweeddale, 8 Feb. 1694; *ib*., fol. 60, same to same, 3 Mar. 1694; *ib*., fol. 74, same to same, 8 Mar. 1694; *ib*., fol. 87, same to same, 17 Mar. 1694.

207. Riley (*King William*, 105, n105) considers this as 'folklore ... border[ing] on fantasy'. However, a letter of 31 March from an Edinburgh cleric to Carstares on 31 March, two days after the Assembly sat, was already thanking him for getting the disastrous order withdrawn (*Carstares S.P.*, 62–3). The curious letter from an English Jacobite Presbyterian to the Scottish ones (*ib*., 52–6) shows one erratic course they might have taken if repulsed. Riley argued that 'William was merely taking the easy way out': if he could have been relied on to do that, his ministers would have had far fewer problems. Story, *Carstares*, 237–42, 244n; *Seafield Corr.*, 142, Steuart to Ogilvie, 30 Apr. 1694; SRO GD 406/1/7488, [Hamilton] to [Duchess], 27 Mar. 1694; *ib*., 6532, [Duchess] to [Hamilton], 29 Mar. 1694; NLS MS 14,408 fol. 283, [Johnston] to Tweeddale, 25 Mar. 1694; *HMCR Hope-Johnstone*, 96, same to Annandale, 29 Mar. [1694].

208. *Annandale Book*, ii, 357, same to same, 9 Apr. [1695]; NLS MS 7028 fol. 107, Tweeddale to Johnston, 31 May 1695; *ib*., MS 14,408 fol. 310, [Johnston] to Tweeddale, 7 June 1694.

209. SRO PC 1/49, 251–8; NLS MS 7016 fol. 12, Stevenson to Tweeddale, 6 Jan. 1693/4; *ib*., fol. 14, William to PCS, 30 Dec. 1693.

210. This assumes that the 'Halket Stirk' for whom a reward was offered in 1700 was the same one; but, as the title seems to have been transferred (see Chapter 1, n.49) it may not have been. *Seafield Corr.*, 121, J. Anderson to Ogilvie, 30 Aug. 1693.

211. Fountainhall, *Decisions*, i, 566, 591; SRO GD 112/39/1292, D. Toshach to Breadalbane, 10 Feb. 1694.

212. *Ib*., 40/4/6/56, ? to same, 10 Apr. 1694; *ib*., PC 1/49, 251–8 (*Highland Papers*, 92, Commission of Justiciary), 342; *HMCR Roxburghe*, 123–4, Hill to Polwarth, 14 July 1694.

213. *Ib*., 143, Culloden to same, 14 Aug. 1693.

214. *Ib*., 142–3; *ib*., 143–4, same to same, 25 Aug. 1693; SRO PC 1/50, 18–19; GD 112/39/1300, Johnston to Breadalbane, 30 Oct. 1694; Blair, Atholl MSS, Box 29 I (7) 88, Commissioners to Murray, 21 Sept. 1694.

215. *Highland Papers*, 94–7, PC register, 19 July 1694; NLS MS 7028 fol. 2, Tweeddale to Johnston, 13 Jan. 1694.

216. Perth, *Letters*, 36–7, Perth to Countess of Erroll, 31 July 1694; PRO PC 1/50, 133–4; NLS MS 14,266 fol. 56 (16, 20 Aug. 1694 (NS)); BL Add. 19,254 fol. 147, ? to Hamilton, [1693–4].

217. *Ib*., fol. 132, ? to Blair Drummond, 15 Jan. 1695; John, Master of Sinclair, *Memoirs of the Insurrection in Scotland in 1715*, ed. Sir W. Scott & J. MacKnight (Abbotsford Club, 1858), 29, 91–2, 260; Blair, Atholl MSS, Box 29 I (9) 138, Countess of Dundonald to Countess of Tullibardine, 17 Mar. 1697; *Memoirs of Locheill*, 328, 330–2.

218. See Chapter 12, pp. 398–9.

219. *Ib*., 249; *CSPD 1697*, 133, Warrant for removing sequestration, 23 Apr. 1697; *Annandale Book*, ii, 117, H. Villiers to Annandale, 25 May 1695; Macdonald, *Clan Donald*, ii, 341; SCA, Blairs Letters, Box C¹, 2, Clanranald to 'cousin', 25 June 1695.

220. NLS Adv. MS 13.1. 8 fol. 79, 'Behaviour of Alexander Robertson of Struan'; SRO PC 1/50, 103.

221. *Ib*., 68–9, 135, 196–7; *HMCR Hope-Johnstone*, 178, Gordon to Crawford, 23 Feb.

1694; SRO GD 406/1/7489, [Hamilton] to [Duchess], 29 Mar. 1694; NLS MS 7028 fol. 137, Tweeddale to Johnston, 25 Aug. 1694.

222. *Ib.*, fols. 124v–125, same to same, 26 July 1694; *ib.*, MS 7029 fol. 69, same to Pringle, 5 Sept. 1695; *ib.*, MS 7018 fol. 28, Annandale to Tweeddale, 27 Jan. [1695]; *ib.*, fols. 30–1, same to same, 22 Jan. [1695]; *ib.*, MS 7019 fol. 44, Pringle to same, 26 Sept. 1695(NS); SRO PC 1/50, 106, 241–2; *ib.*, SP 3/1 fol. 205v, Johnston to Steuart, 2 Nov. 1693; Drumlanrig, Queensberry Papers, Vol. 115, 28, ? to Queensberry, 10 Sept. 1695.

12

The Inquiry (November 1694–February 1696)

As William prepared to return from the 1694 campaign, Johnston mustered his allies in London for another attempt to crush the 'episcopalians'. They had better prospects than ever before, if he was correct in believing that Scottish politics ultimately depended on English ones. His Junto Whig allies, firmly in power since the spring, had governed fairly successfully, and (of more importance to William) could virtually guarantee fresh war supplies. The Junto were concerned to establish similar regimes in Ireland and Scotland, and had also personal debts to repay. Johnston had helped them against Nottingham, and Alexander Johnston, co-operating in an unsuccessful drive against plotters, had been unjustly blamed by Jacobite propagandists for the Duke of Shrewsbury's actions.[1]

Although they were working closely together, Johnston still somewhat mistrusted Tweeddale, less now from memory of the Edinburgh episode than because some of his confidants were close to Carstares, who had turned against Johnston that autumn.[2] However, Carstares's hostility, although chiefly resentment at his independence, included a superstitious belief that Melville, not he, was the Presbyterians' true representative; and fear of Melville, a family enemy, drove Tweeddale closer to Johnston. When summoned to London in November, he was alarmed that Melville, by mustering relatives and 'episcopalians', might be voted acting President of the Council.[3] Fortunately, there was another candidate, Annandale. His mercilessness to Jacobites and the death in France of his old seducer Montgomerie had purged any suspicions arising from the Club Plot, and a large majority elected him acting President.[4] With his usual ingratitude, he pestered Johnston to have William make the post permanent, and denounced Tweeddale and Murray to him.

The 'presbyterians' exploited this majority to overturn what remained of Breadalbane's highland policy. Already in August, Tweeddale had officially declared that William's order not to quarter in the Highlands for taxes before 1691 was a mere suspension, not a remission.[5] A Major Macdonald (Sir Donald's brother-in-law) who had not taken the Indemnity, although protected by Hill since 1690, was seized in Edinburgh carrying his old Jacobite commission. In October, the Council ordered that he be tried for High Treason, which he avoided only by accepting banishment to Ireland.[6] William, predictably, had not answered the Highland Commissioners' question whether Breadalbane's or Murray's interpretation of the Indemnity was correct, and now, with only one other member supporting Breadalbane, they applied to the Council. A committee of judges was appointed. On 29 November, they duly declared the highlanders fully liable for goods stolen, unless they could prove these had been consumed in the Jacobite camp, 'Bredalbin being left alone to flourish upon the pacification he said he had made, tho it was answered they must have given up without terms if their condition had been understood'. To his credit, he continued protesting even when it was clearly useless. Tweeddale smugly noted that he 'did but expose himself more yn ever I saw him'. Among those who immediately exploited the decision in the Session was Lady Glenlyon, who began proceedings against Keppoch.[7]

Johnston thought that the 'episcopalians' would blame any highland disorders on the Council's rigour, but that none were likely. However, three weeks later Mackintosh appeared before the Council demanding a warrant to seize Keppoch. Ignoring the wise example set by Hill, who had refused to arrest him while he attended the Justiciary Commission at Fort William, they granted it. Objectors were told that it was 'a strange politick to protect one corner of a country for murders and robberies ... to keep rascalls in quiet'.[8] This hostile view of the highlanders was the norm among 'presbyterians' just before they undertook the investigation of Glencoe.

Their superiority in the Council partly reflected the fact that more of the 'episcopalians' had succeeded in going to London for Court intrigues than the previous winter. This enabled Dalrymple to employ a dangerous weapon, a promise that the 'episcopalians' could persuade this or a new parliament to grant William eight months' cess for life. No parliament was likely to commit suicide this way, and the proposal dwindled into a pious hope in Tweeddale's secret instructions. Yet William showed such eagerness to regain all James's financial prerogatives, and Johnston and his supporters were so alarmed that an 'episcopalian' — and therefore unpatriotic — parliament might pass such a measure, that they temporarily proposed that the 'presbyterians' should offer the same on condition William dismiss the 'episcopalian' ministers.[9] The lesson that an appeal to the prerogative could revive the prospects of Dalrymple, whom he had written off, and jeopardise his own power and policies, encouraged Johnston towards greater radicalism.

Dalrymple had hoped by this unscrupulous proposal to get his father made Chancellor and Linlithgow Lord President; but soon the 'episcopalians' were struggling, at best, to delay unfavourable changes.[10] Breadalbane later considered Mary's death in December the fatal blow to them.[11] Of their English allies in 1691, there remained only Carmarthen, now Duke of Leeds but rapidly losing power. Early in 1695, to Johnston's joy, the Commons finally discredited him for taking bribes from the East India Company.[12] The card Dalrymple had played so often, the sufferings of the episcopalian clergy, was becoming ineffective. When William told him 'he did not admire any Society made difficulty of accepting members who would not say they had no mind to undo them', he saw the danger signal. The friendly English bishops could not decide whether they wanted the Episcopalians secured by comprehension or toleration as a separate body. 'Ile not burn my fingers for the method of it,' wrote Dalrymple, who now feared that toleration would produce constant disorder, 'altar against altar'. By early March, his memorials were advocating compromise all round, and he warned Breadalbane that only this shift had prevented disastrous ministerial changes.[13]

This enforced moderation brought the 'episcopalians' an incongruous ally,

Carstares, the 'M.' of Johnston's letters.[14] Although he declared violently to Johnston that winter that he would never have anything to do with such 'known knaves' as the 'episcopalians', in January he steered a presbyterian delegation almost exclusively into the company of Dalrymple, Linlithgow and English bishops.[15] By April, he was secretly conferring with Arran (in his capacity as Sunderland's son-in-law), was playing on Melville's resentment against Tweeddale and Johnston and on the presbyterianism (and disloyalty) of Steuart and Ormiston, and was declaring that more 'Jacobites'(his own term) should be brought into the government to broaden its base.[16] In response to this realignment, it was noted, Johnston 'acts more Cavaleerly that is with more assurance and less cringing to the Covenanted Apostles'.[17] As his trust in presbyterian support diminished, his Whig side grew stronger.

Johnston had strong hopes of transforming the ministry in January and February — 'Have patienc, we shall loose the horse or gain the sadle', he wrote. Carstares's and Melville's opposition, William's collapse after Mary's death and his natural procrastination destroyed them. Dalrymple thwarted Tweeddale's efforts for Johnston, often denying him access to William.[18] Even Johnston's most important protégé, Murray, had his request to be put on the Treasury Commission refused. Murray's opponents accused him, with some truth, of irregularities in his regiment, but Johnston, to ease the affront, forced through a grant to him of the sheriffdom of Perthshire.[19] Portland's balance was tilting towards the 'episcopalians', and he tried to make Linlithgow an extraordinary Lord of Session. Tweeddale however, was chosen early as Commissioner of the coming Parliament, and Johnston got Annandale made President of it despite Carstares.[20]

Carstares's casual words about 'Jacobites' partly explain Johnston's failure. He could not, as in 1693, exploit a rational fear of present conspiracy and invasion. William had announced, correctly, that Scotland was in no danger that summer. Johnston reported plots in March and argued in May that the parliamentary opposition must be depending on French promises, but he convinced nobody.[21] James himself admitted to Arran not only that Murray was heartily entering into William's service, but that Queensberry, Linlithgow and Breadalbane were likely to turn to Jacobitism again only if they suffered heavy disappointments.[22] This lack of present plotting probably diverted Johnston's attention to Glencoe and the intrigues before it, not yet covered by indemnity.

Without such concessions, Parliament might become uncontrollable. The only intended favours to 'country' discontent in the instructions Tweeddale carried north in mid-April were vague encouragement for a foreign plantation and an inquiry into the Poll farm. Yet Johnston knew that if the session failed he would be accused of secretly sabotaging it. Carstares, who had gone to Scotland to discover the 'real' dispositions of members, was intercepting his letters; and, if William had authorised this, he was determined to resign.[23] Yet Carstares' and Melville's departure north was an error. On 29 April, Johnston at last obtained 'some oylle to make the lamp burn, rather than risk a breach'. A chiefly 'presbyterian' commission was appointed to audit the Treasury accounts since 1692. Another, headed by Tweeddale, was to investigate the Massacre of Glencoe. Its other members were Annandale, Murray, the Advocate, Solicitor and Justice-Clerk, two Lords of Session and a (lowland) baron for Perthshire.[24]

William admitted later that he 'allowed the Glenco bussiness to be enquired into, because of the noise it had made at home and abroad'. Johnston may have used arguments he mentioned later, that the failure to act on the 1693 report would cause accusations of 'stifling'; and that a 'presbyterian' Parliament would not overlook accusations by those really to blame that the 'presbyterians' were responsible, and might order their own inquiry. He denounced Dalrymple's part in it, saying that only loyalty to a colleague had previously kept him silent; and he probably also played on William's susceptibilities by recalling how anxious the dead Archbishop Tillotson, and, even more, Mary had been to clear his name by establishing the truth. The commission was partly William's performance of a project he had neglected in her lifetime, like Greenwich Hospital.[25] The 'episcopalians' claimed that it was kept secret from Dalrymple, and did not even pass the seals until William had sailed, in mid-May — which indicates that Breadalbane financed Glenlyon's departure for Flanders earlier that month not as a dangerous witness but simply to enable him to keep his commission. Later, the 'managers' told Livingston to stay in Scotland for the session without giving the reason. Some 'episcopalians' tried to blunt their enthusiasm by hinting that William was implicated.[26] The commission, though very advantageous for them, had one major disadvantage. Tweeddale could not, if his employment of it was attacked, appeal to any written or verbal guidelines from William.

Johnston and Tweeddale naturally intended, as parliamentary 'managers', to attack the head of the 'episcopalian' ministry. Yet it was not immediately obvious who this was. Dalrymple might seem the obvious target; Johnston 'would rather be as low as the center [of the earth] than have writen' the letters calling for the Massacre. Yet he bracketed these, for political exploitation, with others of Dalrymple's which were merely indiscreet.[27] His opinion that Dalrymple was a spent force seemed confirmed when William appointed Robert Pringle to accompany him as Undersecretary to Flanders without consulting him. Stair was so ill that he had to visit Bath instead of attending Parliament, and Tweeddale's secret instructions anticipated his death.[28] Queensberry, long inactive and out of touch with the 'episcopalians', died on 28 March. It would take Drumlanrig some time to gather together the family 'interest'. In February, the 'episcopalians' had suspected him of intriguing with Johnston, and his attempt to gain his father's place on the Session was opposed not only by Tweeddale, because he was a soldier, but by Linlithgow as a rival.[29] Linlithgow himself had been temporarily cowed by Johnston's winter campaign, and was very unpopular with the Parliament.[30] Tarbat, temporarily under the illusion that he wanted to retire, was trying to resign as Register in favour of his cousin, Campbell of Aberuchill.[31]

Breadalbane hoped to establish himself as leader, founding his power on the second marriage for Glenorchy he had been arranging since early 1694, to Henrietta, sister of William's mistress Elizabeth Villiers, his favourite Lord Villiers and Portland's wife — the courtier family *par excellence*, a strong contrast with the Newcastles. This indicated that Breadalbane had committed himself to William, since James, the Stuart monarch least susceptible to the Villiers, could never trust a noble with so many 'wrong' connections. This alliance, he claimed, particularly roused Johnston's hostility. Yet, when the marriage took place on 22 May, Mary's death had, unforeseeably, driven William remorsefully to part with Elizabeth. Breadalbane, not understanding how this weakened him, began to act as leader.[32] Previously, Johnston claimed, because

> he never dipped in blood in the late reigns, ... possibly of several men of his ways ... he is the man they [Parliament] would rather have borne with ... had he kept to his character of going along quietly with his party, and making what money he could; but since his late alliance he would needs be the head of the party, and act above board, practising upon the members by threatenings and other undue means, and bidding defiance to all mankind.[33]

He apparently hoped to head a coalition, trying to win over Steuart. However, his new arrogance undermined the hopes that inspired it. He remained at Edinburgh, trying to browbeat the Council into paying him a ridiculous £800 for damage to Finlarig, until 17 April.[34] Arran, through Sunderland, provided an alternative means of applying to William — used, for instance, when Hill was again dangerously ill that winter, by Lieutenant-Colonel Hamilton's friends — but he had temporarily quarrelled with Breadalbane, partly because he too had courted Lady Henrietta.[35] Breadalbane reached London too late to establish himself in William's eyes, and had to return before the wedding to attend Parliament.

The Glencoe Commission seemed, from what was suspected, to be the perfect weapon to attack both Dalrymple and Breadalbane. Yet it would inevitably raise the question of William's involvement. Tweeddale and Johnston had, besides, as royal 'managers', a general obligation to concede only what was overwhelmingly demanded. They intended, therefore, that Breadalbane should be attacked for corruption in the Treasury and Stair, as so often before, for unjust judgements.[36] The 'managers' would avoid taking any action over Glencoe unless the threat of a parliamentary inquiry made it necessary — a delay which caused considerable difficulties with time. If, however, an inquiry was begun, they would exploit it to the limit.

Johnston's aims were — or became — more radical that is usually realised. Eight years later, when his circle could see his policy in perspective — and, admittedly, rationalise it — his former master-spy wrote: 'He is the first who shewed the Commons of that Kingdom their Strength, and to establish them on a Foot independent of the Nobility (to whom they have always been Slaves) as the surest way to make their Constitution lasting, and to make them a flourishing People'.[37] It is an unexpected comment on so flexible a politician, and one who had taken such trouble to win over magnates and their heirs. Yet that policy had failed to secure the triumph of his party and principles. The weight which his social position had given to Hamilton, despite his political ineptitude, had helped destroy the gains of the 1693 session when he reacted against the policy he had executed. Hamilton, besides, had been almost the only major recruit to counterbalance the flow of discontented 'presbyterian' peers such as Melville, with their dependent politicians, into alliance with the 'episcopalians', who, thanks to the link between civil and ecclesiastical hierarchy which had seemed so obvious since the Interregnum, were an immense numerical majority in the nobility.

Johnston, of course, was no doctrinaire, except with regard to 'episcopalians' and Tories. Besides the immense trouble he had taken to rehabilitate his chief Annandale, he greatly valued the one major ally his former policy had secured, Murray, who brought with him much of the Atholl 'interest'. Hamilton's death unexpectedly increased his significance: since Arran's irresponsibility and overt Jacobitism disqualified him from being political head of the family, most of them turned to his brother-in-law, an alliance that lasted at least until 1700.[38] However, Arran himself, after all Johnston's advances and advice, seemed incorrigible, and also opposed his attempts to promote Annandale in early 1695.[39] More significantly, favour for Murray revived his highland interest, naturally driving into the opposite faction Argyll, who, apart from being made an extraordinary Lord of Session, received nothing to reconcile him. He had been concentrating upon establishing an estate, and a mistress, in Northumberland. His attempt to remain incognito there caused his arrest as a Jacobite suspect in late 1694 — a grotesque misadventure which made Johnston underestimate him as an opponent.[40] Johnston probably saw Queensberry, with his strong connections with the English Tories, as more likely than his father to be hostile. When such magnates came to exert their full political strength, Scotland's future would, from Johnston's viewpoint, be bleak. Yet, since 1689, Atholl's and the late Queensberry's evil reputations from the late reign, their and Arran's Jacobitism, and Argyll's apparent personal incapacity for sustained effort, had prevented the magnate interests from dominating politics. The one partial exception was Hamilton's, but his death and Arran's delinquency had united much of that with Atholl's under Murray — a favourable opportunity which might not recur. Nor might the numerical weakness of the nobility as a politically active order: Tarbat estimated that nearly three-fifths of the peers were Jacobites, Nonjurors, Catholics, minors or simply persistent absentees from Parliament.[41]

Johnston's response was largely Fabian, the characteristic of one side of the 1695 session. He and Tweeddale as 'managers' looked on its economic measures, the East India Company, the Bank, agrarian acts for dividing lands held in runrig and commonty (revolutionary in giving an 'improving' minority's desire overriding power)[42] with a double vision, realistic about the immediate effect in a country with so few resources (naturally the side they emphasised when under attack that winter), yet hopeful that the acts would ultimately help to create national prosperity — precisely the type of far-sighted legislation that Fletcher of Saltoun claimed ministers were too selfish to attempt.[43] Johnston may have hoped that broadening the base of the nation's wealth would produce greater social independence, as in England; but he would naturally avoid revealing any such thoughts. One strand of his policy, however, was overt. The prosecution and supporting threats he launched in the 1695 session, relying on the voting power of barons and burghs, shattered the convention by which a great noble involved in Jacobitism, Queensberry or Breadalbane, inevitably escaped punishment, which descended upon lesser men like Montgomerie — or MacIain. And the nobles realised his intention.

A second one, the strengthening of Parliament at the expense of William's prerogative and his advisers' power, was an even greater reversal of his past policy. Sustained by his trust that William's intentions were basically good, if not diverted by premature confrontations, he had willingly worked within his system of government, despite its drawbacks —William's constant delays, frequent irrationalities and reliance on 'rules and often very hidden ones' to which all his ministers must conform, whatever the 'mortifications' ('my dayly bread', wrote Johnston in 1694);[44] the use as intermediaries of Portland (an even worse procrastinator than William)[45] and Carstares; the overall lack of interest in Scottish affairs. Johnston had the warning example of Montgomerie, whom impatience and inflexibility had driven into soul-destroying Jacobitism. Johnston, like him, depended largely on his power over Parliament, but exercised it with careful ambiguity. In 1693, for example, he had exploited a largely concocted danger of invasion and rebellion to obtain excessive supplies which probably no other argument would have procured. Yet he used the allegations to put pressure on William to dismiss the 'episcopalian' leaders. And, indirectly, he slightly strengthened Parliament in relation to the executive by allowing it to examine material on Jacobitism — breaking a cardinal rule observed in England rigidly since mid-1689.[46]

Even among ministerial Williamites strong underground hostility to aspects of his rule existed, often in surprising places. When Johnston was appointed, Dalrymple's Undersecretary, momentarily defying the predictable rivalry between the Secretaries which was to make him also Johnston's enemy, sent him a memorial suggesting that the Secretaries should unite and risk everything to smash the insulting 'slavery' in which Portland held the nation. Receiving no encouragement, he naturally plunged into intrigues against him on Dalrymple's behalf, but Johnston never exploited this dangerous paper against him.[47] Now, when William's susceptibility to the promise of a cess for life and Carstares' mould-breaking intrigues showed how precarious were the advances he had gained, Johnston (according to Dalrymple) asked for Portland's authorisation to attack the 'episcopalians' in Parliament, or at least, if an independent attack succeeded, that would stand by the victors afterwards. On his refusal, Johnston decided (he claimed in 1704) that Portland, though well-intentioned, was ignorant of Scotsmen, and must be prevented from meddling — an attempt that lost him his post.[48]

Loss of support at Court left only one possible alternative power-base for Johnston and his principles, a strengthened Parliament. Not only, however, must the strengthening, to succeed, avoid being too blatant or stressing the breach with the Court; Johnston himself probably saw matters as less clear-cut, and could consider himself a royal servant making only unavoidable concessions, even when he was organising and encouraging the demand for them. His final course was largely a response to events: Breadalbane's unexpected firmness drove him and Tweeddale to extremes they would have shuddered at in the spring. Yet the extremes developed logically from their programme. Tweeddale's bold support for it was in conscious contrast to the trimming of his past career; he said 'that he is going off, and that he is resolved his exit shall be honourable'.[49]

Johnston's strategy depended on William's need, while the war continued, for regular grants of supplies, which forced him to ensure that relations with the Scottish Parliament did not break down. This was the first time it had possessed such leverage: Glenorchy lamented that summer that William 'looks upon a Scots parliament and ane English the same, and therfore is not willing to medle in anything commenced in them'.[50] The session must be held while William was campaigning, unable to exercise even the second-hand control possible from London. Dalrymple knew that his failure to get it held before William's departure or after real campaigning was over was a heavy defeat.[51] The delay before William returned would also give his anger at the 'managers'' more extreme acts time to subside. The wartime realism he had shown over the 1694 Assembly might overcome the bloody-minded clinging to prerogatives which had made his ministers' position in 1689 so hopeless, and make him accept a *fait accompli* which guaranteed future supplies. The alternative, disavowing Parliament's proceedings, Johnston warned in July, would be fatal, confirming suspicions 'that the King undervalues & abandons this nation and that further than to keep us from Rebellions wch might make him uneasy in England, that he Cares not what becomes of it, and therfore leaves the nation in such a state, that come what will the event must be ruine to that handfull of honest men'.[52] His own leadership, encouraging Parliament to go to extremes, had forced this dilemma upon William; but there was enough truth in his warning to show how dangerous a course it was.

However, even if William could afford to alienate the Scottish Parliament, he must conciliate his English one; and English contacts provided the vital security for Johnston's policy. Twenty years earlier, the fear that Lauderdale intended to make Scotland a base for imposing absolutism upon England and the axiom that government encroachments on Scottish rights were trial runs for English ones, had forged a link between the Whigs and the Scottish parliamentarians. This had endured, and Montgomerie had played upon it in late 1689. By 1695, Court and Country Whigs were increasingly divided, but they might temporarily reunite even to attack the prerogative if this were being exploited by Tory, allegedly crypto-Jacobite, ministers. Johnston's and Tweeddale's main correspondent in the Junto, Shrewsbury, was the member who longest retained links with the Country Whigs, and had accepted office (although, typically, Fletcher of Saltoun never forgave him for this) only on condition that William should pass a Triennial Act.[53] Through him and other channels, they could influence the Commons. Their tactics were to imply that the Scottish Parliament had, or should have, like the English one, the right to investigate grave public scandals, particularly Jacobite treason; that the 'episcopalians' were mostly Jacobites; and that those tried or indicted before it for major crimes were not merely (as Breadalbane's legal supporters were to claim) the King's prisoners being prosecuted in but not by

Parliament, whom he could simply pardon according to his personal wish. William's own failure to protest that summer seemed to confirm this. The English Parliament had fought long to gain its equivalent rights, and was jealous of Court attempts to limit them.[54] Although William faced no direct confrontation, he would know that disavowing such Scottish proceedings on his return would greatly alarm them as a possible precedent for similar repression in England — a repercussion he would scarcely dare risk.

Parliament assembled on 9 May. Carstares, unnervingly, hung about during the first sessions before leaving for Flanders, having promised 'presbyterian' members some changes.[55] William's letter requested supplies for the army and a naval force to protect trade, and recommended church union. Yet its reference to Parliament's 1693 letter might, without his realising it, be misconstrued to imply that, had his collapse after Mary's death not delayed all business, he would already have dismissed the 'episcopalians'. The latter claimed that rumours corroborating this had been vigorously spread. The disillusionment among members who found that Johnston had no secret assurances to give them made matters still worse. Both Tweeddale and Johnston reported to William after the first sessions that most members were desperately afraid that, if he were killed in battle, the 'episcopalians' would betray them to James; some were therefore reluctant even to maintain an army.[56] Breadalbane admitted that it would be counterproductive if the 'episcopalians' took the lead in requesting supply. A meeting of fifty to sixty backbenchers planned to address William to dismiss him, Tarbat, Linlithgow and Dalrymple, without giving specific reasons. Johnson admitted that, to divert them from this, he advised them to bring forward charges they could prove. He foresaw a 'backward and discreditable' session which might easily become uncontrollable and have to be adjourned, and in which business would have to be carried on chiefly in committees. Behind this was a widening alienation and apathy that had deeper roots than fear of 'episcopalians' or Jacobites; and yet dismissing the 'episcopalians' would be a step towards recovery.[57] The problem reconciled the two sides of his thinking, as royal servant and Whig: he could organise the 'presbyterians'' preparation of charges against their opponents, while justifying this to himself and the Court as necessary to keep the session from collapse. Carstares noted that one of Johnston's later reports inadvertently showed that he had exaggerated Parliament's original intractability.[58]

Johnston was more willing to offend the nobles' susceptibilities as their initial attendance was poor — only twenty-five — and as Queensberry and Argyll were openly hostile to Tweeddale. In the new Committee for Security, Queensberry, Argyll, Leven, Morton and Lothian were powerless against four 'presbyterian' peers and eighteen barons and burgh members,who showed their independence by electing, for most meetings, Hamilton of Whitelaw to preside. On 21 May, this Committee presented, with its report on supply, a demand for an inquiry into Glencoe. Not even the 'episcopalian' apologists could deny that this attracted massive support.[59] Tweeddale met it by exhibiting the royal commission, and met a strong demand that the findings should be laid before Parliament with vague assurances that William would doubtless do so. Parliament voted its thanks for

William's order 'wherby the honor and justice of the nation might be vindicated', and the Committee immediately prepared proposals for massive supplies.[60] One of the few dissidents was Fountainhall, who thought an inquiry upon oath without due process illegal, but his fellow-'episcopalians' dared not appear to obstruct justice by supporting him. It was immediately reported that Dalrymple would be attacked over Glencoe.[61]

The commission had already passed the seals, but, to conciliate William, nothing was done until 23 May, when Tweeddale displayed it. Annandale immediately summoned Hill and Hamilton (who had recently transferred to Lindsay's regiment by exchange with its lieutenant-colonel, Jackson) to attend, bringing their original orders and select witnesses. Those at hand were examined, Sir Thomas Livingston —enabling him to establish his version unchecked by Hamilton's papers — Major Forbes, the Clerks of Council and Ardkinglas. The horror of the Massacre began to emerge. The Commission met assiduously, often crowding out the Committee for Security.[62]

Annandale presided, and conducted formal correspondence; but Murray gave the inquiry its fire and drive. He was the only commissioner with real knowledge of the Highlands, and, barred from Parliament as Atholl's eldest son, could concentrate undividedly on the investigation. Breadalbane was saying 'that he is sure nothing will be made out against him because the orders and letters ... did come from a freind of his', Dalrymple. To Murray, convinced, like others, that Breadalbane had advised Dalrymple, this seemed shocking cynicism. His genuine determination to have 'that barbarous action ... laied on the true author' conveniently harmonised with his patronage of the Macdonalds and his hatred of Breadalbane. He wrote 'to acquaint the Laird of Glenco, and any of his people that can giv best information of the matter of fact'. He ascertained from his mother-in-law that Hamilton's private conclusion from the 1693 report had been that 'it would light much upon Bredalbin & the Mr of Stair, by whom the warrand was procured'. 'The Government here' was directing the Commission to exceed its warrant and investigate Breadalbane's 'private articles', and Murray concentrated on this. He sent for Glengarry, and had Atholl summon Keppoch, who left Dunkeld under escort lest any of Breadalbane's friends (including Duncan Menzies, summoned himself only after Keppoch was secured) should spirit him away. It was argued that this unauthorised investigation 'will bring the Glenco affaire to be best understood'. Retrospective complaints would be meaningless when Breadalbane's responsibility for the Massacre was proved; nobody foresaw it might not be.[63]

Hill left Fort William early in June. Even before the summons, he had feared trouble from Parliament. The Laird of Grant, one of the most uncontrollable of 'presbyterian' barons, was making trouble. He may already have obtained a paper of complaints the gentry of Badenoch, his enemies and Hill's friends, had imprudently made against the Ruthven garrison. Lieutenant-Colonel Hamilton was in Ireland when the summons arrived, possibly (despite his exchange into Lindsay's regiment) to arrange the illegal shipment of Irish victual to supply the fort, which Hill was unsuccessfully to petition Parliament to allow.[64] Murray, hostile to him from family interests, was to investigate his share in an action he knew to be indefensible. Not surprisingly, he followed the guidelines indicated to him.

Hill can only just have reached Edinburgh on 7 June, and the commissioners' proceedings that day showed their priorities. They imposed on the witnesses and themselves an oath to reveal nothing until the investigation was completed, which they were unscrupulously to break. Glengarry's deposition described Breadalbane's attempt to get certificates of innocence after the Massacre, Barclay's and Menzies's mission — and the drawing up of unsigned 'private articles' at Achallader on 2 July, on which he perjured himself without hesitation. Hill told what he had heard of these 'articles' in 1691. Even if no longer Breadalbane's enemy, he could not soften accusations already on record.[65] The Commission had tried to hide Keppoch's presence in Edinburgh. To make him co-operative, a petition was introduced in Parliament that morning from the town of Inverness for permission to cite him there to refund the 4,000 merks he had extorted in 1689, and was granted. Nevertheless, he denied all knowledge of the 'articles', despite Murray's verbal battering and interrogator's tricks, and he sent Breadalbane a warning.[66]

Business meanwhile proceeded in Parliament, with Johnston taking the lead and speaking indefatigably on all matters.[67] The 'presbyterians' were further alienated in late May when the unpopular Linlithgow received a gift of Dunfermline's forfeited estate which duplicated one to Livingston. Linlithgow reported that the 'managers' were assuring members that their accusations against ministers would be acceptable to William.[68] The first attack, was not on him but on Stair, for an allegedly corrupt judicial decision. Johnston prudently left the 'club' of forty members meeting late on 1 June before they began planning their tactics, but Annandale remained to encourage them. The petition was brought in on 3 June. Stair, of course, was absent, sick at Bath, and Tweeddale disrupted his son Hew's arguments defending him. Most members thought an inquiry justified; but even some 'presbyterians' were uneasy when it was proposed to lay it before the partisan Committee for Security rather than a new one, and the motion passed by only three votes. Despite considerable obstruction, a report was later made; but Johnston claimed that it was not presented because by then Glencoe had sufficiently discredited the Dalrymples.[69]

The 'episcopalians' were awaiting an interim report on this on 10 June, and Breadalbane sat unsuspecting in his place, when Annandale announced an unexpected discovery the Glencoe Commission had obtained from Glengarry and Hill. The 'private articles' and Glengarry's deposition on them were read out in this heightened melodramatic atmosphere, and it was moved to prosecute him for treason. 'This surprize being great, many things might have bein said that did not occurr', although Queensberry, Argyll, Linlithgow, Tarbat, the Melvilles and Hew Dalrymple spoke for Breadalbane. He himself, taken aback, claimed incongruously both that William had authorised the lengths to which he went in negotiation, and that there were never any 'articles', adding that Glengarry was a Papist and his hereditary enemy. Parliament ignored William's August 1691 approbation because he did not then have it in his pocket. Queensberry testified that the accusation had been laid before William and ignored. Melville, the 'episcopalians'' most useful ally, emphasised how persistently he himself had brought it before Mary, and vainly proposed that Breadalbane should be allowed a private interview with Tweeddale to prove his case. Others argued that the Glencoe Commission had no authority to investigate something so many months earlier, but many burgh members assumed (they afterwards claimed) that the charge must be relevant to the Massacre.[70]

Having phrased the question to exclude the alternative of delaying until William could be informed, the accusers carried the vote that the Advocate should immediately start a process of treason against Breadalbane by a fairly small margin — twelve, he claimed, with only five peers supporting it. None of his several lists of those voting for and against him coincides with this, but all have one feature: the great majority of the nobles is for him, and it is the weight of the barons and burghs which is decisive. The fullest list, presumably a survey of all members rather than recording any single vote, reckons as for him 16 dukes, marquesses and earls, 9 viscounts and lords, 33 shire barons and 28 burgh members; against him (besides the 'neutral' Tweeddale and Annandale) 3 earls (another list gives 5), 4 officers of state, 49 barons and 35 burgh members, 'the very tradesmen of these towns', he wrote, 'who generally are brought over with very small promises, [to] what they judge for the time to be the rising side'. As before the attack on Stair, many of these commoners had probably been prepared at a weekend 'club'. The peers voting against him, he claimed, mostly had government pensions; the only 'episcopalian' one was Lovat, evidently directed by his brother-in-law Murray. Carstares had alienated from Johnston some 'presbyterian' peers, such as Belhaven, who might have been expected to support his patriotic policies. Melville, as an Officer of State, abstained from voting. Breadalbane was committed to the Castle.[71]

'I doe desire your Majesties commands . . .', wrote Tweeddale, 'if you will have a stop putt to this procese which will hardly be gott done but by adjourning the parliament'. Though he helped delay further proceedings while awaiting a reply, he knew that William's need for supply made adjournment practically impossible.[72] Breadalbane wrote to Portland emphasising that he had merely listened to the highlanders' 'impertinent proposalls' at Achallader. Queensberry pointed out that such magnifying of old charges would make everybody feel unsafe. To anticipate Breadalbane's other friends, who lamented wildly to William's entourage and English ministers that his life was in imminent danger, Johnston also wrote to Portland — Glenorchy's brother-in-law. He both posed as a royal servant, automatically obliged to follow up any charge of treason, and showed his involvement. There was no design against Breadalbane's life or fortune; it was merely a means to force his resignation from the Treasury.[73] To Shrewsbury, he added that the charge probably could not be proved. Breadalbane's fear arose from knowledge that Johnston had evidence of his Jacobite intrigues since taking office; but all charges would be dropped if he resigned. Johnston was not telling the full truth. His actual warning, via the new Lady Glenorchy, was 'that there was but one way left to save you, which was to throw your Self in the kings mercy before the tryall begun, and this is a preparitory for a pardon which in these cases are never refus'd'. This would have branded the whole 'episcopalian' party with Jacobitism.[74]

Johnston's further attempts to smash the Opposition alliance drove home the social message of the vote. He sent Argyll a message that, if he did not change sides in Parliament,

> he the said SJ had a paper in his pocket under the E hande that would ruin him and his familie, and that whenever he did sie the King he would be upon his knees to beg his Maties pardon for that he ever did speak to the King in favour of the Earle, and that nothing less than the kings pardon could saif his life, and the mangrs had it under ther Consideratne to secure the Earle in prisone in the mean tyme.

Johnston was abusing the confidential information he had inherited as Secretary, for the sequel shows that the paper concerned the dealings with Balcarres in 1691. Argyll confronted Johnston, identified it, and sent him to Melville to confirm that he had acted in William's interest.[75] He afterwards erupted into attacks on the Glencoe Commission, challenging one member to a duel. The attempt increased the nobles' conviction that Johnston was attacking their order, and their determination to retaliate. Argyll was to write that, since 'the mob. intends to make a wondrous weapon shaw ... this winter at London', 'the nob.' must also 'think of drawing a fitt detashment'.[76] Tarbat, who heard in mid-June that he would be attacked (as at least one member was) for the advice he had given the episcopalian clergy, drew the same moral: 'The nobility is the force and pulse of this nation' but 'a burges vote does as much as the Duke of Queensberries or Earle Argyle'.[77] Melville was attacked more legitimately, but inconclusively, for a £3,000 bond he had extorted from Edinburgh in 1690.[78] So many different interests aligned together could not plausibly be dismissed as Jacobite 'malignants' (though Middleton, now seldom in touch with Scotland, later expressed pleasure at the 'good behaviour in the parliament' of Queensberry as well as Tarbat).[79]

The Glencoe Commission's voluntary exposure of the sensational charge against Breadalbane, which violated every rule of parliamentary management, had its foreseeable effect. Parliament on 14, 17 and 20 June moved that Tweeddale should give them a full account of the proceedings, and deliberately slowed its own activities, amid hints that finance would be delayed until they saw the Report — a serious matter when Tweeddale had already had to ask William to authorise extending the session a week or two. He took the other commissioners' opinion in writing to justify himself, and replied to the third motion that the Report was only just completed. He would immediately dispatch a copy to William, and, as a gesture of respect, lay it before them only after four days' delay. Parliament responded by passing an act for six months' cess. The token delay could not compensate William for being deprived of the choice of revealing or concealing the Report's contents — a point which made some 'presbyterians' uneasy. Yet the 'managers'' attack on Breadalbane had made the demand irresistible. Many future 'Country' members (like their ally Andrew Fletcher) saw Glencoe as both a means and a justification for overthrowing the incorrigible pre-Revolution ministers. Tweeddale later rationalised his action as making Parliament's exculpation of William more impressive, since done after a free inquiry.[80]

Parliament's demands had also put pressure on the commissioners to finish the Report. Iain MacIain, his brother and their clansmen probably arrived only on 15 June, when a protection was issued. Murray (presumably the only Gaelic-speaking commissioner) took a major part in obtaining their statements and drafting that section of the Report. Longer time could not have remedied that section's one major weakness: apart from a few transferred soldiers, Glenlyon's and Drummond's companies were with Argyll's regiment (now his son Lord Lorne's) in Flanders.[81]

Political considerations caused deeper distortions elsewhere. Livingston must be protected; and, as he was in some disfavour with William for earlier refusing to accompany him to Flanders, nothing must be left to chance. If Hill had repeated his 1693 testimony that he had informed Livingston of MacIain's submission well before the Massacre, the Commission, remembering that Parliament would be re-examining the evidence, could not have declared him blameless. There was therefore an understanding, probably tacit, that Hill would omit this point and not produce Livingston's letters; in return, they gave full weight to his real excuses for his conduct. Lieutenant-Colonel Hamilton jeopardised this policy by producing all his relevant letters from Livingston, including the fatal order of 23 January — which showed that he knew MacIain had taken the oath after the deadline — and others expressing contempt for the 1693 inquiry. The order was quoted in the Report, but so was his justification that he had only just returned from his abortive London journey and that he knew nothing of the quartering of troops in Glencoe.[82] The commissioners might justify their mildness to him more easily since the report pronounced no judgement on any of the soldiers involved, not even Hamilton for ordering the quartering.

The commissioners also had to prove Breadalbane guilty to justify their meddling with the Achallader negotiations and their denunciation of him. The Report placed these negotiations in July, indicating their preoccupation with Glengarry's charges, and framed its account of the Massacre between Breadalbane's quarrel with MacIain and his offer to the survivors. Yet they could find nothing more. Hamilton was strictly interrogated, and afterwards wrote to Annandale denying 'upon the faith of a Christian having any thing to doe with a party as is alledged, or ever had, more than became me or a person of my station in duety and sivillity'. The 'party' was Breadalbane, whom the Report tried to link with Dalrymple's letters to Hamilton. The commissioners spread the slur that Hamilton was being disingenuous — and, indeed, were convinced that evidence of Breadalbane's guilt was being concealed.[83] Johnston tried to fill the gap for William with *a priori* deduction:

> The Macdonalds and the Campbells being the two great names in the Highlands, and emulous the one of the other, and the Macdonalds having defeated the 12,000l. negotiation, it is evident that dominion and resentment have been at the bottom of the business, and that my Lord Breadalbane has imposed upon the Master of Stair. That which is in the report about Breadalbane amounts only to conjecture.[84]

There was no such difficulty over Dalrymple. His letters provided evidence for all the commissioners' charges, even (probably mistakenly) that he had known beforehand of MacIain's submission. His violence of expression also made it easier to distinguish between his responsibility and the King's. William was, inevitably, declared blameless, without resort to the admission that he was careless in Scottish business. Yet they weakened this conclusion by omitting one basic background fact — that the Court had reason to believe until mid-January that the highland war was continuing. This was largely mere hindsight, but it helped give Dalrymple's December remarks to Hamilton the air of a sinister plot. Hindsight and recent political realignments also encouraged them to present the cancellation of MacIain's certificate as a conspiracy by Stair and the Campbells, including the former 'presbyterian' Aberuchill (now Tarbat's would-be successor as Register) and Sheriff-Clerk Colin (a dependent of Argyll).[85]

Mention of these distortions must not devalue the Report's permanent value and importance. It created a sensation when Tweeddale placed it, with William's instructions and Dalrymple's letters, before Parliament on 24 June. Even the government's friends were surprised that it could vindicate itself so far. The 'episcopalians' argued that they should leave anything further to the Commission, but, weakened by uncertainty over William's real intentions, were naturally defeated. Parliament immediately voted that William's instructions allowed mercy for all who submitted, even after 1 January; and, therefore, that the killings were murder. Crawford and Polwarth immediately proposed an address to William to have Dalrymple sent home for trial as an accessory (which would incapacitate him from acting as Secretary). Yet even some 'presbyterians' decided that Dalrymple, though violent, had made 'the principall instructions ... the regula regulans in everie step of that action', so that the fault must lie lower down. Johnston urged William to send the officers of Lorne's home for trial, since their orders would probably be held to justify them.[86]

On 26 June, Dalrymple's friends tried vainly to have the methods of the killings considered first, to bog down the inquiry, and to address the King on what was already done. The documents were re-read, and there was a violent nine hours' debate on whether Dalrymple's letters exceeded the instructions. Argyll, roused by Johnston's attempted blackmail, led the opposition, but some 'presbyterians' later to join the 'Country Party' probably helped to make the debate the most undutiful Johnston claimed ever to have heard, with attempts to lay the responsibility on William's instructions. However, they hardly dared place this on record, and finally the opponents abstained — 85 against 71 who voted, the 'episcopalians' later claimed.[87] A dishonest *Information* Hew Dalrymple had written defending his brother was printed too late for the vote, and was condemned as calumnious.[88] The vote made the Glencoe men petition Parliament for compensation for their material losses, and, despite one aggrieved member's protest that the young MacIains were murderers and robbers, they were referred to the Committee for Security.[89]

An event the same day was to make all the virtuoso organisation and intrigues futile: the act establishing a Scots East India Company was touched. The earliest planning among merchants in London had made Johnston advise William to insert the (very vague) limitations in his instructions to Tweeddale, and Tweeddale was uneasy at the immense concessions granted to it in committee. Yet, when it passed, Johnston sent merely a note of the date, nothing on the contents, and Tweeddale wrote nothing.[90] Preoccupied with concealing their manipulation of the Glencoe inquiry, the use of blackmail, their activity as Court 'managers' to foster what might be thought a 'Country' programme, they overlooked so apparently uncontroversial a measure. This roused suspicions in hindsight that they had deliberately concealed its signficance from William, or, at least, from the English; even, as was later widely believed, that they had illegally prolonged the session specifically to pass the act.[91] For the murderous ill-luck which constantly made the 'managers' appear more radical than they intended still pursued them. On 27 June (OS), William signed an instruction prolonging Parliament for a month, although it could not reach Scotland exactly on time. When the French captured the packet-boat carrying it, Tweeddale determined, on the strength of reports of its existence, to extend the session for some weeks without formal authority — which was technically High Treason.[92]

On 28 June, Livingston (having failed to get himself summoned to Flanders) had his responsibility considered. Only two of his letters to Hamilton were produced. When Argyll and the 'episcopalians' proposed a vote whether or not he also had exceeded his instructions, it was argued that he might well believe Dalrymple's letters were authorised — although this would not excuse whoever ordered the quartering. It was voted that Livingston had had reason to give the orders. This, and the stronger passage in Parliament's address to William, would have been impossible had Hill produced the same testimony and letters as for the 1693 inquiry. Not surprisingly, Livingston was still uneasy in 1699 at the prospect of a fresh investigation.[93]

Hill was more roughly treated on 2 July, attacked from both sides and forced to undergo interrogation in open Parliament. He was asked whether he had produced any documents before the Commission besides those now shown, why he had delayed and then ordered the Massacre, whether he had told Hamilton that MacIain had taken the oath, who had described the passes out of Glencoe. His answers satisfied them, and he was voted innocent.[94]

Hamilton was summoned for 4 July, but absconded instead. Previous debates had shown that obedience to orders would not justify him. Before fleeing to Flanders, he wrote to Annandale that the spreading of rumours that he was being disingenuous, and the refusal of copies of the letters and orders to him, had frightened him. He had some reason: six years later Captain Kidd, an embarrassment to the English ministers, was hanged for piracy partly because documents he called for were 'unavailable' in official custody. Thus the inquiry did some rough justice. Hamilton had fairly certainly organised the abuse of hospitality in Glencoe, and his previous intrigues had so undermined Hill's authority that he dared not protest. Yet Hamilton had a moral code, and would not save himself by bearing false witness.[95] On 8 July, although the 'episcopalians' defended him, Parliament voted that there were grounds for prosecuting him; that

Major Duncanson should be interrogated, in Flanders or Scotland, on his part; and that Glenlyon, Drummond and their subordinates should be sent home for trial. An address to William summarising Parliament's findings and requesting compensation for the Macdonalds, was passed on the 10th, after Dalrymple's supporters had attempted a last amendment and had been beaten by 41 votes. A speedy reply was evidently hoped for.[96]

Meanwhile, Breadalbane remained in prison, while the shock of his arrest spread through the Highlands. Sir Donald Macdonald, fearing a similar attack on Tarbat for his 1690 negotiations, offered to provide proof that they had been in William's interest.[97] The blow Breadalbane's influence had suffered was shown within a fortnight. Rob Roy Macgregor, who had been successfully on the run from Murray, hastened to Edinburgh and formally submitted to him, with Glengarry and Alasdair MacIain as cautioners for his good behaviour.[98] This benefited Murray's campaign to re-establish Atholl dominance over the Macgregors. The childless chief who died in 1693 had, despite Atholl's pressure, nominated as successor the Laird of Kilmannan, whose chosen alias was Graham and who immediately handed over a Macgregor thief to Breadalbane for execution. When, in 1694, the unstable Kilmannan pointlessly murdered his servant while drunk, Murray, his rigid morality conveniently harmonising with family interest, collected evidence to ensure in advance that sympathetic local courts would not stifle the crime and that William would grant no pardon. Only Kilmannan's potential usefulness as a spy on Jacobites after the Assassination Plot broke Murray's web.[99]

During late June, as it became clear that Breadalbane would not break and resign, the government built a case against him. As Johnston protested, they never intended to execute him; but they clearly intended to convict him, using evidence of his more recent Jacobite intrigues as adminicles. William's order to drop the prosecution had been lost with his permission to continue the session, and nobody in Scotland knew that it had been sent.[100] To blacken Breadalbane's reputation still further, the Countess was roused to petition Parliament over the Caithness land bargains.[101] Lochiel was arrested (which made other highlanders flee to the hills) and brought to Edinburgh. He, Keppoch and Duncan Menzies were interrogated and exhorted by Glengarry to make them confirm his account. On refusing, they were imprisoned in the Tolbooth until Parliament rose.[102] Hill, the other main prosecution witness, secretly gave Carwhin the useful information that Sir Aeneas Macpherson had given him the 'private articles'.[103]

Sir Aeneas himself was in the Tolbooth. He had been arrested in London in early 1694, had retracted a promise to tell all, and (with dubious legality) had been shipped north for examination. Now the Advocate visited him, and suggested that he should testify against his enemy Breadalbane (with whom Steuart himself had held political negotiations two months earlier), citing Glengarry as a respectable precedent. However, this infringed Macpherson's intermittent but genuine sense of honour, and he refused. The Council threatened him with torture — proof of their determination to try Breadalbane — but he persisted, denouncing torture in a petition and claiming to have helped pacify the Highlands in 1691. Breadalbane sent Macnachtan to thank him. In November, the Council retaliated by banishing him.[104]

On 27 June, Breadalbane received his indictment, which gave the date of the treasonable meeting as 2 July.[105] Besides the lawyers formally allotted him, he had untiring help from Tarbat, who gave Glengarry's testimony special consideration, arguing that the past grudges he was now openly declaring disqualified him as a witness.[106] On 1 July, Breadalbane was brought before Parliament. He had prepared, and presumably delivered, a fighting speech emphasising that the charge did not concern Glencoe; that the Court had asked him to negotiate; that he had patriotically attempted to transfer £12,000 from the English Treasury for distribution in Scotland; that the Achallader agreement had dispersed the highlanders, and that his opponents had disrupted it by offering higher terms. His supporters rallied and, despite Johnston's strong protests, gained him a fortnight, close to the time Tweeddale had promised to adjourn, to collect evidence.[107] The next day, two-thirds of the Parliament walked out to avoid the vote for forfaulting Middleton and Melfort as traitors — not merely 'episcopalians' who might now be branded as Jacobites, but also 'presbyterians' plainly reluctant to join in prosecutions which might one day recoil on them. Tarbat was conveniently sick. Annandale, presiding, sarcastically sent to 'tell these Noblemen yt they might come back for the danger was past'. And that had been merely a formality: they would be even less likely, Johnston considered, to support a real and controversial trial. The threats of Court displeasure with which 'presbyterian' members were being bombarded might rouse some to further defiance, but would cow others.[108]

Carwhin prepared Breadalbane's printed *Answer* to the indictment. They and Tarbat had considered discrediting Glengarry by telling the more complex truth behind the story of 'private articles', but so over-subtle a defence might have backfired and was dropped. The *Answer* also indicates uneasiness over Menzies's mission to James, which Johnston alleged he could prove. Howevere, Barcaldine was extremely successful in collecting alibis for 2 July. Feeling in Argyllshire was strongly for Breadalbane. Even Ardkinglas, whose testimony had not directly affected him and who had voted for him, was in local disgrace.[109]

On 15 July, Breadalbane was brought to the bar, and pleaded that the failure to provide him with a list of prosecution witnesses should invalidate the process, but he was given forty-eight hours to give in his defence. However, the government was plainly uncertain which way several witnesses would testify, since Lochiel, Keppoch and Duncan Menzies were also summoned for the defence, as well as which way members would vote.[110] Steuart 'urged for the King's interest that the trial should be expeded in this session', but two days later Tweeddale abruptly ended the session, to prevent the 'presbyterians' from addressing William for the dismissal of ministers, and, he claimed, so 'that the adjournment should anticipate yt diet [Breadalbane's trial] that the processes might be altogether at your Maties disposall'. They were not: the trial was postponed to the next Parliament.[111]

The session had otherwise been successful. Supply had been obtained. At the price of some bad puritanical acts, Johnston had got the time extended in which episcopalian ministers might take the oaths. One main reason for the violent attacks on their patrons had been to convince them that it would be futile to hold out, as in 1693, in hope of something better.[112] Another, of course was to crush the 'episcopalians' so utterly in Parliament that William must dismiss them to remain on terms with it. The letter which Tweeddale frustrated by adjourning would merely have stated crudely what the 'managers'' activities had been directed to proving implicitly all session. Solicitor Ogilvie, a pure careerist, was sufficiently convinced of their success to throw in his lot with them openly. He wrote to Carstares that the majorities obtained against Dalrymple, Stair and Breadalbane proved how little real power their party had: most, though not all, of them should be dismissed. The 'episcopalians' suffered another major blow when Linlithgow, who still had much influence, died unexpectedly in early August.[113]

To cool William's anger, the 'managers' looked to English intermediaries. Their main ally was, of course, Shrewsbury, to whom Johnston hinted that Glencoe and Achallader might be exploited against English Tories; but they sent Annandale south to make sure of Lord Keeper Somers and Archbishop Tenison (to whom Johnston explained the religious settlement) and to hoodwink the Tory Secretary Trumbull. He also ensured that the misrepresentations of a propaganda pamphlet published in London to justify Dalrymple, Stair and Breadalbane were contradicted.[114] The inquiry had better success further afield. Johnston claimed that he had made the Paris *Gazette*, which had first spread the charges internationally against William, retract them. Its occasional reports from Edinburgh accepted the votes exculpating William without comment, although they correctly predicted that neither the senior officers nor the actual killers would be punished.[115]

Johnston journeyed round the North-East for some months to persuade episcopalian clergy to take the oaths, and had considerable success, greatly strengthening his party's position.[116] Keppoch applied to him there for advice on his dispute with Mackintosh. Despite the 'managers'' quarrel with Argyll and the highland witnesses' recalcitrance, the new Act for the Justiciary of the Highlands had been unadventurous, merely renewing for three years the obligation on possessors of private regalities to co-opt the government's commissioners. Things had returned to normal — which included Mackintosh's persecution of Keppoch. Keppoch declared his willingness to submit the whole dispute to the Officers of State, but feared that Mackintosh would appeal directly to William in London. Johnston promised in that case to pass on his offer. Keppoch, however, did not rely totally on Johnston's and Murray's patronage. When a lawsuit called him to Inveraray, he found that his loyalty to Breadalbane had won him Argyll's favour. He willingly responded (although he denied it to the jealous Murray), and in late 1697 mentioned both magnates as his 'friends'.[117] Lochiel also was in favour with Argyll, who, early in 1696 successfully recommended Campbell of Lochnell's daughter as a bride for Lochiel's eldest son John — a match which preserved the links between the clans, helped settle the disputes over Sunart and Ardnamurchan and was politically congenial, since the Lochnell family was the most persistently Jacobite of the Argyllshire Campbells.[118]

The Macdonalds of Glencoe were less fortunate. On 25 July, they petitioned the

Council, stating that they were about to be quartered upon for £305 Scots arrears of cess since Candlemas 1691, which they could not pay. As the Council recommended, the Treasury stayed the quartering until William's pleasure was known. As William did nothing, it is uncertain how long this immunity lasted.[119] It did not relieve their existing poverty. In January, Alasdair MacIain and Glengarry were applying to Murray and Johnston to obtain the compensation for which Parliament had addressed William. Except perhaps at the start of December, before he turned against the 'managers', there was never hope of William's granting it. The Scottish Treasury was in no position to recompense even Williamites who had suffered heavily during the highland war, several of whom, including Grant and Aberuchill, Parliament had also just recommended to William.[120] The failure of revenue in the famine made relief even less likely. The date on the house the new chief built on the site of his father's, 1706, may indicate when prosperity began to return.[121] A grotesque consequence of the publicity was that in 1700 one of the many plot-forgers who wove into their stories everybody supposed, rightly or wrongly, to favour the Jacobites informed Carstares that one of the MacIains, encouraged by second sight, was leading a party to Holland to assassinate William. Even the credulity created by a decade of such allegations probably found this too hard to swallow.[122]

On 18 June, soon after the news of Breadalbane's arrest reached London, Glenorchy and Dalrymple had left London for Flanders. Pushing on without an escort, they arrived on 26 June at William's camp outside Namur, which he was just starting to besiege. To William, Portland and others they denounced the 'Whigs'' misdeeds. The next day, William sent Tweeddale orders to cease the prosecution, but warned them he could go no further until the adjournment.[123] As they hoped, news of Parliament's further misdeeds arrived. As Undersecretary Pringle warned the 'managers', William was increasingly furious at Breadalbane's prosecution, the communication of the Glencoe report, and, above all, the continuing of the session beyond the date allowed — so 'republican' a measure that he could scarcely believe it. Portland particularly blamed Johnston.[124]

Yet William did not act on his displeasure. This sprang partly from lack of time. He was concentrating on a great siege, and constantly forced, in addition, to march and manoeuvre for a possible battle that 'determins the war as wele as this seedg'. In the reports, letters and documents from Scotland, he usually glanced only at passages marked by Carstares. 'I assure you the King hath not writt nor signed all this summer one paper to Scotland', wrote Glenorchy on 26 August.[125] Yet, he admitted, William was as cautious of meddling with the Scottish Parliament as the English one. He would 'have no noyse made' over the affair because he was in the 'managers'' hands, and would not even complain at their ignoring his orders since they could equally easily ignore the complaint.[126] Yet there was no improvement when Parliament rose; 'to press your affair now may ruine it', Glenorchy confessed on 8/18 August.[127] Death and the 'managers' had so shattered the 'episcopalians' that William might well accept the *fait accompli*. Tweeddale confidently informed Pringle, on the spot, that he was mistaken about the King's anger. Both sides put forward candidates for Linlithgow's Treasury seat. Tweeddale's, his son

Yester, was endorsed by Shrewsbury, to whom it was reported that William 'seems inclined, but ... will do nothing in it before his return for England'.[128]

One event in July which angered William, checking Glenorchy's applications, was the shameful surrender to the French of Dixmunde with a large Allied garrison, including three Scottish regiments. Yet this saved William from having to refuse Parliament's address to send home for trial Glenlyon, Drummond and their subordinates; for they, with the rest of Lorne's regiment, were among those captured and recovered only some time after Namur fell.[129] Lieutenant-Colonel Hamilton caused some embarrassment by coming to the camp to throw himself on the King's mercy; but William apparently avoided seeing him. He is last heard of in Holland, threatening to print his story and throw the blame on Hill.[130]

Even after the fall of Namur, William was still reluctant to use his authority in Breadalbane's favour, and Dalrymple drifted away in despair. Glenorchy persevered, and finally on 3 September obtained the order of release. He sent it via Breadalbane to the Advocate, to present to the Council.[131] Steuart, who received it on 16 September, wished to avoid a duty which would set his party against him, and, typically, played a double game. He drew up a formal notification, but, instead of sending it, kept the order secret for ten days, while he urged Breadalbane to offer bail. Breadalbane feared that, if he did, he would be barred from sitting in Treasury and Council. He obtained legal opinions that Steuart must present the order — based largely on 'episcopalian' views of the prerogative, including a denial that the Grievances were binding. Yet Steuart admitted their validity, and himself drew up for Breadalbane a petition, which did offer bail.[132] Once Johnston had gone south, he plucked up courage to request Teeeddale to summon an extraordinary Council meeting. However, after Tweeddale reached Edinburgh on 28 September, Steuart first feigned sickness and then promised not to present the warrant unless ordered. On this understanding, Tweeddale summoned a Council for 1 October.[133]

Breadalbane had prudently sent 'Circular letters' to his supporters, and nearly all came, the dying Stair carried in a litter from Ayrshire. Twenty-four members were present besides Tweeddale, who dragged out some minor business and then rose. Argyll, who had a copy of William's order, demanded that Steuart produce it, but Tweeddale declined to admit its existence until he did. Steuart refused, saying it would be futile since Breadalbane would not offer bail, and when his petition offering it, which he himself had written, was presented, declared it contrary to law. Argyll, Queensberry and Stair continued to argue that Breadalbane had the right to call for the order. They pointed out that Tweeddale's arguments might equally be used to suppress a reprieve of execution; and he had seen enough political upheavals to know how dangerous a precedent he might be setting. Nevertheless, when Breadalbane's friends demanded a vote if they should ask for the letter, he left, breaking up the Council. Breadalbane's supporters, eleven in number, wrote a letter of protest to William.[134]

Breadalbane could not hope for William's immediate intervention to enforce his slighted order. He was making a Midlands progress in preparation for the English elections, and employing it, like Namur, to justify ignoring Scottish business, since he 'has more trouble than profit from that kingdom'.[135] To ensure a sympathetic hearing on his return, Breadalbane sent Carwhin to London to remind Leeds of his sponsorship of the 1691 negotiation. He was also to apply to the English nobility for support against Johnston's threat to the whole order, and to Arran (to whom Argyll had already appealed in June) to use his influence with Murray to prevent him from rising by Breadalbane's ruin. To give the appearance of complete sincerity, Carwhin began an account of Breadalbane's recent career which admitted his Jacobite plotting in 1689-90.[136] Breadalbane's reliance on Leeds emphasised that his political touch was failing. Although he still had destructive power as unofficial head of the East India Company's parliamentary interest (as the Scots found to their cost), his exposure for corruption had destroyed his ministerial credit, and William secretly barred him from the Council. He retired to Wimbledon and began mending his fences with the Jacobites.[137]

He exaggerated the implications of his January 1692 opposition to Dalrymple's plans to Charles Leslie, who was preparing a new pamphlet on Glencoe.[138] Leslie had access to the Report, and his *Gallienus Redivivus* contained many effective quotations from it, besides the reprinted 1692 'Letter'. He set Glencoe in a rational context, unlike the contortions of the *Answer to King*, linking it with illegal executions in Ireland and the lynching of the de Witts in Holland as typical of William's rule. He made the excellent point that Livingston's and Hill's defence that they were only obeying orders was insufficient and alarming.[139] Yet Leslie again showed serious dishonesty, minimising Dalrymple's responsibility not only in order to blame William for everything — legitimate propaganda — but to protect Dalrymple as a supporter of the episcopalian clergy. This produces a ridiculous split. In the few pages on Dalrymple's letters Leslie's comments emphasise their barbarity, but the rest of the Scottish section attacks Johnston, not only for whitewashing William, but for really attacking Dalrymple from presbyterian bigotry, even for bringing about the inquiry.[140]

'Presbyterian' concern over Glencoe did contain some hypocrisy, as the Highland Commission for the northern districts showed by pushing to extremes the Council's hostility to the Indemnity. Failing to hold a much-needed court at Fort William, they summoned most of the gentry of Lochaber, Badenoch, and Ardgour, nearly a thousand in all, to answer charges, mainly for wartime raids, at Inverness. Hill saw 'much Peique ill will and selfe interest in these warme proceedings', but Grant, the chief prosecutor, used the imprudent Badenoch protest over Ruthven to discredit his views. Most of the accused did not appear, giving the commissioners their chance.[141] Keppoch was ordered to pay 30,000 merks to two Stratherrick proprietors for goods taken in 1689. Grant prosecuted Lochiel for the Camerons' notorious raid on Glen Urquhart, although Lochiel claimed that it had been on Dundee's orders and that the Indemnity should cover it. When Lochiel's lawyer pleaded that his lands lay within Argyll's jurisdiction, the 'twentie-five com[missioner]s qrof all wold stope att nothing yt could destroy me and myne' (as Lochiel claimed), 'said they wold fetch men from Inviraray itselfe'.[142] Hill and others wrote to the law officers that the sentences would create chaos, particularly when the troops were called on to enforce them; and the Council perhaps felt that this policy was inconsistent with the concern recently expressed for the Glencoe men. Therefore, when Keppoch's and Lochiel's petitions independently arrived on 10 December they ordered the commissioners 'for the peace of ye countrey' to stop all prosecutions for offences committed before the Indemnity against Lochiel, Keppoch, Appin, Glencoe, and the inhabitants of Lochaber, Moidart, Ardgour, Morvern, Argyll and the Isles. The order still left the Badenoch gentry exposed to the northern commissioners; but it frustrated decrees like the one in which the Cumings of Dulshangie, with a Cuming prosecutor and a Cuming among the judges, were awarded £3,000 Scots against Alasdair MacIain (and his superior Ardsheal) for a raid in October 1689.[143] Some claimants already preferred to settle without ruining, in the highland fashion. Murray himself, the chief advocate of severity, had never intended to sue for the Glenlyon raid, for which Keppoch finally paid a set number of cows, to be sold, or given to 'the pour poppel in Glenlayon'. Breadalbane's recent highland policy had been proved correct.[144]

Meanwhile, his obstinate resistance and the extremist responses to which it forced Tweeddale and Johnston had lengthened the odds against their success. It ensured that Portland would realise that, having 'had that nation once wholly in his hands, ... he had let it go out of his dependence'. He was vowing to withdraw entirely from Scottish affairs — the usual prelude to his most vigorous meddling. By early November, Ogilvie was revising his expectations of 'presbyterian' success: 'something will be done, but not neir so much as our pairtie wishes or expects for'.[145] However, Dalrymple was excluded from his turn in waiting even before his father's death further weakened his interest. Retaining him, Tweeddale wrote, would be condoning his accession to the Massacre. William's easiest option, Dalrymple wrote bitterly, would be to sacrifice the 'episcopalians', knowing that they would remain loyal to the monarch despite neglect.[146]

To secure victory, Tweeddale and Johnston were relying increasingly on support from the English Whigs. Refusing Breadalbane's offer of bail showed that Tweeddale wished not only to prevent his resuming his official powers but secretly to uphold the principle that William could not stop a parliamentary prosecution. His letter to Shrewsbury (who had maintained the principle in England in Carmarthen's case) made the claim explicit: Englishmen pressing William to release Breadalbane 'should know better how such a thing would relish with an English Parliament'. Freeing Breadalbane, Tweeddale had explained, would cause disastrous disillusionment among the regime's strongest supporters, an argument with which he might justify his conduct to William. Yet this, extreme disobedience, imperfectly masked by concentration on protocol, was likely to revive the King's anger at his return. Possibly the need to ensure support from English Whig and Country politicians, several of whom had complained that the prosecution had not been carried through, forced Tweeddale take the risk over a principle they so treasured — a risk which made English support still more necessary.[147]

English fury over the Scottish East India Company shattered every equation the 'managers' had relied on. The merchants' complaints, developing since September, were strongly taken up by the Lords. Leeds, heading the East India Company 'interest', and other Tories created a broad coalition hostile to the Scottish act, the Scottish ministry (perhaps Breadalbane's appeals to fellow-aristocrats had some influence) — and, less overtly, to William, including Country Whigs and even known Jacobites. The unruly Whig Commons majority returned by the election nursed strong suspicions of the Junto, whose position was in jeopardy. They dared not oppose the flood of hostility to the act. After Shrewsbury's last friendly advice to Tweeddale in mid-November, to see William and justify himself, they let the tide carry them — a desertion which surprised and angered Johnston.[148] Rather than, as they expected, creating a position which William could not attack without excessive trouble from the English Parliament, the 'managers' had brought that trouble upon him over an act of which he knew nothing until the complaints arose.[149] Nevertheless, Tweeddale showed an unprecedented determination to fight for the act as the most important passed that session (if only as a lever to force England to grant Scotland commercial rights), and hinted strongly to William that interference with it might turn the Scottish Parliament hostile. Johnston, in contrast, was wishing by late November that the act had never passed, since the depth of English opposition doomed it to failure: if matters came to extremes, the English would sink the Company's ships at sea and incite other nations to attack its factories. He was still complaining in January that Tweeddale failed to grasp the gravity of the crisis.[150]

Riley has argued that the real cause of the major government changes that winter was not the East India Company Act, but William's realisation that only dismissal of both Johnston and Dalrymple would stop their faction-fights, and the heavy pressure which a new generation of magnates, under-represented in government since 1689, brought to bear the Court, even though William and his advisers did not understand its significance.[151] Certainly, there was an incentive for sweeping changes in the state of the Scottish administration, running down slowly as deaths and departures for London deprived Session, Treasury and Exchequer of the necessary quorums: Tweeddale was reluctantly forced to remain in Scotland throughout the crisis to keep some sort of government in existence. Certainly, even some 'presbyterians' considered that the struggles had created such bad blood and mutual fear of the other side's triumph that both Secretaries should be removed.[152] However, Johnston could argue that there would be no further disputes: he had won. The division between 'presbyterian' and 'episcopalian' became indistinct thereafter not because the two factions and their religious connections (however incongruous) had always been illusory, but because the old 'episcopalian' leadership had been smashed and many of their clergy brought to submit. To calm the survivors' fears over his victory, Johnston had ready a candidate acceptable to them, Murray, for Dalrymple's post. The massive ministerial changes arose not from any one Court initiative, conscious or semi-conscious, but from two independent, hostile, intrigues conducted by Johnston and Carstares which succeeded within three weeks of each other. Carstares still saw politics in terms of 'presbyterians' and the long-discredited Melville, although the English laughed away his attempt to make him Chancellor. He did not view the new magnates as distinct, in January considering Argyll and Annandale almost interchangeable for various posts, and ranking Queensberry with other 'episcopalians'. His preferred candidate for Secretary was the mere 'presbyterian' Lord Ross.[153] Yet there was a 'magnate resurgence'; but one strand in it, Murray's promotion, was the fruit of Johnston's persistent toil, and the rest was largely a self-conscious response to his conduct in Parliament and its implications. Argyll, for instance, might well have continued to devote himself to dissipation; but Johnston's threat of denouncing him for treason concentrated his mind wonderfully. Not only magnates but lesser peers had been aroused: Johnston, an observer commented in November, 'hath a great deall of the nobility against him'.[154]

The first debate before William on 2 December, with Dalrymple (now Stair), hysterical from fury, Argyll and Carstares facing Johnston and Annandale, went fairly well for the 'managers'. William showed anger only over the East India Company Act, saying that it granted such powers as if there were no king in Scotland; but even that he discussed rationally. Every claim Stair made about the proceedings over Breadalbane and Glencoe was contradicted as untrue. William 'expressed his horrour at the Glenco bussiness, That it had been verrie near his heart, That it had brought reproach upon him, not only over Scotland and England, but all the world over', and claimed to have had no knowledge of the facts until Hamilton told him in late 1693. Even Carstares felt it prudent to balance, admitting that Parliament had never shown any inclination to give a cess for life.[155]

Over the next few weeks, William's attitude changed. 'All our affaires were right in the Kings mind as I certainly know but now the Trade Act undoes all', lamented Johnston on the 12th. Reports indicated that Tweeddale, as proposer of the Act, was the most likely to be dismissed, although Johnston and Steuart might follow him.[156] The House of Lords made a report on the 9th. Momentarily, Johnston hoped that the Act might be 'the greatest blessing to Scotland that ever befell us for it has excited here a wonderfull disposition to an Union'. A motion for one was made in the Lords by Burnet and Lord Monmouth (who responded to the argument that William had known nothing of the Act: 'there had been murders and Massacres in Scotland, possibly the King knew nothing of them neither.'). Instead, however, the Lords drew up an address denouncing the Act, the Commons concurred, and William on 18 December made his decisive reply: 'I have been ill served in Scotland ... ' Several 'episcopalians' unscrupulously encouraged the English attack. Stair was the most prominent, and was never forgiven in Scotland. He and Carstares won over Portland in early December, and gained another audience for Stair to make fresh attacks on the 'managers'' proceedings over Glencoe. If Carwhin guessed correctly, he also spent considerable effort in poisoning William's mind against the East India Company Act, and by mid-December the King would scarcely speak to the 'presbyterians'.[157] The final blow came later when Steuart (whom Tweeddale should have learned to distrust over the Breadalbane affair) arrived in London and, although he had drawn up the act, denied all involvement in it.[158] The change in William's attitude was comprehensive: a fortnight after expressing his horror at Glencoe, he allowed Argyll to present Lieutenant-Colonel Duncanson to him.[159]

Breadalbane benefited from the change. On 16 December, William signed a remission for him and a direct order to Leven to release him from Edinburgh Castle. The last year had taught Breadalbane the need of an absolutely watertight pardon; it is therefore significant that in all the drafts, which are very full on the 'private articles', there is no mention of Glencoe. Stair's draft of his, in contrast, concentrates upon it, claiming that he could not be to blame because he was many hundred miles away, and adding a pardon for 'any excess of zeal'.[160] Breadalbane was released on 23 December, Tweeddale making difficulties to the last. Reasonably enough after Tweeddale's conduct in October, he played a practical joke on him, coming to the Council next day with the argument that the order of release by itself ended the prosecution and restored his status, provoking a long debate on the question and finally producing his remission. The objections were renewed at the next session, and Breadalbane declared he would sit at his peril.[161] However, he left for London on 31 December with Queensberry and other peers, including Tarbat, with whom, after his six months' loyal support, he was squabbling before they reached Dunbar.[162] He had instigated the highlanders who benefited from the Council's act of 10 December restraining the Justiciary Commissions to send Keppoch to London to ask William to confirm it. They feared that Murray, from anger that the Southern as well as the Northern Commission had been checked, might get it reversed; but MacIain, from loyalty to Murray, would not join them.[163]

Murray had left early on 31 December for London. Johnston had summoned him in William's name on the 21st, an unexpected success which (though by this stage he could only guess at William's intentions) seemed to indicate that he might still emerge victor. When the news reached London, the 'episcopalians' begged William to make no changes until Queensberry, whom Murray easily outstripped, arrived. In early January, however, William announced changes. Stair was dismissed as Secretary, Breadalbane from Treasury and Council, and Tarbat from being Register (though he kept a pension).[164] On 13 January, William appointed Murray Secretary and 'told me I owed it only to himself'. Murray, unfortunately for his political career, took this literally, dismissing the years during which Johnston had been his patron. The Secretary had naturally avoided emphasising the idea to the young magnate; had they become colleagues, he must inevitably have relied partly on luck to preserve good relations between them. On his dismissal, political logic made the 'presbyterian' remnant look to the episcopalian Murray (whose 'conversion' Argyll later placed in early 1696) as leader; but, acting as if William's statement were true, he gave them too little encouragement.[165] Murray did not, however, fail to realise that his power rested not only on his own family interest but that of his Hamilton in-laws, who soon included William's ex-mistress, the Countess of Orkney. Arran felt that, although he was still an overt Jacobite refusing the oaths, this family contribution gave him a right to be consulted on all Murray's activities. His brother Basil, though himself a Jacobite at that time, wrote to strengthen Murray in refusing.[166]

Stair retreated, and was omitted from the new Council. Although there were wild rumours that he and Breadalbane intended to reverse the 1695 acts in the 1696 Parliament, he tried to take his seat only in 1698. Murray (Tullibardine) and other Opposition leaders encouraged him, intending if he accepted to attack him (as even Ormiston, a 1695 'presbyterian' still in the ministry, was determined to do) and disrupt the session. The Commissioner ordered him to stay away.[167] Only in May 1699 did he receive, with some grants, his remission for Glencoe and other crimes he might have committed in office — a reward for his brother Hew's political services. The delay, probably justified as necessary to avoid alienating Parliament unnecessarily, ensured that he could not regain William's sympathy by recalling his struggles to defend the prerogative and pose any threat as a rival to the new ministers. It completed the inquiry's work of destroying his independent power as a politician; afterwards, he was Queensberry's jackal.[168]

Breadalbane accepted defeat with a stylish flourish. Arriving in London only after William had dismissed him, he kissed his hand and congratulated Murray on his appointment. He received a grant of £400 for damage done Finlarig, though the Scottish Treasury had still been unable to pay £200 of it by May 1699. He retreated from public affairs, even for a while from the Highland Justiciary. It was Glenorchy who received a pension, in 1699.[169] Breadalbane returned to Parliament only for the second session of 1700, partly in response to Queensberry's claim that the Opposition were the old 'presbyterian' party, with whom he himself had broken in 1695 for Breadalbane's sake.[170] The violently hostile 1704 'character' written in Johnston's circle showed how much his resistance in 1695 and its consequences still rankled, blaming him (but not Stair) for Glencoe, and claiming that honour and religion in him were mere pretences to cover his absolute self-interest. Predictably, it assumed that his cunning was about to bring him a Marquisate, even a Dukedom. In fact, he stayed almost withdrawn from overt politics (apart from a term as a Scottish Representative Peer in 1713-14), while cautiously entering into Jacobite intrigues —allegedly, after hesitating because St. Germain had become so exclusively catholic. His involvement in the '15 showed his old cunning and cynicism; but it was obvious that Mar was no Dundee. If he had abused his Treasury place, the benefits were short-lived: in 1703, Carwhin was writing that only new Caithness bargains could save the family from ruin.[171] (See Preface, p. xiv)

Having succeeded in bringing in Murray, Johnston, as the days passed, hoped that he had weathered the gale, and Carstares's superficial friendliness apparently confirmed the belief. In fact, William had determined on his dismissal by mid-January and personally selected a successor, Solicitor Ogilvie, likely to carry out royal policies rather than his own. Johnston's activities even provoked a temporary revival of proposals for a permanent Scottish Council at London to counterbalance the Secretaries.[172] Johnston's actual dismissal at the start of February evidently left him surprised and angry, for he apparently hinted strongly to his cousin Burnet that, despite the Report and votes, William or Portland had been involved in the Massacre. His brother Alexander similarly later spread hints of Jacobitism against another former patron, Shrewsbury.[173] Tweeddale's dismissal was delayed until May by the need to keep the Scottish administration running and then by the Assassination Plot emergency, so long that Murray suggested William might ultimately have kept him but for his official statement that he had been ill-served in Scotland.[174] Johnston temporarily hoped to re-establish an independent position at Court, but did not even receive minor office, as Carstares suggested. Instead, he was granted £4,000 out of compounded teinds, the collection of which was inevitably oppressive, to relieve his 'low condition'.[175]

The dispute over the East India Company and the change of ministry marked the decisive turning-point of William's Scottish reign. Previously there had always been a possibility that its disadvantages, the burdens of civil and foreign war and the one black blot of Glencoe, would be outweighed by constitutional reforms consolidating those obtained in 1690, the withering away of some oppressive prerogatives and a development of parliamentary powers and responsibilities under the demands of war parallel, to a lesser extent, to what happened in England. The revolution had created conditions and trends which made such an outcome possible — including even the ramshackle nature and incompetence of William's regime, which caused the lapse of judicial torture.[176] In 1695, Johnston exploited these vague trends and opportunities more systematically, hoping to establish them on a solid foundation —a partial recompense for the failure to introduce more general reforms in the 1689 Convention. It was a less conscious and deliberate programme than those the Country Party proclaimed in later sessions. However, the complicity of government 'managers' like him was necessary for lasting success. Once Parliament was openly polarised into Court or Country, the Country alliance had its poorer or greedier members picked off with bribes or favours. Since the Articles had been abolished, the Country could nevertheless force through measures; but with such disruption and bitterness that the London government ultimately found it easiest to extinguish the Scottish Parliament. Johnston's 1695 policies, with the 'managers' acting more like English party leaders than royal representatives, pointed to another alternative, the assumption by Parliament of positive powers, which would at least have eased the problem when William's death left Scotland visibly dependent on an invalid ruling entirely through English ministers.

In turning vague trends into positive policies, however, Johnston in 1695 was certain to arouse far greater conscious antagonism. He gambled on gaining the power to overcome this, and he lost, totally; and the trends he had fostered were crushed, far more deliberately than they would otherwise have been. William replaced Johnston with the obedient servant Ogilvie, who would not use the King's own authority quietly to undermine his prerogative. The 'antient nobility' returned to power stronger and more conscious than before of possible threats. They kept lesser men, like Lord Chancellor Polwarth, carefully in subordination; and in Parliament the organisation of the burgh members, which Johnston had used in alliance with the shire barons to imprison Breadalbane, was exploited in later sessions to overwhelm barons' Country votes.[177] Even Johnston's one unreversed achievement, ending the overt 'presbyterian'-'episcopalian' struggle by crushing the old 'episcopalian' leadership, contributed to this. The magnates, no longer obliged to align themselves with the political factions, could more freely form personal ones; and the hostility to the pre-Revolution aristocratic dominance in the government, which formed a strong part of 'presbyterian' feeling, could no longer safely be expressed in attacks on the old gang of 'episcopalians' like Breadalbane. Carstares's earlier interventions, though sometimes mistaken, might be justified as intended for the nation's good; the more frequent ones after his feud with Johnston appeared to rest chiefly on personal dislikes and concern for his own influence. As Ormiston warned Murray early in 1696, he would be dangerous until he was firmly thrust into a Scottish parish.[178] The East India Company Act unexpectedly shattered the old sympathy of English Whig and Country politicians for their Scottish equivalents. Although the Country alliance largely dominated William's later English parliaments, and its activities might indirectly benefit the Scottish Country Party, its conscious attitude was xenophobic and opposed to the Darien colony — largely from a hostile desire to involve William in as many difficulties as possible.[179] The Whig Junto of Anne's reign, unscrupulously exploiting Scottish affairs for English advantage, felt merely hatred for 'the Darien ministry' and all its works.[180] This ensured that Johnston, on his brief return to office in 1704, was politically a ghost of his former self. Meanwhile, the failure of his initiative helped determine the ultimate shape of William's reign: the disastrous Darien venture and the immense resentment against England and its King; famine, more difficult to alleviate with the continuing burden on the country of taxation and a large army; an empty Treasury; unscrupulous feuding among ministers weakening still further the already feeble administration of the country.

Cutting across the changes came the exposure on 23 February of the Assassination Plot against William. Louis and the Jacobites had planned a rising around London, to be supported by an army making a surprise crossing from Calais. Sir George Barclay, the proposed London second-in-command, found the would-be rebels hopelessly unready, and instead employed the Catholic officers sent across with him as a gang to attack and kill William while hunting. The intended crime against a ruler shocked Europe. Barclay did not mention Glencoe as a justification for the plan, merely its legitimacy by the laws of war. Having merely obeyed orders did not preserve his subordinates from the gallows.[181]

Scotland was in no danger, and probably no Jacobites there knew of the planned invasion. Sir William Bruce, their chief organiser, emphasised that they were too frightened of Johnston's counterspies to be active. Since January, the Council had, on William's order, been releasing prominent men in prison or under house arrest, such as the Duke of Gordon, Bruce, and Sir William Sharp.[182] Then, on 29 February, arrived the news of the plot, and they immediately began to arrest them and other traditional suspects —unsystematically, Argyll complained.[183] One fresh prisoner was the new Earl of Strathmore, whose Jacobite enthusiasm had recently made him refuse the posts as Privy Councillor and Sheriff of Angus which Johnston and Ogilvie had obtained for him. Murray persuaded him to take the oaths, and he was released. He received both posts under the new regime.[184] Mistaken warnings from London (as in 1692) that a squadron from Dunkirk was sailing to invade Scotland increased the tension, and vigorous precautions were taken.[185] Yet the only hostile action came from Lord Drummond, who was captured about 1 March travelling under an alias, immediately escaped from Stirling Castle and, despite promising to Murray to surrender, remained on the run, claiming to fear prison.[186] There was apparently a meeting of highlanders and lowlanders at Inversnaid beside Loch Lomond in mid-March, but the sensational rumour, as in 1692, that disillusioned ex-Williamites attended was apparently untrue.[187] Arran was in England, and had given his word not to go to Scotland or France.[188] This made easier the most solid result of the plot in Scotland, the strengthening of Murray's position. William sent him down to invigorate the Council. The suspicions which had dogged the family since 1689 seemed over.[189]

Although both Seaforth and Drummond were now on the run in the Highlands, the Council felt little anxiety about danger there. The order of 10 March for the loyal northern clans to be ready to take the field was prompted by a letter from Ogilvie. A committee established to considered how to enforce highland chieftains' bonds to keep the peace was diverted by Argyll into considering lowland problems of security.[190] Hill had been ordered in early March to seize suspect chiefs, but most of these, including, as in 1693, Cluny, simply came in when written to. Lochiel took the opportunity to attempt to establish all three of his grown sons in William's army. Hill had recently seized for banishment some popular catholic priests, but this caused no disturbance.[191] The rumours of invasion and the temporary prohibition of watches led to frequent raiding in the southern Highlands; but Hill restrained the Lochaber men from taking a major part by quartering troops in thieves' home areas until the goods were returned.[192]

Glengarry had apparently avoided submitting at Fort William; but, when the Council summoned the chiefs to Edinburgh for June or July in the traditional way, he was one of the few remoter ones who appeared, to strengthen his patron Murray's influence.[193] Keppoch was on the run in the hills, never spending two nights in the same place, for fear of Mackintosh. He had gone to London to put his case personally, but when in July William's letter arrived ordering the Council to put him in possession of the disputed lands, they prudently ignored it.[194] Drummond surrendered in June, Seaforth at Inverness in early September. In March 1697 they were freed on bail, and the prosecution of Seaforth for his 1690 invasion was finally stopped.[195] The Highlands remained fairly quiet. Nationalist sentiment over the Darien expedition was to give Jacobitism in the Lowlands new life, as the revival of old feuds and creation of new ones did in the Highlands. The Assassination Plot alarm revealed, however, that the movement in both was, for the moment, moribund.

NOTES

1. *Carstares S.P.*, 211, A. Johnston to Carstares, 10 Aug. 1694; Burnet *History*, iv, 284–6; H. Horwitz, *Parliament, Policy and Politics in the reign of William III* (Manchester, 1977), 132–5, 213–14 (hereafter *PPP*); *Annandale Book*, ii, 93–5, Johnston to Annandale, 19 Jan. 1695.

2. *Ib.*, 336, same to same, 19 Jan. 1695; *ib.*, 113–14, same to same, 20 Apr. [1695]; NLS MS 7016 fol. 19, Blackbarony to Tweeddale, 16 Jan. 1695.

3. Riley, *King William,* 92–3; *Annandale Book,* ii. 336, Johnston to Annandale, 19 Jan. [1695].

4. *Ib.*, 68–9, A. Johnston to Annandale, 15 Feb. 1693/4; *ib.*, 73, Annandale to Johnston, 5 Apr. [1694]; NLS MS 7029 fol. 8, Tweeddale to same, 29 Nov. 1694.

5. *Ib.*, MS 7028 fols. 126v–127, same to Queensberry, 1 Aug. 1694.

6. *More Highland Papers,* 214–15, Hill to Culloden, 2 Nov. 1690; SRO PC 1/50, 2, 21, 33.

7. *Ib.*, 53; Fountainhall, *Decisions,* i, 661; *Lairds of Glenlyon,* 57; NLS MS 7029 fol. 9, Tweeddale to Johnston, 29 Nov. 1694; *ib.*, fol. 10v same to same, 5 Dec. 1694.

8. *Ib.*, MS 7017 fol. 131, Steuart to Tweeddale, 22 Dec. 1694; *Annandale Book,* ii, 80, Johnston to Annandale, 6 Dec. 1694.

9. *Ib.*, 87–8, same to same, 28 Dec. 1694; *CSPD 1694–5.* 430, Secret instructions, 17 Apr. 1695; *HMCR Roxburghe,* 125–6, Jerviswood to Polwarth, 8 Nov. 1694; *ib.*, 126, Johnston to same, 4 Dec. 1694; Riley, *King William,* 93; NLS MS 7018 fol. 1, Ormiston to Tweeddale, 2 Jan. 1695.

10. *Annandale Book,* ii, 83, Livingston to Annandale, 16 Dec. 1694.

11. *Earls of Cromartie,* i, 129, Breadalbane to Tarbat, 17 Mar. 1698.

12. *HMCR Hope-Johnstone,* 97, Johnston to Annandale, 27 Apr. [1695].

13. SRO GD 112/40/4/7/104, 'Memorial on the affairs of Scotland', [1695]; *ib.*, 105, [Dalrymple] to [Breadalbane], 7 Mar. 1695; Drumlanrig, Queensberry Papers, Vol. 115, 23, same to Queensberry, 30 Mar. 1695; Blair, Atholl MSS, Box 29 I (7) 114, Anstruther to Murray, 30 Mar. 1695.

14. Historians have accepted Sir William Fraser's suggestion as editor of *HMCR Hope-Johnstone* (p. 76) that 'M' was Lord Murray, but it is certainly wrong. 'M.' was intriguing in London all winter and spring, but the series of letters sent to Murray throughout that period (Blair, Atholl MSS, Box 29 I (7)) make it clear that he did not visit England. 'M.'s' true identity is established by a letter on his most outrageous remarks from Johnston in which, since it was carried by a reliable hand, he could name Carstares. NLS MS 14,408 fols. 386v–387, [Johnston] to Tweeddale, 23 April. 1695; *Annandale Book,* ii, 115, same to Annandale, 23 Apr. [1695].

15. *Ib; HMCR Roxburghe,* 126–7, same to Polwarth, 12 Jan. 1695; *Melvilles & Leslies,* ii, 172, Carstares to Melville, 22 July 1695; Riley, *King William,* 93.

16. *Annandale Book,* ii, 115–16, Johnston to Annandale, 23 Apr. [1695]; *ib,* 110–11, same to same, 13 Apr. 1695; *ib.*, 114, same to same, 20 Apr. [1695]; *ib.*, 334, same to same, 11 Dec. [1694]; *ib.*, 337, same to same, 9 Apr. [1695].

17. NLS MS 1320 fol. 80v, R. Mackenzie to Delvine, 4 Apr. 1695.

18. Riley, *King William,* 93–4; Blair, Atholl MSS, Box 29 I (7) 114, Anstruther to Murray, 30 Mar. 1695; *Annandale Book,* ii. 102, Ogilvie to Annandale, 26 Feb. 1695; *ib.*, 336, Johnston to same, 10 Jan. 1695.

19. *Ib.*, 99, same to same, 7 Feb. 1695; Blair, Atholl MSS, Box 29 I (7) 108, same to Murray, 2 Mar. 1695; Atholl, *Chronicles,* i, 361.

20. Drumlanrig, Queensberry Papers, Vol. 115, 24, Ranelagh to Queensberry, 4 May 1695; *ib.*, 23, Dalrymple to same, 30 Mar. 1695; *Annandale Book,* ii, 114, Johnston to Annandale, 23 Apr. 1695.

21. *Ib.*, 99, same to same, 7 Feb. 1695; *CSPD 1694–5,* 478, [Johnston] to [William], 25–28 May 1695 (for identification of the authorship of this run of reports, *ib. 1695,* 145,

[Carstares], 'Parliamentary memoranda', [July 1695], itself identifiable by internal evidence).

22. The mention of Murray discredits Simon Fraser's allegation that he was then tempting potential officers into his regiment with Jacobite assurances, and suddenly became a Williamite only on appointment as Secretary. Lord James Murray's letters refute Fraser's similar claim about him. Macpherson, *Original Papers*, i, 485, James to A[rran], Feb. [1695]; Lovat, *Memoirs*, 14-16, 24-5; Atholl, *Chronicles*, i, 398, Ld James Murray to Murray, 11 Aug. 1693.

23. *CSPD 1694-5*, 428-30, Instructions, 17 Apr. 1695; Riley, *King William*, 94; NLS MS 7029 fol. 23, Tweeddale to Shrewsbury, 19 Apr. 1695; *Annandale Book*, ii, 114, Johnston to Annandale, 20 Apr. [1695].

24. *Ib.*, 113, same to same, 18 Apr. 1695; *CSPD 1694-5*, 445-6, Commissions of Inquiry, 29 Apr. 1695.

25. *Earls of Cromartie*, i. 112, Tweeddale to Yester, 8 Dec. 1695; NLS MS 7027 fol. 39v [Johnston], 'Our Conference', [Dec. 1695]; *ib.*, MS 14,408 fol. 392, same to Tweeddale, 27 Apr. 1695; *Highland Papers*, 118, 1703 preface to Report.

26. *Ib.*, 154, 'Memorial of some affairs of state', [June 1695]; *HMCR Buccleuch (Montagu)*, ii, 203, Johnston to Shrewsbury, 19 July 1695; *The Lairds of Glenlyon*, 65; NUL, Portland MSS, PwA 714, Livingston to Portland, 25 May 1695.

27. *Annandale Book*, ii, 99, Johnston to Annandale, 7 Feb. 1695.

28. Dalrymple's position in limbo may explain the surprising estimate of him eight years later (in the 'Characters' published with Macky's *Memoirs*, which certainly came from Johnston's circle (see n. 37)) as 'very indolent', and its tone of friendly contempt. *Ib.*, 337, same to same, 9 Apr. [1695]; NLS MS 7018 fol. 76, same to Tweeddale, 11 May 1695; *CSPD 1694-5*, 430, Secret instructions, 17 Apr. 1695.

29. *Ib.*, 466, [Johnston] to [William], 9-17 May 1695; SRO GD 112/40/4/7/105, [Dalrymple] to [Breadalbane], 7 Mar. 1695; NLS MS 7017 fol. 109, Queensberry to Tweeddale, 16 Nov. 1694; Drumlanrig, Queensberry Papers, Vol. 115, 24, Ranelagh to Queensberry, 4 May 1695.

30. *CSPD 1694-5*, 477-8, [Johnston] to [William], 25-28 May 1695; *Annandale Book*, ii, 101, Ormiston to Annandale, 16 Feb. 1694/5.

31. *Carstares S.P.*, 229-31, Tarbat to Carstares, 16 May 1695 (+ draft warrant); *ib.*, 234, same to same, 25 June 1695.

32. *Scots Peerage*, ii, 207; *Annandale Book*, ii, 108, Ormiston to Annandale, 9 Apr. 1695; SRO GD 50/10/148, Glenorchy to Carwhin, Mar. 1694; GD 112/43/1/5/3, Memorandum to Carwhin, Oct. '1696' [1695].

33. *HMCR Buccleuch (Montagu)*, ii, 194-5, Johnston to Shrewsbury, 21 June 1695.

34. *Annandale Book*, ii, Ormiston to Annandale, 2 Apr. 1695; NLS MS 7018 fol. 76, Johnston to Tweeddale, 11 May 1695; *ib.*, MS 7029 fol. 24v, Tweeddale to Johnstone, 21 Apr. 1695; *ib.*, fol. 26, same to same, 4 May 1695.

35. Marshall, *Days of Duchess Anne*, 212; SRO GD 406/1/4056, Breadalbane to Arran, 9 Feb. 1695; *ib.*, 6946, [Ld J. Hamilton] to same, 4 Dec. 1694.

36. *HMCR Buccleuch (Montagu)*, ii, 195, Johnston to Shrewsbury, 21 June 1695; Atholl, *Chronicles*, i, 336, Murray to [Marchioness], 29 May [1695]; *Highland Papers*, 156, 'Memorial ... ', [June 1695].

37. Macky, *Memoirs*, 205. Claims that these famous character sketches are really by Burnet (W. A. Shaw, 'Burnet and the 'Characters' of John Macky', *Times Literary Supplement* (1928), 447,466) or by Shrewsbury, Somers and Johnston (*39th Report of the Deputy Keeper of the Public Records* (1878), 786-7) seem to be groundless (*HMCR Buccleuch*

(*Montagu*), ii, 788; BL Loan 29/45X fol. 29, [J. Drummond] to R. Harley, 21 Apr. 1705). Shaw's argument, that whereas the 'Characters' denounce Carstares and praise Johnston, Macky as a spy belonged to the Carstares faction, seems groundless: a spy reports to whom his orders tell him, Macky served Johnston after Carstares, and all this was before the split. In the early 1700s, Johnston in retirement at Twickenham would naturally attract Macky, a fellow-expatriate and fellow-Whig, into his circle (for Macky's mention of his gardens, *DNB* sub 'Johnston or Johnstone, James').

38. Blair, Atholl MSS, Box 29 I (8) 65, Ld B. Hamilton to Murray, 13 Feb. 1696; *ib.*, bundle 1720, Tullibardine to [Hamilton], 8 Sept. 1698.

39. *Annandale Book*, ii, 114, Johnston to Annandale, 23 Apr. [1695].

40. *CSPD 1695*, 298, newsletter, 25 Dec. 1694; NLS MS 7017 fol. 64, A. Johnston to Tweeddale, 13 Sept. 1694.

41. Riley, *King William*, 107–8; NUL, Portland MSS, PwA 842, Tarbat to Portland, 25 June 1695 + List.

42. The second of these was, admittedly, privately offered; but it was inspired by the first, whose origin (and particularly that of its strikingly doctrinaire preamble) is not clear. *APS*, ix, 421, 462; *ib.*, App., 104, 110, 117; Whyte, *Agriculture & Society*, 105–7.

43. Fletcher, *Select Political Writings*, 114; NLS MS 7029 fol. 95, Tweeddale to Johnston, 19 Oct. 1695; *ib.*, fol. 105, same to William, 13 Nov. 1695; *ib.*, fol. 136, same to Johnston, 14 Dec. 1695. Riley (*King William*, 97–8) sees only the more sceptical part of their views.

44. *HMCR Hope-Johnstone*, 97, Johnston to Annandale, 25 Dec. [1694].

45. Blair, Atholl MSS, Box 29 I (9) 410, Anstruther to Tullibardine, 9 Nov. 1697.

46. Hopkins, 'Sham Plots', *Ideology & Conspiracy*, 97.

47. SRO SP 3/1 fol. 12v, Halsyde's memorial, 15 Mar. 1691/2.

48. *Ib.*, GD 124/10/434/1, 'An Account of what past in the Parliament of Scotland 1704', 16; NLS MS 7027 fol. 39, [Johnston], 'Our Conference', [Dec. 1695].

49. *HMCR Buccleuch (Montagu)*, ii, 203, Johnston to Shrewsbury, 19 July 1695.

50. SRO GD 112/40/4/8/4, [Glenorchy] to Breadalbane, 22 July/1 Aug. 1695.

51. Drumlanrig, Queensberry Papers, Vol. 115, 23, Dalrymple to Queensberry, 30 Mar. 1695; NLS MS 7027 fol. 39, [Johnston], 'Our Conference', [Dec. 1695].

52. Lambeth Palace MS 2020 fol. 23v, Johnston to Tenison, 18 July 1695.

53. Macky, *Memoirs*, 222–3; Horwitz, *PPP*, 132, 181; *HMCR Buccleuch (Montagu)*, ii, 218, Shrewsbury to Tweeddale, 24 Aug. 1695.

54. *Ib.*, 243, Tweeddale to Shrewsbury, 24 Oct. 1695; SRO GD 112/43/1/2/26, Tarbat's opinion, [Sept. 1695]; NLS MS 14,408 fol. 403, [Johnston] to [Tweeddale], 10 Oct. 1695.

55. *CSPD 1694-5*, 478, [same] to [William], 26–8 May, 1695; NLS MS 7029 fol. 30v, Tweeddale to A. Johnston, 11 May 1695.

56. *Ib.*, fol. 33, same to William, 16 May 1695; *APS*, ix, 323, 347, 351; *Highland Papers*, 152, 'Memorial', [June 1695]; *CSPD 1694-5*, 467, [Johnston] to [William], 9–17 May 1695.

57. *Ib.*, 466–8; NUL, Portland MSS, PwA 222, Breadalbane to Portland, 1 June 1695; NLS MS 7027 fol. 39, [Johnston], 'Our Conference', [Dec. 1695].

58. *Ib.*, fol. 39v; *CSPD 1695*, 145, [Carstares], Parliamentary memoranda, [July 1695].

59. *Ib. 1694-5*, 466, [Johnston] to [William], 9–17 May 1695; *Highland Papers*, 152–4, 'Memorial ... ', [June 1695]; *APS*, ix, 354.

60. *Ib; ib.*, App., 98–9; NLS MS 7029 fols. 34v–35, Tweeddale to William, 25 May 1695.

61. *Ib.*, MS 7027 fol. 40, [Johnston], 'Our Conference', [Dec. 1695]; *Highland Papers*, 154, 'Memorial ... ', [June 1695].

62. *Ib.*, 154–5; *Annandale Book*, ii, 116, Annandale to Hill, 23 May 1695; SRO SP 4/17,

368–9; NLS MS 7029 fols. 34v–35, Tweeddale to William, 25 May 1695; Atholl, *Chronicles*, i, 335–6, Murray to [Marchioness], 29 May '1693' [1695]. The original of this last letter (Blair, Atholl MSS, Box 29 I (7) 10) is without a year. The *Chronicles* assign it to 1693, when he was not on the Commission of Inquiry — had not even taken the oaths — and when almost none of the lines of inquiry he mentions were exploited; all were in 1695.

63. *Ib.*, 335–6; Blair, Atholl MSS, Box 29 I (7) 141, Ld B. Hamilton to Murray, 31 May 1695.

64. *APS*, ix, 370; *Culloden Papers*, 22–3, Hill to Culloden, 15 May 1695; *Annandale Book*, ii, 54, same to Annandale, 30 May '1692' [1695]; Macpherson, 'Gleanings', *TGSI*, xx, 242–3, same to [Gentry of Badenoch], 30 Nov. 1695; NLS MS 7027 fol. 40, [Johnston], 'Our Conference', [Dec. 1695].

65. *HMCR Buccleuch (Montagu)*, ii, 195, Johnston to Shrewsbury, 21 June 1695; *Highland Papers*, 154–5, 'Memorial . . . ', [June 1695]; Atholl, *Chronicles*, i, 336, Murray to [Marchioness], 29 May [1695]; NLS MS 7029 fol. 36, Tweeddale to William 11 June 1695; SRO GD 112/43/1/2/10, précis of Glengarry's deposition.

66. *Ib.*, 43/1/5/19, [Keppoch to Breadalbane, ?7 June 1695]; *ib.*, 40/4/8/32, undated note; *APS*, ix, 364–5.

67. The later Jacobite Lockhart of Carnwarth looked back on the 1695 session as 'a mean, servile Parliament . . . to suffer [Johnston] to bully and dictate to them'. *Lockhart Papers*, i, 99; Drumlanrig, Queensberry Papers, Vol. 128, 80, abstract of Philiphaugh's letter, 13 July [1704].

68. NUL, Portland MSS, PwA 713, Linlithgow to Portland, 25 May 1695; *CSPD 1694–5*, 477–8, [Johnston] to [William], 25–28 May 1695.

69. The 'episcopalians' misused the narrowness of the vote to suggest that Parliament was evenly balanced. *HMCR Buccleuch (Montagu)*, ii, 201, same to Shrewsbury, 19 July 1695; *APS*, ix, App., 101; *Marchmont Papers*, iii, 414–15, 'Account of Proceedings'; *Highland Papers*, 156–7, 'Memorial . . . ', [June 1695]; *Impartial Account of some of the transactions in Scotland, Somers Tracts*, xi, 549, 555–7.

70. *Ib.*, 557–8; *APS*, ix, 366; *Highland Papers*, 157–8, 'Memorial . . . ', [June 1695]; *Marchmont Papers*, iii, 415–16, 'Account of Proceedings'; NLS MS 7029 fol. 36, Tweeddale to William, 11 June 1695; SRO GD 112/43/1/2/71, 'Narration of the true matter of fact', 17 Aug. 1695; *ib.*, 76, 'Memd Parliament of Scotland'.

71. Another 'episcopalian' peer mentioned by two lists as hostile (though probably not involved on 10 June) was the Earl of Findlater, directed by his son Solicitor Ogilvie. *Ib; ib.*, 35–6, 38–40, parliamentary lists; *ib.*, GD 26/xiii/94, 4, Melville's apologia; *APS*, ix, 366; *Highland Papers*, 159, 'Memorial . . . ', [June 1695]; *Correspondence of George Baillie of Jerviswood*, ed. Lord Minto, (*Jerviswood Corr:* Bannatyne Club, 1842), 6, Johnston to Jerviswood, 4 Aug. 1702; Riley, *King William*, 99–100; NUL, Portland MSS, PwA 842a, Tarbat's list of peers, June 1695; *Rawdon Papers*, 384, Breadalbane to Rawdon, 19 Aug. 1695.

72. *HMCR Buccleuch (Montagu)*, ii, 195, Johnston to Shrewsbury, 21 June 1695; NLS MS 7029 fol. 37v, Tweeddale to William, 11 June 1695.

73. NUL, Portland MSS, PwA 223, Breadalbane to Portland, 11 June 1695; *ib.*, 364, Queensberry to same, 11 June 1695; *ib.*, 699, Johnston to same, 11 June 1695.

74. *HMCR Buccleuch (Montagu)*, ii, 194–5, Johnston to Shrewsbury, 21 June 1695; SRO GD 112/40/4/8/20, Lady Glenorchy to [Breadalbane], 25 June [1695]; *ib.*, 50, [Glenorchy] to [same, 15 June 1695].

75. *Ib.*, 43/1/2/77–8, 'Memd Parliament of Scotland'; *Carstares S.P.*, 232, Argyll to Carstares, 21 June 1695.

76. *Ib.*, 256, Ormiston to same, 23 July 1695; Drumlanrig, Queensberry Papers, Vol. 115, 25, Boyle of Kelburn to Queensberry, 25 June 1695; *ib.*, 27, Argyll to same, 31 July 1695.

77. NUL, Portland MSS, PwA 841, Tarbat to Portland, 21 June 1695; *ib.*, 842, same to same, 25 June 1695; *Highland Papers*. 159, 'Memorial . . . ', [June 1695].

78. *APS*, ix, 408–10; Riley, *King William*, 72, 96.

79. Macpherson, *Original Papers*, i, 529, Middleton to Sir W. Bruce, 23 Dec. 1695 (NS); NUL, Portland MSS, PwA 842, Tarbat to Portland, 25 June 1695.

80. *APS*, ix, 368–9, 371; *CSPD 1694–5*, 500, [Johnston] to [William], 18–20 June 1695; *ib.*, 503, same to same, 21–25 June 1695; *Highland Papers*, 161–2, 'Memorial of some affairs of state', [June 1695]; *Maxwells of Pollok*, ii, 95, Pollok to Carstares, 25 June 1695; *ib.*, 96, same to same, 7 Nov. 1695; NLS MS 7029 fol. 37v, Tweeddale to William, 11 June 1695; *ib.*, fol. 38, same to same, 20 June 1695; *ib.*, fol. 44v, same to same, 13 July 1695; Fletcher, *Selected Political Writings*, 42–4.

81. Murray's involvement is indicated by the one relevant original document connected with it in in the Atholl MSS, the 'Information of the Murder of the Glenco men, 1692' ([Murray], 'Information'; Box 43/VI/5). It treats the events from the same viewpoint as the 1695 witnesses, although it is more compressed, contains additional details, and makes one major mistake — having Achtriachtan and his companions, rather than the men at Inverrigan, bound before they were killed. This mistake makes it improbable that the document was prepared after copies of the Report began circulating; and Murray's letter of 29 May indicates that the Atholl family did not know the horrific details of the Massacre before the Commission. Atholl, *Chronicles*, i, 336, Murray to [Marchioness], 29 May [1695]; *Highland Papers*, 99, Protection, 15 June 1695; *ib.*, 107–8, Report, 20 June 1695.

82. See Chapter 10, p. 331, Chapter 11, pp. 373–4. *Annandale Book*, ii, 93, Johnston to Annandale, 17 Jan. 1695; *Highland Papers*, 90–1, Livingston to Lt-Col Hamilton, 8 May 1693; *ib.*, 107–8, Report, 20 June 1695.

83. The 'party' was certainly not Livingston, and Hamilton also produced letters vaguely damaging to Dalrymple. The wording implies the vague 'duty' owed to social superiors like Breadalbane; 'sivillity' is the wrong word for the military obedience he owed to Livingston's and Dalrymple's orders. *Ib.*, 101, 109; *Annandale Book*, ii, 118, Lt-Col Hamilton to Annandale, 5 July 1695.

84. *CSPD 1694–5*, 500, [Johnston] to [William], 18–20 June 1695.

85. *Carstares S.P.*, 234–5, Tarbat to Carstares, 25 June 1695; *Highland Papers*, 101, 103–4, 112, 114, Report, 20 June 1695.

86. *APS*, ix, 377; *Maxwells of Pollok*, ii, 94–6, Pollok to Carstares, 25 June 1695; NUL, Portland MSS, PwA 365, Queensberry to Portland, 25 June 1695; *CSPD 1694–5*, 503–4, [Johnston] to [William], 21–25 June 1695.

87. The 'episcopalians" numbers, being given only at the December conference at London in which they lied freely, may not be reliable; but Johnston avoided challenging them head on. *Ib.*, 507–8, [same] to [same], 26–28 June 1695; *APS*, ix, 377; *ib.*, App., 107; *Marchmont Papers*, iii, 416–17, 'Account of Proceedings'; NLS MS 7027 fol. 39, [Johnston], 'Our Conference', [Dec. 1695].

88. *Highland Papers*, 120–31, *'Information for the Master of Stair'; Carstares S.P.*, 236, ? to Carstares, 5 July 1695; *APS*, ix, App., 108.

89. *Ib*; SRO GD 112/43/1/2/77, 'Memd Parliament of Scotland'.

90. *APS*, ix, 377–81; *CSPD 1695*, 145, [Carstares], Parliamentary memoranda, [July 1695]; Foxcroft, *Supplement to Burnet*, 412; Riley, *King William*, 97–8.

91. *Jerviswood Corr.*, 17, Johnston to Jerviswood, 7 Dec. 1704; Drumlanrig, Queensberry Papers, bundle 1156, Carstares to Queensberry, n.d. [c. Jan. 1700[/1]].

92. *HMCR Buccleuch (Montagu)*, ii, 201, Johnston to Shrewsbury, 19 July 1695; NLS 7018 fols. 119-20, Pringle to Tweeddale, July 1695; *ib.*, fol. 45, Tweeddale to William, 13 July 1695; *ib.*, fols. 53v-55, same to Pringle, 26 July 1695; *CSPD 1694-5*, 511, Additional Instruction, 27 June 1695.

93. *Ib.*, 509 [Johnston] to [William], 26-28 June 1695; *APS*, ix, 388, 425; *Annandale Book*, ii, 180, Teviot to Annandale, 9 Feb. 1699; NLS MS 7018 fol. 102, Pringle to Tweeddale, 14 July 1695 (NS); *Marchmont Papers*, iii, 418, 'Account of Proceedings'.

94. *Ib;* *CSPD 1694-5*, 509, [Johnston] to [William], 26-28 June 1695; SRO GD 112/43/1/5/30, Hill's deposition, 2 July 1695; *APS*, ix, 407-8.

95. *Ib;* *Annandale Book*, ii, 118, Lt-Col Hamilton to Annandale, 5 July 1695.

96. *APS*, ix, 421-2, 424-6, 431; *Marchmont Papers*, iii, 418, 'Account of Proceedings'; NLS MS 7027 fol. 39v, [Johnston], 'Our Conference', [Dec. 1695].

97. Dunlop, 'A Chief and his Lawyer', *TGSI*, xlv, 264.

98. Blair, Atholl MSS, Box 29 I (7) 147, A. Menzies to Murray, 5 June 1695; Atholl, *Chronicles*, i, App., xliii-xliv, Murray to Marchioness, 21 May [1695]; *ib.*, xliv-xlv, Rob Roy's submission, 22 June 1695.

99. *Ib.*, 339, Marchioness to Murray, 25 Nov. [1693]; *ib.*, 351-4, Declarations on the murder, c. Oct. 1694; Blair, Atholl MSS, Box 29 I (8) 124, Murray to Steuart, 29 Apr. 1695; *ib.*, 131, Dalrymple to Murray, 14 May 1695; *ib.*, (9) 180, Ormiston to same, 9 May 1696; SRO GD 112/39/1288, 'Macgregor' to D. Toshach, 25 Jan. 1694; *ib.*, 1292, D. Toshach to Breadalbane, 10 Feb. 1694.

100. And nobody in Flanders that it had been lost. *Ib.*, 40/4/8/1, [Glenorchy] to Breadalbane, 27 June 1695(OS); *ib.*, 4, [same] to same, 22 July 1695 (OS); *ib.*, 48, William to Tweeddale, [27 June 1695]; *HMCR Buccleuch (Montagu)*, ii, 202, Johnston to Shrewsbury, 19 July 1695.

101. SRO GD 112/43/1/2/78, 'Memd Parliament of Scotland'.

102. NLS MS 7018 fol. 115, Hill to Tweeddale, 29 July 1695; SRO PC 1/50, 219; GD 112/40/4/8/21, [Tarbat] notes on procedure; *ib.*, 33, [Dalrymple] to [Breadalbane], 4 July 1695; *ib.*, 43/1/2/30, list of prosecution witnesses, 15 July 1695; *ib.*, 72, 'Narration of the true matter of fact', 19 Aug. 1695.

103. *Ib.*, 34, [Carwhin, notes on libel of exculpation].

104. *CSPD 1695*, 241, 249, 294, newsletters, 1 Mar., 7 Apr., 14 Dec., 1694; Luttrell, iii, 336, 362; Macpherson, *Loyall Dissuasive*, 10-13, 201-5; SRO PC 1/50, 1-3, 93, 219, 268-9.

105. *Ib.*, GD 112/43/1/5/16i, Indictment.

106. *Ib.*, 28, 'Memorandum, Viscount Tarbat'; *ib.*, 43/1/5/7, H. Dalrymple, Memorandum, 19 July 1695; *ib.*, 40/4/8/21, [Tarbat], notes on procedure; *APS*, ix, 384; *Marchmont Papers*, iii, 417, 'Account of Proceedings'.

107. *Ib.*, 419; *Rawdon Papers*, 427, Case of the Earl of Breadalbane; *APS*, ix, 389, 407; *ib.*, App., 110; SRO GD 112/40/4/8/4, [Glenorchy] to Breadalbane, 22 July/1 Aug. 1695; *ib.*, 28-30, Breadalbane's draft speeches; NLS MS 7027 fol. 39, [Johnston], 'Our Conference', [Dec. 1695].

108. Large numbers of other Jacobites were remitted to the Justice Court for trial. *Ib.*, fol. 40; *APS*, ix, 408; *ib.*, App., 110-13; *Marchmont Papers*, iii, 419, 'Account of Proceedings'; *Carstares SP.*, 235-6, ? to Carstares, 5 July 1695; *HMCR Buccleuch (Montagu)*, ii, 202, Johnston to Shrewsbury, 19 July 1695.

109. *Ib;* Drumlanrig, Queensberry Papers, Vol. 115, 27, Argyll to Queensberry, 31 July 1695; SRO GD 112/43/1/5/1, *Answers for the Earl of Breadalbane to the Indictment of Treason*, 2-3, 5, 6-7; *ib.*, 32, Barcaldine to Breadalbane, 12 July [1695]; *ib.*, 43/1/2/28,

'Memorandum, Viscount Tarbat'; *ib.*, 34, [Carwhin, notes on libel of exculpation]; *ib.*, 36, parliamentary list.

110. *Ib.*, 30, list of prosecution witnesses, 15 July 1695; *ib.*, 43/1/5/18, list of defence witnesses; *APS*, ix, App., 122-2; *Rawdon Papers*, 427-8, Breadalbane's Case; NLS MS 7029 fol. 47v, Tweeddale to William, 18 July 1695.

111. *Ib.*, fols. 47v-49; *APS*, ix, 122, 124; *Marchmont Papers*, iii, 419, 'Account of Proceedings'.

112. *CSPD 1694-5*, 508-9, [Johnston] to [William], 26-28 June 1695; *HMCR Buccleuch (Montagu)*, ii, 202-3, same to Shrewsbury, 19 July 1695; Riley, *King William*, 95.

113. Another 'episcopalian' noble, the Earl of Strathmore, had died in May, returning to Jacobitism near the end. *Carstares S.P.*, 258, Ogilvie to Carstares, 23 July 1695; Macpherson, *Original Papers*, i, 529, Middleton to Sir W. Bruce, 23 Dec. 1695(NS); *Scots Peerage*, v, 449; *ib.*, viii, 302; NLS MS 7029 fol. 65, Tweeddale to William, 17 Aug. 1695.

114. *HMCR Buccleuch (Montagu)*, ii, 202-3, Johnston to Shrewsbury, 19 July 1695; Lambeth Palace MS 2020 fols. 21-4, same to Tenison, 18 July 1695; *Impartial Account of some of the transactions in Scotland, Somers Tracts*, xi, 547-61; NLS MS 7029 fol. 68, Tweeddale to A. Johnston, 29 Aug. 1695; NLS MS 7018 fols. 128-9, Annandale to Tweeddale, 10 Aug. 1695.

115. *Ib.*, MS 7027 fol. 39v [Johnston], 'Our Conference', [Dec. 1695]; *Gazette de France*, 30 July 1695, 351-2, Edinburgh report, 6 July; *ib.*, 6 Aug. 1695, 366-7, same, 14 July; *ib.*, 13 Aug. 1695, 377, same, 21 July (all NS).

116. Riley, *King William*, 95-6.

117. *APS*, ix, 461-2; NLS MS 7018 fol. 115, Hill to Tweeddale, 29 July 1695; *ib.*, MS 1305 fol. 55, Keppoch to Delvine, 2 Nov. 1697; Blair, Atholl MSS, Box 29 I (8) 48, same to Murray, 29 Jan. 1696; *ib.*, 84, same to same, 26 Feb. 1696.

118. SRO GD 1/658, 30-1, 62-3.

119. Blair, Atholl MSS, Box 29 I (9) 215, Dollery to same 27 Apr. 1697; *Highland Papers*, 149-50, Glencoe men's petition, 25 July 1695; SRO E 7/8, 355.

120. *APS*, ix, 425, 426-7, 464-5; Atholl, *Chronicles*, i, 363-4, A. MacIain to Murray, 6 Jan. 1696; *ib.*, 367, Glengarry to same, 24 Jan. 1696.

121. Paget, *New Examen*, 45.

122. *Carstares S.P.*, 569, ? to Carstares, 16 July 1700; Hopkins, 'Sham Plots & Real Plots', *Ideology & Conspiracy*, 100-2.

123. *CSPD 1694-5*, 498, passes, 18 June 1695; Huygens, *Journaal*, ii. 501; SRO GD 112/40/4/8/1, Glenorchy to Breadalbane, 27 June 1695; *ib.*, 22, [Dalrymple] to same, 27 June 1695.

124. *Melvilles & Leslies*, ii, 172, Carstares to Melville, 11 July 1695; *HMCR Roxburghe*, 128, Pringle to Polwarth, 24 July 1695 (NS); NLS MS 7018 fol. 108, same to Tweeddale, 11 July 1695(NS); *ib.*, fols. 119-20, same to same, [July 1695].

125. *Ib.*, fol. 119, same to same, 1 Aug. 1695(NS); *CSPD 1695*, 144-5, [Carstares], Parliamentary memoranda, [July 1695]; SRO GD 112/40/4/8/8, Glenorchy to Breadalbane, 26 Aug./5 Sept. 1695; *ib.*, 12, [Dalrymple] to same, 31 July 1695 (OS).

126. *Ib.*, 4, Glenorchy to same, 22 July 1695; *ib.*, 42, [same] to same, 1 July 1695; *ib.*, 46, same to [same], 11/21 July 1695.

127. *Ib.*, 2, [same] to same, 8 Aug. 1695(OS).

128. *HMCR Buccleuch (Montagu)*, ii, 216-17, Tweeddale to Shrewsbury, 17 Aug. 1695; *ib.*, 221-2, Shrewsbury to Tweeddale, 5 Sept. 1695; NUL, Portland MSS, PwA 368, Queensberry to Portland, 12 Aug. 1695; NLS MS 7029 fol. 58v, Tweeddale to Pringle, 17 Aug. 1695.

129. Duncanson, who protested at the surrender, was made the regiment's lieutenant-colonel; but it had just been reclothed, and he was imprisoned at Edinburgh for the debt, 1697–c. 1699, when the English Treasury repaid him. Serving again (unlike Hamilton or Drummond) from 1702, he received a regiment in 1705, but was killed that May in Spain. *CTB*, xv, 5, 160, 173, 177; Holden, 'The First Highland Regiment', *SHR*, iii, 38–40; Prebble, *Glencoe*, 292; SRO GD 112/40/4/8/8, Glenorchy to Breadalbane, 26 Aug./5 Sept. 1695; *ib.*, 15, Dalrymple to same, 25 July [1695](OS).

130. *More Culloden Papers*, 223, Hill to Culloden, 9 Sept. 1695; NLS MS 7018 fol. 125, Pringle to Tweeddale, 12 Aug. 1695. But see Bland Burges, *Selections*, 358.

131. SRO GD 112/40/4/8/18, Dalrymple to Breadalbane, 1 Sept. 1695 (OS); *ib.*, 5, Glenorchy to same, 6 Sept. 1695; *ib.*, 43/1/5/13, same to same, 2–3 Sept. 1695; *ib.*, 43/1/2/70, William's order.

132. *Ib.*, 26, Viscount Tarbat's opinion; *ib.*, 44, Arguments, 21 Sept. 1695; *ib.*, 58, Memorandum, [Oct. 1695]; *ib.*, 60, Steuart to Tweeddale, 15 Sept. 1695; *ib.*, 65, Breadalbane's petition; *ib.*, 43/1/5/3, Memorandum for Carwhin, Oct. '1696' [1695].

133. NLS MS 7029 fol. 79, Tweeddale to Johnston, 1 Oct. 1695.

134. *Ib.*, fols. 79–81; *ib.*, fols. 81v–83, same to same, 3 Oct. 1695; *Annandale Book*, ii, 119–20, same to Annandale, 10 Oct. 1695; *Carstares S.P.*, 262, Steuart to Carstares, 17 Oct. 1695; SRO PC 1/50, 247–8; GD 112/43/1/2/31, PCS minority to William, 3 Oct. 1695.

135. Blair, Atholl MSS, Box 29 I (7) 173, ? to Murray, 19 Oct. 1695; SRO GD 112/39/1303, [Dalrymple] to Breadalbane, 18 Oct. 1695.

136. The document's treatment of Achallader indicates that it was intended for a Williamite audience; its shift from frankness to evasion over Breadalbane's Jacobite dealings, that it was written between his remissions of December 1690 and December 1695; its degree of frankness, that it was required for a great emergency. *Ib.*, 43/1/2/55, 'The heads of what I am to discourse upon with the D. of Leeds', Nov. 1695; *ib.*, 98, Carwhin's draft of Breadalbane's 'Life'; *ib.*, 43/1/5/3, Memorandum, Breadalbane to Carwhin, Oct. '1696' [1695]; GD 406/1/4064, Argyll to Arran, 16 June 1695.

137. Riley, *King William*, 99; Horwitz, *PPP*, 159; Ailesbury, *Memoirs*, i, 347–9.

138. Leslie, *Gallienus Redivivus*, 6.

139. *Ib.*, 11, 20.

140. *Ib.*, 3–5, 11.

141. *More Culloden Papers*, 223, Hill to Culloden, 9 Sept. 1695; Macpherson, 'Gleanings', *TGSI*, xx, 242–3, same to [Gentry of Badenoch], 10 Nov. 1695.

142. D. C. Mactavish (ed.), *Inveraray Papers* (Oban, 1939), 17–21, papers on Highland Justiciary persecutions, 1695; SRO GD 112/43/1/4/3, 'A true information of the death of Grant of Shewglie', [Nov. 1695]; NLS MS 7019 fol. 125, Lochiel to Tweeddale, 11 Nov. 1695; Blair, Atholl MSS, Box 29 I (8), 48, Keppoch to Murray, 29 Jan. 1696.

143. *Ib;* *Highland Papers*, 150–1, PC warrant, 10 Dec. 1695; Wimberley, 'Bighouse Papers', *TGSI*, xxi, 134–6, decreet, 20 Dec. 1695.

144. Atholl, *Chronicles*, i, 336, Murray to [Marchioness], 29 May [1695]; Blair, Atholl MSS, Box 29 I (8) 222, Ld James Murray to Murray, 6 June 1696; *ib.*, 268, same to same, 10 July 1696; *ib.*, (11) 212, Campbell of Duneaves to same, 24 Oct. 1698.

145. Foxcroft, *Supplement to Burnet*, 415; *Carstares S.P.*, 263, Ogilvie to Carstares, 26 Oct. 1695; *Seafield Corr.*, 174, same to Findlater, 8 Nov. 1695.

146. *Ib;* SRO GD 112/39/1303, [Dalrymple] to Breadalbane, 18 Oct. 1695, NLS MS 7029 fol. 160, Tweeddale to ?, [1695–6].

147. *HMCR Buccleuch (Montagu)*, ii, 226, same to Shrewsbury, 10 Sept. 1695; *ib.*, 243, same to same, 24 Oct. 1695; Burnet, *History*, iv, 121–2; NLS MS 7018 fol. 129, Annandale

to Tweeddale, 10 Aug. 1695.

148. *Ib.*, MS 7019 fol. 35, A. Johnston to same, 12 Sept. 1695; *CSPD 1695*, 105, Shrewsbury to same, 19 Nov. 1695; *LJ*, xv, 608; Macky, *Memoirs*, 205–6; Riley, *King William*, 99; Horwitz, *PPP*, 158, 161–2.

149. *Ib.*, 204.

150. My understanding of Tweeddale's reason for mentioning that it was a draft brought in by a committee of Parliament is diametrically opposed to Riley's: not that he hoped to pretend that it was passed by mistake, but that this implied that Parliament was behind it. Even when he had begun denying the importance of the act, he still erased from his letters of 14 December the remark that William could quash the Company, NLS MS 7029 fols. 92v–93, Tweeddale to Johnston, 15 Oct. 1695; *ib.*, fol. 95, same to same, 19 Oct. 1695; *ib.*, fol. 136, same to same, 14 Dec. 1695; *ib.*, fol. 105, same to William, 13 Nov. 1695; *ib.*, MS 7030 fol. 2v, same to same, 21 Dec. 1695; *ib.*, MS 14,408 fols. 419–20, [Johnston] to Tweeddale, 21 Nov. 1695; *ib.*, fol. 441, [same] to same, 2 Jan 1696; Riley, *King William*, 99.

151. *Ib.*, 100–2, 107–9.

152. *CSPD 1695*, 124, warrant to Tweeddale, 13 Dec. 1695; *Maxwells of Pollok*, ii, 97–8, Pollok to Carstares, 16 Dec. 1695; NLS MS 7029 fol. 122, Tweeddale to Johnston, 27 Nov. 1695; *ib.*, fol. 135, same to same, 14 Dec. 1695.

153. Story, *Carstares*, 252–4, Carstares, Memorial, [Jan. 1696]; Riley, *King William*, 107; NLS MS 14,408 fol. 444, [Johnston] to Tweeddale, [10 Jan. 1696].

154. *Caldwell Papers*, 193, W. Stewart to W. Hamilton, 27 Nov. 1695.

155. NLS MS 7019 fol. 145, Annandale to Tweeddale, 3 Dec. 1695; *ib.*, fol. 154, same to same, 9 Dec. 1695; *ib.*, MS 7027 fols. 39–40, [Johnston], 'Our Conference', [Dec. 1695].

156. *Ib.*, MS 14,408 fol. 433, [same] to Tweeddale, 12 Dec. 1695; *Seafield Corr.*, 177, J. Baird to Findlater, 2 Jan. 1696; Blair, Atholl MSS, Box 29 I (7) 181, Lady Dundonald to Lady Murray, 19 Dec. 1695; SRO GD 112/39/1305, [Carwhin] to Breadalbane, [16 Dec. 1695].

157. *Ib; ib.*, 1304, same to same, 17 Dec. 1695; *LJ*, xv, 608–11, 614, 616; *Lockhart Papers*, i, 88; *Earls of Cromartie*, i, 119, Tweeddale to Yester, 21 Dec. 1695; NLS MS 7029 fol. 134, same to Johnston, 14 Dec. 1695; *ib.*, MS 7019 fol. 157, Annandale to Tweeddale, 14 Dec. 1695; *ib.*, MS 14,408 fols. 434v–436, [Johnston] to same, 12–13 Dec. 1695.

158. Riley, *King William*, 98–9.

159. SRO GD 112/39/1305, [Carwhin] to Breadalbane, [16 Dec. 1695].

160. *Ib.; ib.*, 43/1/2/62, copy of Remission, 16 Dec. 1695; *ib.*, 43/1/5/5a, 8, drafts of same; *CSPD 1695*, 127, Remission & order to Leven, 16 Dec. 1695; *Highland Papers*, 143, Scroll remission for Stair.

161. SRO PC 1/50, 302–3; NLS MS 7029 fols. 149v–152, Tweeddale to Johnston, 24 Dec. 1695; *ib.*, fol. 156, same to same, 26 Dec. 1695.

162. *Ib.*, MS 7030 fol. 5v, same to Yester, 31 Dec. 1695; Blair, Atholl MSS, Box 29 I (8) 11, Lady Murray to Murray, 9 Jan. 1696.

163. *Ib.*, 48, Keppoch to same, 29 Jan. 1696; Atholl, *Chronicles*, i, 367, Glengarry to same, 24 Jan. 1696.

164. *Ib.*, 361, Johnston to same, 21 Dec. 1695; Blair, Atholl MSS, Box 44/VI/217, same to same, [?Dec. 1695]; *ib.*, Box 29 I (8) 9, Murray to Lady Murray, 9 Jan. 1696; *CSPD 1696*, 62, Pension for Tarbat, 29 Feb. 1696; NLS MS 14,408 fol. 444, [Johnston] to Tweeddale, [10 Jan. 1696].

165. Atholl, *Chronicles*, i, 364 (Blair, Atholl MSS, Box 29 I (8) 13), Murray to Lady Murray, 14 Jan. 1696; *Seafield Corr.*, 177–8, J. Baird to Findlater, 20 Jan. 1696; *Carstares S.P.*, 371, Argyll to Carstares, 26 Feb. 1698.

166. Blair, Atholl MSS, Box 29 I (8) 65, Ld. B. Hamilton to Murray, 13 Feb. 1696; *ib.*, 156, Duchess of Hamilton to Lady Murray, 14 Apr. 1696.

167. *CSPD 1696*, 150, Grant, 28 Apr. 1696; *Annandale Book*, ii, 126, Livingston to Annandale, 8 Sept. 1696; *Marchmont Papers*, iii, 170, Marchmont to William, 3 Sept. 1698; *Carstares S.P.*, 426, Seafield to Carstares, 20 Aug. 1698; *ib.*, 427–8, same to same, 23 Aug. 1698.

168. Yet his personal hatred for 'presbyterians' probably largely explains at least one disastrous policy into which he persuaded Queensberry in 1702. *Ib.*, 477n, Ormiston to same, 4 Apr. 1699; Riley, 'The Abjuration Vote of 27 June 1702 . . . ', *Parliamentary History*, ii (1983), 184–6; *CSPD 1699–1700*, 204, Pardon to Stair, 30 May 1699; *ib.*, 204, 206, Grants to same.

169. *Ib.*, 206, Pension to Glenorchy, 30 May 1699; *ib.*, 302, Grant to same, 30 Nov. 1699; *ib. 1696*, 84, Grant to Breadalbane, 12 Mar. 1696; *ib. 1697*, 77, Commission of Highland Justiciary, 30 Mar. 1697; Blair, Atholl MSS, Box 29 I (8) 9, Murray to Lady Murray, 9 Jan. 1696; *ib.*, 14, same to same, 16 Jan. 1696.

170. *APS*, ix, 196; Drumlanrig, Queensberry Papers, Vol. 111, 42, Queensberry to Breadalbane, [1700].

171. *HMCR Portland*, x, 208–9, 298–9, 303, 349, 353, 414, 427, Papers, 1710–13; *Earls of Cromartie*, i, 129–30, Breadalbane to Tarbat, 17 Mar. 1698; *LJ*, xvii, 405, Sir J. Maclean's discovery; Mr of Sinclair, *Memoirs*, 185–6, 260; SRO GD 50/12/1/12, Carwhin to Lady Glenorchy, 13 Feb. 1703; D. Szechi, *Jacobitism and Tory Politics, 1710–14* (Edinburgh, 1984), 19, 66, 150, 158, 172, 202; Macky, *Memoirs*, 199–200.

172. *Ib.*, 210–11; Story, *Carstares*, 204–7, Carstares, Report on Scottish Council, [?1695–6]; *ib.*, 253, Memorial, [Jan. 1696].

173. *CSPD 1696*, 35, Appointment of Ogilvie, 5 Feb. 1696; Foxcroft, *Supplement to Burnet*, 415; Berkshire RO, Marquess of Downshire's MSS, Trumbull Add. MS 125, 27, 32, diary of Sir W. Trumbull, 1 June, 14 Oct. 1697.

174. Unlike Johnston, Tweeddale tried to maintain the links with the Junto, informing Shrewsbury of the delaying of the Association. NLS MS 7020 fol. 90, J. Dickson to Tweeddale, 6 Sept. 1696; *ib.*, MS 7030 fol. 83, Tweeddale to Johnston, 18 Mar. 1696; *ib.*, fol. 87, same to Shrewsbury, 26 Mar. 1696.

175. *HMCR Hope-Johnstone*, 99–100, Johnston to Annandale, 18 May 1696; Story, *Carstares*, 254, Memorial, [Jan. 1696]; *CSPD 1697*, 78, grant to Johnston, 30 Mar. 1697; *Lockhart Papers*, i, 367–8; Blair, Atholl MSS, Box 29 I (9) 52, Tullibardine to Lady Tullibardine, 16 Feb. 1697.

176. Although Neville Payne in 1690 was the last man actually tortured, Murray still threatened Robert Ferguson with it after the Assassination Plot. *LJ*, xvii, 411, Ferguson's narrative, 27 Dec. 1703.

177. *Annandale Book*, ii, 156, Teviot to Annandale, 15 Feb. 1698; Riley, *King William*, 114, 118, 127.

178. Blair, Atholl MSS, Box 29 I (8) 15, Ormiston to Murray, 16 Jan. 1696.

179. Riley, *King William*, 135, 137, 150.

180. *Jerviswood Corr.*, 17, Johnston to Jerviswood, 7 Dec. 1704; *ib.*, 186, same to same, 7 Feb. [1707].

181. *Life of James*, ii, 547–8; *State Trials*, x, 1302, 1326; *ib.*, xi, 318.

182. Macpherson, *Original Papers*, i, 529–30, Middleton to Sir W. Bruce, 23 Dec. 1695(NS); SRO PC 1/50, 316–18, 322–3, 332, 336, 338–9.

183. *Ib.*, 345–7, 352–3, 365, 402; *Carstares S.P.*, 277, Argyll to Carstares, '16' Mar. 1696.

184. *CSPD 1695*, 127, William to PCS, 18 Dec. 1695; Macpherson, *Original Papers*, i,

529, Middleton to Sir W. Bruce, 23 Dec. 1695 (NS); *Seafield Corr.*, 178, J. Baird to Findlater, 20 Jan. 1696; *Scots Peerage*, viii, 304; SRO PC 1/50, 351, 417-8; NLS MS 7030 fol. 72, Tweeddale to Murray, 29 Feb. 1696; Blair, Atholl MSS, Box 29 I (8) 117, Murray to Lady Murray, 17 Mar. [1696].

185. *Ib.*, 112, William to Ormiston, 12 Mar. 1696; *CSPD 1696*, 65-6, same to PCS, 2 Mar. 1696; SRO PC 1/50, 365.

186. *Ib.*, 352, 389; *Memoirs of Locheill*, 329-30; Blair, Atholl MSS, Box 29 I (8) 101, D. Moncrieff to Murray, 3 Mar. 1696; *ib.*, 117, Murray to Lady Murray, 17 Mar. 1696; *ib.*, 142, Lady Erroll to Murray, 6 Apr. 1696.

187. MacPhail, *Dumbarton Castle*, 127; SRO PC 1/50, 473, 576-7.

188. *HMCR Hamilton Supplement*, 135-6, papers on Arran's promise, [1696].

189. *CSPD 1696*, 65, William to PCS, 2 Mar. 1696.

190. *Carstares S.P.*, 279, Argyll to Carstares, 23 Mar. 1696; *ib.*, 280-1, same to same, 24 Mar. 1696; NLS MS 7020 fol. 34, Ogilvie to Tweeddale, 2 Mar. 1696; SRO PC 1/50, 346, 392, 421, 425, 427.

191. *Ib.*, 520-1; Macpherson, 'Gleanings', *TGSI*, xx, 244, Permission to Cluny, 5 May 1696; *ib.*, 245, Hill to Steuart, 11 May 1696; NLS MS 7030 fol. 77v, Tweeddale to Ogilvie, 7 Mar. 1696; *ib.*, fol. 132v, same to Hill, 13 Mar. 1696; NUL, Portland MSS, PwA 675, Hill to Portland, 30 Apr. 1696.

192. Atholl, *Chronicles*, i, 378, C. Campbell to Murray, 8 July 1696; *ib.*, 379, Ardvorlich to same, 14 July 1696; Blair, Atholl MSS, Box 29 I (8) 286, Hill to same, 15 July 1696.

193. *Ib.*, 182, Glengarry to same, 9 May 1696; *ib.*, 273, same to same, 12 July 1696; SRO PC 1/50, 457-8, 489, 560-1, 571, 587-8.

194. *Ib.*, 612-13; Blair, Atholl MSS, Box 29 I (8) 84, Keppoch to Murray, 26 Feb. 1696; *ib.*, 222, Ld James Murray to same, 6 June 1696.

195. *CSPD 1697*, 48, Warrants to free Drummond and Seaforth, 1 Mar. 1697; *State Trials*, xiii, 1445-50; SRO PC 1/50, 560, 631-2.

13

Magnate Revival and Highland Disorder (1696–1702)

Lord Murray for the moment seemed to possess William's full confidence, and therefore to be the most powerful politician in Scotland. He was supported not only by his own family 'interest' but, since Arran remained beyong the pale, by most of the Hamiltons, who profited from the change. One of his brothers-in-law, Selkirk, became Register, another General of the Mint, a third had married Elizabeth Villiers. Murray, created Earl of Tullibardine to qualify him as Commissioner for a parliamentary session in September 1696, obtained the required supplies despite the nation's hardships, largely through Hamilton of Whitelaw's management of the burghs.

Murray wielded his power with a mixture of normal magnate self-interest and jealousy and of a self-conscious but genuine idealism — shown, for instance, when he assured Tweeddale after his dismissal of protection against the traditional savage attacks on fallen statesmen.[1] He was eager to help reconcile and bring into the government able and powerful men of both parties and all factions, even making advances, before the Assassination Plot, to the old Earl of Aberdeen.[2] Not only did he, like Ogilvie, urge William and Portland to bring in Queensberry and Argyll, and emphasise to Lord Polwarth (made Chancellor largely through his influence) the need to co-operate fully with them; he took a leading part in the elaborate negotiations by which Melville was kicked upstairs to be President of the Council, Queensberry in his place became Lord Privy Seal and Argyll in *his* place second-in-command of the army. He was needlessly laying himself open, since the delays caused by Melville's obstinacy, and his proposal that Queensberry, who held several posts, should draw a reduced salary to help the nation's finances, made Queensberry and Argyll (who had both, admittedly, secretly denounced him before the negotiations) start working as his colleagues to undermine him earlier than they might otherwise have done.[3] He remained blind to the danger from them for an abnormally long time. Even in January 1697, he was trying on principle to avoid committing himself to any party.[4]

He ignored the real danger mainly because he concentrated his suspicions on the possibility of Johnston's regaining power and the survivors of Johnston's 'presbyterians'.[5] The background to his appointment should have made him friendly towards them; but he had taken literally William's claim that he owed it entirely to him. The Association, on the English model, which several of the surviving 'presbyterians' suggested after the Assassination Plot, emphasised the breach which existed, and they complained that Murray had turned to the other party. He, Queensberry and Argyll all opposed a measure which some of their followers would have refused; they could argue that, after the 1695 session, it had a suspicious Covenanting air about it, and that it might well backfire and expose government weaknesses, like the 1692 oaths.[6] Some 'presbyterians' followed Polwarth and Whitelaw in supporting the Court; others (secretly encouraged by Justice-Clerk Ormiston) formed the opposition in the 1696 session, the nucleus of the future 'Country Party'. Murray was particularly hostile towards Annandale as a traitor and turncoat, lost few opportunities to denounce him and repelled his approaches into 1697. In fact, after the Association and a natural period of sulking over losing the presidency of the Council, Annandale came to support him longer than he normally did any leader whose success was so unsure.[7]

The struggle over Whitelaw finally revealed to Murray/Tullibardine his real position. He had promised him the post of President of the Session before the 1696 Parliament in return for organising the burghs and William had actually signed the grant. Yet, although Whitelaw performed his part of the bargain, the King refused to let Tullibardine give him it, secretly influenced by Queensberry, who (like many less biased men) dared not allow an enemy in a position with such power over property rights. Tullibardine, who considered his honour pledged to Whitelaw, discovered that, despite appearances, he had alarmingly little control over appointments or policy, and that Carstares, who had much, was an unscrupulous enemy to him and supporter of Queensberry. This transformed his conduct, driving him from early 1697 into desperate attempts to force William to accept his policies and candidates for office, and into over-reaction when William favoured other men's, which still further reduced his influence with him. Even while still refusing to organise a personal faction, he quarrelled jealously with Ogilvie over their respective powers. After a futile attempt to prise Argyll away from Queensberry, he finally allied with Annandale. He flaunted his influence over his in-laws, once (Argyll claimed) trying to override Ogilvie with a threatening 'What, will you oppose the family of Hamilton'?[8] On the whole, this relationship worked to his disadvantage. If Arran were to submit to William's government, and threw his family interest completely behind the Atholl one, the alliance might well be able to dominate Scottish politics: and Tullibardine's enemies therefore laboured with frenzied determination to tear him down before this could occur.[9]

Behind these factional squabbles, deeper causes were shaping the nation's fortunes. Until September 1697, the war continued to have a burdensome and distorting influence — but only an indirect one, although French preparation of a fleet made the government expect an invasion in December 1696. The usual suspects were arrested and filled Edinburgh Castle.[10] Hill was ordered to detain several highlanders, including Lochiel, Glengarry (specially insisted on by Argyll for being the Atholl family's protégé) and several Macleans in Mull. They surrendered quietly (while Lochiel's eldest son probably, as usual, lurked in the hills in case the invasion did occur) and after their release furnished bonds for good behaviour.[11] The English attempts to sabotage the Scots East India Company were a cause of growing controversy, but this did not reach a crisis until the Darien attempt; and few highlanders were directly involved. (See Preface, pp. x-xiv)

The Highlands were only too deeply involved in the other major event of these years, the series of bad harvests and famines which began in 1695 and began to pass away only with the good harvests of 1700 and 1701 — the last of the blows which made William's reign so catastrophic for Scotland. No regime in those days, of course, could do much to alleviate such a disaster; but the popular memory which referred to it as 'King William's seven ill years' was founded on more than superstitions about God's punishment for accepting usurpation. William's main priority throughout, enforced without consideration for local conditions, was to maintain an experienced Scottish standing army of a size unprecedented in peacetime. In 1697-8, by an unsystematic series of orders which made advance planning impossible, he had the regiments still in Scotland disbanded, often without their arrears and far from the men's homes at a time when this might make the difference between survival and starvation. He then ordered regiment after regiment from Flanders back into the country, to be quartered in badly-hit areas and reduce food-stocks still further. The ministers' main priority was to please William by keeping up the crushing taxation for the army, at a time when the English, though suffering no such catastrophe, were enforcing massive reductions in theirs; and, to justify this, they sometimes publicly ignored or concealed the depth of the crisis. Lord Chancellor Marchmont (formerly Polwarth) as Commissioner in 1698 obtained supplies, suppressed a proposal for poor relief, and declared in his closing speech that there was hope of a good harvest, despite his private knowledge that it would be late and terribly vulnerable — in the event the worst, and the most terrible in its effects, of the entire famine. Johnston complained that the ministers had not even publicly represented matters to William, which would have made the English parliament grant special concessions for corn export to Scotland.[12] Not all that could have been done was done.

The Highlands may not immediately have been affected in 1695. Despite their comparative poverty, their more diverse economy sometimes allowed them to ride out short famines which ravaged the Lowlands. Tarbat, returning defeated to the North Highlands in mid-1696, was still able to imagine himself in a (sour-grapes) Arcadia; by 1698 he could see only suffering and worse to come.[13] The famine apparently began to bite in the Highlands early in 1697, when the Council first asked the Irish government for permission to buy Irish meal for Fort William.[14] There were some deaths from starvation in Lochaber that spring, but the real crisis came that autumn. The harvest, which elsewhere was good but limited, seems to have failed in the Highlands — migrants who traditionally helped in the Lowlands harvest refused to return home, knowing there was no food for them — and was followed by a cruel winter. cattle and horses could not subsist, and the new-fangled crop, potatoes (still of very limited importance), was destroyed by frost. The surviving parish registers for Kilmorack and Kirkhill in the Aird, Fraser country, show that the worst mortality, from hunger or the diseases malnutrition encouraged, in the famine period ocurred in 1697-8, and the reports of Breadalbane's chamberlains emphasise that the South Highlands were equally badly off.[15] As in the great Irish famine, the toll was increased by the people's inability to buy what meal was produced, and by transport difficulties: while one Breadalbane chamberlain was trying to sell all he could gather to the Fort William garrison, the arrival of two boatloads abruptly reduced the price there by 12/- the boll.[16] The terrible weather which wiped out the 1698 harvest was at its worst in the Highlands: what little was saved in Strathardle was uprooted by hand from under snowdrifts. So many goats (on which poorer highlanders largely relied for milk) had to be slaughtered that 100,000 skins were exported to London in 1699. If mortality did not reach new heights, as it did in the Lowlands, it was because the most vulnerable groups had already died; and lack of seed and money probably prolonged the starvation and disease in these remote areas after the Lowlands' recovery was well under way.[17]

Far too little evidence exists about the highland population to allow any firm estimate of how many died. Although famine was universal in the Highlands and Islands, the proportion of deaths probably varied sharply; some areas, including parts of Mull and Speyside, were said to have been totally depopulated. The one general estimate, made by the catholic priests, was that two-thirds of the inhabitants of the North Highlands died; but this is probably too high. The one estimate for a single clan, made by Keppoch (who had brought 2-300 followers to Dundee's rendezvous in 1689), was that over a hundred of them now perished (although they, being on the run from Mackintosh, were even worse off than other clans, and some of the deaths were by sword or gallows).[18] Estimates of his clan's strength suggest that within a few years even this loss was largely made up. The starving highlanders had one slight advantage over lowland tenants or even the Orkney freeholders: their chiefs and landlords on the whole made greater efforts to help them. This was, admittedly, sometimes for lack of alternative. Breadalbane failed to sell his surplus victual to Fort William before having it distributed to select deserving tenants to tide them over, and, when he forgave arrears of rent, the only alternative, seizing tenants' oxen, would make them unable to work the land.[19] He was inevitably torn between a desire to help his tenants and the need to extract as much of this rent as possible, for the crisis made his normal creditors more urgent, bringing ruin very close. The famine had not caused any major breakdown of society, and chiefs and even clan gentry carried on their business dealing and lawsuits almost as usual. Nor, unfortunately, did the famine's worst ravages check clan feuding and forays (with theoretical legal backing), Atholl men against Frasers, Mackintosh against Keppoch Macdonalds; their ravaging added its mite to the misery.

One natural result of the famine was a massive increase in cattle-raiding and robbery. From late 1696 onwards, Lochiel was continually paying compensation for his clansmen's thefts. Breadalbane's lands constantly suffered, particularly from Stewarts and Macgregors (against whom he used Rob Roy as an agent), and in desperation he took to trying raiders certain to be found 'not proven', hoping that at least the fright would act as a deterrent.[20] The crime often went beyond normal raiding. Drovers were murdered for their money. Some Macgregors kidnapped a leading Campbell for ransom. Full-scale attacks were made on gentlemen's homes. Tarbat, whose large expenditure on watches could not preserve his estates, complained that the government had forgotten the North's existence.[21]

The Highland Justiciary, the government's main instrument for tackling the problem, was still in disarray after the 1694 disputes. In the 1696 session, Tullibardine passed an act (which William's advisers, nervous after 1695, had feared Parliament might exploit to gain control over it), prolonging its powers for a year and allowing replacement of the death penalty with some lesser punishment — which came to include, occasionally, perpetual servitude within Scotland. Several supplementary acts were proposed in the 1698 session, but none passed.[22] In March 1697, William issued a new Commission: of the hundred men originally named, and those the Council added, only three, Hill, Lieutenant-Colonel Forbes and Glendessary, resided in Lochaber. Breadalbane and several of his Campbell supporters were dropped, but Atholl (always hostile to the Commission) complained that he still had more influence there than himself.[23]

Besides offering rewards for fugitives, the Council assisted the Justiciary by posting detachments of the regular army to supplement Fort William and its out-garrisons. In June 1697, they had four companies stationed, in Rannoch, the braes of Menteith and Strathearn, Glenshee and Braemar, and (at Tarbat's desire) Kilcumin, at the head of Loch Ness. Hill, who already had eighty of his own garrison on patrols against thieves, sent them provisions and advice. In October, two companies were withdrawn to act more directly under the Justiciary Commission's orders; but all arrangements apparently lapsed that winter in the chaos created by piecemeal disbandment and the Frasers' outrages.[24]

The Council revived them in March 1699, stationing 120 men in six detachments from Blair Atholl to Achallader and south to Drymen by Loch Lomond, and smaller detachments from the Fort William regiment at Kilcumin and Invermoriston. The southern companies were commanded by Captain Alexander Campbell of Fonab, formerly of Argyll's regiment, a distant cousin of Breadalbane's — and an enemy of the Atholl family. The expert local knowledge of the Highlands which helped to gain him the appointment may already have been shown in grimmer circumstances: his brother Robert had apparently been Captain Drummond's lieutenant of grenadiers in 1692, and may have been the officer who gave information on the passes into Glencoe.[25] Within three months, Fonab's other abilities led to his replacement: the Scottish East India Company sent him to command the Darien settlement's armed forces. In late June, the Council had three similar detachments in the braes to protect Aberdeenshire, but by November the raiders had evidently discovered means to bypass them, and they were ordered to shift their posts.[26] The northern garrisons were inadequate to satisfy Tarbat, who protested passionately that the army was lying idle, a crushing burden on the tax-payers, although a detachment 80–100 strong, patrolling from Glenmoriston to the west coast, could prevent raiding into the North. Others echoed his accusations of government neglect. In December, the Council's 'Committie anent the peace off the Highlands' (by now a permanent body) under his chairmanship called for more small garrisons, and suggested that chiefs should not be allowed to evade responsibility for robber clansmen by omitting them from the lists of their tenants they handed in; even that the Council should order the chiefs to bring in known local robbers, and imprison them if they failed.[27]

By then, the Highland Justiciary Commission's own flaws had become conspicuous. Atholl was its most violent critic

> govern'd by persons … very ill chose: … espetialy in ye north, for it is all our enemies there has it … & in ys place there is such a number of insignificant little people, who has neither honnour nor sens, only minds their own interest & their little picks … [and later] I was allwaies agaenst these Justice Courts because I knew by experience they never did good to ye Countrie & to have a number of people who are ignorant & malitious to be Judges of our lives & fortunes is a very ill thing, espetialy wn we are not in ye Governmt.

He had a selfish reason for objecting. As he grew older, his judgements in his regality court were increasingly arbitrary and unjust, and he feared that meddlesome outsiders might expose this.[28] Breadalbane was also critical of the southern commissioners, but was reluctant to see 'the country' openly denounce them: that would incapacitate them for the limited good they were doing, and they might well be replaced by something worse.[29]

The northern commission, however, was the most notorious. Even a just court would have faced problems. Robbery was so widespread and restitution so impossible that decreets for damages would only drive men to desperation and further crime. Sir Donald Macdonald wanted his neighbour Mackinnon to be empowered to try and execute the leading local thieves:

> It is not but that we would send willingly a few to Inverness to be try'd by the sheriffs there but the sending of them wod discover soe many more be the shirrif deputs … as wod goe near to put the half of Mackinnons lands out of tenantrie whereas if they be taken course at home … they that were spar'd wod be terrified to live peacably in tyme comeing.[30]

Several thieves Hill sent to Inverness escaped, returned to Lochaber, and necessarily continued robbing in order to survive, and he desired powers to accept their surrender on bail. Late in 1697, he complained:

> Some partes of the Brae of Lochabbor, and other partes, are beggered, and the land wast, by paying the Justiciary decreits, and nou charitie is soe cold they must either steal or starve; but when they doe, they pay dear for it. Aplecros got 1000 merkes worth of cowes lately from these partes upon a decreit. The courts are sure to doe justice upon highlanders, right or wronge, some of them commonly being judge and partie.

They were less interested in punishing thieves than in obtaining heavy damages, assessed without any examination of witnesses on the real value of the stolen goods, against those formally responsible for them. Hill apparently began to send thieves he caught to Breadalbane, to be hanged by his regality courts, 'as they will not be in this corrupt Northern District … I'me sure weel never live quiet till hanging Come more in fashion'.[31] Instead, they hanged many innocent men.

Not surprisingly, landlords near the Highland Line would accept highlanders as tenants only if they gave rigorous security.[32] Decreets, even those for wartime claims frozen by the December 1695 order, became, even more than ordinary bonds, a secondary paper currency in the North. Yet they soon gained a bad reputation: when a lowlander, the Laird of Glenmoriston's debtor, gained a convenient decreet against him, his own lawyer automatically doubted whether the claim was genuine. Often, the court would let the landlord or chief also escape if he could throw the burden on some 'responsall debtors hands', easier to bring to account than a distant and impoverished highlander.[33] Two of the most notorious examples come from the Middle District. The uncontrollable inhabitants of Rannoch, theoretically under the Tutor of Weem's control, took part in a series of raids on Strachan of Glenkindie's lands. Damages were awarded against the Tutor, but by a contract Glenkindie agreed to remit most of them if the Tutor could build a case against other alleged accessories, in particular Glenkindie's neighbour: 'he is ritch and if there could be information gotten against him as ane outhunder [out-hounder] it Is very proper that he should help . . . to make up the totall . . . the more convenient debtor of all the rest, if once hooked'. In 1699, Lord Forbes, the convener of the Middle District, contracted to pay a man if he would prove against 'responsible' men that they had hounded out the highlanders who raided his lands in 1689. He must have known he would be paying for perjury.[34]

The Commission's ethos appears most clearly in the man who dominated the Northern District, Forbes's comrade-in-arms the Laird of Grant. His wartime appointment as Sheriff of Inverness-shire had become permanent, and a new barony had been created for him. 'His Highland Majesty', as James II had sarcastically called him, 'that Highland Saint' [violent Presbyterian], was an autocratic and ruthless judge; and his mass hangings, carried out in defiance of any threats from the victims' clans, became notorious. One instance of his bias and corruption has been immortalised in a ballad: 'he saved the life of Peter Brown', the head of a band of gipsy-robbers which had operated under his protection, 'and let Macpherson die', although the dashing young vagrant musician was the less guilty. An unscrupulous Strathardle family who falsely accused a neighbour of witchcraft found it worthwhile to kidnap him and carry him to Inverness to obtain a sufficiently unfair trial before Grant.[35]

Contrary to tradition, however, it was apparently not Grant's private vendettas which destroyed the most illustrious victim of the period, the cateran-poet Domhnall Donn of Bohuntin.[36] Instead, the affair emphasises that the courts' bias, damaging to the highlanders as a whole, could save individual robbers if their chiefs and clan gentry would use their influence — to pin the blame, for instance, on some luckless 'responsall debtor'. Clearly even the Macdonalds of Keppoch, although widely regarded as merely a glorified robber-band themselves, had some influence; for when Domhnall Donn was surprised and taken to Inverness, at some time after 1697 (and, presumably, after mid-1700), his prison poem shows that he expected their help. The private hostility of Keppoch (presumably increased by Domhnall's support for Simon Fraser) and Iain Lom frustrated this, and he was beheaded.[37]

Plaintiffs debarred from prosecuting for raids before 1691 in the Commission's courts could still use the older alternatives. The most disruptive instance was in 1697 when Campbell of Barbreck sued Stewart of Ardsheal, former Tutor of

Appin, for plunder his force had taken during the 1685 rebellion. Neither James's indemnity to Atholl and his followers nor the fact that Barbreck had been in rebellion was accepted in defence. Ardsheal's only means of raising the money was to obtain in his turn a decreet in the Argyllshire courts (in 1701) against the chieftains whose men had followed him. As these included young MacIain of Glencoe, the Atholl family concluded that Barbreck's maternal uncle Breadalbane had prompted the prosecution in a further attempt to ruin that clan. In reality, Breadalbane's letters to Barcaldine indicate that his main motive, besides saving Barbreck from total financial ruin, was probably to force Appin to acknowledge the obedience to him his ancestors had paid to the Glenorchy family, to obtain which he exploited more recent thefts.[38]

The Atholl family were ready to expect Breadalbane's malice against any of their dependents because they were in more direct confrontation over Glenlyon. The wretched Robert Campbell had died on campaign at Bruges in 1696, and his young son, whom Breadalbane had been employing in Caithness, negotiated and then sued to have the sale of the estate set aside on equitable grounds. Glenlyon lost the case; Ogilvie later claimed that Tullibardine exploited his political power in the courts, and even Aberuchill, a Campbell, seems to have favoured him unduly.[39] Breadalbane's support for Glenlyon did more harm than good: the Atholl family, which at first seemed willing at least to give him a favourable tack, became convinced that any settlement 'is down right to give it to Bradalbane'. By 1699, Atholl was saying 'he wud rather be banishd Scotld yn yt a Campbell shud have it', and in 1701 it was finally granted to Colonel Menzies's heirs (an eventual compromise exchange gave the Glenlyon family Fortingall). Breadalbane was not reconciled to Tullibardine until 1707.[40] Many others were hostile, warrantably or unwarrantably, to the Atholl family's power and exercise of power in the Highlands; and some were ready to support through thick and thin the man who shook that power to its roots — Captain Simon Fraser of Beaufort.

Simon Fraser's distinctive characteristic, as claimant to and possessor of the chiefship and Lovat title, was intense self-consciousness. Living when the clan structure was still strong and generally accepted as a natural part of Scottish society, he constantly worked to bolster it among the Frasers with all the exaggerated attention to dress and other externals, and the ultimate insecurity, of an antiquarian revivalist trying to recreate a dead system. He resembled in this not his contemporaries, but the tragi-comic Glengarry of Napoleonic times, who was still evicting tenants for refusing to serve under his banner when others were already evicting theirs to make way for sheep. Practically all Simon's actions good and bad, the pennies and kind words bestowed on poor people on the road and the unscrupulous 'judicial' hangings to frighten the Frasers into obedience, were deliberately planned. Contemporaries with these judicial powers — his enemy Atholl, for instance — might likewise abuse them, but from passion as well as calculation; they could not, as he did, imagine such haphazard actions jeopardising their positions.

This self-consciousness (perhaps partly resulting from his being a younger son until 1689) enabled him to play deliberate variations on existing highland patterns of conduct, achieving surprise. His most notorious youthful exploit, the forcible marriage to Lady Lovat, at first resembled a familiar type of riot, in which an heir's friends and highland supporters noisily invaded the family home to compel his predecessor's obstructive widow to leave. Their violence, however alarming, was apparently purely symbolic, and the initial similarity of Simon's attack temporarily encouraged local sympathisers not to intervene; but he carried it through to its extreme conclusion. In reverting with such success from symbolic violence to the real violence it was by degrees replacing he taught the old lesson, often repeated but never learned, that the most barbarous and 'obsolete' features of a society can, with a little skilful adjustment, be extremely effective in the more modern world around it. Breadalbane, the highlander with the greatest reputation for unscrupulous cunning in the previous generation, was clumsy in comparison. Simon would not have pursued policies so lacking in an alternative to fall back on that their collapse left him exposed to his enemies, as Breadalbane was after Allt nam Mearlach and in late 1691; and he, rather than Breadalbane, deserves Macaulay's hostile portrait of the latter:

> He seems to have united two different sets of vices, the growths of two different regions and of two different stages in the progress of society. In his castle among the hills he had learned the barbarian pride and ferocity of a Highland chief. In . . . Edinburgh he had contracted the deep taint of treachery and corruption.[41]

Simon's brain and pen, sharpened in 1691-5 at Aberdeen University, were deeply skilled in lowland methods of thought and argument. Throughout his career, his use of the printing press and his long hypnotic letters, wheedling or denouncing, produced in vast numbers — at some crises, he can scarcely have left his writing-desk for days — were vital elements in his successes. Now he used them to shatter the dichotomy so usual in major highland disputes, with one party having free access to and ability to manipulate the government and law courts, writing its representations and misrepresentations into the official records, while the other, cut off from them by distance, poverty or cultural barriers, stood almost as inarticulate (by Edinburgh standards) as a dumb ox until its opponent's unscrupulous but formally legal goading provoked it into some damning act of violence. Thus Keppoch had been ensnared; but Simon's acts of violence were preceded, accompanied and followed by a stream of plausible, rationalising excuses individually tailored for each sympathiser or foe to Atholl. One of his strongest cards was his ability to lie shamelessly and repeatedly. Almost every statement he made, then or later, about his career to 1702 (including, it would seem, his age) was a lie, and his various accounts of incidents and his motives flatly contradict each other. This is a statement of elementary fact about his political methods (assuming that his lying was always controlled, not partly psychopathic), not a moral denunciation; but it has been shirked by his more recent biographers, who have been willing, if only (like some contemporaries) from exhaustion, to believe the most plausible of his conflicting accounts, and have avoided the main source exposing him, the correspondence of his enemies the Atholl family.[42] That might itself contain pitfalls, since they also had reason to lie if necessary; but it is contemporary, while most of Simon's versions are later, and most of its claims are confirmed by accidental and casual cross-references intended only for the eyes of relatives, while everything Simon wrote was intended for his public.

Fraser grievances arose from Hugh Lord Lovat's marriage in 1685 to Atholl's daughter Amelia, and the family's evident determination to keep a permanent hold on 'ye best feather in our wing'. It was hardly a descent from freedom into slavery; for two generations, virulent Mackenzie women, including the dowager, Tarbat's sister, had dominated and further damaged the family, which was already deep in debt. Atholl may (as Simon claimed) have done likewise, virtually quartering three of his unprovided-for younger sons on the estate.[43] Yet the real damage would be done after Lovat's death. By his marriage contract, if no son survived him, the title and estates (and with them the chiefship) were to go to his eldest daughter rather than the next male heir, his great-uncle and Simon's father, Thomas Fraser of Beaufort. There was no written rule of succession, since the peerage was founded on a writ of summons to Parliament, not a formal charter, and there had been no need to apply Salic law while the family held it (though it was done shortly before).

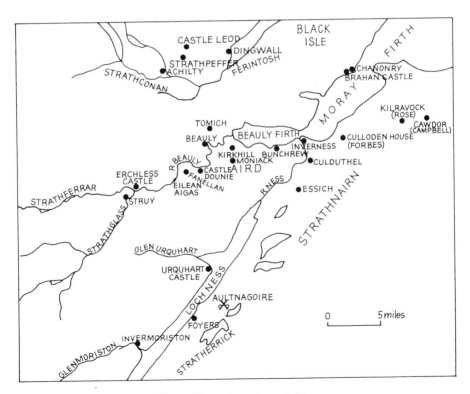

Simon Fraser's early activities

Yet clan tradition and logic were overwhelmingly against the succession of a female whose marriage would convey the chiefship to an outsider. By the marriage contract he must be a Fraser but, if her mother controlled the match, he would probably be an ally of Atholl, strengthening the latter's grip on the clan.[44] Atholl might expect the Frasers, who had by now a reputation as one of the most peaceful and most fully assimilated clans, to accept this. Yet the Macpherson gentry's 1689 bond against Cluny showed how vital such a consideration was to a clan, and in 1680 he himself had encouraged the setting aside of all the normal rules of succession to obtain a satisfactory strong chief for the Glengarry Macdonalds. Simon's 1718 testament gave a hysterical (but sincere) expression to clansmen's most extreme fears: outside chiefs by marriage 'will certainly in less than an age chase you all by slight and might, as well gentlemen as commons, out of your native country . . . ;and you will be like the . . . Jews, scattered and vagabonds throughout the unhappy kingdom of Scotland'.[45] This was a wild exaggeration of the real danger, and he lied in his claim that only three treacherous Frasers supported Atholl after 1696. There was a division in the clan, mainly along the same line as that between the two parts of the Lovat estate. The Fraser gentry holding land in the heart of it, the fertile, low-lying Aird west of Inverness around the River Beauly, were mostly willing to accept a female succession and its consequences; they could prosper without outside assistance. Those in the barren highland areas, particularly Stratherrick along the south-east side of Loch Ness, areas thickly planted with minor gentry by old Lovat policy, probably could not; without assistance from a kindly chief, they would be crushed by their debts, and they became Simon's chief supporters. Some of them were still without written tacks, and a stranger chief might evict them in favour of his own kin: the most obvious example was the next heir Thomas Fraser of Beaufort. 'Of Beaufort' was only a courtesy title, since Lord Lovat's present main seat, Castle Dounie, stood there, and his estate of Tomich, his 'choice of any labouring within the Lordship' in recompense for his exclusion from the tutorship of his great-nephew, was, in the Atholl interpretation, only a tenancy-at-will.[46]

Despite this, Simon's later claim that he had always been openly hostile to Atholl and his sons, out of concern for his clan and his family, was false; had it been true, he would have avoided the first pitfall in his career. Behind all the betrayals for personal advantage, one consistent strand running through his career was an intertwining of anti-Union Scottish patriotism and Jacobitism, which had prompted him to follow Buchan in 1690 and, he claimed, offer to accompany him to France in 1692. In January 1695, after Simon's first application to join Lord Murray's regiment, news came of Queen Mary's death, and he wrote overtly Jacobite letters of rejoicing — 'I doubt not you will be in mourning . . . but I am resolved to buy none till K.W. dies, which perhaps may serve for the next summer suit' — not only to his father but to Atholl's son Mungo and his supporter Glengarry.[47] In 1695, he accepted a lieutenancy of grenadiers, another proof, once his own lies are cleared away, of his outward attitude at the time.[48] What finally stirred him to exert influence over his weak-willed cousin Hugh was, it is claimed, the prospect of his dying and leaving only daughters; in fact, he began his intrigues when there was, for the first time since 1693, an infant Master of Lovat.[49]

Lord Murray had a professional soldier as lieutenant-colonel in his regiment, but, although Lovat remained only a captain, he had obtained for him in early 1695 a lieutenant-colonel's rank and pay.[50] It was not usual for a Secretary to remain a colonel, and on his appointment in January 1696 he called Lovat to London, hoping that William would bestow it on him. Later that month, he authorised Simon, then playing the good soldier and begging for promotion, to accompany him, though secretly hoping that he had already set out. Soon after their arrival in London, the Assassination Plot broke out, and William did not wish Murray, who hastened to take control in Scotland, to demit until the crisis was over.[51] Lovat was exposed for the first time to the luxury and sin of London, and his life soon became a round of all-night debauchery, wine, women and eviction from lodgings. Simon, according to his letters and assurances to the Atholl family, was desperately trying to make him return home, or at least to save him from public exposure or arrest for debt. Murray suspected, probably correctly, that he was deliberately keeping him in London but away from the Murray circle to gain his own ends.[52] If so, he could foresee the probable consequences: the Lovat family in recent generations had shown a fearful hereditary tendency to die young, even without help from London dissipation.

Another interested party tempting Lovat to stay was Tarbat, who had never forgiven the marriage which took the Lovat estate out of his control. He and Simon convinced Lovat that Murray's offer of a regiment was merely the last in a series of tricks and insults, and persuaded him, when summoned to rejoin his regiment at the crisis, to throw up his commission instead. Simon's concern was obvious: Lovat recommended that he receive the company, since he could not support himself without it, and he himself hinted in support that only he could now control the Frasers who composed it. The suggestion was made to William, but he rejected it, while promising him the next vacancy, and Lord James Murray later received the company.[53] A few days after the refusal, Simon persuaded Lovat to sign two bonds. One, declaring that his easy temper had been imposed on to make him, in the marriage contract and later deeds, entail the estate on his daughters if he died without sons, granted it instead to the next male heir, Beaufort. The other showed more clearly how complete a control Simon had established. It granted to him, without any conditions, 50,000 merks scots — £2,750 sterling: if Lovat or the infant Master survived, enforcement of this would plunge the family, already indebted, into total ruin.[54]

In June and July, Lovat crept home, with Simon at every stage claiming credit for their progress and his cousin's repentance. A few days after Lovat reached Dunkeld, Simon received his company, although he apparently had to pay purchase money and fill it with Fraser recruits.[55] Lovat started south to attend Parliament, but fell ill and died at Perth in September, a month after the death of his infant son. According to one of Simon's moving accounts, the Atholl family practically drove the sick man away from Dunkeld, and totally neglected him on his deathbed, alone but for his loyal, grieving cousin. According to another, they were so desperate to have him cancel the grant to Beaufort that they surrounded it like vultures, made him sign a will when already delirious, and passed a new law on deathbed testaments to validate it, only to have him die too soon.[56] Simon wrote to his father to assume the title of Lovat, Tarbat gave the same advice, and he did so. With the help of Fraser of Struy (in Strathglass), he began to disturb Lady Lovat's[57] tenants and collect rents from them. Atholl was eager to crush them, by illegal means if necessary, but Marchmont persuaded him that she had a cast-iron case and should rely on the law.[58] Simon himself pretended to be surprised at his father's actions. Yet they did indicate that the family had a grievance; and, probably that autumn, Simon pretended to reach an agreement with Tullibardine that they should have what income the estate could bear settled on them.[59]

Such agreements are often reached via quarrels, and for his next melodramatic fantasy Simon perhaps conflated one of these with a serious blow suffered by his credit that winter. Glengarry passed on to Tullibardine Simon's compromising Jacobite private letters of January 1695; Simon never forgave him. According to a story he had already circulated by November 1697, Tullibardine, while Commissioner, ordered him to sign a renunciation of all claims to the Lovat inheritance, threatening otherwise to have him condemned for treason by means of the letters; Simon challenged him to fight and threw back his commission; Tullibardine had him tried by court martial, but Livingston protected and acquitted him — justly, since the letters were written before his enlistment.[60] As Simon's own correspondence shows that he was still unaware in February 1697 that Tullibardine knew of the letters, his whole story is a lie. So is the Atholl family's counter-claim that Tullibardine informed William and had Simon dismissed. Whether to protect Simon, seeing him as a fairly loyal dependent of the family, or to avoid reflections on Glengarry and Lord Mungo, he reacted to the letters by suspending Simon without explanation from his regimental duty and pay in January 1697 — on which his Fraser company began to desert. Only when Simon, between protestations of innocence, began claiming that the letter was merely one criticising Tullibardine's failure to transfer the regiment to Lovat did he reveal the truth to Livingston; Simon may then have needed the protection for which he later thanked the Commander-in-Chief. No proceedings were taken, and he was allowed to exchange with a captain in McGill's regiment.[61] He would hardly have escaped had Tullibardine known of his recent activities. During the invasion scare of December 1696, he was on duty at the Castle, and he plotted with Lord Drummond and other prisoners that, if a French force did land, his and another highland company would seize the Castle and free them.[62]

An incident that winter should have been a warning how far the Beaufort party was prepared to go. Fraser of Teankyle was sent to carry away the little heiress, then aged nine, to them from from Castle Dounie, but, having hurried her out half-dressed into the snowdrifts, he repented and took her back. She was removed for safety to Dunkeld. The plan was presumably to marry her to Simon, for a synthetic Fraser tradition survives, telling of their love and suppressing her age.[63] As it failed, Simon did not go north until April. Lacking money for the journey, he visited Dunkeld. Atholl was naturally by now somewhat suspicious of his good faith, but he willingly signed a renunciation of his own claims to the title and estate (which he was later particularly anxious to get back, pretending it had been 'extorted') and was sent on, carrying another to be signed by his father, whom he promised to try to bring back to reason.[64]

Beaufort's supporters had gathered in Stratherrick, where the tenants were refusing their rents to Lady Lovat and collected them for him. Alexander Fraser of Strichen, a landowner there (though his family lived in Aberdeenshire) began raising money to enable him to petition Parliament for his rights. Simon's complicity became increasingly clear to the Atholl family as he ignored his colonel's orders to return to duty, but he still tried to maintain the uncertainty, swearing to Glengarry as late as September that he was not involved. On her side, Lady Lovat was reluctant to push matters openly to extremes against Beaufort. She refused the 120 Atholl men her father offered as certain to cause bloodshed but too few to suppress him. The parties from Invergarry which entered Stratherrick were officially only hunting some horse-thieves who had joined him. Hill promised her further help from the detachment at Inverness whenever she needed it, but she suspected that he and his officers were secretly hostile to her. In August, Lord Saltoun made a proposal which might possibly reunite the clan.[65] He was one of two peers with the family name Fraser living in Aberdeenshire. Although the mother of the other one, Lord Fraser, had been Beaufort's sister, neither was otherwise descended from the Lovat family; their ancestors had migrated north from the Borders some time after it did. Yet if, as Saltoun suggested, his son married the heiress, it would fulfil the 1685 stipulation; this seemed to Atholl a solution which should satisfy both sides. He wrote to the Frasers urging them to hand over 'that rebel' Beaufort and promising to provide them with a Fraser chief. Most of the lowland clan gentry returned thanks, but the highland ones replied 'that they would have no borrowed Chief, tho' he was [a] Fraser'.[66]

There were several valid objections to the Master of Saltoun, an Aberdeenshire stranger, unable to speak Gaelic, of lowland descent and impoverished family. In addition, Simon spread the groundless rumour that the proposal was merely a blind for a plot to marry the heiress to Tullibardine's little son; his own Machiavellian outlook may really have made him believe this.[67] He assembled Fraser gentry and made those he distrusted give oaths of fidelity to his family. In mid-September, he boldly held a similar meeting at Moniack in the Aird, and attempted to seize the clan's Edinburgh lawyer, an Atholl supporter. Displays of popular hostility towards other supporters, especially by women, gave him encouragement. Finally, he summoned an armed muster of horse and foot, attended by 60-70 men, at Essich, only four miles south of Inverness, on 22 September. There he produced a bond of association in the form of a letter for Lord Fraser (who attended, but left early to avoid overt complicity) to pass on to Saltoun. It declared that the Frasers faced ruin but were determined to fight for survival, claimed that the negotiations were a trick played on him to cover an Atholl marriage (in the hope that Saltoun would demand possession of the heiress and later surrender her to them) and warned him not to proceed or even visit

Inverness-shire without their permission. Although Simon was plainly the author, he left the signing to Beaufort and twenty Fraser gentry, mostly from Stratherrick and helf of them members or cadets of three major impoverished families, Foyers, Erchitt and Farraline.[68]

None of Simon's opponents realised the threat implicit in such musters; and the letter came too late to influence Saltoun. Had Atholl seen it, its reference to 'the many good and great friends wee have, in all the places of the kingdome' might have given him some eleventh-hour realisation how precarious was the structure of highland power he had built up.[69] The Lovat interest, its keystone, had been secured when the Campbells, the Frasers' hereditary allies, were at their nadir; now Argyll was again one of Scotland's magnates. Not only did all the neighbouring clans and families, Mackenzies, Chisholms, Rosses, Grants, Culloden, Calder, so fear an expanding Atholl power that they would assist or connive at any attack on it; his own West Highland allies and dependents might be unwilling or unable to assist him. Keppoch remained loyal, despite having links with Argyll, Tarbat and Breadalbane and good grounds for complaint in Tullibardine's failure to quash Mackintosh's proceedings; but these might destroy his power to give help. In August 1696, when the Council ignored William's letter, Mackintosh had planned to make Hill summon Keppoch to Fort William, and there arrest him for debt, but Breadalbane gave him warning.[70] In November, he was expecting through Atholl influence a protection to come to Edinburgh for negotiations. However, Mackintosh had adopted the tactic of taking the decisive steps in his prosecution when Keppoch's main protectors, at this time Tullibardine and Argyll, were absent in attendance on William. The safe-conduct was refused by the Council under Polwarth, whose view of Keppoch as a mere brigand overrode his factional loyalties.[71] He supported Mackintosh's petition that autumn for a renewal of the commission of fire and sword. In November, the Council granted one, then had to cancel it as illegal, but drew up an order for Hill to seize Keppoch, dead or alive. This condition, insisted on by Hill for his own protection, was also illegal, but the Justice Court authorised it on the ground that Keppoch was a madman and a thief, despite Tarbat's protest that they had recently thought him a reputable witness against Breadalbane. However, pressure from Tullibardine and Argyll made Marchmont delay issuing it, and the invasion scare provided the excuse that driving Keppoch to open rebellion then would be too dangerous. Once that was over, the Council again voted for the warrant, and for a price on Keppoch's head, but Tullibardine got William to countermand it. For fear it should be issued, Hill had Keppoch go into hiding, while spreading the news that he had fled to Ireland, and the maddened Mackintosh denounced Hill to Marchmont as a traitor, 'ane sinister, dangerous . . . gheust in the Government'.[72] At Tullibardine's request, William had Polwarth write to both opponents to meet in Edinburgh and try for a compromise. Keppoch came, and until 9 March lurked in the Holyrood debtors' sanctuary; but Mackintosh was kept in the North by a convenient illness until he returned home in despair, and then continued legal proceedings. He might demand of the Council a garrison in Brae-Lochaber, Keppoch warned Tullibardine that summer; the only sure protection for himself would be a particular remission for Mulroy. 'It is not the Improvement of ye Lands of Glenroy' he warned, 'But rather the Exterpatione of my family that he hunts after.'[73]

In contrast, Glengarry, Atholl's chief highland agent, was secretly disaffected. Tullibardine had obtained him a £200 pension (in Lord James Murray's name);[74] but he had failed to get the garrison removed from Invergarry. Not only was Glengarry's home occupied, but the troops, who despite Hill's efforts received no allowance for 'coal and candle', had by mid-1697 destroyed his woods for firing; those in other out-garrisons acted likewise.[75] Even had Tullibardine been willing to solicit on behalf of such a crypto-Jacobite — and when he finally did so in 1703, it was soon exploited as 'proof' of his own Jacobite plotting[76] — there was no chance of success; yet Glengarry was alienated. The Atholl family automatically relied on him, believing that he 'has shoued his wonted zeall in seruing the familie . . . in making the popel senseble of ther Duty' to Lady Lovat. Their faith seemed rational, since he was one of the trustees of the heiress (his niece by marriage), and since Simon would never forgive 'the hireling sycophant of Lord Murray' for his own actions or his clan's possession of former Fraser lands. Yet Simon kept his feelings hidden, and, exploiting friendships he had struck up with Clanranald and Glengarry's father (now living in Moidart), tempted him with the prospect of benefits from Argyll towards a change of sides, or at least neutrality.[77]

Argyll, with whom he corresponded via Clanranald, was naturally the protector on whom Simon relied most. He may, admittedly, have exaggerated his expectations in public; but it is significant that the Frasers were already complaining in mid-November that they had expected Argyll to do more for them.[78] They also claimed to be supported by Tarbat, who, besides his old grievance, was hoping to get Lord Chancellor Polwarth (now Earl of Marchmont) dismissed in favour of himself. If he was one of Simon's supporters, he was the most hypocritical, writing repeated denunciations to the Atholl family equating him with his own *betes noires*, the highland robbers, and urging even after Lady Lovat was released that there must be no remission in pursuit. Yet by December the Atholl family's Edinburgh agent suspected that he was at the bottom of everything.[79] Evidence against other possible patrons was more circumstantial, raised as Atholl thrashed about in a fury looking for his enemies. Grant, the Sheriff of Inverness-shire, conveniently left for Edinburgh just before Simon's outbreak. Livingston (now Lord Teviot) had previously favoured him. He wrote to Ogilvie after seizing Lord Saltoun.[80] The facts are clearer about his West Highland supporters. About the end of September, he met Lochiel, Clanranald and Sir Donald at Inverlochy; and Glengarry, although absent, was informed of what was agreed.[81] It is uncertain whether any of them, even Argyll, realised beforehand how far Simon intended to go, although they had afterwards little choice but to endorse him when a disclaimer would not have been believed. Indeed, despite Simon's obvious intention to carry out some violent stroke in October, when the Privy Council's vacation left government largely paralysed, it is uncertain how far his own plans extended (though the attempt to carry off the heiress forshadowed them). Fairly certainly Hill was dupe rather than accomplice. Hostile to Atholl and misreading Simon as another Keppoch — a figure caught in the contradiction between lowland legal rights and highland custom, breaking out into momentary and unplanned violence only under pressure — he treated him with kid gloves. Had he had foreknowledge, he would hardly have let himself be so publicly outmanoeuvred and fooled as he was.

Simon was with Hill at Fort William when he learned that Saltoun, accompanied by Lord Mungo Murray, was visiting Lady Lovat at Castle Dounie to discuss the marriage.[82] He immediately returned to Stratherrick and began mustering his supporters; he *may*, as he claimed, unsuccessfully have demanded that Saltoun meet him in the Highlands. Reconnaisance among sympathisers in Inverness revealed that Saltoun, Lord Mungo and their friends and servants were returning there on 6 October. Simon, with eight horsemen (on Strichen's horses) and forty foot led by his father, seized them in the wood of Bunchrew (a feat he frequently boasted of, although they had been proceeding as a peaceable party) and carried them round to the house of Fanellan, west of Castle Dounie.[83] He sent out the fiery cross, and within a day several hundred Frasers assembled to be mustered in companies, with colours and pipers, under Simon's chief followers, Stratherrick gentry including Foyers, Erchitt and every member of the Culduthel family except its head, and the Frasers of Guisachan and Struy from the Aird; lesser followers included Grant of Glenmoriston's piper (presumably sent as a gesture of solidarity) and an ex-Jacobite Captain Maclean.[84] He erected a gallows outside Fanellan, and gave warning that he would hang the prisoners (including Frasers who supported Saltoun) if any troops were sent to rescue them, and Lady Lovat wrote to Hill not to send any yet. Simon also wrote, lamenting 'ane unlucky accident that is lyke ... utterly to extirpet ... the wholl name of Frazer', and explaining that he had accidentally met with Saltoun's party, accidentally seized them and accidentally imprisoned them. In a later letter, he blamed his father's rashness. The deliberate impression he gave of anxiously seeking means of drawing back completely deceived Hill, who was also reluctant to drive the Frasers into the hills to augment the chaos caused by existing outlaws. He checked the force he had prepared to send, and passed on Simon's demands to the government; an indemnity, freedom to prosecute others at law, the return of his 'extorted' renunciation of his claims, and the placing of the heiress in neutral hands. His mistake was natural; even the Atholl family were checked in their first impulse to appeal to the Council by the threat that the prisoners would be hanged (or even burned alive) and by a letter from them; instead, they decided to rely for the moment on negotiations, and sent north to Inverness, hoping to sow divisions among the Frasers and, perhaps, apprehend Simon without a conflict, Lord James Murray and one of the family's main local supporters, Leonard Robertson of Straloch.[85]

The negotiations, attended by Culloden, gave all Simon's opponents a sense of false security; apparently not even Lady Lovat realised her vulnerability, unprotected at Castle Dounie with several hundred Frasers at hand. Within a few days, he marched there with a large party, took her prisoner and at once began to make far larger demands. He further lulled the government and the Atholl family by sending letters south reporting that he had disbanded nearly all his men and hoped they were on the brink of an agreement, and Hill by forcing Lady Lovat to write the same to him and having some secret sympathisers send confirmatory reports. Hill repeated them with fatuous satisfaction.[86] The capture more than compensated for one slight setback. Saltoun and Lord Mungo were carried to Eilean Aigas in the River Beauly on the highland edge of the Aird. In the primitive conditions, Saltoun became dangerously ill with dysentery, and Simon, allegedly after consulting on the possible alternative of hanging him, made him sign a promise not to pursue the match and released him.[87]

Leaving Lord James at Inverness, Straloch gained access to Castle Dounie. He negotiated terms for freeing the captives, had Lord James sign them, and returned on 19 October expecting their release. Meanwhile, however, Simon determined (or revealed an existing purpose) to force Lady Lovat into marriage with him. If (as he assumed) shame made her adhere to it afterwards, Atholl could hardly repudiate the concessions, as he would certainly otherwise do, or take further steps against his son-in-law, and he would have control over Lady Lovat's jointure, her chamberlains and, probably, the little heiress, enabling him to have her claims invalidated. He suddenly confined Lady Lovat again and made the demand, which she refused. To her horror and bewilderment, Straloch advised her, even in private, to consent, making her despair by indicating that her relations agreed, and repeating his arguments to Simon. The Atholl family never forgave this, although they hid their resentment because he was a vital witness for any prosecution of the Frasers. However, a careless admission in one of Simon's narratives that on a pretext he was put under arrest partly explains his conduct: he was frightened for his own skin. If Simon had held a dagger to her throat, Lady Lovat said afterwards, it would not have prevailed more than this — a rather odd metaphor if, as the evidence states, a dagger really was held to her throat later, suggesting that she did make some undue concession, possibly a half-promise to marry him at some later date.[88] The final outcome is not in doubt. The Frasers burst into the room to 'force' Simon to marry her on pain of death. She pleaded, offering to bring her daughter back to Castle Dounie if they would only let her alone. But with the bagpipe playing to drown her protests she was 'married' to him by the vagabond episcopalian minister of Abertarff, a specialist in such weddings, and with it still playing to drown her screams, she was raped by Simon, which drove her into a temporary fit of insanity. Next day, Lord Mungo and Straloch were released.[89]

The almost incredible news reached Edinburgh on 30 October. In Marchmont's absence, Tarbat called an emergency Council, and ordered Lord Forbes (the Master of Forbes of the 1689-90 campaigns) to march his dragoon regiment north to Inverness. The Sheriff of Inverness-shire was commissioned to capture the Frasers, and Hill and the Sheriff of Perthshire (Tullibardine) were ordered to send him assistance for this, ... *when* he or his deputes asked for it. The Atholl family denounced this as underhand sabotage, designed to ensure that Simon should go scot-free. Yet those who spoke against directly employing the Atholl men, including Grant and, at first, Tarbat, had one plausible reason. Although the forces Atholl was gathering at Blair were formally a militia regiment, he was acting and thinking as a highland chief determined to wash out this unbearable insult to his family in blood; and they were his vassals, mostly eager to avenge it on the Fraser country, particularly when, as an ally reported, 'in caise of slaughter & blood they are indemnified'. Simon was declaring his eagerness to meet them in battle, and the Council naturally feared a clan war of old-style savagery that would devastate Inverness-shire.[90] Finally, the Atholl men (including Straloch's company of Tullibardine's regiment) marched without orders in early November under the command of Lord Nairne and Lord Edward Murray, although only a select 600 went on from Badenoch. Atholl had written to Glengarry to meet them with the mainland Macdonalds at Ruthven, but there was no sign of him.[91] Possibly to prevent their march, Hill gave warning that the Frasers might slip past the troops and ravage Atholl, and part of Tullibardine's regiment was ordered to Dunkeld to protect it.[92]

William's disbandment policy was a further difficulty. In October, Tullibardine had been dismayed to find that he, although senior Secretary, had no say in choosing which regiments were to go, followed by the news that his was to be among the first three, although it was far better disciplined and equipped than others (such as Lorne's (Argyll's), spared for three months longer). Although the arrival on 27 October of the order, which was also for the disbandment of Forbes's and the reduction of Hill's was coincidence (unless someone at Court forewarned Simon), it benefited him. His younger brother John, a Glasgow student, was arrested for inciting the Frasers and other northerners in Tullibardine's to desert and join him, since they would anyway be disbanded; there was trouble in Forbes's, and Hill's could only send limited assistance. The Council reprieved them for the emergency, explaining the reason; but William repeated his order in mid-November, when Forbes's was engaged in the pursuit, and, for all he knew, Tullibardine's as well, wrecking any chance of catching the Beauforts and making his simultaneous order to the Council to do so a dead letter.[93]

Atholl, politically ruthless himself, secretly accepted that his northern opponents might well count Simon's threat to hang his son legitimate politics; but he was genuinely shocked that they should condone his daughter's rape.[94] Forcible marriages, however, were still fairly common in the Highlands (though increasingly restricted to the poorer classes) and were, on the whole, viewed sympathetically in highland culture. In Ireland, where abduction of heiresses was common among the idle squireens, protestant and catholic, the populace vigorously supported them, and the London mob's reaction to Captain Johnston's execution in 1690 showed that sympathy was not confined to Celtic societies.[95] It rested mainly on the universal popular assumption, which also took gentler forms, that men and women must be paired off, and, provided this was achieved, the means were unimportant. Encouragement was given by surviving wedding rituals of mock-capture and of brides' (often genuine) reluctance, by the usual emphasis on woman's inferiority, whereby a would-be husband might do almost anything to gain her fortune — the important consideration — and any violation of her chastity made her 'damaged goods', and, in the Highlands, by a more general sympathy for raids against rival clans and lowlanders. Forcible marriage might be anything from a 'respectable' facade to cover a woman's elopement with a lover her relatives disliked, through a kidnapping which at least ensured her a husband with the traditional warlike virtues, to a brutal crushing of whatever degree of choice and respect for her individuality new developments in lowland society allowed her. In official correspondence, Hill denounced Simon's 'oppress[ing] a poor lady inhumanely'; privately he wrote to Tarbat on 1 November: 'Wee are all peaceable, the bussenes of Captain Fraser being ended in the marrage of my Lady Lovett'. He fairly certainly had few illusions about the means used, but was confident that everything would now be hushed up, and urged Culloden to persuade Simon to surrender her on assurance of pardon.[96] The fearsome, impermeable clan self-righteousness which justified the Frasers in their own eyes for anything they did was matched among their gentry neighbours. These were ready to ignore all evidence of anything untoward in the marriage as determinedly as the 1750s Fermanagh county society who for twenty years paid normal social visits to a husband holding his rich wife prisoner in her bedroom.[97]

It is not clear what effect this had on Lady Lovat during her captivity. Bred believing in woman's inferiority and in the total degradation which followed female loss of honour, she may at times have seen acceptance of the marriage as the only means of avoiding lifelong shame. Observers gave diametrically opposite reports on her attitude, that she was kept close prisoner or that she went willingly with Simon, according to which side they supported.[98] One of Simon's strongest supporters later wrote that she summoned the parish minister and had the marriage repeated; unfortunately for that story, none of Simon's varied defences mention it. She claimed instead that two Fraser ministers attempted to preach her into the state of whipped-spaniel wifely devotion in which Queen Mary had remained throughout her career, so much to William's advantage. One of these was Rev. James Fraser of Kirkhill and Wardlaw, the historian of the clan, whose adherence gave Simon some symbolic legitimacy; for the sake of his eloquence, the risk was taken of carrying Lady Lovat near Inverness. She was also exposed to respectable ladies, such as his wife and later Lady Chisholm, and to less respectable witches, whose conversation and sorcery respectively would inculcate the same duty.[99]

Lord James, hearing on 23 October that his sister had been brought to Kirkhill, gathered a party to rescue her; but Simon, warned by some of his many supporters at Inverness, carried her off at midnight to Eilean Aigas, raising 400 men from the country with the fiery cross to cover his retreat. Old Beaufort and seven of his leading supporters wrote to Argyll formally announcing the marriage and asking for his help to have the charges against them quashed; with sublime humbug, they lamented her delicate health and expressed dread that fatigue and fear of bloodshed might kill her. Hill sent 200 troops down Stratherrick to Inverness, and the Atholl men arrived on 11 November. They soon discovered that 'Never was creatur so befrinded as he is in yt countrie, either out of kindness to him, or ... hatred to us and the familie of Lovet'. The authorities and local gentry refused to let them go beyond Inverness Bridge.[100] That left the regular troops; but, in that winter, it would be almost impossible for them to approach Eilean

Aigas. A Fraser hostile to Simon offering to guide them was immediately carried off. Captain Maclean refused a reward offered if he would rescue Lady Lovat — only for Simon, with his normal sign-manual of ingratitude, to denounce him throughout the Highlands as a paid assassin.[101] If troops did approach, Simon could simply retreat with his prisoner westwards up Strathfarrar into the remotest Highlands; so Lord James wrote to Glengarry to block it. However, Glengarry, who had secretly retired into Ross on being summoned to the original rendezvous (so that Keppoch, who had raised 200 men, by waiting for his orders reached Ruthven too late), now in his answer dropped the mask, casually assuming that the Beauforts would 'retire until the time their remission is procured, after submission and acknowledgement of their high misdemeanors', and he later wrote that if Lady Lovat wished to uphold the marriage it would be unjust to disturb her resolution.[102]

On 14 November, a herald left a summons to the Frasers to surrender outside Eilean Aigas, and soon afterwards Culloden and Straloch arrived to negotiate. Simon felt that in doing so Culloden was 'betraying' him, and treated Straloch with distrust; but, according to the Atholl family, the latter, having promised to bring Mackenzie pressure on him, again played a double game, drawing up a declaration of adherence to the marriage for Lady Lovat to sign.[103] As the troops advanced through the Aird on the 15th, Simon's party retreated up the Beauly to Erchless, the Chisholm's house, and there on the 16th she signed the document (which declared that she had married him without any compulsion), with the Chisholm, Kilravock and Cuthbert of Castlehill among the witnesses. According to the pro-Atholl witnesses, Simon and 180 followers were about the Castle during this free adherence. An officer's letter suggests that he had actually retired to the hills the previous evening dispersing his men, but that, if she had not signed as his sympathisers ordered, they would not, as they did, have brought her to Forbes at Castle Dounie that evening.[104] When she expressed a wish next day to return with her brothers, they protested that a wife should not be taken from her husband, and spread reports that she was being forced; her signed certificate of her release, being witnessed by her brothers, would hardly convince sceptical outsiders. At Inverness, Lord James was persuaded by Straloch, whom he did not yet mistrust, and by supposedly friendly local gentry that as snowstorms were setting in, making it futile for the Atholl men to pursue Simon and his few remaining followers in the hills, he should not even let them pass Inverness Bridge, but should take them home.[105] At Struy, Simon had dismissed all but forty or fifty of his followers (apparently chosen on some sort of parochial basis), who swore fealty on their dirks. With these he roamed the hills and even the Aird, all Forbes's attempts to trap him being frustrated by snowstorms.[106]

Meanwhile, he sent constant messengers to potential supporters in the south; Atholl declared he had captured more Frasers there than they had in the north.[107] Some of these were actually at Dunkeld. Simon and his supporters so persistently claimed that Atholl imprisoned his daughter there, without pen and paper or communication with outsiders, until she would renounce her husband, that it might be credible — had they not too obviously prepared the story before releasing her, and if letters from her did not exist. Their real contact at Dunkeld, with whom Culduthel's brother was caught, was her waiting maid Macbriar, whom Simon had secretly won over; she had sent him a letter forged by her husband in her mistress's handwriting regretting her departure. Her exposure, after Straloch's, made the Atholl family fear that they might give hostile testimony in any trial; but, in the event, he complied and they avoided using her.[108] Implicit pressure existed — Atholl had disowned one daughter for an 'unsuitable' marriage — but he seems to have shown some delicacy in probing Lady Lovat's feelings. Once her hostility to Simon was clear, he used it as a lever to regain the support of Fraser prisoners. Although a dozen Stratherrick gentry who surrendered at Inverness when Hill's men marched through their country were hurriedly bailed, nine were arrested; and one of Forbes's last actions before disbanding his (mutinous) regiment was to arrest Lord Fraser and Strichen on Marchmont's orders. The latter two were brought to Edinburgh but, despite the Atholl family's efforts, bailed in February and March.[109] Fraser officials in Aberdeenshire allowed two of the others to escape as they were marched south, and Atholl carried off the remainder to Blair for re-indoctrination — a high-handed step which might furnish his enemies with ammunition. He was confident that Lady Lovat's refusal to acknowledge the marriage would make them support the Atholl family, 'for now they know they would be ruind if they did not, wch is ye best argumt to Highlanders'. The sneer was typical, for the affair, like the Atholl men's desertion in 1689, had aroused in the family a very strong dislike and distrust of highlanders and highland mores.[110]

Almost from the moment his sons' party returned, Atholl, who considered that they had bungled the expedition by accepting advice from the family's secret enemies, was planning a second one, and delayed only on account of the greatest snowstorm in memory. Lord James complied without enthusiasm: 'I confess I neither expect honour nor credet by turning a plunderer, for when I goe ther, I can't expect to get any of the chief villanes, tho I shall do my utmost'.[111] The regular forces were having little success on their own; Atholl blamed this largely on the hostility of Hill's officers, but the terrain, the snow and the local support for the Beauforts were sufficient explanation. After premature rumours that Simon had gone south to obtain a remission, he was discovered by spies in mid-December still in upper Strathglass with 50–60 followers, some from Tullibardine's regiment. Old Beaufort had been sent to seek refuge with his Macleod in-laws in Skye. The chief who gave protection to him, and later Simon, despite the government's proclamations, was not Iain Breac, the upholder of Gaelic culture, but his Lowlands-haunting, spendthrift son Rory, maintaining *one* highland tradition.[112] In late December, parties marched from Inverness and Invergarry to trap Simon, but storms delayed them and he simply retired to the woods. In January, when they placed garrisons in Strathglass and Kilcumin, he and a few companions crossed by boat into Stratherrick. Dragoons were to panic them back across into an ambush laid on the north side, but they instead dodged south, re-crossing and reassembling in Strathglass after the troops were gone.[113]

In January 1698, Atholl, his sons and Saltoun planned their strategy. Lord James was to take only a few hundred Atholl men; also two of the Fraser captives,

now supposedly supporting Lady Lovat, to persuade their fellow-clansmen —
Atholl believed that he had by now broken the leading Stratherrick gentry's
support for Simon. Colonel Row's fusilier regiment from Flanders was marching
north, and the Council, prompted by Leven, ordered its lieutenant-colonel to hunt
down the fugitives and plant garrisons. If Lord James and the troops drove Simon
out of the Fraser country, Saltoun was to catch him if he tried to break south
through Aberdeenshire, Keppoch if (as his intercepted letters suggested) he
retired towards the Isles. Keppoch was the only exception to Atholl's present
distrust of all highlanders but his own: he consulted with him at Dunkeld and
promised him a remission for Mulroy. When Tullibardine was reluctant to use his
official position to get one for that public crime passed out of private motives,
Atholl cursed his foolish scruples: Argyll's party, to which Keppoch would
otherwise be forced to apply, would have none, and was applying for a remission
for Simon. Keppoch's unreliable brother Alexander was hired to spy out Simon's
whereabouts.[114]

On 30 January, Lord James marched north from Blair through the frozen,
starving Highlands with 600 Atholl men, deliberately including among his
captains those most reluctant to go, such as young Ballechin, who claimed that his
children were sick (Atholl had recently been hollowly reconciled to his father).
The Duke of Gordon had some of his vassals join them under Mackintosh of
Borlum.[115] Early in February, Lord James sent his brother Mungo with 200 men
up Stratherrick and round Loch Ness to be joined by the Invergarry garrison,
followed by 300 more under Ballechin to block the passes to the West, while he
himself with the rest and the troops advanced through the Aird. Keppoch,
following instructions, joined Lord Mungo with only forty men at Kilcumin. A
few prisoners were taken, but Simon was well-informed in advance and, despite
his previous boasts, fled when Lord Mungo approached to Kintail and Skye,
leaving a self-justifying letter with Calder. The troops pursued him for some
distance. Lord James wanted Keppoch to go further, but he had too few of his own
followers, and Lord James would not risk sending the Atholl men so far. Keppoch
instead returned home, promising to search for Simon and urge Sir Donald
Macdonald not to receive him in Skye. His brother's spying activities failed
miserably.[116] The main achievement of the expedition was to plunder Fraser
lands. Since Atholl declared that he could not afford to maintain the force, and the
Lovat estates were producing no rent, they must have lived off the country; the
Chisholms suffered, and 400 men sent back in late February nearly came to blows
with the inhabitants of 'friendly' Badenoch.[117] Desire to avenge Atholl honour
made them still more destructive in Fraser territory, although few but women,
children and the old remained visible there. Besides plundering, they burned
houses and household goods, cut down trees and killed cattle; some inhabitants
must have died of hunger and cold as a result. The Fraser gentry still openly living
in the area submitted, and Atholl re-educated the fresh prisoners sent to Dunkeld
(except one who died in the dungeon) until he considered he could trust them
more than the Macdonalds. However, Lord Saltoun, terrorised by fear of further
ambushes, was backing out of the agreement. Lord James, who brought south his

remaining men, whom the family could not afford to maintain in arms, in late March, thought that they must find a proper match for the little heiress, since the Frasers 'are inconstant people, as most of ye Highlanders are, that till they have on to head them as their master, their is noe depending upon them'.[118]

In mid-February, the order arrived to replace Hill at Fort William and disband his regiment. He had been convinced since December that Tullibardine was campaigning for his dismissal.[119] This would hardly have been unreasonable, after the way he had let Simon deceive him; but in reality William's general policy of maintaining Flanders regiments determined such matters, not his Secretary. Tullibardine had his own candidate for Governor, but, one witness reported, even urged that Hill and his regiment be kept, to block the candidate William (to fulfil a promise to a Continental ally) intended to appoint, Brigadier Maitland, a supporter of Argyll, who would still further increase his highland influence.[120] His allies all suggested yet another alternative Governor, Colonel Row, experienced, of good character, high in William's favour, later to act as Commander-in-Chief when Livingston and Argyll were absent. Unknown to them, a highly ironic recommendation; for Row had not only made advances to the Jacobites in the past, but still did so in 1699, when the insincere had nearly all fallen silent, and the penetration of St Germain by government spies made mere 'reinsurance' foolish.[121] William may, characteristically, have wavered briefly in his purpose, at first merely making Hill reduce his regiment in size; but on 1 February he issued the final orders. It took several months, of course, for Maitland to march his regiment to Fort William and replace in the outgarrisons the detachments of Hill's, who were to be disbanded on the spot. It was hoped that many soldiers with highland experience would enlist in Maitland's, but the disbandment created great bitterness, and there was even a plot to burn Fort William before Maitland's arrival. Hill, acting with his usual devotion to duty, prevented this (partly by distributing money) and assisted Maitland in establishing himself before he finally retired on half-pay.[122] (See Preface, p. viii)

Maitland, who admitted his inexperience in highland affairs, was expected to rely on Major (now Lieutenant-Colonel) Forbes's contacts and expertise, but was sceptical of their value, preferring local landowners' advice. He began the rebuilding of Fort William in stone, and continued Hill's policy on the outgarrisons, being convinced like him (but unlike their successor at the time of the '15) that maintaining them was vital to its security.[123] He certainly did not copy Hill, who with manifold opportunities for profit had saved only £1,000, in financial honesty. He forced the Maryburgh 'tenendrie' to pay him rent and dues, although the Duke of Gordon was still legal owner of the land, monopolised brewing, and forced all traders by sea to sell their cargoes through him. His exploitation stunted the town's growth, making its intended task of spreading lowland civilisation still more hopeless.[124]

Maitland's first major duty, which, unlike Hill, he carried out willingly, was to help Mackintosh dispossess Keppoch. Mackintosh again pushed ahead proceedings at Edinburgh only when Keppoch's patrons Tullibardine and Argyll were at Court for the winter.[125] Keppoch's involvement in pursuing Simon not only prevented him from soliciting at Edinburgh but weakened support for him. When Calder and other north-eastern allies of Simon informed Argyll, he secretly threw his weight behind Mackintosh, while Atholl, obsessively convinced now that no highlander was really trustworthy, became unreasonably angry at raids by Keppoch's men which he could not have prevented, failed to support him adequately and predicted dismissively afterwards that the 'cunning little fellow' would probably shift his allegiance to Argyll.[126] Tarbat, on whom (next to Atholl) Keppoch most relied, was sick. Some Privy Councillors obviously supported Mackintosh chiefly to punish Keppoch for helping Atholl, and even in the hope of driving him as an outlaw to ally with the Frasers, making it impossible to subdue them. Yet is was Tullibardine's supporter Marchmont, seeing Mackintosh as simply a victim of illegal oppression, who in secrecy on 22 February 1698 persuaded the Council to renew his 1681 commission of fire and sword against Keppoch, his two brothers, and his followers (including the Glencoe bard Aonghus Mac Alasdair Ruaidh); the assistants included Maitland, Grant, Fraser of Culduthel (father of Simon's strongest supporters) and a score of Clan Chattan gentry. The next day, Tarbat sent them a letter he had received from Keppoch (delayed en route, he explained), offering in desperation to renounce all pretensions to the lands if claims for arrears and lawsuits were dropped. Marchmont's faction, including Forbes and Grant, prevented it even from being read.[127]

Despite the ravages of the famine among Clan Chattan, Mackintosh by early summer was preparing a large war party. Keppoch feverishly considered ways at least to protect Inverlair, the one part of his estate held from Gordon — could he nominally transfer the rights before Mackintosh had it comprised for arrears of feu duty? In early May, Maitland unsuccessfully attempted to seize him, and put a price on his head. Flitting about by night, he forced his tenants to swear to remain loyal to him and prevented them from planting any crops, but Maitland and Mackintosh thought they would submit once he was captured. In May, he retired to take refuge with Sir Donald in Skye, but was back by August, when Mackintosh invaded with an overwhelming force. They had neither the money nor the provisions to stay beyond a week or rebuild the fort at the House of Keppoch, but constructed timber huts for a company of Maitland's ordered to lie there as a permanent garrison. Mackintosh sent out raiding parties to seize Keppoch, his followers and their belongings. They captured many cattle, which forced some of the tenants to come in and submit to Mackintosh, but 'the great mists upon the hills did marr that interpryse, since it was impossible while they wer abroad to see man or beast'. In returning, Mackintosh plundered and burned Inverlair. Keppoch, after momentary delusive hopes of obtaining a commission of fire and sword against him for exceeding his powers in this, remained on the run.[128]

A detachment of Maitland's had garrisoned Inverness, and the Council ordered Row's regiment south, partly, Atholl suspected, for co-operating too well with his sons. Maitland at his request placed a small garrison in Castle Dounie, to which more Frasers submitted on bail; but, besides feeling reluctant to assist the family that had opposed his appointment, he was put off guard by the report that Simon was applying for a remission. Atholl heard, more accurately, that he intended to seize the Lovat estates first. In late April, he returned to the mainland with a few men, and marched across into Easter Ross. Balnagown, one of his strongest supporters, met him secretly and raised a contribution for him, and Calder and other supporters declared that Argyll would protect him. In May, he attempted to kidnap Robert Fraser, the clan lawyer, still an Atholl partisan.[129] For the third time, Lord James Murray marched north, with his brother Mungo and a force of 300 men. They may again have made it a punishment battalion for the luke-warm, over-confident because Simon had never yet stood to fight — although Tullibardine was uneasy at how few troops were available to join them. Besides protecting the estate, their task was to muster and protect the witnesses for the prosecution of Simon, who would certainly try to intercept them.[130]

In June, he and a small party crossed into Stratherrick to do so and planted a garrison at Garthmore, and he (by his later account) went incognito to Inverness to consult with friends. Hoping to surprise his party, the Atholl men made a rapid night march into Stratherrick guided by several Frasers, including Thomas of Gortuleg whose brothers were with Simon. Regular troops were supposed to follow soon from Inverness; but detachments had reduced Maitland's garrison at Fort William to 300, and he could give no help even if a crisis occurred. It did; Simon hurried back from Inverness, sent out the fiery cross through Stratherrick, and by the evening of 15 June had gathered 250 men, although the previous Atholl raid had left many of them ill-armed. Lord James had encamped in a strong position, and the Fraser gentry advised Simon to await reinforcements from Abertarff and Glenmoriston. In preparation for a battle next day, he had a few snipers fire all night to prevent the Atholl men from resting. By morning on the 16th, he had received fifty men from Abertarff. His gentry followers included nearly all those indicted for supporting him the previous autumn, and some fresh ones from Upper Stratherrick, several of them descended from the Foyers and Erchitt family — although not Erchitt himself. The calculations of Simon's secret friends who voted for the commission against Keppoch were partly justified: his brother Angus appeared with some Macdonalds, including Alasdair Mor, a leading cateran.[131]

To Alasdair Mor, who had Fraser blood, Simon entrusted the vital task of distracting the Atholl men by a feint attack with fifty men in their front, while Simon, with the main body, worked round their flank and attacked from there. As they advanced, the Atholl men, whose spies had grossly exaggerated Simon's numbers to them, began to retreat towards Inverness. The retreat soon became a disorganised rout, and the Frasers broke into an equally disorganised pursuit. Alasdair Mor realised that the critical point was where the road turned inland through the pass of Aultnagoire, and ran ahead with his fastest followers to secure it. When the Atholl men found their retreat cut off, according to Simon, their morale collapsed, despite Lord James's efforts — the Stewarts under another of Ballechin's sons were the most mutinous — and they sued for terms. Simon and the young men were eager to attack — had he known that Mulroy, ten years earlier, would be remembered as the last private clan battle, he would probably have been deaf to argument — but the older Fraser gentry refused to allow them. If they slaughtered their enemies, it could not, like the forced marriage, be glossed over; it would lose them their vital outside supporters and perhaps bring total destruction upon the clan, while moderation might even persuade Atholl to cut his losses and withdraw. The pledge the Murray brothers were obliged to sign and swear to was even-handed enough to call Simon 'pretended' Master of Lovat. They were not to prosecute Simon for that day's deeds, and neither they nor any other Atholl men should invade the Fraser country except on direct government order. Lady Lovat was to be left free in Edinburgh, with none of her relations allowed to speak to her for twenty days, to decide whether to own the marriage. The witnesses they had collected were taken away, but Simon did no more even to Gortuleg than call him 'ane unkynd kinsman'. As some compensation, he made the Atholl men pass under the yoke in the approved classical fashion before letting them go.[132]

The Atholl family did not honour the terms, considering them extorted. A fresh prosecution was begun against Simon and his present accomplices, the government issued a proclamation, Row's regiment returned north with orders to garrison all Lovat houses and catch Simon, and the aroused detachment of Maitland's hunted him through Stratherrick, forcing his party to take to the hills and live on stolen cattle, while the Stratherrick gentry flocked in to submit on bail.[133] However, Simon's bloodless victory was the climax of eight months during which the Atholl family's failure to catch or crush him had made them seem weak and bungling and had won him widespread support and admiration; that could not be undone.

The blow was fiercer since Tullibardine was no longer in office. From the start, the forcible marriage, which his enemies in London made a jest of, and the drawn-out failure to catch Simon had further weakened his position, and the acceptance of assistance from Keppoch when a commission of fire and sword was impending 'was made a mountain of' against him. The final straw came in March 1698: despite the commission for Whitelaw to be President of the Session which William had actually signed but kept back, he appointed Hew Dalrymple, Stair's brother and Queensberry's friend. Tullibardine resigned: William thought that he was surprised when it was accepted, but he himself constantly declared that he could have done nothing else.[134]

This did not entirely remove the fears of an Atholl-Hamilton dominance which had driven other magnates to such frenzied intriguing. In August, William allowed the transfer to Arran by his mother of the dukedom of Hamilton. However, despite both families' repeated requests, he would not return to Scotland until late 1699. And — a point Tullibardine's influence over the Hamilton interest had tended to obscure —Hamilton was incapable of playing second fiddle to another politician, or following any consistent policy of his own for long: in late 1698, he was making secret advances to Queensberry. Yet for this reason the Atholl family and its connections were hurled from power and attacked afterwards with a violence that had not been seen since the early 1680s, in striking contrast to Melville's demotion by slow stages.[135]

In July, William said that he could not then show Tullibardine the least mark of favour for fear of harming his business, and immediately wrote to the Council

emphasising that his resignation had forfeited his Council and Exchequer places
— a clear invitation to the wolves to attack, as Marchmont unhappily saw.[136]
Besides appeasing Queensberry's and Argyll's jealousy, William probably went to
this extreme because Tullibardine was clearly planning to lead the opposition in
the parliamentary session which began that month, with Marchmont as
Commissioner. He used the declaration of peace which had taken place since he
held that post to justify the reversal of his views on granting massive subsidies for
an army in time of famine. However, he failed to bring over former allies such as
Annandale, or to persuade his father and brother Nairne to take the oaths and join
the budding 'Country Party', which, despite defections among Marchmont's
personal followers, and unscrupulous tricks such as encouraging Stair to sit in
order to denounce the government for condoning his crimes, never came near
gaining a majority.[137] Marchmont too used what weapons came to hand, even
against his recent ally. In August, Tullibardine and his brothers quarrelled with
Ross of Balnagown, who intended to sabotage Simon's trial by petitioning
Parliament as his creditor, and who angered them further by talking of Lady
Lovat's *first* husband. He afterwards denounced them for assaulting him, making
his servants confirm his increasingly wild claims, and Marchmont placed
Tullibardine under house arrest. His pretext was that both sides' highland
followers might otherwise start street-fighting in Edinburgh, but it was generally
recognised as an open affront to the Atholl family. Argyll and other enemies
violently urged on Ross, and the ministers were receptive to charges; but
Tullibardine was bailed within a few days and finally exonerated in November.[138]
By then, however, Queensberry's and Argyll's constant pressure had obtained the
dismissal from office of all the Atholl-Hamilton connection (except Selkirk); and
Argyll was beginning proceedings to recover his family's losses in Argyllshire
during Atholl's lieutenancy.[139]

While their power and influence were torn to pieces around them, the Atholl
family doggedly persisted in one main purpose, the prosecution of Simon Fraser
and his supporters in the Justiciary Court at Edinburgh. The first indictment, on
27 June, was against the Beauforts and twenty-seven others, including twenty-one
Fraser gentry or their relations, for treason, rebellion, rape and kidnapping. A
second, on 12 July, provoked by Aultnagoire, was for treason and convocation
against Simon, Thomas, thirty-seven Frasers or close relations, and sixteen others,
including Angus and Alasdair Mor Macdonald. This was intended partly to apply
pressure on the Frasers to testify: two of the major witnesses at the trial had the
charge hanging over them, and a third over his brothers.[140] The proceedings
placed a strain on the loyalty even of Simon's main supporters. How great a strain
is indicated by the response he thought necessary: in August he gave a bond
promising one-tenth of Stratherrick, once it was reconquered, to Fraser of Foyers
if he remained loyal, and he may have divided up the rest among other Frasers.
Erchitt wrote secretly to his doer seeking means of exculpating himself for 'the late
unhappie disaster at ffannellen'.[141]

The Atholl family also faced defections: Saltoun slipped away from Edinburgh
rather than put himself in possible further danger by being a witness.[142] Their

main problem was Lady Lovat's reluctance to testify in Edinburgh. Besides her private reasons (some still applicable at rape trials today), she faced strong legal reluctance to accept female testimony at all. Her sister-in-law, one of those encouraging her, wrote in August that a too low estimate of her own abilities was her main handicap, but that she would speak out to prove Simon's allegations false. She did not, however, go to Edinburgh, and Atholl claimed to his son that October that she had sunk into a weak condition (presumably provoked by the trial) which she would probably not have survived without her parents' support. Her failure to appear instantly gave Simon's supporters the advantage. Even before the trial, Argyll was writing to Carstares that, if William would pardon the Fraser's convocation (which should not be treated as treason, since highlanders often gathered on slight grounds), Simon was willing to stand trial for the private charges, referring everything to Lady Lovat's oath.[143]

The prosecution made an odd compromise: in early September Simon (but not his father) and nineteen others (seventeen of them Frasers) were tried and convicted, in their absence, solely for treason, but several of the witnesses testified in detail about the forced marriage. Treason was chosen as the only crime for which the Justiciary Court could convict and forfault, rather than merely outlaw, defendants who failed to appear — and that only by Lauderdale's notorious act. The judgement the Atholl family obtained by exploiting it to the limit against private crimes to which it only technically applied was particularly vulnerable to criticism and reversal. To them, of course, the opposite seemed true: if the enormity of Simon's crimes and the massive forces he repeatedly raised to defy law and government did not make it a public crime, what would? The large number forfaulted and made desperate was another point of criticism, and stronger evidence of malice towards the Frasers than anything Simon had originally used to incite them. The family argued in reply that they had prosecuted only ringleaders, sparing their several hundred followers, and that all twenty were inconsiderable men, none worth £100 sterling.[144] Most of those in both indictments who were not prosecuted were outlawed, including Keppoch's brother, a sign that Atholl's anger still outweighed any prudent desire to restore his shattered highland connection. The prosecution was dropped against those who had submitted; but, unless they genuinely turned against Simon, Atholl continued to harass them with expensive yearly summonses.[145]

Atholl himself now became a defendant, in a suit by Argyll to recover the damages done in his invasion of Argyllshire in 1685, and the rents he had received from forfeited Argyll estates as a 'creditor'. The revolutionary implication was that the 1690 restoration of Argyll and James's deposition made invalid the orders and remission Atholl had received; and it soon became clear that the Session would decide so, for political reasons. Ogilivie (now Lord Seafield) was among those encouraging Argyll to proceed, recalling Tullibardine's use of political power against Glenlyon. The inflated claim, for £4,225, was finally settled out of court for £2,670 — still an immense strain on Murray finances.[146] After this defeat, Atholl went downhill rapidly, becoming increasingly arbitrary in his regality courts and excessively suspicious that Tullibardine or others were trying to usurp his authority and vassals' loyalty — characteristics which helped ensure that the Atholl interest would not recover its natural strength until he died in 1703.[147] In one perspective, the lawsuit marked a second logical stage of the Revolution in the Highlands, delayed for a decade by civil war and politics. Two other major pillars of the Restoration regime there, Seaforth and Gordon, were undergoing similar attacks; in 1698, Atholl urged Tullibardine to protect them as the family's natural allies.[148]

In both cases, catholicism was an increasing handicap. The late 1690s saw outbursts of strong religious intolerance and persecution, fuelled by the social pressures of war and famine. The hanging of a student for adolescent blasphemies and an outbreak of witch-hunting are the most notorious instances; but it was the escalating campaign against catholicism, which culminated in an act of 1700 (copied from England) for depriving catholic families of their estates in favour of the nearest protestant heir, w' .ich most affected the Highlands. The presbyterian alarm over the 'growth of popery' had some reason. Converts included Auchinbreck, so active in the Argyllshire protestant 'crusades' of 1685 and 1689–90. A bishop arrived and started to reorganise the Mission, establishing training for native priests; within a few years, there were so many Macdonald priests that they were nicknamed 'the priesthood of Aaron', and it was no longer necessary to rely on Ireland. The episcopalian ministers surviving in highland areas were often demoralised and had no help from their presbyteries in resisting incursions. James's support for the Mission, and the priests' use of Jacobitism to encourage their flocks, were further reasons for the government's hostility. It sent soldiers to hunt down the priests. By 1702, although there were a dozen of them in the Highlands and Islands, the persecution was the worst yet known: the schools were shut, and the priests on the mainland dared not stay more than a night in one place. In 1704, one was to die of ill-treatment as a prisoner in the Invergarry garrison.[149]

When Seaforth was released in 1697, besides Mackenzies his Whig neighbours Culloden and Brodie agreed to sign the bond guaranteeing his good behaviour. Yet the dispute which occurred then in the Council at the news that the local commander had previously allowed him parole should have warned him of a powerful hostile faction there, including the Dowager Countess's brother Tarbat and brother-in-law Campbell of Aberuchill. One threat to his liberty arose from his massive arrears of feu-rents for Lewis; another from a parliamentary decreet for the return of a valuable bond the government had regranted to him after a 1684 forfaulture.[150] The most dangerous, in the anti-catholic atmosphere, was the case of Cornelius Con, the apostate priest and seducer held prisoner on various Hebridean isles by the Mackenzies since 1688 — on Seaforth's direct orders since 1690. The presbyterian Synod of Argyll had long known of his plight, and in mid-1697 the Earl of Argyll as Commander-in-Chief ordered the parties from Fort William collecting public rents in the Western Isles to search for him. They arrived just too late at the islet where he had recently been imprisoned, finding only a petition for help to King William scratched on a mutton-bone.[151]

In early September, the Council ordered Seaforth to produce Con and his captor before them. He did not, gave a false account of the affair, and exacerbated matters by launching a riot in Chanonry against a creditor, making some opponents imagine he might ally with Simon Fraser. In fact, he was summoning the Mackenzie gentry to advise him on organising his affairs.[152] He was again ordered south, despite the winter snowdrifts. His long imprisonment had undermined his health, and he genuinely could not travel, but the Council eagerly set about exacting the penalties from even his Whig sureties. Hearing of this, Seaforth managed to struggle south and present himself in February 1698. He was at first bailed again (Lord Forbes and Grant standing his sureties), and was even allowed to return home in March; but when he appeared again in July without producing Con — the last major mistake of a career filled with them — he was sent to the Castle. His wife arranged for Con to be handed over in August, but he was not released.[153] Tarbat showed his malice towards his chief by warning Queensberry that he was confidently relying on the Atholl-Hamilton interest for his freedom; he claimed merely to want him 'frighted' from this, not 'sore hurt'.[154] Con declared himself a Protestant and eager to testify against Seaforth, but nevertheless prevaricated when questioned, and was himself sent to the Castle. Seaforth's first petitions for release were ignored; but in March 1700 he confidently claimed that no proof had been found linking him with the 1697 riot, and that the government now realised the nature of Con, whom it had now banished the country. He was released, and returned home; but the long imprisonment had finally broken his health, and, before he could fully rebuild his interest among the clan gentry or restore his finances, he died in March 1701. His mother, having prevented his wife from seeing him until he was past setting his affairs in order, battened on the estate. His widow, fearing that her young son would be bred a Protestant, sent him to France. Their actions were to keep the Seaforth family poor, powerless and Jacobite for another quarter-century.[155]

The Duke of Gordon, who remained at Edinburgh forbidden to return to the North-East, suffered directly for his catholicism only a brief imprisonment in 1699, when a congregation worshipping at his lodgings was arrested and he struck a defiant attitude before the Council. Yet it laid him open to worse suspicions: spies were sent to investigate a groundless rumour that he was sheltering Sir George Barclay the Assassin on his estates. In April 1700, William authorised the Council to let him go free.[156] By then, however, he was already the target of the most extreme attempt, for the Highlands, to annul the significance of the Restoration — an attempt by Argyll to reverse his grandfather the Marquess's attainder, which would give him the latter's full pre-1661 rights to the Huntly lands, and would, in effect, totally ruin the Gordon family.

Argyll could rely on support from the descendents of the Marquess's creditors, who saw this as the only means of obtaining repayment, and one of them undertook test cases in the courts. When he introduced into the 1700–1 Parliament a process for reducing the Marquess's forfaulture, it seemed secure of a majority, composed partly of creditors. His determination to push it through at all costs divided and alarmed the other ministers. If enforced rigorously, it would cause chaos, and the Gordons would probably resist in arms any attempt to dispossess the Duke, starting a private war in the most peaceable part of the Highlands at the very time when there was a danger of a full-scale Scottish rebellion over Darien. Admittedly, not all Gordon's major vassals would have risen in his defence; he was oppressing the Macphersons and trying to have Cluny evicted by virtue of his feudal rights. William at first refused to intervene, ignoring a petition which Huntly presented with full backing from his Howard relatives. Unknown to him, the decisive agent in changing his policy was (according to Sir Aeneas Macpherson) the expatriate Jacobite Robert Ferguson. He 'tugged like a Galley slave' to create a party for Gordon, and, exploiting every ounce of his credit in the movement, emphasised to those of William's leading advisers who were 'reinsuring' themselves with St Germain that this would be seen as a test case of their sincerity.[157]

On 10 January, William wrote asking Queensberry and Argyll to bring about an accomodation with Gordon, but agreement proved elusive. It was proposed to reduce the forfaulture and grant Argyll his grandfather's honours, but merely free him from the latter's debts; but, Gordon pointed out, that would enable the creditors to ruin him. Finally, Argyll suspended his process (though keeping the power to resume it) and they submitted the matter to William.[158] Argyll was rewarded with a dukedom; but discontent at being thwarted in what had long been his family's dream was one main reason for the rift which developed between him and Queensberry.[159]

Unlike the Catholics Seaforth and Gordon, Tullibardine could still hope for political power, and he began to rebuild the Atholl influence in the Highlands. Glengarry, for instance, hoped that his conduct towards Simon might enable him to 'settle with' Argyll and gain his favour; but evidently Argyll was no more helpful in getting Invergarry evacuated, and by 1701 he was again soliciting favours as a good Atholl dependant.[160] As the crisis over Darien reached its head in 1700, government supporters feared that Tullibardine might be organising a highland army to support the 'Country Party' if it began a rebellion or called an illegal convention. Argyll, however, reported that the ex-Jacobite western clans 'say, since they have swore alledgiance, their dependance shall be on the court ... their interest as well as duty; and, if they could be seduced it should not be by D. Hamilton', now the obvious 'Country' leader, whom they had never forgiven for failing them when James made him their general in 1690.[161]

The Atholl family was powerless to touch Simon Fraser (who assumed the title of Lord Lovat when his father died in Skye in May 1699). He established good relations with the Fort William garrison, and the detachment at Castle Dounie was withdrawn in December 1698 on Argyll's motion.[162] In February 1699, two of those forfaulted with Simon and therefore liable to immediate execution (one of them an assistant in the rape) were brought to Edinburgh; the embarrassed Council gave them reprieve after reprieve until the mob rioting over Darien in July 1700 obligingly freed them from the Tolbooth.[163] Argyll, encouraged by the Frasers, worked vigorously to obtain a pardon for Simon. Carstares was on his side, and might have obtained one when William was in Holland in 1699 but for the new Secretary Carmichael's protest. Late in 1699, Argyll (and, in one version, Queensberry) summoned Simon, who came secretly to London. Seafield promised Argyll and Carstares to work for his pardon; but he had secretly promised the Atholl family that he would not, and sabotaged it.[164] After Simon had spent several months waiting in London — during which he later untruthfully claimed he had visited St Germain and been well received[165] — he crossed to appeal to William at Loo. There Undersecretary Pringle was under Carstares's thumb, and on 22 August William granted Simon and his accomplices a remission for their treason in assembling in arms and defying the law — that is, for their public crimes only, not the rape.[166] Argyll wrote joyfully to Simon's supporters, including Lochiel and Culloden, that 'Beaufort's (now I may say Lord Lovatt's) pardon' was safe in his possession.[167]

Earlier that summer, Keppoch also had made his peace. Since 1698, he and the loyal remnant of his clan had suffered the hardships of fugitives as well as the famine. They had 'not only Lost the most of their effects to the value of Threttie thousand merks but alssoe above ane hundred of his men uer Lost by ffamin suord gallous and severalls uent to serv abroad who never returned'.[168] Maitland reported, however, that Keppoch found friends in many places. In late 1699, when he was on Macfarlane's lands with eighty followers, a party of the forces nearly captured him, but he escaped by boat. The long failure to crush him seems to have worn down Mackintosh again, and that October Keppoch believed that they were close to settlement; but the negotiations collapsed.[169]

Early in 1700, Mackintosh obtained a licence to treat with the outlaws, and in May, being sick himself, he commissioned some leading members of Clan Chattan, including Invercauld and Borlum the younger, to represent him. On 22 May, they signed an agreement with Keppoch before Maitland at Fort William. The terms were less favourable to Keppoch than those almost agreed on the previous year, and, he felt, betrayed his successors in acknowledging Mackintosh's right at all. He was to cede some land in return for the cancellation of Mackintosh's prior claims against him (excluding arrears of past teinds and cess). He was granted a nineteen year tack of the estate, at a rapidly rising rent, and was to perform a vassal's duties. If his rent became more than two years in arrears, he would forfeit the tack, and, if he harassed any tenants Mackintosh installed afterwards, his cautioner, Sir Donald Macdonald, would forfeit £250. Sir Donald also gave security for Keppoch's good behaviour. 'I engaged something more than I proposed,' he wrote, but he trusted that Keppoch 'is burnt soe as he will not reddily turn outlaw again'. Within a few months, he and some of his Skye tenants had to give bond for the appearance of Keppoch's brother Angus for wounding a Mackinnon.[170]

The settlement would be void if the government disapproved, and old-style 'presbyterians' protested against any favour towards Keppoch. He still had to obtain a remission for Mulroy, and to earn it he co-operated for months with Maitland in suppressing robbery, notably by handing over Alasdair Mor Macdonald. Seafield may have demanded this, but Keppoch probably welcomed the opportunity to dispose of the clansmen who had most openly defied him in his support of Simon. However, although he was several times allowed to visit Edinburgh seeking a remission, he still had not gained it when Anne succeeded:

another agreement then with Mackintosh contained provisions 'if he do not obtain this, or shall suffer death' for Mulroy. It was only in late 1703 that he was finally pardoned, through the efforts of Tarbat, now Secretary and a supporter of the Atholl interest in the Highlands.[171] Within a few years, he fell behind in his payments; he hoped to persuade Mackintosh to sell Brae-Lochaber to Sir Donald, but Mackintosh instead prosecuted Keppoch and Sir Donald; yet the dispute was no longer pushed to violent extremes.[172]

The Highland Justiciary Commission had expired at the start of 1700 and was not immediately renewed. The Highland Committee of the Council advised that it should first be reconstructed with fewer highland members and more lowlanders, and should be compelled to restrict itself to genuine cases of robbery. Some local sufferers now found the garrisons, in their turn, inadequate protection. In Aberdeenshire, Lord Forbes, using his Privy Councillor's authority, encouraged the heritors to organise their own defence, and they offered rewards for the capture of leading robbers, mostly Macdonalds such as Alasdair Mor.[173]

Queensberry's instructions for the abortive May 1700 session included ones to renew the Commission with the usual power over regalities, and to assent to any acts proposed for pacifying the Highlands. Although none was passed (no acts were), the Perthshire heritors' petition showed that one was needed, complaining of 'continuall Murders, Robberies and Depredations which have brought many who might have wrestled with their other difficulties to such a condition that our Countries are now become Desarts and lye absolutely waste'. Some could trace their ruin to the wartime raids; Marchmont, appealing to disgruntled ex-Williamites, even suggested in his opening speech that Parliament might fairly soon compensate them for the ravages of 'our own unnatural Countreymen' — an absurdity at the height of the famine.[174] Despite these tokens of hostility to the cattle-raiding clans, Queensberry, preparing for the more successful 1700-1 session, considered a proposal to allow the Macgregors their name again, and wrote to Argyll promising to concur in it if he considered it for the King's and his own interest. Unless Argyll's attitude had changed since 1691, he must have supported this, but it seems merely to have aroused hostility: the draft act for renewing the Commission included a clause specifically renewing the prohibition. The act's one major innovation was the establishment of two new highland companies of one hundred men each, to be under Council orders; Forbes of Culloden's alternative draft would also have obliged Maitland's regiment to make permanent the ring of small garrisons round Lochaber. However, one of the violent Court-Country disputes over the order of business caught the act at its proposed second reading, with Lord Forbes and Culloden supporting its priority. Queensberry angrily intervened to end the session, and it was lost.[175]

The resolve on the army establishment had already authorised the two highland companies, and in June 1701 William appointed the captains the public wanted: for the northern company a Grant, for the southern one, Campbell of Fonab, whose expedition against the Spaniards (with Thomas Drummond, giving him advice. See Preface, p. xii) was the one success of the disastrous second settlement at Darien. He looked to Breadalbane as his chieftain, and this encouraged the Atholl interest in their (apparently atypical) hostility to the companies, which Tullibardine denounced as 'filled uith all the most notorious rogues and theives in the Highlands'.[176]

In May, William appointed a new Highland Justiciary, which sat from September. There were two commissions, whose jurisdictions covered only the shires from Ross round to Argyllshire. Caithness and Sutherland were omitted, evidently from a lack of parliamentary authority to co-opt members to the hereditary jurisdictions there, but the northern commission nevertheless continued to try cases from those counties, even obvious fabrications: the Session denounced one such verdict as 'iniquous'.[177] Outside their duties, the commissions could bolster the regime slightly with their political support. In late 1701, they responded to the French recognition of the Pretender with addresses promising their support against his enemies. Tullibardine's refusal on a technicality to sign the southern one gave his enemies fresh ammunition (although he organised a rival address), and few signed the northern one because it expressed support for presbyterianism.[178]

The commissions' dubious methods and defiance of higher authority appear most clearly in the trial of Alasdair Mor, which for some reason split the North-East into two factions. The party bent on conviction, headed by Lord Forbes, might merely have been determined not to let slip 'a very special deliverance'; but he had equally persistent supporters (the most important known member of whom was Earl Marischal) who organised his defence and the writing of his long, pathetic petitions to the Council in a language he could not speak. Possibly the assistance he had given Simon inspired this (but Culloden and others of Simon's supporters joined the prosecution); possibly crypto-Jacobitism; possibly his supporters had used him to harass their enemies.[179]

As Alasdair Mor was transported from Fort William to Edinburgh in early 1701, Forbes vainly moved for this trial to be in the North. Instead, it was ordered before the Justiciary Court, and, by the new Act anent wrongeous imprisonment, must take place by November. Forbes and the northern commission wrote again calling for him to be sent north, and complaining 'that the councill did not design that justice should be done upon him', but despite this insolence, and his petition, the Council agreed to send him to Aberdeen for trial. Another petition from Alasdair claimed that the prosecution (as had been foreseen) had pre-engaged all the available lawyers but one, that the blatant bias of some judges had made others walk out in protest, and that a new indictment was being prepared blaming him for all Dundee's ravages. Although many members had promised Forbes not to intervene further, the Council were divided. At first, on Marchmont's casting vote, they allowed the execution to proceed, but a further petition from Alasdair, emphasising that he had never shed blood and offering to go into perpetual banishment persuaded them to commute the sentence, to the fury of the northern commission. However, William refused to grant a remission, since he had made it a rule in England and Holland not to pardon robbery, and Forbes immediately organised a new trial to nullify the commutation, with the Advocate's legal blessing. When Anne on her accession and the Council ordered a reprieve until these proceedings also were examined, they went ahead with a third and even a fourth trial.[180] Finally, Marischal was given custody of Alasdair, on granting a heavy security of £500 that he would never return. He had decided to ship him to Florence or Leghorn. But clan tradition claims that he was merely transported to, and died in Holland.[181]

Despite the defiant attitude and irregular procedure this case revealed, the Highland Justiciary continued its activities in Anne's reign, once more granted parliamentary endorsement by one of the few acts passed in the controversial 1702 session. Caithness and Sutherland remained · outside its jurisdiction. In December, Anne issued a fresh Commission, adding about fifty members, mostly Mackenzies in Ross and ex-Jacobites (or rather crypto-Jacobites) in the East Highlands and Perthshire.[182]

After receiving his pardon, Simon Fraser returned to the North of Scotland in the autumn of 1700. In one account, he claimed that the local gentry gave him a viceregal welcome along his way and offered to pay the family debts. This seems, as usual, to be false, although the Atholl family, who were uncertain until late October even that he had been pardoned, then heard that the Frasers and some of their neighbours had written a letter of thanks to Argyll for it. Simon immediately started preparing a process for criminal libel against Atholl and his vassals for their ravages on Fraser territory and the imprisonment of clansmen at Dunkeld; probably also a civil suit for the estate.[183] Atholl had that year been attempting to marry the little heiress into the Tweeddale family, who suddenly withdrew after terms were agreed, perhaps from fear. He wrote to the Marchioness that he would take care not to expose their daughter to publicity, but that Simon was likely to force her to testify. Not least to forestall these counter-suits Atholl launched a new prosecution, for hamesucken and rape, against Simon and nine other Frasers, his accomplices in the rape and also, presumably the gentry who most persistently ·defied the Atholl family, Erchitt (though he had sought to submit), his brother and young Culduthel.[184] Simon's supporters spread the news that he would confidently stand trial. He journeyed to Edinburgh, bringing witnesses to prove that Lady Lovat had accepted the marriage, appeared openly in Edinburgh, enjoying Argyll's and Leven's countenance — and then, on the morning set for the trial, fled south. According to one of his explanations, his noble friend Argyll had just learned from Aberuchill that Tullibardine had corrupted over half the Session. According to another, his false friend Argyll frightened him into fleeing needlessly, for fear he and the Atholl family should be reconciled! In reality, if the written defence he prepared is any guide, he gambled entirely, until the very last moment, on Lady Lovat's not having the strength of will or self-possession to appear in court, testify and deny the authorship of her alleged letters. When it became clear that she would, it was not surprising that the Advocate warned Argyll that Simon was doomed if he stayed.[185] On 17 February 1701, the Justice-Court outlawed him and his co-defendants for non-appearance, and fined Lord Fraser for failing to present them. Her relations congratulated Lady Lovat on this final vindication.[186]

Simon lurked in London that summer, planning to serve with William as a volunteer if war broke out, and relying on Argyll and the others who promised him support (including Carstares, who offered to lend him money) to obtain him another remission. Seafield was hostile, and, according to the Atholl family, William was approached and refused outright; but Simon constantly complained that his allies had neglected him. From the start, he was anxious to return to Scotland, and in August he set out, carrying letters from Argyll to assist his journey through Argyllshire. To Leven, he wrote that he had the King's favour, and on the Jacobite side greater friends than either Hamilton or Atholl, though he hoped he need never apply to them: both claims were false.[187] In 1703–4, to boost his importance in St Germain's eyes, he was to pretend that William had promised him a regiment if he would exploit his highland influence in his favour; but the despairing tone of his other contemporary letters, which talked of his enlisting merely to subsist, belies this.[188] En route, he seized a major opportunity to establish a more solid claim to the Lovat estates. Lord Elcho (Leven's brother-in-law) had an important interest in them, for which the Atholl family was negotiating with him. He had ignored Simon's letters from London, but, on meeting him in the Lowlands, he agreed to reconsider if he produced Lovat's 1696 conveyance. As their agreement would ruin the Atholl interest, Atholl denounced Elcho as a 'shittlecock' and made attempts to prove the document a forgery.[189]

On 23 September, Simon wrote from Inveraray to Fonab's lieutenant, Campbell of Glendaruel (later his accomplice in the 'Scots Plot' of 1703) asking him and Fonab to prevent his enemies from using the Highland Justiciary against him, 'sinc I resolve to Do no disturbance but get a little money in my Countery'. Going north, he allegedly consulted Brodie, Calder and Gordonstoun on raising Elcho's money. Afterwards, Lady Lovat complained to the Council, he lived openly in Stratherrick surrounded by men in arms, and issuing proclamations in the churches on Sunday that the rest of the clan should be prepared to rise. Meanwhile, he levied contributions from them, 'which many of them out of fear and some out of kindness to him granted', and sent his men to quarter, army style, on the refractory, so that the tenants could not pay their rent.[190]

As this implied, Simon probably had to rely more now on force to control the Frasers, for the continued official and private pressure was wearing away their support for him. When young Lady Lovat's representatives obtained letters of intercommuning against him in February 1702, he felt obliged on 7 March to issue bonds to many of the clan gentry promising them large sums, to be paid in 1708, 'to stand in force upon condition the said   stand faithful to our interest, and no otherwise' — 10,000 merks to Fraser of Struy alone. Forty years later, Simon was to wriggle out of this obligation by arguing that the bonds were issued for a Jacobite purpose (and therefore invalid); and, because William died the next day and Simon soon crossed to St Germain, historians have accepted this. In fact, the bonds resembled the 1698 grant of part of Stratherrick to Foyers; and Simon was gathering Fraser hands to an address to William when news of his death arrived.[191] He several times afterwards claimed that he gathered several hundred men and, expecting an immediate invasion, proclaimed James III — according to the most fantastic of these accounts, at Inverness itself. However, the Atholl family, alert for anything to discredit him, heard only that he had lit bonfires and railed at William as his greatest enemy; and he wrote to Annandale, emphasising that his followers would hold the North for Anne in any emergency.[192] His general attitude to the dead king and his reign was widely shared in the Highlands, and not merely by Jacobites. Traditions long surviving in Glenlyon and Argyllshire recalled William's death almost as the breaking of an evil spell; the cows began to yield plentiful milk again, and the sun's rays once more gave warmth.[193]

Simon also claimed that he visited the major highland chiefs and received their commission to represent them at St Germain. If he made any such preparations, they were on a small, second-string scale; for when, after threatening Captain Grant of the independent company by letter for planning to seize him, Simon again left for London (arriving on 20 April), his main aim was to gain remission and favour at Anne's court. Admittedly, Tullibardine had been her friend before her accession, and Argyll's position seemed insecure, but Queensberry, who remained at the head of the Scottish government, was a far older member of her circle. Simon relied on him and Argyll, and was recommended to Anne's uncle Rochester.[194] Queensberry and Argyll did nothing for him; but the blow that crushed his hopes was the news that the Atholl family had married the little heiress to Alexander, Mackenzie of Prestonhall's son and Tarbat's nephew; at a stroke they transformed their chief opponent in the North — and therefore Simon's main local ally — into a friend. Negotiations began in October 1701 and were concluded by February 1702, although Simon apparently only learned of them after leaving Scotland.[195] Other former supporters, such as the Chisholm, now changed sides. A year later, the policy was carried a stage further to cut off Simon's potential refuge among his Macleod kin: the new chief married the heiress's younger sister, and lived in Lady Lovat's household.[196] The Prestonhall marriage created in Simon a violent hatred against Tarbat — in his 1703 allegations to Queensberry, he was to accuse him of treason even before he named Tullibardine[197] — and it, not William's death, was decisive in shattering and reshaping his plans. In a letter of 2 May, he blamed Argyll for not helping the Frasers, his natural allies, against his natural enemy Tarbat, and lamented that the clan would vanish within a decade. He himself would now push his fortunes elsewhere — plainly meaning St Germain. Yet he retreated to Harwich slowly and reluctantly, frequently attempting to appeal via his London friends to Godolphin and other ministers, and he finally set sail for the Continent only after several weeks' delay.[198]

He had left a worthy deputy, his brother John, who sallied from Stratherrick, still the family's main centre of support, into the Aird, garrisoned Beauly and roamed the country for months with thirty men, threatening the tenants and forcing them to enter into bonds. Much of the estate was lying waste, and the remainder paid no rent; even without clan feeling, the renewal of attempts to collect it would inevitably be unpopular. Prestonhall, who controlled his son's affairs, appointed Mackenzies (with Mackenzie bodyguards) as joint bailie and chamberlain; he doubtless considered it adequate conciliation to the clan that the Fraser ones were continued in tandem with them, but he seemed to be starting to fulfil Simon's prophecies of doom. In July, John Fraser's supporters beat up the

Fraser chamberlain. Lady Lovat's agents appealed to the Highland Justiciary, which sent ten men from Grant's highland company. They drove John back into the Aird, but could not prevent a mob of women and men in women's clothes from stoning the Mackenzie bailie as he was ceremonially installed. He and his Fraser colleague occupied the house of Fanellan, guarded by the soldiers. But John had mustered fifty reliable supporters in Stratherrick, and on 5 August he returned, gathered a further 2–300 male and female supporters at a fair, attacked and burned Fanellan, disarmed the soldiers, and carried the bailies off into several months' captivity.[199] Once again, the Beauforts had pushed violence slightly too far, and some gentry wrote apprehensively denying involvement. The first attack had already made the Atholls and Prestonhall, as Lady Lovat's representatives, obtain letters of intercommuning against the clansmen convicted with Simon in 1701, while still apparently hoping to avoid proceeding to extremes against John, 'a simple young man'. Now, after some opposition, the Council ordered Grant's entire company to patrol Stratherrick and the Aird, and the Fort William outgarrisons to reinforce him. Maitland co-operated vigorously, and Queen Anne wrote ordering that the Frasers be brought to condign punishment.[200]

The diversion of Grant's company to protect exclusively Lovat interests probably caused bitterness, and in February 1703 the Council ordered it back to its normal posts. By then, however, the Frasers' resistance was ebbing. In December, Prestonhall had obtained a Session decreet deciding the dispute over the estate in young Lady Lovat's favour. Simon's stay at St Germain, which he had expected to last only a few weeks, dragged on for over a year.[201] When he returned to Scotland in 1703, it temporarily seemed that he might triumph after all. He appeared to have the full confidence and backing of St Germain, which had entrusted him with an important mission, recognised him as Lord Lovat and granted him an (unsigned) patent for an earldom and a colonel's commission. On the government side, his patrons Argyll, Queensberry and Leven connived at his presence; and he not only carried out his Jacobite mission without hindrance but persuaded the willingly deceived Queensberry to believe in the 'Scots Plot', accusations of treasonable activities, nearly all false, which were intended to ruin all his major enemies, Hamilton, Atholl (Tullibardine), Cromartie (Tarbat) and Prestonhall, Glengarry. 'If we live another year', he wrote to his loyal supporter young Culduthel, 'you will by GOD'S Help, see me the greatest Lord Lovat that ever was.' He wrote to the clan that, although his reluctance to spill Fraser blood had so far prevented him from harming his enemies among them, those who did not submit now would be destroyed.[202] Atholl partisans, however, claimed that by then he had only about fifty supporters left. Nor would Jacobite feeling necessarily increase the number; he was fairly obviously ready to change sides if it benefited him, and one of young Lady Lovat's most reliable officials was a crypto-Jacobite.[203]

Within a few months, Simon's hopes on both sides were destroyed. His most reliable ministerial ally, Argyll, died after a scuffle in his private brothel in Northumberland. Although those accused in the 'Scots Plot' never entirely succeeded in removing the smear on their names, they were able through timely publicity to discredit it widely, and Queensberry temporarily lost office. St

Germain had allowed Simon's mission largely from temporary panic at a Scottish indemnity.[204] On his return, Middleton proved to be his enemy, as much because Simon's schemes clashed with his own Fabian (and futile) plans for restoring James III as because he had lied so brazenly and had abused Jacobite trust so grossly. He was discredited and imprisoned for a decade. In Scotland, his enemies had John Fraser also outlawed for fire raising, forcing him also to flee to France in 1704, and most of the clan soon became uncertain if either brother still lived. Young Prestonhall reigned unchallenged. He had taken the name 'Fraser of Fraserdale', but, by a secret protestation, enabled himself to resume that of Mackenzie. Largely as a result of his own actions, Simon's prophecies of doom were being fulfilled. 'His poor friends [were] persecuted at home, which continued for several years, till the most part of them were reduced to poverty, and garrisons keept in their houses, and themselves and their children exposed to the mountains, and to the charity of good people', while the rest of the Frasers were looked down on by the neighbouring clans and constantly encroached on by the Mackenzies. With their longed-for King Stork detained in France, they were helpless, and therefore remained submissive — for a time.[205]

NOTES

1. Riley, *King William*, 110.

2. Blair, Atholl MSS, Box 29 I (8) 97, Aberdeen to Murray, 2 Mar. 1696.

3. *Ib.*, 204, Queensberry to same, 2 June 1696; *ib.*, 230, Dollery to same, 9 June 1696; *Marchmont Papers*, iii, 103-4, Polwarth to same, 14 May 1696; Riley, *King William*, 112-14; Drumlanrig, Queensberry Papers, Vol. 115, 11, [Murray] to Queensberry, 7 May [1696]; *ib.*, 40, ? to same, 17 May 1696; *ib.*, Vol. 126, 43, [Murray] to same, 23 May 1696; NUL Portland MSS, PwA 952, same to Portland, 12 May 1696. For his part in appointing Polwarth, Blair, Atholl MSS, Box 29 I (10) 208, Countess of Tullibardine (hereafter 'Countess') to Countess of Orkney 13 Sept. 1698.

4. *Ib.*, (8) 281, Sir P. Moray to Tullibardine, 14 July 1696; *ib.*, (9) 6, Countess to same, 7 Jan. 1697; *ib.*, 17, Tullibardine to Countess, 17 Jan. 1697; *ib.*, 25, same to same, 23 Jan. 1697; Drumlanrig, Queensberry Papers, Vol. 115, 12, [same] to Queensberry, 23 Dec. [1696].

5. *HMCR Hope-Johnston*, 99-100, Johnston to Annandale, 18 May 1696; Blair, Atholl MSS, Box 29 I (9) 27, Tullibardine to Countess, 26 Jan. 1697; *ib.*, 34, Countess to Tullibardine, 2 Feb. 1697; *ib.*, (8) 293, Dollery to same, 18 July 1696.

6. Tullibardine later passed an Association, to be subscribed by office-holders, in the 1696 session. *Ib.*, 144, Murray to Lady Murray, 7 Apr. 1696; *ib.*, 152, Ld B. Hamilton to same, 11 Apr. 1696; *ib.*, 156, Duchess of Hamilton to same, 14 Apr. 1696; *ib.*, 148, Reasons offered in Council, Apr. 1696; *APS*, x, 35; Riley, *King William*, 111-112.

7. *Ib.*, 112; *HMCR Hope-Johnstone*, 100, Johnston to Annandale, 22 Aug. 1697; Blair, Atholl MSS, Box 29 I (9) 13, Countess to Tullibardine, 14 Jan. 1697; *ib.*, 160, Annandale to same, 27 Mar. 1697; *ib.*, 40, Tullibardine to Countess, 11 Feb. 1697; *Carstares S.P.*, 316-17, Argyll to Carstares, 10 July 1697.

8. *Ib.*, 327, same to same, 3 Aug. 1697; 297-8, Ogilvie to same, 27 Apr. 1697; *Marchmont Papers*, iii, 120-2, Polwarth to Tullibardine, 5 Jan. 1697; Riley, *King William*, 119-21.

9. Blair, Atholl MSS, bundle 1720, Tullibardine to [Hamilton], 8 Sept. 1698.

10. Hill was sometimes referred to as 'Sir John'. As the first official mention of this mysterious knighthood seems to be in the Council registers for late 1696 (SRO PC1/51, 28, 107), Murray may possibly, using his powers as Commissioner, have knighted him in the hope of reducing his hostility to the Atholl family; but the title is a mystery.

11. *Ib.*, 41-8, 50, 60, 74-5, 91-2, 97-8, 101-3, 107-8; *HMCR Roxburghe,* 134, Hill to Marchmont, 26 Apr. 1697; 'Camerons in the '15', *TGSI*, xxvi, 68; *Marchmont Papers,* iii, 119, Polwarth to Tullibardine, 29 Dec. 1696; SRO GD 158/964, 95, 135-6, same to same, 9 Jan., 9 Feb. 1697; Blair, Atholl MSS, Box 29 I (9) 2, Countess to same, 4 Jan. 1697.

12. *Ib.*, (10) 208, same to Countess of Orkney, 13 Sept. 1698; *APS* x, App., 32; *HMCR Hope-Johnstone,* 107, Johnston to Annandale, 20 Jan, 1699; Flinn, *Scottish Population History,* 169.

13. The example cited (*ib.*, 165) to suggest that the famine already had a grip on the Highlands is of war damage. *Ib.*, 150-1; Drumlanrig, Queensberry Papers, Vol. 115, 47, Tarbat to Queensberry, 21 July 1696; *ib.*, 80, same to same, 31 Oct. 1698.

14. This was repeated yearly; in 1699 it was refused, but the Governor had already secretly smuggled some in. SRO PC 1/51, 107, 421, 572; *ib.*, GD 112/40/4/7/21, Maitland to Breadalbane, 6 Dec. 1698; *HMCR Roxburghe,* 148, Lords Justices to Marchmont, 4 Feb. 1699.

15. *Ib.*, 134, Hill to same, 26 Apr. 1697; Flinn, 172-5, 181; SRO GD 112/40/4/7/17, Breadalbane to ?, 28 Jan. 1698; *ib.*, 18, ? Campbell to Breadalbane, 12 Feb. 1698 (potatoes).

16. *Ib*; Flinn, 171.

17. *Ib.*, 181-2; Fergusson, 'Early History of Strathardle', *TGSI*, xxiv, 202; Drumlanrig, Queensberry Papers, Vol. 115, 80, Tarbat to Queensberry, 31 Oct. 1698; Forbes Leith, *Scottish Catholics,* ii, 178.

18. *Ib.*; Flinn, 171, 181; Blair, Atholl MSS, Box 45 (13) 34, [Lady Keppoch], 'Information of Keppoch's Expeditione ... against Capt Simon Fraser'.

19. Shaw, *Northern & Western Islands,* 106, 195; SRO GD 112/40/4/7/18, ? Campbell to Breadalbane, 12 Feb. 1698; *ib.*, 17, Breadalbane to ?, 28 Jan. 1698; GD 170/629/81, same to Barcaldine, 2 Mar. 1698.

20. *Ib; ib.*, 104, same to same, 19 Dec. 1698; GD 1/658, 44-5; GD 112/39/1309, Rob Roy to Breadalbane, 17 Dec. 1697.

21. *Ib; ib.*, 1308, Cameron of Callart to same, 13 Dec. 1697; *ib.*, PC 1/51. 593; *HMCR Athole,* 55, Tarbat to Tullibardine, 21 Oct. 1697; *Argyll Just. Recs.,* 158-9, 166-7.

22. *APS,* x, 55, 79, 142-3; *Carstares S.P.,* 294, Carstares's notes on Murray's instructions; *CSPD 1698,* 318, Instructions to Marchmont, 24 June 1698; Atholl, *Chronicles,* i, 492-3.

23. *Ib.*, 445, Atholl to Tullibardine, 22 Mar. 1698; *CSPD 1697,* 79-81, Justiciary Commission, 30 Mar. 1697; SRO PC 1/51, 199, 217, 295.

24. *Ib.*, 216-7, 234; Steele, ii, S3129; Blair, Atholl MSS, Box 29 I (9) 268, Hill to Tullibardine, 19 July 1697; *ib.*, Box 42 I (2) 10, PC minute, 6 Oct. 1697.

25. According to early muster-rolls, the only Lt Robert Campbell to begin his service as early as Fonab's brother did was the lieutenant of grenadiers. For his possible part in planning the Massacre, see Chapter 10, p. 332 & n.139. As he left the regiment on 1 March 1692, he might possibly be one of the two officers who refused to take part (see *ib.*, n.141) — or merely a stay-at-home. *HMCR Laing,* ii, 1, Testificate, 30 July 1700; Dalton, *English Army Lists,* iii, 337, iv 44; SRO GD 26/ix/291, Muster-rolls, Jan. 1690.

26. *Ib.*, PC 1/51, 560, 582, 590; *ib.*, 1/52, 38; Lovat, *Memoirs,* 37.

27. *Earls of Cromartie,* i, 136, Tarbat to Marchmont, 15 May 1699; Forbes, *More Culloden*

Papers, 258, Lt Col Forbes to Culloden, 4 Apr. 1699; *Hist Papers*, i, 1–2, Committee report, 6 Dec. 1699; Drumlanrig, Queensberry Papers, Vol. 115, 97, Strathmore to Queensberry, 12 May 1699.

28. Atholl, *Chronicles*, i, 415–16, Robertson of Lude to Dollery, 23 Nov. 1697; *ib.*, 445, Atholl to Tullibardine, 22 Mar. 1698; Blair, Atholl MSS, Box 45 (1) 249, [same] to same, 29 Sept. 1701; *ib.*, (2) 76, Marchioness to [same], 16 Mar. [?1702].

29. SRO GD 50/26/13/124, Breadalbane to Carwhin, 15 Jan. 1698[19].

30. Dunlop, 'A Chief and his Lawyer', *TGSI*, xlv, 274.

31. *Earls of Cromartie*, i, 124–5, Hill to Tarbat, 1 Nov. 1697; SRO GD 112/40/4/7/13, same to Breadalbane, 23 Dec. 1697; *ib.*, 107, same to same, 12 Nov. 1697; *ib.*, 108, same to same, 4 Dec. 1697; Blair, Atholl MSS, Box 29 I (9) 282, same to Tullibardine, 14 Aug. 1697.

32. Doune, Moray MSS, Box 6, 750, Moray to J. Christie, 16 Mar. 1697/8.

33. Fraser-Macintosh, *Letters*, 136, D. Forbes to W. Baillie, 5 Dec. 1699; *More Culloden Papers*, 264, Culloden to Lochiel, 3 Aug. 1699; Mackay, *Urquhart & Glenmoriston*, 217–20.

34. 'The Raid on Glenkindie in 1698', ed. J. Macgregor, *Miscellany of the Third Spalding Club*, ii, ed. W. Douglas Simpson (3rd Spalding Club, 1940), 89–94, 113–14; Tayler, *House of Forbes*, 238, Contract, 12 Apr. 1699.

35. 'The Process against the Egyptians at Banff, 1700', *Spalding Club Misc.* iii, 175–7, 183–4; Fergusson, 'Early History of Strathardle', *TGSI*, xxiv, 202–4; *Lairds of Grant*, i, 301, 323–6.

36. The traditional story is that Domhnall was in love with Grant's daughter Mary (he apparently had none of that name) when Grant was staying at Urquhart Castle (left a ruin by the garrison on withdrawing in 1692), was tricked and captured by the Grants, and invoked Mary in a final poem (a couplet which Sorley Maclean considers clumsy and interpolated). If the legend contains any truth, it probably concerns a lesser Grant gentry family. *Ib.*, 330; Mackay, *Urquhart & Glenmoriston*, 188–90, 211; Mac Gill-Eain, 'Domhnall Don', *TGSI*, xlii, 110.

37. As Sorley Maclean points out, Domhnall's reference to one of Simon Fraser's supporters as his fellow-prisoner indicates a date after 1697. Breadalbane in early 1698 was trying to capture or extort terms for a pardon from a robber, 'Donald Donn' or 'Doun', but this may not be he. His expectation of help from his clan suggests a date after May 1700, when the agreement with Mackintosh in practice (though not law) ended their outlawry. *Ib.*, 102–10; SRO GD 112/40/4/7/17, Breadalbane to ?, 28 Jan. 1698; GD 170/629/76, same to Barcaldine, 15 Jan. 1698.

38. *Ib; ib.*, 81, same to same, 2 Mar. 1698; Mactavish, *Commons of Argyll*, 61–2; NLS MS 1305 fol. 42, MacIain to Delvine, 27 Jan. 1697; *ib.*, fol. 44, same to same, 5 May 1697; Blair, Atholl MSS, Box 29 I (9) 202, Glengarry to Tullibardine, 20 Apr. 1697; *ib.*, 203, Atholl to same, 21 Apr. 1697.

39. *Ib.*, (8) 381, Glenlyon to same, 21 Dec. 1696; *ib.*, (10) 59, J. Flemyng to same, 5 Feb. 1698; Fountainhall, *Decisions*, i, 787 (*ib.*, 789 for a similarly dubious one); *Lairds of Glenlyon*, 65–6, 68–71; Drumlanrig, Queensberry Papers, Vol. 115, 85, Seafield to Argyll, 22 Jan. 1699; SRO GD 170/133/34, Glenlyon to Carwhin, 9 May 1698.

40. He himself was still ruthlessly harrying Campbell of Lawers. *Ib.*, 31, Interrogatories, 1698; Atholl, *Chronicles*, ii, 77; Blair, Atholl MSS, Box 29 I (9) 255, Atholl to Tullibardine, 15 June 1697; *ib.*, (10) 98, J. Flemyng to same, 1 Mar. 1698; *ib.*, Box 45 (1) 222, same to same, 14 Aug. 1701; *ib.*, 146, Ballechin jr to same, 20 July 1700; *ib.*, 2, Marchioness to Countess, 20 Jan. 1699; Cumnock, Dunbar House, Bute MSS, bundle A32, A. Campbell to Lawers, 19 Aug. 1703.

41. Perhaps, in Simon's case, rather than Edinburgh, Aberdeen University, where, he

later claimed, he was asked to become a don. Macaulay, *History*, v, 2144; *Major Fraser's MS*, ii, 199-200.

42. The standard life by W. C. Mackenzie was published in the same year as the Atholl *Chronicles*, but he could presumably have consulted the Blair archives during their preparation. He did not, and failed to use the *Chronicles* for his revised 1934 abbreviation (*Lovat of the '45*). The best means of drawing some truth from Simon's contradictory accounts is to look *not* for the most plausible but for incongruous details, appearing only in one version and suppressed in others.

43. *Wardlaw MS*, 244, 422-3; Atholl, *Chronicles*, i, 445, Atholl to Tullibardine, 22 Mar. 1698; Hooke, *Correspondence*, i, 131, 'A Short Account of the Quarell twixt the Family of Atholl and Lovat', Mar. 1704.

44. *Scots Peerage*, v, 521; Mackenzie, *Lovat*, 3n, 9-10; A. Mackenzie, *History of the Frasers of Lovat* (Inverness, 1896), 210.

45. *Ib.*, 352, Lovat to Frasers, 5 Apr. 1718; *Wardlaw MS*, 467, 511-14.

46. *Ib.*, 250, 253-4, 515; Hooke, *Correspondence*, i, 134, 'Short Account'; *Major Fraser's MS*, i, 102, 107; Mackenzie, *Lovat*, 7-9; *An Account of Captain Simon Fraser of Beaufort*, (1704), *Somers Tracts*, xii, 438.

47. *Ib.*, 439, 441; Hooke, *Correspondence*, i, 134, 'Short Account'; BL Add. 31,249 fol. 9v, 'A Short Account of the life of Simon, Lord Fraser of Lovat'; *ib.*, Add. 31,253 fol. 5, Memorandum for Perth.

48. See Chapter 11, n.204.

49. *Scots Peerage*, v, 535.

50. *Melvilles & Leslies*, ii, 53-4, William to Treasury, 7 Feb. 1695; Blair, Atholl MSS, Box 29 I (7) 104, Lovat to Murray, 11 Feb. 1695.

51. *Ib.*, (8) 13, Murray to Lady Murray, 14 Jan. 1696; *ib.*, 34, same to same, 23 Jan. 1696; Lovat, *Memoirs*, 21-3; Atholl, *Chronicles*, i, 365-6, Simon to Murray, 18 Jan. 1696; *ib.*, 366, Lt Col Hay to same, 22 Jan. 1696.

52. *Ib.*, 374, Murray to Lady Murray, 17 Mar. 1696; *Major Fraser's MS*, i, 103; Blair, Atholl MSS, Box 29 I (8) 115, 135, 145, 218, Simon to Murray, 15 Mar., 31 Mar., 7 Apr., c. 8 June 1696; *ib.*, 134, Lady Lovat to same, 30 Mar. 1696; *ib.*, 105, 113, 116, 132, Lady Murray to same, 6 Mar., 14 Mar., 16 Mar., 28 Mar. 1696.

53. *Ib.*, 105, 116; Atholl, *Chronicles*, i, 374, Lovat to same, 11 Mar. [1696]; *ib.*, 374-5, Simon to same, 15 Mar. 1696; *ib.*, 355; Lovat, *Memoirs*, 23-5.

54. The Atholl family later tried to claim that Simon forged these bonds in 1699-1700. *Ib.*, 25-6; *Account of Cpt. Simon*, *Somers Tracts*, xii, 440; Mackenzie, *Frasers*, 210-11.

55. Atholl, *Chronicles*, i, 355; *ib.*, 377-8, Simon to Murray, 30 June 1696; Blair, Atholl MSS, Box 29 I (8) 268, Ld James Murray to same, 10 July 1696; Lovat, *Memoirs*, 16.

56. Such an act was introduced in the 1696 session, but passed only some days after Lovat's death. *Ib.*, 27-9; APS, x, 12, 33; *Major Fraser's MS*, i, 104; Hooke, *Correspondence*, i, 131, 'Short Account of the Quarell'; BL Add. 31,249 fols. 6v-7, 'A Short Account of ... Simon'.

57. For convenience sake, this title will be given to the Dowager Lady Lovat, and the lands she was administering for her daughter will be referred to as hers.

58. By a retrospective decision (influenced by politics) of 1730, Beaufort was Lord Lovat, and Simon from this point Master of Lovat. He will nevertheless still be called 'Simon', to reflect contemporary reality and annoy his ghost. *Ib.*, fol. 7v; *Major Fraser's MS*, i, 107; SRO GD 158/964, 69-70, Marchmont to Atholl, 5 Dec. 1696; *ib.*, 73, same to Tullibardine, 5 Dec. 1696; Blair, Atholl MSS, Box 44/VI/224, Marchioness to Countess, 16 Oct. [1696].

59. *Ib.*, Box 29 I (9) 215, Dollery to Tullibardine, 27 Apr. 1697.

60. *Ib.*, 471, same to same, 30 Nov. 1697; Lovat, *Memoirs*, 30–7; *Major Fraser's MS*, i, 105–6; Hooke, *Correspondence*, i, 133–4, 'Short Account'; BL Add. 31,249 fols. 8–10, 'Short Account of . . . Simon'.

61. *Account of Captain Simon, Somers Tracts*, xii, 439; Blair, Atholl MSS, Box 29 I (9) 18, Countess to Tullibardine, 19 Jan. 1697; Atholl, *Chronicles*, i, 354–5; *ib.*, 380–1, Simon to same, 22 Feb., 23 Mar. 1697; BL Add. 31,251 fol. 1, same to Teviot, 7 Nov. 1701.

62. As Simon emphasised this to Perth, who would certainly be in close contact with his son, the story may be accepted. *Ib.*, Add. 31,253 fol. 5, Memorandum for Perth; Hooke, *Correspondence*, i, 132–3, 'Short Account'.

63. *Major Fraser's MS*, i, 107–8; Mackenzie, *Frasers*, 213–4.

64. Atholl, *Chronicles*, i, 394, Hill to Advocate, 12 Oct. 1697; Blair, Atholl MSS, Box 29 I (9) 215, Dollery to Tullibardine, 27 Apr. 1697; *ib.*, 366, same to same, 23 Oct. 1697.

65. *Ib.*, 279, Cpt. Steuart to same, 6 Aug. 1697; *ib.*, 297; Atholl to same, 31 Aug. 1697; *ib.*, Box 44/VI/254, [same] to same, 16 July 1697; Atholl, *Chronicles*, i, 389, Lady Lovat to same, 9 Sept. 1697; *ib.*, 389–90, Hill to same, 18 Sept. 1697; *Major Fraser's MS*, i, 107–8.

66. Simon claimed that the original proposal came from Atholl, and that his chief local agent, Fraser of Dunballoch the younger, won over only three inconsiderable Frasers, Kinneries (the Lovat chamberlain) Kyllachy (?) and Achnagairn. *Ib.*, 108–9; Lovat, *Memoirs*, 42–51; BL Add. 31,249 fols. 10v–11, 'Short Account of . . . Simon'; D. Warrand, *Some Fraser Pedigrees*, (Inverness, 1934), 3–4, 19, 28–9.

67. The wording of the 22 September bond makes it clear that the claim was made on *a priori* grounds.

68. *Ib.*, 45, 69, 74, 77, 79–81, 92, 98, 100, 110, 114, 117; *State Trials*, xiv, 352–3, 356–8, 364–6; *Major Fraser's MS*, i, 109–10; *Scots Peerage*, vii, 444; BL Add. 31,249 fols. 10v–11; Blair, Atholl MSS, Box 29 I (9) 494, Dollery to Tullibardine, 13 Dec. 1697.

69. The bond was later found on Fraser, although he claimed to have sent it (?a copy) to Saltoun. *Ib.; ib.*, 489, Sir P. Home to same, 13 Dec. 1697; *State Trials*, xiv, 353, 357.

70. SRO GD 170/629/55, [Breadalbane] to [Barcaldine], 25 Aug. 1696.

71. *Ib.*, 3037, Keppoch to J. Cameron, 14 Nov. 1696; GD 158/1104/6, Mackintosh to Marchmont, 4 Feb. 1698; Blair, Atholl MSS, Box 42 (1) 40–1, Keppoch's submission & petition, 1696; NLS MS 1305 fol. 52, Keppoch to Delvine, 1 Nov. 1696.

72. *Ib.*, fol. 68, same to same, 2 Dec. 1696; *Marchmont Papers*, iii, 117–18, Polwarth to Tullibardine, 28 Nov. 1696; *ib.*, 119–20, same to same, 29 Dec. 1696; *ib.*, 123, same to Ogilvie, 14 Jan. 1696; SRO GD 158/964, 62–3, same to same, 28 Nov. 1696; *ib.*, GD 112/43/1/2/8, [?Tarbat] to [Breadalbane], 2 Dec. 1696; *ib.*, PC 1/51, 28–9, 34–5, 80; *HMCR Roxburghe*, 144, Mackintosh to Polwarth, 30 Dec. 1696.

73. SRO GD 158/1104/4, same to same, 15 Feb. 1697; Blair, Atholl MSS, Box 29 I (9) 103, Keppoch to Tullibardine, 8 Mar. 1697; *ib.*, 258, same to same, 29 June 1697; *ib.*, 281, same to same, 12 Aug. 1697; *ib.*, 70, Dollery to same, 23 Feb. 1697; *ib.*, 112, same to same, 9 Mar. 1697.

74. *CSPD 1696*, 469, Pension, 23 Dec. 1696; *Carstares S.P.*, 466–7, Argyll to Carstares, 14 Mar. 1699.

75. SRO PC 1/51, 34–5; *ib.*, 1/52, 4; NLS MS 3550, Mackintoshes to ?, 19 Aug. 1697; Blair, Atholl MSS, Box 29 I (8) 182, Glengarry to Murray, 9 May 1696; *ib.*, (9) 202, same to same, 20 Apr. 1697; *ib.*, 268, Hill to same, 19 July 1697; *ib.*, 272, Cpt Steuart to same, 27 July, 1697.

76. *Ib.*, Box 45 (4) 123, Sir P. Scott to same, 30 Mar. 1704.

77. *Ib.*, Box 44/VI/243, Ld James Murray to same, 8 [July 1697]; *ib.*, 253, [Atholl] to same, 8 July [1697]; *ib.*, Box 29 I (9) 512, same to same, 20 Dec. 1697; *ib.*, (10) 79, same to

same, 22 Feb. [1698]; Lovat, *Memoirs*, 8–9.

78. Blair, Atholl MSS, Box 29 I (9) 454, Dollery to Tullibardine, 25 Nov. 1697; *ib.*, 457, same to same, 27 Nov. 1697; *ib.*, 471, same to same, 30 Nov. 1697; Atholl, *Chronicles*, i, 401, same to same, 4 Nov. 1697.

79. *Ib; ib.*, 409, same to same, 16 Nov. 1697; Blair, Atholl MSS, Box 29 I (9) 508, same to same, 18 Dec. 1697; *ib.*, 397, Ruglen to same, 4 Nov. 1697; *ib.*, 363 (*HMCR Athole*, 55), 385, 426, 447, Tarbat to same, 21 Oct., 30 Oct., 13 Nov., 23 Nov., 1697.

80. *Ib.*, 454, 457, Dollery to same, 25 Nov., 27 Nov. 1697; *ib.*, (10) 82, same to same, 22 Feb. 1698; Atholl, *Chronicles*, i, 438–9, Atholl to same, 15 Feb. [1698].

81. Blair, Atholl MSS, Box 29 I (9) 512, same to same, 20 Dec. 1697; *ib.*, 414, Dollery to same, 9 Nov. 1697.

82. BL Add. 31,249 fols. 11–12, 'Short Account of . . . Simon'.

83. *Ib*; Atholl, *Chronicles*, i, 391–2, Simon to Hill, etc., 8 Oct. [1697]; *ib.*, 409, Dollery to Tullibardine, 16 Nov. 1697; Lovat, *Memoirs*, 52–60; *Major Fraser's MS*, i, 110–11; *State Trials*, xiv, 353–4, 366, 368.

84. *Ib.*, 352, 354, 364, 366, 368, 370; *Thanes of Cawdor*, 390; NLS MS 1275 fol. 143, Erchitt to Delvine, 12 Aug. 1698 (falsely denying involvement).

85. *State Trials*, xiv, 355, 365, 367–8; *Major Fraser's MS*, i, 111; *HMCR Roxburghe*, 136, Steuart to Marchmont, 18 Oct. 1697; Atholl, *Chronicles*, i, 391–3, Simon to Hill, etc., 8 Oct. [1697]; *ib.*, 393–4, Hill to Tullibardine, 12 Oct. 1697; Blair, Atholl MSS, Box 29 I (9) 351, same to same, 13 Oct. 1697; *ib.*, 449, same to same, 23 Nov. 1697; *ib.*, 355, Nairne to same, 16 Oct. 1697; *ib.*, 354, Dollery to same, 16 Oct. 1697; *ib.*, 414, same to same, 9 Nov. 1697; *ib.*, 457, same to same, 27 Nov. 1697; *ib.*, 362, Steuart to same, 21 Oct. 1697.

86. The indictment claims that Lady Lovat was seized the same night Saltoun was captured, but the family letters in mid-October indicate otherwise; they probably wished at the trial to minimise her negotiations with Simon. *Ib; ib.*, 366, Dollery to same, 23 Oct. 1697; *ib.*, 449, same to same, 23 Nov. 1697; Atholl, *Chronicles*, i, 395, same to same, 19 Oct. 1697, Lady Lovat to Hill, 15 Oct. 1697; *ib.*, 401–2, Tullibardine to Hill, 4 Nov. 1697; *State Trials*, xiv, 354–5, 364–7.

87. *Ib.*, 355, 366–7; Fraser-Macintosh, *Letters*, 133, Saltoun to Robertson of Inches, 15 Oct. 1697; *Major Fraser's MS*, i, 112.

88. Atholl, *Chronicles*, i, 420, Atholl to Tullibardine, 9 Dec. 1697; Blair, Atholl MSS, Box 29 I (9) 507, Lady Nairne to same, 18 Dec. 1697; NLS MS 298 fol. 79v, 'Deffences for Simon Lord Lovitt Against the Accusation of Hamesucken and Rapt'.

89. *Fraser Papers*, 17, 29–33; *Major Fraser's MS*, i, 113–14; NLS MS 3161, Countess of Findlater to D. Crawford, 27 Oct. 1697.

90. SRO PC 1/51, 276–84; *HMCR Roxburghe*, 137, Dollery to Marchmont, 1 Nov. 1697; Atholl, *Chronicles*, i, 464, Tullibardine to Annandale, 9 Nov. 1697; *ib.*, 420, Atholl to Tullibardine, 9 Nov. 1697; *ib.*, 407, Dollery to same, 13 Nov 1697; Blair, Atholl MSS, Box 29 I (9) 408, same to same, 6 Nov. 1697; *ib.*, 385, Tarbat to same, 30 Oct. 1697; *ib.*, 398, Ruglen to same, 4 Nov. 1697; *ib.*, 512, Atholl to same, 20 Dec. 1697.

91. *Ib.*, 417, Ormiston to same, 11 Nov. 1697; *ib.*, Box 45 (13) 34, 'Keppoch's Expeditione'; Atholl, *Chronicles*, i, 406; *ib.*, 416–17, Cpt P. Murray to Tullibardine, 27 Nov. 1697; *ib.*, 407, Dollery to same, 13 Nov. 1697.

92. *Ib.*, 408, same to same, 16 Nov. 1697; SRO PC 1/51, 286–7.

93. *Ib.*, 274–5, 294–5; *CSPD 1697*, 421, 480; Atholl, *Chronicles*, i, 406, Dollery to Tullibardine, 9 Nov. 1697; Blair, Atholl MSS, Box 29 I (9) 392, Ormiston to Tullibardine, 2 Nov. 1697; *ib.*, bundle 1720, Tullibardine to [Selkirk], 15 Oct. 1697.

94. *Ib.*, Box 29 I (10) 158, Atholl to Tullibardine, 29 Apr. 1698.

95. For the Johnston case see Chapter 8, p. 267. Sir Walter Scott, *Rob Roy*, Introduction & App. V; Scott, *Prose Works*, xx, (Edinburgh, 1835), 63-4, Review of *Culloden Papers*; M. Weiner, *Matters of Felony* (London, 1967), 80-98, 139, 169, 188-92.

96. *Earls of Cromartie*, i, 124, Hill to Tarbat, 1 Nov. 1697; SRO GD 158/1108, same to Marchmont, 5 Nov. 1697; *Culloden Papers*, 23-4, same to Culloden, 7 Nov. 1697.

97. *Ib.*, 23, Simon to same, 26 Oct. 1697. At least in Lady Grange's case she was too far off for her husband's acquaintances to free her personally. M. Edgeworth, *Castle Rackrent* (Oxford, 1969), 29-30, 125.

98. *Carstares S.P.*, 362, Ogilvie to Carstares, 5 Nov. 1697; NLS MS 3161 fols. 3v-4, Countess of Findlater to D. Crawford, 27 Oct. 1697; Atholl, *Chronicles*, i, 455.

99. Rev. James Fraser's son joined Simon in the attack on the Atholl men in June 1698. *Ib.*, 419-20, Atholl to Tullibardine, 9 Dec. 1697; *Major Fraser's MS*, i, 114-15; Scott, *Fasti*, vii, 39; NLS MS 298 fols, 75v, 83v-84, 'Deffences'; *State Trials*, xiv, 359.

100. *Ib.*, 368; *HMCR Roxburghe*, 138, Forbes to Marchmont, 19 Nov. 1697; *Carstares S.P.*, 434-6, Frasers to Argyll; Atholl, *Chronicles*, i, 422, Ld James Murray to Tullibardine, 13 Dec. [1697]; Blair, Atholl MSS, Box 29 I (9) 480, Nairne to same, 9 Dec. 1697; NLS MS 3161 fol. 2v, Countess of Findlater to D. Crawford, 27 Oct. 1697. SRO RH 15/13/27 seems to be Argyll's reply to the Frasers' letter.

101. *Thanes of Cawdor*, 390-1, Cpt. McCulloch to Cpt. Maclean, 16 Mar. 1698; Lovat, *Memoirs*, 77; *Major Fraser's MS*, i, 116-19.

102. Blair, Atholl MSS, Box 45 (13) 34, 'Keppoch's Expeditione'; *ib.*, Box 29 I (9) 467, Glengarry to Ld James Murray, 30 Nov. 1697; Atholl, *Chronicles*, i, 407-8, same to same, 14 Nov. 1697.

103. *Ib.*, 422, Ld James Murray to Tullibardine, 13 Dec. [1697]; *HMCR Roxburghe*, 138, Forbes to Marchmont, 19 Nov. 1697; *Culloden Papers*, 24, Simon to Culloden, 23 Nov. 1697; *Fraser Papers*, 29-30; *State Trials*, xiv, 370; *Major Fraser's MS*, i, 119-22.

104. In a passage in his *Memoirs* close to other statements which are certainly lies (ib., 123-6), Major Fraser claims that his brother Culduthel escorted Lady Lovat to Castle Dounie; that she went only under protest, to declare her marriage; and that her brothers beat her up for her pains and imprisoned Culduthel for trying to help her. However, all the other accounts (including Simon's, which would have exploited this), agree that it was his non-Fraser allies who brought her. Macgill, *Old Ross-shire*, ii, 24, Declaration, 16 Nov. 1697; *State Trials*, xiv, 365, 368-9; *Hooke, Negotiations*, i, 138-9, 'Short Account'; NLS MS 298 fols. 77v-78, 'Deffences'; Atholl, *Chronicles*, i, 410, Lt-Col Bruce to Tullibardine, 18 Nov. 1697.

105. *Ib.*, 411; Blair, Atholl MSS, Box 29 I (9) 512, Atholl to same, 20 Dec. 1697; *ib.*, 507, Lady Nairne to Countess, 18 Dec. 1697; *Fraser Papers*, 38-9, Testificate, 18 Nov. 1697; Hooke, *Negotiations*, i 139; *HMCR Roxburghe*, 138, Forbes to Marchmont, 19 Nov. 1697.

106. *Ib.*, 138-9, same to same, 26 Nov. 1697; *Fraser Papers*, 40, same to [same], 4 Dec. 1697; *State Trials*, xiv, 365, 368-70.

107. Blair, Atholl MSS, Box 29 I (9) 512, Atholl to Tullibardine, 20 Dec. 1697.

108. *Ib.*, 494, Dollery to same, 13 Dec. 1697; *ib.*, Box 45 (1) 170, Atholl to Marchioness, [?Nov. 1700]; Atholl, *Chronicles*, i, 420-1, same to Tullibardine, 9 Dec. 1697; *ib.*, 428-9, Lady Lovat to Countess, 7 Jan. 1698; *Culloden Papers*, 24, Simon to Culloden, 23 Nov. 1697; Hooke, *Negotiations*, i, 139; *Major Fraser's MS*, i, 126-7; NLS MS 298 fols. 77v-78, 'Deffences'. For a similar use of forged letters in the most notorious Irish abduction case, Weiner, *Matters of Felony*, 146-8.

109. *HMCR Roxburghe*, 138, Forbes to Marchmont, 19 Nov. 1697; *Fraser Papers*, 39-41, same to [same], 4 Dec. 1697; SRO PC 1/51, 298-9, 312, 323-4, 355-6, 359, 400-2; GD

158/964, 273, Orders, 19 Nov. 1697; *ib.*, 280, Marchmont to Tullibardine, 30 Nov. 1697; Blair, Atholl MSS, Box 29 I (9) 449, Hill to same, 23 Nov. 1697; *ib.*, 466, Dollery to same, 27 Nov. 1697.

110. Atholl, *Chronicles*, i, 430, same to same, 25 Jan. 1698; *ib.*, 432, Atholl to same, 28 Jan. [1698]; *ib.*, 438, same to same, 15 Jan. [1698]; SRO GD 158/964, 305, Marchmont to same, 1 Jan. 1697 [8]; *ib.*, PC 1/51, 353, 367.

111. Atholl, *Chronicles*, i, 428, Ld James Murray to Tullibardine, 7 Jan. 1698; *ib.*, 425, Blair, Atholl MSS, Box 29 I (9) 512, Atholl to same, 20 Dec. 1697.

112. Lovat, *Memoirs*, 73; Grant, *Macleods*, 330-1, 333; Atholl, *Chronicles*, i, 420, Atholl to Tullibardine, 9 Dec. 1697; *ib.*, 423-4, Major Anderson to same, 15 Dec. 1697.

113. *Fraser Papers*, 41-4, same to [same], 27 Dec. 1697, 17 Jan. 1698, 24 Jan. 1698.

114. Atholl, *Chronicles*, i, 420, Atholl to same, 9 Dec. 1697; *ib.*, 432-4, same to same, 28 Jan. [1698]; Blair, Atholl MSS, Box 29 I (9) 512, same to same, 20 Dec. 1697; *ib.*, 520, Dollery to same, 21 Dec. 1697; *ib.*, (10) 20, same to same, 13 Jan. 1698; SRO PC 1/51, 332-3; SRO GD 170/629/76, [Breadalbane] to Carwhin, 15 Jan. 1698 [9].

115. Fergusson, 'Early History of Strathardle', *TGSI*, xxiii, 170; Atholl *Chronicles*, i, 442, same to same, 5 Mar. 1698; *ib.*, 425, Atholl to same, 20 Dec. 1697; *ib.*, 434-5, Marchioness to same, 2 Feb. [1698]; *ib.*, 437, Ld James Murray to same, 14 Feb. 1698.

116. *Ib.*, 436-7; *ib.*, 435-6, same to Atholl, 5 Feb. 1698; *ib.*, 440-1, same to same, 16 Feb. 1698; *ib.*, 441-2, Atholl to Tullibardine, 4 Mar. [1698]; Blair, Atholl MSS, Box 45 (13) 34, 'Keppoch's Expeditione'.

117. Mackenzie, *Frasers*, 232n; Atholl, *Chronicles*, i, 442, Dollery to Tullibardine, 5 Mar. 1698.

118. *Ib.*, 420, Atholl to same, 9 Dec. 1697; *ib.*, 443-5, same to same, 22 Mar. 1698; *ib.*, 447, Ld James Murray to same, 9 Apr. 1698; Hooke, *Negotiations*, i, 137-8, 'Short Account of the Quarell'; NLS MS 298 fol. 67-8, Grounds for raising a criminal libel against Atholl.

119. SRO GD 112/40/4/7/13, Hill to Breadalbane, 23 Dec. 1697; *ib.*, 111, same to same, 22 Dec. 1697.

120. Blair, Atholl MSS, Box 29 I (9) 512, Atholl to Tullibardine, 20 Dec. 1697; *ib.*, 531, Annandale to same, 23 Dec. 1697; *Annandale Book*, ii, 141, Lt- Col Reid to Annandale, 30 Dec. 1697; *ib.*, 143, Tullibardine to same, 31 Dec. 1697; *ib.*, 192, Teviot to same, 4 Dec. '1669' [1697].

121. *Ib.*, 150, same to same, 20 Jan. 1698; *ib.*, 149, Row to same, 18 Jan. 1698; Macpherson, *Original Papers*, i, 473, Memorial, 4 Jan. 1694 (NS); C. Cole, *Historical and Political Memoirs* (London, 1735), 62-3, Manchester to Jersey, 29 Oct. 1699; SRO PC 1/51, 567; Blair, Atholl MSS, Box 29 I (9) 528, Ruglen to Tullibardine, 23 Dec. 1697; *ib.*, (10) 12, Marchmont to same, 10 Jan. 1698.

122. *Ib.*, 128, Ormiston to same, 24 Mar. 1698; *CSPD 1698*, 57, 65; *HMCR Roxburghe*, 146, Ogilvie to Marchmont, 15 Feb. 1698; Dalton, *English Army Lists*, iii, 414-15; SRO PC 1/51, 328-9, 360-1; *Seafield Corr.*, 229-30, Maitland to Seafield, 15 May 1698.

123. *Ib.*, 230; SRO GD 112/40/4/7/25, same to Breadalbane, 4 May 1698; *Carstares S.P.*, 492-3, Seafield to Carstares, 17 Aug. 1699; Cameron, 'Clan Cameron', *TGSI*, xlvii, 408.

124. *Seafield Corr.*, 230; Kilgour, *Lochaber in War & Peace*, 326-8, Information on the Governors' abuses.

125. SRO GD 158/1104/6, Mackintosh to Marchmont, 4 Feb. 1698; NLS MS 1305 fol. 55, Keppoch to Delvine, 2 Nov. 1697.

126. *Ib.*, fol. 56v, same to same, 23 Aug. 1698; SRO GD 170/629/75, [Breadalbane] to

Barcaldine, 14 [?Mar. 1698]; Blair, Atholl MSS, Box 45 (13) 34, 'Keppoch's Expeditione'; Atholl, *Chronicles*, i, 444, Atholl to Tullibardine, 22 Mar. 1698.

127. *HMCR Athole*, 58, Tarbat to same, 1 Mar. 1698; Blair, Atholl MSS, Box 29 I (10) 82, Dollery to same, 22 Mar. 1698; *ib.*, 87, D. Moncreiffe to same, 24 Feb. 1698; *ib.*, 89 [Atholl] to same, 25 Feb. [1698]; *ib.*, 9, Keppoch to [Tarbat], 11 Feb. 1698; SRO PC 1/51, 368-83.

128. *HMCR Roxburghe*, 144-5, Mackintosh to Marchmont, 14 May 1698; *ib.*, 145, same to same, 15 Aug. 1698; NLS MS 1305 fol. 56, Keppoch to Delvine, 23 Aug. 1698; *ib.*, fol. 57, same to same, 7 May 1698; *Seafield Corr.*, 230-1, Maitland to Seafield, 17 May 1698.

129. *Ib.*, 231; PRO PC 1/51, 395-6, 422-3; NLS MS 5136 fol. 52v, Dollery to Ld James Murray, 19 May 1698; Blair, Atholl MSS, Box 44/I/4, T. Ross's declaration, 26 May 1698; *ib.*, Box 29 I (10) 158, Atholl to Tullibardine, 29 Apr. 1698.

130. 300 is Major Fraser's estimate; Simon, typically, makes it 5-600. Atholl, *Chronicles*, i, 450, Ld James Murray to same, '26' June 1698; *Major Fraser's MS*, i, 128; *State Trials*, xiv, 360; NLS MS 298 fol. 65v, Terms accepted by Murrays, 16 June 1698: Lovat, *Memoirs*, 78, 86.

131. *Ib.*, 78-79; Warrand, *Some Fraser Pedigrees*, 13-14, 74, 96, 100; SRO PC 1/51, 440; *State Trials*, xiv, 358-9, 361, 367, 371-2.

132. *Ib.*, 361, 365, 367; Lovat, *Memoirs*, 87-96; *Major Fraser's MS*, i, 129; MS 298 fol. 65, Terms accepted by Murrays, 16 June 1698.

133. SRO PC 1/51, 440-2, 448-9; Steele, ii, S3155; Atholl, *Chronicles*, i, 450, Row to Atholl, 2 July 1698; *ib.*, 451, Cpt Pumphry to same, 6 July 1698; *ib.*, 451-4.

134. *Ib.*, 446, Tullibardine to same, 31 Mar. 1698; *HMCR Hope-Johnstone*, 102, Johnston to Annandale, 27 Nov. 1697; Riley, *King William*, 122-3; *Carstares S.P.*, 610, Ormiston to Carstares, 10 Aug. 1698.

135. *Ib.*, 426, Seafield to same, 20 Aug. 1698; *ib.*, 441, same to same, 10 Sept. 1698; Riley, *King William*, 134; Blair, Atholl MSS, bundle 1720, Tullibardine to [Hamilton], 8 Sept. 1698.

136. *Ib.*, Box 29 I (10) 174, [Countess of Orkney] to Countess, 2 July 1698; *CSPD 1698*, 347, William to PCS, 9 July 1698; Riley, *King William*, 127.

137. *Ib.*, 125-8; *Carstares S.P.*, 391, Seafield to Carstares, 16 July 1698; *ib.*, 398, same to same, 21 July 1698; *ib.*, 426, same to same, 20 Aug. 1698.

138. *Ib.*, 441-2, same to same, 10 Sept. 1698; *ib.*, 431-2, Argyll to same, 3 Sept. 1698; *ib.*, 449, same to same, 27 Sept. 1698; *Marchmont Papers*, iii, 170-1, Marchmont to William, 3 Sept. 1698; Atholl, *Chronicles*, i, 455-6, Tullibardine's report, Aug. 1698; *ib.*, 457-8, same to Atholl, 17 Nov. 1698; SRO PC 1/51, 467-8, 519; Blair, Atholl MSS, bundle 1720, same to [Hamilton], 8 Sept. 1698; Countess to [same], 8 Sept. 1698; same to [Selkirk], 30 Aug. 1698.

139. *Ib.*, Box 29 I (10) 215, J. Flemyng to ?, 5 Dec., 1698; Riley, *King William*, 129.

140. One of the witnesses was referred to as 'of Culbokie' when he testified, but only as 'of Guisachan' (the last remaining family property) when indicted — one example of the prosecution's policy of minimising the status of Simon's supporters. *State Trials*, xiv, 349-52, 356, 358-9, 362-5, 367; Warrand, *Some Fraser Pedigrees*, 6.

141. Mackenzie, *Frasers*, 694, Bond, 9 Aug. 1698; NLS MS 1275 fol. 143, Erchitt to Delvine, 12 Aug. 1698.

142. Blair, Atholl MSS, Box '71' II 18, Tullibardine to Saltoun, 8 'Sept.' [1698].

143. *Ib.*, Box 44/VI/259, Atholl to Tullibardine, 17 Oct. [? 1698]]; Atholl, *Chronicles*, i, 454-5, Lady Nairne to Countess, 16 Aug. 1698; *Just Recs.*, i, xiv; *Carstares S.P.*, 431-3, Argyll to Carstares, 3 Sept. 1698.

144. *Ib.*, 449, same to same, 27 Sept. 1698; *ib.*, 437, Seafield to same, 6 Sept. 1698; *Fraser*

Papers, 23–36; Blair, Atholl MSS, bundle 1720, Tullibardine to Hamilton, 8 Sept. 1698; *State Trials*, xiv, 362–3, 372–8.

145. *Ib.*, 363, 371–2; *Major Fraser's MS*, i, 132–4 (date corrected from mention of Gordon's imprisonment).

146. Fountainhall, *Decisions*, ii, 37, 47–8; SRO GD 50/26/13/124, Breadalbane to Carwhin, 14 Jan. 1698[9]; Drumlanrig, Queensberry Papers, Vol. 115, 85, Seafield to Argyll, 22 Jan. 1699; Blair, Atholl MSS, Box 45 (1) 55, J. Flemyng to Atholl, 7 Dec. 1699; Atholl, *Chronicles*, i, 265–6.

147. *ib.*, 461–6, 477.

148. Blair, Atholl MSS, Box 29 I (10) 125, Atholl to Tullilbardine, 22 Mar. 1698.

149. *APS*, x, 209, 215–18, 223–4; *HMCR Roxburghe*, 149, G. Gordon to Marchmont, 6 May 1699; Forbes Leith, *Scottish Catholics*, ii, 172–6, 177–8, 182–9, 191–2; Lenman, *Jacobite Risings*, 228; Maclean, *Counter-Reformation*, 153–5 (numbers unreliable), 194–5; MacWilliam, 'A Highland Mission', *IR*, xxiv, 85–6; SRO PC 1/52, 217–18.

150. *More Culloden Papers*, 246–7, Lady Seaforth (sr) to Culloden, 24 July 1697; *Earls of Cromartie*, i, 126–7, same to Tarbat, 13 Dec. 1697; *HMCR Roxburghe*, 133, Seaforth to Polwarth, 2 Apr. 1697; Blair, Atholl MSS, Box 29 I (9) 139, Sir G. Elliott to Tullibardine, 18 Mar. 1697; *ib.*, 315, Seaforth to same, 22 Sept. 1697.

151. *Ib; ib.*, 285, Lady Seaforth (sr) to same, 16 Aug. 1697; *ib.*, 377 (*HMCR Athole*, 55), Dollery to same, 27 Oct. 1697; *APS*, ix, 437; *ib.*, x, 84–5, 92; Maclean, *Counter-Reformation*, 308; SRO PC 1/51, 247.

152. *Ib.*, 258; Blair, Atholl MSS, Box 29 I (9) 315, Seaforth to Tullibardine, 22 Sept. 1697; *ib.*, 377, Dollery to same, 27 Oct. 1697; *Earls of Cromartie*, i, 125–6, Mackenzies to Tarbat, 1 Dec. 1697.

153. *Ib.*, 63–4, Seaforth to same, 17 Jan. [1698]; *More Culloden Papers*, 249–50, Culloden to [?Marchmont], 18 Jan. 1698; *ib.*, 250–1, A. Simson to Culloden, 16 Feb. 1698; SRO PC 1/51, 285, 309, 317–18, 325–7, 358–9, 366–7, 389–90, 402, 442, 446, 467.

154. Drumlanrig, Queensberry Papers, Vol.115, 80, Tarbat to Queensberry, 31 Oct. 1698.

155. The claim in the *Scots Peerage* (vii, 510) that the Fourth Earl died in France is groundless.*More Culloden Papers*, 252–7, letters on the Seaforth family, 1701; SRO PC 1/51, 472–3, 475, 562–3; *ib.*, 1/52, 82, 85, 329; NLS MS 1333 fol. 139, C. Mackenzìe to Delvine, 7 Apr. 1701; *ib.*, MS 1356 fol. 13, Lady Seaforth (sr) to same, 5 Mar 1701; *ib.*, fol. 99, Seaforth to same, 22 May 1700; *HMCR Roxburghe*, 147–8, Con to Marchmont, Dec. 1698–May 1699.

156. *Ib.*, 148–9, G. Gordon to same, Apr.–May 1699; *ib.*, 150, Steuart to same, 8 Apr. 1699; *CSPD 1699–1700*, 238; *ib.*, *1700–2*, 1–2; *Carstares S.P.*, 484, Seafield to Carstares, 2 Aug. 1699; SRO PC 1/51, 383, 572–3, 587, 591–2; *ib.*, 1/52, 96–7.

157. *APS*, x, 209, 222, 228–30, 232, 244, 252; Sir D. Hume of Crossriggs, *A Diary of the Proceedings in the Parliament and Privy Council*, ed. J. Hope (Bannatyne Club, 1828), 25, 48, 57–8, 65–6; Fountainhall, *Decisions*, ii, 85, 93–4; *Seafield Corr.*, 318–19, Seafield to Carstares, 1 Jan. 1701; *Spalding Club Misc.*, iv, 165–6, Macphersons' Vindication, 1699; Macpherson, *Loyall Dissuasive*, 170–3.

158. *Ib.*, 174–5; *APS*, x, 265–6, 268; *CSPD 1700–2*, 196, William to Queensberry, Argyll, 10 Jan. 1701; Drumlanrig, Queensberry Papers, Vol. 111, 18, [Gordon's] Declaration; *ib.*, bundle 1154, Pringle to Queensberry, 11 Jan. 1701.

159. Riley, *King William*, 144, 155.

160. SRO GD 50/26/13/124, Breadalbane to Carwhin, 15 Jan. 1698(9); Blair, Atholl MSS, Box 45 (1) 235, Glengarry to [Tullibardine], 4 Sept. 1701; SRO PC 1/51, 590.

161. *Carstares S.P.*, 570, J. Stewart to Carstares, 18 July 1700; *ib.*, 618, Mar to same, 17 Aug. 1700; *ib.*, 647–8, Argyll to same, 15 July 1700.

162. Lovat, *Memoirs*, 97; Mackenzie, *Frasers*, 242–3; Blair, Atholl MSS, Box 29 I (10) 217, Marchioness to Countess, [Dec. 1698]; SRO PC 1/51, 499.

163. *Ib.*, 546, 592; *ib.*, 1/52, 40, 55–6, 62–3, 91, 97–8; *Fraser Papers*, 36–7; *Carstares S.P.*, 482, Seafield to Carstares, 8 July 1699; *ib.*, 598, Argyll to same, 8 Aug. 1700.

164. The Atholl correspondent who reported Simon's arrival thought, apparently wrongly, that he had already been in Holland. *Ib.*, 580, J. Fraser to same, 29 July 1700; Atholl, *Chronicles*, i, 473–4, Graeme to Tullibardine, 11 Nov. 1699; Blair, Atholl MSS, Box 45 (1) 156, Carmichael to same, 26 Sept. 1700; Hooke, *Negotiations*, i, 140, 'Short Account'; Lovat, *Memoirs*, 98–100.

165. Simon's description of his reception (only in his memoirs of c. 1714) is detailed but incredible; and Lockhart denies that he was there in James's lifetime. In 1702, he was to write to the Duke of Perth that he had never had a chance to show his affection for James until then, which seems to imply that he had not risked a visit before. There is no trace of one in surviving Jacobite documents or the reports of the Williamite spies, who had by now so thoroughly penetrated St Germain that it would fairly certainly have wrecked his chances of a remission. *Ib.*, 101–4; *Lockhart Papers*, i, 79; BL Add. 31,253 fol. 5v, [Simon] to [Perth, c. Nov. 1702].

166. Simon's account is, as usual, a lie. *CSPD 1700–2*, 110–11, Remission, 22 Aug. 1700; *Carstares S.P.*, 580, J. Fraser to Carstares, 29 July 1700; *Account of Captain Simon, Somers Tracts*, xii, 439; Lovat, *Memoirs*, 104–5.

167. *Culloden Papers*, 28, Argyll to Culloden, 5 Sept. 1700; SRO GD 1/658, 31.

168. Blair, Atholl MSS, Box 45 (13) 34, 'Keppoch's expeditione'.

169. *Carstares S.P.*, 498–9, Seafield to Carstares, 3 Oct. 1699; NLS MS 1305, fol. 61, Keppoch to Delvine, 6 Oct. 1699.

170. *Ib.*, fol. 62, same to same, 1 June 1700; *ib.*, fol. 63, same to same, 5 July 1700; Macdonald, *Clan Donald*, ii, 788–9, Agreement, 22 May 1700; Fraser-Macintosh, *Letters*, 146–7, Bond, 3 Aug. 1700; Dunlop, 'A Chief and his Lawyer', *TGSI*, xlv, 264; SRO PC 1/52, 86, 118; *Mackintosh Muniments*, 147, Mackintosh's deputation, 18 May 1700 *ib.*, 149, Obligation & articles, 28 Aug. 1702.

171. *Ib.*; *Carstares S.P.*, 608–10, Ormiston to Carstares, 10 Aug 1700; *Seafield Corr.*, 315–16, Maitland to Seafield, 26 Nov. 1700; *More Culloden Papers*, 273, Seafield to Forbes, 8 Jan. 1702; SRO PC 1/52, 136, 143, 272, 386; NLS MS 1305 fol. 66, Keppoch to Delvine, 6 Jan. 1703; *ib.*, fol. 70, same to same, 4 Jan. 1704.

172. Fraser-Macintosh, *Letters*, 148, same to Macphail, 8 Oct. 1708; *ib.*, 147, Sir D. Macdonald to Mackintosh, 15 May 1707; Macdonald, *Clan Donald*, ii, 656; NLS MS 1247 fol. 72, Breadalbane to Delvine, 25 Mar. 1709.

173. *Hist. Papers*, i, 3, Committee report, 3 Dec. 1699; *ib.*, 19, Forbes's commission to Auchintoul, 3 Jan. 1700; *ib.*, 20–2, Heritors' bonds, 26 Apr. 1700; *More Culloden Papers*, 266, Lady Culloden to Culloden, 1700; SRO PC 1/52, 50, 150.

174. *CSPD 1700–2*, 24–6, Instructions, 25 Apr. 1700; SRO PC 1/52, 235–6; *APS*, x, App., 34, 39–40.

175. *Ib.*, 96–7; *APS*, x, 241, 258, 268; *More Culloden Papers*, 267–8, Scroll act; Drumlanrig, Queensberry Papers, Vol. 111, 42, Queensberry to [Argyll, 1700]; Hume of Crossrigg, *Diary*, 66, 73–5.

176. *Ib.*, 61–2; *APS*, x, App. 93–4; *CSPD 1700–2*, 375–7, Commissions, 24 June 1701; *Earls of Cromartie*, i, 185, Tullibardine to Cromartie, 11 Feb. 1703; SRO PC 1/52, 276.

177. *Ib.*, 178, 259, 268, 272, 295; *CSPD 1700–2*, 337–45, Justiciary Commission, 30 May

1701; Fountainhall, *Decisions*, ii, 140, 148.

178. *HMCR Mar & Kellie*, 223-4, Mar to Seafield, 17 Oct. 1701; *ib.*, 224, Seafield to Mar, 25 Oct. 1701; *Culloden Papers*, 28, same to Culloden, 30 Dec. 1701; *HMCR Hamilton Supplement*, 147, J. Hamilton to Hamilton, 30 Oct. 1701; *ib.*, 148, same to same, 13 Dec. 1701; *Seafield Corr.*, 340-1, J. Ogilvie to Findlater, 8 Dec. 1701.

179. *Hist. Papers*, i, 26, Northern commission's petition [1702]; *More Culloden Papers*, 272-3, Brodie to Culloden, 8 Jan. 1702.

180. *Ib.*, 270-7, letters on Alasdair Mor, 1701-2; *Hist. Papers*, i, 24-7, papers on same; *Seafield Corr.*, 341-2, Kintore to Findlater, 8 Dec. 1701; *ib.*, 343, Forbes to same, 10 Dec. 1701; *ib.*, 345, W. Blake to same, 13 Jan. 1702; *ib.*, 346, same to same, 29 Jan. 1702; *CSPD 1702-3*, 15, Warrant, 28 Mar. 1702; SRO PC 1/52, 286-7, 307, 309-10, 323-5, 332-4, 384-5, 422-3, 435.

181. Macdonald, *Clan Donald*, iii, 427; SRO PC1/52, 445-6, 486.

182. *Ib.*, 372, 434; *APS*, xi, 14, 25, 27; *CSPD 1702-3*, 353-5, Justiciary Commission, 31 Dec. 1702.

183. His claim that Lord Advocate Steuart supported him in this is false; he was shortly to write reproaching him as one of his chief persecutors. Hooke, *Correspondence*, i, 138, 140-1, 'Short Account'; BL Add. 31,251 fol. 2, Simon to Steuart, [1701]; NLS MS 298 fols. 67-8, Grounds for a criminal libel; Blair, Atholl MSS, Box 45 (1) 168, Marchioness to Col Stanley, 29 Oct. 1700; *ib.*, Box 44/VI/315, same to Countess, [Oct. 1700].

184. Atholl, *Chronicles*, i, 481, same to same, 1700; *Trials of Simon afterwards Lord Fraser of Lovat, 1698, 1700*, ed. Sir W. A. Fraser (Edinburgh, 18?), 87-9; Blair, Atholl MSS, Box 45 (1) 170, Atholl to Marchioness, [?Nov. 1700].

185. *Ib*; Lovat, *Memoirs*, 106-10; Hooke, *Correspondence*, i, 141-2, 'Short Account'; *Major Fraser's MS*, i, 129-31; NLS MS 298 fols. 75, 78-80, 87, 'Deffences'; BL Add. 31,251 fol. 2, Simon to Steuart, [1701]; *Fraser Papers*, 37.

186. *Ib.*, 37-8; Atholl, *Chronicles*, i, 482-3; Blair, Atholl MSS, Box 45 (1) 182, Lady Nairne to Countess of Tullibardine, 21 Feb. 1701.

187. At St Germain, Middleton was to be his main enemy; and Melfort, Middleton's implacable opponent (just exiled, but still dominating his brother Perth) considered Hamilton one of Jacobitism's main assets. *LJ*, xvi, 599-600; Mackenzie, *Frasers*, 255; *Carstares S.P.*, 695, Simon to Carstares, 20 June 1701; SRO GD 26/xiii/116, same to [Leven], 29 Apr. 1701; *ib.*, 117, same to [same], 29 Aug. 1701; BL Add. 31,251 fols. 1-2, same to Annandale, Teviot, Steuart, Ramsey, [1701].

188. *Ib;* *ib.*, Add. 31,253 fol. 5v, same to Perth, n.d; Hooke, *Correspondence*, i, 142-3, 'Short Account'.

189. *Account of Captain Simon, Somers Tracts*, xii, 440; SRO GD 26/xiii/117, Simon to [Leven], 29 Aug. 1701; Blair, Atholl MSS, Box 45 (1) 264, Countess to Lady Leven, 24 Oct. 1701; *ib.*, 218, R. Fraser to Tullibardine, 11 Aug. 1701; *ib.*, 255, [Atholl] to same, 1 Oct. 1701; *ib.*, Box 44/VI/314, [same] to same, 7 Oct. [?1700]; *ib.*, Box 45 (1) 261, J. Flemyng to same, 21 Oct. 1701.

190. *Ib;* *ib.*, bundle 683, Simon to Glendaruel, 23 Sept. 1701; Mackenzie, *Frasers;* 252-3, 255.

191. *Ib.*, 253-4; Mackenzie, *Lovat*, 51-2; SRO PC 1/52, 346-7; Blair, Atholl MSS, Box 45 (2) 102, Dunmore to Tullibardine, 14 Apr. 1702.

192. One version, written about the same time as the Inverness one, has him gather his men — 1,000! — but be dissuaded by his friends from a public declaration. *Ib; Annandale Book*, ii, 214, Simon to Annandale, 19 Mar. 1702; Lovat, *Memoirs*, 115-16; Hooke, *Correspondence*, i, 143, 'Short Account'; BL Add. 31,250 fol. 1, Memorandum; *ib.*, Add.

31,253 fol. 5v, Memorandum for Perth.

193. *Lairds of Glenlyon*, 83–4; *Account of the Depredations*, 125.

194. *LJ*, xvii, 405, Glendaruel's account, 24 Dec. 1703; Lovat, *Memoirs*, 116–18; BL Add. 31,250 fol. 1, Memorandum; *ib.*, Add. 31,251 fol. 3, Simon to 'Right Hon.'; *ib.*, fol. 4, Memorial to Rochester; Blair, Atholl MSS, Box 45 (2) 102, Dunmore to Tullibardine, 14 Apr. [1702]; *ib.*, 107, P. Scott to same, 17 Apr. 1702.

195. Had he known of it earlier, he would surely have mentioned it in one of his letters. *Ib.*, 128, Lady Nairne to Countess, 'Sunday'; *Scots Peerage*, v, 535–6; BL Add. 31,251 fol. 3, Simon to 'Right Hon'; *ib.*, fol. 5, same to Argyll, 2 May 1702.

196. Grant, *Macleods*, 334–5; NLS MS 1250 fol. 32, Chisholm to Delvine, 25 June 1702.

197. *LJ*, xvii, 451, Queensberry to Anne, 25 Sept. 1703.

198. Mackenzie, *Lovat*, 54–5, 59, 63, 70–1.

199. *Major Fraser's MS*, i, 147–8; Mackenzie, *Frasers*, 264–6; SRO PC 1/52, 428–31; Blair, Atholl MSS, Box 45 (2) 138, Prestonhall to Atholl, 16 June 1702; *ib.*, 163 (Atholl, *Chronicles*, i, 497–8), R. Fraser to Tullibardine, 12 Aug. 1702.

200. *Ib*; NLS MS 1275 fol. 15, Fraser of Balmain to Delvine, 25 Aug. 1702; SRO PC 1/52, 407–8, 442–4, 449–50.

201. *Ib.*, 502; *Scots Peerage*, v, 536; BL Add. 31,253 fol. 3, Simon to Perth, n.d.

202. *LJ*, xvii, 427, Simon to Culduthel jr, 17 Dec. 1703; *ib.*, 428, same to Frasers, 15 Dec. 1703.

203. Macpherson, *Original Papers*, i, 665, James Murray's Report, 22 Feb. 1704.

204. *Ib.*, 630.

205. *Major Fraser's MS*, i, 135, 148–52; Mackenzie, *Frasers*, 291–3; Blair, Atholl MSS, Box 45 (4) 52, Sir P. Home to Atholl, 10 Feb. 1704.

Conclusion

If Montrose's and Alasdair's campaigns had brought the highlanders back into Scottish and British politics, the first Jacobite rising brought them directly into European affairs. France and its Continental enemies took their activities and potential into serious account when planning their own campaigns, and were to do so, although at greater intervals and with growing scepticism, until the '45. For the first time also, the highlanders entered lowland politics not merely as an unpredictable force called upon, usually by the 'Cavaliers', in civil wars and crises, but as one of the subjects of everyday divisions between the new parliamentary factions. Within a few years, James Johnston was arousing the indignation of Whig 'presbyterians' over the massacre of one of the West Highland clans, their traditional enemies (while simultaneously keeping fear of them alive), in his valiant attempt to reduce aristocratic power in politics.

Popular interest in Glencoe will always be primarily in the question of who was to blame for planning, ordering and executing it. This is largely a search for answers 'relevant' to later politics. The Massacre, carried out by one group of Scottish highlanders upon another, upon orders given by a Scottish Secretary and countersigned by a Dutch King, is something for which, naturally, no true Scot will ever forgive the English. In reality, the interests of England and lowland Scotland were for once in harmony during the affair, and it was the Scots who set events in motion throughout. England supplied merely the extra weight behind the joint foreign policy which provided its deadly impetus (since Scotland alone would not have found itself compelled to defeat France or have France forcibly restore its deposed king) — and the money which should have averted tragedy. The general pattern of events was to become more familiar in British imperial history than domestic. A settled, ordered community, perhaps an Indian or African province, confronts a poorer, peripheral society, with a different culture and moral standard. This continually harasses its richer neighbour, making the agreements for a solid peace which the latter's rulers consider sacred and universal, and then casually breaking them; and, though its mosquito persistence cannot inflict vital damages, it finally arouses such irritation against the treacherous 'barbarians' that the 'civilised' power either smashes them altogether or commits glaring atrocities against them. In two points, however, the comparison is favourable to the government of the 1690s. Unlike equivalent Indian or African leaders, the highland chiefs were hardly strangers to lowland society and priorities, and might be expected to foresee the consequences of their actions. Colonial frontier trouble was unlikely to endanger the colonising power directly; but the continuance of the highland rising was a definite encouragement to Louis XIV to invade England or Scotland.

This gulf between lowland and highland attitudes towards a pacification, and the difficulties and dangers to which the highlanders' stupidly cunning ambivalence exposed the nation during a European war, made a bloody outcome more probable but not inevitable. Concentration on the general political and cultural causes of the Massacre makes the same mistake as the popular accounts with their hindsight, oversimplification bred of repetition, and belief in all-powerful villains planning the last detail: it overlooks the large part played by chance. Until the last minute, for instance, the intended victim of government anger was to be Glengarry, to be destroyed by a regular siege of Invergarry. The importance of chance is clearest in late 1691 and early 1692, when at least two, perhaps four, vital letters were suppressed or delayed which might, if delivered in time, have averted the Massacre, and nobody explained MacIain's anomalous situation to Dalrymple because nobody knew of both his intentions and his ignorance. Events resembled a Thomas Hardy novel, where tragedy is often brought about by muddles in delivering messages, and is no less tragic for that.

The two major actors who emerge with most credit from the true story of Glencoe are, ironically, two of the most notoriously unscrupulous Scottish politicians of the period, Tarbat and Breadalbane. This is not particularly surprising. Intriguers of their brains and experience were fully prepared to use extreme violence and treachery when these benefited them, but knew they were at other times counter-productive; it was (then as now) nearly always lesser men, outsiders, who, whether they chose roles as pocket Machiavellis or as ostentatiously 'pure' critics of the Establishment, were convinced that, on the practical level, treachery and violence, however clumsy, are always the sure way to success. Both Tarbat and Breadalbane had good reason to desire a genuine pacification. Tarbat's clan would remain in their enemies' power and suspected of Jacobitism while hostilities lasted, and Breadalbane's estates would suffer still further from raids, while any credit the Campbells' activities gained would benefit only Argyll. Both naturally expected major advantages for themselves from the plans they devised for setting the Highlands, but they deserve credit for linking their self-interest with policies intended to benefit the highlanders, not, like most of the politicians involved, with schemes for destroying them. Tarbat, who throughout his career was attracted to sweeping, 'statesmanlike' plans, unscrupulous or unselfish, practical or visionary, so long as they were novel, was the more disinterested: Fort William under Hill would not have given him any such control over the Highlands as Breadalbane tried for in his militia scheme, and, exceptionally, he worked for Breadalbane's success after his own similar policy was discarded. Yet Breadalbane took increasing risks to make his negotiations succeed, and in late 1691, in strong contrast to his fellow 'episcopalians', gave up what seemed his last chance of office in a final attempt to save them. It is ironic that the Massacre should have made him notorious, for his real actions at the time, and his persistent attempts afterwards to have the promises to the chiefs honoured despite their conduct towards him, form the most creditable part of a long and dubious career.

The irony is not only that Breadalbane is notorious, but that his 'presbyterian' enemies have virtually escaped blame for their part in bringing about the Massacre. In their hatred for the highlanders and hard-core 'episcopalians', they used every available trick throughout the summer and autumn of 1691 to sabotage the pacification, and finally succeeded by making the chiefs extravagant counter-promises which they never intended to keep. The reversal of policy by William and Dalrymple, which prevented them from being brought to book for this, should have involved them in responsibility for the Massacre. Some of them might have been enthusiastic — it was their Clerks of the Council who refused MacIain's submission. Because, however, Dalrymple's justified distrust of the Council made him bypass them in giving orders for the campaign, they were not directly involved, and were afterwards in a position to express horror, while consistently suppressing how deeply their own ally Livingston was implicated. Only in Johnston, absent throughout that period, was the combination of hostility towards the western clans and exploitation of Glencoe merely incongruous rather than hypocritical. Moreover, although ruthless orders generally find Hamiltons and Duncansons ready to execute them and wretched Glenlyons who dare not disobey, they often provoke the conscientious to protest and frustrate them. This was a natural role for Hill, and it was owing to his guilt over joining in the 'presbyterian' intrigues and fear for his job that he instead obeyed. Guilt and fear removed all the normal institutional and personal checks on rash instructions from London.

Breadalbane's notoriety has also conveniently obscured the folly of the leading Jacobite chiefs he negotiated with. His past record admittedly gave them justification for caution, even second thoughts later. Yet his vices were only theirs, selfish intriguing and self-congratulatory vanity, writ large; the fatal difference was that they lacked his sense of reality. That autumn, they listened to every accusation and every attempt to inflame their pride against him. Knowing that the 'presbyterians' were their traditional enemies, they took seriously their incredible unguaranteed promises of better terms. Knowing that they could not possibly fight another campaign, they and their clansmen swaggered and boasted until the government was forced to take them seriously. Of the new European dimension of their activities, they grasped only that the French might send them reinforcements if they could spin out negotiations long enough, not that large-scale strategic considerations might ultimately drive the distant government to crush them as vindictively as any local clan with a blood-feud. They mismanaged matters so completely that over the next few years both political factions remained hostile and contemptuous towards them. It was fortunate for the reputations of Glengarry, Maclean, or even the eleventh-hour deserter Lochiel, that the massacre was perpetrated on a chief and clan who had played almost no part in their irresponsible (but ill-documented) intrigues.

The irresponsibility on the Jacobite side is usually sought elsewhere. The chiefs are portrayed as having remained peaceful and inactive all autumn, failing to gain the protection of the Indemnity only because they awaited with sheep-like loyalty permission from James, who, presumably, delayed sending it until December from sheer superstition and personal inertia.[1] Here at its clearest is the main oversimplification in popular accounts of Glencoe: it is assumed that characters not immediately in the limelight were not doing anything. James acted not as an isolated individual but as the head of a government in exile, with ministers and advisers shaping policy in the light of shifting circumstances and the need to gain French help; the final, fatal delay occurred because the French first made and then withdrew an offer to send help to Scotland. This does not make the outcome for the Macdonalds any less tragic; but a modern equivalent would be British policy on the Singapore garrison until 1942, in which a course was followed fairly certain to lead to disaster because the only real alternatives were, in the circumstances, unthinkable, rather than Hitler's pointless orders to isolated forces to die fighting: reason of state is at least a more tolerable excuse than private whim. Admittedly, this study may have discounted James's personal responsibility too far. The reasons behind Jacobite policy can be logically reconstructed from the fragmentary evidence, the influence of his prejudices cannot; and it is known that the most creditable decision, to let the highlanders submit, was made by Melfort (another notorious Scottish politician whose reputation emerges enhanced). However, the really discreditable incident in James's relations with the clans is not Glencoe but the 1690 negotiations with Montgomerie, in which he abandoned their interests in Argyll's favour. Inevitably, there was a clash of interests within the Jacobite movement: willingness on James's part to negotiate terms for his restoration would be good news for most English and lowland Jacobites, but a blow to highlanders, whose claims would be strongest if they helped restore him by force. If James had abandoned their interests only reluctantly and after tough negotiations, it might have been justified; instead, he seems simply to have overlooked them.

The popular accounts are at their most accurate in describing King William's and Sir John Dalrymple's actions; the main correction here is only to place them in a more accurate context. One particularly ironic feature of the Massacre is that it was a government anxious to enforce a moderate highland policy which was ultimately responsible; but this was not entirely accidental. William's faults in ruling Scotland were the opposite of James's, but proved no less disastrous. James's major decisions were usually swiftly reached, unshakeable and unjust; his more conscientious ministers sacrificed their favour in constant attempts to turn him away from arbitrary measures towards moderation. William's decisions (after his first few months of petulance) were usually based on some sense of principle and his obligation to satisfy Scottish expectations of reform; but, with his normal hatred of making irrevocable choices heightened by his negligence in Scottish business, he would fail to carry them out immediately, and *his* ministers of the opposite faction had ample time to raise opposition, bombard him with misinformation and rouse his anxiety over the prerogative. If decisions were at last hastily implemented, it was in a poisoned atmosphere. William was to lose virtually all independent initiative by the mid-1690s and afterwards do little but respond ineptly to events and the surprises sprung by his own ministers. His turn to the 'episcopalians' in 1691 was inevitably a gamble, but, had he carried it through immediately, he would have had Dalrymple confident and using his full political powers to make it work. By delaying, he allowed the 'presbyterians' to sabotage the highland pacification, one of the main reasons for the change, and his failure to punish their first attempts encouraged them to persevere. By winter, the uncertainty whether William might not change his mind in response to their constant surprise attacks had worn Dalrymple's nerves and temper to rags, and hostile accusations and the chiefs' conduct had poisoned the minds of both (and of most leading 'episcopalians') against the clans. They were determined to end highland resistance for good, and Dalrymple was simultaneously attracted by two contradictory radical solutions. The idea of freeing the ordinary highlanders from the domination of their chiefs and gentry and enabling them to become peaceful peasants appeared intermittently in his instructions, even as late as the fatal order. But the other, the 'rooting out' of incorrigible clans, perhaps the whole Clan Donald, to terrorise the rest, always attracted him more strongly — as it had James VI, swaying between two alternative policies somewhat like his, three generations earlier. Dalrymple channelled his natural vindictiveness and accumulated frustrations against these 'barbarians', letting them override his positive plans for the Highlands, military logic and political prudence, and frightening subordinates into silent acquiescence in a scheme for which he was so obviously eager. Even after the first outcry over Glencoe and his discovery of MacIain's true position, he still hoped to carry it further. Contrary to legend, the Campbells did not trick him, and he did not trick William, who since November had considered an example of harshness necessary and assumed that Dalrymple had selected the most legitimate target. Since religion, not the Highlands, was now the most prominent Scottish business, both saw this as a tying of loose ends and were fairly casual, even careless, in dealing with the Instructions of 16 January. The deeds which have risen in judgement against other rulers also have often been ordered just as casually.

The 1691 scheme for buying out troublesome superiorities would not have solved many of the most deep-rooted highland problems, and was largely extorted by wartime necessity; yet it was a wider, more rational and generous reform than Charles or James had attempted, even after 1681 when Argyll's estate was at their disposal. Once, however, the chiefs' recalcitrance had lost the opportunity, and the Massacre had made William and his advisers reluctant to examine highland affairs too closely, there were no more general schemes; existing institutions and officeholders were relied on to maintain order and the status quo. Emergency wartime appointments fossilised into permanency: as the 'natural' Sheriffs of Inverness-shire and Ross, Moray and Seaforth, were not merely Jacobites but papist converts, whose successors also might be disqualified, Grant and Balnagown continued in these posts throughout the reign, although their notoriously partisan characters made them unsuitable. Their influence helped to blunt and discredit the most effective instrument the Restoration government had created to maintain order and repress theft in the Highlands, the Justiciary Commissions. The attempts in 1694–5 to extract impossibly large damages for wartime raids gave some forewarning; but it was the abuses committed from private interest which did the real damage. In 1724, Simon Lord Lovat recalled that the Williamite Commissions were executed in ane unlimited arbitrary manner, without any effect for the purposes they were established, so as to create in all people ane aversion against such courts ... , which, even in matters of life and death, were confined by no rules of law whatsoever — they made malcontents against the government, and at last were prudently laid aside.

Left to themselves, he claimed, the Independent Companies managed to suppress serious robbery by about 1708, only to see the '15 undo their work. Although his proposals conveniently matched his private interests — he hoped to command an Independent Company and wanted no rival highland jurisdiction which might clash with his regality — they are unusually moderate for him (admitting that the Commission had originally been valuable) and are probably, for once, sincere.[2]

The Commission's role of policing and keeping order had largely been assumed by the new Inverlochy garrison and its outposts, the first significant instrument of direct control the government had possessed in the West Highlands since the Restoration. Its effects were, in the long term, decisive. Never again would Lochaber be so safe a stronghold for rebellion and major crime. Glengarry, who held out so obstinately in 1691, was among the first to surrender after the '15. The Clanranald family became a centre of Jacobite activity — but only after transferring their home to Uist. Lady Grange, unlike some earlier kidnapped wives, was taken to the Western Isles, not Lochaber.[3] From this viewpoint, even the Massacre of Glencoe produced some benefits: although the shaken Macdonalds did not afterwards permanently abandon cattle-raiding as completely as some sources claim, they were never again notorious for it, and some became Protestants — reforms which the unscrupulous Dalrymple would have seen as entirely justifying his orders. In reality, the hatred and distrust engendered by Glencoe blighted Fort William's reputation among the clans from the start. It went far to ensure the ill-success of the more constructive activities expected from the garrison, to encourage the clans to accept lowland authority and civilisation (although aspects of these 'positive' policies, such as the persecution of catholicism, also contributed). It was a tribute to Hill's personal character that, despite his involvement in the Massacre, such policies had considerable success under him. His successors never gained such trust. When a detachment attempted to arrest Glengarry on Simon Fraser's accusations in 1704, his whole clan temporarily absconded because, he claimed, they 'are still in dread of anoyr Massacre ... They uer at home the whole day and [did] all their ordinary work only uer afraid to keep their homes at night'.[4] The hostility was to linger on long after the fort's practical usefulness was over, even into the half-century after 1890, when local pressure encouraged a railway company by degrees to destroy almost every trace of the buildings.

Even the long-term influence which the garrisons by their very existence had in reducing illegal activities temporarily seemed in doubt at William's death, as Simon Fraser's activities increasingly exposed the gaps in the government's control over the Highlands. The success of his outrages, and the eagerness of major politicians to condone them, threatened to undo the surviving gains of the Restoration period, when highlanders declared 'rebels' in private disputes, such as

Lord Macdonell and the Macleans, tended to manoeuvre to bring about armed confrontation but then avoid starting large-scale violence — a restraint which perhaps crippled the Macleans' chances. Only Keppoch pushed defiance as far as open bloodshed, and for this (less deliberate than Simon's atrocities) his clan was savagely punished. The magnates' violent power struggles had made them provide support for these 'outlaws', Argyll for Lochiel in 1664–5, Atholl for the Macleans and Keppoch, but not (so far as is known) so unconditionally as to encourage them to fresh aggressions. The outcome of the disputes, the ruin of Argyll and the near-ruin of Breadalbane, accidentally redressed the highlanders' main grievances against the government, its support for far worse armed aggressions under the colour of law; it could more plausibly claim to be holding an equitable balance. Now Argyll's blatant protection of Simon (in contrast to Tullibardine's over-scrupulous refusal to protect Keppoch) struck an alarming new note and encouraged further violence, the attack on the Lovat chamberlains.[5] Simon's return in 1703 and concoction of the 'Scots Plot' encouraged an unprecedented extension of lowland factional divisions to the Highlands. Clans which supported Atholl were systematically harassed; as most of them were Jacobite, it could be represented as necessary for security. In 1704, for instance, MacIain was coerced into expressing full dependence on the Argyll family; the Council came close to arresting Keppoch when he appeared before it on safe-conduct; and it did arrest Glengarry, who had not intrigued with Simon, while leaving free chiefs who had.[6]

Argyll's lack of concern for highland peace and order in his support for Simon Fraser, and his insatiable greed, made his 1701 prosecution of Gordon particularly alarming. Once again, as in his father's struggle with the Macleans, the government might be obliged to endorse with commissions of fire and sword the aggressor in a highland civil war, of unprecedented scale. Combined with systematic discrimination against chiefs supporting the wrong political factions, this would have produced constant disorder and sharpened the Jacobite threat; the Macleans were long to continue resistance by means from full rebellion down to agrarian sabotage.[7] Instead the dangerous trends proved to be a false dusk. Simon Fraser's decade-long imprisonment in France eased tension between highland supporters of rival factions. The pre-Union government, with its control over the Lowlands increasingly precarious, lacked the strength to impose any systematic highland policy, let alone a divisive factional one. In 1708 came the haphazard abolition of the Scottish Privy Council, which had granted the commissions of fire and sword and organised the necessary support for the recipients. Mackintosh's 1700 compromise with Keppoch ended the last attempt to use one to dispossess a clan. The house of Argyll's creeping encroachment on its neighbours through cunning combination of public and private activities, law and force, at last halted; these methods seemed unnecessary when forfaultures after the '15 made so many highland estates openly available.

The greatest danger to highland society was that the Williamite and presbyterian regime would establish a systematic political and legal discrimination against clans whose support (real or alleged) for Jacobite rebellion confirmed the hostile view that they were incorrigible barbarians, robbers and supporters of popery and Stuart tyranny. Immediately after 1692, this seemed likely to happen. Williamite landowners still smarting under uncompensated losses from highland raids would support a ruthless policy, and exploited the Justiciary Commission to extract ruinous damages from chiefs and lesser men, whatever social chaos this might lead to. They dogmatically denied that the clans had a right to the terms of the 1691 cessation, on the ground that they were by then hopelessly beaten and the offer was an 'episcopalian' trick, Johnston intercepted William's intended favour to the Macleans as unscrupulously as Lauderdale had Charles's, not for the Argyll family's sake but from hostility to them as Jacobite auxiliaries to the 'episcopalians'.

The exposure of the facts about Glencoe was decisive in shattering this polarisation. The 'presbyterians'' reaction was partly a political necessity; the Report would be an effective weapon against the 'episcopalians' only if the massacre of Gaelic-speaking ex-Jacobite highlanders, some of them notorious cattle-raiders, was judged by the standards applied to other Scotsmen. Yet even this consideration influenced their more general attitudes. Dalrymple's orders for the Massacre carried their own hostile highland policy to a fearful extreme, but showed that there was no automatic 'episcopalian' alliance with Jacobite clans. For all the Report's distortions, many 'presbyterians' were genuinely horrified by the treachery of the Massacre and the stain on Scottish good faith. Despite the occasional hanging or starving of highland prisoners, and the Eigg massacre (concealed by its perpetrators), the war had been fought without the atrocities and counter-atrocities — Aberdeen and Lagganmore, Philiphaugh and Dunaverty — which had hardened hearts during Montrose's campaigns. Ironically, the degree of sympathy also reflected the degree to which the 1689–91 rising had failed. It was those risings which never visibly came close to toppling the existing regime, Middleton's and the '15, which were treated with comparative mildness; Montrose's and the '45 were suppressed with an extreme ruthlessness which attracted no such official inquiry. Yet the reception of the Report, largely the result of 'Country' dissatisfaction with William's regime, gave ground for hopes — less fruitless than most 'Country' initiatives of this period — that lowlanders would moderate their traditional hostility towards their highland fellow-Scots. 'I think the murder of Glencoo Is a crying sin that aught publickly to be mourned for,' wrote the Duchess of Hamilton in 1700, as she considered Providence's reasons for allowing the Darien failure.[8] Probably many of the western Presbyterians for whom she was spokeswoman, who had previously considered the clansmen only as the sub-human plunderers of their Highland Host memories, now shared her views.

The most important body which did not, and which still discriminated against the Macdonalds as incorrigible Jacobites, was the Court Party, as finally constituted after Tullibardine's fall, which, as the Duchess complained, refused to allow any discussion of the Massacre. Largely from the personal interest of Queensberry's loyal henchmen, the Dalrymples; the Council imprisoned Glengarry in 1704 mainly because Lord President Hew resented his claim that his clan feared another Glencoe.[9] In 1702, Tullibardine had to search and pay to obtain a copy even of 'Glenlyon's order' (i.e. Duncanson's to Glenlyon). The publication in late 1703 in London of the 1695 Report was clearly inspired by Tullibardine (now Duke of Atholl), Johnston and other opponents of Queensberry (who was simultaneously elaborating the 'Scots Plot'), and the Duchess of Atholl reported from Scotland in February that 'they will not reprint ye accompt of Glenco so yt ... there is but two or 3 of ym I can hear of in Scotland'.[10] Johnston, using his old tactics to support his 'New Party' ministry in the 1704 session, intended to bring the Massacre again before Parliament, as a threat to peers who voted against the Hanoverian succession, whom he probably still thought of as 'episcopalian' traitors. This merely allowed the Dalrymples to use the need to protect themselves from attack as an excuse for voting with the Opposition — which they were determined to do anyway, to help undermine the ministry on Queensberry's behalf.[11]

The Union diluted the influence of the Court Party, always hostile to the Jacobite clans. Since Anne's succession, ministers had occasionally proposed variants on Breadalbane's 1691–2 plan for a permanent highland force, and in 1711 Robert Harley, Earl of Oxford, head of the Tory ministry, at last put one into practice. From 1711 to 1714, after negotiations conducted through Robert Stewart of Appin (notorious as a Jacobite), he paid pensions totalling £3,450 a year to various chiefs, who in return were to be ready to serve the Queen with a specified number of followers. Like Breadalbane's 1691 offer of money, this provoked widespread jealousy (not least from Breadalbane himself), partly justified by the eccentric division of the spoils. Stewart himself received £500, a sum equalled only by Glengarry, and promised a number five times his clan's real strength in Appin, including the Glencoe men, the one major branch of Clan Donald not paid independently (See Preface p. x). The Macdougalls received £100. Harley's real intention in this, as in nearly all his later policies, remains mysterious. His explanation in Parliament, that he was merely continuing at a reduced level pensions instituted by William, was false. Of those selected, only the Macleods and Mackinnons had even been truly neutral in 1689 (with the Frasers and Macdougalls hovering close to rebellion). Sir John Maclean was paid for clansmen most of whom were officially now Argyll's followers. Harley may merely have been bribing these chiefs to remain quiet. He may (a possibility nowadays dismissed too automatically) have reserved them in case — one possibility among several — his tortuous policies led him into Jacobitism — although leading Scottish Jacobites were uncertain of his purpose. He may (perhaps the most plausible reason) have wanted them as a new Highland Host in case of a Scottish Whig-presbyterian rising.[12] Unlike the Highland Host, however, this threat, even when followed by the '15, did not provoke a lowland reaction against the consistently Jacobite clans and in favour of the 'Whig' ones which had done so much to resist them. Scottish lawyers felt an increasing hostility to highland institutions and social structure, but it was the pro-Hanoverian clans which were most weakened by their application of principle — one aspect of that curious withering away of the Scottish state which alone made possible Prince Charles Edward's early successes.[13]

Investigation into the Massacre may have aroused a new feeling of sympathy for highlanders among lowlanders, but the Massacre itself naturally kept alive in the West Highlands hostility towards the Revolution government and consequent support for Jacobitism. In other respects, also, needless government ruthlessness assisted the movement's survival. In 1698, despite Andrew Fletcher's warnings, it made illegal the return from France of any Jacobite without a special licence, at a time when St Germain was near total collapse after the peace. A Scottish indemnity was issued only in 1703, but, despite revival of Jacobite hopes with the new war, many former strong supporters, such as Sir John Maclean, returned or attempted to.[14] Admittedly, harshness had crushed the principles of some leading Jacobites — Balcarres, pardoned in 1700, became a slavish supporter of the Court Party in Parliament[15] — but those who were forced to remain loyal were available to pick up the threads in better times.

The Jacobite movement they reconstructed was very different from its predecessor. This study of the 1689–91 rising, with its evidence on the lords and chiefs who came to the brink of joining, and the part chance played in pushing them over or checking them, teaches one lesson, elementary but still needed: that each Jacobite rising or conspiracy should be studied in its own context. It is too easily assumed that from Montrose's campaigns on, almost all the same clans and individuals took their old sides against each other, from the same motives as before — and that every attempt was foredoomed to the same failure. Undoubtedly, certain clans did have partisan traditions which individual defections could not permanently alter. Although it was not surprising that Lachlan Mackintosh in 1689 chose the side opposed to that taken by his hostile superior Gordon, his rebellious vassal Keppoch and his rival as head of Clan Chattan Cluny, his son brought out the Mackintoshes in the '15, and, when his wavering grandson decided to stick to Hanover as the more profitable, Lady Mackintosh raised much of the clan for Charles Edward. Yet the assumption is unreasonably rigid: Atholl, for instance, defended Blair against the '15, but evidence exists (doubtless deserving sceptical examination, but not mere disregard) that he took part in Jacobite intrigues in the very different circumstances before the Union.[16] It is unwise to assume that motives were static: highland Jacobitism might be a reaction against the increasing economic ties with the Lowlands or be encouraged by them, as in 1705, when the prospect of the Alien Act destroying their profitable cattle trade into England seemed likely to drive Lochiel's and Clanranald's clansmen into a premature rising which they would be unable to prevent.[17] In both cases, the state of the nation was the transforming influence. Jacobitism in England had become (for a while) an irrelevant political backwater; in Scotland, by 1702, it was one of the more logical and hopeful patriotic alternatives, and fuller knowledge of what the other alternatives implied would have made it still more attractive. The nationalist dimension of anti-Union Jacobitism could win support from those normally divided from it by self-interest, religion, Whiggery or hostility to the clans. Even after this best opportunity had been missed, the '15 was the most promising Jacobite rising, in numbers, in breadth of support — in everything but leadership. It provides the clearest refutation of the assumption that hatred of the

Macdonalds would almost mechanically bring the Campbells to the government side (they were united there only in the '45). In the '15, Campbells on different sides naturally tried to avoid, where possible, shedding each others' blood; but, although Argyll was the government commander, Glenlyon fought beside Glengarry at Sheriffmuir, Campbell of Calder came out in open rebellion (dying, luckily for his family, early in 1716), and even the cautious Breadalbane nearly toppled into overt Jacobitism.[18] (See Preface, p. xiv).

Nevertheless, the view of the Campbells as consistently anti-Jacobite has become traditionally accepted; so has the interpretation of the Massacre of Glencoe as basically an episode of the Campbell-Macdonald feud, with Breadalbane tricking the government into disposing of his clan enemies. Among government supporters, it may have become established by the mid-eighteenth century,[19] conveniently hiding the moral that high-handed government policy, enforced from afar without understanding, could produce an atrocity even without malignant private distortion. Although the Macdonalds could never so ignore the government's responsibility, the anti-Campbell version became deeply rooted in clan and West Highland tradition, encouraging constant slight everyday hostility between Campbells and Macdonalds which subsided only within living memory. It was strengthened by the willingness of Campbell apologists to accept that the tradition was factually correct and to attempt to brazen the matter out by denigrating the Glencoe Macdonalds, and by the sinister air which continued to cling round the house of Breadalbane until its mysterious economic collapse in this century.

On the highlanders' side also, this tradition could be an insidious temptation, encouraging in its slight degree a reliance on traditional assumptions which made them that much less prepared for the unprecedented changes of their own time — like Scott's Highland Widow, whose reliance on formulas such as 'the race of Diarmid were ever fair and false' instead of on thought ultimately destroyed her son. An understanding of how far the major chiefs' folly had helped provoke the Massacre might have left the ordinary clansmen slightly less unprepared for their part in the Clearances. Yet the legend of Glencoe survived the relegation of the chiefs to a place among the traditional villains of Scottish history; the modern cultural and political trends that have so determinedly destroyed the myth of Bonnie Prince Charlie have encouraged it. This is partly justified — nationalists of every degree can cite the Massacre as the most notorious example of an order issued from London without any understanding of the Scottish local situation. Such traditional simplification of the course of events is natural enough, but it sometimes results in hopeless oversimplification — 'promising to explain how a motor-car works, and then describing a wheelbarrow' as the first Macdonald to become Prime Minister of Britain put it. The legend of Glencoe (which is not true oral 'popular history' but an odd mixture of tradition and limited exploitation of documents) is such an oversimplification; and a dangerous one, for it awakens the strongest temptation for nations or groups often crushed by overwhelming force, the temptation to see themselves in *every* misfortune of their past history purely as innocent victims, without even the blame a dupe must shoulder for the ignorance and greed which allow him to be swindled. Intended to promote national or group solidarity, such a legend often encourages a despairing irresponsibility as well, a particularly ironic outcome in this instance; for it was just such total irresponsibility among the highland leaders, though over-confident rather than despairing, which made them let slip the best post-Restoration chance of strengthening their social structure, and, unforeseen by them, ultimately brought destruction on the Glencoe Macdonalds.

NOTES

1. Prebble, *Glencoe*, 161, 170-1.

2. Burt, *Letters*, ii, 256, 259-62, Lovat's memorial, 1724; R, Mitchison, 'The Government and the Highlands, 1707-1745', in Phillipson & Mitchison (eds.), *Scotland in the Age of Improvement*, 32-4.

3. *Ib.*, 28; *Memoirs of Lochiell*, 249; SCA, Thompson, 'History', i, fol. 149.

4. *Highlands in 1750*, 80-1; Kilgour, *Lochaber in War & Peace*, 318; Prebble, 'Religion and the Massacre of Glencoe', *SHR*, xlvi, 187.

5. Blair, Atholl MSS, Box 45 (4) 130, Glengarry to Atholl, 4 Apr. 1704; *ib.*, 110, P. Scott to same, 18 Mar. 1704.

6. *Ib.*, 98, same to same, 29 Feb. 1704; *ib.*, 114, same to same, 21 Mar. 1704; *ib.*, 92, Dollery to same, 24 Feb. 1704; *ib.*, 108, Lord Justice Clerk to same, 14 Mar. 1704; *ib.*, (5) 109, Glengarry to same, 24 July 1705.

7. Cregeen, 'Changing Role', *Scotland in the Age of Improvement*, 13-18.

8. Blair, Atholl MSS, Box 45 (1) 75, Duchess of Hamilton to Countess, 26 Feb. 1700.

9. *Ib.*, (4) 114, P. Scott to Atholl, 21 Mar. 1704.

10. *Ib.*, (2) 167, James Murray to Tullibardine, 19 Aug. 1702; *ib.*, (4) 33, Duchess of Atholl to same, 2 Feb. 1704; *Highland Papers*, 117-19.

11. Macpherson, *Original Papers*, i, 685, Father Hall to ?, 8 July 1704; P. W. J. Riley, *The Union of England and Scotland* (Manchester, 1978), 91-2.

12. The distribution: £500 each, Glengarry, Appin; £360 each, Lochiel, Sir Donald Macdonald, Clanranald, Sir John Maclean, Fraser of Fraserdale; £200, Macleod; £150, Cluny; £100 each, Mackinnon, Macdougall. *The Whitefoord Papers*, ed. W.A.S. Hewins (Oxford, 1898), 57, 'List of the clans ... '; Riley, *The English Ministers and Scotland, 1707-1727* (Manchester, 1964), 178, 216-17; *Lockhart Papers*, i, 377, 459; W. Cobbett, *Parliamentary History of England*, vi (London, 1810), 1275, 1339-40; *Letters ... in the Reign of Queen Anne by ... Seafield ...*, ed. P. Hume Brown (SHS, 1915), 131-3; *Thanes of Cawdor*, 409-10, Breadalbane to [Calder], 6 May 1714; Blair Atholl MSS, Box 45 (9) 193, same to Atholl, 30 Nov. 1711; *HMCR Portland*, x, 227-8, 309-12, 338, 367-75, 410, 415-16, 437, Papers, 1711-14.

13. Mitchison, 'Government & Highlands', *Scotland in the Age of Improvement*, 31-44.

14. *APS*, x, 175; Steele, ii, S3138, S3247; Fletcher, *Selected Political Writings*, 44-5.

15. His joining the '15 may signify a genuine revival of his Jacobitism, but the publication in 1714 of his 1690 Jacobite *Memoirs* had destroyed all hope of Hanoverian favour for him.

16. *Lockhart Papers*, i, 72-3; Mr of Sinclair, *Memoirs*, 35.

17. Hooke, *Correspondence*, i, 427, Hooke's Memoire, 17 Oct. 1705.

18. *Lairds of Glenlyon*, 241; *Thanes of Cawdor*, 413.

19. *Highlands in 1750*, 78-81.

Select Bibliography and Abbreviations

Manuscripts

1)   Scotland

Edinburgh.
   SRO: Scottish Record Office.

E 6/5	(Treasury Sederunt).
E 7/8–9	(Treasury Register).
E 100	(Muster-rolls).

GD 1/658	(Inventory of Lochiel Charters).
GD 26	(Leven & Melville Papers).
GD 50	(John Macgregor Collection).
GD 64	(Campbell of Jura Papers).
GD 80	(Macpherson of Cluny Papers).
GD 103	(Society of Antiquaries Collection).
GD 112	(Breadalbane Papers).
GD 124	(Mar & Kellie Papers).
GD 158	(Marchmont Papers).
GD 170	(Campbell of Barcaldine Papers).
GD 201	(Clanranald Papers).
GD 202	(Campbell of Dunstaffnage Papers).
GD 406	(Duke of Hamilton Papers)*

PC 1/47–52	(Privy Council Acta).
PC 2/24	(Privy Council Decreta).
PC 12	(Privy Council Miscellaneous Papers, 1692, 1695).
PC 14/3	(Oaths).

REF 310.044   (GD 44) (Transcripts for a projected HMCR volume of Gordon manuscripts).
RH 15/1/16   (Gordon of Edinglassie Papers).
RH 15/13   (Fraser Papers).
RHP 10560,   10561/1,   11623 (Maps of Dunkeld).
SP 3/1   (James Johnston's Letter-Book).
SP 4/11–13,   15,   17   (Secretaries' Warrant-Books).
National Register of Archives (Scotland): The Buchans of Auchmacoy (typescript).

---

*Still in course of recataloguing.

NLS: National Library of Scotland.
Adv. MS 13.1.8 (Robertson of Struan Papers); Adv. MS 33.7.8 (Minutes of the 1689 Convention).
MSS 295; 298 (Lovat transcripts); 542 (Cameronian Regiment); 599; 975 (Argyll Papers); 1031–2 (Selkirk Correspondence); Mackenzie of Delvine Papers: 1247 (Campbells), 1250 (Chisholm), 1275 (Frasers), 1305 (Glencoe, Keppoch), 1313 (Glengarry), 1316, 1339–40, 1353, 1361 (Mackenzies), 1320 (R. Mackenzie), 1329–33 (Mackenzie of Coul), 1356 (Seaforth), 1384 (Macpherson), 1391 (Munro of Foulis), 1401 (Morison); 1672 (Campbell of Inverawe Papers); 1946 (Justiciary Court Records); 2955 (Menzies of Weem Papers); 3134 (Breadalbane Papers, etc.); 3138 (Argyll Papers); 3161 (Countess of Findlater letter); 3186 (Balhaldie Correspondence); 3194, 3196 (Material for *Memoirs of Locheill*); 3550 (Mackintosh protest); 3740 (Blathwayt Papers); 3741 (Menzies of Weem Papers); 5136 (Atholl Correspondence); 7003–6, 7010–20, 7026–30, 14,407–8 (Tweeddale Papers); 14,266 (Sir D. Nairne's Journal); 17,498 (Saltoun Papers).

MS Wodrow Fol. XXXIV (Miscellaneous Papers).

EUL: Edinburgh University Library.

MS Laing II 212 ('A true account of the late fight betuixt Grall Major Mackay and the Viscount of Dundee, in the plane of Gilliecrankie within the bounds of Atholl'); MS Laing III 354 (Lauderdale Correspondence).

SCA: Scottish Catholic Archives, 16 Drummond Place.
Blairs Letters, Boxes T–F[1] (1688–98)★.
President John Thompson: History of the Scottish Mission, vol. i.

Blair Castle.
Atholl MSS: Manuscripts of the Duke of Atholl.
Cawdor Castle.
Cawdor MSS: Manuscripts of the Earl of Cawdor, bundle 584.
Doune Park, Doune.
Moray MSS: Manuscripts of the Earl of Moray, items from Boxes 6 and 7.
Drumlanrig Castle.
Queensberry Papers: Manuscripts of the Duke of Buccleuch and Queensberry.
Dumfries House, Cumnock.
Bute MSS: Manuscripts of the Marquess of Bute, bundle A517 (Dalrymple papers.)

★At present undergoing a complete renumbering.

Glasgow University Library.
MSS Gen. 1274 (W. Macgregor Stirling transcripts), 1577 (Contemporary copies of letters on the Massacre of Glencoe).
West Highland Museum, Fort William.
Manuscript collection.

2)   England.
London
    PRO: Public Record Office.
ADM 8/2 (Admiralty Disposition Books).
ADM 51 (Ships' Logs): 345/1 (*Fanfan*), 3796/4 (*Conception*), 3890/4 (*Lark*), 4285/1 (*Pembroke*).
ADM 106/399 (Navy Board In-Letters).
SP 44/342 (Warrant book).

    BL: British Library.
MS Lansdowne 1163 A–C (Melfort letter-books).
Add. (Additional Manuscripts): 12,068; 17,677LL (Dutch Ambassadors' transcripts); 19,254 (Perth family transcripts); 20,007 (G. Wharton's diary); 23,113–23,138, 23,242–23,251, 35,125 (Lauderdale Papers); 28,239, 28,251 (Seaforth Papers); 31,249–31,253 (Lovat Papers); 33,924 (Miscellaneous); 37,660–37,662 (Melfort letter-books); 51,511 (Halifax's 'Holland House Notebook').

    Historical Manuscripts Commission, Quality House, Chancery Lane.
HMCR Finch, v: Transcripts for a projected fifth volume of Finch manuscripts.
    HLRO: House of Lords Record Office.
Willcocks MSS, Section VI (Tweeddale Letters).
    Lambeth Palace Library.
MS 2020 (17th c. miscellaneous).
    WDA: Westminster Diocesan Archives, Westminster Cathedral.
Browne MSS (Papers of Jacobite Secretary Henry Browne).
Bodl.: Bodleian Library, Oxford.
MSS Carte 76 (newsletters); 180–181, 208–211, 238, 256 (Nairne Papers).
Buckminster, Grantham.
Tollemache MSS, Lauderdale Papers (extracts in catalogue only).
Northamptonshire Record Office, Northampton.
Buccleuch MSS Vol. 63 (Shrewsbury Papers).
NUL: Nottingham University Library.
Portland MSS, PwA (Papers of the 1st Earl of Portland).

3)   France.

Paris.

AAE: Archives des Affaires Etrangères.

Corr. Pol. (Correspondance Politique), Angleterre, Vol. 172.

Archives Nationales.

Marine, B$_3$ 62 (misc. in-letters, 1690).

BN: Bibliothèque Nationale.

Naf (Nouvelles acquisitions françaises) 7487–7492 (Renaudot Papers).

Printed

Primary Sources.

Account, An, of the Depredations committed upon the Clan Campbell and their followers during the years 1685 and 1686, ed. [A. Kincaid] (Edinburgh, 1816).

Ailesbury, Thomas Earl of, *Memoirs*, ed. W.E. Buckley, 2 vols. (Roxburghe Club, 1890).

Analecta Hibernica, iv (Tyrconnell's Letter-Book), xxi, ed. L. Tate (IMC, 1932, 1959).

Annandale Book: Sir W. Fraser, *The Annandale Family Book, of the Johnstones Earls and Marquises of Annandale*, 2 vols. (Edinburgh, 1894).

APS: Acts of the Parliaments of Scotland, ed. T. Thomson, etc., 12 vols. (Edinburgh, 1814–75).

Archives de la Bastille, ed. F. Ravaisson, 19 vols. (Paris, 1866–1904).

Argyll Just. Recs: The Justiciary Records of Argyll and the Isles, 1664–1705, ed. J. Cameron (Edinburgh, 1949).

Argyll, *Letters: Letters from Archibald Earl of Argyll to John Duke of Lauderdale*, ed. C. K. Sharpe & Sir G. Sinclair (Bannatyne Club, 1829).

Argyll Sasines, The, ed. H. Campbell, 2 vols., (Edinburgh, 1933–4).

Atholl, J. Duke of, *Chronicles of the Atholl and Tullibardine Families*, 5 vols. (Edinburgh, 1908).

Aubrey, J., *Three Prose Works*, ed. J. Buchanan Brown (Fontwell, 1972).

Balcarres, Colin Earl of, *Memoirs touching the Revolution in Scotland*, ed. Lord Lindsay (Bannatyne Club, 1841).

Bernardi, J. *A Short History of the Life of Major John Bernardi* (London, 1729).

Black Book of Taymouth, The, ed. C. Innes (Bannatyne Club, 1855).

Blaeu, J., *Atlas Major*, xii (Scotland) (Amsterdam, 1662).

Bland Burges, Sir J., *Selections from the Correspondence* . . . , ed. J. Hutton (London, 1885).

Blind Harper, The, ed. W. Matheson (Edinburgh, 1970).

Book of Dunvegan, The, ed. Canon R.C. Macleod, 2 vols. (3rd Spalding Club, 1938–9).

Brodie, A., *The Diary of Alexander Brodie of Brodie*, ed. D. Laing (Spalding Club, 1863).

Burnet, G., *A History of his own time*, ed. M. J. Routh, 6 vols. (Oxford, 1833).

Burt, E., *Letters from a Gentleman in the North of Scotland*, ed. R. Jamieson, 2 vols. (London, 1818).

Caldwell Papers: Selections from the Family Papers preserved at Caldwell, ed. W. Mure (Maitland Club, 1854).

'Camerons in the '15': J. Cameron, 'The Camerons in the Rising of 1715', ed. W. Mackay, *TGSI*, xxvi (1904–7).

Campana de Cavelli, Marchesa (ed.), *Les Derniers Stuarts à St Germain en Laye*, 2 vols. (Paris, 1871).

Carleton, Cpt. G., *The Memoirs of an English Officer* (London, 1728).

Carstares S.P.: *State Papers and Letters addressed to William Carstares*, ed. J. M'Cormick (Edinburgh, 1774).

Chiefs of Colquhoun and their country, The, by Sir W. Fraser, 2 vols. (Edinburgh, 1869).

Chiefs of Grant, The, by Sir W. Fraser, 3 vols. (Edinburgh, 1883).

Cleland, Lt.-Col. W., *A Collection of Several Poems and Verses* ([Glasgow], 1697).

Correspondentie van Willem III en van Hans Willem Bentinck, ed. N. Japikse, 5 vols. (The Hague, 1927–37).

Creichton, Cpt. J., & Swift, Jonathan, *Memoirs of Captain John Creichton*, Swift, *Miscellaneous and Autobiographical Pieces*, ed. H. Davis (Oxford, 1962).

CSPD: Calendar of State Papers Domestic

CTB: Calendar of Treasury Books.

Culloden Papers . . . from the year 1625 to 1748, ed. H.R. Duff (London, 1815).

Dalrymple, Sir J., *Memoirs of Great Britain and Ireland*, 3 vols. (London, 1771–88).

Dalton, C., (ed.), *English Army Lists and Commission Registers, 1660*–1714, 6 vols. (London, 1892–1904).

--- *The Scots Army, 1661*–1688 (London, 1909).

D'Avaux, *Négociations: Négociations de M. le Comte d'Avaux en Irelande*, ed. P. Hogan (Irish Manuscripts Commission, 1934).

Delaval Papers, The, ed. J. Robinson (Newcastle, [c.1890]).

Dirleton, *Doubts*: Sir J. Nisbet of Dirleton, *Some Doubts and Questions in the Law* (Edinburgh, 1698).

Dunbar Dunbar, E., *Social Life in Former Days* (Edinburgh, 1865).

Dundee, *Letters: Letters of John Grahame of Claverhouse, Viscount Dundee*, ed. G. Smythe (Bannatyne Club, 1826).

Eachann Bacach and other Maclean Poets, ed. Colm O Baioill (Edinburgh, 1979).

Earls of Cromartie: Sir W. Fraser, *The Earls of Cromartie: their kindred, country and correspondence*, 2 vols. (Edinburgh, 1879).

Edinburgh Records: Extracts from the Records of the Burgh of Edinburgh, 1681–1689, ed. M. Wood & H. Armet (Edinburgh, 1954).

--- *1689–1701*, ed. H. Armet (Edinburgh, 1962).

Erskine, J., *The Journal of John Erskine of Carnock, 1683–7*, ed. Rev. W. Macleod (SHS, 1893).

Est. Procs: An Account of the Proceedings of the Estates in Scotland, 1689–1690, ed. E.W.M. Balfour-Maitland, 2 vols. (SHS, 1954).

Family of Kilravock: A Genealogical Deduction of the Family of Rose of Kilravock, ed. C. Innes (Spalding Club, 1848).

Firth, C.H. (ed.), *Scotland and the Protectorate* (SHS, 1899).

Fletcher, A., *Selected Political Writings and Speeches*, ed. D. Daiches (Edinburgh, 1979).

Fountainhall, Sir J. Lauder of, *The Decisions of the Lords of Council and Session*, 2 vols. (Edinburgh, 1759).

---*Hist. Notices: Historical Notices of Scotish Affairs*, ed. D. Laing, 2 vols. (Bannatyne Club, 1848).

--- *Hist. Observes: Historical Observes of Memorable Occurents in Church and State*, ed. A. Urquhart & D. Laing (Bannatyne Club, 1840).

--- *Journals*, ed. D. Crawford (SHS, 1900).

Foxcroft, H. C. (ed.), *A Supplement to Bishop Burnet's History of his own time* (Oxford, 1902).

Franco-Irish Correspondence, Dec. 1688–Feb. 1692, ed. S. Mulloy, 3 vols. (IMC, 1984).

Fraser Papers: Papers from the Collection of Sir William Fraser, ed. J. R. N. Macphail (SHS, 1924).

Fraser-Macintosh, C., *Letters of Two Centuries* (Inverness, 1890).

From the Farthest Hebrides, ed. D.A. Fergusson (Toronto, 1978).

Gazette de France: Recueil des Nouvelles Ordinaires et Extraordinaires (Paris, 1689–96; yearly reprints of the *Gazette*).

Grameid, The, ed. Rev. A.D. Murdoch (SHS, 1888).

Grant, J., *Legends of the Braes o' Mar* (Aberdeen, n.d.).

Highland Papers: Papers Illustrative of the Political Condition of the Highlands of Scotland, 1689–1696, ed. J. Gordon (Maitland Club, 1845).

Highland Papers, i, ed. J.R.N. Macphail (SHS, 1914).

Highlands in 1750: The Highlands of Scotland in 1750, ed. A. Lang (London, 1898).

Hist. Papers: Historical Papers relating to the Jacobite Period, 1699–1750, ed. Col. J. Allardyce, 2 vols (New Spalding Club, 1895).

HMCR (Historical Manuscripts Commission Reports); 1st–8th Reports, 11th Report Appendix 7, Athole, Buccleuch (Drumlanrig), Buccleuch (Montagu) ii, *Finch*, ii–iv, *Hamilton, Hamilton Supplement, Hope-Johnstone, Laing, Le Fleming, Leyborne-Popham, Lords 1689–90, Mar & Kellie, Portland* x, *Roxburghe, Stuart* i–vii.

Hooke, N., *Correspondence of Colonel Nathaniel Hooke*, ed. W.D. Macray, 2 vols. (Roxburghe Club, 1870–1).

Huygens, C., *Journaal*, 2 vols. (Utrecht, 1876).

IMC: Irish Manuscripts Commission.

Inventory of Lamont Papers (1231–1897), ed. Sir N. Lamont (Edinburgh, 1914).

Johnson, S. & Boswell, J., *A Journey to the Western Islands of Scotland*, etc., ed. R.W. Chapman (Oxford, 1979).

'Journal of a Soldier in the Earl of Eglinton's Troop of Horse', ed. G. Neil, *Transactions of the Glasgow Archaeological Society (TGAS)*, i, (1868).

Just. Recs: Justiciary Records, 1661–78, ed. W.G. Scott-Moncreiff (SHS, 1905).

Kirkton, J., *Secret and True History of the Church of Scotland*, ed. C. K. Sharpe (Edinburgh, 1817).

Laud. Papers: The Lauderdale Papers, ed. O. Airy (Camden Soc., 1884–5).

Law, Rev. R., *Memorialls*, ed. C.K. Sharpe (Edinburgh, 1818).

[Leslie], *Answer to King*: [C. Leslie], *An Answer to a Book, Intituled, The State of the Protestants in Ireland under the Late King James's Government* (by Bishop W. King) (London, 1692 [3]).

[Leslie, C.], *Gallienus Redivivus, or Murther Will Out, Being a True Account of the De Witting of Glencoe, Gaffney, etc.* ('Edinburgh', 1695).

'Letter from the Host about Glasgow, A Copie of a', 1 Feb. 1678, *Blackwood's Magazine*, i, (1817).

Letters . . . to George, Earl of Aberdeen, ed. J. Dunn (Spalding Club, 1851).

Leven and Melville Papers; Letters and State Papers chiefly addressed to George Earl of Melville, ed. W.L. Melville (Bannatyne Club, 1843).

Life of James II, ed. J.S. Clarke, 2 vols. (London, 1816).

LJ: Journals of the House of Lords (London, n.d.).

Lockhart Papers, The, ed. A. Aufrere, 2 vols. (London, 1817).

London Gazette.

Lorne, Marquess of, *Adventures in Legend* (Westminster, 1898).

Lovat, Simon Lord, *Memoirs of the Life of Simon Lord Lovat, written by himself in the French Language* (London, 1797).

Luttrell, N., *A Brief Historical Relation of State Affairs from September 1678 to April 1714*, 6 vols. (Oxford, 1857).

McBane, D., *The Expert Sword Man's Companion* ... (Glasgow, 1728).

Macfarlane, *Gen. Colls*: W. Macfarlane, *Genealogical Collections*, ed. J.T. Clark, 2 vols. (SHS, 1900).

Macgill, W., (ed.), *Old Ross-shire and Scotland*, 2 vols. (Inverness, 1909–11).

Mackay, Major-Gen. H., *Memoirs of the War carried on in Scotland and Ireland 1689–1691*, ed. J.M. Hog, P.F. Tytler & A. Urquhart (Bannatyne Club, 1833).

Mackenzie, Sir G. of Rosehaugh, *Memoirs of the Affairs of Scotland from the restoration of King Charles II A.D. 1660*, ed. T. Thomson (Edinburgh, 1821).

Mackintosh Muniments, The, 1442–1830, ed. H. Paton (Edinburgh, 1903).

Maclean, J. A., The Sources, particularly the Celtic Sources, for the History of the Highlands in the Seventeenth Century, (Aberdeen Ph.D., 1939; translations of many Gaelic poems).

[Macleod], *Second Sight*: [Rev. D. Macleod], 'Theophilus Insulanus', *A treatise on the Second Sight* (Edinburgh, 1763).

Macpherson, 'Gleanings': A. Macpherson (ed.), 'Gleanings from the Charter Chest at Cluny Castle', ii–iii, *TGSI*, xx, xxi (1894–6, 1896–7).

Macpherson, *Loyall Dissuasive*: Sir Ae. Macpherson, *The Loyall Dissuasive and other papers concerning the affairs of Clan Chattan*, ed. Rev. A.D. Murdoch (SHS, 1902).

Macpherson, *Original Papers*: J. Macpherson (ed.), *Original Papers; containing the Secret History of Great Britain* ... , 2 vols. (London, 1775).

Mactavish, D. C. (ed.), *The Commons of Argyll: Name Lists of 1685 and 1692* (Lochgilphead, 1935).

---(ed.), *Inveraray Papers* (Oban, 1939).

Macky, J., *Memoirs of the Secret Service of John Macky* (London, 1733).

Major Fraser's Manuscript, ed. A. Fergusson, 2 vols. (Edinburgh, 1889).

Marchmont Papers: A Selection from the Papers of the Earls of Marchmont, ed. G.H. Rose, 3 vols. (London, 1831).

Martin, M. *A Description of the Western Islands of Scotland*, ed. D.J. Macleod (Stirling, 1934).

Maxwells of Pollok: Sir W. Fraser, *Memoirs of the Maxwells of Pollok*, 2 vols. (Edinburgh, 1863).

Melvilles & Leslies: Sir W. Fraser, *The Melvilles Earls of Melville and the Leslies Earls of Leven*, 3 vols. (Edinburgh, 1890).

Memoirs of Dundee: *Memoirs of the Lord Viscount Dundee, the Highland Clans, and the Massacre of Glencoe*, by an Officer of the Army (London, 1714).

Memoirs of Locheill: [J. Drummond of Balhaldie], *Memoirs of Sir Ewen Cameron of Locheill*, ed. J. MacKnight (Maitland Club, 1842).

Misc. SHS., vi: 'Letters from John, Second Earl of Lauderdale to John, Second Earl of Tweeddale, and others', ed. H.M. Paton, *Miscellany of the Scottish History Society*, vi (1939).

[Moncreiff], 'Macaulay's History', *ER*, cv: [Sir James Moncreiff], Review, '*A History of England* ... by ... Macaulay, Vols III and IV', *Edinburgh Review*, cv (Jan.–Apr. 1857) (containing Breadalbane MSS; author's identity from *Wellesley Index to Victorian Periodicals*).

More Culloden Papers, ed. D. Warrand, i (1626–1704) (Inverness, 1923).

Morer, T., *A Short Account of Scotland* (London, 1702).

Napier, M., *Memorials and Letters* ... *of John Graham of Claverhouse, Viscount Dundee*, 3 vols. (Edinburgh, 1859–62).

Nevil Payn's Letter (London, 1693).

Orain Iain Luim; Songs of John Macdonald, bard of Keppoch, ed. A.M. Mackenzie (Edinburgh, 1964).

Rawdon Papers, The, ed. Rev. E. Berwick (London, 1819).

Records of Invercauld, ed. Rev. J.G. Michie (New Spalding Club, 1901).

Records of Inverness, ii, ed. W. Mackay & G. Smith Laing (New Spalding Club, 1914).

Red Book of Grandtully, The, by Sir W. Fraser, 2 vols. (Edinburgh, 1868).

RGSS: Register of the Great Seal of Scotland, 1660-1668.

Robertson, Rev. J., *The Barons Reid-Robertson of Staloch* (Blairgowrie, 1887).

RPCS: Register of the Privy Council of Scotland, 3rd series.

Scotish Pasquils: A Book of Scotish Pasquils, 1568-1715, ed. J. Maidment (Edinburgh, 1868).

Seafield Correspondence, from 1685 to 1708, ed. J. Grant (SHS, 1912).

SHS: Scottish History Society.

Siege of the Castle of Edinburgh, The, ed. R. Bell (Bannatyne Club, 1828).

'Siege of Edinburgh Castle, 1689, The — 'Bonny Dundee' and 'The Gay Gordon'', ed. J. Dowden, *Northern Notes & Queries (NNQ)*, i, (1886). (The copy of Balcarres' *Memoirs* (1714 ed.) from which these notes are taken, formerly in the library of the Theological College of the Episcopalian Church, Edinburgh, has now vanished.)

Sinclair, John Mr of, *Memoirs of the Insurrection in Scotland in 1715*, ed. Sir Walter Scott & J. Macknight (Abbotsford Club, 1858).

Slezer, J., *Theatrum Scotiae* (London, 1693).

Smith, J.A. (ed.)., 'Notes on Original Letters of King James II ... ', *PSAS*, vii, Part I (1866-7).

Somers Tracts; A Collection of Scarce and Valuable Tracts, selected from ... private libraries; particularly that of the late Lord Somers, ed. Sir Walter Scott, 13 vols. (London, 1809-15).

Sourches, Marquis de, *Mémoires*, ed. Comte de Cosnac & E. Pontal, 13 vols. (Paris, 1882-92).

Spalding Club Misc: Miscellany of the Spalding Club, ed. J. Stuart, ii-v (1842-52).

Spottiswoode Miscellany, The, ed. J. Maidment, 2 vols. (Edinburgh, 1844).

State Trials: A Complete Collection of State Trials, ed. T.B. Howell, 23 vols. (London, 1809-26).

Statistical Account: Sir J. Sinclair, *The Statistical Account of Scotland, 1791-1799*, ed. D. J. Withrington & I.R. Grant, 20 vols. (Wakefield, 1975-83).

Steele, R. (ed.), *Tudor and Stuart Proclamations, 1485*-1714, 2 vols. (Oxford, 1910).

Sutherland Book, The, by Sir W. Fraser, 3 vols. (Edinburgh, 1892).

Thanes of Cawdor: The Book of the Thanes of Cawdor, ed. C. Innes (Spalding Club, 1859).

True and Real Account, A, of the Defeat of General Buchan (London, 1690).

Veitch, W., *Memoirs of Mr William Veitch and George Brysson*, ed. T. M'Crie (Edinburgh, 1825).

Wardlaw MS: Rev. J. Fraser, *Chronicles of the Frasers: the Wardlaw Manuscript*, ed. W. Mackay (SHS, 1905).

Wimberley, 'Bighouse Papers': Cpt. P. Wimberley, 'Selections from the Family Papers of the Mackays of Bighouse', *TGSI*, xxi (1896-7).

Wodrow, R., *Analecta*, 4 vols. (Maitland Club, 1842).

--- *Church History: The History of the Sufferings of the Church of Scotland*, 4 vols. (Glasgow, 1829).

Secondary Works.

Anderson, J. *Historical Account of the Family of Frisel or Fraser ...* (Edinburgh, 1825).

Buckroyd, J., *Church and State in Scotland, 1660-1681* (Edinburgh, 1982).

Campbell, A. 'The Keppoch Murders', *TGSI*, xxxix-xl (1942-50).

Cowan, E.J., 'Clanship, kinship and the Campbell acquisition of Islay', *SHR*, lvii (1979).

Cregeen, E.R., 'The Changing Role of the House of Argyll in the Scottish Highlands', in *Scotland in the Age of Improvement*, ed. R. Mitchison & N.T. Phillipson (Edinburgh, 1970).

--- 'The Tacksmen and their Successors; a study in tenurial reorganisation in Mull, Morvern and Tiree in the early eighteenth century', *Scottish Studies (SS)*, xiii (1969).

Cripps, D., *Elizabeth of the Sealed Knot* (Kineton, 1975).

Cunningham, A., *The Loyal Clans* (Cambridge, 1932).

--- 'The Revolution Government in the Highlands', *SHR*, xvi (1916).

Dow, F.D., *Cromwellian Scotland* (Edinburgh, 1979).

Dunlop, J., 'A Chief and his Lawyer', *TGSI*, xlv (1967-8).

Elder, J.R., *The Highland Host of 1678* (Glasgow, 1914).

Fasti Ecclesiae Scoticanae, ed. H. Scott, 8 vols. (Edinburgh, 1915-50).

Ferguson, W. 'Religion and the Massacre of Glencoe', *SHR*, xlvi (1967), xlvii (1968).

--- *Scotland: 1689 to the Present* (Edinburgh, 1968).

Fergusson, C., 'The Early History, legends and traditions of Strathardle', vi-viii, *TGSI*, xxi, xxiii-xxiv (1896-7, 1898-9, 1899-1900).

Flinn, M. (ed.), *Scottish Population History* (Cambridge, 1977).

Forbes Leith, W., *Memoirs of Scottish Catholics during the XVIIth and XVIIIth Centuries*, 2 vols. (London, 1909).

Foxcroft, H.C., *Life and letters of Sir George Savile, first Marquis of Halifax*, 2 vols. (London, 1898).

Fraser-Macintosh, C., *Antiquarian Notes*, 1st series (Inverness, 1865).

Gillies, W.A., *In Famed Breadalbane* (Perth, 1938).

Graham, *Stairs*; J.M. Graham, *Annals and Correspondence of the Viscount and First and Second Earls of Stair*, 2 vols. (Edinburgh, 1875).

Grant, I.F., *The Macleods, the History of a Clan, 1200-1956* (London, 1959).

Henderson, J., *Caithness Family History* (Edinburgh, 1884).

Hill Burton, J., *A History of Scotland . . . 1689-1748*, 2 vols. (London, 1853)

Holden, Lt-Col R.M., 'The First Highland Regiment: the Argyllshire Highlanders', *SHR*, iii (1906).

Hopkins, P.A., Aspects of Jacobite Conspiracy in England in the Reign of William III, (Cambridge Ph.D., 1981).

---'Sham Plots and Real Plots in the 1690s', *Ideology and Conspiracy: Aspects of Jacobitism, 1689-1759*, ed. E. Cruickshanks (Edinburgh, 1982).

Horwitz, H., *Parliament, Policy and Politics in the reign of William III* (Manchester, 1977).

IJNA: International Journal of Nautical Archaeology.

IR: Innes Review.

Kilgour, W.T., *Lochaber in War and Peace* (Paisley, 1908).

Lairds of Glenlyon: D. Campbell, *The Lairds of Glenlyon. Historical Sketches relating to the district of Appin, Glenlyon and Breadalbane* (Perth, 1886).

Lenman, B., *The Jacobite Risings in Britain, 1689-1746* (London, 1980).

Macaulay, T.B., *A History of England from the Accession of James II*, ed. Sir C. Firth, 6 vols. (London, 1913-15).

Macdonald, Rev. A. & Rev. A. , *The Clan Donald*, 3 vols. (Inverness, 1896-1904).

Macdonald, D.J., *Slaughter under Trust* (London, 1965).

Macgibbon, D., & Ross, T., *The Castellated and Domestic Architecture of Scotland*, 5 vols. (Edinburgh, 1887-92).

Mac Gill-Eain, S. (Sorley Maclean), 'Domhnall Donn of Bohuntin', *TGSI*, xlii (1953–9).

MacInnes, Rev. J., 'Clan Unity and Individual Freedom', *TGSI*, xlvii (1971–2).

Mackay, W., *Urquhart and Glenmoriston* (Inverness, 1914).

Mackenzie, A., *History of the Chisholms* (Inverness, 1891).

---*History of the Frasers of Lovat* (Inverness, 1896).

--- *History of the Munros of Fowlis* (Inverness, 1898).

Mackenzie, W.C., *Simon Fraser, Lord Lovat* (London, 1908).

McKechnie, H., *The Lamont Clan, 1235–1935* (Edinburgh, 1938).

Mackintosh, A.M., *The Mackintoshes and the Clan Chattan* (Edinburgh, 1903).

Maclean D., *The Counter-Reformation in Scotland, 1560–1930* (London, 1931).

Maclean Sinclair, Rev. A., *The Clan Gillean* (Charlottetown, 1899).

MacMillan, S., *Bygone Lochaber* (Glasgow, 1971).

McNaughton, D., *The Clan McNaughton* (Edinburgh, 1977).

MacWilliam, A.C., 'A Highland Mission: Strathglass, 1671–1777', *IR*, xxiv (1973).

--- 'The Jesuit Mission in Upper Deeside, 1671–1737', *IR*, xxiii (1972).

Marshall, R.K., *The Days of Duchess Anne* (London, 1973).

Martin, C.J.M., J.R. Adams, P. McBride, etc., 'The Dartmouth: a British frigate wrecked off Mull ... ', *IJNA*, iii–vii (1974–7).

Middle Ages: Inverness Field Club, *The Middle Ages in the Highlands* (Inverness, 1981).

Mitchison, R., *Lordship to Patronage: Scotland 1603–1745* (London, 1983).

Murray Macgregor, A.G., *History of the Clan Gregor*, 2 vols (Edinburgh, 1898–1901).

Paget, J., *The New Examen* ([London], 1934).

Powley, E. B., *The Naval Side of King William's War* (London, 1972).

Prebble, J., *Glencoe, the story of the Massacre* (London, 1966).

--- 'Religion and the Massacre of Glencoe', *SHR*, xlvi (1967).

PSAS: *Proceedings of the Society of Antiquaries of Scotland*.

RCAHMS Argyll: *Royal Commission on the Ancient and Historical Monuments of Scotland; Argyll*, 4 + vols. (HMSO, 1971–).

Rennie, J.A., *In the Steps of the Clansmen* (London, 1951).

Riley, P.W.J., *King William and the Scottish Politicians* (Edinburgh, 1979).

Scots Peerage, The, ed. Sir J. Balfour Paul, 9 vols. (Edinburgh, 1904–14).

Shaw, F.J., *The Northern and Western Islands of Scotland* (Edinburgh, 1980).

Shaw, L., *History of the Province of Moray* (Edinburgh, 1775).

SHR: *Scottish Historical Review*.

Simpson, W.D., 'The Early Castles of Mar', *PSAS*, lxiii (1928–9).

Stevenson, D., *Alasdair MacColla and the Highland Problem in the Seventeenth Century* (Edinburgh, 1980).

Steuart, R.M., 'The Steuarts of Ballechin, Perthshire', *The Stewarts*, xii (1966).

Stewart, J.H.J. & Lt-Col D., *The Stewarts of Appin* (Edinburgh, 1880).

Story, R. H. *William Carstares. A Character and Career of the Revolutionary Epoch, 1649–1715*

Tayler, A. & H., *The House of Forbes* (3rd Spalding Club, 1937).

--- *Jacobites of Aberdeenshire and Banffshire in the Rising of 1715* (Edinburgh, 1934).

Terry, C.S., *John Graham of Claverhouse, Viscount Dundee* (London, 1905).

TGSI: *Transactions of the Gaelic Society of Inverness*.

Tullibardine, Marchioness of, *A Military History of Perthshire, 1660–1902* (Perth, 1908).

Warrand, D. , *Some Mackenzie Pedigrees* (Inverness, 1965).

Whyte, I., *Agriculture and Society in Seventeenth Century Scotland* (Edinburgh, 1979).

Willcock, J., *A Scots Earl in Covenanting Times* (Edinburgh, 1907).

Index

In treating clans or 'names', I have arranged entries as follows: first, the general entry; then the peers of that surname (except those ennobled in the period covered); then families or groups 'of' or 'in' a place or area; lastly the unattached; cadets without territorial titles are grouped immediately after their families, with the family designation in brackets. Wives are (anachronistically) listed under their husbands' names, with their maiden names, where different, in brackets afterwards.

Apart from obvious abbreviations, I have used the following: in the Army entries, F, H and D for Foot, Horse and Dragoons; elsewhere, Bread. for Braedalbane; EIC for the (Scottish) East India Company; HW for the Highland War of 1689-92; PCS for the Scottish Privy Council; SF for Simon Fraser; and Tull. for the Earl of Tullibardine; P for existing entries also in the new preface to the paperback edition.